Fodor's 2014

FLORIDA

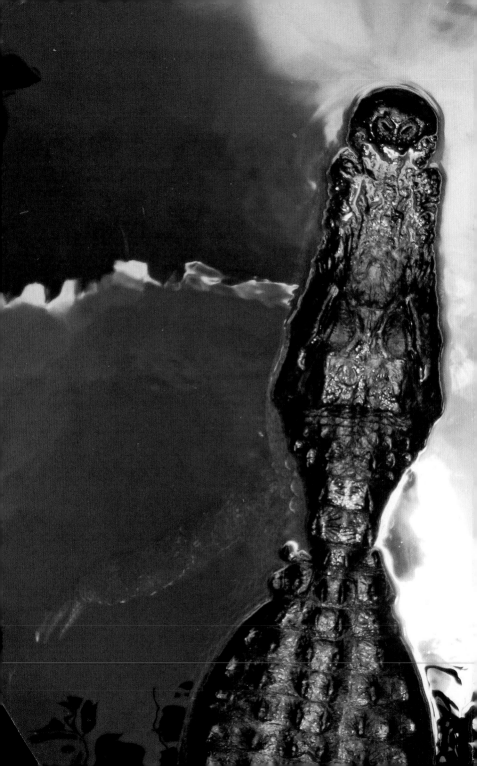

WELCOME TO FLORIDA

With its accessible and varied pleasures, Florida is a favorite of many. Drawn to the colonial charm of St. Augustine, Miami's pulsing nightlife, the glitz of Palm Beach, or the quiet expanse of the Everglades, almost all visitors find something to love here. From the powdery white beaches of the Panhandle to the vibrant coral reefs of the Florida Keys, the ocean is always calling— for sailing, fishing, diving, swimming, and other water sports. Stray off the path a few miles, and you might glimpse a bit of the Florida of old, including cigar-makers and mermaids.

TOP REASONS TO GO

★ **Miami:** A vibrant, multicultural metropolis that buzzes both day and night.

★ **Beaches:** Surf-pounded on the Atlantic coast, powdery and pure white on the Gulf.

★ **Key West:** Quirky, fun, and tacky, it's both family friendly and decidedly not.

★ **Golf:** Oceanfront and inland, some of the country's finest links are found here.

★ **Theme Parks:** The state has some of the biggest and best, not all of them Disney.

★ **Family Fun:** From shelling in Sanibel to meeting astronauts at Kennedy Space Center.

Fodor's FLORIDA 2014

Publisher: Amanda D'Acierno, *Senior Vice President*

Editorial: Arabella Bowen, *Executive Editorial Director*; Linda Cabasin, *Editorial Director*

Design: Fabrizio La Rocca, *Vice President, Creative Director*; Tina Malaney, *Associate Art Director*; Chie Ushio, *Senior Designer*; Ann McBride, *Production Designer*

Photography: Melanie Marin, *Associate Director of Photography*; Jessica Parkhill and Jennifer Romains, *Researchers*

Maps: Rebecca Baer, *Senior Map Editor*; Mark Stroud (Moon Street Cartography), David Lindroth, *Cartographers*

Production: Linda Schmidt, *Managing Editor*; Evangelos Vasilakis, *Associate Managing Editor*; Angela L. McLean, *Senior Production Manager*

Sales: Jacqueline Lebow, *Sales Director*

Marketing & Publicity: Heather Dalton, *Marketing Director*; Katherine Fleming, *Senior Publicist*

Business & Operations: Susan Livingston, *Vice President, Strategic Business Planning*; Sue Daulton, *Vice President, Operations*

Fodors.com: Megan Bell, *Executive Director, Revenue & Business Development*; Yasmin Marinaro, *Senior Director, Marketing & Partnerships*

Writers: Kate Bradshaw, Jennifer Greenhill-Taylor, Rona Grindin, Lynne Helm, Jennie Hess, Sharon Wrightman Hoffmann, Jill Martin, Steve Master, Gary McKechnie, Megan Peck, Paul Rubio, Jamie Wilson, Ashley Wright

Editors: Doug Stallings, Amanda Theunissen

Production Editor: Elyse Rozelle

ISBN 978-0-7704-3256-0

ISSN 0193-9556

All details in this book are based on information supplied to us at press time. Always confirm information when it matters, especially if you're making a detour to visit a specific place. Fodor's expressly disclaims any liability, loss, or risk, personal or otherwise, that is incurred as a consequence of the use of any of the contents of this book.

SPECIAL SALES

This book is available at special discounts for bulk purchases for sales promotions or premiums. For more information, e-mail specialmarkets@randomhouse.com

PRINTED IN COLOMBIA

10 9 8 7 6 5 4 3 2 1

CONTENTS

Fodor's Features

MAPS

ABOUT
THIS GUIDE

Fodor's Recommendations

Everything in this guide is worth doing—
we don't cover what isn't—but exceptional sights, hotels, and restaurants are
recognized with additional accolades.
Fodor's Choice★ indicates our top recommendations; and **Best Bets** call attention to
notable hotels and restaurants in various
categories. Care to nominate a new place?
Visit Fodors.com/contact-us.

Trip Costs

We list prices wherever possible to help
you budget well. Hotel and restaurant
price categories from $ to $$$$ are noted
alongside each recommendation. For
hotels, we include the lowest cost of a
standard double room in high season.
For restaurants, we cite the average price
of a main course at dinner or, if dinner
isn't served, at lunch. For attractions,
we always list adult admission fees; dis-
counts are usually available for children,
students, and senior citizens.

Hotels

Our local writers vet every hotel to recom-
mend the best overnights in each price cat-
egory, from budget to expensive. Unless
otherwise specified, you can expect pri-
vate bath, phone, and TV in your room.
For expanded hotel reviews, facilities, and
deals visit Fodors.com.

Restaurants

Unless we state otherwise, restaurants are
open for lunch and dinner daily. We men-
tion dress code only when there's a specific
requirement and reservations only when
they're essential or not accepted. To make
restaurant reservations, visit Fodors.com.

Credit Cards

The hotels and restaurants in this guide
typically accept credit cards. If not, we'll
say so.

Top Picks
★ Fodor's Choice

Listings
✉ Address
✉ Branch address
☎ Telephone
🖷 Fax
⊕ Website
✉ E-mail
🎫 Admission fee
☉ Open/closed times
Ⓜ Subway
✛ Directions or Map coordinates

Hotels & Restaurants
🏨 Hotel
⇲ Number of rooms
🍽 Meal plans
✗ Restaurant
🍴 Reservations
👔 Dress code
🚫 No credit cards
$ Price

Other
⇨ See also
☞ Take note
⛳ Golf facilities

EXPERIENCE FLORIDA

WHAT'S WHERE

The following numbers refer to chapters.

2 Miami and Miami Beach. Greater Miami is hot—and we're not just talking about the weather. Art deco buildings and balmy beaches set the scene. Vacations here are as much about lifestyle as locale, so prepare for power shopping, club-hopping, and decadent dining.

3 The Everglades. Covering more than 1.5 million acres, the fabled "River of Grass" is the state's greatest natural treasure. Biscayne National Park (95% of which is underwater) runs a close second. It's the largest marine park in the United States.

4 The Florida Keys. This slender necklace of landfalls, strung together by a 113-mile highway, marks the southern edge of the continental United States. It's nirvana for anglers, divers, literature lovers, and Jimmy Buffett wannabes.

5 Fort Lauderdale with Broward County. The town *Where the Boys Are* has grown up. The beaches that first attracted college kids are now complemented by luxe lodgings and upscale entertainment options.

6 Palm Beach with the Treasure Coast. This area scores points for diversity. Palm Beach and environs are famous for their golden sand and glitzy residents, whereas the Treasure Coast has unspoiled natural delights.

7 The Tampa Bay Area. Tampa's Busch Gardens and Ybor City are only part of the area's appeal. Culture vultures flock to St. Petersburg and Sarasota for concerts and museums, and eco-adventurers veer north to the Nature Coast.

8 The Lower Gulf Coast. Blessed with beaches, this was the last bit of coast to be settled. But as Naples's manicured golf greens and Fort Myers's mansions-cum-museums prove, it is far from uncivilized.

9 Orlando and Environs. Theme parks are what draw most visitors to the area, yet downtown Orlando, Kissimmee, and Winter Park have enough sights, shops, and restaurants to make them destinations in their own right.

10 Walt Disney World. The granddaddy of attractions, Disney is four theme parks in one—Magic Kingdom, Animal Kingdom, Epcot, and Hollywood Studios. Plus, it has a pair of water parks and Downtown Disney (an entertainment zone featuring Cirque du Soleil).

11 Universal Orlando. The movies are brought to life at Universal Studios, while Islands of Adventure delivers gravity-defying rides and special-effects surprises—and the Wizarding World of Harry Potter. Nearby Wet 'n Wild is full of watery adventures.

12 SeaWorld Orlando. Marine mammals perform in SeaWorld's meticulously choreographed shows, and thrill seekers find their adrenaline rush on coasters. Sister park Discovery Cove offers a day-long, swim-with-the-dolphins escape. At Aquatica water park, one slide even dips into a dolphin habitat.

13 Northeast Florida. Though time rewinds in historic St. Augustine, it's on fast-forward in Daytona Beach and the Space Coast, where horse-drawn carriages are replaced by race cars and rocket ships.

14 The Panhandle. Southern gentility and redneck rambunctiousness make the Panhandle a colorful place—but it's the green gulf waters and sugar-white sand that keep devotees coming back.

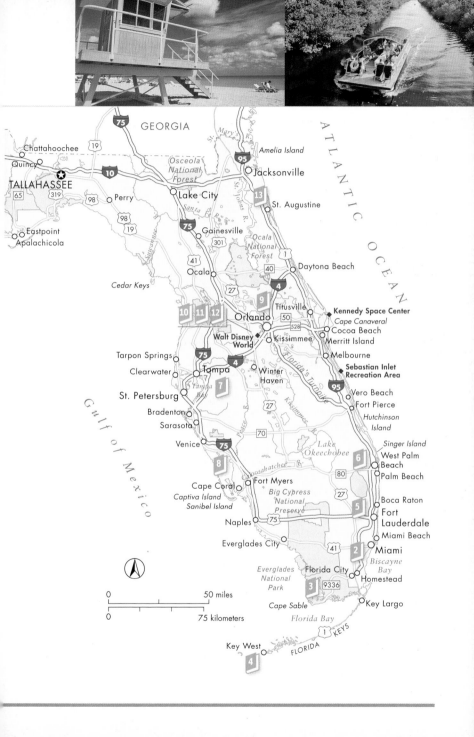

GEORGIA

ATLANTIC OCEAN

Chattahoochee
Quincy
TALLAHASSEE
Perry
Eastpoint
Apalachicola

Osceola
National
Forest

Amelia Island
Jacksonville
Lake City
St. Augustine
Gainesville

Cedar Keys

Ocala
National
Forest

Daytona Beach
Ocala

Titusville
Orlando
Kennedy Space Center
Cape Canaveral
Cocoa Beach
Merritt Island
Melbourne
Sebastian Inlet
Recreation Area

Walt Disney
World
Kissimmee

Tarpon Springs
Clearwater
Tampa
Winter
Haven
St. Petersburg
Bradenton
Sarasota
Vero Beach
Fort Pierce
Hutchinson
Island
Venice

Gulf of Mexico

Lake
Okeechobee
Singer Island
West Palm
Beach
Palm Beach

Cape Coral
Fort Myers
Captiva Island
Sanibel Island
Big Cypress
National
Preserve
Boca Raton
Fort
Lauderdale
Naples
Miami Beach
Everglades City
Miami
Biscayne
Bay
Florida City
Homestead
Everglades
National
Park
Cape Sable
Key Largo
Florida Bay

Key West
FLORIDA KEYS

0   50 miles
0   75 kilometers

FLORIDA TOP ATTRACTIONS

Walt Disney World

(A) Like one of Snow White's dwarfs, Orlando was sleepy until Uncle Walt turned this swampland into the world's most famous tourist attraction. Nowadays Walt Disney World is a 39-square-mile complex and growing, with four separate parks, scores of hotels, and satellite attractions. Thanks to innovative rides and dazzling animatronics, these parks feature prominently in every child's holiday fantasy. Walt Disney World also has grown-up amenities, including championship golf courses, sublime hotels and spas, and fine restaurants. If you have time for only one megapark, choose the original, Walt Disney World's Magic Kingdom ➪ *Chapter 10*.

South Beach

(B) You can't miss the distinctive forms, vibrant colors, and extravagant flourishes of SoBe's architectural gems. The world's largest concentration of art deco edifices is right here. The neighborhood also has enough beautiful people to qualify for the Register of Hippest Places. The glitterati, along with assorted vacationing hedonists, are drawn by über-trendy shops and a surfeit of celeb-studded clubs. Divine eateries are the icing—umm, better make that the ganache—on South Beach's proverbial cake ➪ *Chapter 2*.

Key West

(C) These 800-plus islands in the Florida Keys are at once a unique landmass and a mass of contradictions. At the far end of this island chain, Key West is the main attraction. Its laid-back vibe is intoxicating. Eating, drinking, water sports, sunset cruises, kayaking, and more drinking are high on the agenda. Visitors never grow tired of the walking tours through the gingerbread-house-filled streets and channeling the spirit of Ernest Hemingway, who lived and worked here. Today, touring his former digs and toasting his memory at Sloppy Joe's Bar on Duval Street is almost mandatory ➪ *Chapter 4*.

Shopping in Fort Lauderdale and Miami

(D) The Sunshine State is a shopaholic's dream. Visitors travel from overseas with the sole purpose of shopping weekends at Fort Lauderdale's 2-mile, alligator-shape Sawgrass Mills outlet mall. The alfresco addition to the mall, the Shops at Colonnade, caters to well-heeled patrons with a David Yurman jewelry outlet and other shops, including Valentino, Prada, Burberry, Kate Spade New York, and Barneys New York. For more high-end shoppers, Bal Harbour Shops in the swanky Miami suburb is a collection of 100 haute couture shops, boutiques, and department stores. Restaurants and cafés, in tropical garden settings, overflow with style-conscious diners ⇨ *Chapters 2 and 5.*

Universal Orlando

(E) With rides and attractions more geared toward adults and teens, Universal's two theme parks—Universal Studios and Islands of Adventure—deliver gravity-defying rides and special-effects extravaganzas based on popular television shows and films. The Wizarding World of Harry Potter is the newest "land" at Islands of Adventure, where you'll get to see Hogwarts Castle and drink butter beer! ⇨ *Chapter 11.*

Kennedy Space Center

(F) Though there are enough wide-open expanses to justify the area's moniker, it was NASA that put the "space" in Space Coast—and this is its star attraction. Space memorabilia and aeronautic antiques, ranging from Redstone rockets to the *Apollo XIV* command module, turn an outing here into a trip back in time for anyone who lived through the space race. More down-to-earth types can also visit the Merritt Island National Wildlife Refuge (originally created as a buffer for the space program) and Canaveral National Seashore ⇨ *Chapter 13.*

Tampa Bay

(G) As a vibrant city with exceptional beaches, Tampa Bay is perfect for indecisive folks who want to enjoy surf and sand without sacrificing urban experiences. Families will love Busch Gardens, a major zoo and theme park. Football and hockey fans will relish the chance to see the Buccaneers and Lightning play. Baseball is big, too: the Rays are based here, and the Yankees descend annually for spring training ⇨ *Chapter 7.*

The Dalí Museum

(H) St. Petersburg is home to a museum dedicated to the work of Salvador Dalí, showcasing the most comprehensive collection of the surrealist's artwork. This is the kind of first-class museum you'd expect to find in Paris or Madrid, but instead it's here on the Gulf Coast. The state-of-the-art glass building housing the museum is quite a spectacle in and of itself ⇨ *Chapter 7.*

Sportfishing

(I) Islamorada in the Florida Keys holds steadfast to its claim as Sportfishing Capital of the World. Up in the Panhandle, Destin proves it is the World's Luckiest Fishing Village each October by inviting anglers young and old to compete in the monthlong Destin Fishing Rodeo. However, if you'd prefer to throw fish rather than catch them, head to Pensacola in late April for the Interstate Mullet Toss. (Participants line up to throw dead fish across the Florida–Alabama state line.) ⇨ *Chapter 14.*

Surfing in Cocoa Beach

(J) Cocoa Beach, on the northeast coast, is Surf City for Floridians. Baby boomers may remember it as the place where Major Nelson dreamed of Jeannie. The community is better known today as the hometown of surfing's biggest celeb, Kelly Slater. He has won a record-breaking 10 world championships, and totally

tubular types can learn to emulate him at the Ron Jon Surf School ⇨ *Chapter 13.*

Palm Beach

(K) If money could talk, you'd hardly be able to hear above the din in Palm Beach. The upper crust started calling it home—during winter at least—in the early 1900s. And today it remains a ritzy, glitzy enclave for both old money and the nouveau riche (a coterie led by the Donald himself, who owns the landmark Mar-a-Lago Club). Simply put, Palm Beach is the sort of place where shopping is a full-time pursuit and residents don't just wear Polo—they play it. Ooh and aah to your heart's content; then, for more conspicuous consumption, continue south on the aptly named Gold Coast ⇨ *Chapter 6.*

Broward's Inland Waterways

(L) Mariners should set their compass for Fort Lauderdale (aka the Venice of America), where vessels from around the world moor along some two dozen finger isles between the beach and the mainland. Tourists can cruise Broward County's 300 miles of inland waterways by water taxi and tour boat, or bob around the Atlantic in a chartered yacht. If you're in a buying mood, come in late October for the annual Fort Lauderdale International Boat Show. Billed as the world's largest, it has $3 billion worth of boats in every conceivable size, shape, and price range ⇨ *Chapter 5.*

Little Havana

(M) On the streets of Miami's Little Havana, just west of downtown, salsa tunes blare and the smell of spicy chorizo fills the air. (You can get a good whiff of tobacco, too, thanks to the cigar makers who still hand-roll their products here.) For nearly 50 years, the neighborhood's undisputed heart has been Calle Ocho, the commercial thoroughfare that hosts Carnaval Miami. The roaring 10-day block party each March culminates with the world's longest conga line. Ambience- and amenity-wise, it is as close as you'll get to Cuba without running afoul of the federal government ⇨ *Chapter 2.*

The Everglades

(N) No trip to southern Florida is complete without seeing the Everglades. At its heart is a river—50 miles wide but merely 6 inches deep—flowing from Lake Okeechobee into Florida Bay. For an up-close look, speed demons can board an airboat that careens through the marshy waters. Purists, alternately, may placidly canoe or kayak within the boundaries of Everglades National Park. Just remember to keep your hands in the boat. The critters that call this unique ecosystem home (alligators, Florida panthers, and cottonmouth snakes for starters) can add real bite to your visit! ⇨ *Chapter 3.*

Sanibel Island

(O) Ready to do something slightly more vigorous than applying SPF 45 and rolling over? Trade beach-bumming for beachcombing in Sanibel, the Shell Capital of the World. Conchs, cockles, clams, coquinas—they're all here (the bounty is caused by this barrier island's unusual east–west orientation). Of course, if you'd rather construct sand castles than do the Sanibel Stoop, you need only cross the 3-mile causeway to Fort Myers Beach. It has the finest building material and, every November, professional and

1

amateur aficionados prove it during the American SandSculpting Championship ⇨ *Chapter 8.*

Ringling Center for the Arts

(P) Sarasota, once winter headquarters for Ringling Bros. and Barnum & Bailey, is proud of its circus heritage. Ringling's former 32-room, 15-bathroom mansion is now the site of the Florida State University's Ringling Center for the Cultural Arts. Within this center, visitors who can't get enough of sawdust and sequins can see an impressive collection of vintage costumes, props, and parade wagons at the stunning Ringling Circus Museum. In addition, the center's John and Mable Ringling Museum of Art showcases 500 years of art, including an impressive collection of tapestries and paintings by Rubens. The adjacent Tibbals Learning Center houses a mind-boggling ¾-inch-scale miniature circus with almost a million pieces ⇨ *Chapter 8.*

St. Augustine

(Q) History comes to life in St. Augustine . . . and the same can perhaps be said of the undead. Ghosts are plentiful, thanks to all the pirates, plunderers, and other lost souls who formerly lived in this deceptively quiet city. To hear lurid lore about local haunts, sign on for one of the nightly outings organized by Ghost Tours of St. Augustine. These 90-minute lantern-lighted walks recount spirited stories full of goose bump–inducing details. You can also opt for a trolley ride and enter the old jail if you dare, or take a cruise through the harbor shadows in the summer. Top off your tour with an overnight stay at St. Francis Inn (St. Augustine's oldest hostelry) or the Casablanca Inn: both are reputedly haunted ⇨ *Chapter 13.*

WHEN TO GO

Although Florida is a year-round vacation venue, it divides the calendar into regional tourism seasons. Holidays and school breaks are major factors. However, the clincher is weather, with the best months being designated as peak periods.

High season in southern Florida starts with the run-up to Christmas and continues through Easter. Snowbirds migrate down then to escape frosty weather back home, and festivalgoers flock in because major events are held this time of year to avoid summer's searing heat and high humidity. Winter is also *the* time to visit the Everglades, as temperatures, mosquito activity, and water levels are all lower (making wildlife easier to spot).

Northern Florida, conversely, receives the greatest influx of visitors from Memorial Day to Labor Day. Costs are highest then, but so are temperatures. (In winter, when the mercury dips into the 40s, you'd get a chilly reception on Panhandle beaches.) Specific areas, like Panama City Beach or Daytona Beach, attract throngs—and thongs—during spring break, too. In the latter location, expect revved-up revelers during Speedweeks (late January and February) and Bike Week (early March).

Thanks to its theme parks, Central Florida is a magnet for children, meaning the largest crowds gather, logically enough, whenever class lets out. Lineups at attractions do shrink after they return to school, though this area's hopping all year, with large numbers of international families and kid-free adults coming in the off-season. Spring and fall shoulder seasons are the optimal time to visit, both weatherwise and pricewise.

Climate

Florida is rightly called the Sunshine State—areas like Tampa Bay report 361 days of sunshine a year! But it could also be dubbed the Humid State. From June through September, 90% humidity levels aren't uncommon, nor are accompanying thunderstorms. In fact, more than half of the state's rain falls during these months. Florida's two-sided coastline also makes it a target for tropical storms. Hurricane season officially begins June 1 and ends November 30.

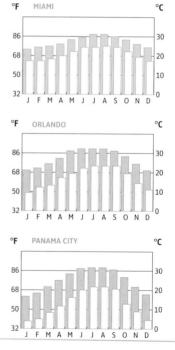

FAQS

I'm not crazy about spending seven nights in hotels. Any affordable alternatives? If you want to pretend you're lucky enough to live here, try a vacation rental. Aside from providing privacy, rentals let you set your own schedule and do your own cooking. The caveat is that you may have to rent in weekly—not nightly—increments. Several companies specialize in the Orlando area, Magical Memories (☎ 866/535–7851 ⊕ *www. magicalmemories.com*) being one reliable bet. But in terms of coverage, geographically and pricewise, HomeAway (☎ 877/228–3145 ⊕ *www.homeaway. com*) wins, listing more than 20,000 Floridian condos, cottages, beach houses, and villas. ⇨ *Apartment and House Rentals under Accommodations in Travel Smart Florida.*

Will I need a car? Public transportation is limited here. So unless you'll be spending your whole vacation on-site at Walt Disney World (where complimentary shuttles are available to resort guests) or in Miami Beach (where dense traffic and limited parking is the norm), having a vehicle is recommended. Renting one on arrival is wise, unless you drive your own. To make car time less tedious, consider occasionally taking the road less traveled. The National Scenic Byways Program website (⊕ *www.byways.org*) spotlights memorable routes within the state, including the Overseas Highway, which has been designated as an "All-American Road" and is one of only 31 roads countrywide to be so honored.

How do I pick between Orlando's parks and Tampa's Busch Gardens? That's a tough call, especially if you haven't yet seen newer attractions like Manta at Sea-World or Jungala at Busch Gardens. The good news is you don't have to choose, because the Busch Gardens Shuttle Express (☎ 407/423–5566 ⊕ *www. mearstransportation.com*) offers same-day round-trip service between designated locations in Orlando and the Tampa venue for free when you buy a ticket to Busch Gardens, but you may arrive at the park as late as 11:30 am and will return whenever the park closes.

Is Miami OK for families? Absolutely. Despite all the attention paid to G-strings, it retains areas with genuine G-rated appeal. Beyond the beaches, attractions like the interactive Children's Museum and MiaSci (a museum of science) draw kids in droves. Want to go wild? Bypass the nightclubs and head instead to Zoo Miami or the Seaquarium. If you dream of being named "best parent ever," sign your offspring up for a sleepover at the former or a dolphin swim at the latter.

What about hurricanes? The hurricane season begins on June 1 and lasts through November 1 (roughly half the year). However, big storms are much more likely in August and September. Chances are, you'll be just fine if you travel to Florida in June or July, though it's always a good idea to buy travel insurance in case something does happen. In the summer, frequent afternoon thunderstorms are common, especially inland in places like Orlando. On the coast, the weather is almost universally hot and muggy, and rain is common, especially later in the summer.

IF YOU LIKE

Animal Encounters

Florida is home to one supersize mouse and makes an ideal habitat for party animals. Yet there are other types of wildlife here, too. In terms of biodiversity, the state ranks third in the country, with approximately 1,200 different kinds of critters.

■ **Alligators.** Florida has more than 1.3 million resident alligators. You can witness them doing inane tricks at places like **Gatorland** (⇨ Chapter 9), but gator spotting in the wild is far more rewarding. Everglades National Park teems with gators. The best place to get up close and personal with them is **Shark Valley** (⇨ Chapter 3), in the north of the national park.

■ **Birds.** Poised on two major migratory routes, Florida draws about 500 species of birds—and the 2,000-mile **Great Florida Birding Trail** (⇨ Chapter 8) helps you track them down. Through detailed guides and highway signs, it identifies sites where you may spy anything from bald eagles to burrowing owls.

■ **Manatees.** They're nicknamed sea cows and resemble walruses. But Florida's official marine mammals are most closely related to elephants, which may account for their slow pace and hefty frames. For a chance at swimming with manatees in the wild, take an organized pontoon ride through **Crystal River** (⇨ Chapter 7), near the Upper Gulf Coast.

■ **Sea Turtles.** Ready for a late-night rendezvous with the massive leatherbacks and loggerheads that lumber onto Floridian beaches to lay their eggs between March and October? **Archie Carr National Wildlife Refuge** (⇨ Chapter 6), the Western Hemisphere's largest loggerhead nesting site, organizes free turtle watches in June and July.

Life in the Fast Lane

The Sunshine State has been satisfying visitors' need for speed ever since Henry Ford and his snowbird buddies started using Ormond Beach as a test track. Today roller coasters, stock cars, supersonic jets, and spaceships add momentum to your vacation.

■ **Daytona Beach.** Daytona 500, NASCAR's most prestigious event, pulls in legions of devotees each February. But any time of year you can slip into a driving suit and then into the driver's seat of a Winston Cup–style stock car, courtesy of the Richard Petty Driving Experience at **Daytona International Speedway.** See ⇨ Chapter 13.

■ **Kennedy Space Center.** Whether you admire Buzz Aldrin or Buzz Lightyear, this spot has the right stuff. See a rocket launch or take your own giant leap with the **Astronaut Training Experience.** The half-day program consists of realistic training exercises culminating in a simulated mission. See ⇨ Chapter 13.

■ **Pensacola.** The **National Museum of Naval Aviation** displays 150-plus military aircraft and has motion-based simulators that let you "fly" an F/A-18. Better yet, the U.S. Navy Precision Flight Team (familiar to most of us as the Blue Angels) is based here, so you may get to observe them in action at 700 mph. See ⇨ Chapter 14.

■ **Tampa.** If you think the pursuit of happiness is a high-speed activity, head for **Busch Gardens,** Florida's premier roller-coaster location. SheiKra is one of the world's tallest dive coasters, Kumba features one of the world's largest vertical loops, and Montu (a gut-churning inverted coaster) delivers a g-force of 3.85. See ⇨ Chapter 7.

Something Old, Something New

You don't have to look far for "New Florida." It's evident in skyscrapers and sprawling suburbs, in malls, multiplexes, and the ubiquitous condo complexes that obscure parts of the coast. Yet it is easy enough to find reminders of the state's rich past.

■ **Apalachicola.** A booming cotton-and-lumber industry turned this Panhandle town into a bustling port in the 19th century. Now it's part of the Forgotten Coast. Hundreds of preserved buildings, ranging from antebellum warehouses to gracious Victorian-style homes, give it a time-warped appeal. See ⇨ *Chapter 14.*

■ **Coral Gables.** You can soak up 1920s architecture in Miami Beach. But in nearby Coral Gables you can soak *in* it at the **Venetian Pool**, a vintage municipal lagoon fashioned from a quarry. Back in the day it attracted Johnny Weissmuller, Esther Williams, and other legendary swimmers. See ⇨ *Chapter 2.*

■ **Cross Creek.** You can tour the Cracker-style house where Marjorie Kinnan Rawlings wrote The Yearling at **Marjorie Kinnan Rawlings Historic State Park** from October through July and visit the surrounding farm and grove year-round. See ⇨ *Chapter 13.*

■ **St. Augustine.** Fortify yourself at **Castillo de San Marcos.** Built by the Spanish to defend *La Florida*, this formidable 17th-century structure is America's oldest masonry fort. Even kids whose interest in architecture stops at Cinderella Castle will be impressed by its turrets, moat, and double drawbridge. See ⇨ *Chapter 13.*

Hitting the Greens

With more courses than any other state and weather that allows for year-round play, Florida is a dream destination for golfers. Ready to go for it? The tourism board's new, dedicated golf site (⊕ *www. golf.visitflorida.com*) will point you in the right direction.

■ **The Breakers.** Floridians' fascination with golf began in 1897 when the state's first course opened at this Palm Beach resort. (Rockefellers, Vanderbilts, and Astors are all listed in the guest book.) Today, the original 70-par **Ocean Course** offers spectacular Atlantic views and challenging shots on 140 acres. See ⇨ *Chapter 6.*

■ **Doral Golf Resort & Spa.** The **Blue Monster** understandably grabs the spotlight here: the par-72 course has been a stop on the PGA tour for more than 45 years. But the Miami resort has four other championship courses (including the new Jim McLean Signature Course) as well as McLean's own golf school. See ⇨ *Chapter 2.*

■ **PGA Village.** Owned and operated by the PGA, this Port St. Lucie venue boasts three championship courses designed by Tom Fazio and Pete Dye, plus a 35-acre **Golf Learning and Performance Center** that can turn weekend duffers into scratch players. A free museum of golf memorabilia is also on-site. See ⇨ *Chapter 6.*

■ **Reunion Resort.** This spot near Orlando just keeps upping its game. Not content with having courses laid out by Tom Watson, Arnold Palmer, and Jack Nicklaus, it recently added the Annika Academy, a golf school named for LPGA phenom Annika Sörenstam and overseen by her coach, Henri Reis. See ⇨ *Chapter 9.*

FLORIDA
BEST BEACHES

Bahia Honda State Park

Though the Florida Keys aren't renowned for beautiful sandy beaches, this is an exception. The 524-acre park has three superb beaches over 2.5 miles of sandy coastline at the crossroads of the Atlantic and the gulf, idyllic for swimming, snorkeling, kayaking, and fishing. Atlantic-facing Sandspur beach flaunts long stretches of powdery sands. See ⇨ *Chapter 4.*

Bowman's Beach, Sanibel Island

On Sanibel's secluded northwest end, this beach doubles as a shell hunter's paradise and a beach wanderer's great escape. For the former, the likelihood of leaving with a bag full of gorgeous shells is high. For the latter, the chance of serene, inspiring vistas is guaranteed. See ⇨ *Chapter 8.*

Caladesi Island State Park

Accessible only by ferry from Honeymoon Island State Recreation Area, this park offers pure white beaches, beautiful sunsets, and excellent bird-watching. See ⇨ *Chapter 7.*

Clearwater Beach

At what is arguably the state's best beach for families, kids and parents alike love the white stands and shallow, clear, warm waters by day, followed by sunset celebrations nightly, complete with musicians and artists. See ⇨ *Chapter 7.*

Fort de Soto Beach

Another winner of "America's Best Beach," the 1,136-acre park lies at the mouth of Tampa Bay, spread over five islands and housing 7 miles of beach, two fishing piers, and a 4-mile hiking/skating trail. The beaches are super packed on weekends but splendidly quiet on weekdays. See ⇨ *Chapter 7.*

Fort Lauderdale Beach

The former spring break capital now plays host to a reinvented, more upscale beachfront; however, the downy sands and crystalline waters from the days of

Where the Boys Are haven't changed. The beach "scene" is found between Las Olas and Sunrise boulevards. See ⇨ *Chapter 5.*

John Pennekamp Coral Reef State Park

Florida's best bet for diving and snorkeling, this state park adjacent to the Florida Keys National Marine Sanctuary encompasses 78 square miles of ecological treasures, the majority of which are found underwater. Although the beaches here do attract families, the real draw is experiencing the underwater world of the 600 varieties of fish that call this park home. See ⇨ *Chapter 4.*

Panama City Beach

It may be Spring Break Capital of the World come March and April, but the rest of the year this 17-mile expanse of snowy-white sand and sparking emerald-green water attracts families from all across the Southeast to enjoy some awesome fun in the sun. Pier Park offers great shopping and watering holes on the streets opposite the beachfront hotels. See ⇨ *Chapter 14.*

Siesta Key Beach

Crowned "America's Best Beach" in 2012, this one boasts the finest quartz sands in the world. The sand is so fine and powdery it appears like piles of flour and squeaks under your feet when you walk on it. The 40-acre beach park of this island is exceptionally wide and long, providing ample space for families, romantics, and Sunday's Drum Circle celebration. See ⇨ *Chapter 8.*

South Beach

The legend of beautiful people is very much a reality on the sands parallel to deco-drenched Ocean Drive from 5th to 15th street, and upscale Collins Avenue from 15th to 23rd Street. Expect diesel bodies, plastic surgery, hunky gay guys, pretentious partygoers, and random families coming to see what the fuss is all about. See ⇨ *Chapter 2.*

GREAT ITINERARIES

Florida is a long, lean peninsula anchored to the mainland by a "panhandle," so the distances between destinations may surprise you. Panama City, for example, is closer to New Orleans than to Orlando, and Tallahassee, though only 8 miles from the Georgia border, is a whopping 465 miles from Miami Beach. Key West, similarly, is 494 miles from Jacksonville, yet only 90 miles from Cuba. When plotting your dream trip, study a map to determine how easy it will be to connect the dots—or simply follow one of these tried-and-true itineraries. If you have two or more weeks to drive through the state, you can do them all.

3 to 4 Days: Orlando

Anyone can easily spend a week doing the attractions. (Remember, Walt Disney World alone is roughly the size of San Francisco.) But unless you're a die-hard ride hound, a few days will let you sample them and still enjoy some of Orlando's other amenities. The hard part is deciding where to start. The Magic Kingdom has the greatest concentration of classic sites, and Epcot proves this really is a small world. Film buffs can get reel at Disney's Hollywood Studios or Universal Studios, and thrill seekers can get their hearts pumping at Islands of Adventure. As for wildlife encounters, you can go like Dolittle at Disney's Animal Kingdom or SeaWorld. On top of all that, there's a sufficient number of water parks—including both old favorites such as Wet 'n Wild and newer entries like Aquatica—to make you forget you're inland. In the city itself, art connoisseurs can survey the collection of modern paintings at the Orlando Museum of Art, and flower fans can check out Orlando blooms in the 50-acre Harry P. Leu Gardens. Boaters can take advantage of the area's numerous lakes, and golfers can link up on courses designed by the sport's biggest stars.

2 to 3 Days: Panhandle

Let's be honest: people come to Florida's Panhandle primarily for those white-sand beaches. Some of the best in the country are along this coastline, affectionately known as the Redneck Riviera. But it's possible to work on a tan and still work in some sightseeing. At Gulf Islands National Seashore, for instance, you can soak up the sun, cast a fishing net, take a hike, tour centuries-old forts, and have time left for a trip into historic Pensacola. After beach time around Apalachicola Bay, head north through the canopied roads around Apalachicola National Forest. Then get a true taste of the Old South in moss-draped Tallahassee. Yet another day could be devoted to glorious Grayton Beach, where diving and kayaking can be followed up with a relaxing drive along Route 30A to cute, nostalgia-inducing communities like WaterColor and Seaside. When planning your trip, bear in mind that the Panhandle not only has its own time zone but its own tourism season—summer, and that's prime time for beach-going.

2 to 3 Days: Space Coast

If you need proof that Florida was the first part of the United States to be settled, look no farther than St. Augustine. It was founded by the Spanish in 1565, and visiting Castillo de San Marcos (its colonial-era fortress) or strolling the streets of the Old City that grew up around it allows you to experience life in the past lane. Taking in the stellar sites at the 150,000-acre Kennedy Space Center has just the opposite effect. Although it may seem centuries removed, the nation's oldest continuously inhabited city is less than two hours by car from our launch pad to the moon. Between them, you can hear the call of the wild at Merritt Island National

Wildlife Refuge, catch a wave like local surfing legend Kelly Slater, or blissfully hit the beach at Canaveral National Seashore. (The 24-mile preserve remains undeveloped, so you lounge in the shelter of dunes, not the shadow of high-rises.) Racier options also await—just reset your GPS for Daytona Beach. Its International Speedway, which has hosted NASCAR's Daytona 500 every February since 1959, is a must-see for stock-car enthusiasts, and there's plenty to do here year-round even if it's not a race day.

2 to 3 Days: Gold Coast and Treasure Coast

The opulent mansions of Palm Beach's Ocean Boulevard give you a glimpse of how the richer half lives. For exclusive boutique shopping, art gallery browsing, and glittery sightseeing, sybarites should wander down "The Avenue" (that's Worth Avenue to non–Palm Beachers). The sporty set will find dozens of places to tee up (hardly surprising given that the PGA is based here), along with tennis courts, polo clubs, even a croquet center. Those who'd like to see more of the Gold Coast can continue traveling south through Boca Raton to Fort Lauderdale (justifiably known as the Yachting Capital of the World). But to balance the

highbrow with the low-key, turn northward for a tour of the Treasure Coast. Notable for its outdoor opportunities and Old Florida ambience, this region was named for the booty spilled by a fleet of Spanish galleons shipwrecked here in 1715, and for centuries treasure kept washing ashore south of Sebastian Inlet. These days you're more likely to discover manatees and golden surfing opportunities. You can also look for the sea turtles that lay their own little treasures in the sands from March through October.

2 to 3 Days: Miami Area

Greater Miami lays claim to the country's most celebrated strand—South Beach—and lingering on it tops most tourist itineraries. (The Ocean Drive section, lined with edgy clubs, boutiques, and eateries, is where the see-and-be-seen crowd gathers.) Once you've checked out the candy-color art deco architecture, park yourself to ogle the parade of stylish people. Or join them in browsing Lincoln Road Mall, and be sure to check out its latest addition, the glittering Frank Gehry–designed New World Symphony. Later, merengue over to Calle Ocho, the epicenter of Miami's Cuban community. Elsewhere in the area, Coconut Grove, Coral Gables, and the Miami Design District (an 18-block area crammed with showrooms and galleries) warrant a visit as well. Because Miami is the sole U.S. city with two national parks and a national preserve in its backyard, it is also a convenient base for eco-excursions. You can take a day trip to the Everglades; get a spectacular view of the reefs from a glass-bottom boat in Biscayne National Park; and then spot some rare wood storks in Big Cypress Swamp, which is best explored via Alligator Alley (Interstate 75).

2 to 3 Days: Florida Keys

Some dream of "sailing away to Key Largo," others of "wasting away again in Margaritaville." In any case, almost everybody equates the Florida Keys with relaxation. And they live up to their reputation, thanks to offbeat attractions and that fabled come-as-you-are, do-as-you-please vibe. Key West, alternately known as the Conch Republic, is a good place to get initiated. The Old Town has a funky, laid-back feel. So take a leisurely walk, pay your respects to Ernest Hemingway, and then (if you haven't imbibed too much at one of the renowned watering holes) rent a moped to tour the rest of the island. Clear waters and abundant marine life make underwater activities another must. After scoping out the parrotfish, you can head back into town and join local Parrotheads in a Jimmy Buffett sing-along. When retracing your route to the mainland, plan a last pit stop at Bahia Honda State Park (it has ranger-led activities plus the Keys' best beach) or John Pennekamp Coral Reef State Park, which offers unparalleled snorkeling and scuba diving.

TIPS

Now that one-way airfares are commonplace, vacationers visiting multiple destinations can fly into and out of different airports. Rent a car in between, picking it up at your point of arrival and leaving it at your point of departure. If you do this itinerary as an entire vacation, your best bet is to fly into and out of Orlando and rent a car from there.

Inquire about scheduled activities when visiting national and state parks or preserves. Many of them run free or low-cost ranger-led programs that run the gamut from walks and talks to campfires and canoe trips.

2 to 3 Days: Tampa Bay Area

Whether you bypassed Orlando's theme parks or simply want to add another one to your list, Busch Gardens is a logical starting point. With hair-raising rides and more than 2,000 animals, it appeals to adrenaline junkies and 'fraidy cats alike. Later you can catch a pro-sporting event (Tampa has Major League baseball, football, and hockey teams) or catch an act in the Spanish-inflected Ybor City entertainment district. If you're more interested in catching some rays, try Caladesi Island State Park to the west of the city or Fort De Soto Park at the mouth of Tampa Bay. After exploring the Riverwalk's new museums, culture vultures can take day trips to the galleries in St. Petersburg and to Sarasota's thriving arts scene. Nature lovers proceed north to Crystal River, where you can snorkel with the manatees that congregate in the warm water November through March.

MIAMI AND
MIAMI BEACH

2

Visit Fodors.com for advice, updates, and bookings

WELCOME TO MIAMI AND MIAMI BEACH

TOP REASONS TO GO

★ **The beach:**
Miami Beach has been rated as one of the 10 best in the world. White sand, warm water, and bronzed bodies everywhere provide just the right mix of relaxation and people-watching.

★ **Dining delights:**
Miami's eclectic residents have transformed the city into a museum of epicurean wonders, ranging from Cuban and Argentine fare to fusion haute cuisine.

★ **Wee-hour parties:**
A 24-hour liquor license means clubs stay open until 5 am, and after-parties go until noon the following day.

★ **Picture-perfect people:**
Miami is a watering hole for the vain and beautiful of South America, Europe, and the Northeast. Watch them—or join them—as they strut their stuff and flaunt their tans on the white beds of renowned art deco hotels.

★ **Art deco district:**
Iconic pastels and neon lights accessorize the architecture that first put South Beach on the map in the 1930s.

1 Downtown Miami.
Weave through the glass-and-steel labyrinth of new condo construction to catch a Miami Heat game at the AmericanAirlines Arena or a show at the Adrienne Arsht Center for the Performing Arts.

2 Coconut Grove. Catch dinner and a movie, listen to live music, or cruise the bohemian shops and locals' bars in this hip neighborhood.

3 Coral Gables. Dine and shop on family-friendly Miracle Mile, and take a driving tour of the Mediterranean-style mansions in the surrounding neighborhoods.

4 Key Biscayne. Pristine parks and tranquillity make this upscale enclave a total antithesis to the South Beach party.

5 Wynwood/Midtown/Design District. These three trendy, creative neighborhoods north of downtown have shops and galleries, see-and-be-seen bars, and slick restaurants.

6 Miami Beach. People-watch from sidewalk cafés and party 'til dawn at the nation's hottest clubs in South Beach. Experience the booming restaurant scene and trendy hotels of Mid-Beach. Shop and relax in posh Bal Harbour and quieter North Beach.

2

GETTING ORIENTED

Long considered the gateway to Latin America, Miami is as close to Cuba and the Caribbean as you can get within the United States. The 36-square-mile city is at the southern tip of the Florida peninsula, bordered on the east by Biscayne Bay. Over the bay lies a series of barrier islands, the largest being a thin 18-square-mile strip called Miami Beach. To the east of Miami Beach is the Atlantic Ocean. To the south are the Florida Keys.

CUBAN FOOD

If the tropical vibe has you hankering for Cuban food, you've come to the right place. Miami is the top spot in the country to enjoy authentic Cuban cooking.

The flavors and preparations of Cuban cuisine are influenced by the island nation's natural bounty (yucca, sugarcane, guava), as well as its rich immigrant history, from near (Caribbean countries) and far (Spanish and African traditions). Chefs in Miami tend to stick with the classic versions of beloved dishes, though you'll find some variation from restaurant to restaurant, as recipes have often been passed down through generations of home cooks. For a true Cuban experience, try either the popular **Versailles** (⌧ *3555 S.W. 8th St.* ☎ *305/444–0240* ⊕ *www. versaillesrestaurant.com*) or classic **La Carreta** (⌧ *3632 S.W. 8th St.* ☎ *305/444–7501*) in Little Havana, appealing to families seeking a home-cooked, Cuban-style meal. For a modern interpretation of Cuban eats, head to Coral Gable's **Havana Harry's** (⌧ *4612 S. Le Jeune Rd.* ☎ *305/661–2622*). The South Beach late-night institution **David's Café** (⌧ *1058 Collins Ave.* ☎ *305/534–8736*) is the beach's favorite Cuban hole-in-the-wall.

THE CUBAN SANDWICH

A great *cubano* (Cuban sandwich) requires pillowy Cuban bread layered with ham, garlic-citrus-marinated slow-roasted pork, Swiss cheese, and pickles (plus salami, in Tampa; lettuce and tomatoes in Key West), with butter and/or mustard. The sandwich is grilled in a sandwich press until the cheese melts and all the elements are fused together. Try one at **Enriqueta's Sandwich Shop** (⌧ *2830 N.E. 2nd Ave.* ☎ *305/573–4681* ☾ *Weekdays 6 am–4 pm, Sat. 6 am–2 pm*) in the Wynwood Arts District, or **Exquisito Restaurant** (⌧ *1510 S.W. 8th St.* ☎ *305/643–0227* ☾ *Daily 7 am–11 pm*) in Little Havana.

KEY CUBAN DISHES

ARROZ CON POLLO

This chicken-and-rice dish is Cuban comfort food. Found throughout Latin America, the Cuban version is typically seasoned with garlic, paprika, and onions, then colored golden or reddish with saffron or achiote (a seed paste), and enlivened with a sizable splash of beer near the end of cooking. Green peas and sliced, roasted red peppers are a standard topping.

BISTEC DE PALOMILLA

This thinly sliced sirloin steak is marinated in lime juice and garlic, and fried with onions. The steak is often served with chimichurri sauce, an olive oil, garlic, and cilantro sauce that sometimes comes with bread (slather bread with butter and dab on the chimichurri). Also try *ropa vieja*, a slow-cooked, shredded flank steak in a garlic-tomato sauce.

DESSERTS

Treat yourself to a slice of *tres leches* cake. The "three milks" come from the sweetened condensed milk, evaporated milk, and heavy cream that are poured over the cake until it's an utterly irresistible gooey mess. Also, don't miss the *pastelitos*, Cuban fruit-filled turnovers. Traditional flavors include plain guava, guava with cream cheese, and cream cheese with coconut. Yum!

DRINKS

Sip *guarapo* (gwa-RA-poh), a fresh sugarcane juice that isn't really as sweet as you might think, or grab a straw and enjoy a frothy *batido* (bah-TEE-doe), a Cuban-style milk shake made with tropical fruits like mango, *piña* (pineapple), or *mamey* (mah-MAY, a tropical fruit with a melon-cherry taste). For a real twist, try the *batido de trigo*—a wheat shake that will remind you of sugar-glazed breakfast cereal.

FRITAS

If you're in the mood for an inexpensive, casual Cuban meal, have a *frita*—a hamburger with distinctive Cuban flair. It's made with ground beef that's mixed with ground or finely chopped chorizo, spiced with pepper, paprika, and salt, topped with sautéed onions and shoe-string potato fries, and then served on a bun slathered with a special tomato-based ketchuplike sauce.

LECHON ASADO

Fresh ham or an entire suckling pig marinated in *mojo criollo* (parsley, garlic, sour orange, and olive oil) is roasted until fork tender and served with white rice, black beans, and *tostones* (fried plantains) or yucca (pronounced YU-kah), a starchy tuber with a mild nut taste that's often sliced into fat sticks and deep-fried like fries.

Updated by
Paul Rubio

Three-quarters of a century after the art deco movement, Miami remains one of the world's trendiest and flashiest hot spots. Luckily for visitors, South Beach is no longer the only place to stand and pose in Miami. North of downtown Miami's megamakeover, the growing Wynwood and Design districts—along with nearby Midtown—are home to Miami's hipster and fashionista scenes, and South Beach continues to extend both north and west, with the addition of new venues north of 20th Street and along the bay on West Avenue. Following the reopening of the mammoth Fontainebleau and its enclave of nightclubs and restaurants along Mid-Beach, other globally renowned resorts have moved into the neighborhood, like the Soho Beach House and Canyon Ranch.

Visit Miami today and it's hard to believe that 100 years ago it was a mosquito-infested swampland, with an Indian trading post on the Miami River. Then hotel builder Henry Flagler brought his railroad to the outpost known as Fort Dallas. Other visionaries—Carl Fisher, Julia Tuttle, William Brickell, and John Sewell, among others—set out to tame the unruly wilderness. Hotels were erected, bridges were built, the port was dredged, and electricity arrived. The narrow strip of mangrove coast was transformed into Miami Beach—and the tourists started to come. They haven't stopped since!

Greater Miami is many destinations in one. At its best it offers an unparalleled multicultural experience: melodic Latin and Caribbean tongues, international cuisines and cultural events, and an unmistakable joie de vivre—all against a beautiful beach backdrop. In Little Havana the air is tantalizing with the perfume of strong Cuban coffee. In Coconut Grove,

Caribbean steel drums ring out during the Miami/Bahamas Goombay Festival. Anytime in colorful Miami Beach, restless crowds wait for entry to the hottest new clubs.

Many visitors don't know that Miami and Miami Beach are really separate cities. Miami, on the mainland, is South Florida's commercial hub. Miami Beach, on 17 islands in Biscayne Bay, is sometimes considered America's Riviera, luring refugees from winter with its warm sunshine; sandy beaches; graceful, shady palms; and tireless nightlife. The natives know well that there's more to Greater Miami than the bustle of South Beach and its Art Deco District. In addition to well-known places such as Ocean Drive and Lincoln Road, the less reported spots—like the burgeoning Design District in Miami, the historic buildings of Coral Gables, and the secluded beaches of Key Biscayne—are great insider destinations.

PLANNING

WHEN TO GO

Miami and Miami Beach are year-round destinations. Most visitors come November through April, when the weather is close to perfect; hotels, restaurants, and attractions are busiest; and each weekend holds a festival or event. The "Season" kicks off in December with Art Basel Miami Beach, and hotel rates don't come down until after the college kids have left after spring break in late March.

It's hot and steamy from May through September, but nighttime temperatures are usually pleasant. Also, summer is a good time for the budget traveler. Many hotels lower their rates considerably, and many restaurants offer discounts—especially during **Miami Spice** in August and September, when slews of top restaurants offer special tasting menus at a steep discount. (Check ⊕ *www.iLoveMiamiSpice.com* for details.)

FESTIVALS AND ANNUAL EVENTS

Art Basel Miami Beach. The most prestigious art show in the United States is held every December, with plenty of fabulous parties to go along with the pricey art. This is a who's-who of the art world where collectors, emerging artists, renowned artists, curators, gallerists, and art aficionados convene alongside novices and trendsetters. While the main exhibition is held at the Miami Beach Convention Center, dozens of smaller exhibitions are set up on the beach, downtown, and in Wynwood. ⊕ *www.artbaselmiamibeach.com*.

Art Deco Weekend. This annual weekend of all things art deco was started by the Miami Preservation League in the 1970s to draw attention to and celebrate Miami Beach's Art Deco Historic District. Tours, lectures, film screenings, and dozens of other 1930s-themed events are on tap over this January weekend. Festivities—many of them free—begin on Friday, followed by a Saturday morning parade and street fair. More than a quarter of a million people join in the action, which centers on Ocean Drive between 5th and 15th streets. ⊕ *www.ArtDecoWeekend.com*.

South Beach Wine and Food Festival. The Food Network's star-studded four-day weekend each February, presented by *Food & Wine*, showcases the flavors and ingenuity of the country's top chefs and wine and spirits producers. Personalities like Paula Dean, Bobby Flay, and Rachel Ray headline brunches, lunches, dinners, and seminars. The festival attracts more than 60,000 attendees annually. To avoid disappointment, book your choice events far in advance. ☎ 877/762–3933 *for ticketed events* ⊕ *www.sobefest.com.*

Winter Music Conference. The largest DJ showcase in the world rocks Miami every March, when South Beach truly turns into one big ole party. The latest and greatest in electronic music takes over the lobbies and pools of Miami's most iconic hotels. ⊕ *www.wintermusicconference.com.*

Winter Party Festival. An extended weekend of GLBT beach parties and raging nightlife attracts more than 10,000 in early March, benefiting the National Gay and Lesbian Task Force. More than 20 years strong, this long weekend is the ultimate pageantry of big muscles and hard bodies. ⊕ *www.winterparty.com.*

GETTING HERE AND AROUND

Greater Miami resembles Los Angeles in its urban sprawl and traffic. You'll need a car to visit many attractions and points of interest. If possible, avoid driving during the rush hours of 7–9 am and 5–7 pm—the hour just after and right before the peak times also can be slow going. During rainy weather, be especially cautious of flooding in South Beach and Key Biscayne.

AIR TRAVEL

Miami is serviced by Miami International Airport (MIA), 8 miles northwest of downtown, and Fort Lauderdale–Hollywood International Airport (FLL), 26 miles northeast. Many discount carriers, like Spirit Airlines, Southwest Airlines, and JetBlue, fly into FLL, making it a smart bargain if you're renting a car. Otherwise, look for flights to MIA on American Airlines, Delta, and United. MIA recently underwent an extensive face-lift, improving facilities, common spaces, and the overall aesthetic of the airport.

CAR TRAVEL

Interstate 95 is the major expressway connecting South Florida with points north; State Road 836 is the major east–west expressway and connects to Florida's Turnpike, State Road 826, and Interstate 95. Seven causeways link Miami and Miami Beach, with Interstate 195 and Interstate 395 offering the most convenient routes; the Rickenbacker Causeway extends to Key Biscayne from Interstate 95 and U.S. 1. The high-speed lanes on the left-hand side of I–95 require a prepaid toll gadget called a "Sunpass," available in most drug and grocery stores.

Remember U.S. 1 (aka Biscayne Boulevard)—you'll hear it often in directions. It starts in Key West, hugs South Florida's coastline, and heads north straight through to Maine.

PUBLIC TRANSPORTATION

Some sights are accessible via the public transportation system, run by the **Metro-Dade Transit Agency,** which maintains 740 Metrobuses on 90 routes; the 23-mile Metrorail elevated rapid-transit system; and the Metromover, an elevated light-rail system. Those planning to use public transportation should get an EASY Card or EASY Ticket available at any Metrorail station and most supermarkets. Fares are discounted, and

2

transfer fees are nominal. The bus stops for the **Metrobus** are marked with blue-and-green signs with a bus logo and route information. The fare is $2 (exact change only if paying cash). Cash-paying customers must pay for another ride if transferring. Some express routes carry a surcharge of 35¢. Elevated **Metrorail** trains run from downtown Miami north to Hialeah and south along U.S. 1 to Dadeland. The system operates daily 5 am–midnight. The fare is $2; 50¢ transfers to Metrobus are available only for EASY Card and EASY Ticket holders. **Metromover** resembles an airport shuttle and runs on two loops around downtown Miami, linking major hotels, office buildings, and shopping areas. The system spans 4 miles, including the 1-mile Omni Loop and the 1-mile Brickell Loop. There is no fee to ride.

Tri-Rail, South Florida's commuter-train system, stops at 18 stations north of MIA along a 71-mile route. There's a Metrorail transfer station two stops north of MIA. Prices range from $2.50 to $6.90 for a one-way ticket.

Contacts Metro-Dade Transit Agency ☎ *305/891–3131, 3-1-1* ⊕ *www.miamidade.gov/transit.* **Tri-Rail** ☎ *800/874–7245* ⊕ *www.tri-rail.com.*

TAXI TRAVEL

Except in South Beach, it's difficult to hail a cab on the street; in most cases you'll need to call a cab company or have a hotel doorman hail one for you. Fares run $2.50 for the first 1/6th of a mile and $2.40 every mile thereafter; flat-rate fares are also available from the airport to a variety of zones, including Miami Beach for $32. Expect a $2 surcharge on rides leaving from Miami International Airport or the Port of Miami. For those heading from MIA to downtown, the 15-minute, 7-mile trip costs around $22. Many cabs now accept credit cards; inquire before you get in the car.

Taxi Companies Central Cabs ☎ *305/532–5555.* **Tropical Taxi** ☎ *305/945– 1025* ☞ *Serving Miami Beach only.* **Yellow Cab** ☎ *305/888–8888.*

TRAIN TRAVEL

Amtrak provides service from 500 destinations to the Greater Miami area. The trains make several stops along the way; north–south service stops in the major Florida cities of Jacksonville, Orlando, Tampa, West Palm Beach, and Fort Lauderdale. Note that these stops are often in less than ideal locations for immediate city access. For extended trips, or if you want to visit other areas in Florida, you can come via Auto Train (where you bring your car along) from Lorton, Virginia, just outside Washington, D.C., to Sanford, Florida, just outside Orlando. From there it's less than a four-hour drive to Miami. Fares vary, but expect to pay between around $275 and $350 for a basic sleeper seat and car passage each way. ▦ TIP→ You must be traveling with an automobile to purchase a ticket on the Auto Train.

VISITOR INFORMATION

For additional information about Miami and Miami Beach, contact the city's visitor bureaus. You can also pick up a free Miami Beach INcard at the Miami Beach Visitors Center 10 am–4 pm seven days a week, entitling you to discounts and offers at restaurants, shops, galleries, and more.

Contacts **Coconut Grove Chamber of Commerce** ⊠ *2820 McFarlane Rd., Coconut Grove* ☎ *305/444–7270* ⊕ *www.coconutgrovechamber.com.* **Coral Gables Chamber of Commerce** ⊠ *224 Catalonia Ave., Coral Gables* ☎ *305/446–1657* ⊕ *www.coralgableschamber.org.* **Greater Miami Convention & Visitors Bureau** ⊠ *701 Brickell Ave., Suite 2700* ☎ *305/539–3000, 800/933–8448 in U.S.* ⊕ *www.miamiandbeaches.com.* **Key Biscayne Chamber of Commerce and Visitors Center** ⊠ *88 W. McIntyre St., Suite 100, Key Biscayne* ☎ *305/361–5207* ⊕ *www.keybiscaynechamber.org.* **Visit Miami Beach Visitors Center** ⊠ *1901 Convention Center Dr., Hall C, Miami Beach* ☎ *786/276–2763, 305/673–7400 Miami Beach Tourist Hotline* ⊕ *www.miamibeachguest.com.*

EXPLORING MIAMI AND MIAMI BEACH

If you'd arrived here 50 years ago with a guidebook in hand, chances are you'd be thumbing through listings looking for alligator wrestlers and you-pick strawberry fields or citrus groves. Things have changed. While Disney sidetracked families in Orlando, Miami was developing a unique culture and attitude that's equal parts beach town/big business, Latino/Caribbean meets European/American—all of which fuels a great art and food scene, as well as exuberant nightlife and myriad festivals.

To find your way around Greater Miami, learn how the numbering system works (or better yet, use a GPS). Miami is laid out on a grid with four quadrants—northeast, northwest, southeast, and southwest—that meet at Miami Avenue and Flagler Street. Miami Avenue separates east from west, and Flagler Street separates north from south. Avenues and courts run north–south; streets, terraces, and ways run east–west. Roads run diagonally, northwest–southeast. But other districts—Miami Beach, Coral Gables, and Hialeah—may or may not follow this system, and along the curve of Biscayne Bay the symmetrical grid shifts diagonally. It's best to buy a detailed map, stick to the major roads, and ask directions early and often. However, make sure you're in a safe neighborhood or public place when you seek guidance; cabdrivers and cops are good resources.

DOWNTOWN MIAMI

Downtown Miami dazzles from a distance. The skyline is fluid, thanks to the sheer number of sparkling glass high-rises between Biscayne Boulevard and the Miami River. Business is the key to downtown Miami's daytime bustle. However, the influx of massive, modern, and affordable condos has lured a young and trendy demographic to the areas in and around downtown, giving Miami much more of a "city" feel come nightfall. In fact, downtown has become a nighttime hot spot in recent years, inciting a cultural revolution that has fostered burgeoning areas north in Wynwood, Midtown, and the Design District, and south along Brickell Avenue. The pedestrian streets here tend to be very restaurant-centric, complemented by lounges and nightclubs.

The free, 23-mile, elevated commuter system known as the Metromover runs inner and outer loops through downtown and to nearby neighborhoods south and north. Many attractions are conveniently located within a few blocks of a station.

Note that if you have a vehicle, you can combine a visit to this neighborhood with one to Little Havana, which is just southwest of downtown. ⇨ *See the illustrated feature "Caribbean Infusion" for a map of Little Havana as well as one of Little Haiti in north Miami.*

TOP ATTRACTIONS

Adrienne Arsht Center. Culture vultures and other artsy types are drawn to this stunning performing arts center, home of the Florida Grand Opera, Miami City Ballet, New World Symphony, Concert Association of Florida, and other local and touring groups, which have included Broadway hits like *Wicked* and *Jersey Boys*. Think of it as a sliver of savoir faire to temper Miami's often-over-the-top vibe. Designed by architect César Pelli, the massive development contains a 2,400-seat opera house, a 2,200-seat concert hall, a black-box theater, and an outdoor Plaza for the Arts. Restaurateur Barton G. presents his pretheater dining extravaganza at the Arsht Center's restaurant, **Prelude by Barton G.**, with a two-course, $29 prix-fixe menu (☎ *305/357–7900* ⊕ *www.preludebybartong.com*). ⊠ *1300 Biscayne Blvd., at N.E. 13th St., Downtown* ☎ *305/949–6722* ⊕ *www.arshtcenter.org.*

Freedom Tower. In the 1960s this ornate Spanish-baroque structure was the Cuban Refugee Center, processing more than 500,000 Cubans who entered the United States after fleeing Fidel Castro's regime. Built in 1925 for the *Miami Daily News*, it was inspired by the Giralda, an 800-year-old bell tower in Seville, Spain. Preservationists were pleased to see the tower's exterior restored in 1988. Today, it is owned by Miami Dade College (MDC), functioning as a cultural and educational center, principally for premiere exhibitions of MDC's Art Gallery System. ⊠ *600 Biscayne Blvd., at N.E. 6th St., Downtown* ☎ *305/237–7700* ⊙ *Hrs vary.*

HistoryMiami. Discover a treasure trove of colorful stories about the region's history at HistoryMiami, formerly known as the Historical Museum of Southern Florida. Exhibits celebrate the city's multicultural heritage, including an old Miami streetcar and unique items chronicling the migration of Cubans to Miami. ⊠ *101 W. Flagler St., between N.W. 1st and 2nd Aves., Downtown* ☎ *305/375–1492* ⊕ *www.historymiami. org* ⊞ *$8* ⊙ *Tues.–Fri. 10–5, weekends noon–5.*

WORTH NOTING

Bayfront Park. This pedestrian-friendly waterfront park sits on a 32-acre site smack in the heart of downtown Miami on Biscayne Bay, with three major event spaces: Bicentennial Park, Tina Hills Pavilion, and Klipsch Amphitheater at Bayfront Park. It also has a lovely bay walk and a number of monuments. In the park's southwest corner is the white *Challenger* Memorial, commemorating the space shuttle that exploded in 1986. A little north is Plaza Bolivar, a tribute by Cuban immigrants to their adopted country, and the JFK Torch of Friendship, a plaza with plaques representing all South and Central American countries except Cuba. To the north, the park ends with the colossal Bayside Marketplace entertainment, dining, and retail complex, which is particularly popular with cruise passengers as well as visitors from South America. ⊠ *301 N. Biscayne Blvd., Downtown* ⊕ *www.bayfrontparkmiami.com.*

Downtown
Miami

KEY

Ⓜ Metromover Staion

--- Metromover

FAMILY **Jungle Island.** Originally located deep in south Miami and known as Parrot Jungle, South Florida's original tourist attraction opened in 1936 and moved closer to Miami Beach in 2003. Located on Watson Island, a small stretch of land off I–395 between Downtown Miami and South Beach, Jungle Island is far more than a park where cockatoos ride tricycles; this interactive zoological park is home to just about every unusual and endangered species you would want to see, including a rare albino alligator, a liger (lion and tiger mix), and myriad exotic birds. The most intriguing offerings are the VIP animal tours, including the Lemur Experience ($79.95), in which the highly social primates make themselves at home on your lap or shoulders. Jungle Island offers complimentary shuttle service to most Downtown Miami and South Beach hotels. ✉ *1111 Parrot Jungle Trail, off MacArthur Causeway (I–395), Downtown* ☎ *305/400–7000* ⊕ *www.jungleisland.com* ✉ *$34.95, plus $8 parking* ⊘ *Weekdays 10–5, weekends 10–6.*

FAMILY **Miami Children's Museum.** This Arquitectonica-designed museum, both imaginative and geometric in appearance, is directly across the MacArthur Causeway from Jungle Island. Twelve galleries house hundreds of interactive, bilingual exhibits. Children can scan plastic groceries in the supermarket, scramble through a giant sand castle, climb a rock wall, learn about the Everglades, and combine rhythms in the world-music studio. ✉ *980 MacArthur Causeway, off I–395, Downtown* ☎ *305/373–5437* ⊕ *www.miamichildrensmuseum.org* ✉ *$16, parking $1/hr* ⊘ *Daily 10–6.*

COCONUT GROVE

Eclectic and intriguing, Miami's Coconut Grove can be considered a loose tropical equivalent of New York's Greenwich Village. A haven for writers and artists, the neighborhood has never quite outgrown its image as a small village. During the day it's business as usual in Coconut Grove, much as in any other Miami neighborhood. But in the evening, especially on weekends, it seems as if someone flips a switch and the streets come alive. Locals and tourists jam into small boutiques, sidewalk cafés, and stores lodged in two massive retail-entertainment complexes. For blocks in every direction, students, families, and prosperous retirees flow in and out of a mix of galleries, restaurants, bars, bookstores, comedy clubs, and theaters. With this weekly influx of traffic, parking can pose a problem. There's a well-lighted city garage at 3315 Rice Street (behind the Mayfair hotel and CocoWalk), or look for police to direct you to parking lots where you'll pay $10 and up for an evening's slot. If you're staying in the Grove, leave the car behind, and your night will get off to an easier start.

Nighttime is the right time to see Coconut Grove, but in the day you can take a casual drive around the neighborhood to see its diverse architecture. Posh estates mingle with rustic cottages, modest frame homes, and stark modern dwellings, often on the same block. If you're into horticulture, you'll be impressed by the Garden of Eden–like foliage that seems to grow everywhere without care. In truth, residents are determined to keep up the Grove's village-in-a-jungle look, so they lavish attention on exotic plantings even as they battle to protect any remaining native vegetation.

TOP ATTRACTIONS

Barnacle Historic State Park. A pristine bay-front manse sandwiched between cramped luxury developments, Barnacle is Miami's oldest house still standing on its original foundation. To get here, you'll hike along an old buggy trail through a tropical hardwood hammock and landscaped lawn leading to Biscayne Bay. Built in 1891 by Florida's first snowbird—New Yorker Commodore Ralph Munroe—the large home, built of timber that Munroe salvaged from wrecked ships, has many original furnishings, a broad sloping roof, and deeply recessed verandas that channel sea breezes into the house. If your timing is right, you may catch one of the monthly Moonlight Concerts, and the old-fashioned picnic on July 4 is popular. ✉ *3485 Main Hwy.* ☎ *305/442–6866* ⊕ *www.floridastateparks.org/thebarnacle* ☞ *$2 park entry, tours $3, concerts $7* ⊗ *Fri.–Mon. 9–5; tours at 10, 11:30, 1, and 2:30; concerts monthly Sept.–May 6–9, call or check website for dates.*

FAMILY **Miami Museum of Science and Planetarium.** This small fun museum is chock-full of hands-on sound, gravity, and electricity displays for children and adults alike. For animal lovers, its wildlife center houses native Florida snakes, turtles, tortoises, and birds of prey. Check the museum's schedule for traveling exhibits that appear throughout the year. If you're here the first Friday of the month—called Fabulous First Fridays—stick around for the free star show at 7 pm and then gaze at the planets through two powerful Meade telescopes at the Weintraub Observatory. Also enjoy a laser-light rock-and-roll show nightly at 8, 9, 10, or 11 to the tunes of the Doors, the Beatles, or Pink Floyd to name a few. ✉ *3280 S. Miami Ave.* ☎ *305/646–4200* ⊕ *www.miamisci. org* ☞ *$14.95* ⊗ *Museum daily 10–6; planetarium varies.*

Fodor's Choice **Vizcaya Museum and Gardens.** Of the 10,000 people living in Miami
★ between 1912 and 1916, about 1,000 of them were gainfully employed by Chicago industrialist James Deering to build this European-inspired residence. Once comprising 180 acres, this National Historic Landmark now occupies a 30-acre tract that includes a rockland hammock (native forest) and more than 10 acres of formal gardens with fountains overlooking Biscayne Bay. The house, open to the public, contains 70 rooms, 34 of which are filled with paintings, sculpture, antique furniture, and other fine and decorative arts. The collection spans 2,000 years and represents the Renaissance, baroque, rococo, and neoclassical periods. The 90-minute self-guided Discover Vizcaya Audio Tour is available in multiple languages for an additional $5. Moonlight tours, offered on evenings that are nearest the full moon, provide a magical look at the gardens; call for reservations. ✉ *3251 S. Miami Ave.* ☎ *305/250–9133* ⊕ *www.vizcayamuseum.org* ☞ *$15* ⊗ *Wed.–Mon. 9:30–4:30.*

CORAL GABLES

You can easily spot Coral Gables from the window of a Miami-bound jetliner—just look for the massive orange tower of the Biltmore Hotel rising from a lush green carpet of trees concealing the city's gracious homes. The canopy is as much a part of this planned city as its distinctive architecture, all attributed to the vision of George E. Merrick nearly 100 years ago.

The story of this city began in 1911, when Merrick inherited 1,600 acres of citrus and avocado groves from his father. Through judicious investment he nearly doubled the tract to 3,000 acres by 1921. Merrick dreamed of building an American Venice here, complete with canals and homes. Working from this vision, he began designing a city based on centuries-old prototypes from Mediterranean countries. Unfortunately for Merrick, the devastating no-name hurricane of 1926, followed by the Great Depression, prevented him from fulfilling many of his plans. He died at 54, an employee of the post office. Today Coral Gables has a population of about 45,000. In its bustling downtown more than 150 multinational companies maintain headquarters or regional offices, and the University of Miami campus in the southern part of the Gables brings a youthful vibrancy to the area. A southern branch of the city extends down the shore of Biscayne Bay through neighborhoods threaded with canals.

TOP ATTRACTIONS

Biltmore Hotel. Bouncing back stunningly from its dark days as an army hospital, this hotel has become the jewel of Coral Gables—a dazzling architectural gem with a colorful past. First opened in 1926, it was a hot spot for the rich and glamorous of the Jazz Age until it was converted to an army–air force regional hospital in 1942. Until 1968, the Veterans Administration continued to operate the hospital after World War II. The Biltmore then lay vacant for nearly 20 years before it underwent extensive renovations and reopened as a luxury hotel in 1987. Its 16-story tower, like the Freedom Tower in downtown Miami, is a replica of Seville's Giralda Tower. The magnificent pool is reportedly the largest hotel pool in the continental United States. Because it functions as a full-service hotel, your ticket in—if you aren't staying here—is to patronize one of the hotel's several restaurants or bars. Sunday champagne brunch is a local legend; try to get a table in the courtyard. ✉ *1200 Anastasia Ave., near De Soto Blvd.* ☏ *855/311–6903* ⊕ *www.biltmorehotel.com.*

FAMILY
Fodor's Choice
★

Fairchild Tropical Botanic Garden. With 83 acres of lakes, sunken gardens, a 560-foot vine pergola, orchids, bellflowers, coral trees, bougainvillea, rare palms, and flowering trees, Fairchild is the largest tropical botanical garden in the continental United States. The tram tour highlights the best of South Florida's flora; then you can set off exploring on your own. A 2-acre rain-forest exhibit showcases tropical plants from around the world complete with a waterfall and stream. The conservatory, Windows to the Tropics, is home to rare tropical plants, including the Titan Arum (*Amorphophallus titanum*), a fast-growing variety that attracted thousands of visitors when it bloomed in 1998. (It was only the sixth documented bloom in this country in the 20th

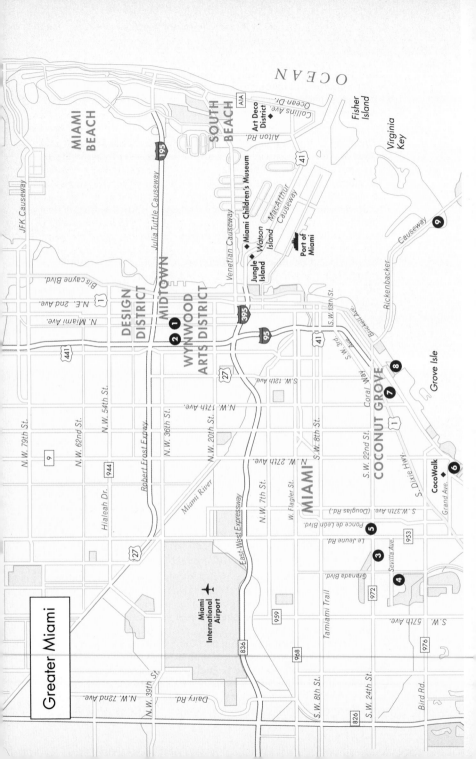

Greater Miami

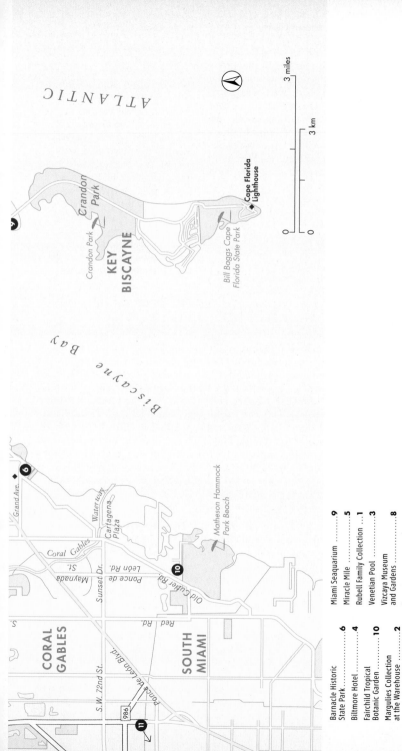

ATLANTIC

Biscayne Bay

KEY BISCAYNE

Crandon Park

Crandon Park

Bill Baggs Cape
Florida State Park

Cape Florida
Lighthouse

0   3 km
0   3 miles

CORAL GABLES

S.W. 72nd St.

Ponce de León Blvd.

Grand Ave.

Coral Gables

Maynada St.

Sunset Dr.

Ponce de León Rd.

Red Rd.

Old Cutler Rd.

Waterway

Cartagena
Plaza

SOUTH MIAMI

Matheson Hammock
Park Beach

century.) The Keys Coastal Habitat, created in a marsh and mangrove area in 1995 with assistance from the Tropical Audubon Society, provides food and shelter to resident and migratory birds. Check out the Montgomery Botanical Center, a research facility devoted to palms and cycads. Spicing up Fairchild's calendar are plant sales, afternoon teas, and genuinely special events year-round, such as the International Mango Festival the second weekend in July. The excellent bookstore–gift shop carries books on gardening and horticulture, and the Garden Café serves sandwiches and, seasonally, smoothies made from the garden's own crop of tropical fruits. ⊠ *10901 Old Cutler Rd.* ☎ *305/667–1651* ⊕ *www. fairchildgarden.org* ⊠ *$25* ⊙ *Daily 9:30–4:30.*

> ### SAIL AWAY
>
> If you can sail in Miami, do. Blue skies, calm seas, and a view of the city skyline make for a pleasurable outing—especially at twilight, when the fabled "moon over Miami" casts a soft glow on the water. Key Biscayne's calm waves and strong breezes are perfect for sailing and windsurfing, and although Dinner Key and the Coconut Grove waterfront remain the center of sailing in Greater Miami, sailboat moorings and rentals sit along other parts of the bay and up the Miami River, too.

FAMILY **Venetian Pool.** Sculpted from a rock quarry in 1923 and fed by artesian wells, this 820,000-gallon municipal pool had a major face-lift in 2010. It remains quite popular because of its themed architecture—a fantasy version of a waterfront Italian village—created by Denman Fink. The pool has earned a place on the National Register of Historic Places and showcases a nice collection of vintage photos depicting 1920s beauty pageants and swank soirees held long ago. Paul Whiteman played here, Johnny Weissmuller and Esther Williams swam here, and you should, too (but no kids under 3). A snack bar, lockers, and showers make this must-see user-friendly as well. ⊠ *2701 De Soto Blvd., at Toledo St.* ☎ *305/460–5306* ⊕ *www.gablesrecreation.com* ⊠ *$11; free parking across De Soto Blvd.* ⊙ *Usually open Tues.–Sun. 11–4:30, but best to call ahead.*

WORTH NOTING

Miracle Mile. Even with competition from some impressive malls, this half-mile stretch of colorful retail stores continues to thrive because of its intriguing mixture of unique boutiques, bridal shops, art galleries, charming restaurants, and upscale nightlife venues. It attracts Latin America's power players as well as the kinds of women you might see on *The Real Housewives of Miami.* ⊠ *Coral Way, between S.W. 37th and S.W. 42nd Aves.* ⊕ *www.shopcoralgables.com.*

OFF THE
BEATEN
PATH

Zoo Miami. Don't miss a visit to this top-notch zoo, 14 miles southwest of Coral Gables, in the Miami suburbs. The only subtropical zoo in the continental United States, it has 320-plus acres that are home to more than 2,000 animals, including 40 endangered species, which roam on islands surrounded by moats. Amazon & Beyond encompasses 27 acres of simulated tropical rain forests showcasing 600 animals indigenous to the region, such as giant river otters, harpy eagles, anacondas, and jaguars. The Wings of Asia aviary has about 300 exotic birds representing

Miami Beach is dotted with lifeguard towers.

70 species flying free within the junglelike enclosure. In 2014 ZooMiami unveils Florida: Mission Everglades, showcasing the diverse wildlife of native Florida ecosystems. There's also a petting zoo with a meerkat exhibit and interactive opportunities, such as those at Wacky Barn and Dr. Wilde's World and the Ecology Theater, where kids can touch animals like alligators and opossums. An educational and entertaining wildlife show is given three times daily. ⊠ *12400 S.W. 152nd St., Richmond Heights, Miami* ☏ *305/251–0400* ⊕ *www.miamimetrozoo. com* ⌑ *$15.95, $11.95 children ages 3 to 12; 45-min tram tour $4.95* ⊙ *Daily 9:30–5:30, last admission 4.*

KEY BISCAYNE

Once upon a time, the two barrier islands that make up the village of Key Biscayne (Key Biscayne itself and Virginia Key) were outposts for fishermen and sailors, pirates and salvagers, soldiers and settlers. The 95-foot Cape Florida Lighthouse stood tall during Seminole Indian battles and hurricanes. Coconut plantations covered two-thirds of Key Biscayne, and there were plans as far back as the 1800s to develop the picturesque island as a resort for the wealthy. Fortunately, the state and county governments set much of the land aside for parks, and both keys are now home to top-ranked beaches and golf, tennis, softball, and picnicking facilities. The long and winding bike paths that run through the islands are favorites for in-line skaters and cyclists. Incorporated in 1991, the village of Key Biscayne is a hospitable community of about 12,500, even though Virginia Key remains undeveloped at the moment. These two playground islands are especially family-friendly.

TOP ATTRACTIONS

FAMILY   **Miami Seaquarium.** This classic family attraction stages shows with sea lions, dolphins, and Lolita the killer whale. The Crocodile Flats exhibit has 26 Nile crocodiles. Discovery Bay, an endangered mangrove habitat, is home to sea turtles, alligators, herons, egrets, and ibis. You can also visit a shark pool, a tropical reef aquarium, and West Indian and Florida manatees. A popular interactive attraction is the Stingray Touch Tank, where you can touch and feed cow-nose rays and southern stingrays. Another big draw is the Dolphin Interaction program, including the quite intensive Dolphin Odyssey ($199) experience and the lighter shallow-water Dolphin Encounter ($139). Make reservations for either experience. ⊠ *4400 Rickenbacker Causeway, Virginia Key, Miami* ☎ *305/361–5705* ⊕ *www.miamiseaquarium.com* ⊡ *$39.95, parking $8 (cash only)* ⊗ *Daily 9:30–6, last admission 4:30.*

WYNWOOD/MIDTOWN/DESIGN DISTRICT

These three trendy, creative neighborhoods are 3 to 4 miles north of downtown and have developed an impressive mix of one-of-a-kind shops and galleries, see-and-be-seen bars, and slick restaurants. **Midtown** (⊕ *midtownmiami.com*) lies between Northeast 29th and 36th streets, from North Miami Avenue to Northeast 2nd Avenue.

Just southwest, the funky and edgy **Wynwood Art District** (⊕ *www.wyn-woodmiami.com)* is peppered with galleries, art studios, and private collections accessible to the public. Though the neighborhood hasn't completely shed its dodgy past, artist-painted graffiti walls and reinvented urban, industrial buildings have transformed the area from grimy and gritty to fresh and trendy. The Wynwood Walls on Northwest 2nd Avenue between Northeast 25th and 26th streets are a cutting-edge enclave of modern urban murals. Visit during Wynwood's monthly gallery walk on the second Saturday evening of each month, when studios and galleries are all open at the same time.

To reach the **Design District** (⊕ *www.miamidesigndistrict.net*), head north up Miami Avenue just beyond Interstate 195. From about Northeast 38th to Northeast 42nd streets, east to North Federal Highway, you'll find 18 blocks of clothiers, antiques shops, design stores, and bars and eateries.

TOP ATTRACTIONS

Margulies Collection at the Warehouse. Make sure a visit to Wynwood includes a stop at the Margulies Collection at the Warehouse. Martin Margulies's collection of vintage and contemporary photography, videos, and installation art in a 45,000-square-foot space makes for eye-popping viewing. Admission proceeds go to the Lotus House, a local homeless shelter for women and children. ⊠ *591 N.W. 27th St., between N.W. 5th and 6th Aves., Wynwood, Miami* ☎ *305/576–1051* ⊕ *www.marguglieswarehouse.com* ⊡ *$10* ⊗ *Oct.–Apr., Wed.–Sat. 11–4.*

Rubell Family Collection. Fans of edgy art will appreciate the Rubell Family Collection. Mera and Don Rubell have accumulated work by artists from the 1970s to the present, including Jeff Koons, Cindy

Sherman, Damien Hirst, and Keith Haring. Admission includes a complimentary audio tour. ✉ 95 N.W. 29th St., between N. Miami and N.W. 1st Aves., Wynwood, Miami ☏ 305/573–6090 ⊕ www. rfc.museum ✈ $10 ☼ Wed.–Sat. 10–6.

2

SOUTH BEACH

The hub of Miami Beach is South Beach (better known as SoBe), with its energetic Ocean Drive, Collins Avenue, and Washington Avenue. Here life unfolds 24 hours a day. Beautiful people pose in hotel lounges and sidewalk cafés, bronzed cyclists zoom past palm trees, and visitors flock to see the action. On Lincoln Road, café crowds spill onto the sidewalks, weekend markets draw all kinds of visitors and their dogs, and thanks to a few late-night lounges, the scene is just as alive at night. To the north, a Mid-Beach renaissance is unfolding on Collins Avenue, with swanky new hotels and restaurants popping up between 40th and 60th streets.

Quieter areas still farther north on Collins Avenue are Surfside (from 88th to 96th streets), fashionable Bal Harbour (beginning at 96th Street), and Sunny Isles (between 157th and 197th streets).

TOP ATTRACTIONS

Española Way. There's a bohemian feel to this street lined with Mediterranean-revival buildings constructed in 1925. Al Capone's gambling syndicate ran its operations upstairs at what is now the Clay Hotel, a youth hostel. At a nightclub here in the 1930s, future bandleader Desi Arnaz strapped on a conga drum and started beating out a rumba rhythm. Visit this quaint avenue on a weekend afternoon, when merchants and craftspeople set up shop to sell everything from handcrafted bongo drums to fresh flowers. Between Washington and Drexel avenues the road has been narrowed to a single lane and Miami Beach's trademark pink sidewalks have been widened to accommodate sidewalk cafés and shops selling imaginative clothing, jewelry, and art. ✉ Española Way, between 14th and 15th Sts. from Washington to Jefferson Aves., South Beach.

Holocaust Memorial. A bronze sculpture depicts refugees clinging to a giant bronze arm that reaches out of the ground and 42 feet into the air. Enter the surrounding courtyard to see a memorial wall and hear the music that seems to give voice to the 6 million Jews who died at the hands of the Nazis. It's easy to understand why Kenneth Treister's dramatic memorial is in Miami Beach: the city's community of Holocaust survivors was once the second-largest in the country. ✉ 1933–1945 Meridian Ave., at Dade Blvd., South Beach ☏ 305/538–1663 ⊕ www. holocaustmmb.org ✈ Free ☼ Daily 9–sunset.

Continued on page 55

CARIBBEAN INFUSION

by Michelle Delio

Miami has sun, sand, and sea, but unlike some of Florida's other prime beach destinations, it also has a wave of cultural traditions that spice up the city.

It's with good reason that people in Miami fondly say that the city is an easy way for Americans to visit another country without ever leaving the United States. According to the U.S. Census Bureau, approximately half of Miami's population is foreign born and more than 70% speak a language other than English at home (in comparison, only 35.7% of New York City residents were born in another country). The city's Latin/Caribbean immigrants and exiles make up the largest segments of the population.

Locals merrily merge cultural traditions, speaking "Spanglish" (a mix of Spanish and English), sipping Cuban coffee with Sicilian pastries, eating Nuevo Latino fusion food, and dancing to the beat of other countries' music. That said, people here are just as interested in keeping to their own distinct ways—think of the city as a colorful mosaic composed of separate elements rather than a melting pot.

Miami's diverse population creates a city that feels alive in a way that few other American cities do. And no visit to the city would be complete without a stop at one of the two neighborhoods famed for their celebrations of cultural traditions—Little Haiti and Little Havana—places that have a wonderful foreign feel even amid cosmopolitan Miami.

⚠ Safety can be an issue in Little Haiti. Exercise special caution and do not visit at night.

Playing dominoes is a favorite pastime at Maximo Gomez Park in Little Havana (left).

LA PETITE HAÏTI—LITTLE HAITI

Little Haiti is a study in contrasts. At first glance you see the small buildings painted in bright oranges, pinks, reds, yellows, and turquoises, with signs, some handwritten, touting immigration services, lunch specials with *tassot* (fried cubed goat), and voodoo supplies.

But as you adjust to this dazzle of color, you become aware of the curious juxtapositions of poverty and wealth in this evolving neighborhood. Streets dip with potholes in front of trendy art galleries, and dilapidated houses struggle to survive near newly renovated soccer fields and arts centers.

Miami's Little Haiti is the largest Haitian community outside of Haiti itself, and while people of different ethnic backgrounds have begun to move to the neighborhood, people here tend to expect to primarily see other Haitians on these streets. Obvious outsiders may be greeted with a few frozen stares on the streets, but owners of shops and restaurants tend to be welcoming. Creole is commonly spoken, although some people—especially younger folks—also speak English.

WHEN TO GO

The neighborhood is best visited during the daytime, combined with a visit to the nearby Miami Design District, an 18-block section of art galleries, interior design showrooms, and restaurants between N.E. 41st Street and N.E. 36th Street, Miami Avenue, and Biscayne Boulevard.

CREOLE EXPRESSIONS

Creole, one of Haiti's two languages (the other is French), is infused with French, African, Arabic, Spanish, and Portuguese words.

Komon ou ye? How are you? *(also spelled Kouman)
N'ap boule! Great!
Kisa ou ta vla? What would you like?
Mesi. Thanks.
Souple. Please.

MANGÉ KRÉYOL (HAITIAN FOOD)

Traditional Caribbean cuisines tend to combine European and African culinary techniques. Haitian can be a bit spicier—though never mouth-scorching hot—than many other island cuisines. Rice and beans are the staple food, enlivened with a little of whatever people might have: fish, goat, chicken, pork, usually stewed or deep-fried, along with peppers, plantains, and tomatoes.

Chez Le Bebe (⊠ *114 N.E. 54th St.* ☎ *305/751–7639* ⊕ *www.chezlebebe.com*) offers Haitian home cooking—if you want to try stewed goat, this is the place to do it. Chicken, fish, oxtail, and fried pork are also on the menu; each plate comes with rice, beans, plantains, and salad for less than $12.

Tap Tap restaurant (⊠ *819 Fifth St.* ☎ *305/672–2898*) is outside of Little Haiti, but this Miami institution will immerse you in the island's culture with an extensive collection of Haitian folk art displayed everywhere in the restaurant. On the menu is pumpkin soup, *spageti kreyol* (pasta, shrimp, and a Creole tomato sauce), goat stewed in Creole sauce (a mildly spicy tomato-based sauce), conch, and "grilled goat dinner." You can eat well here for $15 or less.

GETTING ORIENTED

Little Haiti, once a small farming community outside of Miami proper, is the heart and soul of Haitian society in the U.S. Its northern and southern boundaries are 85th Street and 42nd Street, respectively, with Interstate–95 to the west and Biscayne Boulevard to the east. The best section to visit is along North Miami Avenue from 54th to 59th streets. Driving is the best way to get here; parking is easy to find on North Miami Avenue. Public transit (☎ *305/891–3131*) is limited.

SHOPPING

The cluster of botanicas at N.E. 54th Street and N.E. 2nd Avenue offer items intended to sway the fates, from candles to plastic and plaster statues of Catholic saints that, in the voodoo tradition, represent African deities. While exploring, don't miss **Sweat Records** (⊠ *5505 N.E. 2nd Ave.* ☎ *786/693–9309* ⊕ *www.sweatrecordsmiami. com*). Sweat sells a wide range of music—rock, pop, punk, electronic, hip-hop, and Latino. Check out the vegan-friendly organic coffee bar at the store, which is open from noon to 10 PM every day but Sunday.

LITTLE HAVANA

First settled en masse by Cubans in the early 1960s, after Cuba's Communist revolution, Little Havana is a predominantly working-class area and the core of Miami's Hispanic community. Spanish is the main language, but don't be surprised if the cadence is less Cuban than Salvadoran or Nicaraguan: the neighborhood is now home to people from all Latin American countries.

If you come to Little Havana expecting the Latino version of New Orleans's French Quarter, you're apt to be disappointed—it's not that picturesque. But if great, inexpensive food (not just Cuban; there's Vietnamese, Mexican, and Argentinean here as well), distinctive, affordable art, cigars, and coffee interest you, you'll enjoy your time in Little Havana. It's not a prefab tourist destination, so don't expect Disneyland with a little Latino flair—this is real life in Miami.

WHEN TO GO

The absolute best time to visit Calle Ocho is the last Friday evening of every month, between 6:30 and 11 PM on 8th Street from 14th to 17th avenues. Known as **Viernes Culturales** (⊕ www.viernes-culturales.org), it's a big block party that everyone is welcome to attend. Art galleries, restaurants, and stores stay open late, and music, mojitos, and avant-garde street performances bring a young, hip crowd to the neighborhood where they mingle with locals.

If you come in mid-March, your visit may coincide with the annual **Calle Ocho festival** (⊕ www.carnavalmiami.com), which draws more than a million visitors in search of Latin music, food, and shopping.

LITTLE HAVANA

S. W. 6th St.

S.W. 16th Ave.

S.W. 14th Ave.

S.W. 19th Ave.

S. W. 12th Ave.

S.W. 10th Ave.

S. W. 7th St.

Lily's Records ◆

Calle Ocho

El Titan de Bronze ◆

S. W. 8th St.

Tamiami Trail

Casa Panza ✕ ✕
Restaurant El Pub
Restaurant

◆ Domino
Park

Los Pinareños
Fruteria

S.W. 9th St.

S. W. 17th Ave.

S.W. 16th Ave.

S.W. 15th Ave.

S.W. 14th Ave.

S.W. 13th Ave.

S.W. 11th Ave.

S.W. 10th St.

S.W. 11th St.

0 ————— 1/8 mile

0 ————— 1/8 km

GETTING ORIENTED

Little Havana's semi-official boundaries are 27th Avenue to 4th Avenue on the west, Miami River to the north, and S.W. 11th Street to the south. Much of the neighborhood is residential, but its heart and tourist hub is Calle Ocho (8th Street), between 12th and 17th avenues.

The best way to get here is by car. Park on the side streets off **Calle Ocho** (some spots have meters; most don't). Other options include the free **Metromover** (☎ *305/891– 3131*) and a cab ride. From Miami Beach the 15-minute ride should cost just under $30 each way.

THE SIGHTS

Little Havana is not chock full of "sights." Rather, it's a place to soak in the atmosphere. Make sure you're hungry. Grazing is one of the the best things to do here.

Stroll down Calle Oche from 12th to 17th avenues and look around you: cafés are selling guava pastries and rose petal flan, a botanica brims with candles and herbs to heal whatever ails you. Small galleries showcasing modern art jostle up next to mom-and-pop food shops and high-end Cuban clothes and crafts. At Domino Park (officially Maximo Gomez Park), guayabera-clad seniors bask in the sun and play dominoes, while at corner bodegas and coffee shops (particularly Versailles) regulars share neighborhood gossip and political opinions.

At SW 13th Street, the Cuban Memorial Boulevard fills 2 blocks with monuments to Cuba's freedom fighters.

SPANISH EXPRESSIONS

Algo más? Anything else?

Muchas gracias! Thank you very much!

No hay de qué. / De nada. You're welcome.

No entiendo. I don't understand.

Oye! All-purpose word used to get attention or express interest, admiration, and appreciation.

Calle Ocho Carnaval

Rolling cigars by hand in a Little Havana factory.

THE SOUNDS

Salsa and merengue pour out of storefronts and restaurants, while other businesses cater to the snap and shuffles of flamenco performances and Sevillaña *tablaos* (dances performed on a wood-plank stage, using castanets). If you want to join in the merriment along Calle Ocho, dance with locals on the patio of **El Pub Restaurant** (near 15th Avenue), or snack on tapas at **Casa Panza Restaurant** (near 16th), where the background music is the restaurant owner's enthusiastic singing. Any time of day, you can hear the constant backbeat of people speaking Spanish and the occasional crowing of a stray, time-confused rooster. To take these sounds home with you, wander over to **Lily's Records** (✉ *1419 S.W. 8th St, near 14th* ☎ *305/856–0536*), for its huge selection of Latin music.

THE SCENTS

Bottled, the essence of Little Havana would be tobacco, café cubano, and a whiff of tropical fruit. To indulge your senses in two of these things, head to **Los Pinareños Frutería** on Calle Ocho just west of 13th Avenue. Here you can sip a sweet, hot *cortadito* (coffee with milk), a *cafecito* (no milk), or a cool *coco frio* (coconut water). For more subsistence, dig into a Cuban-style tamale. There are stools out front of the shop, or take your drink to go and wander over to S.W. 13th Avenue, which has monuments to Cuban heroes, and sit under the ceiba trees. For cigars, head to Calle Ocho near 11th Avenue and visit **El Titan de Bronze**. At this family-owned business employees deftly hand-roll millions of stogies a year.

TOURS

If a quick multicultural experience is your goal, set aside an hour or two to do your own self-guided walking tour of the neighborhood. For real ethnic immersion, allow more time; eating is a must, as well as a peek at the area's residential streets lined with distinctive homes.

Especially illuminating are **HistoryMiami, Little Havana Neighborhood Architecture Walk** (✉ *101 W. Flagler St.* ☎ *305/375–1621* ⊕ *www.historymiami.org/tours*). Those led by Dr. Paul George, a history professor at Miami Dade College and historian for History Miami, cover architecture and community history. These take place only a few times a year.

Private three-hour tours are available for groups of up to 20 people for $400 ($20 per person above 20 people).

HistoryMiami's Web site has up-to-date information on tour dates and times.

For customized offerings, try **Miami Cultural Community Tours** (✉ *305/416-6868* ⊕ *www.miamiculturaltours.com*), interactive tours that introduce people to Little Havana and Little Haiti. Group and private tours are available, with prices ranging from $39 to $79 a person.

FAMILY
Fodor's Choice
★

Lincoln Road Mall. This open-air pedestrian mall flaunts some of Miami's best people-watching. The eclectic interiors of myriad fabulous restaurants, colorful boutiques, art galleries, lounges, and cafés are often upstaged by the bustling outdoor scene. It's here among the prolific alfresco dining enclaves that you can pass the hours easily beholding the beautiful people. Indeed, outdoor restaurant and café seating take center stage along this wide pedestrian road adorned with towering date palms, linear pools, and colorful broken-tile mosaics. Some of the shops on Lincoln Road are owner-operated boutiques carrying a smart variety of clothing, furnishings, jewelry, and decorative elements. You'll also find typical upscale chain stores—H & M, Banana Republic, and so on. Lincoln Road is fun, lively, and friendly for people–old, young, gay, and straight—and their dogs.

> **DID YOU KNOW?**
>
> The Miami Circle, an archaeological site and a National Historic Landmark, halted a multimillion-dollar development when work on the site led to the discovery of a circular stone formation and other ancient artifacts. Archaeologists believe they belonged to the Tequesta Indians.

Two landmarks worth checking out at the eastern end of Lincoln Road are the massive 1940s keystone building at 420 Lincoln Road, which has a 1945 Leo Birchanky mural in the lobby, and the 1921 Mission-style Miami Beach Community Church, at Drexel Avenue. The Lincoln Theatre (No. 541–545), at Pennsylvania Avenue, is a classical four-story art deco gem with friezes. At Euclid Avenue there's a monument to Morris Lapidus, the brains behind Lincoln Road Mall, who in his 90s watched the renaissance of his whimsical South Beach creation. At Lenox Avenue, a black-and-white art deco movie house with a Mediterranean barrel-tile roof is now the Colony Theater (1040 Lincoln Road), where live theater and experimental films are presented. ⊠ *Lincoln Rd., between Washington Ave. and Alton Rd., South Beach* ⊕ *www.lincolnroad.org.*

QUICK
BITES

Lincoln Road is a great place to cool down with an icy treat while touring South Beach. If you visit on a Sunday, stop at one of the many juice vendors, who'll whip up made-to-order smoothies from mangoes, oranges, and other fresh local fruits.

Frieze Ice Cream Factory. Delight in mouthwatering homemade ice cream and sorbets, including Indian mango, key lime pie, cashew toffee crunch, and chocolate decadence. This could very well be the best ice cream in Florida! ⊠ *1626 Michigan Ave., just south of Lincoln Rd., South Beach* ☏ *305/538–0207* ⊕ *www.thefrieze.com.*

Gelateria 4D. Authentic Italian gelato is scooped up with plenty of authentic Miami attitude at this sleek glass-and-stainless-steel sweet spot. The gelato is delicious despite the not-so-sweet service. ⊠ *670 Lincoln Rd., between Euclid and Pennsylvania Aves., South Beach* ☏ *786/276–9475* ⊕ *www.gelateria4d.com.*

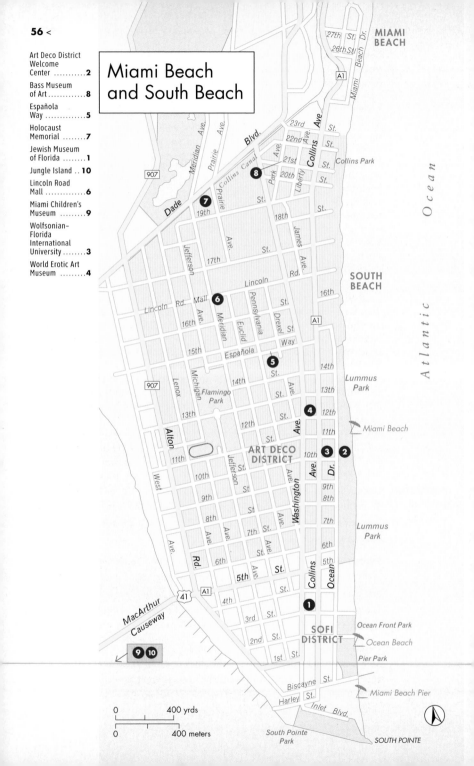

Miami Beach and South Beach

WORTH NOTING

Art Deco District Welcome Center. Run by the Miami Design Preservation League, the center provides information about the buildings in the district. An improved gift shop sells 1930s–1950s art deco memorabilia, posters, and books on Miami's history. Several tours—covering Lincoln Road, Española Way, North Beach, and the entire Art Deco District, among others—start here. You can choose from a self-guided iPod audio tour or join one of the regular morning walking tours at 10:30 every day. On Thursday a second tour takes place at 6:30 pm. Arrive at the center 15 minutes beforehand and prepurchase tickets online. All of the options provide detailed histories of the art deco hotels as well as an introduction to the art deco, Mediterranean revival, and Miami Modern (MiMo) styles found within the Miami Beach Architectural Historic District. Don't miss the special boat tours during Art Deco Weekend, in early January. (⇨ *For a map of the Art Deco District and info on some of the sites there, see the "A Stroll Down Deco Lane" in-focus feature.*) ⊠ *1001 Ocean Dr., South Beach* ☎ *305/672–2014* ⊕ *www.mdpl.org* ⊠ *Tours $20* ☉ *Daily 9:30–7.*

Bass Museum of Art. Special exhibitions join a diverse collection of European art at this museum whose original building is constructed of keystone and has unique Maya-inspired carvings. An expansion designed by Japanese architect Arata Isozaki houses another wing and an outdoor sculpture garden. Works on permanent display include *The Holy Family,* a painting by Peter Paul Rubens; *The Tournament,* one of several 16th-century Flemish tapestries; and works by Albrecht Dürer and Henri de Toulouse-Lautrec. Docent tours are by appointment but free with entry. ⊠ *2100 Collins Ave., South Beach* ☎ *305/673–7530* ⊕ *www. bassmuseum.org* ⊠ *$8* ☉ *Wed.–Sun. noon–5.*

Jewish Museum of Florida. Listed on the National Register of Historic Places, this former synagogue, built in 1936, contains art deco chandeliers, 80 impressive stained-glass windows, and a permanent exhibit, MOSAIC: Jewish Life in Florida, which depicts more than 235 years of the Florida Jewish experience. The museum, which includes a store filled with books, jewelry, and other souvenirs, also hosts traveling exhibits and special events. ⊠ *301 Washington Ave., at 3rd St., South Beach* ☎ *305/672–5044* ⊕ *www.jewishmuseum.com* ⊠ *$6, free on Sat.* ☉ *Tues.–Sun. 10–5. Museum store closed Sat.*

Wolfsonian–Florida International University. An elegantly renovated 1926 storage facility is now a research center and museum showcasing a 120,000-item collection of modern design and "propaganda arts" amassed by Miami native Mitchell ("Micky") Wolfson Jr., a world traveler and connoisseur. Broad themes of the 19th and 20th centuries—nationalism, political persuasion, industrialization are addressed in permanent and traveling shows. Included in the museum's eclectic holdings, which represent art deco, art moderne, art nouveau, Arts and Crafts, and other aesthetic movements, are 8,000 matchbooks collected by Egypt's King Farouk. ⊠ *1001 Washington Ave., South Beach* ☎ *305/531–1001* ⊕ *www.wolfsonian.org* ⊠ *$7, free after 6 pm Fri.* ☉ *Daily noon–6, Fri. noon–9.*

World Erotic Art Museum (WEAM). The sexy collection of more than 4,000 erotic items, all owned by millionaire Naomi Wilzig, unfolds with unique art of varying quality—fertility statues from around the globe and historic Chinese *shunga* books (erotic art offered as gifts to new brides on the wedding night) share the space

with some kitschy knickknacks. If this is your thing, an original phallic prop from Stanley Kubrick's *A Clockwork Orange* and an over-the-top Kama Sutra bed is worth the price of admission, but the real standout is "Miss Naomi," who is usually on hand to answer questions and provide behind-the-scenes anecdotes. Kids 17 and under are not admitted. ✉ *1205 Washington Ave., at 12th St., South Beach* ☎ *305/532–9336* ⊕ *www. weam.com* ✉ *$15* ☉ *Mon.–Thurs. 11–10, Fri.–Sun. 11–midnight.*

BEACHES

CORAL GABLES

FAMILY   **Matheson Hammock Park Beach.** Kids love the gentle waves and warm water of this beach in Coral Gables suburbia, near Fairchild Tropical Botanic Garden. But the beach is only part of the draw—the park includes a boardwalk trail, a playground, and a golf course. Plus the park is a prime spot for kite-boarding. The man-made lagoon, or "atoll pool," is perfect for inexperienced swimmers, and it's one of the best places in mainland Miami for a picnic. But the water can be a bit murky, and with the emphasis on families, it's not the best place for singles. **Amenities:** parking (fee); toilets. **Best for:** swimming. ✉ *9610 Old Cutler Rd.* ☎ *305/665–5475* ✉ *$6 per vehicle* ☉ *Daily 8–sunset.*

KEY BISCAYNE

Fodor'sChoice   **Bill Baggs Cape Florida State Park.** Thanks to inviting beaches, sunsets, ★   and a tranquil lighthouse, this park at Key Biscayne's southern tip is worth the drive. In fact, the 1-mile stretch of pure beachfront has been named several times in Dr. Beach's revered America's Top 10 Beaches list. It has 18 picnic pavilions available as daily rentals, two cafés that serve light lunches (Lighthouse Café, overlooking the Atlantic Ocean, and the Boater's Grill, on Biscayne Bay), and plenty of space to enjoy the umbrella and chair rentals. A stroll or ride along walking and bicycle paths provides wonderful views of Miami's dramatic skyline. From the southern end of the park you can see a handful of houses rising over the bay on wooden stilts, the remnants of Stiltsville, built in the 1940s and now protected by the Stiltsville Trust. The nonprofit group was established in 2003 to preserve the structures, because they showcase the park's rich history. Bill Baggs has bicycle rentals, a playground, fishing piers, and guided tours of the **Cape Florida Lighthouse,** South Florida's oldest structure. The lighthouse was erected in 1845 to replace an earlier one damaged in an 1836 Seminole attack, in which the keeper's helper was killed. Free tours are offered at the restored cottage and lighthouse at 10 am and 1 pm Thursday to Monday. Be there a half hour beforehand. **Amenities:** food and drink; lifeguards; parking; showers; toilets. **Best for:** solitude; sunsets; walking. ⊠ *1200 S. Crandon Blvd., Key Biscayne* ☎ *305/361–5811* ⊕ *www.floridastateparks.org/capeflorida* ◳ *$8 per vehicle; $2 per person on bicycle, bus, motorcycle, or foot* ☉ *Daily 8–sunset.*

FAMILY **Crandon Park Beach.** This relaxing oasis in northern Key Biscayne is dotted with palm trees, which provide a respite from the steamy sun until it's time to take a dip in the blue waters. Families really enjoy the beaches here—the sand is soft, there are no rip tides, there's a great view of the Atlantic, and parking is both inexpensive and plentiful. However, on weekends, be prepared for a long hike from your car to the beach. There are bathrooms, outdoor showers, plenty of picnic tables, concession stands, and golf and tennis facilities. The family-friendly park offers abundant options for kids who find it challenging to simply sit and build sand castles. **Crandon Gardens** at Crandon Park was once the site of a zoo. There are swans, waterfowl, and dozens of huge iguanas running loose. Nearby you'll find a restored carousel (it's open weekends and major holidays 10–5, until 6 in summer, and you get three rides for $1), an old-fashioned outdoor roller rink, a dolphin-shape spray fountain, and a playground. **Amenities:** food and drink; lifeguards; parking (fee); showers; toilets. **Best for:** swimming; walking. ⊠ *6747 Crandon Blvd., Key Biscayne* ☎ *305/361–5421* ⊕ *www.biscaynenaturecenter.org* ◳ *$5 per vehicle* ☉ *Daily 8–sunset.*

Marjory Stoneman Douglas Biscayne Nature Center. At the north end of the beach is the free Marjory Stoneman Douglas Biscayne Nature Center, where you can explore sea-grass beds on a tour with a naturalist; see red, black, and white mangroves; and hike along the beach and hammock in the Bear Cut Preserve. The park also sponsors hikes and tours. ⊠ *Key Biscayne* ☎ *305/361–6767* ⊕ *www.biscaynenaturecenter.org* ☉ *Daily 10–4.*

SOUTH BEACH

Fodor'sChoice **South Beach.** A 10-block stretch of white sandy beach hugging the tur-
★ quoise waters along Ocean Drive—from 5th to 15th streets—is one of the most popular in America, known for drawing unabashedly modelesque sunbathers and posers. With the influx of new luxe hotels and hotspots from 1st to 5th and 16th to 25th streets, the South Beach stand-and-pose scene is now bigger than ever and stretches yet another dozen plus blocks. The beaches crowd quickly on the weekends with a blend of European tourists, young hipsters, and sun-drenched locals offering Latin flavor. Separating the sand from the traffic of Ocean Drive

is palm-fringed **Lummus Park**, with its volleyball nets and chickee huts (huts made of palmetto thatch over a cypress frame) for shade. The beach at **12th Street** is popular with gays, in a section often marked with rainbow flags. Locals hang out on 3rd Street beach, in an area called **SoFi** (South of Fifth) where they watch fit Brazilians play foot volley, a variation of volleyball that uses everything but the hands. Because much of South Beach leans toward skimpy sunning—women are often in G-strings and casually topless—many families prefer the tamer sections of Mid- and North Beach. Metered parking spots next to the ocean are a rare find. Instead, opt for a public garage a few blocks away and enjoy the people-watching as you walk to find your perfect spot on the sand. **Amenities:** food and drink; lifeguards; parking (fee); showers; toilets. **Best for:** partiers; sunrise; swimming; walking. ✉ *Ocean Dr., from 5th to 15th Sts., then Collins Ave. to 25th St., South Beach, Miami Beach.*

THE OCEAN DRIVE HUSTLE

As you stroll by the sidewalk restaurants lining Ocean Drive, don't be surprised if you're solicited by a pretty hostess, who'll literally shove a menu in your face to entice you to her café—which is exactly like every other eatery on the strip. Be warned that reputable restaurants refrain from these aggressive tactics. If you're indeed enticed by the fishbowl drinks, use the chance to bargain. A request for free drinks with dinner may very well be accommodated!

2

NORTH BEACH AND AVENTURA

Haulover Beach Park. This popular clothing-optional beach is embraced by naturists of all ages, shapes, and sizes; there are even sections primarily frequented by families, singles, and gays. However, Haulover has more claims to fame than its casual attitude toward swimwear—it's also the best beach in the area for bodyboarding and surfing, as it gets what passes for impressive swells in these parts. Plus the sand here is fine-grain white, unusual for the Atlantic coast. Once you park in the North Lot, you'll walk through a short tunnel covered with trees and natural habitat until you emerge on the unpretentious beach, where nudity is rarely met by gawkers. There are volleyball nets, and plenty of beach chair and umbrella rentals to protect your birthday suit from too much exposure—to the sun, that is. The sections of beach requiring swimwear are popular, too, given the park's ample parking and relaxed atmosphere. Lifeguards stand watch. More active types might want to check out the kite rentals, or charter-fishing excursions. **Amenities:** food and drink; lifeguards; parking (fee); showers; toilets. **Best for:** nudists; surfing; swimming; walking. ✉ *10800 Collins Ave., north of Bal Harbour, North Beach and Aventura, Miami Beach* ☎ *305/944–3040* 🌐 *www.hauloverbeach.org* 🎟 *$6 per vehicle if parking in lot* ⏲ *Daily 8–sunset.*

FAMILY **Oleta River State Park.** Tucked away in North Miami Beach, this urban park is a ready-made family getaway. Nature lovers will find it easy to embrace the 1,128 acres of subtropical beauty along Biscayne Bay. Swim in the calm bay waters and bicycle, canoe, kayak, and bask among egrets, manatees, bald eagles, and fiddler crabs. Dozens of picnic tables, along with 10 covered pavilions, dot the stunning natural habitat, which was restored with red mangroves to revitalize the ecosystem and draw endangered birds, like the roseate spoonbill. There's a playground for tots, a mangrove island accessible only by boat, 15 miles of mountain-bike trails, a half-mile exercise track, concessions, and outdoor showers. **Amenities:** food and drink; parking (fee); showers; toilets; water sports. **Best for:** solitude; sunrise; sunset; walking. ⊠ *3400 N.E. 163rd St., North Beach and Aventura, Miami* ☎ *305/919–1846* ⊕ *www. floridastateparks.org/oletariver* ⚍ *$6 per vehicle; $2 per person on foot or bike* ⊙ *Daily 8–sunset.*

WHERE TO EAT

Miami's restaurant scene has exploded in the last few years, with dozens of great new restaurants springing up left and right. The melting pot of residents and visitors has brought an array of sophisticated, tasty cuisine. Little Havana is still king for Cuban fare, and Miami Beach is swept up in a trend of fusion cuisine, which combines Asian, French, American, and Latin cooking with sumptuous—and pricey—results. Locals spend the most time in downtown Miami, Wynwood, Midtown, and the Design District, where the city's ongoing foodie and cocktail revolution is most pronounced. Since Miami dining is a part of the trendy nightlife scene, most dinners don't start until 8 or 9 pm, and may go well into the night. To avoid a long wait among the late-night partiers at hot spots, come before 7 or make reservations. Attire is usually casual-chic, but patrons like to dress to impress. Don't be surprised to see large tables of women in skimpy dresses—this is common in Miami. Prices tend to stay high in hot spots like Lincoln Road, but if you venture off the beaten path you can find delicious food for reasonable prices. When you get your bill, check whether a gratuity is already included; most restaurants add between 15% and 20% (ostensibly for the convenience of, and protection from, the many Latin American and European tourists who are used to this practice in their homelands), but supplement it depending on your opinion of the service.

Use the coordinate (✚ C2) at the end of each review to locate a property on the Where to Eat in the Miami Area map.

DOWNTOWN MIAMI

$$$$
ECLECTIC
Fodor's Choice
★

✕ **Azul.** A restaurant known for producing celebrity chefs and delivering dining fantasies of Food Network proportions, Azul is a Miami foodie institution. With its award-winning team, Azul offers a haute-cuisine experience on par with a two- or three-Michelin-star restaurant. Chefs fuse disparate ingredients, merging as decadent, gastronomic art. Headliners include the House Cured Salmon, Grilled Spanish Octopus, and Lobster "Pot Pie" stuffed with vegetables and foie gras. Dine here and you'll undoubtedly experience bold new taste sensations while enjoying one of the finest wine lists in the city and an incomparable skyline

BEST BETS FOR MIAMI DINING

2

Fodor's writers and editors have selected their favorite restaurants by price, cuisine, and experience in the Best Bets lists below. In the first column, Fodor's Choice designations represent the "best of the best" in every price category. Find specific details about a restaurant in the full reviews, listed alphabetically by neighborhood.

Fodor's Choice★

Azul, Downtown Miami, p. 62

Bourbon Steak, North Miami and Aventura, p. 78

Cantina Beach, Key Biscayne, p. 67

CATCH Miami, South Beach, p. 69

1500°, Mid-Beach, p. 76

Florida Cookery, South Beach, p. 72

Hakkasan, Mid-Beach, p. 77

Hy-Vong Vietnamese Cuisine, Little Havana, p. 65

Joe's Stone Crab Restaurant, South Beach, p. 72

Khong River House, South Beach, p. 73

Pied à Terre, South Beach, p. 74

Rusty Pelican, Key Biscayne, p. 67

Sugarcane Raw Bar Grill, Midtown Miami, p. 68

Tosca Miami, South Beach, p. 76

Yardbird Southern Table & Bar, South Beach, p. 76

By Price

$

Palacio de los Jugos, Coral Gables, p. 66

$$

Peacock Garden Café, Coconut Grove, p. 66

Yardbird, Southern Table & Bar, South Beach, p. 76

$$$

Cantina Beach, Key Biscayne, p. 67

$$$$

Azul, Downtown Miami, p. 62

Cioppino, Key Biscayne, p. 67

The Forge, Mid-Beach, p. 77

Juvia, South Beach, p. 73

By Cuisine

AMERICAN

Florida Cookery, South Beach, p. 72

Michael's Genuine Food & Drink, Design District, p. 68

ASIAN

Hakkasan, Mid-Beach, p. 77

Makoto, North Miami and Aventura, p. 78

SushiSamba Dromo, South Beach, p. 75

CUBAN

Havana Harry's, Coral Gables, p. 66

Versailles, Little Havana, p. 65

ITALIAN

Cioppino, Key Biscayne, p. 67

Il Mulino New York, North Miami and Aventura, p. 78

SEAFOOD

CATCH Miami, South Beach, p. 69

Joe's Stone Crab Restaurant, South Beach, p. 72

STEAKHOUSE

Gotham Steak, Mid-Beach, p. 77

Meat Market, South Beach, p. 74

Prime One Twelve, South Beach, p. 74

By Experience

CHILD-FRIENDLY

Cantina Beach, Key Biscayne, p. 67

HOT SPOTS

Meat Market, South Beach, p. 74

Wynwood Kitchen & Bar, Wynwood, p. 68

view. $ *Average main: $48* ⊠ *Mandarin Oriental, Miami, 500 Brickell Key Dr., Downtown* ☎ *305/913–8358* ⊕ *www.mandarinoriental.com/miami* ⚐ *Reservations essential* ☽ *Closed Sun. No lunch* ✛ *E5.*

$$$$ ✕ **db Bistro Moderne Miami.** One of America's most celebrated French
FRENCH chefs, Daniel Boulud brings his renowned cooking to the Miami scene. The menu of Boulud's latest outpost pays homage to the different cuisines and specialties of his homeland and surrounding regions, beginning with a fabulous raw bar alongside regional tasting plates such as the "Assiette Provencale" with mackerel escabeche, black olive tapenade, goat cheese with pear, and Swiss chard *barbajuan*. Moving on to the second course, choose from a dozen hot and cold small plates, like the signature "Daniel Boulud's Smoked Salmon," escargots persillade with wild burgundy snails simmered in parsley, garlic, salted butter with yellow tomatoes and wild mushrooms, and the tomato *tarte tatin*. For the main course, the authentic coq au vin and the *moules piquante* are guaranteed crowd pleasers, channeling images and/or memories of France through the tastes and smells of the restaurant's flagship dishes. $ *Average main: $42* ⊠ *JW Marriott Marquis Miami, 255 Biscayne Blvd. Way, Downtown* ☎ *305/421–8800* ⊕ *www.danielnyc.com* ✛ *D4.*

$$$ ✕ **Edge, Steak & Bar.** It's farm-to-table surf-and-turf at this elegantly
STEAKHOUSE understated restaurant in the Four Seasons, where hefty portions of the finest cuts and freshest seafood headline the menu, prepared by renowned chef Aaron Brooks. The innovative tartares are a surefire way to start the night right—try the corvina with baby cucumber and green apple in a celery-leaf, yellow-pepper sauce, or ahi tuna with pickled shallots, watermelon, and mint. For the main event, Edge offers a variety of small, medium, and large cuts from the infrared grill, the most popular being the black Angus filet mignon. For a more casual experience, enjoy your meal and the restaurant's artisan cocktails under the skies in the alfresco section. $ *Average main: $30* ⊠ *Four Seasons Miami, 1435 Brickell Ave., Downtown* ☎ *305/381–3190* ⊕ *www.edgerestaurantmiami.com* ✛ *D5.*

$$$$ ✕ **NAOE.** Once in a rare while, you discover a restaurant so authentic,
JAPANESE so special, yet still undiscovered by the masses. By virtue of its petite size (less than two-dozen max) and strict seating times (twice per night at 6 and 9:30), the Japanese gem, NAOE, will forever remain intimate and original. The all-inclusive menu changes daily, based on the day's best and freshest seafood, but always includes a Bento Box, soup, nigirizushi, and dessert. Every visit ushers in a new exploration of the senses. Chef Kevin Cory prepares the gastronomic adventure a few feet from his patrons, using only the best ingredients and showcasing family treasures, like the renowned products of his centuries'-old family shoyu (soy sauce) brewery and sake brewery. From start to finish, you'll be transported to Japan through the stellar service, the tastes of bizarre sea creatures, the blanching of live scallops, and the smoothness of spectacular sakes. $ *Average main: $85* ⊠ *661 Brickell Key Dr., Downtown* ☎ *305/947–6263* ⊕ *www.naoemiami.com* ⚐ *Reservations essential* ✛ *E5.*

$$ ✕ **Perricone's Marketplace and Café.** Brickell Avenue south of the Miami
ITALIAN River is a haven for Italian restaurants, and this lunch place for local bigwigs is the biggest and most popular among them. It's housed partially

outdoors and partially indoors in an 1880s Vermont barn. Recipes were handed down from generation to generation, and the cooking is simple and good. Buy your wine from the on-premises deli, and enjoy it (for a small corking fee) with homemade minestrone; a generous antipasto; linguine with a sauté of jumbo shrimp, scallops, and calamari; or gnocchi with four cheeses. The homemade tiramisu and cannoli are top-notch. [$] *Average main: $22* ✉ *Mary Brickell Village, 15 S.E. 10th St., Downtown* ☎ *305/374–9449* 🌐 *www.perricones.com* ✥ *D5.*

2

LITTLE HAVANA

$$ VIETNAMESE Fodor's Choice ★

🍴 **Hy-Vong Vietnamese Cuisine.** Florida's best Vietnamese food in the heart of Little Havana? It may sound bizarre, but Hy-Vong will have you rethinking your drive to Calle Ocho for Cuban cuisine. In fact, people are willing to wait on the sidewalk for hours to sample the *cha gio* (Vietnamese spring rolls), fish panfried with mango or with *nuoc man* (a garlic-lime fish sauce), not to mention the pork *thit kho* (caramelized braised pork) stewed in coconut milk. Beer-savvy proprietors Kathy Manning and Tung Nguyen serve a half-dozen top brews (Double Grimbergen, Peroni, and Spaten, among them) to further inoculate the experience from the ordinary. Arrive early to avoid long waits. [$] *Average main: $16* ✉ *3458 S.W. 8th St.* ☎ *305/446–3674* 🌐 *www.hyvong.com* 🕒 *Closed Mon.* ✥ *C5.*

$$ CUBAN

🍴 **Versailles.** *¡Bienvenido a Miami!* To the area's Cuban population, Miami without Versailles is like rice without black beans. First-timer Miami visitors looking for that "Cuban food on Calle Ocho" experience, look no further. The storied eatery, where old émigrés opine daily about all things Cuban, is a stop on every political candidate's campaign trail, and it should be a stop for you as well. Order a heaping platter of *lechon asado* (roasted pork loin), *ropa vieja* (shredded beef), or *picadillo* (spicy ground beef), all served with rice, beans, and fried plantains. Battle the oncoming food coma with a cup of the city's strongest *cafecito,* which comes in the tiniest of cups but packs a lot of punch. Versailles operates a bakery next door as well—take some *pastelitos* home. [$] *Average main: $13* ✉ *3555 S.W. 8th St., between S.W. 35th and S.W. 36th Aves.* ☎ *305/444–0240* ✥ *C5.*

COCONUT GROVE

$$$ PERUVIAN

🍴 **Jaguar Ceviche Spoon Bar & Latam Grill.** A fabulous fusion of Peruvian and Mexican flavors, Jaguar is a gastronomic tour of Latin America in a single restaurant. As the name implies, there is a heavy emphasis on ceviches. The best option for experiencing this delicacy is the spoon sampler, which includes six distinct Peruvian and Mexican ceviches served in oversized spoons. Meals come with blue corn tortilla and pita chips served with authentic Mexican salsa. Dishes, such the Mexican Tortilla Lasagna (chicken, poblano peppers, corn, tomato sauce, and cream, topped with melted cheese), are colorful, flavorful, and innovative. [$] *Average main: $20* ✉ *3067 Grand Ave.* ☎ *305/444–0216* 🌐 *www.jaguarspot.com* ✥ *C5.*

$$ ✕ **Peacock Garden Café.** Reinstating the artsy and exciting vibe of Coco-
AMERICAN nut Grove circa once-upon-a-time, this lovely spot offers an indoor-
FAMILY outdoor, tea-time setting for light bites. By day, it's one of Miami's
most serene lunch spots. The lushly landscaped courtyard is lined with
alfresco seating, drawing some of Miami's most fabulous ladies who
lunch. Come evening, the café buzzes with a multigenerational crowd,
enjoying the South Florida zephyrs and the delicious flatbreads, sal-
ads, homemade soups, and entrées. Breakfast is also excellent. $ *Av-
erage main: $19* ⊠ *2889 McFarlane Rd.* ☎ *305/774–3332* ⊕ *www.
peacockspot.com* ✛ *C5.*

CORAL GABLES

$ ✕ **El Palacio de los Jugos.** To the northwest of Coral Gables proper, this
CUBAN joint is one of the easiest and truest ways to see Miami's local Latin
life in action. It's also one of the best fruit-shake shacks you'll ever
come across (ask for a tropical juice of mamey or guanabana). Besides
the rows of fresh tropical fruits and vegetables, and the shakes you
can make with any of them, this boisterous indoor-outdoor market
has numerous food counters where you can get just about any Cuban
food—tamales, rice and beans, a *pan con lechón* (roast pork on Cuban
bread for $4), fried pork rinds, or a coconut split before you and served
with a straw. Order your food at a counter and eat it along with local
families at rows of outdoor picnic-style tables next to the parking lot.
It's disorganized, chaotic, and not for those cutting calories, but it's
delicious and undeniably the real thing. $ *Average main: $5* ⊠ *5721 W.
Flagler St., Flagami, Miami* ☎ *305/262–0070* ▭ No credit cards ✛ *B4.*

$$ ✕ **Havana Harry's.** When Cuban families want an affordable home-
CUBAN cooked meal with a twist but don't want to cook it themselves or go
supercheap at the Cuban fast-food joint, Pollo Tropical, they come
to this big, unassuming restaurant. In fact, you're likely to see whole
families here representing multiple generations. The fare is traditional
Cuban: long thin steaks known as *bistec palomilla* (a panfried steak),
roast chicken with citrus marinade, and fried pork chunks; contemporary flourishes—mango sauce and guava-painted pork roast—are kept
to a minimum. Most dishes come with white rice, black beans, and
a choice of ripe or green plantains. The sweet ripe ones offer a good
contrast to the savory dishes. Start with the $5.25 *mariquitas* (plantain
chips) with mojo. Finish with the acclaimed flan. $ *Average main: $14*
⊠ *4612 Le Jeune Rd.* ☎ *305/661–2622* ⊕ *www.havanaharrys.net* ✛ *C5.*

$$$ ✕ **Ortanique on the Mile.** Cascading *ortaniques*, a Jamaican hybrid
CARIBBEAN orange, are hand-painted on columns in this warm, welcoming yel-
low dining room. Food is vibrant in taste and color, as delicious as it
is beautiful. Though there is no denying that the strong, full flavors are
imbued with island breezes, chef-partner Cindy Hutson's personal "cui-
sine of the sun" goes beyond Caribbean refinements. The menu centers
on fish, since Hutson has a special way with it, and the West Indian
Style Bouillabaisse is not to be missed. Ceviches and soups change
nightly. The mojitos here—and the cocktails in general—are amazing!
$ *Average main: $32* ⊠ *278 Miracle Mile* ☎ *305/446–7710* ⊕ *www.
cindyhutsoncuisine.com* ☯ *No lunch weekends* ✛ *C5.*

KEY BISCAYNE

$$$
MEXICAN
Fodor's Choice
★

X**Cantina Beach.** Leave it to the Ritz-Carlton Key Biscayne, Miami to bring a small, sumptuous piece of coastal Mexico to Florida's fabulous beaches. The pool- and ocean-side Cantina Beach showcases authentic and divine Mexican cuisine, including fresh guacamole made tableside. The restaurant also boasts the region's only *tequilier*, mixing and matching 110 high-end tequilas. It's no surprise then that Cantina Beach has phenomenal margaritas. And the best part is that you can enjoy them with your feet in the sand, gazing at the ocean. $ *Average main: $21* ✉ *Ritz-Carlton Key Biscayne, Miami, 455 Grand Bay Dr., Key Biscayne* ☎ *305/365–4622* ⊕ *www. ritzcarlton.com/keybiscayne* ✛ *E6.*

> ## FULL-MOON DINNERS
>
> The Full Moon Dinner Series at Cioppino is fun, romantic, geeky, and one of Miami's most memorable experiences. Held from October to May on the exact night of the full moon, the dinner is a four-course Italian gastronomic extravaganza under the magical path of the rising full moon. Tabletop telescopes serve as centerpieces. The restaurant's Constellation Concierge visits each table to point out key stars and constellations, and then invites guests to look at the moon through the mega-telescope. Meanwhile highly attentive staff members serve the divine creations of Chef de Cuisine Ezio Gamba.

$$$$
ITALIAN

X**Cioppino.** Few visitors think to venture out to the far end of Key Biscayne for dinner, but making the journey to the soothing grounds of this quiet Ritz-Carlton property on the beach is well worth it. Choose your view: the ornate dining room near the exhibition kitchen or the alfresco area with views of landscaped gardens or breeze-brushed beaches. Choosing your dishes may be more difficult, given the many rich, luscious Italian options, including imported cheeses, olive oils, risottos, and fresh fish flown in daily. Items range from the creamy *burrata* mozzarella and authentic pasta dishes to tantalizing risotto with organic spinach and roasted quail, all expertly matched with fine, vintage, rare, and boutique wines. An after-dinner drink and live music at the old-Havana-style RUMBAR inside the hotel is another treat. $ *Average main: $36* ✉ *Ritz-Carlton Key Biscayne, Miami, 455 Grand Bay Dr., Key Biscayne* ☎ *305/365–4156* ⊕ *www.ritzcarlton. com/keybiscayne* ✛ *E6.*

$$$$
MODERN
AMERICAN
Fodor's Choice
★

X**Rusty Pelican.** Whether you're visiting Miami for the first or 15th time, a meal at the Rusty Pelican could easily stand out as your most memorable experience. The legendary Key Biscayne restaurant's $7 million reinvention is nothing short of spectacular. Vistas of the bay and Miami skyline are sensational—whether you admire them through the floor-to-ceiling windows or from the expansive outdoor seating area, lined with alluring fire pits. The menu is split between tropically inspired small plates and heartier entrées from land and sea. Standouts include sea bass ceviche; baked crab cakes; and the fried, whole local red snapper. $ *Average main: $38* ✉ *3201 Rickenbacker Causeway, Key Biscayne* ☎ *305/361–3818* ⊕ *www.therustypelican.com* ✛ *E5.*

WYNWOOD/MIDTOWN/DESIGN DISTRICT

$$$
FRENCH
✕**Georges Kitchen & The Loft.** French restaurateur George Eric Farge has joined forces with Michelin-starred Executive Chef Steven Rojas to create a chic and trendy restaurant/lounge combo in the heart of Miami's burgeoning Midtown area. Downstairs at Georges Kitchen, Rojas shows off his award-winning skills in the open kitchen, crafting such masterpieces as short-rib tartare and a tasty grilled pork cheek with diver scallops. Upstairs at the Loft, the party rages until late as the young, sophisticated crowd toasts to Midtown's magic and the design-savvy surroundings. $ *Average main: $26* ⊠ *3404 N. Miami Ave., Midtown* ☎ *305/438–9199* ⊕ *www.georgeskitchenmidtown.com* ✛ *D4.*

$$$
AMERICAN
✕**Michael's Genuine Food & Drink.** Michael's is often cited as Miami's top restaurant, and it's not hard to see why. This indoor-outdoor bistro in Miami's Design District relies on fresh ingredients and a hip but unpretentious vibe to lure diners. Beautifully arranged combinations like crispy, sweet-and-spicy pork belly with kimchi explode with unlikely but satisfying flavor. Owner and chef Michael Schwartz aims for sophisticated American cuisine with an emphasis on local and organic ingredients. He gets it right. Portions are divided into small, medium, and large plates, and the smaller plates are more inventive, so you can order several and explore. Reserve two weeks in advance for weekend tables; also, consider brunch. $ *Average main: $26* ⊠ *130 N.E. 40th St.* ☎ *305/573–5550* ⊕ *www.michaelsgenuine.com* ⬥ *Reservations essential* ✛ *D3.*

$$$$
JAPANESE
Fodor's Choice
★
✕**Sugarcane Raw Bar Grill.** Midtown's most popular restaurant rages seven nights a week; and it's not hard to see why. The vibrant, casually elegant restaurant perfectly captures Miami's Latin vibe while serving eclectic tapas and modern Japanese delights from three separate kitchens (robata, raw bar, and hot kitchen). This trio engineers some 60 small bites that include everything from sushi to bacon-wrapped dates and maple-glazed sweet potatoes. Sugarcane has its fair share of awesome foodie fear factor dishes (think: Pig's ear in bbq spice and crispy Florida frogs' legs) but it's the specialty sushi rolls—like the night crab with snow crab, shrimp tempura, and caper mustard, and the shrimp ceviche in passion fruit and coconut milk—that get the most attention. $ *Average main: $38* ⊠ *3252 N.E. 1st Ave., Midtown* ☎ *786/369–0353* ⊕ *sugarcanerawbargrill.com* ⬥ *Reservations essential* ✛ *D4.*

$$
ECLECTIC
✕**Wynwood Kitchen & Bar.** At the center of Miami's artsy gallery-driven neighborhood, Wynwood Kitchen & Bar offers an experience completely different from anything else in the state. While you enjoy Latin-inspired small plates, you can marvel at the powerful, hand-painted murals characterizing the interiors and exteriors, which also spill out onto the captivating Wynwood Walls. Designed for sharing, tapas-style dishes include wood-grilled baby octopus skewers, lemon-pepper calamari, roasted beets, bacon-wrapped dates, and ropa vieja empanadas. It's best to allot a good chunk of time to thoroughly enjoy the creative food, the artist-inspired cocktails, and the coolio crowd, and to venerate the sensational works of art all around you. $ *Average main: $22* ⊠ *2550 N.W. 2nd Ave., Wynwood Art District* ☎ *305/722–8959* ⊕ *www.wynwoodkitchenandbar.com* ✛ *D4.*

SOUTH BEACH

$$$$
ITALIAN

✕ **Bianca.** In a hotel where style reigns supreme, this high-profile restaurant provides both glamour and solid cuisine. The main attraction of dining here is to see and be seen, but you may leave talking about the food just as much as the outfits, hairdos, and celebrity appearances. This Italian restaurant doles out some amazing fare, including a shaved baby-artichoke salad and truffle tagliatelle—perfection in every bite. The dessert menu may seem a bit back-to-basics, with tiramisu and cheesecake among the favorites, but these sweet classics are done right. For something a bit more casual at the Delano, try sushi from the Philippe Starck countertop sushi bar, Umi, at the front of the hotel. $ *Average main: $45* ⊠ *Delano Hotel, 1685 Collins Ave., South Beach* ☎ *305/674–5752* ⊕ *www.delano-hotel.com* ⌂ *Reservations essential* ✛ *H2.*

$$$$
STEAKHOUSE

✕ **BLT Steak.** This Ocean Drive favorite, renowned for seriously divine Gruyère cheese popovers and succulent steak and fish dishes, illuminates the vibrant, open lobby of the snazzy Betsy Hotel. It has the distinction among all of Miami's steak houses of serving breakfast daily and consistently impressing even the most finicky eaters. You can count on the highest-quality cuts of USDA prime, certified Black Angus, and American Wagyu beef, in addition to blackboard specials, and sushi and raw-bar selections. Though the name may say steak, the fresh fish is arguably the highlight of the entire menu—the sautéed Dover sole with soy-caper brown butter is legendary. $ *Average main: $32* ⊠ *Betsy Hotel, 1440 Ocean Dr., South Beach* ☎ *305/673–0044* ⊕ *www.bltrestaurants.com* ✛ *H2.*

$$$$
MODERN ASIAN
Fodor'sChoice
★

✕ **CATCH Miami.** *Top Chef* winner, Executive Chef Hung Huynh made his Miami debut in a big and bold way. Modeled after his restaurant of the same name in New York City, CATCH Miami brings Asian fusion fantasies to life in a design-savvy art deco building that commingles the big city vibe of the Big Apple with South Beach sultriness. The seafood-centric menu pushes the envelope on just about every fruit from the sea, with avante-garde sushi rolls, dumplings, crispy whole snapper, sizzling lobster, and baked shrimp. Unique to CATCH Miami are items like the Shorecrest Roll (spicy tuna, cucumber, and salsa verde) and Po "Little Rich" Boys (potato rolls stuffed with fried oysters, caviar, and spicy remoulade). Experiential artisan drinks match experiential eats. $ *Average main: $43* ⊠ *James Royal Palm, 1545 Collins Ave., South Beach* ☎ *786/224–7200* ⊕ *www.jameshotels.com/miami/eat-drink/catch* ✛ *H2.*

$$$$
MODERN
AMERICAN

✕ **The Dutch Miami.** Loft meets cozy-kitchen at the Miami outpost of Chef Andrew Carmellini's NYC foodie hot spot. Located in the swank W South Beach Hotel, the Dutch takes on a personality all its own, adorned with cute tchotchkes and ornamental objects set along white bookshelves. There's a bit of everything on the "roots-inspired American menu," from local line-caught fish to homemade pastas and the full gamut of steaks. Dinner begins with a twist on a Southern classic—a corn-bread loaf with a hint of jalapeño. Two dishes that may blow your mind are the Maine sea scallops with heirloom cauliflower and citrus, and the yellowtail crudo with watermelon and jalapeño. It's worth coming here for this dish alone. $ *Average main: $36* ⊠ *W South Beach, 2201 Collins Ave., South Beach* ☎ *305/938–3111* ⊕ *www.thedutchmiami.com* ✛ *H1.*

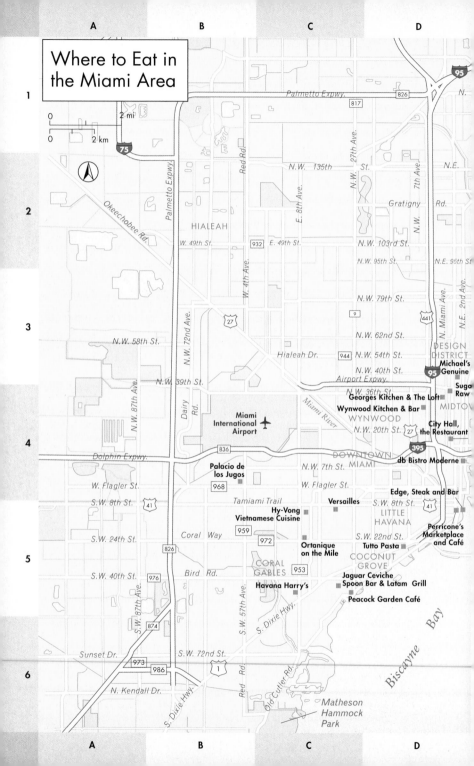

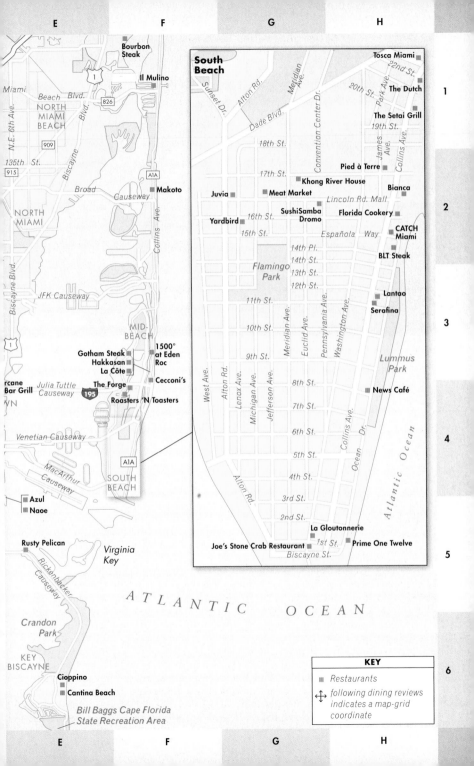

South Beach

Bourbon Steak

Il Mulino

Tosca Miami

The Dutch

The Setai Grill

Pied à Terre

Khong River House

Bianca

Juvia

Meat Market

Makoto

SushiSamba Dromo

Florida Cookery

Yardbird

CATCH Miami

BLT Steak

Lantao

Serafina

Gotham Steak
Hakkasan
La Côte

1500°
at Eden
Roc

Cecconi's

The Forge

Roasters 'N Toasters

News Café

Azul

Naoe

Rusty Pelican

La Gloutonnerie

Joe's Stone Crab Restaurant

Prime One Twelve

Cioppino

Cantina Beach

Miami

NORTH
MIAMI
BEACH

Beach Blvd.

NORTH
MIAMI

Broad Causeway

Collins Ave.

JFK Causeway

MID-
BEACH

Julia Tuttle
Causeway

Venetian Causeway

MacArthur
Causeway

SOUTH
BEACH

Virginia
Key

Rickenbacker
Causeway

Crandon
Park

KEY
BISCAYNE

Bill Baggs Cape Florida
State Recreation Area

N.E. 6th Ave.

Biscayne Blvd.

rcane
Bar Grill
WN

Sunset Dr.

Alton Rd.

Meridian Ave.

Dade Blvd.

Convention Center Dr.

18th St.

17th St.

Lincoln Rd. Mall

16th St.

Española Way

15th St.

14th Pl.
14th St.
Flamingo   13th St.
Park   12th St.

11th St.

West Ave.

Alton Rd.

Lenox Ave.

Michigan Ave.

Jefferson Ave.

Meridian Ave.

Euclid Ave.

Pennsylvania Ave.

Washington Ave.

10th St.

9th St.

8th St.

7th St.

6th St.

5th St.

4th St.

3rd St.

2nd St.

Alton Rd.

Collins Ave.

Ocean Dr.

Atlantic Ocean

Lummus
Park

22nd St.

Park Ave.

20th St.

19th St.

James Ave.

Collins Ave.

1st St.

Biscayne St.

ATLANTIC   OCEAN

KEY

Restaurants

following dining reviews
indicates a map-grid
coordinate

CATCH Miami

$$$ ✕ **Florida Cookery.** Award-winning Miami chef Kris Wessel (of *Chopped*
AMERICAN fame) has reinvented Florida cuisine with this sensational restaurant. In
Fodor's Choice a vintage luxe dining room designed by Laura Rottet of Rottet Studios,
★ Wessel delivers mind-boggling taste sensations crafted from just about
all things Florida—from local fish, conch, and spiny lobster to frog's
legs, alligator, and wild boar from the Everglades, and Indian River
County grapefruit, hearts of palm, and kumquats. Each course is a new
experience. Start with the conch chowder and "fritter dipper," Wessel's
family recipe since 1948. Then move on to the oxtail, oyster, and alli-
gator empanadas, the sweet-and-sour "Kris's Biscayne Blvd." shrimp,
and the spiny lobster pan-braised in a sherry bisque. Even if you're full
after appetizers and mains, order dessert. The hot banana-pecan pud-
ding in a jar is simply heaven on Earth. $ *Average main: $26* ⊠ *James
Royal Palm, 1545 Collins Ave, South Beach* ☎ *786/276–0333* ⊕ *www.
florida-cookery.com* ⊹ *H2.*

$$$$ ✕ **Joe's Stone Crab Restaurant.** In South Beach's decidedly new-money
SEAFOOD scene, the stately Joe's Stone Crab is an old-school testament to good
Fodor's Choice food and good service. South Beach's most storied restaurant started
★ as a turn-of-the-century eating house when Joseph Weiss discovered
succulent stone crabs off the Florida coast. Almost a century later,
the restaurant stretches a city block and serves 2,000 dinners a day
to local politicians and moneyed patriarchs. Stone crabs, served with
legendary mustard sauce, crispy hash browns, and creamed spinach,
remain the staple. Though stone-crab season runs from October 15 to
May 15, Joe's remains open year-round (albeit with a limited sched-
ule) serving other phenomenal seafood dishes. Finish your meal with
tart key lime pie, baked fresh daily. ▬TIP➔ Joe's famously refuses

reservations, and weekend waits can be three hours long—yes, you read that correctly—so come early or order from Joe's Take Away next door. [$] *Average main: $42* ✉ *11 Washington Ave., South Beach* ☎ *305/673–0365, 305/673–4611 for takeout* 🌐 *www.joesstonecrab.com* ✍ *Reservations not accepted* 🕓 *No lunch Sun. and Mon. and mid-May–mid-Oct.* ✥ *G5.*

$$$$ JAPANESE FUSION
🍴 **Juvia.** High atop South Beach's design-driven 1111 Lincoln Road parking garage, Juvia commingles urban sophistication with South Beach seduction. Towering over the beach's art deco district, the restaurant rises as a bold amalgamation of steel, glass, hanging gardens, and purple accents—a true work of art high in the sky. Three renowned chefs unite to deliver an amazing eating experience that screams Japanese, Peruvian, and French all in the same breath, focusing largely on raw fish and seafood dishes. The see-and-be-seen crowd can't get enough. [$] *Average main: $42* ✉ *1111 Lincoln Rd., South Beach* ☎ *305/763–8272* 🌐 *www.juviamiami.com* ✍ *Reservations essential* ✥ *G2.*

$$$ ASIAN Fodor's Choice ★
🍴 **Khong River House.** A James Beard Foundation semifinalist as America's Best New Restaurant 2013, Khong River House brings the exotic flavors of rural Thailand to Miami's storied Lincoln Road. Don't expect pad Thai here. Unlike your typical American Thai restaurant, Khong doles out hefty portions of lesser-known dishes common to the Mekong River and Golden Triangle region, where Myanmar, Thailand, Laos, and Vietnam converge. Ambush your senses with *Kuay Teaw Hor Phama* (Burmese noodle wraps stuffed with chilis, roasted peanuts, palm sugar, and cilantro), *Gang Pah Gai* (northeastern-style jungle curry), or *Pad Ped Grob Prik Thai On* (Thai-style crispy duck). The restaurant is also a visual feast for the senses with seductive hardwood walls and furnishings, tastefully placed Buddhist statues, as well as a clandestine second-floor dining room. [$] *Average main: $27* ✉ *1661 Meridian Ave., South Beach* ☎ *305/763–8147* 🌐 *www.khongriver.com* ✍ *Reservations essential* ✥ *G2.*

$$$ MODERN FRENCH
🍴 **La Gloutonnerie.** Far removed from South Beach's mass-market deco drive strip, this intimate "vintage kitchen" brings the best of French old-school cuisine to the beach's more refined SoFi (South of Fifth) neighborhood. The chef presents everything you'd desire from a renowned French kitchen from *escargots Bourgogne* to *chateubriand* while adding new-world flavors and fusions to the mix with dishes such as the shrimp carpaccio Santa Margherita (cured in peach and citrus juice) and an assortment of fresh pasta entrées. Within the restaurant, a retro mini-market offers cheese, cold cuts, and imported French products. Add stylish black and white decor, stellar service, and a hip crowd, and you have the perfect recipe for keeping history in style. [$] *Average main: $28* ✉ *81 Washington Ave., South Beach* ☎ *305/503–3811* 🌐 *www.lagloutonnerie.com* ✥ *G5.*

$$$ MODERN ASIAN
🍴 **Lantao.** Inside the Kimpton Group's trendy Surfcomber Hotel, Lantao brings the best of Asian street food to America's sexiest city. Forget food trucks—this is a one-stop shop for touring the food stalls of an entire continent. Transport yourself to Southeast Asia with the Singapore chili prawns and crispy kale, or head to the Land of the Morning Calm, Korea, for barbecue pork ribs. The cocktails are equally impressive and colorful. It's not every day you're able to knock back

a Hibiki Highball (Hibiki Japanese Whiskey with Fever-Tree soda) and gawk at Miami's profusion of pretty people. [$] *Average main: $28* ✉ *Surfcomber Hotel, 1717 Collins Ave., South Beach* ☎ *305/604–1800* 🌐 *www.lantaorestaurant.com* ✥ *H3.*

$$$$ STEAKHOUSE 🍴 **Meat Market.** On Lincoln Road, where most of the restaurants emphasize people-watching over good food, this is one spot where you can find the best of both. Indeed, this is a meat market in every sense of the phrase, with great cuts of meat and plenty of sexy people passing by in skimpy clothes and enjoying fruity libations at the bar. Hardcore carnivores go wild over the the 14-ounce center-cut prime New York steak as well as the "mixed-grill special," a creative trio of meats and seafood that changes nightly. The tuna tartare is exceptional here, lightly tossed in ginger and soy with mashed avocados and mango mole. Also consider the wood-grilled blackened local snapper cooked to perfection and topped with a light sun-dried-tomato pesto and dollops of black-garlic sauce. The broccolini side makes a nice complement to any meal. [$] *Average main: $34* ✉ *915 Lincoln Rd., South Beach* ☎ *305/532–0088* 🌐 *www.meatmarketmiami.com* 🕒 *No lunch* ✥ *G2.*

$$ AMERICAN 🍴 **News Café.** No trip to Miami is complete without a stop at this Ocean Drive landmark. The 24-hour café attracts a crowd with snacks, light meals, drinks, periodicals, and the people-parade on the sidewalk out front. Most prefer sitting outside, where they can feel the salt breeze and gawk at the human scenery. Sea-grape trees shade a patio where you can watch from a quiet distance. Offering a little of this and a little of that—bagels, pâtés, chocolate fondue, sandwiches, and a terrific wine list—this joint has something for everyone. Although service can be indifferent to the point of laissez-faire and the food is mediocre at best, News Café is just one of those places visitors love. [$] *Average main: $18* ✉ *800 Ocean Dr., South Beach* ☎ *305/538–6397* 🌐 *www.newscafe.com* ✍ *Reservations not accepted* ✥ *H4.*

$$$$ MODERN FRENCH Fodor's Choice ★ 🍴 **Pied à Terre.** This cozy, 36-seat French Contemporary restaurant with Mediterranean influence resides in the heart of South Beach, but it's everything the beach is not. Quiet, classic, and elegant, this hidden gastro-sanctuary within the Cadet Hotel forgoes glitz and gimmicks for taste and sophistication. The restaurant recalls the ambience of an intimate Parisian eatery—the kind you'd randomly discover on a side street in the City of Light's 5th or 6th arrondissement—and doles out succulent French contemporary cuisine enhanced by an excellent and reasonably priced wine list. [$] *Average main: $36* ✉ *Cadet Hotel, 1701 James Ave., South Beach* ☎ *305/672–6688* 🌐 *www.piedaterrerestaurant.com* ✍ *Reservations essential* 🕒 *Closed Sun. and Mon. No lunch* ✥ *H2.*

$$$$ STEAKHOUSE 🍴 **Prime One Twelve.** This wildly busy steak house is particularly renowned for its highly marbleized prime beef, creamed corn, truffle macaroni and cheese, and buzzing scene: while you stand at the bar awaiting your table (everyone has to wait—at least a little bit), you'll clamor for a drink with all facets of Miami's high society, from the city's top real estate developers and philanthropists to striking models and celebrities (Lenny Kravitz, Jay-Z, and Matt Damon are among a big list of celebrity regulars). [$] *Average main: $42* ✉ *112 Ocean Dr., South Beach* ☎ *305/532–8112* 🌐 *www.mylesrestaurantgroup.com* 🕒 *No lunch weekends* ✥ *H5.*

CHEAP EATS ON SOUTH BEACH

Miami Beach is notorious for overpriced eateries, but locals know better. **Pizza Rustica** (✉ *8th St. and Washington Ave., 14th St. and Washington Ave., and at 667 Lincoln Rd.*) serves up humongous slices overflowing with mozzarella, steak, olives, and barbecue chicken until 4 am. **La Sandwicherie** (✉ *14th St. between Collins and Washington Aves.*) is a South Beach classic that's been here since 1988, serving gourmet French sandwiches, a delicious prosciutto salad, and healthful smoothies from a walk-up bar. **Lime Fresh Mexican Grill** (✉ *1439 Alton Rd., at 14th St.*) serves fresh and tangy fish tacos and homemade guacamole.

$$ ✕ **Serafina.** The 15th outpost of this Northern Italian restaurant resides
NORTHERN in the heart of South Beach, off Collins Avenue and 11th Street. Serv-
ITALIAN ing up the full gamut of pastas, risottos, and thin-crust pizzas from a wood-fired oven, Serafina is all about classic done right and at an affordable price. Similar to the original Serafina restaurants in New York, the tried and true recipes of Serafina South Beach are already staples in Miami, most notably the Pizza al Tartufo, a white pizza with black truffle shavings. $ *Average main: $20* ✉ *1111 Collins Ave, South Beach* ☎ *305/534–8455* ✛ *H3.*

$$$$ ✕ **The Setai Grill.** If there's such a thing as an haute steakhouse, the
STEAKHOUSE Setai Grill is it. Executive Chef Mathias Gervais reinterprets Ameri-
can classics using the Rolls Royces of the food industry (think: Pat LaFrieda beef, Cinco Jotas's Jamón Ibérico, and Marky's caviar) and adding a French, contemporary twist. While the LaFrieda prime cuts and the braised meats exemplify tradition perfected, Gervais goes more avante-garde with his "Butcher's Cuts," starters, and salads. The Roseval salad, for example, is a sensational taste explosion, as the flavors of warm shallot-marinated potatoes, cold arugula, chives, and truffle vinaigrette unite. The signature "Caviar Tin"—a tower of extra-large Florida stone crab claws, crème fraîche, and a choice of three fabulous caviars—is pure decadence. $ *Average main: $70* ✉ *Setai Hotel, 101 20th St., South Beach* ☎ *305/520–6800* ⊕ *www.thesetaihotel.com/dining* ⚭ *Reservations essential* ☉ *Closed Mon. and Tues.* ✛ *H1.*

$$$ ✕ **SushiSamba Dromo.** This sibling to the New York City SushiSamba
JAPANESE makes an eclectic pairing of Japanese, Peruvian, and Brazilian cuisines.
The results are fabulous if a bit mystifying: miso-marinated sea bass, hamachi *taquitos* (basically a yellowtail tartare), *mocqueca mista* (Brazilian seafood stew), and caramel–passion fruit sponge cake. Loaded with customers in the heart of pedestrian Lincoln Road, colorful SushiSamba has a vibe that hurts the ears but warms the trendy heart. $ *Average main: $32* ✉ *600 Lincoln Rd., South Beach* ☎ *305/673–5337* ⊕ *www.sushisamba.com* ✛ *G2.*

$$$$
EUROPEAN
Fodor'sChoice
★

✗ **Tosca Miami.** If you're looking to find out where Miami's A-list splurges on dinner, look no further. Extravagance and decadence are indeed on the menu as Tosca's dishes feature some of the finest and most expensive ingredients in the world—literally. Think rare blue lobster from Brittany, 100-year-aged balsamic vinegar, vintage Valrhona chocolate, Kaviari caviar, and truffles flown in daily from Alba, Italy. The divine fettucine with mascarpone cheese is tossed tableside in a larger-than-life parmesan wheel and topped with fresh black Périgord truffles. Going *à la carte* requires deep pockets; but given the quality and taste, the five-course, $75 prix-fixe menu is a bargain. Dress to impress. $ *Average main: $75* ⊠ *210 23rd St., South Beach* ☎ *786/216–7230* ⊕ *www. toscamiami.com* ♨ *Reservations essential* ✛ *H1.*

$$
SOUTHERN
Fodor'sChoice
★

✗ **Yardbird Southern Table & Bar.** *Top Chef* contestant Jeff McInnis brings a helluva lot of Southern lovin' (from the Lowcountry to South Beach) to this lively and funky spot. Miami's A-list puts calorie-counting aside for decadent nights filled with comfort foods and innovative drinks. The family-style menu is divided between "small shares" and "big shares," but let's not kid ourselves—all the portions are huge (and surprisingly affordable). You'll rave about Mama's chicken biscuits, the Atlantic fried oysters, the fried-green-tomato BLT, the grilled-mango salad, the 27-hour-fried chicken, and the shrimp and grits. Oh, and then there are the sides, like "caviar"-topped deviled eggs, house-cut fries with a buttermilk dipping sauce and bacon salt, and the super-creamy macaroni-and-cheese. Don't plan on hitting the beach in a bikini the next day. $ *Average main: $18* ⊠ *1600 Lenox Ave., South Beach* ☎ *305/538–5220* ⊕ *www.runchickenrun.com* ✛ *G2.*

MID-BEACH

$$$
ITALIAN

✗ **Cecconi's.** The wait for a table at this outpost of the iconic Italian restaurant is just as long as its West Hollywood counterpart, and the dining experience just as fabulous. Eating here is a real scene of who's who and who's eating what. Without a doubt, the truffle pizza, which servers shave huge hunks of black or white truffle onto table-side, is the restaurant's most talked about dish. The fish carpaccios are light and succulent while the classically hearty pastas and risottos provide authentic Italian fare. $ *Average main: $28* ⊠ *Soho Beach House, 4385 Collins Ave., Mid-Beach* ☎ *786/507–7900* ⊕ *www.cecconismiamibeach. com* ♨ *Reservations essential* ✛ *F4.*

$$$$
BRAZILIAN
Fodor'sChoice
★

✗ **1500°.** Thanks to the superb vision and prowess of Executive Chef Paula DaSilva, 1500° launches the farm-to-table revolution into an entirely new dimension. The menu changes seasonally, many items daily, but a few staples remain over the passing months, including the mouthwatering, tender steaks broiled to perfection (at 1500°, natch), and the delicate Florida wahoo ceviche. All side dishes (you have a whopping 17 to choose from) are beyond robust in flavor and ingenuity—the Vidalia onion–and–potato gratin is an entire, mammoth sweet onion stuffed and baked with potatoes, cheese, cream, and grilled onions. The restaurant's interiors scream modern luxury, flaunting showroom elegance spiced with trendy design elements. $ *Average main: $32* ⊠ *Eden Roc Renaissance Miami Beach, 4525 Collins Ave., Mid-Beach* ☎ *305/674–5594* ⊕ *www.1500degreesmiami.com* ✛ *F3.*

$$$$
STEAKHOUSE

✕ **The Forge.** Legendary for its opulence, this restaurant has been wowing patrons since 1968. After a renovation, The Forge reemerged in 2010 more decadent than ever; and it hasn't looked back since. It is a steak house, but a steak house the likes of which you haven't seen before. Antiques, gilt-framed paintings, a chandelier from the Paris Opera House, and Tiffany stained-glass windows from New York's Trinity Church are the fitting background for some of Miami's best cuts. The tried-and-true menu also includes prime rib, bone-in fillet, lobster *thermidor*, chocolate soufflé, and sinful side dishes like creamed spinach and roasted-garlic mashed potatoes. For its walk-in humidor alone, the over-the-top Forge is worth visiting. Automated wine machines span the perimeter of the restaurant and allow you to pick your own pour and sample several wines throughout your meal. $ *Average main: $38 ✉ 432 Arthur Godfrey Rd., Mid-Beach ☎ 305/538–8533 ⊕ www. theforge.com ⚠ Reservations essential ⊗ No lunch ✛ F4.*

$$$$
STEAKHOUSE

✕ **Gotham Steak.** The Miami outpost of this NYC institution—set inside the fabulous Fontainebleau resort—is often cited as the best steak house in South Florida's oversaturated meat market. It's not hard to see why. The apps, meats, seafood, and sides are all stellar. The Gotham Raw bar presents top-of-the-line stone crabs, succulent sashimis, excellent ceviches, and a fantastic chilled Maine lobster salad with fresh avocado, orange, fennel and citrus vinaigrette. Classic cuts from the grill, namely the Kansas City Strip and Porterhouse, wow even hard-core carnivores—these can be prepared simply or with one of six sauces, such as bearnaise. Naturally, Gotham offers the full gamut of decadent sides, including the must-try creamed corn with Manchego cheese and jalapeño. $ *Average main: $54 ✉ Fontainebleau Hotel, 4441 Collins Ave, Mid-Beach ☎ 305/538–2000 ⊕ www.fontainebleau.com ✛ F3.*

$$$$
CANTONESE
Fodor'sChoice
★

✕ **Hakkasan.** This stateside sibling of the Michelin-star London restaurant brings the haute-Chinese-food movement to South Florida, adding Pan-Asian flair to even quite simple and authentic Cantonese recipes, and producing an entire menu that can be classified as blow-your-mind delicious. Seafood and vegetarian dishes outnumber meat options, with the scallop-and-shrimp dim sum, Szechuan-style braised eggplant, and charcoal-grilled silver cod with champagne and Chinese honey reaching new heights of excellence. Superb eats notwithstanding, another reason to experience Hakkasan is that it's arguably the sexiest, best-looking restaurant on Miami Beach. Intricately carved, lacquered-black-wood Chinois panels divide seating sections, creating a deceptively cozy dining experience for such a large restaurant. Dress to impress. $ *Average main: $40 ✉ Fontainebleau Hotel, 4441 Collins Ave., 4th fl., Mid-Beach ☎ 305/538–2000 ⊕ www.fontainebleau.com ⚠ Reservations essential ⊗ No lunch weekdays ✛ F3.*

$$
FRENCH

✕ **La Côte.** With clean white lines, colorful bursts of aqua-blue cushions, and elegant umbrellas, La Côte at the Fontainebleau whisks you away to the coast of southern France. The two-level, predominantly al fresco restaurant snuggled between the beach and the Fontainebleau's pools opens its arms in a generous embrace while flirting with your taste buds, and maybe your man: the female waitstaff wear bikinis and flip-flops. Depending on your tastes, this may or may not foster a relaxed atmosphere that complements the simple elegant menu. Try the popular fruits de mer, or order a variety of oysters on the half shell. The vegetable pissaladière is a great vegetarian option for the table. Eating lunch here is an inexpensive way to get a good peek at the Fontainebleau while having a nice meal. [$] *Average main: $18* ✉ *Fontainebleau Hotel, 4441 Collins Ave., Mid-Beach* ☎ *305/538–2000* 🌐 *www.fontainebleau.com* ⏲ *No dinner Sun.–Wed.* ✥ *F3.*

$ DELI FAMILY 🍴 **Roasters 'N Toasters.** Formerly the longtime family establishment Arnie and Richie's, Roasters 'N Toasters Miami Beach has preserved an intimate, Jewish deli feel that would make Arnie and Richie proud. The prices are slightly higher than back in the day, but the faithful still come for the onion rolls and smoked whitefish salad, as well as the new "Corky's Famous Zaftig Sandwich," a deliciously juicy skirt steak served on twin challah rolls with a side of apple sauce. Service can be brusque, but it sure is quick. [$] *Average main: $10* ✉ *525 Arthur Godfrey Rd., Mid-Beach* ☎ *305/531–7691* 🌐 *www.roastersntoasters.com* ⏲ *Daily 6 am–3:30 pm* ⏲ *No dinner* ✥ *F4.*

NORTH BEACH AND AVENTURA

$$$$ STEAKHOUSE Fodor's Choice ★ 🍴 **Bourbon Steak.** Michael Mina's sole restaurant in the southeastern United States is one of his best. The restaurant design is seductive, the clientele sophisticated, the wine list outstanding, the service phenomenal, and the food exceptional. Dinner begins with a skillet of fresh potato focaccia and chive butter. Mina then presents a bonus starter—his trio of famous fries (fried in duck fat) with three robust sauces. Appetizers are mainly seafood. The raw bar impresses and classic appetizers like the ahi tuna tartare are delightful and super fresh. Entrees like the Maine lobster pot pie and any of the dozen varieties of butter-poached, wood-grilled steaks (from prime cuts to American wagyu) are cooked to perfection. [$] *Average main: $35* ✉ *Turnberry Isle Miami, 19999 W. Country Club Dr., Aventura, Miami* ☎ *786/279–6600* 🌐 *www.michaelmina.net* ✍ *Reservations essential* ✥ *F1.*

$$$$ ITALIAN 🍴 **Il Mulino New York.** For more than two decades, Il Mulino New York has ranked among the top Italian restaurants in Gotham, so it's no surprise that the Miami outpost is similarly venerable. Even before the antipasti arrive, you may find yourself in a phenomenal carb coma from the fresh breads and the bruschetta. Everything that touches your palate is prepared to perfection, from simply prepared fried calamari and gnocchi pomodoro to the more complex scampi oregenata and ever-changing risottos. The restaurant is seductive, quiet, and intimate, and a favorite hangout of A-list celebs seeking a refined spot where crowds won't gawk over their presence. [$] *Average main: $52* ✉ *Acqualina Resort, 17875 Collins Ave., Sunny Isles* ☎ *305/466–9191* 🌐 *www.acqualinaresort.com* ✍ *Reservations essential* ✥ *F1.*

$$$$ JAPANESE 🍴 **Makoto.** Stephen Starr's Japanese headliner is one of the most popular restaurants in the swanky and prestigious Bal Harbor Shops. The ambience, service, and food all impress; and given its location in haute-couture central, the patrons definitely dress to impress. There are two menus, one devoted solely to sushi, sashimi, and maki; the other to Japanese hot dishes like tempuras, meats, and vegetables grilled over

Japanese charcoal (robata), rice and noodle dishes, and steaks and fish inspired by the Land of the Rising Sun. [$] *Average main: $34* ✉ *Bal Harbour Shops, 9700 Collins Ave., North Beach and Aventura, Bal Harbour* ☎ *305/864–8600* 🌐 *www.makoto-restaurant.com* ✥ *F2.*

WHERE TO STAY

Room rates in Miami tend to swing wildly. In high season, which is January through May, expect to pay at least $150 per night, even at low-budget hotels. In summer, however, prices can be as much as 50% lower than the dizzying winter rates. You can also find great deals between Easter and Memorial Day, which is actually a delightful time in Miami. Business travelers tend to stay in downtown Miami, and most vacationers stay on Miami Beach, as close as possible to the water. South Beach is no longer the only "in" place to stay. Mid-Beach and downtown have taken the hotel scene by storm in the past few years, and become home to some of the region's most avant-garde and luxurious properties to date. If money is no object, stay in one of the glamorous hotels lining Collins Avenue between 15th and 23rd streets. Otherwise, stay on the quiet beaches farther north, or in one of the small boutique hotels on Ocean Drive, Collins, or Washington avenues between 10th and 15th streets. Two important considerations that affect price are balcony and view. If you're willing to have a room without an ocean view, you can sometimes get a much lower price than the standard rate.

For expanded reviews, facilities, and current deals, visit Fodors.com.

Use the coordinate (✥ C2) at the end of each review to locate a property on the Where to Stay in the Miami Area map.

DOWNTOWN MIAMI

$$$ HOTEL 🏨 **Casa Moderna.** In the Marquis high-rise residential building downtown, Casa Moderna (formerly Tempo Miami, a Rock Resort) offers a splendid boutique experience of contemporary luxury, with LCD TV screens built into bathroom mirrors and floor-to-ceiling windows peering over downtown. **Pros:** spacious rooms; quiet respite; amazing bathrooms. **Cons:** some open-floor-plan bathrooms lack privacy; windy pool area; amenities shared with condo residents. [$] *Rooms from: $319* ✉ *1100 Biscayne Blvd.* ☎ *786/369–0300* 🌐 *www.casamodernamiami.com* 🛏 *56 rooms* 🍴 *No meals* ✥ *D4.*

$$$ HOTEL 🏨 **Conrad Miami.** Occupying floors 16 to 26 of a 36-story skyscraper in Miami's Financial District, this chic hotel mixes business with pleasure, offering easy access to the best of Downtown Miami. **Pros:** central downtown location; excellent service. **Cons:** Poor views from some rooms; expensive parking. [$] *Rooms from: $309* ✉ *Espirito Santo Plaza, 1395 Brickell Ave.* ☎ *305/503–6500* 🌐 *www.conradhotels.com* 🛏 *189 rooms, 14 suites* 🍴 *No meals* ✥ *D5.*

$ HOTEL 🏨 **Doubletree Grand Hotel Biscayne Bay.** Near the Port of Miami at the north end of downtown, this waterfront hotel offers basic, spacious rooms and convenient access to and from the cruise ships and downtown, making it a good crash pad for budget-conscious cruise passengers.

BEST BETS FOR MIAMI LODGING

Fodor's offers a selective listing of high-quality lodging experiences in every price range, from the city's best budget beds to its most sophisticated luxury hotels. Here, we've compiled our top recommendations by price and experience. The very best properties are designated in the listings with the Fodor's Choice logo. Find specific details about a hotel in the full reviews, listed alphabetically by neighborhood.

Fodor's Choice ★

**Acqualina Resort &
Spa on the Beach,**
North Beach and Aventura, p. 92

Cadet Hotel, South Beach, p. 85

Epic Hotel, Downtown, p. 81

The James Royal Palm, South Beach, p. 86

Mandarin Oriental, Miami, Downtown, p. 81

Ritz-Carlton, South Beach, p. 90

St. Regis Bal Harbour Resort, North Beach and Aventura, p. 93

Surfcomber Miami, South Beach, p. 90

W South Beach, South Beach, p. 91

By Price

$

Circa 39 Hotel, Mid-Beach, p. 91

Townhouse Hotel, South Beach, p. 90

$$

The Standard, Belle Isle, p. 85

$$$

Biltmore Hotel, Coral Gables, p. 84

Fontainebleau Miami Beach, Mid-Beach, p. 92

The Ritz-Carlton Key Biscayne, Key Biscayne, p. 84

$$$$

Four Seasons Hotel Miami, Downtown, p. 81

The Setai, South Beach, p. 90

W South Beach, South Beach, p. 91

By Experience

BEST HOTEL BAR

National Hotel, South Beach, p. 87

Viceroy Miami (rooftop bar), Downtown, p. 81

BEST-KEPT SECRET

Acqualina Resort & Spa on the Beach, North Beach and Aventura, p. 92

Soho Beach House, Mid-Beach, p. 92

BEST LOCATION

The Betsy Hotel, South Beach, p. 85

Surfcomber Miami, South Beach, p. 90

BEST POOL

Biltmore Hotel, Coral Gables, p. 84

Delano Hotel, South Beach, p. 86

Raleigh Hotel, South Beach, p. 90

Viceroy Miami, Downtown, p. 81

BEST SERVICE

Acqualina Resort & Spa on the Beach, North Beach and Aventura, p. 92

The Ritz-Carlton Key Biscayne, Key Biscayne, p. 84

St. Regis Bal Harbour Resort, North Beach and Aventura, p. 93

BEST VIEWS

Epic Hotel, Downtown, p. 81

St. Regis Bal Harbour Resort, North Beach and Aventura, p. 93

W South Beach, South Beach, p. 91

HIPSTER HOTELS

Catalina Hotel & Beach Club, South Beach, p. 86

Shore Club, South Beach, p. 90

Soho Beach House, Mid-Beach, p. 92

Pros: marina; proximity to port. **Cons:** need a cab to get around; dark lobby and neighboring arcade of shops; worn rooms. Ⓢ *Rooms from: $171* ✉ *1717 N. Bayshore Dr.* ☎ *305/372–0313, 800/222–8733* ⊕ *www. doubletree.com* ↝ *152 rooms, 56 suites* ⭑○⭑ *No meals* ✛ *E4.*

$$$
HOTEL
Fodor'sChoice
★

🖼 **Epic Hotel.** In the heart of downtown, Kimpton's pet-friendly, freebie-heavy Epic Hotel has 411 guest rooms, each with a spacious balcony (many of them overlook Biscayne Bay) and fabulous modern amenities—Frette linens, iPod docks, spa-inspired luxury bath products—that match the modern grandeur of the trendy common areas, which include a super sexy rooftop pool. **Pros:** sprawling rooftop pool deck; balcony in every room; complimentary wine hour, coffee, and Wi-Fi. **Cons:** some rooms have inferior views; congested valet area. Ⓢ *Rooms from: $389* ✉ *270 Biscayne Blvd. Way* ☎ *305/424–5226* ⊕ *www.epichotel. com* ↝ *411 rooms* ⭑○⭑ *No meals* ✛ *D4.*

$$$$
HOTEL

🖼 **Four Seasons Hotel Miami.** A favorite of business travelers visiting downtown's busy, business-centric Brickell Avenue, this plush sanctuary offers a respite from the nine-to-five mayhem—a soothing water wall greets you, the understated rooms impress you, and the seventh-floor, 2-acre-pool terrace relaxes you. **Pros:** rooms renovated in 2011; sensational service; amazing gym and pool deck. **Cons:** no balconies; caters mostly to business travelers; not near beach. Ⓢ *Rooms from: $459* ✉ *1435 Brickell Ave.* ☎ *305/358–3535* ⊕ *www.fourseasons.com/ miami* ↝ *182 rooms, 39 suites* ⭑○⭑ *No meals* ✛ *D5.*

$$$
HOTEL

🖼 **JW Marriott Marquis Miami.** The marriage of Marriott's JW and Marquis brands has created a truly tech-savvy, contemporary, and stylish business-minded hotel—you may never have seen a Marriott quite like this one. **Pros:** entertainment center; amazing technology; pristine rooms. **Cons:** swimming pool receives limited sunshine; lots of conventioneers on weekdays. Ⓢ *Rooms from: $389* ✉ *255 Biscayne Blvd. Way* ☎ *305/421–8600* ⊕ *www.jwmarriottmarquismiami.com* ↝ *257 rooms, 56 suites* ⭑○⭑ *No meals* ✛ *D5.*

$$$$
HOTEL
Fodor'sChoice
★

🖼 **Mandarin Oriental, Miami.** Clandestinely situated at the tip of prestigious Brickell Key in Biscayne Bay, the Mandarin Oriental feels as exclusive as it does glamorous, with luxurious rooms, exalted restaurants, and the city's top spa, all of which marry the brand's signature Asian style with Miami's bold tropical elegance. **Pros:** man-made beach; intimate vibe; ultraluxurious. **Cons:** small infinity pool; few beach cabanas. Ⓢ *Rooms from: $519* ✉ *500 Brickell Key Dr.* ☎ *305/913– 8288, 866/888–6780* ⊕ *www.mandarinoriental.com* ↝ *326 rooms, 31 suites* ⭑○⭑ *No meals* ✛ *E5.*

$$$
HOTEL

🖼 **Viceroy Miami.** This hotel cultivates a brash, supersophisticated Miami attitude, likely stemming from its flawless guest rooms decked out with dramatic Kelly Wearstler, Asian-inspired interiors and larger-than-life common areas designed by Philippe Starck. **Pros:** amazing design elements; exceptional pool deck and spa; sleek rooms. **Cons:** poor views from rooms; tiny lobby; some amenities shared with ICON Miami residents. Ⓢ *Rooms from: $319* ✉ *485 Brickell Ave.* ☎ *305/503–4400, 866/781–9923* ⊕ *www.viceroymiami.com* ↝ *150 rooms, 18 suites* ⭑○⭑ *No meals* ✛ *D5.*

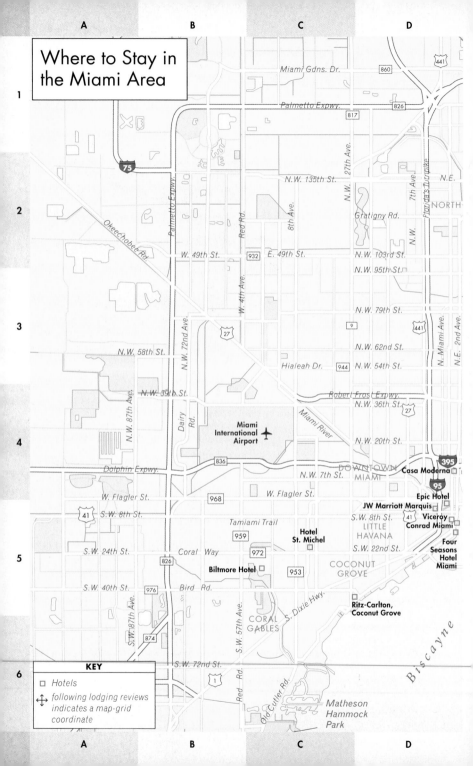

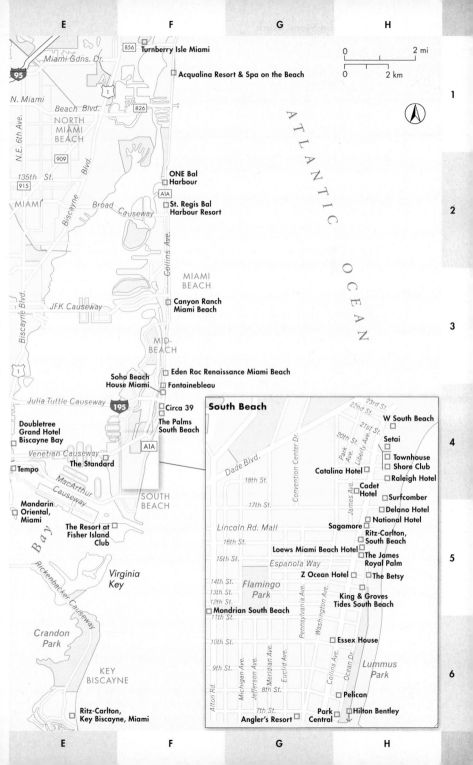

COCONUT GROVE

Coconut Grove is blessed with a number of excellent luxury properties. All are within walking distance of its principal entertainment center, CocoWalk, as well as its marinas. Although this area certainly can't replace the draw of Miami Beach or the business convenience of downtown, about 20 minutes away, it's an exciting bohemian-chic neighborhood with a gorgeous waterfront.

$$$ **The Ritz-Carlton Coconut Grove, Miami.** Overlooking Biscayne Bay, this business-centric Ritz-Carlton hotel in the heart of Coconut Grove received a face-lift in 2012 that gave its lobby and lounge a refreshed, livelier look that complements its sophisticated guest rooms—all with marble baths and private balconies. **Pros:** elevated pool deck; high-quality spa; excellent service. **Cons:** near residential area; more business than leisure oriented. $ *Rooms from: $329* ✉ *3300 S.W. 27th Ave.* ☎ *305/644–4680, 800/241–3333* ⊕ *www.ritzcarlton.com* ⤢ *88 rooms, 27 suites* ❙⊘❙ *No meals* ✛ *D5.*
HOTEL

CORAL GABLES

Beautiful Coral Gables is set around its beacon, the national landmark Biltmore Hotel. It also has a couple of big business hotels and one smaller boutique property. The University of Miami is nearby.

$$$ **Biltmore Hotel.** Built in 1926, this landmark hotel has had several incarnations over the years—including a stint as a hospital during World War II—but through it all, this grande dame has remained an opulent reminder of yesteryear, with its palatial lobby and grounds, enormous pool (largest in the lower 48), and distinctive 315-foot tower, which rises above the canopy of trees shading Coral Gables. **Pros:** historic property; gorgeous pool; great tennis and golf. **Cons:** in the suburbs; a car is necessary to get around. $ *Rooms from: $343* ✉ *1200 Anastasia Ave.* ☎ *855/311–6903* ⊕ *www.biltmorehotel.com* ⤢ *241 rooms, 39 suites* ❙⊘❙ *No meals* ✛ *C5.*
HOTEL

$ **Hotel St. Michel.** This charming European bed-and-breakfast–inspired hotel dates to 1926 and is right off the Miracle Mile in Coral Gables. **Pros:** personal service; free continental breakfast; European sensibility. **Cons:** small rooms; could use a renovation; far from the Miami action. $ *Rooms from: $159* ✉ *162 Alcazar Ave., Coral Gables, Miami* ☎ *305/444–1666, 800/848–4683* ⊕ *www.hotelstmichel.com* ⤢ *29 rooms* ❙⊘❙ *Breakfast* ✛ *C5.*
B&B/INN

KEY BISCAYNE

There's probably no other place in Miami where slowness is lifted to a fine art. On Key Biscayne there are no pressures, there's no nightlife outside of the Ritz-Carlton's great live Latin music weekends, and the dining choices are essentially limited to the hotel (which has four dining options, including the languorous, Havana-style RUMBAR).

$$$ **The Ritz-Carlton Key Biscayne, Miami.** In this ultra-laid-back Key Biscayne setting, it's natural to appreciate the Ritz brand of pampering with luxurious rooms, attentive service, and ample recreational activities for the
RESORT
FAMILY

whole family. **Pros:** on the beach; quiet; luxurious family retreat. **Cons:** far from South Beach and downtown; beach sometimes seaweed strewn; rental car almost a necessity. $ *Rooms from: $340* ☒ *455 Grand Bay Dr., Key Biscayne* ☎ *305/365–4500, 800/241–3333* ⊕ *www.ritzcarlton.com/ keybiscayne* ⤳ *365 rooms, 37 suites* ⧠ *No meals* ✚ *E6.*

FISHER AND BELLE ISLANDS

$$$$
RESORT
The Resort at Fisher Island Club. An exclusive private island, just south of Miami Beach but accessible only by ferry, Fisher Island houses an upscale residential community that includes a small inventory of overnight accommodations, including opulent cottages, villas, and junior suites, which surround the island's original 1920s-era Vanderbilt mansion. **Pros:** great private beaches; never crowded; varied on-island dining choices. **Cons:** ferry ride to get on and off island; limited cell service. $ *Rooms from: $1,037* ☒ *1 Fisher Island Dr., Fisher Island* ☎ *305/535–6000, 800/537–3708* ⊕ *www.fisherislandclub.com* ⤳ *50 condo units, 7 villas, 3 cottages* ⧠ *No meals* ✚ *E5.*

$$
RESORT
The Standard. An extension of André Balazs's trendy and hip yet budget-conscious hotel chain, the shabby-chic Standard is a mile from South Beach on an island just over the Venetian Causeway and boasts one of South Florida's most renowned spas and hottest pool scenes. **Pros:** free bike and kayak rentals; swank pool scene; great spa; inexpensive. **Cons:** slight trek to South Beach; small rooms with no views. $ *Rooms from: $269* ☒ *40 Island Ave., Belle Isle* ☎ *305/673–1717* ⊕ *www.standardhotel.com* ⤳ *104 rooms, 1 suite* ⧠ *No meals* ✚ *E4.*

SOUTH BEACH

$$
HOTEL
Angler's Boutique Resort. This enclave of upscale studios, bi-level duplexes, and villas captures the feel of a sophisticated private Mediterranean villa community, making it easy to forget that the hotel is on busy Washington Avenue, two blocks from the beach. **Pros:** gardened private retreat; excellent service. **Cons:** on busy Washington Avenue; beach is a 10-minute walk. $ *Rooms from: $289* ☒ *660 Washington Ave.* ☎ *305/534–9600* ⊕ *www.theanglersresort.com* ⤳ *24 rooms, 20 suites* ⧠ *No meals* ✚ *G6.*

$$$
HOTEL
The Betsy Hotel. An art deco treasure elegantly refurbished and totally retro-chic, the Betsy sits directly on world-famous Ocean Drive and delivers the full-throttle South Beach experience with style and pizzazz. **Pros:** unbeatable location; super-fashionable; great beach club. **Cons:** some small rooms; service can be hit or miss; no pool scene (but there's a rooftop scene). $ *Rooms from: $389* ☒ *1440 Ocean Dr.* ☎ *305/531–6100* ⊕ *www.thebetsyhotel.com* ⤳ *41 rooms, 20 suites* ⧠ *No meals* ✚ *H5.*

$$
HOTEL
Fodor's Choice
★
Cadet Hotel. A former home to World War II air force cadets, this gem has been reimagined as an oasis in South Beach, offering the antithesis of the sometimes maddening jet-set scene with 34 distinctive rooms exuding understated luxury. **Pros:** excellent service; lovely garden and spa pool; originality. **Cons:** tiny swimming pool; limited appeal for the party crowd. $ *Rooms from: $187* ☒ *1701 James Ave.* ☎ *305/672–6688, 800/432–2338* ⊕ *www.cadethotel.com* ⤳ *32 rooms, 3 suites* ⧠ *Breakfast* ✚ *H4.*

> **WORD OF MOUTH**
>
> "I just returned from a trip to the Keys and spent the last night of the trip at the Cadet Hotel (in Miami). Just around the corner from the Delano, it is a little jewel. The rooms are small but immaculate, and the furnishings are very tasteful."
>
> —bon_voyage

$ HOTEL **Catalina Hotel & Beach Club.** The Catalina is the budget party spot in the heart of South Beach's hottest block and attracts plenty of twentysomethings with its free nightly drink hour, airport shuttles, bike rentals, two fun pools, and beach chairs, all for around $200 a night. **Pros:** free drinks; free bikes; free airport shuttle; good people-watching. **Cons:** service not a high priority; loud; rooms not well-maintained. [$] *Rooms from: $198* ✉ *1732 Collins Ave.* ☎ *305/674–1160* 🌐 *www.catalinahotel.com* 🛏 *200 rooms* 🍴 *No meals* ✣ *H4.*

$$$ HOTEL **Delano Hotel.** The decor of this grand hotel is inspired by Lewis Carroll's *Alice in Wonderland*, and as you make your way from the sparse, busy, spacious lobby past cascading white curtains and through rooms dotted with strange, whimsical furniture pieces, you will feel like you are indeed falling down a rabbit hole. **Pros:** electrifying design; lounging among the beautiful and famous. **Cons:** crowded; scene-y; small rooms; expensive. [$] *Rooms from: $361* ✉ *1685 Collins Ave.* ☎ *305/672–2000, 800/555–5001* 🌐 *www.delano-hotel.com* 🛏 *184 rooms, 24 suites* 🍴 *No meals* ✣ *H5.*

$$ HOTEL **Essex House.** This restored art deco gem is a favorite with Europeans desiring good location and a somewhat no-frills practical base—expect average-size rooms with midcentury-style red furniture and marble tubs. **Pros:** a social, heated pool; great art deco patio. **Cons:** small pool; not on the beach. [$] *Rooms from: $275* ✉ *1001 Collins Ave.* ☎ *305/534–2700* 🌐 *www.essexhotel.com* 🛏 *61 rooms, 15 suites* 🍴 *No meals* ✣ *G6.*

$$$ HOTEL FAMILY **Hilton Bentley Miami/South Beach.** One of the area's only kid-friendly boutique hotels, this contemporary, design-driven, and artsy Hilton in the emerging and trendy SoFi (South of 5th) district offers families just the right mix of South Beach flavor and wholesome fun while still providing couples a romantic base without any party madness. **Pros:** quiet location; style and grace; family-friendly. **Cons:** small pool; small lobby. [$] *Rooms from: $360* ✉ *101 Ocean Dr* ☎ *305/938–4600* 🌐 *www.hilton.com* 🛏 *104 rooms, 5 suites* 🍴 *No meals* ✣ *H6.*

$$$ RESORT Fodor's Choice ★ **The James Royal Palm.** The latest "it" hotel to grace South Beach, the James Royal Palm is a daily celebration of art deco, Art Basel, modernity, and design detail, dutifully embodying the mantra of the James brand—"luxury liberated." **Pros:** multiple pools; complimentary James beach boxes; unbeatable location. **Cons:** occasional noise from in-house nightclub; small driveway for entering. [$] *Rooms from: $359* ✉ *1545 Collins Ave.* ☎ *786/276–0100* 🌐 *www.jameshotels.com/miami* 🛏 *234 studios, 159 suites* 🍴 *No meals* ✣ *H5.*

$$$ HOTEL **King & Groves Tides South Beach.** Formerly the crown jewel of the Viceroy Hotel Group—now managed by King & Grove Hotels, known for their intimate Hamptons properties—the Tides is an exclusive Ocean Drive art deco hotel of just 45 ocean-facing suites adorned with soft pinks and

corals, gilded accents, and marine-inspired decor. **Pros:** superior service; great beach location; ocean views from all suites plus the terrace restaurant. **Cons:** tiny elevators; mediocre restaurant. $ *Rooms from: $339* ✉ *1220 Ocean Dr.* ☎ *305/604–5070* ⊕ *www.kingandgrove.com/tides-south-beach* ⥽ *45 suites* ⓧ *No meals* ✛ *H5.*

$$$ 🏨 **Loews Miami Beach Hotel.** Loews
HOTEL Miami Beach, a two-tower 800-room megahotel with top-tier amenities, a massive spa, a great pool, and direct beachfront access, is good for families, businesspeople, groups, and pet-lovers. **Pros:** top-notch amenities; immense spa; pets welcome. **Cons:** insanely large size; constantly crowded. $ *Rooms from: $399* ✉ *1601 Collins Ave.* ☎ *305/604–1601, 800/235–6397* ⊕ *www.loewshotels.com/miamibeach* ⥽ *733 rooms, 57 suites* ⓧ *No meals* ✛ *H5.*

$$$ 🏨 **Mondrian South Beach.** The Mondrian South Beach has infused life into
HOTEL the beach's lesser-known western perimeter and rises as a poster child of SoBe design glam—head to toe, the hotel is a living and functioning work of art, an ingenious vision of provocateur Marcel Wanders. **Pros:** trendy; perfect sunsets; party vibe. **Cons:** busy lobby; doses of South Beach attitude; no direct beach access. $ *Rooms from: $280* ✉ *1100 West Ave.* ☎ *305/514–1500* ⊕ *www.mondrian-miami.com* ⥽ *233 rooms, 102 suites* ⓧ *No meals* ✛ *F5.*

$$$ 🏨 **National Hotel.** Unlike its neighbors, the National Hotel has maintained
HOTEL its distinct art deco heritage while also keeping up with SoBe's glossy newcomers with its beautifully renovated cabana wing and art deco tower. **Pros:** stunning pool; perfect location. **Cons:** two floors of main tower not renovated; neighboring hotels can be noisy on the weekends. $ *Rooms from: $305* ✉ *1677 Collins Ave.* ☎ *305/532–2311, 800/327–8370* ⊕ *www.nationalhotel.com* ⥽ *143 rooms, 9 suites* ⓧ *No meals* ✛ *H5.*

$ 🏨 **Park Central.** This seven-story, oft-photographed 1937 archetypal
HOTEL art deco building on Ocean Drive offers a wide range of somewhat dated, Old Florida–style rooms complete with wicker chairs and black-and-white photos of old beach scenes. **Pros:** spacious rooftop sundeck; comfy beds; good location. **Cons:** dated furnishings; small bathrooms; most rooms have limited views. $ *Rooms from: $160* ✉ *640 Ocean Dr.* ☎ *305/538–1611* ⊕ *www.theparkcentral.com* ⥽ *113 rooms, 12 suites* ⓧ *No meals* ✛ *H6.*

$$ 🏨 **Pelican Miami Beach.** Each awesome room of this Ocean Drive boutique
HOTEL hotel is completely different, fashioned from a mix of antique and garage-sale furnishings selected by the designer of Diesel's clothing-display windows. **Pros:** unique, over-the-top design; central Ocean Drive location. **Cons:** rooms are so tiny that the quirky charm wears off quickly; not smoke-free. $ *Rooms from: $225* ✉ *826 Ocean Dr.* ☎ *305/673–3373* ⊕ *www.pelicanhotel.com* ⥽ *28 rooms, 4 suites* ⓧ *No meals* ✛ *H6.*

Acqualina Resort & Spa on the Beach

Cadet Hotel

Ritz-Carlton, South Beach

Epic Hotel, Miami

W South Beach

The Surfcomber South Beach

The St. Regis Bal Harbour Resort

Mandarin Oriental

$$$ HOTEL **Raleigh Hotel.** This classy art deco gem balances the perfect amount of style, comfort, and South Beach sultriness, highlighted by the beach's sexiest pool, which was created for champion swimmer Esther Williams. **Pros:** amazing swimming pool; elegance. **Cons:** lobby is a bit dark; not as social as other South Beach hotels. *Rooms from: $400 ⊠ 1775 Collins Ave. ☎ 305/534–6300 ⊕ www.raleighhotel.com 95 rooms, 10 suites No meals ✣ H4.*

$$$$ HOTEL Fodor's Choice ★ **Ritz-Carlton, South Beach.** Completely revamped and renovated for 2013, the smoking hot, art deco Ritz-Carlton, South Beach is a surprisingly trendy, beachfront bombshell, with a dynamite staff, a snazzy Club Lounge, a "tanning butler," and a long pool deck that leads right out to the beach. **Pros:** luxurious renovated rooms; great service; pool with VIP cabanas; great location. **Cons:** not as small and intimate as other properties. *Rooms from: $629 ⊠ 1 Lincoln Rd. ☎ 786/276–4000, 800/241–3333 ⊕ www.ritzcarlton.com/southbeach 375 rooms No meals ✣ H5.*

$$ HOTEL **Sagamore, the Art Hotel.** This supersleek, all-white, all-suite hotel in the middle of the action looks and feels like an edgy art gallery, filled with brilliant contemporary works, the perfect complement to the posh, gargantuan, 500-square-foot crash pads. **Pros:** sensational pool; great location; good rate specials. **Cons:** can be quiet on weekdays; patchy Wi-Fi. *Rooms from: $295 ⊠ 1671 Collins Ave. ☎ 305/535–8088 ⊕ www.sagamorehotel.com 93 suites No meals ✣ H5.*

$$$$ RESORT **The Setai.** This opulent, all-suite hotel feels like an Asian museum, serene and beautiful, with heavy granite furniture lifted by orange accents, warm candlelight, and the soft bubble of seemingly endless ponds complemented by three oceanfront infinity pools (heated to 75, 85, and 95 degrees) that further spill onto the beach's sands. **Pros:** quiet and classy; beautiful grounds. **Cons:** TVs are far from the beds; high price point. *Rooms from: $775 ⊠ 101 20th St. ☎ 305/520–6000 ⊕ www.thesetaihotel.com 121 suites No meals ✣ H4.*

$$$ HOTEL **Shore Club.** In terms of lounging, people-watching, partying, and poolside glitz, the Shore Club ranks among the ultimate South Beach adult playgrounds, despite rather basic guest rooms. **Pros:** hip crowd; good restaurants and bars; nightlife in your backyard. **Cons:** spartan rooms; late-night music. *Rooms from: $330 ⊠ 1901 Collins Ave. ☎ 305/695–3100, 877/640–9500 ⊕ www.shoreclub.com 309 rooms, 79 suites No meals ✣ H4.*

$$$ HOTEL Fodor's Choice ★ **Surfcomber Miami, South Beach.** In 2012 the legendary Surfcomber joined the hip Kimpton Hotel group, spawning a fantastic nip-and-tuck that's rejuvenated the rooms and common spaces to reflect vintage luxe and oceanside freshness, and offering a price point that packs the place with a young, sophisticated, yet unpretentious crowd. **Pros:** stylish but not pretentious; pet-friendly; on the beach. **Cons:** small bathrooms; front desk often busy. *Rooms from: $319 ⊠ 1717 Collins Ave. ☎ 305/532–7715 ⊕ www.surfcomber.com 182 rooms, 4 suites No meals ✣ H4.*

$ HOTEL **Townhouse Hotel.** Though sandwiched between the Setai and the Shore Club—two of the coolest hotels on the planet—the Townhouse doesn't try to act all dolled up: it's comfortable being the shabby-chic, lighthearted, relaxed fun hotel on South Beach (and rates include a

2

Parisian-style breakfast). **Pros:** a great budget buy for the style-hungry; direct beach access; hot rooftop lounge. **Cons:** no pool; small rooms not designed for long stays. $ *Rooms from: $156* ✉ *150 20th St., east of Collins Ave.* ☎ *305/534–3800* ⊕ *www.townhousehotel.com* ⇌ *69 rooms, 2 suites* ✧◯✧ *Breakfast* ✢ *H4.*

$$$$
HOTEL
Fodor's Choice
★

W South Beach. Fun, fresh, and funky, the W South Beach is also the flagship for the brand's evolution toward young sophistication, which means less club music in the lobby, more lighting, and more attention to the multimillion dollar art collection lining the lobby's expansive walls. **Pros:** pool scene; masterful design; ocean-view balconies in each room. **Cons:** not a classic art deco building; hit-or-miss service. $ *Rooms from: $450* ✉ *2201 Collins Ave.* ☎ *305/938–3000* ⊕ *www. whotels.com/southbeach* ⇌ *312 rooms* ✧◯✧ *No meals* ✢ *H4.*

$$
HOTEL

Z Ocean Hotel South Beach. The lauded firm of Arquitectonica designed the rooms and suites at this glossy and bold hideaway, including 27 rooftop suites endowed with terraces, each complete with Jacuzzi, plush chaise lounges, and a view of the South Beach skyline. **Pros:** incredible balconies; huge rooms; space-maximizing closets. **Cons:** gym is tiny and basic; not much privacy on rooftop suite decks. $ *Rooms from: $287* ✉ *1437 Collins Ave.* ☎ *305/672–4554* ⊕ *www.zoceanhotelsouthbeach. com* ⇌ *79 suites* ✧◯✧ *No meals* ✢ *H5.*

MID-BEACH

Where does South Beach end and Mid-Beach begin? With the massive amount of money being spent on former 1950s pleasure palaces like the Fontainebleau and Eden Roc, it could be that Mid-Beach will soon just be considered part of South Beach. North of 24th Street, Collins Avenue curves its way to 44th Street, where it takes a sharp left turn after running into the Soho House Miami and then the Fontainebleau resort. The area between these two points—24th Street and 96th Street—is Mid-Beach. This stretch is undergoing a renaissance, as formerly run-down hotels are renovated and new hotels and condos are built.

$$$$
RESORT

Canyon Ranch Miami Beach. Physical and mental well-being top the agenda at this 150-suite beachfront hotel, defined by its 70,000-square-foot wellness spa, including a rock-climbing wall, 54 treatment rooms, and 30 exercise classes daily. **Pros:** directly on the beach; spacious suites (minimum 720 square feet); spa treatments exclusive to hotel guests. **Cons:** far from nightlife; not a very gregarious clientele. $ *Rooms from: $420* ✉ *6801 Collins Ave.* ☎ *305/514–7000* ⊕ *www.canyonranch.com* ⇌ *150 suites* ✧◯✧ *No meals* ✢ *F3.*

$
HOTEL

Circa 39 Hotel. This stylish yet affordable boutique hotel pays attention to every detail and gets them all right. **Pros:** affordable; chic; intimate; beach chairs provided; art deco fireplace. **Cons:** not on the beach side of Collins Avenue. $ *Rooms from: $169* ✉ *3900 Collins Ave.* ☎ *305/538–4900, 877/824–7223* ⊕ *www.circa39.com* ⇌ *96 rooms* ✧◯✧ *No meals* ✢ *F4.*

$$$$
RESORT

Eden Roc Renaissance Miami Beach. This grand 1950s hotel designed by Morris Lapidus retains its old glamour even as $230 million in renovations and expansions has added sparkle to the rooms and grounds, renewing the allure and swagger of a stay at the Eden Roc. **Pros:** modern rooms; great pools; revival of Golden Age glamour. **Cons:** expensive parking; taxi needed to reach South Beach. $ *Rooms from: $469* ✉ *4525 Collins Ave.* ☎ *305/531–0000, 800/327–8337* ⊕ *www. edenrocmiami.com* ⤴ *535 rooms, 92 suites* ⦿ *No meals* ✣ *F3.*

$$$ ⊡ **Fontainebleau Miami Beach.** Vegas meets art deco at this colossal clas-
RESORT   sic, deemed Miami's biggest hotel after its $1 billion reinvention, which spawned more than 1,500 rooms (split among 658 suites in two new all-suite towers and 846 rooms in the two original buildings), 11 renowned restaurants and lounges, LIV nightclub, several sumptuous pools with cabana islands, a state-of-the-art fitness center, and a 40,000-square-foot spa. **Pros:** excellent restaurants; historic design mixed with all-new facilities; fabulous pools. **Cons:** away from the South Beach pedestrian scene; massive size; bizarre mix of guests. $ *Rooms from: $369* ✉ *4441 Collins Ave.* ☎ *305/538–2000, 800/548–8886* ⊕ *www.fontainebleau. com* ⤴ *846 rooms, 658 suites* ⦿ *No meals* ✣ *F4.*

$$$ ⊡ **The Palms Hotel & Spa.** Stay here if you're seeking an elegant, relaxed
HOTEL   property away from the noise but still near South Beach. **Pros:** tropical garden; relaxed and quiet. **Cons:** standard rooms do not have balconies (but suites do). $ *Rooms from: $359* ✉ *3025 Collins Ave.* ☎ *305/534–0505, 800/550–0505* ⊕ *www.thepalmshotel.com* ⤴ *220 rooms, 22 suites* ⦿ *No meals* ✣ *F4.*

$$$ ⊡ **Soho Beach House.** The Soho Beach House is a throwback to swanky
HOTEL   vibes of bygone decades, bedazzled in faded color palates, maritime ambience, and circa-1930s avant-garde furnishings, luring A-listers and wannabes to indulge in the amenity-clad, retro-chic rooms. **Pros:** trendy; two pools; fabulous restaurant; full spa. **Cons:** patchy Wi-Fi; members have priority for rooms; lots of pretentious patrons. $ *Rooms from: $375* ✉ *4385 Collins Ave., Mid-Beach, Miami Beach* ☎ *786/507–7900* ⊕ *www.sohobeachhouse.com* ⤴ *55 rooms* ⦿ *No meals* ✣ *F4.*

NORTH BEACH AND AVENTURA

Nearing the 100th Street mark on Collins Avenue, Mid-Beach gives way to North Beach. In particular, at 96th Street, the town of Bal Harbour takes over Collins Avenue from Miami Beach. The town runs a mere 10 blocks to the north before the bridge to Sunny Isles. Bal Harbour is famous for its outdoor high-end shops. If you take your shopping seriously, you'll probably want to stay in this area. At 106th Street, the town of Sunny Isles is an appealing, calm, predominantly upscale choice for families looking for a beautiful beach. There's no nightlife to speak of in Sunny Isles, and yet the half-dozen megaluxurious skyscraper hotels that have sprung up here in the past decade have created a niche-resort town from the demolished ashes of much older, affordable hotels. Farther west are the high-rises of Aventura.

$$$$ ⊡ **Acqualina Resort & Spa on the Beach.** Acqualina raises the bar on Miami
RESORT   beachfront luxury, delivering a fantasy of Mediterranean opulence, with
FAMILY   oceanfront lawns and pools that evoke Vizcaya. **Pros:** excellent beach;
Fodor's Choice   in-room check-in; luxury amenities; huge spa. **Cons:** no nightlife near
★   hotel; hotel's towering height shades the beach by early afternoon.

Ⓢ *Rooms from: $625* ✉ *17875 Collins Ave., Sunny Isles, Miami Beach* ☎ *305/918–8000* ⊕ *www.acqualinaresort.com* ↩ *54 rooms, 43 suites* �🍽|*No meals* ✛ *F1.*

$$$$
RESORT

🏨 **ONE Bal Harbour.** In one of South Florida's poshest neighborhoods, ONE Bal Harbour exudes contemporary beachfront luxury design with decadent mahogany-floor guest rooms featuring large terraces with panoramic views of the water and city, over-the-top bathrooms with 10-foot floor-to-ceiling windows, and LCD TVs built into the bathroom mirrors. **Pros:** proximity to Bal Harbour Shops; beachfront; great contemporary-art collection. **Cons:** narrow beach is a bit disappointing; far from nightlife. Ⓢ *Rooms from: $525* ✉ *10295 Collins Ave., North Beach and Aventura, Bal Harbour* ☎ *305/455–5400* ⊕ *www.onebalharbourresort.com* ↩ *124 rooms, 63 suites* �🍽|*No meals* ✛ *F2.*

$$$$
RESORT
Fodor's Choice
★

🏨 **St. Regis Bal Harbour Resort.** With the 2012 opening of this $1 billion–plus resort, Miami's North Beach entered a new era of glamour, with A-list big spenders rushing to stay in this 27-story, 243-room, triple-glass-tower masterpiece. **Pros:** beachfront; beyond glamorous; large rooms. **Cons:** limited lounge space around main pool; limited privacy on balconies. Ⓢ *Rooms from: $659* ✉ *9703 Collins Ave., North Beach and Aventura, Bal Harbour* ☎ *305/993–3300* ⊕ *www.stregisbalharbour. com* ↩ *190 rooms, 53 suites* ⟡|*No meals* ✛ *F2.*

$$$
RESORT
FAMILY

🏨 **Turnberry Isle Miami.** Golfers and families favor this service-oriented, 300-acre tropical resort with jumbo-size rooms and world-class amenities, including a majestic lagoon pool (winding waterslide and lazy river included), an acclaimed three-story spa and fitness center, and celeb chef Michael Mina's Bourbon Steak restaurant. **Pros:** great golf, pools, and restaurants; free shuttle to Aventura Mall; situated between Miami and Fort Lauderdale. **Cons:** not on the beach; no nightlife. Ⓢ *Rooms from: $379* ✉ *19999 W. Country Club Dr., North Beach and Aventura, Aventura* ☎ *305/932–6200, 866/612–7739* ⊕ *www.turnberryislemiami. com* ↩ *408 rooms, 29 suites* ⟡|*No meals* ✛ *F1.*

NIGHTLIFE

One of Greater Miami's most popular pursuits is bar-hopping. Bars range from intimate enclaves to showy see-and-be-seen lounges to loud, raucous frat parties. There's a New York–style flair to some of the newer lounges, which are increasingly catering to the Manhattan party crowd who escape to South Beach for long weekends. No doubt, Miami's pulse pounds with nonstop nightlife that reflects the area's potent cultural mix. On sultry, humid nights with the huge full moon rising out of the ocean and fragrant night-blooming jasmine intoxicating the senses, who can resist Cuban salsa with some disco and hip-hop thrown in for good measure? When this place throws a party, hips shake, fingers snap, bodies touch. It's no wonder many clubs are still rocking at 5 am. If you're looking for a relatively nonfrenetic evening, your best bet is one of the chic hotel bars on Collins Avenue.

Cars whizz by Avalon hotel and other art deco architecure on Ocean Drive, Miami South Beach.

The *Miami Herald* (⊕ *www.miamiherald.com*) is a good source for information on what to do in town. The Weekend section of the newspaper, included in the Friday edition, has an annotated guide to everything from plays and galleries to concerts and nightclubs. The "Ticket" column of this section details the week's entertainment highlights. Or, you can pick up the *Miami New Times* (⊕ *www.miaminewtimes.com*), the city's largest free alternative newspaper, published each Thursday. It lists nightclubs, concerts, and special events; reviews plays and movies; and provides in-depth coverage of the local music scene. *MIAMI* (⊕ *www.modernluxury.com/miami*) and *Ocean Drive* (⊕ *www. oceandrive.com*), Miami's model-strewn, upscale fashion and lifestyle magazines, squeeze club, bar, restaurant, and events listings in with fashion spreads, reviews, and personality profiles. Paparazzi photos of local party people and celebrities give you a taste of Greater Miami nightlife before you even dress up to paint the town.

The Spanish-language *El Nuevo Herald* (⊕ *www.elnuevoherald.com*), published by the *Miami Herald,* has extensive information on Spanish-language arts and entertainment, including dining reviews, concert previews, and nightclub highlights.

DOWNTOWN MIAMI
BARS AND LOUNGES

Gordon Biersch. This popular brewhouse chain in Downtown Miami's Financial District has glass-enclosed copper pots cranking out tasty ales and lagers, an inspired menu, live music on Thursday and Friday, and a steady happy-hour crowd. The garlic fries are a must-try! ⊠ *1201 Brickell Ave., Downtown* ☎ *786/425–1130* ⊕ *www.gordonbiersch.com.*

THE VELVET ROPES

How to get past the velvet ropes at the hottest South Beach nightspots? First, if you're staying at a hotel, use the concierge. Decide which clubs you want to check out (consult *Ocean Drive* magazine celebrity pages if you want to be among the glitterati), and the concierge will email, fax, or call in your names to the clubs so you'll be on the guest list when you arrive. This means much easier access and usually no cover charge (which can be upward of $20) if you arrive before midnight. Guest list or no guest list, follow these pointers: Make sure there are more women than men in your group. Dress up—casual chic is the dress code. For men this means no sneakers, no shorts, no sleeveless vests, and no shirts unbuttoned past the top button. For women, provocative and seductive is fine; overly revealing is not. Black is always right. At the door: don't name-drop—no one takes it seriously. Don't be pushy while trying to get the doorman's attention. Wait until you make eye contact, then be cool and easygoing. If you decide to tip him (which most bouncers don't expect), be discreet and pleasant, not big-bucks obnoxious—a $10 or $20 bill quietly passed will be appreciated, however. With the right dress and the right attitude, you'll be on the dance floor rubbing shoulders with South Beach's finest clubbers in no time.

Hyde AAA. The Miami outpost of the wildly popular Hyde Lounge is situated within the AmericanAirlines Arena (AAA) for use during Miami Heat games and arena concerts. The 250-person venue debuted during the Heat's 2012–2013 season and quickly became a Miami institution. Located court-level on the south end of the arena, Hyde AAA provides a full-blown, big pimpin' dining, lounge, and nightlife experience before and after arena events. ⊠ *AmericanAirlines Arena, 601 Biscayne Blvd., Downtown* ☎ *855/777-HYDE* ⊕ *www.hydeaaarena.com.*

Fodor's Choice
★

Tobacco Road. Opened in 1912, this classic holds Miami's oldest liquor license: No. 0001. Upstairs, in a space that was occupied by a speakeasy during Prohibition, local and national blues bands perform nightly. There is excellent bar food, a dinner menu, and a selection of single-malt scotches, bourbons, and cigars. This is the hangout of grizzled journalists, bohemians en route to or from nowhere, and club kids seeking a way station before the real parties begin. Live blues, R&B, and jazz bands are on tap, along with food and drink, seven days a week. If you like your food and drink the way you like your blues—gritty, honest, and unassuming—then this vintage joint will quickly earn your respect. ⊠ *626 S. Miami Ave., Downtown* ☎ *305/374–1198* ⊕ *www.tobacco-road.com.*

DANCE CLUBS

Space Miami. Want 24-hour partying? Here's the place. Space revolutionized the Miami party scene over a decade ago and still gets accolades as one of the country's best dance clubs. But depending on the month, Space wavers between trendy and empty, so make sure you get the up-to-date scoop from your hotel concierge. Created from four downtown warehouses, it has two levels (one blasts house music; the other reverberates with hip-hop), an outdoor patio, a New York–style industrial look, and a 24-hour liquor license. It's open on weekends only, and you'll need to look good to be allowed past the velvet ropes. Note that the crowd can sometimes be sketchy, and take caution walking around the surrounding neighborhood. ⊠ *34 N.E. 11th St., Downtown* ☎ *305/375–0001* ⊕ *www.clubspace.com.*

WYNWOOD/MIDTOWN/DESIGN DISTRICT

BARS AND LOUNGES

Cafeina Wynwood Lounge. This awesome Wynwood watering hole takes center stage during the highly social Gallery Night and Artwalk through the Wynwood Art District, the second Saturday of every month, which showcases the cool and hip art galleries between Northwest 20th and Northwest 36 streets west of North Miami Avenue. For those in the know, the evening either begins or ends at Cafeina, a seductive, design-driven lounge with a gorgeous patio and plenty of art on display. Other weekends, this is still a great place to hang out and get a true feel for Miami's cultural revolution. Open only Thursday–Saturday. ⊠ *297 N.W. 23rd St., Wynwood, Miami* ☎ *305/438–0792* ⊕ *www. cafeinamiami.com; www.wynwoodartwalk.com.*

SOUTH BEACH

BARS AND LOUNGES

Fodor's Choice
★ **FDR at the Delano.** The Delano's famous Florida Room was reinvented and reopened in spring 2012 as FDR, an über-exclusive subterranean lounge, developed by Las Vegas's Light Group. The world's hottest DJs are on tap for a stylish see-and-be-seen crowd. Seductive lighting illuminates the two-room, 200 person watering hole, decked out in dark and sexy decor. Bottle service is available for high rollers. ⊠ *1685 Collins Ave., Miami* ☎ *305/672–2000* ⊕ *www.delano-hotel.com.*

Lost Weekend. Slumming celebs and locals often patronize this pool hall–dive bar on quaint Española Way. The hard-core locals are serious about their pastime, so it can be challenging to get a table on weekends. However, everyone can enjoy the pin-ball machines and the full bar, which has 150 kinds of beer. Each night, Lost Weekend draws an eclectic crowd, from yuppies to drag queens to celebs on the down-low. So South Beach! ⊠ *218 Española Way* ☎ *305/672–1707.*

MOVA. Formerly known as Halo Lounge, this gay bar and lounge off Lincoln Road is where most GLBT South Beach nights begin (and some end), with ample eye candy to whet the palate for a scintillating night of drinking and partying. The minimalist lounge gives off an undeniably sexy vibe, augmented by the handsome bartenders muddling fresh fruits for the ever-changing avant-garde drink menu. The place gets packed on Friday and Saturday; other nights are hit-or-miss. ⊠ *1625 Michigan Ave.* ☎ *305/534–8181* ⊕ *www.movalounge.com.*

Fodor's Choice
★ **Mynt Lounge.** This is the quintessential celeb-studded, super-VIP, South Beach party where you may or may not be let in, depending on what you wear or who you know. It's the kind of place where LiLo acts out, Brit-Brit chills out, and Paris Hilton zones out, namely because of the club's "no paparazzi" policy. Admittedly, owner Romain Zago says that "Mynt is for the famous and fabulous." Every summer the lounge

undergoes renovations to stay at the top of its game, revealing a slightly different look. ✉ *1921 Collins Ave., Miami Beach* ☎ *305/532–0727* ⊕ *www.myntlounge.com.*

Fodor's Choice ★ **National Hotel.** Dedicate at least one night of your Miami vacation to an art deco pub crawl, patronizing the hotel bars and lounges of South Beach's most iconic buildings, including the National Hotel. Though it's a low-key affair, the nifty wooden bar here is well worth a stop. The bar is one of many elements original to the 1939 building that give it such a sense of its era that you'd expect to see Ginger Rogers and Fred Astaire hoofing it along the polished lobby floor. The adjoining Blues Bar has a great collection of cigars, old airline stickers, and vintage Bacardi ads on the walls. ✉ *National Hotel, 1677 Collins Ave., Miami Beach* ☎ *305/532–2311* ⊕ *www.nationalhotel.com.*

> ## CULTURAL FRIDAYS
>
> On the last Friday of every month Little Havana takes its culture to the streets for *Viernes Culturales* (Cultural Friday ⊕ *www.viernesculturales.org*), held between 7 and 11 pm on 8th Street from 14th to 17th avenues. Art galleries and stores stay open late, and music, mojitos, and avant-garde street performances bring a young, hip crowd to the neighborhood, where they mingle with locals. The annual Calle Ocho festival, held in March, draws more than a million visitors in search of Latin music, food, and shopping.

The Regent Cocktail Club. This classic cocktail bar recalls an intimate gentleman's club (and not the stripper kind) with strong masculine cocktails, dark furnishings, bartenders dressed to the nines, and the sounds of jazz legends in the background. The intimate space exudes elegance and timelessness. It's a welcome respite from South Beach's predictable nightlife scene. Cocktails—each with bespoke ice cubes—change daily and are posted on the house blackboard. ✉ *Gale South Beach, 1690 Collins Ave.* ☎ *305/673–0199* ⊕ *www.galehotel.com.*

Rose Bar at the Delano. Tucked away inside the chic Delano hotel, the Rose Bar is a South Beach mainstay and an essential stop on any South Beach bar crawl. Now managed by Las Vegas's Light Group, the Rose Bar mixes classic art deco architecture with the best in mixology (and a bit of Vegas bling). The bar pushes the envelope on creative cocktails. ✉ *Delano Hotel, 1685 Collins Ave.* ☎ *305/672–2000* ⊕ *www.delano-hotel.com.*

Skybar at the Shore Club. An entire enclave dedicated to alcohol-induced fun for grown-ups, the Skybar is actually a collection of adjoining lounges at the Shore Club, including a chic outdoor lounge, the indoor Red Room, and the areas in between, which teem with party-hungry visitors. Splendor-in-the-garden is the theme in the outdoor lounge, accessorized with daybeds and glowing Moroccan lanterns. Groove to dance music in the Red Room, enjoy an aperitif at Nobu, or have a cocktail at the Italian restaurant Terrazza. ✉ *Shore Club Hotel, 1901 Collins Ave., Miami Beach* ☎ *305/695–3100* ⊕ *www.shoreclub.com.*

DANCE CLUBS

Cameo. One of Miami's ultimate dance clubs, Cameo is constantly rein-venting itself, but the result always seems to be the same—long lines filled with everyone claiming to be on the guest list, hoochie mamas wearing far too little clothing, and some unsuspecting tourists trying to see what all the fuss is about. The combination makes for some insane partying, especially if the night is headlined by an all-star DJ. You'll find both plentiful dance space and plush VIP lounges. If you can brave the velvet rope, the sometimes thuggish crowd, and the nonsense described above, Saturday-night parties are the best. ⌂ *1445 Washington Ave.* ☎ *786/235–5800* ⊕ *www.cameomiami.com.*

Fodor's Choice
★

The Rec Room. Entering the Rec Room is like stumbling upon an awe-some basement party that just happens to be packed with the hottest people ever. This underground space of the Gale Hotel pays homage to everything 1977 (memorabilia included) and features a collection of over 3,000 vinyl records at the disposal of resident DJs. The vibe is totally speakeasy meets modern day—the easy-on-the-eyes crowd lets loose, free of inhibitions, jamming out to old-school hip-hop and eight-ies and nineties throwbacks. ⌂ *Gale South Beach, 1690 Collins Ave.* ☎ *305/673–0199* ⊕ *www.galehotel.com.*

Score. Since the 1990s, Score has been the see-and-be-seen HQ of Miami's gay community, with plenty of global hotties coming from near and far to show off their designer threads and six-pack abs. And this South Beach institution shows no signs of slowing down. DJs spin every night of the week, but Planeta Macho Latin Tuesday is exception-ally popular, as are the upstairs parties on Thursday and the weekend dance-offs. Dress to impress (and then be ready to go shirtless). ⌂ *727 Lincoln Rd.* ☎ *305/535–1111* ⊕ *www.scorebar.net.*

Twist. Twist is a gay institution in South Beach, having been the late-night go-to place for decades, filling to capacity around 2:30 am after the beach's fly-by-night bars and more established lounges begin to die down. There's never a cover here—not even on holidays or during gay pride events. The dark club has several rooms spread over two lev-els and patios, pumping out different tunes and attracting completely disparate groups. It's not uncommon to have young college boys par-tying to Top 40 in one room and strippers showing off their stuff to the straight girls in another area, while an all-out hip-hop throwdown is taking place upstairs. ⌂ *1057 Washington Ave.* ☎ *305/538–9478* ⊕ *www.twistsobe.com.*

LIVE MUSIC

Jazid. If you're looking for an unpretentious alternative to the velvet-rope nightclubs, this unassuming, live-music hot spot is a standout on the SoBe strip. Eight-piece bands play danceable Latin rhythms, as well as reggae, hip-hop, and fusion sounds. Each night caters to a differ-ent genre. Get ready for a late night though, as bands are just getting started at 11 pm. Call ahead to reserve a table. ⌂ *1342 Washington Ave.* ☎ *305/673–9372* ⊕ *www.jazid.net.*

MID-BEACH
DANCE CLUBS

Fodor's Choice ★ **LIV Nightclub.** Since its 2009 opening, the Fontainebleau's LIV Nightclub has garnered plenty of attention. It's not hard to see why—if you can get in, that is. LIV is notorious for lengthy lines, so don't arrive fashionably late. Past the velvet ropes, the dance palladium impresses with its lavish decor, well-dressed international crowd, sensational light-and-sound system, and seductive bi-level club experience. Sometimes the lobby bar, filled with LIV's overflow (and rejects), is just as fun as the club itself. Men beware: Groups of guys entering LIV are often coerced into insanely priced bottle service. ⊠ *Fontainebleau Miami Beach, 4441 Collins Ave., Mid-Beach* ☎ *305/674-4680* ⊕ *www.livnightclub.com.*

SHOPPING

Miami teems with sophisticated shopping malls and the bustling avenues of commercial neighborhoods. But this is also a city of tiny boutiques tucked away on side streets—such as South Miami's Red, Bird, and Sunset roads intersection—and outdoor markets touting unusual and delicious wares. Stroll through Spanish-speaking neighborhoods where shops sell clothing, cigars, and other goods from all over Latin America. At an open-air flea-market stall, score an antique glass shaped like a palm tree and fill it with some fresh Jamaican ginger beer from the table next door. Or stop by your hotel gift shop and snap up an alligator magnet for your refrigerator, an ashtray made of seashells, or a bag of gumballs shaped like Florida oranges. Who can resist?

People fly to Miami from all over the world just to shop, and the malls are high on their list of spending spots. Stop off at one or two of these climate-controlled temples to consumerism, many of which double as mega-entertainment centers, and you'll understand what makes Miami such a vibrant shopping destination.

If you're over the climate-controlled slickness of shopping malls and can't face one more food-court "meal," you've got choices in Miami. Head out into the sunshine and shop the city streets, where you'll find big-name retailers and local boutiques alike. Take a break at a sidewalk café to power up on some Cuban coffee or fresh-squeezed OJ and enjoy the tropical breezes.

Beyond the shopping malls and the big-name retailers, Greater Miami has all manner of merchandise to tempt even the casual browser. For consumers on a mission to find certain items—art deco antiques or cigars, for instance—the city streets burst with a rewarding collection of specialty shops.

Pass the mangoes! Greater Miami's farmers' markets and flea markets take advantage of the region's balmy weather and tropical delights to lure shoppers to open-air stalls filled with produce and collectibles.

LITTLE HAVANA

SPECIALTY SHOPS

CIGARS

Sosa Family Cigars. Like most of the cigar shops lining Calle Ocho, Sosa offers a wide selection of premium and house cigars in a humidified shop. There's a selection of wines for purchase, too. Humidors and other accessories are also available. ⊠ *3475 S.W. 8th St., Little Havana* ☎ *305/446–2606.*

ONLY IN MIAMI

La Casa de las Guayaberas. Open since 1971, this shop sells custom-made guayaberas, the natty four-pocket dress shirts favored by Latin men. Hundreds are also available off the rack. ⊠ *5840 S.W. 8th St., Little Havana* ☎ *305/266–9683.*

FAMILY **La Casa de los Trucos (The House of Costumes).** This popular costume store first opened in Cuba in the 1930s; the exiled owners reopened it here in the 1970s. They have cartoon costumes, rock star costumes, pet costumes, couples costumes, you name it. If you come any time near Halloween, expect to stand in line just to enter the tiny store. ⊠ *1343 S.W. 8th St., Little Havana* ☎ *305/858–5029* ⊕ *www.crazyforcostumes.com.*

COCONUT GROVE

MALLS

CocoWalk. This popular three-story indoor-outdoor mall has three floors of nearly 40 shops that stay open almost as late as its popular restaurants. Typically 1990s chain stores like Victoria's Secret and Gap blend with a few specialty shops like Guayabera World; the space mixes the bustle of a mall with the breathability of an open-air market. Touristy kiosks with cigars, beads, incense, herbs, and other small items are scattered around the ground level, and commercial restaurants and nightlife (Cheesecake Factory, Fat Tuesday, and Paragon Grove 13—a multiscreen, state-of-the-art movie theater with a wine bar and lounge) line the upstairs perimeter. Hanging out and people-watching is something of a pastime here. ⊠ *3015 Grand Ave.* ☎ *305/444–0777* ⊕ *www.cocowalk.net.*

OUTDOOR MARKETS

Coconut Grove Organic Farmers' Market. This pricey, outdoor organic market is a Saturday ritual for locals. It specializes in a mouthwatering array of local produce as well as such ready-to-eat, raw vegan goodies as cashew butter, homemade salad dressings, and fruit pies. If you are looking for a downright granola crowd and experience, pack your Birkenstocks, because this is it. It's open Saturday from 10 to 7, rain or shine. ⊠ *3300 Grand Ave.* ☎ *305/238–7747* ⊕ *www.glaserorganicfarms.com.*

SPECIALTY STORES

ANTIQUES

Worth Galleries. Find an enormous selection of fine European antiques (especially lighting and chandeliers) as well as large and eclectic items—railroad crossing signs, statues, English roadsters. There's also vintage furniture, modern art, oil paintings, and silverware, all in a cluttered setting that makes shopping an adventure. ⊠ *2520 S.W. 28th La.* ☎ *305/285–1330* ⊕ *www.worthgalleries.com.*

CORAL GABLES

MALLS

Fodor's Choice ★ **Village of Merrick Park.** At this Mediterranean-style, tri-level, shopping-and-dining venue, Neiman Marcus and Nordstrom anchor 115 specialty shops. Designers such as Etro, Tiffany & Co., Burberry, CH Carolina Herrera, and Gucci fulfill most high-fashion needs, and haute-decor shopping options include Brazilian contemporary-furniture designer Artefacto. International food favorite C'est Bon and pampering specialist Elemis Day-Spa offer further indulgences. ✉ *358 San Lorenzo Ave.* ☎ *305/529–0200* ⊕ *www.villageofmerrickpark.com.*

SHOPPING DISTRICTS

Miracle Mile. The centerpiece of the downtown Coral Gables shopping district, lined with trees and busy with strolling shoppers, is home to men's and women's boutiques, jewelry and home-furnishings stores, and a host of exclusive couturiers and bridal shops. Running from Douglas Road to LeJeune Road and Aragon Avenue to Andalusia Avenue, more than 30 first-rate restaurants offer everything from French to Indian cuisine, and art galleries and the Actors' Playhouse at the Miracle Theater give the area a cultural flair. ✉ *Miracle Mile (Coral Way), Douglas Rd. to LeJeune Rd., and Aragon Ave. to Andalusia Ave.* ⊕ *www.shopcoralgables.com.*

SPECIALTY SHOPS

ANTIQUES

Alhambra Antiques. The collection of high-quality antique furniture and decorative pieces are acquired on annual jaunts to France. Expect a wide range of classic chandeliers, clocks, chairs, daybeds, tables, and mirrors. ✉ *2850 Salzedo St.* ☎ *305/446–1688* ⊕ *www.alhambraantiques.com.*

Valerio Antiques. This shop carries fine French art deco furniture, bronze sculptures, shagreen boxes, and original art glass by Gallé and Loetz, among others. ✉ *250 Valencia Ave.* ☎ *305/448–6779* ⊕ *www. valerioartdeco.com.*

BOOKS

Fodor's Choice ★ **Books & Books, Inc.** Greater Miami's only independent English-language bookshops specialize in contemporary and classical literature as well as in books on the arts, architecture, Florida, and Cuba. At any of its half-dozen locations you can lounge at the old-fashioned in-store café or, at the Coral Gables store, browse the photography gallery. Stores host regular book signings, literary events, poetry, and other readings. Long live the classic book store! ✉ *265 Aragon Ave.* ☎ *305/442–4408* ⊕ *www.booksandbooks.com* ✉ *927 Lincoln Rd., South Beach, Miami Beach* ☎ *305/532–3222* ✉ *9700 Collins Ave., Bal Harbour, Bal Harbour* ☎ *305/864–4241.*

CLOTHING

Koko & Palenki. Shoe shopaholics come here for the well-edited selection of trendy footwear by Alexandre Birman, Giuseppe Zanotti, Emilia Castillo, Rachel Zoe, Rebecca Minkoff, and others. Handbags and belts add to the selection. Clothing hails from designers like Catherine Malandrino, Issa, J Brand, and Citizens of Humanity.

Koko & Palenki also has a store in Aventura Mall. ⊠ *Village of Merrick Park, 342 San Lorenzo Ave., Suite 1090, Coral Gables, Miami* ☎ *305/444–0626* ⊕ *www.kokopalenki.com* ⊠ *Aventura Mall, 19501 Biscayne Blvd., Suite 779, Aventura, Miami* ☎ *305/792–9299.*

Silvia Tcherassi. The Colombian designer's signature boutique in the Village of Merrick Park features ready-to-wear, feminine, and frilly dresses and separates accented with chiffon, tulle, and sequins. A neighboring atelier at 4101 Ponce de Leon Boulevard showcases the designer's bridal collection. ⊠ *350 San Lorenzo Ave., No. 2140* ☎ *305/461–0009* ⊕ *www.silviatcherassi.com.*

JEWELRY

Jose Roca Fine Jewelry Designs. Jose Roca designs fine jewelry from precious metals and stones. If you have a particular piece that you would like to create, this is the place to have it meticulously executed. ⊠ *297 Miracle Mile* ☎ *305/448–2808.*

WYNWOOD/MIDTOWN/DESIGN DISTRICT

SHOPPING NEIGHBORHOODS

Miami Design District. Miami is synonymous with good design, and this visitor-friendly shopping district—from N.E. 38th to N.E. 42nd streets, between N. Miami Ave. and N.E. 2nd Avenue—is an unprecedented melding of public space and the exclusive world of design. There are more than 200 showrooms and galleries, including Kartell, Ann Sacks, Poliform USA, and Luminaire Lab. Upscale retail outlets have recently entered the district. Cartier, En Avance, Louis Vuitton, Prada, and Scotch & Soda now neighbor the design showrooms. Meanwhile, restaurants like Michael's Genuine Food & Drink also make this trendy neighborhood a hip place to dine. Unlike most showrooms, which are typically the beat of decorators alone, the Miami Design District's showrooms are open to the public and occupy windowed, street-level spaces. Although in some cases you'll need a decorator to secure your purchases, browsers are encouraged to consider for themselves the array of rather exclusive furnishings, decorative objects, antiques, and art. ⊠ *N.E. 2nd Ave. and N.E. 40th St., Miami Design District* ⊕ *www.miamidesigndistrict.net.*

SPECIALTY SHOPS

ANTIQUES

Artisan Antiques. These purveyors of china, crystal, mirrors, and armoires from the French–art deco period also draw customers in with an assortment of 1930s radiator covers, which can double as funky sideboards. The shop is open weekdays. ⊠ *110 N.E. 40th St., Miami Design District* ☎ *305/573–5619* ⊕ *www.artisanartdeco.com.*

ONLY IN MIAMI

ABC Costume Shop. ABC Costume Shop is a major costume source for TV, movie, and theatrical performances. Open to the public, it has more than 30,000 costumes in stock—outfits range from Venetian kings and queens to Tarzan and Jane. Hundreds of these costumes and accessories, such as wigs, masks, gloves, tights, and makeup, are available to buy off the rack; others are available to rent. ⊠ *575 N.W. 24th*

St., Wynwood ☎ *305/573–5657* ⊕ *www.abccostumeshop.com.*

Genius Jones. This is a modern design store for kids and parents. It's the best—and one of the few—places to buy unique children's gifts on South Beach. Pick up furniture, strollers, clothing, home accessories, and playthings, including classic wooden

toys, vintage-rock T-shirts by Claude and Trunk, and toys designed by Takashi Murakami and Keith Haring. ✉ *2800 N.E. 2nd Ave., South Beach, Miami Beach* ☎ *866/436–4875* ⊕ *www.geniusjones.com.*

SOUTH BEACH

SHOPPING DISTRICTS

Fodor'sChoice ★ **Collins Avenue.** Give your plastic a workout in South Beach shopping at the many high-profile tenants on this densely packed stretch of Collins between 5th and 10th streets, with stores like Steve Madden, Club Monaco, M.A.C., Kenneth Cole, Barneys Co-Op, and A/X Armani Exchange. Sprinkled among the upscale vendors are hair salons, spas, cafés, and such familiar stores as the Gap, Diesel, and Urban Outfitters. Be sure to head over one street east to Ocean Drive or west to Washington Avenue for a drink or a light bite, in between shopping on Collins Avenue and Lincoln Road. ✉ *Collins Ave. between 5th and 10th Sts., South Beach, Miami Beach.*

Fodor'sChoice ★ **Lincoln Road Mall.** The eight-block-long pedestrian mall is the trendiest place on Miami Beach. Home to more than 150 shops, 20-plus art galleries and nightclubs, about 50 restaurants and cafés, and the renovated Colony Theatre, Lincoln Road, between Alton Road and Washington Avenue, is like the larger, more sophisticated cousin of Ocean Drive. The see-and-be-seen theme is furthered by outdoor seating at every restaurant, where well-heeled patrons lounge and discuss the people (and pet) parade passing by. An 18-screen movie theater anchors the west end of the street, which is where most of the worthwhile shops are; the far east end is mostly discount and electronics shops. Sure, there's a Gap, a Williams-Sonoma, and an H&M, but the emphasis is on emporiums with unique personalities, like Chroma, Base, and Fly Boutique. ✉ *Lincoln Rd. between Alton Rd. and Washington Ave., South Beach, Miami Beach* ⊕ *www.lincolnroad.org.*

SPECIALTY SHOPS

CLOTHING

Base. This is the quintessential South Beach fun-and-funky boutique experience. Stop here for men's eclectic clothing, shoes, jewelry, and accessories that mix Japanese design with Caribbean-inspired materials. Constantly evolving, this shop features an intriguing magazine section and groovy home accessories. The often-present house-label designer may help select your wardrobe's newest addition. The boutique has small outposts in the Delano Hotel and the Mondrian South Beach, as well as an haute vending machine in the latter. ✉ *939 Lincoln Rd., South Beach, Miami Beach* ☎ *305/531–4982* ⊕ *www.baseworld.com.*

Miami Beach residential buildings tower over the sand.

Fly Boutique. Fly Boutique is where South Beach hipsters flock for the latest arrival of used clothing. At this resale boutique '80s glam designer pieces fly out at a premium price, but vintage camisoles and Levi's corduroys are still a resale deal. Be sure to look up—the eclectic lanterns are also for sale. ⊠ *650 Lincoln Rd., South Beach, Miami Beach* ☎ *305/604–8508* ⊕ *www.flyboutiquevintage.com.*

Intermix. This modern New York–based boutique has the variety of a department store. You'll find fancy dresses, stylish shoes, slinky accessories, and trendy looks by sassy and somewhat pricey designers like Chloé, Stella McCartney, Marc Jacobs, Moschino, and Diane von Furstenberg. ⊠ *634 Collins Ave., South Beach, Miami Beach* ☎ *305/531–5950* ⊕ *www.intermixonline.com* ⊠ *Bal Harbour Shops, 9700 Collins Ave., North Beach and Aventura, Bal Harbour* ☎ *305/993–1232* ⊕ *www.intermixonline.com.*

ONLY IN MIAMI

Dog Bar. Just north of Lincoln Road's main drag, this over-the-top pet boutique caters to enthusiastic animal owners with a variety of unique items for the super-pampered pet (luxurious pet sofas imported from Italy, bling-bling-studded collars, and chic poopy bag holders). ⊠ *1684 Jefferson Ave., South Beach, Miami Beach* ☎ *305/532–5654* ⊕ *www.dogbar.com.*

OUTDOOR MARKETS

The Lincoln Road Outdoor Antique & Collectible Market of Miami Beach. Interested in picking up samples of Miami's ever-present modern and moderne furniture and accessories? About 125 vendors take over outdoor Lincoln Road Mall every other Sunday, selling multifarious goods that should satisfy postimpressionists, deco-holics, Edwardians, Bauhausers, Goths, and '50s junkies. ⊠ *Lincoln Rd. Mall, South Beach, Miami Beach* ⊕ *www.antiquecollectiblemarket.com.*

NORTH BEACH AND AVENTURA

MALLS

Fodor'sChoice **Aventura Mall.** This three-story megamall offers the ultimate in South
★ Florida retail therapy. Aventura houses many global top performers such as the most lucrative Abercrombie & Fitch in the United States, a massive Crate & Barrel, a supersize Nordstrom and Bloomingdale's, and 250 other shops like Façonnable, Dior, and Braccialini, which together create the fifth-largest mall in the United States. This is the one-stop, shop-'til-you-drop retail palladium for locals, out-of-towners, and—frequently—celebrities. ⊠ *19501 Biscayne Blvd., Aventura* ☎ *305/935–1110* ⊕ *www.aventuramall.com.*

Fodor'sChoice **Bal Harbour Shops.** Beverly Hills meets the South Florida sun at this
★ swank collection of 100 high-end shops, boutiques, and department stores, which include such names as Alexander McQueen, Gucci, Hermès, Salvatore Ferragamo, Tiffany & Co., and Valentino. Many European designers open their first North American signature store at this outdoor, pedestrian-friendly mall, and many American designers open their first boutique outside of New York here. Restaurants and cafés, in tropical garden settings, overflow with style-conscious diners. People-watching on the terrace of the Japanese restaurant Makoto is the best in town. The ambience is oh-so-Rodeo Drive. ⊠ *9700 Collins Ave., Bal Harbour* ☎ *305/866–0311* ⊕ *www.balharbourshops.com.*

SPORTS AND THE OUTDOORS

Sun, sand, and crystal-clear water mixed with an almost nonexistent winter and a cosmopolitan clientele make Miami and Miami Beach ideal for year-round sunbathing and outdoor activities. Whether the priority is showing off a toned body, jumping on a Jet Ski, or relaxing in a tranquil natural environment, there's a beach tailor-made to please. But tanning and water sports are only part of this sun-drenched picture. Greater Miami has championship golf courses and tennis courts, miles of bike trails along placid canals and through subtropical forests, and skater-friendly concrete paths amidst the urban jungle. For those who like their sports of the spectator variety, the city offers up a bonanza of pro teams for every season. There's even a crazy ball-flinging game called jai alai that's billed as the fastest sport on earth.

In addition to contacting venues directly, get tickets to major events from **Ticketmaster** (☎ *800/745–3000* ⊕ *www.ticketmaster.com*).

BASEBALL

FAMILY **Miami Marlins.** Miami's baseball team, formerly known as the Florida Marlins, moved into a new home in 2012, Marlins Park—a 37,442-seat retractable-roof baseball stadium on the grounds of Miami's famous

Orange Bowl. Go see the team that came out of nowhere to beat the New York Yankees and win the 2003 World Series. Home games are April through early October. ⊠ *Marlins Park, Marlin Way, N.W. 7th St. and N.W. 14th Ave., 2 miles west of downtown, Little Havana* ☎ *305/626–7378, 877/627–5467 for tickets* ⊕ *www.marlins.com* ⊠ *$10–$395; parking from $20 and should be prepurchased online.*

BICYCLING

Perfect weather and flat terrain make Miami–Dade County a popular place for cyclists; however, biking here can also be quite dangerous. Be very vigilant when biking on Miami Beach, or better yet, steer clear and bike the beautiful paths of Key Biscayne instead.

Key Cycling. Rent bikes for $15 for two hours, $24 for the day, and $80 for the week. ⊠ *Galleria Shopping Center, 328 Crandon Blvd., Suite 121, Key Biscayne* ☎ *305/361–0061* ⊕ *www.keycycling.com.*

Miami Beach Bicycle Center. The easiest and most economical place for a bike rental on Miami Beach is this shop near Ocean Drive. Rent a bike for $5 per hour, $14 per day, or $60 for the week. All bike rentals include locks, helmets, and baskets. ⊠ *601 5th St., South Beach, Miami Beach* ☎ *305/674–0150* ⊕ *www.bikemiamibeach.com.*

BOATING AND SAILING

Boating, whether on sailboats, powerboats, luxury yachts, WaveRunners, or windsurfers, is a passion in Greater Miami. The Intracoastal Waterway, wide and sheltered Biscayne Bay, and the Atlantic Ocean provide ample opportunities for fun aboard all types of watercraft.

The best windsurfing spots are on the north side of the Rickenbacker Causeway at Virginia Key Beach or to the south at, go figure, Windsurfer Beach. Kite surfing adds another level to the water sports craze.

OUTFITTERS AND EXPEDITIONS

Club Nautico. You can rent 18- to 34-foot powerboats and 52- to 54-foot yachts through this national boat rental company with two Miami locations. Half- to full-day rentals range from $399 to $3,600. ⊠ *Miami Beach Marina, 300 Alton Rd., #112, Miami Beach* ☎ *305/673–2502* ⊕ *www.club-nautico.com* ⊠ *Crandon Park Marina, 4000 Crandon Blvd., Key Biscayne.*

Florida Yacht Charters & Sales. The family-owned Coconut Grove outfit will give you the requisite checkout cruise and paperwork. Then you can take off for the Keys or the Bahamas on a catamaran, sailboat, or motor yacht. Charts, lessons, and captains are available if needed. ⊠ *Bayshore Landing Marina, 2550 S. Bayshore Dr., Suite 207, Coconut Grove* ☎ *305/532–8600* ⊕ *www.floridayacht.com.*

Playtime Watersports. All types of boat rentals are available from this company, but a regularly scheduled evening sunset cruise through Biscayne Bay departs nightly at 6:30 pm from Maribella Marina in downtown. ⊠ *Maribella Marina, 801 Brickell Ave., Downtown* ☎ *305/216–6967* ⊕ *www.playtimewatersport.com.*

Continued on page 112

A STROLL DOWN DECO LANE

by Susan MacCallum Whitcomb

"It was an age of miracles, it was an age of art,

it was an age of excess, and it was an age of satire."

—F. Scott Fitzgerald, *Echoes of the Jazz Age*

The 1920s and '30s brought us flappers and gangsters, plunging stock prices and soaring skyscrapers, and plenty of headline-worthy news from the arts scene, from talking pictures and the jazz craze to fashions where pearls piled on and sequins dazzled. These decades between the two world wars also gave us an art style reflective of the changing times: art deco.

Distinguished by geometrical shapes and the use of industrial motifs that fused the decorative arts with modern technology, art deco became the architectural style of choice for train stations and big buildings across the country (think New york's Radio City Music Hall and Empire State Building).

Using a steel-and-concrete box as the foundation, architects dipped into art deco's grab bag of accessories, initially decorating facades with spheres, cylinders, and cubes. They later borrowed increasingly from industrial design, stripping elements used in ocean liners and automobiles to their streamlined essentials.

The style was also used in jewelry, furniture, textiles, and advertising. The fact that it employed inexpensive materials, such as stucco or terrazzo, helped art deco thrive during the Great Depression.

MIAMI BEACH'S ART DECO DISTRICT

With its warm beaches and tropical surroundings, Miami Beach in the early 20th century was establishing itself as America's winter playground. During the roaring '20s luxurious hostelries resembling Venetian palaces, Spanish villages, and French châteaux sprouted up. In the 1930s, middle-class tourists started coming, and more hotels had to be built. Designers like Henry Hohauser chose art deco for its affordable yet distinctive design.

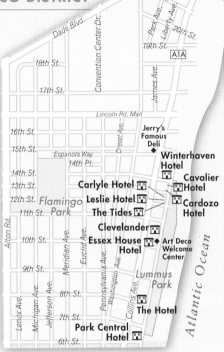

An antidote to the gloom of the Great Depression, the look was cheerful and tidy. And with the whimsical additions of portholes, colorful racing bands, and images of rolling ocean waves painted or etched on the walls, these South Beach properties created an oceanfront fantasy world for travelers.

Many of the candy-colored hotels have survived and been meticulously restored. They are among the more than 800 buildings of historical significance in South Beach's art deco district. Composing much of South Beach, the 1-square-mi district is bounded by Dade Boulevard on the north, the Atlantic Ocean on the east, 6th Street on the south, and Alton Road on the west.

Because the district as a whole was developed so rapidly and designed by like-minded architects—**Henry Hohauser, L. Murray Dixon, Albert Anis,** and their colleagues—it has amazing stylistic unity. Nevertheless, on this single street you can trace the evolution of period form from angular, vertically emphatic early deco to aerodynamically rounded Streamline Moderne. The relatively severe Cavalier and more curvaceous Cardozo are fine examples of the former and latter, respectively.

To explore the district, begin by loading up on literature in the **Art Deco Welcome Center** (✉ *1001 Ocean Dr.* ☎ *305/763–8026* ⊕ *www.mdpl.org*). If you want to view these historic properties on your own, just start walking. A four-block stroll north on Ocean Drive gets you up close to camera-ready classics: the **Clevelander** (1020), the **Tides** (1220), the **Leslie** (1244), the **Carlyle** (1250), the **Cardozo** (1300), the **Cavalier** (1320), and the **Winterhaven** (1400).

ART DECO TOURS

See the bold looks of classic Art Deco architecture along Ocean Drive.

SELF-GUIDED AUDIO TOURS

Expert insight on the architecture and the area's history is yours on the Miami Design Preservation League's (MDPL) 90-minute self-guided walks that use an iPod or iphone and include a companion map. You can pick up the iPod version and companion map at the Art Deco Welcome Center from 9:30 AM to 5 PM daily; the cost is $15.

WALKING TOURS

The tour offers a primer in the three predominate styles found in the Art Deco District: Art Deco, Meditteranean Revival, and Miami Modern (MiMo).

The MDPL's 90-minute "Ocean Drive and Beyond" group walking tour gives you a guided look at area icons, inside and out. (A number of interiors are on the itinerary, so it's a good chance to peek inside spots that might otherwise seem off-limits.) Morning tours depart daily at 10:30 AM from the Art Deco Welcome Center Gift Shop. An additional evening tour departs at 6:30 PM on Thursdays. Buy tickets in advance at ⊕ *mdpl.org*, or arrive 15–20 minutes early to buy tickets ($20).

BIKE TOURS

Rather ride than walk? Half-day cycling tours of the city's art deco history are organized daily for groups (5 or more) by **South Beach Bike Tours** (☎ *305/673–2002* ⊕ *www.southbeachbiketours. com*). The $59 cost includes equipment, snacks, and water.

ART DECO WEEKEND

Tours, lectures, film screenings, and dozens of other '30s-themed events are on tap in mid-January, during the annual **Art Deco Weekend** (☎ *305/672-2014*, ⊕ *www. ArtDecoWeekend.com*). Festivities—many of them free—kick off with a Saturday morning parade and culminate in a street fair. More than a quarter of a million people join in the action, which centers on Ocean Drive between 5th and 15th streets.

Celebrate the 1930s during Art Deco Weekend.

ARCHITECTURAL HIGHLIGHTS

Cavalier Hotel

FRIEZE DETAIL, CAVALIER HOTEL
The decorative stucco friezes outside the Cavalier Hotel at 1320 Ocean Drive are significant for more than aesthetic reasons. Roy France used them to add symmetry (adhering to the "Rule of Three") and accentuate the hotel's verticality by drawing the eye upward. The pattern he chose also reflected a fascination with ancient civilizations engendered by the recent rediscovery of King Tut's tomb and the Chichén Itzá temples.

LOBBY FLOOR, PARK CENTRAL HOTEL
Terrazzo—a compound of cement and stone chips that could be poured, then polished—is a hallmark of deco design. Terrazzo floors typically had a geometric pattern, like this one in the Park Central Hotel, a 1937 building by Henry Hohauser at 640 Ocean Drive.

Park Central Hotel

CORNER FACADE, ESSEX HOUSE HOTEL
Essex House Hotel, a 1938 gem that appears permanently anchored at 1001 Collins Avenue, is a stunning example of Maritime deco (also known as Nautical Moderne). Designed by Henry Hohauser to evoke an ocean liner, the hotel is rife with marine elements, from the rows of porthole-style windows and natty racing stripes to the towering smokestack-like sign. With a prow angled proudly into the street corner, it seems ready to steam out to sea.

Essex House Hotel

NEON SPIRE, THE HOTEL
The name spelled vertically in eye-popping neon on the venue's iconic aluminum spire—Tiffany—bears evidence of the hotel's earlier incarnation. When the L. Murray Dixon–designed Tiffany Hotel was erected at 801 Collins Avenue in 1939, neon was still a novelty. Its use, coupled with the spire's rocket-like shape, combined to create a futuristic look influenced by the sci-fi themes then pervasive in popular culture.

The Hotel

ENTRANCE, JERRY'S FAMOUS DELI
Inspired by everything from car fenders to airplane noses, proponents of art deco's Streamline Moderne look began to soften buildings' hitherto boxy edges. But when Henry Hohauser designed Hoffman's Cafeteria in 1940 he took moderne to the max. The landmark at 1450 Collins Avenue (now Jerry's Famous Deli) has a sleek, splendidly curved facade. The restored interior echoes it through semicircular booths and rounded chair backs.

Jerry's Famous Deli

ARCHITECTURAL TERMS

The Rule of Three: Early deco designers often used architectural elements in multiples of three, creating tripartite facades with triple sets of windows, eyebrows, or banding.

Eyebrows: Small shelf-like ledges that protruded over exterior windows were used to simultaneously provide much-needed shade and serve as a counterpoint to a building's strong vertical lines.

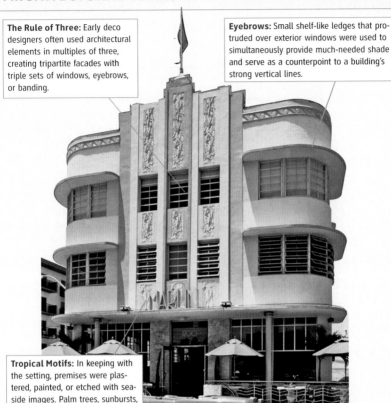

Tropical Motifs: In keeping with the setting, premises were plastered, painted, or etched with seaside images. Palm trees, sunbursts, waves, flamingoes, and the like were particularly common.

Banding: Enhancing the illusion that these immobile structures were rapidly speeding objects, colorful horizontal bands (also called "racing stripes") were painted on exteriors or applied with tile.

Stripped Classic: The most austere version of art deco (sometimes dubbed Depression Moderne) was used for buildings commissioned by the Public Works Administration.

(top) Hotel Marlin; (left) Sherbrooke Hotel; (right) U.S. Post Office in Miami Beach.

Fodor's Choice
★

Sailboards Miami. Rent paddle boards and kayaks or learn how to wind-surf. These friendly folks say they teach more windsurfers each year than anyone in the United States and promise to teach you to windsurf within two hours—for $79. Open Friday–Tuesday only. ⊠ *Mile 6.5 on Rickenbacker Causeway, Key Biscayne* ☎ *305/892–8992* ⊕ *www. sailboardsmiami.com* ☉ *Fri.–Tues. 10–6.*

GOLF

Greater Miami has more than 30 private and public courses. Costs at most courses are higher on weekends and in season, but you can save by playing on weekdays and after 1 or 3 pm, depending on the course. Call ahead to find out when afternoon-twilight rates go into effect. For information on most courses in Miami and throughout Florida, you can visit ⊕ *www.floridagolferguide.com.*

Biltmore Golf Course. The 18-hole, par-71 championship course, known for its scenic layout, has been restored to its original Donald Ross design, circa 1925. Greens fees in season range from $162 to $189 for nonresidents. The optional cart is $27. You can reserve your tee time online. ⊠ *Biltmore Hotel, 1210 Anastasia Ave., Coral Gables* ☎ *855/311–6903* ⊕ *www.biltmorehotel.com.*

Crandon Golf Key Biscayne. Overlooking the bay, this top-rated 18-hole, par-72 public course comes with a beautiful tropical setting. Nonresidents should expect to pay $225 for a round in season (December 15–April) and roughly half that off-season. Deeply discounted twilight rates of $50 apply after 2 pm. ⊠ *6700 Crandon Blvd., Key Biscayne* ☎ *305/361–9129* ⊕ *www.crandongolfclub.com.*

Fodor's Choice
★

Doral Golf Resort and Spa. Just west of Miami proper, Doral Golf Resort and Spa is best known for the par-72 Blue Monster course and the World Golf Championships-Cadillac Championship. The week of festivities planned around this March tournament, which offers $8.5 million in prize money, brings hordes of pro-golf aficionados to South Florida. But there's far more to Doral than the Blue Monster and the Cadillac Championship. There are four other renowned golf courses and numerous other tournaments throughout the year; hence, golf enthusiasts flock here year-round. Greens fees range from $75 to $350. Carts are not required. ⊠ *4400 N.W. 87th Ave., 36th St. Exit off Rte. 826, Doral* ☎ *800/713–6725* ⊕ *www.doralresort.com.*

The Senator Course at Shula's Golf Club. In the suburbs of North Miami, the Senator Course at Shula's Golf Club boasts the longest championship course in the area (7,055 yards, par 72), a lighted par-3 course, and a golf school. Greens fees are $38–$125, depending on the season and time. You'll pay in the lower range on weekdays, more on weekends, and $40 after 2 pm. Golf carts are included. The club hosts more than 75 tournaments a year. ⊠ *7601 Miami Lakes Dr., 154th St. Exit off Rte. 826, Miami Lakes* ☎ *305/820–8088* ⊕ *www. shulasgolfclub.com.*

GUIDED TOURS

BOAT TOURS

Duck Tours Miami. Amphibious vehicles make daily 90-minute tours of Miami that combine land and sea views. Comedy and music are part of the mix. Tickets are $18 for children 4–12. ⊠ *1661 James Ave., South Beach, Miami Beach* ☎ *305/673–2217* ⊕ *www.ducktourssouthbeach. com* ⊠ *$32.*

Island Queen, Island Lady, and Miami Lady. Double-decker, 140-passenger tour boats docked at Bayside Marketplace set sail daily for 90-minute narrated tours of the Port of Miami and Millionaires' Row, Miami's waterfront homes of the rich and famous. ⊠ *401 Biscayne Blvd., Downtown* ☎ *305/379–5119* ⊕ *www.islandqueencruises.com* ⊠ *$27.*

RA Charters. For something a little more private and luxe, sail out of the Dinner Key Marina in Coconut Grove on the sailing *Vessel RA*, a 45-foot sailing yacht. Full- and half-day charters include sailing lessons, with occasional extended trips to the Florida Keys. For a romantic night, have Captain Masoud pack some gourmet fare and sail sunset to moonlight while you enjoy Biscayne Bay's spectacular skyline view of Miami. ⊠ *Dinner Key Marina: Pier 7 Slip 8, Coconut Grove* ☎ *305/989–3959* ⊕ *www.racharters.com* ⊠ *Call for prices.*

WALKING TOURS

Art Deco District Tour. Operated by the Miami Design Preservation League, this is a 90-minute guided walking tour that departs from the league's welcome center at Ocean Drive and 10th Street. It starts at 10:30 am daily, with an extra tour at 6:30 pm Thursday. Alternatively, you can go at your own pace with the league's self-guided iPod audio tour, which also takes roughly an hour and a half. ⊠ *1001 Ocean Dr., South Beach, Miami Beach* ☎ *305/763–8026* ⊕ *www.mdpl.org* ⊠ *$20 guided tour, $15 audio tour.*

Miami Urban Tours. For something different and to experience Miami's diverse, urban areas, try Miami's cultural community tours through the "Urban Tour Host," an outfitter that specializes in group and private excursions. They put together interactive tours (read: you actually step into each locale) that cover all the urban enclaves between Little Havana and Little Haiti, providing a perspective on Miami's Caribbean, African-American, and Hispanic heritage. ⊠ *Ingraham Bldg., 25 S.E. 2nd Ave., Suite 1048, Downtown* ☎ *305/416–6868* ⊕ *www. miamiculturaltours.com.*

SCUBA DIVING AND SNORKELING

Diving and snorkeling on the offshore coral wrecks and reefs on a calm day can be very rewarding. Chances are excellent that you'll come face-to-face with a flood of tropical fish. One option is to find Fowey, Triumph, Long, and Emerald reefs in 10- to 15-foot dives that are perfect for snorkelers and beginning divers. On the edge of the continental shelf a little more than 3 miles out, these reefs are just a ¼ mile away from depths greater than 100 feet. Another option is to paddle around the tangled prop roots of the mangrove trees that line the coast, peering at the fish, crabs, and other creatures hiding there. ⇨ *For the best snorkeling in Miami-Dade, head to Biscayne National Park. See the Everglades chapter for more information.*

Artificial Reefs. Perhaps the area's most unusual diving options are its artificial reefs. Since 1981, Miami-Dade County's Department of Environmental Resources Management has sunk tons of limestone boulders and a water tower, army tanks, and almost 200 boats of all descriptions to create a "wreckreational" habitat where divers can swim with yellow tang, barracudas, nurse sharks, snapper, eels, and grouper. The website offers an interactive map of wreck locations. Dive outfitters are familiar with most of these artificial reefs and can take you to the best ones. ⊠ *Miami Beach* ⊕ *www.miamidade.gov/development/reef-locator.asp.*

OUTFITTERS

Divers Paradise of Key Biscayne. This complete dive shop and diving-charter service next to the Crandon Park Marina, includes equipment rental and scuba instruction with PADI and NAUI affiliation. Four-hour dive trips are offered Tuesday through Friday at 10:30, weekends 8:30 and 1:30. The trip is $60. Night dives are offered Saturday at 5:30. ⊠ *4000 Crandon Blvd., Key Biscayne* ☎ *305/361–3483* ⊕ *www.keydivers.com.*

South Beach Dive and Surf Center. Dedicated to all things ocean, this center offers diving and snorkeling trips (at least four times weekly) as well as surfboard rentals and lessons. The Discover Scuba course trains diving newcomers on Tuesday, Thursday, and Saturday at 8 am at a PADI-affiliated dive shop. Advance classes follow at 9:45 am. Night dives take place each Wednesday at 5, and wreck and reef dives on Sundays at 7:30 am. The center also runs dives in Key Largo's Spiegel Grove, the second-largest wreck ever to be sunk for the intention of recreational diving, and in the Neptune Memorial Reef, inspired by the city of Atlantis and created in part using the ashes of cremated bodies. Boats depart from marinas in Miami Beach and Key Largo, in the Florida Keys. ⊠ *850 Washington Ave., South Beach, Miami Beach* ☎ *305/531–6110* ⊕ *www.southbeachdivers.com.*

THE EVERGLADES

WELCOME TO THE EVERGLADES

TOP REASONS TO GO

★ **Fun fishing:** Cast for some of the world's fightingest game fish—600 species of fish in all—in the Everglades' backwaters.

★ **Abundant birdlife:** Check hundreds of birds off your life list, including—if you're lucky—the rare Everglades snail kite.

★ **Cool kayaking:** Do a half-day trip in Big Cypress National Preserve or reach for the ultimate—the 99-mile Wilderness Trail.

★ **Swamp cuisine:** Hankering for alligator tail and frogs' legs? Or how about swamp cabbage, made from hearts of palm? Better yet, try stone-crab claws fresh from the traps.

★ **Gator-spotting:** This is ground zero for alligator viewing in the United States, and there's a good bet you'll leave having spotted your quota.

1 Everglades National Park. Alligators, Florida panthers, black bears, manatees, dolphins, bald eagles, and roseate spoonbills call this vast habitat home.

2 Biscayne National Park. Mostly under water, this is where the string of coral reefs and islands that form the Florida Keys begins.

GETTING ORIENTED

3

The southern third of the Florida peninsula is largely taken up by protected government land that includes Everglades National Park, Big Cypress National Preserve, and Biscayne National Park. Miami lies to the northeast, and Naples and Marco Island are northwest. Land access to Everglades National Park is primarily by two roads. The park's main road traverses the southern Everglades from the gateway towns of Homestead and Florida City to the outpost of Flamingo, on Florida Bay. To the north, Tamiami Trail (U.S. 41) cuts through the Everglades from the Greater Miami area on the east coast or from Naples on the west coast to the western park entrance in Everglades City at Route 29.

3 **Big Cypress National Preserve.** Neighbor to Everglades National Park, it's an outdoor-lover's paradise.

THE FLORIDA
EVERGLADES

by Lynne Helm

Alternately described as elixir of life or swampland muck, the Florida Everglades is one of a kind—a 50-mi-wide "river of grass" that spreads across hundreds of thousands of acres. It moves at varying speeds depending on rainfall and other variables, sloping south from the Kissimmee River and Lake Okeechobee to estuaries of Biscayne Bay, Florida Bay, and the Ten Thousand Islands.

Today, apart from sheltering some 70 species on America's endangered list, the Everglades also embraces more than 7 million residents, 50 million annual tourists, 400,000 acres of sugarcane, and the world's largest concentration of golf courses.

Demands on the land threaten the Everglades' finely balanced ecosystem. Irrigation canals for agriculture and roadways disrupt natural water flow. Drainage for development leaves wildlife scurrying for new territory. Water runoff, laced with fertilizers, promotes unnatural growth of swamp vegetation. What remains is a miracle of sorts, given decades of these destructive forces.

Creation of the Everglades required unique conditions. South Florida's geology, linked with its warm, wet subtropical climate, is the perfect mix for a marshland ecosystem. Layers of porous, permeable limestone create water-bearing rock, soil, and aquifers, which in turn affects climate, weather, and hydrology.

This rock beneath the Everglades reflects Florida's geologic history—its crust was once part of the African region. Some scientists theorize that continental shifting merged North America with Africa, and then continental rifting later pulled North America away from the African continent but took part of northwest Africa with it—the part that is today's Florida. The Earth's tectonic plates continued to migrate, eventually placing Florida at its current location as a land mass jutting out into the ocean, with the Everglades at its tip.

EXPERIENCING THE ECOSYSTEMS

Eight distinct habitats exist within Everglades National Park, Big Cypress National Preserve, and Biscayne National Park.

Carnestown ○   Ochopee ○
29   41
Gulf Coast   ○ Everglades City
Visitor Center •
○ Chokoloskee

TEN THOUSAND ISLANDS

ECOSYSTEMS	EASY WAY	MORE ACTIVE WAY
COASTAL PRAIRIE: An arid region of salt-tolerant vegetation lies between the tidal mud flats of Florida Bay and dry land. **Best place to see it: The Coastal Prairie Trail**	Take a guided boat tour of Florida Bay, leaving from Flamingo Marina.	Hike the Coastal Prairie Trail from Eco Pond to Clubhouse Beach.
CYPRESS: Capable of surviving in standing water, cypress trees often form dense clusters called "cypress domes" in natural water-filled depressions. **Best place to see it: Big Cypress National Preserve**	Drive U.S. 41 (also known as Tamiami Trail—pronounced Tammy-Amee), which cuts across Southern Florida, from Naples to Miami.	Hike (or drive) the scenic Loop Road, which begins off Tamiami Trail, running from the Loop Road Education Center to Monroe Station.
FRESH WATER MARL PRAIRIE: Bordering deeper sloughs are large prairies with marl (clay and calcium carbonate) sediments on limestone. Gators like to use their toothy snouts to dig holes in prairie mud. **Best place to see it: Pahayokee Overlook**	Drive there from the Ernest F. Coe Visitor Center.	Take a guided tour, either through the park service or from permitted, licensed guides. You also can set up camp at Long Pine Key.
FRESH WATER SLOUGH AND HARDWOOD HAMMOCK: Shark River Slough and Taylor Slough are the Everglades' two sloughs, or marshy rivers. Due to slight elevation amid sloughs, dense stands of hardwood trees appear as teardrop-shaped islands. **Best place to see it: The Observation Tower**	Take a two-hour guided tram tour from the Shark Valley Visitor Center to the tower and back.	Walk or bike (rentals available) the route to the tower via the tram road and (walkers only) Bobcat Boardwalk trail and Otter Cave Hammock Trail.
MANGROVE: Spread over South Florida's coastal channels and waterways, mangrove thrives where Everglades fresh water mixes with salt water. **Best place to see it: The Wilderness Waterway**	Picnic at the area near Long Pine Key, which is surrounded by mangrove, or take a water tour at Biscayne National Park.	Boat your way along the 99-mi Wilderness Waterway. It's six hours by motorized boat, seven days by canoe.
MARINE AND ESTUARINE: Corals, sponges, mollusks, seagrass, and algae thrive in the Florida Bay, where the fresh waters of the Everglades meet the salty seas. **Best place to see it: Florida Bay**	Take a boat tour from the Flamingo Visitor Center marina.	Canoe or kayak on White Water Bay along the Wilderness Waterway Canoe Trail.
PINELAND: A dominant plant in dry, rugged terrain, the Everglades' diverse pinelands consist of slash pine forest, saw palmettos, and more than 200 tropical plant varieties. **Best place to see it: Long Pine Key trails**	Drive to Long Pine Key, about 6 mi off the main road from Ernest F. Coe Visitor Center.	Hike or bike the 28 mi of Long Pine Key trails.

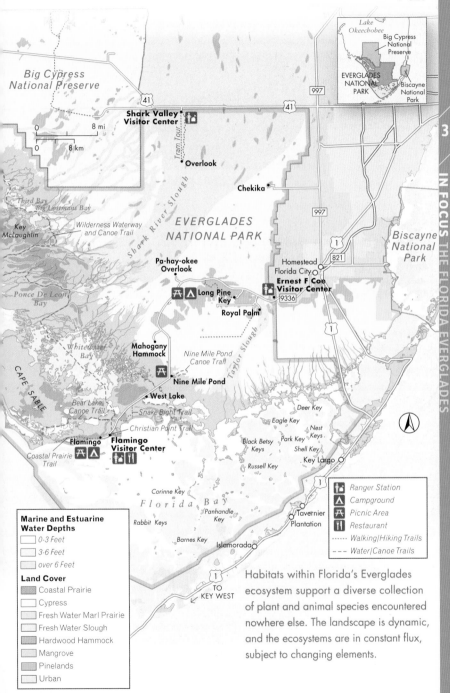

Big Cypress National Preserve

Lake Okeechobee

Big Cypress National Preserve

EVERGLADES NATIONAL PARK

Biscayne National Park

41

997

41

Shark Valley Visitor Center

Tram Tour

• **Overlook**

• **Chekika**

Third Bay
Big Lostmans Bay

Key McLaughlin

Wilderness Waterway and Canoe Trail

EVERGLADES NATIONAL PARK

Shark River Slough

997

Homestead Florida City

Ernest F Coe Visitor Center

9336

Biscayne National Park

821

1

Pa-hay-okee Overlook

Ponce De Leon Bay

🅿️ ⛺ **Long Pine Key**

Royal Palm

Taylor Slough

1

Mahogany Hammock

Whitewater Bay

🅿️

Nine Mile Pond Canoe Trail

Nine Mile Pond

CAPE SABLE

• **West Lake**

Bear Lake Canoe Trail

Snake Bight Trail

Christian Point Trail

Flamingo 🅿️ ⛺ **Flamingo Visitor Center** 🛈🍴

Coastal Prairie Trail

Deer Key

Eagle Key

Nest Keys

Black Betsy Keys

Park Key

Shell Key

Russell Key

Key Largo

1

Corinne Key

Florida Bay

Panhandle Key

Rabbit Keys

Tavernier Plantation

🛈 *Ranger Station*
⛺ *Campground*
🅿️ *Picnic Area*
🍴 *Restaurant*
········· *Walking/Hiking Trails*
--- *Water/Canoe Trails*

Barnes Key

Islamorada

1

TO KEY WEST

Marine and Estuarine Water Depths
☐ *0-3 Feet*
☐ *3-6 Feet*
☐ *over 6 Feet*

Land Cover
☐ Coastal Prairie
☐ Cypress
☐ Fresh Water Marl Prairie
☐ Fresh Water Slough
☐ Hardwood Hammock
☐ Mangrove
☐ Pinelands
☐ Urban

0 ——— 8 mi
0 ——— 8 km

Habitats within Florida's Everglades ecosystem support a diverse collection of plant and animal species encountered nowhere else. The landscape is dynamic, and the ecosystems are in constant flux, subject to changing elements.

FLORA

❶ Cabbage Palm

It's virtually impossible to visit the Everglades and not see a cabbage palm, Florida's official state tree. The cabbage palm (or sabal palm), graces assorted ecosystems and grows well in swamps. **Best place to see them:** At Loxahatchee National Wildlife Refuge (embracing the northern part of the Everglades, along Alligator Alley), throughout Everglades National Park, and at Big Cypress National Preserve.

❷ Sawgrass

With spiny, serrated leaf blades resembling saws, sawgrass inspired the term "river of grass" for the Everglades. **Best place to see them:** Both Shark Valley and Pahayokee Overlook provide terrific vantage points for gazing over sawgrass prairie; you also can get an eyeful of sawgrass when crossing Alligator Alley, even when doing so at top speeds.

❸ Mahogany

Hardwood hammocks of the Everglades live in areas that rarely flood because of the slight elevation of the sloughs, where they're typically found. **Best place to see them:** Everglades National Park's Mahogany Hammock Trail (which has a boardwalk leading to the nation's largest living mahogany tree).

❹ Mangrove

Mangrove forest ecosystems provide both food and protected nursery areas for fish, shellfish, and crustaceans. **Best place to see them:** Along Biscayne National Park shoreline, at Big Cypress National Preserve, and within Everglades National Park, especially around the Caple Sable area.

❺ Gumbo Limbo

Sometimes called "tourist trees" because of peeling reddish bark (not unlike sunburns). **Best place to see them:** Everglades National Park's Gumbo Limbo Trail and assorted spots throughout the expansive Everglades.

FAUNA

❶ American Alligator

In all likelihood, on your visit to the Everglades you'll see at least a gator or two. These carnivorous creatures can be found throughout the Everglades swampy wetlands.

Best place to see them: Loxahatchee National Wildlife Refuge (also sheltering the endangered Everglades snail kite) and within Everglades National Park at Shark Valley or Anhinga Trail. Sometimes (logically enough) gators hang out along Alligator Alley, basking in early morning or late-afternoon sun along four-lane I–75.

❷ American Crocodile

Crocs gravitate to fresh or brackish water, subsisting on birds, fish, snails, frogs, and small mammals.

Best place to see them: Within Everglades National Park, Big Cypress National Preserve, and protected grounds in or around Billie Swamp Safari.

❸ Eastern Coral Snake

This venomous snake burrows in underbrush, preying on lizards, frogs, and smaller snakes.

Best place to see them: Snakes typically shy away from people, but try Snake Bight or Eco Pond near Flamingo, where birds are also prevalent.

❹ Florida Panther

Struggling for survival amid loss of habitat, these shy, tan-colored cats now number around 100, up from lows of near 30.

Best place to see them: Protected grounds of Billie Swamp Safari sometimes provide sightings during tours. Signage on roadway linking Tamiami Trail and Alligator Alley warns of panther crossings, but sightings are rare.

❺ Green Tree Frog

Typically bright green with white or yellow stripes, these nocturnal creatures thrive in swamps and brackish water.

Best place to see them: Within Everglades National Park, especially in or near water.

● *=Extremely Common* ● *=Very Common* ● *=Somewhat Common* ● *=Rare*

BIRDS

❶ Anhinga
The lack of oil glands for waterproofing feathers helps this bird to dive as well as chase and spear fish with its pointed beak. The Anhinga is also often called a "water turkey" because of its long tail, or a "snake bird" because of its long neck.
Best place to see them: The Anhinga Trail, which also is known for attracting other wildlife to drink during especially dry winters.

❷ Blue-Winged Teal
Although it's predominantly brown and gray, this bird's powder-blue wing patch becomes visible in flight. Next to the mallard, the blue-winged teal is North America's second most abundant duck, and thrives particularly well in the Everglades.
Best place to see them: Near ponds and marshy areas of Everglades National Park or Big Cypress National Preserve.

❸ Great Blue Heron
This bird has a varied palate and enjoys feasting on everything from frogs, snakes, and mice to shrimp, aquatic insects, and sometimes even other birds! The all-white version, which at one time was considered a separate species, is quite common to the Everglades.
Best place to see them: Loxahatchee National Wildlife Refuge or Shark Valley in Everglades National Park.

❹ Great Egret
Once decimated by plume hunters, these monogamous, long-legged white birds with S-shaped necks feed in wetlands, nest in trees, and hang out in colonies that often include heron or other egret species.
Best place to see them: Throughout Everglades National Park, along Alligator Alley, and sometimes even on the fringes of Greater Fort Lauderdale.

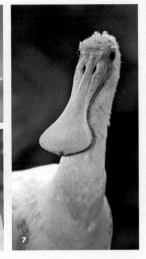

❺ Greater Flamingo

Flocking together and using long legs and webbed feet to stir shallow waters and mud flats, color comes a couple of years after hatching from ingesting shrimplike crustaceans along with fish, fly larvae, and plankton.

Best place to see them: Try Snake Bight or Eco Pond, near Flamingo Marina.

❻ Osprey

Making a big comeback from chemical pollutant endangerment, ospreys (sometimes confused with bald eagles) are distinguished by black eyestripes down their faces. Gripping pads on feet with curved claws help them pluck fish from water.

Best place to see them: Look near water, where they're fishing for lunch in the shallow areas. Try the coasts, bays, and ponds of Everglades National Park. They also gravitate to trees You can usually spot them from the Gulf Coast Visitor Center, or you can observe them via boating in the Ten Thousand Islands.

❼ Roseate Spoonbill

These gregarious pink-and-white birds gravitate toward mangroves, feeding on fish, insects, amphibians, and some plants. They have long, spoon-like bills, and their feathers can have a touch of red and yellow. These birds appear in the Everglades year-round.

Best place to see them: Sandy Key, southwest of Flamingo, is a spoonbill nocturnal roosting spot, but at sunrise these colorful birds head out over Eco Pond to favored day hangouts throughout Everglades National Park.

❽ Wood Stork

Recognizable by featherless heads and prominent bills, these birds submerge in water to scoop up hapless fish. They are most common in the early spring and often easiest to spot in the morning.

Best place to see them: Amid the Ten Thousand Island areas, Nine Mile Pond, Mrazek Pond, and in the mangroves at Paurotis Pond.

● =Extremely Common ● =Very Common ● =Somewhat Common ● =Rare

THE BEST EVERGLADES ACTIVITIES

HIKING

Top experiences: At Big Cypress National Preserve, you can hike along designated trails or push through unmarked acreage. (Conditions vary seasonally, which means you could be tramping through waist-deep waters.) Trailheads for the Florida National Scenic Trail are at Loop Road off U.S. 41 and Alligator Alley at mile marker 63.

What will I see? Dwarf cypress, hardwood hammocks, prairies, birds, and other wildlife.

For a short visit: A 6.5-mi section from Loop Road to U.S. 41 crosses Robert's Lake Strand, providing a satisfying sense of being out in the middle nowhere.

With more time: A 28-mile stretch from U.S. 41 to I–75 (Alligator Alley) reveals assorted habitats, including hardwood hammocks, pinelands, prairie, and cypress.

Want a tour? Big Cypress ranger-led exploration starts from the Oasis Visitor Center, late November through mid-April.

WALKING

Top experiences: Everglades National Park magnets: wheelchair accessible walkways at Anhinga Trail, Gumbo Limbo Trail, Pahayokee Overlook, Mahogany Hammock, and West Lake Trail.

What will I see? Birds and alligators at Anhinga; tropical hardwood hammock at Gumbo Limbo; an overlook of the River of Grass from Pahayokee's tower; a subtropical tree island with massive mahogany growth along Mahogany Hammock; and a forest of mangrove trees on West Lake Trail.

For a short visit: Flamingo's Eco Pond provides for waterside wildlife viewing.

With more time: Shark Valley lets you combine the quarter-mile Bobcat Boardwalk (looping through sawgrass prairie and a bayhead) with the 1-mi-long round-trip Otter Cave, allowing you to steep in subtropical hardwood hammock.

Want a tour? Pahayokee and Flamingo feature informative ranger-led walks.

The Anhinga Trail near the Royal Palm Visitor Center at Everglades National Park

BOATING

Top experiences: Launch a boat from the Gulf Coast Visitors Center or Flamingo Marina. Bring your own watercraft or rent canoes or skiffs at either location.

What will I see? Birds from bald eagles to roseate spoonbills, plus plenty of mangrove and wildlife—and maybe even some baby alligators with yellow stripes.

For a short visit: Canoe adventurers often head for Hells Bay, a 3-mile stretch about 9 mi north of Flamingo. Or put in at the Turner River alongside the Tamiami Trail in the Big Cypress National Preserve and paddle all the way (about eight hours) to Chocoloskee Bay at Everglades City.

With more time: Head out amid the Ten Thousand Islands and lose yourself in territory once exclusively the domain of only the hardiest pioneers and American Indians. If you've got a week or more for paddling, the 99-mile Wilderness Waterway stretches from Flamingo to Everglades City.

Want a tour? Sign on for narrated boat tours at the Gulf Coast or Flamingo visitor center.

BIRD WATCHING

Top experiences: Anhinga Trail, passing over Taylor Slough.

What will I see? Anhinga and heron sightings are a nearly sure thing, especially in early morning or late afternoon. Also, alligators can be seen from the boardwalk.

For a short visit: Even if you're traveling coast to coast at higher speeds via Alligator Alley, chances are you'll spot winged wonders like egrets, osprey, and heron.

With more time: Since bird-watching at Flamingo can be a special treat early in the morning or late in the afternoon, try camping overnight even if you're not one for roughing it. Reservations are recommended. (Flamingo Lodge remains closed after 2005 hurricane damage.)

Want a tour? Ranger-led walks at Pahayokee and from Everglades National Park visitor centers provide solid birding background for novices.

(top left) Tourists cruise the Everglades by airboat; (bottom left) Green Heron; (right) Eastern Meadowlark

THE BEST EVERGLADES ACTIVITIES

BIKING

Top experiences: Shark Valley (where bicycling is allowed on the tram road) is great for taking in the quiet beauty of the Everglades. Near Ernest F. Coe Visitor Center, Long Pine Key's 14-mile nature trail also can be a way to bike happily away from folks on foot.

What will I see? At Shark Valley, wading birds, turtles, and, probably alligators. At Long Pine Key, shady pinewood with subtropical plants and exposed limestone bedrock.

For a short visit: Bike on Shark Valley tram road but turn around to fit time schedule.

With more time: Go the entire 15-mi tram road route, which has no shortcuts. Or try the 22-mile route of Old Ingraham Highway near the Royal Palm Visitor Center, featuring mangrove, sawgrass, and birds (including hawks).

Want a tour? In Big Cypress National Preserve, Bear Island Bike Rides (8 mile round-trip over four to five hours) happen on certain Saturdays.

SNORKELING

Top experiences: Biscayne National Park, where clear waters incorporate the northernmost islands of the Florida Keys.

What will I see? Dense mangrove swamp covering the park shoreline, and, in shallow waters, a living coral reef and tropical fish in assorted colors.

For a short visit: Pick a sunny day to optimize your snorkeling fun, and be sure to use sunscreen.

With more time: Advanced snorkel tours head out from the park on weekends to the bay, finger channels, and around shorelines of the barrier islands. Biscayne National Park also has canoe and kayak rentals, picnic facilities, walking trails, fishing, and camping.

Want a tour? You can swim and snorkel or stay dry and picnic aboard tour boats that depart from Biscayne National Park's visitor center.

(top left) Biking near the Shark Valley Visitor Area. (top right) Snorkeling on the surface in the Atlantic Ocean.

DID YOU KNOW?

You can tell you're looking at a crocodile if you can see its lower teeth protruding when its jaws are shut, whereas an alligator shows no teeth when his mouth is closed. Gators are much darker in color—a gray-ish black—compared with the lighter tan color of crocodiles. Alligators' snouts are also much broader than their long, thin crocodilian counterparts.

THE STORY OF THE EVERGLADES

Dreams of draining southern Florida took hold in the early 1800s, expanding in the early 1900s to convert large tracts from wetlands to agricultural acreage. By the 1920s, towns like Fort Lauderdale and Miami boomed, and the sugar indus-try—which came to be known as "Big Sugar"—established its first sugar mills. In 1947 Ever-glades National Park opened as a refuge for wildlife.

Meanwhile, the sugar industry grew. In its infancy, about 175,000 tons of raw sugar per year was produced from fields totaling about 50,000 acres. But once the U.S. embargo stopped sugar imports from Cuba in 1960 and laws restricting acreage were lifted, Big Sugar took off. Less than five years later, the industry produced 572,000 tons of sugar and occupied nearly a quarter of a million acres.

Fast-forward to 2008, to what was hailed as the biggest conservation deal in U.S. history since the creation of the national parks. A trailblazing restora-tion strategy hinged on creating a water flow-way between Lake Okeechobee and the Everglades by buying up and flooding 187,000 acres of land. The country's largest producers of cane sugar agreed to sell the necessary 187,000 acres to the state of Florida for $1.75 billion. Environmentalists cheered.

But within months, news broke of a scaled-back land acquisition plan: $1.34 billion to buy 180,000 acres. By spring 2009, the restoration plan had shrunk to $536,000 to buy 73,000 acres. With the purchase still in limbo, critics claim the state might overpay for acreage appraised at pre-recession values and proponents fear dwindling revenues may derail the plan altogether.

The Big Sugar land deal is part of a larger effort to preserve the Everglades. In 2010, two separate lawsuits charged the state, along with the United States Environmental Protection Agency, with stalling Everglades cleanup that was supposed to begin in 2006. "Glacial delay" is how one judge put it. The state must reduce phosphorus levels in water that flows to the Everglades or face fines and sanctions for violating the federal Clean Water Act. The fate of the Ever-glades remains in the balance.

3

Updated by
Lynne Helm

More than 1.5 million acres of South Florida's 4.3 million
acres of subtropical, watery wilderness were given national-
park status and protection in 1947 with the creation of
Everglades National Park. It's one of the country's largest
national parks and is recognized by the world community
as a Wetland of International Importance, an International
Biosphere Reserve, and a World Heritage Site. Come here
if you want to spend the day biking, hiking, or boating in
deep, raw wilderness with lots of wildlife.

To the east of Everglades National Park, Biscayne National Park
brings forth a pristine, magical, subtropical Florida. It's the nation's
largest marine park and the largest national park within the continental United States boasting living coral reefs. A small portion of
the park's 172,000 acres consists of mainland coast and outlying
islands, but 95% remains under water. Of particular interest are the
mangroves and their tangled masses of stiltlike roots that thicken
the shorelines. These "walking trees," as some locals call them, have
curved prop roots, which arch down from the trunk, and aerial roots
that drop from branches. The trees draw fresh water from salt water
and create a coastal nursery that sustains myriad types of marine life.
You can see Miami's high-rise buildings from many of Biscayne's 44
islands, but the park is virtually undeveloped and large enough for
escaping everything that Miami and the Upper Keys have become. To
truly escape, don scuba-diving or snorkeling gear and lose yourself in
the wonders of the coral reefs.

On the northern edge of Everglades National Park is Big Cypress
National Preserve, one of South Florida's least-developed watersheds.
Established by Congress in 1974 to protect the Everglades, it com-
prises extensive tracts of prairie, marsh, pinelands, forested swamps,
and sloughs. Hunting is allowed, as is off-road-vehicle use. Come here
if you like alligators. Stop at the Oasis Visitor Center's boardwalk with

alligators lounging underneath, and then drive Loop Road for a back-woods experience. If time permits, kayak the Turner River.

Surrounding the parks and preserve are several communities where you'll find useful outfitters: Everglades City, Florida City, and Homestead.

PLANNING

WHEN TO GO

Winter is the best, and busiest, time to visit the Everglades. Temperatures and mosquito activity are more tolerable, low water levels concentrate the resident wildlife, and migratory birds swell the avian population. In late spring the weather turns hot and rainy, and tours and facilities are less crowded. Migratory birds depart, and you must look harder to see wildlife. Summer brings intense sun and afternoon rainstorms. Water levels rise and mosquitoes descend, making outdoor activity virtually unbearable, unless you swath yourself in netting. Mosquito repellent is a necessity any time of year.

GETTING HERE AND AROUND

Miami International Airport (MIA) is 34 miles from Homestead and 47 miles from the eastern access to Everglades National Park. ⇨ *For MIA airline carrier information, refer to the Miami chapter.* Shuttles run between MIA and Homestead. Southwest Florida International Airport (RSW), in Fort Myers, a little over an hour's drive from Everglades City, is the closest major airport to the Everglades' western entrance. On-demand taxi transportation from the airport to Everglades City is available from MBA Airport Transportation and costs $150 for up to three passengers ($10 each for additional passengers).

Contacts MBA Airport Transportation ☎ *239/225–0428* ⊕ *www.mbaairport.com.*

HOTELS

Accommodations near the parks range from inexpensive to moderate and offer off-season rates in summer, when rampant mosquito populations discourage spending time outdoors, especially at dusk. If you're devoting several days to exploring the east coast Everglades, stay in park campgrounds; 11 miles away in Homestead–Florida City, where there are reasonably priced chain motels and RV parks; in the Florida Keys; or in the Greater Miami–Fort Lauderdale area. Lodgings and campgrounds are also plentiful on the Gulf Coast (in Everglades City, Marco Island, and Naples, the latter of which has the most upscale area accommodations).

RESTAURANTS

Dining in the Everglades area centers on mom-and-pop places serving hearty home-style food, and small eateries specializing in fresh local fare: alligator, fish, stone crab, frogs' legs, and Florida lobster from the Keys. American Indian restaurants serve local favorites as well as catfish, Indian fry bread (a flour-and-water flatbread), and pumpkin bread. A growing Hispanic population around Homestead means plenty of authentic, inexpensive Latin cuisine, with an emphasis on

Cuban and Mexican dishes. Restaurants in Everglades City, especially those along the river, have fresh seafood including particularly succulent, sustainable stone crab. These places are casual to the point of rustic, and are often closed in late summer or fall. For finer dining, go to Marco Island or Naples.

HOTEL AND RESTAURANT COSTS

Prices in the restaurant reviews are the average cost of a main course at dinner or, if dinner isn't served, at lunch. Prices in the hotel reviews are the lowest cost of a standard double room in high season. Prices don't include taxes (6%, more in some counties, and 1%–5% tourist tax for hotel rooms).

ABOUT ACTIVITIES

⇨ *While outfitters are listed with the parks and preserve, see our What's Nearby section later in this chapter for information about each town.*

EVERGLADES NATIONAL PARK

45 miles southwest of Miami International Airport.

If you're heading across South Florida on U.S. 41 from Miami to Naples, you'll breeze right through the Everglades. Also known as Tamiami Trail, this mostly two-lane road skirts the edge of Everglades National Park and cuts across the Big Cypress National Preserve. You'll also be near the park if you're en route from Miami to the Florida Keys on U.S. 1, which cuts through Homestead and Florida City—communities east of the main park entrance. Basically, if you're in South Florida, you can't escape at least fringes of the Everglades. With tourist strongholds like Miami, Naples, and the Florida Keys so close, travelers from all over the world typically make day trips to the park.

Everglades National Park has three main entry points: the park headquarters at Ernest F. Coe Visitor Center, southwest of Homestead and Florida City; the Shark Valley area, accessed by Tamiami Trail (U.S. 41); and the Gulf Coast Visitor Center, south of Everglades City to the west and closest to Naples.

Explore on your own or participate in free ranger-led hikes, bicycle or bird-watching tours, and canoe trips. The variety of these excursions is greatest from mid-December through Easter, and some adventures (canoe trips, for instance) typically aren't offered in sweltering summer. Among the more popular are the Anhinga Amble, a 50-minute walk around the Taylor Slough (departs from the Royal Palm Visitor Center), and the Early Bird Special, a 90-minute walk centered on birdlife (departs from Flamingo Visitor Center). Check with the visitor centers for details.

PARK ESSENTIALS

Admission Fees The fee is $10 per vehicle; and $5 per pedestrian, bicycle, or motorcycle. Payable at gates, the admission is good for seven consecutive days at all park entrances. Annual passes are $25.

Admission Hours The park is open daily, year-round. Both the main entrance near Florida City and Homestead, and the Gulf Coast entrance are open 24 hours. The Shark Valley entrance is open 8:30 am to 6 pm.

War on Pythons

In 2013, Florida launched its first Python Challenge™ to put the kibosh on Burmese pythons, those deadly snakes literally squeezing the life out of Everglades wonders, from colorful birds to full-grown deer to gators.

The state-sponsored winter competition was a trailblazer, attracting amateurs and professionals alike from 38 states and Canada to help decimate this growing environmental threat. Sadly, only 68 pythons were captured out of the thousands estimated to live in the Everglades.

Even experienced 'Gladesmen with special permits to regularly stalk these predators had trouble finding them—partly because tan, splotchy skin provides natural camouflage for slithering about and causing mayhem within the ecosystem. Unseasonably warm winter weather also left the pythons, which grow up to 26-feet long, without incentive to boldly sun themselves.

In 2012, the U.S. Department of the Interior—hailing a milestone in Everglades protection—announced a nationwide ban on the import of Burmese pythons and other non-native, large constrictor snakes, including both northern and southern African pythons and the yellow anaconda.

No matter what the future of the state's Python Challenge™, its war against invasive species and the efforts to protect Everglades wildlife continue unabated.

—By Lynne Helm

COE VISITOR CENTER TO FLAMINGO

About 30 miles from Miami.

The most popular access to Everglades National Park is via the park headquarters entrance southwest of Homestead and Florida City. If you're coming to the Everglades from Miami, take Route 836 West to Route 826/874 South to the Homestead Extension of Florida's Turnpike, U.S. 1, and Krome Avenue (Route 997/old U.S. 27). To reach the Ernest F. Coe Visitor Center from Homestead, go right (west) from U.S. 1 or Krome Avenue onto Route 9336 (Florida's only four-digit route) in Florida City and follow signage to the park entrance.

EXPLORING

To explore this section of the park, follow Route 9336 from the park entrance to Flamingo; you'll find many opportunities to stop along the way, and an assortment of activities to pursue in the Flamingo area. The following is arranged in geographic order.

Ernest F. Coe Visitor Center. Get your park map here, but don't just grab and go; this visitor center's numerous interactive exhibits and films are well worth your time. The 15-minute film *River of Life*, updated frequently, provides a succinct park overview. A movie on hurricanes and a 35-minute wildlife film for children are available on request. A bank of telephones offers differing viewpoints on the Great Water Debate, detailing how last century's gung ho draining of swampland for residential and agricultural development also cut off water-supply routes for precious wetlands in the Everglades ecosystem. You'll also

find a schedule of daily ranger-led
activities, mainly walks and talks;
information on the popular Nike
missile site tour (harking back
to the Cuban missile crisis era);
and details about canoe rentals
and boat tours at Flamingo. The
Everglades Discovery Shop stocks
books, kids' stuff, and jewelry
including bird-oriented earrings,
and you can pick up extra water,
insect repellent, or sunscreen. Coe
Visitor Center, which has rest-
rooms, is outside park gates, so you can stop in without paying park
admission. ✉ *11 miles southwest of Homestead, 40001 State Rd.
9336, Homestead* ☎ *305/242–7700* ☉ *Daily 9–5, subject to change.*

WORD OF MOUTH

"Sign up at the Ernest Coe Visitor
Center or call the Flamingo Visitor Center for the free ranger-led
canoe tour.... No experience
necessary—maneuvering the long
canoe through the twists and
turns of the mangroves was a
challenge, but very fun."
—JC98

Main road to Flamingo. Route 9336 travels 38 miles from the Ernest
F. Coe Visitor Center southwest to the Florida Bay at Flamingo. It
crosses a section of the park's eight distinct ecosystems: hardwood
hammock, freshwater prairie, pinelands, freshwater slough, cypress,
coastal prairie, mangrove, and marine-estuarine. Route highlights
include a dwarf cypress forest, the transition zone between sawgrass
and mangrove forest, and a wealth of wading birds at Mrazek and
Coot Bay ponds—where in early morning or late afternoon you can
observe them feeding. Be forewarned, however, that flamingo sightings are extremely rare. Boardwalks, looped trails, several short spurs,
and observation platforms help you stay dry. You may want to stop
along the way to walk several short trails (each takes about 30 minutes): the wheelchair-accessible **Anhinga Trail,** which cuts through
sawgrass marsh and allows you to see lots of wildlife (be on the
lookout for alligators and the trail's namesake water birds: anhingas);
the junglelike—yet, also wheelchair-accessible—**Gumbo-Limbo Trail;**
the **Pinelands Trail,** where you can see the park's limestone bedrock;
the **Pahayokee Overlook Trail,** ending at an observation tower; and
the **Mahogany Hammock Trail** with its dense growth. ■**TIP➔ Before
heading out on the trails, inquire about insect and weather conditions
and plan accordingly, stocking up on bug repellent, sunscreen, and
water as necessary. Even on seemingly sunny days, it's probably smart
to bring rain gear.** ✉ *Homestead.*

Royal Palm Visitor Center. Ideal for when there's limited time to experience the Everglades, this small center with a bookstore and vending
machines permits access to the **Anhinga Trail boardwalk,** where in
winter spotting alligators congregating in watering holes is almost
guaranteed. The neighboring **Gumbo Limbo Trail** takes you through
a hardwood hammock. Combining these short strolls (½ mile or so)
allows you to experience two Everglades ecosystems. Rangers conduct daily Anhinga Ambles in season (call ahead for times). A Glades
Glimpse program takes place afternoons daily in season, as do starlight walks and bike tours. If you have a mind for history, ask about
narrated Nike missile site tours, stemming from the '60s-era Cuban

missile crisis. ⊠ *4 miles west of Ernest F. Coe Visitor Center on Rte. 9336, Everglades National Park* ☎ *305/242–7700* ⊘ *Daily 8–4:15.*

NEED A BREAK?

Good spots to pull over for a picnic lunch are **Paurotis Pond**, about 10 miles north of Florida Bay, or **Nine Mile Pond**, less than 30 miles from the main visitor center. Another option is along **Bear Lake**, 2 miles north of the Flamingo Visitor Center.

Flamingo. At the far end of the main road to the Flamingo community along Florida Bay, you'll find a marina with a gift shop, visitor center, and campground, with nearby hiking and nature trails. Despite the name, what you are unlikely to find here are flamingos. To improve your luck for glimpsing these flamboyant pink birds with toothpick legs, check out Snake Bight Trail, starting about 5 miles from the Flamingo outpost. Before hurricanes Katrina and Wilma washed them away in 2005, a lodge, cabins, and restaurant facilities in Flamingo provided Everglades National Park's only accommodations. Rebuilding of Flamingo Lodge, long projected, has yet to materialize. For now, you can still pitch tents or bring RVs to the campground, where improvements include solar-heat showers and electricity for RV sites. In 2010, a houseboat rental concession returned, now offering a pair of 35-footers each sleeping six and equipped with shower, toilet, bedding, kitchenware, stereo, and depth finder. The houseboats (thankfully air-conditioned) have 60-horsepower outboards and rent for $350 per night, plus a $200 fuel deposit. ⊠ *Flamingo.*

Flamingo Marina Store—Everglades National Park Boat Tours 2. Next to the Flamingo Visitor Center, the only general store within Everglades National Park stocks limited groceries, snacks, souvenirs, bait, tackle, firewood, tents, and camping supplies, as well as fuel for boats and vehicles. It's a sister operation to Everglades National Park Boat Tours in Everglades City. ⊠ *Everglades National Park* ☎ *239/695–3101* ⊘ *Daily 7–7.*

Flamingo Visitor Center. Check the schedule here for ranger-led activities, such as naturalist discussions, trail hikes, and evening programs in the 100-seat campground amphitheater, replacing the old gathering spot destroyed by 2005 hurricanes. The center's Buttonwood Cafe serves sandwiches, salads, and pizza. You'll find natural history exhibits and pamphlets on canoe, hiking, and biking trails in the second-floor Florida Bay Flamingo Museum, accessible only by stairway and a steep ramp. ⊠ *1 Flamingo Lodge Hwy., Flamingo* ☎ *239/695–2945, 239/695–3101 marina* ⊘ *Exhibits always open, staffed mid-Nov.–mid-Apr., daily 8–4:30.*

SPORTS AND THE OUTDOORS

BIRD-WATCHING

Some of the park's best birding is in the Flamingo area.

BOATING

The 99-mile inland **Wilderness Trail** between Flamingo and Everglades City is open to motorboats as well as canoes, although, depending on the water level, powerboats may have trouble navigating above Whitewater Bay. Flat-water canoeing and kayaking are best in winter, when temperatures are moderate, rainfall diminishes, and mosquitoes back off—a little, anyway. You don't need a permit for day trips, although there's a seven-day, $5 launch fee for all motorized boats brought into the park. The Flamingo area has well-marked canoe trails, but be sure to tell someone where you're going and when you expect to return. Getting lost is easy, and spending the night without proper gear can be unpleasant, if not dangerous.

Flamingo Lodge, Marina, and Everglades National Park Tours. Everglades National Park's official concessionaire—up again for bid in late 2013—operates a marina, runs tours, and rents canoes, kayaks, and skiffs, secured by credit cards. A one-hour, 45-minute backcountry cruise aboard the 50-passenger *Pelican* ($32.50) winds under a heavy canopy of mangroves, revealing abundant wildlife—from alligators, crocodiles, and turtles to herons, hawks, and egrets. Renting a 17-foot, 40-hp skiff from 7 am runs $195 per day (eight hours, if returned by 4 pm), $150 per half day, or $80 for two hours. Canoes for up to three paddlers rent for $16 for two hours (minimum), $22 for four hours, $32 for eight hours, and $40 overnight. Family canoes for up to four go for $20 for two hours, $30 for four hours, $40 for eight hours, and $50 for 24 hours. The concessionaire also rents bikes, binoculars, rods, reels, and other equipment by the half or full day. Feeling sticky after a day in the 'Glades? Hot showers are $3. (Flamingo Lodge, a victim of massive hurricane damage in 2005, remains closed pending a fresh start.) ■ TIP→ An experimental Eco Tent of canvas and wood, unveiled in winter 2012–13, was immediately booked solid for the season. Built by University of Miami architecture students, Eco Tent sleeps four, has a table and chairs, and wins rave reviews from designers, park officials, and campers. It's a prototype for up to 40 more units, once funding is secured. ⊠ *1 Flamingo Lodge Hwy., on Buttonwood Canal, Flamingo* ☎ *239/695–3101, 239/695–0124 Eco Tent reservations* ⊕ *www.evergladesnationalparkboattoursflamingo.com.*

GULF COAST ENTRANCE

To reach the park's western gateway, take U.S. 41 west from Miami for 77 miles, turn left (south) onto Route 29, and travel another 3 miles through Everglades City to the Gulf Coast Ranger Station. From Naples on the Gulf Coast, take U.S. 41 east for 35 miles, and then turn right onto Route 29.

Gulf Coast Visitor Center. The best place to bone up on Everglades National Park's watery western side is at this center just south of Everglades City (5 miles south of Tamiami Trail) where rangers can give you the park lowdown and address your questions. In winter, backcountry campers purchase permits here and canoeists check in for trips to the Ten Thousand Islands and 99-mile Wilderness Waterway Trail. Nature lovers view interpretive exhibits on local flora and fauna while waiting for naturalist-led boat trips. In season (Christmas through Easter), rangers lead bike tours and canoe trips. A selection of about 30 nature presentations on DVDs or VHS tapes are available by request for view on a big screen. Admission is free only to this section, and no direct roads from here link to other parts of the park. ⊠ *Rte. 29, 815 Oyster Bar La., Everglades City* ☎ *239/695–3311* ⊗ *Mid-Nov.–mid-Apr., daily 8–4:30; mid-Apr.–mid-Nov., daily 9–4:30.*

SPORTS AND THE OUTDOORS

BOATING AND KAYAKING

Everglades National Park Boat Tours. In conjunction with boat tours at Flamingo, this operation runs 1½-hour trips ($30) through the Ten Thousand Islands National Wildlife Refuge. Adventure-seekers often see dolphins, manatees, bald eagles, and roseate spoonbills. In peak season (November–April), 49-passenger boats run on the hour and half-hour daily. Mangrove wilderness tours ($40) on smaller boats are for up to six passengers. These one-hour, 45-minute trips are the best option to see alligators. The outfitter also rents canoes ($24 per day) and kayaks (from $45 per day). Taxes are additional. ⊠ *Gulf Coast Visitor Center, 815 Oyster Bar La., Everglades City* ☎ *239/695–2591, 866/628–7275* ⊕ *www.evergladesnationalpar kboattoursgulfcoast.com/index.php.*

Fodor'sChoice
★
Everglades Rentals & Eco Adventures. Ivey House Inn houses this established, year-round source for guided Everglades paddling tours and rentals. Canoes cost $35 the first day, $27 daily thereafter. Day-long kayak rentals are from $45. Shuttles deliver you to major launching areas such as Turner River ($25.60 to $32, one-way for up to two people) and Collier-Seminole State Park ($56 to $70, one-way). Highlights include bird and gator sightings, mangrove forests, no-man's-land beaches, and spectacular sunsets. Longer adventures include equipment rental, guide, and meals. ⊠ *Ivey House, 107 Camellia St., Everglades City* ☎ *877/567–0679, 239/695–3299* ⊕ *www. evergladesadventures.com.*

SHARK VALLEY

23½ miles west of Florida's Turnpike, off Tamiami Trail. Approximately 45 minutes west of Miami.

You won't see sharks at Shark Valley. The name comes from the Shark River, also called the River of Grass, flowing through the area. Several species of shark swim up this river from the coast (about 45 miles south of Shark Valley) to give birth, though not at this particular spot. Young sharks (called pups), vulnerable to being eaten by adult sharks and other predators, gain strength in waters of the slough before heading out to sea.

Much skill is required to navigate boats through the shallow, muddy waters of the Everglades.

EXPLORING

Although Shark Valley is the national park's north entrance, no roads here lead directly to other parts of the park. However, it's still worth stopping to take the two-hour narrated tram tour (reservations recommended; see listing below). Stop at the halfway point and ascend to the top of the observation tower via a ramp.

Prefer to do the trail on foot? It takes nerve to walk the paved 15-mile loop in Shark Valley, because in the winter months alligators lie alongside the road, basking in the sun—most, however, do move quickly out of the way.

You also can ride a bicycle (the outfitter here rents one-speed, well-used bikes daily 8:30–4 for $8.50 per hour). Behind the bike-rental area a short boardwalk trail meanders through sawgrass, and another passes through a tropical hardwood hammock. An underwater live camera in the canal behind the center (viewed from the gift shop) lets visitors sporadically see the alligators and otters.

Observation Tower. At the Shark Valley trail's end (really, the halfway point of the 15-mile loop), you can pause to navigate this tower, first built in 1984, spiraling 50 feet upward. Once on top, you'll find the River of Grass gloriously spreads out as far as you can see. Observe water birds as well as alligators, and maybe even river otters crossing the road. The tower has a wheelchair-accessible ramp to the top. ⊠ *Shark Valley Loop Rd., Miami.*

Shark Valley Visitor Center. This small center has rotating exhibits, an underwater camera, a bookstore (run by the Everglades Association) with hats, postcards, and other souvenir items, and park rangers ready for your questions. ✉ *23½ miles west of Florida's Tpke., off Tamiami Trail, 36000 S.W. 8th St., Miami* ☎ *305/221–8776* ⊙ *Daily 9:15–5:15.*

SPORTS AND THE OUTDOORS

BOATING

Many Everglades-area tours operate only in season, roughly November through April.

Buffalo Tiger's Airboat Tours. A former chief of Florida's Miccosukee tribe heads up this Shark Valley area tour operation, although at 90-plus years, the chief no longer skippers the boat. Savvy guides narrate the trip to an old Indian camp on the north side of Tamiami Trail from the American Indian perspective. Don't worry about airboat noise, since engines are shut down during informative talks. The 45-minute tours go 10–5 Saturday through Thursday at $27.50 per person. Look online for discount coupons. Reservations are not required, and credit cards are now accepted at this once cash-only outpost. ✉ *29708 S.W. 8th St., 5 miles east of Shark Valley, 25 miles west of Florida's Tpke., Miami* ☎ *305/559–5250* ⊕ *www. buffalotigersairboattours.com.*

GUIDED TOURS

Shark Valley Tram Tours. Starting at the Shark Valley visitor center, these popular two-hour, narrated tours ($20) on bio-diesel trams follow a 15-mile loop road—great for viewing gators—into the interior, stopping at a 50-foot observation tower. Bring your own water. Reservations are strongly recommended December through April. ✉ *Shark Valley Visitor Center, Shark Valley Loop Rd., Miami* ☎ *305/221–8455* ⊕ *www.sharkvalleytramtours.com* ⊙ *Tours Dec.–Apr., hourly 9–4; May–Nov., hourly 9–3.*

> ### THE EVERGLADES WITH KIDS
>
> Although kids of all ages can enjoy the park, those six and older will get the most out of the experience. Consider how much you as a supervising adult will enjoy keeping tabs on tiny ones around so much water and so many teeth. Some children are frightened by sheer wilderness.

BIG CYPRESS NATIONAL PRESERVE

Through the early 1960s the world's largest cypress-logging industry prospered in Big Cypress Swamp until nearly all the trees were cut down. With the death of the industry, government entities began buying parcels. Now more than 729,000 acres, or nearly half of the swamp, form this national preserve. "Big" refers not to the new-growth trees but to the swamp, jutting into the north edge of Everglades National Park like a jigsaw-puzzle piece. Size and strategic location make Big Cypress an important link in the region's hydrological system, where rainwater first flows through the preserve, then south into the park, and eventually into Florida Bay. Its variegated pattern of wet prairies, ponds, marshes, sloughs, and strands provides a wildlife sanctuary, and thanks to a policy of balanced land use—"use without abuse"—the watery wilderness is devoted to recreation as well as research and preservation.

Bald cypress trees that may look dead are actually dormant, with green needles springing to life in spring. The preserve allows—in limited areas—hiking, hunting, and off-road vehicle use (airboat, swamp buggy, four-wheel drive) by permit. Compared with Everglades National Park, the preserve is less developed and hosts fewer visitors. That makes it ideal for naturalists, birders, and hikers preferring to see more wildlife than people.

Several scenic drives link from Tamiami Trail, some requiring four-wheel-drive vehicles, especially in wet summer months. A few lead to camping areas and roadside picnic spots. Apart from the Oasis Visitor Center, popular as a springboard for viewing alligators, the newer Big Cypress Swamp Welcome Center features a platform for watching manatees. Both centers, along Tamiami Trail between Miami and Naples, feature a top-notch 25-minute film on Big Cypress.

> ### WORD OF MOUTH
>
> "We drove from Ft. Lauderdale to the Everglades and rented bikes to do the loop at Shark Valley. Lots of wildlife to see! It took us the morning. I think you get better views of the wildlife on the bikes than the tram and of course since you can stop anytime you want, better pics. It's a very easy ride since it's flat and paved."
>
> —klam_chowder

PARK ESSENTIALS

Admission Fees There's no admission fee to visit the preserve.

Admission Hours The park is open 24 hours daily, year-round. Accessible only by boat, Adams Key is for day use only.

Contacts Big Cypress National Preserve ☎ *239/695–1201* ⊕ *www.nps.gov/bicy.*

EXPLORING

Big Cypress Swamp Welcome Center. As a sister to the Oasis Visitor Center, the newer Big Cypress Swamp Welcome Center on the preserve's western side has lots of information, restrooms, picnic facilities, and a 70-seat auditorium. An outdoor breezeway showcases an interactive Big Cypress watershed exhibit, illustrating Florida water flow. ■ TIP➔ **Love manatees? Here you'll find a platform for viewing these intriguing mammals that are attracted to warm water. (They were possibly once mistaken for mermaids by thirsty or love-starved ancient sailors.)** ✉ *33000 Tamiami Trail E, 5 miles east of SR29, Ochopee* ☎ *239/695–4758* ⊕ *www.nps.gov/bicy/planyourvisit/visitorcenters.htm* 🎫 *Free* ⊙ *Daily 9–4:30.*

Clyde Butcher's Big Cypress Gallery. For taking home swamp memories in stark black and white, you can't do better than picking up a postcard, calendar, or more serious piece of artwork by photographer Clyde Butcher at his namesake trailside gallery. Butcher, a big guy with an even bigger beard, is an affable personality renowned for his knowledge of the 'Glades and his ability to capture its magnetism through a large format lens. Even if you can't afford his big stuff, you're warmly invited to gaze. Out back, Butcher and his wife Niki also rent a bungalow ($150 per night) and a cottage ($225 per night) year-round. **TIP→ Ask about Clyde's muck-abouts or Saturday Swamp Walks ($50), September through March. You'll need a hat, long pants, old sneakers, and—because you will get wet—a spare set of clothing.** ✉ *52388 Tamiami Trail, at mile marker 54.5, Ochopee* ☎ *239/695–2428* 🌐 *www.clydebutchersbigcypressgallery.com* 🕒 *Daily 10–5.*

Oasis Visitor Center. The big attraction at **Oasis Visitor Center**, on the east side of Big Cypress Preserve, is the observation deck for viewing fish, birds, and other wildlife. A small butterfly garden's native plants seasonally attract winged wonders. Inside, you'll find an exhibit area, bookshop, and a theater showing an updated, informative 25-minute film on Big Cypress Preserve swamplands. Leashed pets only. **TIP→ Get your gator watch on at the center's observation deck where big alligators congregate.** ✉ *24 miles east of Everglades City, 50 miles west of Miami, 20 miles west of Shark Valley, 52105 Tamiami Trail, Ochopee* ☎ *239/695–1201* 🌐 *www.nps.gov/bicy/planyourvisit/visitorcenters* 🎟 *Free* 🕒 *Daily 9–4:30.*

FAMILY **Ochopee Post Office.** North America's smallest post office is a former irrigation pipe shed on the Tamiami Trail's south side. Blink and you'll risk missing it. To support this picturesque outpost during an era of postal service closures and layoffs, why not buy a postcard of this one-room shack for mailing to whoever would appreciate it? You can mail packages or buy money orders here, too. ✉ *4 miles east of Rte. 29, 38000 E. Tamiami Trail, Ochopee* ☎ *239/695–2099* 🕒 *Weekdays 10–noon and 1–4, Sat. 10–11:30.*

WHERE TO EAT

$ SEAFOOD 🍴 **Joanie's Blue Crab Cafe.** West of the nation's tiniest post office by a quarter mile or so, you'll find this red barn of a place dishing out catfish, frogs' legs, gator, grouper, burgers, salads, and (no surprise here) an abundance of soft-shell crabs, crab cakes, and she-crab soup. Entrées run from $12.95 to market priced. Grab a beer from the cooler and eat at one of the tables out front or on the back patio—keep an eye out for Gertrude, a neighborhood gator on the loose. Joanie's doors are open from 10 am to 5 pm, so don't be late for supper. [$] *Average main: $13* ✉ *About 3.5 miles east of Hwy. 29, and west of Ochopee post office, 39395 Tamiami Trail, Ochopee* ✣ *On Tamiami Trail, less than a mile west of post office* ☎ *239/695–2682* 🌐 *www.joaniesbluecrabcafe.com* 🕒 *Closed Mon. (varies seasonally; call to confirm).*

SPORTS AND THE OUTDOORS

There are three types of trails—walking (including part of the extensive Florida National Scenic Trail), canoeing, and bicycling. All three trail types are easily accessed from the Tamiami Trail near the preserve visitor center, and one boardwalk trail departs from the center. Canoe and bike equipment can be rented from outfitters in Everglades City, 24 miles west, and Naples, 40 miles west.

Hikers can tackle the Florida National Scenic Trail, which begins in the preserve and is divided into segments 6.5 to 28 miles each. Two 5-mile trails, Concho Billy and Fire Prairie, can be accessed off Turner River Road, a few miles east. Turner River Road and Birdon Road form a 17-mile gravel loop drive that's excellent for birding. Bear Island has about 32 miles of scenic, flat, looped trails that are ideal for bicycling. Most trails are hard-packed lime rock, but a few miles are gravel. Cyclists share the road with off-road vehicles, most plentiful from mid-November through December.

To see the best variety of wildlife from your car, follow 26-mile Loop Road, south of U.S. 41 and west of Shark Valley, where alligators, raccoons, and soft-shell turtles crawl around beside the gravel road, often swooped upon by swallowtail kites and brown-shouldered hawks. Stop at H. P. Williams Roadside Park, west of the Oasis, and walk along the boardwalk to spy gators, turtles, and garfish in the river waters.

RANGER PROGRAMS

From the Oasis Visitor Center you can get in on the seasonal ranger-led or self-guided activities, such as campfire and wildlife talks, hikes, slough slogs, and canoe excursions. The 8-mile Turner River Canoe Trail begins nearby and crosses through Everglades National Park before ending in Chokoloskee Bay, near Everglades City. Rangers lead four-hour canoe trips and two-hour swamp walks in season; call for days and times. Bring shoes and long pants for the swamp walks and be prepared to wade at least knee-deep in water. Ranger program reservations are accepted up to 14 days in advance.

BISCAYNE NATIONAL PARK

Occupying 172,000 acres along the southern portion of Biscayne Bay, south of Miami and north of the Florida Keys, Biscayne National Park is 95% submerged, its terrain from 4 feet above sea level to 60 feet below. Contained within are four distinct zones: Biscayne Bay, undeveloped upper Florida Keys, coral reefs, and coastal mangrove forest. Mangroves line the mainland shore much as they do elsewhere along South Florida's protected waters. Biscayne Bay serves as a lobster sanctuary and a nursery for fish, sponges, crabs, and other sea life. Manatees and sea turtles frequent its warm, shallow waters. The park hosts legions of boaters and landlubbers gazing in awe over the bay.

GETTING HERE

To reach Biscayne National Park from Homestead, take Krome Avenue to Route 9336 (Palm Drive) and turn east. Follow Palm Drive about 8 miles until it becomes S.W. 344th Street, and follow signs to park headquarters in Convoy Point. The entry is 9 miles east of Homestead and 9 miles south and east of Exit 6 (Speedway Boulevard/S.W. 137th Avenue) off Florida's Turnpike.

PARK ESSENTIALS

Admission Fees There's no fee to enter Biscayne National Park, and you don't pay a fee to access the islands, but there's a $20 overnight camping fee that includes a $5 dock charge to berth vessels at some island docks. The park concession charges for trips to the coral reefs and islands.

Admission Hours The park is open daily, year-round.

Contact Information Biscayne National Park ⊠ *Dante Fascell Visitor Center, 9700 S.W. 328th St., Homestead* ☎ *305/230–7275* ⊕ *www.nps.gov/bisc.*

3

EXPLORING

Biscayne is a magnet for diving, snorkeling, canoeing, birding, and to some extent (if you have a private boat), camping. Elliott Key is the best place to hike *(⇨ see Islands).*

THE CORAL REEF

Biscayne's corals range from soft, flagellant fans, plumes, and whips found chiefly in shallow patch reefs to the hard brain corals, elkhorn, and staghorn forms that can withstand depths and heavier shoreline wave action.

THE ISLANDS

To the east, about 8 miles off the coast, 44 tiny keys stretch 18 nautical miles north to south, and are reached only by boat. No mainland commercial transportation operates to the islands, and only a handful are accessible: Elliott, Boca Chita, Adams, and Sands keys, lying between Elliott and Boca Chita. The rest are wildlife refuges or have rocky shores or waters too shallow for boats. December through April, when the mosquito population is less aggressive, is the best time to explore. Bring repellent, sunscreen, and water.

Adams Key. A stone's throw from the western tip of Elliott Key and 9 miles southeast of Convoy Point, the island is open for day use. It was the onetime site of the Cocolobo Club, a yachting retreat famous for hosting presidents Harding, Hoover, Johnson, and Nixon as well as other luminaries. Hurricane Andrew blew away what remained of club facilities in 1992. Adams Key has picnic areas with grills, restrooms, dockage, and a short trail running along the shore and through a hardwood hammock. Rangers live on-island. Access is by private boat, with no pets or overnight docking allowed. ⊕ *www.nps.gov/bisc/planyourvisit/adamskey.*

Boca Chita Key. Ten miles northeast of Convoy Point and about 12 miles south of the Cape Florida Lighthouse on Key Biscayne, this key once was owned by the late Mark C. Honeywell, former president of Honeywell Company, and is on the National Register of Historic Places for its 10 historic structures. A ½-mile hiking trail curves around the island's south side. Climb the 65-foot-high ornamental lighthouse (by ranger tour only) for a panoramic view of Miami or check out the cannon from the HMS *Fowey.* There's no freshwater, access is by private boat only, and no pets are allowed. Only portable toilets are on-site, with no sinks or showers. A $20 fee for overnight docking (6 pm to 6 am) covers a campsite; pay at the harbor's automated kiosk.

Elliott Key. The largest of the islands, 9 miles east of Convoy Point, Elliott Key has a mile-long loop trail on the bay side at the north end of the campground. Boaters may dock at any of 36 slips (call ahead; Hurricane Sandy forced closure of the boardwalk and harbor in 2012, and at this writing, docks remained closed). A $20 fee for stays between 6 pm and 6 am covers a campsite. Head out on your own to hike the 6-mile trail along so-called Spite Highway, a 225-foot-wide swath of green that developers mowed down in hopes of linking this key to the mainland. Luckily the federal government stepped in, and now it's a hiking trail through tropical hardwood hammock. Facilities include restrooms, picnic tables, fresh drinking water, cold (occasionally lukewarm) showers, grills, and a campground. Leashed pets are allowed in developed areas only, not on trails. A 30-foot-wide sandy shoreline about a mile north of the harbor on the west (bay) side of the key is the only one in the national park, and boaters like to anchor off here to swim. The beach, fun for families, is for day use only; it has picnic areas and a short trail that cuts through the hammock.

> ### BISCAYNE IN ONE DAY
>
> Most visitors come to snorkel or dive. Divers should plan to spend the morning on the water and the afternoon exploring the visitor center. The opposite is true for snorkelers, as snorkel trips (and one-tank shallow-dive trips) depart in the afternoon. If you want to hike as well, turn to the trails at Elliott Key—just be sure to apply insect repellent (and sunscreen, too, no matter what time of year).

VISITOR CENTER

FAMILY **Dante Fascell Visitor Center.** Go outside on the wide veranda to soak up views across mangroves and Biscayne Bay at this Convoy Point visitor center. Inside the museum, artistic vignettes and on-request videos including the 11-minute *Spectrum of Life* explore the park's four ecosystems, while the Touch Table gives both kids and adults a feel for bones, feathers, and coral. Facilities include the park's canoe and tour concession, restrooms with showers, a ranger information area, gift shop with books, and vending machines. Various ranger programs take place daily during busy fall and winter seasons. On the second Sunday monthly (December through April), the free Family Fun Fest offers three hours of hands-on activities. Rangers also give informal tours on Boca Chita key; arrange in advance. A short trail and boardwalk lead to a jetty, and there are picnic tables and grills. This is the only area of the park accessible without a boat. ✉ *9700 S. W. 328th St., Homestead* ☎ *305/230–7275* ⊕ *www.nps.gov/bisc* ✉ *Free* ☉ *Daily 9–5.*

SPORTS AND THE OUTDOORS

BIRD-WATCHING

More than 170 species of birds have been identified around the park. Expect to see flocks of brown pelicans patrolling the bay—suddenly rising, then plunging beak first to capture prey in their baggy pouches. White ibis probe exposed mudflats for small fish and crustaceans.

Although all the keys are excellent for birding, Jones Lagoon (south of Adams Key, between Old Rhodes Key and Totten Key) is outstanding. It's approachable only by nonmotorized craft.

DIVING AND SNORKELING

Diving is great year-around but best in summer, when calmer winds and smaller seas result in clearer waters. Ocean waters, 3 miles east of the keys, showcase the park's main attraction—the northernmost section of Florida's living tropical coral reefs. Some are the size of an office desk, others as large as a football field. Glass-bottom-boat rides, when operating, showcase this underwater wonderland, but you really should snorkel or scuba dive to fully appreciate it.

A diverse population of colorful fish—angelfish, gobies, grunts, parrot fish, pork fish, wrasses, and many more—flits through the reefs. Shipwrecks from the 18th century are evidence of the area's international maritime heritage, and a Maritime Heritage Trail is being developed to link six of the major shipwreck and underwater cultural sites. Thus far, three sites, including a 19th-century wooden sailing vessel, have been plotted with GPS coordinates and marked with mooring buoys. Plastic dive cards are being developed that will contain navigational and background information.

WHAT'S NEARBY

EVERGLADES CITY

35 miles southeast of Naples and 83 miles west of Miami.

Aside from a chain gas station or two, Everglades City is perfect Old Florida. No high-rises (other than an observation tower) mar the landscape at this western gateway to Everglades National Park, just off the Tamiami Trail. It was developed in the late 19th century by Barron Collier, a wealthy advertising entrepreneur, who built it as a company town to house workers for his numerous projects, including construction of the Tamiami Trail. It grew and prospered until the Depression and World War II. Today this ramshackle town draws adventure-seekers heading to the park for canoeing, fishing, and bird-watching excursions. Airboat tours, though popular, are banned within the preserve and park because of the environmental damage they cause to the mangroves. The Everglades Seafood Festival, going strong for about 40 years and held the first full weekend of February, draws crowds of more than 50,000 for delights from the sea, music, and craft displays. At quieter times, dining choices are limited to a handful of basic eateries. The town is small, fishing-oriented, and unhurried, making it excellent for boating, bicycling, or just strolling around. You can pedal along the waterfront on a 2-mile strand out to Chokoloskee Island.

Visitor Information Everglades Area Chamber of Commerce Welcome Center. Pick up brochures and pamphlets for area lodging, restaurants, and attractions, and ask for additional information from friendly staffers. ⊠ *32016 E. Tamiami Trail, at Rte. 29* ☎ *239/695–3941* ⊕ *www. evergladeschamber.net.*

Native plants along the Turner River Canoe Trail hem paddlers in on both sides, and alligators lurk nearby.

EXPLORING

Fakahatchee Strand Preserve State Park. The ½-mile Big Cypress Bend boardwalk through this linear swamp forest provides opportunity to see rare plants, nesting eagles, and Florida's largest stand of native royal palms co-existing—unique to Fakahatchee Strand—with bald cypress under the forest canopy. Fakahatchee Strand, about 20 miles long and 5 miles wide, is also the orchid and bromeliad capital of the continent with 44 native orchids and 14 native bromeliads, many blooming most extravagantly in hotter months. It's particularly famous for its ghost orchids (as featured in Susan Orlean's novel *The Orchid Thief*), visible on guided hikes. In your quest for ghost orchids, keep alert for white-tailed deer, black bears, bobcats, and the Florida panther. For park nature on parade, take the 12-mile-long (one-way) W. J. Janes Memorial Scenic Drive. Hike its spur trails if you have time. Rangers lead swamp walks and canoe trips November through April. ⊠ *Boardwalk on north side of Tamiami Trail, 7 miles west of Rte. 29; W. J. Janes Scenic Dr., ¾ mile north of Tamiami Trail on Rte. 29; ranger station on W. J. Janes Scenic Dr., 137 Coastline Dr., Copeland* ☎ *239/695–4593* ⊕ *www.floridastateparks.org/ fakahatcheestrand* ⊠ *Free* ☉ *Daily 8 am–sunset.*

Collier-Seminole State Park. The opportunity to try biking, hiking, camping, and canoeing into Everglades territory make this park a prime introduction to this often forbidding land. Of historical interest, a Seminole War blockhouse has been re-created to hold the interpretative center, and one of the "walking dredges"—a towering black machine invented to carve the Tamiami Trail out of the muck—stands silent on grounds

OFF THE
BEATEN
PATH

amid tropical hardwood forest. Campsites ($22 per night plus tax) include electricity, water, and picnic tables. Restrooms have hot water showers, and one has a couple of washers and dryers outside. ✉ *20200 E. Tamiami Trail, Naples* ☎ *239/394–3397* 🌐 *www.floridastateparks.org/collier-seminole* 🎟 *$5 per car, $4 with lone driver, $2 for pedestrians or bikers* 🕒 *Daily 8–sunset.*

3

Florida Panther National Wildlife Refuge. When this refuge opened in 1989, it was off-limits to the public to protect endangered cougar subspecies. In 2005, responding to public demand, the 26,400-acre refuge opened two short loop trails in a region lightly traveled by panthers so visitors could get tastes of wet prairies, tropical hammocks, and pine uplands where panthers roam and wild orchids thrive. The 1.3-mile trail is rugged and often thigh-high under water during summer and fall; it's closed when completely flooded. The shorter 0.3-mile Leslie M. Duncan Memorial Trail is wheelchair-accessible and open year-round. For either, bring drinking water and insect repellent. Although sightings are rare, you may spot deer, black bears, and the occasional panther—or their tracks. Annual events include the Save the Panther Week in March, with an open house, plant walks, and tours. ✉ *Off Rte. 29, between U.S. 41 and I–75* ☎ *239/353–8442* 🌐 *www.fws.gov/floridapanther* 🎟 *Free* 🕒 *Daily dawn–dusk; trails may be closed July–Nov. because of rain.*

Museum of the Everglades. Through artifacts and photographs you can meet American Indians, pioneers, entrepreneurs, and anglers who played roles in southwest Florida development. Exhibits and a short film chronicle the tremendous feat of building the Tamiami Trail across mosquito-ridden, gator-infested Everglades wetlands. Permanent displays and monthly exhibits rotate works of local artists. The museum is housed in the Laundry Building, completed in 1927 and once used for washing linens from the Rod and Gun Club and Everglades Inn. ✉ *105 W. Broadway* ☎ *239/695–0008* 🎟 *Free* 🕒 *Tues.–Sat. 9–4.*

WHERE TO EAT

$$ SEAFOOD 🍴 **City Seafood.** Owner Richard Wahrenberger serves up gems from the sea delivered fresh from his own boats. Even better, you can chow down on his delectable, sustainable stone crabs— medium, large, jumbo, and colossal based on weight—with clear conscience. After removal of meaty claws, crabs are returned to waters where they grow new ones. Enjoy breakfast, lunch, or dinner inside this rustic haven, or sit outdoors to watch pelicans, gulls, tarpon, manatee, and the occasional gator play off the dock in the Barron River. Relax with a beer or wine by the glass. Appetizers run from deep-fried corn to conch, and sandwiches from hot dogs to pulled pork. Big draws, however, remain stone crabs and baskets of smoked mullet, grouper, shrimp, oysters, blue crab, gator, or frogs' legs. Got a cooler? City Seafood can wrap for the road, and also ships. A gift shop sells cutesy crabby-style tanks, boxers, and tees. [$] *Average main: $15* ✉ *702 Begonia St.* ☎ *239/695–4700* 🌐 *www.cityseafood1.com.*

$$ SEAFOOD 🍴 **Everglades Seafood Depot.** Count on tasty, affordable meals in a scenic setting at this storied 1928 Spanish-style stucco structure fronting Lake Placid. Beginning life as the original Everglades train depot, the building later was deeded to the University of Miami for marine research, and appeared in the 1958 film *Winds across the Everglades* (starring Christopher Plummer, Peter Falk, Gypsy Rose Lee, and Burl Ives). Seafood is the star here now including lobster, frogs' legs, crab, and alligator. Steak, seafood, and combo entrées include salad or soup, or an extra-charge option for a salad bar with steamed shrimp. All-you-can-eat specials—fried chicken, a taco bar, or a seafood buffet—are staged on selected nights. Save room for "secret family recipe" coconut guava cake, mango cheesecake, or key lime pie. Ask for a back porch table or for a lake-view window seat. [$] *Average main: $20* ✉ *102 Collier Ave.* ☎ *239/695–0075* 🌐 *www.evergladesseafooddepot.com.*

$$ CUBAN 🍴 **Havana Cafe.** Cuban specialties are a tasty change from the seafood houses of Everglades City. Brightly painted walls and floral tablecloths add cheer to this eatery with a dozen or so tables and more on the porch. Service is order-at-the-counter for breakfast and lunch (7 am–3 pm), with dinner in season on Friday and Saturday nights. Jump-start your day with *café con leche* and a pressed-egg sandwich. For lunch, you'll find the ubiquitous Cuban sandwich, burgers, shrimp, grouper, steak, and pork plates with rice and beans and yucca. [$] *Average main: $15* ✉ *191 Smallwood Dr., Chocoloskee* ☎ *239/695–2214* 🌐 *www.myhavanacafe.com* 💳 *No credit cards* 🕒 *No dinner Apr.–Oct. No dinner Sun.–Thurs. Nov.–Mar.*

$$$ SEAFOOD FAMILY 🍴 **Oyster House Restaurant.** One of the town's oldest fish houses, Oyster House serves all the local staples—shrimp, gator tail, frogs' legs, oysters, stone crab, and grouper—in a lodgelike setting with mounted wild game on walls and rafters. Deep-frying remains an art in these parts, so if you're going to indulge, do it here where you can create your own fried platter from $21.95. Try to dine at sunset for golden rays with your watery view. Outside, a 75-foot observation tower affords a terrific overview of the Ten Thousand Islands. [$] *Average main: $20* ✉ *Rte. 29 S* ☎ *239/695–2073* 🌐 *www.oysterhouserestaurant.com.*

$$$ SEAFOOD 🍴 **Rod and Gun Club.** Striking, polished pecky-cypress woodwork in this historic building dates from the 1920s, when wealthy hunters, anglers, and yachting parties arrived for the winter season. Presidents Hoover, Roosevelt, Truman, Eisenhower, and Nixon stopped by here, as did Ernest Hemingway, Burt Reynolds, and Mick Jagger. The main dining room holds overflow from the expansive screened porch overlooking the river. Like life in general here, friendly servers move slowly and upkeep is minimal. Fresh seafood dominates, from stone crab in season (October 15–May 15) to a surf-and-turf combo of steak and grouper or a swamp-and-turf duet of frogs' legs and steak (each $26.95), or pasta pairings, from $19.95. For $14.95 you can have your own catch fried, broiled, or blackened, served with salad, veggies, and potato. Pie choices are key lime and chocolate–peanut butter. Separate checks are discouraged at this cash-only venue, and there's a $5 plate-sharing charge. Yesteryear's main lobby is well worth a look—even if you're eating elsewhere. Arrive by boat

or land. Ⓢ *Average main: $25* ✉ *200 Riverside Dr.* ☎ *239/695–2101* ⊕ *www.evergladesrodandgun.com* ▭ *No credit cards* ☾ *Sometimes shuts down in summer. Call ahead.*

$$
SEAFOOD
✕ **Triad Seafood.** Along the Barron River, seafood houses, fishing boats, and crab traps populate one shoreline; mangroves the other. Selling fresh off the boat, some seafood houses added picnic tables and eventually grew into restaurants. Family-owned Triad Seafood Market & Cafe is one, with a screened dining area, and additional outdoor seating under a breezeway and on a deck (heated in winter) overhanging the river. Here you can savor fresh seafood at its finest, or have it shipped. Nothing fancy (although smoked fish and blue crab salad are on the menu), but you'd be hard-pressed to find a better grouper sandwich. An all-you-can-eat fresh stone crab feast with butter or mustard sauce (October 15 to May 15; market prices fluctuate wildly) can thin out your wallet, especially for the jumbos. Lunch starts at 10:30 am with fried shrimp, oyster, crab cake, and soft-shell blue crab baskets, plus Reubens, Philly cheesesteaks, burgers, and kid meals. Ⓢ *Average main: $15* ✉ *401 School Dr.* ☎ *239/695–0722* ⊕ *www. triadseafoodmarketcafe.com* ☾ *Closed May 16–Oct. 15.*

WHERE TO STAY

For expanded reviews, facilities, and current deals, visit Fodors.com.

$
HOTEL
▢ **Glades Haven Cozy Cabins.** Bob Miller wanted to build a Holiday Inn next to his Oyster House Restaurant on marina-channel shores, but when that didn't fly, he sent for cabin kits and set up mobile-home-size units around a pool on his property. **Pros:** great nearby food options; convenient to ENP boating; free docking; marina. **Cons:** trailer-park crowded feel with a noisy bar nearby; no phones, no pets. Ⓢ *Rooms from: $95* ✉ *801 Copeland Ave.* ☎ *239/695–2746, 888/956–6251* ⊕ *www.gladeshaven.com* ⤳ *24 cabins, 2 3-bedroom houses* �“Ol *No meals.*

$$$
B&B/INN
Fodor'sChoice
★
▢ **Ivey House.** A remodeled 1928 boardinghouse originally built for crews working on the Tamiami Trail, Ivey House (originally operated by Mr. and Mrs. Ivey) now fits adventurers on assorted budgets. **Pros:** historic; pleasant; affordable. **Cons:** not on water; some small rooms. Ⓢ *Rooms from: $169* ✉ *107 Camellia St.* ☎ *877/567–0679, 239/695–3299* ⊕ *www.iveyhouse.com* ⤳ *30 rooms, 18 with bath; 1 2-bedroom cottage* ❚Ol *Breakfast.*

SPORTS AND THE OUTDOORS

AIR TOURS

Wings Ten Thousand Islands Aero-Tours. These 20-minute to 2-hour scenic flightseeing tours of the Ten Thousand Islands National Wildlife Refuge, Big Cypress National Preserve, Everglades National Park, and Gulf of Mexico operate November through April. Aboard an Alaskan Bush plane, you can see sawgrass prairies, American Indian shell mounds, alligators, and wading birds. Rates start at $46 (Everglades tour) and go up to $224 for a two-hour regional tour (per person with groups of three or four). Flights can be booked to the Florida Keys. ✉ *Everglades Airpark, 650 Everglades City Airpark Rd.* ☎ *239/695–3296.*

BOATING AND CANOEING

On the Gulf Coast explore the nooks, crannies, and mangrove islands of Chokoloskee Bay and Ten Thousand Islands National Wildlife Refuge, as well as the many rivers near Everglades City. The Turner River Canoe Trail, a pleasant day trip with almost guaranteed bird and alligator sightings, passes through the mangrove, dwarf cypress, coastal prairie, and freshwater slough ecosystems of Everglades National Park and Big Cypress National Preserve.

Glades Haven Marina. Get out on Ten Thousand Islands waters in a 19-foot Sundance or a 17-foot Flicker fishing boat. Rates start at $150 a day, plus fuel, with half-day and hourly options. The outfitter also rents kayaks and canoes and has a 24-hour boat ramp and dockage for up to 24-foot vessels. Launch your own boat for $15. ⊠ *801 Copeland Ave. S* ☎ *239/695–2628* ⊕ *www.gladeshaven.com.*

FLORIDA CITY

3 miles southwest of Homestead on U.S. 1.

Florida's Turnpike ends in Florida City, the southernmost town on the peninsula, spilling thousands of vehicles onto U.S. 1 and eventually west to Everglades National Park, east to Biscayne National Park, or south to the Florida Keys. Florida City and Homestead run into each other, but the difference couldn't be more noticeable. As the last outpost before 18 miles of mangroves and water, this stretch of U.S. 1 is lined with fast-food eateries, service stations, hotels, bars, dive shops, and restaurants. Hotel rates increase significantly during NASCAR races at the nearby Homestead-Miami Speedway. Like Homestead, Florida City is rooted in agriculture, with expanses of farmland west of Krome Avenue and a huge farmers' market that ships produce nationwide.

VISITOR INFORMATION

Tropical Everglades Visitor Center. Run by the nonprofit Tropical Everglades Visitor Association, this pastel pink center with teal signage offers abundant printed material plus tips from volunteer experts on exploring south Dade County, Homestead, Florida City, and the Florida Keys. ⊠ *160 U.S. 1* ☎ *305/245–9180, 800/388–9669* ⊕ *www. tropicaleverglades.com.*

WHERE TO EAT

$$$
SEAFOOD

✕ **Captain's Restaurant and Seafood Market.** A comfortable place where the chef prepares seafood with flair, this is among the town's best bets. Choose between the dining room or the covered patio. Chalkboards showcase a varied menu of sandwiches, pasta, seafood, steak, and nightly specials including hogfish, plus stone crabs in season. Inventive offerings sometimes include a lobster Reuben sandwich, pan-seared tuna topped with balsamic onions and shallots, or crawfish pasta. Top things off with key lime pie or a white chocolate brownie. $ *Average main: $23* ⊠ *404 S.E. 1st Ave.* ☎ *305/247–9456.*

$
SEAFOOD

✕ **Farmers' Market Restaurant.** Although this eatery is within the farmers' market on the edge of town and is big on serving fresh vegetables, seafood figures prominently on the menu. A family of anglers runs the place, so fish and shellfish are only hours from the sea, and there's a fish fry on Friday nights. Catering to farmers, the restaurant opens at 5:30 am, serving pancakes, jumbo eggs, and fluffy omelets with home fries or grits in a pleasant dining room with checkered tablecloths. For lunch or dinner, choose among fried shrimp or conch, seafood pasta, country-fried steak, and roast turkey, as well as salads, burgers and sandwiches. [$] *Average main: $13* ✉ *300 N. Krome Ave.* ☎ *305/242–0008.*

SHUTTLES FROM MIAMI

Super Shuttle. This 24-hour service runs air-conditioned vans between MIA and the Homestead-Florida City area; pickup is outside baggage claim and costs around $61 per person depending on your destination. For a return to MIA, reserve 24 hours in advance and know your pickup zip code for a price quote. ☎ *305/871–2000* 🌐 *www.supershuttle.com.*

$$ SEAFOOD 🍴 **Mutineer Wharf Restaurant.** Families and older couples flock to this kitschy roadside outpost with a fish-and-duck pond. Built in 1980 to look like a ship—back when Florida City barely got on maps—etched glass divides bi-level dining rooms, with velvet-upholstered chairs, an aquarium, and nautical antiques. Florida lobster tails, stuffed grouper, shrimp, and snapper top the menu, along with another half-dozen daily seafood specials. Add to that steaks, ribs, and chicken. Seafood sandwiches are hot for lunch. You also can relax for dinner in the restaurant's Wharf Lounge. Friday and Saturday nights feature live entertainment and dancing. [$] *Average main: $18* ✉ *11 S.E. 1st Ave. (U.S. 1), at Palm Dr.* ☎ *305/245–3377* 🌐 *www.mutineerrestaurant.com.*

WHERE TO STAY

For expanded reviews, facilities, and current deals, visit Fodors.com.

$$ HOTEL 🏨 **Best Western Gateway to the Keys.** For easy access to Everglades and Biscayne national parks as well as the Keys, you'll be well-situated at this sprawling, two-story lodging spot two blocks off Florida's Turnpike. **Pros:** convenient to parks, outlet shopping, and dining; business services; attractive pool area. **Cons:** traffic noise; fills up fast in high season. [$] *Rooms from: $135* ✉ *411 S. Krome Ave.* ☎ *305/246–5100, 888/981–5100* 🌐 *www.bestwestern.com/gatewaytothekeys* 🛏 *114 rooms* 🍽 *Breakfast.*

$ HOTEL 🏨 **Econo Lodge.** Close to Florida's Turnpike and with access to the Keys, this is a good overnight pullover spot with a complimentary breakfast and free coffee in the lobby. **Pros:** laundry facility on property; pool; proximity to mall outlet shopping. **Cons:** urban-ugly location; noisy. [$] *Rooms from: $89* ✉ *553 N.E. 1st Ave.* ☎ *305/248–9300, 800/553–2666* 🌐 *www.econolodge.com* 🛏 *42 rooms* 🍽 *Breakfast.*

$ HOTEL 🏨 **Everglades International Hostel.** Stay in clean, spacious private or dorm-style quarters (generally six to a room), relax in indoor or outdoor quiet areas, and watch videos or TV on a big screen. **Pros:** affordable; Everglades tours; free services. **Cons:** communal living; no elevator; old structure. [$] *Rooms from: $28* ✉ *20 S.W. 2nd Ave.* ☎ *305/248–1122, 800/372–3874* 🌐 *www.evergladeshostel.com* 🛏 *46 beds in dorm-style rooms with shared bath, 2 private rooms with shared bath, 2 suites* 🍽 *No meals.*

3

$ HOTEL 🏨 **Fairway Inn.** With a waterfall pool, this two-story motel with exterior room entry has some of the area's lowest chain rates, and it's next to the Chamber of Commerce visitor center so you'll have easy access to reading and planning material. **Pros:** affordable; convenient to restaurants, parks, and raceway. **Cons:** dated, plain, small rooms; no-pet policy. [$] *Rooms from: $89* ✉ *100 S.E. 1st Ave.* ☎ *305/248–4202, 888/340–4734* 🛏 *160 rooms* 🍴 *Breakfast.*

$$ HOTEL 🏨 **Ramada Inn.** If you're looking for an uptick from other chains, this pet-friendly property offers more amenities and comfort, such as 32-inch flat-screen TVs, duvet-covered beds, closed closets, and stylish furnishings. **Pros:** extra room amenities; convenient location. **Cons:** chain anonymity. [$] *Rooms from: $99* ✉ *124 E. Palm Dr.* ☎ *305/247–8833* 🌐 *www.hotelfloridacity.com* 🛏 *123 rooms* 🍴 *Breakfast.*

SHOPPING

FAMILY **Robert Is Here.** Want gifts to take home? This remarkable fruit stand sells more than 100 types of jams, jellies, honeys, and salad dressings along with its vegetables, juices, fresh-fruit milk shakes (try the key lime), and some 30 kinds of tropical fruits, including (in season) carambola, lychee, egg fruit, monstera, sapodilla, dragonfruit, genipa, sugar apple, and tamarind. Back in 1960, the stand got started when seven-year-old Robert sat at this spot selling his father's bumper cucumber crop. Now Robert (still on the scene daily with his wife and kids), ships nationwide and donates seconds to needy area families. An assortment of animals out back—goats to emus—creates entertainment value for kids. Picnic tables, benches, and a waterfall with a koi pond add serenity. On the way to Everglades National Park, Robert opens at 8 am, operating until at least 7, and shutting down from Labor Day until November. ✉ *19200 S.W. 344th St.* ☎ *305/246–1592.*

HOMESTEAD

30 miles southwest of Miami.

Since recovering from Hurricane Andrew in 1992, Homestead has redefined itself as a destination for tropical agro- and ecotourism. At a crossroads between Miami and the Keys as well as Everglades and Biscayne national parks, the area has the added dimension of shopping centers, residential development, hotel chains, and the Homestead-Miami Speedway—when car races are scheduled, hotels hike up their rates and require minimum stays. The historic downtown has become a preservation-driven Main Street. Krome Avenue, where it cuts through the city's heart, is lined with restaurants, an arts complex, antiques shops, and low-budget, sometimes undesirable, accommodations. West of north–south Krome Avenue, miles of fields grow fresh fruits and vegetables. Some are harvested commercially, and others beckon with "U-pick" signs. Stands selling farm-fresh produce and nurseries that grow and sell orchids and tropical plants abound. In addition to its agricultural legacy, the town has an eclectic flavor, attributable to its population mix: descendants of pioneer Crackers, Hispanic growers and farm workers, professionals escaping the Miami hubbub, and latter-day northern retirees.

Are baby alligators more to your liking than their daddies? You can pet one at Gator Park.

EXPLORING

Fruit & Spice Park. Because it officially qualifies for tropical status, this 37-acre park in Homestead's Redland historic agricultural district is the only public botanical garden of its type in the United States. More than 500 varieties of fruit, nuts, and spices typically grow here, and there are 75 varieties of bananas alone, plus 160 of mango. Tram tours (included in admission) run three times daily, and you can sample fresh fruit at the gift shop, which also stocks canned and dried fruits plus cookbooks. The Mango Café, open daily, serves mango salsa, smoothies, and shakes along with salads, wraps, sandwiches, and a yummy Mango Passion Cheesecake. Picnic in the garden at provided tables or on your own blankets. Annual park events include January's Redland Heritage Festival and June's Summer Fruit Festival. ⊠ *24801 S.W. 187th Ave.* ☎ *305/247–5727* ⊕ *www.fruitandspicepark.org* ☜ *$8* ☉ *Daily 9–5; guided tram tours at 11, 1:30, and 3.*

Schnebly Redland's Winery. Enjoy Homestead's fruity bounty in liquid form at this winery that began producing wines of lychee, mango, guava, and other fruits as a way to avoid waste from family groves each year—bounty not perfect enough for shipping. Over the years, the winery has expanded with a reception/tasting indoor area serving snacks and a lush plaza area landscaped in coral rock, tropical plants, and waterfalls—topped with an Indian thatched chickee roof. Tours and tastings are offered daily. The Ultimate Tasting ($9.95) includes five wines, and an etched Schnebly glass you can keep. ⊠ *30205 S.W. 217th Ave.* ☎ *305/242–1224, 888/717–9463 (WINE)* ⊕ *www. schneblywinery.com* ☉ *Weekdays 10–5, Sat. 10–6, Sun. noon–5.*

WHERE TO EAT

$ MEXICAN 🍴 **NicaMex.** Among the local Latin population this 68-seat eatery is a low-budget favorite for Nicaraguan and Mexican flavors. It helps if you know Spanish, but the menu is bilingual and some staffers speak English. Although they term it *comidas rapidas* (fast food), the cuisine is not Americanized. You can get authentic huevos rancheros or *chilaquiles* (corn tortillas cooked in red-pepper sauce) for breakfast. Specialties include *chicharron en salsa verde* (fried pork skin in hot-green-tomato sauce). Hearty seafood and beef soups are top sellers. If you want (or dare), Mexican plates from tacos to tostadas can be made with beef tongue. Choose among domestic or imported beers, and escape south of the border. [$] *Average main: $10* ✉ *32 N.W. 1st St., across from Krome Ave. bandstand* ☎ *305/247–0727.*

WHERE TO STAY

For expanded hotel reviews, visit Fodors.com.

$ HOTEL 🏨 **Hotel Redland.** Of downtown Homestead's smattering of mom-and-pop lodging options, this historic inn, now under new ownership, is by far the most desirable with its Victorian-style rooms done up in pastels and reproduction antique furniture. **Pros:** historic character; convenient to downtown and near antique shops; well maintained; smoke-free. **Cons:** traffic noise; some small rooms. [$] *Rooms from: $100* ✉ *5 S. Flagler Ave.* ☎ *305/246–1904, 800/595–1904* 🌐 *www.hotelredland.com* 🛏 *13 rooms* 🍽 *No meals.*

SPORTS AND THE OUTDOORS

AUTO RACING

Homestead-Miami Speedway. The speedway buzzes more than 280 days each year with racing, manufacturer testing, car-club events, driving schools, and ride-along programs. The facility has 65,000 grandstand seats, club seating eight stories above racing action, and two tracks—a 2.21-mile continuous road course and a 1.5-mile oval. A packed schedule includes GRAND-AM and NASCAR events. Two tunnels on the grounds are below sea-level. ✉ *One Speedway Blvd.* ☎ *866/409–7223* 🌐 *www.homesteadmiamispeedway.com.*

WATER SPORTS

Homestead Bayfront Park. Boaters, anglers, and beachgoers give high ratings to facilities at this recreational area adjacent to Biscayne National Park. The 174-slip marina, accommodating up to 50-foot vessels, has a ramp, dock, bait-and-tackle shop, fuel station, ice, and dry storage. The park also has a snack bar, tidal swimming area, a beach with lifeguards, playground, ramps for people with disabilities, and a picnic pavilion with grills, showers, and restrooms. ✉ *9698 S.W. 328th St.* ☎ *305/230–3033* 🎟 *$6 per passenger vehicle; $12 per vehicle with boat Mon.–Thurs., $15 Fri.–Sun.; $15 per RV or bus* 🕒 *Daily sunrise–sunset.*

TAMIAMI TRAIL

U.S. 41, between Naples and Miami

An 80-mile stretch of U.S. 41 (known as the Tamiami Trail) traverses the Everglades, Big Cypress National Preserve, and Fakahatchee Strand Preserve State Park. The road was conceived in 1915 to link Miami to Fort Myers and Tampa. When it finally became a reality in 1928, it cut through the Everglades and altered the natural flow of water as well as the lives of the Miccosukee Indians, who were try-ing to eke out a living fishing, hunting, farming, and frogging here. The landscape is surprisingly varied, changing from hardwood ham-mocks to pinelands, then abruptly to tall cypress trees dripping with Spanish moss and back to saw-grass marsh. Slow down to take in the scenery and you'll likely be rewarded with glimpses of alligators sun-ning themselves along the banks of roadside canals, and hundreds of waterbirds, especially in the dry winter season. The man-made land-scape includes Native American villages, chickee huts, and airboats parked at roadside enterprises. Between Miami and Naples the road goes by several names, including Tamiami Trail, U.S. 41, 9th Street in Naples, and, at the Miami end, S.W. 8th Street. ▉TIP➔ Businesses along the trail give their addresses based on either their distance from Krome Avenue, Florida's Turnpike, or Miami on the east coast or Naples on the west coast.

EXPLORING

Everglades Safari Park. A perennial favorite with tour-bus operators, this family-run park has an arena, seating up to 300, for alligator wrestling demonstrations and shows. Before and after, get a closer look at both alligators and crocodiles on Gator Island, follow a jungle trail, walk through a small wildlife museum, or climb aboard an airboat for a 40-minute ride on the River of Grass (included in admission). There's also a restaurant, gift shop, and an observation platform looking out over the Glades. Smaller, private airboats can be chartered for tours lasting 40 minutes to 2 hours. Check online for coupons. ✉ *26700 S.W. 8th St., 15 miles west of Florida's Tpke., Miami* ☎ *305/226–6923, 305/223–3804* ⊕ *www.evergladessafaripark.com* ✉ *$23* 🕙 *Daily 9–5, last tour departs 3:30.*

FAMILY **Gator Park.** Here you can get face-to-face with and even touch an alli-gator—albeit a baby one—during the park's Wildlife Show. You also can squirm in a "reptilium" of venomous and nonpoisonous native snakes or learn about American Indians of the Everglades through a reproduction of a Miccosukee village. The park, open rain or shine, also has 35-minute airboat tours as well as a gift shop and restaurant serving fare from burgers to gator tail. ✉ *24050 Tamiami Trail, 12 miles west of Florida's Tpke., Miami* ☎ *305/559–2255, 800/559–2205* ⊕ *www.gatorpark.com* ✉ *Tours, wildlife show, airboat ride $22.99* 🕙 *Daily 9–5.*

FAMILY **Miccosukee Indian Village and Gift Shop.** Showcasing the skills and lifestyle of the Miccosukee Tribe of Florida, this cultural center offers crafts demonstrations and insight into the interaction between alligators and the American Indians. Narrated 30-minute airboat rides take you into the wilderness where natives hid after the Seminole Wars and Indian Removal Act of the mid-1800s. In modern times, many of the Miccosukee have relocated to this village along Tamiami Trail, but most still maintain their hammock farming and hunting camps. The village museum shows a film and displays chickee structures and artifacts. Guided tours run throughout the day, and a gift shop stocks dolls, apparel, silver jewelry, beadwork, and other handcrafts. The Miccosukee Everglades Music and Craft Festival falls on a July weekend, and the 10-day Miccosukee Indian Arts Festival is in late December. ✉ *U.S. 41, just west of Shark Valley entrance, 25 miles west of Florida's Tpke. at MM 70, Miami* ☎ *305/552–8365* 🌐 *www.miccosukee.com* 🎟 *Village $8, airboat rides $10* 🕒 *Daily 9–5.*

CROCS OR GATORS?

You can tell you're looking at a crocodile, not an alligator, if you can see its lower teeth protruding when its jaws are shut. Gators are much darker in color—a grayish black—compared with the lighter tan color of crocodiles. Alligator snouts—sort of U-shape—are also much broader than their long, thin A-shape crocodilian counterparts. South Florida is the world's only place where the two coexist. Alligators are primarily found in freshwater habitats, whereas crocodiles (better at expelling salt from water) are typically in coastal estuaries.

WHERE TO EAT

$ AMERICAN 🍴 **Coopertown Restaurant.** Make this a pit stop for local color and cuisine fished straight from the swamp. Started a half century ago as a sandwich stand, this eatery inside an airboat concession storefront has long attracted the famous and the humbly hungry. House specialties are frogs' legs and alligator tail breaded in cornmeal and deep-fried, served with a lemon wedge and Tabasco. Additional options include catfish, shrimp, burgers, hot dogs, and grilled cheese sandwiches. [$] *Average main: $12* ✉ *22700 S.W. 8th St., 11 miles west of Florida's Tpke., Miami* ☎ *305/226–6048* 🌐 *www.coopertownairboats.com* 🕒 *No dinner.*

$$ SOUTHWESTERN 🍴 **Miccosukee Restaurant.** For breakfast or lunch (or dinner until 9 pm, November–April), this roadside cafeteria a quarter mile from the Miccosukee Indian Village provides the best menu variety along Tamiami Trail in Everglades territory. Atmosphere comes from the view overlooking the River of Grass, servers wearing traditional Miccosukee patchwork vests, and a mural depicting American Indian women cooking while men powwow. Catfish and frogs' legs are breaded and deep-fried. Besides Indian fry bread and pumpkin bread, you'll also find burgers, salads, and south-of-the-border dishes. The Miccosukee Platter ($24.95) offers a sampling of local favorites, including gator bites. [$] *Average main: $15* ✉ *U.S. 41, 18 miles west of Miccosukee Resort & Gaming; 25 miles west of Florida's Tpke., Miami* ☎ *305/894–2374* 🕒 *No dinner May–Oct.*

$ BARBECUE FAMILY 🍴 **Pit Bar-B-Q.** This old-fashioned roadside eatery along Tamiami Trail near Krome Avenue was launched in 1965 by the late Tommy Little, who wanted to provide easy access to cold drinks and rib-sticking fare for folks heading into or out of the Everglades. His backwood heritage vision remains a popular, affordable family option. Order at the counter, pick up your food, and eat at picnic tables on the screened porch or outdoors. Specialties include barbecued chicken and ribs with a tangy sauce, fries, coleslaw, and a fried biscuit, plus burgers and fish sandwiches. The whopping double-decker beef or pork sandwich with slaw requires multiple napkins. Latin specialties include deep-fried pork and fried green plantains. Beer is by the bottle or pitcher. Locals flock here with kids on weekends for pony rides. $ *Average main: $12* ✉ *16400 S.W. 8th St., 5 miles west of Florida's Tpke., Miami* ☎ *305/226–2272* ⊕ *www.thepitbarbq.com.*

WHERE TO STAY

For expanded reviews, facilities, and current deals, visit Fodors.com.

$$$

RESORT

🏨 **Miccosukee Resort & Gaming.** Like an oasis on the horizon of endless sawgrass, this nine-story resort at the southeastern edge of the Everglades can't help but attract attention, even if you're not on the look-out for 24-hour gaming action. **Pros:** casino; most modern resort in these parts; golf. **Cons:** smoky lobby; hotel guests find parking lot fills with gamblers; feels incompatible with the Everglades. $ *Rooms from: $149* ✉ *500 S.W. 177th Ave., 6 miles west of Florida's Tpke., Miami* ☎ *305/925–2555, 877/242–6464* ⊕ *www.miccosukee.com* ⤴ *256 rooms, 46 suites* ⦿| *No meals.*

SPORTS AND THE OUTDOORS

BOAT TOURS

Many Everglades-area tours operate only in season, roughly November through April.

Coopertown Airboats. In business since 1945, the oldest airboat operator in the Everglades offers 35- to 40-minute tours ($20) that take you 9 miles to hammocks and alligator holes. You also can book private charters of up to two hours. ✉ *22700 S.W. 8th St., 11 miles west of Florida's Tpke., Miami* ☎ *305/226–6048* ⊕ *www.coopertownairboats.com.*

Everglades Alligator Farm. Near the entrance to Everglades National Park, this working farm—home of the 14-foot "Grandpa" alligator—runs a 4-mile, 30-minute airboat tour with departures 25 minutes after the hour. The tour ($23) includes free hourly alligator, snake, and wildlife shows; or see only the gator farm and show ($15.50). Alligator feedings are at noon and 3. Look for online coupons. ✉ *40351 S.W. 192nd Ave., Homestead* ☎ *305/247–2628* ⊕ *www.everglades.com.*

Everglades Safari Park. A 30-minute eco-adventure airboat ride costs $23, while longer, smaller, private airboat adventures, like the eco-adventure and sunset tours, cost more. All prices include the alligator show and access to walking trails and exhibits. Look for online discounts. ✉ *26700 S.W. 8th St., 15 miles west of Florida's Tpke., Miami* ☎ *305/226–6923, 305/223–3804* ⊕ *www.evergladessafaripark.com.*

Gator Park Airboat Tours. Open daily rain or shine, Gator Park conducts 45-minute narrated airboat tours ($22.99), including a park tour and wildlife show. Look for significant online discounts. ✉ *24050 S.W. 8th St., 12 miles west of Florida's Tpke., Miami* ☎ *305/559–2255, 800/559–2205* ⊕ *www.gatorpark.com.*

FAMILY **Wooten's Everglades Airboat Tour.** This classic Florida roadside attraction runs airboat tours through the Everglades for up to 18 people and swamp-buggy rides through the Big Cypress Swamp for up to 25 passengers. Each lasts approximately 30 minutes. (Swamp-buggies are giant tractorlike vehicles with huge rubber wheels.) More personalized airboat tours on smaller boats, seating six to eight, last about an hour. An on-site animal sanctuary shelters the typical Everglades array of alligators, snakes, and other creatures. Ask about packages that include an airboat ride, swamp-buggy adventure, and sanctuary access. Rates change frequently. ⊠ *32330 Tamiami Trail E, 1½ miles east of Rte. 29, Ochopee* ☎ *239/695–2781, 800/282–2781* ⊕ *www.wootenseverglades. com* ⊗ *Daily 8:30–5; last ride departs at 4:30.*

THE FLORIDA KEYS

WELCOME TO THE FLORIDA KEYS

TOP REASONS TO GO

★ **John Pennekamp Coral Reef State Park:** A perfect introduction to the Florida Keys, this nature reserve offers snorkeling, diving, camping, and kayaking. An underwater highlight is the massive Christ of the Deep statue.

★ **Under the sea:** Whether you scuba dive, snorkel, or ride a glass-bottom boat, don't miss gazing at the coral reef and its colorful denizens.

★ **Sunset at Mallory Square:** Sure, it's touristy, but just once while you're here, you've got to witness the circuslike atmosphere of this nightly event.

★ **Duval crawl:** Shop, eat, drink, repeat. Key West's Duval Street and the nearby streets make a good day's worth of window-shopping and people-watching.

★ **Get on the water:** From angling for trophy-size fish to zipping out to the Dry Tortugas, a boat trip is in your future. It's really the whole point of the Keys.

1 The Upper Keys. As the doorstep to the islands' coral reefs and blithe spirit, the Upper Keys introduce all that's sporting and sea-oriented about the Keys. They stretch from Key Largo to the Long Key Channel (MM 105–65).

2 The Middle Keys. Centered on the town of Marathon, the Middle Keys hold most of the chain's historic and natural attractions outside of Key West. They go from Conch (pronounced *konk*) Key through Marathon to the south side of the Seven Mile Bridge, including Pigeon Key (MM 65–40).

3 The Lower Keys. Pressure drops another notch in this laid-back part of the region, where wildlife and the fishing lifestyle peak. The Lower Keys go from Little Duck Key west through Big Coppitt Key (MM 40–9).

```
0          10 mi
0          10 km
```

Gulf of

National Key
Deer Refuge

3 THE LOWER KEYS

Big Torch Key
Little Torch Key
Cudjoe Key
Mud Keys
Saddlebunch Keys
Big Pine Key
Summerland Key
Ramrod Key
Sugarloaf Key
Big Coppitt Key
No Name Key
Bahia Honda Key

Key West
Key West
Stock Island
Boca Chica Key
Key West International Airport

4 Key West. The ultimate in Florida Keys craziness, the party town Key West isn't the place for those seeking a quiet retreat. The Key West area encompasses MM 9–0.

4

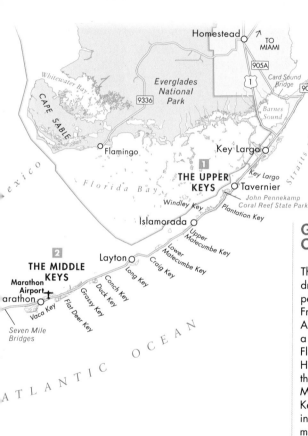

Homestead
TO MIAMI

905A

Card Sound Bridge

905

Everglades National Park

9336

Barnes Sound

Whitewater Bay

CAPE SABLE

Flamingo

Key Largo

1 THE UPPER KEYS

Key Largo

Tavernier

John Pennekamp Coral Reef State Park

Windley Key

Plantation Key

Islamorada

Upper Matecumbe Key

Lower Matecumbe Key

2 THE MIDDLE KEYS

Layton

Craig Key

Long Key

Conch Key

Duck Key

Grassy Key

Flat Deer Key

Marathon Airport

arathon

Vaca Key

Seven Mile Bridges

Florida Bay

exico

Straits of Florida

ATLANTIC OCEAN

GETTING ORIENTED

The Florida Keys are the dribble of islands off the peninsula's southern tip. From Miami International Airport, Key Largo is a 56-mile drive via the Florida Turnpike and Highway 1. The rest of the keys—Islamorada, Marathon, Bahia Honda Key, and Big Pine Key—fall in succession for the 85 miles between Key Largo and Key West along the Overseas Highway. At their north end, the Florida Keys front Florida Bay, part of Everglades National Park. The Middle and Lower Keys front the Gulf of Mexico; the Atlantic Ocean borders the length of the chain on its eastern shores.

SEAFOOD IN THE FLORIDA KEYS

Fish. It's what's for dinner in the Florida Keys. The Keys' runway between the Gulf of Mexico or Florida Bay, and Atlantic warm waters means fish of many fin. Restaurants take full advantage by serving it fresh, whether you caught it or a local fisherman did.

Menus at a number of colorful waterfront shacks such as **Snapper's** (✉ *139 Seaside Ave., Key Largo* ☎ *305/852–5956*) in Key Largo and **Half Shell Raw Bar** (✉ *231 Margaret St., Key West* ☎ *305/294–7496*) range from basic raw, steamed, broiled, grilled, or blackened fish to some Bahamian and New Orleans–style interpretations. Other seafood houses dress up their fish in creative haute-cuisine styles, such as **Pierre's** (✉ *MM 81.5 BS, Islamorada* ☎ *305/664–3225* ⊕ *www.pierres-restaurant.com*) hogfish *meunière*, or yellowtail snapper with pear-ricotta pasta purses with caponata and red pepper coulis at **Café Marquesa** (✉ *600 Fleming St., Key West* ☎ *305/292–1244* ⊕ *www.marquesa.com*). Try a Keys-style breakfast of "grits and grunts"—fried fish and grits—at the **Stuffed Pig** (✉ *3520 Overseas Hwy., Marathon* ☎ *305/743–4059*).

BUILT-IN FISH

You know it's fresh when you see a fish market as soon as you open the door to the restaurant where you're dining. It happens all the time in the Keys. You can even peruse the seafood showcases and pick the fish fillet or lobster tail you want.

Many of the Keys' best restaurants are found in marina complexes, where the commercial fishermen bring their catches straight from the sea. Those in **Stock Island** (one island north of Key West) and at **Keys Fisheries Market & Marina** (✉ MM 49 BS, end of 35th St., Marathon ☎ 305/743–4353 or 866/743–4353) take some finding.

CONCH

One of the tastiest legacies of the Keys' Bahamian heritage, conch shows up on nearly every restaurant menu. It's so prevalent in local diets that natives refer to themselves as Conchs. Conch fritter is the most popular culinary manifestation, followed by cracked (pounded, breaded, and fried) conch, and conch salad, a ceviche-style refresher. Since the harvesting of queen conch is now illegal, most of the islands' conch comes from the Bahamas.

FLORIDA LOBSTER

What happened to the claws? Stop looking for them: Florida spiny lobsters don't have 'em, never did. The sweet tail meat, however, makes up for the loss. Commercial and sports divers harvest these glorious crustaceans from late July through March. Check with local dive shops on restrictions, and then get ready for a fresh feast. Restaurants serve them broiled with drawn butter or in creative dishes such as lobster Benedict, lobster sushi rolls, lobster Reuben, and lobster tacos.

GROUPER

Once central to Florida's trademark seafood dish—fried grouper sandwich—its populations have been overfished in recent years, meaning that the state has exerted more control over bag regulations and occasionally closes grouper fishing on a temporary basis during the winter season. Some restaurants have gone antigrouper to try to bring back the abundance, but most grab it when they can. Black grouper is the most highly prized of the several varieties.

STONE CRAB

In season October 15 through May 15, it gets its name from its rock-hard shell. Fishermen take only the claws, which can regenerate in a sustainable manner. Connoisseurs prefer them chilled with tangy mustard sauce. Some restaurants give you a choice of hot claws and drawn butter, but this means the meat will be cooked twice, because it's usually boiled or steamed as soon as its taken from its crab trap.

YELLOWTAIL SNAPPER

The preferred species of snappers, it's more plentiful in the Keys than in any other Florida waters. As pretty as it is tasty, it's a favorite of divers and snorkelers. Mild, sweet, and delicate, its meat lends itself to any number of preparations. It's available pretty much year-round, and many restaurants will give you a choice of broiled, baked, fried, or blackened. Chefs top it with everything from key lime beurre blanc to mango chutney. **Ballyhoo's** in Key Largo (⊠ *MM 97.8, in median* ☎ *305/852–0822*) serves it 10 different ways.

Updated by Jill
Martin

Being a Conch is a condition of the heart, and foreclosure on the soul. Many throughout the Florida Keys wear that label proudly, yet there's anything but a shared lifestyle here.

To the south, Key West has a Mardi Gras mood with Fantasy Festivals, Hemingway look-alike contests, and the occasional threat to secede from the Union. It's an island whose melting-pot character allows crusty natives to mingle (more or less peacefully) with eccentrics and escape artists who lovingly call this 4-mile sandbar "Paradise." Although life elsewhere in the island chain isn't quite as offbeat, it's nearly as diverse. Flowering jungles, shimmering seas, and mangrove-lined islands are also, conversely, overburdened. Key Largo, nearest the mainland, is becoming more congested as it evolves into a bed-room community and weekend hideaway for residents of Miami and Fort Lauderdale.

A river of tourist traffic gushes along Overseas Highway, the 110-mile artery linking the inhabited islands. But that doesn't mean you can't enjoy the ride as you cruise along the islands. Gaze over the silvery blue-and-green Atlantic and its still-living reef, with Florida Bay, the Gulf of Mexico, and the backcountry on your right (the Keys extend southwest from the mainland). At a few points the ocean and gulf are as much as 10 miles apart; in most places, however, they're from 1 to 4 miles apart, and on the narrowest landfill islands they're separated only by the road. Try to get off the highway. Once you do, rent a boat, anchor, and then fish, swim, or marvel at the sun, sea, and sky. In the Atlantic, dive spectacular coral reefs or pursue grouper, blue marlin, mahimahi, and other deepwater game fish. Along Florida Bay's coastline, kayak and canoe to secluded islands and bays or seek out the bonefish, snap-per, snook, and tarpon that lurk in the grass flats and in the shallow, winding channels of the backcountry.

With virtually no distracting air pollution or obstructive high-rises, sunsets are a pure, unadulterated spectacle that each evening attract thousands to the waterfront.

The Keys were only sparsely populated until the early 20th century. In 1905, however, railroad magnate Henry Flagler began building the extension of his Florida railroad south from Homestead to Key West.

His goal was to establish a Miami–Key West rail link to his steamships that sailed between Key West and Havana, just 90 miles across the Straits of Florida. The railroad arrived at Key West in 1912, and remained a lifeline of commerce until the Labor Day hurricane of 1935 washed out much of its roadbed. The Overseas Highway, built over the railroad's old roadbeds and bridges, was completed in 1938.

PLANNING

WHEN TO GO

High season in the Keys falls between Christmas and Easter. November to mid-December crowds are thinner, the weather is wonderful, and hotels and shops drastically reduce their prices. Summer, which is hot and humid, is becoming a second high season, especially among Floridians, families, and European travelers. If you plan to attend the wild Fantasy Fest in October, book your room at least six months in advance. Accommodations are also scarce during the last consecutive Wednesday and Thursday in July (lobster sport season) and starting the first weekend in August, when the commercial lobster season begins.

Winter is typically 10°F warmer than on the mainland; summer is usually a few degrees cooler. The Keys also get substantially less rain, around 40 inches annually, compared with an average 55–60 inches in Miami and the Everglades. Most rainfalls are quick downpours on summer afternoons, except in June through October, when tropical storms can dump rain for two or more days. Winter cold fronts occasionally stall over the Keys, dragging overnight temperatures down to the low 50s.

GETTING HERE AND AROUND

AIR TRAVEL

About 450,000 passengers use the **Key West International Airport (EYW)** each year; its most recent renovation includes a beach where travelers can catch their last blast of rays after clearing security. Because flights are few, many prefer flying into Miami International Airport (MIA) and driving the 110-mile Overseas Highway (aka U.S. 1).

Contact Key West International Airport (EYW) ☎ 305/296–5439 ⊕ www.keywestinternationalairport.com.

BOAT AND FERRY TRAVEL

Key West can be reached by high-speed catamaran ferry from Fort Myers and Marco Island through Key West Express.

Boaters can travel to and along the Keys either along the Intracoastal Waterway through Card, Barnes, and Blackwater sounds and into Florida Bay or along the deeper Atlantic Ocean route through Hawk Channel. The Keys are full of marinas that welcome transient visitors, but there aren't enough slips for all the boats heading to these waters. Make reservations far in advance and ask about channel and dockage depth—many marinas are quite shallow.

Contact Key West Express ✉ 100 Grinnell St., Key West ☎ 888/539–2628 ⊕ www.seakeywestexpress.com.

BUS TRAVEL

Those unwilling to tackle the route's 42 bridges and peak-time traffic can take **Greyhound's** Keys Shuttle, which has multiple daily departures from Miami International Airport.

Contact **Greyhound** ☏ *800/231–2222* ⊕ *www.greyhound.com.*

CAR TRAVEL

By car, from Miami International Airport, follow signs to Coral Gables and Key West, which puts you on LeJeune Road, then Route 836 west. Take the Homestead Extension of Florida's Turnpike south (toll road), which ends at Florida City and connects to the Overseas Highway (U.S. 1). Tolls from the airport run approximately $3. Payment is collected via SunPass, a prepaid toll program, or with Toll-By-Plate, a system that photographs each vehicle's license plate and mails a monthly bill for tolls, plus a $2.50 administrative fee, to the vehicle's registered owner. Vacationers traveling in their own cars can obtain a mini-SunPass sticker via mail before their trip for $4.99 and receive the cost back in toll credits and discounts. The pass also is available at many major Florida retailers and turnpike service plazas. It works on all Florida toll roads and many bridges. For details on purchasing a mini-SunPass, call or visit the website. For visitors renting cars in Florida, most major rental companies have programs allowing customers to use the Toll-By-Plate system. Tolls, plus varying service fees, are automatically charged to the credit card used to rent the vehicle. For details, including pricing options at participating rental-car agencies, check the program website. Under no circumstances should motorists attempt to stop in high-speed electronic tolling lanes. Travelers can contact Florida's Turnpike Enterprise for more information about the all-electronic tolling on Florida's Turnpike.

The alternative from Florida City is Card Sound Road (Route 905A), which has a bridge toll of $1. SunPass isn't accepted. Continue to the only stop sign and turn right on Route 905, which rejoins Overseas Highway 31 miles south of Florida City. The best Keys road map, published by the Homestead–Florida City Chamber of Commerce, can be obtained for $5.50 from the Tropical Everglades Visitor Center.

Contacts **Florida's Turnpike Enterprise** ☏ *800/749–7453* ⊕ *www.floridasturnpike.com.* **SunPass** ☏ *888/865–5352* ⊕ *www.sunpass.com.* **TOLL-BY-PLATE** ⊕ *www.sunpass.com/rentalcar.*

THE MILE MARKER SYSTEM

Getting lost in the Keys is almost impossible once you understand the unique address system. **Many addresses are simply given as a mile marker (MM) number.** The markers are small, green, rectangular signs along the side of the Overseas Highway (U.S. 1). They begin with MM 126, 1 mile south of Florida City, and end with MM 0, in Key West. **Keys residents use the abbreviation BS for the bay side of Overseas Highway and OS for the ocean side.** From Marathon to Key West, residents may refer to the bay side as the gulf side.

HOTELS

Throughout the Keys, the types of accommodations are remarkably varied, from 1950s-style motels to cozy inns to luxurious resorts. Most are on or near the ocean, so water sports are popular. Key West's lodging portfolio includes historic cottages, restored Conch houses, and large resorts. Some larger properties throughout the Keys charge a mandatory daily resort fee of $15 or more, which can cover equipment rental, fitness-center use, and other services. You can expect another 12.5% (or more) in state and county taxes. Some guesthouses and inns don't welcome children, and many don't permit smoking.

RESTAURANTS

Seafood rules in the Keys, which is full of chef-owned restaurants with not-too-fancy food. Things get more exotic once you reach Key West. Restaurants serve cuisine that reflects the proximity of the Bahamas and Caribbean. Tropical fruits figure prominently—especially on the beverage side of the menu. Florida spiny lobster should be local and fresh from August to March, and stone crabs from mid-October to mid-May. And don't dare leave the islands without sampling conch, be it in a fritter or in ceviche. Keep an eye out for authentic key lime pie—yellow custard in a graham-cracker crust. If it's green, just say "no." Note: Particularly in Key West and particularly during spring break, the more affordable and casual restaurants can get loud and downright rowdy, with young visitors often more interested in drinking than eating. Live music contributes to the decibel levels. If you're more of the quiet, intimate dining type, avoid such overly exuberant scenes by eating early or choosing a restaurant where the bar isn't the main focus.

HOTEL AND RESTAURANT COSTS

Prices in the restaurant reviews are the average cost of a main course at dinner or, if dinner isn't served, at lunch. Prices in the hotel reviews are the lowest cost of a standard double room in high season. Prices don't include taxes (6%, more in some counties, and 1%–5% tourist tax for hotel rooms).

VISITOR INFORMATION

Contact **Monroe County Tourist Development Council** ☎ *800/352–5397* ⊕ *www.Fla-Keys.com.* **Tropical Everglades Visitor Association** ☎ *305/245–9180, 800/388–9669* ⊕ *www.tropicaleverglades.com.*

THE UPPER KEYS

Diving and snorkeling rule in the Upper Keys, thanks to the tropical coral reef that runs a few miles off the seaward coast. Divers of all skill levels benefit from accessible dive sites and an established tourism infrastructure. Fishing is another huge draw, especially around Islamorada, known for its sportfishing in both deep offshore waters and in the backcountry. Offshore islands accessible only by boat are popular destinations for kayakers. In short, if you don't like the water, you might get bored here.

Other nature lovers won't feel shortchanged. Within 1½ miles of the bay coast lie the mangrove trees and sandy shores of Everglades National Park, where naturalists lead tours of one of the world's few saltwater forests. Here you'll see endangered manatees, curious dolphins, and other underwater creatures. Although the number of birds has dwindled since John James Audubon captured their beauty on canvas, the rare Everglades snail kite, bald eagles, ospreys, and a colorful array of egrets and herons delight bird-watchers. At sunset, flocks take to the skies as they gather to find their night's roost, adding a swirl of activity to an otherwise quiet time of day.

The Upper Keys are full of low-key eateries where the owner is also the chef and the food is tasty and never too fussy. The one exception is Islamorada, where you'll find more upscale restaurants. Places to eat may close for a two- to four-week vacation during the slow season between mid-September and late October.

In the Upper Keys the accommodations are as varied as they are plentiful. The majority of lodgings are in small waterfront complexes with furnished one- or two-bedroom units. These places offer dockage and often arrange boating, diving, and fishing excursions. There are also larger resorts with every type of activity imaginable and smaller boutique hotels where the attraction is personalized service.

Depending on which way the wind blows and how close the property is to the highway, there may be some noise from Overseas Highway. If this is an annoyance for you, ask for a room as far from the traffic as possible. Some properties require two- or three-day minimum stays during holiday and high-season weekends. Conversely, discounts may apply for midweek, weekly, and monthly stays.

GETTING HERE AND AROUND

Airporter operates scheduled van and bus pickup service from all Miami International Airport (MIA) baggage areas to wherever you want to go in Key Largo ($50) and Islamorada ($55). Groups of three or more passengers receive discounts. There are three departures daily; reservations are required 48 hours in advance. The SuperShuttle charges about $165 for two passengers for trips from Miami International Airport to the Upper Keys; reservations are required. For a trip to the airport, place your request 24 hours in advance.

Contacts Airporter ☎ 305/852–3413, 800/830–3413.
SuperShuttle ☎ 305/871–2000 ⊕ www.supershuttle.com.

KEY LARGO

56 miles (90 km) south of Miami International Airport.

The first of the Upper Keys reachable by car, 30-mile-long Key Largo is also the largest island in the chain. Key Largo—named Cayo Largo ("Long Key") by the Spanish—makes a great introduction to the region. The history of Largo is similar to that of the rest of the Keys, with its succession of native people, pirates, wreckers, and developers. The first settlement on Key Largo was named Planter, back in the days of pineapple, and later, key lime plantations. For a time it was a convenient shipping port, but when the railroad arrived, Planter died on the vine.

Today three communities—North Key Largo, Key Largo, and Tavernier—make up the whole of Key Largo.

If you've never tried diving, Key Largo is the perfect place to learn. Dozens of companies will be more than happy to show you the ropes. Nobody comes to Key Largo without visiting John Pennekamp Coral Reef State Park, one of the jewels of the state-park system. Also popular is the adjacent Key Largo National Marine Sanctuary, which encompasses about 190 square miles of coral reefs, seagrass beds, and mangrove estuaries. Both are good for underwater exploration.

Fishing is the other big draw, and world records are broken regularly. There are plenty of charter operations to help you find the big ones and teach you how to hook the elusive (but inedible) bonefish, sometimes known as the ghost fish. On land, restaurants will cook your catch or dish up their own offerings with inimitable style.

Key Largo offers all the conveniences of a major resort town, with most businesses lined up along Overseas Highway (U.S. 1), the four-lane highway that runs down the middle of the island. Cars whiz past at all hours—something to remember when you're booking a room. Most lodgings are on the highway, so you'll want to be as far from the road as possible.

GETTING HERE AND AROUND

Key Largo is 56 miles south of Miami International Airport, with the mile markers going from 106 to 91. The island runs northeast–southwest, with Overseas Highway running down the center. If the highway is your only glimpse of the island, you're likely to feel barraged by its tacky commercial side. Make a point of driving Route 905 in North Key Largo and down side streets to the marinas to get a better feel for it.

VISITOR INFORMATION

Contact **Key Largo Chamber of Commerce** ⊠ MM 106 BS, 10600 Overseas Hwy. ☎ 305/451–4747, 800/822–1088 ⊕ www.keylargochamber.org.

EXPLORING

Dagny Johnson Key Largo Hammock Botanical State Park. American crocodiles, mangrove cuckoos, white-crowned pigeons, Schaus swallowtail butterflies, mahogany mistletoe, wild cotton, and 100 other rare critters and plants inhabit these 2,400 acres, sandwiched between Crocodile Lake National Wildlife Refuge and Pennekamp Coral Reef State Park. The park is also a user-friendly place to explore the largest remaining stand of the vast West Indian tropical hardwood hammock and mangrove wetland that once covered most of the Keys' upland areas. Interpretive signs describe many of the tropical tree species along a wide 1-mile paved road (2-mile round-trip) that invites walking and biking. There are also more than 6 miles of nature trails accessible to bikes and wheelchairs. Pets are welcome if on a leash no longer than 6 feet. You'll also find restrooms, information kiosks, and picnic tables. ■TIP→ Rangers recommend not visiting when it's raining as the trees can drip poisonous sap. ⊠ 0.5 mile north of Overseas Hwy., Rte. 905 OS, North Key Largo ☎ 305/451–1202 ⊕ www.floridastateparks.org/keylargohammock ☎ $2.50 (exact change needed) ⊙ Daily 8–sundown.

FAMILY **Dolphin Cove.** This educational program begins at the facility's lagoon with a get-acquainted session from a platform. After that, you slip into the water for some frolicking with your new dolphin pals. The cost is $155 for a Shallow Water Swim and $195 for a Hands-on Structured Swim. Spend the day shadowing a dolphin trainer for $670. Admission for nonparticipants is $10 for adults. ✉ *MM 101.9 BS, 101900 Overseas Hwy.* ☎ *305/451–4020, 877/365–2683* 🌐 *www.dolphinscove.com.*

FAMILY **Dolphins Plus.** A sister property to Dolphin Cove, Dolphin Plus offers some of the same programs. Costing $150, the Natural Swim program begins with a one-hour briefing; then you enter the water to become totally immersed in the dolphins' world. In this visual orientation, participants snorkel but are not allowed to touch the dolphins. For tactile interaction (kissing, fin tows, etc.), sign up for the Structured Swim program ($195). The same concept with different critters, the sea lion swim costs $140. ✉ *MM 99, 31 Corrine Pl.* ☎ *305/451–1993, 866/860–7946* 🌐 *www.dolphinsplus.com.*

FAMILY **Jacobs Aquatic Center.** Take the plunge at one of three swimming pools: an 8-lane, 25-meter lap pool with a diving well; a 3- to 4-foot-deep pool accessible to people with mobility problems; and an interactive play pool with a waterslide, pirate ship, waterfall, and sloping zero entry instead of steps. ✉ *MM 99.6 OS, 320 Laguna Ave., at St. Croix Pl. (at Key Largo Community Park)* ☎ *305/453–7946* 🌐 *www.jacobsaquaticcenter.org* 🎟 *$8–$10* ⏲ *Daily 10–6 (10–7 in summer).*

BEACHES

FAMILY
Fodor's Choice ★
John Pennekamp Coral Reef State Park. This state park is on everyone's list for easy access to the best diving and snorkeling in Florida. The underwater treasure encompasses 78 square miles of coral reefs and seagrass beds. It lies adjacent to the Florida Keys National Marine Sanctuary, which contains 40 of the 52 species of coral in the Atlantic Reef System and nearly 600 varieties of fish, from the colorful parrot fish to the demure cocoa damselfish. Whatever you do, get in the water. Snorkeling and diving trips ($30 and $55, respectively, equipment extra) and glass-bottom-boat rides to the reef ($24) are available, weather permitting. One of the most popular snorkel trips is to see *Christ of the Deep,* the 2-ton underwater statue of Jesus. The park also has nature trails, two man-made beaches, picnic shelters, a snack bar, and a campground. **Amenities:** food and drink; parking (fee); showers; toilets; water sports. **Best for:** snorkeling; swimming. ✉ *MM 102.5 OS, 102601 Overseas Hwy.* ☎ *305/451–1202 for park, 305/451–6300 for excursions* 🌐 *www.pennekamppark.com, www.floridastateparks.org/pennekamp* 🎟 *$4.50 for 1 person in vehicle, $8 for 2–8 people, $2 for pedestrians and cyclists or extra people (plus a 50¢ per-person county surcharge)* ⏲ *Daily 8–sunset.*

WHERE TO EAT

$$
SEAFOOD
🍴 **Buzzard's Roost Grill and Pub.** The views are nice at this waterfront restaurant but the food is what gets your attention. Burgers, fish tacos, and seafood baskets are lunch faves. Dinner is about seafood and steaks, any way you like them. Try the smoked-fish dip, served with Armenian heart-shape lavash crackers. Look for the big signs on U.S. 1 that direct you where to turn—it's worth finding. [$] *Average main: $21*

DID YOU KNOW?

The bronze *Christ of the Deep* (also called *Christ of the Abyss*) statue of Jesus Christ underwater near John Pennekamp Coral Reef State Park is modeled after one in the Mediterranean Sea near where Italian Dario Gonzatti died while scuba diving.

✉ *At Garden Cove Marina, 21 Garden Cove Dr., Northernmost Key Largo* ☎ *305/453–3746* 🌐 *www.buzzardsroostkeylargo.com.*

WORD OF MOUTH

"The Keys are definitely a get out on the water type place instead of a driving up and down U.S. 1 kind of place. Bars and restaurants open early and close early. Get out over the water. That is where the most amazing things in the Keys are."

—GoTravel

$$$ SEAFOOD 🍴 **The Fish House.** Restaurants not on the water have to produce the highest quality food to survive in the Keys. That's how the Fish House has succeeded since the 1980s—so much so that it built the Fish House Encore (a fancier version) next door to accommodate fans. The pan-sautéed catch of the day is a long-standing favorite, as is the "Matecumbe-style" preparation—baked with tomatoes, capers, olive oil, and lemon juice, it will make you moan with pleasure. Prefer shellfish? Choose from shrimp, lobster, and (mid-October to mid-May) stone crab. The only thing bland is their side dishes: simple boiled red potatoes, a hunk of corn on the cob, or black beans and rice. For a sweet ending, the homemade key lime pie is award-winning. [$] *Average main: $21* ✉ *MM 102.4 OS, 102341 Overseas Hwy.* ☎ *305/451–4665* 🌐 *www.fishhouse.com* ✍ *Reservations not accepted* ⏲ *Closed Sept.* ☞ *American Express not accepted.*

$ AMERICAN 🍴 **Harriette's Restaurant.** If you're looking for comfort food—like melt-in-your-mouth buttermilk biscuits—try this refreshing throwback. The kitchen makes fresh muffins daily, in flavors like mango, chocolate, and key lime. Little has changed over the years in this yellow-and-turquoise eatery. Owner Harriette Mattson often personally greets guests who come for steak and eggs with hash browns or old-fashioned hotcakes with sausage or bacon. Stick to simple dishes; the eggs Benedict are a disappointment. At lunch- and dinnertime, Harriette's shines in the burger department, but there are also hot meals such as chicken-fried steak and a fried shrimp basket. [$] *Average main: $8* ✉ *MM 95.7 BS, 95710 Overseas Hwy.* ☎ *305/852–8689* ✍ *Reservations not accepted* ⏲ *No dinner Fri.–Sun.* ☞ *American Express not accepted.*

$$ SEAFOOD 🍴 **JJ's Big Chill.** Owned by former NFL coach, Jimmy Johnson, this waterfront establishment offers three entertaining experiences, and all are big winners. You'll find the best sports bar in the Upper Keys complete with the coach's Super Bowl trophies, a main restaurant with all-glass indoor seating and a waterfront deck, and an enormous outdoor tiki bar with entertainment seven nights a week. There's even a pool and cabana club where (for an entrance fee) you can spend the day sunning. Menu favorites are the Parmesan-crusted snapper and brick-oven roasted chicken wings, but don't miss the tuna nachos—as delicious as they are artfully presented. As the sun sets over the bay, enjoy the views and a slice of white chocolate–macadamia cheesecake. [$] *Average main: $16* ✉ *MM104 BS, 104000 Overseas Hwy.* ☎ *305/453–9066* 🌐 *www.jjsbigchill.com.*

$ AMERICAN 🍴 **Key Largo Conch House.** Tucked into the trees along the Overseas Highway, this Victorian-style home and its true-to-the-Keys style of cooking is worth seeking out—at least the Food Network and the Travel

Channel have thought so in the past. Family-owned since 2004, it feels welcoming either indoors around the coffee bar or on the Old South veranda. Raisin pecan French toast and eight varieties of benedicts, including conch, are reason enough to rise early and get your fresh coffee fix. Lunch and dinner menus cover all bases from the conch chowder bread bowl and vegetarian wraps to lobster and conch ceviche, andouille Alfredo, and yellowtail Florentine. $ *Average main: $15* 305/453–4844 *www.keylargoconchhouse.com* *Reservations essential.*

$
SEAFOOD ✕ **Mrs. Mac's Kitchen.** Townies pack the counters and booths at this tiny eatery, where license plates are stuck on the walls and made into chandeliers. Got a hankering for meat loaf or crab cakes? You'll find them here, along with specials like grilled yellowfin tuna. Bring your appetite for the all-you-can-eat catfish special on Tuesday and all-you-can-eat spaghetti on Thursday. There's also champagne breakfast, an assortment of tasty Angus beef burgers and sandwiches, a famous chili, and key lime freeze (somewhere between a shake and a float). In season, ask about the hogfish special du jour. A second location, Mrs. Mac's Kitchen 2, is about half a mile south, also on the Overseas Highway (99020 Overseas Hwy., MM99 Center) in Key Largo. $ *Average main: $15* MM 99.4 BS, 99336 Overseas Hwy. 305/451–3722 *www. mrsmacskitchen.com* *Reservations not accepted* *Closed Sun.*

$$$
AMERICAN ✕ **Sundowners.** The name doesn't lie. If it's a clear night and you can snag a reservation, this restaurant will treat you to a sherbet-hue sunset over Florida Bay. If you're here in mild weather—anytime other than the dog days of summer or the rare winter cold snap—the best seats are on the patio. The food is excellent: try the key lime seafood, a happy combo of sautéed shrimp, lobster, and lump crabmeat swimming in a tangy sauce spiked with Tabasco served over penne or rice. Wednesday and Saturday are all about prime rib, and Friday draws the crowds with an all-you-can-eat fish fry ($17.99). Vegetarian and gluten-free menus are available. $ *Average main: $22* MM 104 BS, 103900 Overseas Hwy. 305/451–4502 *sundownerskeylargo.com* *Reservations essential.*

WHERE TO STAY
For expanded reviews, facilities, and current deals, visit Fodors.com.

$$$
B&B/INN ⌂ **Azul del Mar.** The dock points the way to many beautiful sunsets at this adults-only boutique hotel. **Pros:** great garden; good location; sophisticated design. **Cons:** small beach; close to highway; high-priced. $ *Rooms from: $189* MM 104.3 BS, 104300 Overseas Hwy. 305/451–0337, 888/253–2985 *www.azulkeylargo.com* 2 studios, 3 1-bedroom suites, 1 2-bedroom suite *No meals.*

$$
RESORT ⌂ **Coconut Bay Resort & Bay Harbor Lodge.** Some 200 feet of waterfront is the main attraction at this property, a combination of two lodging options. **Pros:** bay front; neatly kept gardens; walking distance to restaurants; complimentary kayak and paddleboat use. **Cons:** a bit dated; small sea-walled sand beach. $ *Rooms from: $105* MM 97.7 BS, 97702 Overseas Hwy. 305/852–1625, 800/385–0986 *www. coconutbaykeylargo.com* 7 rooms, 5 efficiencies, 2 suites, 1 2-bedroom villa, 6 1-bedroom cottages *No meals.*

$$$$ B&B/INN **Dove Creek Lodge.** With its sherbet-hued rooms and plantation-style furnishings, these tropical-style units (21 in all) range in size from simple lodge rooms to luxury two-bedroom suites. **Pros:** luxurious rooms; walk to Snapper's restaurant. **Cons:** loud music next door. [$] *Rooms from: $229* ✉ *MM 94.5 OS, 147 Seaside Ave.* ☎ *305/852–6200, 800/401–0057* 🌐 *www.dovecreeklodge.com* 🛏 *4 room, 10 suites* 🍴 *Breakfast.*

$$$ RESORT **Hilton Key Largo Resort.** Nestled within a hardwood hammock (localese for uplands habitat where hardwood trees such as live oak grow) near the southern border of Everglades National Park, this sprawling resort—fresh off a $12-million renovation—offers a full slate of amenities in a woodsy setting. **Pros:** nice nature trail on bay side; pretty pools with waterfalls; awesome trees; bicycles available for rent. **Cons:** some rooms overlook the parking lot; pools near the highway; $14 per night for parking. [$] *Rooms from: $159* ✉ *MM 97 BS, 97000 Overseas Hwy.* ☎ *305/852–5553, 888/871–3437* 🌐 *www.keylargoresort.com* 🛏 *190 rooms, 10 suites* 🍴 *No meals.*

$$$$ RESORT Fodor's Choice ★ **Kona Kai Resort, Gallery & Botanic Gardens.** Brilliantly colored bougainvilleas, coconut palms, guava trees, and a new botanical garden of rare species make this 2-acre adult hideaway one of the prettiest places to stay in the Keys. **Pros:** free custom tours of botanical gardens for guests; free use of sports equipment; knowledgeable staff. **Cons:** expensive; some rooms are very close together. [$] *Rooms from: $269* ✉ *MM 97.8 BS, 97802 Overseas Hwy.* ☎ *305/852–7200, 800/365–7829* 🌐 *www.konakairesort.com* 🛏 *8 suites, 3 rooms* ⏲ *Closed Sept.* 🍴 *No meals.*

$$$ B&B/INN **Largo Lodge.** Tucked away on more than two waterfront acres, this peaceful lodge boasts an island environment that feels untouched by time and the cares of the outside world. **Pros:** lush grounds; great sunset views; affordable rates; boat docking. **Cons:** no pool, some traffic noise outdoors. [$] *Rooms from: $175* ✉ *MM 101.7 BS, 101740 Overseas Hwy.* ☎ *305/451–0424, 800/468–4378* 🌐 *www.largolodge.com* 🛏 *2 rooms, 6 cottages* 🍴 *No meals.*

$$ RESORT FAMILY **Marriott's Key Largo Bay Beach Resort.** This 17-acre bayside resort has plenty of diversions, from diving to parasailing to a day spa. **Pros:** lots of activities; free covered parking; dive shop on property; free Wi-Fi. **Cons:** rooms facing highway can be noisy; thin walls; unspectacular beach. [$] *Rooms from: $139* ✉ *MM 103.8 BS, 103800 Overseas Hwy.* ☎ *305/453–0000, 866/849–3753* 🌐 *www.marriottkeylargo.com* 🛏 *132 rooms, 20 2-bedroom suites, 1 penthouse suite* 🍴 *No meals.*

$ HOTEL **The Pelican.** This 1950s throwback is reminiscent of the days when parents packed the kids into the station wagon and headed to no-frills seaside motels, complete with an old-timer fishing off the dock. **Pros:** free use of kayaks and a canoe; well-maintained dock; reasonable rates. **Cons:** some small rooms; basic accommodations and amenities. [$] *Rooms from: $60* ✉ *MM 99.3, 99340 Overseas Hwy.* ☎ *305/451–3576, 877/451–3576* 🌐 *www.hungrypelican.com* 🛏 *13 rooms, 4 efficiencies, 4 suites, 2 trailers* 🍴 *No meals.*

NIGHTLIFE

The semiweekly *Keynoter* (Wednesday and Saturday), weekly *Reporter* (Thursday), and Friday through Sunday editions of the *Miami Herald* are the best sources of information on entertainment and nightlife. Daiquiri bars, tiki huts, and seaside shacks pretty well summarize Key Largo's bar scene.

Breezers Tiki Bar & Grille. Mingle with locals over cocktails and sunsets at Marriott's Key Largo Bay Beach Resort. ✉ *MM 103.8 BS, 103800 Overseas Hwy.* 🕾 *305/453–0000.*

Caribbean Club. Walls plastered with Bogart memorabilia remind customers that the classic 1948 Bogart–Bacall flick *Key Largo* has a connection with this club. It draws boaters, curious visitors, and local barfly types, all of whom happily mingle and shoot pool. Postcard-perfect sunsets and live music draw revelers on weekends. No food is served. ✉ *MM 104 BS, 10404 Overseas Hwy.* 🕾 *305/451–4466.*

SHOPPING

For the most part, shopping is sporadic in Key Largo, with a couple of shopping centers and fewer galleries than you find on the other big islands. If you're looking to buy scuba or snorkeling equipment, you'll have plenty of places from which to choose.

Bluewater Potters. Bluewater Potters creates functional and decorative pieces ranging from signature vases and kitchenware to one-of-a-kind pieces where the owners' creative talent at the wheel blazes. In addition to their main gallery location in Key Largo, find them in the new Morada Way Arts and Culture District in Islamorada at MM 81.5. ✉ *MM 102.9 OS, 102991 Overseas Hwy.* 🕾 *305/453–1920* ⊕ *www. bluewaterpotters.com.*

Randy's Florida Keys Gift Co. Since 1989, Randy's has been "the" place for unique gifts. Owner Randy and his wife Lisa aren't only fantastic at stocking the store with a plethora of items, they're well respected in the community for their generosity and dedication. Stop in and say hello then browse the tight aisles and loaded shelves filled with key lime candles, books, wood carvings, jewelry, clothing, T-shirts, and eclectic, tropical decor items. This friendly shop prides itself on carrying wares from local craftsmen and there's something for every budget. At press time, Randy's was planning to move to a new, yet-to-be-determined Key Largo location in late 2013. Call ahead for new address details. ✉ *1102421 Overseas Hwy* ✛ *Right on U.S. 1, next to Sandal Factory Outlet* 🕾 *305/453–9229* ⊕ *www.keysmermaid.com.*

SPORTS AND THE OUTDOORS

BOATING

Everglades Eco-Tours. Captain Sterling operates Everglades and Florida Bay ecology tours ($50 per person) and sunset cruises ($75 per person). You can see dolphins, manatees, and birds from the casual comfort of his pontoon boat, equipped with PVC chairs. Bring your own food and drinks. ✉ *MM 104 BS, Sundowners Restaurant, 103900 Overseas Hwy.* 🕾 *305/853–5161, 888/224–6044* ⊕ *www.captainsterling.com.*

M.V. *Key Largo Princess.* Two-hour glass-bottom-boat trips and sunset cruises on a luxury 70-foot motor yacht with a 280-square-foot glass viewing area (each $30) depart from the Holiday Inn docks three times a day. ⊠ *MM 100 OS, 99701 Overseas Hwy.* ☎ *305/451–4655, 877/648–8129* ⊕ *www.keylargoprincess.com.*

CANOEING AND KAYAKING

Sea kayaking continues to gain popularity in the Keys. You can paddle for a few hours or the whole day, on your own or with a guide. Some outfitters even offer overnight trips. The **Florida Keys Overseas Paddling Trail,** part of a statewide system, runs from Key Largo to Key West. You can paddle the entire distance, 110 miles on the Atlantic side, which takes 9–10 days. The trail also runs the chain's length on the bay side, which is a longer route.

Coral Reef Park Co. At John Pennekamp Coral Reef State Park, this operator has a fleet of canoes and kayaks for gliding around the 2½-mile mangrove trail or along the coast. It also rents powerboats. ⊠ *MM 102.5 OS, 102601 Overseas Hwy.* ☎ *305/451–6300* ⊕ *www.pennekamppark.com.*

Florida Bay Outfitters. Rent canoes or sea kayaks from this company, which sets up self-guided trips on the Florida Keys Overseas Paddling Trail, helps with trip planning, and matches equipment to your skill level. It also runs myriad guided tours around Key Largo. Take a full-moon paddle or a one- to seven-day canoe or kayak tour to the Everglades, Lignumvitae Key, or Indian Key. Trips start at $60 for a three hours. ⊠ *MM 104 BS, 104050 Overseas Hwy.* ☎ *305/451–3018* ⊕ *www.kayakfloridakeys.com.*

FISHING

Private charters and big head boats (so named because they charge "by the head") are great for anglers who don't have their own vessel.

Sailors Choice. Fishing excursions depart twice daily ($40 cash for half-day trips). The 65-foot boat leaves from the Holiday Inn docks. Rods, bait, and license are included. ⊠ *MM 100 OS, Holiday Inn Resort & Marina, 99701 Overseas Hwy.* ☎ *305/451–1802, 305/451–0041* ⊕ *www.sailorschoicefishingboat.com.*

SCUBA DIVING AND SNORKELING

Much of what makes the Upper Keys a singular dive destination is variety. Places like Molasses Reef, which begins 3 feet below the surface and descends to 55 feet, have something for everyone, from novice snorkelers to experienced divers. The *Spiegel Grove*, a 510-foot vessel, lies in 130 feet of water, but its upper regions are only 60 feet below the surface. On rough days, Key Largo Undersea Park's Emerald Lagoon is a popular spot. Expect to pay about $80 for a two-tank, two-site-dive trip with tanks and weights, or $35–$40 for a two-site-snorkel outing. Get big discounts by booking multiple trips.

Amy Slate's Amoray Dive Resort. This outfit makes diving easy. Stroll down to the full-service dive shop (NAUI, PADI, TDI, and BSAC certified), then onto a 45-foot catamaran. The rate for a two-dive trip is $85. ✉ *MM 104.2 BS, 104250 Overseas Hwy.* ☎ *305/451–3595, 800/426–6729* ⊕ *www.amoray.com.*

Conch Republic Divers. Book diving instruction as well as scuba and snorkeling tours of all the wrecks and reefs of the Upper Keys. Two-location dives are $85 with tank and weights or $65 without the equipment. ✉ *MM 90.8 BS, 90800 Overseas Hwy.* ☎ *305/852–1655, 800/274–3483* ⊕ *www.conchrepublicdivers.com.*

Coral Reef Park Co. At John Pennekamp Coral Reef State Park, this company gives 3½-hour scuba ($55) and 2½-hour snorkeling ($30) tours of the park. In addition to the great location and the dependability it's also suited for water adventurers of all levels. ✉ *MM 102.5 OS, 102601 Overseas Hwy.* ☎ *305/451–6300* ⊕ *www.pennekamppark.com.*

Ocean Divers. The PADI five-star facility offers day and night dives, a range of courses, and dive-lodging packages. The cost is $85 for a two-tank reef dive with tank and weight rental. Snorkel trips cost $35 with equipment. ✉ *MM 100 OS, 522 Caribbean Dr.* ☎ *305/451–1113, 800/451–1113* ⊕ *www.oceandivers.com.*

Quiescence Diving Services. This operator sets itself apart in two ways: it limits groups to six to ensure personal attention and offers day and night dives, as well as twilight dives when sea creatures are most active. Two-dive day trips are $85; twilight/night dives are $75. ✉ *MM 103.5 BS, 103680 Overseas Hwy.* ☎ *305/451–2440* ⊕ *www.quiescence.com.*

ISLAMORADA

Islamorada is between mile markers 90.5 and 70.

Early settlers named this key after their schooner, *Island Home,* but to make it sound more romantic they translated it into Spanish: *Isla Morada.* The chamber of commerce prefers to use its literal translation "Purple Island," which refers either to a purple-shelled snail that once inhabited these shores or to the brilliantly colored orchids and bougainvilleas.

Early maps show Islamorada as encompassing only Upper Matecumbe Key. But the incorporated "Village of Islands" is made up of a string of islands that the Overseas Highway crosses, including Plantation Key, Windley Key, Upper Matecumbe Key, Lower Matecumbe Key, Craig Key, and Fiesta Key. In addition, two state-park islands accessible only by boat—Indian Key and Lignumvitae Key—belong to the group.

Islamorada (locals pronounce it *eye*-la-mor-*ah*-da) is one of the world's top fishing destinations. For nearly 100 years, seasoned anglers have fished these clear, warm waters teeming with trophy-worthy fish. There are numerous options for those in search of the big ones, including chartering a boat with its own crew or heading out on a vessel rented from one of the plethora of marinas along this 20-mile stretch of the Overseas Highway. Islamorada is one of the more affluent resort areas of the Keys. Sophisticated resorts and restaurants meet the needs of those in search of luxury, but there's also plenty for those looking for something

Islamorada's warm waters attract large fish and the anglers and charter captains who want to catch them.

more casual and affordable. Art galleries and boutiques make Islamorada's shopping scene the best in the Upper Keys, but if you're shopping for groceries, head to Marathon or Key Largo.

ESSENTIALS

Visitor Information Islamorada Chamber of Commerce & Visitors Center
⊠ *MM 83.2 BS, 83224 Overseas Hwy., Upper Matecumbe Key* ☎ *305/664–4503, 800/322–5397* ⊕ *www.islamoradachamber.com.*

EXPLORING

History of Diving Museum. Adding to the region's reputation for world-class diving, this museum plunges into the history of man's thirst for undersea exploration. Among its 13 galleries of interactive and other interesting displays are a submarine and helmet re-created from the film *20,000 Leagues Under the Sea*. Vintage U.S. Navy equipment, diving helmets from around the world, and early scuba gear explore 4,000 years of diving history. For the grand finale, spend $4 for a mouthpiece and sing your favorite tune at the helium bar. ⊠ *MM 83 BS, 82990 Overseas Hwy., Upper Matecumbe Key* ☎ *305/664–9737* ⊕ *www.divingmuseum.org* 🖃 *$12* ☉ *Daily 10–5.*

Islamorada Founder's Park. This public park is the gem of Islamorada and boasts a palm-shaded beach, swimming pool, marina, skate park, tennis, and plenty of other facilities. If you want to rent a boat or learn to sail, businesses here can help you. If you're staying in Islamorada, admission is free. Those staying elsewhere pay $8 to enter the park. Either way, you pay an additional $3 to use the Olympic-size pool. A spiffy amphitheater hosts concerts, plays, and shows. The shallow water beach is ideal for swimming and families with little ones. Showers and bathrooms are beachside. ⊠ *MM 87 BS, 87000 Overseas Hwy., Planta-tion Key* ☎ *305/853–1685.*

FAMILY **Robbie's Marina.** Huge, prehistoric-looking denizens of the not-so-deep, silver-sided tarpon congregate around the docks at this marina on Lower Matecumbe Key. Children—and lots of adults—pay $3 for a bucket of sardines to feed them and $1 each for dock admission. Spend some time hanging out at this authentic Keys community, where you can grab a bite to eat indoors or out, shop at a slew of artisans' booths, or charter a boat, kayak, or other water craft. ⊠ *MM 77.5 BS, 77522 Overseas Hwy., Lower Matecumbe Key* ☎ *305/664–9814, 877/664–8498* ⊕ *www.robbies.com* 🖳 *Dock access $1* ⊙ *Daily sunrise–sunset.*

FAMILY **Theater of the Sea.** The second-oldest marine-mammal center in the world doesn't attempt to compete with more modern, more expensive parks. Even so, it's among the better attractions north of Key West, especially if you have kids in tow. In addition to marine life exhibits and shows, you can make reservations for up-close-and-personal encounters like a swim with a dolphin or sea lion, or stingray and turtle feedings ($55–$185, which includes general admission; reservations required). These are popular, so reserve in advance. Ride a "bottomless" boat to see what's below the waves and take a guided tour of the marine-life exhibits. Nonstop animal shows highlight conservation issues. You can stop for lunch at the grill, shop in the extensive gift shop, or sunbathe and swim at their private beach. This easily could be an all-day attraction. ⊠ *MM 84.5 OS, 84721 Overseas Hwy., Windley Key* ☎ *305/664–2431* ⊕ *www. theaterofthesea.com* 🖳 *$29.95* ⊙ *Daily 9:30–5 (last ticket sold at 3:30).*

Upper Matecumbe Key. This was one of the first of the Upper Keys to be permanently settled. Early homesteaders were so successful at grow-ing pineapples in the rocky soil that at one time the island yielded the country's largest annual crop. However, foreign competition and the hurricane of 1935 killed the industry. Today, life centers on fishing and tourism, and the island is filled with bait shops, marinas, and charter-fishing boats. ⊠ *MM 84–79.*

OFF THE
BEATEN
PATH

Indian Key Historic State Park. Mystery surrounds 10-acre Indian Key, on the ocean side of the Matecumbe islands. Before it became one of the first European settlements outside of Key West, it was inhabited by American Indians for several thousand years. The islet served as a base for 19th-century shipwreck salvagers until an Indian attack wiped out the settlement in 1840. Dr. Henry Perrine, a noted botanist, was killed in the raid. Today his plants grow in the town's ruins. Most people kayak or canoe here from Indian Key Fill or Robbie's Marina (about 20 minutes away by paddle) to tour the nature trails and the town ruins or to snorkel. There are no restrooms or picnic facilities on Indian Key. ☎ *305/664–2540 park* ⊕ *www.floridastateparks.org/ indiankey* 🖳 *Free* ⊙ *Daily 8–5.*

OFF THE
BEATEN
PATH

Lignumvitae Key Botanical State Park. On the National Register of Historic Places, this 280-acre bay-side island is the site of a virgin hardwood forest and the 1919 home of chemical magnate William Matheson. His caretaker's cottage serves as the park's visitor center. Access is by boat—your own, a rented vessel, or a tour operated from Robbie's

Marina. The tour leaves at 8:30 am Friday through Sunday and takes in both Lignumvitae and Indian keys (reservations required). Paddling here from Indian Key Fill, at MM 78.5, is a popular pastime. The only way to do the trails is by a guided ranger walk, offered at 10 am and 2 pm Friday to Sunday. Wear long sleeves and pants, and bring mosquito repellent. On the first Saturday in December is the Lignumvitae Christmas Celebration, when the historic home is decorated 1930s-style. ☎ *305/664–2540 park, 305/664–8070 boat tours* 🌐 *www.floridastateparks.org/lignumvitaekey* 🎫 *$1 for ranger tours; $35 for boat tours* 🕒 *Park Thurs.–Mon. 8–5; house tours Fri.–Sun at 10 and 2.*

Windley Key Fossil Reef Geological State Park. The fossilized-coral reef, dating back about 125,000 years, demonstrates that the Florida Keys were once beneath the ocean. Excavation of Windley Key's limestone bed by the Florida East Coast Railway exposed the petrified reef, full of beautifully fossilized brain coral and sea ferns. Visitors can see the fossils along a 300-foot quarry wall when hiking the park's three trails. There are guided (Friday, Saturday, and Sunday only) and self-guided tours along the trails, which lead to the railway's old quarrying equipment and cutting pits, where you can make rubbings of the quarry walls. The **Alison Fahrer Environmental Education Center** holds historic, biological, and geological displays about the area, including videos. The first Saturday in March is Windley Key Day, when the park sells native plants and hosts environmental exhibits. ✉ *MM 84.9 BS, Windley Key* ☎ *305/664–2540* 🌐 *www.floridastateparks.org/windleykey* 🎫 *Education center free, $2.50 for park self-tours, $1 for ranger-guided tours* 🕒 *Education center Fri.–Sun. 9–5 (tours at 10 and 2).*

BEACHES

Anne's Beach Park. On Lower Matecumbe Key this popular village park is named for a local environmental activist. Its "beach" (really a typical Keys-style sand flat) is best enjoyed at low tide. The nicest feature here is an elevated, wooden half-mile boardwalk that meanders through a natural wetland hammock. Covered picnic areas along the way give you places to linger and enjoy the view. Restrooms are at the north end. Weekends are packed with Miami day-trippers as it's the only public beach until you reach Marathon. **Amenities:** parking (no fee); toilets. **Best for:** partiers; snorkeling; swimming; windsurfing. ✉ *MM 73.5 OS, Lower Matecumbe Key* ☎ *305/853–1685.*

WHERE TO EAT

$$$ SEAFOOD

🍴 **Green Turtle Inn.** This circa-1928 landmark inn and its vintage neon sign is a slice of Florida Keys history. Period photographs decorate the wood-paneled walls. Breakfast and lunch options include surprises like coconut French toast made with Cuban bread, and a yellowtail po' boy. Executive Chef Billy McCrossin lends a "Floribbean" flair to the menu with a healthy dose of new American cuisine: think turtle chowder (don't gasp; it's made from farm-raised freshwater turtles), drunken scallops, and a chipotle skirt steak. For dessert, the seventh generation pound cake gets a standing ovation. [$] *Average main: $24* ✉ *MM 81.2 OS, 81219 Overseas Hwy., Upper Matecumbe Key* ☎ *305/664–2006* 🌐 *www.greenturtlekeys.com* ✍ *Reservations essential* 🕒 *Closed Mon.*

$ SEAFOOD FAMILY 🍴 **Islamorada Fish Company.** When a restaurant is owned by Bass Pro Shops, you know the seafood is as fresh as you can get it. The fun begins in the parking lot with painted white fish marking the parking spaces. The restaurant is housed in an open-air, oversized tiki hut right on Florida Bay, making this the quintessential Keys experience. There's a small, low-key tiki bar area if you prefer a stool to a table. Menu highlights include cracked conch beaten 'til tender and fried crispy, and Grouper Portofino, which will keep you coming back for more. Each afternoon, the staff feed the fish in the bay. Jump out of your seat and walk over for a close-up view of snapper, large tarpon, and even sharks. [$] *Average main: $15* ✉ *MM 81.5 BS, 81532 Overseas Hwy., Windley Key* ☎ *305/664–9271* 🌐 *restaurants.basspro.com/fishcompany/Islamorada/* 🕒 *Daily 11–10.*

4

$ SEAFOOD 🍴 **Island Grill.** Don't be fooled by appearances; this shack on the waterfront takes island breakfast, lunch, and dinner up a notch. The eclectic menu tempts you with such dishes as its famed "original tuna nachos," lobster rolls, and a nice selection of seafood and sandwiches. Southern-style shrimp and andouille sausage with grits join island-style specialties such as grilled ribs with guava barbecue sauce on the list of entrées. There's an air-conditioned dining room and bar as well as open seating under a vaulted porch ceiling. The outdoor bar hosts live entertainment Wednesday to Sunday. [$] *Average main: $12* ✉ *MM 85.5 OS, 85501 Overseas Hwy., Windley Key* ☎ *305/664–8400* 🌐 *www.keysislandgrill.com* ✍ *Reservations not accepted.*

$$$ SEAFOOD 🍴 **Marker 88.** A few yards from Florida Bay, this seafood restaurant has been popular since the late '60s. Large picture windows offer great sunset views, but the bay is lovely no matter what time of day you visit. Chef Bobby Stoky serves such irresistible entrées as onion-crusted mahi-mahi, crispy yellowtail snapper, and mangrove-honey-and-chipotle–glazed rib eye. In addition, there are a half-dozen burgers and sandwiches, and you can't miss the restaurant's famous key lime baked Alaska dessert. The extensive wine list is an oenophile's delight. [$] *Average main: $28* ✉ *MM 88 BS, 88000 Overseas Hwy., Plantation Key* ☎ *305/852–9315* 🌐 *www.marker88.info* ✍ *Reservations essential.*

$$$ ECLECTIC FAMILY 🍴 **Morada Bay Beach Café.** This bayfront restaurant wins high marks for its surprisingly stellar cuisine, tables planted in the sand, and tiki torches that bathe the evening in romance. Entrées feature alluring combinations like fresh fish of the day sautéed with Meyer lemon butter and whole fried snapper with coconut rice. Seafood takes center stage, but you can always get roasted organic chicken or prime rib. Tapas and raw bar menus cater to smaller appetites or those who can't decide with offerings like fried calamari, conch fritters, and Wagyu beef sliders. Lunch adds interesting sandwiches to the mix, plus there's breakfast Friday through Sunday. Sit in a dining room outfitted with surfboards, or outdoors on a beach, where the sunset puts on a mighty show and kids (and your feet) play in the sand. [$] *Average main: $27* ✉ *MM 81 BS, 81600 Overseas Hwy., Upper Matecumbe Key* ☎ *305/664–0604* 🌐 *www.moradabay-restaurant.com* 🕒 *Closed Tues. No breakfast Mon.–Thurs.*

$$$$ ✕**Pierre's.** One of the Keys' most elegant restaurants, Pierre's marries
FRENCH colonial style with modern food trends. Full of interesting architec-
Fodor'sChoice tural artifacts, the place oozes style, especially the wicker chair–strewn
★ veranda overlooking the bay. Save your best "tropical chic" duds for
dinner here, so you don't stand out from your surroundings. The food,
drawn from French and Floridian influences, is multilayered and beautifully presented. Among the seasonally changing appetizer choices,
you might find smoked hogfish chowder and foie gras sliders with a
butternut squash milk shake. A changing list of entrées might include
hogfish meunière and scallops with pork belly tortellini. The downstairs
bar is a perfect spot for catching sunsets, sipping martinis, and enjoying
light eats. $ *Average main: $35* ✉ *MM 81.5 BS, 81600 Overseas Hwy.,
Upper Matecumbe Key* ☎ *305/664–3225* ⊕ *www.pierres-restaurant.
com* ⌕ *Reservations essential* ☾ *No lunch.*

$$$ ✕**Uncle's Restaurant.** Former fishing guide Joe LePree adds Italian flair to
ITALIAN standard seafood dishes. Here you can have your seafood almandine,
Milanese (breaded and fried), LePree (with artichokes, mushrooms, and
lemon-butter wine sauce), or any of five other preparations. For start-
ers, feast on mussels or littleneck clams in a marinara or garlic sauce.
Specials sometimes combine game (bison, caribou, or elk) with seafood.
Portions are huge, so share dishes or take home a doggie bag. Alterna-
tively arrive early (between 5 and 7) for the lighter menu, priced $12.95
to $17.95. Weather permitting, sit outdoors in the garden; poor acous-
tics make dining indoors unusually noisy. $ *Average main: $21* ✉ *MM
81 OS, 80939 Overseas Hwy., Upper Matecumbe Key* ☎ *305/664–4402*
⊕ *www.unclesrestaurant.com* ☾ *Closed Mon.*

WHERE TO STAY

For expanded reviews, facilities, and current deals, visit Fodors.com.

$$$$ ▦**Casa Morada.** This relic from the 1950s has been restyled into a suave,
B&B/INN design-forward, all-suites property with outdoor showers and Jacuzzis
Fodor'sChoice in some of the suites. **Pros:** cool design; complimentary snacks and
★ bottled water; complimentary use of bikes, kayaks, and snorkel gear.
Cons: trailer park across the street; beach is small and inconsequential.
$ *Rooms from: $299* ✉ *MM 82 BS, 136 Madeira Rd., Upper Mate-
cumbe Key* ☎ *305/664–0044, 888/881–3030* ⊕ *www.casamorada.com*
⌕ *16 suites* ◉*Breakfast.*

$$$$ ▦**Cheeca Lodge & Spa.** In the main lodge, West Indian–style rooms boast
RESORT luxurious touches like elegant balcony tubs that fill from the ceiling.
Pros: beautifully landscaped grounds; new designer rooms; dive shop
on property. **Cons:** expensive rates; $39 resort fee for activities; busy.
$ *Rooms from: $299* ✉ *MM 82 OS, Box 527, Upper Matecumbe Key*
☎ *305/664–4651, 800/327–2888* ⊕ *www.cheeca.com* ⌕ *60 1-bedroom
suites, 64 junior suites* ◉*No meals.*

$$ ▦**Drop Anchor Resort and Marina.** It's easy to find your unit here, as
HOTEL they are painted in an array of Crayola colors. **Pros:** bright and color-
ful; attention to detail; laid-back charm. **Cons:** noise from the highway; beach is better for fishing than swimming. $ *Rooms from: $129*
✉ *MM 85 OS, 84959 Overseas Hwy., Windley Key* ☎ *305/664–4863,
888/664–4863* ⊕ *www.dropanchorresort.com* ⌕ *18 suites* ◉*No meals.*

$$$$ HOTEL Fodor's Choice ★ **The Moorings Village.** This tropical retreat is everything you imagine when you think of the Keys—from hammocks swaying between towering trees to sugar-white sand (arguably the Keys' best resort beach) lapped by aqua-green waves. **Pros:** romantic setting; good dining options with room-charging privileges; beautiful beach. **Cons:** no room service; extra fee for housekeeping; daily resort fee for activities. [$] *Rooms from: $375* ✉ *MM 81.6 OS, 123 Beach Rd., Upper Matecumbe Key* ☎ *305/664–4708* 🌐 *www.themooringsvillage.com* 🛏 *6 cottages, 12 houses* 🍴 *No meals.*

$$$$ HOTEL Fodor's Choice ★ **Ocean House.** Islamorada's newest adult boutique hotel is situated right on the Atlantic, yet it's hidden from passersby amid lush gardens. **Pros:** complimentary use of paddle boards, snorkel equipment, and bicycles; luxurious facilities and amenities. **Cons:** limited number of units means they're often booked solid; luxury comes at a price. [$] *Rooms from: $299* ✉ *MM 82 OS, 82885 Old Hwy., Windley Key* ☎ *866/540–5520* 🌐 *www.oceanhousefloridakeys.com* 🛏 *8 suites* 🍴 *Some meals.*

$$$ RESORT **Postcard Inn Beach Resort & Marina at Holiday Isle.** After an $11-million renovation that encompassed updating everything from the rooms to the public spaces, this iconic property (formerly known as the Holiday Isle Beach Resort) has found new life. **Pros:** large private beach; heated pools; on-site restaurants including Shula Burger. **Cons:** rooms near Tiki bar are noisy; minimum stay required during peak times. [$] *Rooms from: $215* ✉ *MM 84 OS, 84001 Overseas Hwy., Plantation Key* ☎ *305/664–2321* 🌐 *www.holidayisle.com/Islamorada-beachclub* 🛏 *143 rooms.*

$ HOTEL **Ragged Edge Resort.** Tucked away in a residential area at the ocean's edge, this hotel is big on value but short on style. **Pros:** oceanfront location; boat docks and ramp; cheap rates. **Cons:** dated decor; off the beaten path. [$] *Rooms from: $100* ✉ *MM 86.5 OS, 243 Treasure Harbor Rd., Plantation Key* ☎ *305/852–5389, 800/436–2023* 🌐 *www.ragged-edge.com* 🛏 *6 studios, 1 efficiency, 3 2-bedroom suites* 🍴 *No meals.*

NIGHTLIFE

Islamorada isn't known for its raging nightlife, but for local fun Lorelei's is legendary. Others cater to the town's sophisticated clientele and fishing fervor.

Lorelei Restaurant & Cabana Bar. Behind a larger-than-life mermaid, this is the kind of place you fantasize about during those long cold winters up north. It's all about good drinks, tasty pub grub, and beautiful sunsets set to live bands playing island tunes and light rock nightly. ✉ *MM 82 BS, 81924 Overseas Hwy., Upper Matecumbe Key* ☎ *305/664–2692* 🌐 *www.loreleicabanabar.com.*

SHOPPING

Art galleries, upscale gift shops, and the mammoth World Wide Sportsman (if you want to look the part of a local fisherman, you must wear a shirt from here) make up the variety and superior style of Islamorada shopping.

Banyan Tree. A sharp-eyed husband-and-wife team successfully combines antiques and contemporary gifts for the home and garden with plants, pots, and trellises in a stylishly sophisticated indoor–outdoor setting. ⊠ *MM 81.2 OS, 81197 Overseas Hwy., Upper Matecumbe Key* ☎ *305/664–3433* ⊕ *www.banyantreegarden.com.*

Gallery Morada. The go-to destination for one-of-a-kind gifts beautifully displays blown-glass objects, original sculptures, paintings, lithographs, and jewelry by 200 artists. ⊠ *MM 81.6 OS, 81611 Old Hwy., Upper Matecumbe Key* ☎ *305/664–3650* ⊕ *www.gallerymorada.com.*

Rain Barrel Artisan Village. This is a natural and unhurried shopping showplace. Set in a tropical garden of shady trees, native shrubs, and orchids, the crafts village has shops with works by local and national artists and resident artists in studios. The Main Gallery up front showcases the craftsmanship of the resident artisans, who create marine-inspired artwork while you watch. Have your photo taken with "Betsy" the giant Florida lobster roadside. ⊠ *MM 86.7 BS, 86700 Overseas Hwy., Plantation Key* ☎ *305/852–3084* ⊕ *www.seefloridaonline.com/ rainbarrel/index.html.*

Redbone Gallery. One of the largest sportfishing–art galleries in Florida stocks hand-stitched clothing and giftware, in addition to work by wood and bronze sculptors such as Kendall van Sant; watercolorist C.D. Clarke; and painters Daniel Caldwell, David Hall, Steven Left, and Stacie Krupa. Proceeds benefit cystic fibrosis research. ⊠ *MM 81.5 OS, 200 Industrial Dr., Upper Matecumbe Key* ☎ *305/664–2002* ⊕ *www.redbone.org.*

World Wide Sportsman. This two-level retail center sells upscale and everyday fishing equipment, resort clothing, sportfishing art, and other gifts. When you're tired of shopping, relax at the Zane Grey Long Key Lounge, located above the store—but not before you step up and into *Pillar*, a replica of Hemingway's boat. ⊠ *MM 81.5 BS, 81576 Overseas Hwy., Upper Matecumbe Key* ☎ *305/664–4615, 800/327–2880.*

SPORTS AND THE OUTDOORS

BOATING

Marinas pop up every mile or so in the Islamorada area, so finding a rental or tour is no problem. Robbie's Marina is a prime example of a salty spot where you can find it all—from fishing charters and kayaking rentals to lunch and tarpon feeding.

Bump & Jump. Fishing and deck boats rentals (from 15 to 29 feet) are $165 to $495 per day, and weekly rates go from $745 to $2,490. ⊠ *MM 81.2 OS, 81197 Overseas Hwy., Upper Matecumbe Key* ☎ *305/664–9404, 877/453–9463* ⊕ *www.keysboatrental.com.*

Houseboat Vacations of the Florida Keys. See the islands from the comfort of your own boat (captain's cap optional). The company maintains a fleet of 42- to 55-foot boats that accommodate up to 10 people and come outfitted with everything you need besides food. (You may provision yourself at a nearby grocery store.) The three-day minimum starts at $1,112; one week costs $1,950 and up. Kayaks, canoes, and skiffs suitable for the ocean are also available. ⊠ *MM 85.9 BS, 85944 Overseas Hwy., Plantation Key* ☎ *305/664–4009* ⊕ *www.floridakeys. com/houseboats.*

Robbie's Boat Rentals & Charters. This full-service company will even give you a crash course on how not to crash your boat. The rental fleet includes an 18-foot skiff with a 60-horsepower outboard for $150 for four hours and $200 for the day to a 23-foot deck boat with a 130-horsepower engine for $185 for a half day and $235 for eight hours. Robbie's also rents fishing and snorkeling gear (there's good snorkeling nearby) and sells bait, drinks and snacks, and gas. Want to hire a guide who knows the local waters and where the fish lurk? Robbie's offers offshore-fishing trips, patch-reef trips, and party-boat fishing. Backcountry flats trips are a specialty. ✉ *MM 77.5 BS, 77522 Overseas Hwy., Lower Matecumbe Key* ☎ *305/664–9814, 877/664–8498* ⊕ *www.robbies.com.*

Treasure Harbor Marine. Captains Pam and Pete Anderson provide everything you'll need for a bareboat sailing vacation at sea. They also give excellent advice on where to find the best anchorages, snorkeling spots, or lobstering sites. Vessels range from a 19-foot Cape Dory to a 41-foot Morgan Out Island. Rates start at $125 a day; $500 a week. Captained sails are $550 a day, $3,250 a week aboard the 41-footer. Marina facilities are basic—water, electric, ice machine, laundry, picnic tables, and restrooms with showers. A store sells snacks, beverages, and sundries. ✉ *MM 86.5 OS, 200 Treasure Harbor Dr., Plantation Key* ☎ *305/852–2458, 800/352–2628* ⊕ *www.treasureharbor.com.*

FISHING

Here in the self-proclaimed "sportfishing capital of the world," sailfish is the prime catch in the winter and dolphinfish (mahimahi) in the summer. Buchanan Bank just south of Islamorada is a good spot to try for tarpon in the spring. Blackfin tuna and amberjack are generally plentiful in the area, too. ▮TIP→ The Hump at Islamorada ranks highest among anglers' favorite fishing spots in Florida because of the incredible offshore marine life.

Captain Ted Wilson. Go into the backcountry for bonefish, tarpon, redfish, snook, and shark aboard a 17-foot boat that accommodates up to three anglers. For two people, half-day trips run $400, full-day trips $575, two-hour sunset bonefishing $250, and evening excursions $400. There's a $100 charge for an extra person. ✉ *MM 79.9 OS, 79851 Overseas Hwy., Upper Matecumbe Key* ☎ *305/942–5224, 305/664–9463* ⊕ *www.captaintedwilson.com.*

Florida Keys Fly Fish. Like other top fly-fishing and light-tackle guides, Captain Geoff Colmes helps his clients land trophy fish in the waters around the Keys ($450–$550). ✉ *105 Palm La., Upper Matecumbe Key* ☎ *305/853–0741* ⊕ *www.floridakeysflyfish.com.*

Florida Keys Outfitters. Long before fly-fishing became popular, Sandy Moret was fishing the Keys for bonefish, tarpon, and redfish. Now he attracts anglers from around the world on a quest for the big catch. Weekend fly-fishing classes, which include classroom instruction, equipment, and daily lunch, cost $695. Add $1,070 for two additional days of fishing. Guided fishing trips cost $450 for a half day, $600 for a full day. Packages combining fishing and accommodations at Islander Resort are available. ✉ *MM 81.2, Green Turtle, 81219 Overseas Hwy., Upper Matecumbe Key* ☎ *305/664–5423* ⊕ *www.floridakeysoutfitters.com.*

Kayak ready to be used on the beach in the Florida Keys

Hubba Hubba Charters. Captain Ken Knudsen has fished the Keys waters for more than 40 years. A licensed backcountry guide, he's ranked among Florida's top 10 by national fishing magazines. He offers four-hour sunset trips for tarpon ($450) and two-hour sunset trips for bone-fish ($200), as well as half- ($425) and full-day ($600) outings. Prices are for one or two anglers, and tackle and bait are included. ⊠ *MM 79.8 OS, Upper Matecumbe Key* ☎ *305/664–9281.*

Miss Islamorada. This 65-foot party boat has full-day trips for $65. Bring your lunch or buy one from the dockside deli. ⊠ *Bud n' Mary's Marina, MM 79.8 OS, 79851 Overseas Hwy., Upper Matecumbe Key* ☎ *305/664–2461, 800/742–7945* ⊕ *www.budnmarys.com.*

SCUBA DIVING AND SNORKELING

San Pedro Underwater Archaeological Preserve State Park. About 1¼ nautical miles south of Indian Key is the San Pedro Underwater Archaeological Preserve State Park, which includes the remains of a Spanish treasure-fleet ship that sank in 1733. The state of Florida protects the site for divers; no spearfishing or souvenir collecting is allowed. Seven replica cannons and a plaque enhance what basically amounts to a 90-foot-long pile of ballast stones. Resting in only 18 feet of water, its ruins are visible to snorkelers as well as divers and attract a colorful array of fish. ⊠ *MM 85.5 OS* ☎ *305/664–2540* ⊕ *www.floridastateparks.org/sanpedro.*

Florida Keys Dive Center. Dive from John Pennekamp Coral Reef State Park to Alligator Light with this outfitter. The center has two 46-foot Coast Guard–approved dive boats, offers scuba training, and is one of the few Keys dive centers to offer Nitrox and Trimix (mixed gas) diving. Two-tank dives cost $65 with no equipment; two-location snorkeling is $38. ✉ *MM 90.5 OS, 90451 Overseas Hwy., Plantation Key* ☎ *305/852–4599, 800/433–8946* ⊕ *www.floridakeysdivectr.com.*

Holiday Isle Dive Shop. This one-stop dive shop has a resort, pool, restaurant, lessons, and twice-daily dive and snorkel trips. Rates start at $50 for a two-tank dive or one-tank night dive without equipment. Snorkel trips are $30. ✉ *MM 84 OS, 84001 Overseas Hwy., Windley Key* ☎ *305/664–3483, 800/327–7070* ⊕ *www.diveholidayisle.com.*

WATER SPORTS

The Kayak Shack. Rent kayaks for trips to Indian (about 20 minutes one-way) and Lignumvitae (about 45 minutes one-way) keys, two favorite destinations for paddlers. Kayak rental half-day rates (and you'll need plenty of time to explore those mangrove canopies) are $40 for a single kayak and $55 for a double. Pedal kayaks are available for $50 single and $65 double. The company also offers guided three-hour tours, including a snorkel trip to Indian Key ($45). It also rents stand-up paddleboards, at $50 for a half-day including lessons, and canoes. ✉ *MM 77.5 BS, Robbie's Marina, 77522 Overseas Hwy., Lower Matecumbe Key* ☎ *305/664–4878* ⊕ *www.kayakthefloridakeys.com*

EN ROUTE **Long Key Viaduct.** As you cross Long Key Channel, look beside you at the old viaduct. The second-longest bridge on the former rail line, this 2-mile-long structure has 222 reinforced-concrete arches. The old bridge is popular with cyclists and anglers, who fish off the sides day and night.

THE MIDDLE KEYS

Most of the activity in this part of the Florida Keys centers on the town of Marathon—the region's third-largest metropolitan area. On either end of it, smaller keys hold resorts, wildlife research and rehab facilities, a historic village, and a state park. The Middle Keys make a fitting transition from the Upper Keys to the Lower Keys not only geographically but mentally. Crossing Seven Mile Bridge prepares you for the slow pace and don't-give-a-damn attitude you'll find a little farther down the highway. Fishing is one of the main attractions—in fact, the region's commercial-fishing industry was founded here in the early 1800s. Diving is another popular pastime. There are many beaches and natural areas to enjoy in the Middle Keys, where mainland stress becomes an ever more distant memory.

If you get bridge fever—the heebie-jeebies when driving over long stretches of water—you may need a pair of blinders (or a couple of tranquilizers) before tackling the Middle Keys. Stretching from Conch Key to the far side of the Seven Mile Bridge, this zone is home to the region's two longest bridges: Long Key Viaduct and Seven Mile Bridge, both historic landmarks.

Overseas Highway takes you from one end of the region to the other in a direct line that takes in most of the sights, but you'll find some interesting resorts and restaurants off the main drag.

Continued on page 199

DID YOU KNOW?

The coral making up the Barrier Reef is living and provides an ecosystem for small marine creatures. Bumping against or touching the coral can kill these creatures as well as damage the reef itself.

UNDER THE SEA
SNORKELING AND DIVING
IN THE FLORIDA KEYS by Lynne Helm

Up on the shore they work all day...

While we devotin',

Full time to floatin',

Under the sea...

—"Under the Sea,"
from Disney's *Little Mermaid*

All Floridians—even those long-accustomed to balmy breezes and swaying palms—turn ecstatic at the mere thought of tripping off to the Florida Keys. Add the prospect of underwater adventure, and hot diggity, it's unparalleled bliss.

Perennially laid back, the Keys annually attract nearly 800,000 snorkeling and scuba diving aficionados, and why not? There's arguably no better destination to learn these sports that put you up close to the wonders of life under the sea.

THE BARRIER REEF
The continental United States' only living coral barrier reef stretches 5 mi offshore of the Keys and is a teeming backbone of marine life, ranging from brilliant corals to neon-colored fish from blue-striped grunts to green moray eels. This is the prime reason why the Keys are where you descend upon intricate natural coral formations and encrusted shipwrecks, some historic, others sunk by design to create artificial reefs that attract divers

and provide protection for marine life. Most diving sites have mooring buoys (nautical floats away from shore, sometimes marking specific sites); these let you tie up your boat so you don't need to drop anchor, which could damage the reef. Most of these sites also are near individual keys, where dozens of dive operators can cater to your needs.

Reef areas thrive in waters as shallow as 5 feet and as deep as 50 feet. Shallow reefs attract snorkelers, while deeper reefs suit divers of varying experience levels. The Keys' shallow diving offers two benefits: longer time safely spent on the bottom exploring, and more vibrant colors because of sunlight penetration. Most divers log maximum depths of 20 to 30 feet.

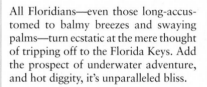

(left) Shallow-water coral reef, (top) Nine Foot Stake is a popular site for underwater photography.

WHERE TO SNORKEL AND DIVE

KEY WEST
Mile Marker 0–4

You can soak up a mesmerizing overview of submerged watery wonders at the **Florida Keys Eco-Discovery Center**, opened in 2007 on Key West's Truman

Nine Foot Stake

Annex waterfront. Both admission and parking are free at the 6,000 square–foot center (⌚ 9–4 Tues.–Sat. ☎ 305/809–4750); interactive exhibits here focus on Keys marine life and habitats. Key West's offshore reefs are best accessed via professional charters, but it's easy to snorkel from shore at **Key West Marine Park**. Marked by a lighthouse, **Sand Key Reef** attracts snorkelers and scuba divers. **Joe's Tug**, at 65-foot depths, sets up encounters with Goliath grouper. **Ten-Fathom Ledge**, with coral caves and

dramatic overhangs, shelters lobster. The **Cayman Salvor**, a buoy tender sunk as an artificial reef in 1985, shelters baitfish. Patch reef **Nine Foot Stake**, submerged 10 to 25 feet, has soft corals and juvenile marine life. **Kedge Ledge** features a pair of coral-encrusted anchors from 18th-century sailing vessels. 🚩 *Florida Keys main visitor line at* ☎ *800/FLA-KEYS (352-5397).*

BIG PINE KEY/LOWER KEYS
Mile Marker 4–47

Many devotees feel a Florida dive adventure would not be complete without heading 5 mi from Big Pine Key to **Looe Key National Marine Sanctuary**, an underwater preserve named for the HMS Looe running aground in 1744. If you time your visit for July, you might hit the one-day free underwater music festival for snorkelers

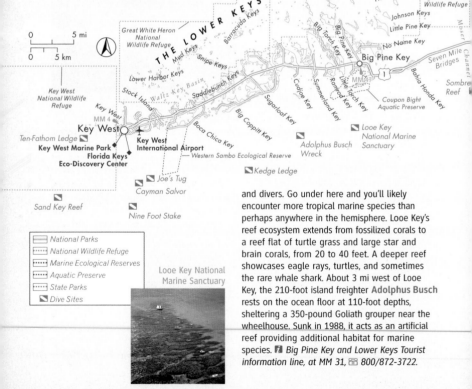

Looe Key National Marine Sanctuary

and divers. Go under here and you'll likely encounter more tropical marine species than perhaps anywhere in the hemisphere. Looe Key's reef ecosystem extends from fossilized corals to a reef flat of turtle grass and large star and brain corals, from 20 to 40 feet. A deeper reef showcases eagle rays, turtles, and sometimes the rare whale shark. About 3 mi west of Looe Key, the 210-foot island freighter **Adolphus Busch** rests on the ocean floor at 110-foot depths, sheltering a 350-pound Goliath grouper near the wheelhouse. Sunk in 1988, it acts as an artificial reef providing additional habitat for marine species. 🚩 *Big Pine Key and Lower Keys Tourist information line, at MM 31,* ☎ *800/872-3722.*

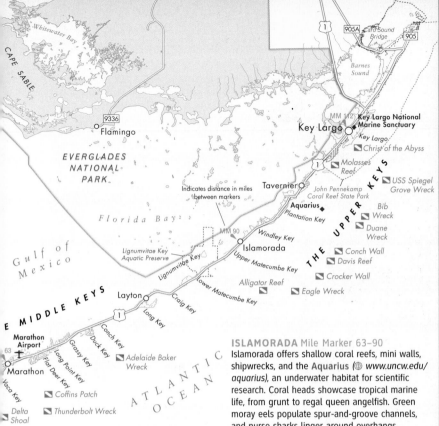

Whitewater Bay

CAPE SABLE

9336
Flamingo

EVERGLADES NATIONAL PARK

Florida Bay

Gulf of Mexico

Indicates distance in miles between markers

MM 90

Lignumvitae Key Aquatic Preserve

Lignumvitae Key

THE MIDDLE KEYS

Layton

Long Key

Craig Key

Conch Key

Duck Key

Marathon Airport

63

Marathon

Long Point Key

Grassy Key

Flat Deer Key

Vaca Key

Delta Shoal

ATLANTIC OCEAN

Adelaide Baker Wreck

Coffins Patch

Thunderbolt Wreck

905A Card Sound Bridge 905

Barnes Sound

MM 112 **Key Largo National Marine Sanctuary**
Key Largo

Key Largo

Christ of the Abyss

Molasses Reef

Tavernier

John Pennekamp Coral Reef State Park

USS Spiegel Grove Wreck

Aquarius
Plantation Key

Bib Wreck

Windley Key

Duane Wreck

Islamorada

Upper Matecumbe Key

Conch Wall

Davis Reef

Lower Matecumbe Key

Crocker Wall

Alligator Reef

Eagle Wreck

THE UPPER KEYS

4

IN FOCUS UNDER THE SEA

MARATHON/MIDDLE KEYS
Mile Marker 47–63

The Middle Keys yield a marine wilderness of a spur-and-groove coral and patch reefs. The **Adelaide Baker** historic shipwreck has a pair of stacks in 25 feet of water.

Sombrero Reef

Popular **Sombrero Reef**, with coral canyons and archways, is marked by a 140-foot lighted tower. Six distinct patch reefs known as **Coffin's Patch** have shallow elkhorn forests. **Delta Shoals**, a network of coral canyons fanning seaward from a sandy shoal, attracts divers to its elkhorn, brain, and star coral heads. Marathon's **Thunderbolt**, a 188-foot ship sunk in 1986, sits upright at 115-foot depths, coated with sponge, coral, and hydroid, and attracting angelfish, jacks, and deep-water pelagic creatures. 🚩 *Greater Marathon Chamber and visitors center at MM 53.5,* ☎ *800/262-7284.*

ISLAMORADA Mile Marker 63–90
Islamorada offers shallow coral reefs, mini walls, shipwrecks, and the **Aquarius** (🌐 *www.uncw.edu/ aquarius*), an underwater habitat for scientific research. Coral heads showcase tropical marine life, from grunt to regal queen angelfish. Green moray eels populate spur-and-groove channels, and nurse sharks linger around overhangs. Submerged attractions include the **Eagle**, a 287-foot ship in 110 feet of water; **Davis Reef**, with gorgonian coral; **Alligator Reef**, where the *USS Alligator* sank while fighting pirates; the sloping **Conch Wall**, with barrel sponges and gorgonian; and **Crocker Wall**, featuring spur-and-groove and block corals. 🚩 *Islamorada Chamber and visitor center at MM 83.2,* ☎ *800/322-5397.*

KEY LARGO Mile Marker 90–112
Key Largo marine conservation got a big leg up with creation of **John Pennekamp Coral Reef State Park** in 1960, the nation's first undersea preserve, followed by 1975's designation of the **Key Largo National Marine Sanctuary**. A popular underwater attraction is the bronze statue of **Christ of the Abyss** between coral formations. Explorers with a "lust for rust" can dive down to 60 to 90 feet and farther to see the murky cemetery for two twin 327-foot U.S. Coast Guard cutters, *Duane* and *Bibb*, used during World War II; *USS Spiegel Grove*, a 510-foot Navy transport ship sunk in 2002 to create an artificial reef; and **Molasses Reef**, showcasing coral heads. 🚩 *Key Largo Chamber at MM 106,* ☎ *800/822-1088.*

SCUBA DIVING

A diver explores the coral reef in the Florida Keys National Marine Sanctuary off Key Largo.

Florida offers wonderful opportunities to spend your vacation in the sun and become a certified diver at the same time. In the Keys, count on setting aside three to five days for entry-level or so-called "Open Water" certification offered by many dive shops. Basic certification (covering depths to about 60 feet) involves classroom work and pool training, followed by one or more open-water dives at the reef. After passing a knowledge test and completing the required water training (often starting in a pool), you become a certified recreational scuba diver, eligible to rent dive gear and book dive trips with most operations worldwide. Learning through video or online computer programs can enable you to complete classroom work at home, so you can more efficiently schedule time in the Keys for completing water skills and getting out to the reef for exploration.

Many would-be divers opt to take the classroom instruction and pool training at home at a local dive shop and then spend only two days in the Keys completing four dives. It's not necessarily cheaper, but it can be far more relaxing to commit to only two days of diving.

Questions you should ask: Not all dive shops are created equal, and it may be worthwhile to spend extra money for a better diving experience. Some of the larger dive shops take out large catamarans that can carry as many as 24 to 40 people. Many people prefer the intimacy of a smaller boat.

Good to know: Divers can become certified through PADI *(www.padi.com)*, NAUI *(www.naui.org)*, or SSI *(www.divessi.com)*. The requirements for all three are similar, and if you do the classroom instruction and pool training with a dive shop associated with one organization, the referral for the open water dives will be honored by most dive shops. Note that you are not allowed to fly for at least 24 hours after a dive, because residual nitrogen in the body can pose health risks upon decompression. While there are no rigid rules on diving after flying, make sure you're well-hydrated before hitting the water.

Cost: The four-day cost can range from $300 to $475, but be sure to ask if equipment, instruction manuals, and log books are extra. Some dive shops have relationships with hotels, so check for dive/stay packages. Referral dives (a collaborative effort among training agencies) run from $285 to $300 and discover scuba runs around $175 to $200.

SNUBA

Beyond snorkeling or the requirements of scuba, you also have the option of "Snuba." The word is a trademarked portmanteau or combo of snorkel and scuba. Marketed as easy-to-learn family fun, Snuba lets you breathe underwater via tubes from an air-supplied vessel above, with no prior diving or snorkel experience required.

NOT CERTIFIED?

Not sure if you want to commit the time and money to become certified? Not a problem. Most dive shops and many resorts will offer a discover scuba day-long course. In the morning, the instructor will teach you the basics of scuba diving: how to clear your mask, how to come to the surface in the unlikely event you lose your air supply, etc. In the afternoon, instructors will take you out for a dive in relatively shallow water—less than 30 feet. Be sure to ask where the dive will take place. Jumping into the water off a shallow beach may not be as fun as actually going out to the coral. If you decide that diving is something you want to pursue, the open dive may count toward your certification.

■**TIP→** You can often book the discover dives at the last minute. It may not be worth it to go out on a windy day when the currents are stronger. Also the underwater world looks a whole lot brighter on sunny days.

(top) Scuba divers; (bottom) Diver ascending line.

SNORKELING

Snorkling lets you see the wonders of the sea from a new perspective.

The basics: Sure, you can take a deep breath, hold your nose, squint your eyes, and stick your face in the water in an attempt to view submerged habitats . . . but why not protect your eyes, retain your ability to breathe, and keep your hands free to paddle about when exploring underwater? That's what snorkeling is all about.

Equipment needed: A mask, snorkel (the tube attached to the mask), and fins. In deeper waters (any depth over your head), life jackets are advised.

Steps to success: If you've never snorkeled before, it's natural to feel a bit awkward at first, so don't sweat it. Breathing through a mask and tube, and wearing a pair of fins take getting used to. Like any activity, you build confidence and comfort through practice.

If you're new to snorkeling, begin by submerging your face in shallow water or a swimming pool and breathing calmly through the snorkel while gazing through the mask.

Next you need to learn how to clear water out of your mask and snorkel, an essential skill since splashes can send water into tube openings and masks can leak. Some snorkels have built-in drainage valves, but if a tube clogs, you can force water up and out by exhaling through your mouth. Clearing a mask is similar: lift your head from water while pulling forward on mask to drain. Some masks have built-in purge valves, but those without can be cleared underwater by pressing the top to the forehead and blowing out your nose (charming, isn't it?), allowing air to bubble into the mask, pushing water out the bottom. If it sounds hard, it really isn't. Just try it a few times and you'll soon feel like a pro.

Now your goal is to get friendly with fins—you want them to be snug but not too tight—and learn how to propel yourself with them. Fins won't help you float, but they will give you a leg up, so to speak, on smoothly moving through the water or treading water (even when upright) with less effort.

Flutter stroking is the most efficient underwater kick, and the farther your foot bends forward the more leg power you'll be able to transfer to the water and the farther you'll travel with each stroke. Flutter kicking movements involve alternately separating the legs and then drawing them back together. When your legs separate, the leg surface encounters drag from the water, slowing you down. When your legs are drawn back together, they produce a force pushing you forward. If your kick creates more forward force than it causes drag, you'll move ahead.

Submerge your fins to avoid fatigue rather than having them flailing above the water when you kick, and keep your arms at your side to reduce drag. You are in the water—stretched out, face down, and snorkeling happily away—but that doesn't mean you can't hold your breath and go deeper in the water for a closer look at some fish or whatever catches your attention. Just remember that when you do this, your snorkel will be submerged, too, so you won't be breathing (you'll be holding your breath). You can dive head-first, but going feet-first is easier and less scary for most folks, taking less momentum. Before full immersion, take several long, deep breaths to clear carbon dioxide from your lungs.

If your legs tire, flip onto your back and tread water with inverted fin motions while resting. If your mask fogs, wash condensation from lens and clear water from mask.

TIPS FOR SAFE SNORKELING

- ■ Snorkel with a buddy and stay together.

- ■ Plan your entry and exit points prior to getting in the water.

- ■ Swim into the current on entering and then ride the current back to your exit point.

- ■ Carry your flippers into the water and then put them on, as it's difficult to walk in them.

- ■ Make sure your mask fits properly and is not too loose.

- ■ Pop your head above the water periodically to ensure you aren't drifting too far out, or too close to rocks.

- ■ Think of the water as someone else's home—don't take anything that doesn't belong to you, or leave any trash behind.

- ■ Don't touch any sea creatures; they may sting.

- ■ Wear a T-shirt over your swimsuit to help protect you from being fried by the sun.

- ■ When in doubt, don't go without a snorkeling professional; try a guided tour.

Cayman Salvor

4

IN FOCUS UNDER THE SEA

TOP OUTFITTERS

COMPANY	ADDRESS & PHONE	COST	DESCRIPTION
AMY SLATE'S AMORAY DIVE CENTER ⊕ www.amoray.com	⊠ 104250 Overseas Hwy. (MM 104.2), Key Largo ☎ 305/451-3595	⊙ Daily 🤿 Scuba classes for kids ages 8 and up and adults $100-$200.	Sign up for dive/snorkel trips, scuba instruction and kid programs.
DIVE KEY WEST ⊕ www.divekeywest.com	⊠ 3128 N. Roosevelt Blvd., Key West ☎ 305/296-3823	🤿 Snorkel from $49, dive from $69	Operating nearly 40 years. Has charters, instruction, and gear.
FLORIDA KEYS DIVE CENTER ⊕ www.floridakeys-divectr.com	⊠ 90451 Old Hwy. (MM 90.5), Tavernier ☎ 305/852-4599	⊙ Daily 🤿 Classes from $175.	Charters for snorkerlers and divers go to Pennekamp, Key Largo, and Islamorada.
HORIZON DIVERS ⊕ www.horizondivers.com	⊠ 100 Ocean Dr. #1, Key Largo ☎ 305/453-3535	⊙ Daily 🤿 Snorkel from $50, scuba from $80.	Take customized dive/snorkel trips on a 45-foot catamaran.
ISLAND VENTURES ⊕ www.islandventure.com	⊠ 103900 Overseas Hwy. (MM 103.9), Key Largo ☎ 305/451-4957	⊙ Two trips daily 🤿 Snorkel $45, scuba from $80.	Go on snorkeling and scuba explorations to the Key Largo reef and shipwrecks.
KEYS DIVER SNORKEL TOURS ⊕ www.keysdiver.com	⊠ 99696 Overseas Hwy. (MM 99.6), Key Largo ☎ 305/451-1177	🤿 Three daily snorkel tours from $28. Includes gear.	Family-oriented snorkel-only tours head to coral reefs such as Pennekamp.
LOOE KEY REEF RE-SORT & DIVE CENTER ⊕ www.diveflakeys.com	⊠ 27340 Overseas Hwy. (MM 27.5), Ramrod Key ☎ 305/872-2215	⊙ Daily 🤿 Snorkel from $44, scuba from $85.	Beginner and advanced scuba instruction, a photographer course, and snorkel gear rental.
RON JON SURF SHOP ⊕ www.ronjons.com	⊠ 503 Front St., Key West ☎ 305/293-8880	⊙ Daily 🤿 Sells snorkel gear.	Several locations in Florida; its HQ is in Cocoa Beach.
SCUBA-DO DIVE COMPANY ⊕ www.scuba-do.com	⊠ 102670 Overseas Hwy. (MM 102.7), Key Largo ☎ 305/451-3446	⊙ Daily 🤿 Snorkel from $50, scuba from $85.	Small groups, instruc-tion, gear rental, and charters.
SNUBA OF KEY WEST ⊕ www.snubakeywest.com	⊠ 600 Palm Ave., Key West ☎ 305/292-4616	⊙ Daily 🤿 $99 per person, $44 for ride-alongs.	Swimmers ages 8 and up can try Snuba.
TILDENS SCUBA CENTER ⊕ www.tildensscuba-center.com	⊠ 4650 Overseas Hwy. (MM 49.5), Marathon ☎ 305/743-7255	⊙ Daily 🤿 Snorkel from $35.99, scuba from $60.99.	Operating for 25 years. Has lessons, tours, snorkeling, scuba, snuba, gear, and a kids club.

DUCK KEY

Duck Key is at mile marker 61.

Duck Key holds one of the region's nicest marina resorts, Hawks Cay, plus a boating-oriented residential community.

EXPLORING

Dolphin Connection. Hawk's Cay Resort's Dolphin Connection offers three programs, including Dockside Dolphins, a 30-minute encounter from the dry training docks ($60); Dolphin Discovery, an in-water program that lasts about 45 minutes and lets you kiss, touch, and feed the dolphins ($175); and Trainer for a Day, a three-hour session with the animal training team ($325). ✉ *MM 61 OS, 61 Hawks Cay Blvd.* ☎ *305/743–7000* 🌐 *www.dolphinconnection.com.*

4

WHERE TO EAT AND STAY

For expanded hotel reviews, visit Fodors.com.

$$$ LATIN AMERICAN 🍴 **Alma.** A refreshing escape from the Middle Keys' same-old menus, Alma serves expertly prepared Florida and Latin-Caribbean dishes in an elegant setting. Nightly changing menus might include a trio of ceviche, ahi tuna with a wonderful garbanzo bean tomato sauce, gnocchi and exotic mushroom ragout, or pan-seared Wagyu steak. Finish your meal with the silky, smooth, passion fruit crème brûlée, which has just the right amount of tartness to balance the delicate caramelized crust. [$] *Average main: $28* ✉ *Hawks Cay Resort, 61 Hawks Cay Blvd.* ☎ *305/743–7000, 888/432–2242* 🌐 *www.hawkscay.com* 🕒 *No lunch.*

$$$$ RESORT FAMILY Fodor's Choice ★ 🏨 **Hawks Cay Resort.** The 60-acre, Caribbean-style retreat has plenty to keep the kids occupied (and adults happy). **Pros:** huge rooms; restful spa; full-service marina and dive shop. **Cons:** no real beach; far from Marathon's attractions. [$] *Rooms from: $240* ✉ *MM 61 OS, 61 Hawks Cay Blvd.* ☎ *305/743–7000, 888/432–2242* 🌐 *www.hawkscay.com* 🛏 *161 rooms, 16 suites, 225 2- and 3-bedroom villas* 🍽 *No meals.*

GRASSY KEY

Grassy Key is between mile markers 60 and 57.

Local lore has it that this sleepy little key was named not for its vegetation—mostly native trees and shrubs—but for an early settler by the name of Grassy. The key is inhabited primarily by a few families operating small fishing camps and roadside motels. There's no marked definition between it and Marathon, so it feels sort of like a suburb of its much larger neighbor to the south. Grassy Key's sights tend toward the natural, including a worthwhile dolphin attraction and a small state park.

GETTING HERE AND AROUND

Most visitors arriving by air drive to this destination either from Miami International Airport or Key West International Airport. Rental cars are readily available at both, and in the long run, are the most convenient means of transportation for getting here and touring around the Keys.

DID YOU KNOW?

Dolphins in Florida are predominantly of the Atlantic
bottlenose variety. These
playful and smart creatures
love to leap out of the water
and synchronize their movements with others. By swimming next to boats, dolphins
can conserve energy.

EXPLORING

Curry Hammock State Park. Looking for a slice of the Keys that's far removed from tiki bars? On the ocean and bay sides of Overseas Highway are 260 acres of upland hammock, wetlands, and mangroves. On the bay side, there's a trail through thick hardwoods to a rocky shoreline. The ocean side is more developed, with a sandy beach, a clean bathhouse, picnic tables, a playground, grills, and a 28-site campground. Locals consider the paddling trails under canopies of arching mangroves one of the best kayaking spots in the Keys. Manatees frequent the area, and it's a great spot for bird-watching. Herons, egrets, ibis, plovers, and sanderlings are commonly spotted. Raptors are often seen in the park, especially during migration periods. ✉ *MM 57 OS, 56200 Overseas Hwy., Little Crawl Key* ☎ *305/289–2690* 🌐 *www.floridastateparks.org/curryhammock* 🎟 *$4.50 for 1 person, $6 for 2, 50¢ per additional person* 🕒 *Daily 8–sunset.*

4

FAMILY **Dolphin Research Center.** The 1963 movie *Flipper* popularized the notion of humans interacting with dolphins, and Milton Santini, the film's creator, also opened this center, which is home to a colony of dolphins and sea lions. The nonprofit center has educational sessions and programs that allow you to greet the dolphins from dry land or play with them in their watery habitat. You can even paint a T-shirt with a dolphin—you pick the paint, the dolphin "designs" your shirt ($65 plus admission). The center also offers five-day programs for children and adults with disabilities. ✉ *MM 59 BS, 58901 Overseas Hwy.* ☎ *305/289–1121 information, 305/289–0002 reservations* 🌐 *www.dolphins.org* 🎟 *$20* 🕒 *Daily 9–4:30.*

WHERE TO EAT

$$$$ AMERICAN 🍴 **Hideaway Café.** The name says it all. Tucked between Grassy Key and Marathon, it's easy to miss if you're barnstorming through the middle islands. When you find it (upstairs at Rainbow Bend Resort), you'll discover a favorite of locals who appreciate a well-planned menu, lovely ocean view, and quiet evening away from the crowds—fancy with white tablecloths, but homey with worn carpeting. For starters, dig into escargots à la Edison (sautéed with vegetables, pepper, cognac, and cream). Then feast on several specialties, such as a rarely found chateaubriand for one, a whole roasted duck, or the seafood medley combining the catch of the day with scallops and shrimp in a savory sauce. [$] *Average main: $30* ✉ *MM 58 OS, Rainbow Bend Resort, 57784 Overseas Hwy.* ☎ *305/289–1554* 🌐 *www.hideawaycafe.com* 🕒 *No lunch.*

MARATHON

Marathon is between mile markers 53 and 47.5.

Marathon is a bustling town, at least compared with other communities in the Keys. As it leaves something to be desired in the charm department, Marathon will probably not be your first choice of places to stay. But there are a number of good dining options, so you'll definitely want to stop for a bite even if you're just passing through on the way to Key West.

If you stop a while, you'll find Marathon has the most historic attractions outside of Key West, and the well-worth-visiting Sombrero Beach—though fishing, diving, and boating are the main events here. The town throws tarpon tournaments in April and May, more fishing tournaments in June and September, a seafood festival in March, and lighted boat parades around the winter holidays.

New Englanders founded this former fishing village in the early 1800s. The community on Vaca Key subsequently served as a base for pirates, salvagers (also known as "wreckers"), spongers, and, later, Bahamian farmers who eked out a living growing cotton and other crops. More Bahamians arrived in hopes of finding work building the railroad. According to local lore, Marathon was renamed when a worker commented that it was a marathon task to position the tracks across the 6-mile-long island. During the building of the railroad, Marathon developed a reputation for lawlessness that rivaled that of the Old West. It's said that to keep the rowdy workers from descending on Key West for their off-hours endeavors, residents would send boatloads of liquor up to Marathon. Needless to say, things have quieted down considerably since then. Grassy Key segues into Marathon with little more than a slight increase in traffic and higher concentration of commercial establishments. Marathon's roots are anchored to fishing and boating, so look for marinas to find local color, fishing charters, and good restaurants. At its north end, Key Colony Beach is an old-fashioned island neighborhood worth a visit for its shops and restaurants. Nature lovers shouldn't miss the attractions on Crane Point. Other good places to leave the main road are at Sombrero Beach Road (MM 50), which leads to the beach, and 35th Street (MM 49), which takes you to a funky little marina and restaurant. Overseas Highway hightails through Hog Key and Knight Key before the big leap over Florida Bay and Hawk's Channel via the Seven Mile Bridge.

GETTING HERE AND AROUND

The SuperShuttle charges $102 per passenger for trips from Miami International Airport to the Upper Keys. To go farther into the Keys, you must book an entire 11-person van, which costs about $250 to Marathon. For a trip to or from the airport, place your request 24 hours in advance.

Miami Dade Transit provides daily bus service from MM 50 in Marathon to the Florida City Walmart Supercenter on the mainland. The bus stops at major shopping centers as well as on-demand anywhere along the route during daily round-trips on the hour from 6 am to 10 pm. The cost is $2 one-way, exact change required. The Lower Keys Shuttle bus runs from Marathon to Key West ($4 one-way), with scheduled stops along the way.

ESSENTIALS

Transportation Contacts **Lower Keys Shuttle** ☎ 305/809–3910
⊕ www.kwtransit.com. **Miami Dade Transit** ☎ 305/770–3131
⊕ www.miamidade.gov/transit. **SuperShuttle** ☎ 305/871–2000, 800/258–3826
⊕ www.supershuttle.com.

Visitor Information **Greater Marathon Chamber of Commerce and Visitor Center** ⊠ *MM 53.5 BS, 12222 Overseas Hwy.* ☎ *305/743–5417, 800/262–7284* ⊕ *www.floridakeysmarathon.com.*

EXPLORING

FAMILY **Crane Point Museum, Nature Center, and Historic Site.** Tucked away from the highway behind a stand of trees, Crane Point—part of a 63-acre tract that contains the last-known undisturbed thatch-palm hammock—is delightfully undeveloped. This multiuse facility includes the **Museum of Natural History of the Florida Keys,** which has displays about local wildlife, a seashell exhibit, and a marine-life display that makes you feel you're at the bottom of the sea. Kids love the replica 17th-century galleon and pirate dress-up room where they can play, and the re-created **Cracker House** filled with insects, sea-turtle exhibits, and children's activities. On the 1-mile indigenous loop trail, visit the **Laura Quinn Wild Bird Center** and the remnants of a Bahamian village, site of the restored **George Adderly House.** It is the oldest surviving example of Bahamian tabby (a concretelike material created from sand and seashells) construction outside of Key West. A boardwalk crosses wetlands, rivers, and mangroves before ending at Adderly Village. From November to Easter, docent-led tours are available; bring good walking shoes and bug repellent during warm weather. ⊠ *MM 50.5 BS, 5550 Overseas Hwy.* ☎ *305/743–9100* ⊕ *www.cranepoint.net* ☞ *$12.50* ⊙ *Mon.–Sat. 9–5, Sun. noon–5; call to arrange trail tours.*

Pigeon Key. There's much to like about this 5-acre island under the Old Seven Mile Bridge. You can reach it via a ferry that departs from behind the visitors center (look for the old red railroad car on Knight's Key, MM 47 OS). Once there, tour the island on your own or join a guided tour to explore the buildings that formed the early-20th-century work camp for the Overseas Railroad that linked the mainland to Key West in 1912. Later the island became a fish camp, a state park, and then government-administration headquarters. Exhibits in a small museum recall the history of the Keys, the railroad, and railroad baron Henry M. Flagler. The ferry ride with tour lasts two hours; visitors can self-tour and catch the ferry back in a half hour. ⊠ *MM 45 OS, 1 Knights Key Blvd., Pigeon Key* ☎ *305/743–5999* ⊕ *www.pigeonkey.net* ☞ *$12* ⊙ *Daily 9:30–2:30; ferry departures at 10, noon and 2.*

Seven Mile Bridge. This is one of the most photographed images in the Keys. Actually measuring slightly less than 7 miles, it connects the Middle and Lower Keys and is believed to be the world's longest segmental bridge. It has 39 expansion joints separating its various concrete sections. Each April runners gather in Marathon for the annual Seven Mile Bridge Run. The expanse running parallel to Seven Mile Bridge is what remains of the **Old Seven Mile Bridge,** an engineering and architectural marvel in its day that's now on the National Register of Historic Places. Once proclaimed the Eighth Wonder of the World, it rested on a record 546 concrete piers. No cars are allowed on the old bridge today.

FAMILY **The Turtle Hospital.** More than 100 injured sea turtles check in here every year. The 90-minute guided tours take you into recovery and surgical areas at the world's only state-certified veterinary hospital for sea turtles. In the "hospital bed" tanks, you can see recovering patients and others that are permanent residents due to their injuries. After the tour, you can feed some of the "residents." Call ahead—space is limited and tours are sometimes cancelled due to medical emergencies. The turtle ambulance out front makes for a memorable souvenir photo. ✉ *MM 48.5 BS, 2396 Overseas Hwy.* ☎ *305/743–2552* 🌐 *www.turtlehospital.org* 🎟 *$15* 🕘 *Daily 9–5.*

BEACHES

FAMILY **Sombrero Beach.** No doubt one of the best beaches in the Keys, here you'll find pleasant, shaded picnic areas that overlook a coconut palm–lined grassy stretch and the Atlantic Ocean. Roped-off areas allow swimmers, boaters, and windsurfers to share the narrow cove. Facilities include barbecue grills, a large playground, a pier, a volleyball court, and a paved, lighted bike path off Overseas Highway. Sunday afternoons draw lots of local families toting coolers. The park is accessible for those with disabilities and allows leashed pets. Turn east at the traffic light in Marathon and follow signs to the end. **Amenities:** showers; toilets. **Best for:** families; swimming; windsurfing. ✉ *MM 50 OS, Sombrero Beach Rd.* ☎ *305/743–0033* 🎟 *Free* 🕘 *Daily 8–sunset.*

WHERE TO EAT

$ SEAFOOD 🍴 **Fish Tales Market and Eatery.** This roadside eatery with its own seafood market serves signature dishes such as snapper on grilled rye with coleslaw and melted Muenster cheese and a fried fish burrito. You also can slurp luscious lobster bisque or tomato-based conch chowder. There are burgers, chicken, and dogs for those who don't do seafood. Plan to dine early; it's only open until 6:30 pm. This is a no-frills kind of place with a loyal local following, unfussy ambiance, a couple of outside picnic tables, and friendly service. [$] *Average main: $8* ✉ *MM 52.5 OS, 11711 Overseas Hwy.* ☎ *305/743–9196, 888/662–4822* 🌐 *www.floridalobster.com* ✍ *Reservations not accepted* 🕘 *Closed Sun.*

$ AMERICAN 🍴 **Herbie's.** Since 1972, this has been the go-to spot for quick-and-affordable comfort food from cheeseburgers and fried oysters to shrimp scampi and filet mignon. You'll find all the local staples—conch, lobster tail, and fresh fish—to enjoy at picnic tables in the screened-in porch or inside where it's air-conditioned. Its shack-like appearance gives it an old-Keys feel. [$] *Average main: $10* ✉ *MM 50.5, 6350 Overseas Hwy.* ☎ *305/743–6373* ✍ *Reservations not accepted* 💳 *No credit cards* 🕘 *Closed Sun. and Mon.*

$$ ITALIAN 🍴 **Key Colony Inn.** The inviting aroma of an Italian kitchen pervades this family-owned favorite with a supper-club atmosphere. As you'd expect, the service is friendly and attentive. For lunch there are fish and steak entrées served with fries, salad, and bread in addition to Italian specialties. At dinner you can't miss with traditional dishes like veal Oscar and New York strip, or such specialties as seafood *Italiano,* a dish of scallops and shrimp sautéed in garlic butter and served with marinara sauce over a bed of linguine. The place is renowned for its Sunday brunch, served from November to April. [$] *Average main: $19* ✉ *MM 54 OS, 700 W. Ocean Dr., Key Colony Beach* ☎ *305/743–0100* 🌐 *www.kcinn.com.*

$$ SEAFOOD FAMILY 🍴 **Keys Fisheries Market & Marina.** From the parking lot, you can't miss the enormous, stilted tiki bar but the walk-up window on the ground floor is the heart of this warehouse-turned restaurant. Order at the window, pick up your food, then dine at one of the waterfront tables outfitted with rolls of paper towels. The menu is comprised of fresh seafood and a token hamburger and chicken sandwich. A huge lobster Reuben ($14.95) served on thick slices of toasted bread is the signature dish. Other delights include the shrimp burger, very rich whiskey-peppercorn snapper, and the Keys Kombo (grilled lobster, shrimp, scallops, and mahi-mahi for $29). The adults-only upstairs tiki bar offers a sushi and raw bar for eat-in only. Bring quarters for fish food—you can feed the tarpon while you wait for your food. [$] *Average main: $16* ✉ *MM 49 BS, 3390 Gulfview Ave., at end of 35th St. (turn right on 35th St. off Gulfview Ave.)* ☎ *305/743–4353, 866/743–4353* 🌐 *www.keysfisheries.com* ✍ *Reservations not accepted.*

$$$ SEAFOOD 🍴 **Lazy Days South.** Tucked into Marathon Marina a half-mile north of the Seven Mile Bridge, this restaurant offers views just as spectacular as its highly lauded food. A spin-off of an Islamorada favorite, here you'll find a wide range of daily offerings from fried- or sautéed conch and a coconut-fried fish du jour sandwich to seafood pastas and beef tips over rice. Choose a table on the outdoor deck, or inside underneath paddle fans and surrounded by local art. [$] *Average main: $22* ✉ *MM 47.3 OS, 725 11th St.* ☎ *305/289–0839* 🌐 *www.keysdining.com/lazydays.*

$ AMERICAN 🍴 **The Stuffed Pig.** With only nine tables and a counter inside, this breakfast-and-lunch place is always hopping. When the weather's right, grab a table out back. The kitchen whips up daily lunch specials like burgers, seafood platters, or pulled pork with hand-cut fries, but a quick glance around the room reveals that the all-day breakfast is the main draw. You can get the usual breakfast plates, but most newcomers opt for oddities like the lobster omelet, alligator tail and eggs, or "grits and grunts" (that's fish, to the rest of us). [$] *Average main: $9* ✉ *MM 49 BS, 3520 Overseas Hwy.* ☎ *305/743–4059* 🌐 *www.thestuffedpig.com* ✍ *Reservations not accepted* 💳 *No credit cards* 🕒 *No dinner.*

WHERE TO STAY

For expanded reviews, facilities, and current deals, visit Fodors.com.

$$$$ RESORT FAMILY 🏨 **Tranquility Bay.** Ralph Lauren could have designed the rooms at this luxurious beach resort. **Pros:** secluded setting; gorgeous design; lovely crescent beach. **Cons:** a bit sterile; no real Keys atmosphere; cramped building layout. [$] *Rooms from: $399* ✉ *MM 48.5 BS, 2600 Overseas Hwy.* ☎ *305/289–0888, 866/643–5397* 🌐 *www.tranquilitybay.com* 🛏 *45 2-bedroom suites, 41 3-bedroom suites* 🍽 *No meals.*

SPORTS AND THE OUTDOORS

BIKING

Tooling around on two wheels is a good way to see Marathon. There's easy cycling on a 1-mile off-road path that connects to the 2 miles of the Old Seven Mile Bridge leading to Pigeon Key.

Bike Marathon Bike Rentals. "Have bikes, will deliver" could be the motto of this company, which gets beach cruisers to your hotel door for $35 per week, including a helmet and basket. They also rent kayaks. Note that there's no physical location, but services are available Monday through Saturday 9–4 and Sunday 9–2. ☎ *305/743–3204* ⊕ *www. bikemarathonbikerentals.com.*

Bubba's. Book a custom biking tour through the Keys along the heritage trail. A van accompanies tours to carry luggage and tired riders. Operated by former police officer Bubba Barron, Bubba's hosts an annual one-week ride down the length of the Keys every November. Riders can opt for tent camping ($675 early-bird registration) or motel-room accommodations (prices vary). Meals are included on the annual ride and bike rentals are extra. ☎ *321/759–3433* ⊕ *www. bubbafestbiketours.com.*

Overseas Outfitters. Aluminum cruisers and hybrid bikes are available for rent at this outfitter for $10 to $30 per day. It's open weekdays 9–5:30 and Saturday 9–3. ⊠ *MM 48 BS, 1700 Overseas Hwy.* ☎ *305/289–1670* ⊕ *www.overseasoutfitters.com.*

BOATING

Sail, motor, or paddle—whatever your choice of modes, boating is what the Keys are all about. Brave the Atlantic waves and reefs or explore the backcountry islands on the calmer gulf side. If you don't have a lot of boating and chart-reading experience, it's a good idea to tap into local knowledge on a charter.

Captain Pip's. This operator rents 20- to 24-foot outboards, $195–$330 per day, as well as tackle and snorkeling gear. Fishing charters are also available with a captain and a mate from $450–$550 for a half day and $700–$800 for a full day. Ask about multiday deals, or try one of their accommodation packages and walk right from your bayfront room to your boat. ⊠ *MM 47.5 BS, 1410 Overseas Hwy.* ☎ *305/743–4403, 800/707–1692* ⊕ *www.captainpips.com.*

Fish 'n Fun. Get out on the water on 19- to 26-foot powerboats starting at $175 for a half day, $200 for a full day. The company offers free delivery in the Middle Keys. You also can rent jet skis, kayaks, fishing and snorkel gear. ⊠ *MM 49.5 OS, 4590 Overseas Hwy., at Banana Bay Resort & Marina* ☎ *305/743–2275, 800/471–3440* ⊕ *www.fishnfunrentals.com.*

FISHING

For recreational anglers, the deepwater fishing is superb in the ocean. Marathon West Hump, one good spot, has depths ranging from 500 to more than 1,000 feet. Locals fish from a half-dozen bridges, including Long Key Bridge, the Old Seven Mile Bridge, and both ends of Tom's Harbor. Barracuda, bonefish, mahimahi, and tarpon all frequent local waters. Party boats and private charters are available.

Marathon Lady. Morning, afternoon, and night, fish for mahimahi, grouper, and other tasty catch aboard this 73-footer, which departs on half-day ($45) excursions from the Vaca Cut Bridge (MM53), north of Marathon. Join the crew for night fishing ($55) from 6:30 to midnight from Memorial Day to Labor Day; it's especially beautiful on a full-moon night. ⊠ *MM 53 OS, at 117th St.* ☎ *305/743–5580* ⊕ *www. marathonlady.net.*

Sea Dog Charters. Captain Jim Purcell, a deep-sea specialist for ESPN's *The American Outdoorsman,* provides one of the best values in Keys fishing. Next to the Seven Mile Grill, his company offers half- and full-day offshore, reef and wreck, and backcountry fishing trips, as well as fishing and snorkeling trips aboard 30- to 37-foot boats. The cost is $60 per person for a half day, regardless of whether your group fills the boat, and includes bait, light tackle, ice, coolers, and fishing licenses. If you prefer an all-day private charter on a 37-foot boat, he offers those, too, for $600 for up to six people. A fuel surcharge may apply. ⊠ *MM 47.5 BS, 1248 Overseas Hwy.* ☎ *305/743–8255* ⊕ *www.seadogcharters.net.*

SCUBA DIVING AND SNORKELING

Local dive operations take you to Sombrero Reef and Lighthouse, the most popular down-under destination in these parts. For a shallow dive and some lobster-nabbing, Coffins Patch, off Key Colony Beach, is a good choice. A number of wrecks such as *Thunderbolt* serve as artificial reefs. Many operations out of this area will also take you to Looe Key Reef.

Hall's Diving Center & Career Institute. The institute has been training divers for more than 40 years. Along with conventional twice-a-day snorkel and two-tank dive trips ($40–$65) to the reefs at Sombrero Lighthouse and wrecks like the *Thunderbolt,* the company has more unusual offerings like photography and nitrox courses. ⊠ *MM 48.5 BS, 1994 Overseas Hwy.* ☎ *305/743–5929, 800/331–4255* ⊕ *www.hallsdiving.com.*

Spirit Snorkeling. Join snorkeling excursions to Sombrero Reef and Lighthouse Reef on this company's comfortable catamaran at a cost of $30 a head. They also offer sunset cruises ($35), private charters, and new-age yoga cruises. ⊠ *MM 47.5 BS, 1410 Overseas Hwy., Slip No. 1* ☎ *305/289–0614* ⊕ *www.spiritsnorkeling.net.*

THE LOWER KEYS

Beginning at Bahia Honda Key, the islands of the Florida Keys become smaller, more clustered, and more numerous—a result of ancient tidal water flowing between the Florida Straits and the gulf. Here you're likely to see more birds and mangroves than other tourists, and more refuges, beaches, and campgrounds than museums, restaurants, and hotels. The islands are made up of two types of limestone, both denser than the highly permeable Key Largo limestone of the Upper Keys. As a result, freshwater forms in pools rather than percolating through the rock, creating watering holes that support alligators, snakes, deer, rabbits, raccoons, and migratory ducks. Many of these animals can be seen in the National Key Deer Refuge on Big Pine Key. Nature was generous with her beauty in the Lower Keys, which have both Looe Key Reef, arguably the Keys' most beautiful tract of coral, and Bahia Honda State Park, considered one of the best beaches in the world for its fine-sand dunes, clear warm waters, and panoramic vista of a historic bridge, hammocks, and azure sky and sea. Big Pine Key is fishing headquarters for a laid-back community that swells with retirees in the winter. South of it, the dribble of islands can flash by in a blink of an eye if you don't take the time to stop at a roadside eatery or check out tours and charters at the little marinas. In truth, the Lower Keys include Key West, but since it's as different from the rest of the Lower Keys as peanut butter is from jelly, it's covered in its own section.

GETTING HERE AND AROUND

The Lower Keys in this section include the keys between MM 37 and MM 9. The Seven Mile Bridge drops you into the lap of this homey, quiet part of the Keys.

Heed speed limits in these parts. They may seem incredibly strict given that the traffic is lightest of anywhere in the Keys, but the purpose is to protect the resident Key deer population, and officers of the law pay strict attention and will readily issue speeding tickets.

BAHIA HONDA KEY

Bahia Honda Key is between mile markers 38 and 36.

All of Bahia Honda Key is devoted to its eponymous state park, which keeps it in a pristine state. Besides the park's outdoor activities, it offers an up-close look at the original railroad bridge.

EXPLORING

FAMILY

Fodor's Choice

★

Bahia Honda State Park. Most first-time visitors to the region are dismayed by the lack of beaches—but then they discover Bahia Honda Key. The 524-acre park sprawls across both sides of the highway, giving it 2½ miles of fabulous sandy coastline. The snorkeling isn't bad, either; there's underwater life (soft coral, queen conchs, random little fish) just a few hundred feet offshore. Although swimming, kayaking, fishing, and boating are the main reasons to visit, you shouldn't miss biking along the 2½ miles of flat roads or hiking the Silver Palm Trail, with rare West Indian plants and several species found nowhere else in the nation. Along the way you'll be treated to a variety of butterflies. Seasonal ranger-led nature programs take place at or depart from the Sand and Sea Nature Center. There are rental cabins, a campground, snack bar, gift shop, 19-slip marina, nature center, and facilities for renting kayaks and arranging snorkeling tours. Get a panoramic view of the island from what's left of the railroad—the Bahia Honda Bridge. ⊠ *MM 37 OS, 36850 Overseas Hwy.* ☎ *305/872-2353* ⊕ *www.floridastateparks.org/bahiahonda* ⊠ *$4.50 for single occupant vehicle, $9 for vehicle with 2–8 people* ⊗ *Daily 8–sunset.*

BEACHES

Sandspur Beach. Bahia Honda Key State Beach contains three beaches in all—on both the Atlantic Ocean and the Gulf of Mexico. Sandspur Beach, the largest, is regularly declared the best beach in the Florida Keys, and you'll be hard-pressed to argue. The sand is baby-powder soft, and the aqua water is warm, clear, and shallow. With their mild currents, the beaches are great for swimming, even with small fry. **Amenities:** food and drink; showers; toilets; water sports. **Best for:** snorkeling; swimming. ⊠ *MM 37 OS, 36850 Overseas Hwy.* ☎ *305/872-2353* ⊕ *www.floridastateparks.org/bahiahonda* ⊠ *$4.50 for single occupant vehicle, $9 for vehicle with 2–8 people* ⊗ *Daily 8–sunset.*

DID YOU KNOW?

An old railroad bridge connected Bahia Honda Key with Key West until a hurricane destroyed it in 1935. Although it's no longer in operation, the bridge is used by hikers as a place from which to view the island and waters.

WHERE TO STAY

For expanded reviews, facilities, and current deals, visit Fodors.com.

$$$

RENTAL

🖼 **Bahia Honda State Park.** Elsewhere you'd pay big bucks for the wonderful water views available at these cabins on Florida Bay. **Pros:** great bayfront views; beachfront camping; affordable rates. **Cons:** books up fast; area can be buggy. $ *Rooms from: $183* ⊠ *MM 37 OS, 36850 Overseas Hwy.* ☎ *305/872–2353, 800/326–3521* ⊕ *www.reserveamerica. com* ↪ *80 partial hook-up campsites, 6 cabin units* ⦿ *No meals.*

SPORTS AND THE OUTDOORS

SCUBA DIVING AND SNORKELING

Bahia Honda Dive Shop. The concessionaire at Bahia Honda State Park manages a 19-slip marina; rents wet suits, snorkel equipment, and corrective masks; and operates twice-a-day offshore-reef snorkel trips ($30 plus $9 for equipment). Park visitors looking for other fun can rent kayaks ($12 per hour for a single, $18 for a double) and beach chairs. ⊠ *MM 37 OS, 36850 Overseas Hwy.* ☎ *305/872–3210* ⊕ *www. bahiahondapark.com.*

BIG PINE KEY

Big Pine Key runs from mile marker 32 to 30.

Welcome to the Keys' most natural hold out, where wildlife refuges protect rare and endangered animals. Here you've left behind the commercialism of the Upper Keys for an authentic backcountry atmosphere.

How could things get more casual than Key Largo? Find out by exiting Overseas Highway to explore the habitat of the charmingly diminutive Key deer or cast a line from No Name Bridge. Tours explore the expansive waters of National Key Deer Refuge and Great White Heron National Wildlife Refuge, one of the first such refuges in the country. Along with Key West National Wildlife Refuge, it encompasses more than 200,000 acres of water and more than 8,000 acres of land on 49 small islands. Besides its namesake bird, the Great White Heron National Wildlife Refuge provides habitat for uncounted species of birds and three species of sea turtles. It's the only U.S. breeding site for the endangered hawksbill turtle.

ESSENTIALS

Visitor Information Big Pine and the Lower Keys Chamber of Commerce ⊠ *MM 31 OS, 31020 Overseas Hwy.* ☎ *305/872–2411, 800/872–3722* ⊕ *www.lowerkeyschamber.com.*

EXPLORING

National Key Deer Refuge. This 84,824-acre refuge was established in 1957 to protect the dwindling population of the Key deer, one of more than 22 animals and plants federally classified as endangered or threatened, including five that are found nowhere else on earth. The Key deer, which stands about 30 inches at the shoulders and is a subspecies of the Virginia white-tailed deer, once roamed throughout the Lower and Middle Keys, but hunting, destruction of their habitat, and a growing human population caused their numbers to decline to 27 by 1957. The deer have made a comeback, increasing their numbers to approximately

750. The best place to see Key deer in the refuge is at the end of Key Deer Boulevard and on No Name Key, a sparsely populated island just east of Big Pine Key. Mornings and evenings are the best time to spot them. Deer may turn up along the road at any time of day, so drive slowly. They wander into nearby yards to nibble tender grass and bougainvillea blossom, but locals do not appreciate tourists driving into their neighborhoods after them. Feeding them is against the law and puts them in danger.

A quarry left over from railroad days, the **Blue Hole** is the largest body of freshwater in the Keys. From the observation platform and nearby walking trail, you might see the resident alligator, turtles, and other wildlife. There are two well-marked trails, recently revamped: the Jack Watson Nature Trail (.6 mile), named after an environmentalist and the refuge's first warden; and the Fred Mannillo Nature Trail, one of the most wheelchair-accessible places to see an unspoiled pinerockland forest and wetlands. The visitor center has exhibits on Keys biology and ecology. The refuge also provides information on the Key West National Wildlife Refuge and the Great White Heron National Wildlife Refuge. Accessible only by water, both are popular with kayak outfitters. ⊠ *MM 30.5 BS, Visitor Center–Headquarters, Big Pine Shopping Center, 28950 Watson Blvd.* ☎ *305/872–2239* ⊕ *www. fws.gov/nationalkeydeer* ⊒ *Free* ☉ *Daily sunrise–sunset; headquarters weekdays 8–5.*

WHERE TO EAT

$ ✗ **Good Food Conspiracy.** Like good wine, this small natural-foods eatery
VEGETARIAN and market surrenders its pleasures a little at a time. Step inside to the aroma of brewing coffee, and then pick up the scent of fresh strawberries or carrots blending into a smoothie, the green aroma of wheatgrass juice, followed by the earthy odor of hummus. Order raw or cooked vegetarian and vegan dishes, organic soups and salads, and organic coffees and teas. Bountiful sandwiches (available halved) include the popular tuna melt or hummus and avocado. If you can't sit down for a bite in the back courtyard, stock up on healthful snacks like dried fruits, raw nuts, and carob-covered almonds. $ *Average main: $7* ⊠ *MM 30.2 OS, 30150 Overseas Hwy.* ☎ *305/872–3945* ⊕ *www.goodfoodconspiracy. com* ⌂ *Reservations not accepted* ☉ *No dinner Sun.*

$ ✗ **No Name Pub.** This no-frills honky-tonk has been around since 1936,
AMERICAN delighting inveterate locals and intrepid vacationers who come for the excellent pizza, cold beer, and *interesting* companionship. The decor, such as it is, amounts to the autographed dollar bills that cover every inch of the place. The full menu printed on place mats includes a tasty conch chowder, a half-pound fried-grouper sandwich, spaghetti and meatballs, and seafood baskets. The lighting is poor, the furnishings are rough, and the music is oldies. This former brothel and bait shop is just before the No Name Key Bridge in the midst of a residential neighborhood. It's a bit hard to find, but worth the trouble if you want a singular Keys experience. $ *Average main: $15* ⊠ *MM 30 BS, turn west on Wilder Rd., left on South St., right on Ave. B, right on Watson Blvd.* ☎ *305/872–9115* ⊕ *www.nonamepub.com* ⌂ *Reservations not accepted.*

WHERE TO STAY

For expanded reviews, facilities, and current deals, visit Fodors.com.

$ HOTEL **Big Pine Key Fishing Lodge.** There's a congenial atmosphere at this lively family-owned lodge-campground-marina—a happy mix of tent campers (who have the fabulous waterfront real estate), RVers (who look pretty permanent), and motel dwellers (rooms start at $109) who like to mingle at the rooftop pool and challenge each other to a game of poker. **Pros:** local fishing crowd; nice pool; great price. **Cons:** RV park is too close to motel; deer will eat your food if you're camping. [$] *Rooms from: $39* ✉ *MM 33 OS, 33000 Overseas Hwy.* ☎ *305/872–2351* 🛏 *16 efficiencies, 97 campsites with full hook-ups, 61 campsites without hook-ups* 🍴 *No meals.*

$$$$ B&B/INN **Deer Run Bed & Breakfast.** Key deer wander the grounds of this beachfront bed-and-breakfast, set on a quiet street lined with buttonwoods and mangroves. **Pros:** quiet location; healthy breakfasts; complimentary bike, kayak, and state park passes use. **Cons:** price is a bit high; hard to find. [$] *Rooms from: $235* ✉ *MM 33 OS, 1997 Long Beach Dr.* ☎ *305/872–2015* 🌐 *www.deerrunfloridabb.com* 🛏 *4 rooms* 🍴 *Breakfast.*

SPORTS AND THE OUTDOORS

BIKING

A good 10 miles of paved roads run from MM 30.3 BS, along Wilder Road, across the bridge to No Name Key, and along Key Deer Boulevard into the National Key Deer Refuge. Along the way you might see some Key deer. Stay off the trails that lead into wetlands, where fat tires can do damage to the environment.

Big Pine Bicycle Center. Owner Marty Baird is an avid cyclist and enjoys sharing his knowledge of great places to ride. He's also skilled at selecting the right bike for the journey, and he knows his repairs, too. His old-fashioned single-speed, fat-tire cruisers rent for $8 per half day and $10 for a full day. Helmets, baskets, and locks are included. ✉ *MM 30.9 BS, 31 County Rd.* ☎ *305/872–0130.*

BOATING AND FISHING EXCURSIONS

Those looking to fish can cast from No Name Key Bridge or hire a charter to take them into backcountry or deep waters for fishing year-round. If you're looking for a good snorkeling spot, stay close to Looe Key Reef, which is prime scuba and snorkeling territory. One resort caters to divers with dive boats that depart from their own dock. Others can make arrangements for you.

Strike Zone Charters. Glass-bottom-boat excursions venture into the backcountry and Atlantic Ocean. The five-hour Island Excursion ($59 plus fuel surcharge) emphasizes nature and Keys history; besides close encounters with birds, sea life, and vegetation, there's a fish cookout on an island. Snorkel and fishing equipment, food, and drinks are included. This is one of the few nature outings in the Keys with wheelchair access. Deep-sea charter rates for up to six people are $650 for a half day, $850 for a full day. It also offers flats fishing in the Gulf of Mexico. Dive excursions head to the wreck of the 110-foot *Adolphus Busch* ($59), and scuba ($48) and snorkel ($38) trips to Looe Key Reef, prime scuba and snorkeling territory, aboard glass-bottom boats. ⊠ *MM 29.6 BS, 29675 Overseas Hwy.* ☎ *305/872–9863, 800/654–9560* ⊕ *www.strikezonecharter.com.*

KAYAKING

There's nothing like the vast expanse of pristine waters and mangrove islands preserved by national refuges from here to Key West. The maze-like terrain can be confusing, so it's wise to hire a guide at least the first time out.

Big Pine Kayak Adventures. There's no excuse to skip a water adventure with this convenient kayak rental service, which delivers them to your lodging or anywhere between Seven Mile Bridge and Stock Island. The company, headed by *The Florida Keys Paddling Guide* author Bill Keogh, will rent you a kayak and then ferry you—called taxi-yakking—to remote islands with clear instructions on how to paddle back on your own. Rentals are by the half day or full day. Group kayak tours ($50 each for three hours) explore the mangrove forests of Great White Heron and Key Deer National Wildlife Refuges. Custom tours ($125 each and up, four hours) transport you to exquisite backcountry areas teeming with wild-life. Kayak fishing charters are also popular. ⊠ *MM 30 BS, Old Wooden Bridge Fishing Camp, turn right at traffic light, continue on Wilder Rd. toward No Name Key* ☎ *305/872–7474* ⊕ *www.keyskayaktours.com.*

LITTLE TORCH KEY

Little Torch Key is between mile markers 29 and 10.

Little Torch Key and its neighbor islands, Ramrod Key and Summerland Key, are good jumping-off points for divers headed for Looe Key Reef. The islands also serve as a refuge for those who want to make forays into Key West but not stay in the thick of things.

The undeveloped backcountry at your door makes Little Torch Key an ideal location for fishing and kayaking. Nearby **Ramrod Key,** which also caters to divers bound for Looe Key, derives its name from a ship that wrecked on nearby reefs in the early 1800s.

NEED A BREAK?

Baby's Coffee. The aroma of rich roasting coffee beans arrests you at the door of "the Southernmost Coffee Roaster." Buy it by the pound or by the cup along with sandwiches and sweets. ⊠ *MM 15 OS, 3178 Overseas Hwy.* ☎ *305/744–9866, 800/523–2326* ⊕ *www.babyscoffee.com.*

WHERE TO EAT

$ ╳ **Geiger Key Smokehouse Bar & Grill.** There's a strong hint of the Old
AMERICAN Keys at this oceanside marina restaurant, which came under new man-agement in 2010 by the same folks who own Hogfish Grill on Stock Island. "On the backside of paradise," as the sign says, its tiki struc-tures overlook quiet mangroves at an RV park marina. Locals usually outnumber tourists. The all-day menu spans an ambitious array of sandwiches, tacos, and seafood. Local fishermen stop here for break-fast before heading out in search of the big one. Don't miss the Sunday barbecue from 4 to 9. $ *Average main: $12* ⊠ *MM 10, 5 Geiger Key Rd., off Boca Chica Rd., on Geiger Key, Key West* ☎ *305/296–3553, 305/294–1230* ⊕ *www.geigerkeymarina.com.*

$$$$
ECLECTIC

✕ **Little Palm Island Restaurant.** The oceanfront setting calls to mind St. Barts and other high-end destinations of the Caribbean. Keep that in mind as you reach for the bill, which can also make you swoon. The restaurant at the exclusive Little Palm Island Resort—its dining room and adjacent outdoor terrace lit by candles and warmed by live music—is one of the most romantic spots in the Keys. The seasonal menu is a melding of French and Caribbean flavors, with exotic little touches. Think shrimp and yellowtail ceviche or coconut lobster bisque as a starter, followed by mahimahi with creamy cilantro polenta. The Sunday brunch buffet, the full-moon dinners with live entertainment, and the Chef's Table Dinner are popular. The dining room is open to nonguests on a reservations-only basis. No children under 16 are allowed. $ *Average main: $65* ✉ *MM 28.5 OS, 28500 Overseas Hwy.* ☎ *305/872–2551* ⊕ *www.littlepalmisland.com* ⌂ *Reservations essential.*

$$
ITALIAN

✕ **Zaza Pizzeria Neopolitana.** Besides artisan pizzas such as béchamel with ham, you'll find hand-rolled fried risotto balls filled with ground beef, mozzarella, and peas; risotto infused with fresh lobster; pasta; bruschetta; and fried calzones. There's even pizza for breakfast (or try a frittata with ricotta and spinach or buffalo mozzarella, baby arugula, and prosciutto). Everything's fresh, most of it imported from Italy. ZaZa adds a bit of elegance to the pizza scene, not only with its menu, but also with its blue-tiled wood-fired pizza oven. $ *Average main: $18* ✉ *MM 17 BS, 17015 Overseas Hwy.* ☎ *305/745–2717* ⊕ *www.zazapizzeria.com.*

WHERE TO STAY
For expanded reviews, facilities, and current deals, visit Fodors.com.

$$$$
RESORT
Fodor's Choice
★

⌂ **Little Palm Island Resort & Spa.** *Haute tropicale* best describes this luxury retreat, and "second mortgage" might explain how some can afford the extravagant prices. **Pros:** secluded setting; heavenly spa; easy wildlife viewing. **Cons:** expensive; might be too quiet for some. $ *Rooms from: $1,590* ✉ *MM 28.5 OS, 28500 Overseas Hwy.* ☎ *305/872–2524, 800/343–8567* ⊕ *www.littlepalmisland.com* ⇨ *30 suites* ¶⊙¶ *Some meals.*

$
HOTEL

⌂ **Looe Key Reef Resort & Center.** If your Keys vacation is all about diving, you'll be well served at this scuba-obsessed operation—the closest place to stay to the stellar reef (and affordable to boot). **Pros:** guests get discounts on dive and snorkel trips; fun bar. **Cons:** small rooms; unheated pool; close to road. $ *Rooms from: $89* ✉ *MM 27.5 OS, 27340 Overseas Hwy., Ramrod Key* ☎ *305/872–2215, 877/816–3483* ⊕ *www.diveflakeys.com* ⇨ *23 rooms, 1 suite* ¶⊙¶ *No meals.*

$$
HOTEL

⌂ **Parmer's Resort.** Almost every room at this budget-friendly option has a view of South Pine Channel, with the lovely curl of Big Pine Key in the foreground. **Pros:** bright rooms; pretty setting; good value. **Cons:** a bit out of the way; housekeeping costs extra; little shade around the pool. $ *Rooms from: $134* ✉ *MM 28.7 BS, 565 Barry Ave.* ☎ *305/872–2157* ⊕ *www.parmersresort.com* ⇨ *18 rooms, 12 efficiencies, 15 apartments, 1 penthouse, 1 2-bedroom cottage* ¶⊙¶ *Breakfast.*

SPORTS AND THE OUTDOORS

BOATING AND KAYAKING

Dolphin Marina. Dolphin Marina rents 19- and 22-foot boats with 150 horsepower for up to eight people by the half day (from $200) and full day (from $250). ⊠ 28530 Overseas Hwy. ☎ 305/872–2685 ⊕ www. dolphinmarina.net.

Sugarloaf Marina. Rent a paddle-propelled vehicle for exploring local gulf waters. Rates for one-person kayaks start at $15 for one hour to $35 for a full day. Two-person kayaks are also available. Delivery is free for rentals of three days or more. They can also hook you up with a day of offshore or backcountry fishing as well as ultra light air tours. ⊠ MM 17 BS, 17015 Overseas Hwy., Sugarloaf Key ☎ 305/745–3135 ⊕ www.sugarloafkeymarina.com.

SCUBA DIVING AND SNORKELING

Looe Key Reef. In 1744 the HMS *Looe*, a British warship, ran aground and sank on one of the most beautiful coral reefs in the Keys. Today the key owes its name to the ill-fated ship. The 5.3-square-nautical-mile reef, part of the **Florida Keys National Marine Sanctuary,** has strands of elkhorn coral on its eastern margin, purple sea fans, and abundant sponges and sea urchins. On its seaward side, it drops almost vertically 50 to 90 feet. In its midst, **Shipwreck Trail** plots the location of nine historic wreck sites in 14 to 120 feet of water. Buoys mark the sites, and underwater signs tell the history of each site and what marine life to expect. Snorkelers and divers will find the sanctuary a quiet place to observe reef life—except in July, when the annual Underwater Music Festival pays homage to Looe Key's beauty and promotes reef awareness with six hours of music broadcast via underwater speakers. Dive shops, charters, and private boats transport about 500 divers and snorkelers to hear the spectacle, which includes classical, jazz, new age, and Caribbean music, as well as a little Jimmy Buffett. There are even underwater Elvis impersonators. ⊠ MM 27.5 OS, 216 Ann St., Key West ☎ 305/292–0311.

Looe Key Reef Resort & Dive Center. This center, the closest dive shop to Looe Key Reef, offers two affordable trips daily, 7:30 am or 12:15 pm ($69 for divers, $39 for snorkelers, $25 for bubble watchers). The maximum depth is 30 feet, so snorkelers and divers go on the same boat. On Wednesday it runs a trip that visits a wreck and reefs in the area for the same price for either snorkeling or diving. The dive boat, a 45-foot catamaran, is docked at the full-service Looe Key Reef Resort. ⊠ MM 27.5 OS, Looe Key Reef Resort, 27340 Overseas Hwy., Ramrod Key ☎ 305/872–2215, 877/816–3483 ⊕ www.diveflakeys.com.

EN ROUTE The huge object that looks like a white whale floating over Cudjoe Key (MM 23–21) isn't a figment of your imagination. It's Fat Albert, a radar balloon that monitors local air and water traffic.

KEY WEST

Situated 150 miles from Miami, 90 miles from Havana, and an immeasurable distance from sanity, this end-of-the-line community has never been like anywhere else. Even after it was connected to the rest of the country—by the railroad in 1912 and by the highway in 1938—it maintained a strong sense of detachment.

Key West reflects a diverse population: Conchs (natives, many of whom trace their ancestry to the Bahamas), freshwater Conchs (long-time residents who migrated from somewhere else years ago), Hispanics (primarily descendants of Cuban immigrants), recent refugees from the urban sprawl of mainland Florida, military personnel, and an assortment of vagabonds, drifters, and dropouts in search of refuge. The island was once a gay vacation hot spot, and it remains a decidedly gay-friendly destination. Some of the most renowned gay guesthouses, however, no longer cater to an exclusively gay clientele. Key Westers pride themselves on their tolerance of all peoples, all sexual orientations, and even all animals. Most restaurants allow pets, and it's not surprising to see stray cats, dogs, and chickens roaming freely through the dining rooms. The chicken issue is one that government officials periodically try to bring to an end, but the colorful iconic fowl continue to strut and crow, particularly in the vicinity of Old Town's Bahamian Village.

Although the rest of the Keys are known for outdoor activities, Key West has something of a city feel. Few open spaces remain, as promoters continue to churn out restaurants, galleries, shops, and museums to interpret the city's intriguing past. As a tourist destination, Key West has a lot to sell—an average temperature of 79°F, 19th-century architecture, and a laid-back lifestyle. Yet much has been lost to those eager for a buck. Duval Street looks like a miniature Las Vegas lined with garish signs for T-shirt shops and tour-company offices. Cruise ships dwarf the town's skyline and fill the streets with day-trippers gawking at the hippies with dogs in their bike baskets, gay couples walking down the street holding hands, and the oddball lot of locals, some of whom bark louder than the dogs.

GETTING HERE AND AROUND

Between mile markers 4 and 0, Key West is the one place in the Keys where you could conceivably do without a car, especially if you plan on staying around Old Town. If you've driven the 106 miles down the chain, you're probably ready to abandon your car in the hotel parking lot anyway. Trolleys, buses, bikes, scooters, and feet are more suitable alternatives. To explore the beaches, New Town, and Stock Island, you'll probably need a car.

Greyhound Lines runs a special Keys shuttle two times a day (depending on the day of the week) from Miami International Airport (departing from Concourse E, lower level) and stops throughout the Keys. Fares run about $45 for Key West (3535 S. Roosevelt, Key West International Airport). Keys Shuttle runs scheduled service six times a day in 15-passenger vans between Miami Airport and Key West with stops throughout the Keys for $70 to $90 per person. Key West

KEY WEST'S COLORFUL HISTORY

The United States acquired Key West from Spain in 1821, along with the rest of Florida. The Spanish had named the island Cayo Hueso, or Bone Key, after the Native American skeletons they found on its shores. In 1823 President James Monroe sent Commodore David S. Porter to chase pirates away. For three decades the primary industry in Key West was wrecking—rescuing people and salvaging cargo from ships that foundered on the nearby reefs. According to some reports, when pickings were lean, the wreckers hung out lights to lure ships aground. Their business declined after 1849, when the federal government began building lighthouses.

In 1845 the army began construction on Fort Taylor, which kept Key West on the Union side during the Civil War, even though most of Florida seceded. After the fighting ended, an influx of Cubans unhappy with Spain's rule brought the cigar industry here. Fishing, shrimping, and sponge gathering became important industries, as did pineapple canning. Through much of the 19th century and into the 20th, Key West was Florida's wealthiest city in per-capita terms. But in 1929 the local economy began to unravel. Cigar making moved to Tampa, Hawaii dominated the pineapple industry, and the sponges succumbed to blight. Then the Depression hit, and within a few years half the population was on relief.

Tourism began to revive Key West, but that came to a halt when a hurricane knocked out the railroad bridge in 1935. To help the tourism industry recover from that crushing blow, the government offered incentives for islanders to turn their charming homes—many of them built by shipwrights—into guesthouses and inns. The wise foresight has left the town with more than 100 such lodgings, a hallmark of Key West vacationing today. In the 1950s the discovery of "pink gold" in the Dry Tortugas boosted the economy of the entire region. Harvesting Key West shrimp required a fleet of up to 500 boats and flooded local restaurants with sweet luscious shrimp. The town's artistic community found inspiration in the colorful fishing boats.

Express operates air-conditioned ferries between the Key West Terminal (Caroline and Grinnell streets) and Marco Island and Fort Myers Beach. The trip from Fort Myers Beach takes at least four hours each way and costs $86 one-way, $146 round-trip. Ferries depart from Fort Myers Beach at 8:30 am and from Key West at 6 pm. The Marco Island ferry costs $86 one-way and $146 round-trip, and departs at 8:30 am (the return trip leaves Key West at 5 pm). A photo ID is required for each passenger. Advance reservations are recommended. The SuperShuttle charges $102 per passenger for trips from Miami International Airport to the Upper Keys. To go farther into the Keys, you must book an entire 11-person van, which costs about $350 to Key West. You need to place your request for transportation back to the airport 24 hours in advance.

The City of Key West Department of Transportation has six color-coded bus routes traversing the island from 6:30 am to 11:30 pm. Stops have signs with the international bus symbol. Schedules are available on buses and at hotels, visitor centers, and shops. The fare is $2 one-way. The Lower Keys Shuttle bus runs from Marathon to Key West ($4 one way), with scheduled stops along the way.

Old Town Key West is the only place in the Keys where parking is a problem. There are public parking lots that charge by the hour or day (some hotels and bed-and-breakfasts provide parking or discounts at municipal lots). If you arrive early, you can sometimes find a spot on side streets off Duval and Whitehead, where you can park for free—just be sure it's not marked for residential parking only. Your best bet is to bike or take the trolley around town if you don't want to walk. You can disembark and reboard the trolley at will.

ESSENTIALS

Transportation Contacts City of Key West Department of Transportation ☎ *305/809–3910* ⊕ *www.kwtransit.com.* **Greyhound Lines** ☎ *800/410–5397 Local information, 800/231–2222* ⊕ *www.greyhound.com.* **Keys Shuttle** ☎ *305/289–9997, 888/765–9997* ⊕ *www.floridakeysshuttle.com.* **Key West Express** ✉ *100 Grinnell St.* ☎ *888/539–2628* ⊕ *www.seakeywestexpress.com.* **Lower Keys Shuttle** ☎ *305/809–3910* ⊕ *www.kwtransit.com.* **SuperShuttle** ☎ *305/871–2000, 800/258–3826* ⊕ *www.supershuttle.com.*

Visitor Information Gay & Lesbian Community Center ✉ *513 Truman Ave.* ☎ *305/394–4603* ⊕ *www.gaykeywestfl.com.* **Greater Key West Chamber of Commerce** ✉ *510 Greene St.* ☎ *305/294–2587, 800/527–8539* ⊕ *www.keywestchamber.org.*

EXPLORING

OLD TOWN

The heart of Key West, the historic Old Town area runs from White Street to the waterfront. Beginning in 1822, wharves, warehouses, chandleries, ship-repair facilities, and eventually in 1891 the U.S. Custom House sprang up around the deep harbor to accommodate the navy's large ships and other sailing vessels. Wreckers, merchants, and sea captains built lavish houses near the bustling waterfront. A remarkable number of these fine Victorian and pre-Victorian structures have been restored to their original grandeur and now serve as homes, guesthouses, shops, restaurants, and museums. These, along with the dwellings of famous writers, artists, and politicians who've come to Key West over the past 175 years, are among the area's approximately 3,000 historic structures. Old Town also has the city's finest restaurants and hotels, lively street life, and popular night spots.

TOP ATTRACTIONS

Audubon House and Tropical Gardens. If you've ever seen an engraving by ornithologist John James Audubon, you'll understand why his name is synonymous with birds. See his works in this three-story house, which was built in the 1840s for Captain John Geiger and filled with period furniture. It now commemorates Audubon's 1832 stop in Key West

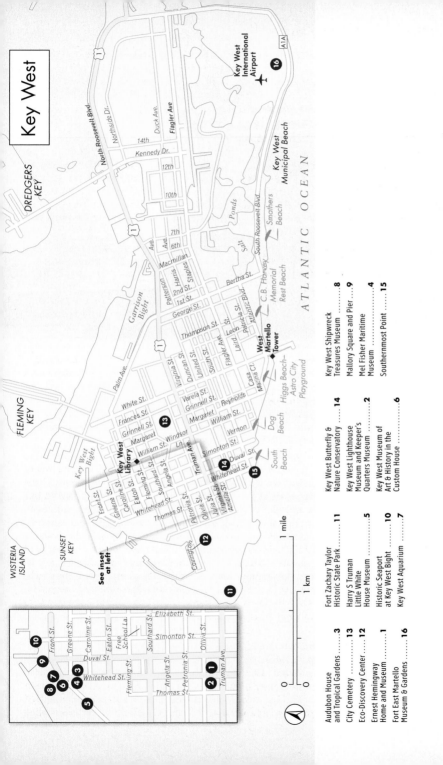

Key West

DREDGERS KEY

FLEMING KEY

WISTERIA ISLAND

SUNSET KEY

Key West Bight

See inset at left

Key West Library

Key West International Airport

Garrison Bight

ATLANTIC OCEAN

Key West Municipal Beach

Smathers Beach

Atlantic Rest Beach

West Martello Tower ◆

Higgs Beach– Astro City Playground

Dog Beach

South Beach

North Roosevelt Blvd.

Northside Dr.

Duck Ave.

Flagler Ave.

14th
Kennedy Dr.
12th
10th

Ponds

7th
6th
Ave.
Macmillan

Patterson
2nd St.
1st St.
2nd Harris
Staples
George St.

Palm Ave.

Thompson St.

Virginia St.
Duncan St.
United St.
South St.
Flagler Ave.
Leon St.
Laird St.
Patricia St.
Atlantic Blvd.

Bertha St.

Salt

C.B. Harvey Memorial

South Roosevelt Blvd.

Casa Ct.
Marina Ave.

White St.
Frances St.
Grinnell St.
Margaret
Windsor Ln.
Truman Ave.
Simonton St.
Vernon
William St.
Reynolds
Margaret
Grinnell St.
Frances St.

Virginia St.
Varela St.

Duval St.
Whitehead St.

Front St.
Greene St.
Caroline St.
Eaton St.
Fleming St.
Angela St.
Southard St.
Whitehead St.
Thomas St.
Petronia St.
Olivia St.
Julia St.
Virginia St.
Amelia St.

13

15

14

12

11

Inset:
Elizabeth St.
Olivia St.
Simonton St.
Southard St.
Caroline St.
Eaton St.
Free School La.
Greene St.
Front St.
Duval St.
Fleming St.
Whitehead St.
Angela St.
Petronia St.
Thomas St.
Truman Ave.

10
9
8 7 6
4 3
5
2 1
16

0 _____ 1 mile
0 _____ 1 km

See the typewriter Hemingway used at his home office in Key West. He lived here from 1931 to 1942.

while he was traveling through Florida to study birds. After an introduction by a docent, you can do a self-guided tour of the house and gardens (or just the gardens). An art gallery sells lithographs of the artist's famed portraits. ✉ *205 Whitehead St.* ☎ *305/294–2116, 877/294–2470* ⊕ *www.audubonhouse.com* ✉ *$7.50 gardens only; $12 house and gardens* ☉ *Daily 9:30–5, last tour starts at 4:30.*

Ernest Hemingway Home and Museum. Amusing anecdotes spice up the guided tours of Ernest Hemingway's home, built in 1801 by the town's most successful wrecker. While living here between 1931 and 1942, Hemingway wrote about 70% of his life's work, including classics like *For Whom the Bell Tolls*. Few of his belongings remain aside from some books, and there's little about his actual work, but photographs help you visualize his day-to-day life. The famous six-toed descendants of Hemingway's cats—many named for actors, artists, authors, and even a hurricane—have free rein of the property. Tours begin every 10 minutes and take 30 minutes; then you're free to explore on your own. ✉ *907 Whitehead St.* ☎ *305/294–1136* ⊕ *www.hemingwayhome.com* ✉ *$13* ☉ *Daily 9–5.*

Fort Zachary Taylor Historic State Park. Construction of the fort began in 1845 but was halted during the Civil War. Even though Florida seceded from the Union, Yankee forces used the fort as a base to block Confederate shipping. More than 1,500 Confederate vessels were detained in Key West's harbor. The fort, finally completed in 1866, was also used in the Spanish-American War. Take a 30-minute guided walking tour of the redbrick fort, a National Historic Landmark, at noon and 2, or self-tour anytime between 8 and 5. In February a celebration called

Hemingway Was Here

In a town where Pulitzer Prize–winning writers are almost as common as coconuts, Ernest Hemingway stands out. Bars and restaurants around the island claim that he ate or drank there (except Bagatelle, where a sign in the bar reads "Hemingway never liked this place").

Hemingway came to Key West in 1928 at the urging of writer John dos Passos and rented a house with wife number two, Pauline Pfeiffer. They spent winters in the Keys and summers in Europe and Wyoming, occasionally taking African safaris. Along the way they had two sons, Patrick and Gregory. In 1931 Pauline's wealthy uncle Gus gave the couple the house at 907 Whitehead Street. Now known as the Ernest Hemingway Home & Museum, it's Key West's number-one tourist attraction. Renovations included the addition of a pool and a tropical garden.

In 1935, when the visitor bureau included the house in a tourist brochure, Hemingway promptly built the brick wall that surrounds it today. He wrote of the visitor bureau's offense in a 1935 essay for *Esquire,* saying, "The house at present occupied by your correspondent is listed as number eighteen in a compilation of the forty-eight things for a tourist to see in Key West. So there will be no difficulty in a tourist finding it or any other of the sights of the city, a map has been prepared by the local F.E.R.A. authorities to be presented to each arriving visitor. This is all very flattering to the easily bloated ego of your correspondent but very hard on production."

During his time in Key West, Hemingway penned some of his most important works, including *A Farewell to Arms, To Have and Have Not, Green Hills of Africa,* and *Death in the Afternoon.* His rigorous schedule consisted of writing almost every morning in his second-story studio above the pool, and then promptly descending the stairs at midday. By afternoon and evening he was ready for drinking, fishing, swimming, boxing, and hanging around with the boys.

One close friend was Joe Russell, a craggy fisherman and owner of the rugged bar Sloppy Joe's, originally at 428 Greene Street but now at 201 Duval Street. Russell was the only one in town who would cash Hemingway's $1,000 royalty check. Russell and Charles Thompson introduced Hemingway to deep-sea fishing, which became fodder for his writing. Another of Hemingway's loves was boxing. He set up a ring in his yard and paid local fighters to box with him, and he refereed matches at Blue Heaven, then a saloon at 729 Thomas Street.

Hemingway honed his macho image, dressed in cutoffs and old shirts, and took on the name Papa. In turn, he gave his friends new names and used them as characters in his stories. Joe Russell became Freddy, captain of the *Queen Conch* charter boat in *To Have and Have Not.*

Hemingway stayed in Key West for 11 years before leaving Pauline for wife number three. Pauline and the boys stayed on in the house, which sold in 1951 for $80,000, 10 times its original cost.

—Jim and Cynthia Tunstall

Civil War Heritage Days includes costumed reenactments and demonstrations. From mid-January to mid-April the park serves as an open-air gallery for pieces created for Sculpture Key West. One of its most popular features is its man-made beach, a rest stop for migrating birds in the spring and fall; there are also picnic areas, hiking and biking trails and a kayak launch. ✉ *Box 6565, end of Southard St., through Truman Annex* ☎ *305/292–6713* ⊕ *www.floridastateparks.org/forttaylor* 💲 *$4 for single occupant vehicles, $6 for 2–8 people in a vehicle, plus a 50¢ per person county surcharge* ☼ *Daily 8–sunset.*

NEED A BREAK?
Key West Library. Check out the pretty palm garden next to the Key West Library at 700 Fleming Street, just off Duval. This leafy, outdoor reading area, with shaded benches, is the perfect place to escape the frenzy and crowds of downtown Key West. There's free Internet access in the library, too. ✉ *700 Fleming St.* ☎ *305/292–3595.*

Harry S Truman Little White House Museum. Renovations to this circa-1890 landmark have restored the home and gardens to the Truman era, down to the wallpaper pattern. A free photographic review of visiting dignitaries and presidents—John F. Kennedy, Jimmy Carter, and Bill Clinton are among the chief executives who passed through here—is on display in the back of the gift shop. Engaging 45-minute tours begin every 20 minutes until 4:30. They start with an excellent 10-minute video on the history of the property and Truman's visits. On the grounds of **Truman Annex,** a 103-acre former military parade grounds and barracks, the home served as a winter White House for presidents Truman, Eisenhower, and Kennedy. ▄TIP➔ **The house tour does require climbing steps. Visitors can do a free self-guided botanical tour of the grounds with a brochure from the museum store.** ✉ *111 Front St.* ☎ *305/294–9911* ⊕ *www.trumanlittlewhitehouse.com* 💲 *$16.13* ☼ *Daily 9–5, grounds 7–6.*

Historic Seaport at Key West Bight. What was once a funky—in some places even seedy—part of town is now an 8½-acre historic restoration of 100 businesses, including waterfront restaurants, open-air bars, museums, clothing stores, bait shops, dive shops, docks, a marina, and water-sports concessions. It's all linked by the 2-mile waterfront **Harborwalk,** which runs between Front and Grinnell streets, passing big ships, schooners, sunset cruises, fishing charters, and glass-bottom boats. ✉ *100 Grinnell St.* ☎ *305/293–8309* ⊕ *www.keywestseaport.com.*

FAMILY **Key West Butterfly and Nature Conservatory.** This air-conditioned refuge for butterflies, birds, and the human spirit gladdens the soul with hundreds of colorful wings—more than 45 species of butterflies alone—in a lovely glass-encased bubble. Waterfalls, artistic benches, paved pathways, birds, and lush, flowering vegetation elevate this above most butterfly attractions. The gift shop and gallery are worth a visit on their own. ✉ *1316 Duval St.* ☎ *305/296–2988, 800/839–4647* ⊕ *www.keywestbutterfly. com* 💲 *$12* ☼ *Daily 9–5, gallery and shop open until 5:30.*

Key West Lighthouse Museum and Keeper's Quarters Museum. For the best view in town, climb the 88 steps to the top of this 1847 lighthouse. The 92-foot structure has a Fresnel lens, which was installed in the 1860s at

Divers examine the intentionally scuttled 327-foot former U.S. Coast Guard cutter Duane in 120 feet of water off Key Largo.

a cost of $1 million. The keeper lived in the adjacent 1887 clapboard house, which now exhibits vintage photographs, ship models, nautical charts, and lighthouse artifacts from all along the Key reefs. A kids' room is stocked with books and toys. ⊠ *938 Whitehead St.* ☎ *305/295–6616* ⊕ *www.kwahs.com* ✉ *$10* ⊘ *Daily 9:30–4:30.*

Fodor'sChoice
★
Key West Museum of Art & History in the Custom House. When Key West was designated a U.S. port of entry in the early 1820s, a custom-house was established. Salvaged cargoes from ships wrecked on the reefs were brought here, setting the stage for Key West to become—for a time—the richest city in Florida. The imposing redbrick-and-terra-cotta Richardsonian Romanesque–style building reopened as a museum and art gallery in 1999. Smaller galleries have long-term and changing exhibits about the history of Key West, including a Hemingway room and a fine collection of folk artist Mario Sanchez's wood paintings. In 2011, to commemorate the 100th anniversary of the railroad's arrival to Key West in 1912, a new permanent Flagler exhibit opened. ⊠ *281 Front St.* ☎ *305/295–6616* ⊕ *www.kwahs.com* ✉ *$7* ⊘ *Daily 9:30–4:30.*

Mallory Square and Pier. For cruise-ship passengers, this is the disembarkation point for an attack on Key West. For practically every visitor, it's the requisite venue for a nightly sunset celebration that includes street performers—human statues, sword swallowers, tightrope walkers, musicians, and more—plus craft vendors, conch fritter fryers, and other regulars who defy classification. (Wanna picture with my pet iguana?) With all the activity, don't forget to watch the main show: a dazzling tropical sunset. ⊠ *Mallory Sq.*

The Southernmost Point. Possibly the most photographed site in Key West (even though the actual geographic southernmost point in the continental United States lies across the bay on a naval base, where you see a satellite dish), this is a must-see. Who wouldn't want his picture taken next to the big striped buoy that marks the southernmost point in the continental United States? A plaque next to it honors Cubans who lost their lives trying to escape to America and other signs tell Key West history. ⊠ *Whitehead and South Sts.*

WORTH NOTING

City Cemetery. You can learn almost as much about a town's history through its cemetery as through its historic houses. Key West's celebrated 20-acre burial place may leave you wanting more, with headstone epitaphs such as "I told you I was sick," and, for a wayward husband, "Now I know where he's sleeping at night." Among the interesting plots are a memorial to the sailors killed in the sinking of the battleship USS *Maine*, carved angels and lambs marking graves of children, and grand aboveground crypts that put to shame many of the town's dwellings for the living. There are separate plots for Catholics, Jews, and refugees from Cuba. You're free to walk around the cemetery on your own, but the best way to see it is on a 90-minute tour given by the staff and volunteers of the Historic Florida Keys Foundation. Tours leave from the main gate, and reservations are required. ⊠ *Margaret and Angela Sts.* ☎ *305/292–6718* ⊕ *www.historicfloridakeys.org* ☞ *Tours $15* ⊙ *Daily sunrise–6 pm; tours Tues. and Thurs. at 9:30 year-round, call for additional times.*

FAMILY **Eco-Discovery Center.** While visiting Fort Zachary Taylor Historic State Park, stop in at this 6,400-square-foot interactive attraction, which encourages visitors to venture through a variety of Florida Keys habitats from pinelands, beach dunes, and mangroves to the deep sea. Walk through a model of NOAA's (National Oceanic and Atmospheric Administration) Aquarius, a unique underwater ocean laboratory 9 mile off Key Largo, to virtually discover what lurks beneath the sea. Touchscreen computer displays, a dramatic movie, a 2,450-gallon aquarium, and live underwater cameras show off North America's only contiguous barrier coral reef. ⊠ *35 E. Quay Rd., at end of Southard St. in Truman Annex* ☎ *305/809–4750* ⊕ *www.floridakeys.noaa.gov* ☞ *Free, donations accepted* ⊙ *Tues.–Sat. 9–4.*

FAMILY **Key West Aquarium.** Pet a nurse shark and explore the fascinating underwater realm of the Keys without getting wet at this historic aquarium. Hundreds of tropical fish and enormous sea creatures live here. A touch tank enables you to handle starfish, sea cucumbers, horseshoe and hermit crabs, even horse and queen conchs—living totems of the Conch Republic. Built in 1934 by the Works Progress Administration as the world's first open-air aquarium, most of the building has been enclosed for all-weather viewing. Guided tours, included in the admission price, feature shark feedings. ⊠ *1 Whitehead St.* ☎ *305/296–2051* ⊕ *www.keywestaquarium. com* ☞ *$15.05* ⊙ *Daily 10–8; tours at 11, 1, 2, 4:30, and 6:30.*

FAMILY **Key West Shipwreck Treasures Museum.** Much of Key West's history, early prosperity, and interesting architecture come from ships that ran aground on its coral reef. Artifacts from the circa-1856 *Isaac Allerton*, which

THE CONCH REPUBLIC

Beginning in the 1970s, pot smuggling became a source of income for islanders who knew how to dodge detection in the maze of waterways in the Keys. In 1982 the U.S. Border Patrol threw a roadblock across the Overseas Highway just south of Florida City to catch drug runners and undocumented aliens. Traffic backed up for miles as Border Patrol agents searched vehicles and demanded that the occupants prove U.S. citizenship. Officials in Key West, outraged at being treated like foreigners by the federal government, staged a protest and formed their own "nation," the so-called Conch Republic. They hoisted a flag and distributed mock border passes, visas, and Conch currency. The embarrassed Border Patrol dismantled its roadblock, and now an annual festival recalls the city's victory. You can even "apply" for a Conch Republic passport (for entertainment purposes, and not travel!). It'll set you back $100 but those who hold one think it's priceless. Begin your journey online at ⊕ www.conchrepublic.com.

yielded $150,000 worth of wreckage, comprise the museum portion of this multifaceted attraction. Actors and films add a bit of Disneyesque drama. The final highlight is climbing to the top of the 65-foot lookout tower, a reproduction of the 20 or so towers used by Key West wreckers during the town's salvaging heydays. ⊠ *1 Whitehead St.* ☎ *305/292–8990* ⊕ *www.shipwreckhistoreum.com* ☞ *$15.05* ⊙ *Daily 9:40–5.*

Mel Fisher Maritime Museum. In 1622 two Spanish galleons laden with riches from South America foundered in a hurricane 40 miles west of the Keys. In 1985 diver Mel Fisher recovered the treasures from the lost ships, the *Nuestra Señora de Atocha* and the *Santa Margarita.* Fisher's incredible adventure tracking these fabled hoards and battling the state of Florida for rights is as amazing as the loot you'll see, touch, and learn about in this museum. Artifacts include a 77.76-carat natural emerald crystal worth almost $250,000. Exhibits on the second floor rotate and might cover slave ships, including the excavated 17th-century *Henrietta Marie,* or the evolution of Florida maritime history. ⊠ *200 Greene St.* ☎ *305/294–2633* ⊕ *www.melfisher.org* ☞ *$12.50* ⊙ *Weekdays 8:30–5, weekends 9:30–5.*

NEW TOWN

The Overseas Highway splits as it enters Key West, the two forks rejoining to encircle New Town, the area east of White Street to Cow Key Channel. The southern fork runs along the shore as South Roosevelt Boulevard (Route A1A), skirting Key West International Airport. Along the north shore, North Roosevelt Boulevard (U.S. 1) leads to Old Town. Part of New Town was created with dredged fill. The island would have continued growing this way had the Army Corps of Engineers not determined in the early 1970s that it was detrimental to the nearby reef.

Fort East Martello Museum & Gardens. This redbrick Civil War fort never saw a lick of action during the war. Today it serves as a museum, with historical exhibits about the 19th and 20th centuries. Among the latter

WORD OF MOUTH

"The historic Key West Garrison Bight Marina is crowded with pleasure and commercial boats. We always skip the 'short cut' around the harbor and take the long walk by the boats. We never tire of seeing the variety and arrangement of boats."

—photo by John Franzis, Fodors.com member

are relics of the USS *Maine,* cigar factory and shipwrecking exhibits, and the citadel tower you can climb to the top. The museum, operated by the Key West Art and Historical Society, also has a collection of Stanley Papio's "junk art" sculptures inside and out, and a gallery of Cuban folk artist Mario Sanchez's chiseled and painted wooden carvings of historic Key West street scenes. ⊠ *3501 S. Roosevelt Blvd.* ☎ *305/296–3913* ⊕ *www.kwahs.com* ☒ *$7* ⊘ *Daily 9:30–4:30.*

BEACHES

OLD TOWN

Dog Beach. Next to Louie's Backyard, this tiny beach—the only one in Key West where dogs are allowed unleashed—has a shore that's a mix of sand and rocks. **Amenities:** none. **Best for:** walking. ⊠ *Vernon and Waddell Sts.* ☒ *Free* ⊘ *Daily sunrise–sunset.*

FAMILY **Fort Zachary Taylor Beach.** The park's beach is the best and safest place to swim in Key West. There's an adjoining picnic area with barbecue grills and shade trees, a snack bar, and rental equipment, including snorkeling gear. A café serves sandwiches and other munchies. **Amenities:** food and drink; showers; toilets; water sports. **Best for:** swimming; snorkeling. ⊠ *Box 6565, end of Southard St., through Truman Annex* ☎ *305/292–6713* ⊕ *www.floridastateparks.org/forttaylor* ☒ *$4 for one-occupant vehicles, $6 for 2–8 people in vehicle, plus 50¢ per person county surcharge* ⊘ *Daily 8–sunset tours noon and 2.*

FAMILY **Higgs Beach–Astro City Playground.** This Monroe County park with its groomed pebbly sand is a popular sunbathing spot. A nearby grove of Australian pines provides shade, and the West Martello Tower provides shelter should a storm suddenly sweep in. Kayak and beach-chair rentals are available, as is a volleyball net. The beach also has a marker and cultural exhibit commemorating the gravesite of 295 enslaved Africans who died after being rescued from three South America–bound slave ships in 1860. Across the street, **Astro City Playground** is popular with young children. **Amenities:** parking; toilets; water sports. **Best for:** swimming; snorkeling. ⊠ *Atlantic Blvd., between White and Reynolds Sts.* ☒ *Free* ⊘ *Daily 6 am–11 pm.*

NEW TOWN

C.B. Harvey Memorial Rest Beach. This beach and park were named after Cornelius Bradford Harvey, former Key West mayor and commissioner. Adjacent to Higgs Beach, it has half a dozen picnic areas across the street, dunes, a pier, and a wheelchair and bike path. **Amenities:** none. **Best for:** walking. ⊠ *Atlantic Blvd., east side of White St. Pier* ☒ *Free* ⊘ *Daily 6 am–11 pm.*

Smathers Beach. This wide beach has nearly 1 mile of nice white sand, plus beautiful coconut palms, picnic areas, and volleyball courts, all of which make it popular with the spring-break crowd. Trucks along the road rent rafts, windsurfers, and other beach "toys." **Amenities:** parking; toilets; water sports. **Best for:** partiers. ⊠ *S. Roosevelt Blvd.* ☒ *Free* ⊘ *Daily 7 am–11 pm.*

South Beach. On the Atlantic, this stretch of sand, also known as City Beach, is popular with travelers staying at nearby motels. It is now part of the new Southernmost Hotel on the Beach resort, but is open to the public with a fun beach bar and grill. There's little parking however, so visitors must walk or bike to the beach. **Amenities:** food and drink; parking; toilets. **Best for:** partiers; sunrise; sunset. ✉ *Duval St. at South St.* 🎟 *Free* ⏲ *Daily 7 am–11 pm.*

WHERE TO EAT

Bring your appetite, a sense of daring, and a lack of preconceived notions about propriety. A meal in Key West can mean overlooking the crazies along Duval Street, watching roosters and pigeons battle for a scrap of food that may have escaped your fork, relishing the finest in what used to be the dining room of some 19th-century Victorian home, or gazing out at boats jockeying for position in the marina. And that's just the diversity of the setting. Seafood dominates local menus, but the treatment afforded that fish or crustacean can range from Cuban and American to Asian and Continental.

$$ JAPANESE 🍴 **Ambrosia.** Ask any savvy local where to get the best sushi on the island and you'll undoubtedly be pointed to this tiny wood-and-tatami-paneled dining room with indoor waterfall tucked away into a resort near the beach. Grab a seat at the sushi bar and watch owner and head sushi chef Masa prepare an impressive array of superfresh sashimi delicacies. Sushi lovers can't go wrong with the Ambrosia special ($40): miso soup served with a sampler of 15 kinds of sashimi, seven pieces of sushi, and sushi rolls. There's an assortment of lightly fried tempura and teriyaki dishes and a killer bento box at lunch. Enjoy it all with a glass of premium sake or a cold glass of Sapporo beer. [$] *Average main: $20* ✉ *Santa Maria Resort, 1401 Simonton St.* ☎ *305/293–0304* 🌐 *www.keywestambrosia.com* ⏲ *No lunch weekends. Closed 2 wks after Labor Day.*

$$$ ECLECTIC 🍴 **Azur Restaurant.** Fuel up on the finest fare at this former gas station, now part of the Eden House complex. In a contemporary setting with indoor and outdoor seating, welcoming staff serves breakfast, lunch, and dinner that stand out from the hordes of Key West restaurants by virtue of originality. For instance, key lime-stuffed French toast and yellowtail snapper Benedict make breakfast a pleasant wake-up call. The fennel-roasted pork sandwich with Fontina cheese, crab cake BLT, and charred marinated octopus command notice on the lunch menu. Four varieties of homemade gnocchi are a dinner-time specialty, along with tasting plates, "almost entrées" like braised lamb ribs over Moroccan-spiced chick peas, and main courses that include seafood risotto with chorizo and grilled sea bass. [$] *Average main: $26* ✉ *425 Grinnell St.* ☎ *305/292–2987* 🌐 *www.azurkeywest.com* ✍ *Reservations essential.*

$$$ CARIBBEAN 🍴 **Blue Heaven.** The outdoor dining area here is often referred to as "the quintessential Keys experience," and it's hard to argue. There's much to like about this historic restaurant where Hemingway refereed boxing matches and customers cheered for cockfights. Although these events are no more, the free-roaming chickens and cats add that "what-a-hoot" factor. Nightly specials include black bean soup, Caribbean

BBQ shrimp, bison strip steak with blackberry salad, and jerk chicken. Desserts and breads are baked on the premises; the banana bread and lobster Benedict with key lime hollandaise are hits during breakfast, the signature meal here. Bring patience as there is always a wait. $ *Average main: $24* ⊠ *729 Thomas St.* ☎ *305/296–8666* ⊕ *www.blueheavenkw. com* ♨ *Reservations not accepted* ☉ *Closed after Labor Day for 6 wks.*

$ × **B.O.'s Fish Wagon.** What started out as a fish house on wheels appears
SEAFOOD to have broken down on the corner of Caroline and William streets and is today the cornerstone for one of Key West's junkyard-chic dining institutions. Step up to the wood-plank counter window and order the specialty: a grouper sandwich fried or grilled and topped with key lime sauce. Other choices include fish nuts (don't be scared, they're just fried nuggets), hot dogs, cracked conch sandwich, and shrimp or soft-shell-crab sandwich. Talk sass with your host and find a picnic table or take a seat at the plank. Grab some paper towels off one of the rolls hanging around and busy yourself reading graffiti, license plates, and irreverent signs. It's a must-do Key West experience. $ *Average main: $10* ⊠ *801 Caroline St.* ☎ *305/294–9272* ⊕ *www.bosfishwagon.com* ♨ *Reservations not accepted* ▭ *No credit cards.*

$ × **The Café.** You don't have to be a vegetarian to love this new-age café
VEGETARIAN decorated with bright artwork and a corrugated tin–fronted counter. Local favorites include homemade soup, veggie sandwiches and burgers (order them with a side of sweet potato fries), grilled portobello mushroom salad, seafood, vegan specialties, stir-fry dinners, and grilled Gorgonzola pizza. There's also a nice selection of draft beer and wines by the glass, plus daily desserts (including vegan selections). $ *Average main: $11* ⊠ *509 Southard St.* ☎ *305/296–5515* ⊕ *www.thecafekw.com* ♨ *Reservations not accepted.*

$$$ × **Café Marquesa.** Chef Susan Ferry presents seven or more inspired
EUROPEAN entrées on her changing menu each night; delicious dishes can include
Fodor'sChoice yellowtail snapper with pear, ricotta pasta purses with caponata, and
★ Australian rack of lamb crusted with goat cheese and a port-fig sauce. End your meal on a sweet note with key lime napoleon with tropical fruits and berries. There's also a fine selection of wines and custom martinis such as the key limetini and the Irish martini. Adjoining the intimate Marquesa Hotel, the dining room is equally relaxed and elegant. $ *Average main: $29* ⊠ *600 Fleming St.* ☎ *305/292–1244* ⊕ *www. marquesa.com* ♨ *Reservations essential* ☉ *No lunch.*

$$$ × **Café Solé.** This little corner of France hides behind a high wall in a
FRENCH residential neighborhood. Inside, French training intertwines with local ingredients, creating delicious takes on classics, including a must-try conch Carpaccio, yellowtail snapper with mango salsa, and some of the best bouillabaisse that you'll find outside of Marseilles. Hog snapper, aka hogfish, is a house specialty here, prepared several ways by Chef John Correa, including with beurre blanc or red pepper custard sauce. From the land, there is filet mignon with a wild-mushroom demi-glaze. Lunch is served from 11 to 2, dinner from 5 to 10. $ *Average main: $27* ⊠ *1029 Southard St.* ☎ *305/294–0230* ⊕ *www.cafesole.com* ♨ *Reservations essential.*

$$$
MODERN
AMERICAN

✕ Camille's Restaurant. Break out the stretchy pants because everything on the menu at this affordable hot spot not only sounds scrumptious, it is. Start your day with a shrimp, lobster, or crab-cake Benedict—the latter was voted best in the Florida Keys. Lunch brings dishes like hand-pulled chicken salad or a mahimahi wrap. Evenings will have you swooning for the famous grilled stone-crab cakes with an addictive Captain Morgan spiced-rum mango sauce. Locals have tried to keep this place a secret for more than 20 years, but the word is out. Line up beneath the bright pink awning and happily wait for your seat. Be sure to ask your server about the Barbie dolls—they have a most unique collection, many with a Key West flair. $ *Average main: $21* ⊠ *Corner of Simonton and Catherine Sts., 1202 Simonton St.* ☎ *305/296–4811* ⊕ *www.camilleskeywest.com* ⌕ *Reservations essential.*

$$
CUBAN

✕ El Meson de Pepe. If you want to get a taste of the island's Cuban heritage, this is the place. Perfect for after watching a Mallory Square sunset, you can dine alfresco or in the dining room on refined versions of Cuban classics. Begin with a megasized mojito while you enjoy the basket of bread and savory sauces. The expansive menu offers *tostones rellenos* (green plantains with different traditional fillings), ceviche (raw fish "cooked" in lemon juice), and more. Choose from Cuban specialties such as roasted pork in a cumin mojo sauce and *ropa vieja* (shredded beef stew). At lunch, the local Cuban population and cruise-ship passengers enjoy Cuban sandwiches and smaller versions of dinner's most popular entrées. A Latin band performs outside at the bar during sunset celebration. $ *Average main: $19* ⊠ *Mallory Sq., 410 Wall St.* ☎ *305/295–2620* ⊕ *www.elmesondepepe.com.*

$
CUBAN

✕ El Siboney. Dining at this family-style restaurant is like going to Mom's for Sunday dinner—if your mother is Cuban. The dining room is noisy, and the food is traditional *cubano*. There are well-seasoned black beans, a memorable paella, traditional ropa vieja (shredded beef), and local seafood served grilled, stuffed, and breaded. Dishes come with plantains and beans and rice or salad and fries. To make a good thing even better, the prices are very reasonable. $ *Average main: $10* ⊠ *900 Catherine St.* ☎ *305/296–4184* ⊕ *www.elsiboneyrestaurant.com* ⌕ *Reservations not accepted.*

$$
SEAFOOD
FAMILY

✕ Half Shell Raw Bar. Smack-dab on the docks, this legendary institution gets its name from the oysters, clams, and peel-and-eat shrimp that are a departure point for its seafood-based diet. It's not clever recipes or fine dining (or even air-conditioning) that packs 'em in; it's fried fish, po'boy sandwiches, and seafood combos. For a break from the deep fryer, try the fresh and light conch ceviche "cooked" with lime juice. The potato salad is flavored with dill, and the "PamaRita" is a new twist in Margaritaville. $ *Average main: $16* ⊠ *Lands End Village at Historic Seaport, 231 Margaret St.* ☎ *305/294–7496* ⊕ *www.halfshellrawbar.com* ⌕ *Reservations not accepted.*

$
AMERICAN
FAMILY

✕ Lobo's Mixed Grill. Famous for its selection of wrap sandwiches, Lobo's has a reputation among locals for its 8-ounce, charcoal-grilled ground chuck burger—thick and juicy and served with lettuce, tomato, and pickle on a toasted bun. Mix it up with toppings like Brie, blue cheese, or portobello mushroom. The menu of 30 wraps includes rib eye, oyster, grouper, Cuban, and chicken Caesar. The menu includes salads and quesadillas, as well as a fried-shrimp-and-oyster combo. Beer and wine are served. This courtyard food stand closes around 5, so eat early. Most of Lobo's business is takeout (it has a half-dozen outdoor picnic tables), and it offers free delivery within Old Town. [$] *Average main: $9* ✉ *5 Key Lime Sq., east of intersection of Southard and Duval Sts.* ☎ *305/296–5303* 🌐 *www.lobosmixedgrill.com* ✍ *Reservations not accepted* 🕓 *Closed Sun. Apr.–early Dec.*

WORD OF MOUTH

"My favorite fine dining restaurant is Louie's Backyard, though we always go for lunch rather than dinner. The food is just as good, the view is wonderful during the day, and the prices are reasonable."

—SusanCS

$$$$ ECLECTIC 🍴 **Louie's Backyard.** Feast your eyes on a steal-your-breath-away view and beautifully presented dishes prepared by executive chef Doug Shook. Once you get over sticker shock on the seasonally changing menu (appetizers cost around $10–$18; entrées can hover around the $38 mark), settle in on the outside deck and enjoy dishes like grilled scallops with portobello relish, grilled king salmon with fried risotto, and mint-rubbed pork chop with salsa verde. A more affordable option upstairs is the Upper Deck, which serves tapas such as flaming ouzo shrimp, roasted olives with onion and feta, and Gruyère and duck confit pizza. If you come for lunch, the menu is less expensive but the view is just as fantastic. For night owls, the tin-roofed Afterdeck Bar serves cocktails on the water until the wee hours. [$] *Average main: $36* ✉ *700 Waddell Ave.* ☎ *305/294–1061* 🌐 *www.louiesbackyard.com* ✍ *Reservations essential* 🕓 *Closed Labor Day to mid-Sept. Upper Deck closed Sun. and Mon. No lunch at Upper Deck.*

$$ ITALIAN 🍴 **Mangia Mangia.** This longtime favorite serves large portions of homemade pastas that can be matched with any of their homemade sauces. Tables are arranged in a brick garden hung with twinkling lights and in a cozy, casual dining room in an old house. Everything out of the open kitchen is outstanding, including the *bollito misto di mare* (fresh seafood sautéed with garlic, shallots, white wine, and pasta) or the memorable spaghettini "schmappellini," homemade pasta with asparagus, tomatoes, pine nuts, and Parmesan. The wine list—with more than 350 offerings—includes old and rare vintages, and also has a good by-the-glass selection. [$] *Average main: $16* ✉ *900 Southard St.* ☎ *305/294–2469* 🌐 *www.mangia-mangia.com* ✍ *Reservations not accepted* 🕓 *No lunch.*

$$$ AMERICAN 🍴 **Michaels Restaurant.** White tablecloths, subdued lighting, and romantic music give Michaels the feel of an urban eatery. Garden seating reminds you that you are in the Keys. Chef–owner Michael Wilson flies in prime rib, cowboy steaks, and rib eyes from Allen Brothers in Chicago, which has supplied top-ranked steak houses for more than a century. Also on the menu is a melt-in-your-mouth grouper stuffed with jumbo lump crab, Kobe and tenderloin meat loaf, veal saltimbocca, and a variety of made-to-order fondue dishes (try the pesto pot, spiked with hot pepper and basil). To lighten up, smaller portions of many of the favorites

are available until 7:30 Sunday through Thursday. The Hemingway (mojito-style) and the Third Degree (raspberry vodka and white crème de cacao) top the cocktail menu. $ *Average main: $25* ✉ *532 Margaret St.* ☎ *305/295–1300* ⊕ *www.michaelskeywest.com* ⚐ *Reservations essential* ☾ *No lunch.*

$$$ ✕ **Nine One Five.** Twinkling lights draped along the lower- and upper-
ECLECTIC   level outdoor porches of a 100-year-old Victorian mansion set an elegant—though unstuffy—stage here. If you like to sample and sip, you'll appreciate the variety of smaller plate selections and wines by the glass. Starters include a cheese platter, crispy duck confit, a tapas platter, and the signature "tuna dome" with fresh crab, lemon-miso dressing, and an ahi tuna–sashimi wrapping. There are also larger plates if you're craving something like seafood soup or steak au poivre frites. Dine outdoors and people-watch along upper Duval, or sit at a table inside while listening to light jazz. $ *Average main: $28* ✉ *915 Duval St.* ☎ *305/296–0669* ⊕ *www.915duval.com* ⚐ *Reservations essential* ☾ *No lunch.*

$$$$ ✕ **Pisces.** In a circa-1892 former store and home, chef William Arnel
EUROPEAN   and staff create a contemporary setting with a stylish granite bar, Andy Warhol originals, and glass oil lamps. Favorites include "lobster tango mango," flambéed in cognac and served with saffron butter sauce and sliced mangoes; Pisces Aphrodite (seafood in puff pastry); fillet *au poivre*; and black grouper braised in champagne. $ *Average main: $35* ✉ *1007 Simonton St.* ☎ *305/294–7100* ⊕ *www.pisceskeywest.com* ⚐ *Reservations essential* ☾ *No lunch.*

$$ ✕ **Salute Ristorante at the Beach.** This colorful restaurant sits on Higgs
ITALIAN   Beach, giving it one of the island's best lunch views—and a bit of sand and salt spray on a windy day. Owners of the popular Blue Heaven restaurant took it over and have designed an intriguing dinner menu that includes linguine with mussels, lasagna, and white bean soup. At lunch the gazpacho refreshes with great flavor and texture, and the calamari marinara, antipasti sandwich, and yellowtail sandwich do not disappoint. Plans are under way to expand the kitchen and serve breakfast. $ *Average main: $20* ✉ *1000 Atlantic Blvd., Higgs Beach* ☎ *305/292–1117* ⊕ *www.saluteonthebeach.com* ⚐ *Reservations not accepted.*

$$ ✕ **Sarabeth's.** Named for the award-winning jam-maker and pastry
AMERICAN   chef Sarabeth Levine, who runs the kitchen, it naturally is proclaimed for its all-morning, all-afternoon breakfast, best enjoyed in the picket-fenced front yard of this sweet circa-1870 cottage. Lemon ricotta pancakes, pumpkin waffles, omelets, and homemade jams make the meal. Lunch offerings range from a griddled smoked mozzarella sandwich to poached salmon "Cobb" salad. Start dinner with the signature velvety cream of tomato soup, or roasted red beets and Gorgonzola salad. The daily special augments the short entrée listing that includes meatloaf, green chile pepper macaroni with three cheeses, and grilled mahi with tomatillo sauce. In the mood for dessert? The warm orange-apricot bread pudding takes its cues from Sarabeth's most popular flavor of jam. $ *Average main: $20* ✉ *530 Simonton St.* ☎ *305/293–8181* ⊕ *www.sarabethskeywest.com* ⚐ *Reservations not accepted* ☾ *Closed Mon. Easter through Christmas, no dinner Mon. Christmas through Easter, closed Tues.*

$$$ SEAFOOD 🍴 **Seven Fish.** A local hot spot, this intimate, off-the-beaten-track eatery is good for an eclectic mix of dishes like tropical shrimp salsa, wild-mushroom quesadilla, seafood marinara, and old-fashioned meat loaf with real mashed potatoes. For dessert, the sweet potato pie provides an added measure of down-home comfort. Those in the know reserve for dinner early to snag one of the 20 or so tables clustered in the bare-bones dining room. [$] *Average main: $21* ✉ *632 Olivia St.* ☎ *305/296–2777* 🌐 *www.7fish.com* ✍ *Reservations essential* 🕒 *Closed Tues. No lunch.*

$$ SEAFOOD FAMILY 🍴 **Turtle Kraals.** Named for the kraals, or corrals, where sea turtles were once kept until they went to the cannery, this place calls to mind the island's history. The lunch–dinner menu offers an assortment of marine cuisine that includes seafood enchiladas, mesquite-grilled fish of the day, and mango crab cakes. The slow-cook wood smoker results in wonderfully tender ribs, brisket, mesquite-grilled oysters with Parmesan and cilantro, and mesquite grilled chicken sandwich. The open restaurant overlooks the marina at the Historic Seaport. Turtle races entertain during happy hour on Monday and Friday at 6 pm. [$] *Average main: $16* ✉ *231 Margaret St.* ☎ *305/294–2640* 🌐 *www.turtlekraals.com* ✍ *Reservations not accepted.*

WHERE TO STAY

Historic cottages, restored century-old Conch houses, and large resorts are among the offerings in Key West, the majority charging from $100 to $300 a night. In high season, Christmas through Easter, you'll be hard-pressed to find a decent room for less than $200, and most places raise prices considerably during holidays and festivals. Many guesthouses and inns don't welcome children under 16, and most don't permit smoking indoors. Rates often include an expanded continental breakfast and afternoon wine or snack.

For expanded reviews, facilities, and current deals, visit Fodors.com.

$$$$ B&B/INN 🏨 **Ambrosia Key West.** If you desire personal attention, a casual atmosphere, and a dollop of style, stay at these twin inns spread out on nearly 2 acres. **Pros:** spacious rooms; poolside breakfast; friendly staff. **Cons:** on-street parking can be tough to come by; a little too spread out. [$] *Rooms from: $319* ✉ *615, 618, 622 Fleming St.* ☎ *305/296–9838, 800/535–9838* 🌐 *www.ambrosiakeywest.com* 🛏 *6 rooms, 3 town houses, 1 cottage, 10 suites* 🍽 *Breakfast.*

$$ B&B/INN 🏨 **Angelina Guest House.** In the heart of Old Town, this home away from home offers simple, clean, attractively priced accommodations. **Pros:** good value; nice garden; friendly staff. **Cons:** thin walls; basic rooms; shared balcony. [$] *Rooms from: $109* ✉ *302 Angela St.* ☎ *305/294–4480, 888/303–4480* 🌐 *www.angelinaguesthouse.com* 🛏 *13 rooms* 🍽 *Breakfast.*

$$$$ B&B/INN 🏨 **Azul Key West.** The ultramodern—nearly minimalistic—redo of this classic circa-1903 Queen Anne mansion is a break from the sensory overload of Key West's other abundant Victorian guesthouses. **Pros:** lovely building; marble-floored baths; luxurious linens. **Cons:** on a busy street. [$] *Rooms from: $239* ✉ *907 Truman Ave.* ☎ *305/296–5152, 888/253–2985* 🌐 *www.azulhotels.us* 🛏 *11 rooms, 1 suite* 🍽 *Breakfast.*

4

$$$
RESORT
FAMILY

Casa Marina Resort & Beach Club. At any moment, you expect the landed gentry to walk across the oceanfront lawn, just as they did when this 13-acre resort was built back in the 1920s. **Pros:** nice beach; historic setting; away from the crowds. **Cons:** long walk to central Old Town; $25 resort fee. *$ Rooms from: $159 ✉ 1500 Reynolds St. ☎ 305/296–3535, 866/203–6392 ⊕ www.casamarinaresort.com ⤳ 241 rooms, 70 suites ⫯◯⫯ No meals.*

$$$$
B&B/INN

Courtney's Place. If you like kids, cats, and dogs, you'll feel right at home in this collection of accommodations ranging from cigar-maker cottages to shotgun houses. **Pros:** near Duval Street; fairly priced. **Cons:** small parking lot; small pool; minimum stay requirements. *$ Rooms from: $229 ✉ 720 Whitmarsh La., off Petronia St. ☎ 305/294–3480, 800/869–4639 ⊕ www.courtneysplacekeywest.com ⤳ 6 rooms, 2 suites, 2 efficiencies, 8 cottages ⫯◯⫯ Breakfast.*

$$$
HOTEL

Crowne Plaza Key West–La Concha. History and franchises can mix, as this 1920s-vintage hotel proves with its handsome faux-palm atrium lobby and sleep-conducive rooms. **Pros:** restaurant and Starbucks in-house; close to downtown attractions; free Wi-Fi. **Cons:** high-traffic area; confusing layout; $20/night valet-only parking. *$ Rooms from: $199 ✉ 430 Duval St. ☎ 305/296–2991 ⊕ www.laconchakeywest.com ⤳ 160 rooms, 8 rooms with balconies, 10 suites ⫯◯⫯ No meals.*

$$$
HOTEL

Eden House. From the vintage metal rockers on the street-side porch to the old neon hotel sign in the lobby, this 1920s rambling Key West mainstay hotel is high on character, low on gloss. **Pros:** free parking; hot tub is actually hot; daily happy hour around the pool; discount at excellent Azur restaurant. **Cons:** pricey; a bit of a musty smell in some rooms; no TV in some rooms. *$ Rooms from: $200 ✉ 1015 Fleming St. ☎ 305/296–6868, 800/533–5397 ⊕ www.edenhouse.com ⤳ 36 rooms, 8 suites ⫯◯⫯ No meals.*

$$$$
HOTEL
Fodor's Choice
★

The Gardens Hotel. Built in 1875, this gloriously shaded, award-winning property covers a third of a city block in Old Town, among orchids, ponytail palms, black bamboo, walks, fountains, and earthen pots (called tinajones) imported from Cuba. **Pros:** luxurious bathrooms; secluded garden seating; free domestic phone calls and Wi-Fi. **Cons:** hard to get reservations; expensive; $20 per night secure parking fee. *$ Rooms from: $385 ✉ 526 Angela St. ☎ 305/294–2661, 800/526–2664 ⊕ www.gardenshotel.com ⤳ 17 rooms ⫯◯⫯ Breakfast.*

$$$$
RESORT
FAMILY

Hyatt Key West Resort and Spa. With its own man-made beach, the Hyatt Key West is one of few resorts where you can dig your toes in the sand, then walk a short distance away to the streets of Old Town. **Pros:** a little bit away from the bustle of Old Town; plenty of activities. **Cons:** beach is small; cramped-feeling property. *$ Rooms from: $290 ✉ 601 Front St. ☎ 305/809–1234 ⊕ www.keywest.hyatt.com ⤳ 118 rooms ⫯◯⫯ No meals.*

$$$
B&B/INN

Key Lime Inn. This 1854 Grand Bahama–style house on the National Register of Historic Places succeeds by offering amiable service, a great location, and simple rooms with natural-wood furnishings. **Pros:** free parking; some rooms have private outdoor spaces. **Cons:** standard rooms are pricey; pool faces a busy street; mulch-covered paths. $ *Rooms from: $179* ✉ *725 Truman Ave.* ☎ *305/294–5229, 800/549–4430* ⊕ *www.keylimeinn.com* ⇋ *37 rooms* ⦿ *Breakfast.*

$

B&B/INN

⬚ **Key West Bed and Breakfast/The Popular House.** There are accommodations for every budget, but the owners reason that budget travelers deserve as pleasant an experience (and lavish a tropical Continental breakfast) as their well-heeled counterparts. **Pros:** lots of art; tiled outdoor shower; hot tub and sauna area is a welcome hangout. **Cons:** some rooms are small. $ *Rooms from: $99* ✉ *415 William St.* ☎ *305/296–7274, 800/438–6155* ⊕ *www.keywestbandb.com* ⇋ *10 rooms, 6 with private bath* ⦿ *Breakfast.*

$$$$

HOTEL

⬚ **Key West Marriott Beachside Hotel.** This hotel vies for convention business with one of the biggest ballrooms in Key West, but it also appeals to families with its spacious condo units decorated with impeccable good taste. **Pros:** private beach; poolside cabanas. **Cons:** small beach; long walk to Old Town; cookie-cutter facade. $ *Rooms from: $228* ✉ *3841 N. Roosevelt Blvd., New Town* ☎ *305/296–8100, 800/546–0885* ⊕ *www.keywestmarriottbeachside.com* ⇋ *93 rooms, 93 1-bedroom suites, 10 2-bedroom suites, 26 3-bedroom suites* ⦿ *No meals.*

$$$$

HOTEL

Fodor's Choice

★

⬚ **Marquesa Hotel.** In a town that prides itself on its laid-back luxury, this complex of four restored 1884 houses stands out. **Pros:** elegant setting; romantic atmosphere; turndown service. **Cons:** street-facing rooms can be noisy; expensive rates. $ *Rooms from: $330* ✉ *600 Fleming St.* ☎ *305/292–1919, 800/869–4631* ⊕ *www.marquesa.com* ⇋ *27 rooms* ⦿ *No meals.*

$$$$

B&B/INN

⬚ **Merlin Guesthouse.** Key West guesthouses don't usually welcome families, but this laid-back jumble of rooms and suites is an exception. **Pros:** good location near Duval Street; good rates. **Cons:** neighbor noise; street parking. $ *Rooms from: $279* ✉ *811 Simonton St.* ☎ *305/296–3336, 800/642–4753* ⊕ *www.merlinguesthouse.com* ⇋ *10 rooms, 6 suites, 4 cottages* ⦿ *Breakfast.*

$$$$

B&B/INN

⬚ **Mermaid & the Alligator.** An enchanting combination of flora and fauna makes this 1904 Victorian house a welcoming retreat. **Pros:** hot plunge pool; massage pavilion; island-getaway feel. **Cons:** minimum stay required (length depends on season); dark public areas; plastic lawn chairs. $ *Rooms from: $248* ✉ *729 Truman Ave.* ☎ *305/294–1894, 800/773–1894* ⊕ *www.kwmermaid.com* ⇋ *9 rooms* ⦿ *Breakfast.*

$$$$

RESORT

⬚ **Ocean Key Resort & Spa.** A pool and lively open-air bar and restaurant sit on Sunset Pier, a popular place to watch the sun sink into the horizon. **Pros:** well-trained staff; lively pool scene; best spa on the island. **Cons:** $20 per night valet parking; too bustling for some; pricey. $ *Rooms from: $348* ✉ *Zero Duval St.* ☎ *305/296–7701, 800/328–9815* ⊕ *www. oceankey.com* ⇋ *64 rooms, 36 suites* ⦿ *No meals.*

$$$

HOTEL

⬚ **Parrot Key Resort.** This revamped destination resort feels like an old-fashioned beach community with picket fences and rocking-chair porches. **Pros:** four pools; finely appointed units; access to marina and other facilities at three sister properties in Marathon. **Cons:** outside of walking distance to Old Town; no transportation provided; hefty resort fee. $ *Rooms from: $199* ✉ *2801 N. Roosevelt Blvd., New Town* ☎ *305/809–2200* ⊕ *www.parrotkeyresort.com* ⇋ *74 rooms, 74 suites, 3 3-bedroom cottages* ⦿ *No meals.*

Sunset Key cottages are right on the water's edge, far away from the action of Old Town.

$$$$
RESORT
🏠 **Pier House Resort and Caribbean Spa.** The location—on a quiet stretch of beach at the foot of Duval—is ideal as a buffer from and gateway to the action. **Pros:** beautiful beach; good location; nice spa. **Cons:** lots of conventions; poolside rooms are small; not really suitable for children under 16. $ *Rooms from: $339* ✉ *1 Duval St.* ☎ *305/296–4600, 800/327–8340* ⊕ *www.pierhouse.com* ⋙ *116 rooms, 26 suites* ⊖*No meals.*

$$$$
RESORT
🏠 **The Reach Resort.** Embracing Key West's only natural beach, this full-service resort has its roots in the 1980s when locals rallied against the loss of the topless beach it displaced. **Pros:** removed from Duval hubbub; great sunrise views; pullout sofas in most rooms. **Cons:** $25 per day per room resort fee; expensive. $ *Rooms from: $279* ✉ *1435 Simonton St.* ☎ *305/296–5000, 888/318–4316* ⊕ *www.reachresort.com* ⋙ *72 rooms, 78 suites* ⊖*No meals.*

$$$$
B&B/INN
🏠 **Simonton Court.** A small world all its own, this adult lodging makes you feel deliciously sequestered from Key West's crasser side, but close enough to get there on foot. **Pros:** lots of privacy; well-appointed accommodations; friendly staff. **Cons:** minimum stays required in high season. $ *Rooms from: $260* ✉ *320 Simonton St.* ☎ *305/294–6386, 800/944–2687* ⊕ *www.simontoncourt.com* ⋙ *17 rooms, 6 suites, 6 cottages* ⊖*Breakfast.*

$$$
B&B/INN
🏠 **Speakeasy Inn.** During Prohibition, Raul Vasquez made this place popular by smuggling in rum from Cuba; today its reputation is for having reasonably priced rooms within walking distance of the beach. **Pros:** good location; reasonable rates; kitchenettes. **Cons:** no pool; on busy Duval. $ *Rooms from: $149* ✉ *1117 Duval St.* ☎ *305/296–2680* ⊕ *www.speakeasyinn.com* ⋙ *4 suites* ⊖*Breakfast.*

$$$$ RESORT Fodor's Choice ★ **Sunset Key.** This private island retreat feels completely cut off from the world, yet you're just minutes away from the action. **Pros:** peace and quiet; roomy verandas; free 24-hour shuttle; free Wi-Fi. **Cons:** luxury doesn't come cheap. [$] *Rooms from: $695* ✉ *245 Front St.* ☎ *305/292–5300, 888/477–7786* 🌐 *www.westinsunsetkeycottages.com* 🛏 *40 cottages* 🍴 *Breakfast.*

NIGHTLIFE

Rest up: Much of what happens in Key West does so after dark. Open your mind and have a stroll. Scruffy street performers strum next to dogs in sunglasses. Brawls tumble out the doors of Sloppy Joe's. Drag queens strut across stages in Joan Rivers garb. Tattooed men lick whipped cream off women's body parts. And margaritas flow like a Jimmy Buffett tune.

4

BARS AND LOUNGES

Capt. Tony's Saloon. When it was the original Sloppy Joe's in the mid-1930s, Hemingway was a regular. Later, a young Jimmy Buffett sang here and made this watering hole famous in his song "Last Mango in Paris." Captain Tony was even voted mayor of Key West. Yes, this place is a beloved landmark. Stop in and take a look at the 'hanging tree' that grows through the roof, listen to live music seven nights a week, and play some pool. ✉ *428 Greene St.* ☎ *305/294–1838* 🌐 *www.capttonyssaloon.com.*

Durty Harry's. This megasize entertainment complex is home to eight different bars and clubs, both indoor and outdoor. Their motto is, "Eight Famous Bars, One Awesome Night," and they're right. You'll find pizza, dancing, live music, a martini bar, and the infamous Red Garter strip club. ✉ *208 Duval St.* ☎ *305/296–5513.*

Green Parrot Bar. Pause for a libation in the open-air and breathe in the spirit of Key West. Built in 1890 as a grocery store, this property has been many things to many people over the years It's touted as the oldest bar in Key West and the sometimes-rowdy saloon has locals outnumbering out-of-towners, especially on nights when bands play. ✉ *601 Whitehead St., at Southard St.* ☎ *305/294–6133* 🌐 *www.greenparrot.com.*

Hog's Breath Saloon. Belly up to the bar for a cold mug of the signature Hog's Breath Lager at this infamous joint, a must-stop on the Key West bar crawl. Live bands play daily 1 pm–2 am (except when the game's on TV). ✉ *400 Front St.* ☎ *305/296–4222* 🌐 *www.hogsbreath.com.*

Margaritaville Café. A youngish, touristy crowd mixes with aging Parrot Heads. It's owned by former Key West resident and recording star Jimmy Buffett, who has been known to perform here. The drink of choice is, of course, a margarita, made with Jimmy's own brand of Margaritaville tequila. There's live music nightly, as well as lunch and dinner. ✉ *500 Duval St.* ☎ *305/292–1435* 🌐 *www.margaritaville.com.*

Pier House. The party here begins with a steel-drum band to celebrate the sunset on the beach (on select Thursdays and Fridays), then moves indoors to the Wine Galley piano bar for live jazz. ✉ *1 Duval St.* ☎ *305/296–4600, 800/327–8340* 🌐 *www.pierhouse.com.*

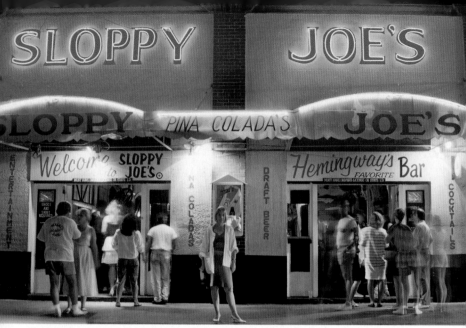

Sloppy Joe's is one must-stop on most Key West visitors' barhop stroll, also known as the Duval Crawl.

Schooner Wharf Bar. This open-air waterfront bar and grill in the historic seaport district retains its funky Key West charm and hosts live entertainment daily. Its margaritas rank among Key West's best, as does the bar itself, voted Best Local's Bar six years in a row. For great views, head up to the second floor and be sure to order up some fresh seafood and fritters. ✉ *202 William St.* ☎ *305/292–3302* ⊕ *www.schoonerwharf.com.*

Sloppy Joe's. There's history and good times at the successor to a famous 1937 speakeasy named for its founder, Captain Joe Russell. Decorated with Hemingway memorabilia and marine flags, the bar is popular with travelers and is full and noisy all the time. A Sloppy Joe's T-shirt is a de rigueur Key West souvenir, and the gift shop sells them like crazy. Grab a seat (if you can) and be entertained by the bands and by the parade of people in constant motion. ✉ *201 Duval St.* ☎ *305/294–5717* ⊕ *www.sloppyjoes.com.*

The Top. On the seventh floor of the Crowne Plaza Key West La Concha, this is one of the best places in town to view the sunset and enjoy live entertainment on Friday and Saturday nights. ✉ *430 Duval St.* ☎ *305/296–2991* ⊕ *www.laconchakeywest.com.*

Virgilio's Martini Bar. In the best traditions of a 1950s cocktail lounge, this bar serves chilled martinis to the soothing tempo of live jazz and blues. Locals love the late night dancing. ✉ *524 Duval St.* ☎ *305/296–8118* ⊕ *www.virgilioskeywest.com.*

SHOPPING

On these streets you'll find colorful local art of widely varying quality, key limes made into everything imaginable, and the raunchiest T-shirts in the civilized world. Browsing the boutiques—with frequent pub stops along the way—makes for an entertaining stroll down Duval Street.

MALLS AND SHOPPING CENTERS

Bahama Village. Where to start your shopping adventure? This cluster of spruced-up shops, restaurants, and vendors is responsible for the restoration of the colorful historic district where Bahamians settled in the 19th century. The village lies roughly between Whitehead and Fort streets and Angela and Catherine streets. Hemingway frequented the bars, restaurants, and boxing rings in this part of town. ⊠ *Between Whitehead and Fort Sts. and Angela and Catherine Sts.*

ARTS AND CRAFTS

Key West is filled with art galleries, and the variety is truly amazing. Much is locally produced by the town's large artist community, but many galleries carry international artists from as close as Haiti and as far away as France. Local artists do a great job of preserving the island's architecture and spirit.

Alan S. Maltz Gallery. The owner, declared the state's official wildlife photographer by the Wildlife Foundation of Florida, captures the state's nature and character in stunning portraits. Spend four figures for large-format images on canvas or save on small prints and closeouts. ⊠ *1210 Duval St.* ☎ *305/294–0005* ⊕ *www.alanmaltz.com.*

Art@830. This inviting gallery carries a little bit of everything, from pottery to paintings and jewelry to sculptures. Most outstanding is its selection of glass art, particularly the jellyfish lamps. Take time to admire all that is here. ⊠ *830 Caroline St., Historic Seaport* ☎ *305/295–9595* ⊕ *www.art830.com.*

Cuba, Cuba!. Check out this shop's stock of cigars, coffee, and paintings, sculptures, pottery, and photos by Cuban artists and artisans. ⊠ *814 Duval St.* ☎ *305/295–9442, 800/621–3596* ⊕ *www.cubacubastore.com.*

Gallery on Greene. This is the largest gallery–exhibition space in Key West and it showcases 37 museum-quality artists. They pride themselves on being the leader in the field of representational fine art, painting, sculptures, and reproductions from the Florida Keys and Key West. You can see the love immediately from gallery curator Nancy Frank, who aims to please everyone, from the casual buyer to the established collector. ⊠ *606 Greene St.* ☎ *305/294–1669* ⊕ *www.galleryongreene.com.*

Gingerbread Square Gallery. The oldest private art gallery in Key West represents local and internationally acclaimed artists on an annually changing basis, in mediums ranging from graphics to art glass. ⊠ *1207 Duval St.* ☎ *305/296–8900* ⊕ *www.gingerbreadsquaregallery.com.*

KW Light Gallery. Historian, photographer, and painter Sharon Wells opened this gallery to showcase her own fine-art photography and painted tiles and canvases, as well as the works of other national artists. You can find historic photos here as well. ⊠ *1203 Duval St.* ☎ *305/294–0566* ⊕ *www.keywestlightgallery.com.*

Nightlife, shops, and some interesting street art can all be found on Key West's Duval Street.

Lucky Street Gallery. High-end contemporary paintings are the focus at this gallery with more than 30 years of experience and a passionate staff. There are also a few pieces of jewelry by internationally recognized Key West–based artists. Changing exhibits, artist receptions, and special events make this a lively venue. ⊠ *1130 Duval St.* ☎ *305/294–3973* ⊕ *www.luckystreetgallery.com.*

Pelican Poop Shoppe. Caribbean art sells in a historic building (with Hemingway connections, of course). For $2 admission or a $10 purchase, you can stroll the tropical courtyard garden. The owners buy directly from the artisans every year, so the prices are very attractive. ⊠ *314 Simonton St.* ☎ *305/292–9955* ⊕ *www.pelicanpoopshoppe.com.*

Whitehead St. Pottery. Potters Charles Pearson and Tim Roeder display their porcelain stoneware and raku-fired vessels. The setting, around two koi ponds with a burbling fountain, is as sublime as the art. ⊠ *322 Julia St.* ☎ *305/294–5067* ⊕ *www.whiteheadstreetpottery.com.*

BOOKS

Key West Island Bookstore. This home away from home for the large Key West writers' community carries new, used, and rare titles. It specializes in Hemingway, Tennessee Williams, and South Florida mystery writers. ⊠ *513 Fleming St.* ☎ *305/294–2904* ⊕ *www.keywestislandbooks.com.*

CLOTHING AND FABRICS

Fairvilla Megastore. Don't leave town without a browse through the legendary shop, where you'll find an astonishing array of fantasy wear, outlandish costumes (check out the pirate section), and other "adult" toys. ⊠ *520 Front St.* ☎ *305/292–0448* ⊕ *www.fairvilla.com.*

Kino Sandals. A pair of Kino Sandals was once a public declaration that you'd been to Key West. The attraction? You can watch these inexpensive items being made. The factory has been churning out several styles since 1966. Walk up to the counter, grab a pair, try them on, and lay down some cash. It's that simple. ⊠ *107 Fitzpatrick St.* ☏ *305/294–5044* ⊕ *www.kinosandalfactory.com* ⊘ *Closed Sun. in off-season.*

FOOD AND DRINK

Fausto's Food Palace. Since 1926 Fausto's has been the spot to catch up on the week's gossip and to chill out in summer—it has groceries, organic foods, marvelous wines, a sushi chef on duty 8 am–3 pm, and box lunches to go. There are two locations you can shop at in Key West, plus a recently opened online store. ⊠ *522 Fleming St.* ☏ *305/296–5663* ⊕ *www.faustos.com* ✉ *1105 White St.* ☏ *305/294–5221.*

Kermit's Key West Lime Shoppe. You'll see Kermit himself standing on the corner every time a trolley passes, pie in hand. Besides pie, his shop carries a multitude of key lime products from barbecue sauce to jellybeans. His prefrozen pies, dressed with a special long-lasting whipped cream instead of meringue, travels well. This is a must-stop shop while in Key West. The key lime pie is the best on the island; once you try it frozen on a stick, dipped in chocolate, you may consider quitting your job and moving here. Savor every bite on their outdoor patio/garden area. Heaven. ⊠ *200 Elizabeth St., Historic Seaport* ☏ *305/296–0806, 800/376–0806* ⊕ *www.keylimeshop.com.*

GIFTS AND SOUVENIRS

Cayo Hueso y Habana. Part museum, part shopping center, this circa-1879 warehouse includes a hand-rolled cigar shop, one-of-a-kind souvenirs, a Cuban restaurant, and exhibits that tell of the island's Cuban heritage. Outside, a memorial garden pays homage to the island's Cuban ancestors. ⊠ *410 Wall St., Mallory Sq.* ☏ *305/293–7260.*

Cocktails! Key West. Could there possibly be a better location to celebrate the art of the drink than Key West? This celebratory shop carries everything you need for cocktails including beautiful hand-painted stemware, hi-ball, martini, and shot glasses, mugs, accessories, and art that blends perfectly. Most of the designs are made on the island. ⊠ *808 Duval St.* ☏ *305/292–1190* ⊕ *www.cocktailskeywest.com.*

Montage. For that unique (but slightly overpriced) souvenir of your trip to Key West head here, where you'll discover hundreds of handcrafted signs of popular Key West guesthouses, inns, hotels, restaurants, bars, and streets. If you can't find what you're looking for, they'll make it for you. ⊠ *291 Front St.* ☏ *305/395–9101, 877/396–4278* ⊕ *www.montagekeywest.com.*

SPORTS AND THE OUTDOORS

Unlike the rest of the region, Key West isn't known primarily for outdoor pursuits. But everyone should devote at least half a day to relaxing on a boat tour, heading out on a fishing expedition, or pursuing some other adventure at sea. The ultimate excursion is a boat trip to Dry Tortugas National Park for snorkeling and exploring Fort Jefferson. Other excursions cater to nature lovers, scuba divers and snorkelers, anglers, and those who would just like to get out in the water and enjoy the scenery and sunset. For those who prefer their recreation land based, biking is the way to go. Hiking is limited, but walking the streets of Old Town provides plenty of exercise.

BIKING

Key West was practically made for bicycles, but don't let that lull you into a false sense of security. Narrow and one-way streets along with car traffic result in several bike accidents a year. Some hotels rent or lend bikes to guests; others will refer you to a nearby shop and reserve a bike for you. Rentals usually start at about $10 a day, but some places also rent by the half day. ▓TIP➔ Lock up! Bikes—and porch chairs!—are favorite targets for local thieves.

A&M Rentals. Rent beach cruisers with large baskets for $15 a day. Rates for scooters start at $35 a day. Look for the huge American flag on the roof, or call for free airport, ferry, or cruise ship pick-up. ⊠ *523 Truman Ave.* ☎ *305/294–0399* ⊕ *www.amscooterskeywest.com.*

Eaton Bikes. Tandem, three-wheel, and children's bikes are available in addition to the standard beach cruisers ($18 for first day) and hybrid bikes ($25). Delivery is free for all Key West rentals. ⊠ *830 Eaton St.* ☎ *305/294–8188* ⊕ *www.eatonbikes.com.*

Lloyd's Original Tropical Bike Tour. Explore the natural, noncommercial side of Key West at a leisurely pace, stopping on backstreets and in backyards of private homes to sample native fruits and view indigenous plants and trees with a 30-year Key West veteran. The behind-the-scenes tours run two hours and cost $39, including bike rental. ⊠ *Truman Ave. and Simonton St.* ☎ *305/304–4700, 305/294–1882* ⊕ *www.lloydstropicalbiketour.com.*

Moped Hospital. This outfit supplies balloon-tire bikes with yellow safety baskets for adults and kids ($12 for the first day, $8 for extra days), as well as scooters ($35) and double-seater scooters ($55). ⊠ *601 Truman Ave.* ☎ *305/296–3344, 866/296–1625* ⊕ *www.mopedhospital.com.*

BOAT TOURS

Dancing Dolphin Spirit Charters. Victoria Impallomeni, a wilderness guide and environmental marine science expert, invites up to six nature lovers—especially children—aboard the *Imp II*, a 25-foot Aquasport, for four-hour ($500) and seven-hour ($700) ecotours that frequently include encounters with wild dolphins. While island-hopping, you visit underwater gardens, natural shoreline, and mangrove habitats. For her Dolphin Day for Humans tour, Impallomeni pulls you through the water, equipped with mask and snorkel, on a specially designed "dolphin water massage board" that simulates dolphin swimming motions. Sometimes dolphins follow the boat and swim among participants. All equipment is supplied. ⊠ *MM 5 OS, Murray's Marina, 5710 Overseas Hwy.* ☎ *305/304–7562, 888/822–7366* ⊕ *www.captainvictoria.com.*

White Knuckle Thrill Boat Ride. For something with an adrenaline boost, book with this specially designed jet boat. It holds up to 10 people and does amazing maneuvers like 360s, fishtails, and other water stunts. The cost is $59 per person, and includes pickup shuttle. Another unique experience is their Sea Spi Eco Tour. These individual glass bottom boats are electric powered so they glide quietly, giving you a peek below the sea without getting in the water. Tours are 90 min for $69 plus tax. ⊠ *Sunset Marina, 555 College Rd.* ☎ *305/797–0459* ⊕ *www. whiteknucklethrillboatride.com.*

BUS AND TROLLEY TOURS

City View Trolley Tours. In 2010, City View Trolley Tours began service, offering a little competition to the Conch Train and Old Town Trolley, which are owned by the same company. Its rates are more affordable at $19 per adult. Tours depart every 30 minutes from 9:30 to 4:30. Passengers can board and disembark at any of nine stops, and can reboard at will. ☎ *305/294–0644* ⊕ *www.cityviewtrolleys.com.*

Gay & Lesbian Trolley Tour. Decorated with a rainbow, the Gay and Lesbian Trolley Tour rumbles around the town beginning at 4 pm every Saturday afternoon. The 70-minute tour highlighting Key West's gay history costs $25. ⊠ *513 Truman Ave.* ☎ *305/294–4603* ⊕ *www.gaykeywestfl.com.*

Old Town Trolley. Old Town Trolley operates trolley-style buses, departing from the Mallory Square every 30 minutes from 9 to 4:30, for 90-minute narrated tours of Key West. The smaller trolleys go places the larger Conch Tour Train won't fit and you can ride a second consecutive day for free. You may disembark at any of 12 stops and reboard a later trolley. The cost is $30, but you can save $3 by booking online. It also offers package deals with Old Town attractions. ⊠ *201 Front St.* ☎ *305/296–6688, 888/910–8687* ⊕ *www.trolleytours.com.*

FISHING

Any number of local fishing guides can take you to where the big ones are biting, either in the backcountry for snapper and snook or to the deep water for the marlin and sharks that brought Hemingway here in the first place.

Key West Bait & Tackle. Prepare to catch a big one with the live bait, frozen bait, and fishing equipment provided here. They even offer rod and reel rentals (starting at $15 for 24 hours). Stop by their on-site Live Bait Lounge where you can sip ice-cold beer while telling fish tales. ⊠ *241 Margaret St.* ☎ *305/292–1961* ⊕ *www.keywestbaitandtackle.com.*

Key West Pro Guides. Trips include flats and backcountry fishing ($400–$450 for a half day) and reef and offshore fishing (starting at $550 for a half day). ⊠ *G-31 Miriam St.* ☎ *866/259–4205* ⊕ *www. keywestproguides.com.*

KAYAKING

Key West Eco-Tours. Key West is surrounded by marinas, so it's easy to find what you're looking for, whether it's sailing with dolphins or paddling in the mangroves. These sail-kayak-snorkel excursions take you into backcountry flats and mangrove forests without the crowds. The 4½-hour trip costs $99 per person and includes lunch. Private sunset sails ($295) and private charters ($545) are also available. ⊠ *Historic Seaport, 100 Grinnell St.* ☎ *305/294–7245* ⊕ *www.keywestecotours.com.*

Lazy Dog Kayak Guides. Take a two- or four-hour guided sea kayak–snorkel tour around the mangrove islands just east of Key West. The $40 or $60 charge, respectively, covers transportation, bottled water, a snack, and supplies, including snorkeling gear. Paddleboard tours are $40. Rentals for self-touring are also available. ✉ *5114 Overseas Hwy.* ☎ *305/295–9898* ⊕ *www.lazydog.com.*

SCUBA DIVING AND SNORKELING

The Florida Keys National Marine Sanctuary extends along Key West and beyond to the Dry Tortugas. Key West National Wildlife Refuge further protects the pristine waters. Most divers don't make it this far out in the Keys, but if you're looking for a day of diving as a break from the nonstop party in Old Town, expect to pay about $65 and upward for a two-tank dive. Serious divers can book dive trips to the Dry Tortugas.

Captain's Corner. This PADI–certified dive shop has classes in several languages and twice-daily snorkel and dive trips ($40–$65) to reefs and wrecks aboard the 60-foot dive boat *Sea Eagle.* Use of weights, belts, masks, and fins is included. ✉ *125 Ann St.* ☎ *305/296–8865* ⊕ *www. captainscorner.com.*

Dive Key West. Operating over 40 years, Dive Key West is a full-service dive center that has charters, instruction, gear rental, sales, and repair. Snorkel excursions are $59; scuba trips start at $75. ✉ *3128 N. Roosevelt Blvd.* ☎ *305/296–3823* ⊕ *www.divekeywest.com.*

Snuba of Key West. Safely dive the coral reefs without getting a scuba certification. Ride out to the reef on a catamaran, then follow your guide underwater for a one-hour tour of the coral reefs. You wear a regulator with a breathing hose that is attached to a floating air tank on the surface. No prior diving or snorkeling experience is necessary, but you must know how to swim. The $99 price includes beverages. ✉ *Garrison Bight Marina, Palm Ave., between Eaton St. and N. Roosevelt Blvd.* ☎ *305/292–4616* ⊕ *www.snubakeywest.com.*

WALKING TOURS

Historic Florida Keys Foundation. In addition to publishing several good guides on Key West, the foundation conducts tours of the City Cemetery Tuesday and Thursday at 9:30. ✉ *510 Greene St., Old City Hall* ☎ *305/292–6718* ⊕ *www.historicfloridakeys.org.*

DRY TORTUGAS NATIONAL PARK

70 miles southwest of Key West.

History buffs might remember long-deactivated Fort Jefferson as the prison that held Dr. Samuel Mudd for his role in the Lincoln assassination. But today's "guests" are much more captivated by this sanctuary's thousands of birds and marine life.

GETTING HERE AND AROUND

At this writing, the ferryboat *Yankee Freedom II* departs from a marina in Old Town and does day trips to Garden Key. Key West Seaplane Adventures has half- and full-day trips to the Dry Tortugas, where you can explore Fort Jefferson, built in 1846, and snorkel on the beautiful protected reef. Departing from the Key West airport, the flights include soft drinks and snorkeling equipment for $280 (half day) and $495 (full day), plus there's a $5 (cash only) park fee. If you want to explore the park's other keys, look into renting a boat or hiring a private charter. *For more information on the two ferries and the seaplane, see* ⇨ *Exploring.*

ESSENTIALS

Visitor Information Dry Tortugas National Park ☎ *305/242–7700* ⊕ *www.nps.gov/drto.*

EXPLORING

Dry Tortugas National Park. This park, 70 miles off the shores of Key West, consists of seven small islands. Tour the fort; then lay out your blanket on the sunny beach for a picnic before you head out to snorkel on the protected reef. Many people like to camp here ($3 per person per night, eight sites plus group site and overflow area; first come, first served), but note that there's no freshwater supply and you must carry off whatever you bring onto the island.

The typical visitor from Key West, however, makes it no farther than the waters of Garden Key. Home to 19th-century Fort Jefferson, it is the destination for seaplane and fast ferry tours out of Key West. With 2½ to 6½ hours to spend on the island, visitors have time to tour the mammoth fort-come-prison and then cool off with mask and snorkel along the fort's moat wall.

History buffs might remember long-deactivated Fort Jefferson, the largest brick building in the western hemisphere, as the prison that held Dr. Samuel Mudd, who unwittingly set John Wilkes Booth's leg after the assassination of Abraham Lincoln. Three other men were also held there for complicity in the assassination. Original construction on the fort began in 1846 and continued for 30 years, but was never completed because the invention of the rifled cannon made it obsolete. That's when it became a Civil War prison and later a wildlife refuge. In 1935 President Franklin Roosevelt declared it a national monument for its historic and natural value.

The brick fort acts as a gigantic, almost 16-acre reef. Around its moat walls, coral grows and schools of snapper, grouper, and wrasses hang out. To reach the offshore coral heads requires about 15 minutes of swimming over seagrass beds. The reef formations blaze with the color and majesty of brain coral, swaying sea fans, and flitting tropical fish. It takes a bit of energy to swim the distance, but the water depth pretty much measures under 7 feet all the way, allowing for sandy spots to stop and rest. (Standing in seagrass meadows and on coral is detrimental to marine life.)

Serious snorkelers and divers head out farther offshore to epic formations, including Palmata Patch, one of the few surviving concentrations of elkhorn coral in the Keys. Day-trippers congregate on the sandy beach to relax in the sun and enjoy picnics. Overnight tent campers have use of restroom facilities and achieve a total getaway from noise, lights, and civilization in general. Remember that no matter how you get here, the park's $5 admission fee must be paid in cash.

The park has set up with signage a self-guided tour that takes about 45 minutes. You should budget more time if you're into photography, because the scenic shots are hard to pass up. Ranger-guided tours are also available at certain times. Check in at the visitor center for a schedule. The small office also shows an orientation video, sells books and other educational materials, and, most importantly, provides a blast of air-conditioning on hot days.

Birders in the know bring binoculars to watch some 100,000 nesting sooty terns at their only U.S. nesting site, Bush Key, adjacent to Garden Key. Noddy terns also nest in the spring. During winter migrations, birds fill the airspace so thickly they literally fall from the sky to make their pit stops, birders say. Nearly 300 species have been spotted in the park's seven islands, including frigatebirds, boobies, cormorants, and broad-winged hawks. Bush Key is closed to foot traffic during nesting season, January through September. ⊠ *Key West* ⊕ *www.nps.gov/drto* ✉ *$5.*

Yankee Freedom II. The fast, sleek, 100-foot catamaran *Yankee Freedom II* travels to the Dry Tortugas in 2¼ hours. The time passes quickly on the roomy vessel equipped with three restrooms, two freshwater showers, and two bars. Stretch out on two decks: one an air-conditioned salon with cushioned seating, the other an open sundeck with sunny and shaded seating. Continental breakfast and lunch are included. On arrival, a naturalist leads a 40-minute guided tour, which is followed by lunch and a free afternoon for swimming, snorkeling (gear included), and exploring. The vessel is ADA–certified for visitors using wheelchairs. ■TIP→ The Dry Tortugas lies in the central time zone. ⊠ *Lands End Marina, 240 Margaret St., Key West* ☎ *305/294–7009, 800/634–0939* ⊕ *www.yankeefreedom.com* ✉ *$165, parking $5* ☉ *Trips daily at 8 am; check in 7:15 am.*

FORT LAUDERDALE

with Broward County

WELCOME TO FORT LAUDERDALE

TOP REASONS TO GO

★ **Blue waves:** Sparkling Lauderdale beaches spanning Broward County's entire coast were Florida's first to capture Blue Wave Beach status from the Clean Beaches Council.

★ **Inland waterways:** More than 300 miles of inland waterways, including downtown Fort Lauderdale's historic New River, create what's known as the Venice of America.

★ **Everglades access:** Just minutes from luxury hotels and golf courses, the rugged Everglades tantalize with alligators, colorful birds, and other wildlife.

★ **Vegas-style gaming:** Since slots and blackjack tables hit Hollywood's glittering Seminole Hard Rock Hotel & Casino in 2008, smaller competitors have followed this lucrative trend on every square inch of Indian Territory.

★ **Cruise gateway:** Port Everglades—home port for *Allure* and *Oasis of the Seas,* the world's largest cruise vessels—hosts cruise ships from major lines.

1 **Fort Lauderdale.** Anchored by the fast-flowing New River and its attractive Riverwalk, Fort Lauderdale embraces high-rise condos along with single-family homes, museums, parks, and attractions. Las Olas Boulevard, lined with boutiques, sidewalk cafés, and restaurants, links downtown with 20 miles of sparkling beaches.

2 **North on Scenic A1A.** Stretching north on Route A1A, old-school seaside charm abounds, from high-rise Galt Ocean Mile to quiet, low-rise resort communities farther north.

3 **South Broward.** From Hollywood's beachside Broadwalk and historic Young Circle (the latter transformed into an Arts Park) to Seminole gaming, South Broward provides grit, glitter, and diversity in attractions.

441

Coconut
Creek

Sample Rd.
7 **Butterfly ◆
World**

Margate

Coconut Cr.
Pkwy.

**North
Lauderdale**

91

Powerline Rd.

834

Dixie Hwy.

Atlantic Blvd.

95

Cypress Creek Rd.

Commercial Blvd.

Oakland Park Blvd.

**Lauderdale
Lakes**
441

Sunrise Blvd.

Broward Blvd.

Davie Blvd.

**Melrose
Park**

7

84

595

Griffin Rd.

Stirling Rd.

Sheridan St.

95

Hollywood Blvd.

Pembroke Rd.

Hallandale Blvd.

Seminole Dr.

S.W. 31st Ave.

N. Andrews Ave.

Four
th
Track

811

811

Federal Hwy.

1

**Fort
Lauderdale**

1 Las Olas
Blvd.

S.E. 17th St.
Causeway

◆ **Port Everglades**

✈ **Fort Lauderdale-Hollywood
International Airport**

1

Dania Beach
Blvd.

**Dania
Beach**

A1A

822

Dixie Hwy.

Hollywood

3

Hallandale

○ **Deerfield
A1A Beach**

○ Hillsboro
Beach

**● Hillsboro
Lighthouse**

○ **Pompano
Beach**

1

Lauderdale-
by-the-Sea

2

A1A

A T L A N T I C   O C E A N

⊕

0		3 mi
0		3 km

GETTING
ORIENTED

Along the southeast's Gold
Coast, Fort Lauderdale and
Broward County anchor
a delightfully chic middle
ground between the posh
and elite Palm Beaches and
the international hubbub
of Miami. From downtown
Fort Lauderdale it's about
a four-hour drive to either
Orlando or Key West,
but there's plenty to keep
you in Broward. All told,
Broward boasts 31 com-
munities from Deerfield
Beach to Hallandale
Beach along the coast,
and from Coral Springs
to Southwest Ranches
closer to the Everglades.
Big—in fact, huge—shop-
ping options await in
the western suburbs,
home of Sawgrass Mills,
the upscale Colonnade
Outlets at Sawgrass,
and IKEA Sunrise.

5

Revised and
updated by
Paul Rubio

Collegians of the 1960s returning to Fort Lauderdale would be hard-pressed to recognize the onetime "Sun and Suds Spring Break Capital of the Universe." Back then, Fort Lauderdale's beachfront was lined with T-shirt shops, and downtown consisted of a lone office tower and dilapidated buildings waiting to be razed.

The beach and downtown have since exploded with upscale shops, restaurants, and luxury resort hotels equipped with enough high-octane amenities to light up skies all the way to western Broward's Alligator Alley. At risk of losing small-town 45-rpm magic in iPod times—when hotel parking fees alone eclipse room rates of old—Greater Fort Lauderdale somehow seems to meld disparate eras into nouveau nirvana, seasoned with a lot of Gold Coast sand.

The city was named for Major William Lauderdale, who built a fort at the river's mouth in 1838 during the Seminole Indian wars. It wasn't until 1911 that the city was incorporated, with only 175 residents, but it grew quickly during the Florida boom of the 1920s. Today's population hovers around 165,000, and suburbs keep growing—1.75 million live in Broward County's 31 municipalities and unincorporated areas.

As elsewhere, many speculators busily flipping property here got caught when the sun-drenched real-estate bubble burst, leaving Broward's foreclosure rate to skyrocket. But the worst is far behind us. By the time the city began celebrating its centennial in 2011, it had resumed the renaissance that began before the economic crisis. The 20-mile shoreline—with wide ribbons of golden sand for beachcombing and sunbathing—remains the anchor draw for Fort Lauderdale and Broward County, but amazing beaches are now complemented by show-stopping hotels, an exploding foodie scene, and burgeoning cultural scene. In a little more than 100 years, Fort Lauderdale has grown into Fort Fabulous.

PLANNING

WHEN TO GO

Peak season runs Thanksgiving through April, when concert, art, and entertainment seasons go full throttle. Expect heat and humidity and some rain in summer. Hurricane winds come most notably in August and September. Golfing tee-time waits are longer on weekends year-round. Regardless of season, remember that Fort Lauderdale sunshine can burn even in cloudy weather.

ANNUAL FESTIVALS AND EVENTS

Fort Lauderdale International Boat Show. In late October, Fort Lauderdale hosts the world's largest boat show, the end-all, be-all of marine envy, with more than $2 billion worth of boats, yachts, superyachts, electronics, engines, and thousands of accessories from every major marine manufacturer and builder worldwide. The city buzzes with parties and cocktail hours to celebrate the bling bling water toy mania. ☏ 954/764–7642 ⊕ *www.showmanagement.com.*

Fort Lauderdale International Film Festival. Beginning in late October, this annual event showcases more than 100 feature, documentary, and short films from around the world at downtown's Cinema Paradiso and other local venues. In addition to 21 days of screenings, you can expect seminars and parties; but don't expect the glitterati of a big city film festival. ☏ 954/760–9898 ⊕ *www.fliff.com.*

Seminole Hard Rock Winterfest Boat Parade. Weeks of pre-events culminate in the largest one-day spectator event in Florida each December, drawing a crowd of 1 million onlookers as a stampede of 1,500 jaw-dropping yachts cruise 10 miles of Fort Lauderdale's waterways, complete with original themes and decorations. Over the years, celebrity grand marshals have included Joan Rivers, Brooke Burke, Kim Kardashian, and Deborah Norville. ☏ 954/767–0686 ⊕ *www.winterfestparade.com.*

GETTING HERE AND AROUND

AIR TRAVEL

Serving more than 23 million travelers a year, **Fort Lauderdale–Hollywood International Airport** is 3 miles south of downtown Fort Lauderdale, just off U.S. 1 between Fort Lauderdale and Hollywood, and near Port Everglades and Fort Lauderdale Beach. Other options include **Miami International Airport,** about 32 miles to the southwest, and the far less chaotic **Palm Beach International Airport,** about 50 miles to the north. All three airports link to **Tri-Rail,** a commuter train operating seven days through Palm Beach, Broward, and Miami-Dade counties.

Airport Information Fort Lauderdale–Hollywood International Airport (*FLL*) ☏ 866/435-9355 ⊕ www.broward.org/airport. **Miami International Airport** (*MIA*) ☏ 305/876-7000 ⊕ www.miami-airport.com. **Palm Beach International Airport** (*PBI*) ☏ 561/471-7420 ⊕ www.pbia.org. **Tri-Rail** ☏ 800/874-7245 ⊕ www.tri-rail.com.

BUS TRAVEL

Broward County Transit operates bus route No. 1 between the airport and its main terminal at Broward Boulevard and Northwest 1st Avenue, near downtown Fort Lauderdale. Service from the airport is every 20 minutes and begins at 5:22 am on weekdays, 5:37 am Saturday, and 8:41 am Sunday; the last bus leaves the airport at 11:38 pm Monday–Saturday and 9:41 pm Sunday. The fare is $1.50 (cash only). △ The Northwest 1st Avenue stop is in a crime-prone part of town. Exercise special caution there, day or night. Better yet, take a taxi to and from the airport. Broward County Transit (BCT) also covers the county on 303 fixed routes. The fare is $1.50 (cash only). Service starts around 5 am and continues to 11:30 pm, except on Sunday.

Bus Contact Broward County Transit ☎ 954/357–8400 ⊕ www.broward.org/BCT.

CAR TRAVEL

Renting a car to get around Broward County is highly recommended. Taxis are scarce and costly. Public transportation is rarely used.

By car, access to Broward County from north or south is via Florida's Turnpike, Interstate 95, U.S. 1, or U.S. 441. Interstate 75 (Alligator Alley, requiring a toll despite being part of the nation's interstate-highway system) connects Broward with Florida's west coast and runs parallel to State Road 84 within the county. East–west Interstate 595 runs from westernmost Broward County and links Interstate 75 with Interstate 95 and U.S. 1, providing handy access to the airport and seaport. Route A1A, designated a Florida Scenic Highway by the state's Department of Transportation, parallels the beach.

TRAIN TRAVEL

Amtrak provides daily service to Fort Lauderdale and stops at Deerfield Beach and Hollywood.

HOTELS

Back-to-back openings of luxury beachfront hotels have created Fort Lauderdale's upscale "hotel row"—with the Atlantic Resort & Spa, the Hilton Beach Resort, the Ritz-Carlton, the W, and the Westin all less than a decade old. More upscale places to hang your hat are on the horizon, whereas smaller family-run lodging spots are disappearing. You can also find chain hotels along the Intracoastal Waterway. If you want to be *on* the beach, be sure to ask specifically when booking your room, since many hotels advertise "waterfront" accommodations that are along inland waterways or overlooking the beach from across Route A1A.

RESTAURANTS

References to "Fort Liquordale" from spring-break days of old have given way to au courant allusions for the decidedly cuisine-oriented "Fork Lauderdale." Greater Fort Lauderdale offers some of the finest, most varied dining of any U.S. city its size, spawned in part by the advent of new luxury hotels and upgrades all around. From among more than 4,000 wining-and-dining establishments in Broward, choose from basic Americana or cuisines of Asia, Europe, or Central and South America, and enjoy more than just food in an atmosphere with subtropical twists.

HOTEL AND RESTAURANT COSTS

Prices in the restaurant reviews are the average cost of a main course at dinner or, if dinner is not served, at lunch. Prices in the hotel reviews are the lowest cost of a standard double room in high season. Prices do not include taxes (6%, more in some counties and 1%–5% tourist tax for hotel rooms).

FORT LAUDERDALE

Like many southeast Florida neighbors, Fort Lauderdale has long been revitalizing. In a state where gaudy tourist zones often stand aloof from workaday downtowns, Fort Lauderdale exhibits consistency at both ends of the 2-mile Las Olas corridor. The sparkling look results from upgrades both downtown and on the beachfront. Matching the downtown's innovative arts district, cafés, and boutiques is an equally inventive beach area, with hotels, cafés, and shops facing an undeveloped shoreline, and new resort-style hotels replacing faded icons of yesteryear. Despite wariness of pretentious overdevelopment, city leaders have allowed a striking number of glittering high-rises. Nostalgic locals and frequent visitors fret over the diminishing vision of sailboats bobbing in waters near downtown; however, Fort Lauderdale remains the yachting capital of the world, and the water toys don't seem to be going anywhere. Sharp demographic changes are also altering the faces of Greater Fort Lauderdale communities, increasingly cosmopolitan with more minorities, including Hispanics and people of Caribbean descent, as well as gays and lesbians. In Fort Lauderdale, especially, a younger populace is growing, whereas longtime residents are heading north, to a point where one former city commissioner likens the change to that of historic New River—moving with the tide and sometimes appearing at a standstill: "The river of our population is at still point, old and new in equipoise, one pushing against the other."

GETTING HERE AND AROUND

The Fort Lauderdale metro area is laid out in a grid system, and only myriad canals and waterways interrupt the mostly straight-line path of streets and roads. Nomenclature is important here. Streets, roads, courts, and drives run east–west. Avenues, terraces, and ways run north–south. Boulevards can (and do) run any which way. For visitors, boutique-lined Las Olas Boulevard is one of the most important east–west thoroughfares from the beach to downtown, whereas Route A1A—referred to as Atlantic Boulevard, Ocean Boulevard, and Fort Lauderdale Beach along some stretches—runs along the north–south oceanfront. These names can confuse visitors, since there are separate streets called Atlantic and Ocean in Hollywood and Pompano Beach. Boulevards, composed of either pavement or water, give Fort Lauderdale its distinct "Venice of America" character.

The city's transportation system, though less congested than elsewhere in South Florida, suffers from traffic overload. I-595 connects the city and suburbs and provides a direct route to the Fort Lauderdale–Hollywood International Airport and Port Everglades, but lanes slow to a crawl during rush hours. The Intracoastal Waterway, paralleling Route

This couple tours Fort Lauderdale via a three-wheeled scooter; photo by rockindom, Fodors.com member.

A1A, is the nautical equivalent of an interstate highway. It runs north–south between downtown Fort Lauderdale and the beach and provides easy boating access to neighboring beach communities.

Catch an orange-bottomed, yellow-topped Sun Trolley, running every 15 minutes, for as little as 50¢ each way. Sun Trolley's *Convention Connection* runs round-trip from Cordova Road's Harbor Shops near Port Everglades (where you can park free) to past the Convention Center, over the 17th Street Causeway, and north along Route A1A to Beach Place. Sun Trolley's Las Olas Beaches route passes from downtown through Las Olas and then north on A1A. Wave at trolley drivers—yes, they'll stop—for pickups anywhere along the route.

Meters in Yellow Cab taxis run at rates of $4.50 for the first mile and $2.40 for each additional mile; waiting time is 40¢ per minute. There's a $10-fare minimum to or from seaport or airport, and an additional $2 service charge when you are collected from the airport. All Yellow Cab vehicles accept major credit cards.

Transportation Contacts Sun Trolley ☎ 954/761–3543
⊕ *www.suntrolley.com.* **Yellow Cab** ☎ 954/777–7777.

TOURS

Honeycombed with some 300 miles of navigable waterways, Fort Lauderdale is the home port for about 44,000 privately owned vessels, but you don't need to be a boat owner to ply the waters. For a scenic way to really see this canal-laced city, take a relaxing boat tour or simply hop on a Water Taxi, part of Fort Lauderdale's water-transportation system. See why the city is called the "Venice of America."

Carrie B. Board a 300-passenger day cruiser for a 90-minute tour on the New River and Intracoastal Waterway. Cruises depart at 11, 1, and 3 daily November through May and Thursday–Monday between June and October. The cost is $22.95. ✉ *440 N. New River Dr. E, off Las Olas Blvd.* ☎ *954/768–9920* ⊕ *www.carriebcruises.com.*

FAMILY **Fort Lauderdale Duck Tours.** Quack, quack! The famous 45-passenger amphibious Hydra-Terra tours, which first gained popularity in Boston, have arrived in Fort Lauderdale. Ninety-minute tours include lots of land/water family fun, cruising and driving through Venice of America neighborhoods, historic areas, and the Intracoastal Waterway. Several tours depart daily and cost $32. Schedule varies and ducks sometimes don't run in low season, so check ahead of time. ✉ *17 S. Fort Lauderdale Beach Blvd., at Beach Pl.* ☎ *954/761–4002* ⊕ *www.fortlauderdaleducktours.com.*

Jungle Queen Riverboat. The kitsch *Jungle Queen* riverboat seats more than 550 and cruises up the New River through the heart of Fort Lauderdale, as it has for more than 75 years. It's old school and totally touristy but that's half the fun! The sightseeing cruises at 9:30 and 1:30 cost $19.95, and the 6 pm all-you-can-eat BBQ dinner cruise costs $42.95. ✉ *Bahia Mar Beach Resort, 801 Seabreeze Blvd.* ☎ *954/462–5596* ⊕ *www.junglequeen.com.*

Water Taxi. A great way to experience the multimillion-dollar homes, hotels, and seafood restaurants along Fort Lauderdale's waterways is via the public Water Taxi, which runs every 30 minutes beginning at 10 am and ending at midnight. An unlimited day pass serves as both a tour and a means of transportation between Fort Lauderdale's hotels and hot spots, though Water Taxi is most useful when viewed as a tour. It's possible to cruise all afternoon while taking in the waterfront sights. Captains and helpers indulge guests in fun factoids about Fort Lauderdale, white lies about the city's history, and bizarre tales about the celebrity homes along the Intracoastal. A day pass is $20. There are 10 regularly scheduled pickup stations in Fort Lauderdale. Water Taxi also connects Fort Lauderdale to Hollywood, where there are seven scheduled stops. ⊕ *www.watertaxi.com.*

VISITOR INFORMATION

Greater Fort Lauderdale Convention and Visitors Bureau ☎ *954/765–4466* ⊕ *www.sunny.org.*

EXPLORING

DOWNTOWN AND LAS OLAS

The jewel of downtown along New River is the small Arts and Entertainment District, with Broadway shows, ballet, and theater at the riverfront Broward Center for the Performing Arts. Clustered within a five-minute walk are the Museum of Discovery & Science, the

Fort Lauderdale

Hugh Taylor Birch State
Recreation Area

E. Sunrise Blvd.   838

8

S. Ocean Blvd.

Sunrise Key Blvd.

1A

Fort Lauderdale
Beach

E. Las Olas Blvd.

New River

7

Harbour
Beach

1A

17th St. Causeway

Stranahan
River

0   1 mi

0   1 km

expanding Fort Lauderdale Historical Museum, and the Museum of Art—home to stellar touring exhibits. Restaurants, sidewalk cafés, bars, and dance clubs flourish along Las Olas and its downtown extension. Tying these areas together is the Riverwalk, extending 2 miles along the New River's north and south banks. Tropical gardens with benches and interpretive displays fringe the walk on the north, boat landings on the south.

TOP ATTRACTIONS

Fort Lauderdale History Center. Surveying city history from the Seminole era to more recent times, the Fort Lauderdale Historical Society's museum has expanded into several adjacent buildings, including the historic King-Cromartie House (typical early 20th-century style Fort Lauderdale home), the 1905 New River Inn (Broward's oldest remaining hotel building), and the Hoch Heritage Center, a public research facility archiving original manuscripts, maps, and more than 250,000 photos. Daily docent-led tours run on the hour 1 pm–3 pm. ⊠ *231 S.W. 2nd Ave.* ☎ *954/463–4431* ⊕ *www.oldfortlauderdale.org* 🖃 *$10* ☉ *Tues.–Sun. noon–4.*

Las Olas Boulevard. What Lincoln Road is to South Beach, Las Olas Boulevard is to Fort Lauderdale. The terrestrial heart and soul of Broward County, Las Olas is the premier street for restaurants, art galleries, shopping, and people-watching. From west to east the landscape of Las Olas transforms from modern downtown high-rises to original boutiques and ethnic eateries. Beautiful mansions and traditional Floridian homes line the Intracoastal and define Fort Lauderdale. The streets of Las Olas connect to the pedestrian friendly Riverwalk, which continues to the edge of the New River on Avenue of the Arts. ⊕ *www.lasolasboulevard.com.*

Museum of Art Fort Lauderdale. Currently in an Edward Larrabee Barnes–designed building that's considered an architectural masterpiece, activists started this museum in a nearby storefront about 50 years ago. MOAFL now coordinates with Nova Southeastern University to host world-class touring exhibits and has an impressive permanent collection of 20th-century European and American art, including works by Picasso, Calder, Dalí, Mapplethorpe, Warhol, and Stella, as well as works by celebrated Ashcan School artist William Glackens. The lobby-level bookstore and cafe combo, Books & Books/Museum Cafe often hosts book signings, author visits, and special events. ⊠ *1 E. Las Olas Blvd., Downtown and Las Olas* ☎ *954/525–5500* ⊕ *www.moafl.org* 🖃 *$14* ☉ *Mon.–Wed., Fri., and Sat. 10–5, Thurs. 10–7, Sun. noon–5.*

FAMILY

Fodor'sChoice
★

Museum of Discovery & Science/AutoNation IMAX Theater. With more than 200 interactive exhibits, the aim here is to entertain children—*and* adults—with the wonders of science and the wonders of Florida. In 2012, the museum doubled in size, meaning twice the fun! Exhibits include the Ecodiscovery Center with an Everglades Airboat Adventure ride, resident otters, and an interactive Florida storm center. Florida Ecoscapes has a living coral reef, plus sharks, rays, and eels. Runways to Rockets offers stimulating trips to Mars and the moon while nine different cockpit simulators let you try out your pilot skills. The AutoNation IMAX theater, part of the complex, shows films, some in 3-D, on an 80-foot by 60-foot

THE GHOSTS OF STRANAHAN HOUSE

These days the historic Stranahan House is as famous for its nighttime ghost tours as it is for its daytime history tour. Originally built as a trading post in 1901 and later expanded into a town hall, a post office, a bank, and the personal residence of Frank Stranahan and wife, Ivy Cromartie, the historic Stranahan House was more than plagued by a number of tragic events and violent deaths, including Frank's tragic suicide. After financial turmoil, Stranahan tied himself to a concrete sewer grate and jumped into New River, leaving his widow to carry on. Sunday night at 7:30, house staff reveal the multiple tragic tales from the Stranahan crypt during the River House Ghost Tour ($25) and help visitors communicate with "the other side." Using special tools and snapping photos to search for orbs, guests are encouraged to field energy from the supposed five ghosts in the house. Given the high success rate of reaching out to the paranormal, the Stranahan House has become a favorite campground for global ghost hunters and television shows. Advance reservations are required.

screen with 15,000 watts of digital surround sound broadcast from 42 speakers. ⊠ *401 S.W. 2nd St., Downtown and Las Olas* ☎ *954/467–6637 museum, 954/463–4629 IMAX* ⊕ *www.mods.org* ⊠ *Museum $14, $19 with one IMAX show* ☉ *Mon.–Sat. 10–5, Sun. noon–6.*

Riverwalk. Lovely views prevail on this paved promenade on the New River's north bank. On the first Sunday of every month a free jazz festival attracts visitors. From west to east, the Riverwalk begins at the residential New River Sound, passes through the Arts and Science District, then the historic center of Fort Lauderdale, and wraps around the New River until it meets with Las Olas Boulevard's shopping district.

Stranahan House. The city's oldest residence, on the National Register of Historic Places, and increasingly dwarfed by high-rise development, was once home to businessman Frank Stranahan, who arrived in 1892. With his wife, Ivy, the city's first schoolteacher, he befriended and traded with Seminole Indians, and taught them "new ways." In 1901 he built a store that would later become his home after serving as a post office, a general store, and a restaurant. Frank and Ivy's former residence is now a museum, with many period furnishings, and tours. The historic home remains Fort Lauderdale's principal link to its brief history. Note that self-guided tours are not allowed. ⊠ *335 S.E. 6th Ave., at Las Olas Blvd., Downtown and Las Olas* ☎ *954/524–4736* ⊕ *www. stranahanhouse.org* ⊠ *$12* ☉ *Tours Oct.–Aug., daily at 1, 2, and 3.*

QUICK
BITES

Kilwin's Ft. Lauderdale. The sweet smell of waffle cones lures pedestrians to an old-fashioned confectionery in the heart of Las Olas Boulevard that also sells hand-paddled fudge and scoops of homemade ice cream. ⊠ *809 E. Las Olas Blvd., Downtown and Las Olas* ☎ *954/523–8338* ⊕ *www.kilwins.com/ftlauderdale.*

ALONG THE BEACH

Bonnet House Museum & Gardens. A 35-acre oasis in the heart of the beach area, this subtropical estate on the National Register of Historic Places stands as a tribute to the history of Old South Florida. This charming home, built in the 1920s, was the winter residence of the late Frederic and Evelyn Bartlett, artists whose personal touches and small surprises are evident throughout. If you're interested in architecture, artwork, or the natural environment, this place is worth a visit. After admiring the fabulous gardens, be on the lookout for playful monkeys swinging from trees. ⊠ *900 N. Birch Rd., Along the beach* ☎ *954/563–5393* ⊕ *www.bonnethouse.org* ⊜ *$20 for house tours, $10 for gardens only* ⊙ *Tues.–Sun. 9–4; tours hourly 9:30–3:30.*

International Swimming Hall of Fame Museum. This monument to underwater accomplishments has photos, medals, and other souvenirs from major swim events, and the Huizenga Theater provides an automated video experience where you can select vintage-Olympic coverage or old films such as Esther Williams's *Million Dollar Mermaid.* Connected to the museum, the **Fort Lauderdale Aquatic Complex** (⊕ *www.ci.ftlaud.fl.us/flac*) has two 50-meter pools plus a dive pool open daily to the public (except mid-December to mid-January). ⊠ *501 Sea Breeze Blvd., 1 block south of Las Olas at Rte. A1A, Along the beach* ☎ *954/462–6536, 954/828–4580* ⊕ *www.ishof.org* ⊜ *Museum $8, pool $5* ⊙ *Museum weekdays 9–5, weekends 9–2; pool daily 8–2, plus 6 pm–7:30 pm weekdays.*

NEED A BREAK?

Casablanca Café. For respite from the sun, duck in for a nice glass of chardonnay or a light bite. ⊠ *3049 Alhambra St., Along the beach* ☎ *954/764–3500.*

Steak 954. Recover from a long day in the sun with a much-deserved, refreshing cocktail. ⊠ *401 N. Fort Lauderdale Beach Blvd., Along the beach* ☎ *954/414–8333.*

WESTERN SUBURBS AND BEYOND

West of Fort Lauderdale is ever-growing suburbia, with most of Broward's golf courses, shopping, casinos, and chain restaurants. As you head farther west, the terrain takes on more characteristics of the Everglades, and you'll occasionally see alligators sunning on canal banks. Eventually, you reach the Everglades themselves after hitting the airboat outfitters on the park's periphery. Tourists flock to these airboats, but the best way of seeing the Everglades is to visit the Everglades National Park itself.

FAMILY **Ah-Tah-Thi-Ki Museum.** A couple of miles from Billie Swamp Safari is Ah-Tah-Thi-Ki Museum, whose name means "a place to learn, a place to remember." This museum documents the traditions and culture of the Seminole Tribe of Florida through artifacts, exhibits, and reenactments of rituals and ceremonies. The 60-acre site includes a living-history Seminole village, nature trails, and a wheelchair-accessible boardwalk through a cypress swamp. Guided tours are available daily at 2:30; self-guided audio tours are available anytime. There are also children's programs. ⊠ *34725 W. Boundary Rd., Western Suburbs and Beyond, Clewiston* ☎ *877/902–1113* ⊕ *www.ahtahthiki.com* ⊜ *$9* ⊙ *Wed.–Sun. 9–5.*

FAMILY **Billie Swamp Safari.** At the Billie Swamp Safari, experience the majesty of the Everglades firsthand. Daily tours of wildlife-filled wetlands and hammocks yield sightings of deer, water buffalo, raccoons, wild hogs, hawks, eagles, and alligators. Animal and reptile shows entertain audiences. Ecotours are conducted aboard motorized swamp buggies, and airboat rides are available, too. The on-site Swamp Water Café serves gator nuggets, frogs' legs, catfish, and Indian fry bread with honey. ⊠ *Big Cypress Seminole Indian Reservation, 30000 Gator Tail Trail, Western Suburbs and Beyond, Clewiston* ☎ *863/983–6101, 800/949–6101* ⊕ *www.swampsafari.com* ✉ *Swamp Safari Day Package (ecotour, shows, exhibits, and airboat ride) $49.95* ☉ *Daily 9–6.*

FAMILY **Butterfly World.** As many as 80 butterfly species from South and Central America, the Philippines, Malaysia, Taiwan, and other Asian nations are typically found within the serene 3-acre site inside Tradewinds Park in the northwest reaches of Broward County. A screened aviary called North American Butterflies is reserved for native species. The Tropical Rain Forest Aviary is a 30-foot-high construction, with observation decks, waterfalls, ponds, and tunnels filled with thousands of colorful butterflies. There are lots of birds, too; and kids love going in the lorikeet aviary, where the colorful birds land on every limb! ⊠ *3600 W. Sample Rd., Western Suburbs and Beyond, Coconut Creek* ☎ *954/977–4400* ⊕ *www.butterflyworld.com* ✉ *$24.95* ☉ *Mon.–Sat. 9–5, Sun. 11–5.*

FAMILY **Everglades Holiday Park.** This 30-acre park provides a decent glimpse of the Everglades and Florida's wild west circa 1950. Take an hour-long airboat tour, look at an 18th-century-style American Indian village, or catch the alligator wrestling. The airboats tend to be supersize and the experience very commercialized. Most episodes of Animal Planet's Gator Boys are filmed here. ⊠ *21940 Griffin Rd., Western Suburbs and Beyond* ☎ *954/434–8111* ⊕ *www.evergladesholidaypark.com* ✉ *Park free; airboat tour $25* ☉ *Daily 9–5.*

FAMILY **Flamingo Gardens.** Gators, crocodiles, river otters, and birds of prey lie in wait at Flamingo Gardens, with a walk-through aviary, plant house, and Everglades museum in the pioneer Wray Home. A half-hour guided tram ride winds through a citrus grove and wetlands area; and the gift shop helps you ship oranges, grapefruit and tangerines home. ⊠ *3750 S. Flamingo Rd., Western Suburbs and Beyond, Davie* ☎ *954/473–2955* ⊕ *www.flamingogardens.org* ✉ *$18, tram ride $4* ☉ *Daily 9:30–5.*

FAMILY **Sawgrass Mills.** Twenty-six million visitors a year flock to this mall, 10 miles west of downtown Fort Lauderdale, making it Florida's second-biggest tourist attraction (after the one with the mouse). The ever-growing complex has a basic alligator shape, and walking it all amounts to about a 2-mile jaunt. Count on 11,000 self-parking spaces (note your location, or you'll be working those soles), valet parking, and two information centers. More than 400 shops—many manufacturer's outlets, retail outlets, and name-brand discounters—include Gucci, Guess, Gap, and Ron Jon Surf Shop. Chain restaurants such as P.F. Chang's, the Cheesecake Factory, Grand Lux Cafe,

and Rainforest Café are on-site. The Shops at Colonnade cater to well-heeled patrons with a David Yurman jewelry outlet and other shops including Valentino, Prada, Burberry, Kate Spade New York, and Barneys New York. Nonlocals are entitled to a free coupon book at guest services. ⊠ *12801 W. Sunrise Blvd., at Flamingo Rd., Western Suburbs and Beyond, Sunrise* ☎ *954/846–2350* ⊕ *www.sawgrassmills. com* ⊙ *Mon.–Sat. 10–9:30, Sun. 11–8.*

FAMILY **Sawgrass Recreation Park.** A half-hour airboat ride through the Everglades allows you to view a good variety of plants and wildlife, from ospreys and alligators to turtles, snakes, and fish. Besides the ride, your entrance fee covers admission to an Everglades nature exhibit; a native Seminole village; and exhibits on alligators, other reptiles, and birds of prey. Super cool airboat nights tours are offered on Wednesday and Saturday at 8:30 pm to experience the nocturnal world of the 'glades. Reservations required for night tours. ⊠ *1006 N. U.S. Hwy. 27, Western Suburbs and Beyond, Weston* ☎ *888/424–7262* ⊕ *www.evergladestours.com* ⊠ *$19.50; $40 night tours* ⊙ *Airboat rides daily 9–5.*

Sand can sometimes be forgiving if you fall, and bicyclists also appreciate the ocean views.

BEACHES

Fodor's Choice
★ **Fort Lauderdale Beach.** The same downy sands that once welcomed America's youth-gone-wild (aka wild spring breakers) now frame a multimile shoreline of beachside sophistication. Alone among Florida's major beachfront communities, Fort Lauderdale's principal beach remains gloriously open and uncluttered. Walkways line both sides of the beach roadway, and traffic has been trimmed to two gently curving northbound lanes. Fort Lauderdale Beach unofficially begins between the Sheraton Fort Lauderdale and the Bahia Mar Resort, starting with the quiet **South Beach Park,** where picnic tables and palm trees rule. Going north, the younger, barely legal crowd gravitates toward the section of sand at the mouth of Las Olas Boulevard. The beach is actually most crowded between Las Olas and Sunrise Boulevards, directly in front of the major hotels and condominiums, namely in front of **Beach Place,** home to the Marriott time-share building and touristy places like Hooters and Fat Tuesday (and a beach-themed CVS Pharmacy). Gay men and women get their fix of vitamin D along **Sebastian Beach,** on Sebastian Street, just north of the Ritz-Carlton, Fort Lauderdale. Families with children enjoy hanging out between Seville Street and Vistamar Street, between the Westin Fort Lauderdale Beach and the Atlantic Resort and Spa. **Amenities:** food and drink; lifeguards; parking (fee). **Best for:** sunrise; swimming; walking. ⊠ *A1A from Holiday Dr. to Sunrise Blvd., Along the beach.*

Harbor Beach. The posh neighborhood of Harbor Beach boasts Fort Lauderdale's most opulent homes along the Intracoastal Waterway. Due east of this community, and just south of Fort Lauderdale's South Beach Park, a stunning swath of beach has adopted the name of its neighborhood—Harbor Beach. This section offers some of the few private beaches in Fort Lauderdale, most of which belong to big hotel names like the Marriott Harbor Beach and the Lago Mar. (Only hotel guests can access these beaches.) Such status permits the hotels to offer full-service amenities and eating and drinking outlets on their bespoke slices of sugarloafed heaven. **Amenities:** water sports. **Best for:** solitude; swimming; walking. ⊠ *S. Ocean La. and southern tip of Holiday Dr., Along the beach.*

Hugh Taylor Birch State Recreation Area. North of Fort Lauderdale's bustling beachfront, past Sunrise Boulevard, the quieter sands of Fort Lauderdale beach run parallel to Hugh Taylor Birch State Recreation Area, a nicely preserved patch of primeval Florida. The 180-acre tropical park sports lush mangrove areas along the Intracoastal waterway, and lovely nature trails. Visit the Birch House Museum, enjoy a picnic, play volleyball, or paddle a rented canoe. Since parking is limited on Route A1A, park here and take a walkway underpass to the beach (which can be accessed 9–5, daily). **Amenities:** toilets. **Best for:** solitude; walking. ⊠ *3109 E. Sunrise Blvd., Along the beach* ☎ *954/564–4521* ⊕ *www.floridastateparks.org* ☞ *$6 per vehicle, $2 per pedestrian* ⊙ *Daily 8–sunset.*

5

WHERE TO EAT

DOWNTOWN AND LAS OLAS

$$$
ECLECTIC
FAMILY
Fodor'sChoice
★

✕ **Big City Tavern.** A Las Olas landmark, Big City Tavern is the boulevard's most consistent spot for good food, good spirits, and good times. The diverse menu commingles Asian entrées like pad Thai, Italian options like homemade meatballs and cheese ravioli in a toasted garlic marinara, and American dishes like the grilled skirt-steak Cobb salad. Don't forget to ask about the crispy flatbread of the day, and make sure to save room for the homemade desserts. The pistachio brown-butter bundt cake with honey-roasted spiced peaches and pistachio gelato, the caramelized banana sundae in a Mason jar, and the devil's-food-cake ice-cream sandwich are all heaven on earth. Big City is open late into the night for drinks, desserts, and even offers a special late-night menu. $ *Average main: $24* ⊠ *609 E. Las Olas Blvd., Downtown and Las Olas* ☎ *954/727–0307* ⊕ *www.bigtimerestaurants.com.*

$$
AMERICAN

✕ **The Floridian.** This classic diner is plastered with photos of Monroe, Nixon, and local notables past and present in a succession of brightly painted rooms with funky chandeliers. The kitchen dishes up typical grease-pit breakfast favorites (no matter the hour), with oversized omelets that come with biscuits, toast, or English muffins, plus a choice of grits or tomatoes. The restaurant also has good hangover eats, but don't expect anything exceptional (besides the location). It's open 24 hours—even during hurricanes, as long as the power holds out. $ *Average main: $18* ⊠ *1410 E. Las Olas Blvd., Downtown and Las Olas* ☎ *954/463–4041* ⊟ *No credit cards.*

$
CAFÉ

✕ **Gran Forno Cafe.** The gamble of importing an entire Italian bakery direct from Brescia, Italy definitely paid off. Most days, the sandwiches, fresh baked breads, and pastries sell out even before lunchtime. All products are made fresh daily (except Monday), beginning at 4 am, by a team of bakers who can be seen hard at work through the café's glass windows. Customers line up at the door early in the morning to get their piping-hot artisanal breads, later returning for the scrumptious paninis and decadent desserts. A second branch, five blocks east on Las Olas, called Gran Forno Pronto, offers full service and a more extensive menu seven days a week, but it's only open until 7 pm. [$] *Average main: $10* ✉ *1235 E. Las Olas Blvd., Downtown and Las Olas* ☎ *954/467–2244* 🌐 *www.granforno.com* ⏲ *Closed Mon.* [$] *Average main: $10* ✉ *704 E. Las Olas Blvd., Downtown and Las Olas* ☎ *954/533–6276.*

$$$ STEAKHOUSE Fodor's Choice ★ 🍴 **Grille 401.** Enveloped in panes of wine bottles, floor-to-ceiling glass windows, and masculine wood panels, seductive Grille 401 is part avant-garde steak house, part pan-Asian eatery, part chic lounge—all together 100% fabulous. With a diverse menu that includes Osaka-style pressed sushi, classic filet mignon, crispy crab fritters, wood-grilled lobster, as well as a "light and healthy" menu for the lithe and calorie-conscious, there's something special for just about everyone. For the not-so-calorie-conscious, the homemade desserts, including a white-chocolate brioche bread pudding and, arguably, the world's best carrot cake are must tries. By day, Grille 401 caters to a power-lunch crowd escaping the ordinary in the Las Olas financial district; by night, Grille 401 is all about sophisticated dining, excellent cocktails, and feeding your wildest foodie fantasies. [$] *Average main: $28* ✉ *401 E. Las Olas Blvd., Downtown and Las Olas* ☎ *954/767–0222* 🌐 *www.grille401.com.*

$$$ MODERN MEXICAN Fodor's Choice ★ 🍴 **Rocco's Tacos & Tequila Bar.** The busiest spot on the Las Olas strip, Rocco's is more of a scene than just a restaurant. With pitchers of margaritas a-flowin', the middle-age crowd is boisterous and fun, recounting (and reliving) the days of spring break debauchery from their preprofessional years. In fact, Rocco's drink menu is even larger than its sizeable food menu. Guacamole is made tableside, and Mexican dishes such as chimichangas and enchiladas have been reinvented (and made far less spicy) for the American palate. Expect a wild night and lots of fun! [$] *Average main: $23* ✉ *1313 E. Las Olas Blvd., Downtown and Las Olas* ☎ *954/524–9550* 🌐 *www.roccostacos.com.*

$$ CAJUN Fodor's Choice ★ 🍴 **Royal Pig Pub.** Fort Lauderdale's coolest gastro-pub revels in doling out hefty portions of cajun comfort cuisine and potent, creative libations. As the name implies, this is indeed a place to pig out on the beer and butter-soaked New Orleans–style BBQ shrimp, grilled fish-of-the-day atop cheese grits, mussel étouffée, sweet-potato fries with honey-cider drizzle, and grilled free-range turkey burgers loaded with exotic condiments. Plenty of folks come here just for the awesome drinks. In fact, it's one of Fort Lauderdale's busiest joints come midnight. The pub's arched ceilings are lined with flat-screen TVs, and the bar occupies nearly half the restaurant. Rub elbows with Fort Lauderdale's yuppies and hotties over blood-orange caipiroskas and lemonade with cucumber, mint, and blueberries. [$] *Average main: $20* ✉ *350 E. Las Olas Blvd., Downtown and Las Olas* ☎ *954/617–7447* 🌐 *www.royalpigpub.com.*

$$$ ITALIAN 🍴 **Timpano Italian Chophouse.** Combine the likes of a high-end steak house with a typical Italian-American trattoria, and you've got yourself a successful recipe for an Italian chophouse. Timpano's Italian-centric

offerings include fresh pastas, flatbreads, and the full gamut of parmesans, marsalas, and fra diavolos. Its steak-house identity plays out through a wide selection of aged beef and chops with decadent sides (including truffle mac-and-cheese). Regardless of whether you go carb or carnivore for the main event, the blow-your-mind delicious salads are an essential component to the Timpano experience, namely the watercress and arugula salad and the chopped salad. $ *Average main: $25* ⊠ *450 Las Olas Blvd., Downtown and Las Olas* ☎ *954/462–9119* ⊕ *www.timpanochophouse.net.*

$$$$
SEAFOOD
× **Wild Sea.** In the heart of tony Las Olas Boulevard, this oyster bar and grille keeps things simple with a small menu focused on a beautiful raw bar and ever-changing preparations of diverse catches from Florida, Hawaiian, and New England waters. With everything filleted and/or shucked in house, the just-caught freshness is evident in each bite. Make sure to try the *poke* of the day (Hawaiian raw fish salad), which is made tableside, as well as the seared popcorn-crusted big eye tuna (if it's in season). $ *Average main: $31* ⊠ *Riverside Hotel, 620 E. Las Olas Blvd, Downtown and Las Olas* ☎ *954/467–0671* ⊕ *www. WildSeaLasOlas.com* ☉ *No lunch. Closed Sun. and Mon.*

$$$
AMERICAN
× **YOLO.** YOLO stands for "You Only Live Once," but you will definitely want to eat here more than once. For Fort Lauderdale's bourgeoisie, this is the place to see and be seen and to show off your hottest wheels in the driveway. For others, it's an upscale restaurant with affordable prices and a great ambience. The restaurant serves the full gamut of new American favorites like tuna sashimi, fried calamari, garden burgers, and short ribs with a sophisticated spin. For example, the Szechuan calamari is flash-fried, and then covered in garlic-chili sauce, chopped peanuts, and sesame seeds; the garden burger is made from bulgur wheat, cremini mushrooms, and cashews and served with thin-cut fries. $ *Average main: $22* ⊠ *333 E. Las Olas Blvd., Downtown and Las Olas* ☎ *954/523–1000* ⊕ *www.yolorestaurant.com.*

ALONG THE BEACH

$$
ECLECTIC
× **Casablanca Cafe.** Located along A1A in the heart of Fort Lauderdale's hotel row, Casablanca Cafe offers alfresco and indoor dining with a fabulous ocean view. The historic two-story Moroccan-style villa was built in the 1920s by local architect Francis Abreu. The menu at this piano bar and restaurant showcases a global potpourri of American, Mediterranean, and Asian flavors; however, the recommended "house favorites" focus on eclectic preparations of Florida's best fish. Prepare for long waits to eat in the outdoor section; it's wildly popular morning, noon, and night with tourists and locals alike. $ *Average main: $18* ⊠ *3049 Alhambra St., Along the beach* ☎ *954/764–3500* ⊕ *www. casablancacafeonline.com.*

$$$$
ITALIAN
× **da Campo Osteria.** On the ground floor of the sleek Il Lugano hotel, this stylish Italian restaurant features "mozzarella baristas," who knead mouthwatering cheese fresh at your table from raw ingredients of buttermilk, hot water, and salt. The warm cheese is then served with a choice of four toppings, including heirloom tomatoes and sweet basil, and tapenade made of green and black olives. The cheese course is followed by an array of antipasti, *primi,* and *secondi* that include pastas,

meats, and seafood. Most notably, four pastas are handcrafted in-house daily, usually two special ones and the two staples—spaghetti, tagliatelle—plus risotto. $ *Average main: $33* ⊠ *Il Lugano Suite Hotel, 3333 N.E. 32nd Ave., Intracoastal and Inland* ☎ *954/226–5002* ⊕ *www.dacampoosteria.com.*

$$$ ✕ **Ocean 2000.** This waterfront restaurant and lounge at the Pelican
SEAFOOD   Grand Beach Resort is a favorite of locals in the know, renowned for its stunning Atlantic ocean views and excellent fish and seafood (prepared with a Latin flair). Expect succulent and savory dishes that include local fish ceviche, Gulf-shrimp Cobb salad, and Florida yellowtail snapper *á la plancha* (skillet-grilled). If indulging in the wildly popular Sunday brunch or a casual seaside lunch, make sure to request seating on the oceanfront patio, arguably the best seats in any house in Fort Lauderdale. Come nightfall, the slick dining room comes to life, illuminated by futuristic chandeliers, ubiquitous candles, and the moonlight over the ocean through oversized windows. $ *Average main: $29* ⊠ *Pelican Grand Beach Resort, 2000 N. Ocean Blvd., Along the beach* ☎ *954/556–7667* ⊕ *www.pelicanbeach.com/ocean2000.*

$$$$ ✕ **SAIA Sushi.** The superlative locale for getting your sushi fix in Fort
SUSHI   Lauderdale, SAIA offers innovative rolls and perfectly executed classics
Fodor's Choice as well as a great selection of hot Thai and Japanese dishes. SAIA's master
★   chef, Subin Chenkosorn, hails from the renowned Blue Sea at the Delano in Miami and has brought his amazing skill set to the Fort Lauderdale shoreline. The stylish restaurant doubles as a gregarious lounge come late evening, perfect for enjoying another round of saketinis, soju-based cocktails, and other specialty drinks like the divine SAIA-rita and Ruby Foo, after a fabulous dinner. $ *Average main: $35* ⊠ *B Ocean Fort Lauderdale, 999 N. Fort Lauderdale Beach Blvd., Along the beach* ☎ *954/302–5252.*

$$$$ ✕ **Shula's on the Beach.** For anyone who gets positively misty-eyed at the
STEAKHOUSE mere mention of Don Shula's Miami Dolphins 17–0 Perfect Season of 1972, the good news is that this beachfront spot also turns out culinary winners just as handily. Despite dozens of new, trendy steak houses in Miami and Fort Lauderdale, Shula's on the Beach remains staunch competition. Carnivores rejoice over the aged premium Black Angus beef grilled over a super-hot fire for quick charring. The seafood is excellent, too, and served in generous portions. The jumbo sea scallops and jumbo lump crab cakes are indeed "jumbo" and über-delicious. For a more casual affair, check out the lively bar area adorned with sports memorabilia and large-screen TVs. $ *Average main: $38* ⊠ *Westin Beach Resort & Spa, Fort Lauderdale, 321 N. Fort Lauderdale Beach Blvd., Along the beach* ☎ *954/355–4000* ⊕ *www.donshula.com.*

$$$$ ✕ **Steak 954.** It's not just the steaks that impress at Stephen Starr's super-
STEAKHOUSE star restaurant. The lobster and crab-coconut ceviche and the red snap-
Fodor's Choice per tiradito are divine; the butter-poached Maine lobster is perfection;
★   and the raw bar showcases only the best and freshest seafood on the market. Located on the first floor of the swanky W Fort Lauderdale, Steak 954 offers spectacular views of the ocean for those choosing outdoor seating; inside, there's a sexy, sophisticated ambience for those choosing to dine in the main dining room, with bright tropical colors balanced with dark woods and an enormous jellyfish tank spanning

the width of the restaurant. Sunday brunch is very popular, so arrive early for the best views. [$] *Average main: $35* ✉ *W Fort Lauderdale, 401 N. Fort Lauderdale Beach Blvd., Along the beach* ☎ *954/414–8333* 🌐 *www.steak954.com.*

$$$$ SEAFOOD Fodor's Choice ★ 🍴 **3030 Ocean.** Celebrity chef Dean James Max's fish and seafood restaurant has been the talk of the town for decades. Constantly evolving with new flavors and fusions, 3030 Ocean gives plenty of great reasons to return time and time again. The ahi tuna coconut ceviche, a kind of tuna tartare served in one-half of a shelled coconut, is so fresh, it melts in your mouth. The apricot-glazed mahi and wild gulf shrimp ravioli in butternut-squash puree are nothing short of experiential. The martini menu is also heaven-sent, advancing mixology with basil-and-passion-fruit martinis, Bellini martinis, and acai-and-sage martinis. If you treat yourself to only one nice dinner in Fort Lauderdale, do it here! [$] *Average main: $32* ✉ *Marriott's Harbor Beach Resort & Spa, 3030 Holiday Dr., Along the beach* ☎ *954/765–3030* 🌐 *www.3030ocean.com.*

$$$ MEDITERRANEAN Fodor's Choice ★ 🍴 **Via Luna.** Fort Lauderdale's newest masterpiece by the beach, Via Luna, is both a visual and gastronomic tour de force. The elegantly appointed restaurant, located within the Ritz-Carlton, Fort Lauderdale, exudes serenity and modern luxury with white marble floors, striking chandeliers, and towering floor-to-ceiling windows overlooking the ocean. The menu is a grand celebration of the beautiful flavors of the Mediterranean. Start, for example, with melt-in-your-mouth, thinly sliced ahi tuna over fennel and grapefruit, topped with virgin olive oil and smoked sea salt. Then move on to hearty mains like fusilli and braised octopus or Maine-lobster risotto mixed with sweet corn and wilted baby arugula. There's also alfresco seating for those wanting to feel the ocean zephyrs. Sunday brunch is the be-all and end-all of extravagant brunches in Fort Lauderdale. [$] *Average main: $29* ✉ *Ritz-Carlton, Fort Lauderdale, 1 N. Fort Lauderdale Beach Blvd., Along the beach* ☎ *954/465–2300* 🌐 *www.ritzcarlton.com* ✍ *Reservations essential.*

INTRACOASTAL AND INLAND

$$$$ SOUTHWESTERN 🍴 **Canyon Southwest Cafe.** Southwestern fusion fare helps you escape the ordinary at this small, magical enclave, managed hands-on by executive chef Chris Wilber. Order, for example, bison medallions with scotch bonnets, a tequila-jalapeño smoked salmon tostada, coriander-crusted tuna, or blue-corn fried oysters. Chipotle, wasabi, mango, and red chilies accent fresh seafood and wild game. If you drink alcohol, start off with a signature prickly pear margarita or choose from a well-rounded wine list or beer selection. Save room for the divine chocolate bread pudding. [$] *Average main: $35* ✉ *1818 E. Sunrise Blvd., Intracoastal and Inland* ☎ *954/765–1950* 🌐 *www.canyonfl.com* ⏲ *No lunch.*

$$$$ STEAKHOUSE 🍴 **The Capital Grille, Fort Lauderdale.** The Capital Grille is a rare example of a restaurant chain that has managed to uphold the superlative food quality and stellar service on which it was founded, regardless of expansion. Indeed, the Fort Lauderdale outpost of this American darling never fails to impress, every dish cooked being to perfection and meticulously presented. The dining room feels warm and welcoming, buzzing with the constant chatter of patrons raving about the food and ordering another round of Stoli dolis (Stoli vodka marinating in a

tub of fresh-cut pineapples for two weeks and then served as a smooth martini). Though the steaks and sides are the main draw, the calamari appetizer, shrimp cocktail, sushi-grade tuna steak, and salmon should not be overlooked. They are all phenomenal. $ *Average main: $34* ✉ *2430 E. Sunrise Blvd., Intracoastal and Inland* ☎ *954/446–2000* ⊕ *www.thecapitalgrille.com.*

$$$$ ✕ **Casa D'Angelo Ristorante.** Owner-chef Angelo Elia has created a gem of
ITALIAN   a Tuscan-style white-tablecloth restaurant, tucked in the Sunrise Square shopping center. Casa D'Angelo's oak oven turns out marvelous seafood and beef dishes. The pappardelle with porcini mushrooms takes pasta to pleasant heights. Another favorite is antipasto "Angelo," an assortment of seasonal grilled vegetables and mozzarella. Ask about the oven-roasted fish of the day at market price. Expect long waits. Casa D'Angelo is packed year-round. $ *Average main: $38* ✉ *1201 N. Federal Hwy., Intracoastal and Inland* ☎ *954/564–1234* ⊕ *www.casa-d-angelo.com* ⊘ *No lunch.*

$$$$ ✕ **China Grill.** China Grill takes the best of Asian cuisine and adds an
ASIAN   American flair to create a pan-Asian eating extravaganza. This concept of global Asian fusion draws inspiration from Marco Polo and his descriptions of the Far East and its riches. While Marco Polo's travels are imprinted on the restaurant floor, the flavors of his destinations are all over the menu. Try the crackling calamari salad—a taste explosion of zest with crispy lettuce, calamari, and citrus in lime-miso dressing—or the Shanghai lobster—a 2.5-pound female lobster, unbelievably soft and tender, drenched in ginger and curry and accompanied by crispy spinach. $ *Average main: $40* ✉ *Hilton Ft. Lauderdale Marina, 1881 S.E. 17th St., Intracoastal and Inland* ☎ *954/759–9950* ⊕ *www. chinagrillmgt.com.*

$$$ ✕ **d.b.a./café.** Expect the unexpected at this small, eclectic, and artsy
MODERN   eatery that serves food with both modern American and modern French
AMERICAN   accents. With a dozen or so tables in a dimly lit space lined with exposed brick and adorned with family photos, this neighborhood restaurant exudes a true one-of-a-kind flair and serves up some pretty amazing food, too. Entrées are served in either half or full portions, catering to either those who like hearty mains or those who want to have a variety of small plates. Enjoy simple sensations like pan-seared sea scallops with porcini-mushroom butter and fresh ricotta gnocchi with gorgonzola sauce, or dive into personality-driven dishes like the flavorful onion-crusted Florida grouper with saffron-vanilla beurre blanc, mushroom risotto, and spinach. A full roster of nightly specials and the desserts of the evening are posted on the restaurant's blackboard menu. $ *Average main: $23* ✉ *2364 N. Federal Hwy., Intracoastal and Inland* ☎ *954/565–3392* ⊕ *www.dba2z.com* ⚓ *Reservations essential* ⊘ *Closed Mon. No lunch Tues.–Sat.*

$$$ ✕ **15th Street Fisheries & Dockside Cafe.** A prime Intracoastal Waterway
SEAFOOD   view is a big part of the allure at this two-story seafood landmark; the
FAMILY   fresh seafood is the other. The old 15th carries on solidly with spicy conch chowder, grilled fish dishes, and homemade breads. There are two separate menus: a dinner menu for more formal upstairs dining and a casual dockside menu served day and night. Kids love feeding

the families of giant tarpon circling around the dock. $ *Average main: $25* ⊠ *1900 S.E. 15th St., Intracoastal and Inland* ☎ *954/763–2777* ⊕ *www.15streetfisheries.com.*

$$

PIZZA

✕**Giorgio's 17th Street.** The delicious brick-oven pizza lures customers to this tiny restaurant, but it's really the salads and sandwiches that provide the wow factor. The blackened chicken Caesar salad and the monstrous grilled chicken sandwiches (with grilled peppers and fresh mozzarella on freshly baked bread) are both memorable. Nevertheless, the homemade seafood salad is still Giorgio's best seller, a healthy mix of tender squid, shrimp, and scallops in a light vinaigrette. All meals are served with piping hot rolls and homemade hummus. $ *Average main: $18* ⊠ *1499 S.E. 17th St., Intracoastal and Inland* ☎ *954/767–8300* ⊕ *www.letseat.at/giorgios.*

$$$

ITALIAN

✕**Kitchenetta.** A modern Italian-American trattoria serving fresh Mediterranean favorites in a chic, loft-inspired setting, Kitchenetta has been pleasing Fort Lauderdale foodies since 2000. The outdoor seating area welcomes pet-lovers, who often dine with pooch in tow. Popular items fresh out of the open kitchen include the fried calamari, fusilli with escarole and cannellini beans, penne puttanesca, pollo scarpariello Siciliano, and a wide range of daily mouthwatering specials. $ *Average main: $24* ⊠ *2850 N. Federal Hwy., Intracoastal and Inland* ☎ *954/567–3333* ⊕ *www.kitchenetta.com.*

$$$

MODERN AMERICAN

✕**Market 17.** Using only the best ingredients from regional farmers and local fishermen, Market 17 leads the organic farm-to-table revolution in South Florida. The menu at this chic restaurant shifts seasonally, lending to an ever-changing kaleidoscope of mouthwatering creations. The Florida wahoo crudo in citrus marinade and the pan-basted Florida yelloweye snapper with leek puree are two local favorites. The desserts, too, are outstanding and include homemade ice creams in flavors like bananas Foster, chocolate cake batter, and ginger and honey. For something awesome and different with a small group, Market 17 offers "dining in the dark," where dinner is served in a blacked-out room, forcing you to rely on your senses of touch, taste, and smell to figure out what you're eating and drinking. $ *Average main: $36* ⊠ *1850 S.E. 17th St., Suite 109, Intracoastal and Inland* ☎ *954/835–5507* ⊕ *www. market17.net* ⟡ *Reservations essential.*

$$

SEAFOOD

Fodor's Choice

★

✕**Pelican Landing.** In this age of globalization and instant information, it's nearly impossible to remain the city's "best-kept secret," but somehow Pelican Landing has managed to do exactly that. Located on a second-story terrace in the Pier Sixty-Six Marina, the serene outdoor restaurant serves mouthwatering beach-shack-style eats surrounded by picturesque panoramas of boats, sea, and sunset. The fish is caught daily, served blackened or grilled, presented with sides, on a salad, or in a burrito. The ceviches and conch fritters are some of the best in South Florida. And matched with frozen drinks and pitchers of mojitos, you'll quickly reach a state of "paradise found!" $ *Average main: $18* ⊠ *Hyatt Regency Pier Sixty Six, 2301 S.E. 17th St. Causeway, at end of main dock, Intracoastal and Inland* ☎ *954/525–6666* ⊕ *www. pier66.hyatt.com.*

$$ SEAFOOD 🍴 **Southport Raw Bar.** You can't go wrong at this unpretentious spot where the motto, on bumper stickers for miles around, proclaims, "eat fish, live longer, eat oysters, love longer, eat clams, last longer." Raw or steamed clams, raw oysters, and peel-and-eat shrimp are market priced. Sides range from Bimini bread to key lime pie, with conch fritters, beer-battered onion rings, and corn on the cob in between. Order wine by the bottle or glass, and beer by the pitcher, bottle, or can. Eat outside overlooking a canal, or inside at booths, tables, or in the front or back bars. Limited parking is free, and a grocery-store parking lot is across the street. [$] *Average main: $18* ✉ *1536 Cordova Rd., Intracoastal and Inland* ☎ *954/525–2526* 🌐 *www.southportrawbar.com.*

$$$ VEGETARIAN 🍴 **Sublime.** Pamela Anderson and her celebrity pals are not the only vegetarians who love this vegan powerhouse. The vegan sushi, the portobello stack, and innovative pizzas and pastas surprisingly can satisfy even carnivore cravings. All dishes are organic and void of any animal by-products, showing the world how vegan eating does not compromise flavor or taste. Even items like the key lime cheesecake, and chicken scaloppini use alternative ingredients and headline an evening of health-conscious eating. [$] *Average main: $30* ✉ *1431 N. Federal Hwy., Intracoastal and Inland* ☎ *954/539–9000* 🌐 *www.sublimerestaurant.com* 🕒 *Closed Mon.*

$$$$ GREEK 🍴 **Thasos Greek Taverna.** A small, heavenly slice of the Greek Isles has floated ashore between Fort Lauderdale's beach and the Intracoastal Waterway. Upon entering Thasos Greek Taverna, you'll immediately think Greek chic, with the white-washed walls, blue trim, streaming images of Greece on the walls, and the easy-on-the-eyes crowd. Plan on eating family style. Start with a variety of *pikilia* (Greek spreads), which include spicy whipped feta, divine *tzatziki* (a garlicky yogurt-cucumber dip), and melt-in-your-mouth taramosalata. Then move onto the *mezedes* (hot shared plates) that include shrimp *Saganaki* (fried with tomatoes, olives, and feta), stuffed grape leaves, and the oh-so-tender fire-grilled octopus. Finally, expand your waistline with a main course, including such specialties as pumpkin swordfish with caramelized root vegetables and traditional moussaka. [$] *Average main: $34* ✉ *3330 E. Oakland Park Blvd., between N. Ocean Blvd and N.E. 33rd Ave., Intracoastal and Inland* ☎ *954/200–6006* 🌐 *www.thasostaverna.com* ✍ *Reservations essential.*

$ MEXICAN Fodor's Choice ★ 🍴 **Zona Fresca.** A local favorite on the cheap, Zona Fresca serves healthful, Mexican fast food with the best chips, salsas, burritos, and quesadillas in town. Everything is made fresh on the premises, including the authentic salsas, presented in a grand salsa bar. Zona is busy seven days a week for both lunch and dinner and offers both indoor and outdoor seating. It's likely to be your best (and cheapest) lunch in Fort Lauderdale. [$] *Average main: $8* ✉ *1635 N. Federal Hwy., Intracoastal and Inland* ☎ *954/566–1777* 🌐 *www.zonafresca.com.*

WESTERN SUBURBS

$$$ PIZZA FAMILY 🍴 **D' Angelo: Pizza, Wine Bar, and Tapas.** Expanding the D'Angelo restaurant empire, Florida's famous restaurateur and Tuscan chef Angelo Elia has opened a second outpost of his casual pizza, tapas, and wine bar in the western suburbs of Fort Lauderdale. D'Angelo serves affordable small plates, salads, ceviches, and pizzas (based with either red or white

sauce) and has quickly become a neighborhood favorite. Both kids and adults love the rotating selections of homemade gelatos. Don't miss the zucchini flowers stuffed with mozzarella, the spinach gnocchi with four cheeses and pine nuts, and the sorrentina pizza with eggplant, mozzarella, fresh tomato, and basil oil. This is superb Italian comfort food! [$] *Average main: $22* ✉ *Country Isle Shopping Center, 1370 Weston Rd., Western Suburbs and Beyond, Weston* ☎ *954/306–0037* 🌐 *www.dangelopizza.com.*

$$ AMERICAN 🍴 **East City Grill.** Try the lamb lollipop appetizer or truffle-crusted sea scallops at this casual yet sophisticated spot with a lake view (no beaches here—this is the 'burbs!). Entrées include crab-crusted grouper and nut-crusted pork tenderloin. Among desserts, East City dark chocolate soufflé is a standout. Martinis—chocolate, butterscotch, mango, or cappuccino—provide liquid-dessert finales. [$] *Average main: $21* ✉ *1800 Bell Tower La., Western Suburbs and Beyond, Weston* ☎ *954/659–3339* 🌐 *www.eastcitygrill.com* 🕑 *No lunch Sun.*

$$$$ STEAKHOUSE 🍴 **Ireland's Steakhouse.** Don't let the name fool you. Ireland's Steakhouse is not particularly Irish nor is it just a steak house. In fact, this restaurant is most popular for its sustainable seafood menu. Promoting a holistic philosophy of green eating, the restaurant meticulously chooses its ingredients and the purveyors that supply them, while staying true to the international "Seafood Watch" guide. The restaurant is a warm and woodsy enclave in the back corner of the Bonaventure Resort & Spa. In keeping with trends of other steak houses, hearty mains (like the cherry balsamic yellowfin tuna and the 20-ounce bone-in rib eye) are paired with loads of decadent sides made for sharing (like lobster mac 'n' cheese and lobster fries). [$] *Average main: $42* ✉ *Bonaventure Resort & Spa, 250 Racquet Club Rd., Western Suburbs and Beyond, Weston* ☎ *800/327–8090* 🌐 *www.bonaventure.hyatt.com* 🕑 *Closed Sun. and Mon. No lunch.*

WILTON MANORS AND OAKLAND PARK

$$$ PIZZA FAMILY 🍴 **D'Angelo Pizza, Wine Bar, and Tapas.** D'Angelo serves affordable small plates, salads, ceviches, and pizzas (based with either white or red sauce) and has quickly become a neighborhood favorite. Both kids and adults love the rotating selections of homemade gelatos, a very necessary end to an evening at D'Angelo. Don't miss the zucchini flowers stuffed with mozzarella, the spinach gnocchi with four cheeses and pine nuts, and the sorrentina pizza with eggplant, mozzarella, fresh tomato, and basil oil. This is superb Italian comfort food! Expanding the D'Angelo restaurant empire, regionally famous restaurateur and Tuscan chef Angelo Elia has opened a second outpost of his casual pizza, tapas, and wine bar in the western suburbs of Fort Lauderdale. [$] *Average main: $22* ✉ *4215 N. Federal Hwy., Wilton Manors and Oakland Park, Oakland Park* ☎ *954/306–0037* 🌐 *www.dangelopizza.com.*

$$$$ SOUTH PACIFIC 🍴 **Mai-Kai.** Cheesy and super touristy to some yet exciting to others, the South Pacific meets South Florida at this torch-lit landmark. It's undeniably gimmicky, but droves arrive for the popular Polynesian dance review and fire shows, Peking duck, and umbrella-garnished exotic tropical drinks. The Pacific allure is maintained with freshly planted palms, thatch, and bamboo, and a wood-planked bridge rebuilt

to make arriving cars sound like rumbling thunder. An expanded wine list embraces boutique vintages from around the world. Valet parking is available. [$] *Average main: $45* ✉ *3599 N. Federal Hwy., Wilton Manors and Oakland Park* ☎ *954/563–3272* 🌐 *www.maikai.com.*

$ CAFÉ 🍴 **Stork's Café.** Wilton Manors' legendary Stork's Café stands out as a gay-friendly, straight-friendly, and just plain friendly coffeehouse and café, ideal for chilling out or catching up on a good read. Sit indoors or outside under tables with red umbrellas and indulge in a coffee and a sweet. The white-chocolate-pistachio cheesecake is a must-try. Baked goods range from croissants, tortes, cakes, and pies to "monster cookies," including gingersnap and snickerdoodle. For lunch, try the Pilgrim (think Thanksgiving in a wrap) or the Hello Kitty (tuna salad on sourdough), or a made-from-scratch soup like vegan split pea. [$] *Average main: $10* ✉ *2505 N.E. 15th Ave., Wilton Manors and Oakland Park, Wilton Manors* ☎ *954/567–3220* 🌐 *storksbakery.com.*

$$$ SEAFOOD 🍴 **Sunfish Grill.** The former Pompano Beach institution migrated south in 2009 and hasn't looked back since. Quickly establishing itself in the Oakland Park area (albeit in a quiet strip mall), Sunfish Grill doles out beautifully presented contemporary American cuisine, namely well-executed, outside-the-box seafood and fish dishes. The spaghetti Bolognaise is made with ground tuna instead of beef; the Sunfish Caesar with Maytag Blue Cheese instead of Parmesan; the "not the usual" key lime pie with coconut sorbet instead of whipped cream. The results of this ingenuity are fantastic. [$] *Average main: $27* ✉ *2775 E. Oakland Park Blvd., Wilton Manors and Oakland Park* ☎ *954/561–2004* 🌐 *www.sunfishgrill.com.*

WHERE TO STAY

For expanded reviews, facilities, and current deals, visit Fodors.com.

DOWNTOWN AND LAS OLAS

$$$ B&B/INN Fodor's Choice ★ 🏨 **Pineapple Point.** Tucked a few blocks behind Las Olas Boulevard in the residential neighborhood of Victoria Park, Pineapple Point is a magnificent maze of posh tropical cottages and dense foliage catering to the gay community and is nationally renowned for its stellar service. **Pros:** superior service; tropical setting. **Cons:** difficult to find at first; need a vehicle for beach jaunts. [$] *Rooms from: $289* ✉ *315 N.E. 16th Terr., Downtown and Las Olas* ☎ *954/527–0094* 🌐 *www.pineapplepoint.com* 🛏 *25 rooms* 🍴 *Breakfast.*

$$ HOTEL 🏨 **Riverside Hotel.** On Las Olas Boulevard, just steps from boutiques, restaurants, and art galleries, Fort Lauderdale's oldest hotel (circa 1936) evokes a time bygone with historical photos gracing hallways, and guest rooms outfitted with antique oak furnishings, ornamental palm trees, and a bold tropical color palate with a Tommy Bahamas throwback flair. **Pros:** historic appeal; in the thick of Las Olas action; nice views. **Cons:** questionable room decor; dated lobby; small bathrooms. [$] *Rooms from: $195* ✉ *620 E. Las Olas Blvd., Downtown and Las Olas* ☎ *954/467–0671, 800/325–3280* 🌐 *www.riversidehotel.com* 🛏 *208 rooms, 6 suites* 🍴 *No meals.*

ALONG THE BEACH

$$$ **The Atlantic Resort & Spa.** The hotel that catalyzed Fort Lauderdale's
HOTEL luxe revolution continues to be a beautiful and well-run gem, and
the skyscraping, oceanfront beauty seems well positioned to stay at
the top of her contemporary game for years to come. **Pros:** sophisticated lodging option; rooms have high-tech touches; hotel received full
renovation in 2011. **Cons:** no complimentary water bottles in room;
expensive parking. $ *Rooms from: $219 ✉ 601 N. Fort Lauderdale
Beach Blvd., Along the beach ☎ 954/567–8020, 877/567–8020 ⊕ www.
atlantichotelfl.com ⇥ 61 rooms, 58 suites, 4 penthouses ⦿ No meals.*

$ **Bahia Mar Fort Lauderdale Beach Hotel.** This nicely situated Fort Lau-
HOTEL derdale beachfront classic received a long-overdue nip/tuck in 2011
before rebranding as a DoubleTree hotel. **Pros:** crosswalk from hotel
to beach; on-site yacht center. **Cons:** dated exteriors; small bathrooms;
popcorn ceilings. $ *Rooms from: $162 ✉ 801 Seabreeze Blvd., Along
the beach ☎ 954/764–2233 ⊕ www.bahiamarhotel.com ⇥ 296 rooms
⦿ No meals.*

$$ **B Ocean Fort Lauderdale.** The first hotel launched by the new "B" hotel
HOTEL brand merges trendiness with affordability in a 13-story U-shape tower
overlooking the ocean. **Pros:** all rooms have ocean views; trendy but
affordable; nightime fire pits. **Cons:** small pool area; lackluster exterior.
$ *Rooms from: $185 ✉ 999 N. Fort Lauderdale Beach Blvd., Along
the beach ☎ 954/564–1000 ⊕ www.boceanfortlauderdale.com ⇥ 240
rooms ⦿ No meals.*

$$ **Hilton Fort Lauderdale Beach Resort.** This 26-story oceanfront sparkler
RESORT features 374 tastefully appointed guest rooms and a fabulous 6th-floor
FAMILY pool deck, colorfully and whimsically decorated. **Pros:** excellent gym;
most rooms have balconies. **Cons:** charge for Wi-Fi; no outdoor bar.
$ *Rooms from: $254 ✉ 505 N. Fort Lauderdale Beach Blvd., Along
the beach ☎ 954/760–7177 ⊕ www.fortlauderdalebeachresort.hilton.
com ⇥ 374 rooms ⦿ No meals.*

$$$ **Lago Mar Resort and Club.** The sprawling, kid-friendly Lago Mar,
RESORT owned by the Banks family since the early 1950s, retains its sparkle
FAMILY and a refreshed old Florida feel thanks to frequent renovations. **Pros:**
secluded setting; plenty of activities; on the beach. **Cons:** not easy to
find; far from restaurants and beach action. $ *Rooms from: $280
✉ 1700 S. Ocean La., Along the beach ☎ 954/523–6511, 800/524–
6627 ⊕ www.lagomar.com ⇥ 52 rooms, 160 suites ⦿ No meals.*

$$$ **Marriott Harbor Beach Resort.** Bill Marriott's personal choice for his
RESORT annual four-week family vacation, the Marriott Harbor Beach Resort
FAMILY sits on a quarter-mile swath of private beach and bursts with the luxe
Fodor's Choice beachfront personality of an upscale Caribbean resort. **Pros:** excel-
★ lent gym; all rooms have balconies; great eating outlets; no resort fees.
Cons: Wi-Fi isn't free; expensive parking; interiors are new but feel a
little cookie-cutter. $ *Rooms from: $399 ✉ 3030 Holiday Dr., Along
the beach ☎ 954/525–4000 ⊕ www.marriottharborbeach.com ⇥ 650
rooms, 31 suites ⦿ No meals.*

$$$ **Pelican Grand Beach Resort.** Smack on Fort Lauderdale beach, this
RESORT yellow-spired, Key West–style property maintains its heritage of Old
FAMILY Florida seaside charm with rooms adorned in florals, pastels, and

wicker; an old-fashioned empo-rium; and a small circulating lazy-river pool that allows kids to float 'round and 'round. **Pros:** free popcorn in the Postcard Lounge; directly on the beach; Ocean 2000 restaurant. **Cons:** high tide can swallow most of beach area; decor appeals to older generations. $ *Rooms from: $224* ⊠ *2000 N. Atlantic Blvd., Along the beach* ☎ *954/568–9431, 800/525–6232* ⊕ *www.pelicanbeach.com* ⇨ *135 rooms* ⦁⊙⦁ *No meals.*

> **WORD OF MOUTH**
>
> "Loved Lago Mar. The rooms are spacious and clean, nice pools and nice beach. Restaurant is very good. You would need a car to get to other places in Fort Lauderdale but I think it is worth it."
>
> —lindafromNJ

$$$ **The Pillars Hotel.** Once a "small secret" kept by locals in the know, this
B&B/INN   elegant boutique gem, sandwiched between Fort Lauderdale beach and the Intracoastal Waterway, rarely falls below capacity since it invariably lands on reader's choice lists. **Pros:** attentive staff; lovely decor; idyllic pool area. **Cons:** small rooms; not for families with young kids given proximity to dock and water with no lifeguard on duty. $ *Rooms from: $309* ⊠ *111 N. Birch Rd., Along the beach* ☎ *954/467–9639* ⊕ *www. pillarshotel.com* ⇨ *13 rooms, 5 suites* ⦁⊙⦁ *No meals.*

$$$$ **The Ritz-Carlton, Fort Lauderdale.** Inspired by the design of an opulent
HOTEL   luxury liner, 24 dramatically tiered, glass-walled stories rise from the
Fodor'sChoice   sea, forming a sumptuous Ritz-Carlton hotel with guest rooms that
★   reinvent a golden era of luxury travel, a lavish tropical sundeck and infinity-edge pool peering over the ocean, and a Club Lounge that spans an entire floor. **Pros:** prime beach location; modern seaside elegance deviates dramatically from traditional Ritz-Carlton decor; sensational Club Lounge. **Cons:** no complimentary Wi-Fi; popularity with locals leads to waits at Via Luna. $ *Rooms from: $329* ⊠ *1 N. Fort Lauderdale Beach Blvd., Along the beach* ☎ *954/465–2300* ⊕ *www.ritzcarlton. com* ⇨ *138 rooms, 54 suites* ⦁⊙⦁ *No meals.*

$$$ **Sheraton Fort Lauderdale Beach Hotel.** As part of its global rebrand-
HOTEL   ing, Sheraton has reinvented (and renamed) its Fort Lauderdale landmark—once the Sheraton Yankee Clipper Hotel—with updated interiors and public spaces throughout its four towers of rooms and suites. **Pros:** Friday night retro mermaid show in swimming pool; proximity to beach; excellent gym. **Cons:** small rooms; low ceilings in lobby; faded exteriors. $ *Rooms from: $167* ⊠ *1140 Seabreeze Blvd., Along the beach* ☎ *954/524–5551* ⊕ *www.sheratonftlauderdalebeach. com* ⇨ *486 rooms* ⦁⊙⦁ *No meals.*

$$$ **The Westin Beach Resort & Spa, Fort Lauderdale.** Smack dab in the center
RESORT   of Fort Lauderdale Beach and connected directly to the beach through a
FAMILY   private overpass, the hotel once known as the Sheraton Yankee Trader has been completely transformed into a modern Westin. **Pros:** direct beach access; heavenly beds and spa. **Cons:** lengthy walks to get to some rooms; fee for Wi-Fi; lot of conventioneers. $ *Rooms from: $239* ⊠ *321 N. Fort Lauderdale Beach Blvd., Along the beach* ☎ *954/467–1111* ⊕ *www.westin.com/fortlauderdalebeach* ⇨ *433 rooms* ⦁⊙⦁ *No meals.*

$$$$ HOTEL Fodor's Choice ★ **W Fort Lauderdale.** Fort Lauderdale's trendiest hotel—equipped with a rooftop see-through swimming pool, a wide range of spectacular contemporary rooms and suites, and an easy-on-the-eyes youthful crowd—boasts a vibe highly reminiscent of South Beach. **Pros:** trendy and flashy; tony scene; amazing pool; great spa. **Cons:** party atmosphere not for everyone; impersonal service. [$] *Rooms from: $305* ✉ *435 N. Fort Lauderdale Beach Blvd., Along the beach* ☎ *954/462–1633* 🌐 *www.starwood.com* 🛏 *346 hotel rooms, 171 condominiums* 🍴 *No meals.*

$$$ B&B/INN **Worthington Guest House.** This hotel is one of Fort Lauderdale Beach's 27 clothing-optional guesthouses for gay men. **Pros:** fresh-squeezed orange juice in the morning; nice pool area. **Cons:** not on the beach; windows open toward fence or other buildings. [$] *Rooms from: $165* ✉ *543 N. Birch Rd., Along the beach* ☎ *954/563–6819* 🌐 *www.theworthington.com* 🛏 *14 rooms* 🍴 *Breakfast.*

INTRACOASTAL AND INLAND

$ HOTEL **Gallery ONE by DoubleTree.** A condo hotel favored by vacationers preferring longer stays, the residential-style Gallery ONE rises over the Intracoastal, within short walking distance of both Fort Lauderdale Beach and the city's popular Galleria Mall. **Pros:** walking distance to both beach and supermarket; easy water taxi access; good for longer stays. **Cons:** pool area needs refurbishment; kitchens don't have stoves; no bathtubs. [$] *Rooms from: $195* ✉ *2670 E. Sunrise Blvd., Intracoastal and Inland* ☎ *954/565–3800* 🌐 *www.doubletree.com* 🛏 *231 rooms* 🍴 *No meals.*

$$ RESORT FAMILY Fodor's Choice ★ **Hilton Fort Lauderdale Marina.** After a $72-million renovation in 2011, the mammoth, 589-room, 20-boat-slip Hilton Fort Lauderdale Marina infused luxury and modernity into its charming Key West style. **Pros:** sexy fire pit; outdoor bar popular with locals; easy water taxi access. **Cons:** no bathtubs in tower rooms; small fitness center. [$] *Rooms from: $199* ✉ *1881 S.E. 17th St., Intracoastal and Inland* ☎ *954/463–4000* 🌐 *www.fortlauderdalemarinahotel.com* 🛏 *589 rooms* 🍴 *No meals.*

$$ RESORT **Hyatt Regency Pier Sixty-Six Resort & Spa.** Don't let the 1970s exterior of the iconic 17-story tower fool you; this lovely 22-acre resort teems with contemporary interior-design sophistication and remains one of Florida's few hotels where a rental car isn't necessary. **Pros:** great views; plenty of activities; free shuttle to beach; easy Water Taxi access. **Cons:** tower rooms are far less stylish than Lanai rooms; totally retro rotating rooftop is used exclusively for private events. [$] *Rooms from: $189* ✉ *2301 S.E. 17th St. Causeway, Intracoastal and Inland* ☎ *954/525–6666* 🌐 *www.pier66.com* 🛏 *384 rooms* 🍴 *No meals.*

$$ HOTEL **Il Lugano Luxury Suite Hotel.** This all-suite condo hotel on Fort Lauderdale's northern Intracoastal waterway offers all the comforts of home (washer, dryer, kitchenette, fridge, sleeper sofa, huge terraces) with all the glamour of a hyper-modern trendsetting hotel. **Pros:** 800-square-foot rooms; easy water taxi access; good for longer stays. **Cons:** limited sunlight in pool area; need wheels to reach main beach and downtown area. [$] *Rooms from: $249* ✉ *3333 N.E. 32nd Ave., Intracoastal and Inland* ☎ *954/564–4400* 🌐 *www.illugano.com* 🛏 *28 suites* 🍴 *No meals.*

Lago Mar Resort and Club in Fort Lauderdale has its own private beach on the Atlantic Ocean.

WESTERN SUBURBS

$ · HOTEL · FAMILY · **Bonaventure Resort & Spa.** This suburban enclave—formerly a Hyatt Regency-flagged resort—targets conventioneers and business executives as well as vacationers who value golf, the Everglades, and shopping over beach proximity; factor in the allure of the huge and soothing ALaya Spa and you'll understand why. **Pros:** lush landscaping; pampering spa. **Cons:** difficult to find; in the suburbs; poor views from some rooms. $ *Rooms from: $185* ⊠ *250 Racquet Club Rd., Western Suburbs and Beyond, Westin* ☎ *800/327–8090* ⊕ *www.bonaventureresortandspa. com* ⊷ *501 rooms* ⦿| *No meals.*

NIGHTLIFE AND THE ARTS

For the most complete weekly listing of events, check "Showtime!," the *South Florida Sun-Sentinel's* tabloid-size entertainment section and events calendar published on Friday. "Weekend," in the Friday Broward edition of the *Herald,* also lists area happenings. The weekly *City Link* and *New Times Broward* are free alternative newspapers, detailing plenty of entertainment and nightlife options. For the latest happenings in GLBT nightlife, visit **Mark's List** (⊕ *jumponmarkslist.com*), the online authority of all things GLBT in South Florida or pick up one of the weekly gay rags, *MARK* or *Hot Spots.*

THE ARTS

Broward Center for the Performing Arts. More than 500 events unfold annually at this 2,700-seat architectural gem, including Broadway-style musicals, plays, dance, symphony, opera, rock, film, lectures, comedy, and children's theater. An expansion and a series of upgrades throughout 2013 (to the tune of $20 million) made the Broward Center more fabulous than ever. An enclosed elevated walkway links the centerpiece of Fort Lauderdale's arts district to a parking garage across the street. ⊠ *201 S.W. 5th Ave., Downtown and Las Olas* ☎ *954/462–0222* ⊕ *www.browardcenter.org.*

Cinema Paradiso. This art-house movie theater operates out of a former church, south of New River near the county courthouse. The space doubles as headquarters for FLIFF, the Fort Lauderdale International Film Festival, while still playing films year-round. FLIFF's website is the easiest way to see what's playing on any given evening at the cinema. Just click on the "Cinema Events" tab on the homepage. ⊠ *503 S.E. 6th St., Downtown and Las Olas* ☎ *954/525–3456* ⊕ *www.fliff.com.*

NIGHTLIFE

DOWNTOWN AND LAS OLAS

The majority of Fort Lauderdale nightlife takes place near downtown, beginning on Himmarshee Street (2nd Street) and continuing on to the Riverfront, and then to Las Olas Boulevard. The downtown Riverfront tends to draw a younger demographic somewhere between underage teens and late twenties. On Himmarshee Street, a dozen rowdy bars and clubs entice a wide range of partygoers, ranging from the seedy to the sophisticated. Approaching East Las Olas Boulevard, near the financial towers and boutique shops, bars cater to the yuppie crowd.

Maguire's Hill 16. With the requisite lineup of libations and pub-style food, this classic Irish pub is good for no-frills fun, fried eats, and daily live music. It's famous locally as the oldest award-winning Traditional Irish Pub and Restaurant in Fort Lauderdale. ⊠ *535 N. Andrews Ave., Downtown and Las Olas* ☎ *954/764–4453* ⊕ *www. maguireshill16.com.*

O Lounge. This lounge and two adjacent establishments, **Yolo** and **Vibe,** on Las Olas and under the same ownership, cater to Fort Lauderdale's sexy yuppies, business men, desperate housewives, and hungry cougars letting loose during happy hour and on the weekends. Crowds alternate between Yolo's outdoor fire pit, O Lounge's chilled atmosphere and lounge music, and Vibe's more intense beats. Expect flashy cars in the driveway and a bit of plastic surgery. ⊠ *333 E. Las Olas Blvd., Downtown and Las Olas* ☎ *954/523–1000* ⊕ *www.yolorestaurant.com.*

Off the Hookah. After a $21-million renovation in 2012, the downtown space formerly home to NV (and before that Voodoo Lounge) has returned as Off the Hookah. Totally revamped from top to bottom and filled with VIP areas, Hookah attempts to reinstate the late-night electro and pop parties that made downtown Fort Lauderdale famous circa 2006. The club also regularly hosts local and national talent. The long-running Sunday gay-straight mixer, Life's a Drag, continues on from its Voodoo days. It's a fun-filled night of drag performances and incriminating debauchery. ⊠ *111 S.W. 2nd Ave., Downtown and Las Olas* ☎ *954/761–8686* ⊕ *www.offthehookah.com.*

ROK: BRG. Downtown Fort Lauderdale warmly welcomed this personality-driven burger bar and gastro-pub in early 2011, giving the grown-ups something to enjoy in teenage-infested downtown. The long and narrow venue, adorned with exposed-brick walls and flatscreen TVs is great for watching sports and for mingling on weekends. Locals come here for the great cocktails and beer selection. ⊠ *208 S.W. 2nd St., Downtown and Las Olas* ☎ *954/525–7656* ⊕ *www. rokbrgr.com.*

Tap 42 Bar and Kitchen. With 42 rotating draft beers from around the USA, 50-plus bourbons, a few dozen original cocktails (including beer cocktails), and 66 bottled craft beers, awesome drinks and good times headline a typical evening at classy cool Tap 42. Although the indoor/outdoor gastro-pub is a bit off the beaten path, it's well worth the detour. The 42 drafts protrude from a stylish wall constructed of pennies, surfacing more like a work of art than a beer-filling station. The venue attracts large crowds of young professionals for nights of heavy drinking and highly caloric new-age bar eats. ⊠ *1411 S. Andrews Ave., Downtown and Las Olas* ☎ *954/463–4900* ⊕ *www.tap42.com.*

Tarpon Bend. This casual two-story restaurant transforms into a jovial resto-bar in the early evening, ideal for enjoying a few beers, mojitos, and some great bar food. It's consistently busy, day, night, and late night with young professionals, couples, and large groups of friends. It's one place that has survived all the ups and downs of downtown Fort Lauderdale. ⊠ *200 S.W. 2nd St., Downtown and Las Olas* ☎ *954/523–3233* ⊕ *www.tarponbend.com.*

ALONG THE BEACH

Given its roots as a beachside party town, it's hard to believe that Fort Lauderdale Beach offers very few options in terms of nightlife. A few dive bars are at opposite ends of the main strip, near Sunrise Boulevard and A1A as well as Las Olas Boulevard and A1A. On the main thoroughfare between Las Olas and Sunrise, a few high-end bars at the beach's show-stopping hotels have become popular, namely those at the W Fort Lauderdale.

Elbo Room. You can't go wrong wallowing in the past, lifting a drink, and exercising your elbow at the Elbo, a noisy, suds-drenched hot spot since 1938. It seems like nothing has changed here since Fort Lauderdale's spring break heyday, and the clientele still includes far too many scantily clad girls that will do anything for booze. At least the bathrooms were redone in 2011. The watering hole phased out food (except for light nibbles) ages ago, but kept a hokey sense of humor: upstairs a sign proclaims "We don't serve women here. You have to bring your own." ⊠ *241 S. Fort Lauderdale Blvd., Along the beach* ☎ *954/463–4615* ⊕ *www.elboroom.com.*

Living Room at the W. The large living-room-like space next to the lobby of the W Fort Lauderdale transforms into a major house-party-style event, mainly on weekends. There are plenty of plush couches, but it's usually standing-room-only early for this South Beach–style throwdown, with great DJs, awesome libations, and an easy-on-the-eyes crowd. A breezy and beautiful outdoor area is idyllic for the overflow, as is the downstairs lounge, Whiskey Blue. ⊠ *W Fort Lauderdale, 401 N. Fort Lauderdale Beach Blvd., Along the beach* ☎ *954/414–8200* ⊕ *www.wfortlauderdalehotel.com/living-room.*

Parrot Lounge. An old-school Fort Lauderdale hangout, this dive bar/ sports bar is particularly popular with Philadelphia Eagles fans, those longing to recall *Where the Boys Are,* and folks reminiscing about Fort Lauderdale's big-hair, sprayed-tan, Sun-In-bright 1980s heyday. This place is stuck in the past, but it's got great libations, wings, fingers, poppers, and skins. 'Nuff said. ⊠ *911 Sunrise La., Along the beach* ☎ *954/563–1493* ⊕ *www.parrotlounge.com.*

INTRACOASTAL AND INLAND

Bars and pubs along Fort Lauderdale's Intracoastal cater to the city's large, transient boating community. Heading inland along Sunrise Boulevard, the bars around Galleria Mall target thirty- and fortysomething singles.

Blue Martini Fort Lauderdale. A hot spot for thirtysomething-plus adults gone wild, Blue Martini's menu is filled with tons of innovative martini creations and lots of cougars on the prowl, searching for a first, second, or even third husband. And the guys aren't complaining! The drinks are great and the scene is fun for everyone, even those who aren't single and looking to mingle. ⊠ *Galleria Fort Lauderdale, 2432 E. Sunrise Blvd., Intracoastal and Inland* ☎ *954/653–2583* ⊕ *www. bluemartinilounge.com.*

Kim's Alley Bar. Around since 1948, Kim's Alley Bar is the ultimate no-frills South Florida dive bar, a neighborhood spot in a strip mall near the Intracoastal. It has two bar areas, a jukebox, and pool tables that provide endless entertainment (if the patrons aren't providing enough diversion). ⊠ *The Gateway, 1920 E. Sunrise Blvd., Intracoastal and Inland* ☎ *954/763–2143.*

WILTON MANORS AND OAKLAND PARK

Fort Lauderdale's gay nightlife is most prevalent in Wilton Manors, affectionately termed Fort Lauderdale's "gayborhood." Wilton Drive has dozens of bars, clubs, and lounges that cater to all types of GLBT subcultures.

Georgie's Alibi. A Fort Lauderdale GBLT institution, Georgie's Alibi is an anchor for the Wilton Manors gay community. The gargantuan pub fills to capacity for $3, 32-ounce Long Island Iced Tea Thursdays (from 9 pm 'til close). Any night of the week, Alibi stands out as a kind of gay Cheers of Fort Lauderdale—a neighborhood bar with darts, pool, libations, and some eye candy, offering a no-frills, laid-back attitude. ⊠ *2266 Wilton Dr., Wilton Manors and Oakland Park* ☎ *954/565–2526* ⊕ *www.alibiwiltonmanors.com.*

The Manor. Inspired by the Abbey in West Hollywood, the Manor offers a one-stop gay party shop in the heart of the Wilton Manors gayborhood. The multifaceted two-story enclave mixes the likes of a massive dance club, a martini bar, a restaurant, a lounge, a small sports bar, and a beer garden with 24 beers on tap. The Manor attracts both gay men and women of all ages to indulge in the neighborhood funhouse. It's most popular on weekends. ⊠ *2345 Wilton Dr., Wilton Manors and Oakland Park* ☎ *954/626–0082* ⊕ *www.themanorcomplex.com.*

Rosie's Bar and Grill. Rosie's is consistently lively, pumping out tons of pop tunes and volumes of joyous laughter to surrounding streets. The former Hamburger Mary's has become an institution in South Florida as the go-to gay-friendly place for cheap drinks, decent bar food, and great times. Most of the fun at Rosie's is meeting new friends and engaging in conversation with the person seated next to you. Drink specials change daily. Sunday brunch with alternating DJs is wildly popular. ⊠ *2449 Wilton Dr., Wilton Manors and Oakland Park, Fort Lauderdale* ☎ *954/567–1320* ⊕ *www.rosiesbarandgrill.com.*

WESTERN SUBURBS AND BEYOND

Florida's cowboy country, Davie, offers country western fun out in the 'burbs. In addition, South Florida's Native American tribes have long offered gambling on Indian Territory near Broward's western suburbs. With new laws, Broward's casinos offer Vegas-style slot machines and even blackjack. Hollywood's Seminole Hard Rock Hotel & Casino offers the most elegant of Broward's casino experiences. ⇨ *See Nightlife in Hollywood.*

SHOPPING

MALLS

Galleria Fort Lauderdale. Fort Lauderdale's most upscale mall is just west of the Intracoastal Waterway. The split-level emporium entices with Neiman Marcus, Dillard's, Macy's, an Apple Store plus 150 specialty shops for anything from cookware to exquisite jewelry. Upgrades in 2010 included marble floors and fine dining options. Chow down at Capital Grille, Truluck's, Blue Martini, P.F. Chang's, or Seasons 52, or head for the food court, which will defy expectations with its international food-market feel. Galleria is open 10–9 Monday through Saturday, noon–5:30 Sunday. ⊠ *2414 E. Sunrise Blvd., Intracoastal and Inland* ☎ *954/564–1015* ⊕ *www.galleriamall-fl.com.*

FAMILY   **Sawgrass Mills.** This alligator-shape megamall draws 26 million shoppers a year to its collection of 400 outlet stores and name-brand discounters. The mall claims to be the second-largest attraction in Florida—second only to Disney World. Though that claim is probably an exaggeration, you should prepare for insane crowds even during nonpeak hours and seasons. ⊠ *12801 W. Sunrise Blvd., at Flamingo Rd., Western Suburbs and Beyond, Sunrise* ⊕ *www.sawgrassmills.com.*

Swap Shop. For those who grew up in Fort Lauderdale, the Swap Shop's cheesy commercials of yesteryear will forever remain. "Where's the bargains?" "At the Swap Shop!" The South's largest flea market, with 2,000 vendors, is open daily. Thankfully, they've done away with the awful circus after years of protests by animal-rights activists. While exploring this indoor–outdoor entertainment-and-shopping complex, hop on the carousel, try some fresh sugarcane juice, or stick around for movies at the 14-screen Swap Shop drive-in. ⊠ *3291 W. Sunrise Blvd., Western Suburbs and Beyond* ⊕ *www.floridaswapshop.com.*

SHOPPING DISTRICTS

The Gallery at Beach Place. Just north of Las Olas Boulevard on Route A1A, this shopping gallery is attached to the mammoth Marriot Beach Place timeshare. Spaces are occupied by touristy shops that sell everything from sarongs to alligator heads, chain restaurants like Hooter's, bars serving frozen drinks, and a super-size CVS pharmacy, which sells everything you need for the beach. ▓ TIP→ **Beach Place has covered parking, and usually has plenty of spaces, but you can pinch pennies by using a nearby municipal lot that's metered.** ⊠ *17 S. Fort Lauderdale Beach Blvd., Along the beach* ⊕ *www.galleryatbeachplace.com.*

Las Olas Riverfront. Largely unoccupied, Las Olas Riverfront is a shopping and entertainment complex in downtown, along the city's serene riverfront. A movie theater remains, as do a few budget eateries and nightclubs. The complex's popularity quickly waned in the late 1990s and news of its demolition has been circulating for a decade. ⊠ *300 S.W. 1 Ave., Downtown and Las Olas.*

Las Olas Boulevard. Las Olas Boulevard is the heart and soul of Fort Lauderdale. Not only are the city's best boutiques, top restaurants, and art galleries found along this beautifully landscaped street, but Las Olas links Fort Lauderdale's growing downtown with its superlative beaches. Though you'll find a Cheesecake Factory on the boulevard, the thoroughfare tends to shun chains and welcomes one-of-a-kind clothing boutiques, chocolatiers, and ethnic eateries. Window shopping allowed. ⊠ *East Las Olas Boulevard, Downtown and Las Olas* ⊕ *www.lasolasboulevard.com.*

FOOD

Chef Jean-Pierre Cooking School. Catering to locals, seasonal snowbirds, and folks winging in for even shorter stays, Jean-Pierre Brehier (former owner of the Left Bank Restaurant on Las Olas) teaches the basics, from boiling water onward. The enthusiastic Gallic transplant has appeared on NBC's *Today* among other shows. For souvenir hunters, this fun cooking facility also sells nifty pots, pastas, oils, and other great items. ⊠ *1436 N. Federal Hwy., Intrcoastal and Inland* ☎ *954/563–2700* ⊕ *www.chefjp.com* 🖃 *$65 per demonstration class, $125 hands-on class* ☉ *Store Mon.–Sat. 10–7, class schedules vary.*

SPORTS AND THE OUTDOORS

BIKING

Among the most popular routes are Route A1A and Bayview Drive, especially in early morning before traffic builds, and a 7-mile bike path that parallels State Road 84 and New River and leads to Markham Park, which has mountain-bike trails. ▓ TIP→ **Alligator alert: Do not dangle your legs from seawalls.**

Broward B–cycle. The big-city trend of "pay and ride" bicycles has now reached Broward County. With 40 station locations over 20 scenic miles, from as far south as Hallandale to as far north as Pompano Beach and Coconut Creek, bikes can be rented for as little as 30 minutes or as long as a week, and can be picked up and dropped off at any and all stations in Broward County. Most stations are found downtown and along the beach. This is an excellent green and health-conscious way to explore Fort Lauderdale. Please note, however, that helmets are not provided at the kiosks. ⊕ *www.broward.bcycle.com.*

FISHING

Bahia Mar Marina. If you're interested in a saltwater charter, check out the offerings at the marina of the Bahia Mar, a DoubleTree hotel. Sportfishing and drift-fishing bookings can be arranged. A number of snorkeling outfitters also leave from here, as does the famous *Jungle Queen* steamboat. ⊠ *Bahia Mar, 801 Seabreeze Blvd., Along the beach* ☎ *800/755–9558 Dock Master* ⊕ *www.bahiamarhotel.com/marina.*

RODEOS

Davie Pro Rodeo. It may sound strange, but South Florida has a rather large cowboy scene, concentrated in the western suburb of Davie. And for over four decades, the Bergeron Rodeo Grounds has surfaced as Davie's biggest tourist attraction. Throughout the year, the Rodeo hosts national tours and festivals as well as the annual Southeaster Circuit Finals. Check the website for the exact dates of these rodeos. ⊠ *Davie Pro Rodeo Arena, 4271 Davie Rd., Western Suburbs and Beyond, Davie* ☎ *954/680–8005* ⊕ *www.davieprorodeo.com.*

SCUBA DIVING AND SNORKELING

Lauderdale Diver. A PADI 5-Star Certification Agency, this dive center facilitates daily day-trips on a variety of dive boats up and down Broward's shoreline. Trips typically last four hours. Nonpackage reef trips are open to divers for around $50; scuba gear is extra. ⊠ *1334 S.E. 17th St., Intracoastal and Inland* ☎ *954/467–2822* ⊕ *www.lauderdalediver.com.*

Pro Dive. The area's oldest diving operation offers daily trips for scuba divers to Broward's natural coral reefs or over two-dozen shipwrecks including the famous "Mercedes I." Expect to pay $55 if using your own gear or $115 with full scuba gear for a 2-tank, half-day charter, lasting 4 hours and heading to two different diving destinations. Pro Dive also offers the full gamut of PADI dive training courses. ⊠ *Bahia Mar, 801 Seabreeze Blvd., Along the beach* ☎ *954/776–3483* ⊕ *www.prodiveusa.com.*

Sea Experience Glassbottom Snorkel Tours. The *Sea Experience I* leaves daily at 10:15 am and 2:15 pm for two-hour glass-bottom-boat and snorkeling combination trips that explore Fort Lauderdale's offshore reefs. The tour costs $28; $7 more to snorkel, equipment provided. ⊠ *Bahia Mar Beach Resort, 801 Seabreeze Blvd.* ☎ *954/770–3483* ⊕ *www.seaxp.com.*

SEGWAY TOURS

M.Cruz Rentals. M.Cruz Rentals offers Segway Tours of Fort Lauderdale Beach four times per day and bicycle rentals by the hour. The rental facility is at the beach entrance of Hugh Taylor Birch State Park, just north of hotel row. The Segway Tours leave from here as well. ⊠ *Hugh Taylor Birch State Park, 3109 E. Sunrise Blvd., Along the beach* ☎ *954/235–5082* ⊕ *www.mcruzrentals.com.*

TENNIS

Jimmy Evert Tennis Center. With 22 courts (18 lighted clay courts, 3 hard courts, and a low-compression sand "beach" court), this is the crown jewel of Fort Lauderdale's public tennis facilities. Legendary champ Chris Evert learned her two-handed backhand here under the watchful eye of her now-retired father, Jimmy, the center's tennis pro for 37 years. ⊠ *Holiday Park, 701 N.E. 12th Ave., Intracoastal and Inland* ☎ *954/828–5378* ⊕ *www.fortlauderdale.gov/tennis/jetc.htm* ✉ *$18 day pass (for Broward nonresidents)* ⊗ *Weekdays 7:45 am–9 pm, weekends 7:45 am–6 pm.*

NORTH ON SCENIC A1A

North of Fort Lauderdale's Birch Recreation Area, Route A1A edges away from the beach through a stretch known as Galt Ocean Mile, and a succession of oceanside communities line up against the sea. Traffic can line up, too, as it passes through a changing pattern of beach-blocking high-rises and modest family vacation towns and back again. As far as tourism goes, these communities tend to cater to a different demographic than Fort Lauderdale. Europeans and cost-conscious families head to Lauderdale-by-the-Sea, Pompano, and Deerfield for fewer frills and longer stays.

Towns are shown on the Broward County map.

LAUDERDALE-BY-THE-SEA

Lauderdale-by-the-Sea is 5 miles north of Fort Lauderdale.

Just north of Fort Lauderdale's northern boundary, this low-rise family resort town traditionally digs in its heels at the mere mention of high-rises. The result is choice shoreline access that's rapidly disappearing in nearby communities. Without a doubt, Lauderdale-by-the-Sea takes delight in embracing its small beach-town feel and welcoming guests to a different world of years gone by.

GETTING HERE AND AROUND

Lauderdale-by-the-Sea is just north of Fort Lauderdale. If you're driving from Interstate 95, exit east onto Commercial Boulevard and head over the Intracoastal Waterway. From U.S. 1 (aka Federal Highway), turn east on Commercial Boulevard. If coming from A1A, just continue north from Fort Lauderdale Beach.

ESSENTIALS

Visitor Information Lauderdale-by-the-Sea Chamber of Commerce ☎ *954/776–1000* ⊕ *www.lbts.com.*

BEACHES

FAMILY **Lauderdale-by-the-Sea Beach.** Especially popular with divers and snorkelers, this laid-back stretch of sand provides great access to lovely coral reefs. When you're not underwater, look up and you'll likely see a pelican flying by. Gentle trade winds make this an utterly relaxing retreat from the hubbub of Fort Lauderdale's busier beaches. That said, the southern part of the beach at Commercial Boulevard and A1A is often busy due to a concentrated number of restaurants at the intersection, including the wildly popular Aruba Beach Cafe. Going north from Commercial Boulevard the beach is lined with no-frills hotels and small inns for families and vacationers visiting Fort Lauderdale for longer periods of time, mainly Europeans. Look for metered parking around Commercial Boulevard and A1A. **Amenities:** food and drink; lifeguards; parking (fee). **Best for:** solitude; snorkeling; swimming. ✉ *Commercial Blvd. at Hwy. A1A.*

WHERE TO EAT

$$ CAFÉ FAMILY 🍴 **Aruba Beach Café.** This casual beachfront eatery is always crowded and always fun. One of Lauderdale-by-the-Sea's most famous restaurants, Aruba Beach serves a wide range of American and Caribbean cuisine, including Caribbean conch chowder and conch fritters. There are also fresh tropical salads, sandwiches, and seafood. The café is famous for its divine fresh-baked Bimini bread with Aruba glaze (think challah with donut glaze). A band performs day and night, so head for the back corner with excellent views of the beach if you want conversation while you eat and drink. Sunday breakfast buffet starts at 9 am. [$] *Average main: $18* ✉ *1 Commercial Blvd.* ☎ *954/776–0001* 🌐 *www.arubabeachcafe.com.*

$$$ SEAFOOD 🍴 **Blue Moon Fish Company.** Most tables have stellar views of the Intracoastal Waterway, but Blue Moon East's true magic comes from the kitchen, where the chefs create moon-and-stars-worthy seafood dishes. It's also the best deal in town with a two-for-one word-of-mouth lunch special Monday through Saturday. Start with whole roasted garlic and bread and continue on to the mussels, the langostino salad (with pecan-crusted goat cheese, spinach, and caramelized onions) or pan-seared fresh-shucked oysters. For Sunday's champagne brunch book early, even in the off-season. [$] *Average main: $34* ✉ *4405 W. Tradewinds Ave.* ☎ *954/267–9888* 🌐 *www.bluemoonfishco.com.*

$ AMERICAN 🍴 **LaSpada's Original Hoagies.** The crew at this seaside hole-in-the-wall puts on quite a show of ingredient-tossing flair while assembling take-out hoagies, subs, and deli sandwiches. Locals rave that they are the best around. LaSpada's popularity has resulted in the addition of four other South Florida locations, taking away from the joint's former one-of-a-kind appeal. Fill up on the foot-long "Monster" (ham, cheese, roast beef, and turkey piled high), "Hot Meatballs Marinara," or an assortment of salads. [$] *Average main: $12* ✉ *4346 Seagrape Dr.* ☎ *954/776–7893* 🌐 *www.laspadashoagies.com.*

WHERE TO STAY

For expanded reviews, facilities, and current deals, visit Fodors.com.

$ HOTEL 🏨 **Blue Seas Courtyard.** Husband and wife team Cristie and Marc Furth run this quaint Mexican-theme motel across the street from Lauderdale-by-the-Sea's family-friendly beaches. **Pros:** south-of-the-border vibe; friendly owners; vintage stoves from 1971; memory foam mattress toppers. **Cons:** rooms lack ocean views; old bath tubs in some rooms. [$] *Rooms from: $158* ✉ *4525 El Mar Dr.* ☎ *954/772–3336* 🌐 *www.blueseascourtyard.com* 🛏 *12 rooms* 🍽 *Breakfast.*

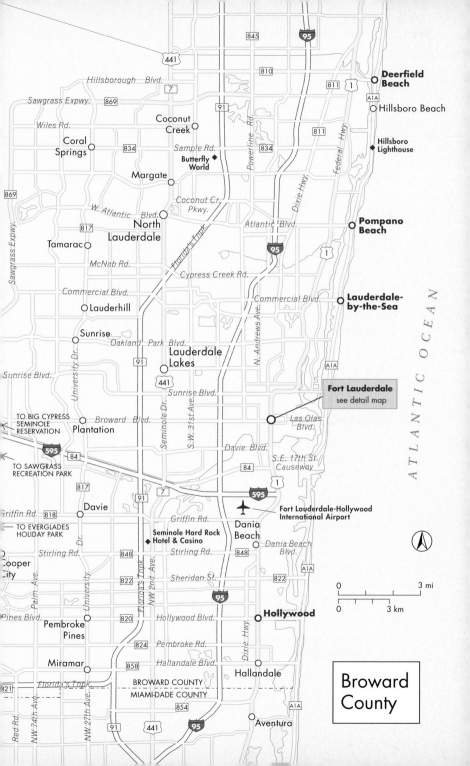

$ HOTEL 🏨 **High Noon Beach Resort.** Family-run since 1961, this hotel sits on 300 feet of beautiful beach, with plenty of cozy spots and an old-school homey ambience that keeps repeat visitors coming back for more. **Pros:** smack on the beach; friendly vibe. **Cons:** early booking required. [$] *Rooms from: $173* ✉ *4424 El Mar Dr.* ☎ *954/776–1121, 800/382–1265* 🌐 *www.highnoonresort.com* 🛏 *40 rooms* 🍴 *Breakfast.*

$ HOTEL 🏨 **Sea Lord Hotel & Suites.** This attractive ocean-side hotel received major upgrades in 2010, including a new pool deck, restaurant, lobby, sundeck, entranceway, small fitness center, and room enhancements. **Pros:** terrific beach location; void of the moldy smell in nearby older hotels. **Cons:** shaky elevators; limited parking. [$] *Rooms from: $155* ✉ *4140 El Mar Dr.* ☎ *954/776–1505, 800/344–4451* 🌐 *www.sealordhotel.com* 🛏 *47 rooms* 🍴 *Breakfast.*

$$ HOTEL FAMILY 🏨 **Tropic Seas Resort Motel.** This two-story property has an unbeatable location—directly on the beach, flanking 150 feet of pristine sands and sparkling blues—and is a favorite of annual European vacationers looking for longer stays. **Pros:** family-owned friendliness; great lawn furniture. **Cons:** must reserve far ahead; dated bathrooms. [$] *Rooms from: $225* ✉ *4616 El Mar Dr.* ☎ *954/772–2555, 800/952–9581* 🌐 *www.tropicseasresort.com* 🛏 *16 rooms* 🍴 *Breakfast.*

SPORTS AND THE OUTDOORS

Anglin's Fishing Pier. This longtime favorite for 24-hour fishing has a fresh, renovated appearance after shaking off repeated storm damage that closed the pier at intervals during the past decade. ✉ *2 Commercial Blvd.* ☎ *954/491–9403* 🌐 *www.boatlessfishing.com/anglins.htm.*

HOLLYWOOD

Hollywood is 8 miles south of Fort Lauderdale.

Hollywood has had a face-lift, with more nips and tucks to come. Young Circle, once down-at-heel, has become Broward's first Arts Park. On Hollywood's western outskirts the flamboyant Seminole Hard Rock Hotel & Casino has enlivened this previously downtrodden section of the State Road 7/U.S. 441 corridor, drawing local weekenders, architecture buffs, and gamblers. But Hollywood's redevelopment effort don't end there: new shops, restaurants, and art galleries open at a persistent clip, and the city has spiffed up its Broadwalk—a wide pedestrian walkway along the beach—where rollerbladers are as commonplace as snowbirds from the north.

GETTING HERE AND AROUND

From Interstate 95, exit east on Sheridan Street or Hollywood Boulevard.

ESSENTIALS

Visitor Information **Hollywood Office of Tourism** ☎ *877/672–2468* 🌐 *www.goHollywoodFLA.com.*

DID YOU KNOW?

Fort Lauderdale's harbor is home to myriad sailboats as well as two of the largest cruise ships in the world, Royal Caribbean's *Allure of the Seas* and *Oasis of the Seas.*

EXPLORING

Downtown Hollywood Art & Design District. From 21st Avenue to Young Circle on Hollywood Boulevard and Harrison Street, the streets are peppered with boutiques, bistros, sidewalk cafés, and galleries featuring original artwork (eclectic paintings, sculpture, photography, and mixed media).

IGFA Fishing Hall of Fame and Museum. This creation of the International Game Fishing Association is a shrine to the sport. It has an extensive museum and research library where seven galleries feature fantasy fishing and other interactive displays. At the Catch Gallery, you can cast off virtually to reel in a marlin, sailfish, trout, tarpon, or bass. (If you suddenly get an urge to gear up for your own adventures, a Bass Pro Shops Outdoor World is next door.) ⊠ *300 Gulf Stream Way* ☎ *954/922–4212* ⊕ *www.igfa.org* ⊠ *$10* ☉ *Mon.–Sat. 10–6, Sun. noon–6.*

FAMILY **West Lake Park.** Rent a canoe, kayak, or take the 40-minute boat tour at this park bordering the Intracoastal Waterway. At 1,500 acres, it is one of Florida's largest urban nature facilities. Extensive boardwalks traverse mangrove forests that shelter endangered and threatened species. A 65-foot observation tower showcases the entire park. At the free **Anne Kolb Nature Center,** named after Broward's late environmental advocate, there's a 3,500-gallon aquarium. The center's exhibit hall has 27 interactive displays. ⊠ *1200 Sheridan St.* ☎ *954/357–5161* ⊕ *www. broward.org/parks/WestLakePark* ⊠ *Weekends $1.50, weekdays free* ☉ *Park daily 9–6:30; Nature Center daily 9–5.*

BEACHES

FAMILY
Fodor'sChoice
★

Hollywood Beach and Broadwalk. The name might be Hollywood, but there's nothing hip or chic about **Hollywood North Beach Park,** which sits at the north end of Hollywood (Route A1A and Sheridan Street), before the pedestrian Broadwalk begins. And that's a good thing. It's just a laid-back, old-fashioned place to enjoy the sun, sand, and sea. The film *Marley & Me,* starring Jennifer Aniston and Owen Wilson and filmed in Greater Fort Lauderdale, spurred a comeback for dog beaches in South Florida, and ever since then, the year-round **Dog Beach of Hollywood** in North Beach Park has allowed dogs to enjoy fun in the sun from 3 pm to 7 pm Friday–Sunday (4 pm to 8 pm during Daylight Savings Time). Farther south on Hollywood beach, the 2.5-mile **Broadwalk** is a delightful throwback to the '50s, with mom-and-pop stores, ice cream parlors, elderly couples going for long strolls, and families building sand castles on the beach. Thanks to millions in investment, this popular stretch of beach has spiffy features like a pristine pedestrian walkway, a concrete bike path, a crushed-shell jogging path, an 18-inch decorative wall separating the Broadwalk from the sand, and places to shower off after a dip. Expect to hear French spoken throughout Hollywood, since its beaches have long been a favorite getaway for Quebecois. **Amenities:** food and drink; lifeguards; parking (fee); toilets. **Best for:** sunrise; swimming; walking. ⊠ *Rte. A1A from Dania Beach Blvd. to Halladale Beach Blvd.* ⊠ *Parking in public lots is $1.75 per hr.*

John U. Lloyd Beach State Recreation Area. The once pine-dotted natural area was restored to its natural state, thanks to government-driven efforts to pull out all but indigenous plants. Now native sea grape, gumbo-limbo, and other native plants offer shaded ambience. Nature trails and a marina are large draws as is canoeing on Whiskey Creek. The beaches are also excellent, but beware of mosquitoes in summer! **Amenities:** parking (fee); toilets. **Best for:** solitude; sunrise. ✉ *6503 N. Ocean Dr.* ☎ *954/923–2833* 🌐 *www.floridastateparks.org/lloydbeach* 🎫 *$6 per vehicle for 2 to 8 passengers, $4 for lone driver* 🕒 *Daily 8–sunset.*

WHERE TO EAT

$$$$ ITALIAN 🍴 **Café Martorano.** Located within Seminole Hard Rock's adjoining entertainment and restaurant zone, this Italian-American institution pays homage to anything and everything that has to do with the "Godfather" and impresses with humungous family-style portions. Dishes run the full Italian-American gamut, from the classic parmigianas to the lobster and snapper francaise. The homemade mozzarella and fried calamari are excellent choices for starters. It's easy to gorge here since each dish is so succulent and savory. The ever-present "Godfather" motif is taken to the extreme—dinner is interrupted hourly with clips from the movie played on the surrounding flat screens. There's another outlet in Fort Lauderdale proper. [$] *Average main: $31* ✉ *5751 Seminole Way* ☎ *954/584–4450* 🌐 *www.cafemartorano.com.*

$ AMERICAN FAMILY 🍴 **Jaxson's Ice Cream Parlour & Restaurant.** This 1950s landmark whips up malts, shakes, and jumbo sundaes from ice creams prepared daily on premises, plus sandwiches and salads, amid an antique-license-plate decor. Owner Monroe Udell's trademarked Kitchen Sink—a small sink full of ice cream, topped by sparklers—for parties of four or more goes for $12.75 per person (no sharing). For those wanting a sample, think again. The oh-so-popular Jaxson's doesn't give samples! [$] *Average main: $13* ✉ *128 S. Federal Hwy.* ☎ *954/923–4445* 🌐 *www.jaxsonsicecream.com.*

$$ ECLECTIC 🍴 **Las Brisas.** Next to the beach, this cozy bistro offers seating inside or out, and the food is Argentine with Italian flair. A small pot, filled with *chimichurri*—a paste of oregano, parsley, olive oil, salt, garlic, and crushed pepper—for spreading on steaks, sits on each table. Grilled fish is a favorite, as are pork chops, chicken, and pasta entrées. Desserts include a flan like *mamacita* used to make. [$] *Average main: $19* ✉ *600 N. Surf Rd.* ☎ *954/923–1500.*

$$ AMERICAN 🍴 **LeTub.** Once a Sunoco gas station, this quirky waterside saloon has an enduring affection for claw-foot bathtubs. Hand-painted porcelain is everywhere—under ficus, sea grape, and palm trees. Despite molasses-slow service and an abundance of flies at sundown, this eatery is favored by locals, and management seemed genuinely appalled when hordes of trend-seeking city slickers started jamming bar stools and tables after Oprah declared its thick, juicy Angus burgers the best around. A 13-ounce sirloin burger and large fries will run you around $16. ⚠ **There's no children's menu, and no children allowed after 8 pm.** [$] *Average main: $16* ✉ *1100 N. Ocean Dr.* ☎ *954/921–9425* 🌐 *www.theletub.com.*

WHERE TO STAY

For expanded reviews, facilities, and current deals, visit Fodors.com.

$$ RENTAL **Manta Ray Inn.** Canadians Donna and Dwayne Boucher run this immaculate, affordable, two-story complex of apartment units that sits right on the beach. **Pros:** on the beach; low-key atmosphere. **Cons:** no restaurant; no pool (but access to one next door is included). [$] *Rooms from: $189* ✉ *1715 S. Surf Rd.* ☎ *954/921–9666, 800/255–0595* 🌐 *www.mantarayinn.com* 🛏 *12 units* 🍴 *No meals.*

$$$ HOTEL **Seminole Hard Rock Hotel & Casino.** On the industrial flatlands of western Hollywood, the Seminole Hard Rock Hotel & Casino serves as a magnet for pulsating Vegas-style entertainment and folks looking for 24 hours of casino, clubbing, and hedonism. **Pros:** nonstop entertainment; plenty of activities; rooms renovated in 2012. **Cons:** in an unsavory neighborhood; no tourist sights in close proximity; endless entertainment can be exhausting. [$] *Rooms from: $289* ✉ *1 Seminole Way* ☎ *866/502–7529, 800/937–0010* 🌐 *www.seminolehardrockhollywood.com* 🛏 *395 rooms, 86 suites* 🍴 *No meals.*

$$$$ RESORT FAMILY Fodor's Choice ★ **The Westin Diplomat Resort & Spa.** This colossal 39-story contemporary property has been instrumental in bringing style and pizzazz to Hollywood Beach with its massive, 60-foot-high atrium and casual-chic guest rooms. **Pros:** heavenly beds for adults and kids; excellent gym; eye-popping architecture. **Cons:** large complex; numerous conventioneers. [$] *Rooms from: $349* ✉ *3555 S. Ocean Dr.* ☎ *954/602–6000, 800/327–1212* 🌐 *www.diplomatresort.com* 🛏 *902 rooms, 96 suites* 🍴 *No meals.*

NIGHTLIFE

Seminole Hard Rock Casino. The glitzy, Vegas-style Seminole Hard Rock Casino in Hollywood has bingo, poker, blackjack, more than 2,500 gaming machines, and 89 tables over a 130,000-square-foot casino. It's open 24/7 and is connected to a hotel and an entire nightlife and entertainment complex. The Seminole Hard Rock is not to be confused with its neighbor, the smoky and seedy Seminole Casino of Hollywood. ✉ *1 Seminole Way* ☎ *866/502–7529* 🌐 *www.seminolehardrockhollywood.com.*

SPORTS AND THE OUTDOORS

FISHING

Sea Leg's III. Sea Legs III goes out three times daily, fishing for wahoo, yellowtail, grouper, and king fish. Two 4½ hour drift-fishing trips run during the day (one at 8 am, the other at 1:30 pm), and bottom-fishing trips run nightly from 7 pm to midnight. Day trips cost $38, night trips $40, both including rod rental. ✉ *5398 N. Ocean Dr.* ☎ *954/923–2109* 🌐 *www.deepseafishingsealegs.com.*

PALM BEACH AND THE TREASURE COAST

WELCOME TO PALM BEACH

TOP REASONS TO GO

★ **Exquisite resorts:**
Two grandes dames, the Breakers and the Boca Raton Resort & Club, perpetually draw the rich, the famous, and anyone else who can afford the luxury. The Ritz-Carlton and Four Seasons sparkle with service fit for royalty.

★ **Beautiful beaches:**
From Jupiter, where dogs run free, to Stuart's tubular waves, to the broad stretches of sand in Delray Beach and Boca Raton, swimmers, surfers, sunbathers—and sea turtles looking for a place to hatch their eggs—all find happiness.

★ **Top-notch golf:**
The Bear Trap at PGA National Resort & Spa alone is worth a round; pros sharpen up at PGA Village.

★ **Horse around:**
Wellington, with its popular polo season, is often called the winter equestrian capital of the world.

★ **Excellent fishing:**
The Atlantic Ocean, teeming with kingfish, sailfish, and wahoo, is a treasure chest for anglers.

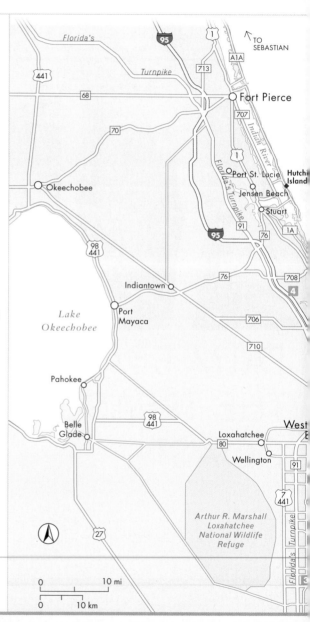

1 Greater Palm Beach.
With Gatsby-era architecture, stone-and-stucco estates, and extravagant dining, Palm Beach is a must-see for travelers to the area. Plan to spend time on Worth Avenue, also known as the Mink Mile, a collection of more than 200 chic shops, and Whitehall, the palatial retreat for Palm Beach's founder, Henry

Flagler. West Palm Beach and its environs—Lake Worth, Palm Beach Gardens, and Singer Island—are bustling with their own identities. Culture fans have plenty to cheer about with the Kravis Center and Norton Museum of Art; sports enthusiasts will have a ball golfing or boating; and kids love Lion Country Safari.

2 Delray Beach. Its lively downtown, with galleries, independent boutiques, and trendy restaurants right by the water, is perfect for strolling. To the west is the unique Morikami Museum and Japanese Gardens.

3 Boca Raton. An abundance of modern shopping plazas mix with historic buildings from the 1920s, masterpieces by renowned architect Addison Mizner. Parks line much of the oceanfront.

4 Treasure Coast.
Northern Palm Beach County and beyond remains blissfully low-key, with fishing towns, spring-training stadiums, and ecotourism attractions until you hit the cosmopolitan—yet understated—Vero Beach.

GETTING ORIENTED

This diverse region extends 120 miles from laid-back Sebastian to tony Boca Raton. The area's glitzy epicenter, Palm Beach, attracts socialites, the well-heeled, and interested onlookers. The northernmost cities are only about 100 miles from Orlando, making that area an ideal choice for families wanting some beach time to go with a visit to Mickey Mouse. Delightfully funky Delray Beach is only an hour north of Miami. The Intracoastal Waterway runs parallel to the ocean and transforms from a canal to a tidal lagoon separating islands from the mainland, starting with Palm Beach and moving northward to Singer Island (Palm Beach Shores and Riviera Beach), Jupiter Island, Hutchinson Island (Stuart, Jensen Beach, and Fort Pierce), and Orchid Island (Vero Beach and Sebastian).

6

Updated by
Paul Rubio

A golden stretch of the Atlantic shore, the Palm Beach area resists categorization, and for good reason: the territory stretching south to Boca Raton, appropriately coined the Gold Coast, defines old-world glamour and new-age sophistication.

To the north you'll uncover the comparatively undeveloped Treasure Coast—liberally sprinkled with seaside gems and wide-open spaces along the road awaiting your discovery. Speaking of discovery, its moniker came from the 1715 sinking of a Spanish fleet that dumped gold, jewels, and silver in the waters; today the *Urca de Lima*, one of the original 11 ships and now an undersea "museum," can be explored by scuba divers.

Altogether, there's a delightful disparity between Palm Beach, pulsing with old-money wealth, and under-the-radar Hutchinson Island. Seductive as the gorgeous beaches, eclectic dining, and leisurely pursuits can be, you should also take advantage of flourishing commitments to historic preservation and the arts, as town after town yields intriguing museums, galleries, theaters, and gardens.

Palm Beach, proud of its status as America's first luxe resort destination and still glimmering with its trademark Mediterranean-Revival mansions, manicured hedges, and highbrow shops, can rule supreme as the focal point for your sojourn any time of year. From there, head off in one of two directions: south toward Delray Beach and Boca Raton along an especially scenic estate-dotted route known as A1A, or back north to the beautiful barrier islands of the Treasure Coast. For rustic inland activities such as bass fishing and biking on the dike around Lake Okeechobee, head west.

PLANNING

WHEN TO GO

The weather is optimal from November through May, but the trade-off is that roadways and hotels are more crowded and prices higher. If the scene is what you're after, try the early weeks of December when "season" isn't yet in full swing. However, be warned that after Easter, the crowd relocates to the Hamptons, and Palm Beach feels like another universe. For some, that's a blessing—and a great time to take advantage of lower summer lodging rates (the Breakers runs promos at a fourth its regular cost). Hurricanes can show up from June to November, but there's always plenty of notice. More important, you'll need to bring your tolerance for heat, humidity, and afternoon downpours.

GETTING HERE AND AROUND

AIR TRAVEL

If you're flying into the area, the most convenient airport is Palm Beach International Airport in West Palm, but it's possible (and sometimes cheaper) to fly to Fort Lauderdale or Orlando. Try to rent a car if you plan on exploring. Interstate 95 runs north–south, linking West Palm Beach with Fort Lauderdale and Miami to the south and with Daytona, Jacksonville, and the rest of the Atlantic Coast to the north. Florida's turnpike runs from Miami north through West Palm Beach before angling northwest to reach Orlando. U.S. 1 threads north–south along the coast, connecting most coastal communities, whereas the more scenic Route A1A, also called Ocean Boulevard or Ocean Drive, depending on where you are, ventures out onto the barrier islands. I–95 runs parallel to U.S. 1, but a few miles inland.

From the airport, call Southeastern Florida Transportation Group, a local hotline for cabs, airport shuttles, and private sedans.

Airport Palm Beach International Airport (PBI) ✉ 1000 Turnage Blvd., West Palm Beach ☎ 561/471–7420 ⊕ www.pbia.org.

Airport Transfers Southeastern Florida Transportation Group ☎ 561/777–7777 ⊕ www.yellowcabflorida.com.

BUS TRAVEL

The county's bus service, Palm Tran, runs two routes (numbers 44 and 40) that offer daily service connecting the airport, the Tri-Rail stop near it, and locations in central West Palm Beach. A network of 34 routes joins towns all across the area; regular fares are $1.50. The free Downtown Trolley connects the West Palm Beach Amtrak station and the Tri-Rail stop in West Palm. It makes continuous loops down Clematis Street, the city's main stretch of restaurants and watering holes interspersed with stores, and through CityPlace, a shopping-dining-theater district. Hop on and off at any of the seven stops. The trolleys run Sunday to Wednesday 11–9 and Thursday to Saturday 11–11.

Contacts Downtown Trolley ☎ 561/833–8873 ⊕ www.westpalmbeachdda. com/transportation. **Palm Tran** ☎ 561/841–4287 ⊕ www.palmtran.org.

TRAIN TRAVEL

Amtrak has daily trains that connect West Palm Beach and Delray Beach with Miami, Orlando, Tampa, and cities in the Northeast, ending with New York. The West Palm Beach station is at the same location as the Tri-Rail stop, so the same free shuttle, the Downtown Trolley (⊕ *www. wpbgo.com*), is available.

Tri-Rail Commuter Service is a rail system with 18 stops altogether between West Palm Beach and Miami; tickets can be purchased at each stop, and a one-way trip from the first to the last point is $6.90 weekdays, $5 weekends. Three stations—West Palm Beach, Lake Worth, and Boca—have free shuttles to their downtowns, and taxis are on call at others.

Contacts Amtrak ☎ *800/872–7245* ⊕ *www.amtrak.com.*
Tri-Rail ☎ *800/874–7245* ⊕ *www.tri-rail.com.*

HOTELS

Palm Beach has a number of smaller hotels in addition to the famous Breakers. Lower-priced hotels and bed-and-breakfasts can be found in West Palm Beach and Lake Worth. Heading south, the oceanside town of Manalapan has the Ritz-Carlton, Palm Beach. The Seagate Hotel & Spa sparkles in Delray Beach, and the posh Boca Beach Club lines the superlative swathe of shoreline in Boca Raton. In the opposite direction there's the PGA National Resort & Spa, and across from it by the water is the Marriott on Singer Island, a well-kept secret for spacious, sleek suites. Even farther north, Vero Beach has a collection of luxury boutique hotels, as well as more modest options along the Treasure Coast. To the west, towns close to Lake Okeechobee offer country-inn accommodations.

RESTAURANTS

Numerous elegant establishments offer upscale American, Continental, and international cuisine, but the area also is chock-full of casual waterfront spots serving affordable burgers and fresh seafood feasts. Grouper, fried or blackened, is especially popular here, along with the ubiquitous shrimp. Happy hours and early-bird menus, Florida hallmarks, typically entice the budget-minded with several dinner entrées at reduced prices offered during certain hours, usually before 5 or 6.

HOTEL AND RESTAURANT COSTS

Prices in the restaurant reviews are the average cost of a main course at dinner or, if dinner isn't served, at lunch. Prices in the hotel reviews are the lowest cost of a standard double room in high season. Prices don't include taxes (6%, more in some counties, and 1%–5% tourist tax for hotel rooms).

VISITOR INFORMATION

Contacts Palm Beach County Convention and Visitors Bureau
✉ *1555 Palm Beach Lakes Blvd., Suite 800, West Palm Beach* ☎ *800/554–7256* ⊕ *www.palmbeachfl.com.*

PALM BEACH

70 miles north of Miami, off I–95.

Long reigning as the place where the crème de la crème go to shake off winter's chill, Palm Beach, which is actually on a barrier island, continues to be a seasonal hotbed of platinum-grade consumption. The town celebrated its 100th birthday in 2011, and there's no competing with its historic social supremacy. It's been the winter address for heirs of the iconic Rockefeller, Vanderbilt, Colgate, Post, Kellogg, and Kennedy families. Even newer power brokers, with names like Kravis, Peltz, and Trump, are made to understand that strict laws govern everything from building to landscaping, and not so much as a pool awning gets added without a town council nod. Only three bridges allow entry, and huge tour buses are a no-no.

To learn who's who in Palm Beach, it helps to pick up a copy of the *Palm Beach Daily News*—locals call it the Shiny Sheet because its high-quality paper avoids smudging society hands or Pratesi linens—for, as it's said, to be mentioned in the Shiny Sheet is to be Palm Beach.

All this fabled ambience started with Henry Morrison Flagler, Florida's premier developer, and cofounder, along with John D. Rockefeller, of Standard Oil. No sooner did Flagler bring the railroad to Florida in the 1890s than he erected the famed Royal Poinciana and Breakers hotels. Rail access sent real-estate prices soaring, and ever since, princely sums have been forked over for personal stationery engraved with 33480, the zip code of Palm Beach (which didn't actually get its status as an independent municipality until 1911). Setting the tone in this town of unparalleled Florida opulence is the ornate architectural work of Addison Mizner, who began designing homes and public buildings here in the 1920s and whose Moorish-Gothic Mediterranean Revival style has influenced virtually all landmarks.

But the greater Palm Beach area is much larger and encompasses several communities on the mainland and to the north and south. To provide Palm Beach with servants and other workers, Flagler created an off-island community across the Intracoastal Waterway (also referred to as Lake Worth in these parts). West Palm Beach, now cosmopolitan and noteworthy in its own right, evolved into an economically vibrant business hub and a sprawling playground with some of the best nightlife and cultural attractions around, including the glittering Kravis Center for the Performing Arts, the region's principal entertainment venue. The mammoth Palm Beach County Judicial Center and Courthouse and the State Administrative Building underscore the breadth of the city's governmental and corporate activity.

The burgeoning equestrian development of Wellington, with its horse shows and polo matches, lies a little more than 10 miles west of downtown, and is the site of much of the county's growth.

Spreading southward from the Palm Beach/West Palm Beach nucleus set between the two bridges that flow from Royal Poinciana Way and Royal Palm Way into Flagler Drive on the mainland are small cities like Lake Worth, with its charming artsy center, Lantana, and Manalapan (home to a fabulous Ritz-Carlton beach resort). All three have turf that's technically on the same island as Palm Beach, and at its bottom edge across the inlet is Boynton Beach, a 20-minute drive from Worth Avenue.

Most visitors don't realize that West Palm Beach itself doesn't have any beaches, so locals and guests hop over to Palm Beach or any of the communities just mentioned—or they head 15 minutes north to the residential Singer Island towns of Palm Beach Shores and Riviera Beach, known for their marinas and laid-back vibe. Another option is Peanut Island, which sits in the Intracoastal between Palm Beach and Singer Island, and to Juno Beach. Suburban Palm Beach Gardens, a paradise for golfers and shoppers (malls abound), is inland from Singer Island and 15 minutes northwest of downtown West Palm Beach. Because of its upscale slant, it has a ton of restaurants and bars (both independents and chains).

GETTING HERE AND AROUND

Palm Beach is 70 miles north of Miami. To access Palm Beach off I–95, exit east at Southern Boulevard, Belvedere Road, or Okeechobee Boulevard. To drive from Palm Beach to Lake Worth, Lantana, Manalapan, and Boynton Beach, head south on Ocean Boulevard/A1A; Lake Worth is roughly 6 miles south, and Boynton is another 6. Similarly, to reach them from West Palm Beach, take U.S. 1 or I–95. To travel between Palm Beach and Singer Island, you must cross over to West Palm before returning to the beach. Once there, go north on U.S. 1 and then cut over on Blue Heron Boulevard/Route 708. If coming straight from the airport or somewhere farther west, take I–95 up to the same exit and proceed east. The main drag in Palm Beach Gardens is PGA Boulevard/Route 786, which is 4 miles north on U.S. 1 and I–95; A1A merges with it as it exits the top part of Singer Island. Continue on A1A to reach Juno Beach.

TOURS

FAMILY **DivaDuck Amphibious Tours.** Running 75 minutes, these duck tours go in and out of the water on USCG-inspected amphibious vessels around West Palm Beach and Palm Beach. The tours depart two or three times most days for $25 per person (adults); there are big discounts for kids. ✉ *CityPlace, 600 S. Rosemary Ave., corner of Hibiscus St. and Rosemary Ave., West Palm Beach* ☎ *877/844–4188* ⊕ *www.divaduck.com.*

Island Living Tours. Book a private mansion-viewing excursion around Palm Beach, and hear the storied past of the island's upper crust. Owner Leslie Diver also hosts an Antique Row Tour and a Worth Avenue Shopping Tour. All vehicle tours are three hours and from $60 per person to $150 per person, depending on the vehicle used. Leslie also runs 90-minute bicycle tours through Palm Beach ($35, not including bike rental). One bicycle tour explores the Estate Section and historic Worth Avenue; another explores the island's lesser known North End. Call in advance for location and to reserve. ☎ *561/868–7944* ⊕ *www. islandlivingpb.com.*

Draped in European elegance, the Breakers in Palm Beach sits on 140 acres along the oceanfront.

EXPLORING

PALM BEACH

Most streets around major attractions and commercial zones have free parking as well as metered spaces. If you can stake out a place between a Rolls Royce and a Bentley, do so, but beware of the "Parking by Permit Only" signs, as a $25 ticket might take the shine off your spot. Better yet, if you plan to spend an entire afternoon strolling Worth Avenue, valet-park at the garage next to Saks Fifth Avenue that's a block in from Ocean Boulevard (if you've reached South County Road you've gone too far); some stores validate the fare.

TOP ATTRACTIONS

Bethesda-by-the-Sea. Donald Trump and his wife, Melania were married here in 2005, but this gothic-style Episcopal church had a claim to fame upon its creation in 1926: it was built by the first Protestant congregation in southeast Florida. Church lecture tours, covering Bethesda's history, architecture, and more, are offered at 12:15 on the second and fourth Sunday each month from September to May (excluding December) and at 11:15 on the fourth Sunday each month from June to August. Adjacent is the formal, ornamental Cluett Memorial Garden. ⊠ *141 S. County Rd.* ☎ *561/655–4554* ⊕ *www.bbts.org* ✉ *Free* ⊙ *Church and gardens daily 9–5.*

Fodor's Choice ★ **The Breakers.** Built by Henry Flagler in 1896 and rebuilt by his descendants after a 1925 fire, this magnificent Italian Renaissance–style resort helped launch Florida tourism with its Gilded Age opulence, attracting influential wealthy Northerners to the state. The hotel, still owned by Flagler's heirs, is a must-see even if you aren't staying here. Walk through the 200-foot-long lobby, which has soaring arched ceilings painted by 72 Italian artisans and hung with crystal chandeliers, and the ornate Florentine Dining Room, decorated with 15th-century Flemish tapestries. ■TIP→ Book a pampering spa treatment or dine on top of the Seafood Bar's whimsical aquarium counter, where leggy green starfish prance below your plate, and the $20 parking is free. ✉ 1 S. County Rd. ☎ 561/655–6611 ⊕ www.thebreakers.com.

Fodor's Choice
★
Henry Morrison Flagler Museum. The worldly sophistication of Florida's Gilded Age lives on at Whitehall, the plush 55-room "marble palace" Henry Flagler commissioned in 1901 for his third wife, Mary Lily Kenan. Architects John Carrère and Thomas Hastings were instructed to create the finest home imaginable—and they outdid themselves. Whitehall rivals the grandeur of European palaces and has an entrance hall with a baroque ceiling similar to Louis XIV's Versailles. Here you'll see original furnishings; a hidden staircase Flagler used to sneak from his bedroom to the billiards room; an art collection; a 1,200-pipe organ; and Florida East Coast Railway exhibits, along with Flagler's personal railcar, No. 91, showcased in an 8,000-square-foot beaux arts–style pavilion behind the mansion. Docent-led tours and audio tours are included with admission. The museum's Café des Beaux-Arts, open from Thanksgiving through March, offers a Gilded Age–style early afternoon tea for $40 (noon–2:30); the price includes museum admission. ✉ 1 Whitehall Way ☎ 561/655–2833 ⊕ www.flagler.org ✉ $18 ☉ Tues.–Sat. 10–5, Sun. noon–5.

Fodor's Choice
★
Worth Avenue. Called "the Avenue" by Palm Beachers, this half-mile-long street is synonymous with exclusive shopping. Nostalgia lovers recall an era when faces or names served as charge cards, purchases were delivered home before customers returned from lunch, and bills were sent directly to private accountants. Times have changed, but a stroll amid the Spanish-accented buildings, many designed by Addison Mizner, offers a tantalizing taste of the island's ongoing commitment to elegant consumerism. In 2010, a clock tower was added on the beach to mark the entrance from Route A1A. Definitely explore the labyrinth of nine pedestrian "vias" off each side that wind past boutiques, tiny plazas, bubbling fountains, and bougainvillea-festooned balconies; this is where the smaller, unique shops are. The Worth Avenue Association holds historic walking tours on Wednesday at 11 during "season" (after Thanksgiving to late April). The $10 fee benefits local nonprofit organizations. ✉ Worth Ave., between Cocoanut Row and S. Ocean Blvd. ☎ 561/659–6909 ⊕ www.worth-avenue.com.

WORTH NOTING

El Solano. No Palm Beach mansion better represents the town's luminous legacy than the Spanish-style home built by Addison Mizner as his own residence in 1925. Mizner later sold El Solano to Harold Vanderbilt, and the property was long a favorite among socialites for parties and photo shoots. Vanderbilt held many a gala fund-raiser here. Beatle John Lennon and his wife, Yoko Ono, bought it less than a year before Lennon's death. It's still privately owned and not open to the public, but it's well worth a drive-by on any Palm Beach mansion tour. ✉ 720 S. Ocean Blvd.

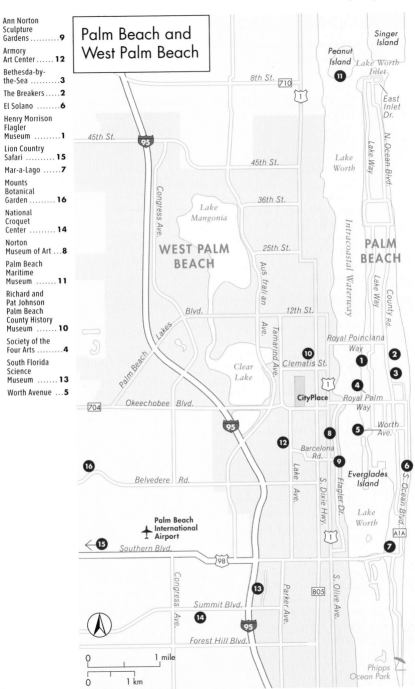

Palm Beach and
West Palm Beach

Singer
Island

Peanut
Island

Lake Worth
Inlet

East
Inlet
Dr.

8th St.

710

1

N. Ocean Blvd.

Lake Way

45th St.

95

45th St.

Lake
Worth

Lake
Mangonia

36th St.

25th St.

WEST PALM
BEACH

Australian Ave.

PALM
BEACH

Lake Way

County Rd.

Intracoastal Waterway

6

Palm Beach Lakes Blvd.

12th St.

Royal Poinciana
Way

1

2

3

Tamarind Ave.

Clear
Lake

Clematis St.

10

1

CityPlace

4

Royal Palm
Way

Okeechobee Blvd.

704

95

12

8

5

Worth
Ave.

Barcelona
Rd.

16

Belvedere Rd.

9

Everglades
Island

6

S. Ocean Blvd.

Lake
Worth

A1A

Palm Beach
International
Airport

Lake Ave.

S. Dixie Hwy.

Flagler Dr.

1

15

Southern Blvd.

98

7

Congress Ave.

13

Parker Ave.

S. Olive Ave.

805

Summit Blvd.

14

95

Forest Hill Blvd.

0   1 mile

0   1 km

Phipps
Ocean Park

CLOSE UP

The Mansions of Palm Beach

Whether you aspire to be a Kennedy, Donald Trump, or Rod Stewart—all onetime or current Palm Beach residents—no trip to the island is complete without gawking at the mega-mansions lining its perfectly manicured streets.

No one is more associated with how the island took shape than Addison Mizner, architect extraordinaire and society darling of the 1920s. But what people may not know is that a Fab Four was really the force behind the residential streets as they appear today: Mizner, of course, plus Maurice Fatio, Marion Sims Wyeth, and John Volk.

The four architects dabbled in different genres, some more so than others, but the unmissable style is Mediterranean Revival, a Palm Beach hallmark mix of stucco walls, Spanish red-tile roofs, Italianate towers, Moorish-Gothic carvings, and the uniquely Floridian use of coquina, a grayish porous limestone made of coral rock with fossil-like imprints of shells. As for Mizner himself, he had quite the repertoire of signature elements, including using differently sized and shaped windows on one façade, blue tile work inside and out, and tiered roof lines (instead of one straight-sloping panel across, having several sections overlap like scales on a fish).

The majority of preserved estates are clustered in three sections: along Worth Avenue; the few blocks of South County Road after crossing Worth and the streets shooting off it; and the 5-mile stretch of South Ocean Boulevard from Barton Avenue to near Phipps Ocean Park, where the condos begin cropping up.

If 10 miles of riding on a bike while cars zip around you isn't intimidating, the two-wheeled trip may be the best way to fully take in the beauty of the mansions and surrounding scenery. Many hotels have bicycles for guest use. Another option is the dependable Palm Beach Bicycle Trail Shop (☎ 561/659–4583 ⊕ www.palmbeach-bicycle.com). Otherwise, driving is a good alternative. Just be mindful that Ocean Boulevard is a one-lane road and the only route on the island to cities like Lake Worth and Manalapan, so you can't go too slowly, especially at peak travel times.

If gossip is more your speed, in-the-know concierges rely on Leslie Diver's "Island Living Tours" (☎ 561/868–7944 ⊕ www.islandliv-ingpb.com); she's one of the town's leading experts on architecture *and* dish, both past and present.

Top 10 Self-Guided Stops: (1) Casa de Leoni, 450 Worth Avenue (Addison Mizner); (2) Villa des Cygnes, 456 Worth Avenue (Addison Mizner and Marion Sims Wyeth); (3) 17 Golfview Road (Marion Sims Wyeth); (4) 220 and 252 El Bravo Way (John Volk); (5) 126 South Ocean Boulevard (Marion Sims Wyeth); (6) El Solano, 720 South Ocean Boulevard (Addison Mizner); (7) Casa Nana, 780 South Ocean Boulevard (Addison Mizner); (8) 920 and 930 South Ocean Boulevard (Maurice Fatio); (9) Mar-a-Lago, 1100 South Ocean Boulevard (Joseph Urban); (10) Il Palmetto, 1500 South Ocean Boulevard (Maurice Fatio).

—Dorothea Hunter Sönne

Mar-a-Lago. Breakfast-food heiress Marjorie Merriweather Post commissioned a Hollywood set designer to create Ocean Boulevard's famed Mar-a-Lago, a 114-room, 110,000-square-foot Mediterranean-revival palace. Its 75-foot Italianate tower is visible from many areas of Palm Beach and from across the Intracoastal Waterway in West Palm Beach. Owner Donald Trump has turned it into a private membership club. So you'll have to enjoy the view from the car window unless you have a membership. ⊠ *1100 S. Ocean Blvd.* ☎ *561/832–2600* ⊕ *www.maralagoclub.com.*

Society of the Four Arts. Despite widespread misconceptions of its members-only exclusivity, this privately endowed institution—founded in 1936 to encourage appreciation of art, music, drama, and literature—is funded for public enjoyment. Members do have special privileges like free admission, but anyone can enjoy the special programming that goes on here throughout the year. A gallery building artfully melds an exhibition hall that houses traveling exhibits with a 700-seat theater. A library designed by prominent Mizner-peer Maurice Fatio, a children's library, a botanical garden, and the Philip Hulitar Sculpture Garden, round out the facilities and are open daily. In addition to the winter art shows, the organization offers films, lectures, workshops, and concerts; a complete schedule is available on the society's website. ⊠ *2 Four Arts Plaza* ☎ *561/655–7227* ⊕ *www.fourarts.org* ⊠ *$5 gallery, special program costs vary* ⊙ *Gallery, Dec.–Apr., Mon.–Sat. 10–5, Sun. 1–5; gardens, daily 10–5; children's library, weekdays 10–4:45, also Sat. 10–12:45 Nov.–Apr. (closed Aug.).*

WEST PALM BEACH

Long considered Palm Beach's less privileged stepsister, West Palm Beach has come into its own over the past 30 years, and just in this millennium the $30-million Centennial Square waterfront complex at the eastern end of Clematis Street, with piers, a pavilion, and an amphitheater, has transformed West Palm into an attractive, easy-to-walk downtown area—not to mention there's the Downtown Trolley that connects the shopping-and-entertainment mecca CityPlace with restaurant-and-lounge-lined Clematis Street. West Palm is especially well regarded for its arts scene, with unique museums and performance venues.

The city's outskirts, vast flat stretches with fast-food outlets and car dealerships, may not inspire, but are worth driving through to reach attractions scattered around the southern and western reaches. Several sites are especially rewarding for children and other animal and nature lovers.

TOP ATTRACTIONS

Ann Norton Sculpture Gardens. This landmarked complex is a testament to the creative genius of the late American sculptor Ann Weaver Norton (1905–82), who was the second wife of Norton Museum founder, industrialist Ralph H. Norton. A set of art galleries in the studio and main house where she lived is surrounded by two acres of gardens with 300 species of rare palm trees, eight brick megaliths, a monumental figure in Norwegian granite, and plantings designed to attract native birds. ⊠ *253 Barcelona Rd.* ☎ *561/832–5328* ⊕ *www.ansg.org* ⊠ *$7* ⊙ *Wed.–Sun. 10–4. Closed Aug.*

The Armory Art Center in West Palm Beach helps students of all ages create works of art in various mediums.

FAMILY **Lion Country Safari.** Drive your own vehicle along four miles of paved roads through a cageless zoo with free-roaming animals (chances are you'll have a giraffe nudging at your window) and then let loose in a 55-acre fun-land with camel rides, bird feedings, and a pontoon-boat cruise past islands with monkeys. A CD included with admission narrates the winding trek past white rhinos, zebras, and ostriches grouped into exhibits like Gir Forest that's modeled after a sanctuary in India and has native twisted-horned blackbuck antelope and water buffalo. (For obvious reasons, lions are fenced off, and no convertibles or pets are allowed.) Aside from dozens more up-close critter encounters after debarking, including a petting zoo, kids can go paddleboating, do a round of mini-golf, climb aboard carnival rides, or have a splash in a 4,000-square-foot aquatic playground (some extra fees apply). ⊠ *2003 Lion Country Safari Rd., at Southern Blvd.* W ☎ *561/793–1084* ⊕ *www.lioncountrysafari.com* ⊠ *$28.50, $6 parking* ⊙ *Mid-Dec.–Aug., daily 9:30–5:30 (last entry 4:30); Sept.–Dec., daily 10–5 (last entry 4).*

Mounts Botanical Garden. The oldest public green space in the county is, unbelievably, across the road from the West Palm Beach airport; but the planes are the last thing you notice while walking around and relaxing amid the nearly 14 acres of exotic trees, rain-forest flora, and butterfly and water gardens. The gift shop contains a selection of rare gardening books on tropical climes. ⊠ *531 N. Military Trail* ☎ *561/233–1757* ⊕ *www.mounts.org* ⊠ *$5 (suggested donation)* ⊙ *Mon.–Sat. 8:30–4, Sun. noon–4.*

National Croquet Center. The world's largest croquet complex, the 10-acre center is also the headquarters for the U.S. Croquet Association. Vast expanses of orderly lawns are the stage for fierce competitions. There's also a clubhouse with a pro shop and the Croquet Grille, with verandas for dining and viewing (armchair enthusiasts can enjoy the games for no charge). You don't have to be a member to try your hand out on the lawns, and on Saturday morning, there's a free group lesson with an introduction to the game, and open play; call in advance to reserve a spot. ⊠ *700 Florida Mango Rd., at Summit Blvd.* ☎ *561/478–2300* ⊕ *www.croquetnational.com* ✉ *Center free; full day of croquet $25* ⊙ *Tues.–Sun. 9–5.*

Fodor'sChoice
★
Norton Museum of Art. Constructed in 1941 by steel magnate Ralph H. Norton and his wife, Elizabeth, it has grown to become one of the most impressive museums in South Florida with an extensive collection of 19th- and 20th-century American and European paintings—including works by Picasso, Monet, Matisse, Pollock, Cassatt, and O'Keeffe—plus Chinese art, earlier European art, and photography. There is a sublime outdoor sculpture garden, a glass ceiling by Dale Chihuly, a gift shop, and a schedule of lectures, programs, and concerts for adults and children. Galleries showcase traveling exhibits, too. ■TIP→ One of the city's best-kept secrets is the gourmet restaurant fratelli Lyon in the West Courtyard of the Museum. Lunch is served Tuesday to Sunday; a prix-fixe dinner with wine is served on Thursday evenings. ⊠ *1451 S. Olive Ave.* ☎ *561/832–5196* ⊕ *www.norton.org* ✉ *$12* ⊙ *Tues., Wed., Fri., and Sat. 10–5, Thurs. 10–9, Sun. 11–5.*

WORTH NOTING

Armory Art Center. Built by the Work Progress Administration (WPA) in 1939, this art deco facility is now a nonprofit art school hosting rotating exhibitions and art classes throughout the year. The Armory Art Center became an institution for art instruction, when the Norton Museum Gallery and School of Art dropped the latter part of its name in 1986 and discontinued art instruction classes. ⊠ *1700 Parker Ave.* ☎ *561/832–1776* ⊕ *www.armoryart.org* ✉ *Free* ⊙ *Weekdays 9–4:30, Sat. 9–2.*

Richard and Pat Johnson Palm Beach County History Museum. A beautifully restored 1916 courthouse in downtown opened its doors in 2008 as the permanent home of the Historical Society of Palm Beach County's collection of artifacts and records dating back before the town's start—a highlight is furniture and decorative objects from Mizner Industries (a real treat since many of his mansions are not open to the public). ⊠ *300 N. Dixie Hwy.* ☎ *561/832–4164* ⊕ *www.historicalsocietypbc.org* ✉ *Free* ⊙ *Tues.–Sat. 10–5.*

FAMILY
South Florida Science Museum. Aside from permanent exhibits with outta-this-world finds like moon and Mars rocks and a 232-pound meteorite, there are fresh- and saltwater aquariums, daily planetarium shows, and even 9 holes of mini-golf. On the second Saturday of each month, the planetarium offers three separate laser shows (6:30, 7:30, and 8:30 pm) incorporating music from the likes of Dave Matthews, Pink Floyd, and Michael Jackson. ⊠ *4801 Dreher Trail N* ☎ *561/832–1988* ⊕ *www.sfsm.org* ✉ *$9, laser show $10* ⊙ *Weekdays 10–5, Sat. 10–6, Sun. noon–6.*

LAKE WORTH

For years, tourists looked here mainly for inexpensive lodging and easy access to Palm Beach, since a bridge leads from the mainland to a barrier island with Lake Worth's beach. Now Lake Worth has several blocks of restaurants, nightclubs, shops, and art galleries, making this a worthy destination on its own.

Museum of Polo and Hall of Fame. Start here in Lake Worth for an introduction to polo. See memorabilia, art, and a film on the history of the sport. ⊠ *9011 Lake Worth Rd.* ☎ *561/969–3210* ⊕ *www.polomuseum. com* 🖃 *Free (donation accepted)* ⊗ *Jan.–Apr., weekdays 10–4, Sat. 10–2; May–Dec., weekdays 10–4.*

LANTANA

Lantana—just a bit farther south from Palm Beach than Lake Worth—has inexpensive lodging and a bridge connecting the town to its own beach on a barrier island. Tucked between Lantana and Boynton Beach is **Manalapan,** a tiny but posh residential community.

BOYNTON BEACH

In 1884, when fewer than 50 settlers lived in the area, Nathan Boynton, a Civil War veteran from Michigan, paid $25 for 500 acres with a mile-long stretch of beachfront thrown in. How things have changed, with today's population at about 118,000 and property values still on an upswing. Far enough from Palm Beach to remain low-key, Boynton Beach has two parts, the mainland and the barrier island—the town of Ocean Ridge—connected by two bridges.

FAMILY **Arthur R. Marshall Loxahatchee National Wildlife Refuge.** The most robust part of the northern Everglades, this 221-square-mile refuge is one of two huge water-retention areas accounting for much of the River of Grass outside the national park near Miami. Start at the visitor center, which got a million-dollar face-lift in 2009 and has fantastic interactive exhibits and videos like Night Sounds of the Everglades and an airboat simulator. From there, you can take a marsh trail to a 20-foot-high observation tower, or stroll a ½-mile boardwalk lined with educational signage through a dense cypress swamp. There are also guided nature walks (including some specifically for bird-watching), and there's great bass fishing (bring your own poles and bait) and a 5½-mile canoe trail loop (a rental kiosk is by the fishing pier). ⊠ *10216 Lee Rd., off U.S. 441 between Rte. 804 and Rte. 806* ☎ *561/734–8303* ⊕ *www. loxahatcheefriends.com* 🖃 *$5 per vehicle; $1 per pedestrian* ⊗ *Daily sunrise–sunset; visitor center daily 9–4.*

SINGER ISLAND

Across the inlet from the northern end of Palm Beach is Singer Island, which is actually a peninsula that's big enough to pass for a barrier island, rimmed with mom-and-pop motels and high-rises. Palm Beach Shores occupies its southern tip (where tiny Peanut Island is a stone's throw away); farther north are Riviera Beach and North Palm Beach, which also straddle the inlet and continue on the mainland.

Palm Beach Maritime Museum. You can take a guided tour of the restored "Kennedy Bunker," a bomb shelter built for President John F. Kennedy, and a historic Coast Guard station at the southern end of Peanut Island.

The posh Palm Beach area has its share of luxury villas on the water; many are Mediterranean in style.

The museum has a nice little gift shop, outdoor deck on the water, and a lawn where you can play games including horseshoes. To get there, catch a water taxi from Riviera Beach Municipal Marina (⊕ *www. peanutislandwatertaxi.com*) or Sailfish Marina (⊕ *www.sailfishma-rina.com/water_taxi*). ⊠ *Peanut Island, Riviera Beach* ☎ *561/848–2960* ⊕ *www.pbmm.org* 💵 *$12 (not including water transportation)* ⊗ *Thurs.–Sun. 11–4.*

PALM BEACH GARDENS
About 15 minutes northwest of Palm Beach is this relaxed, upscale residential community known for its high-profile golf complex, the PGA National Resort & Spa. Although not on the beach, the town is less than a 15-minute drive from the ocean.

JUNO BEACH
This small town east of Palm Beach Gardens has 2 miles of shoreline that becomes home to thousands of sea turtle hatchlings each year, making it one of the world's densest nesting sites. A 990-foot-long pier lures fishermen and beachgoers seeking a spectacular sunrise.

Fodor's Choice
★

Loggerhead Park Marine Life Center of Juno Beach. Located in a certified green building in Loggerhead Park—and established by Eleanor N. Fletcher, the "turtle lady of Juno Beach"—the center focuses on the conservation of sea turtles with three core competencies of education, research, and rehabilitation. The education center houses displays of coastal natural history, detailing Florida's marine ecosystems and the life and plight of the various species of sea turtles found on Florida's shores. You can visit recovering turtles in their tanks out back; volunteers are happy to tell you the turtles' heroic tales of survival. The center has regularly scheduled activities, such as Kid's Story Time and Junior Vet Lab, and most are free of charge. During nesting season, the center hosts night walks to experience turtle nesting in action. Given that the adjacent beach is part of the second biggest nesting ground for loggerhead turtles in the world, your chances of seeing this natural phenomenon is pretty high (over 13,000 loggerheads nested here in 2012). ⊠ *14200 U.S. 1* ☏ *561/627–8280* ⊕ *www.marinelife.org* 🎟 *Free* ☉ *Mon.–Sat. 10–5, Sun. noon–4.*

OFF THE BEATEN PATH

Forty miles west of West Palm Beach, amid the farms and cattle pastures rimming the western edges of Palm Beach and Martin counties, is **Lake Okeechobee,** the second-largest freshwater lake completely within the United States. It's girdled by 120 miles of road yet remains shielded from sight for almost its entire circumference. Lake Okeechobee—the Seminole's Big Water and the gateway of the great Everglades watershed—measures 730 square miles, at its longest roughly 33 miles north–south and 30 miles east–west, with an average natural depth of only 10 feet (flood control brings the figure up to 12 feet and deeper). Six major lock systems and 32 separate water-control structures manage the water. Encircling the lake is a 34-foot-high grassy levee that locals call "the wall," and the Lake Okeechobee Scenic Trail, a segment of the Florida National Scenic Trail that's an easy, flat ride for bikers. Anglers have a field day here as well, with great bass and perch catches. ▇TIP➡ There's no shade, so wear a hat, sunscreen, and bug repellent. Be sure to bring lots of bottled water, too, because restaurants and stores are few and far between.

BEACHES

PALM BEACH

Palm Beach Municipal Beach. You know you're here if you see Palm Beach's younger generation frolicking on the sands and nonxenophobic locals setting up chairs as the sun reflects off their gleaming white veneers. The Worth Avenue clock tower is within sight, but the gateways to the sand are actually on Chilean Avenue, Brazilian Avenue, and Gulfstream Road. It's definitely the most central and longest lifeguarded strip open to everyone and a popular choice for hotel guests from the Colony and Chesterfield. Lifeguards are present from Brazilian Avenue down to Chilean Avenue. It's also BYOC (bring your own chair). You'll find no water-sport or food vendors here; however, casual eateries are a quick walk away. Metered spots line A1A. **Amenities:** lifeguards; showers. **Best for:** swimming; sunsets. ⊠ *S. Ocean Blvd. from Brazilian Ave. to Gulfstream Rd.* ☉ *Daily 8–8.*

Phipps Ocean Park. About 2 miles south of "Billionaire's Row" on Ocean Boulevard sits this public oceanside park, with two metered parking lots separated by a fire station. The north side is better for beachgoers and currently houses the sole entry point to the beach itself (the other three entry points are closed for repairs). At the southern entrance, there is a six-court tennis facility. The beach is narrow and has natural rock formations dotting the shoreline. There are picnic tables and grills on-site, as well as the Little Red Schoolhouse, an 1886 landmark that hosts educational workshops for local kids. If a long walk floats your boat, venture north to see the mega-mansions, but don't go too far inland, because private property starts just a few feet from the surf. There's a two-hour time limit for free parking. **Amenities:** parking (no fee); toilets; showers; lifeguards. **Best for:** walking; solitude. ✉ *2185 S. Ocean Blvd.* ☎ *561/227–6450 tennis reservations* 🎫 *Free* ⊘ *Daily 8–8.*

LAKE WORTH

FAMILY **Lake Worth Beach.** This public beach bustles with beachgoers of all ages thanks to the profic family offerings. The waterfront retail promenade—the old fashioned Lake Worth "casino"—has a Mulligan's Beach House Bar & Grill, a T-shirt store, a pizzeria, and a Kilwin's ice cream shop. The beach also has a municipal Olympic-size public swimming pool, a playground, a fishing pier—not to mention the pier's wildly popular daytime eatery, Benny's on the Beach. Omphoy and Four Seasons guests are steps away from the action. **Amenities:** food and drink; lifeguards; parking (no fee); showers; toilets; water sports. **Best for:** sunsets; swimming. ✉ *10 S. Ocean Blvd., at A1A and Lake Ave.* 🎫 *$1 to enter pier, $3 to enter and fish, $2 per hr for parking.*

LANTANA

Town of Lantana Public Beach. Ideal for quiet ambles, this sandy stretch is also noteworthy for a casual restaurant, the no-frills breezy Dune Deck Café, which is perched above the waterline and offers great views for an oceanfront breakfast or lunch. The beach's huge parking lot is directly adjacent to the Ritz-Carlton, Palm Beach, and diagonally across the street is a sizeable strip mall with all sorts of conveniences, including more eateries. Note: The beach is very narrow and large rocks loom in the water. However, these are some of the clearest waters along the Florida coastline, and they make an idyllic background for long walks and great photos. Bring plenty of quarters for the old school parking meters. **Amenities:** food and drink; lifeguards; parking (fee); showers; toilets. **Best for:** walking. ✉ *100 E. Ocean Ave.* 🎫 *$1.50 per hr for parking.*

SINGER ISLAND

FAMILY **John D. MacArthur Beach State Park.** If getting far from rowdy crowds is
Fodor'sChoice your goal, this spot on the north end of Singer Island is a good choice.
★ Encompassing 2 miles of beach and a lush subtropical coastal habitat, inside you'll find a great place for kayaking, snorkeling at natural reefs, bird-watching, fishing, and hiking. A 4,000-square-foot nature center renovated in 2011 has aquariums and displays on local flora and fauna, and there's a long roster of monthly activities, such as surfing clinics, art lessons, and live bluegrass music. Guided sea turtle walks are available at night in season, and daily nature walks depart at 10 am. Check the website for times and costs of activities. **Amenities:** water sports; parking (fee); toilets; showers. **Best for:** swimming; walking; solitude; surfing. ✉ *10900 Jack Nicklaus Dr., North Palm Beach* ☎ *561/624–6952* ⊕ *www.macarthurbeach.org* 🎫 *Parking $5, bicyclists and pedestrians $2* ⊘ *Park daily 8–sunset; nature center and gift shop daily 9–5.*

6

Peanut Island Park. Partiers, families, and overnight campers all have a place to go on the 79 acres here. The island, in a wide section of the Intracoastal between Palm Beach Island and Singer Island with an open channel to the sea, is accessible only by private boat or water taxi, two of which set sail regularly from the Riviera Beach Municipal Marina (⊕ *www.peanutislandwatertaxi.com*) and the Sailfish Marina (⊕ *www.sailfishmarina.com/water_taxi*). Fun-loving seafarers looking for an afternoon of Jimmy Buffett and brewskis pull up to the day docks or the huge sandbar on the north—float around in an inner tube, and it's spring break déjà vu. Walk along the 20-foot-wide paver-lined path encircling the island, and you'll hit a 170-foot fishing pier, a campground, the lifeguarded section to the south that is particularly popular with families because of its artificial reef, and last but not least, the Palm Beach Maritime Museum's "Kennedy Bunker" (a bomb shelter prepared for President John F. Kennedy that was restored and opened to the public in 1999). There are picnic tables and grills, but no concessions. ⚠ **A new ordinance means alcohol possession and consumption is restricted to permit areas. Amenities:** lifeguards (summer only); toilets; showers. **Best for:** partiers; walking; swimming; sunrise. ⊠ *6500 Peanut Island Rd., Riviera Beach* ☎ *561/845–4445* ⊕ *www.pbcgov.com/parks/peanutisland* ⌨ *Beach free; water taxi $10.*

JUNO BEACH

FAMILY **Juno Beach Ocean Park.** An angler's dream, this beach has a 990-foot pier that's open daily, like the beach, from sunrise to sunset—but from November through February, pier gates open at 6 am and don't close until 10 pm on weeknights and midnight on weekends, making it an awesome place to catch a full sunrise and sunset (that is, if you don't mind paying the small admission fee). A concession stand on the pier sells fish food as well as such human favorites as burgers, sandwiches, and ice cream. Families adore this shoreline because of the amenities and vibrant atmosphere. There are plenty of kids building castles but also plenty of teens having socials and hanging out along the beach. **Amenities:** lifeguards; food and drink; parking (free); showers; toilets. **Best for:** sunrise; sunset; swimming. ⊠ *14775 S. U.S. 1* ☎ *561/799–0185 for pier* ⊕ *www.pbcgov.com/parks/locations/junobeach.htm* ⌨ *$4 to fish, $1 to enter pier* ☉ *Daily sunrise–sunset.*

WHERE TO EAT

PALM BEACH

$$$$ ✕ **Bice Ristorante.** The bougainvillea-laden trellises set the scene at the
ITALIAN   main entrance on Peruvian Way, off posh Worth Avenue. Weather
Fodor'sChoice   permitting, many patrons prefer to dine on the outdoor terrace on
★   the narrow pedestrian walkway, where "walking models" showcase jewelry and apparel of nearby boutiques. This is a favorite of Palm Beach society, and both the restaurant and the bar become packed and noisy during high season. The aroma of basil, chives, and oregano fills the air as waiters carry out home-baked *pizzaccia* (a pizzalike bread) to accompany delectable dishes such as seafood risotto and roasted duck breast with sweet potatoes and apricot sauce. $ *Average*

main: $35 ✉ *313½ Worth Ave., Palm Beach* ☎ *561/835–1600* 🌐 *www.palmbeach.bicegroup.com* ✍ *Reservations essential.*

$$$ ECLECTIC Fodor's Choice ★ 🍴 **bûccan.** Lanterns cast a soft glow as young bluebloods rocking D&G jeans slip into tightly packed copper-topped tables alongside groups of silver-haired oil scions. It's island casual in its trendiest, most boisterous, yet still refined incarnation, with a menu to match. Chef-owner Clay Conley's small plates to share (wood-fired wild mushroom pizza with black truffle vinaigrette) with unfussy presentations (house-made squid-ink orecchiette stewed with sausage, conch, and chilies in a mini–Le Creuset cocotte) and inventive, sophisticated flavor combinations and textures (hamachi sashimi with yuzu and crisped lotus root) make this the place to see and be seen—and the best-tasting meal at a price more expected of the mainland. [$] *Average main: $23* ✉ *350 S. County Rd., Palm Beach* ☎ *561/833–3450* 🌐 *www.buccanpalmbeach.com* ✍ *Reservations essential* 🕓 *No lunch.*

$$$$ FRENCH Fodor's Choice ★ 🍴 **Café Boulud.** Celebrated chef Daniel Boulud opened this outpost of Café Boulud in the Brazilian Court hotel. The warm and welcoming French-American venue is casual yet elegant, with a palette of honey, gold, and citron. Plenty of natural light spills through arched glass doors opening to a lush courtyard that's just the place to be on a warm evening. Lunch and dinner entrées on the restaurant's signature four-section menu include classic French, seasonal, vegetarian, and a rotating roster of international dishes. The lounge, with its illuminated amber glass bar, is the perfect perch to take in the jet-set crowd that comes for a hint of the south of France in South Florida. [$] *Average main: $38* ✉ *Brazilian Court Hotel & Beach Club, 301 Australian Ave., Palm Beach* ☎ *561/655–6060* 🌐 *www.cafeboulud.com* ✍ *Reservations essential.*

$$$$ ECLECTIC 🍴 **Café L'Europe.** Since 1980, the favorite spot of society's movers and shakers has remained a regular stop on foodie itineraries. The management pays close attention to service and consistency, a big reason for its longevity. Best sellers include sea bass *en papillote* and traditional Wiener schnitzel, along with such inspired creations as crispy sweetbreads with wild mushrooms and asparagus. Depending on your mood, the champagne-caviar bar can serve up appetizers or desserts. The place has an extensive, award-winning wine list with many by-the-glass options. A pianist plays nightly from 7 to 9:30, and the lively crowd gracefully sways to the music. [$] *Average main: $43* ✉ *331 S. County Rd., Palm Beach* ☎ *561/655–4020* 🌐 *www.cafeleurope.com* ✍ *Reservations essential* 🕓 *No lunch Sat.–Tues. Closed Mon. June–Nov.*

$$$$ FRENCH Fodor's Choice ★ 🍴 **Chez Jean-Pierre.** With walls adorned with avant garde Dalí- and Picasso-like art, this bistro is where the Palm Beach old guard likes to let down its hair, all the while partaking of sumptuous French cuisine and an impressive wine selection. Forget calorie or cholesterol concerns, and indulge in scrambled eggs with caviar or homemade foie gras, along with desserts like frozen hazelnut soufflé or profiteroles au chocolat. Jackets are not required, although many men wear them. The main entrance is through a courtyard in the back. [$] *Average main: $39* ✉ *132 N. County Rd., Palm Beach* ☎ *561/833–1171* 🌐 *www.chezjean-pierre.com* ✍ *Reservations essential* 🕓 *Closed Sun. No lunch.*

$$$
ASIAN

✕ Echo. Palm Beach's window on Asia has a sleek sushi bar and floor-to-ceiling glass doors separating the interior from the popular terrace dining area. Chinese, Japanese, Thai, and Vietnamese selections are neatly categorized: Wind (small plates starting your journey), Water (seafood mains), Fire (open-flame wok creations), Earth (meat dishes), and Flavor (desserts, sweets). Pick from dim sum to sashimi, pad Thai to Szechuan beef, steamed sea bass to shrimp lo mein. $ *Average main: $30 ⊠ 230-A Sunrise Ave., Palm Beach* 🕾 *561/802–4222* ⊕ *www.echopalmbeach.com* ⊘ *Closed Mon. No lunch.*

$$
PIZZA

✕ Pizza Al Fresco. The secret-garden setting is the secret to the success of this European-style pizzeria, where you can dine under a canopy of century-old banyans in an intimate courtyard. Specialties are 12-inch hand-tossed brick-oven pizzas with such interesting toppings as prosciutto, arugula, and caviar. There's even a carbonara breakfast pizza (part of a small morning menu) and a Nutella dessert pizza. Piping-hot calzones, salads, and baked pastas round out the choices. Next to the patio, look for the grave markers of Addison Mizner's beloved pet monkey, Johnnie Brown, and Rose Sachs's dog, Laddie (she and husband Morton bought Mizner's villa and lived there 47 years). Delivery is available. This bistro is dog-friendly. $ *Average main: $17 ⊠ 14 Via Mizner, at Worth Ave., Palm Beach* 🕾 *561/832–0032* ⊕ *www.pizzaalfresco.com.*

$$$
AMERICAN
FAMILY

✕ Testa's Palm Beach. Attracting a loyal clientele since 1921, this restaurant is still owned by the Testa family. Lunches range from burgers to crab salad, and dinner specialties include snapper Florentine and jumbo lump-crab cakes. You can dine inside in an intimate pine-paneled room with cozy bar, out back in a gazebo-style room for large groups, or outside at tables that are pet-friendly. Don't miss the signature strawberry pie made with fresh Florida berries. $ *Average main: $28 ⊠ 221 Royal Poinciana Way, Palm Beach* 🕾 *561/832–0992* ⊕ *www.testasrestaurants.com.*

WEST PALM BEACH

$
AMERICAN

✕ Hamburger Heaven. A favorite with locals since 1945, this famous burger joint has relocated from Palm Beach island to downtown West Palm Beach. Patrons rave that they have the best burgers in the Palm Beaches, not to mention great breakfasts. Omelets come with grits, oats, or home fries, and there are griddle items like French toast and buttermilk pancakes. Later on, fresh salads, homemade pastries, daily soups, and grilled sandwiches join the mix. This diner serves breakfast and lunch until 8 pm on weekdays and 4 pm on Saturday. The staff are friendly and efficient. $ *Average main: $10 ⊠ 1 N. Clematis St., West Palm Beach* 🕾 *561/655–5277* ⊘ *Closed Sun.*

$
AMERICAN

✕ Howley's. Since 1950 this diner's eat-in counter and "cooked in sight, it must be right" motto have made it a congenial setting for meeting old friends and making new ones. Nowadays, Howley's prides itself on its kitsch factor and old-school eats like turkey potpie and a traditional Thanksgiving feast, as well as its retro-redux dishes like potato-and-brisket burrito. Forgo the counter for the retro tables or sit out on the covered patio. The café attracts a loyal clientele into the wee hours (it's open weekdays until 2 am and weekends until 5 am and has a full bar). $ *Average main: $13 ⊠ 4700 S. Dixie Hwy., West Palm Beach* 🕾 *561/833–5691* ⊕ *www.sub-culture.org/howleys/.*

$$$ ITALIAN 🍴 **Il Bellagio.** In the heart of CityPlace, this European-style eatery offers Italian specialties and a wide variety of fine wines. The menu includes classics like chicken parmigiana, risotto, and fettuccine alfredo. Pizzas from the wood-burning oven are especially good. Service is friendly and efficient, but the overall noise level tends to be high. Sit at the outdoor tables next to the main plaza's dancing fountains if you can. [$] *Average main: $21* ✉ *CityPlace, 600 S. Rosemary Ave., West Palm Beach* ☎ *561/659–6160* 🌐 *www.ilbellagiocityplace.com.*

$$$ FRENCH 🍴 **Pistache French Bistro.** Although "the island" is no doubt a bastion of French cuisine, this cozy bistro across Lake Worth on the Clematis Street waterfront entices a lively crowd looking for a good meal with pretention checked at the door. The outdoor terrace can't be beat, and hearty classics with slight twists, such as roasted sliced duck with lingonberry sauce rather than the ubiquitous *à l'orange,* are a delight. Save room for dessert: the house-made pudding Breton, a fluffy, raisin-accented brioche bread pudding paired with Crème Anglaise, could be straight out of a Parisian café. [$] *Average main: $23* ✉ *101 N. Clematis St., West Palm Beach* ☎ *561/833–5090* 🌐 *www.pistachewpb.com.*

$$$$ AMERICAN Fodor's Choice ★ 🍴 **Top of the Point.** As you walk through the 1980s-era Phillips Point office tower at the foot of Royal Park Bridge, you may half expect Gordon Gekko to pop out. This trepidation belies what awaits at the penthouse. Spacious and somehow intimate, the dining room's floor-to-ceiling windows and adjacent observation deck offer gorgeous panoramic views. The menu, modern American with a focus on meats and seafood, has several winners like the locally caught snapper with citrus broth and a salad of petite greens, English peas, asparagus, and marcona almonds. But, truth be told, the views underscore any visit to this restaurant. Sit back with a glass of wine and take in the boats dotting the Intracoastal Waterway, the Breakers' iconic twin spires, and the ocean beyond. [$] *Average main: $39* ✉ *777 S. Flagler Dr., Club Level, Palm Beach* ☎ *561/832–2710* 🌐 *www.topofthepoint.com* 🕒 *Closed Sun. No lunch.*

LAKE WORTH

$ AMERICAN 🍴 **Benny's on the Beach.** Perched on the Lake Worth Pier, Benny's has a walk-up bar, a take-out window, and a full-service, no-frills restaurant serving diner-style food that's cheap and filling. Eat-in diners come here for long afternoons of beer and cocktails, enjoying prolific alfresco seating and a spectacular view of the sun glistening on the water and the waves crashing directly below. [$] *Average main: $12* ✉ *Lake Worth Beach, 10 S. Ocean Blvd., Lake Worth* ☎ *561/582–9001* 🌐 *www.bennysonthebeach.com* 🕒 *No dinner.*

$$ ECLECTIC 🍴 **Bizaare Ave Café.** Decorated with a mix of artwork and antiques, this cozy bistro housed in a circa-1926 building and inspired by TV's *Friends,* fits right into downtown Lake Worth's groovy, eclectic scene. Artwork and furnishings can be purchased. Daily specials are available on both the lunch and dinner menus, where crepes, pizzas, pastas, and salads are the staples. A more formal dining space is now open on the second floor. [$] *Average main: $18* ✉ *921 Lake Ave., Lake Worth* ☎ *561/588–4488* 🌐 *www.bizaareavecafe.com.*

LANTANA

$$
SEAFOOD
FAMILY

✕ **Old Key Lime House.** An informal seafood spot covered by a chickee-hut roof built by Seminole Indians, it's perched on the Intracoastal Waterway and is open and airy, with observation decks that wrap around the back. In 1889, the Lyman family, some of the earliest settlers in Lantana, built this as their house, and it has grown over the years into the popular island-style eatery it is today. Kids love feeding the fish below. Of course, order the namesake key lime pie—the house specialty has been featured in *Bon Appétit.* ⓢ *Average main: $20* ✉ *300 E. Ocean Ave., Lantana* ☎ *561/582–1889* ⊕ *www.oldkeylimehouse.com.*

PALM BEACH GARDENS

$$$$
AMERICAN

✕ **Café Chardonnay.** At the end of a strip mall, Café Chardonnay is surprisingly elegant and has some of the most refined food in the suburban town of Palm Beach Gardens. Soft lighting, warm woods, white tablecloths, and cozy banquettes set the scene for a quiet lunch or romantic dinner. The place consistently receives praise for its innovative, continually changing menu and outstanding wine list. Starters can include wild-mushroom strudel and pancetta-wrapped diver scallops. Entrées might be grilled filet mignon or a pan-roasted veal chop with Parmesan risotto and brandy morel sauce. ⓢ *Average main: $34* ✉ *Gardens Square Shoppes, 4533 PGA Blvd., Palm Beach Gardens* ☎ *561/627–2662* ⊕ *www.cafechardonnay.com* ☾ *No lunch weekends.*

$$$$
STEAKHOUSE

✕ **Ironwood Steak & Seafood.** Located in the PGA National Resort & Spa, this eatery draws guests, locals, and tourists alike eager for a taste of its fired-up Vulcan steaks (Vulcan to meat-eaters is like Titelist to golfers—the best equipment around). The she-crab soup with sherry is a favorite from the sea, as are the raw bar items, like the jumbo shrimp cocktail and tuna tartare. Bright red banquettes, slate-tile walls, private rooms, and an impressive glass-walled wine cellar create a relaxed, contemporary setting that spills out onto the equally chic adjoining lobby bar, which becomes quite the scene on weekend nights when a DJ spins. ⓢ *Average main: $38* ✉ *PGA National Resort & Spa, 400 Ave. of the Champions, Palm Beach Gardens* ☎ *561/627–4852* ⊕ *www.ironwoodgrille.com.*

$$$
SEAFOOD

✕ **Spoto's Oyster Bar.** If you love oysters and other raw bar nibbles, head here, where black-and-white photographs of oyster fisherman adorn the walls. The polished tables give the eatery a clubby look. Spoto's serves up a delightful bowl of New England clam chowder and a truly impressive variety of oysters and clams. The Caesar salad with crispy croutons and anchovies never disappoints. Sit outside on the patio to take advantage of the area's perfect weather. ⓢ *Average main: $26* ✉ *PGA Commons, 4560 PGA Blvd., Palm Beach Gardens* ☎ *561/776–9448* ⊕ *www.spotosoysterbar.com.*

WHERE TO STAY

For expanded reviews, facilities, and current deals, visit Fodors.com.

PALM BEACH

$$$$ HOTEL Fodor's Choice ★ **The Brazilian Court Hotel & Beach Club.** This posh boutique hotel's yellow facade, dramatic white-draped entry, red-tile roof, and lobby with cypress ceilings underscore its "Roaring '20s" origins; and modern touches like plush rooms and access to a shared oceanfront facility at the sleek Omphoy Resort (plus being a short stroll from Worth Avenue) present guests with the best of both worlds. **Pros:** hip crowd; charming courtyard; free beach shuttle. **Cons:** small fitness center; nondescript pool; 10-minute ride to ocean and suggested 24-hour advance reservation. [$] *Rooms from: $489* ✉ *301 Australian Ave., Palm Beach* ☎ *561/655–7740* 🌐 *www.thebraziliancourt.com* 🛏 *80 rooms* 🍴 *No meals.*

$$$$ RESORT FAMILY Fodor's Choice ★ **The Breakers Palm Beach.** More than an opulent hotel, the Breakers is a 140-acre self-contained jewel of a resort built in an Italian Renaissance style and loaded with amenities, from a 20,000-square-foot luxury spa and grandiose beach club to 10 tennis courts and two 18-hole golf courses—not to mention Henry Flagler's heirs still run the place and invest $20 million a year to keep it at the cutting edge. **Pros:** impeccable attention to detail; fantastic service; beautiful room views; extensive activities for families. **Cons:** big price tag; short drive to reach off-property attractions. [$] *Rooms from: $539* ✉ *1 S. County Rd., Palm Beach* ☎ *561/655–6611, 888/273–2537* 🌐 *www.thebreakers.com* 🛏 *608 rooms* 🍴 *No meals.*

$$$ HOTEL **The Chesterfield Palm Beach.** A distinctly upper-crust northern European feel pervades the peach stucco walls and elegant rooms here; the hotel sits just north of the western end of Worth Avenue, and high tea, a cigar parlor, and daily turndown service recall a bygone, more refined era. **Pros:** gracious, attentive staff; Leopard Lounge entertainment; free Wi-Fi and valet parking. **Cons:** long walk to beach; only one elevator; to some, can come off as a bit stuffy. [$] *Rooms from: $389* ✉ *363 Cocoanut Row, Palm Beach* ☎ *561/659–5800, 800/243–7871* 🌐 *www.chesterfieldpb.com* 🛏 *41 rooms, 11 suites* 🍴 *No meals.*

$$$$ HOTEL **The Colony.** This legendary British colonial-style hotel has sunny rooms, suites, and villas with traditional furnishings and a slight Caribbean flair in a particularly convenient location, just one block from Worth Avenue and one block from a pretty beach on the Atlantic Ocean. **Pros:** unbeatable location; famous polo bar; pillow-top mattresses; full English breakfast included. **Cons:** lobby is small; elevators are tight. [$] *Rooms from: $440* ✉ *155 Hammon Ave., Palm Beach* ☎ *561/655–5430, 800/521–5525* 🌐 *www.thecolonypalmbeach.com* 🛏 *83 rooms, 7 villas* 🍴 *Breakfast.*

$$$$ RESORT FAMILY **Four Seasons Resort Palm Beach.** Couples and families seeking relaxed seaside elegance in a ritzy, yet understated, setting will love this manicured 6-acre oceanfront escape at the south end of Palm Beach, with serene, bright, airy rooms in a cream-color palette and spacious marble-lined baths. **Pros:** accommodating service; all rooms have balconies; outstanding complimentary kids' program. **Cons:** 10-minute drive to downtown Palm Beach (but can walk to Lake Worth); pricey. [$] *Rooms*

from: $499 ✉ *2800 S. Ocean Blvd., Palm Beach* ☎ *561/582–2800, 800/432–2335* ⊕ *www.fourseasons.com/palmbeach* ⤳ *210 rooms* ⍢ *No meals.*

$$$$ ⌂ **The Omphoy Ocean Resort.** From the monumental entrance and the
RESORT   lobby's exotic ebony pillars to a lounge with Balinese art and a pool table to the bronze-infused porcelain tile floors, this Zen-like boutique hotel has a sexy, sophisticated look and a loyal following with young, hip travelers. **Pros:** most rooms have beautiful views of the private beach; ultra-contemporary vibe; luxury setting. **Cons:** a hike from shopping and nightlife; the infinity pool is across the driveway. $ *Rooms from: $425* ✉ *2842 S. Ocean Blvd., Palm Beach* ☎ *561/540–6440, 888/344–4321* ⊕ *www.omphoy.com* ⤳ *144 rooms* ⍢ *No meals.*

WEST PALM BEACH

$$$$ ⌂ **Casa Grandview West Palm Beach.** In West Palm's charming Grandview
B&B/INN   Heights historic district—and just minutes away from both downtown
Fodor'sChoice   and the beach—this warm and personalized B&B offers a wonderful
★   respite from South Florida's big-hotel norm. **Pros:** daily dry cleaning of all linens; complimentary soft drinks, coffee, and snacks (and lots of them) in lobby; simple keyless entry (number code lock system). **Cons:** cottages and suites have seven-day minimum; free breakfast in B&B rooms only; art deco suites don't have air-conditioning; in a residential area. $ *Rooms from: $225* ✉ *1410 Georgia Ave., West Palm Beach* ☎ *561/655–8932* ⊕ *www.casagrandview.com* ⤳ *17 rooms* ⍢ *Multiple meal plans.*

$$$ ⌂ **Grandview Gardens Bed & Breakfast.** Defining the Florida B&B experi-
B&B/INN   ence, this 1925 Mediterranean Revival home overlooks a serene court-
Fodor'sChoice   yard pool and oozes loads of charm and personality, while the fabulous
★   owners provide heavy doses of bespoke service. **Pros:** multilingual owners; outside private entrances to rooms; innkeepers offer historic city tours. **Cons:** not close to the beach; in a residential area. $ *Rooms from: $209* ✉ *1608 Lake Ave., West Palm Beach* ☎ *561/833–9023* ⊕ *www. grandview-gardens.com* ⤳ *5 rooms, 2 cottages* ⍢ *Breakfast.*

$$ ⌂ **Hampton Inn & Suites Wellington.** The lobby of this four-story chain
HOTEL   hotel, about 10 miles west of downtown—and the only hotel near the polo fields in the equestrian mecca of Wellington—feels a bit like a tony clubhouse, with rich wood paneling, hunt prints, and elegant chandeliers. **Pros:** complimentary hot breakfast; free Wi-Fi; outdoor swimming pool; close to a large shopping center. **Cons:** no restaurant; Intracoastal Waterway is a 30-minute drive, and beach is farther. $ *Rooms from: $219* ✉ *2155 Wellington Green Dr., Wellington* ☎ *561/472–9696* ⊕ *hamptoninn3.hilton.com* ⤳ *122 rooms, 32 suites* ⍢ *Breakfast.*

$ ⌂ **Hotel Biba.** In the El Cid historic district, this 1940s-era motel has got-
HOTEL   ten a fun stylish revamp from designer Barbara Hulanicki: each room has a vibrant mélange of colors, along with handcrafted mirrors, mosaic bathroom floors, and custom mahogany furnishings. **Pros:** cool, punchy design and luxe fixtures; popular wine bar; free continental breakfast with Cuban pastries. **Cons:** water pressure is weak; bathrooms are tiny; noisy when the bar is open late; not all rooms have central a/c. $ *Rooms from: $139* ✉ *320 Belvedere Rd., West Palm Beach* ☎ *561/832–0094* ⊕ *www.hotelbiba.com* ⤳ *43 rooms* ⍢ *Breakfast.*

LAKE WORTH

$ B&B/INN **Sabal Palm House.** Built in 1936, this romantic, two-story B&B is a short walk from Lake Worth's downtown shops, eateries, and the Intracoastal Waterway, and each room is decorated with antiques and inspired by a different artist, including Renoir, Dalí, Norman Rockwell, and Chagall. **Pros:** on quiet street; hands-on owners; chairs and totes with towels provided for use at nearby beach. **Cons:** no pool; peak times require a two-night minimum stay; no parking lot. [$] *Rooms from: $159* ✉ *109 N. Golfview Rd., Lake Worth* ☎ *561/582–1090, 888/722–2572* 🌐 *www.sabalpalmhouse.com* 🛏 *5 rooms, 2 suites* 🍴 *Breakfast.*

SOUTH PALM BEACH AND MANALAPAN

$$$$ RESORT FAMILY Fodor's Choice ★ **The Ritz-Carlton, Palm Beach.** In the coastal town of Manalapan (just south of Palm Beach), this sublime, glamorous destination resort showcases a newer, younger face of Ritz-Carlton luxury, including a 3,000-square-foot oceanfront terrace, two sleek pools, a huge fitness center, a deluxe spa, and richly upholstered furnishings with contemporary, beachy patterns. **Pros:** magnificent aesthetic details throughout; indulgent pampering services; excellent on-site dining; kids love the cool cyber-lounge just for them. **Cons:** golf course is off property; 15-minute drive to Palm Beach. [$] *Rooms from: $459* ✉ *100 S. Ocean Blvd., Manalapan* ☎ *561/533–6000, 800/241–3333* 🌐 *www.ritzcarlton.com* 🛏 *310 rooms* 🍴 *No meals.*

SINGER ISLAND

$$$ RESORT FAMILY **Palm Beach Marriott Singer Island Beach Resort & Spa.** Families with a yen for the cosmopolitan but requiring the square footage and comforts of home revel in these spacious marble-tiled, granite-topped, Kitchen Aid–outfitted condos; couples wanting a private beach without the same level of sticker shock or bustle found 10 minutes to the south also appreciate the infinity pool and quiet sundeck. **Pros:** wide beach; genuinely warm service; plenty of kids' activities; sleek spa. **Cons:** no upscale dining or shopping nearby; unspectacular room views for an oceanside hotel. [$] *Rooms from: $269* ✉ *3800 N. Ocean Dr., Singer Island, Riviera Beach* ☎ *561/340–1700, 877/239–5610* 🌐 *www.marriott.com* 🛏 *202 suites* 🍴 *No meals.*

$ HOTEL **Sailfish Marina Resort.** A marina with deepwater slips—and prime location at the mouth to the Atlantic Ocean on the Intracoastal Waterway across from Peanut Island—lures boaters and anglers here to these rather basic rooms, studios, and efficiencies. **Pros:** inexpensive rates; great waterfront restaurant; has a water taxi; pretty grounds. **Cons:** no real lobby; not directly on beach; area attracts a party crowd and can be noisy; dated decor. [$] *Rooms from: $115* ✉ *98 Lake Dr., Palm Beach Shores* ☎ *561/844–1724* 🌐 *www.sailfishmarina.com* 🛏 *30 units* 🍴 *No meals.*

PALM BEACH GARDENS

$$ RESORT Fodor's Choice ★ **PGA National Resort & Spa.** A soup-to-nuts renovation completed in 2012 elevated this golfer's paradise (five championship courses and the site of the yearly Honda Classic pro-tour tournament) from its Caddyshack-style beginnings to a sleek modern playground with a gorgeous zero-entry lagoon pool, seven different places to eat, and a

full-service spa with unique mineral-salt therapy pools. **Pros:** dream golf facilities; affordable rates for top-notch amenities; close to shopping malls. **Cons:** no beach shuttle; difficult to get around if you don't have a car; long drive to Palm Beach proper. $ *Rooms from: $279* ⊠ *400 Ave. of the Champions, Palm Beach Gardens* ☎ *561/627–2000, 800/633–9150* ⊕ *www.pgaresort.com* ⇆ *280 rooms, 59 suites* ⍩ *No meals.*

NIGHTLIFE AND THE ARTS

PALM BEACH

NIGHTLIFE

Palm Beach is teeming with restaurants that turn into late-night hot spots, plus hotel lobby bars perfect for tête-à-têtes.

bûccan. A hip Hamptons-esque scene with society darlings crowds the lounge, throwing back killer cocktails like the Basil Rathbone and the Astro-Pop. ⊠ *350 S. County Rd., Palm Beach* ☎ *561/833–3450* ⊕ *www.buccanpalmbeach.com.*

Café Boulud. Happy hours from 4 to 7:30 spiked by creative drinks from Café Boulud draw locals to the lobby lounge and outdoor courtyard. ⊠ *301 Australian Ave., Palm Beach* ☎ *561/655–6060* ⊕ *www.cafeboulud.com/palmbeach.*

Cucina Dell' Arte. Though this spot is popular for lunch and dinner, it's even more popular later in the night. The younger, trendier set comes late to dance and mingle and have a great time. ⊠ *257 Royal Poinciana Way, Palm Beach* ☎ *561/655–0770* ⊕ *www.cucinadellarte.com.*

The Leopard Lounge. In the Chesterfield hotel, this enclave feels like an exclusive club, particularly since a major face-lift in 2011. The trademark ceiling and spotted floors are still there, but the rest of the decor has received a major glam upgrade. Though it starts each evening as a restaurant, as the night progresses the Leopard is transformed into a popular nightclub with live music for Palm Beach's old guard. Expect dancing until the wee hours. ⊠ *Chesterfield Palm Beach, 363 Cocoanut Row, Palm Beach* ☎ *561/659–5800* ⊕ *www.chesterfieldpb.com.*

WEST PALM BEACH

NIGHTLIFE

West Palm is known for its exuberant nightlife—Clematis Street and CityPlace are the prime party destinations. In fact, downtown rocks every Thursday from 6 pm on with Clematis by Night, a celebration of music, dance, art, and food at Centennial Square.

Blue Martini. CityPlace comes alive at this popular South Florida bar, where eclectic music and a mix of DJs and live bands, attracts a diverse crowd. ⊠ *CityPlace, 550 S. Rosemary Ave., #244, West Palm Beach* ☎ *561/835–8601* ⊕ *www.bluemartinilounge.com.*

ER Bradley's Saloon. People of all ages congregate to hang out and socialize at this kitschy open-air restaurant and bar to gaze at the Intracoastal Waterway; the mechanical bull is a hit on Saturday. Enough said. ⊠ *104 Clematis St., West Palm Beach* ☎ *561/833–3520* ⊕ *www.erbradleys.com.*

Feelgoods Rock Bar. There are guitars hanging from the ceiling and a DJ booth made of a 1957 Chevy at this club, and Vince Neil, Mötley Crüe's lead singer, is a partner. ⊠ *219 Clematis St., West Palm Beach* ☎ *561/833–6500* ⊕ *www.feelgoodswestpalm.com.*

Rocco's Tacos and Tequila Bar. In the last few years, Rocco's has taken root in numerous South Florida downtowns and become synonymous with wild nights of chips 'n' guac, margaritas, and intoxicating fun. Get your party started here with more than 220 choices of tequila. There's another branch at 5250 Town Center Circle in Boca Raton. ⊠ *224 Clematis St., West Palm Beach* ☎ *561/650–1001* ⊕ *www.roccostacos.com.*

THE ARTS

Palm Beach Dramaworks (pbd). Housed in an intimate venue with only 218 seats in downtown West Palm Beach, their modus operandi is "theater to think about" with plays by Pulitzer Prize-winners like Arthur Miller and Eugene O'Neill on rotation. ⊠ *201 Clematis St., West Palm Beach* ☎ *561/514–4042* ⊕ *www.palmbeachdramaworks.org.*

Palm Beach Opera. The organization celebrated its 50th anniversary with the 2011–2012 season. Five productions, including the Grand Finals Concert of its yearly vocal competition, are staged from December to April at the Kravis Center with English translations projected above the stage. There's an annual family opera weekend matinee performance, such as *Romeo and Juliet.* Tickets start at $20 and can be purchased at either the company's administrative offices or at the Kravis Center. ⊠ *415 S. Olive Ave., administrative office, West Palm Beach* ☎ *561/833–7888* ⊕ *www.pbopera.org.*

Fodor's Choice **Raymond F. Kravis Center for the Performing Arts.** This is the crown jewel
★ amid a treasury of local arts attractions, and its marquee star is the 2,195-seat Dreyfoos Hall, a glass, copper, and marble showcase just steps from the restaurants and shops of CityPlace. The center also boasts the 289-seat Rinker Playhouse, 170-seat Persson Hall, and the Gosman Amphitheatre, which holds 1,400 total in seats and on the lawn. A packed year-round schedule features a blockbuster lineup of Broadway's biggest touring productions, concerts, dance, dramas, and musicals; Miami City Ballet and the Palm Beach Pops perform here. ⊠ *701 Okeechobee Blvd., West Palm Beach* ☎ *561/832–7469* ⊕ *www.kravis.org.*

SHOPPING

As is the case throughout Florida, many of the smaller boutiques in Palm Beach close in the summer, and most stores are closed on Sunday. Consignment stores in Palm Beach are definitely worth a look; you'll often find high-end designer clothing in impeccable condition.

PALM BEACH

SHOPPING AREAS

Royal Poinciana Way. Cute shops like resort-wear favorite Joy of Palm Beach (⊕ *www.joyofpalmbeach.com*) dot the north side of Royal Poinciana Way between Bradley Place and North County Road. Wind through the courtyards past upscale consignment stores to Sunset Avenue, then stroll down Sunrise Avenue: this is the place for specialty items like out-of-town newspapers, health foods, and rare books. ⊠ *Worth Ave., between Bradley Pl. and N. County Rd., Palm Beach.*

South County Road. The six blocks of South Country Road north of Worth Avenue have interesting and somewhat less expensive stores. ⊠ *South County Rd., between Seaspray Ave. and Worth Ave., Palm Beach.*

Fodor's Choice
★

Worth Avenue. One of the world's premier showcases for high-quality shopping runs half a mile from east to west across Palm Beach, from the beach to Lake Worth. The street has more than 200 shops (more than 40 of them sell jewelry), and many upscale chain stores (Gucci, Hermès, Pucci, Saks Fifth Avenue, Neiman Marcus, Louis Vuitton, Chanel, Cartier, Tiffany & Co., and Tourneau) are represented—their merchandise appealing to the discerning tastes of the Palm Beach clientele. Don't miss walking around the vias, little courtyards lined with smaller boutiques; historic tours are available each month during "season" from the Worth Avenue Association. ⊠ *Worth Ave., between Cocoanut Row and S. Ocean Blvd., Palm Beach* ⊕ *www.worth-avenue.com.*

RECOMMENDED STORES

Betteridge at Greenleaf & Crosby. Jewelry is very important in Palm Beach, and for more than 100 years the diverse selection here has included investment pieces. ⊠ *236 Worth Ave., Palm Beach* ☎ *561/655–5850* ⊕ *www.betteridge.com.*

Calypso St. Barth. For those boutiques that are represented in the wealthiest cities across the country, having an outpost here on Via Encantada on Worth Avenue is almost obligatory. For its Palm Beach store, Calypso has curated a lively collection of resort wear like beautifully embroidered tunics and patterned bikinis as well as shoes, fragrances, and accessories for the pampered lady. ⊠ *247-B Worth Ave., Palm Beach* ☎ *561/832–5006* ⊕ *www.calypsostbarth.com.*

The Church Mouse. Many high-end resale boutique owners grab their merchandise at this thrift store run by the Episcopal Church of Bethesda-by-the-Sea. Proceeds go to regional non-profits. ⊠ *378 S. County Rd., Palm Beach* ☎ *561/659–2154* ⊕ *www.bbts.org/churchmouse.*

Déjà Vu. There are so many gently used, top-quality pieces from Chanel here that this could be a resale house for the brand. There's no digging through piles here; clothes are in impeccable condition and are well organized. ⊠ *Via Testa, 219 Royal Poinciana Way, Palm Beach* ☎ *561/833–6624.*

Giorgio's. Over-the-top indulgence comes in the form of 50 colors of silk and cashmere sweaters and 22 colors of ostrich and alligator adorning everything from bags to bicycles. ⊠ *230 Worth Ave., Palm Beach* ☎ *561/655–2446* ⊕ *www.giorgiosofpalmbeach.com.*

Spring Flowers. Specializing in European labels, beautiful children's clothing starts with newborn gown sets by Petit Bateau and grows into fashions by Léon and Fleurisse. ⊠ *320 Worth Ave., Palm Beach* ☎ *561/832–0131* ⊕ *www.springflowerschildren.com.*

Van Cleef & Arpels. This international chain has held court here since 1940. The renowned shop is where legendary members of Palm Beach society shop for tiaras and formal jewels. ⊠ *202 Worth Ave., Palm Beach* ☎ *561/655–6767* ⊕ *www.vancleefarpels.com.*

Worth Avenue is the place in Palm Beach for high-end shopping, from international boutiques to independent jewelers.

WEST PALM BEACH

Fodor's Choice ★ **Antique Row.** West Palm's U.S. 1, "South Dixie Highway," is the destination for those who are interested in interesting home decor. From thrift shops to the most exclusive stores, it is all here—museum-quality furniture, lighting, art, junk, fabric, frames, tile, and rugs. So if you're looking for an art deco, French-provincial, or Mizner pièce de résistance, big or small, schedule a few hours for an Antique Row stroll. You'll find bargains during the off-season (May to November). Antique Row runs north–south from Belvedere Road to Forest Hill Boulevard, although most stores are bunched between Belvedere Road and Southern Boulevard. ⊠ *U.S. 1, between Belvedere Rd. and Forest Hill Blvd., West Palm Beach* ⊕ *www.westpalmbeachantiques.com.*

CityPlace. The 72-acre, four-block-by-four-block commercial and residential complex centered on Rosemary Avenue attracts people of all ages to with restaurants, a 20-screen Muvico and IMAX, the Harriet Himmel Theater, and a 36,000-gallon water fountain and light show. The dining, shopping, and entertainment are all family-friendly; at night a lively crowd likes to hit the outdoor bars. Among CityPlace's stores are such popular national retailers as Macy's, Pottery Barn, Banana Republic, and Restoration Hardware. There are also shops unique to Florida: Behind the punchy, brightly colored clothing in the front window of **C. Orrico** (☏ *561/832–9203*) are family fashions and accessories by Lily Pulitzer. ⊠ *700 S. Rosemary Ave., West Palm Beach* ☏ *561/366–1000* ⊕ *www.cityplace.com.*

Clematis Street. If lunching is just as important as window-shopping, the renewed downtown West Palm around Clematis Street that runs west to east from South Rosemary Avenue to Flagler Drive is the spot for you. Centennial Park by the waterfront has an attractive design—and fountains where kids can cool off—which adds to the pleasure of browsing and resting at one of the many outdoor cafés. Hip national retailers such as Design Within Reach mix with local boutiques, and both blend in with restaurants and bars. ⊠ *Clematis St., between S. Rosemary Ave. and Flagler Dr., West Palm Beach* ⊕ *www.westpalmbeach.com/clematis.*

PALM BEACH GARDENS

Downtown at the Gardens. This open-air pavilion down the street from the Gardens Mall has boutiques, chain stores, day spas, a 16-screen movie theater, and a lively restaurant and nighttime bar scene that includes the Dirty Martini and Cabo Flats, which both feature live music. ⊠ *11701 Lake Victoria Gardens Ave., Palm Beach Gardens* ☎ *561/340–1600* ⊕ *www.downtownatthegardens.com.*

Fodor'sChoice
★

The Gardens Mall. One of the most refined big shopping malls in America, the Gardens Mall in northern Palm Beach County has stores like Burberry, Chanel, Gucci, Louis Vuitton, and David Yurman. There are also plenty of reasonably priced national retailers like H&M and Abercrombie & Fitch. This beautiful mall has prolific seating pavilions, making it a great place to spend a humid summer afternoon. ⊠ *3101 PGA Blvd., Palm Beach Gardens* ☎ *561/775–7750* ⊕ *www.thegardensmall.com.*

SPORTS AND THE OUTDOORS

You can have a baseball bonanza while on vacation in the greater Palm Beach area by venturing up to the Treasure Coast's spring-training facilities, winter home to several major league teams and minor leagues the rest of the year. Northern towns like Palm Beach Gardens are only minutes away.

PALM BEACH

Palm Beach Island has two good golf courses, but there are more on the mainland, as well as myriad other outdoor sports opportunities.

BIKING

Bicycling is a great way to get a closer look at Palm Beach. Only 14 miles long, half a mile wide, flat as the top of a billiard table, and just as green, it's a perfect biking place.

Lake Trail. This palm-fringed trail, about 4 miles long, skirts the backyards of mansions and the edge of Lake Worth. The start ("south trail" section) is just up from Royal Palm Way behind the Society of the Four Arts; follow the signs and you can't miss it. As you head north, the trail gets a little choppy around the Flagler Museum, so most people just enter where the "north trail" section begins at the very west end of Sunset Avenue. The path stops just short of the tip of the island, but people follow the quiet residential streets until they hit North Ocean Boulevard and the dock there with lovely views of Peanut Island and Singer Island, and then follow North Ocean Boulevard the 4 miles back for a change of scenery. ⊠ *Parallel to Lake Way, Palm Beach.*

Palm Beach Bicycle Trail Shop. Open daily year-round, the shop rents bikes by the hour or day, and it's about a block from the north Lake Trail entrance. The shop has maps to help you navigate your way around the island, or you can download the main map from the shop's website. ⊠ *223 Sunrise Ave., Palm Beach* ☎ *561/659–4583* ⊕ *www. palmbeachbicycle.com.*

GOLF

The Breakers Ocean Course. The historic par-70 Ocean Course, the oldest 18 holes in all of Florida, as well as its contemporary off-site counterpart the Breakers Rees Jones Course, are open to members and hotel guests only. A $190 greens fee for each includes range balls, cart, and bag storage; the John Webster Golf Academy at the Breakers offers private and group lessons. ⊠ *1 S. County Rd., Palm Beach* ☎ *561/655–6611* ⊕ *www.thebreakers.com/golf.*

Palm Beach Par 3 Golf Course. The 18 holes—redesigned in 2009 by Hall-of-Famer Raymond Floyd—include six directly on the ocean, with some holes over 200 yards. Greens fees are $46; cart is an extra $20, but walking is encouraged. Nine holes are allowed (and cheaper) before 8:30 am and after 2 pm. ⊠ *2345 S. Ocean Blvd., Palm Beach* ☎ *561/547–0598* ⊕ *www.golfontheocean.com.*

WEST PALM BEACH

POLO

Fodor'sChoice **International Polo Club Palm Beach.** Attend matches and rub elbows with
★ celebrities who make the pilgrimage out to Palm Beach polo country (the western suburb of Wellington) during the January-through-April season. The competition is not just among polo players. High society dresses in their best polo couture week after week, each outfit more fabulous than the next. An annual highlight at the polo club is the U.S. Open Polo Championship at the end of season. ⊠ *3667 120th Ave. S, Wellington* ☎ *561/204–5687* ⊕ *www.internationalpoloclub.com.*

LAKE WORTH

GOLF

Palm Beach National Golf and Country Club. This classic course has 18 holes and a Joe Lee championship layout; greens fees are $75 for 18 holes, $49 for 9 holes. The Steve Haggerty Golf Academy is based here. ⊠ *7500 St. Andrews Rd., Lake Worth* ☎ *561/965–3381 pro shop* ⊕ *www.palmbeachnational.com.*

SINGER ISLAND

FISHING

Sailfish Marina. Book a full or half day of deep-sea fishing for up to six people with the seasoned captains and large fleet of 28- to 65-foot boats. ⊠ *Sailfish Marina Resort, 98 Lake Dr., Palm Beach Shores* ☎ *561/844–1724* ⊕ *www.sailfishmarina.com.*

PALM BEACH GARDENS

GOLF

PGA National Resort & Spa. If you're the kind of traveler who takes along a set of clubs, this is the place for you. The five championship courses are open only to hotel guests and club members, and the Champion Course, redesigned by Jack Nicklaus and famous for its Bear Trap holes, is the site of the yearly Honda Classic pro tournament (greens fees are $301 for 18 holes and $146 for 9 holes). The four other challenging courses each carry the same greens fees ($182 and $95): the Palmer, named for its architect, the legendary Arnold Palmer; the Haig, the resort's first course, and the Squire, both from Tom and George Fazio; and the Karl Litten–designed Estates, the sole course not on the property. Lessons are available at the David Leadbetter Golf Academy. ⊠ *400 Ave. of the Champions, Palm Beach Gardens* ☎ *561/627–1800* ⊕ *www.pgaresort.com/golf/pga-national-golf.*

DELRAY BEACH

15 miles south of West Palm Beach.

A onetime artists' retreat with a small settlement of Japanese farmers, Delray has grown into a sophisticated beach town. Delray's current popularity is caused in large part by the fact that it has the feel of an organic city rather than a planned development or subdivision—and it's completely walkable. Atlantic Avenue, the once-dilapidated main drag, has evolved into a more-than-a-mile-long stretch of palm-dotted sidewalks, lined with stores, art galleries, and dining establishments. Running east–west and ending at the beach, it's a happening place for a stroll, day or night. Another active pedestrian area, the Pineapple Grove Arts District, begins at Atlantic and stretches northward on Northeast 2nd Avenue about half a mile, and yet another active pedestrian way begins at the eastern edge of Atlantic Avenue and runs along the big, broad swimming beach that extends north to George Bush Boulevard and south to Casuarina Road.

GETTING HERE AND AROUND

To reach Delray Beach from Boynton Beach, drive 2 miles south on I–95, U.S. 1, or A1A.

ESSENTIALS

VISITOR INFORMATION

Contacts **Palm Beach County Convention and Visitors Bureau** ⊠ *1555 Palm Beach Lakes Blvd., Suite 800, West Palm Beach* ☎ *800/554–7256* ⊕ *www.palmbeachfl.com.*

EXPLORING

Colony Hotel. The chief landmark along Atlantic Avenue since 1926 is this sunny Mediterranean revival–style building, which is a member of the National Trust's Historic Hotels of America. Walk through the lobby to the parking lot where original garages still stand—relics of the days when hotel guests would arrive via chauffeured cars and stay there the whole season. ⊠ *525 E. Atlantic Ave.* ☎ *561/276–4123* ⊕ *www.thecolonyhotel.com.*

FAMILY   **Delray Beach Center for the Arts at Old School Square.** Instrumental in the revitalization of Delray Beach circa 1995, this cluster of galleries and event spaces were established in restored school buildings dating from 1913 and 1925. The **Cornell Museum of Art & American Culture**

CLOSE UP

The Morikami: Essence of Japan in Florida

A magical 200-acre garden where the Far East meets the South lies just beyond Palm Beach's allure of sun, sea, and glittering resorts. It's called the Morikami Museum and Japanese Gardens and is a testament to one man's perseverance. One of the largest Japanese gardens outside of Japan, it's also a soothing destination for reflection, with a pine forest, trails, and lakes.

In 1904, Jo Sakai, a New York University graduate, returned to his homeland of Miyazu, Japan, to recruit hands for farming what is now northern Boca Raton. With help from Henry Flagler's East Coast Railroad subsidiary they colonized as Yamato, an ancient name for Japan. When crops fell short, everyone left except for George Sukeji Morikami, who carried on cultivating local crops, eventually donating his land to memorialize the Yamato Colony in the mid-1970s to Palm Beach County. His dream took on a new dimension with the 1977 opening of the Morikami complex,

a living monument bridging cultural understanding between Morikami's two homelands.

The original Yamato-kan building chronicles the Yamato Colony, and a 32,000-square-foot main museum that opened in 1993 has rotating exhibits with 7,000 art objects and artifacts from the permanent collection, including 200 examples of textiles and a 500-piece collection of tea-ceremony items. No visit is complete without exploring the expansive Japanese gardens that have strolling paths, a tropical bonsai collection, and lakes teeming with koi. Enjoy a demonstration of *sado*, the Japanese tea ceremony, in the Seishin-an teahouse (check website for schedule), learn about Japanese history in the 5,000-book library, or register in advance for classes like calligraphy, bonsai, art, and intro to sushi-making. The gift shop has some great finds for the whole family, and the Cornell Café has excellent pan-Asian fare and a relaxing terrace that overlooks the gardens.

6

offers ever-changing exhibits on fine arts, crafts, and pop culture, plus a hands-on children's gallery. From November to April, the 323-seat **Crest Theatre** showcases national-touring Broadway musicals, cabaret concerts, dance performances, and lectures. ⊠ *51 N. Swinton Ave.* ☎ *561/243–7922* ⊕ *www.oldschool.org* ✉ *$10 for museum* ☉ *Museum Tues.–Sat. 10:30–4:30, Sun. 1–4:30.*

Morikami Museum and Japanese Gardens. The boonies west of Delray Beach seems an odd place to encounter one of the region's most important cultural centers, but this is exactly where you can find a 200-acre cultural and recreational facility heralding the Yamato Colony of Japanese farmers that settled here in the early 20th century. A permanent exhibit details their history, and all together the museum's collection has more than 7,000 artifacts and works of art on rotating display. Traditional tea ceremonies ($) are conducted monthly from October to June, along with educational classes ($) on topics like calligraphy and sushi-making (these require advance registration). The six main gardens are inspired by famous historic periods in Japanese garden design and have South Florida accents (think tropical bonsai), and the

Morikami Museum and Japanese Gardens gives a taste of the Orient through its exhibits and tea ceremonies.

on-site Cornell Café serves light Asian fare at affordable prices and was recognized by the Food Network as being one of the country's best museum eateries. ✉ *4000 Morikami Park Rd.* ☎ *561/495–0233* ⊕ *www.morikami.org* ✉ *$13* ⊘ *Tues.–Sun. 10–5.*

BEACHES

Fodor'sChoice
★ **Delray Municipal Beach.** If you're looking for a place to see and be seen, head for this wide expanse of sand, the heart of which is where Atlantic Avenue meets A1A, close to restaurants, bars, and quick-serve eateries. Singles, families, and water sports enthusiasts alike love it here. Lounge chairs and umbrellas can be rented every day, and lifeguards man stations half a mile out in each direction. The most popular section of beach is south of Atlantic Ave. on A1A, where the street parking is found. There are also two metered lots with restrooms across from A1A at Sandoway Park and Anchor Park (bring quarters if parking here!). On the beach by Anchor Park, north of Casuarina Rd., are six volleyball nets and a kiosk that offers Hobie Wave rentals, surfing lessons, and snorkeling excursions to the 1903 SS *Inchulva* shipwreck half a mile offshore. The beach itself is open 24 hours, if you're at a nearby hotel and fancy a moonlight stroll. **Amenities:** water sports; food and drink; lifeguards; parking (fee); toilets; showers. **Best for:** windsurfing; partiers; swimming. ✉ *Rte. A1A and E. Atlantic Ave.* ✉ *$1.50 per 1 hr parking* ⊘ *Daily 24 hrs.*

WHERE TO EAT

$$$ SEAFOOD Fodor's Choice ★ 🍴 **City Oyster & Sushi Bar.** This trendy restaurant mingles the personalities and flavors of a New England oyster bar, a modern sushi eatery, an eclectic seafood grill, and an award-winning dessert bakery to create a can't-miss foodie haven in the heart of Delray's bustling Atlantic Avenue. With fruits of the sea delivered fresh daily and a winning culinary team, dishes like the New England clam chowder, New Orleans–style shrimp and crab gumbo, tuna crudo, and lobster fried rice are simply sublime. What's more? The restaurant's colossal bakery adds an unexpected element of carb bliss with a full roster of house-made breads and desserts, including the decadent, seasonal pies (ranging from chocolate–peanut butter to mixed berries) and the insanely divine pecan pie in a glass, smothered in salted caramel, pecan brittle, butter-pecan ice cream, and topped with whipped cream. Pastas are also made in-house. The wine list and craft beer menus are also off the charts. [$] *Average main: $23* ✉ *213 E. Atlantic Ave.* ☎ *561/272–0220* 🌐 *www.cityoysterdelray.com.*

$$$ ITALIAN 🍴 **D'Angelo Trattoria.** One of South Florida's most renowned Italian chefs, Angelo Elia, has once again expanded his empire with this lively trattoria off Atlantic Avenue in Delray Beach. In a refurbished and reinvented beach house, the restaurant delivers hefty portions of original Italian favorites—such as gnocchi *quattro formaggi* (four cheeses) and seafood risotto—as well as American-Italian delights, like jumbo-shrimp parmigiana over spicy linguini. The wood oven also commands a lot of attention for its excellent pizzas, from the more traditional margherita to the more avant-garde, like the Integrale made with whole-wheat flour and topped with mozzarella, brie, zucchini, and smoked salmon. Come hungry and prepare yourself for a major food hangover that's worth every bite. [$] *Average main: $28* ✉ *9 S.E. 7th Ave.* ☎ *561/330–1237* 🌐 *www.dangelotrattoria.com* 🕒 *No lunch.*

$$$ MODERN AMERICAN Fodor's Choice ★ 🍴 **Max's Harvest.** A few blocks off Atlantic Avenue in the artsy Pineapple Grove neighborhood, a tree-shaded, fenced-in courtyard welcomes foodies eager to dig into its "farm-to-fork" offerings. The menu encourages people to experiment with "to share," "start small," and "think big" plates. An ideal sampling: organic deviled eggs with chives and truffle sea salt; tequila-cured salmon; ricotta gnocchi, boiled then sautéed with porcini mushrooms and truffle tremor (goat cheese with truffles); and a pork chop over mustard spaetzle. Sunday brunch is wildly popular and includes an unlimited interactive Bloody Mary bar and champagne cocktails. [$] *Average main: $27* ✉ *169 N.E. 2nd Ave.* ☎ *561/381–9970* 🌐 *www.maxsharvest.com* 🕒 *No lunch Mon.–Sat.*

$$$ AMERICAN 🍴 **The Office.** Scenesters line the massive indoor-outdoor bar from noon 'til the wee hours at this cooler-than-thou retro library restaurant, but it's worth your time to stop here for the best burger in town. There's a whole selection, but the Prime CEO steals the show: Maytag bleu cheese and Gruyere with tomato-onion confit, arugula, and bacon. It's so juicy, you'll quickly forget the mess you're making. Other upscale renditions of comforting classics like nachos (a delicate puff of whipped crab per chip served with jicama slaw), fried green tomatoes (panko-and-cornmeal crusted with crisped bits of Serrano ham),

6

and "naughty" alcoholic shakes are worth every indulgent calorie. [$] *Average main: $24* ✉ *201 E. Atlantic Ave.* ☎ *561/276–3600* 🌐 *www.theofficedelray.com.*

$ AMERICAN Fodor's Choice ★ 🍴 **Old School Bakery.** This place concentrates on sandwich making at its best, and it is known for freshly baked breads (the owner spent time in three-star Michelin restaurants before opening up shop). Particularly worthy is the cherry chicken salad sandwich with brie on multigrain bread. Apart from sandwiches and soups served for lunch every day, you can order from a diverse menu of baked goods that include artisan breads, pastries, several kinds of cookies, and even biscotti. The bakery is really just for takeout, but there are a few small tables in an adjacent open-air courtyard. [$] *Average main: $8* ✉ *814 E. Atlantic Ave.* ☎ *561/243–8059* 🌐 *www.oldschoolbakery.com.*

> **WORD OF MOUTH**
>
> "If you really want to be close to restaurants and shops in the Palm Beach area, check out the Marriott in Delray Beach or even the adjacent Residence Inn by Marriott . . . about 30 minutes south of Palm Beach."
>
> —rattravlers

$$$ AMERICAN Fodor's Choice ★ 🍴 **32 East.** Although restaurants come and go on a trendy street like Atlantic Avenue, 32 East remains one of the best in Delray Beach. An ever-changing daily menu defines modern American cuisine. Depending on what is fresh and plentiful, you might indulge in oak-fired organic black mission figs wrapped in ham or perfectly prepared snapper over autumn vegetables. Medium-tone wood accents and dim lighting make this brasserie seem cozy. There's a packed bar in front, an open kitchen in back, and patio seating on the sidewalk. [$] *Average main: $29* ✉ *32 E. Atlantic Ave.* ☎ *561/276–7868* 🌐 *www.32east.com* ⏲ *No lunch.*

WHERE TO STAY

For expanded reviews, facilities, and current deals, visit Fodors.com.

$$ HOTEL 🏨 **Colony Hotel & Cabaña Club.** In the heart of downtown Delray, this charming hotel dates back to 1926, and although it's landlocked, it does have a pool and private beach for hotel guests only. **Pros:** pet-friendly; full breakfast buffet included with rooms; free use of cabanas, umbrellas, and hammocks. **Cons:** no pool at main hotel building; must walk to public beach for water sport rentals. [$] *Rooms from: $189* ✉ *525 E. Atlantic Ave.* ☎ *561/276–4123, 800/552–2363* 🌐 *www.thecolonyhotel.com* 🛏 *48 rooms, 22 suites* 🍽 *Breakfast.*

$$$ HOTEL FAMILY 🏨 **Delray Beach Marriott.** By far the largest hotel in Delray Beach, the Marriott has two towers on a stellar plot of land at the east end of Atlantic Avenue—it's the only hotel that directly overlooks the water, yet it is still within walking distance of restaurants, shopping, and nightlife. **Pros:** fantastic ocean views; pampering spa; two pools. **Cons:** chain-hotel feel; charge for parking; must rent beach chairs. [$] *Rooms from: $279* ✉ *10 N. Ocean Blvd.* ☎ *561/274–3200* 🌐 *www.delraybeachmarriott.com* 🛏 *181 rooms, 88 suites* 🍽 *No meals.*

$$$$
RESORT
Fodor's Choice
★

The Seagate Hotel & Spa. Those who crave 21st-century luxury in its full glory (ultraswank tilework and fixtures, marble vanities, seamless shower doors) will love this LEED-certified hotel that offers a subtle Zen coastal motif throughout. **Pros:** two swimming pools; fabulous beach club; exceptionally knowledgeable concierge team. **Cons:** main building not directly on beach; daily resort fee; separate charge for parking. $ *Rooms from: $359* ⊠ *1000 E. Atlantic Ave.* ☎ *561/665–4800, 877/577–3242* ⊕ *www.theseagatehotel.com* 🖙 *154 rooms* ⦿ *No meals.*

$
B&B/INN
Fodor's Choice
★

Sundy House. Just about everything in this bungalow-style B&B is executed to perfection—especially its tropical, verdant grounds, which are actually a nonprofit botanical garden (something anyone can check out during free weekday tours) with a natural, freshwater swimming pool where your feet glide along limestone rocks and mingle with fish. **Pros:** charming eclectic decor; each room is unique; renowned restaurant with popular indoor-outdoor bar and free breakfast; in quiet area off Atlantic Avenue. **Cons:** need to walk through garden to reach rooms (i.e., no covered walkways); beach shuttle requires roughly half-hour advance notice; no private beach facilities. $ *Rooms from: $189* ⊠ *106 Swinton Ave.* ☎ *561/272–5678, 877/434–9601* ⊕ *www.sundyhouse. com* 🖙 *11 rooms* ⦿ *Breakfast.*

NIGHTLIFE

Boston's on the Beach. You'll find beer flowing and the ocean breeze blowing at this beach bar and eatery, a local watering hole since 1983. The walls are laden with paraphernalia from the Boston Bruins, New England Patriots, and Boston Red Sox, including a shrine to Ted Williams. Boston's can get loud and rowdy (or lively, depending on your taste) later at night. Groove to reggae on Monday, live blues music on Tuesday, and other live music from rock to country on Friday, Saturday, and Sunday. ⊠ *40 S. Ocean Blvd.* ☎ *561/278–3364* ⊕ *www.bostonsonthebeach.com.*

Dada. Bands play in the living room of a historic house. It's a place where those who don't drink will also feel comfortable, and excellent gourmet nibbles are a huge bonus (a full dinner menu is available, too). ⊠ *52 N. Swinton Ave.* ☎ *561/330–3232* ⊕ *www.sub-culture.org.*

Jellies Bar at the Atlantic Grille. The Delray over-30 set floats over to the stunning bar in the Atlantic Grille to shimmy to live music Tuesday to Saturday; the namesake jellyfish tank never fails to entertain as well. ⊠ *Seagate Hotel & Spa, 1000 E. Atlantic Ave.* ☎ *561/665–4900* ⊕ *www.theatlanticgrille.com.*

SHOPPING

Atlantic Avenue and Pineapple Grove, both charming neighborhoods for shoppers, have maintained Delray Beach's small-town integrity. Atlantic Avenue is the main drag, with art galleries, boutiques, restaurants, and bars lining it from just west of Swinton Avenue all the way east to the ocean. The up-and-coming Pineapple Grove Arts District is centered on the half-mile strip of Northeast 2nd Avenue that goes northward from Atlantic.

Furst. This studio-shop gives you the chance to watch the two designers at work—and then purchase their handcrafted bags and fine jewelry. ⊠ *123 N.E. 2nd Ave.* ☎ *561/272–6422* ⊕ *www.flaviefurst.com* ☽ *Closed Sun.*

Snappy Turtle. Jack Rogers sandals and Trina Turk dresses mingle with other fun resort fashions for the home and family at this family-run store. ⊠ *1100 E. Atlantic Ave.* ☎ *888/762–7798* ⊕ *www.snappy-turtle.com.*

SPORTS AND THE OUTDOORS

BIKING

There's a bicycle path in Barwick Park, but the most popular place to ride is up and down the special oceanfront bike lane along Route A1A. The city also has an illustrated and annotated map on key downtown sights available through the Palm Beach Convention and Visitors Bureau.

Richwagen's Bike & Sport. Rent bikes by the hour, day, or week (they come with locks, baskets, and helmets); Richwagen's also has copies of city maps on hand. A 7-Speed Cruiser rents for $55 per week. ⊠ *298 N.E. 6th Ave.* ☎ *561/276–4234* ⊕ *www.delraybeachbicycles.com.*

TENNIS

Delray Beach Tennis Center. Each year this complex hosts simultaneous professional tournaments where current stars like Andy Roddick and Juan Martin del Potro along with legends like Ivan Lendl and Michael Chang duke it out (⊕ *www.yellowtennisball.com*), as well as Chris Evert's Pro-Celebrity Tennis Classic charity event (⊕ *www.chrisevert. org*). The rest of the time, you can practice or learn on 14 clay courts and 7 hard courts; private lessons and clinics are available, and it's open from 7:30 am to 9 pm weekdays and until 6 pm weekends. Since most hotels in the area do not have courts, tennis players visiting Delray Beach often come here to play. ⊠ *201 W. Atlantic Ave.* ☎ *561/243–7360* ⊕ *www.delraytennis.com.*

BOCA RATON

6 miles south of Delray Beach.

Less than an hour south of Palm Beach and anchoring the county's south end, upscale Boca Raton has much in common with its fabled cousin. Both reflect the unmistakable architectural influence of Addison Mizner, their principal developer in the mid-1920s. The meaning of the name Boca Raton (pronounced boca rah-*tone*) often arouses curiosity, with many folks mistakenly assuming it means "rat's mouth." Historians say the probable origin is Boca Ratones, an ancient Spanish geographical term for an inlet filled with jagged rocks or coral. Miami's Biscayne Bay had such an inlet, and in 1823 a mapmaker copying Miami terrain confused the more northern inlet, thus mistakenly labeling this area Boca Ratones. No matter what, you'll know you've arrived in the heart of downtown when you spot the historic town hall's gold dome on the main street, Federal Highway. Much of the Boca landscape was heavily planned, and many of the bigger sights are clustered in the area around town hall and Lake Boca, a wide stretch of the Intracoastal Waterway between Palmetto Park Road and Camino Real (two main east–west streets at the southern end of town).

GETTING HERE AND AROUND

To get to Boca Raton from Delray Beach, drive south 6 miles on Interstate 95, Federal Highway (U.S. 1), or A1A.

ESSENTIALS

VISITOR INFORMATION

Contacts Palm Beach County Convention and Visitors Bureau ⊠ *1555 Palm Beach Lakes Blvd., Suite 800, West Palm Beach* ☎ *800/554–7256* ⊕ *www.palmbeachfl.com.*

EXPLORING

FAMILY **Boca Raton Museum of Art.** Changing-exhibition galleries on the first floor showcase internationally known artists—both past and present—at this museum in a spectacular building that's part of the Mizner Park shopping center; the permanent collection upstairs includes works by Picasso, Degas, Matisse, Klee, Modigliani, and Warhol, as well as notable African and pre-Columbian art. Daily tours are included with admission. In addition to the treasure hunts and sketchbooks you can pick up from the front desk, there's a roster of special programs that cater to kids, including studio workshops and gallery walks. Another fun feature is the cell phone audio guide—certain pieces of art have a corresponding number you dial to hear a detailed narration. ⊠ *501 Plaza Real, Mizner Park* ☎ *561/392–2500* ⊕ *www.bocamuseum.org* ⊠ *$15* ⊙ *Tues., Thurs., and Fri. 10–5, Wed. 10–9, weekends noon–5.*

FAMILY **Gumbo Limbo Nature Center.** A big draw for kids, this stellar spot has four huge saltwater tanks brimming with sea life, from coral to stingrays to spiny lobsters, plus a sea turtle rehabilitation center. Nocturnal walks in spring and early summer, when staffers lead a quest to find nesting female turtles coming ashore to lay eggs, are popular; so are the hatching releases in August and September. Call to purchase tickets in advance as there are very limited spaces. Gumbo Limbo is one of only a handful of centers that offer the chance to observe the babies departing into the ocean. There is also a nature trail and butterfly garden, a ¼-mile boardwalk, and a 40-foot observation tower, where you're likely to see brown pelicans and osprey. ⊠ *1801 N. Ocean Blvd.* ☎ *561/544–8605* ⊕ *www.gumbolimbo.org* ⊠ *Free ($5 suggested donation); turtle walks $15* ⊙ *Mon.–Sat. 9–4, Sun. noon–4.*

Old Floresta. This residential area was developed by Addison Mizner starting in 1925 and is beautifully landscaped with palms and cycads. Its houses are mainly Mediterranean in style, many with balconies supported by exposed wood columns. Explore by driving northward on Paloma Avenue from Palmetto Park Road, then weave in and out of the side streets. ⊠ *Paloma Ave., north of W. Palmetto Park Rd.*

BEACHES

Boca's three city beaches (South Beach, Red Reef Park, and Spanish River Park, south to north, respectively) are beautiful and hugely popular; but unless you're a resident or enter via bicycle, parking can be expensive. Save your receipt if you care to go in and out, or park-hop—most guards at the front gate will honor a same-day ticket from another location if you ask nicely. Another option is the county-run South Inlet Park that's walking distance from the Boca Raton Bridge Hotel at the southern end of Lake Boca; it has a metered lot for a fraction of the cost, but not quite the same charm as the others.

FAMILY **Red Reef Park.** The ocean with its namesake reef that you can wade up to is just one draw: a fishing zone on the Intracoastal Waterway across the street, a 9-hole golf course next door, and the Gumbo Limbo Environmental Education Center at the northern end of the park can easily make a day at the beach into so much more. But if pure old-fashioned fun-in-the-sun is your focus, to that end there are tons of picnic tables and grills, and two separate playgrounds. Pack snorkels and explore the reef at high tide when fish are most abundant. Swimmers, be warned: once lifeguards leave at 5, anglers flock to the shores and stay well past dark. **Amenities:** lifeguards; parking (fee); showers; toilets. **Best for:** snorkeling; swimming; walking. ⊠ *1400 N. Rte. A1A* ☎ *561/393–7974, 561/393–7989 for beach conditions* ⊕ *www.ci.boca-raton.fl.us/rec/parks/redreef.shtm* 🅿 *$16 parking (weekdays), $18 parking (weekends)* ⊙ *Daily 8 am–10 pm.*

South Beach Park. Perched high up on a dune, a large open-air pavilion at the east end of Palmetto Park Road offers a panoramic view of what's in store below on the sand that stretches up the coast. Serious beachgoers need to pull into the main lot ¼-mile north on the east side of A1A, but if a short-but-sweet visit is what you're after, the 15 or so one-hour spots with meters in the circle driveway will do. During the day, pretty young things blanket the shore, and windsurfers practice tricks in the waves. Quiet quarters are farther north. **Amenities:** lifeguards; parking (fee); toilets; showers. **Best for:** sunsets; windsurfing; walking; swimming. ⊠ *400 N. Rte A1A* ⊕ *www.ci.boca-raton.fl.us/rec/parks/southbeach.shtm* 🅿 *$15 parking (weekdays), $17 parking (weekends)* ⊙ *Daily 8–sunset.*

Spanish River Park. At 76 acres and including extensive nature trails, this is by far one of the largest ocean parks in the southern half of Palm Beach County and a great pick for people who want more space and fewer crowds. Big groups, including family reunions, favor it because of the number of covered picnic areas for rent, but anyone can snag a free table (there are plenty!) under the thick canopy of banyan trees. Even though the vast majority of the park is separated from the surf, you never actually have to cross A1A to reach the beach, because tunnels run under it at several locations. **Amenities:** lifeguards; parking (fee); showers; toilets. **Best for:** swimming; walking; solitude. ⊠ *3001 N. Rte. A1A* ☎ *561/393–7815* ⊕ *www.ci.boca-raton.fl.us/rec/parks/spanishriver.shtm* 🅿 *$16 parking (weekdays), $18 parking (weekends)* ⊙ *Daily 8–sunset.*

WHERE TO EAT

$$$$ TUSCAN Fodor's Choice ★ 🍴 **Casa D'Angelo Ristorante.** The lines are deservedly long at Chef Angelo Elia's upscale Tuscan restaurant in tony Boca Raton. The third outpost of his renowned Casa D'Angelo chain impresses with an outstanding selection of antipasti, carpaccios, pastas, and specialties from the wood-burning oven. From staples like the antipasto *angelo* (grilled vegetables and buffalo mozzarella) and linguine with white-water clams and garlic, to the ever-changing gnocchi, risotto, veal scaloppine, and fish specials of the day, Angelo's dishes deliver pure perfection in every bite. The wine list is also exceptional with hundreds of Italian and American wines to choose from. [$] *Average main: $38* ✉ *171 E. Palmetto Park Rd.* ☎ *561/996–1234* 🌐 *www.casa-d-angelo.com* ✍ *Reservations essential* ⏲ *No lunch.*

$$ ITALIAN Fodor's Choice ★ 🍴 **Ovenella.** Celebrating the flavors and fusions of the Mediterranean, executive chef Mennan Tekeli dishes out a menu of European staples and reinvented Italian classics, a successful hybrid with both Turkish and Brazilian influences. Almost everything here is made from scratch—from the tender gnocchi to the aromatic tomato sauces and ragouts to the caramel that tops the wood oven–baked apple tart and the lace cookie that binds the crispy toasted-almond basket. Of course, the center of attention is the wood-burning oven; hence the name. The oven is filled to the brim with piping hot artisan pizzas, roasted beets, balsamic mushrooms, and more. The service here is as excellent as the wine list. [$] *Average main: $18* ✉ *499 S. Federal Hwy.* ☎ *561/672–7553* 🌐 *www.ovenella.com* ⏲ *No lunch weekends.*

$$$ AMERICAN 🍴 **Racks Downtown Eatery & Tavern.** Whimsical indoor–oudoor decor and comfort food with a twist help define this popular eatery in tony Mizner Park. Instead of dinner rolls, pretzel bread and mustard get things started. Share plates like bacon-wrapped shrimp and sea bass lettuce cups to promote convivial social dining. Happy hour at the bar is 4–7 and offers half-price drinks and appetizers. [$] *Average main: $23* ✉ *402 Plaza Real, Mizner Park* ☎ *561/395–1662* 🌐 *www.racksboca.com.*

$$$$ SEAFOOD Fodor's Choice ★ 🍴 **Truluck's.** This popular Florida and Texas seafood chain is so serious about its fruits of the sea that it supports its own fleet of 16 fishing boats. Stone crabs are the signature dish, and you can have all you can eat on Monday night from October to May. Other recommended dishes include salmon topped with blue crab and shrimp, hot-and-crunchy trout, crab cakes, and blackened Florida grouper. Portions are huge, so you might want to make a meal of appetizers. And don't miss the warm carrot cake. The place comes alive each night with its popular piano bar. [$] *Average main: $35* ✉ *351 Plaza Real, Mizner Park* ☎ *561/391–0755* 🌐 *www.trulucks.com.*

$$$ CHINESE 🍴 **Uncle Tai's.** The draw at this upscale eatery is some of the best Hunan cuisine on Florida's east coast. Specialties include sliced duck with snow peas and water chestnuts in a tangy plum sauce, and orange beef delight—flank steak stir-fried until crispy and then sautéed with pepper sauce, garlic, and orange peel. They'll go easy on the heat on request. The service is quietly efficient. [$] *Average main: $21* ✉ *5250 Town Center Circle* ☎ *561/368–8806* 🌐 *www.uncletais.com.*

WHERE TO STAY

For expanded reviews, facilities, and current deals, visit Fodors.com.

$$$
RESORT
FAMILY
Fodor'sChoice
★

Boca Beach Club. Dotted with turquoise lounge chairs, ruffled umbrellas, and white-sand beaches, this newly reconceived and rebranded hotel is now part of the Waldorf-Astoria collection and looks as if it was carefully replicated from a retro-chic postcard. **Pros:** great location on the beach; kids' activity center. **Cons:** pricey; shuttle ride away from the main building. $ *Rooms from: $399* ⊠ *900 S. Ocean Blvd.* ☎ *888/564–1312* ⊕ *www.bocabeachclub.com* ⤳ *212 rooms* ⦿ *No meals.*

$
HOTEL

Boca Raton Bridge Hotel. This boutique hotel on the Intracoastal Waterway near the Boca Inlet has views of Lake Boca and the ocean that can't be beat, especially from higher-up floors and the penthouse restaurant, Carmen's at the Top of the Bridge. **Pros:** lively pool bar scene; affordable rates; great location and short walk to beach; pet-friendly. **Cons:** can be noisy if you're near the bridge; rooms are nondescript; building is on the older side. $ *Rooms from: $179* ⊠ *999 E. Camino Real* ☎ *561/368–9500, 866/909–2622* ⊕ *www.bocaratonbridgehotel.com* ⤳ *142 rooms* ⦿ *No meals.*

$$
RESORT
FAMILY
Fodor'sChoice
★

Boca Raton Resort & Club. Addison Mizner built this Mediterranean-style hotel in 1926, and additions over time have created a sprawling, sparkling resort, one of the most luxurious in all of South Florida and now part of the Waldorf-Astoria collection. **Pros:** super-exclusive—grounds are closed to the public; decor strikes the right balance between historic roots and modern comforts; plenty of activities. **Cons:** daily resort charge; conventions often crowd common areas. $ *Rooms from: $299* ⊠ *501 E. Camino Real* ☎ *561/447–3000, 888/543–1277* ⊕ *www.bocaresort.com* ⤳ *635 rooms* ⦿ *No meals.*

NIGHTLIFE

Fodor'sChoice
★

Rustic Cellar. Warm and intimate, this dark cozy nook is modeled after a Napa Valley tasting room and is perhaps the best wine bar in Palm Beach County. More than 300 hand-selected vintages, most from top domestic and rare vinters, are served—and nearly all are available by the glass. There's also an impressive collection of craft beers. ⊠ *Royal Palm Pl., 409 S.E. Mizner Blvd.* ☎ *561/392–5237* ⊕ *www.rusticcellar.com.*

SHOPPING

Mizner Park. This distinctive 30-acre shopping center off Federal Highway, one block north of Palmetto Park Road, intersperses apartments and town houses among its gardenlike commercial areas. Some three dozen national and local retailers line the central axis that's peppered with fountains and green space, restaurants, galleries, a movie theater, the Boca Raton Museum of Art, and an amphitheater that hosts major concerts as well as community events. ⊠ *327 Plaza Real* ☎ *561/362–0606* ⊕ *www.miznerpark.com.*

Royal Palm Place. The retail enclave of Royal Palm is filled with independent boutiques selling fine jewelry and apparel. By day, stroll the walkable streets and have your pick of sidewalk cafés for lunch alongside Boca's ladies who lunch. Royal Palm Place assumes a different personality come nightfall, as its numerous restaurants and lounges attract throngs of patrons for great dining and fabulous libations. ⊠ *101 Plaza Real S* ☎ *561/392–8920* ⊕ *www.royalpalmplace.com.*

Town Center at Boca Raton. Over on the west side of Boca, this indoor megamall has more than 220 stores, with anchor stores including Saks and Neiman Marcus and just about every major high-end designer, including Bulgari and Anne Fontaine. But not every shop here requires deep pockets. The Town Center at Boca Raton is also firmly rooted with a variety of more affordable national brands like Gap and Guess. ⊠ *6000 Glades Rd.* ☎ *561/368–6000* ⊕ *www.simon.com.*

SPORTS AND THE OUTDOORS

GOLF

Boca Raton Resort & Club. Legendary Sam Snead was the head pro here in the 1960s when the Resort Course (greens fee with cart $163) was the hotel's only option; nowadays there's a second one off-site, the Country Club Course (greens fee with cart $163), with a Dave Pelz Scoring Game School that is open to the public—course play is just for guests and members. ⊠ *501 E. Camino Real* ☎ *561/447–3078* ⊕ *www. bocaresort.com.*

Red Reef Park Executive Golf Course. These 9 Intracoastal- and oceanfront holes, between 54 and 227 yards each, are great for a quick round. The greens fees range from $16.25 to walk in the off-season to $25.75 with a cart in season. Park in the lot across the street from the main beach entrance, and put the greens fees receipt on the dash; that covers parking. ⊠ *1221 N. Ocean Blvd.* ☎ *561/391–5014* ⊕ *www.bocacitygolf.com.*

SCUBA AND SNORKELING

Force-E. This company rents, sells, and repairs scuba and snorkeling equipment—and organizes about 80 dive trips a week throughout the region. The PADI–affiliated five-star center has instruction for all levels and offers private charters, too. ⊠ *2181 N. Federal Hwy.* ☎ *561/368– 0555, 866/307–3483* ⊕ *www.force-e.com.*

TREASURE COAST

In contrast to the glitzy, über-planned Gold Coast that includes Greater Palm Beach and Boca Raton, the more bucolic Treasure Coast stretches from northernmost Palm Beach County into Martin, St. Lucie, and Indian River counties. Along the east are barrier islands all the way to Sebastian and beyond, starting with Jupiter Island, then Hutchinson Island, and finally Orchid Island—and reefs, too. Those reefs are responsible for the region's nickname: they've caused ships carrying riches dating back as far as 1715 to fall asunder and cast their treasures ashore. The Intracoastal Waterway here is called the Indian River starting at the St. Lucie Inlet in Stuart and morphs into a broad tidal lagoon with tiny uninhabited islands and wildlife galore. Inland, there's cattle ranching and tracts of pine and palmetto scrub, along with sugar and citrus production.

Despite a growing number of malls and beachfront condominiums, much of the Treasure Coast remains untouched, something not lost on ecotourists, game fishers, and people who want a break from the over-saturated digital age. Consequently, there are fewer lodging options in this region of Florida, but if 30 minutes in the car sounds like a breeze, culture vultures can live in the lap of luxury in Vero Beach and detour south to Fort Pierce's galleries and botanical gardens. Likewise, families will revel in every amenity imaginable at the Hutchinson Island Marriott and be able to swing northwest to hit up the Mets spring-training stadium in Port St. Lucie or down to Jupiter for the Cardinals and the Marlins.

JUPITER AND VICINITY

12 miles north of West Palm Beach.

Jupiter is one of the few towns in the region not fronted by an island, and it's still quite close to the fantastic hotels, shopping, and dining of the Palm Beach area. The beaches here are on the mainland, and Route A1A runs for almost 4 miles along the beachfront dunes and beautiful homes.

Northeast across the Jupiter Inlet from Jupiter is the southern tip of Jupiter Island, which stretches about 15 miles to the St. Lucie Inlet. Here expansive and expensive estates often retreat from the road behind screens of vegetation, and the population dwindles the farther north you go. At the very north end, sea turtles come to nest. To the west, on the mainland, is the little community of Hobe Sound.

GETTING HERE AND AROUND
If you're coming from the airport in West Palm Beach, take I–95 to Route 706. Otherwise, Federal Highway (U.S. 1) and A1A are usually more convenient.

Contacts Palm Beach County Convention and Visitors Bureau
✉ *1555 Palm Beach Lakes Blvd., Suite 800, West Palm Beach* ☏ *800/554–7256* ⊕ *www.palmbeachfl.com.*

EXPLORING

Fodor's Choice
★

Blowing Rocks Preserve. Managed by the Nature Conservancy, this protected area on Jupiter Island is headlined by an almost otherworldly looking limestone shelf that fringes South Florida's most turquoise waters. Also protected within its 73 acres are plants native to beachfront dunes, coastal strand (the landward side of the dunes), mangrove swamps, and tropical hardwood forests. There are two short walking trails on the Intracoastal side of the preserve, as well as an education center and a butterfly garden. The best time to come and seeing the "blowing rocks" is when a storm is brewing: If high tides and strong offshore winds coincide, the sea blows spectacularly through the holes in the eroded outcropping. During a calm summer day, you can swim in crystal clear waters on the mile-long beach and climb around the rock formations at low tide. Park in one of the two lots because police ticket cars on the road. ✉ *574 S. Beach Rd., CR 707, Hobe Sound* ☏ *561/744–6668* ⊕ *www.nature.org/blowingrocks* ✉ *$2* ☼ *Daily 9–4:30.*

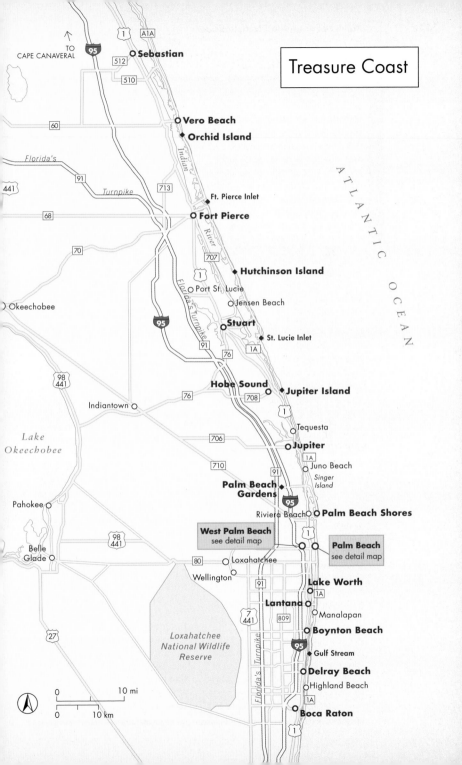

Treasure Coast

TO CAPE CANAVERAL

95 1 A1A

512 Sebastian
510

60 Vero Beach
Orchid Island

Florida's

91 Turnpike

441

713

68

70 Ft. Pierce Inlet

Fort Pierce

707

Florida's Turnpike

95

1 Port St. Lucie
Hutchinson Island

Jensen Beach

Okeechobee Stuart

91 St. Lucie Inlet
76 1A

Hobe Sound

76 Jupiter Island
708

Indiantown 1
Tequesta

706

Lake Okeechobee Jupiter
710 1A
Juno Beach

91 Singer Island

Pahokee Palm Beach
Gardens
95

Belle Riviera Beach Palm Beach Shores
Glade 98
441
West Palm Beach
see detail map

80 Loxahatchee Palm Beach
Wellington see detail map

91 Lake Worth
1A

7 Lantana
441 809 Manalapan

Loxahatchee Boynton Beach
National Wildlife 95
Reserve Gulf Stream

27 Delray Beach

Highland Beach
1A

0   10 mi

0   10 km Boca Raton
1

ATLANTIC OCEAN

Florida's Turnpike

CLOSE UP

Florida's Sea Turtles: The Nesting Season

From May to October turtles nest all along the Florida coast. Female loggerhead, Kemp's ridley, and other species living in the Atlantic Ocean or Gulf of Mexico swim as much as 2,000 miles to the Florida shore. By night they drag their 100- to 400-pound bodies onto the beach to the dune line. Then each digs a hole with her flippers, drops in 100 or so eggs, covers them up, and returns to sea.

The babies hatch about 60 days later. Once they burst out of the sand, the hatchlings must get to sea rapidly or risk becoming dehydrated from the sun or being caught by crabs, birds, or other predators.

Instinctively, baby turtles head toward bright light, probably because for millions of years starlight or moonlight reflected on the waves was the brightest light around, serving to guide hatchlings to water. But now light from beach development can lead the babies in the wrong direction, toward the street rather than the water. To help, many coastal towns enforce light restrictions during nesting months. Florida homeowners are asked to dim their lights on behalf of baby sea turtles.

At night, volunteers walk the beaches, searching for signs of turtle nests. Upon finding telltale scratches in the sand, they cordon off the sites, so beachgoers will leave the spots undisturbed. Volunteers also keep watch over nests when babies are about to hatch and assist if the hatchlings get disoriented.

It's a hazardous world for baby turtles. They can die after eating tar balls or plastic debris, or they can be gobbled by sharks or circling birds. Only about one in a thousand survives to adulthood. After reaching the water, the babies make their way to warm currents. East Coast hatchlings drift into the Gulf Stream, spending years floating around the Atlantic.

Males never return to land, but when females attain maturity, in 15–20 years, they return to shore to lay eggs. Remarkably, even after migrating hundreds and even thousands of miles out at sea, most return to the very beach where they were born to deposit their eggs. Each time they nest, they come back to the same stretch of beach. In fact, the more they nest, the more accurate they get, until eventually they return time and again to within a few feet of where they last laid their eggs. These incredible navigation skills remain for the most part a mystery despite intense scientific study.

Several local organizations offer nightly turtle walks during nesting season. Most are in June and July, starting around 8 pm and sometimes lasting until midnight. Expect a $10 to $15 fee. Call in advance to confirm times and to reserve a spot—places usually take reservations as early as April. If you're in southern Palm Beach County, contact Boca Raton's **Gumbo Limbo Nature Center** (☎ 561/338–1473 ⊕ www.gumbolimbo.org). The **John D. MacArthur Beach State Park** (☎ 561/624–6952 ⊕ www.macarthurbeach.org) is convenient for Palm Beach–area visitors at the northern end of Singer Island. **Hobe Sound Nature Center** (☎ 772/546–2067 ⊕ www.hobesoundnaturecenter.com) is farther up. Treasure Coasters in or near Vero Beach can go to **Sebastian Inlet State Park** (☎ 321/984–4852 ⊕ www.floridastateparks.org/sebastianinlet).

Away from developed shorelines, Blowing Rocks Preserve on Jupiter Island lets you wander the dunes.

FAMILY **Hobe Sound Nature Center.** Though located in the Hobe Sound National Wildlife Refuge, this nature center is an independent organization. The exhibit hall houses live baby alligators, crocodiles, a scary-looking tarantula, and more—and is a child's delight. Among the center's more popular events are the annual nighttime sea turtle walks, held between May and June; reservations are accepted as early as April 1. Just off the center's entrance is a mile-long nature trail loop that snakes through three different kinds of habitats: coastal hammock, estuary beach, and sand pine scrub, which is one of Florida's most unusual and endangered plant communities and what composes much of the refuge's nearly 250 acres. ✉ *13640 S.E. U.S. 1, Hobe Sound* ☎ *772/546–2067* ⊕ *www.hobesoundnaturecenter.com* ✆ *Free (donation requested)* ⊙ *Mon.–Sat. 9–3.*

Jonathan Dickinson State Park. This serene state park provides a glimpse of predevelopment "real" Florida. A beautiful showcase of Florida inland habitat, the park teems with endangered gopher tortoises and manatees. From Hobe Mountain, an ancient dune topped with a tower, you are treated to a panoramic view of this park's more than 11,000 acres of varied terrain and the Intracoastal Waterway. The Loxahatchee River, which cuts through the park, is home to plenty of charismatic manatees in winter and alligators year-round; two-hour boat tours of the river depart daily (see ⇨ *Jonathan Dickinson State Park River Tours*). Kayak rentals are available, as is horseback riding (it was reintroduced after a 30-year absence). Among the amenities are a dozen newly redone cabins for rent, tent sites, bicycle and hiking trails, two established campgrounds and some primitive campgrounds, and a snack bar. Don't skip the Elsa Kimbell Environmental Education and Research Center, which has interactive displays, exhibits, and a short film on the natural history of the area. The park is also a fantastic birding location, with about 150 species to spot. ⊠ *16450 S.E. U.S. 1, Hobe Sound* ☎ *772/546–2771* ⊕ *www.floridastateparks.org/jonathandickinson* 🚗 *Vehicles $6, bicyclists and pedestrians $2* ☉ *Daily 8–sunset; Elsa Kimbell Environmental Education and Research Center daily 9–5.*

Fodor'sChoice ★ **Jupiter Inlet Lighthouse & Museum.** Designed by Civil War hero Lieutenant George Gordon Meade, this brick lighthouse has been under the Coast Guard's purview since 1860. Tours of the 108-foot-tall landmark are held approximately every half-hour and are included with admission. (Children must be at least 4 feet tall to go to the top.) The museum tells about efforts to restore this graceful spire to the way it looked from 1860 to 1918; its galleries and outdoor structures, including a pioneer home, also showcase local history dating back 5,000 years. ⊠ *Lighthouse Park, 500 Capt. Armour's Way* ☎ *561/747–8380* ⊕ *www. jupiterlighthouse.org* 🚗 *$9* ☉ *Jan.–Apr., daily 10–5; May–Dec., Tues.– Sun. 10–5. Last tour at 4.*

BEACHES

Carlin Park. About ½ mile south of the Jupiter Beach Resort and Indiantown Road, the quiet beach here is just one draw; otherwise, the manicured park, which straddles A1A, is chock-full of activities and amenities. Two bocce ball courts, six lighted tennis courts, a baseball diamond, a wood-chip-lined running path, and an amphitheater that hosts free concerts and Shakespeare productions are just some of the highlights. Locals also swear by the Lazy Loggerhead Café that's right off the seaside parking lot for a great casual breakfast and lunch. **Amenities:** lifeguards; food and drink; parking (free); toilets; showers. **Best for:** swimming; walking. ⊠ *400 S. Rte. A1A* ⊕ *www.pbcgov.com/parks/ locations/carlin.htm.*

Fodor'sChoice ★ **Jupiter Beach.** Famous throughout all of Florida for a unique pooch-loving stance, the town of Jupiter's beach welcomes Yorkies, Labs, pugs—you name it—along its 2½-mile oceanfront. Dogs can frolic unleashed or join you for a dip. Free parking spots line A1A in front of the sandy stretch, and there are multiple access points and continuously refilled dog-bag boxes (29 to be exact). The dog beach starts on Marcinski Road (Beach Marker #25) and continues north until Beach Marker #5. Before going, read through the guidelines posted on the Friends of Jupiter Beach website; the biggest things to note are be sure to clean up after your dog and to steer clear of lifeguarded areas to the north and south. **Amenities:** toilets; showers. **Best for:** walking. ⊠ *2188 Marcinski Rd., across street from parking lot* ☎ *561/748–8140* ⊕ *www. friendsofjupiterbeach.com.*

Hobe Sound National Wildlife Refuge. Nature lovers seeking to get as far as possible from the madding crowds will feel at peace at this refuge managed by the U.S. Fish & Wildlife service. It's a haven for people who want some quiet while they walk around and photograph the gorgeous coastal sand dunes, where turtle nests and shells often wash ashore. The beach has been severely eroded by high tides and strong winds (surprisingly, surfing is allowed and many do partake). You can't actually venture within most of the 735 protected acres, so if hiking piques your interest, head to the refuge's main entrance a few miles away on Hobe Sound (✉ *13640 S.E. U.S. 1 in Hobe Sound*) for a mile-long trek close to the nature center, or to nearby Jonathan Dickinson State Park (*16450 S.E. U.S. 1 in Hobe Sound*). **Amenities:** parking (fee); toilets. **Best for:** solitude; surfing; walking. ✉ *198 N. Beach Rd., at end of N. Beach Rd., Jupiter Island* ☎ *772/546–6141* ⊕ *www.fws. gov/hobesound* ☞ *$5.*

WHERE TO EAT

$$ ✕ **Guanabanas.** Expect a wait for dinner, which is not necessarily a bad

SEAFOOD thing at this island paradise of a waterfront restaurant and bar. Take the wait time to explore the bridges and trails of the open-air tropical oasis and nibble on some conch fritters at the large tiki bar until your table is ready. Try the lemon-butter hogfish for dinner and stick around for the live music (a full concert calendar is on the website). Breakfast, offered only on weekends, is good, too. That said, it's more about the view than the food here. $ *Average main: $18* ✉ *960 N. Rte. A1A* ☎ *561/747–8878* ⊕ *www.guanabanas.com* ☜ *Reservations not accepted.*

$$ ✕ **Little Moir's Food Shack.** This local favorite is not much to look at and

SEAFOOD a bit tricky to find, but worth the search. The fried-food standards you

Fodor's Choice might expect at such a casual place that uses plastic utensils are not

★ found on the menu; instead there are fried tuna rolls with basil, and panko-crusted fried oysters with spicy fruit salad. A variety of beers are fun to pair with the creatively prepared seafood dishes that include wahoo, mahimahi, and snapper. $ *Average main: $17* ✉ *103 S. U.S. 1* ☎ *561/741–3626* ⊕ *www.littlemoirs.com/food-shack* ☜ *Reservations not accepted* ⊘ *Closed Sun.*

$$$ ✕ **Sinclairs Ocean Grill.** Remodeled in late 2012 to give it a slick, con-

SEAFOOD temporary look, this upscale restaurant at the Jupiter Beach Resort & Spa is a favorite of locals in the know. The menu has a daily selection of fresh fish, such as Atlantic black grouper over lemon crab salad, sesame-seared tuna, and mahimahi with fruit salsa. There are also thick, juicy cuts of meat, including New York strip steak and beef tenderloin, as well as mouthwatering chicken and lamb dishes. The new Sinclairs Lounge is idyllic for a predinner aperitif. For something more casual, dine outside on the terrace to hear the waves lapping and take in the beachscape. $ *Average main: $21* ✉ *Jupiter Beach Resort, 5 N. Rte. A1A* ☎ *561/746–2511* ⊕ *www.jupiterbeachresort.com.*

$$ ✕ **Taste Casual Dining.** Located in the center of historic Hobe Sound, this

AMERICAN cozy dining spot with a pleasant, screened-in patio offers piano dinner music on Fridays. Locals like to hang out at the old, English-style wine bar; however, the food itself is the biggest draw here. Try a lobster roll and the signature Gorgonzola salad for lunch, and any fish dish for dinner. On weekend nights, order the excellent, slow-cooked prime rib, another specialty. $ *Average main: $16* ✉ *11750 S.E. Dixie Hwy., Hobe Sound* ☎ *772/546–1129* ⊕ *www.tastehobesound.com* ⊘ *May– Oct., closed Sun.*

6

WHERE TO STAY

For expanded reviews, facilities, and current deals, visit Fodors.com.

$$$$ RESORT **Jupiter Beach Resort & Spa.** Families love this nine-story hotel filled with rich Caribbean-style rooms containing mahogany sleigh beds and armoires; all rooms have balconies, and many have stunning views of the ocean and local landmarks like the Jupiter Lighthouse and Juno Pier. **Pros:** fantastic beachside pool area with hammocks and a fire pit; marble showers; great restaurant. **Cons:** $25 nightly resort fee; no covered parking; bathtubs only in suites. [$] *Rooms from: $309* ✉ *5 N. Rte. A1A* ☎ *561/746–2511, 800/228–8810* 🌐 *www.jupiterbeachresort.com* 🛏 *134 rooms, 34 suites* 🍴 *No meals.*

SPORTS AND THE OUTDOORS

BASEBALL

Roger Dean Stadium. It's a spring training doubleheader! Both the St. Louis Cardinals and the Miami Marlins call this 6,600-seat facility home base from February to April. The rest of the year two minor league teams (Jupiter Hammerheads and Palm Beach Cardinals) share its turf. In the Abacoa area of Jupiter, the grounds are surrounded by a mix of restaurants and sports bars for pre- and postgame action. ✉ *4751 Main St.* ☎ *561/775–1818* 🌐 *www.rogerdeanstadium.com.*

BOATING AND CANOEING

Fodor's Choice ★ **Canoe Outfitters of Florida.** See animals, from otters to eagles, along 8 miles of the Loxahatchee River in Riverbend County Park daily except Tuesday and Wednesday. Canoe and kayak rentals are $26.50 for four hours. Bike rentals are available, too. ✉ *Riverbend County Park, 9060 W. Indiantown Rd.* ☎ *561/746–7053* 🌐 *www.canoeoutfittersofflorida.com.*

Jonathan Dickinson State Park River Tours. Boat tours of the Loxahatchee River and guided horseback rides, along with canoe, kayak, bicycle, and boat rentals are offered daily. The popular Wilderness Guided Boat Tour leaves four times daily at 9, 11, 1, and 3 pm and costs $18.87 (for best wildlife photos take the 11 or 1 tour). The pontoon cruises up the Loxahatchee in search of manatees, herons, osprey, alligators, and more. The skipper details the region's natural and cultural history; and from Thursday to Monday the boat also stops at the Trapper Nelson Interpretive Site for a tour of the home of a local legend, the so-called "Wildman" of the Loxahatchee. ✉ *Jonathan Dickinson State Park, 16450 S.E. U.S. 1, Hobe Sound* ☎ *561/746–1466* 🌐 *www.floridaparktours.com.*

GOLF

Abacoa Golf Club. This Joe Lee-designed 18-hole course with range is on par with nearby private courses; the greens fee ranges from $30 to $89 (including cart), depending on time of year, time of day, and weekday versus weekend. ✉ *105 Barbados Dr.* ☎ *561/622–0036* 🌐 *www.abacoagolfclub.com.*

Golf Club of Jupiter. There are 18 holes of varying difficulty at this championship, public course; the greens fee ranges from $29 to $69 (including cart). ✉ *1800 S. Central Blvd.* ☎ *561/747–6262* 🌐 *www.golfclubofjupiter.com.*

STUART AND JENSEN BEACH

10 miles north of Hobe Sound.

The compact town of Stuart lies on a peninsula that juts out into the St. Lucie River off the Indian River and has a remarkable amount of shoreline for its size. It scores huge points for its charming historic district and is the self-described "Sailfish Capital of the World." On the southern end, you'll find Port Salerno and its waterfront area, the Manatee Pocket, which are a skip away from the St. Lucie Inlet.

Immediately north of Stuart is down-to-earth Jensen Beach. Both Stuart and Jensen Beach straddle the Indian River and occupy Hutchinson Island, the barrier island that continues into the town of Fort Pierce. Between late April and August, hundreds, even thousands, of turtles come here to nest along the Atlantic beaches. Residents have taken pains to curb the runaway development that has created commercial crowding to the north and south, although some high-rises have popped up along the shore.

GETTING HERE AND AROUND

To get to Stuart and Jensen Beach from Jupiter and Hobe Sound, drive north on Federal Highway (U.S. 1). Route A1A crosses through downtown Stuart and is the sole main road throughout Hutchinson Island. Route 707 runs parallel on the mainland directly across the tidal lagoon.

ESSENTIALS

Visitor Information Martin County Convention & Visitors Bureau ⊠ *101 S.W. Flagler Ave.* ☎ *772/288–5451, 877/585–0085* ⊕ *www.discovermartin.com.*

EXPLORING

Strict architectural and zoning standards guide civic-renewal projects in the heart of Stuart. Antiques stores, restaurants, and more than 50 specialty shops are rooted within the two-block area of Flagler Avenue and Osceola Street north of where A1A cuts across the peninsula (visit ⊕ *www.stuartmainstreet.org* for more information). A self-guided walking-tour pamphlet is available at assorted locations to clue you in on this once-small fishing village's early days.

Elliott Museum. Opened in March 2013, the museum's glittering new, green-certified 48,000-square-foot facility is double its previous size and houses a permanent collection along with traveling exhibits. The original museum was founded in 1961 in honor of Sterling Elliott, an inventor of an early automated-addressing machine, the egg crate, and a four-wheel bicycle, and it celebrates history, art, and technology, much of it viewed through the lens of the automobile's effect on American society. There's an impressive array of antique cars, plus paintings, historic artifacts, and nostalgic goods like vintage baseball cards and toys. ⊠ *825 N.E. Ocean Blvd., Jensen Beach* ☎ *772/225–1961* ⊕ *www. elliottmuseumfl.org* ⏴ *$12* ⏲ *Daily 10–5.*

FAMILY **Florida Oceanographic Coastal Center.** This hydroland is the place to go for an interactive marine experience and live the center's mission "to inspire environmental stewardship of Florida's coastal ecosystems through education and research." Petting and feeding stingrays can be done at various times; in the morning, a sea turtle program introduces you to three full-time residents. Make sure to catch the "feeding frenzy" when keepers toss food into the 750,000-gallon lagoon tank and sharks, tarpon, and snook swarm the surface. Join a 1-mile guided walk through the coastal hardwood hammock and mangrove swamp habitats, or explore the trails on your own—you may see a dolphin or manatee swim by. ✉ *890 N.E. Ocean Blvd.* ☎ *772/225–0505* 🌐 *www.floridaocean.org* 🎟 *$10* 🕒 *Mon.–Sat. 10–5, Sun. noon–4. Nature trails close at 4.*

Gilbert's House of Refuge Museum. Built in 1875 on Hutchinson Island, this is the only remaining example of ten such structures that were erected by the U.S. Life-Saving Service (a predecessor of the Coast Guard) to aid stranded sailors. The displays here include antique life-saving equipment, maps, artifacts from nearby wrecks, and boatbuilding tools. The museum is affiliated with the nearby Elliott Museum. ✉ *301 S.E. MacArthur Blvd., Jensen Beach* ☎ *772/225–1875* 🌐 *www.houseofrefugefl.org* 🎟 *$8* 🕒 *Mon.–Sat. 10–4, Sun. 1–4.*

Stuart Heritage Museum. What started off in 1901 as the tin-roofed George W. Parks General Merchandise Store and in 1946 became Stuart's feed and garden store (the name is still emblazoned on the pine facade) is now the Stuart Heritage Museum, an interesting trip down nostagia lane with Americana artifacts and goods detailing the town's history, just steps from city hall. ✉ *161 S.W. Flagler Ave.* ☎ *772/220–4600* 🌐 *www.stuartheritagemuseum.com* 🎟 *Free* 🕒 *Daily 10–3.*

BEACHES

FAMILY **Stuart Beach.** When the waves robustly roll in, the surfers are rolling in, too. Beginning surfers are especially keen on Stuart Beach because of its ever-vigilant lifeguards, and pros to the sport like the challenges that the choppy waters here bring. Families enjoy the snack bar known for its chicken fingers, the basketball courts, the large canopy-covered playground, and the three walkways interspersed throughout the area for easy ocean access. For those who like a dose of culture with their day in the sand, the Elliott Museum is steps from the beach. **Amenities:** lifeguards; food and drink; parking (free); showers; toilets. **Best for:** surfing; swimming. ✉ *889 N.E. Ocean Blvd.* 🕒 *Daily 24 hrs.*

WHERE TO EAT

$$$ SEAFOOD 🍴 **Conchy Joe's.** Like a hermit crab sliding into a new shell, Conchy Joe's moved up from West Palm Beach in 1983 to its current home, a 1920s rustic stilt house on the Indian River. It's full of antique fish mounts, gator hides, and snakeskins and is a popular tourist spot—but the waterfront location, casual vibe, and delicious seafood lures locals, too. Grouper marsala, coconut shrimp, and fried Bahamian cracked conch are menu fixtures, and live reggae gets people out of their shells Thursday through Sunday. [$] *Average main: $27* ✉ *3945 N.E. Indian River Dr., Jensen Beach* ☎ *772/334–1130* 🌐 *www.conchyjoes.com.*

$$$ FRENCH 🍴 **Courtine's.** A husband-and-wife team oversees this quiet and hospitable restaurant under the Roosevelt Bridge. French and American influences are clear in the Swiss chef's dishes, from rack of lamb with Dijon mustard to grilled filet mignon stuffed with Roquefort and fresh spinach. The formal dining room has subtle, elegant touches, such as votive

candlelight and white tablecloths. A more casual menu is available at the bar. $ *Average main: $25* ⊠ *514 N. Dixie Hwy.* ☎ *772/692–3662* ⊕ *www.courtines.com* ☾ *Closed Sun. and Mon. No lunch.*

$$$
ECLECTIC

✕ **11 Maple Street.** This cozy spot is as good as it gets on the Treasure Coast. Soft music and a friendly staff set the mood in the antiques-filled dining room, which holds only 21 tables. An extensive list of small plates can be ordered as starters or mains and include tasty treats like black-rice calamari fritters with Thai sauce and Wagyu hanger steak with onion rings and salsa verde. The limited but superb selection of entrées include wood-grilled venison with onion-potato hash and beef tenderloin with white-truffle-and-chive butter. All desserts are made from scratch and are also seductive, including white-chocolate custard with blackberry sauce. $ *Average main: $22* ⊠ *3224 N.E. Maple Ave., Jensen Beach* ☎ *772/334–7714* ⊕ *www.11maplestreet.net* ⌦ *Reservations essential* ☾ *Closed Mon. and Tues. No lunch.*

WHERE TO STAY

For expanded reviews, facilities, and current deals, visit Fodors.com.

$$
RESORT
FAMILY

⌂ **Hutchinson Island Marriott Beach Resort & Marina.** With a 77-slip marina, a full water sports program, a golf course, tons of tennis courts, and children's activities, this self-contained resort is excellent for families, most of whom prefer to stay in the tower directly on the ocean. **Pros:** attentive, warm staff; rooms are comfortable and casually chic; all rooms have balconies. **Cons:** only one sit-down indoor restaurant; common areas are a bit dated; no spa; extra charge for parking. $ *Rooms from: $249* ⊠ *555 N.E. Ocean Blvd., Hutchinson Island* ☎ *772/225–3700, 800/775–5936* ⊕ *www.marriott.com* ⟿ *204 rooms, 70 suites* ⦙◯⦙ *No meals.*

$
RESORT

⌂ **Pirate's Cove Resort & Marina.** This cozy enclave on the banks of the Manatee Pocket with ocean access at the southern end of Stuart is the perfect place to set forth on a day at sea or wind down after one—it's relaxing and casual, and has amenities like a swimming pool courtyard, restaurant, and fitness center. **Pros:** spacious tropical-themed rooms; great for boaters, with a 50-slip full-service marina; each room has a balcony overlooking the water; free Wi-Fi and parking. **Cons:** lounge gets noisy at night; decor and furnishings are pretty but not luxurious; pool is on the small side. $ *Rooms from: $160* ⊠ *4307 S.E. Bayview St., Port Salerno* ☎ *772/287–2500* ⊕ *www.piratescoveresort.com* ⟿ *50 rooms* ⦙◯⦙ *Breakfast.*

SHOPPING

More than 60 restaurants and shops with antiques, art, and fashion have opened downtown along Osceola Street.

B&A Flea Market. A short drive from downtown and operating for more than two decades, the oldest and largest flea market on the Treasure Coast has a street-bazaar feel, with shoppers happily scouting the 500 vendors for the practical and unusual. ⊠ *2885 S.E. U.S. 1* ☎ *772/288–4915* ⊕ *www.bafleamarket.com* ▱ *Free* ☾ *Weekends 8–3.*

SPORTS AND THE OUTDOORS

FISHING

Sailfish Marina of Stuart. Nab a deep-sea charter here, the closest public marina to the St. Lucie Inlet. ⊠ *3565 S.E. St. Lucie Blvd.* ☎ *772/283–1122* ⊕ *www.sailfishmarinastuart.com.*

FORT PIERCE AND PORT ST. LUCIE

11 miles north of Jensen Beach.

About an hour north of Palm Beach, Fort Pierce has a distinctive rural feel—but it has a surprising number of worthwhile attractions for a town of its size, including those easily seen while following Route 707 on the mainland (A1A on Hutchinson Island). A big draw is an inlet that offers fabulous fishing and excellent surfing. Nearby Port St. Lucie is largely landlocked southwest of Fort Pierce and is almost equidistant from there and Jensen Beach. It's not a big tourist area except for two sports facilities near I–95: the Mets' training grounds, Tradition Field, and the PGA Village. If you want a hotel directly on the sand or crave more than simple, motel-like accommodations, stay elsewhere and drive up for the day.

GETTING HERE AND AROUND

You can reach Fort Pierce from Jensen Beach by driving 11 miles north on Federal Highway (U.S. 1), Route 707, or A1A. To get to Port St. Lucie, continue north on U.S. 1 and take Prima Vista Boulevard west. From Fort Pierce, Route 709 goes diagonally southwest to Port St. Lucie, and I–95 is another choice.

ESSENTIALS

Visitor Information St. Lucie County Tourist Development Council ✉ *2300 Virginia Ave.* ☎ *800/344–8443* ⊕ *www.visitstluciefla.com.*

EXPLORING

A.E. Backus Museum & Gallery. Works by one of Florida's foremost landscape artists, Albert Ernest Backus (1906–90), are on display at this museum. It also mounts changing exhibits and offers exceptional buys on paintings, pottery, and jewelry by local artists. ✉ *500 N. Indian River Dr.* ☎ *772/465–0630* ⊕ *www.backusgallery.com* 🖼 *$2* ⊙ *Oct.–June, Wed.–Sat. 10–4, Sun. noon–4; summer hrs by appointment.*

Heathcote Botanical Gardens. Stroll through this 3½-acre green space, which includes a palm walk, a Japanese garden, and a collection of 100 bonsai trees. There is also a gift shop with whimsical and botanical knickknacks. Guided tours are available by appointment for an extra fee. ✉ *210 Savannah Rd.* ☎ *772/464–4672* ⊕ *www.heathcotebotanicalgardens.org* 🖼 *$6* ⊙ *Tues.–Sat. 9–5, Sun. 1–5 (Nov.–Apr.).*

National Navy UDT-SEAL Museum. Commemorating the more than 3,000 troops who trained on these shores during World War II when this elite military unit got its start, there are weapons, vehicles, and equipment on view. Exhibits honor all frogmen and underwater demolition teams and depict their history. The museum houses the lifeboat from which SEALs saved the *Maersk Alabama* captain from Somali pirates in 2009. ✉ *3300 N. Rte. A1A* ☎ *772/595–5845* ⊕ *www.navysealmuseum.com* 🖼 *$8* ⊙ *Tues.–Sat. 10–4, Sun. noon–4.*

FAMILY   **Savannas Recreation Area.** Once a reservoir, the 550 acres have been returned to their natural wetlands state. Today the wilderness area has trails and a boat ramp; camping along with canoe and kayak rentals are available October through May. ✉ *1400 E. Midway Rd.* ☎ *772/464–7855* ⊕ *www.stlucieco.gov/parks/savannas.htm* 🖼 *Free* ⊙ *Daily 6 am–7:30 pm.*

BEACHES

Fort Pierce Inlet State Park. Across the inlet at the northern side of Hutchinson Island, a fishing oasis lures beachgoers who can't wait to reel in snook, flounder, and bluefish, among others. The park is also known as a prime wave-riding locale, thanks to a reef that lies just outside the jetty. Summer is the busiest season by a long shot, but don't be fooled: it's a laid-back place to sun and surf. There are covered picnic tables but no concessions; however, from where anglers perch, a bunch of casual restaurants can be spotted on the other side of the inlet that are a quick drive away. **Amenities:** toilets; showers; parking (fee); lifeguards (summer only). **Best for:** surfing; walking; solitude. ✉ *905 Shorewinds Dr.* ☎ *772/468–3985* 🌐 *www.floridastateparks.org/fortpierceinlet* 🎟 *Vehicle $6, bicyclists and pedestrians $2* 🕒 *Daily 8–sunset.*

WHERE TO EAT

$$ SEAFOOD 🍴 **Mangrove Mattie's.** This no-frills spot on Fort Pierce Inlet provides dazzling waterfront views and delicious seafood. Dine on the terrace or in the dining room, and don't forget to try the coconut-fried shrimp or the shrimp scampi. Happy hour (daily 3 to 7) features roast beef or ham sandwiches, or oysters, clams and shrimp. Many locals come by for the Champagne Sunday brunch. [$] *Average main: $20* ✉ *1640 Seaway Dr.* ☎ *772/466–1044* 🌐 *www.mangrovematties.com.*

WHERE TO STAY

For expanded reviews, facilities, and current deals, visit Fodors.com.

$ 🏨 **Dockside Inn.** This hotel is the best of the lodgings lining the scenic Fort Pierce Inlet on Seaway Drive (and that's not saying much); it's a practical base for fishing enthusiasts with nice touches like two pools and a waterfront restaurant. **Pros:** good value; overnight boat docking available; reasonable rates at marina; parking included. **Cons:** basic decor; some steps to climb; grounds are nothing too fancy but have great views. [$] *Rooms from: $99* ✉ *1160 Seaway Dr.* ☎ *772/468–3555, 800/286–1745* 🌐 *www.docksideinn.com* 🛏 *35 rooms* 🍽 *Breakfast.*

SPORTS AND THE OUTDOORS

BASEBALL

Tradition Field. Out west by I–95, this Port St. Lucie baseball stadium, formerly known as Digital Domain Park as well as Thomas J. White Stadium, is where the New York Mets train; it's also the home of the St. Lucie Mets minor league team. ✉ *525 N.W. Peacock Blvd., Port St. Lucie* ☎ *772/871–2115.*

GOLF

PGA Village. Owned and operated by the PGA of America, the national association of teaching pros, it's the winter home to many Northern instructors along with permanent staff. The facility is a little off the beaten path and the clubhouse is basic, but serious golfers will appreciate the three championship courses by Pete Dye and Tom Fazio (greens fee $119/$55 including cart), and the chance to sharpen their skills at the 35-acre PGA Center for Golf Learning and Performance that has nine practice bunkers mimicking sands and slopes from around the globe. ✉ *1916 Perfect Dr., Port St. Lucie* ☎ *772/467–1300, 800/800–4653* 🌐 *www.pgavillage.com.*

6

SCUBA DIVING

The region's premier dive site is actually on the National Register of Historic Places. The *Urca de Lima* was part of the storied treasure fleet bound for Spain that was destroyed by a hurricane in 1715. It's now part of an underwater archaeological preserve about 200 yards from shore, just north of the National Navy UDT-SEAL Museum and under 10 to 15 feet of water. The remains contain a flat-bottom, round-bellied ship and cannons that can be visited on an organized dive trip.

Dive Odyssea. This shop offers tank rentals and scuba lessons; guided excursions can be arranged to dive sites like nearby reefs or the *Urca de Lima Underwater Archaeological Preserve*, a shipwreck from 1715 that's listed on the National Register of Historic Places. ⊠ *621 N. 2nd St.* ☎ *772/460–1771* ⊕ *www.diveodyssea.com.*

VERO BEACH AND SEBASTIAN

12 miles north of Fort Pierce.

Tranquil and picturesque, these Indian River County towns have a strong commitment to the environment and culture, particularly the upscale yet low-key Vero Beach, which is home to eclectic galleries and even trendy restaurants. Sebastian, a coastal fishing village that feels as remote as possible between Jacksonville and Miami Beach, has plenty of outdoor activities—including those at the Sebastian Inlet State Park, one of Florida's biggest and best recreation areas (and a paradise for surfers). It's actually within the boundaries of the federal government's massive protected Archie Carr National Wildlife Refuge, which encompasses several smaller parks within its boundaries. Downtown Vero is centered on the historic district on 14th Avenue, but much of the fun takes place across the Indian River (aka the Intracoastal Waterway) around Orchid Island's beaches.

GETTING HERE AND AROUND

To get here, you have two basic options—Route A1A along the coast (not to be confused with Ocean Drive, an offshoot on Orchid Island), or either U.S. 1 or Route 605 (also called Old Dixie Highway) on the mainland. As you approach Vero on the latter, you pass through an ungussied-up landscape of small farms and residential areas. On the beach route, part of the drive bisects an unusually undeveloped section of the Florida coast. If flying in, consider Orlando International Airport, which is larger (more flights and lower prices) and a smidge closer than Palm Beach International Airport.

ESSENTIALS

Visitor Information **Indian River County Chamber of Commerce** ⊠ *1216 21st St.* ☎ *772/567–3491* ⊕ *www.indianriverchamber.com.* **Sebastian River Area Chamber of Commerce** ⊠ *700 Main St., Sebastian* ☎ *772/589–5969* ⊕ *www.sebastianchamber.com.*

EXPLORING

Environmental Learning Center. Off of Wabasso Beach Road, the 64 acres here are almost compeletely surrounded by water. In addition to a 600-foot boardwalk through the mangrove shoreline and a 1-mile canoe trail, there are aquariums filled with Indian River creatures. Boat and kayak trips to see the historic Pelican Island rookery are also on offer. Call or check the center's website for times. ✉ *255 Live Oak Dr.* ☎ *772/589–5050* ⊕ *www.discoverelc.org* ✉ *$5* ☉ *Tues.–Fri. 10–4, Sat. 9–4, Sun. 1–4 (summer hrs can vary).*

Fodor'sChoice
★

McKee Botanical Garden. On the National Register of Historic Places, the 18-acre plot is a tropical jungle garden—one of the most lush and serene around. This is *the* place to see spectacular water lilies, and the property's original 1932 Hall of Giants, a rustic wooden structure that has stained-glass and bronze bells, contains the world's largest single-plank mahogany table at 35 feet long. There's a Seminole bamboo pavilion, a gift shop, and café, which serves especially tasty snacks and sandwiches. ✉ *350 U.S. 1* ☎ *772/794–0601* ⊕ *www.mckeegarden.org* ✉ *$10* ☉ *Tues.–Sat. 10–5, Sun. noon–5.*

McLarty Treasure Museum. On a National Historic Landmark site on the southern boundary of Sebastian Inlet State Park, this museum underscores the credo: "Wherever gold glitters or silver beckons, man will move mountains." It has displays of coins, weapons, and tools salvaged from the fleet of Spanish treasure ships that sank here in the 1715 storm, leaving some 1,500 survivors struggling to shore between Sebastian and Fort Pierce. The museum sits on the site of the survivors' camp. The museum's last video showing of "The Queen's Jewels and the 1715 Fleet" begins at 3:15. ✉ *Sebastian Inlet State Park, 13180 Rte. A1A, Sebastian* ☎ *772/589–2147* ⊕ *www.floridastateparks.org/ sebastianinlet/activities.cfm* ✉ *$2* ☉ *Daily 10–4.*

Mel Fisher's Treasure Museum. You'll really come upon hidden loot when you enter this place operated by the family of late treasure hunter Mel Fisher. See some of what he recovered in 1985 from the Spanish *Atocha* that sank in 1622 and dumped 100,000 gold coins, Colombian emeralds, and 1,000 silver bars into Florida's high seas—and what his team still salvages each year off the Treasure Coast. The museum certainly piques one's curiosity about what is still buried, and the website is all about the quest for more booty. ✉ *1322 U.S. 1, Sebastian* ☎ *772/589–9875* ⊕ *www.melfisher.com* ✉ *$6.50* ☉ *Mon.–Sat. 10–5, Sun. noon–5* ☉ *Closed Sept.*

Pelican Island National Wildlife Refuge. Founded in 1903 by President Theodore Roosevelt as the country's first national wildlife refuge, the park encompasses the historic Pelican Island rookery itself—a small island in the Indian River Lagoon and important nesting place for 16 species of birds such as endangered wood storks and, of course, brown pelicans—and the land surrounding it overlooking Sebastian. The rookery is a closed wilderness area, so there's no roaming alongside animal kingdom friends; however, there is an 18-foot observation tower across from it with direct views and more than 6 miles of nature trails in the refuge. Another way to explore is via guided kayak tours from the Florida Outdoor Center. ✉ *Rte. A1A, 1 mile north of Treasure Shores Park* ⊹ *Take A1A and turn on Historic Jungle Trail* ☎ *772/581–5557* ⊕ *www.fws.gov/pelicanisland* ✉ *Free* ☉ *Daily 7:30–sunset.*

6

BEACHES

Most of the hotels in the Vero Beach area are clustered around South Beach Park or line Ocean Drive around Beachland Boulevard just north of Humiston Park. Both parks have lifeguards daily. South Beach, at the end of East Causeway Boulevard, is one of the widest, quietest shores on the island, and has plenty of hammock shade before the dunes to picnic in, plus volleyball nets on the beach. Humiston Park is smack-dab in the main commercial zone with restaurants galore, including the lauded Citrus Grillhouse at its southern tip.

Humiston Park. Just south of the Driftwood Resort on Ocean Drive sits Humiston Park, one of the best beaches in town. Parking is free and plentiful, as there's a large lot on Easter Lily Lane and there are spots all over the surrounding business district. The shore is somewhat narrow and there isn't much shade, but the vibrant scene and other amenities make it a great choice for people who crave lots of activity. With lifeguards on call daily, there's a children's playground, plus a ton of hotels, restaurants, bars, and shops within walking distance. **Amenities:** lifeguards; food and drink; toilets; showers. **Best for:** swimming; partiers; sunsets; walking. ⊠ *3000 Ocean Dr., at Easter Lily La.* ☎ *772/231–5790.*

Sebastian Inlet State Park. The 578-acre park, which spans from the tip of Orchid Island across the passage to the barrier island just north, is one of the Florida park system's biggest draws, especially because of the inlet's highly productive fishing waters. Views from either side of the tall bridge are spectacular, and a unique hallmark is that the gates never close—an amazing feature for die-hard anglers who know snook bite better at night. The park has two entrances, the entrance in Vero Beach and the main entrance in Melbourne (⊠ *9700 Rte. A1A*). Within its grounds, you'll discover a wonderful two-story restaurant built in 2012 that overlooks the ocean, a fish and surfing shop (by the way, this place has some of the best waves in the state, but there are also calmer zones for relaxing swims), two museums, guided sea turtle walks in season, 51 campsites with water and electricity, and a marina with powerboat, kayak, and canoe rentals. **Amenities:** food and drink; parking (fee); showers; toilets; water sports. **Best for:** surfing; sunrise; sunset; walking. ⊠ *14251 N. Rte. A1A* ☎ *321/984–4852* ⊕ *www.floridastateparks.org/ sebastianinlet* ⊠ *$8 vehicles with up to 8 people, $4 single drivers, $2 bicyclists and pedestrians* ☉ *Daily 24 hrs (gates never close).*

FAMILY **Wabasso Beach Park.** A favorite for local surfboarding teens and the families at the nearby Disney's Vero Beach Resort, the park is nestled in a residential area at the end of Wabasso Road about 8 miles up from the action on Ocean Drive and 8 miles below the Sebastian Inlet. Aside from regular amenities like picnic tables, restrooms, and a dedicated parking lot (which really is the "park" here—there's not much green space—and it's quite small, so arrive early), the Disney crowd walks there for its lifeguards (the strip directly in front of the hotel is unguarded) and the local crowd appreciates its conveniences, like a pizzeria and a store that sells sundries, snacks, and beach supplies. **Amenities:** food and drink; lifeguards; parking (free); toilets; showers. **Best for:** swimming; surfing. ⊠ *1820 Wabasso Rd.* ☉ *Daily 7–sunset.*

6

WHERE TO EAT

$$$ MODERN AMERICAN Fodor's Choice ★ 🍴 **Citrus Grillhouse.** There are rooms with a view, and then there's this view: uninterrupted sea from a wraparound veranda at the southern end of Humiston Park. Even better, the food here is a straightforward, delicious celebration of fresh and fabulous. One such dish—the fire-roasted baby squid with grilled lemon, garlic, toasted crouton—is an exercise in restraint that you can't help but gobble up. Speaking of gobble-gobble, the herb-roasted breast of turkey sandwich with arugula, tomato, red onion, and red-wine vinaigrette on a toasted sesame roll is the idyllic light lunch on the beach. Sunset lovers (and bargain hunters) rejoice over the three-course prix-fixe menu Monday through Thursday from 5 to 6:30 pm. [$] *Average main: $24* ✉ *Humiston Park, 1050 Easter Lily La.* ☎ *772/234–4114* 🌐 *www.citrusgrillhouse.com.*

$$ DINER FAMILY 🍴 **The Lemon Tree.** If Italy had old school luncheonettes, this is what they'd look like: a storefront of yellow walls, dark-green booths, white linoleum tables, and cascading sconces of faux ivy leaves and hand-painted Tuscan serving pieces for artwork. It's self-described by the husband-wife owners (who are always at the front) as an "upscale diner," and locals swear by it for breakfast, lunch, and dinner (breakfast only on Sunday), so expect a short wait in season at peak hours. There's always a treat on the house, like a glass of sorbet to finish lunch; and don't miss the shrimp scampi after 11 am—the sauce is so good, you'll want to dip every bit of the fresh focaccia in it. [$] *Average main: $19* ✉ *3125 Ocean Dr.* 🌐 *www.lemontreevero.com* 🕒 *No lunch or dinner Sun. No dinner June–Sept.*

$$$ ECLECTIC Fodor's Choice ★ 🍴 **The Tides.** A charming cottage restaurant west of Ocean Drive prepares some of the best food around—not just in Vero Beach, but all of South Florida. The chefs, classically trained, present a trip around the globe through food, but the setting, although effortlessly elegant (think pale blue coral-printed fabrics and a brick fireplace), is down-to-earth. Putting the crab in crab cake, an appetizer's two jumbo patties have scarcely anything but sweet, fresh flesh; the Southern-inspired corn-and-pepper sauce surrounding them is heavenly. For dinner, the inside-out chicken saltimbocca (rolled up, stuffed, and sliced) hits a high note, and the English pudding dessert is perfectly sticky and sweet. To boot, there's a notable wine list. [$] *Average main: $27* ✉ *3103 Cardinal Dr.* ☎ *772/234–3966* 🌐 *www.tidesofvero.com* ✍ *Reservations essential* 🕒 *No lunch.*

WHERE TO STAY

For expanded reviews, facilities, and current deals, visit Fodors.com.

$ RESORT 🏨 **Costa d'Este Beach Resort.** This stylish, contemporary boutique hotel in the heart of Vero's bustling Ocean Drive area has a gorgeous infinity pool overlooking the ocean and a distinctly Miami Beach vibe—just like its famous owners, singer Gloria Estefan and producer Emilio Estefan, who bought the property in 2004. **Pros:** all rooms have balconies or secluded patios; huge Italian marble showers; complimentary signature mojitos on arrival. **Cons:** spa is on small side; rooms have only blackout shades; daily resort fee. [$] *Rooms from: $179* ✉ *3244 Ocean Dr.* ☎ *772/562–9919* 🌐 *www.costadeste.com* 🛏 *94 rooms* 🍽 *No meals.*

$$ RESORT FAMILY **Disney's Vero Beach Resort.** This oceanfront, family-oriented retreat tucked away in a residential stretch of Orchid Island has a retro Old Florida design and not too much Mickey Mouse, which is a welcome surprise for adults. **Pros:** a great pool with waterslide; campfire circle; several dining options on property. **Cons:** far from shopping and dining options; minimal Disney-themed decor. [$] *Rooms from: $245* ✉ *9250 Island Grove Terr.* ☎ *772/234–2000, 407/939–7540* 🌐 *www.disneybeachresorts.com/vero-beach-resort/* 🛏 *181 rooms* 🍴 *No meals.*

$ RESORT FAMILY **The Driftwood Resort.** On the National Register of Historic Places, the two original buildings of this 1935 inn were built entirely from ocean-washed timbers; over time more buildings were added, and all are now decorated with such artifacts as ship's bells, Spanish tiles, and a cannon from a 16th-century Spanish galleon, which create a quirky, utterly charming landscape. **Pros:** central location and right on the beach; free Wi-Fi; laundry facilities; weekly treasure hunt is a blast. **Cons:** older property; rooms can be musty; no-frills furnishings. [$] *Rooms from: $150* ✉ *3150 Ocean Dr.* ☎ *772/231–0550* 🌐 *www.verobeachdriftwood.com* 🛏 *100 rooms* 🍴 *No meals.*

$$$ RESORT Fodor's Choice ★ **Vero Beach Hotel & Spa.** With a sophisticated, relaxed British West Indies feel, this luxurious five-story beachfront hotel at the north end of Ocean Drive is an inviting getaway and, arguably, the best on the Treasure Coast. **Pros:** beautiful pool; complimentary daily wine hour with hors d'oeuvres. **Cons:** separate charge for valet parking; some rooms overlook parking lot. [$] *Rooms from: $309* ✉ *3500 Ocean Dr.* ☎ *772/231–5666* 🌐 *www.verobeachhotelandspa.com* 🛏 *102 rooms* 🍴 *No meals.*

SHOPPING

The place to go when in Vero Beach is **Ocean Drive.** Crossing over to Orchid Island from the mainland, the Merrill P. Barber Bridge turns into Beachland Boulevard; its intersection with Ocean Drive is the heart of a commercial zone with a lively mix of upscale clothing stores, specialty shops, restaurants, and art galleries.

Just under 3 miles north of that roughly eight-block stretch on A1A is a charming outdoor plaza, the **Village Shops.** It's a delight to stroll between the brightly painted cottages that have more unique, high-end offerings.

Back on the mainland, take 21st Street westward and you'll come across a small, modern shopping plaza with some independent shops and national chains. Keep going west on 21st Street, and then park around 14th Avenue to explore a collection of art galleries and eateries in the historic downtown.

SHOPPING CENTERS AND MALLS

Vero Beach Outlets. Just west of I–95 off Route 60 is a discount shopping destination with 50 high-end brand-name stores, including Ann Taylor, Polo Ralph Lauren, Restoration Hardware, White House/Black Market, and Jones New York. ✉ *1824 94th Dr.* ✥ *On Rte. 60, West of I–95 at Exit 147* ☎ *772/770–6097* 🌐 *www.verobeachoutlets.com.*

6

SPORTS AND THE OUTDOORS

BOATING AND FISHING

Most of the region's fishing outfitters are based at the Capt. Hiram's Resort marina in Sebastian.

Big Easy Fishing Charters. Big Easy offers Sebastian off-shore fishing, including guided backwater and deep-sea excursions. ⊠ *Capt. Hiram's Resort, 1606 N. Indian River Dr., Sebastian* ☎ *772/538–1072* ⊕ *www.bigeasyfishingcharter.com.*

Incentive Fishing Charters. These experts on bottom-fishing do ocean trolling as well. ⊠ *Capt. Hiram's Resort, 1606 N. Indian River Dr., Sebastian* ☎ *321/676–1948* ⊕ *www.incentivecharters.com.*

Sebastian Watercraft Rentals. Their fleet ranges from 16-passenger pontoons to jet skis, and the company also organizes fishing charters. ⊠ *Capt. Hiram's Resort, 1606 N. Indian River Dr., Sebastian* ☎ *772/589–5560* ⊕ *www.floridawatercraftrentals.com.*

Skipper Sportfishing Charters. This company offers full- and half-day ocean and river fishing trips. ⊠ *Capt. Hiram's Resort, 1606 N. Indian River Dr., Sebastian* ☎ *772/589–8505* ⊕ *www.skipperfish.com.*

GOLF

Sandridge Golf Club. These two public 18-hole courses designed by Ron Garl allow walking and nine holes in the early morning and later afternoon. Green fees with cart at peak times in winter season are $50; lessons and clinics are also available. ⊠ *5300 73rd St.* ☎ *772/770–5000* ⊕ *www.sandridgegc.com.*

GUIDED TOURS

Florida Outdoor Center. Guided tours explore the area's natural wonders like the Pelican Island National Wildlife Refuge and begin at only $35 per person. The company is mobile and, therefore, flexible; excursions can be done by foot, bike, kayak, or paddleboard. ☎ *772/202–0220* ⊕ *www.floridaoutdoorcenter.com.*

THE TAMPA
BAY AREA

WELCOME TO THE TAMPA BAY AREA

TOP REASONS TO GO

★ **Art gone wild:**
Whether you take the guided tour or chart your own course, experience the one-of-a-kind collection at the Salvador Dalí Museum, which has relocated to a gorgeous waterfront building in downtown St. Petersburg.

★ **Cuban roots:**
You'll find great food and vibrant nightlife in historic Ybor City, just east of downtown Tampa.

★ **Beachcomer bonanza:**
Caladesi Island State Park has some of the best shelling on the Gulf Coast, and its five-star sunsets are a great way to end the day.

★ **Culture fix:** If you love the arts, there's no finer offering in the Bay Area than at the Florida State University Ringling Center for the Cultural Arts in Sarasota.

1 Tampa. Situated on a large bay of the same name, Tampa is a growing waterfront metropolis that's packed with state-of-the-art zoos, plenty of museums, and inviting shopping districts. Among the main draws is Busch Gardens, which doubles as a theme park and a zoo.

2 St. Petersburg.
Although downtown St. Petersburg can be rowdy, there are also pockets of culture. The mellow but pricey Pinellas County beach towns include St. Pete Beach and Treasure Island.

3 Clearwater and Vicinity. Quiet during the winter, the beach areas north of St. Petersburg buzz all spring and summer. In addition to Clearwater, the area includes Dunedin and Tarpon Springs.

4 Sarasota and Vicinity. Sarasota County's barrier islands lure travelers to a battery of white-sand beaches, but Sarasota's cultural treasures are the true draw for many of its visitors.

GETTING ORIENTED

On the east side of the bay, Tampa is a sprawling cosmopolitan city offering attractions like Busch Gardens and Ybor City. To the west, St. Petersburg and Clearwater boast lovely barrier island beaches. Moving to the south, Sarasota's arts scene is among the finest in Florida.

7

BUSCH GARDENS

Busch Gardens was opened in Tampa on March 31, 1959, by the Anheuser-Busch company. It was originally designed as an admission-free animal attraction to accompany the brewing plant, but it eventually was turned into a theme park, adding more exotic animals, tropical landscaping, and rides to entertain its guests.

Today the 335-acre park has nine distinct territories packed with roller coasters, rides, eateries, shops, and live entertainment. The park is best known for its incredible roller coasters and water rides, which draw thrill seekers from around the globe. These rides tend to cater to those over the age of 10. With this in mind, Busch Gardens created the **Sesame Street Safari of Fun,** which is designed solely with children under five in mind. There's a lot packed into this area: junior thrill rides, play areas (some with water), and shows—all of which make it exciting for the kids.

GETTING ORIENTED

The park is set up on a north–south axis, with Nairobi being in the center.

Your first encounter at the park is the Moroccan market (grab a map here). There are several small eateries and souvenir shops in this area. If you head west from Morocco, you'll get to the Bird Gardens, Sesame Street Safari of Fun, Stanleyville, and Jungala. Heading north you'll find Nairobi, Timbuktu, and the Congo. Heading east takes you to Egypt and the Serengeti Plain. If you get lost, there are team members available almost everywhere to help you.

TOP ATTRACTIONS

FOR AGES 7 AND UP

Cheetah Hunt. Riders zoom over 4,000 feet of Serengeti-like landscape and down through a rocky cave.

Gwazi. The largest, fastest wooden dueling roller coaster in the world boasts crossing speeds of 100 mph.

Kumba. Riders on this coaster experience weightlessness, cobra rolls, corkscrews, and inverted rolls.

Montu. This 150-foot-tall inverted coaster reaches speeds of 60 mph, and has a zero-G roll and seven inversions.

Rhino Rally. A Land Rover takes you on an off-road safari with up-close animal encounters and a raging river adventure.

Sand Serpent. It's a pint-size roller coaster with twists and turns throughout.

SheiKra. This coaster is 200 feet tall with a 200-foot vertical descent, and isn't for the faint of heart.

Wild Surge. You're shot out of a mountain crater up 40 feet and then bounced up and down, creating a free-fall experience.

FOR AGES 6 AND UNDER

Air Grover. Take a ride on Grover's plane and soar through the Sahara on this junior coaster.

Bert and Ernie's Watering Hole. It's a water adventure filled with bubblers, geysers, jets, dumping buckets, and more.

Rosita's Djembe Fly-Away. Rosita takes you on a swing ride that sends you above the African canopy.

Walkabout Way. You don't have to be a kid to enjoy this Australian-theme attraction, which allows you and the little ones to hand-feed a bunch of cuddly kangaroos.

Zoe-Petra & the Hippos of the Nile. A kid-size flume ride with Zoe's hippo friends gives children a river glimpse of Africa.

VISITING TIPS

■ The park is least crowded during the week, with weekends bringing in a lot of locals. Summer and the holidays also are crowded.

■ Ride the thrill rides as early in the day as possible. Think about purchasing a Quick Queue pass for $14.95, which grants you no-wait access. It's good only once per ride but ensures you'll hit all the big rides quickly.

■ Bring extra quarters for all the locker rentals at each of the coasters.

■ You can pick up a map at the entrance, which lists showtimes, meet-the-keeper times, and special hours for attractions and restaurants.

■ Vegetarians will enjoy the veggie burgers at **Zagora Café** or the **Colony House's** delicious vegetable platter. A money-saver is the All Day Dining Deal, which costs $32.99 per adult and $14.99 per child. It's accepted at most dining venues. If eating at the Colony House, you'll want to make your reservations immediately upon entering the park.

Updated
by Kate
Bradshaw

If you seek a destination that's no one-trick pony, the
Tampa Bay region is a spot you can't miss. Encompassing an area from Tarpon Springs to Tampa proper and
all the way south to Sarasota, it's one of those unsung
places as dynamic as it is appealing—and word has definitely started to spread about its charms. With its long list
of attractions—from pristine beaches to world-class museums—it's easy to see why.

First and foremost, Tampa Bay's beaches are some of the best in the
country. Whether you want coarse or fine sand, and whether you seek
a mellow day of shelling or a raucous romp on a crowded stretch of
waterfront, this place has it all. Of course, you can choose from a range
of water activities, including charter fishing, parasailing, sunset cruises,
kayaking, and more.

The region has its share of boutique districts spotted with shops and
sidewalk cafés. Tampa's Hyde Park Village and downtown St. Petersburg's Beach Drive are among the top picks if you're looking to check
out some upscale shops and dine alfresco while getting the most of
the area's pleasant climate. Vibrant nightlife tops off Tampa Bay's
list of assets. Ybor City attracts the club set, and barrier islands like
St. Pete Beach offer loads of live music and barefoot dancing into the
wee hours.

Tampa Bay has lots of family-friendly attractions, too. You can check
out Busch Gardens, Adventure Island, and the Clearwater Marine
Aquarium, to name a few. And art fanatics will find an astonishing array
of attractions, including Sarasota's Ringling Museum of Art, St. Petersburg's enrapturing Salvador Dalí and Dale Chihuly collections (both
permanent and housed in exquisite new digs), and Tampa's Museum of
Art. Come prepared to explore and see for yourself what a compelling,
unforgettable place the Tampa Bay area really is.

PLANNING

WHEN TO GO

Winter and spring are high season, and the amount of activity during this time is double that of the off-season. Beaches do stay pretty packed throughout the sweltering summer, which is known for massive, almost-daily afternoon thunderstorms. Summer daytime temperatures hover around or above 90°F. Luckily the mercury drops to the mid-70s at night, and the beaches have a consistent onshore breeze that starts just before sundown, which enabled civilization to survive here before air-conditioning arrived.

GETTING HERE AND AROUND

AIR TRAVEL

Tampa International Airport, the area's largest and busiest airport, with 19 million passengers per year, is served by most major carriers and offers ground transportation to surrounding cities. Many of the large U.S. carriers also fly into and out of Sarasota–Bradenton International Airport. St. Petersburg–Clearwater International Airport, 9 miles west of downtown St. Petersburg, is much smaller than Tampa International and has limited service.

Airport Transfers: SuperShuttle is one of the easiest ways to get to and from the airport if you forgo a rental car. All you need to do is call or visit the SuperShuttle website to book travel—they'll pick you up and/or drop you off wherever you're staying at any hour. Basic service costs around $28.

Blue One Transportation provides service to and from Tampa International Airport for areas including Hillsborough (Tampa, Plant City), Pinellas (St. Petersburg, St. Pete Beach, Clearwater), and Polk (Lakeland) counties. Rates vary by pickup location/destination and fuel costs.

Airport Sarasota–Bradenton International Airport ☏ 941/359–2777 ⊕ www.srq-airport.com. **St. Petersburg–Clearwater International Airport** ☏ 727/453–7800 ⊕ www.fly2pie.com. **Tampa International Airport** ☏ 813/870–8700 ⊕ www.tampaairport.com.

Airport Transfers Blue One Transportation ☏ 813/282–7351 ⊕ www.blueonetransportation.com. **SuperShuttle** ☏ 800/258–3826 ⊕ www.supershuttle.com.

BOAT TRAVEL

Dolphin Landings Charter Boat Center has daily four-hour cruises to unspoiled Egmont Key at the mouth of Tampa Bay. Hubbard's Marina also operates a ferry to Egmont Key on most days. Climb aboard the glass-bottom boats of St. Nicholas Boat Line to take a sightseeing cruise of Tarpon Springs' historic sponge docks and see a diver at work.

On Captain Memo's Pirate Cruise, crew members dressed as pirates take you on sightseeing and sunset cruises in a replica of a 19th-century sailing ship. Starlite Cruises operates two very different ships for lunch, sightseeing, and dinner cruises: the *Starlite Majesty*, a sleek, yacht-style vessel; and *Starlite Princess*, an old-fashioned paddle wheeler that sails out of St. Pete Beach.

Tour Operators **Captain Memo's Pirate Cruise** ⊠ *Clearwater Beach Marina, Clearwater Beach* ☎ *727/446–2587* ⊕ *www.captainmemo.com*. **Dolphin Landings Charter Boat Center** ⊠ *4737 Gulf Blvd., St. Pete Beach* ☎ *727/360–7411* ⊕ *www.dolphinlandings.com*. **Hubbard's Marina** ⊠ *150 John's Pass, Madeira Beach* ☎ *727/867–6569* ⊕ *www.hubbardsmarina.com*. **St. Nicholas Boat Line** ⊠ *693 Dodecanese Blvd., Tarpon Springs* ☎ *727/942–6425*. *Starlite Cruises* ⊠ *Clearwater Beach Marina, at end of Rte. 60, Clearwater Beach* ☎ *727/462–2628* ⊕ *www.starlitecruises.com*.

BUS AND TROLLEY TRAVEL

Hillsborough Area Regional Transit and TECO Line Street Cars replicate Tampa's first electric streetcars, transporting cruise-ship passengers to Ybor City and downtown Tampa. Pinellas Suncoast Transit Authority offers bus service throughout Pinellas County, from the county's inland parts out to the beaches. PSTA also runs the Suncoast Beach Trolley, which takes passengers up and down the beaches—from Pass-A-Grille all the way up to Clearwater Beach and downtown Clearwater—for $2 each way.

Manatee County Area Transit (MCAT) has buses throughout Bradenton and the nearby towns of Palmetto and Ellenton, as well as connections to Sarasota attractions. Service is inexpensive, but it's really no substitute for a car.

St. Petersburg Trolley will get you to key destinations throughout downtown St. Pete, and even offers free service between the Chamber of Commerce Visitor's Bureau and certain destinations.

Contacts **Hillsborough Area Regional Transit** ☎ *813/254–4278* ⊕ *www.gohart.org*. **Pinellas Suncoast Transit Authority** ☎ *727/540–1900* ⊕ *www.psta.net*. **St. Petersburg Trolley** ☎ *727/821–5166* ⊕ *www.stpetetrolley.com*. **TECO Line Street Cars** ☎ *813/254–4278* ⊕ *www.tecolinestreetcar.org*.

CAR TRAVEL

Interstates 75 and 275 span the Bay Area from north to south. Coming from Orlando, you're likely to drive west into Tampa on Interstate 4. Along with Interstate 75, U.S. 41 (the Tamiami Trail) stretches the length of the region and links the business districts of many communities; avoid this route during rush hours (7–9 am and 4–6 pm).

TRAIN TRAVEL

Amtrak trains run from the Northeast, the Midwest, and much of the South into Tampa; the Tampa station is at 601 N. Nebraska Avenue.

Train Contacts **Amtrak** ☎ *800/872-7245* ⊕ *www.amtrak.com*.

HOTELS

Many convention hotels in the Tampa Bay area double as family-friendly resorts—taking advantage of nearby beaches, marinas, spas, tennis courts, and golf links. However, unlike Orlando and some other parts of Florida, the area has been bustling for more than a century, and its accommodations often reflect a sense of its history.

You'll find a turn-of-the-20th-century beachfront resort where Zelda and F. Scott Fitzgerald stayed, a massive all-wood building from the 1920s, plenty of art deco, and Spanish-style villas. But one thing they all have in common is a certain Gulf Coast charm.

RESTAURANTS

Fresh gulf seafood is plentiful—raw bars serving oysters, clams, and mussels are everywhere. Tampa's many Cuban and Spanish restaurants serve paella with seafood and chicken, *boliche criollo* (sausage-stuffed eye-round roast) with black beans and rice, *ropa vieja* (shredded flank steak in tomato sauce), and other treats. Tarpon Springs adds classic Greek specialties. In Sarasota the emphasis is on ritzier dining, though many restaurants offer extra-cheap early-bird menus.

HOTEL AND RESTAURANT COSTS

Prices in the restaurant reviews are the average cost of a main course at dinner or, if dinner is not served, at lunch. Prices in the hotel reviews are the lowest cost of a standard double room in high season. Prices do not include taxes (6%, more in some counties, and 1%–5% tourist tax for hotel rooms).

VISITOR INFORMATION

Contacts **Bradenton Area Convention and Visitors Bureau.** This organization has all you need to know about everything Bradenton, Anna Maria Island, Palmetto, and Ellenton have to offer. ☎ 941/729-9177 ⊕ www.bradentongulfislands.com. **Manatee County Area Transit** ✉ Bradenton ⊕ www.mymanatee.org. **Sarasota Convention and Visitors Bureau.** This organization has the skinny on South Tampa Bay. ✉ 701 N. Tamiami Trail, U.S. 41, Sarasota ☎ 800/348-7250 ⊕ www.sarasotafl.org. **Tampa Bay Beaches Chamber of Commerce.** The staff here will give you the lowdown on the Pinellas County beaches. ✉ 6990 Gulf Blvd., St. Pete Beach ☎ 727/360-7957 ⊕ www.tampabaybeaches.com. **Tampa Bay & Company** ✉ 401 E. Jackson St., Suite 2100, Tampa ☎ 800/448-2672, 813/223-1111 ⊕ www.visittampabay.com.

TAMPA

84 miles southwest of Orlando via I–4.

Tampa, the west coast's business-and-commercial hub, has a sprinkling of high-rises and heavy traffic. A concentration of restaurants, nightlife, stores, and cultural events is amid the bustle. The city has really come into its own in recent years. The downtown Tampa waterfront features stunning views and excellent museums. Animal lovers flock here for attractions like Lowry Park Zoo, Busch Gardens, Big Cat Rescue, and Giraffe Ranch. Revelers will enjoy the strip of bars and clubs that constitutes Ybor City, a historic area with a heavy Cuban influence. The city also abounds with art museums, shops, and a wide array of restaurants. Downtown and Ybor City are both excellent spots to look for live music. Not too far out of town are some great golf courses and nature trails. Tampa is also a short drive from a long stretch of gorgeous Gulf Coast beaches.

GETTING AROUND

Downtown Tampa's Riverwalk, on Ashley Drive at the Hillsborough River, connects waterside entities such as the Florida Aquarium, the Channelside shopping-and-entertainment complex, and Marriott Waterside. The landscaped park is 6 acres and extends along the Garrison cruise-ship channel and along the Hillsborough River downtown. The walkway is being expanded as waterside development continues.

Although downtown Tampa, the Channelside District, and Ybor City are easy to navigate without a car, you'll want to rent one if you plan on hitting the beaches or heading to Busch Gardens, Hyde Park, International Plaza, or any of the zoos.

VISITOR INFORMATION

Contacts Tampa Bay & Company ⊠ *401 E. Jackson St., Suite 2100* ☏ *800/448–2672, 813/223–1111* ⊕ *www.visittampabay.com.* **Tampa Bay Beaches Chamber of Commerce.** The staff here will give you the lowdown on the Pinellas County beaches. ⊠ *6990 Gulf Blvd., St. Pete Beach* ☏ *727/360– 7957* ⊕ *www.tampabaybeaches.com.* **Ybor City Chamber Visitor Bureau** ⊠ *1600 E. 8th Ave., Suite B104* ☏ *813/241–8838* ⊕ *www.ybor.org.*

EXPLORING

TOP ATTRACTIONS

Fodors Choice ★   **Big Cat Rescue.** Suburban Citrus Park in North Tampa is probably the last place you'd expect to be able to get face-to-face with an 800-pound tiger. Yet at the end of a shaded road just yards off the Veterans' Expressway, you can do just that. This rescue center is home base for a nonprofit organization that serves as a sanctuary for tigers, ocelots, bobcats, cougars, and members of any other large cat species you can imagine. Each and every one of these marvelous creatures has a unique story. Some arrived here after narrowly avoiding becoming an expensive coat. Others were kept as pets until the owners realized how pricey 15 pounds of meat per day (what it takes to feed some of these creatures) can be. They're all kept in large enclosures. A volunteer guide will lead you around the property and tell you every cat's story. You'll also get an earful of little-known facts about these big cats, from the true origin of the white tiger to why some cats have white spots on the backs of their ears. Tours (no unescorted visits are allowed) are every day but Thursday, but kids under 10 are only allowed on a special kids' tour at 9 am on weekends. ⊠ *12802 Easy St., Citrus Park* ☏ *813/920–4130* ⊕ *bigcatrescue.org* ✉ *$29* ⊙ *Mon.–Wed. and Fri. at 3, weekends at 10 and 1; kids' tour weekends at 9. Other special tours available by reservation only, at varying costs.*

FAMILY
Fodors Choice ★   **Busch Gardens.** The Jungala exhibit at Busch Gardens brings Bengal tigers to center stage and puts them at eye level—allowing you to view them from underground caves and underwater windows. The big cats are just one of the reasons the theme park attracts some 4½ million visitors each year. This is a world-class zoo, with more than 2,000 animals, and a live entertainment venue that provides a full day (or more) of fun for the whole family. If you want to beat the crowds, start in the back of the park and work your way around clockwise.

The 335-acre adventure park's habitats offer views of some of the world's most endangered and exotic animals. For the best animal sightings, go to their habitats early, when it's cooler. You can experience up-close animal encounters on the Serengeti Plain, a 65-acre

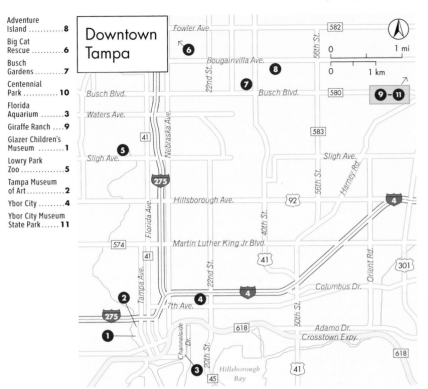

Downtown Tampa

free-roaming habitat, home to reticulated giraffes, Grevy's zebras, white rhinos, bongos, impalas, and more. Myombe Reserve allows you to view lowland gorillas and chimpanzees in a lush, tropical-rain-forest environment. Down Under–themed Walkabout Way offers those ages five and up an opportunity to hand-feed kangaroos and wallabies (a cup of vittles is $5).

Interested in watching a tiger get a dental check-up? Then head over to the Animal Care & Nutrition Center, where you can observe veterinary care for many of the park's animals.

Many consider the seven roller coasters to be the biggest lure. On the wings of an African hawk, SheiKra—North America's first dive coaster—takes riders on a three-minute journey 200 feet up, then (gulp!) plunges 90 degrees straight down at 70 mph. The park's coaster lineup also includes steel giants Kumba, Scorpion, and Montu; a double, wooden roller coaster called Gwazi; and Sand Serpent, a five-story family coaster full of hairpin turns and breathtaking dips. The Cheetah Hunt, the park's latest thrill ride, is an absolutely exhilarating 4,429-foot-high launch coaster. With three different launch points, this coaster takes you through the Serengeti and into a rocky gorge with a top speed of 60 mph.

The off-road-safari Rhino Rally brings you face-to-face with zebras, elephants, and white rhinos. Catering to the shorter set, the Sesame Street Safari of Fun is a 5-acre kids' playground with Sesame-themed rides, shows, and water adventures. The Air Grover Rollercoaster takes kids (and parents) on minidives and twisty turns over the Sahara, while Rosita's Djembe Fly-Away (a swing ride) and Elmo's Safari Go-Round (carousel) get them swinging and screeching. If you're looking to cool off, your best bets are Oscar's Swamp Stomp, Zoe-Patra & the Hippos of the Nile (a flume ride), or Bert & Ernie's Water Hole—complete with bubblers, geysers, water jets, and dumping buckets. Character lunches are available (but you might want to wait until after your rides). ⊠ *3000 E. Busch Blvd., 8 miles northeast of downtown Tampa and 2 miles east of I–275 Exit 50, Central Tampa* ☏ *813/987–5000, 888/800–5447* ⊕ *www.buschgardens.com* ⊒ *$85; parking $13* ☉ *Daily 9:30–6.*

FAMILY   **Florida Aquarium.** Although eels, sharks, and stingrays are the headliners, the Florida Aquarium is much more than a giant fishbowl. This architectural landmark features an 83-foot-high, multitier, glass dome; 250,000 square feet of air-conditioned exhibit space; and more than 20,000 aquatic plants and animals representing species native to Florida and the rest of the world—from black-tip sharks to leafy sea dragons.

Floor-to-ceiling interactive displays, behind-the-scenes tours, and in-water adventures allow kids to really get hands-on—and even get their feet wet. Adventurous types (certified divers age 15 and up) can dive with mild-mannered sharks and sea turtles, participate in shark-feeding programs (age 12 and up), or shallow-water swim with reef fish such as eels and grouper (age 6 and up).

However, you don't have to get wet to have an interactive experience: the Ocean Commotion exhibit offers virtual dolphins and whales and multimedia displays and presentations, and even allows kids to upload video to become part of the exhibit. The Coral Reef Gallery is a 500,000-gallon tank with viewing windows, an awesome 43-foot-wide panoramic opening, and a walk-through tunnel that gives the illusion of venturing into underwater depths. There you see a thicket of elkhorn coral teeming with tropical fish, and a dark cave reveals sea life you would normally see only on night dives.

If you have two hours, try the Wild Dolphin Adventure Cruise, which takes up to 130 passengers onto Tampa Bay in a 72-foot catamaran for an up-close look at bottlenose dolphins and other wildlife. The outdoor Explore a Shore exhibit, which gives younger kids a chance to release some energy, is an aquatic playground with a waterslide, water-jet sprays, and a climbable replica pirate ship. Last but not least, two black-footed South African penguins make daily appearances in the Coral Reef Gallery. For an extra cost, you can get an up-close look at the daily lives of these penguins during the half-hour-long Penguins: Backstage Pass demonstration. ⊠ *701 Channelside Dr., Downtown* ☏ *813/273–4000* ⊕ *www.flaquarium.org* ⊒ *Aquarium $21.95; Aquarium/Adventure Cruise combo $37.95; Penguins: Backstage Pass combo $48.95; Behind the Scenes Combo $29.95; Dive with the Sharks, $175; Swim with the Fishes, $75; parking $6* ☉ *Daily 9:30–5.*

OFF THE
BEATEN
PATH

Giraffe Ranch. Rural Dade City is known mostly for its strawberries, but word is quickly spreading about something else that makes people flock here: giraffes. These graceful creatures are the headliners at this nearly 50-acre ranch. You can view them as part of a safari-style vehicle tour or from the back of a camel; on either tour, you can hand-feed them cabbage leaves. You'll also see tons of zebras, a pair of pygmy hippos, an impala, ostriches, and many other animal species roaming the grounds. Near the ranch's welcome center and gift shop is a corral of enclosures where you can watch guinea pigs chomp on sweet-potato chunks, hold a baby goat, and, for a little extra cash, feed grapes to lemurs. The ranch's proprietors have encyclopedic knowledge of the animal kingdom, and the overall experience is meant to impart a sense of connection to the animal world—and the environment—on those who visit. Tours take about two hours, and reservations are required. Credit cards are not accepted. ⊠ *38650 Mickler Rd., Dade City* ☎ *813/482–3400* ⊕ *www.gifferranch.com* ✉ *$59 for tour in safari van; $150 for tour by camelback* ☉ *Tours daily at 11 and 2, by reservation only.*

FAMILY **Glazer Children's Museum.** It's all about play here, and with 53,000-square-feet, 12 themed areas, and 175 "interactives," there's plenty of opportunity for it. Areas designed to nurture imagination and strengthen confidence allow children and families to experience everything from flying an airplane to shopping for groceries. Kids can also create art, control the weather, navigate a mini–shipping channel, and "drive" a miniature (stationary) fire truck through Tampa. A Water's Journey Tree lets kids climb the tree to the second floor and mimics the water cycle. ⊠ *110 W. Gasparilla Plaza, Downtown* ☎ *813/443–3861* ⊕ *www.glazermuseum.org* ✉ *$15 adult; $9.50 children* ☉ *Weekdays 10–5, Sat. 10–6, Sun. 1–6.*

FAMILY **Lowry Park Zoo.** Natural-habitat exhibits featuring clouded leopard cubs in Asia Gardens make the 56-acre Lowry Park Zoo one of the best mid-size zoos in the country. Safari Africa is the home of a herd of African elephants, and residents of the nearby Ituri Forest include cheetahs and lovably plump pygmy hippos. The stars at Primate World range from cat-size lemurs to a family of heavyweight Bornean orangutans that love to ham for the camera. As you stroll through, keep an eye out for okapis, a rare forest giraffe from Central Africa.

For hands-on experiences, Lowry has more options than most large parks, including chances to ride a camel, feed a giraffe, or touch a slippery stingray. Majestic red-tailed hawks and other raptors put on a show at the Birds of Prey Center. You can come face-to-face with Florida manatees at the Manatee Aquatic Center, the only nonprofit manatee rehab center on the planet. Dwindling native species like Florida panthers, black bears, and red wolves may be tough to find in the wild, but you can easily find them at the Florida Wildlife Center. Kookaburras, emus, and wallabies populate the Wallaroo Station children's zoo. There are also water-play areas, rides (all of which are included with zoo admission), shows, and restaurants. ⊠ *1101 W. Sligh Ave., Central Tampa* ☎ *813/935–8552* ⊕ *www.lowryparkzoo.com* ✉ *$24.95* ☉ *Daily 9:30–5.*

7

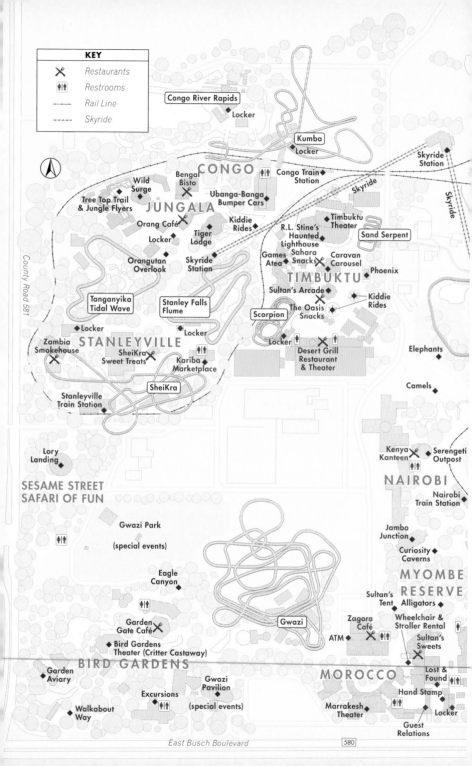

KEY

✗ Restaurants
🚻 Restrooms
┼┼┼┼ Rail Line
······ Skyride

Congo River Rapids

Locker

Kumba
Locker

Skyride Station

CONGO

🚻 Congo Train Station

Skyride

Skyride

Wild Surge
Bengal Bisto ✗
Tree Top Trail & Jungle Flyers
Ubanga-Banga Bumper Cars
JUNGALA
Orang Café ✗
Kiddie Rides
Locker
Tiger Lodge
Timbuktu Theater
R.L. Stine's Haunted Lighthouse
Sand Serpent
Orangutan Overlook
Skyride Station
Games Atea
Sahara Snacks
Caravan Carousel
Phoenix
TIMBUKTU
Sultan's Arcade
Kiddie Rides
Tanganyika Tidal Wave
Stanley Falls Flume
Scorpion
The Oasis Snacks
Locker
Locker
Zambia Smokehouse
Locker
STANLEYVILLE
🚻
SheiKra Sweet Treats ✗
Kariba Marketplace
Locker
Locker
Desert Grill Restaurant & Theater ✗
Elephants
SheiKra
Stanleyville Train Station
Camels

County Road 581

Lory Landing

SESAME STREET SAFARI OF FUN

Kenya Kanteen ✗
Serengeti Outpost
🚻
NAIROBI
Nairobi Train Station

Gwazi Park
(special events)

Jambo Junction

Eagle Canyon

Curiosity Caverns

MYOMBE RESERVE

🚻

Garden Gate Café ✗
Gwazi

Sultan's Tent
Alligators
Zagora Café ✗
Wheelchair & Stroller Rental 🚻
ATM 🚻
Sultan's Sweets

Bird Gardens Theater (Critter Castaway)

BIRD GARDENS

MOROCCO
Lost & Found 🚻

Garden Aviary
Gwazi Pavilion
(special events)
Hand Stamp

Excursions 🚻

Marrakesh Theater
🚻
Locker

Walkabout Way

Guest Relations

East Busch Boulevard   580

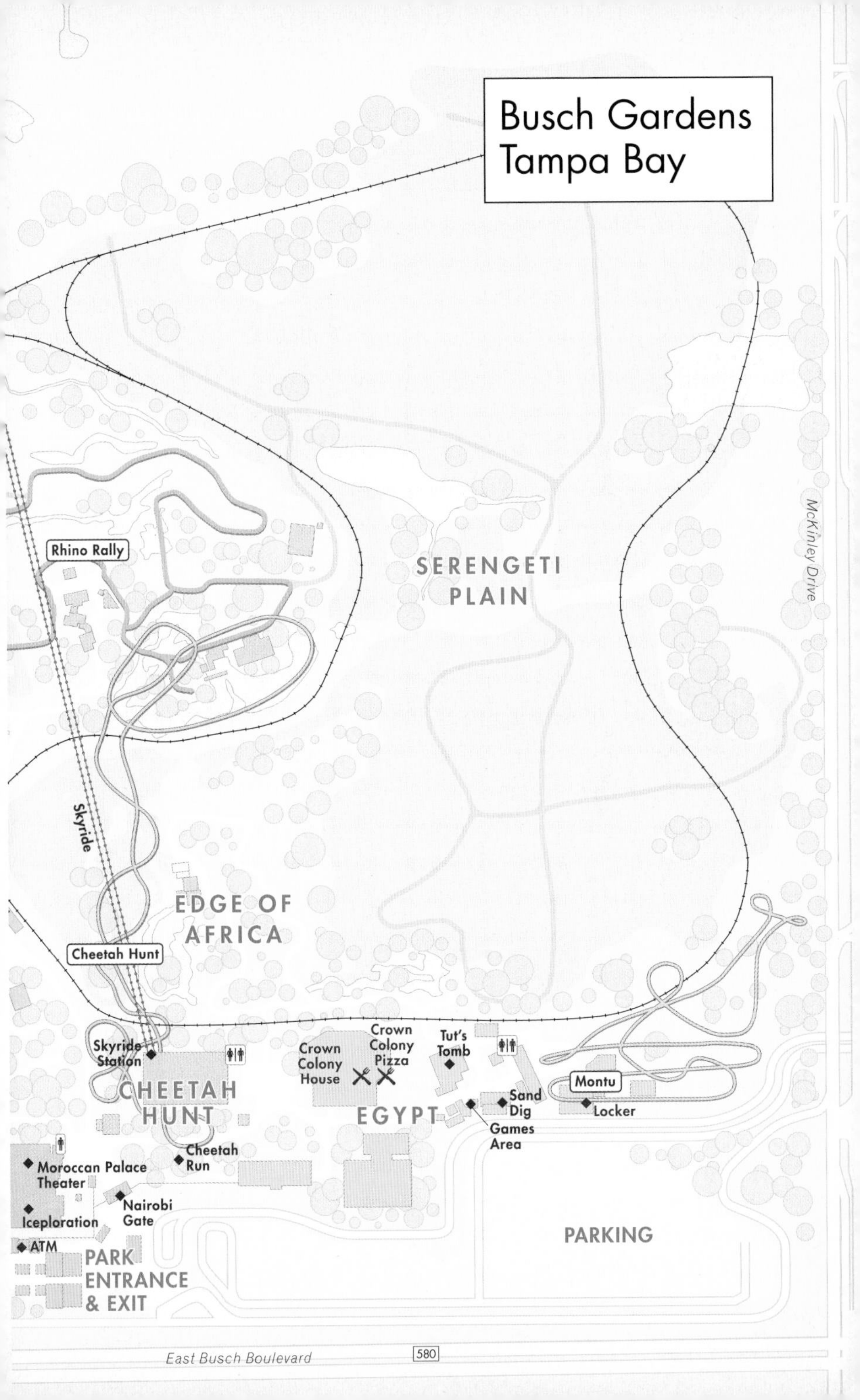
Busch Gardens Tampa Bay
Rhino Rally
SERENGETI PLAIN
McKinley Drive
Skyride
EDGE OF AFRICA
Cheetah Hunt
Skyride Station
CHEETAH HUNT
Crown Colony House
Crown Colony Pizza
Tut's Tomb
Sand Dig
Games Area
EGYPT
Montu
Locker
Cheetah Run
Moroccan Palace Theater
Nairobi Gate
Iceploration
ATM
PARK ENTRANCE & EXIT
PARKING
East Busch Boulevard
580

BUSCH GARDENS

NAME	Min. Height	Type of Entertainment	Duration	Suits	Crowds	Strategy
Egypt						
Montu	54"	Thrill ride	3 min.	14 and up	Yes!	Go here first
Skyride	n/a	Ride	5 min.	All	Yes	Can get busy
Tut's Tomb	n/a	Walk thru	10 min.	All	OK	Go after Montu
Edge of Africa	n/a	Walk thru	Up to you	All	OK	Go after lunch
Morocco						
Gwazi	48"	Thrill ride	2.5 min.	10 and up	Yes!	Expect to wait
Myombe Reserve	n/a	Walk thru	Up to you	All	OK	Before noon photo op
Iceploration	n/a	Show	30 min.	All	Yes	Arrive 15 min. early
Bird Gardens						
Critter Castaway	n/a	Show	25 min.	All	Yes	Do after Gwazi
Lory Landing	n/a	Walk thru	Up to you	All	OK	Bring money to feed
Garden Aviary	n/a	Walk thru	Up to you	All	OK	Go after lunch
Backyard Wildlife Habitat	n/a	Walk thru	Up to you	All	Yes	Good anytime
Sesame Street Safari of Fun						
Air Grover	n/a	Junior thrill ride	2 min.	Under 6	Yes!	Expect a wait
Zoe-Petra & the Hippos of the Nile	n/a	Junior thrill ride	3 min.	Under 6	Yes	Good cool-off spot
Elmo's Treehouse Trek	n/a	Play area	Up to you	Under 6	OK	May be hard to keep track of toddlers
Rosita's Djembe Fly-Away	n/a	Junior thrill ride	2 min.	Under 6	Yes	Older toddlers may enjoy this more
The Count's Zambezi Rally	n/a	Ride	Up to you	Under 6	Yes	Go early in the day
Elmo's Safari Go-Round	n/a	Ride	3 min.	Under 6	Yes	Good anytime
Oscar's Swamp Stomp	n/a	Play area	Up to you	All	OK	Bring a towel
Bert and Ernie's Watering Hole	n/a	Play area	Up to you	All	OK	Bring a bathing suit
Slimey's Sahara Sand	n/a	Play area	Up to you	All	OK	Chance for parents to relax
Big Bird's Whirly Birdy	n/a	Ride	3 min.	Under 6	OK	Excellent for toddlers
Cookie Monster's Canopy Crawl	n/a	Play area	Up to you	Under 6	OK	Good for energetic children
Telly's Jungle Jam	n/a	Play area	Up to you	All	OK	Slow- paced area
Big Bird's 123-Smile With Me	n/a	Walk thru	Up to you	All	Yes	Photo/autograph op

Stanleyville

Attraction	Height	Type	Duration	Age	Rating	Tips
SheiKra	54"	Thrill ride	2.5 min.	14 and up	Yes!	Use the lockers
Stanley Falls Flume	46"	Thrill ride	3 min.	10 and up	Yes	Lengthy lines
Tanganyika Tidal Wave	48"	Thrill ride	2 min.	10 and up	Yes	Bring a change of clothes or poncho

Jungala

Attraction	Height	Type	Duration	Age	Rating	Tips
Jungle Flyers	48"	Junior thrill ride	3 min.	6 to 13	Yes	Skip for other rides
Wild Surge	38"	Thrill ride	2 min.	5 and up	Yes!	
Tree Top Trails	n/a	Walk thru	Up to you	All	Yes	Gets crowded
Tiger Lodge	n/a	Walk thru	Up to you	All	Yes	Close-up views
Orangutan Overlook	n/a	Walk thru	Up to you	All	Yes	Morning photo op
Jungala Stiltwalkers	n/a	Show	15 min.	All	OK	Very entertaining

Congo

Attraction	Height	Type	Duration	Age	Rating	Tips
Congo River Rapids	42"	Thrill ride	6 min.	10 and up	Yes!	Bring extra clothes or poncho
Kumba	54"	Thrill ride	3 min.	14 and up	Yes!	Go early or before closing
Ubanga-Banga Bumper Cars	42"	Ride	2 min.	8 and up	Yes	Long wait times

Timbuktu

Attraction	Height	Type	Duration	Age	Rating	Tips
Animal Care Center	n/a	Educational Exhibit	n/a	5 and up	No	Slow-paced ride
Carousel Caravan	n/a	Ride	3 min.	All	OK	Newer ride, expect lines
Cheetah Hunt	48"	Thrill ride	3.5 min.	12 and up	Yes!	Arrive 15 min. early
Pirate 4-D Movie	n/a	Show	15 min.	All	OK	Go after Scorpion
Phoenix	48"	Thrill ride	2 min.	12 and up	Yes	Very popular
Sand Serpent	46"	Junior thrill ride	2 min.	All	Yes	Go during Dance to the Music show
Scorpion	42"	Thrill ride	2 min.	14 and up	Yes	Arrive 15 min. before show
Dance to the Music	n/a	Seasonal show	20 min.	All	Yes	Good break from the sun
Sesame Street Presents Lights, Camera, Action!	n/a	Show	20 min.	All	OK	

Nairobi

Attraction	Height	Type	Duration	Age	Rating	Tips
Rhino Rally	39"	Vehicle ride	10 min.	10 and up	Yes	This ride is bumpy—hold on to your valuables
Serengeti Express	n/a	Vehicle ride	12–35 min.	All	No	Great way to relax and see the park
Curiosity Caverns	n/a	Walk thru	Up to you	All	No	Good to get out of the sun
Elephant Habitat	n/a	Walk thru	Up to you	All	OK	Go during Meet the Keeper
Rhino Habitat	n/a	Walk thru	Up to you	All	Yes	Earlier the better
Edge of Africa	n/a	Walk thru	Up to you	All	OK	Great break from the crowds

DID YOU KNOW?

One of six roller coasters at Busch Gardens, the steel, 60-foot-tall Scorpion twists and turns at speeds near 50 mph and then throws you into a 360-degree vertical loop. During the 2-minute ride you'll experience a 3.5 g-force.

Fodor's Choice
★

Ybor City. Tampa's lively Latin quarter is one of only a few National Historic Landmark districts in Florida. Bordered by I-4 to the north, 22nd Street to the east, Adamo Drive to the south, and Nebraska Avenue to the West, it has antique-brick streets and wrought-iron balconies. Cubans brought their cigar-making industry to Ybor (pronounced *ee-bore*) City in 1886, and the smell of cigars—hand-rolled by Cuban immigrants—still wafts through the heart of this east Tampa area, along with the strong aroma of roasting coffee. These days the neighborhood is one of Tampa's hot spots, if at times a rowdy one, as empty cigar factories and historic social clubs have been transformed into trendy boutiques, art galleries, restaurants, and nightclubs. ⊠ *Ybor City.*

WORTH NOTING

FAMILY **Adventure Island.** From spring until fall, rides named Calypso Coaster, Gulf Scream, and Key West Rapids promise heat relief at Busch Gardens' water park. Tampa's most popular "wet" park features waterslides and artificial wave pools, along with tranquil "beaches" in a 30-acre package. One of the attraction's headliners, Riptide, challenges you to race three other riders on a sliding mat through twisting tubes and hairpin turns. Planners of this park also took the younger kids into account, with offerings such as Fabian's Funport, which has a scaled-down pool and interactive water gym. Along with a volleyball complex and a rambling river, there are cafés, snack bars, picnic and sunbathing areas, changing rooms, and private cabanas. ⊠ *10001 N. McKinley Dr., less than 1 mile north of Busch Gardens, Central Tampa* ☎ *813/987–5660, 888/800–5447* ⊕ *www.adventureisland.com* ⊠ *$46; parking $12* ⊗ *Mid-Mar.–Aug., daily 10–5; Sept. and Oct., weekends only 10–5.*

Centennial Park. You can step back into the past at Centennial Park, which re-creates a period streetscape and hosts a farmer's market called the "Fresh Market" every Saturday. ⊠ *8th Ave. and 19th St., Ybor City.*

Tampa Museum of Art. Housed in an exquisitely designed new building, the Tampa Museum of Art is emblematic of the city's efforts to revitalize the downtown riverfront. The facility overlooks Curtis Hixon Park, the towering minarets of the University of Tampa, and the Hillsborough River. The museum's 66,000 square feet of gallery space displays an impressive permanent collection of 20th- and 21st-century sculpture as well as Greek and Roman antiquities. Five additional galleries host traveling exhibits ranging from the classics to some of the most prominent artists working today. Also notable is Sono, the museum's café, which is operated by Mise en Place, one of Tampa's top restaurants. ⊠ *120 W. Gasparilla Plaza, Downtown* ☎ *813/274–8130* ⊕ *www.tampamuseum. org* ⊠ *$10* ⊗ *Mon.–Thurs. 11–7, Fri. 11–8, weekends 11–5.*

Ybor City Museum State Park. This park provides a look at the history of the cigar industry. Admission includes a tour of La Casita, one of the shotgun houses occupied by cigar workers and their families in the late 1890s, held every half-hour between 10 and 3. ⊠ *1818 E. 9th Ave., between Nuccio Pkwy. and 22nd St. from 7th to 9th Aves., Ybor City* ☎ *813/247–6323* ⊕ *www.ybormuseum.org* ⊠ *$4* ⊗ *Daily 9–5.*

7

WHERE TO EAT

$$$$
STEAKHOUSE
Fodor'sChoice
★

✕**Bern's Steak House.** With the air of an exclusive club, this is one of Florida's finest steak houses. Rich mahogany paneling and ornate chandeliers define the legendary Bern's, where the chef ages his own beef, grows his own organic vegetables, and roasts his own coffee. There's also a Cave Du Fromage, housing a discriminating selection of artisanal cheeses from around the world. Cuts of topmost beef are sold by weight and thickness. There's a 60-ounce strip steak that's big enough to feed your pride (of lions), but for most appetites the veal loin chop or 8-ounce chateaubriand is more than enough. The wine list includes approximately 7,000 selections (with 1,000 dessert wines). After dinner, tour the kitchen and wine cellar before having dessert upstairs in a cozy booth. The dessert room is a hit. For a real jolt, try the Turkish coffee with an order of Mississippi mud pie. Casual business attire is recommended. $ *Average main: $32* ⊠ *1208 S. Howard Ave., Hyde Park* ☎ *813/251–2421* ⊕ *www.bernssteakhouse.com* ⌖ *Reservations essential* ⌂ *Jacket and tie.*

$$$
ASIAN FUSION

✕**BT.** Local restaurateur B. T. Nguyen has earned quite a following since opening her first eatery more than two decades ago. The latest locale is supermodern, and the cuisine features fresh herbs grown on-site and a drink list that includes organic sake martinis—some flavored with herbs from a garden on the property. With a motto like "eat local, think global," the menu is inevitably sophisticated yet simple, with creative offerings like Deconstructed Kobe Stroganoff James, which consists of a grass-fed filet mignon, chanterelle mushrooms, and a Burgundy reduction served over fresh pasta. Vegetarians and vegans can rest easy here with options such as Food Karma (braised tofu, edamame, eggplant, and ginger in coconut broth over rice). $ *Average main: $28* ⊠ *2507 S. MacDill Ave., Suite B, Hyde Park* ☎ *813/258–1916* ⊕ *www.restaurantbt.com.*

$$
ECLECTIC

✕**Café Dufrain.** Dogs can tag along if you dine on the front patio at pet-friendly Café Dufrain, a waterfront eatery with an upscale crowd. Creative menu items, which vary by season, include fried chicken and waffles (a Southern classic) and ceviche with sweet potato and toasted macadamia nuts. In mild weather, opt for the waterfront view of downtown Tampa. $ *Average main: $20* ⊠ *707 Harbour Post Dr., Downtown* ☎ *813/275–9701* ⊕ *www.cafedufrain.com.*

$
PIZZA
FAMILY

✕**Cappy's Pizza.** Chicago may be the first place you think of when you hear the words "deep dish pizza," which is why the high-quality pies this place offers may surprise (and please) you. The menu at this family-friendly spot is pretty simple: choose either a Chicago- or New York–style crust, and select your toppings. The "Cappy" features a blend of pepperoni, ham, onions, green pepper, sausage, and mushrooms. You can also go with a calzone. There's no hostess here, so put your name on the (usually long) list you see when you first walk in. If it's not too packed, try to get garden seating. The feel inside is very nostalgic—vintage signs and an old toy train set adorn the walls. You'll find a lengthy list of craft brews, and the kids might enjoy an IBC root beer. Keep in mind that it's cash only. $ *Average main: $12* ⊠ *4910 N. Florida Ave., Seminole Heights* ☎ *813/238–1516* ⌖ *Reservations not accepted* ▭ *No credit cards.*

$$ ✕ **Columbia.** Make a date for some of the best Latin cuisine in Tampa.
SPANISH A fixture since 1905, this magnificent structure with an old-world air
Fodor'sChoice and spacious dining rooms takes up an entire city block and seems to
★ feed the entire city—locals as well as visitors—throughout the week, but
especially on weekends. The paella, bursting with seafood, chicken, and
pork, is arguably the best in Florida, and the 1905 salad—with ham,
olives, cheese, and garlic—is legendary. The menu has Cuban classics
such as *boliche criollo* (tender eye of round stuffed with chorizo sau-
sage), *ropa vieja* (shredded beef with onions, peppers, and tomatoes),
and *arroz con pollo* (chicken with yellow rice). Don't miss the flamenco
dancing show every night but Sunday. This place is also known for
its sangria. If you can, walk around the building and check out the
elaborate, antique decor along every inch of the interior. $ *Average
main: $19* ⊠ *2117 E. 7th Ave., Ybor City* ☎ *813/248–4961* ⊕ *www.
columbiarestaurant.com.*

$ ✕ **Estela's.** On the quaint Davis Islands near Downtown Tampa, Este-
MEXICAN la's is a favorite among those who enjoy authentic Central American
cuisine and Mexico's best beers. Expect the usual entrées (enchiladas,
fajitas, and chiles rellenos) mixed with delightful starters (chicken soup
with guacamole). The margaritas aren't bad, either. The place gets very
crowded for weekday lunches. $ *Average main: $12* ⊠ *209 E. Davis
Blvd., Downtown* ☎ *813/251–0558* ⊕ *www.estelas.com.*

$$ ✕ **Kojak's House of Ribs.** Few barbecue joints can boast the staying power
SOUTHERN of this family-owned and -operated pit stop. Located along a shaded
stretch in South Tampa, it debuted in 1978 and has since earned a following of sticky-fingered regulars who have turned it into one of the
most popular barbecue stops in central Florida. It's in a 1927 house
complete with veranda, pillars supporting the overhanging roof, and
brick steps. Day and night, three indoor dining rooms and an outdoor
dining porch have a steady stream of hungry patrons digging into tender pork spareribs that are dry-rubbed and tanned overnight before
visiting the smoker for a couple of hours. Then they're bathed in the
sauce of your choice. Kojak's also has a nice selection of sandwiches,
including chopped barbecue chicken and country-style sausage. This is
definitely not the kind of place you'd want to bring a vegan. $ *Aver-
age main: $14* ⊠ *2808 Gandy Blvd., South Tampa* ☎ *813/837–3774*
⊕ *www.kojaksbbq.net* ☉ *Closed Mon.*

$ ✕ **Mel's Hot Dogs.** This is a must after a long day of riding roller coasters
HOT DOG and scoping out zebras at Busch Gardens. Visitors as well as passersby
usually are greeted by a red wiener-mobile parked on the north side of
the highway near Busch Gardens. Venture inside to find walls dotted
with photos from fans and a hot-diggity menu that's heaven for tube-
steak fans. You can order a traditional dog, but try something with a
little more pizzazz, such as a bacon-cheddar Reuben-style bowwow on
a poppy-seed bun, or the Mighty Mel, a quarter-pounder decked out
with relish, mustard, and pickles. Herbivores, fear not: there's a vegan
option on the menu, and it's mighty tasty. To avoid lunch crowds, arrive
before 11:30 or after 1:30. $ *Average main: $8* ⊠ *4136 E. Busch Blvd.,
Central Tampa* ☎ *813/985–8000* ⊕ *www.melshotdogs.com* ▭ *No credit
cards* ☉ *Closed Sun.*

7

Where to Eat and Stay in Tampa

KEY

❶ *Restaurants*

① *Hotels*

$$$ MODERN AMERICAN 🍴 **Mise en Place.** Known to locals as "Mise" (pronounced *meez*), this upscale, modern downtown space is a popular lunch spot for Tampa's political and social elite. At night, it transforms into an elegant, understated dining destination with a menu that offers adventurous yet meticulously crafted modern American cuisine. The menu changes every week, save for staples like the shiitake-pear port-mousse pâté and the rack of lamb. Another thing that doesn't change is the intricacy of every item listed—whether it's tandoori-crusted tofu or pumpkin-spiced rubbed scallops. The long list of boutique wines and specialty cocktails further demonstrate the intelligence and imagination that go into the crafting of the menu. This place is on the western edge of downtown, just across the street from University of Tampa's shining minarets. Parking and entry are behind the building. [$] *Average main: $29* ✉ *442 W. Kennedy Blvd., Suite 110, Downtown* ☎ *813/254–5373* 🌐 *www.miseonline.com.*

$$$ ASIAN 🍴 **Roy's.** Chef Roy Yamaguchi's pan-Asian restaurant has fresh ingredients flown in every day from around the Pacific. Regular dishes include roasted macadamia-nut-crusted mahimahi with lobster sauce and blackened ahi tuna with spicy soy-mustard sauce. Can't decide? Try the prix-fixe menu, usually under $40 for three courses. For dessert, choices include chocolate soufflé and the pear tart. [$] *Average main: $28* ✉ *4342 Boy Scout Blvd., Airport Area* ☎ *813/873–7697* 🌐 *www.roysrestaurant.com* 🕒 *No lunch.*

$ MEXICAN 🍴 **Taco Bus.** It's a Mexican joint with a simple name in a less-than-magnificent location, but that matters not to anyone who's ever eaten here. You have a long list of meat, seafood, and vegetarian options, which employees will stuff into the casing of your choice and hand to you through the window of a stationary bus. Don't let the low-key nature of this establishment fool you—the menu features classier items like ceviche, butternut-squash tostadas, and chicken mole among the quesadillas and carne asada. The flagship location is open 24 hours, seven days a week. [$] *Average main: $7* ✉ *913 E. Hillsborough Ave., Central Tampa* ☎ *813/232–5889* [$] *Average main: $7* ✉ *2324 Central Ave., St. Petersburg* ☎ *727/322–5000* 🌐 *www.tampatacobus.com.*

WHERE TO STAY

For expanded reviews, facilities, and current deals, visit Fodors.com.

$$$ B&B/INN Fodor's Choice ★ 🏨 **Don Vicente de Ybor Historic Inn.** Built as a home in 1895 by town founder Don Vicente de Ybor, this inn shows that the working-class cigar city had an elegant side, too. **Pros:** elegant rooms; rich in history; walking distance to nightlife. **Cons:** rowdy neighborhood on weekend nights. [$] *Rooms from: $150* ✉ *1915 Republica de Cuba, Ybor City* ☎ *813/241–4545, 866/206–4545* 🌐 *www.donvicenteinn.com* 🛏 *13 rooms, 3 suites* 🍽 *Breakfast.*

$$$$ HOTEL 🏨 **Floridan Palace Hotel.** This newly restored 1926 hotel at the northern end of downtown Tampa offers a well-manicured glimpse into a bygone era amid a bustling modern urban core. **Pros:** great downtown location; historic hotel. **Cons:** far from beaches. [$] *Rooms from: $249*

✉ *905 Florida Ave., Downtown, Tampa* ☎ *813/225–1700* 🌐 *www.floridanpalace.com* 🛏 *195 rooms, 18 suites* 🍴 *No meals.*

$$$ RESORT Fodor's Choice ★ 🏨 **Grand Hyatt Tampa Bay.** Situated on the western edge of Tampa, near the airport and overlooking the Courtney Campbell Causeway, the Grand Hyatt has a lot to offer—both in its guest rooms and on the property. **Pros:** extensive amenities; amazing views; world-class dining. **Cons:** far from beach; getting here can be tough due to traffic and awkward road layout. [$] *Rooms from: $169* ✉ *2900 Bayport Dr., West Tampa, Tampa* ☎ *813/874–1234* 🌐 *www.grandtampabay.hyatt.com* 🛏 *442* 🍴 *No meals.*

$$$ HOTEL 🏨 **Hilton Garden Inn Tampa Ybor Historic District.** Although its modern architecture makes it seem out of place in this historic district, this chain hotel's location across from Centro Ybor is a plus. **Pros:** good location for business travelers; reasonable rates. **Cons:** chain-hotel feel; far from downtown. [$] *Rooms from: $179* ✉ *1700 E. 9th Ave., Ybor City* ☎ *813/769–9267* 🌐 *www.hiltongardeninn.com* 🛏 *84 rooms, 11 suites* 🍴 *No meals.*

$$$$ RESORT 🏨 **Saddlebrook Resort Tampa.** If you can't get enough golf and tennis, here's your fix. **Pros:** away from urban sprawl; great choice for the fitness minded. **Cons:** a bit isolated. [$] *Rooms from: $249* ✉ *5700 Saddlebrook Way, Wesley Chapel* ☎ *813/973–1111, 800/729–8383* 🌐 *www.saddlebrookresort.com* 🛏 *540 rooms, 407 suites* 🍴 *No meals.*

$$$ HOTEL 🏨 **Tampa Marriott Waterside Hotel & Marina.** Across from the Tampa Convention Center, this downtown hotel was built for conventioneers but is also convenient to tourist spots such as the Florida Aquarium and the Ybor City and Hyde Park shopping and nightlife districts. **Pros:** great downtown location; near shopping. **Cons:** gridlock during rush hour; streets tough to maneuver; area sketchy after dark. [$] *Rooms from: $190* ✉ *700 S. Florida Ave., Downtown* ☎ *888/268–1616* 🌐 *www.marriott.com* 🛏 *683 rooms, 36 suites* 🍴 *No meals.*

$$$$ HOTEL 🏨 **Westin Tampa Harbour Island.** Few folks think of the islands when visiting Tampa, but this 12-story hotel on a 177-acre man-made islet is a short drive from downtown Tampa and even closer to the cruise terminal. **Pros:** close to downtown; nice views; on the TECO streetcar line. **Cons:** a bit far from the action; chain-hotel feel. [$] *Rooms from: $169* ✉ *725 S. Harbour Island Blvd., Harbour Island* ☎ *813/229–5000* 🌐 *www.starwoodhotels.com* 🛏 *299 rooms, 19 suites* 🍴 *No meals.*

NIGHTLIFE AND THE ARTS

When it comes to entertainment, there's never a dull moment in Tampa. Colorful Ybor City, a heavily Cuban-influenced area minutes from downtown, is a case in point. It has by far the biggest concentration of nightclubs (too many to list here), all situated along 7th and 8th avenues. Ybor comes alive at night and on weekends, when a diverse array of bars and clubs open their doors to throngs of partygoers. Whether it's bumping house music or some live rock and roll you seek, you'll find it here. Downtown Tampa is also becoming a formidable nightlife destination. When it comes to the arts—visual, musical, performing, or otherwise—Tampa is one of the South's leading spots.

THE ARTS

Straz Center. With 335,000 square feet, this is the second largest arts complex south of the Kennedy Center in Washington, D.C. Among the facilities are the 2,500-seat Carol Morsani Hall, a 1,047-seat playhouse, the 200-seat TECO Theater, a 300-seat cabaret theater, and a 120-seat black-box theater. Opera, concerts, drama, and ballet performances are presented here. ✉ *1010 North W.C. MacInnes Pl., Downtown* ☎ *813/229–7827* ⊕ *www.strazcenter.org.*

Tampa Theatre. This ornate vintage 1926 movie palace hosts films, concerts, and special events. If you catch a flick here, go early to see a set from an old-school organ player. ✉ *711 N. Franklin St., Downtown* ☎ *813/274–8286* ⊕ *www.tampatheatre.org.*

BARS

Blue Martini Lounge. This spot in International Plaza has live entertainment nightly, except Sunday, and a menu of killer martinis. ✉ *2223 N. West Shore Blvd., West Tampa* ☎ *813/873–2583.*

Centro Cantina. There are lots of draws here: a balcony overlooking the crowds on 7th Avenue, live music Thursday through Sunday nights, a large selection of margaritas, and more than 30 brands of tequila. Food is served until 2 am. ✉ *1600 E. 8th Ave., Ybor City* ☎ *813/241–8588.*

Cigar City Brewing Tasting Room. Offering the fruits of the adjacent Cigar City brewery, the tasting room here puts Tampa on the map for craft beer enthusiasts. On tap, it offers mainstay brews like Jai Alai IPA and Maduro Brown Ale as well as an interesting rotation of seasonal beers. It's a cozy spot with friendly staff and generally good music. But beware: happy hour can be packed. Brewery tours are available on the hour Wednesday through Saturday between 11 am and 2 pm for a nominal fee. ✉ *3924 W. Spruce St., Suite A, Central Tampa* ☎ *813/348–6363* ⊗ *Sun.–Thurs. 11–10, Fri. and Sat. 11 am–midnight.*

Fly Bar. A happy hour mecca for hip young professionals, Fly Bar and Restaurant offers an intriguing selection of creative cocktails. Consider the Huck Cinn, made from huckleberry vodka, cinnamon syrup, and fresh lemon. East of Eden is a cocktail consisting of bison grass vodka, Calvados, and chai syrup. The list goes on. If you're hungry, you'll find a food menu to match. There's live music on weekends and occasionally during the week. A huge draw is the rooftop deck, which offers views of surrounding downtown Tampa. ✉ *1202 N. Franklin St., Downtown* ☎ *813/275–5000* ⊕ *www.flybarandrestaurant.com.*

Gaspar's Grotto. Spanish pirate Jose Gaspar was known for swashbuckling up and down Florida's west coast in the late 18th and early 19th century. His legend has inspired a massive, raucous street festival each winter. This Ybor City drinkery has adopted his name, and rightly so. Decked out in tons of pirate memorabilia, it's the cornerstone to any night spent barhopping on the Ybor strip. The sangria is a good choice, but the aged rums may be a better fit here. You'll also find a food menu that goes well beyond standard bar fare. ✉ *1805 E. 7th Ave., Ybor City* ☎ *813/248–5900* ⊕ *www.gasparsgrotto.com.*

Hub. Considered something of a dive—but a lovable one—by a loyal and young local following that ranges from esteemed jurists to nose-ring-wearing night owls, the Hub is known for strong drinks and a jukebox that goes well beyond the usual. ✉ *719 N. Franklin St., Downtown* ☎ *813/229–1553.*

CASINOS

Seminole Hard Rock Hotel & Casino. In addition to playing one of the hundreds of Vegas-style slot machines, gamers can get their kicks at the casino's poker tables and video-gaming machines. The lounge serves drinks 24 hours a day. Hard Rock Cafe, of course, has live music, dinner, and nightlife. There is a heavy smell of cigarette smoke here, as with most casinos. ✉ *5223 N. Orient Rd., off I–4 at N. Orient Rd. exit, East Tampa* ☎ *813/627–7625, 866/502–7529* ⊕ *www.seminolehardrock. com* ⊡ *Free* ⊙ *Daily 24 hrs.*

COMEDY CLUBS

Side Splitters. Comedians perform Thursday through Sunday nights (and other nights, sporadically, throughout the week). ✉ *12938 N. Dale Mabry Hwy., Central Tampa* ☎ *813/960–1197* ⊕ *www. sidesplitterscomedy.com.*

Tampa Improv. Top comedians perform here Wednesday through Sunday. ✉ *Centro Ybor, 1600 E. 8th Ave., Ybor City* ☎ *813/864–4000* ⊕ *www. improvtampa.com.*

MUSIC CLUBS

Skippers Smokehouse. A junkyard-style restaurant and oyster bar, Skippers has live reggae on Wednesday, Uncle John's Band (a long-running Grateful Dead cover act) on Thursday, and great smoked fish every night. Check their calendar for exceptional musical lineups on the weekends. ✉ *910 Skipper Rd., Northeast Tampa* ☎ *813/971–0666* ⊕ *www. skipperssmokehouse.com.*

SHOPPING

MALLS

Centro Ybor. Ybor City's destination within a destination is this dining-and-entertainment palace. It has shops, trendy bars and restaurants, and a 20-screen movie theater. ✉ *1600 E. 8th Ave., Ybor City* ⊕ *www. centroybor.com.*

International Plaza. If you want to grab something at Neiman Marcus or Nordstrom, this is the place. You'll also find Juicy Couture, J.Crew, LUSH, Louis Vuitton, Tiffany & Co., and many other upscale shops. Stick around after hours, when watering holes in the mall's courtyard become a high-end club scene. ✉ *2223 N. West Shore Blvd., Airport Area* ⊕ *www.shopinternationalplaza.com.*

Old Hyde Park Village. It's a typical upscale shopping district in a quiet, shaded neighborhood near the water. Williams-Sonoma and Brooks Brothers are mixed in with bistros and sidewalk cafés. ✉ *1602 W. Swann Ave., Hyde Park* ⊕ *www.hydeparkvillage.net.*

SPECIALTY SHOPS

King Corona Cigar Factory. If you are shopping for hand-rolled cigars, head to Ybor City, where a few hand-rollers practice their craft in small shops. This is one of the more popular places thanks to its plentiful outdoor seating, perfect if you want to grab some nibbles and a Cuban coffee or a beer. ✉ *1523 E. 7th Ave., Ybor City* ☎ *813/251–9109* ⊕ *www.kingcoronacigars.com.*

La France. One of the landmark vintage shops in the Tampa Bay area, La France stocks such items as antique beaded wedding gowns, psychedelic mini-dresses, and period costumes that will make you a hit should you sport one at the Gasparilla Pirate Fleet parade. If you're in any way a vintage clothing buff, prepare to spend a solid couple of hours (and a good chunk of change) here. ✉ *1612 E. 7th Ave., Ybor City* ☎ *813/248–1381.*

Squaresville. From the mildly unusual to the downright bizarre this store has it all—from the mid-20th century, that is. Among the finds are Cuban clothing, Elvis posters, and Bettie Page clocks. ✉ *508 S. Howard Ave., Hyde Park* ☎ *813/259–9944* ⊕ *www.squaresvilletampa.com* ⊗ *Weekdays 11–6, Sat. 11–5:30, Sun. 1–4.*

SPORTS AND THE OUTDOORS

BASEBALL

George M. Steinbrenner Field. Locals and tourists flock each March to see the New York Yankees play about 17 spring training games at this 11,000-seat facility. (Call for tickets.) From April through September, the stadium belongs to a Yankee farm team, the Tampa Yankees, who play 70 games against the likes of the Daytona Cubs and the Sarasota Red Sox. ✉ *3802 Dr. Martin Luther King Jr. Blvd., near corner of Dale Mabry Hwy., off I–275 Exit 41B, Central Tampa* ☎ *813/879–2244* ⊕ *www.steinbrennerfield.com.*

FOOTBALL

Tampa Bay Buccaneers. Seeing the National Football League play isn't easy without connections, since the entire stadium is booked by season-ticket holders years in advance. But tickets can be found in the classifieds of newspapers such as the *Tampa Tribune* and *Tampa Bay Times.* ✉ *Raymond James Stadium, 4201 N. Dale Mabry Hwy., Central Tampa* ☎ *813/879–2827* ⊕ *www.buccaneers.com.*

GOLF

Babe Zaharias Golf Course. The greens fees are $17–$40 at this challenging par-70, 18-hole public course with water hazards on eight holes. A pro is on hand to give lessons. ✉ *11412 Forest Hills Dr., Northeast Tampa* ☎ *813/631–4374* ⊕ *www.tbgolf.com.*

Bloomingdale Golfers Club. In addition to an 18-hole, par-72 course, this club has a two-tiered driving range, a 1-acre putting green, and a restaurant. Green fees are $30–$80. ✉ *4113 Great Golfers Pl., Valrico* ☎ *813/685–4105* ⊕ *www.bloomingdalegolf.com.*

The Claw at USF. Named for its many doglegged fairways, the 18-hole, par-71 course is on a preserve with moss-draped oaks and towering pines. Greens fees are $20–$45. ⊠ *13801 N. 46th St., North Tampa* ☎ *813/632–6893* ⊕ *www.theclawatusfgolf.com.*

Saddlebrook Resort. There's a lot on offer at this resort, which is half an hour northeast of Tampa: 36 holes and 70- and 71-par courses, a driving range, a golf shop, on-site pros, and a resort spa. The greens fees range from $50 to $105, depending on the season. ⊠ *5700 Saddlebrook Way, Wesley Chapel* ☎ *813/973–1111* ⊕ *www.saddlebrook.com.*

Tournament Players Club of Tampa Bay. This public 18-hole 71-par course 15 miles north of Tampa was designed by Bobby Weed and Chi Chi Rodriguez; greens fees $79/$159. ⊠ *5300 W. Lutz Lake Fern Rd., Lutz* ☎ *813/949–0090* ⊕ *www.tpctampabay.com.*

WALKING

Bayshore Boulevard Trail. Considered the world's longest continuous sidewalk, this 4.5-mile trail is a good spot for just standing still and taking it all in, with its spectacular views of downtown Tampa and the Hillsborough Bay area. Of course, you can also walk, talk, jog, bike, and in-line skate with locals. The trail is open from dawn to dusk daily. ⊠ *Bayshore Blvd.* ☎ *813/274–8615.*

ST. PETERSBURG

21 miles west of Tampa.

Nicknamed the Sunshine City, St. Pete is much more than a mass of land between the airport and the beaches. In recent years it's seen a fierce arts and cultural revival, which you can plainly see as you stroll through the city's lively downtown area. The new Salvador Dalí Museum building is a testament to the great pride residents of the 'Burg take in their waterfront city. But the city has other arts-oriented attractions, including the Dale Chihuly Collection, the Fine Arts Museum, and the burgeoning young artist hub known as the 600 Block, where eateries and bars attract crowds in the evening. Beach Drive offers some upscale options, whereas Central Avenue appeals more to night owls. The Grand Central District offers some unique vintage and antiques shopping. Gulfport is a stylishly low-key suburb southwest of St. Petersburg. The long strip of barrier islands lining St. Pete's west coast offer miles of gorgeous white beaches as well as dining, nightlife, and phenomenal sunsets. Beach towns here include St. Pete Beach, Treasure Island, Madeira Beach, and Redington Shores. No trip to this area is complete without a visit to the remote, pristine beaches of Fort De Soto.

GETTING HERE AND AROUND

Interstate 275 heads west from Tampa across Tampa Bay to St. Petersburg, swings south, and crosses the bay again on its way to Terra Ceia, near Bradenton. U.S. 19 is St. Petersburg's major north–south artery; traffic can be heavy, and there are many lights, so try to avoid it. Alternatives include 66th and 4th streets. One key thing to remember about St. Pete is that the roads form an easy-to-navigate grid: streets run north to south; avenues run east to west. Central Avenue connects downtown to the beaches.

Around St. Petersburg, Pinellas Suncoast Transit Authority serves Pinellas County. Look for buses that cover the beaches and downtown exclusively.

Contacts Pinellas Suncoast Transit Authority ☎ *727/540–1800* ⊕ *www.psta.net.*

TOURS

All About Fun Tours. What sets this tour apart from others is you are not going by bus or boat—your self-guided chariot is a motorized Segway. Each tour starts with an easy 15- to 20-minute training session. Tours are 60 or 90 minutes and are offered up to three times daily. It's a carefree way to see downtown St. Petersburg, the park system, and the waterfront while learning about local history. Reservations are required. ⊠ *335 N.E. 2nd Ave.* ☎ *727/896–3640* ⊕ *www.gyroglides. com* ⊠ *Tours $35–$50* ☉ *Tues.–Sat. 10:30 and 2, Sun. 12:30 and 2:30, Mon. call for availability.*

Dolphin Landings Tours. This operation runs a four-hour shelling trip, a two-hour dolphin-sighting excursion powered mostly by sail, backbay or party-boat fishing, and other outings to Egmont Key and Shell Key. It's not easy to spot from the road: the boats are docked behind a strip mall. ⊠ *4737 Gulf Blvd., St. Pete Beach* ☎ *727/360–7411* ⊕ *www.dolphinlandings.com.*

VISITOR INFORMATION

Contacts St. Petersburg Area Chamber of Commerce ⊠ *100 2nd Ave. N* ☎ *727/821–4069* ⊕ *www.stpete.com.* **St. Petersburg/Clearwater Area Convention and Visitors Bureau** ⊠ *13805 58th St. N, Suite 2-200, Clearwater* ☎ *727/464–7200, 877/352–3224* ⊕ *www.visitstpeteclearwater.com.*

EXPLORING

TOP ATTRACTIONS

Fodor'sChoice
★

Chihuly Collection. For the uninitiated, those passing this collection's polished exterior may think it's a gallery like any other. Yet what's contained inside is an experience akin to *Alice in Wonderland*. This, the first permanent collection of world-renowned glass sculptor Dale Chihuly's work, has such impossibly vibrant, larger-than-life pieces as "Float Boat" and "Ruby Red Icicle." You can tour the museum independently or with one of its volunteer docents (no added cost; tours are given hourly on the half-hour during the week). Each display is perfectly lit, which adds to the drama of Chihuly's designs. After passing under a hallway with a semi-transparent ceiling through which a brilliant array of smaller glass pieces shine, you'll wind up at the breathtaking finale, "Mille Fiore" ("Thousand Flowers"), a spectacular, whimsical glass montage mimicking a wildflower patch, critters and all. Check out the gift shop at the end if you'd like to take some of the magic home with you. A combination ticket gets you a glimpse into Morean Arts Center's off-site glass-blowing studio, where you can watch resident artisans create a unique glass piece before your eyes. ⊠ *400 Beach Dr., Downtown* ☎ *727/822–7872* ⊕ *www.moreanartscenter.com.* ⊠ *$15* ☉ *Mon.–Sat. 10–5, Sun. noon–5.*

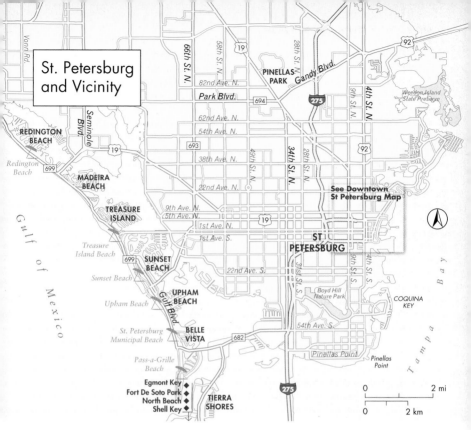

St. Petersburg
and Vicinity

The Dalí Museum. Inside and out, the waterfront Dalí Museum, which opened on 1/11/11 (Dalí is said to have been into numerology), is almost as remarkable as the Spanish surrealist's work. The state-of-the-art building has a surreal geodesic-like glass structure called the Dalí Enigma, as well as an outdoor labyrinth and a DNA-inspired spiral staircase leading up to the collection. All this, before you've even seen the collection, which is one of the most comprehensive of its kind—courtesy of Ohio magnate A. Reynolds Morse, a friend of Dalí's.

Here, you can scope out his early impressionistic works and see how the painter evolved into the visionary he's now seen to be. The mind-expanding paintings in this downtown headliner include *Eggs on a Plate Without a Plate*, *The Hallucinogenic Toreador*, and more than 90 other oils. You'll also discover more than 2,000 additional works including watercolors, drawings, sculptures, photographs, and objets d'art. Free hour-long tours are led by well-informed docents. ⌂ *1 Dali Blvd.* ☎ *727/823–3767* ⊕ *www.thedali.org* ⛁ *$21* ⊙ *Mon.–Wed., Fri., and Sat. 10–5:30, Thurs. 10–8, Sun. noon–5:30.*

Egmont Key. In the middle of the mouth of Tampa Bay lies the small (350 acres), largely unspoiled but critically eroding island Egmont Key, now a state park, national wildlife refuge, national historic site, and bird sanctuary. On the island are the ruins of Fort De Soto's sister fortification, Fort Dade, built during the Spanish-American War to protect Tampa Bay. The primary inhabitants of the less-than-2-mile-long island are the threatened gopher tortoise and box turtles. The only way to get here is by boat—you can catch a ferry from Fort De Soto. Nature lovers will find the trip well worth it—the beach here is excellent for shelling, secluded beach bathing, wildlife viewing, and snorkeling. Hubbard's Marina operates a ferry to Egmont Key from Fort DeSoto most days.

FAMILY **Sunken Gardens.** A cool oasis amid St. Pete's urban clutter, this lush 4-acre plot was created from a lake that was drained in 1903. Explore the cascading waterfalls and koi ponds, and walk through the butterfly house and exotic gardens where more than 50,000 tropical plants and flowers from across the globe thrive amid groves of some of the area's most spectacular palm trees. The on-site restaurant and hands-on kids' museum make this place a family favorite. ⊠ *1825 4th St. N* ☎ *727/551–3102* ⊕ *www.sunkengardens.org* ⬚ *$8* ⊙ *Mon.–Sat. 10–4:30, Sun. noon–4:30.*

WORTH NOTING

Florida Holocaust Museum. The downtown Florida Holocaust Museum is one of the largest of its kind in the United States. It has the permanent History, Heritage, and Hope exhibit, an original boxcar, and an extensive collection of photographs, art, and artifacts. One compelling display includes portraits and biographies of Holocaust survivors. The museum, which also has a series of rotating exhibits, was conceived as a learning center for children, so many of the exhibits avoid overly graphic content; signs are posted outside galleries if the subject matter might be too intense for kids. ⊠ *55 5th St. S* ☎ *727/820–0100* ⊕ *www. flholocaustmuseum.org* ⬚ *$16* ⊙ *Daily 10–5.*

FAMILY **Fort De Soto Park.** Spread over five small islands, 1,136-acre Fort De Soto Park lies at the mouth of Tampa Bay. It has 7 miles of waterfront (much of it beach), two fishing piers, a 4-mile hiking and skating trail, picnic-and-camping grounds, and a historic fort that kids of any age can explore. The fort for which it's named was built on the southern end of Mullet Key to protect sea lanes in the gulf during the Spanish-American War. Roam the fort or wander the beaches of any of the islands within the park. Kayaks and beach cruisers are available for rental. ⊠ *3500 Pinellas Bayway St., Tierra Verde* ☎ *727/582–2267* ⊕ *www. pinellascounty.org/park/05_ft_desoto.htm* ⬚ *$5* ⊙ *Beaches, daily sunrise–sunset; fishing and boat ramp, 24 hrs.*

FAMILY **Great Explorations.** "Don't touch" are words never spoken here. The museum is hands-on through and through, with a Robot Lab, Climb Wall, Lie Detector, Fire House, Vet's Office, and other interactive play areas. Smart exhibits like the Tennis Ball Launcher, which uses compressed air to propel a ball through a series of tubes, and Sound Waves, where Styrofoam pellets in a clear tube show differences in sound frequencies, employ low-tech to teach high-tech principles. ⊠ *1925 4th St. N* ☎ *727/821–8992* ⊕ *www.greatexplorations.org* ⬚ *$10* ⊙ *Tues.–Sat. 10–4:30, Sun. noon–4:30* ⊙ *Closed Mon.*

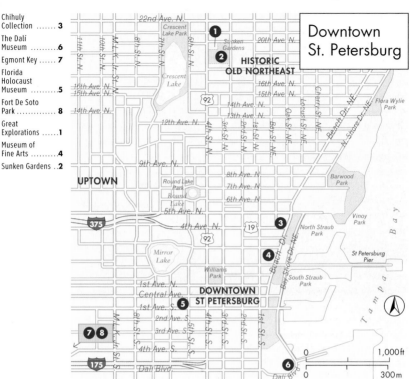

Museum of Fine Arts. One of the city's cornerstones, this museum is a gorgeous Mediterranean-revival structure that houses outstanding collections of Asian, African, Native American, European, and American art. Major works here by American artists range from Hassam to O'Keeffe to Bellows and Morisot, but the museum is known for its collection of French artists, including Cézanne, Monet, Rodin, Gauguin, and Renoir. There are also photography exhibits that draw from a permanent collection of more than 14,000 works. The recent Hazel Hough Wing more than doubled the museum's exhibit space. A café offers visitors a lunch respite and a beautiful view of the bay. Docents give narrated gallery tours. ⊠ *255 Beach Dr. NE* ☎ *727/896–2667* ⊕ *www.fine-arts.org* ☑ *$17* ⊙ *Mon.–Wed., Fri., and Sat. 10–5, Sun. noon–5, Thurs. 10–8.*

BEACHES

Egmont Beach. An undeveloped island teeming with birds, shells, and native plants is a short ferry ride away. You'll find serene lengths of beach, abandoned former military buildings, and a lighthouse. You can grab a ferry here from Fort De Soto for as little as $15. **Amenities:** none. **Best for:** solitude; walking. ⊠ *Accessible by boat only, Tierra Verde* ☎ *727/867–6569.*

A St. Petersburg pelican stares down passersby on the wharf; photo by Seymour Levy, Fodors.com member.

Madeira Beach. Known to locals as "Mad Beach," this lively barrier island town occupies the southern tip of Shell Key. The beachfront consists of a long stretch of soft, shell-strewn sand, and it's often crowded with families as well as clusters of twentysomething beachgoers. You can get to the beach via numerous public access points, but your best bet is to park at the municipal beach parking lot and head to the sand from there. It's easily accessible from Treasure Island, northern St. Petersburg, and Clearwater Beach. **Amenities:** food and drink; parking; showers; toilets. **Best for:** partiers; swimming; walking. ⊠ *14400 Gulf Blvd., Madeira Beach.*

North Beach, Fort De Soto. Pretty much anywhere you go in this county park can make you feel like you're hundreds of miles from civilization, but the beach on the northern tip of this island chain has perhaps the most remote feel. Sure, it gets pretty packed with weekend revelers and family reunions, but you can easily find your own space on this award-winning beach. It starts out wide at the entrance, and narrows as you go north, so it's perfect for those who enjoy a good stroll. There are some striking panoramic views of the park's undeveloped wetlands. Be warned that once you get past a certain point, the beach becomes clothing optional. **Amenities:** food and drink; parking; showers; toilets. **Best for:** solitude; sunset; swimming; walking. ⊠ *3500 Pinellas Bayway, head right at flag, Tierra Verde.*

FAMILY
Fodor'sChoice
★
Pass-a-Grille Beach. At the southern tip of St. Pete Beach (past the Don Cesar), this is the epitome of Old Florida. One of the most popular beaches in the area, it skirts the west end of charming, historic Pass-a-Grille, a neighborhood that draws tourists and locals alike with its stylish yet low-key mom-and-pop motels and restaurants. On weekends,

check out the Art Mart, an open-air market off the boulevard between 9th and 10th avenues that showcases the work of local artisans. **Amenities:** food and drink; parking; showers; toilets. **Best for:** sunset; windsurfing. ⊠ *1000 Pass-a-Grille Way, St. Pete Beach.*

Redington Beach. Sand Key, the landmass that is home to Madeira Beach at the south end and Belleaire Beach in the north, is spotted with public beach access points. This particular spot has a bigger parking area than the others, though it's not free. It's also within walking distance of the Redington Pier, one of the most popular areas for fishing. **Amenities:** food and drink; parking; toilets. **Best for:** solitude; swimming; walking. ⊠ *160th Ave. at Gulf Blvd., Redington Beach.*

Shell Key. If you want to find the most pristine beach possible without heading to some remote outpost, this is your best bet. The shuttle to this seemingly remote paradise runs out of Pass-A-Grille. You can catch it most days at 10, noon, and 2. If you do, expect some amazing snorkeling, shelling, and bird-watching. You can also kayak or canoe here from a launch near Fort DeSoto. **Amenities:** none. **Best for:** solitude; swimming; walking. ⊠ *801 Pass-A-Grille Way, Pass-A-Grille, St. Pete Beach* ☎ *727/360–1348.*

St. Petersburg Municipal Beach. Though the beach is technically in the city of Treasure Island, the city of St. Pete Beach owns and maintains this stretch. Due in part to a concession stand and playground, it's excellent for families. The beach here is very, very wide, near hotels, and great for beach volleyball. **Amenities:** food and drink; parking; showers; toilets. **Best for:** solitude; partiers; sunset; swimming. ⊠ *11260 Gulf Blvd., Treasure Island.*

FAMILY **Sunset Beach.** Technically part of Treasure Island, this 2-mile-long outcrop is one of Tampa Bay's best-kept secrets. The northern end has a mixed crowd—from bikers to spring breakers—the middle portion is good for families (there's a pavilion and playground at around 78th and West Gulf Boulevard), and the southern tip attracts the LGBT crowd. Surfers hit up Sunset Beach on the rare occasion that the gulf has some swells to offer. Once you turn onto West Gulf, you can find parking on the side streets, but make sure you park legally—it's all too easy to unwittingly get a barrage of parking tickets here. There are several pay lots starting to your right just south of 82nd Avenue. **Amenities:** parking; toilets. **Best for:** solitude; partiers; sunset. ⊠ *West Gulf Blvd., Treasure Island.*

Treasure Island. Large, wide swaths of sand that are sans crowd abound, but you can also find some good crowds, especially on weekends. The Sunday-evening drum circle, which happens around sunset just southwest of the Bilmar, makes for some interesting people-watching. It's also the only beach that allows alcohol, as long as it's not contained in glass. Plus, getting here is super easy—just head west on St. Petersburg's Central Avenue, which dead-ends smack-dab in the middle of T.I. (that's what the locals call it), where the iconic Thunderbird Beach Resort sign towers over the boulevard. Hang a left at the light. There's a Publix right across the street if you're up for an impromptu picnic or don't want to pay beach-bar prices for a beer. **Amenities:** food and drink; parking; showers; toilets. **Best for:** solitude; partiers; sunsets. ⊠ *10400 Gulf Blvd., Treasure Island.*

Upham Beach. One of the most notable things about this popular beach is the series of large objects that look like yellow school buses buried in the sand. These are actually designed to stabilize the shoreline (this beach is known for rapid erosion). The structures, called T-groins, may not please the eye, but that doesn't keep locals from flocking here. Upham is a wide beach with tons of natural landscaping, and it's near Postcard Inn and the TradeWinds. **Amenities:** food and drink; showers; toilets. **Best for:** partiers; sunset; swimming; walking. ⊠ *900 Gulf Way, St. Pete Beach.*

WHERE TO EAT

$$$

TAPAS

✕ **Ceviche.** A choice romantic destination as well as an excellent launch-pad for a night out, this tapas bar offers an astonishing spate of pleasant sensations for those with savvy taste buds. You can't go wrong with a huge order of seafood or chicken paella. The ceviche, *solomillo a la parilla* (prime fillet with wild mushrooms and brandy cream sauce), and super-garlicky spinach (sautéed with figs) are good bets for tapas. In the cata-comb-like bar downstairs, there's jazz, salsa, and flamenco every night but Monday. While you're here, the sangria is a must. $ *Average main: $25* ⊠ *10 Beach Dr., Downtown* ☎ *727/209–2299* ⊕ *www.ceviche.com.*

$$$

SEAFOOD

✕ **Crabby Bill's.** Nothin' fancy about the crab-man's place—just some of the area's tastiest seafood served family-style (picture long picnic-style tables). Crustaceans are the house specialty, meaning your choice of blue or soft-shell, and, from October to May, delicious—though costly—stone crabs, among others. There's also a good selection of other treats, including scallops and farm-raised oysters. Seafood aficionados will want to stick with items for which this place is best known, as the menu can be hit-or-miss. The views alone are a great reason to check it out. This restaurant sits on the beach front, something that turns the rooftop deck into prime real estate at sunset. Diners usually dress in the official uniform of the gulf coast beaches: shorts, T-shirts, and flip-flops. $ *Average main: $18* ⊠ *5100 Gulf Blvd.* ☎ *727/360–8858* ⊕ *www.crabbybills.com.*

$

SEAFOOD

Fodor's Choice

★

✕ **Hurricane Seafood Restaurant.** Sunsets and gulf views are the bait that hooks regulars as well as travelers who find their way to this somewhat hidden pit stop in historic Pass-A-Grille. Dating to 1977, it's mainly her-alded as a watering hole where you can hoist a cold one while munching on one of the area's better grouper sandwiches. (Speaking of this sweet white fish, it's the real deal here, which—be warned—isn't always a guar-antee in some restaurants.) There's also a range of seafood and steak entrées, and the crab cakes are legendary. The aforementioned sunsets are best seen from the rooftop sundeck. $ *Average main: $15* ⊠ *809 Gulf Way, St. Pete Beach* ☎ *727/360–9558* ⊕ *www.thehurricane.com.*

$$$

ECLECTIC

✕ **Marchand's Bar & Grill.** Opened in 1925, this wonderful restaurant in the posh Renaissance Vinoy Resort has frescoed ceilings and a spec-tacular view of Tampa Bay. Upscale and special-occasion diners are drawn to Marchand's by an imaginative menu, which changes often, though mainstays include the crab cakes and calamari. There's always the salmon, too. For early birds, the 1925 menu (named for the year the hotel originally opened) offers a four-course meal for just, as you may have guessed, $19.25. Sushi is available Thursday through Saturday.

The wine list is extensive, including a number of by-the-glass selections. [$] *Average main: $28* ✉ *Renaissance Vinoy Resort, 501 5th Ave. NE* ☎ *727/824–8072* 🌐 *www.marchandsbarandgrill.com.*

$ MODERN MEXICAN 🍴 **Peg's Cantina.** A favorite watering hole for Tampa Bay's craft beer enthusiasts, Peg's also offers a variety of specialty pizzas and healthy Mexican options. Housed in an old bungalow along Gulfport's famed Beach Boulevard, it features excellent outdoor seating, and, in perfect Gulfport form, hospitable service for the canine set. Cyclists enjoy cruising here from the Pinellas Trail. Tap beers include house-brand brews as well as options from regional and national breweries. [$] *Average main: $15* ✉ *3038 Beach Blvd. S, Gulfport* ☎ *727/328–2720* 🌐 *www.pegscantina.com* ⏲ *Closed Mon. No lunch weekdays.*

$$$ SEAFOOD 🍴 **Salt Rock Grill.** This hot spot is where tourists and locals converge to enjoy a fun and lively waterfront atmosphere. The rock-solid (if slightly less than imaginative) menu is the best reason to come. Don't believe the Caribbean lobster is a "monster"—at 1¼ pounds it's on the small side, but it's twice cooked—including a finish on the grill—and quite tasty. The showstopper is the cioppino (shrimp, king crab, lobster, mussels, fish, and clams with a sourdough crust). In fair weather, dine on the dock; otherwise ask for a table with a view of the water. [$] *Average main: $25* ✉ *19325 Gulf Blvd., Indian Shores* ☎ *727/593–7625* 🌐 *www.saltrockgrill.com.*

$ SEAFOOD 🍴 **Sloppy Joe's on the Beach.** A sister to the famous Hemingway haunt in Key West, this breezy spot is less gritty than the original and a little more focused on food than drink (although you will find a full menu of tasty tropical concoctions here as well). It's right on the beach, in the Bilmar Beach Resort, and the location affords diners amazing views. On particularly stunning beach days, you'll want to make reservations. Try to get seated on the sizable wooden deck that overlooks Treasure Island's massive beach. As you might imagine, seafood is big here, and the menu includes heaping portions of such favorites as lobster mac-and-cheese and gulf-caught shrimp. The salads are also a huge hit. If you come on a Sunday evening, look a little bit to the south, where a weekly drum circle turns into a huge beach bash come sunset. [$] *Average main: $15* ✉ *Bilmar Beach Resort, 10650 Gulf Blvd., Treasure Island* ☎ *727/367–1600* 🌐 *www.sloppyjoesonthebeach.com.*

$ CAFÉ 🍴 **Steam & Chill.** This eatery is a bit of a rare gem on St. Pete Beach offering creative breakfast options that tend to be a bit healthier than their greasy spoon counterparts (think: vegan hash and berry-and-brie crepes). It's also pretty much the only neighborhood spot where you'll find proper espresso drinks. At night, the dining room transforms into a tapas bar with live music and flowing sangria. If you plan on eating here, give yourself extra time as service can be slow (but oh, so worth it). [$] *Average main: $12* ✉ *7400 Gulf Blvd., St. Pete Beach* ☎ *727/360–8080* 🌐 *www.steamandchill.com.*

$ SEAFOOD Fodor's Choice ★ 🍴 **Ted Peters Famous Smoked Fish.** Picture this: flip-flop-wearing anglers and beach-towel-clad bathers lolling on picnic benches, sipping a beer, and devouring oak-smoked salmon, mullet, mahimahi, and mackerel. Dinner comes to the table with heaped helpings of potato salad and coleslaw. If you're industrious enough to have hooked your own fish, the crew will smoke it for about $1.50 per pound. If not, there's always what many consider to be the best burger in the region. The popular smoked fish spread and Manhattan clam chowder are available to go. There's also indoor seating at Ted's, which has been a south-side fixture for more than six decades. Closing time is 7:30 pm, so dinner is only for early diners. [$] *Average main: $12* ✉ *1350 Pasadena Ave. S, South Pasadena* ☎ *727/381–7931* ✍ *Reservations not accepted* 💳 *No credit cards* ⏲ *Closed Tues.*

WHERE TO STAY

For expanded reviews, facilities, and current deals, visit Fodors.com.

$$ RESORT 🏨 **Dolphin Beach Resort.** If you don't want to stay at a chain but can't afford a huge resort, this beachfront spot is probably a good choice. **Pros:** good bargain; on the beach. **Cons:** decor seems a little dated. [$] *Rooms from: $159* ✉ *4900 Gulf Blvd., St. Pete Beach* ☎ *727/360–7011* 🌐 *www.dolphinbeach.com* 🛏 *173 rooms* 🍴 *No meals.*

$$$ RESORT 🏨 **Doubletree Beach Resort Tampa Bay.** This hotel from the Hilton family offers the chain's well-known luxury without diminishing the mellow charm of the surrounding area. **Pros:** lauded facility; quiet, beachfront location. **Cons:** few attractions nearby. [$] *Rooms from: $159* ✉ *17120 Gulf Blvd., N. Redington Beach* ☎ *727/391–4000* 🌐 *www.doubletreeresort.com* 🛏 *126 rooms* 🍴 *No meals.*

$$$ HOTEL 🏨 **Island's End Resort.** We love this converted 1950s-vintage motel because it has some of the area's best sunrise and sunset views and, like the rest of historic Pass-A-Grille, is totally friendly and totally Old Florida. **Pros:** good value; nice views; near restaurants and shops. **Cons:** access via a traffic-clogged road, parking can be tricky. [$] *Rooms from: $199* ✉ *1 Pass-A-Grille Way, St. Pete Beach* ☎ *727/360–5023* 🌐 *www.islandsend.com* 🛏 *6 cottages* 🍴 *Breakfast.*

$$$$ RESORT Fodor's Choice ★ 🏨 **Loews Don CeSar Hotel.** Today the "Pink Palace," as it's called thanks to its paint job, is a storied resort and gulf-coast architectural landmark, with exterior and public areas oozing turn-of-the-20th-century elegance. **Pros:** romantic destination; great beach; tasty dining options. **Cons:** small rooms, can be quite pricey. [$] *Rooms from: $269* ✉ *3400 Gulf Blvd., St. Pete Beach* ☎ *727/367–6952, 800/282–1116* 🌐 *www.doncesar.com* 🛏 *277 rooms, 40 suites, 70 condos* 🍴 *No meals.*

$$$ HOTEL Fodor's Choice ★ 🏨 **Postcard Inn.** Take a Waikiki surf shack from back in Duke's day, shake it up with a little Miami chic (circa 1955), and give it a clean modern twist—that's this ultrahip beachfront hotel to a T. **Pros:** lively fresh feel; on the beach; walking distance to restaurants and nightlife; friendly staff. **Cons:** not for squares. [$] *Rooms from: $169* ✉ *6300 Gulf Blvd., St. Pete Beach* ☎ *727/367–2611, 800/237–8918* 🌐 *www.postcardinn.com* 🛏 *196 rooms* 🍴 *Breakfast.*

$$$ RESORT FAMILY 🏨 **TradeWinds Islands Resorts.** The only resort on the beach offering up its own fireworks display, the island-chic TradeWinds is popular with foreign travelers and the go-to place for beach weddings; it's also one of the few pet-friendly resorts in the area, boasting a play area and a room-service menu for dogs and cats. **Pros:** great beachfront location; close to restaurants. **Cons:** large, sprawling complex; lots of conventions;

pesky resort fee. $ *Rooms from: $219* ⊠ *5500 Gulf Blvd., St. Pete Beach* ☎ *727/363–2212* ⊕ *www.justletgo.com* ⟿ *584 rooms, 103 suites* ⊠*No meals.*

$$$$ ⊞ **Vinoy Renaissance Resort & Golf Club.** Built in 1925, (making it the
RESORT same vintage as the Don CeSar), the Vinoy is a luxury resort in St.
Fodor'sChoice Petersburg's gorgeous Old Northeast. **Pros:** charming property; friendly
★ service; close to downtown museums. **Cons:** pricey; small rooms.
$ *Rooms from: $269* ⊠ *501 5th Ave. NE* ☎ *727/894–1000* ⊕ *www. vinoyrenaissanceresort.com* ⟿ *346 rooms, 15 suites* ⊠*No meals.*

NIGHTLIFE

Daiquiri Shak. If frozen DayGlo concoctions spinning around in washing mashine–like mechanisms are your thing, this place should certainly be on your list. If not, this is still a good go-to weekend watering hole on Madeira Beach (technically, it's across the street from the beach). In addition to selections like the Grape Ape and the Voodoo Loveshake, there's a respectable selection of beer on tap and a full bar. Entertainment ranges from a weekly pub quiz to full-on funk and rock bands on weekends. The menu includes loads of seafood, of course (oysters are a winner), and the late-night menu is served until 1:30 am. There are several sister locations throughout the area, including one in Sarasota. ⊠ *14995 Gulf Blvd., Madeira Beach* ☎ *727/292–2706* ⊕ *www.daiquirishak.com.*

The Garden. This multifaceted drinkery is a good place to start if you plan on barhopping in downtown St. Petersburg, which gets packed on weekends—especially for the monthly first Friday festivities. There are essentially three parts to this establishment: the ground-level area, which offers craft beer and infused vodkas; the courtyard, where you can hear some excellent live jazz on the right night; and the Lobby, which turns into a booming club on weekend nights. ⊠ *217 Central Ave.* ☎ *727/896–3800* ⊕ *www.thegardendtsp.com.*

Jimmy B's. The default beach bar for tourists and locals alike overlooks the vast dunes leading down to the beach. There's live music virtually every night. ⊠ *6200 Gulf Blvd., behind Beachcomber Resort, St. Pete Beach* ☎ *727/367–1902.*

The Mandarin Hide. Perhaps the epitome of downtown St. Pete's bold transformation into a stylish nightlife destination, this place exudes a classy yet jubilant speakeasy vibe. A claw-foot bathtub is one of the first things you see when you walk in the door. Just as vintage as the decor is the drinks menu, which features numerous classic cocktails (made the old-fashioned way), tasty concoctions you'll find nowhere else, and craft beers. You'll find either live music or a DJ most nights. On Sunday they open early to serve up a mean bloody Mary. Closed Monday and Tuesday. ⊠ *231 Central Ave., Downtown* ☎ *727/231–4007* ⊕ *www.mandarinhide.com.*

Ruby's Elixir. If you want to scope out some vintage jazz, blues, or swing, this is the place to do it. It has much better ventilation than most other bars downtown, and you can bring your beverages to one of the outdoor tables—if you can snag one. It's also a great place to find a unique cocktail. ⊠ *15 3rd St. N, Downtown* ☎ *727/798–9829* ⊕ *www.rubyselixir.com.*

World of Beer. The name says it all. This local chain is less than a decade old, but it's starting to get some national attention. There are now locations throughout the state, including outlets in Tampa and West Palm Beach, but this one fits right in with the downtown St. Pete vibe. A new and improved version of the neighborhood pub, WOB offers bottle and draft beers from as far away as New Zealand and as nearby as Tampa. There's live music on weekends. ⊠ *100 4th St. S, Downtown* ☎ *727/823–2337* ⊕ *www.wobusa.com.*

SHOPPING

There's no need for a trip to the mall here. Few places in the Tampa Bay area offer so many eclectic shopping options as the St. Petersburg area. Downtown St. Petersburg's Beach Drive is sprinkled with tons of smart yet pricey boutiques. The Grand Central district has plenty of antiques and vintage clothing shops. Beach shopping hubs John's Pass Village and 8th Avenue offer souvenir shopping that goes well beyond the norm. Each of these is also packed with a range of enticing eateries, many with outdoor seating and live entertainment.

Epitomizing St. Petersburg's cultural rebirth, the block-long stretch of Central Avenue between 6th and 7th streets has loads of art galleries and indie shops, as well as dive bars frequented by tattooed hipsters. The central point is Crislip Arcade, where you'll find a vintage cloth-ing shop (Ramblin' Rose), local art galleries (eve-N-odd and Olio, to name a couple), and a unique jewelry shop (Kathryn Cole). Local busi-nesses line the street, including one that specializes in Moroccan imports (Treasures of Morocco), one that hawks colorfully hand-painted Chuck Taylors (1 of 1 Customs With Rasta), and a smoky bar specializing in craft beer and punk rock (Fubar). Local 662 and the State Theater are two music venues on this block that attract national indie music acts.

Art Village. It's hard to believe that the low-key yet vibrant artist enclave of Gulfport was once a blighted fishing village. Now, it's a colorful waterfront community that's friendly to the LGBT community. It's pretty much in between St. Pete Beach and St. Petersburg proper, and Beach Boulevard's Art Village sports a high volume of locally owned boutiques. Highlights include Hula Hula, a shop dealing in vintage tropical attire and decor, and Domain, where you can find items—Flo-ridiana or otherwise—you'll find nowhere else, given that much of it was forged at the hands of local artisans. An Art Walk occurs every first Friday and third Saturday of the month, and there's a farmer's market every Tuesday. Keep an eye out for cool local events, as there are many here. ⊠ *Beach Blvd. at Shore Dr., Gulfport.*

Florida Craftsmen Galleries. Downtown St. Pete's bursting art revival is epitomized at Florida Craftsmen Galleries, a nonprofit that gives 125 local crafts people a chance to exhibit glassware, jewelry, furniture, and more. (Think: a vivid coral reef seascape made entirely out of yarn. Stuff like that.) While you're here, take a stroll along Central Avenue's 600 block for a real glimpse into downtown St. Pete's fresh, burgeoning art scene. ⊠ *501 Central Ave.* ☎ *727/821–7391* ⊕ *www. floridacraftsmen.net.*

Haslam's. One of the state's most notable bookstores is a family-owned emporium that's been doing business just west of downtown St. Petersburg for more than 70 years. Rumored to be haunted by the ghost of *On the Road* author Jack Kerouac (indeed the renowned Beat Generation author used to frequent Haslam's before he died in St. Pete in 1969), the store carries some 300,000 volumes, from cutting-edge best-sellers to ancient tomes. If you value a good book or simply like to browse, you could easily spend an afternoon here. ⊠ *2025 Central Ave.* ☎ *727/822–8616* ⊕ *www.haslams.com.*

John's Pass Village and Boardwalk. This collection of shops and restaurants is in an old-style fishing village, where you can watch pelicans cavorting and dive-bombing for food or check out some mellow island music. There's even a live gator attraction here, where patrons can pay to feed the enormous Florida icons large slabs of meat. ⊠ *12901 Gulf Blvd., Madeira Beach* ⊕ *www.johnspass.com.*

Pass-a-Grille 8th Avenue. Pass-A-Grille, the extremely laid-back portion of St. Pete Beach, is well known for its serene beaches, historic buildings, and small-town vibe. What many visitors—and locals—don't know is that eight blocks north of the island's southern tip lies a strip of upscale local shops and art galleries. Favorites include Evander Preston's (who also brews a beer sold locally), Paradiso (resortwear, etc.), and Mountcastle International Trading Company (featuring hand-crafted items from across the globe). An interesting variety of restaurants and bars, including a sweets shop, an all-vegan eatery, and Shadrack's, a quintessential beach dive, also line the street. ⊠ *8th Ave., St. Pete Beach.*

SPORTS AND THE OUTDOORS

BASEBALL

Tampa Bay Rays. Major League Baseball's Tampa Bay Rays completed an improbable worst-to-first turnaround when they topped the American League Eastern Division in 2008, and again in 2010. Then there was that dramatic end-of-season comeback in 2011. Tickets are available at the box office for most games, but you may have to rely on the classifieds sections of the *Tampa Tribune* and *Tampa Bay Times* for popular games. Get here early; parking is often at a premium (pregaming at Ferg's is always a safe bet). ⊠ *Tropicana Field, 1 Tropicana Dr., off I–175* ☎ *727/825–3137* ⊕ *www.tampabay.rays.mlb.com.*

CLEARWATER AND VICINITY

Clearwater is 12 miles north of St. Petersburg via U.S. 19.

In Clearwater itself, residential areas are a buffer between the commercial zone that centers on U.S. 19 and the beach, which is moderately quiet during winter but buzzing with life during spring break and in summer. There's a quaint downtown area on the mainland, just east of the beach. You'll find a nightly sunset celebration on the beach and tons of options for dining and entertainment. Among this area's celebrity residents is Winter, the young dolphin who was fitted with a prosthetic tail and depicted in the 2011 film Dolphin Tale; she's helping put this place and its renowned beaches on the map.

If you're up for a day trip, you have two good options if you head north on U.S. 19. One is Dunedin, a Scottish settlement that's packed with cute shops, restaurants, and craft beer bars. You'll find some gorgeous beaches to the west.

Farther north is charming Tarpon Springs, which has a highly Greek-influenced downtown. Here, you'll find historic sponge docks, a Greek restaurant or two, and some great beaches for watching the sunset.

GETTING HERE AND AROUND
Clearwater is due west from Tampa International Airport via State Road 60, and it's about 45 minutes north of St. Petersburg. If you want to fly directly to Clearwater instead of Tampa, though, St. Pete/Clearwater International Airport is another option. From St. Pete you can get here via U.S. 19, which is notorious for its congestion, Alternate U.S. 19, or County Road 1. If you're up for a scenic yet slower drive, Gulf Boulevard takes you all the way to Clearwater from St. Pete Beach—as does a beach trolley that runs along that route.

VISITOR INFORMATION
Contacts **Clearwater Regional Chamber of Commerce** ✉ *600 Cleveland St., Suite 200* ☎ *727/461–0011* ⊕ *www.clearwaterflorida.org.* **Greater Dunedin Chamber of Commerce** ✉ *301 Main St., Dunedin* ☎ *727/733-3197* ⊕ *www.dunedin-fl.com.* **Tarpon Springs Chamber of Commerce** ✉ *111 E. Tarpon Ave., Tarpon Springs* ☎ *727/937–6109* ⊕ *www.tarponspringschamber.com.*

EXPLORING

Clearwater Marine Aquarium. This aquarium gives you the opportunity to participate in the work of saving and caring for endangered marine species. Many of the sea turtles, dolphins, and other animals living at the aquarium were brought here to be rehabilitated from an injury or saved from danger. The dolphin exhibit has an open-air arena giving the dolphins plenty of room to jump during their shows. This aquarium is also home to Winter, a dolphin fitted with a prosthetic tail that was the subject of the 2011 film *Dolphin Tale*. The aquarium conducts tours of the bays and islands around Clearwater, including a daily cruise on a pontoon boat (you might just see a wild dolphin or two), and kayak tours of Clearwater Harbor and St. Joseph Sound. ✉ *249 Windward Passage* ☎ *727/441–1790* ⊕ *www.seewinter.com* 🎟 *$20* ⊙ *Daily 10–6.*

Konger Tarpon Springs Aquarium. Although it's not on par with larger facilities in Tampa and Clearwater, this is certainly an entertaining attraction. There are some good exhibits, including a 120,000-gallon shark tank complete with a coral reef. (Divers feed the sharks several times daily.) Also look for tropical fish exhibits and a tank where you can touch baby sharks and stingrays. ✉ *850 Dodecanese Blvd., off U.S. 19, Tarpon Springs* ☎ *727/938–5378* ⊕ *www.tarponspringsaquarium. com* 🎟 *$7.75* ⊙ *Mon.–Sat. 10–5, Sun. noon–5.*

Continued on page 404

SPRING TRAINING, FLORIDA-STYLE

by Jim Tunstall and Connie Sharpe

Sunshine, railroads, and land bargains were Florida's first tourist magnets, but baseball had a hand in things, too. The Chicago Cubs led the charge when they opened spring training in Tampa in 1913— the same year the Cleveland Indians set up camp in Pensacola.

Over the next couple of decades, World War I and the Great Depression interrupted normal lives, but the Sunshine State became a great fit for the national pastime. Soon, big-league teams were flocking south to work off the winter rust.

At one point, the Florida "Grapefruit League" held a monopoly on spring training, but in 1947 Arizona's "Cactus League" started cutting into the action.

Today, roughly half of Major League Baseball's 30 teams arrive in Florida in February for six weeks of calisthenics, tryouts, and practice games. The clubs range from the Detroit Tigers, who have been in the same city (Lakeland) longer than any other team (since 1934), to the Tampa Bay Rays, who moved to a new spring home (Port Charlotte) in 2009.

The Los Angeles Dodgers play the Washington Nationals in Viera during a spring training game.

HERE COME THE FANS

Fan appreciate the relative intimacy of Spring Training stadiums.

Florida's spring training teams play 25 or 30 home and away games, to the delight of 1.68 million annual ticker buyers. Diehards land as soon as the first troops—pitchers and catchers—come to practice around the third week of February. Inter-squad games start in the fourth week, while the real training schedule begins by the end of February or first of March and lasts until the end of the month or early April. These games don't count in the regular season, but they give managers and fans a good idea of which players will be on the opening-day rosters, and who will be traded, sent to the teams' minor leagues, or told it's time to find a regular day job.

Spring training games provide a great excuse for local baseball fans to cut out of work early, while visitors from the North can leave ice, snow, and sleet behind. And who doesn't want a few chili dogs,

brats, burgers, and brews on a March day? Spring training's draw is more than just a change of venue with an early sample of concession-stand staples. There is also the ample choice of game sites. Teams are scattered around most of the major tourist areas of central and southern Florida, so those coming to watch the games can try a different destination each spring—or even make a road trip to several. Baseball fans also like that it's a melting pot—teams from more than a dozen cities are represented here.

Finally, you can't beat the price—tickets are usually cheaper than during the regular season—nor the access you have to baseball celebrities. In fact, the relaxed atmosphere of spring training makes most players more willing to sign your ball, glove, or whatever. You can get autographs during pregame workouts (practice sessions), which are free, as well as after the game.

4 TIPS

■ **Have a game plan.** Don't just show up. Most teams only have about 15 home games, and those involving popular teams often sell out weeks in advance. Consider buying tickets ahead of time, and if needed, make hotel room reservations at the same time.

■ **Beat the crowds.** The best chance to do this is to go to a weekday game. You'll still encounter lots of fans, but weekday games generally aren't as well attended as weekenders. Also, each team only has a few night games.

■ **Pack a picnic.** Some stadiums let you bring coolers through the turnstiles. Many game attendees also gather for a tailgate party, grilling burgers and sipping a lemonade or beer while jawing with fellow fans (have a chair in tow).

■ West coast games get a lot of sun. Seats in the shade are premium.

(above) Hammond Stadium in Ft. Myers is where the Minnesota Twins practice.
(right) St. Louis Cardinals Chris Duncan is tagged out at Roger Dean Stadium in Jupiter.

Atlanta Braves	2	New York Yankees	4
Baltimore Orioles	7	Philadelphia Phillies	1
Boston Red Sox	14	Pittsburgh Pirates	10
Detroit Tigers	9	St. Louis Cardinals/	
Houston Astros	11	Florida Marlins	12
Minnesota Twins	8	Tampa Bay Rays	3
New York Mets	6	Toronto Blue Jays	5
		Washington Nationals	13

PLAY BALL!

Spring training schedules are determined around Thanksgiving. Ticket prices change each year. For all of these teams, you also can order spring training tickets through Ticketmaster (☎ 866/448–7849 ⊕ www.ticketmaster.com) or through the respective team's box office or team Web site. For more information about any of the teams, visit ⊕ www.florida-grapefruitleague.com.

SPRING TRAINING GUIDE
Order a free Guide to *Florida Spring Training* from the **Florida Sports Foundation** (✉ 2930 Kerry Forest Parkway, Tallahassee, FL ☎ 850/488–8347 ⊕ www.flasports.com). Published in February each year, it's packed with information about teams, sites, tickets, and more.

New York Mets catcher Ramon Castro.

ATLANTA BRAVES
Home Field: Champion Stadium, Walt Disney World Wide World of Sports, 700 S. Victory Way, Lake Buena Vista. **Tickets:** $10–$49 ☎ 407/939–4263 ⊕ www.braves.mlb.com

BALTIMORE ORIOLES
Home Field: Ed Smith Stadium, 2700 12th St., Sarasota. **Tickets:** $8–$32
☎ 941/954–4101 ⊕ www.orioles.mlb.com

BOSTON RED SOX
Home Field: JetBlue Park, 11500 Fenway South Dr., Fort Myers. **Tickets:** $10–$46
☎ 239/334–4700, 888/733–7696 ⊕ www.redsox.mlb.com

DETROIT TIGERS
Home Field: Joker Marchant Stadium, 2301 Lakeland Hills Blvd., Lakeland. **Tickets:** $10–$32
☎ 863/686–8075 ⊕ www.tigers.mlb.com

HOUSTON ASTROS
Home Field: Osceola County Stadium, 631 Heritage Parkway, Kissimmee. **Tickets:** $15–$27
☎ 321/697–3200 ⊕ www.astros.mlb.com

MIAMI MARLINS
Home Field: Roger Dean Stadium (shared with St. Louis Cardinals), 4751 Main St., Jupiter. **Tickets:** $15–$28
☎ 561/775–1818 ⊕ www.marlins.mlb.com

MINNESOTA TWINS
Home Field: Lee County Sports Complex, 14100 Six Mile Cypress Parkway, Fort Myers. **Tickets:** $13–$29
☎ 800/338-9467 ⊕ www.twins.mlb.com

NEW YORK METS
Home Field: Mets Field, 525 NW Peacock Blvd., Port St. Lucie. **Tickets:** $8–$25
☎ 772/871-2115 ⊕ www.mets.mlb.com

NEW YORK YANKEES
Home Field: George M. Steinbrenner Field, 1 Steinbrenner Dr., Tampa. **Tickets:** $17–$33
☎ 813/879-2244 ⊕ www.yankees.mlb.com

PHILADELPHIA PHILLIES
Home Field: Bright House Networks Field, 601 N. Old Coachman Rd., Clearwater. **Tickets:** $14–$39
☎ 727/467-4457 ⊕ www.phillies.mlb.com

PITTSBURGH PIRATES
Home Field: McKechnie Field, 1611 9th St. W, Bradenton. **Tickets:** $12–$22
☎ 941/747-3031 ⊕ www.pirates.mlb.com

ST. LOUIS CARDINALS
Home Field: Roger Dean Stadium (shared with Miami Marlins), 4751 Main St., Jupiter. **Tickets:** $15–$28
☎ 561/630-1828 ⊕ www.cardinals.mlb.com

TAMPA BAY RAYS
Home Field: Charlotte County Sports Park, 2300 El Jobean Rd., Port Charlotte. **Tickets:** $10–$27
☎ 888/326-7297 ⊕ www.rays.mlb.com

TORONTO BLUE JAYS
Home Field: Florida Auto Exchange Park, 373 Douglas Ave., Dunedin. **Tickets:** $15–$30
☎ 727/733-0429 ⊕ www.bluejays.mlb.com

WASHINGTON NATIONALS
Home Field: Space Coast Stadium, 5800 Stadium Parkway, Viera. **Tickets:** $12–$26
☎ 321/633-4487 ⊕ www.nationals.mlb.com

FAMILY **Pier 60.** This spot is the terminus of State Road 60 (hence the name), which runs under various names between Vero Beach on the east coast and Clearwater Beach on the west coast. Around 3:30 each day, weather permitting, the area surrounding the pier starts to liven up. Local artists and craftspeople populate their folding tables with beaded jewelry, handmade skincare products, and beach landscape paintings. Jugglers, musicians, break-dancers, and fire breathers put on some lively shows for those in attendance. And the grand finale is the sun setting over the Gulf of Mexico. On weekends when the weather is mild, there are also free, family-friendly movie screenings. ⊠ *10 Pier 60 Dr., Clearwater Beach* ☎ *727/449–1036* ⊕ *www.sunsetsatpier60.com.*

> ### WORD OF MOUTH
>
> "Tampa has a great aquarium, Ybor City, and Busch Gardens, of course, but the Gulf beaches are beautiful and full of fun things to do. No matter where you stay, you should include a trip to the Sponge docks in Tarpon Springs and a visit to Fort De Soto Park."
>
> —stpetereb

The Sponge Factory. This shop, museum, and cultural center reveals more than you ever imagined about how a lowly sea creature created the industry that built this village. See a film about these much-sought-after creatures from the phylum *porifera* and how they helped the town prosper in the early 1900s. You'll come away converted to (and loaded up with) natural sponges. ⊠ *15 Dodecanese Blvd., off U.S. 19, Tarpon Springs* ☎ *727/938–5366* ⊕ *www.spongedocks.net* ☞ *Free* ⊗ *Daily 9–6.*

FAMILY **Suncoast Primate Sanctuary.** You may not be able to find monkeys in the wild in the Tampa Bay area (at least not naturally), but you can catch them bouncing around in their cages at this low-key facility. The alleged final home of Cheetah, the chimp who played Tarzan's sidekick for a couple of years in the 1930s, the sanctuary houses a whole slew of primates. One of the first you'll meet is Pongo, a massive Bornean orangutan; if he's in the right mood, he will greet you when you walk up. The sanctuary also hosts baboons, lemurs, spider monkeys, macaques—you name it—many of them former pets or onetime laboratory test subjects. There are also a few reptiles (you can get a picture of yourself holding a baby alligator) and a colorful array of birds. You may find the colorful plastic toys in the primate enclosures odd, but they actually serve to enhance the animals' senses. Veterans receive free admission here. ⊠ *4600 Alt. Hwy. 19, Palm Harbor* ☎ *727/943–5897* ⊕ *www.suncoastprimate.org* ☞ *$10* ⊗ *Thurs.–Sun. 10–4.*

BEACHES

Caladesi Island State Park. Quiet, secluded, and still wild, this 3½-mile-long barrier island is one of the best shelling beaches on the Gulf Coast, second only to Sanibel. The park also has plenty of sights for birders—from common sandpipers to majestic blue herons to rare black skimmers—and miles of trails through scrub oaks, saw palmettos, and cacti (with tenants such as armadillos, rabbits, and raccoons). The landscape

Clearwater's Bait House lures in those heading to the pier to fish; photo by watland, Fodors.com member.

also features mangroves and dunes, and the gradual slope of the sea bottom makes this a good spot for novice swimmers and kids. You have to get to Caladesi Island by private boat (there's a 108-slip marina) or through its sister park, Honeymoon Island State Recreation Area, where you take the hourly ferry ride across to Caladesi. Ferry rides cost $14 per person. **Amenities:** food and drink; showers; toilets. **Best for:** solitude; swimming. ⊠ *Dunedin Causeway, Dunedin* ☎ *727/469–5942* ☞ *$5 per car* ☉ *Daily 10–4:30.*

Fodor's Choice ★ **Clearwater Beach.** On a narrow island between Clearwater Harbor and the gulf is a stretch of sand with a widespread reputation for beach volleyball. It's also the site of a nightly sunset celebration, complete with musicians and artisans. It's one of the area's nicest and busiest beaches, especially on weekends and during spring break, but it's also one of the costliest in terms of parking fees, which can reach $2 per hour. **Amenities:** food and drink; showers; toilets. **Best for:** partiers; sunset; walking. ⊠ *Western end of Rte. 60, 2 miles west of downtown Clearwater.*

Honeymoon Island State Park. If you're seeking an almost completely undeveloped beach that's still easily accessible by car, this is one of your best bets. Northwest of Clearwater, this large state park offers some of the best shell hunting you'll find, as well as thousands of feet of serene beachfront. If you head north along the park road, you find extensive hiking trails, along which you'll see an astonishing array of birds. **Amenities:** food and drink; showers; toilets. **Best for:** solitude; swimming; walking. ⊠ *1 Causeway Blvd., Dunedin* ☞ *Single occupant vehicle $4, vehicle with 2–8 people $8.*

Howard Park Beach. It comes in two parts: a shady mainland picnic area with barbecues and a white-sand beach island. The causeway is a popular hangout for windsurfers, and the entire area is great for birding. **Amenities:** showers; toilets. **Best for:** sunset; swimming; windsurfing. ⊠ *1700 Sunset Dr., Tarpon Springs* 🅿 *$5.*

Indian Rocks Beach. This beach community is a mellow alternative to the oft-crowded shorelines of Clearwater and St. Pete Beach along the gulf coast. This is a town in which the road narrows to two lanes and is lined with upscale residential condos instead of busy hotels. There are quite a few beach access points, though your best bet is a landscaped facility offering ample parking, nearby food and drink, and an occasional event. **Amenities:** food and drink; parking; showers; toilets. **Best for:** solitude; swimming; walking. ⊠ *Indian Rocks Beach Nature Preserve, 1700 Gulf Blvd., Indian Rocks Beach* ⊕ *www. indian-rocks-beach.com.*

Sand Key Park. This is a mellow counterpart to often-crowded Clearwater Beach to the north. It has a lovely beach, plenty of green space, a playground, and a picnic area in an otherwise congested area. **Amenities:** food and drink; lifeguards; showers; toilets. **Best for:** solitude; sunset; swimming. ⊠ *1060 Gulf Blvd.* ☎ *727/588–4852.*

Sunset Beach. As the name suggests, this beach park is known as one of the best places in North Pinellas County to watch the sunset. It's a small beach but a great place to barbecue. From April through November there's a weekly concert. **Amenities:** toilets. **Best for:** sunset; swimming. ⊠ *1800 Gulf Rd., Tarpon Springs.*

WHERE TO EAT

$$$
AMERICAN

✕ **Bob Heilman's Beachcomber.** The Heilman family has fed hungry diners since 1920. Although it's popular with tourists, you'll also rub shoulders with devoted locals. Despite the frequent crowds, the service is fast and friendly. The sautéed chicken is an American classic—arriving with mashed spuds, gravy, veggie du jour, and fresh-baked bread. Or try the New Bedford sea scallops, broiled with lemon and capers, or pan-seared with roasted peppers. $ *Average main: $25* ⊠ *447 Mandalay Ave., Clearwater Beach* ☎ *727/442–4144* ⊕ *www.bobheilmans.com.*

$$$
EUROPEAN

✕ **Bon Appétit.** Known for its creative fare, this waterfront restaurant has a menu that changes frequently, offering such entrées as broiled rack of lamb in herbed walnut crust, and red snapper on a bed of lobster hash. The sautéed grouper, when available, gets well-deserved plaudits from many patrons. Bon Appétit has staying power, having served at the same location for more than three decades. It's a great place to catch a sunset over the Gulf of Mexico. There's a pianist Wednesday through Sunday evenings and a Sunday brunch. $ *Average main: $25* ⊠ *150 Marina Plaza, Dunedin* ☎ *727/733–2151* ⊕ *www.bonappetitrestaurant.com.*

$
MEXICAN
Fodor'sChoice
★

✕ **Casa Tina.** At this colorful Dunedin institution, vegetarians can veg out on roasted chiles rellenos (cheese-stuffed peppers), enchiladas with vegetables, and a cactus salad that won't prick your tongue but will tickle your taste buds with the tantalizing flavors of tender pieces of cactus, cilantro, tomatoes, onions, lime, and *queso fresco* (a mild white cheese). The stuffed sapote squash also makes the grade. Tamales, tacos, and tortillas are prepared in dozens of ways. The place is often crowded, and service can be slow as a result, but there's a reason everyone's eating here. $ *Average main: $15* ⊠ *365 Main St., Dunedin* ☎ *727/734–9226.*

$
SEAFOOD
✕**Frenchy's Rockaway Grill.** Quebec native Mike "Frenchy" Preston runs four eateries in the area, including the fabulous Rockaway Grill. Visitors and locals alike keep coming back for the grouper sandwiches that are moist and not battered into submission. (It's also real grouper, something that's not a given these days.) Frenchy also gets a big thumbs-up for the she-crab soup, and, on the march-to-a-different-drummer front, the grouper eggrolls. In mild weather, eat on the deck, though the screaming yellow awning can be nearly as blinding as the sun. $ *Average main: $15* ⊠ *7 Rockaway St.* ☎ *727/446–4844* ⊕ *www. frenchysonline.com.*

$$
SEAFOOD
✕**Palm Pavilion Beachside Grill & Bar.** Long heralded as one of the best spots for watching sunsets, this place also gets high marks for its fresh seafood offerings. The grouper sandwich in particular gets rave reviews. The restaurant is casual but not too casual. It's got a bit of a Tommy Bahama feel to it, so you may want to ditch the beach attire if you plan to dine here. Be advised that it gets pretty packed around sunset, when a live band plays island music and the margaritas flow. $ *Average main: $15* ⊠ *10 Bay Esplande, Clearwater Beach* ☎ *727/446–2642* ⊕ *www. palmpavilion.com.*

WHERE TO STAY

For expanded reviews, facilities, and current deals, visit Fodors.com.

$$$
HOTEL
⊞**Hilton Clearwater Beach.** Some $26 million in renovations have given this marquee property a clean, modern look without losing the Clearwater Beach vibe, and staying here may be a little less pricey than you might expect. **Pros:** on the beach; about as modern as you can get. **Cons:** chain hotel feel; lots of conventions. $ *Rooms from: $199* ⊠ *400 Mandalay Ave., Clearwater Beach* ☎ *727/298–1486* ⊕ *www.hilton.com* ⌁ *416 rooms, 12 suites* ⦿| *No meals.*

$$$$
RESORT
⊞**Hyatt Regency Clearwater Beach.** One of the more recent additions to the Clearwater Beach skyline, this upscale resort towers above almost everything else in the immediate area, both in terms of height and luxury. **Pros:** gorgeous facility; plenty of amenities; near the action. **Cons:** beach is across busy street; some floors are residential; expensive. $ *Rooms from: $450* ⊠ *301 S. Gulfview Blvd.* ☎ *727/373–1234* ⊕ *www.clearwaterbeach.hyatt.com* ⌁ *250 suites* ⦿| *No meals.*

$$$
RESORT
⊞**Innisbrook Resort & Golf Club.** A massive pool complex with a 15-foot waterfall, two winding waterslides, and a sandy beach are part of the allure of this sprawling resort, but it may be the 72 holes of golf, including the challenging Copperhead course, that are the real draw. **Pros:** great for serious golfers; varied dining options. **Cons:** far from attractions. $ *Rooms from: $149* ⊠ *36750 U.S. 19 N, Palm Harbor* ☎ *727/942–2000, 888/794–8627* ⊕ *www.innisbrookgolfresort.com* ⌁ *50 rooms, 550 suites* ⦿| *No meals.*

7

$$$$ RESORT 🏨 **Safety Harbor Resort & Spa.** Those who enjoy old-school pampering love this hotel's 50,000-square-foot spa, which has the latest in therapies and treatments. **Pros:** charm to spare; good choice for pampering. **Cons:** far from beach; not ideal for families with children. [$] *Rooms from: $269* ✉ *105 N. Bayshore Dr., Safety Harbor* ☎ *727/726–1161, 877/784–6835* 🌐 *www.safetyharborspa.com* 🛏 *175 rooms, 16 suites* 🍴 *No meals.*

$$$$ RESORT 🏨 **Sheraton Sand Key Resort.** Expect something special when you stay here, including a modern property and one of the few uncluttered beaches in the area. **Pros:** private beach; great views; no resort fee and parking is also free. **Cons:** near crowded Clearwater Beach; views come with a high price tag. [$] *Rooms from: $230* ✉ *1160 Gulf Blvd., Clearwater Beach* ☎ *727/595–1611* 🌐 *www.sheratonsandkey.com* 🛏 *375 rooms, 15 suites* 🍴 *No meals.*

THE ARTS

Ruth Eckerd Hall. This 73,000-square-foot hall hosts national artists and companies performing ballet, opera, and pop, classical, or jazz music. ✉ *1111 N. McMullen Booth Rd.* ☎ *727/791–7400* 🌐 *www.rutheckerdhall.com.*

SPORTS AND THE OUTDOORS

BASEBALL

Philadelphia Phillies. The Phillies get ready for the season with spring training here (late February to early April). The stadium also hosts the Phillies' farm team. Check out their minor league team, the Clearwater Threshers, at Bright House Field during the summer months. ✉ *Bright House Networks Field, 601 N. Old Coachman Rd.* ☎ *727/441–8638* 🌐 *philadelphia.phillies.mlb.com.*

Toronto Blue Jays. The Jays play around 15–20 spring training games here, starting in February. ✉ *Florida Auto Exchange Stadium, 373 Douglas Ave., north of Hwy. 580, Dunedin* ☎ *727/733–0429.*

BIKING

Pinellas Trail. This 42-mile paved route spans Pinellas County, from near the southernmost point all the way north to Tarpon Springs. Along a former railway line, the trail runs adjacent to major thoroughfares, no more than 10 feet from the roadway, so you can access it from almost any point. The trail, also popular with in-line skaters, has spawned trailside businesses such as repair shops and health-food cafés. There are also many lovely rural areas to bike through and plenty of places to rent bikes. Be wary of traffic in downtown Clearwater and on the congested areas of the Pinellas Trail, which still needs more bridges for crossing over busy streets, and avoid the trail at night. To start riding from the route's south end, park at Trailhead Park (37th Street South at 8th Avenue South) in St. Petersburg. To ride south from the north end, park your car in downtown Tarpon Springs (East Tarpon Avenue at North Stafford Avenue). ☎ *727/549–6099* 🌐 *www.pinellascounty.org/trailgd.*

SURFING

FlowRider at Surf Style. Surf Style, in the towering Hyatt, is a chain store that sells beach essentials like sarongs, sunblock, and souvenirs. But what sets this particularly enormous store apart is a new FlowRider, an outdoor pool that generates artificial waves suitable for surfing; for $20 a half hour, you and the kids can surf or learn to surf, something you can't usually do out in the gulf. An instructor is on hand to show you the ropes. ⊠ *SurfStyle, 311 S. Gulfview Blvd.* ☎ *727/446–6566* ⊕ *www.surf-style.com.*

EXCURSIONS FROM CLEARWATER

The coastal and western inland areas north of Tampa and St. Petersburg are sometimes called the Nature Coast, and aptly so. Flora and fauna have been well preserved in this area, and West Indian manatees are showstoppers. These gentle vegetarian marine mammals, distantly related to elephants, remain an endangered species, though their numbers have grown to 3,500 or more today. Many manatees have massive scars on their backs from run-ins with boat propellers. Extensive nature preserves and parks have been created to protect them and other wildlife indigenous to the area, and these are among the best spots to view manatees in the wild. Although they're far from mythical beauties, it's believed that manatees inspired ancient mariners' tales of mermaids. This is one of the only spots in the world where you can legally swim with—and even touch—these gentle creatures.

GETTING HERE AND AROUND

U.S. 19 and the Suncoast Parkway, a toll road, are the prime north–south routes through this rural region, and traffic flows freely once you've left the congestion of St. Petersburg, Clearwater, and Port Richey. In most cases, the Suncoast Parkway is a far quicker drive than U.S. 19, though you'll have to pay several dollars in tolls. If you're planning a day trip from the Bay Area, pack a picnic lunch before leaving, since most of the sights are outdoors.

HOMOSASSA SPRINGS

65 miles north of St. Petersburg on U.S. 19.

A little more than an hour north of Clearwater, you'll come upon this small and friendly hub for water lovers. Along with a phenomenal manatee-centric state park, you'll find more than a handful of charming restaurants, some featuring live music in the evening. This and Crystal River provide you with the once-in-a-lifetime chance to swim with manatees, something best done in winter. Summer's scallop season is also a massive draw.

EXPLORING

FAMILY **Homosassa Springs Wildlife State Park.** Here you can see many manatees and several species of fish through a floating glass observatory known as the Fish Bowl—except in this case the fish are outside the bowl and you are inside it. The park's wildlife walk trails lead you to excellent manatee, alligator, and other animal programs. Among the species are bobcats, a western cougar, white-tailed deer, a black bear, pelicans, herons, snowy egrets, river otters, whooping cranes, and even a hippopotamus named Lu, a keepsake from the park's days as an exotic-animal attraction. Boat cruises on Pepper Creek lead you to the Homosassa wildlife park (which takes its name from a Creek Indian word meaning "place where wild peppers grow"). ✉ *4150 S. Suncoast Blvd., U.S. 19* ☎ *352/628–2311* 🌐 *www.hswsp.com* 🎟 *$13* 🕒 *Daily 9–5:30; last boat departs at 3:15.*

Yulee Sugar Mill Ruins Historic State Park. This state park has the remains of a circa-1851 sugar mill and other remnants of a 5,100-acre sugar plantation owned by Florida's first U.S. senator, David Levy Yulee. It makes for pleasant picnicking, although it is somewhat lacking visually. ✉ *Rte. 490(Yulee Dr.), 3 miles off U.S. 19/98* ☎ *352/795–3817* 🌐 *www.floridastateparks.org* 🎟 *Free* 🕒 *Daily 8 am–sunset.*

WHERE TO EAT

$ SEAFOOD 🍴 **Dan's Clam Stand.** Four reasons to go: the fried grouper sandwich, the clam "chowda," anything else seafood, and the beef burgers. The original location is about 2 miles east of Homosassa Springs State Wildlife Park. It's very popular among locals—just check out the packed parking lot at lunch and dinner. New England–style seafood is a house specialty, including whole-belly clams and lobster, but the grouper and mahimahi are fresh from local waters. Best of all, Dan's won't bust your budget. [$] *Average main: $10* ✉ *7364 Grover Cleveland Blvd.* ☎ *352/628–9588* 💳 *No credit cards* 🕒 *Closed Sun.* [$] *Average main: $10* ✉ *2315 N. Sunshine Path, off Rte. 44, Crystal River* ☎ *352/795–9081.*

$ CUBAN 🍴 **Museum Cafe.** A short trip west of Homosassa Springs State Wildlife Refuge, this tiny eatery housed in the Olde Mill House Printing Museum is known for its Cuban sandwiches. It's only open for lunch, but it's well worth making room for a visit here in your itinerary. You can sit at a table within the museum itself or one of the tables in the very casual main dining room. Another option is to get your lunch to go and picnic at nearby Yulee Sugar Mill Ruins State Park. [$] *Average main: $10* ✉ *10466 W. Yulee Dr.* ☎ *352/628–1081.*

$$ SEAFOOD 🍴 **Neon Leon's Zydeco Steakhouse.** If you couldn't already tell, the Nature Coast is about as Southern as you can get. This place is a case in point. This roadhouse-style eatery is co-owned by family members of former Lynyrd Skynyrd bassist Leon Wilkeson. Legend has it that Wilkeson had long dreamed of opening a restaurant serving Southern and Cajun food, with music to match. You'll hear nightly live zydeco here, and the menu offers Dixieland staples like jambalaya (a favorite here), frog legs, and catfish. It may have a roadhouse feel and plenty of musical memorabilia, but it's also smoke-free and pretty family-friendly. [$] *Average main: $15* ✉ *10350 Yulee Dr.* ☎ *352/621–3663* 🌐 *www.neonleonszydecosteakhouse.com.*

CRYSTAL RIVER

6 miles north of Homosassa Springs on U.S. 19.

Situated along the peaceful Nature Coast, this area is *the* low-key getaway spot in one of the most pristine and beautiful areas in the state. It's also one of the only places on the planet where you can legally swim with manatees. The river's fed by a spring that's a constant 72°F, which is why manatees enjoy spending their winters here. Boating and snorkeling are popular, as is scalloping in the summer. This is a true paradise for nature lovers, and absolutely worth making room for in your vacation itinerary.

EXPLORING

Crystal River National Wildlife Refuge. This is a U.S. Fish and Wildlife Service sanctuary for the endangered manatee. Kings Spring, around which manatees congregate in winter (generally from November to March), feeds crystal-clear water into the river at 72°F year-round. This is one of the sure-bet places to see manatees in winter since hundreds congregate near this 90-acre refuge. The small visitor center has displays about the manatee and other refuge inhabitants. If you want to get an even closer look at these gentle giants, several dive companies provide opportunities for you to swim among them—if you don't mind shelling out some extra cash, donning a wetsuit, and adhering to some strict interaction guidelines. In warmer months, when most manatees scatter, the main spring is fun for a swim or scuba diving. ✉ *1502 S.E. Kings Bay Dr.* ☎ *352/563–2088* 🌐 *www.fws.gov/crystalriver* 🎟 *Free* 🕒 *Daily 7:30–4.*

BEACHES

Fort Island Gulf Beach. This is one of the most remote beaches you will find north of Fort De Soto, the isolated beach south of St. Petersburg. One of the best parts of coming here is the drive. The beach sits as the terminus of Fort Island Trail, the same road where you'll find the Plantation Inn & Golf Resort. A 9-mile drive through the wetlands gets you here, offering sweeping views along the way (though the Crystal River nuclear plant looms to the north). The beach itself is raw and subdued, though there are picnic shelters, barbecues and a fishing pier. Don't expect many frills, but if you need to relax after a long day of playing in the water, this is your place. **Amenities:** showers; toilets. **Best for:** solitude, sunset. ✉ *16000 W. Fort Island Trail.*

WHERE TO STAY

$$ HOTEL 🏨 **Best Western Crystal River Resort.** Divers favor this cinder-block roadside motel close to the manatee population at Kings Bay. **Pros:** great location; bargain rates. **Cons:** chain-motel feel; few amenities; no restaurant or bar. [$] *Rooms from: $99* ✉ *614 N.W. U.S. 19* ☎ *352/795–3171, 800/435–4409* 🌐 *www.crystalriverresort.com* 🛏 *96 rooms, 18 efficiencies* 🍴 *Breakfast.*

$$ RESORT 🏨 **Plantation Inn & Golf Resort.** On the shore of Kings Bay, this two-story plantation-style resort is on 232 acres near nature preserves and rivers. **Pros:** good location; perfect for nature lovers. **Cons:** lots of conventions; basic rooms. [$] *Rooms from: $130* ✉ *9301 W. Fort Island Trail* ☎ *352/795–4211* 🌐 *www.plantationinn.com* 🛏 *196 rooms, 12 villas* 🍴 *No meals.*

MANATEE DIVES

American Pro Diving Center. This is one of several local operators in the area conducting manatee tours of Crystal River National Wildlife Refuge or Homosassa River, something they say you can't legally do pretty much anywhere else. ✉ *821 S.E. U.S. 19* ☎ *352/563–0041* 🌐 *www.americanprodiving.com.*

Crystal Lodge Dive Center. This dive center is one of the more popular operators offering dives, swims, and snorkel trips to see manatees. ✉ *525 N.W. 7th Ave.* ☎ *352/795–6798* ⊕ *www.manatee-central.com.*

Plantation Dive Shop. An obvious choice if you're staying at the Plantation Inn, this dive tour company stands on its own as a manatee tour operator. The guides bring you out to various spots along the river to interact with manatees, and tend to be long-time residents who know their subject well. If the weather is warm, that means no manatees, so opt for a sunset cruise instead. ✉ *9301 Fort Island Trail* ☎ *352/795–4211* ⊕ *www.crystalriverdivers.com* 🏷 *$30 plus equipment.*

SARASOTA AND VICINITY

Widely thought of as one of the best places in Florida to live, Sarasota County anchors the southern end of Tampa Bay. A string of barrier islands borders it with 35 miles of gulf and bay beaches. Sarasota County has something for anyone, from the athletic to the artistic. Thirteen public beaches, two state parks, 22 municipal parks, plus more than 60 public and private golf courses will help keep the active in motion. Spring training was an original destination attraction that now shares the stage with international rowing, swimming, and sailing events. Add to that a plentiful cultural scene dating to the era of circus magnate John Ringling, who chose this area for the winter home of his circus and his family.

BRADENTON

49 miles south of Tampa.

In 1539 Hernando de Soto landed near this Manatee River city, which has some 20 miles of beaches. Bradenton is well situated for access to fishing, both fresh- and saltwater, and it also has its share of golf courses and historic sites dating to the mid-1800s. Orange groves and cattle ranches mix with farmlands between Bradenton's beaches and I–75.

GETTING HERE AND AROUND
You can get to Bradenton via I–75, I–275, and U.S. 41/301. West Manatee Avenue gets you out to the beaches. Manatee County Area Transit (MCAT) has buses throughout Bradenton and the nearby towns of Palmetto and Ellenton, as well as connections to Sarasota attractions. Fares for local bus service range from $1.25 to $3 (for an all-day pass); exact change is required. A $30 monthly "M-Card" is available for unlimited rides on all MCAT routes. However, if you want to get around efficiently—and want access to more places—you're best off renting a car.

Contacts Manatee County Area Transit ⊕ *www.mymanatee.org.*

VISITOR INFORMATION
Contacts Bradenton Area Convention and Visitors Bureau.
This organization has all you need to know about everything Bradenton, Anna Maria Island, Palmetto, and Ellenton have to offer. ☎ *941/729-9177* ⊕ *www.bradentongulfislands.com.*

DID YOU KNOW?

Sometimes called "sea cows," manatees are aquatic relatives of elephants. They can weigh more than 1,500 pounds and live 50-plus years. There are more than 3,000 in Florida's coastal waters.

EXPLORING

Fodor'sChoice **De Soto National Memorial.** One of the first Spanish explorers to land
★ in North America, Hernando de Soto came ashore with his men and
200 horses near what is now Bradenton in 1539; this federal park
commemorates De Soto's expedition and the Native Americans he
and his crew encountered. During the height of tourist season, from
mid-December to late April, park staff and volunteers dress in period
costumes at Camp Uzita, demonstrate the use of 16th-century weapons, and show how European explorers prepared and preserved food
for their overland journeys. The season ends with a reenactment of
the explorer's landing. The site also offers a film and short nature trail
through the mangroves. ⊠ *8300 De Soto Memorial Hwy.* ☏ *941/792–
0458* ⊕ *www.nps.gov/deso* ⊠ *Free* ☉ *Visitor center daily 9–5, grounds
daily dawn–dusk.*

■ OFF THE
BEATEN
PATH

Gamble Plantation Historic State Park. Built in the 1840s, this antebellum
mansion five miles northeast of Bradenton was home to Major Robert
Gamble and is the headquarters of an extensive sugar plantation. It is
the only surviving plantation house in South Florida. The Confederate secretary of state took refuge here when the Confederacy fell to
Union forces. Picnic tables are available. ⊠ *3708 Patten Ave., Ellenton*
☏ *941/723–4536* ⊠ *Free, tours $6* ☉ *Thurs.–Mon. 8–4:30.*

Pine Avenue. Anna Maria Island's newly restored "Main Street" features
numerous pricey mom-and-pop boutiques, including upscale yet beach-
appropriate clothiers, beach-inspired home decor stores, and antique
furniture shops. You can also find shops offering items such as quality vintage clothing and infused olive oil. ⊠ *Pine Ave., Anna Maria*
☏ *941/592–6642* ⊕ *www.pineavenueinfo.com.*

■ OFF THE
BEATEN
PATH

Solomon's Castle. For a visit to the wild and weird side, particularly fun
for children, head to this castle about 45 minutes east of Bradenton
through orange groves and cattle farms. Artist and Renaissance man
Howard Solomon began building the 12,000-square-foot always-in-
progress work out of thousands of aluminum offset printing plates.
Inside, you'll find tons of intrigues—everything from a knight assembled
with Volkswagen parts to a chair fashioned out of 86 beer cans to an elephant made from seven oil drums. A restaurant serves sit-down lunches
in a full-scale model of a Spanish galleon. It is also open Friday and
Saturday nights in season. ⊠ *4585 Solomon Rd., Ona* ☏ *863/494–6077*
⊕ *www.solomonscastle.org* ⊠ *$10* ☉ *Tues.–Sun 11–4; closed July–Sept.*

FAMILY **South Florida Museum and Parker Manatee Aquarium.** Snooty, the oldest
manatee in captivity, is the headliner here. Programs about the endangered marine mammals run four times daily. View changing exhibits
such as digital images of water and other natural resources in the East
Gallery; glass cases and roll-out drawers on the second floor allow
you to look at exhibits normally out of public view. At the Bishop
Planetarium (with a domed theater screen), programs presented range
from black holes to Jimi Hendrix, Pink Floyd, and other rockers.
⊠ *201 10th St. W* ☏ *941/746–4131* ⊕ *www.southfloridamuseum.org*
⊠ *$15.95* ☉ *Mon.–Sat. 10–5, Sun. noon–5. Closed Mon. May and June
and Aug.–Dec.*

BEACHES

Anna Maria Island, Bradenton's 7-mile barrier island to the west, has a number of worthwhile beaches, as does Longboat Key. Manatee Avenue connects the mainland to the island via the Palma Sola Causeway, adjacent to which is a long, sandy beach fronting Palma Sola Bay. There are boat ramps, a dock, and picnic tables.

Anna Maria Bayfront Park. This secluded beach fronts Tampa Bay at Passage Key Inlet and the Gulf of Mexico. It's also situated between two fishing piers. Don't forget to bring the picnic gear to this unforgettably scenic stretch of shoreline. **Amenities:** lifeguards; showers; toilets. **Best for:** solitude; sunset. ⊠ *310 North Bay Blvd., adjacent to a municipal pier, Anna Maria Island.*

Coquina Beach. Singles and families flock to Coquina Beach, which is at the southern end of Anna Maria Island. Beach walkers love this stretch since it's Anna Maria's longest beach, and it also attracts crowds of young revelers. **Amenities:** food and drink; lifeguards; showers; toilets. **Best for:** solitude; swimming; walking. ⊠ *1800 Gulf Dr. S, Anna Maria Island.*

Cortez Beach. Towering Australian pines greet you at the entrance of this popular beach park, a favorite among locals and visitors alike. **Amenities:** lifeguards; showers; toilets. **Best for:** solitude; swimming; walking. ⊠ *Gulf Blvd., between 5th and 13th Aves., Bradenton Beach.*

Greer Island Beach. Just across the inlet on the northern tip of Longboat Key, Greer Island Beach is accessible by boat or by car via North Shore Boulevard. You'll also hear this place referred to as Beer Can Island. The secluded peninsula has a wide beach and excellent shelling, but no facilities. **Amenities:** None. **Best for:** solitude; walking. ⊠ *Longboat Key.*

Manatee Beach Park. In the middle of Anna Maria Island, Manatee County Beach is popular with beachgoers of all ages. Paid parking is in the gravel lot next to the beach. **Amenities:** food and drink; parking; showers; toilets. **Best for:** solitude; swimming; walking. ⊠ *400 S.R. 64 and Gulf Dr., Holmes Beach.*

WHERE TO EAT

$$$$
STEAKHOUSE
Fodor's Choice
★

╳ **Euphemia Haye.** A lush tropical setting on the barrier island of Longboat Key, this is one of the most romantic restaurants around. The staff is friendly and gracious, the food delightful, and the atmosphere contagious. Its popular dessert display is a sweet ending to the pricey menu items that feature signature dishes such as crisp roast duckling with bread, and flambéed prime peppered steak. The upstairs Haye Loft, once the home of the original owner's grandson, has been converted into a bistro and lounge. $ *Average main: $35* ⊠ *5540 Gulf of Mexico Dr., Longboat Key* ☎ *941/383–3633* ⊕ *www.euphemiahaye.com* ☾ *No lunch.*

$
AMERICAN

╳ **Gulf Drive Café & Tiki.** Especially popular for breakfast (served all day), this unassuming landmark squats on the beach and serves cheap sit-down eats: mostly sandwiches, but also a sampling of entrées after 4 pm. $ *Average main: $14* ⊠ *900 N. Gulf Dr. N, Bradenton Beach* ☎ *941/778–1919.*

$$$
AMERICAN

╳ **Sandbar Seafood & Spirits.** If the grouper is not fresh, it is not on the menu at this newly renovated beachfront restaurant. Ordered blackened, it can hold its own against the Island Salad made with mangoes,

Ringling Mansion Sarasota

Gorgonzola, passion fruit, and pralines. The popular fish also goes over well here in taco form. Other fresh seafood options include a spicy Szechuan tilapia sandwich, and crab cakes and crab-crusted sea scallops, a blend of the Chesapeake and the Gulf. The outside deck sits on the beach—the view is spectacular and a great place to watch the sunset. $ *Average main: $22* ⊠ *100 Spring Ave., Anna Maria Island* ☎ *941/778-0444* ⊕ *www.groupersandwich.com.*

WHERE TO STAY

For expanded reviews, facilities, and current deals, visit Fodors.com.

$$$
RENTAL
BridgeWalk. This circa-1947 Caribbean colonial-style property is across from the beach and a community within itself. **Pros:** great location; variety of lodging and dining experiences. **Cons:** can be pricey. $ *Rooms from: $210* ⊠ *100 Bridge St., Bradenton Beach* ☎ *941/779-2545, 866/779-2545* ⊕ *www.silverresorts.com* ⤳ *28 apartments* ⦿ *No meals.*

$$$$
RESORT
Longboat Key Club & Resort. This spectacularly landscaped property is one of the best places to play golf in the state, and among the top tennis resorts in the country. **Pros:** upscale vibe; lovely grounds; most rooms have private balcony. **Cons:** service can feel snooty. $ *Rooms from: $379* ⊠ *220 Sands Point Rd., Longboat Key* ☎ *941/383-8821, 888/237-5545* ⊕ *www.longboatkeyclub.com* ⤳ *219 rooms and suites* ⦿ *No meals.*

$$$
RESORT
Silver Surf Gulf Beach Resort. A sister to BridgeWalk, the Silver Surf has the air of a well-maintained 1960s motel, offering both studios and full apartments. **Pros:** location; good value for your money. **Cons:** rooms are motel-basic. $ *Rooms from: $160* ⊠ *1301 Gulf Dr. N, Anna Maria Island, Bradenton Beach* ☎ *941/778-6626, 800/441-7873* ⊕ *www.silverresorts.com* ⤳ *50 rooms* ⦿ *No meals.*

GOLF

Buffalo Creek Golf Course. The excellent county-owned 18-hole Buffalo Creek Golf Course, designed by Ron Garl, resembles a Scottish links course. Greens fees are $26–$54. ⊠ *8100 Erie Rd., Palmetto* ☎ *941/776–2611* ⊕ *www.golfmanatee.com.*

SARASOTA

30 miles south of Tampa and St. Petersburg.

Sarasota is a year-round destination and home to some of Florida's most affluent residents. Circus magnate John Ringling and his wife, Mable, started the city on the road to becoming one of the state's hotbeds for the arts. Today sporting and cultural events can be enjoyed anytime of the year, and there's a higher concentration of upscale shops, restaurants, and hotels here than in other parts of the Tampa Bay area. Across the water from Sarasota lie the barrier islands of Siesta Key and Lido Key, with myriad beaches, shops, hotels, condominiums, and houses.

GETTING HERE AND AROUND

Sarasota is accessible from I–75, I–275, and U.S. 41. The town's public transit company is Sarasota County Area Transit (SCAT). Fares for local bus service range from 75¢ to $3 (for an all-day pass); exact change is required. A $60 monthly "R-Card" is available for unlimited rides on all SCAT and Manatee County Area Transit (MCAT) routes. If you want to make it to the farther reaches of the area, though, renting a car is probably your best bet.

Contacts Sarasota County Area Transit (SCAT) ☎ *941/861–1234* ⊕ *www.scgov.net/scat.*

VISITOR INFORMATION

Contacts Sarasota Convention and Visitors Bureau. This organization has the skinny on South Tampa Bay. ⊠ *701 N. Tamiami Trail, U.S. 41* ☎ *800/348–7250* ⊕ *www.sarasotafl.org.*

EXPLORING

TOP ATTRACTIONS

FAMILY

Fodor's Choice

★

John and Mable Ringling Museum of Art. Administered by Florida State University, the museum encompasses the entire Ringling estate, far more than just the art museum; there's also the Tibbals Learning Center and Circus Museums as well as Ca' d'Zan Mansion, the original Ringling home, and its expansive gardens. The entire compound covers 20 waterfront acres and also has the Historic Asolo Theater, restaurants, and a research library.

The **Art Museum** was a dream long in the making for John Ringling (of Ringling Brothers fame). Finally finshed in 1931 after setbacks including a land bust and the the death of his wife Mable, this enormous museum was originally built to house Ringling's mindblowingly expansive art collection. You'll find works ranging from Indian doorways elaborately carved with Jain deities to opulescent Baroque paintings from the likes of Rubens. There seems to be an endless number of rooms, themselves decorated in an appropriately gorgeous manner,

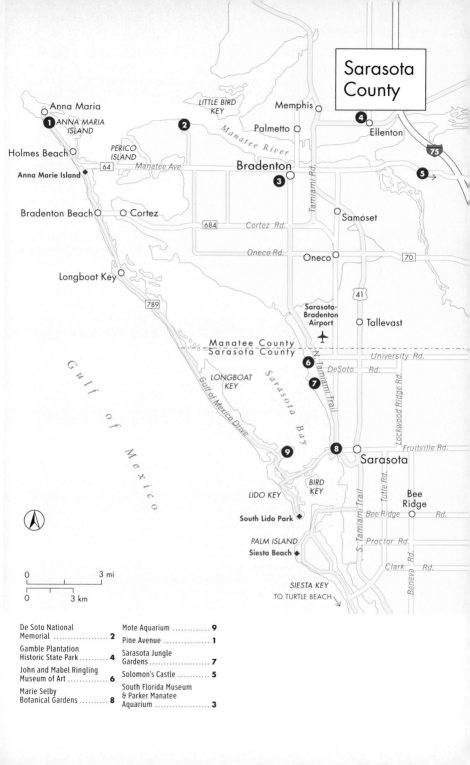

Sarasota County

Anna Maria

1 ANNA MARIA ISLAND

LITTLE BIRD KEY

Memphis

Palmetto ○

4 Ellenton

2

Manatee River

Holmes Beach ○

PERICO ISLAND

Manatee Ave

75

♦ Anna Marie Island

64

Bradenton

Tamiami Rd.

3 ○

5

Bradenton Beach ○   ○ Cortez

Cortez Rd.

Samoset ○

684

Oneco Rd.

Oneco ○

70

Longboat Key ○

789

Sarasota-Bradenton Airport ✈

LONGBOAT KEY

Gulf of Mexico Drive

Sarasota Bay

41

Tallevast ○

G u l f

Manatee County
Sarasota County

University Rd.

6

7

N Tamiami Trail

DeSoto Rd.

Lockwood Ridge Rd.

o f

9

8 ○ Sarasota

Fruitville Rd.

M e x i c o

BIRD KEY

LIDO KEY

Bee Ridge

Tutte Rd.

South Lido Park ♦

Bee Ridge ○   Rd.

S. Tamiami Trail

Proctor Rd.

PALM ISLAND

Siesta Beach ♦

Clark Rd.

Beneva Rd.

SIESTA KEY
TO TURTLE BEACH ↘

0   3 mi

0   3 km

housing these masterpieces. A wing that features traveling exhibits serves as a temporary home to many thought-provoking pieces throughout the year. The museum's exit opens out into an enormous courtyard, over which a towering statue of David replica presides, flanked by royal palms.

Circus magnate John Ringling's grand home, **Ca' d'Zan,** which was built along Sarasota Bay, was patterned after Doge's Palace in Venice. This exquisite mansion of 32 rooms, 15 bathrooms, and a 61-foot Belvedere Tower was completed in 1925, and today is the crowning jewel at the site of the Ringling Estate. Its 8,000-square-foot terrace overlooks the dock where Ringling's wife, Mable, moored her gondola. Mansion tours occur on the hour, and last half an hour. If you don't want a guided tour, show up on the half-hour for a self-guided your.

Allot some extra time to wander around in the Mable Ringling's **Rose Garden,** a lush labyrinth surrounded by towering banyans and full of rare roses and haunting statues.

Don't let the name **Tibbals Learning Center** fool you. This Ringling estate attraction offers a colorful glimpse into a most wondrous element of a bygone era: the traveling circus. The center focuses on the history of the American circus and the collection of Howard Tibbals, master model builder, who spent 40 years building the world's largest miniature circus. Perhaps the center's main attraction, this impressive to-scale replica of the circa 1920s and '30s Ringling Bros. and Barnum & Bailey Circus is an astonishingly accurate portrayal of a circus coming through town—the number of pancakes the circus cooks are flipping, the exact likenesses and costumes of the performers, the correct names of the animals marked on the miniature mess buckets—you name it. Tibbals's passion to re-create every exact detail continues in his on-site workshop, where kids can ask him questions and watch him carving animals and intricate wagons.

If you're looking for clown noses, ringmaster hats, and circus-themed T-shirts, don't leave before checking out the **Ringling Museum of Art Store.**

The **Historic Asolo Theater** is also on the estate grounds and is home to the Asolo Repertory Company. ⊠ *5401 Bay Shore Rd., ½ mile west of Sarasota-Bradenton Airport* ☎ *941/359–5700* ⊕ *www.ringling.org* 🖼 *$25 (art museum only free Mon.)* ⊗ *Grounds daily 9:30–6; museums and mansion daily 10–5 (until 8 Thurs.).*

Marie Selby Botanical Gardens. Orchids make up nearly a third of the 20,000 species of flowers and plants here. You can stroll through the Tropical Display House, home of orchids and colorful bromeliads gathered from rain forests, and wander the garden pathway past plantings of bamboo, ancient banyans, and mangrove forests along Little Sarasota Bay. Although spring sees the best blooms, the greenhouses make this an attraction for all seasons. The added bonus is a spectacular view of downtown. There are rotating exhibits of botanical art and photography in a 1934 restored Southern Colonial mansion. Enjoy lunch at the Selby Café. ⊠ *811 S. Palm Ave.* ☎ *941/366–5731* ⊕ *www.selby.org* 🖼 *$17* ⊗ *Daily 10–5.*

WORTH NOTING

FAMILY **Mote Aquarium.** The latest edition to this world-class marine research facility is a handful of South African penguins, whose daily feasting you are free to observe. Another key feature here is something not so cuddly—the preserved body of a giant squid, which is one of the most mysterious and rare marine species out there. A 135,000-gallon shark tank lets you view various types of sharks from above and below the surface. Other tanks show off eels, rays, and other marine creatures native to the area. There's also a touch tank where you can get friendly with horseshoe crabs, conchs, and other creatures. Hugh and Buffett are the resident manatees and, though not as venerable as Snooty at the Parker Manatee Aquarium, they have lived here since 1996 as part of a research program. There's also a permanent sea-turtle exhibit. Sarasota Bay Explorers offers boat tours from the museum's dock (reservations required), and a combination ticket that includes both admission into the museum and the boat tour is available. ⊠ *1600 Ken Thompson Pkwy., City Island* ☎ *941/388–4441* ⊕ *www.mote.org* ⊠ *Aquarium $17, combined aquarium and boat tour $36* ⊙ *Aquarium daily 10–5; boat tours daily 11, 1:30, and 4.*

Sarasota Bay Explorers. Many visitors to the Mote Aquarium take the 105-minute boat trip onto Sarasota Bay. Conducted by Sarasota Bay Explorers, all boat trips are done in conjunction with the aquarium and leave from the aquarium's dock. The crew brings marine life on board, explains what it is, and throws it back to swim away. You are almost guaranteed to see bottlenose dolphins. Reservations are recommended. You can also charter a power or sailboat or take a guided kayak or nature tour. ⊠ *1600 Ken Thompson Pkwy.* ☎ *941/388–4200* ⊕ *www.sarasotabayexplorers.com* ⊠ *Boat tour $27, kayak tour $55, nature tour $45; call for charter prices* ⊙ *Tours daily at 11, 1:30, and 4 (reservations required).*

FAMILY **Sarasota Jungle Gardens.** One of Old Florida's charming, family-owned and -operated attractions, Sarasota Jungle Gardens fills 10 acres with native and exotic animals as well as tropical plants. The lush gardens date to 1939, and still have the small-world feel of yesterday's Florida. You'll find red-tailed hawks and great horned owls in the birds of prey show, American alligators and a variety of snakes in the reptile encounter, and bugs of many varieties in a show called Critters and Things. You can talk to trainers and get to know such plants as the rare Australian nut tree and the Peruvian apple cactus in the gardens. Also on-site are flocks of flamingos that guests can hand-feed, plus reptiles and a butterfly garden. ⊠ *3701 Bay Shore Rd.* ☎ *941/355–5305* ⊕ *www.sarasotajunglegardens.com* ⊠ *$15* ⊙ *Daily 10–5.*

BEACHES

Fodor's Choice **Siesta Beach.** With 40 acres of nature trails, this park is popular; you'll
★ find tons of amenities. This beach has fine, powdery quartz sand that squeaks under your feet, very much like the sand along the state's northwestern coast. Don't forget to bring a volleyball—or a tennis racket. **Amenities:** food and drink; lifeguards; toilets. **Best for:** partiers; sunset; swimming; walking. ⊠ *948 Beach Rd., Siesta Key.*

South Lido Park. At the southern tip of the island, South Lido Park has one of the best beaches in the region, but there are no lifeguards. The 100-acre park interacts with four significant bodies of water: the Gulf of Mexico, Big Pass, Sarasota Bay, and Brushy Bayou. The sugar-sand beach has plenty of early morning sand dollars and is a popular place to fish. Take a dip in the gulf, or picnic as the sun sets through the Australian pines into the water. Facilities include nature trails, canoe and kayak trails, restrooms, and picnic grounds. This park was purchased by John Ringling in 1920 as part of his ambitious plan to develop island properties. His plan collapsed with the great Florida Land bust of 1926. **Amenities:** showers; toilets. **Best for:** solitude; swimming; walking. ✉ *2201 Ben Franklin Dr., Lido Key.*

Turtle Beach. A 14-acre beach-park that's popular with families, Turtle has 2,600 linear feet of beach frontage and is more secluded than most gulf beaches. It's known for abundant sea turtles. It has covered picnic shelters, grills, and a volleyball court. Locals like the 40-site campground that is also open to visitors with advance reservations. Fittingly enough, this beach is near the über-mellow Turtle Beach Resort. **Amenities:** toilets. **Best for:** solitude; sunset; swimming; walking. ✉ *8918 Midnight Pass Rd., Siesta Key* ☎ *941/349–3839.*

WHERE TO EAT

$$ CAFÉ Fodor's Choice ★

🍴 **Bijou Café.** Once a 50-seat 1920 gas station–turned-restaurant, the Bijou is now a 140-seat restaurant with the type of enchanting decor you might expect in a quaint, modern European café—think French windows and doors, sparkling glassware, bouquets of freshly picked flowers, and the soft glow of candlelight. Lunches begin with an inspired soup, salads, or sandwiches such as the Waldorf Chicken Salad Croissant. Dinners emphasize fresh local produce and sustainable seafood. Opera season—typically February and March—is the only time Sunday dinner is served. [$] *Average main: $30* ✉ *1287 1st St.* ☎ *941/366–8111* 🌐 *www.bijoucafe.net* 🕒 *Apr.–Jan., closed Sun. No lunch weekends.*

$$ ITALIAN

🍴 **Café Baci.** Specializing in Tuscan and Roman cuisine, Café Baci appeals to loyal locals and savvy travelers alike. Its menu highlights original family recipes; specialties range from fresh, succulent seafood dishes and homemade pastas to traditional veal recipes such as *piccata de vitella* simmered with white wine, lemon, and capers or grilled salmon served on spinach pesto risotto. From the moment you walk through the door, you'll enjoy the peaceful, elegant, Italian-inspired atmosphere. [$] *Average main: $18* ✉ *4001 S. Tamiami Trail* ☎ *941/921–4848* 🌐 *www.cafebaci.net* 🕒 *No lunch Sat.; closed Sun.*

$$$$ CAFÉ

🍴 **Café L'Europe.** Located in St. Armand's Circle, this sidewalk and indoor café has a spectacular menu featuring tableside specialties such as chateaubriand for two. Other popular entrées range from potato-crusted grouper and brandied duck to rack of lamb. There's also a nice choice of wines by the glass. Veranda tables are a great place to watch shoppers and strollers. [$] *Average main: $33* ✉ *431 St. Armands Circle, Lido Key* ☎ *941/388–4415* 🌐 *www.cafeleurope.net* 🕒 *Closed Sun.*

$$$ AMERICAN 🍴**Michael's on East.** Not only do the lounge and piano bar, with their extensive wines and vintage cocktails, lure the after-theater set, but inspired cuisine and superior service also entice. Inside its Midtown Plaza shopping center location, you'll find a decor similar to New York's better bistros of the 1930s and '40s, but there is plenty of veranda seating for enjoying Sarasota's balmy weather. The fare ranges from bow-tie pasta with sun-dried tomatoes to porcini-rubbed rack of lamb to roasted swordfish with red potatoes. The pecan-graham-crusted key lime tart served under a cloud of baked meringue is only one of the creative combinations for concluding your cuisine adventure. [$] *Average main: $26* ✉ *1212 East Ave. S* ☎ *941/366–0007* 🌐 *www.michaelsoneast.com* 🕒 *Closed Sun. No lunch Sat.*

$$ AMERICAN 🍴**The Old Salty Dog.** A menu of steamer and raw-bar options has been added to the much-enjoyed old favorites, including quarter-pound hot dogs, fish-and-chips, wings, and burgers. With views of New Pass between Longboat and Lido Keys, this is a popular stop for locals and visitors en route from Mote Aquarium and the adjoining bay-front park. Open-air dining area is comfortable even in summer, thanks to a pleasant breeze. Its bar is shaped from the hull of an old boat. [$] *Average main: $15* ✉ *1601 Ken Thompson Pkwy., City Island* ☎ *941/388–4311* 🌐 *www.theoldsaltydog.com* ✍ *Reservations not accepted* [$] *Average main: $15* ✉ *5023 Ocean Blvd., Siesta Key* ☎ *941/349–0158* 🌐 *www.theoldsaltydog.com* ✍ *Reservations not accepted.*

$$$$ AMERICAN 🍴**Ophelia's on the Bay.** Florida the way it should be: you can watch as dolphins swim past while blue herons lounge on the dock. Enjoy the flowering gardens while dining alfresco on the outdoor patio on its dock at Market #48 or in one of two casually elegant dining rooms. An ever-evolving menu highlights the Florida surroundings with selections such as Gulf of Mexico hog snapper with cracked pepper and orange honey, and Chilean salmon with blueberry lavendar sauce. The tuna (bigeye, yellowfin, and more) is flown in from Hawaii thanks to owner Jane Ferro, who is also the grandniece of the restaurant's namesake. [$] *Average main: $32* ✉ *9105 Midnight Pass Rd., Siesta Key* ☎ *941/349–2212* 🌐 *www.opheliasonthebay.net* 🕒 *No lunch.*

$ AMERICAN 🍴**Yoder's.** Lines for meals stretch well beyond the hostess podium here. Pies—key lime, egg custard, banana cream, peanut butter, strawberry rhubarb, and others—are the main event at this family restaurant in the heart of Sarasota's Amish community. Daily specials typically include zesty goulash, chicken and dumplings, and pulled smoked pork. For breakfast, choose from French toast stuffed with cream cheese or perhaps a hearty stack of pancakes. Sandwiches include Manhattans (roast beef, turkey, or meat loaf on homemade bread with mashed potatoes and gravy). The entire village is always crowded, but there's plenty of waitstaff who keep tables clean and cleared, so the flow is steady. The decor retains its Old Florida efficiency appearance. [$] *Average main: $10* ✉ *3434 Bahia Vista* ☎ *941/955–7771* 🌐 *www.yodersrestaurant.com* ✍ *Reservations not accepted* 🕒 *Closed Sun.*

WHERE TO STAY

For expanded reviews, facilities, and current deals, visit Fodors.com.

$$$$
B&B/INN
Fodor's Choice
★

The Cypress, a Bed & Breakfast Inn. The only bed-and-breakfast in downtown Sarasota, the inn has a delightful assortment of themed rooms. **Pros:** friendly staff; convenient to downtown; a five-minute drive (or a pleasant walk) from the beaches at Lido Key. **Cons:** no in-room phones. *§ Rooms from: $279 ✉ 621 Gulfstream Ave. S ☎ 941/955–4683 ⊕ www.cypressbb.com ⤴ 2 rooms, 3 suites ⏽⊙⏽ Multiple meal plans.*

$$
RENTAL

Gulf Beach Resort. Lido Key's first motel, this beachfront condo complex has been designated a historic property. **Pros:** near shopping; well maintained; lots of beach; free Wi-Fi. **Cons:** basic rooms; motel feel. *§ Rooms from: $140 ✉ 930 Ben Franklin Dr., Lido Key ☎ 941/388–2127, 800/232–2489 ⊕ www.gulfbeachsarasota.com ⤴ 8 rooms, 41 suites ⏽⊙⏽ No meals.*

$$$$
HOTEL

Hyatt Regency Sarasota. Popular among business travelers, the Hyatt Regency is contemporary in design and sits in the heart of the city across from the Van Wezel Performing Arts Hall. **Pros:** great location; stellar views. **Cons:** chain-hotel feel. *§ Rooms from: $300 ✉ 1000 Blvd. of the Arts ☎ 941/953–1234, 800/233–1234 ⊕ www.sarasota.hyatt.com ⤴ 294 rooms, 12 suites ⏽⊙⏽ Multiple meal plans.*

$$$
RENTAL

Lido Beach Resort. Superb gulf views can be found at this stylish beachfront resort. **Pros:** beachfront location; many rooms have kitchens. **Cons:** bland furnishings. *§ Rooms from: $210 ✉ 700 Ben Franklin Dr., Lido Key ☎ 941/388–2161, 800/441–2113 ⊕ www.lidobeachresort.com ⤴ 158 rooms, 64 suites ⏽⊙⏽ No meals.*

$$$$
HOTEL

Ritz-Carlton, Sarasota. With a style that developers like to say is circus magnate John Ringling's realized dream, The Ritz is appointed with fine artwork and fresh-cut flowers. **Pros:** Ritz-style glitz; lots of amenities; attentive staff. **Cons:** long distance to golf course; not on the beach. *§ Rooms from: $450 ✉ 1111 Ritz-Carlton Dr. ☎ 941/309–2000, 800/241–3333 ⊕ www.ritzcarlton.com/sarasota ⤴ 266 rooms, 30 suites ⏽⊙⏽ No meals.*

$$$$
HOTEL
Fodor's Choice
★

Turtle Beach Resort. Reminiscent of a quieter time, many of the cottages at this friendly, affordable, family- and pet-friendly resort date to the 1940s, a romantic plus for yesteryear lovers. **Pros:** nice location; romantic setting; self-serve laundry and Wi-Fi included. **Cons:** far from the area's cultural attractions. *§ Rooms from: $299 ✉ 9049 Midnight Pass Rd., Siesta Key ☎ 941/349–4554 ⊕ www.turtlebeachresort.com ⤴ 16 rooms, 4 cottages ⏽⊙⏽ No meals.*

NIGHTLIFE AND THE ARTS

NIGHTLIFE

Blase Cafe and Lounge. Siesta Key Village doesn't shut down after the dinner crowd vacates its eateries. To the contrary, there are quite a few places to grab a beverage or two. Blase is a good pick if you're in a martini mood. While the café has some pretty sophisticated fare, you can be dressed casual if you want to belly up to the circular bar. ✉ 5263 Ocean Blvd., Siesta Key ☎ 941/349–9822 ⊕ www.theblasecafe.com.

5 O'clock Club. If you find yourself in Southside Village after dinner and are looking for a watering hole that offers live music, look no further. This spot has been one of Sarasota's key music venues for years.

Musical offerings differ by night, but you can expect to hear blues, jazz, or rock covers on a given night. If you're looking for a more upscale club, look elsewhere; this is a no-frills kind of place. ⊠ *1930 Hillview St.* ☎ *941/366–5555* ⊕ *www.5oclockclub.net.*

Gator Club. A famous nightclub located in a beautifully restored, brick historic cornerstone building downtown, the Gator Club has live music and dancing 365 days a year. ⊠ *1490 Main St.* ☎ *941/366–5969* ⊕ *www.thegatorclub.com.*

Straight Up Night Club @ 15 South. St. Armand's Circle is a pretty bustling place in the daytime, but the action continues into the wee hours—if you know where to find it. This bar, which is upstairs from an upscale restaurant of the same name, has an excellent martini list and plenty of live music, especially salsa. ⊠ *15 S. Blvd. of the Presidents, Lido Key* ☎ *941/388–1555* ⊕ *www.15southristorante.com.*

THE ARTS

Asolo Repertory Theatre. One of the best theaters in Sarasota stages productions from November to June in varying venues, which include the Historic Asolo Theater in the Ringling Estate. ⊠ *5555 Tamiami Trail* ☎ *941/351–8000* ⊕ *www.asolorep.org.*

The Players Theatre. A long-established community theater, having launched such actors as Montgomery Clift and Paul Reubens, this troupe performs comedies, special events, live concerts, and musicals. ⊠ *838 N. Tamiami Trail, U.S. 41 and 9th St.* ☎ *941/365–2494* ⊕ *www. theplayers.org.*

Sarasota Opera. Performing in a historic 1,122-seat downtown theater, the Sarasota Opera features internationally known artists singing the principal roles, supported by a professional chorus of young apprentices. ⊠ *Edwards Theater, 61 N. Pineapple Ave.* ☎ *941/328–1300* ⊕ *sarasotaopera.org.*

SHOPPING

St. Armand's Circle has a cluster of oh-so-exclusive shops and laid-back restaurants. It's just east of Lido Beach.

SHOPPING AREAS

Siesta Key Village. Not too far from Siesta Key's wildly popular beaches is a cluster of shops, restaurants, and watering holes you won't want to miss. This is a great place to shop and grab a bite after a the beach—or earlier if it's not a beach day. Park in the municipal lot at the end of Avenida Madera, then stroll down Ocean Boulevard, where you'll find clusters of upscale shops and a range of restaurants and bars. ⊠ *Ocean Blvd., between Beach Rd. and Av. Madera, Siesta Key* ⊕ *www. siestakeyvillage.org.*

Southside Village. This is one of Sarasota's newer spots, with tons of sidewalk cafés, hip boutiques, jewelry stores, and an excellent gourmet market. This place hasn't gotten as much attention as St. Armand's Circle, but it's also got a much shorter history. It's popular among locals and is now starting to get on the radar for visitors. ⊠ *Osprey Ave. at Hillview St.* ☎ *941/366–0771.*

St. Armand's Circle. No visit to Sarasota is complete without a visit to this busy yet laid-back shopping and dining hub. One can literally refer to it as a hub because it's arranged around a large traffic circle in the middle of Lido Key. You'll find a sprinkling of upscale retail chains, including White House Black Market, but the area's small, imaginative boutiques are the real draw. Among them is Foxy Lady, which sells trendy women's clothing. The Met is also a good option for women's fashion. Carmen's is a good choice for shoes, and Taffy's offers some stylish menswear. St. Armand's Circle also offers plenty of dining/desert (especially ice cream) options, nightlife, and just plain people watching. Some days you can even spot a busker or two performing on one of the area's many street corners. ⊠ *300 Madison Dr.* ☎ *941/388–1554* ⊕ *www.starmandscircleassoc.com.*

RECOMMENDED STORES

Elysian Fields Bookstore. This independent store carries a diverse selection of books and periodicals, as well as gifts, candles, and jewelry, and hosts various events and art fairs. ⊠ *Midtown Plaza, 1273 S. Tamiami Trail* ☎ *941/361–3006* ⊕ *www.elysianfieldsonline.com.*

Lotus. The specialties here include women's denim and fashion, cute handbags, perfumes, and lingerie. ⊠ *1451 Main St.* ☎ *941/906–7080* ⊕ *www.lotussarasota.com.*

L. Boutique. Find the trendiest fashions and most stylish handbags and shoes from top designers in this downtown Sarasota shop. Attached is a swanky spa. ⊠ *556 S. Pineapple Ave.* ☎ *941/906–1350* ⊕ *www.lboutiques.com.*

SPORTS AND THE OUTDOORS

FISHING

Flying Fish Fleet. Several boats can be chartered for deep-sea fishing, and there are daily group trips on a "party" fishing boat. ⊠ *2 Marina Plaza, U.S. 41, on bay front at Marina Jack* ☎ *941/366–3373* ⊕ *www.flyingfishfleet.com.*

GOLF

Bobby Jones Golf Course. There are 45 holes and a driving range; greens fees are $17–$37. ⊠ *1000 Circus Blvd.* ☎ *941/365–2200* ⊕ *www.bobbyjonesgolfclub.com.*

KAYAKING

Siesta Sports Rentals. Up for rent here are kayaks, bikes, beach chairs, scooters, and beach wheelchairs and strollers. Guided kayaking trips are also available. ⊠ *6551 Midnight Pass Rd., Siesta Key* ☎ *941/346–1797* ⊕ *www.siestasportsrentals.com.*

THE LOWER
GULF COAST

With Fort Myers, Naples, and
the Coastal Islands

WELCOME TO
THE LOWER GULF COAST

TOP REASONS
TO GO

★ **Heavenly beaches:**
Whether you go to the
beach to sun, swim,
gather shells, or watch
the sunset, the region's
Gulf of Mexico beaches
rank among the best.

★ **Edison & Ford Winter
Estates:** A rare complex
of two famous inventors'
winter homes comes
complete with botanical-
research gardens, Edison's
lab, and a museum.

★ **Island hopping:**
Rent a boat or jump aboard
a charter for lunch, picnicking, beaching, or shelling
on a subtropical island
adrift from the mainland.

★ **Naples shopping:**
Flex your buying power
in downtown Naples's
charming shopping dis-
tricts or in lush outdoor
centers around town.

★ **Watch for wildlife:**
On the edge of Everglades
National Park, the region
protects vast tracts of
fragile land and water
where you can see alliga-
tors, manatees, dolphins,
roseate spoonbills, and
hundreds of other birds.

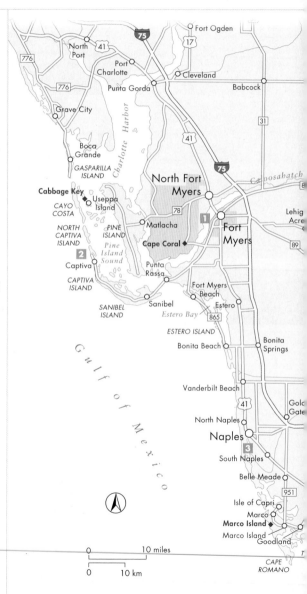

1 Fort Myers and Vicinity.
Don't miss the Edison &
Ford Winter Estates along
royal-palm-lined McGregor
Boulevard. For museums,
theater, and art, the up-
and-coming downtown
River District rules.

2 The Coastal Islands.
Shells and wildlife refuges
bring nature-lovers to
Sanibel and Captiva islands.
Fort Myers Beach is known
for its lively clubs and
shrimp fleet. For true seclusion, head to the area's
unbridged island beaches.

3 Naples and Vicinity.
Some of the region's best
shopping and dining take up
residence in historic buildings trimmed with blossoms
and street sculptures in Old
Naples. Hit Marco Island
for the boating lifestyle
and funky fishing-village
character.

GETTING
ORIENTED

The Lower Gulf Coast of
Florida, as its name sug-
gests, occupies a stretch of
coastline along southern-
most west Florida, bordered
by the Gulf of Mexico. It
lies south of Tampa and
Sarasota, directly on the
other side of the state from
West Palm Beach and Fort
Lauderdale. In between the
two coasts stretch heartland
agricultural areas and
Everglades wilderness.
The region encompasses
the major resort towns of
Fort Myers, Fort Myers
Beach, Sanibel Island,
Naples, and Marco Island,
along with a medley of
suburban communities
and smaller islands.

8

Updated by Kate Bradshaw and Jill Martin

With its subtropical climate and beckoning family-friendly beaches known for their powdery sand, calm surf, and nary a freighter in sight, the Lower Gulf Coast, also referred to as the state's southwestern region, is a favorite vacation spot of Florida residents as well as visitors. Vacationers tend to spend most of their time outdoors—swimming, sunning, shelling, fishing, boating, and playing tennis or golf.

The region has several distinct travel destinations. Small and historic downtown Fort Myers rises inland along the Caloosahatchee River, and the rest of the town sprawls in all directions. It got its nickname, the City of Palms, from the hundreds of towering royal palms that inventor Thomas Edison planted between 1900 and 1917 along McGregor Boulevard, a historic residential street and site of his winter estate. Edison's idea caught on, and more than 2,000 royal palms now line 14-mile-long McGregor Boulevard. Museums and educational attractions are the draw here. Across the river, Cape Coral has evolved from a mostly residential community to a resort destination for water sports enthusiasts.

Off the coast west of Fort Myers are more than 100 coastal islands in all shapes and sizes. Connected to the mainland by a 3-mile causeway, Sanibel is known for its superb shelling, fine fishing, beachfront resorts, and wildlife refuge. Here and on Captiva, to which it is connected by a short bridge, multimillion-dollar homes line both waterfronts. Just southwest of Fort Myers is Estero Island, home of busy Fort Myers Beach, and farther south, Lovers Key State Park and Bonita Beach.

Farther down the coast lies Naples, once a small fishing village and now a thriving and sophisticated enclave. It's like a smaller, more understated version of Palm Beach, with fine restaurants, chichi shopping areas, luxury resorts, and—locals will tell you—more golf holes per capita than anywhere else in the world. A half hour south basks Marco Island, best known for its beaches and fishing. See a maze of pristine miniature mangrove islands when you take a boat tour from the island's marinas into Ten Thousand Islands National Wildlife Refuge. Although high-rises line much of Marco's waterfront, the tiny fishing village of Goodland, an outpost of Old Florida, tries valiantly to stave off new development.

PLANNING

WHEN TO GO

In winter this is one of the warmest areas of the United States. Occasionally temperatures drop in December or January, but rarely below freezing. From February through April you may find it next to impossible to find a hotel room.

Numbers drop the rest of the year, but visitors within driving range, European tourists, and convention clientele still keep things busy. Temperatures and humidity spike, but discounted room rates make summer attractive. Summer is also rainy season, but most storms occur in the afternoon and last for a flash. Hurricane season runs from June through November.

GETTING HERE AND AROUND

AIR TRAVEL

The area's primary airport is in Fort Myers, where many airlines offer flights; private pilots land at both RSW and Page Field, also in Fort Myers. Gulf Coast Airways to Key West and a couple of private charter services also land at Naples Municipal Airport, and North Captiva Island has a private airstrip.

Contacts **Naples Municipal Airport** ⊠ *160 Aviation Dr. N, Naples* ☎ *239/643–0733* ⊕ *www.flynaples.com.* **Southwest Florida International Airport** *(RSW).* ⊠ *11000 Terminal Access Rd., Fort Myers* ☎ *239/590-4800* ⊕ *www.flylcpa.com.*

Ground Transportation Contacts **Aaron Airport Transportation** ☎ *239/768–1898* ⊕ *www.aarontaxi.com.* **Sanibel Taxi** ☎ *239/472-4160, 888/527-7806* ⊕ *www.sanibeltaxi.com.*

CAR TRAVEL

If you're driving, U.S. 41 (the Tamiami Trail) runs the length of the region. Sanibel Island is accessible from the mainland via the Sanibel Causeway (toll $6 round-trip). Captiva Island lies across a small pass from Sanibel's north end, accessible by bridge.

Be aware that the destination's popularity, especially during winter, means traffic congestion at peak times of day. Avoid driving when the locals are getting to and from work and visitors to and from the beach.

HOTELS

Lodging in Fort Myers, the islands, and Naples can be pricey, but there are affordable options even during the busy winter season. If these destinations are too rich for your pocket, consider visiting in the off-season, when rates drop drastically, or look to Fort Myers Beach and Cape Coral for better rates. Beachfront properties tend to be more expensive; to spend less, look for properties away from the water. In high season—Christmastime and Presidents' Day through Easter—always reserve ahead for the top properties. Fall is the slowest season: rates are low and availability is high, but this is also hurricane season (June 1–November 30).

8

RESTAURANTS

In this part of Florida fresh seafood reigns supreme. Succulent native stone-crab claws, a particularly tasty treat, in season from mid-October through mid-May, are usually served hot with drawn butter or chilled with tangy mustard sauce. Supplies are typically steady, since claws regenerate in time for the next season. Other seafood specialties include fried grouper sandwiches and Sanibel pink shrimp. In Naples's highly hailed restaurants and sidewalk cafés, mingle with locals, winter visitors, and other travelers, and catch up on the latest culinary trends.

HOTEL AND RESTAURANT COSTS

Prices in the restaurant reviews are the average cost of a main course at dinner or, if dinner isn't served, at lunch. Prices in the hotel reviews are the lowest cost of a standard double room in high season. Prices don't include taxes (6%, more in some counties, and 1%–5% tourist tax for hotel rooms).

TOURS

Captiva Cruises. Shelling, dolphin, luncheon, beach, sunset, and history cruises run to and around the out islands of Cabbage Key, Useppa Island, Cayo Costa, and Gasparilla Island. Night sky cruises and excursions also go to the Edison and Ford Winter Estates. Excursions cost $27 to $70 each. ⊠ *McCarthy's Marina, 11401 Andy Rosse La., Captiva* ☎ *239/472–5300* ⊕ *www.captivacruises.com.*

Manatee Sightseeing Adventure. Tours to sight these gentle creatures run near Marco Island. ⊠ *525 Newport Dr., Naples* ☎ *239/642–8818* ⊕ *www.see-manatees.com.*

Tarpon Bay Explorers. One of the best ways to see the J.N. "Ding" Darling National Wildlife Refuge is by taking one of these guided or self-guided nature tours. There are many options to choose depending on your activity level and desire—including a sea life cruise, open-air tram tours, and nature cruises, to name a few. Rentals of kayaks, canoes, stand-up paddleboards, bikes, and pontoon boats are right on-site. Charter boats are also available. ⊠ *900 Tarpon Bay Rd., Sanibel* ☎ *239/472–8900* ⊕ *www.tarponbayexplorers.com.*

FORT MYERS AND VICINITY

In parts of Fort Myers, old Southern mansions and their modern-day counterparts peek out from behind stately palms and blossomy foliage. Views over the broad Caloosahatchee River, which borders the city's small but businesslike cluster of office buildings downtown, soften the look of the area. These days it's showing the effects of age and urban sprawl, but planners work at reviving what has been termed the River District at the heart of downtown. North of Fort Myers are small fishing communities and new retirement towns, including Boca Grande on Gasparilla Island; Englewood Beach on Manasota Key; and Port Charlotte, north of the Peace River.

FORT MYERS

80 miles southeast of Sarasota, 125 miles west of Palm Beach

The city core lies inland along the banks of the Caloosahatchee River, a half hour from the nearest beach. The town is best known as the winter home of inventors Thomas A. Edison and Henry Ford.

GETTING HERE AND AROUND

The closest airport to Fort Myers is Southwest Florida International Airport (RSW), about 15 miles southeast of town. A taxi for up to three passengers costs about $20–$40. Extra people are charged $10 each. LeeTran bus service serves most of the Fort Myers area.

If you're driving here from Florida's East Coast, consider Alligator Alley, a toll section of Interstate 75 that runs from Fort Lauderdale to Naples. I–75 then runs north–south the length of the region. U.S. 41 (the Tamiami Trail, also called South Cleveland Avenue in Fort Myers) runs parallel to the interstate to the west and goes through downtown Naples and Fort Myers. McGregor Boulevard (Route 867) and Summerlin Road (Route 869), Fort Myers's main north–south city streets, head toward Sanibel and Captiva islands. San Carlos Boulevard (Route 865) runs southwest from Summerlin Road to Fort Myers Beach, and Pine Island–Bayshore Road (Route 78) leads from North Fort Myers through northern Cape Coral onto Pine Island.

Key West Express operates a ferry from Fort Myers Beach (year-round) to Key West.

Bus Contacts LeeTran ☎ *239/275–8726, 239/533–8726* ⊕ *www.rideleetran.com.*

Ferry Contacts Key West Express ✉ *1200 Main St., Fort Myers Beach* ☎ *239/394–9700, 888/539–2628* ⊕ *www.keywestexpress.us.*

VISITOR INFORMATION

Contacts Lee County Visitor & Convention Bureau ✉ *2201 2nd St., Suite 600* ☎ *239/338–3500, 800/237–6444* ⊕ *www.fortmyers-sanibel.com.*

EXPLORING

TOP ATTRACTIONS

Art of the Olympians. Opened in January 2010, this institution was the vision of the late Al Oerter, four-time gold medalist and Fort Myers Beach resident. Based on the original Greek standard of well-rounded achievement in athletics and art, the gallery upstairs overlooks the river and displays artwork created by Olympian athletes including Oerter, Florence Griffith-Joyner, Peggy Fleming, Rink Babka, and Bob Beamon; exhibits on the first floor inspire children and other visitors toward high achievement in sports with interactive displays, Olympic videos, memorabilia, traveling exhibits, and guest Olympic programs. This is the only facility other than Olympic training and competition centers that the U.S. Olympic Committee allows to use the "Olympian" name and display its five-ring logo. ✉ *1300 Hendry St.* ☎ *239/332–5055* ⊕ *www.artoftheolympians.org* 🖼 *$5* ⊘ *Tues.– Sat. 10–4.*

8

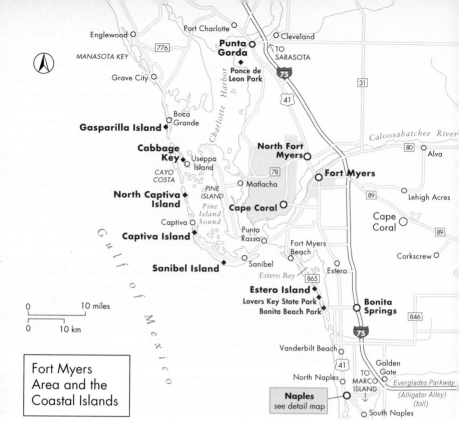

Fort Myers
Area and the
Coastal Islands

Fodor's Choice **Edison & Ford Winter Estates.** Fort Myers's premier attraction pays homage
★ to two of America's most ingenious inventors: Thomas A. Edison, who
gave the world the stock ticker, the incandescent lamp, and the phono-
graph, among other inventions; and his friend and neighbor, automaker
Henry Ford. Donated to the city by Edison's widow, his once 12-acre
estate has been expanded into a remarkable 25 acres, with three homes,
two caretaker cottages, a laboratory, botanical gardens, and a museum.
The laboratory contains the same gadgets and gizmos as when Edison
last stepped foot into it. Visitors can see many of his inventions, along
with historic photographs and memorabilia, in the museum. Edison
traveled south from New Jersey and devoted much of his time here
to inventing things (there are 1,093 patents to his name), experiment-
ing with rubber for friend and frequent visitor Harvey Firestone, and
planting hundreds of plant species collected around the world. Next
door to Edison's two identical homes is Ford's "Mangoes," the more
modest seasonal home of Edison's fellow inventor. The property's oldest building, the Edison Caretaker's House, dates to 1860. Tours are
guided or audio self-guided. One admission covers homes of both men;
museum and laboratory-only tickets and botanical-garden tour tickets
are also available. ⊠ 2350 McGregor Blvd. ☎ 239/334–7419 ⊕ www.
edisonfordwinterestates.org ⊒ Complete Estate Tour $20; other tours
available ☉ Daily 9–5:30; hourly tours 10–4.

FAMILY

Fodor's Choice
★

Imaginarium Science Center. Kids can't wait to get their hands on the wonderful interactive exhibits at this lively museum–aquarium combo that explores technology, physics, weather, and other science topics. Check out the stingrays and other marine life in the aquariums, touch tanks, and the living-reef tank; feed the fish, turtles, and swans in the outdoor lagoon; visit a tarantula, python, hissing cockroach, juvenile alligator, and other live critters in the Animal Lab; dig for dinosaur bones; score in the Sporty Science sports simulator; watch a 3-D movie in the theater; take part in a hands-on Animal Encounter demonstration; and touch a cloud, then prepare to get blown away in the Hurricane Experience. Other highlights include the Tiny Town early childhood area, Backyard Nature, Discovery Lab exploration station, Idea Lab engineering design center, as well as Build-Your-Own-Coaster and Science of Motion. ⊠ *2000 Cranford Ave.* ☎ *239/321–7420* ⊕ *www.imaginariumfortmyers.com* ⊠ *$12* ⊙ *Tues.–Sat. 10–5, Fri. 10–8, Sun. noon–5.*

FAMILY

Manatee Park. Here you may glimpse Florida's most famous, yet often hard to spot, marine mammal. When gulf waters drop to 68 degrees F or below—usually from November to March—the sea cows congregate in these waters, which are warmed by the outflow of a towering nearby power plant. Pause at any of the three observation decks (the first nearest the outflow and last at the lagoon usually yield the most sightings, as does the Fishing Pier) and watch for bubbles. Hydrophones on the last deck allow you to eavesdrop on their songs. Periodically, one of these gentle giants—mature adults weigh an average of 1,000 pounds—will surface. Calusa Blueway Outfitters (see ⇨ *Kayaking in Sports and the Outdoors*) run the visitor center/gift shop and offer kayak and canoe rentals, as well as clinics and tours to paddle the canals and get a closer look. ⊠ *10901 Palm Beach Blvd., 1¼ miles east of I–75 Exit 141* ☎ *239/690–5030* ⊕ *www.leeparks.org* ⊠ *Park free. Parking Apr.–Nov. $1 per hr, $5 daily; Dec.–Mar. $2 per hr, $5 daily* ⊙ *Park daily 8–sunset; visitor center Nov.–Mar., daily 9–4; Apr.–Oct., weekends 9–1.*

WORTH NOTING

FAMILY

Calusa Nature Center & Planetarium. Get a look at Florida's native animals and habitats. Boardwalks and trails lead through subtropical wetlands, a birds-of-prey aviary, and a screened-in butterfly house. There are snake, alligator, butterfly, and other live-animal demonstrations several times daily. Museum exhibits include an Exotic Species room and the Insectarium. The domed, state-of-the-art, 90-seat planetarium hosts astronomy shows daily and special laser shows. ⊠ *3450 Ortiz Ave.* ☎ *239/275–3435* ⊕ *www.calusanature.org* ⊠ *$10* ⊙ *Mon.–Sat. 10–5, Sun. 11–5.*

Southwest Florida Museum of History. A restored railroad depot serves as a showcase for the area's history dating to 800 BC. Displays include prehistoric animals and Calusa artifacts, a reconstructed *chickee* hut, a dugout canoe, clothing and photos from Seminole settlements, historical vignettes, changing exhibits, and a replicated Florida Cracker house. A favorite attraction is the *Esperanza,* a private, restored 1929 Pullman rail car. ⊠ *2031 Jackson St.* ☎ *239/321–7430* ⊕ *www. swflmuseumofhistory.com* ⊠ *$9.50* ⊙ *Tues.–Sat. 10–5.*

8

View 200 phonographs, an invention Thomas Edison patented in 1878, at his Fort Myers winter estate.

WHERE TO EAT

$$$ **AMERICAN** 🍴 **Bistro 41.** Shoppers and businesspeople meet here for some of the town's most dependable and inventive cuisine. Amid brightly painted, textured walls and a display kitchen, the menus roam from "41 Prime Dip" sandwich and the popular bistro salad with portobellos and a pesto drizzle to a delicious pork pot roast. To experience the kitchen at its imaginative best, check the night's specials, which often include daringly done seafood (crabmeat-crusted triple-tail fish with caramelized plantains and passion-fruit beurre blanc, for instance). Half portions and small plates are on offer. When weather permits, ask for a table on the patio. [$] *Average main: $23* ✉ *13499 S. Cleveland Ave.* ☎ *239/466–4141* 🌐 *www.bistro41.com* ✍ *Reservations essential.*

$ **MEXICAN** 🍴 **Chile Ranchero.** Latinos and gringos alike converge on this authentic little corner of Mexicana in a strip mall along busy Tamiami Trail. The decor is humble, but you can't beat the prices or the portions. The warm and inviting staff speaks Spanish and so does the menu, with English subtitles. The intensely flavorful dishes appeal to American and Latin palates, with a range from fajitas and steak ranchero to seafood soup and excellent nachos con ceviche. [$] *Average main: $12* ✉ *11751 S. Cleveland Ave., No. 18* ☎ *239/275–0505.*

$$$ **ITALIAN** 🍴 **Cibo.** Its flavor-bursting Italian food and its propensity for fresh, quality ingredients keep Cibo at the head of the class for local Italian restaurants. In contrast to the sophisticated black-and-white setting, the menu comes in colors from the classic Cesare salad with shaved Grana Padano and spaghetti and meatballs to salmon piccata and veal porterhouse with porcini risotto. The lasagna Napoletana is typical of the standards set here—a generous square of pasta layered with fluffy ricotta, meat ragu, mozzarella, and garlicky pomodoro sauce. [$] *Average main: $24* ✉ *12901 McGregor Blvd.* ☎ *239/454–3700* 🌐 *www.cibofortmyers.com* ✍ *Reservations essential* ⏲ *No lunch.*

$$$ VIETNAMESE 🍴 **Saigon Paris Bistro.** Irish omelets, Belgian waffles, crêpes, steak au poivre, Vietnamese sea bass, Waldorf chicken salad: this eatery's extensive menu clearly travels farther abroad than its name implies. And it does so with utmost taste and flavor, as its faithful local clientele will attest. The best deals are the lunchtime Vietnamese entrées and chicken egg-drop soup. The restaurant is known for its gigantic bowls of *pho* (traditional soup), which can be ordered any time of day (some people have them for breakfast). It also offers three-course Vietnamese or Parisian dinners for $30. Leave room for crêpes à la Grand Marnier, prepared tableside. The interior is pleasant if a bit old-fashioned. [$] *Average main: $21* ✉ *12995 S. Cleveland. Ave., No. 118* ☎ *239/936–2233* 🌐 *www.saigonparisbistro.com* ⏲ *Closed Mon. June–Sept.*

$ SEAFOOD FAMILY 🍴 **Shrimp Shack.** Seafood lovers, families, and retired snowbirds flock to this venue with its vivacious staff, bustle, and colorful, cartoonish wall murals. There's a wait for lunch in winter season and a brisk take-out business with drive-through. Southern-style deep frying prevails—whole-belly clams, grouper, shrimp, onion rings, hush puppies, and fried pork loins—though you can get certain selections broiled or blackened, and there's some New England flavor with seafood rolls at lunch. Create your own combo by selecting two or three fried, broiled, or blackened choices. Kids love this place for the buzzing atmosphere and parents love the inexpensive kids meals. For more savings, print out the restaurant's "Kids Eat Free" coupon from the website. [$] *Average main: $13* ✉ *13361 Metro Pkwy.* ☎ *239/561–6817* 🌐 *www.shrimpshackusa.com.*

$$$$ SOUTHERN 🍴 **The Veranda.** Restaurants come and go quickly as downtown reinvents itself, but this one has endured since 1978. A favorite of business and government bigwigs at lunch (the fried green tomato salad is signature), it serves imaginative Continental fare with a trace of a Southern accent for dinner. Notable are tournedos with smoky sour-mash-whiskey sauce, rack of lamb with rosemary-merlot sauce, herb-crusted honey-grilled salmon, and a grilled seafood sampler with saffron fettuccine, all served with homemade honey-drizzled bread and corn muffins with pepper jelly. The restaurant is a combination of two turn-of-the-20th-century homes, with a two-sided central brick fireplace, and sconces and antique oil paintings on its pale-yellow walls. Ask for an outdoor courtyard table when weather permits. [$] *Average main: $34* ✉ *2122 2nd St.* ☎ *239/332–2065* 🌐 *www.verandarestaurant.com* ⏲ *Closed Sun. No lunch Sat.*

WHERE TO STAY

For expanded reviews, facilities, and current deals, visit Fodors.com.

$$$ HOTEL 🏨 **Crowne Plaza Hotel Fort Myers at the Bell Tower Shops.** Baseball fans often make this hotel home base since spring training and other sports parks are just a few miles away, while singles love the sports bar downstairs and being a stroll from the Bell Tower Shops, and families appreciate the mini-refrigerators and microwaves in the rooms. **Pros:** free airport shuttle; complimentary transportation within a

3-mile radius; laundry facilities. **Cons:** showing signs of age; rooms a bit tight; meeting traffic crowds the lobby. [$] *Rooms from: $159* ✉ *13051 Bell Tower Dr.* ☎ *239/482–2900* 🌐 *www.cpfortmyers.com* 🛏 *225 rooms* 🍴 *No meals.*

$$$ HOTEL 🏨 **Hilton Garden Inn Fort Myers.** This compact, prettily landscaped low-rise is near Fort Myers's cultural and commercial areas, and a business clientele favors it for its convenience. **Pros:** near performing-arts center; enjoyable restaurant; large rooms. **Cons:** chain feel; small pool; at busy intersection. [$] *Rooms from: $199* ✉ *12600 University Dr.* ☎ *239/790–3500* 🌐 *www.fortmyers.stayhgi.com* 🛏 *126 rooms* 🍴 *Breakfast.*

$$$ HOTEL 🏨 **Hotel Indigo, Ft. Myers Downtown River District.** The only modern boutique hotel downtown, it attracts a cosmopolitan set that wants to be in the center of the River District's art, dining, and shopping scene—and just minutes from other attractions. **Pros:** sleek design; walking distance to restaurants and nightlife; tower built in 2009 and lobby part of historic arcade; rooftop bar. **Cons:** must drive to beach; no suites have full kitchens. [$] *Rooms from: $169* ✉ *1520 Broadway* ☎ *239/337–3446* 🌐 *www.hotelindigo.com* 🛏 *60 rooms, 7 suites* 🍴 *No meals.*

$$$$ RESORT FAMILY Fodor's Choice ★ 🏨 **Sanibel Harbour Marriott Resort & Spa.** Vacationing families and businesspeople who want luxury pick this sprawling resort complex that towers over the island-studded San Carlos Bay at the last mainland exit before the Sanibel Causeway. **Pros:** top-notch accommodations; full amenities; updated spa. **Cons:** daily-parking fee added to rate; unspectacular beach. [$] *Rooms from: $369* ✉ *17260 Harbour Pointe Dr.* ☎ *239/466–4000, 800/767–7777* 🌐 *www.sanibel-resort.com* 🛏 *283 rooms, 64 suites, 37 condominiums* 🍴 *No meals.*

NIGHTLIFE AND THE ARTS

THE ARTS

Broadway Palm Dinner Theatre. Buffet dinners come along with some of Broadway's best comedies and musicals. There's also a 98-seat black-box theater that hosts smaller-scale productions. ✉ *1380 Colonial Blvd.* ☎ *239/278–4422* 🌐 *www.broadwaypalm.com.*

Florida Rep. In the restored circa-1915 Arcade Theatre downtown, this top professional company stages Tony- and Pulitzer-winning plays and musicals. There's also an adjacent, more intimate space for edgier works and a Lunchbox Theatre Series for children. ✉ *2267 1st St.* ☎ *239/332–4488* 🌐 *www.floridarep.org.*

NIGHTLIFE

Bratta's Seafood, Steaks & Pasta. Steaks grilled to order, truly dazzling seafood creations, and 15 different pasta dishes make for an enticing menu. For dessert, their signature chocolate piano filled with silky mousse is worth every calorie. Full bar available, and there is entertainment most nights. ✉ *12984 S. Cleveland Ave.* ☎ *239/433–4449* 🌐 *www.brattasristorante.com* 🕒 *Mon.–Thurs. 4–11, Sun 4–9.*

Crü. Trendsters in the mood for a drink and excellent global tapas crowd the lounge area of this cutting-edge restaurant. The lounge serves food until midnight on weekends. ✉ *13499 S. Cleveland Ave., Suite 241* ☎ *239/466–3663* 🌐 *www.eatcru.com.*

Groove Street Grille & Discotheque. Dance to those fabulous songs of the 1970s and hot hits from today. Happy hour, ladies' night, and good food add to the fun atmosphere. ⊠ *College Plaza, 8595 College Pkwy., #300* ☎ *239/437–2743* ⊕ *www.groovestreet.com* ☽ *Thurs. 9 pm–2 am, Fri. 5 pm–2 am, Sat. 8 pm–2 am.*

The Happy Buddha. A giant gold statue of his Zen-ness out front greets fans—a fun mix of frat boys, retirees, and young professionals—who crowd the casual, smoky bar and groove to hits from live bands and DJs. This is a local favorite. ⊠ *12701 McGregor Blvd.* ☎ *239/482–8565.*

Laugh-In Comedy Cafe. South of downtown comedians perform Friday and Saturday. ⊠ *College Plaza, 8595 College Pkwy., #300* ☎ *239/479–5233* ⊕ *www.laughincomedycafe.com.*

Stevie Tomato's Sports Page. Five miles up on I–75 from the buzzing Gulf Coast Town Center bars, this is a low-key spot to catch a late game and feast on good munchies; earlier in the evening it's very family-friendly. ⊠ *9510 Market Place Rd.* ☎ *239/939–7211* ⊕ *www. stevietomatossportspage.com.*

SHOPPING

Bell Tower Shops. This open-air shopping center has about 40 stylish boutiques and specialty shops, a Saks 5th Avenue, some of Fort Myers's best restaurants and bars, as well as 20 movie screens. ⊠ *S. Cleveland Ave. at Daniels Pkwy.* ☎ *239/489–1221* ⊕ *www.thebelltowershops.com.*

Edison Mall. The largest air-conditioned indoor mall in Fort Myers houses several major department stores and some 160 specialty shops. ⊠ *4125 Cleveland Ave.* ☎ *239/939–1933* ⊕ *www.edison-mall-fl.com.*

Fleamasters Fleamarket. Just east of downtown, more than 900 vendors sell new and used goods Friday through Sunday 9–5. Its music hall hosts live entertainment. ⊠ *4135 Dr. Martin Luther King Jr. Blvd., 1.7 miles west of I–75 Exit 138* ☎ *239/334–7001* ⊕ *www.fleamall.com.*

Gulf Coast Town Center. This megamall of stores and chain restaurants includes a 130,000-square-foot Bass Pro Shops, Ron Jon Surf Shop, Best Buy, Costco, Golf Galaxy, and movie theaters. ⊠ *9903 Gulf Coast Main St.* ☎ *239/267–0783* ⊕ *www.gulfcoasttowncenter.com.*

Sanibel Tanger Factory Outlets. Its boardwalks are lined with outlets for Van Heusen, Maidenform, Coach, Coldwater Creek, Bath & Body Works, and Samsonite, among others. ⊠ *20350 Summerlin Rd.* ☎ *888/471–3939* ⊕ *www.tangeroutlet.com/fortmyers.*

SPORTS AND THE OUTDOORS
BASEBALL

Boston Red Sox. The Sox settled into new digs in 2012 at JetBlue Park at Fenway South, a new $77 million, 10,823-capacity stadium and 106-acre training facility. The field itself is an exact duplicate of their famous home turf, with a Green Monster wall and manual scoreboard. ⊠ *JetBlue Park, 11581 Daniels Pkwy.* ☎ *239/334–4700, 888/733–7696* ⊕ *boston.redsox.mlb.com.*

Minnesota Twins. The team plays exhibition games in town during March and early April. From April through September, the Miracle (⊕ *www. miraclebaseball.com*), a Twins single-A affiliate, plays home games at

Hammond Stadium. ⊠ *Lee County Sports Complex, 14100 6 Mile Cypress Pkwy.* ☎ *800/338–9467* ⊕ *minnesota.twins.mlb.com.*

BIKING

One of the longest bike paths in Fort Myers is along Summerlin Road. It passes commercial areas and gets close to Sanibel through dwindling wide-open spaces. Linear Park, which runs parallel to Six Mile Cypress Parkway, offers more natural, less congested views. Trailhead Park is linked to the new John Yarbrough Linear Park to create a 30-mile path-way, the longest in Lee County.

Bike Route. Come here for a good selection of rentals. ⊠ *8595 College Pkwy., Suite 200* ☎ *239/481–3376* ⊕ *www.thebikeroute.com.*

BOATING AND SAILING

Southwest Florida Yachts. Charter a sailboat or powerboat, or take lessons. With 30 years in the business, they can help you explore Southwest Florida like a native. ⊠ *3444 Marinatown La. NW, North Fort Myers* ☎ *239/656–1339, 800/262–7939* ⊕ *www.swfyachts.com.*

FISHING

Anglers head for the gulf, its bays, and the estuaries for saltwater fish-ing—snapper, sheepshead, mackerel, grouper, and other species. The Caloosahatchee River, Orange River, canals, and small lakes offer fresh-water alternatives.

GOLF

Eastwood Golf Course. The driving range and 18-hole course are afford-able, especially if you don't mind playing at unfavorable times (midday in summer, for example). Many golfers enjoy the lack of development around the course, which poses challenges with its water hazards and doglegs. Fees include cart and tax; fees without cart are available at cer-tain times; greens fee are $65/$35. ⊠ *4600 Bruce Herd La.* ☎ *239/321–7487* ⊕ *www.cityftmyers.com/eastwood.*

Fort Myers Country Club. Eighteen holes challenge golfers with its small greens. It's the town's oldest course. Lessons are available. Its clubhouse holds a lively restaurant and bar; greens fees $35/$20 without cart, $55/$30 with cart. ⊠ *3591 McGregor Blvd.* ☎ *239/321–7488* ⊕ *www.cityftmyers.com/countryclub.*

Shell Point Golf Club. Head here for an 18-hole course and a driving range; greens fee $99/$55 (including cart and taxes). ⊠ *17401 On Par Blvd.* ☎ *239/433–9790* ⊕ *www.shellpointgolf.com.*

KAYAKING

Calusa Blueway Outfitters. Paddling enthusiasts can rent kayaks to explore the Manatee Park environs daily from Thanksgiving to Easter and on weekends in the summer; clinics and guided tours are also available, but go in winter if spotting sea cows is your aim. ⊠ *Manatee Park, 10901 Palm Beach Blvd., 1¼ mile east of I–75 Exit 141* ☎ *239/481–4600* ⊕ *www.calusabluewayoutfitters.com.*

CAPE CORAL, PINE ISLAND, AND NORTH FORT MYERS

13 miles from downtown Fort Myers.

Cape Coral is determinedly trying to move from its pigeonhole as a residential community by attracting tourism with its downtown reconfiguration, The Resort at MarinaVillage, and destination restaurants at the Cape Harbour residential marina development.

GETTING HERE AND AROUND

Four bridges cross from Fort Myers to Cape Coral and North Fort Myers. Pine Island–Bayshore Road (Route 78) leads from North Fort Myers through northern Cape Coral onto off-the-beaten path Pine Island, known for its art galleries, fishing, and exotic fruit farms.

EXPLORING

Calusa Heritage Trail. Affiliated with the University of Florida's natural history museum in Gainesville, this 7/10th-mile interpretive walkway explores the site of an ancient Amerindian village—more than 1,500 years old—with excellent signage, two intact shell mounds you can climb, the remains of a complex canal system, and ongoing archaeological research. Guided tours are given 3 times a week from January to April. Check the website for special tours and lecture events. ⊠ *Randell Research Center, 13810 Waterfront Dr., Bokeelia, Pine Island, Pineland* ☎ *239/283–2157* ⊕ *www.flmnh.ufl.edu/rrc* ✏ *$7 (suggested donation)* ☉ *Daily 10–4. Restrooms and gift shop closed Sun.*

FAMILY **Shell Factory & Nature Park.** This entertainment complex, once just a quirky shopping destination and a survivor from Florida's roadside-attraction era, now contains eateries, museum displays, an arcade, bumper boats, miniature golf, and a mining sluice where kids can pan for shells, fossils, and gemstones. Strolling the grounds is free, but some activities carry individual fees, and a separate admission is required to enter the Nature Park, which has the feel of a small zoo. There you can find llamas and a zebra to ogle; a petting farm with sheep, pigs, and goats; a walk-through aviary; an EcoLab with reptiles and small animals; and a gator slough. The Shell Factory also hosts annual events such as the Gumbo Fest in January. ⊠ *2787 N. Tamiami Trail, North Fort Myers* ☎ *239/995–2141* ⊕ *www.shellfactory.com* ✏ *Shell Factory free, attractions starting at $2 each; Nature Park $12* ☉ *Shell Factory daily 9–7, Nature Park daily 10–5.*

FAMILY
Fodor'sChoice ★
Sun Splash Family Waterpark. Head here to cool off when summer swelters. Nearly two dozen wet and dry attractions include ten thrill waterslides; the Sand Dollar Walk, where you step from one floating "sand dollar" to another; pint-sized Pro Racer flumes; a professional sand volleyball court; a family pool and Tot Spot; and a river-tube ride. Rates go down after 2 pm, plus the park offers Family Fun Night specials. ⊠ *400 Santa Barbara Blvd.* ☎ *239/574–0558* ⊕ *www.sunsplashwaterpark.com* ✏ *$17.95* ☉ *Mar.–Sept., weekends and some weekdays 10–5; call or visit the website for specific open hrs.*

8

PUNTA GORDA DAY TRIP

A half hour (23 miles) north of Fort Myers, the small, old town of Punta Gorda merits a day trip for its restaurants and historic sites. If you're driving to Boca Grande via U.S. 41, it also makes a nice stop along the way. On the mouth of the Peace River, where it empties into Charlotte Harbor, a new riverfront park, water views, and murals enliven the compact downtown historic district. Away from the downtown area, a classic-car museum, wildlife rehabilitation center, and waterfront shopping complex built into an old fish-packing plant fills out a day of sightseeing. Fishing and nature-watching tours also depart from the Fishermen's Village complex.

OFF THE BEATEN PATH

Babcock Wilderness Adventures. To see what Florida looked like centuries ago, visit Babcock's Crescent B Ranch, northeast of Fort Myers. During the 90-minute swamp-buggy-style excursion you ride in a converted school bus through several ecosystems, including the unusual and fascinating Telegraph Cypress Swamp. Along the way an informative and typically amusing guide describes the area's social and natural history while you keep an eye peeled for alligators, wild pigs, all sorts of birds, Florida panthers, and other denizens of the wild. The tour also takes in the ranch's resident cattle and cougar in captivity. Reservations are needed for tours. An on-site restaurant servers "Cracker" chow in season. ☒ *8000 Rte. 31, Punta Gorda* ☎ *800/500–5583* ⊕ *www.babcockwilderness.com* ☒ *Eco-tour $22, call or visit website for specialty tours* ☒ *Reservations essential* ☉ *Oct.–May tours daily; June–Sept., tours Tues.–Sat. All tours by reservation only; some specialty tours are offered only monthly or seasonally.*

WHERE TO EAT

$ ✕ **Bert's Bar & Grill.** Looking to hang out with the locals of Pine Island?
AMERICAN Here you'll find cheap eats, live entertainment, a pool table, and a water view to boot. Speaking of boots, you're likely to see some of the clientele wearing white rubber fishing boots, known here as Pine Island Reeboks. Order fried oysters, a burger, pizza, or a grouper Reuben melt from the no-nonsense menu, and enjoy live music most days. $ *Average main: $9* ☒ *4271 Pine Island Rd., Matlacha* ☎ *239/282–3232* ⊕ *www.bertsbar.com* ☒ *Reservations not accepted.*

$ ✕ **Rumrunners.** Cape Coral's best casual cuisine is surprisingly afford-
AMERICAN able, considering the luxury condo development that rises around it and the size of the yachts that pull up to the docks. Caribbean in spirit, with lots of indoor and outdoor views of a mangrove-fringed waterway, it serves bistro specialties such as conch fritters, seafood potpie, bronzed salmon, and a warm chocolate bread pudding that is addictive. Bar staff is affable and welcoming. $ *Average main: $13* ☒ *Cape Harbour Marina, 5848 Cape Harbour Dr., off Chiquita Blvd.* ☎ *239/542–0200* ⊕ *www.capeharbourdining.com.*

DID YOU KNOW?

Marco Island is the northernmost of the so-called
"Ten Thousand Islands." Its
powdery soft beaches are
made more accessible by two
bridges connecting Marco to
the mainland.

$ ✗**Siam Hut.** Lunch and dinner menus at this Cape Coral fixture let you
THAI design your own stir-fry, noodle, or fried-rice dish. Dinner specialties
include fried crispy frogs' legs with garlic and black pepper, a sizzling
shrimp platter, fried whole tilapia with curry sauce, salads, and pad thai
(rice noodles, egg, ground peanuts, vegetables, and choice of protein).
Two traditional Thai tables allow you to sit on floor pillows (conveniently with backs), or you can opt for a more conventional table or
booth. $ *Average main: $12* ✉ *4521 Del Prado Blvd.* ☎ *239/945–4247*
⊕ *www.siamhutcapecoral.com* ⊗ *Closed Sun. No lunch Sat.*

WHERE TO STAY

For expanded reviews, facilities, and current deals, visit Fodors.com.

$$ ☷**Casa Loma Motel.** Stay at this pretty little motel, 15 minutes from Fort
HOTEL Myers at the end of the Croton Canal, to be close to Cape Coral's attrac-
tions and escape the sticker shock of beachfront lodgings. **Pros:** kitchen
facilities in rooms; free Wi-Fi; large sundeck with canal access. **Cons:** must
drive to beach; on a busy street; decor a bit dated; no restaurant. $ *Rooms
from: $105* ✉ *3608 Del Prado Blvd.* ☎ *239/549–6000, 877/227–2566*
⊕ *www.casalomamotel.com* ⤳ *48 efficiencies, 1 suite* ⦿*No meals.*

$$$$ ☷**The Westin Cape Coral Resort at MarinaVillage.** Cape Coral's only luxury
RESORT resort, this modern 19-story tower sits alongside a marina fringed with
mangroves and caters to families and water sports enthusiasts. **Pros:**
full-service marina; designer appointments; three pools; great kayak-
ing. **Cons:** 45-minute ferry to beach; high-rise. $ *Rooms from: $255*
✉ *5951 Silver King Blvd.* ☎ *239/541–5000, 888/372–9256* ⊕*www.
marinavillageresort.com* ⤳ *83 studios, 83 1-bedroom condos, 82
2-bedroom condos, 16 3-bedroom condos* ⦿*No meals.*

THE COASTAL ISLANDS

A maze of islands in various stages of habitation fronts Fort Myers
mainland, separated by the Intracoastal Waterway. Some are accessible
via a causeway; to reach others, you need a boat. If you cut through
bay waters, you have a good chance of being escorted by bottlenose
dolphins. Mostly birds and other wild creatures inhabit some islands,
which are given over to state parks. Traveler-pampering hotels on Sani-
bel, Captiva, and Fort Myers Beach give way to rustic cottages, old
inns, and cabins on quiet Cabbage Key and Pine Island, which have no
beaches because they lie between the barrier islands and mainland. Oth-
ers are devoted to resorts. When exploring barrier island beaches, keep
one eye on the sand: collecting seashells is a major pursuit in these parts.

GASPARILLA ISLAND (BOCA GRANDE)

43 miles northwest of Fort Myers.

Before roads to the Lower Gulf Coast were even talked about, wealthy
Northerners came by train to spend the winter at the Gasparilla Inn.
The inn was completed in 1913 in Boca Grande on Gasparilla Island,
named, legend has it, for a Spanish pirate who set up headquarters in
these waters. Although condominiums and modern mansions occupy
the rest of Gasparilla, much of the town of Boca Grande evokes another

era. The mood is set by the Old Florida homes and tree-framed roadways. The island's calm is disrupted in the spring when anglers descend with a vengeance on Boca Grande Pass, considered among the best tarpon-fishing spots in the world.

GETTING HERE AND AROUND

Boca Grande is more than an hour's drive northwest of Fort Myers. Day-trippers can catch a charter boat or rent a boat, dock at a marina, and rent a bike or golf cart for a day of exploring and lunching. North of it stretches a long island, home to Don Pedro Island State Park and Palm Island Resort, both accessible only by boat. Also nearby is the off-the-beaten-path but car-accessible island of Manasota Key and its fishing resort community of Englewood Beach.

EXPLORING

Gasparilla Island State Park and Port Boca Grande Lighthouse Museum. The island's beaches are its greatest prize and lie within the state park at the south end. The long, narrow beach ends at Boca Grande Pass, famous for its deep waters and tarpon fishing. The pretty, two-story, circa-1890 lighthouse once marked the pass for mariners. In recent years it has been restored as a museum that explores the island's fishing and railroad heritage. The lighthouse is closed in August. ✉ *880 Belcher Rd., Boca Grande* ☎ *941/964–0060* 🌐 *www.floridastateparks.org/gasparillaisland* 🎟 *$3 per vehicle; $2 suggested donation to lighthouse (exact change only)* ⏲ *Park daily 8–sunset. Lighthouse Nov.–Apr., Mon.–Sat. 10–4, Sun. noon–4; May–July, Sept., and Oct., Wed.–Sat. 10–4, Sun. noon–4.*

WHERE TO EAT

$$$ AMERICAN 🍴 **The Loose Caboose.** Revered by many—including Katharine Hepburn in her time—for its homemade ice cream, this is also a good spot for solid, affordable fare, from burgers and a Thanksgiving wrap (turkey and cranberry sauce) to chicken potpie and crispy duck with orange-teriyaki sauce. Housed in the town's historic depot, it offers indoor and patio seating in an all-American setting. [$] *Average main: $24* ✉ *433 W. 4th St.* ☎ *941/964–0440* 🌐 *www.loosecaboose.biz* ⏲ *No dinner Wed. or Apr.–Dec.*

WHERE TO STAY

For expanded reviews, facilities, and current deals, visit Fodors.com.

$$$$ HOTEL 🏨 **Gasparilla Inn & Club.** Once the playground of social-register members such as the Vanderbilts and DuPonts, the gracious pale-yellow wooden hotel was built by shipping industrialists in the early 1900s. **Pros:** historic property; nicely renovated. **Cons:** expensive rates; the quirks of a very old building. [$] *Rooms from: $385* ✉ *500 Palm Ave., Boca Grande* ☎ *941/964–2201, 800/996–1913* 🌐 *www.gasparillainn.com* 🛏 *137 rooms, 18 cottages* 🍽 *Multiple meal plans.*

SPORTS AND THE OUTDOORS

CANOEING AND KAYAKING

FAMILY **Grande Tours.** Kayaking excursions travel along the creeks and open waters around Charlotte Harbor. The cost is $55 for two hours. Also available are kayaking lessons, kayak fishing excursions, stand-up paddleboarding, and rentals. ✉ *12575 Placida Rd., Placida* ☎ *941/697–8825* 🌐 *www.grandetours.com.*

8

CABBAGE KEY

5 miles south of Boca Grande.

Cabbage Key is the ultimate island-hopping escape in these parts. Some say Jimmy Buffett was inspired to write "Cheeseburger in Paradise" after a visit to its popular restaurant.

GETTING HERE AND AROUND

You'll need to take a boat—from Bokeelia or Pineland, on Pine Island, or from Captiva Island—to get to this island, which sits at Mile Marker 60 on the Intracoastal Waterway. Local operators offer day trips and luncheon cruises.

WHERE TO STAY

For expanded reviews, facilities, and current deals, visit Fodors.com.

$$　　**Cabbage Key Inn.** Atop an ancient Calusa Indian shell mound and
HOTEL　accessible only by boat, the friendly, somewhat quirky inn built by novelist and playwright Mary Roberts Rinehart in 1938 welcomes guests seeking quiet and isolation. **Pros:** plenty of solitude; Old Florida character. **Cons:** two-night minimum stay; accessible only by boat; limited amenities, some rooms have no TV. $ *Rooms from: $119* ☎ *239/283–2278* ⊕ *www.cabbagekey.com* 6 *rooms, 7 cottages* ❍ *No meals.*

SANIBEL AND CAPTIVA ISLANDS

23 miles southwest of downtown Fort Myers.

Sanibel Island is famous as one of the world's best shelling grounds, a function of the unusual east–west orientation of the island's south end. Just as the tide is going out and after storms, the pickings can be superb, and shell seekers performing the telltale "Sanibel stoop" patrol every beach carrying bags of conchs, whelks, cockles, and other bivalves and gastropods. (Remember, it's unlawful to pick up live shells.) Away from the beach, flowery vegetation decorates small shopping complexes, pleasant resorts and condo complexes, mom-and-pop motels, and casual restaurants. But much of the two-lane road down the spine of the island is bordered by nature reserves that have made Sanibel as well known among bird watchers as it is among seashell collectors.

Captiva Island, connected to the northern end of Sanibel by a bridge, is quirky and engaging. At the end of a twisty road lined with million-dollar mansions lies a delightful village of shops, eateries, and beaches.

GETTING HERE AND AROUND

Sanibel Island is approximately 23 miles southwest of downtown Fort Myers, and Captiva lies north of 12-mile-long Sanibel. If you're flying into Southwest Florida International Airport, an on-demand taxi for up to three passengers to Sanibel or Captiva costs about $60–$68; additional passengers are charged $10 each. Sanibel Island is accessible from the mainland via the Sanibel Causeway (toll $6 round-trip). Captiva Island lies across a small pass from Sanibel's north end, accessible by bridge.

8

ESSENTIALS

Visitor Information **Sanibel and Captiva Islands Chamber of Commerce**
✉ *1159 Causeway Rd., Sanibel* ☎ *239/472–1080* ⊕ *www.sanibel-captiva.org.*

EXPLORING

FAMILY
Fodor'sChoice
★

Bailey-Matthews Shell Museum. More than 25 vignettes and exhibits explore shells in the environment, art, and history, including a life-size display of native Calusa and how they used shells for tools and vessels and new exhibits on cowrie shells and the biggest shells in the world. Visit the shell-identifier wheel, which categorizes specimens from local waters in sizes ranging from tiny to huge. Handle shell specimens and play games in the colorful kids' lab. A six-foot globe at the center of the museum rotunda highlights shells from around the world. ✉ *3075 Sanibel–Captiva Rd., Sanibel* ☎ *239/395–2233, 888/679–6450* ⊕ *www.shellmuseum.org* ✉ *$9* ☽ *Daily 10–5.*

Clinic for the Rehabilitation of Wildlife (C.R.O.W). In existence for more than 40 years, the clinic currently cares for more than 4,000 wildlife patients each year. The center offers a look inside the world of wildlife medicine through exhibits, videos, interactive displays, touch screens, and critter cams that feed live footage from four different animal spaces. ✉ *3883 Sanibel–Captiva Rd., Sanibel* ☎ *239/472–3644* ⊕ *www.crowclinic.org* ✉ *$5* ☽ *Tues.–Sat. 10–4.*

FAMILY
Fodor'sChoice
★

J.N. "Ding" Darling National Wildlife Refuge. More than half of Sanibel is occupied by the subtly beautiful 6,300 acres of wetlands and jungly mangrove forests named after a conservation-minded Pulitzer prize-winning political cartoonist. The masses of roseate spoonbills and ibis and the winter flock of white pelicans here make for a good show even if you're not a die-hard bird-watcher. Birders have counted some 230 species, including herons, ospreys, and the timid mangrove cuckoo. Raccoons, otters, alligators, and a lone American crocodile also may be spotted. The 4-mile Wildlife Drive is the main way to explore the preserve; drive, walk, or bicycle along it, or ride a specially designed open-air tram with an on-board naturalist. New QR codes signs link to interactive You Tube videos. There are also a couple of short walking trails, including one to a Calusa shell mound. Or explore from the water via canoe or kayak (guided tours are available). The best time for bird-watching is in the early morning and about an hour before or after low tide; the observation tower along the road offers prime viewing. Interactive exhibits in the free visitor center, at the entrance to the refuge, demonstrate the refuge's various ecosystems and explain its status as a rest stop along a major bird-migration route. A new manatee exhibit was recently unveiled, too. Wildlife Drive is closed to vehicular traffic on Friday, but you can still kayak and do tours from the Tarpon Bay Recreation Area. ✉ *1 Wildlife Dr., off Sanibel–Captiva Rd. at MM 2, Sanibel* ☎ *239/472–1100 for refuge, 239/472–8900 for kayaking and tours* ⊕ *www.fws.gov/dingdarling* ✉ *$5 per car, $1 for pedestrians and bicyclists, tram $13* ☽ *Education Center Jan.–Apr., daily 9–5; May–Dec., daily 9–4; Wildlife Drive Sat.–Thurs. 7:30–½ hr before sunset.*

Continued on page 452

SHELL-BENT ON SANIBEL ISLAND
by Chelle Koster Walton

Sanibel Island beachgoers are an unusual breed: they pray for storms; they muck around tidal pools rather than play in the waves; and instead of lifting their faces to the sun, they have their heads in the sand—almost literally—as they engage in the so-called "Sanibel Stoop."

Odd? Not when you consider that this is Florida's prime shelling location, thanks to the island's east-west bend (rather than the usual north-south orientation of most beaches along the coastline). The lay of the land means a treasure trove of shells—more than 400 species—wash up from the Caribbean.

These gifts from the sea draw collectors of all levels. Come winter, when the cold and storms kill the shellfish and push them ashore, a parade of stoopers forms on Sanibel's shores.

The reasons people shell are as varied as the shellers themselves. The hardcore compete and sell, whereas others collect simply for the fun of discovery, for displaying, for use in gardens, or for crafts. The typical Sanibel tourist who comes seeking shells is usually looking for souvenirs and gifts to take home.

WHERE TO SHELL

Shelling is good anywhere along Sanibel's gulf-front. Remote **Bowman's Beach** (*off Sanibel-Captiva Road at Bowman's Beach Rd.*) offers the least competition. Other public accesses include **Lighthouse Beach** (Periwinkle Way), **Tarpon Bay Beach** (Tarpon Bay Rd.), and **Turner Beach** (Sanibel-Captiva Rd.). If you want to ditch your car (and crowds), walk or bike using **resident access beaches** (along the Gulf drives). If you want to search with others and get a little guidance, you can join shelling cruises from Sanibel and Captiva islands to the unbridged island of Cayo Costa. For information contact, **Captiva Cruises** (☎ 239/472-5300, ⊕ www.captivacruises.com) or **Adventures in Paradise** (☎ 239/472–8443, ⊕ www.adventureinparadiseinc.com).

Captiva
Island

Captiva

Turner
Beach

Bowman's
Beach

SANIBEL ISLAND

Lighthouse
Beach

○ **Sanibel**

Tarpon Bay
Beach

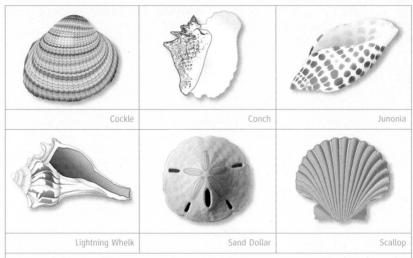

Cockle | Conch | Junonia
Lightning Whelk | Sand Dollar | Scallop

TYPES OF SHELLS

Cockles: The common Sanibel bivalve (hinged two-shelled mollusk), the heart cockle (named for its Valentine shape) is larger and more bowl-like than the scallop, which makes it a popular, colorful find for soap dishes, ashtrays, and catch-alls.

Conchs: Of the large family of conchs, fighting conchs are most commonly found on Sanibel. Contrary to its macho name, the fighting conch is one of the few vegetarian gastropods. While alive, the shell flames brilliant orange; it fades under tropical sunshine.

Junonias: These olive-shaped, spotted gastropods (single-shell mollusks) are Sanibel's signature, though somewhat rare, finds. People who hit upon one get their picture in the local paper. Resorts have been accused of planting them on their beaches for publicity.

Lightning Whelks: The lightning variety of whelk is "left-handed"—opening on the opposite side from most gastropods. Early islanders used them for tools. The animals lay their miniature shell eggs in papery egg-case chains on the beach.

Sand Dollars: Classified as an echinoderm not a mollusk, the thin sand dollar is brown and fuzzy while alive, studded with tiny tubes for breathing and moving. Unoccupied shells bleach to a beautiful white textured pattern, ideal for hanging on Christmas trees.

Scallops: No surprise that these pretty little bivalves have "scalloped" edges. They invented the word. Plentiful on Sanibel beaches, they come in a variety of colors and sizes.

SHELLING LIKE A PRO

Veteran shell-seekers go out before the sun rises so they can be the first on the beach after a storm or night of high tides. (Storms and cold fronts bring in the best catches.)

Most shellers use a bag to collect their finds. But once you're ready to pack shells for transit, wash them thoroughly to remove sand and debris. Then wrap fragile species such as sand dollars and sea urchins in tissue paper or cotton, then newspaper. Last, place your shells in a cardboard or plastic box. To display them, restore the shell's luster by brushing it with baby oil.

Sanibel shops sell books and supplies for identifying your finds and turning them into craft projects.

FAMILY **Sanibel–Captiva Conservation Foundation.** For a good look at night herons and other inhabitants of Sanibel's interior wetlands, follow the 4½ miles of walking trails and climb the observation tower. See island research projects, Nature Center exhibits including live turtles, snakes and a touch tank, and visit a butterfly house. Guided walks are available seasonally on and off property. ⊠ *3333 Sanibel–Captiva Rd., Sanibel* ☎ *239/472–2329* ⊕ *www.sccf.org* ⬛ *$5* ⊙ *Oct.–May, weekdays 8:30–4; June–Sept., weekdays 8:30–3.*

Sanibel Historical Museum & Village. Charming buildings from the island's past include a general store, a one-room schoolhouse, 1927 post office, a tea room, 1925 winter-vacation cottage, a 1898 fishing cottage, and the 1913 Rutland House Museum, containing old documents and photographs, artifacts, and period furnishings. All buildings are authentic and have been moved from their original locations to the museum grounds. ⊠ *950 Dunlop Rd., Sanibel* ☎ *239/472–4648* ⊕ *www.sanibelmuseum. org* ⬛ *$5* ⊙ *Nov.–Apr., Wed.–Sat. 10–4; May–mid-Aug., Wed.–Sat. 10–1; closed mid-Aug.–Oct.*

BEACHES

Red tide, an occasional natural beach occurrence that kills fish, also has negative effects on the human respiratory system. It causes scratchy throats, runny eyes and noses, and coughing. Although the effects aren't long-term, it's a good idea to avoid the beach when red tide is in the vicinity (look for posted signs).

SANIBEL

FAMILY **Bowman's Beach.** This long, wide beach on Sanibel's northwest end is the island's most secluded strand, but it also has the most amenities. Park facilities include a playground, a fitness trail, picnic tables, and a canoe launch. It is famed for its shell collecting and spectacular sunsets at the north end—try to spot the green flash, said to occur just as the sun sinks below the horizon. For utmost seclusion, walk north from the two main access points where bridges cross an estuary to reach the beach. It's a long walk from the parking lot over the estuary to the beach, so pack accordingly and plan on a long stay. Tall Australian pines provide shade behind the white sands. Typically gentle waves are conducive to swimming and wading with kids. **Amenities:** parking (fee); showers; toilets. **Best for:** sunsets; swimming; walking. ⊠ *Bowman Beach Rd., at Blind Pass, Sanibel* ☎ *239/472–3700* ⬛ *Parking $2 per hr.*

FAMILY **Gulfside Park Preserve.** The beach is quiet, safe from strong currents, and good for solitude, bird-watching, and shell-finding. There are restrooms, and long stretches to stroll. The white sand is slightly coarse and borders a park with shade, picnic tables, and a loop nature trail. Low-rise resorts and homes lie to the east and west of the parking lot accesses. **Amenities:** parking (fee); toilets. **Best for:** swimming; walking. ⊠ *Algiers La., off Casa Ybel Rd., Sanibel* ☎ *239/472–3700* ⬛ *Parking $2 per hr.*

Lighthouse Beach. At Sanibel's eastern tip, the beach is guarded by the frequently photographed Sanibel Lighthouse, built in 1884, before the island was settled. The lighthouse is not currently open to the public, but there's talk of refurbishing the tower so visitors can climb to the top. The park rounds the island's east end for waterfront on both the gulf and bay, where a fishing pier draws avid anglers. Shaded nature trails connect the two shores; the park is listed on the Great Florida Birding Trail because of its fall and spring migration fall-outs. A pair of ospreys frequently perch on the lighthouse railing, look for these local residents while you're there. **Amenities:** parking (fee); toilets. **Best for:** sunrise; walking; windsurfing. ⊠ *East end of Periwinkle Way, Sanibel* ☎ *239/472–3700* 🅿 *Parking $2 per hr.*

Tarpon Bay Beach. This centrally located beach is safer for swimming than beaches at the passes, where waters move swiftly. It is, however, one of the more populated beaches, lined with low-rise condos and resorts set back behind vegetation. Casa Ybel Resort lies east of the public access; other smaller resorts can be found along the stretch to the west. The parking lot is a five-minute walk from the beach, so drop off your gang and gear before you park (the lot is open daily from 7 am to 7 pm). At the beach, you can walk for miles in either direction on soft white sand studded with shells. **Amenities:** parking (fee); toilets. **Best for:** swimming; walking. ⊠ *Off Sanibel–Capriva Rd., Tarpon Bay Rd. at Gulf Dr., Sanibel* ✛ *Drive to end of West Gulf Dr. and east to Casa Ybel Rd.* ☎ *239/472–3700* 🅿 *Parking $2 per hr.*

CAPTIVA

FAMILY **Alison Hagerup Beach Park.** This park, once called Captiva Beach, is acclaimed as one of the nation's most romantic beaches for its fabulous sunsets—the best view on Sanibel and Captiva. Shells stud the white, wide sands. The parking lot is small, so arrive early, and bring an umbrella if you need shade. The beach can get crowded, especially in the busy winter/spring season. Facilities are limited to portable restrooms and a volleyball net, but stores and restaurants are nearby. South Seas Island Resort lines the north end of the beach. **Amenities:** parking (fee); toilets. **Best for:** sunsets; swimming; walking. ⊠ *Captiva Dr., at north end, Captiva* 🅿 *Parking $2 per hr, $10 for 8 hrs.*

Turner Beach. Looking for some romance? This is a prime sunset-watching spot on the southern point of Captiva. Strong currents through Blind Pass make swimming tricky but shelling amazing, and parking is limited. Surfers head here when winds whip up the waves. The beach is narrower than in other parts of the island. No buildings sit on the beach, but 'Tween Waters Resort is across the road to the north of the public access, and Castaways Beach & Bay Cottages is beachfront across the bridge on the Sanibel side of Blind Pass. Restaurants are nearby. **Amenities:** parking (fee); toilets. **Best for:** sunsets; surfing; walking. ⊠ *Captiva Dr. at Blind Pass, Captiva* 🅿 *Parking $2 per hr.*

WHERE TO EAT

SANIBEL

$ ✕ **Lazy Flamingo.** At two Sanibel locations, plus two more in neighbor-
AMERICAN ing Fort Myers and Pine Island Sound, this is a friendly neighborhood
FAMILY hangout enjoyed by locals and visitors alike. All of these restaurants have a funky nautical look à la Key West and a popular following for their Dead Parrot Wings (buffalo wings coated with tongue-scorching hot sauce), mesquite-grilled grouper sandwiches, burgers, and steamer pots. The Flamingo garlic bread is always a hit, and the grouper caesar salad is cheesy and award-winning. Kids' meals are served on a Frisbee

8

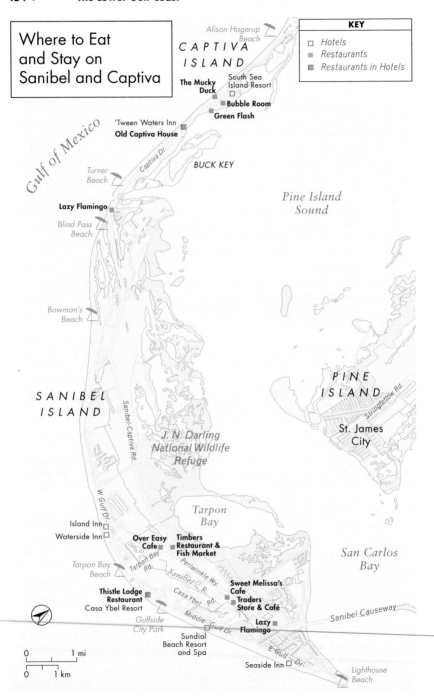

Where to Eat and Stay on Sanibel and Captiva

KEY

☐ *Hotels*
■ *Restaurants*
■ *Restaurants in Hotels*

Alison Hagerup Beach

CAPTIVA ISLAND

South Sea Island Resort

The Mucky Duck

Bubble Room

Green Flash

'Tween Waters Inn
Old Captiva House

Gulf of Mexico

Turner Beach

Lazy Flamingo

Blind Pass Beach

Captiva Dr.

BUCK KEY

Pine Island Sound

Bowman's Beach

PINE ISLAND

Sanibel-Captiva Rd.

SANIBEL ISLAND

St. James City

Stringfellow Rd.

J. N. Darling National Wildlife Refuge

Tarpon Bay

W Gulf Dr.

Island Inn
Waterside Inn

Over Easy Cafe

Timbers Restaurant & Fish Market

San Carlos Bay

Tarpon Bay Beach

Tarpon Bay Rd.

Periwinkle Wy.

Sanibel R. R.

Sweet Melissa's Cafe

Thistle Lodge Restaurant
Casa Ybel Resort

Casa Ybel Rd.

Traders Store & Café

Lazy Flamingo

Sanibel Causeway

Gulfside City Park

Middle Gulf Dr.

Sundial Beach Resort and Spa

E Gulf Dr.

Seaside Inn

Lighthouse Beach

0   1 mi

0   1 km

that makes not only a great souvenir but also a cool new beach toy. The second Sanibel location is at 1036 Periwinkle Way (☎ 239/472–6939). [$] *Average main: $12* ✉ *6520C Pine Ave., Sanibel* ☎ *239/472–5353* 🌐 *www.lazyflamingo.com* ✍ *Reservations not accepted.*

$$ AMERICAN 🍴 **Over Easy Café.** Locals head to this chicken-theme eatery mainly for breakfast and lunch, although it also serves dinner in season. Kick-start the day with the egg Reuben sandwich, veggie Benedict, pancakes, or omelets such as crab and asparagus or "meat-lovers." Breakfast is available until 3 pm. The lunch and dinner menu includes a vast variety of salads, sandwiches, wraps, and seafood. Indoor dining is cheerful; outdoors, and pet-friendly. While waiting for a table, you can shop for gifts next door. [$] *Average main: $16* ✉ *630-1 Tarpon Bay Rd., Sanibel* ☎ *239/472–2625* 🌐 *www.overeasycafesanibel.com* ✍ *Reservations not accepted* 🕓 *No dinner.*

$$$ MODERN AMERICAN Fodor's Choice ★ 🍴 **Sweet Melissa's Cafe.** You've seen them before, those people who take photos of their food: you'll become one of them when you eat here. Choose from full portions or small plates, but the latter are recommended so that you can savor more outstanding dishes in one sitting. For starters, the cured Japanese yellowtail is delicately placed atop avocado puree with jalapeños, cilantro, and ponzu. Even if you don't like duck, you'll love it here. Fish stew, grilled smoked beef tenderloin, fresh cobia: they all are good choices for people who don't mind sharing. Chef Melissa also makes her own sorbet. Dine indoors, on the patio, at the bar, or at the chef's bar overlooking the exhibition kitchen. Live guitar music adds to the experience. [$] *Average main: $25* ✉ *1625 Periwinkle Way, Sanibel* ☎ *239/472–1956* 🌐 *www.sweetmelissascafe.com* ✍ *Reservations essential* 🕓 *No lunch weekends.*

$$$$ CONTEMPORARY Fodor's Choice ★ 🍴 **Thistle Lodge Restaurant.** Now this is romance: the Lodge was built as a wedding gift from a husband to his wife and is now a gift to those lucky enough to dine here. Lush green grounds are right outside the window, then just beyond is the Gulf of Mexico and Sanibel's seashell-laden shores. But it's more than the views that will lull you into a dreamy mood. The food is fresh, elegant, and flavorful. Entrées include everything from mojito-glazed black grouper to brûléed Gorgonzola fillet. Frequent patrons back in the day included Thomas Edison and Henry Ford. [$] *Average main: $35* ✉ *Casa Ybel Resort, 2255 West Gulf Dr., Sanibel* ☎ *239/472–9200* 🌐 *www.thistlelodge.com.*

$$$ SEAFOOD 🍴 **Timbers Restaurant & Fish Market.** One of Sanibel's longest-running restaurants successfully satisfies visitors and residents with consistent quality and a full net of nightly catches and specials. The fish market inside the door is a sure sign of freshness, and most of the dishes showcase seafood simply and flavorfully. The oysters Romanoff with caviar, shallots, and sour cream are a nice twist on oyster "sliders." Corn flakes grant the crunchy grouper and shrimp rights to their names. Choose to have your fresh catch blackened, fried, or broiled, or go for a sirloin or beef filet. House salad or soup du jour comes with each entrée, or you can upgrade to the crab bisque, which is tasty but a bit on the salty side. For lighter fare and a sports bar vibe, Sanibel Grill shares the same space. [$] *Average main: $21* ✉ *703 Tarpon Bay Rd., Sanibel* ☎ *239/472–3128* 🌐 *www.prawnbroker.com* ✍ *Reservations not accepted.*

$$$
AMERICAN

✕ **Traders Store & Café.** In the midst of a warehouse-size store, this bistro, accented with artifacts from exotic places, is a favorite of locals. The marvelous sesame-seared tuna lunch salad with Asian slaw and wasabi vinaigrette exemplifies the creative fare. For dinner, try the barbecued baby back ribs, macadamia-crusted grouper, or any of the day's finely crafted specials. A local band entertains two nights a week. The bar serves light nibbles and happy-hour twofers. $ *Average main: $26* ⊠ *1551 Periwinkle Way, Sanibel* ☎ *239/472–7242* ⚑ *Reservations not accepted.*

CAPTIVA

$$$
AMERICAN
FAMILY

✕ **Bubble Room.** This lively, kitschy visitors' favorite is fun for families and nostalgic types with fat wallets. Servers wear scout uniforms and funny headgear. Electric trains circle overhead, glossies of Hollywood stars past and present line the walls, and glass tabletops showcase old-time toys. There's so much going on that you might not notice your food is not quite as happening, and somehow that's okay. After grazing your basket of cheesy bubble bread and sweet, yeasty sticky buns, go for slow-cooked prime rib or shrimp sautéed in spicy tequila garlic butter. The homemade triple-layer cakes, delivered in hefty wedges, are notorious, and the gooey orange crunch cake is a signature favorite. Kids are welcome and will love to gawk at the Christmas Room before or after they gobble up the hand-breaded chicken fingers. Be prepared to wait for a table in season. $ *Average main: $25* ⊠ *15001 Captiva Dr., Captiva* ☎ *239/472–5558* ⊕ *www.bubbleroomrestaurant.com* ⚑ *Reservations not accepted.*

$$$
SEAFOOD

✕ **Green Flash.** Good food and sweeping views of quiet waters and a mangrove island keep boaters and others coming back to this casual indoor-outdoor restaurant. Seafood dominates, but there's a bit of everything on the menu, from barbecued shrimp and bacon to grilled swordfish to pork tenderloin wrapped in prosciutto and puff pastry. For lunch, try the Green Flash sandwich (smoked turkey and prosciutto or vegetables, both with cheese on grilled focaccia). Grouper tacos are filling and dripping with freshness. On cool, sunny days, grab a table out back dockside. $ *Average main: $23* ⊠ *15183 Captiva Dr., Captiva* ☎ *239/472–3337* ⊕ *www.greenflashcaptiva.com.*

$$$
SEAFOOD

✕ **The Mucky Duck.** A longtime fixture on Captiva's beach, it parodies British pubs with its name and sense of humor. Since 1975, it has consistently drawn crowds that occupy themselves with walking the beach and watching sunset while waiting for their name to be called for a table indoors or out. A little Brit, a lot Florida, the recently revamped menu has kept some favored specialties such as barbecued shrimp wrapped in bacon appetizer, crab cakes, fish-and-chips, and frozen key lime pie. $ *Average main: $24* ⊠ *11546 Andy Rosse La., Captiva* ☎ *239/472–3434* ⊕ *www.muckyduck.com* ⚑ *Reservations not accepted.*

$$$$
SEAFOOD
Fodor'sChoice
★

✕ **Old Captiva House.** This wonderfully romantic restaurant is casual, comfortable, and considered by many to be the best fine-dining restaurant on Captiva Island. Executive Chef Jason Miller adds a fresh, Florida flair to seafood dishes like the island snapper wrap (moist snapper wrapped in crispy phyllo then drizzled with an aged balsamic glaze). Tempting appetizers, creative salads, juicy steaks, and tantalizing desserts round out the menu. The restaurant has its own baker on-site for sweet and savory breads and cakes. No need to dress up; island casual is welcome. Make time to enjoy the fantastic sunsets just across the street at the beach. $ *Average main: $32* ✉ *'Tween Waters Inn, 15951 Captiva Dr., Captiva* ☎ *239/472–5161* ⊕ *www.tween-waters.com/dining. php* ⌖ *Reservations essential.*

WHERE TO STAY

For expanded reviews, facilities, and current deals, visit Fodors.com.

SANIBEL

$$$$
RESORT
FAMILY
Fodor'sChoice
★

Casa Ybel Resort. Palm trees, quiet ponds, and gazebos set the mood at this resort on 23 acres of gulf-facing grounds. **Pros:** on the beach; good restaurants; lots of recreational opportunities. **Cons:** spa treatments in-room only; minimum stay requirement in some units. $ *Rooms from: $559* ✉ *2255 W. Gulf Dr., Sanibel* ☎ *239/472–3145, 800/276–4753* ⊕ *www.casaybelresort.com* ⇆ *40 1-bedroom units, 74 2-bedroom units* ⦿ *No meals.*

$$$
RESORT

Island Inn. Choose from your own cottage on the beach, or take your pick from six different styles of modernized hotel rooms at the most established inn on Sanibel. **Pros:** right on the beach; free breakfast; laundry facilities. **Cons:** minimum stays in season; furniture and bathrooms are dated in some units. $ *Rooms from: $220* ✉ *3111 W. Gulf Dr., Sanibel* ☎ *239/472–1561* ⊕ *www.islandinn.com* ⇆ *60 rooms* ⦿ *Breakfast.*

$$$$
HOTEL

Seaside Inn. Tucked among the tropical greenery, this beachfront inn is a pleasant alternative to the area's larger resorts. **Pros:** intimate feel; lots of character; beautiful beachfront. **Cons:** no on-site restaurant; cramped parking lot. $ *Rooms from: $279* ✉ *541 E. Gulf Dr., Sanibel* ☎ *239/472–1400, 866/565–5092* ⊕ *www.seasideinn.com* ⇆ *32 rooms, 6 cottages, 4 suites* ⦿ *Breakfast.*

$$$$
RESORT
FAMILY

Sundial Beach Resort and Spa. Newly renovated in 2013 to the tune of $5 million, Sanibel's largest resort encompasses 400 privately owned studio, one-, two-, and three-bedroom low-rise condo units, about half of which are in its rental program. **Pros:** great beach; plenty of amenities; no charge for beach chairs. **Cons:** conference crowds; packed pool area, $30 per night resort fee. $ *Rooms from: $279* ✉ *1451 Middle Gulf Dr., Sanibel* ☎ *239/472–4151, 866/565–5093* ⊕ *www. sundialresort.com* ⇆ *184 1-, 2-, and 3-bedroom units (varies according to rental program participants)* ⦿ *No meals.*

$$$$
HOTEL

Waterside Inn. Palm trees, sea-grape trees, pastel cottages, and white sand set the scene at this quiet beachside vacation spot. **Pros:** beachfront location; intimate feel; small pets allowed in most cottages. **Cons:** no restaurants within walking distance; office closes at night. $ *Rooms from: $255* ✉ *3033 W. Gulf Dr., Sanibel* ☎ *239/472–1345, 800/741–6166* ⊕ *www.watersideinn.net* ⇆ *4 rooms, 10 efficiencies, 13 cottages* ⦿ *No meals.*

CAPTIVA

$$$$
RESORT
FAMILY
Fodor'sChoice
★

South Seas Island Resort. This 330-acre resort feels as lush as its name suggests and is full-service with 18 swimming pools (one with two tubular slides), private restaurants and shops, a nature center stocked with small live animals, a family interactive center, and a 9-hole golf course with attractive water features. **Pros:** full range of amenities; exclusive feel; car-free transportation. **Cons:** high rates in season; a bit

8

isolated; spread out. $ *Rooms from: $239* ✉ *5400 Plantation Rd., Captiva* ☎ *239/472–5111, 888/222–7848* ⊕ *www.southseas.com* ↪ *106 rooms, 365 suites* ¶○¶ *No meals.*

$$$$
B&B/INN
🔳 **'Tween Waters Inn.** Besides its great beach-to-bay location, this inn has historic value and in 2011 was listed in the National Register of Historic Places. **Pros:** great views; lots of water-sports options; free Wi-Fi. **Cons:** beach is across the road. $ *Rooms from: $250* ✉ *Captiva Dr., Captiva* ☎ *239/472–5161, 800/223–5865* ⊕ *www.tween-waters.com* ↪ *48 rooms, 24 studios, 41 1-bedroom suites, 4 2-bedroom suites, 2 3-bedroom suites, 19 cottages* ¶○¶ *Breakfast.*

SHOPPING

SANIBEL

Periwinkle Place. The largest complex of outdoor Sanibel shopping has about 25 shops in a parklike setting. ✉ *2075 Periwinkle Way, Sanibel* ☎ *734/769–2289* ⊕ *www.periwinkleplace.com.*

Sanibel Seashell Industries. Among the island's cache of shell shops, this one is favored by serious collectors and crafters because of its reasonable prices and the knowledgeable family that runs it. For shell gifts, the family operates another little shop right behind the warehouse-size one. ✉ *905 Fitzhugh St., Sanibel* ☎ *239/472–1603* ⊕ *www.seashells.com.*

She Sells Sea Shells. At She Sells Sea Shells, everything imaginable is made from shells, from mirrors to lamps to Christmas ornaments. The owner wrote the book on shell art, and you can buy it here. ✉ *1157 Periwinkle Way, Sanibel* ☎ *239/472–6991* ⊕ *www.sanibelshellcrafts.com.*

CAPTIVA

Fodor's Choice
★
Jungle Drums. Expect the unexpected in wildlife art, where fish, sea turtles, and other wildlife are depicted with utmost creativity and touches of whimsy. If you're looking for souvenirs above and beyond the usual, or unique jewelry, paintings, sculptures, and pottery—this is the place. ✉ *11532 Andy Rosse La., Captiva* ☎ *239/395–2266* ⊕ *www.jungledrumsgallery.com.*

SPORTS AND THE OUTDOORS

BIKING

Everyone bikes around flat-as-a-pancake Sanibel and Captiva—on bikeways that edge the main highway in places, on the road through the wildlife refuge, and along side streets. Free maps are available at bicycle liveries.

Billy's Bikes. Rent by the hour or the day from this Sanibel outfitter, which also rents motorized scooters and leads Segway tours. ✉ *1470 Periwinkle Way, Sanibel* ☎ *239/472–5248* ⊕ *www.billysrentals.com.*

Jim's Rentals. Bikes (and water-sport recreation rentals) of all kinds are available at this Captiva operator. ✉ *11534 Andy Rosse La., Captiva* ☎ *239/472–1296* ⊕ *www.yolowatersports.com.*

CANOEING AND KAYAKING

Tarpon Bay Explorers. One of the best ways to scout out the wildlife refuge is by paddle. Rent a canoe or kayak from the refuge's official concessionaire and explore at your leisure. The kayak water trail is easy to follow, simply paddle your way along 17 markers and see a bevy of birds and other wildlife. Guided tours by kayak or pontoon boat are also offered and worthwhile for visitors unfamiliar with the ecosystem. Their on-site touch tank gives a hands-on learning experience about local sea life. ✉ *900 Tarpon Bay Rd., Sanibel* ☎ *239/472–8900* ⊕ *www.tarponbayexplorers.com.*

FISHING

Local anglers head out to catch mackerel, pompano, grouper, snook, snapper, tarpon, and shark.

Sanibel Marina. To find a charter captain on Sanibel, ask around the marina. ✉ *634 N. Yachtsman Dr., Sanibel* ☎ *239/472–2723* ⊕ *www. sanibelmarina.com.*

'Tween Waters Marina. On Captiva, this is the place to look for guides. You can also rent kayaks, canoes, stand-up paddleboards, and other recreational watercrafts. ✉ *'Tween Waters Inn, 15951 Captiva Dr., Captiva* ☎ *239/472–5161* ⊕ *www.tween-waters.com/marina.php.*

GOLF

Dunes Golf & Tennis Club. Rent clubs and take lessons as well as test your skills against the water hazards on the 18-hole course; greens fees $75/$120 (including cart). The club also has 6 Har-Tru tennis courts. ✉ *949 Sandcastle Rd., Sanibel* ☎ *239/472–2535* ⊕ *www.dunesgolfsanibel.com.*

FORT MYERS BEACH (ESTERO ISLAND)

18 miles southwest of Fort Myers.

Crammed with motels, hotels, and restaurants, Estero Island is one of Fort Myers's more frenetic gulf playgrounds. Dolphins frequently frolic in Estero Bay, part of the Intracoastal Waterway, and marinas provide a starting point for boating adventures, including sunset cruises, sightseeing cruises, and deep-sea fishing. At the southern tip, a bridge leads to Lovers Key State Park.

GETTING HERE AND AROUND

San Carlos Boulevard in Fort Myers leads to Fort Myers Beach's high bridge, Times Square, and Estero Boulevard, the island's main drag. Estero Island is 18 miles southwest of Fort Myers.

BEACHES

Lovers Key State Park. Once a little-known secret, this out-of-the-way park encompassing 1,616 acres on four barrier islands and several uninhabited islets is popular among beachgoers and birders. Bike, hike, walk, or paddle the park's trails (rentals available); go shelling on its 2½ miles of white-sand beach; take a boat tour; or have a beach picnic under the trees. Trams run regularly from 9 to 4:30 to deliver you and your gear to South Beach. The ride is short but often dusty. North Beach is a five-minute walk from the concession area and parking lot. Watch for osprey, bald eagles, herons, ibis, pelicans, and roseate spoonbills, or sign up for a free excursion to learn fishing and nature photography. On the park's bay side, across the road from the beach entrance, playgrounds and a picnic area cater to families, plus there are boat ramps, kayak rentals, and a bait shop. **Amenities:** food and drink; parking (fee); showers; toilets; water sports. **Best for:** swimming; walking. ✉ *8700 Estero Blvd.* ☎ *239/463–4588* ⊕ *www.floridastateparks.org/loverskey* 🎫 *$4–$8 per vehicle, $2 for pedestrians and bicyclists* ☉ *Daily 8–sunset.*

FAMILY **Lynn Hall Memorial Park.** At the 17-acre park in the commercial northern part of Estero Island, the wide, sandy shore slopes gradually into the usually tranquil and warm gulf waters, providing safe swimming for children. And since houses, restaurants, condominiums, and hotels (including the Best Western Beach Resort and Pink Shell Resort north of the parking lot) line most of the beach, you're never far from civilization. There are picnic pavilions and barbecue grills, as well as playground equipment and a free fishing pier. The park is part of a pedestrian mall with a number of beach shops and restaurants steps away. The parking lot fills early on sunny days. **Amenities:** food and drink; parking (fee); showers; toilets; water sports. **Best for:** partiers; sunsets; walking. ⊠ *Estero Blvd. at San Carlos Blvd., to Bowditch Point Park* 📞 *239/463–1116* ⊕ *www.leeparks.org* 🚗 *Parking $2 per hr* ☉ *Daily 7 am–11 pm.*

WHERE TO EAT

$$ ✕ **Doc Ford's Rum Bar & Grille.** For dependably well-prepared food with
MODERN a water view, Doc Ford's is the top choice in Fort Myers Beach. A
AMERICAN spinoff of a Sanibel Island original, its name and theme come from a murder-mystery series by local celebrity author Randy Wayne White. The Yucatan shrimp—steamed in the shell with spicy key lime butter—has earned acclaim. Other choice picks include the beach bread, pulled pork sandwich, banana leaf–wrapped snapper, shrimp and grits with tomatillo sauce, and penne with rock shrimp. Live bands play weekend and Wednesday nights. $ *Average main: $20* ⊠ *708 Fisherman's Wharf* 📞 *239/765–9660* ⊕ *www.docfordsfortmyersbeach.com* 🍴 *Reservations not accepted.*

$$ ✕ **Matanzas Inn.** Watch boats coming and going whether you sit inside
SEAFOOD or out at this rustic Old Florida–style restaurant right on the docks alongside the Intracoastal Waterway. When the weather cooperates, enjoy the view from the shaded outdoor tables. Inside, a rustic shack gives way to a more formal dining area in the back; there's a bar upstairs with sweeping views, pizza, and live music nightly. You can't miss with shrimp from the local fleets—delicately cornmeal-breaded, stuffed, or dipped in rum and coconut. Landlubbers can choose from ribs and steak. Note that service can be a bit gruff—and slow. $ *Average main: $18* ⊠ *416 Crescent St.* 📞 *239/463–3838* ⊕ *www.matanzas.com* 🍴 *Reservations not accepted.*

$$ ✕ **Parrot Key Caribbean Grill.** For something more contemporary than
SEAFOOD Fort Myers Beach's traditional shrimp and seafood houses, head to San Carlos Island on the east side of the high bridge where the shrimp boats dock. Parrot Key sits marina-side near the shrimp docks and exudes merriment with its Floribbean cuisine and island music. The all-day menu takes tropical cues with dishes such as habanero-pepper wings; corned beef, turkey, or grouper Reuben; fillet topped with blue cheese; and day's catch with your choice of sauce. There's live entertainment most nights. $ *Average main: $20* ⊠ *2500 Main St.* 📞 *239/463–3257* ⊕ *www.myparrotkey.com* 🍴 *Reservations not accepted.*

$ ✕ **The Plaka.** A casual longtimer and a favorite for a quick breakfast,
GREEK lunch breaks, and sunset dinners, Plaka—Greek for "fun"—has typical Greek fare such as moussaka, pastitsio, gyros, and roast lamb, as well as

burgers, sandwiches, fried seafood, and strip steak. It lies along a row of casual sidewalk restaurants in a pedestrian mall near the beach. There's indoor dining, but grab a seat on the porch or under an umbrella on the patio for the best people-watching and sunset view. $ *Average main: $13* ⊠ *1001 Estero Blvd.* ☏ *239/463–4707* ⌾ *Reservations not accepted.*

$$
AMERICAN
✕ **Shoals Restaurant & Wine Bar.** Recently renamed, this large restaurant is part of the Sandy Butler (its former name) gourmet market and deli; it seats 150 diners next door. Although its bar serves full liquor, it touts its select wine list, which is extremely affordable by the bottle or glass. If you find a bottle you like better in the market, they'll uncork it for a reasonable $5 fee. The all-day menu has come down in price considerably as well. Snack on jerk Angus beef sliders with roasted pineapple or pepper-jack-and-corn-salsa flatbread. Or have a full meal starting with Florida sweet onion soup or citrus crab salad and moving on to local seafood, pasta, or steak. There's also a burger and other sandwiches and orange glaze sponge cake or key lime tart for dessert. $ *Average main: $16* ⊠ *17650 San Carlos Blvd.* ☏ *239/482–6765* ⊕ *www. shoalswinebar.com.*

WHERE TO STAY

For expanded reviews, facilities, and current deals, visit Fodors.com.

$$$$
RESORT
FAMILY
DiamondHead. This 12-story resort sits on the beach, and many of the suites, especially those on higher floors, have stunning views. **Pros:** on the beach; nice views; kitchen facilities. **Cons:** heavy foot and car traffic; tiny fitness center; not the best value on the beach. $ *Rooms from: $269* ⊠ *2000 Estero Blvd.* ☏ *239/765–7654, 888/765–5002* ⊕ *www. diamondheadfl.com* ⇆ *121 suites* ⦿ *No meals.*

$$$
RENTAL
Harbour House. This condo-hotel adds a degree of beach luxury with brightly painted and sea-motif studios and one- and two-bedroom condos, all privately owned. **Pros:** close to lots of restaurants; roomy units; all have private balconies or lanais; free covered parking. **Cons:** a walk to the beach; not great views from most rooms. $ *Rooms from: $152* ⊠ *450 Old San Carlos Blvd.* ☏ *239/463–0700, 866/998–9250* ⊕ *www.harbourhouseattheinn.com* ⇆ *6 studios, 15 1-bedroom condos, 13 2-bedroom condos* ⦿ *No meals.*

$$$$
RENTAL
Lovers Key Resort. Views can be stupendous from upper floors in this 14-story tower just north of Lovers Key State Park. **Pros:** excellent views; off the beaten path; spacious accommodations. **Cons:** not a true beach; far from shopping and restaurants; limited amenities. $ *Rooms from: $270* ⊠ *8771 Estero Blvd.* ☏ *239/765–1040, 877/798–4879* ⊕ *www.loverskey.com* ⇆ *100 condominiums* ⦿ *No meals.*

$$$
RESORT
FAMILY
Outrigger Beach Resort. On a wide gulf beach, this casual resort has rooms and efficiencies with configurations to suit different guests' needs. **Pros:** beautiful beach; water-sports rentals; family-friendly vibe. **Cons:** can be noisy; crowded pool area; old-school feel. $ *Rooms from: $163* ⊠ *6200 Estero Blvd.* ☏ *239/463–3131, 800/657–5659* ⊕ *www. outriggerfmb.com* ⇆ *76 rooms, 68 efficiencies* ⦿ *No meals.*

8

SPORTS AND THE OUTDOORS

BIKING

Fort Myers Beach has no designated trails, so most cyclists ride along the road.

Fun Rentals. Bike-rentals are available from anywhere between two hours and a week. ⊠ *1901 Estero Blvd.* ☎ *239/463–8844* ⊕ *www. funrentals.org.*

Lover's Key Adventures and Events. This company rents one-speed bikes, kayaks, canoes and concessions in Lovers Key State Park. Fees for adult bikes are $18 for a half day, $25 for a full day. ⊠ *8700 Estero Blvd.* ☎ *239/765–7788* ⊕ *www.loverskeyadventures.com.*

CANOEING

Lover's Key Adventures and Events. Lovers Key State Park offers kayak and canoe rentals and guided kayaking tours of its bird-filled estuary. Guided tours cost $55 (call for dates and times). Rentals begin at $38 for a half day. ⊠ *8700 Estero Blvd.* ☎ *239/765–7788* ⊕ *www. loverskeyadventures.com.*

FISHING

Getaway Deep Sea Fishing. Arrange anything from half-day party-boat charters to full-day excursions, fishing equipment included. Rates start at $60 for a half-day trip. ⊠ *18400 San Carlos Blvd.* ☎ *800/641–3088, 239/466–3600* ⊕ *www.getawaymarina.com.*

FAMILY   **SoulMate Charters.** Local "REEL Talk" radio host Captain Rob Modys takes care of everything from the fishing license to the rods and bait on the half-, three-quarter-, and full-day fishing charters he offers around the scenic back bays and tiny islands near Fort Myers Beach. He's a local guide who knows every "honey hole" and will no doubt find fish for you to catch. As a father himself, he's great with kids and has the patience to teach budding anglers. He is based out of Fish Tale Marina. ⊠ *7225 Estero Blvd.* ☎ *239/851–1242* ⊕ *www.soulmatecharters.com.*

GOLF

Fort Myers Beach Golf Course. Eighteen holes and a practice range sit in the midst of a condo community filled with birds; greens fees $53/$25. ⊠ *4200 Bay Beach La., off Estero Blvd.* ☎ *239/463–2064* ⊕ *www.fmbgc.com.*

NAPLES AND VICINITY

As you head south from Fort Myers on U.S. 41, you soon come to Estero and Bonita Springs, followed by the Naples and Marco Island areas, which are sandwiched between Big Cypress Swamp and the Gulf of Mexico. East of Naples the land is largely undeveloped and mostly wetlands, all the way to Fort Lauderdale. Naples itself is a major vacation destination that has sprouted pricey high-rise condominiums and golfing developments, plus a spate of restaurants and shops to match. A similar but not as thorough evolution has occurred on Marco Island, the largest of the Ten Thousand Islands.

ESTERO/BONITA SPRINGS

10 miles south of Fort Myers via U.S. 41.

Towns below Fort Myers have started to flow seamlessly into one another since the opening of Florida Gulf Coast University in San Carlos Park and as a result of the growth of Estero and Bonita Springs, which were agricultural communities until the 1990s. In recent years the area has become a shopping mecca of mega-outdoor malls mixing big-box stores, smaller chains, and restaurants. Bonita Beach, the closest beach to Interstate 75, has evolved from a fishing community into a strip of upscale homes and beach clubs built to provide access for residents of inland golf developments.

GETTING HERE AND AROUND

U.S. 41 (Tamiami Trail) runs right through the heart of these two adjacent communities. You can also reach them by exits 123 and 116 off Interstate 75.

EXPLORING

FAMILY **Everglades Wonder Gardens.** Opened in 1936 and one of the first attractions of its kind in the state, this garden captures the beauty of untamed Florida. The old-fashioned, rather cramped zoological gardens have Florida panthers, black bears, crocodiles and alligators, tame Florida deer, flamingos, otters, and birds. There's also a funky natural history museum. Tours, which include otter and alligator feedings, run continuously, the last starting at 4:15. The swinging bridge over the alligator pit is a real thrill. ⊠ *27180 Old U.S. 41* ☎ *239/992–2591* ⊕ *www. evergladeswondergardens.com* ⊠ *$15* ⊙ *Daily 9–5.*

Koreshan State Historic Site. Tour one of Florida's quirkier chapters from the past. Named for a religious cult that was active at the turn of the 20th century, Koreshan preserves a dozen structures where the group practiced arts, worshipped a male-female divinity, and created its own branch of science called cosmogony. The cult floundered when leader Cyrus Reed Teed died in 1908, and in 1961 the four remaining members deeded the property to the state. Rangers and volunteers lead tours and demonstrations, and the grounds are lovely for picnicking and camping. Canoeists paddle the Estero River, fringed by a forest of exotic vegetation the Koreshans planted. ⊠ *3800 Corkscrew Rd., at U.S. 41 (Tamiami Trail), Estero* ☎ *239/992–0311* ⊕ *www. floridastateparks.org/koreshan* ⊠ *$5 per vehicle with up to 8 passengers; $4 for single motorist; $2 per bicyclist, pedestrian, or extra passenger* ⊙ *Daily 8–sunset.*

BEACHES

Barefoot Beach Preserve. This one is not exactly easy to find since it's accessible only by a quiet neighborhood road around the corner from buzzing Bonita Beach Park, but it's still well worth the trip if you're looking to commune with nature—and have some fun while you're at it. Shells here are bountiful, as are adorable gopher tortoises that may cross in front of your car. Stop by the nature center and see if you can join a ranger-led walk through the trails and gardens, or take up a paddle and go canoeing. There's no towel-jockeying here along the wide-open space (the preserve

8

as a whole is 342 acres), and refreshments and beach rentals provide ample comfort while you unwind in the pristine sands. **Amenities:** parking (fee); food and drink; showers; toilets; water sports. **Best for:** solitude; walking. ✉ *5901 Bonita Beach Rd., Barefoot Beach Rd. off Bonita Beach Rd.* ☎ *239/591–8596* 🌐 *www.collierparks.com* 🎟 *Parking $8.*

Bonita Beach Park. The joint is always jumping on this rowdy stretch of coast, the easiest by far to reach from the inland areas south of Fort Myers. Local favorite hangout Doc's Beach House, open from breakfast until the wee hours of the night, keeps bellies full and libations flowing. Other food and sports vendors camp out here, too, making it nearly impossible to resist an ice cream or a ride on a Jet Ski. Shaded pavilions between the parking lot and dunes are a great way to cool off from the sweltering heat—just don't sit too close to the picnickers barbecuing. **Amenities:** showers; toilets; parking (fee); food and drink; water sports. **Best for:** partiers; windsurfing. ✉ *27954 Hickory Blvd., at Bonita Beach Rd.* ☎ *239/949–4615* 🌐 *www.leeparks.org* 🎟 *Parking $2 per hr.*

WHERE TO EAT

$$$ ITALIAN Fodor's Choice ★ 🍴 **Angelina's Ristorante.** Here it's all about the experience—one of the most indulgent, pampered meals you'll ever eat. Formally trained waitstaff attend to your every need in this temple of traditional Italian cuisine. A dramatic wine tower hovers over the main room; the plush private booths surrounding it are the best tables (call early to snag one). The taste circus begins with an amuse bouche. Pick between antipasti, crispy flatbreads, and wholesome soups before moving on to homemade pastas and grilled meats. Absolutely try the butternut squash ravioli, an inventive version with citrus-tomato butter and truffled almonds. The evening ends with a complimentary nightcap. There is also a great prix-fixe menu. **TIP→ This is an upscale restaurant. Don't show up in flip-flops, jeans, or shorts; the staff may be too polite to turn you away, but you will be uncomfortable.** [$] *Average main: $25* ✉ *24041 U.S. 41* ☎ *239/390–3187* 🌐 *www.angelinasofbonitasprings.com* ✍ *Reservations essential* ⏲ *No lunch.*

$$$ SEAFOOD 🍴 **Blue Water Bistro.** For the convenience of shoppers at Coconut Point, several excellent restaurants cluster in the midst of the shopping center. Most are hooked to a chain. This one, although part of a Naples–Bonita Springs dining dynasty, has a personality all its own with a suave indoor–outdoor bar scene and seafood that's anything but timid. Its specialty is grilled fish from around the globe that you can mix and match with a choice of sauces and sides. For instance, try swordfish with a sweet-and-sour mango sauce and coconut sticky rice. Other specialties include a classic burger, Thai lobster, and excellent shrimp scampi taglioni. [$] *Average main: $22* ✉ *Coconut Point, 23151 Village Shops Way, Estero* ☎ *239/949–2583* 🌐 *www.bluewaterbistro.net* ⏲ *No lunch.*

$ AMERICAN FAMILY 🍴 **Doc's Beach House.** Right next door to the public access point for Barefoot Beach, Doc's has fed hungry beachgoers for decades. Come barefoot and grab a quick libation or meal downstairs, outside on the beach, or in the courtyard. When the thermometer reaches "searing," take refuge on the air-conditioned second floor, with its great view of beach action. Basic fare on the breakfast and all-day menu includes a popular Angus burger, Chicago-style pizza, and seafood plates. The conch chowder is some of the best in these parts, with just the right amount of fire. $ *Average main: $10* ✉ *27908 Hickory Blvd.* ☎ *239/992–6444* ⊕ *www.docsbeachhouse.com* ⌂ *Reservations not accepted* ▭ *No credit cards.*

$ ✕ **Old 41 Restaurant.** Locals vote this "best breakfast" and "best Philly
AMERICAN cheesesteak," and mostly locals populate its cheery dining room with its Philadelphia allegiance. For breakfast, don't miss the incredible Texas French toast with homemade caramel and pecans, Carbon's malted Belgian waffles, or eggs and homemade hash with Boar's Head meat. Besides cheesesteak, lunch specialties include Boar's Head hoagies, burgers, in-house-roasted beef or turkey sandwiches, and other comfort food it serves until 3 pm. $ *Average main: $7* ✉ *25091 Bernwood Dr.* ☎ *239/948–4123* ⊕ *www.old41.com* ⌂ *Reservations not accepted* ☉ *No dinner.*

WHERE TO STAY

For expanded reviews, facilities, and current deals, visit Fodors.com.

$$$$ ▦ **Hyatt Regency Coconut Point Resort & Spa.** This secluded luxury resort,
RESORT with its marble-and-mahogany lobby and championship golf course,
FAMILY makes a lovely sanctuary for families who want a refined atmosphere,
Fodor'sChoice plus fun features like a 140-foot waterslide, a rock climbing wall, and a
★ s'mores fire pit. **Pros:** pampering spa; great ceviche bar; rooms upgraded in 2012. **Cons:** need water shuttle to reach the beach; expensive restaurants. $ *Rooms from: $259* ✉ *5001 Coconut Rd.* ☎ *239/444–1234, 800/554–9288* ⊕ *www.coconutpoint.hyatt.com* ⇱ *454 rooms and suites* ⵏ◯⵿ *No meals.*

$$$ ▦ **Trianon Bonita Bay.** Convenient to Bonita Springs's best shopping and
HOTEL dining, this branch of a refined downtown Naples favorite has a peace-ful, sophisticated feel and a poolside–lakeside alfresco bar and grill. **Pros:** spacious rooms; intimate atmosphere; complimentary breakfast. **Cons:** sometimes less-than-friendly staff; far from beach; slightly stuffy. $ *Rooms from: $149* ✉ *3401 Bay Commons Dr.* ☎ *239/948–4400, 800/859–3939* ⊕ *www.trianon.com* ⇱ *100 rooms* ⵏ◯⵿ *Breakfast.*

SHOPPING

FAMILY **Coconut Point.** A 500-acre planned community tops the Gulf Coast Town Center with even more upscale and big-box stores and restaurants. There's a boardwalk for a breather between impulse purchases, and a castle-theme kids' play area. ✉ *23106 Fashion Dr., Estero* ☎ *239/992–9966* ⊕ *www.shopcoconutpoint.com.*

Miromar Outlets. The complex includes Adidas, Coach, Michael Kors, Nike, Nautica, and more than 140 other stores and eateries, plus a free Playland for kids. ✉ *10801 Corkscrew Rd., at I–75 Exit 123, near Germain Arena, Estero* ☎ *239/948–3766* ⊕ *www.miromaroutlets.com.*

SPORTS AND THE OUTDOORS

BIRDING

The last leg of the Great Florida Birding Trail has more than 20 stops in the Lower Gulf Coast. Go to ⊕ *www.floridabirdingtrail.com* for a complete list.

8

CANOEING

The meandering Estero River is pleasant for canoeing as it passes through Koreshan State Historic Site to the bay.

Estero River Outfitters. The company rents canoes, kayaks, and equipment. ✉ *20991 Tamiami Trail S, Estero* ☎ *239/992–4050* ⊕ *www.esteroriveroutfitters.com.*

NAPLES

21 miles south of Bonita Springs, on U.S. 41.

Poised between the Gulf of Mexico and the Everglades, Naples belies its wild setting and Indian past with the trappings of wealth—neo-Mediterranean-style mansions, neatly manicured golfing developments, revitalized downtown streets lined with galleries and one-of-a-kind shops, and a reputation for lively and eclectic dining. Visitors come for its luxury hotels—including two Ritz-Carltons—its fabulous white-sand beaches, fishing, shopping, theater and arts, and a lofty reputation for golf. Yet with all the highfalutin living, Naples still appeals to families, especially with its water park and the new Golisano Children's Museum of Naples that opened in 2012.

Old Naples, the historic downtown section, has two main commercial areas, 5th Avenue South and 3rd Street South, and there's also a small cluster of restaurants right by City Dock on Naples Bay. Farther north on U.S. 41 (the Tamiami Trail, or 9th Street here), hotels, shopping centers, and developments have fast been filling in the area around and south of Vanderbilt Beach, including the dining and shopping meccas Waterside Shops, and the Village on Venetian Bay.

GETTING HERE AND AROUND

The Naples Municipal Airport is a small facility east of downtown principally serving private planes, commuter flights, and charters. A taxi for up to three passengers is about $60–$90 from Southwest Florida International Airport (RSW) in Fort Myers to Naples; each additional person is charged $10. If you prefer to book a car or limo pickup in advance, three major companies are Aaron Airport Transportation, Naples Taxi & Limo Services, and Naples Airport Shuttle. In Naples and Marco Island, Collier Area Transit runs regular routes.

Downtown Naples is 15 miles south of Bonita Springs, on U.S. 41. If you're driving here from Florida's east coast, consider Alligator Alley, a toll section of Interstate 75 that's a straight shot from Fort Lauderdale to Naples. In Naples, east–west county highways exiting off Interstate 75 include, from north to south, Immokalee Road (Route 846), Pine Ridge Road (Route 896), and Collier Boulevard (Route 951), which actually goes north–south and takes you also to Marco Island.

Contacts Aaron Airport Transportation ☎ *239/768–1898* ⊕ *www.aarontaxi.com.* **Collier Area Transit (CAT)** ☎ *239/252–7777* ⊕ *www.colliergov.net.* **Naples Airport Shuttle** ☎ *239/430–4747, 888/569–2227* ⊕ *www.naplesairportshuttle.com.* **Naples Taxi & Limo Services** ☎ *239/435–0000, 800/472–1371* ⊕ *www.naplestaxiflorida.com.*

TOURS

If you want someone to be your guide as you go about town, Naples Trolley Tours offers eight narrated tours daily, covering more than 100 points of interest in town. The tour ($25) lasts about two hours, but you can get off and on at no extra cost.

Contacts Naples Trolley Tours ⊠ *1010 6th Ave. S* ☎ *239/262–7300, 800/592–0848* ⊕ *www.naplestrolleytours.com* ⊗ *Daily 9:30–5:30.*

VISITOR INFORMATION

Contacts Naples, Marco Island, Everglades Convention and Visitors Bureau ⊠ *2800 Horseshoe Dr. N* ☎ *800/688–3600, 239/225–1013* ⊕ *www.paradisecoast.com.*

EXPLORING

TOP ATTRACTIONS

FAMILY **Collier County Museum.** To get a feel for local history, stroll the nicely presented indoor vignettes and traveling exhibits and outdoor parklike displays at this museum. A Seminole *chickee* village, native plant garden, swamp buggy, reconstructed 19th-century fort, steam logging locomotive, and more capture important Naples-area developments from prehistoric times to the World War II era. ⊠ *3331 Tamiami Trail E* ☎ *239/252–8476* ⊕ *www.colliermuseums.com* ⊠ *Free* ⊗ *Weekdays 9–5.*

FAMILY **Conservancy of Southwest Florida Nature Center.** On 21 acres bordering a tidal lagoon teeming with wildlife, the center finished a massive makeover in 2013. Kids of all ages will love the new Dalton Discovery Center, which will have interactive exhibits on six Florida ecosystems, a sea turtle tank, and other live wildlife exhibits with roughly 150 animals, including a saltwater touch tank. The opening of the wildlife hospital will more than triple the space of the old one, and this time sections will be open to the public, including a nursery viewing area where you can go gaga over baby animals. Guided walks through an endangered gopher tortoise preserve and boat tours (for ages two and older) on the mangrove-bordered Gordon River will depart several times daily. Kayaks will be available for rent. Call or check the website ahead of time to confirm open attractions and hours. ⊠ *1450 Merrihue Dr.* ☎ *239/262–0304* ⊕ *www.conservancy.org* ⊠ *$12.95* ⊗ *Mon.–Sat. 9–4:30.*

Fodor'sChoice **Corkscrew Swamp Sanctuary.** To get a feel for what this part of Florida
★ was like before civil engineers began draining the swamps, drive 17 miles east of North Naples to these 14,000 acres of pine flatwood and cypress, grass-and-sedge "wet prairie," saw-grass marshland, and lakes and sloughs filled with water lettuce. Managed by the National Audubon Society, the sanctuary protects North America's largest remaining stand of ancient bald cypress, 600-year-old trees as tall as 130 feet, as well as endangered birds, such as wood storks, which often nest here. This is a favorite destination for serious birders and is the gateway to the Great Florida Birding and Wildlife Trail. If you spend a couple of hours to take the 2¼-mile self-guided tour along the boardwalk, you'll spot ferns, orchids, and air plants, as well as wading birds and possibly alligators and river otters. A nature center educates you about this precious, unusual habitat with a dramatic re-creation of

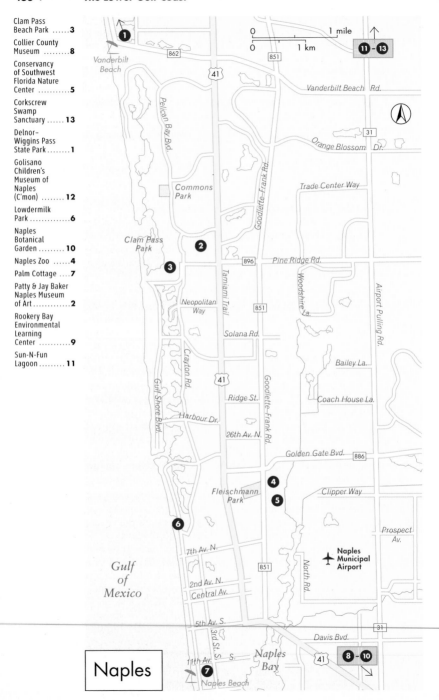

Naples

the preserve and its creatures in the Swamp Theater. ⊠ *375 Sanctuary Rd. W, 17 miles east of I–75 on Rte. 846* ☎ *239/348–9151* ⊕ *www. corkscrew.audubon.org* ⊠ *$12* ☾ *Daily 7–5:30.*

FAMILY **Golisano Children's Museum of Naples.** This bright, cheery 30,000-square-foot ode to playful learning burst onto Naples's cultural scene in 2012 after a decade of much-anticipated planning, and its 12 state-of-the-art permanent galleries do not disappoint. Kids of many ages and abilities (exhibits were designed to be accessible for children with special needs, too) will love the gigantic Banyan Tree, a focal point at 45 feet tall and a climbing obstacle of sorts; the Farm & Market, a cooperative playground where roles are assigned (a harvester or cashier, for example) to subtly enforce team building and math skills; and the Green Construction zone, where hard hats and ecofriendly building materials will inspire future architects. ∎∎TIP➔ It's in the same park as Sun-N-Fun Lagoon, and it's possible to do both in one day. ⊠ *North Collier Regional Park, 15080 Livingston Rd.* ☎ *239/514–0084* ⊕ *www.cmon. org* ⊠ *$10* ☾ *Tues.–Sat. 10–5, Sun. 11–4.*

Naples Botanical Garden. An expansion and renovation of the botanical gardens that finished in 2010 elevated this attraction to one of Naples's most culturally and botanically exciting. Its "gardens with latitude" flourish with plants and architectural and decorative elements from Florida and other subtropical locales including Asia, Brazil, and the Caribbean. Highlights of the 170 acres include a Children's Garden with a butterfly house, treehouse, waterfall, cave, Cracker house, and hidden garden; an infinity water lily pool; an aromatic Enabling Garden; and a dramatic waterfall feature. ⊠ *4820 Bayshore Dr.* ☎ *239/643–7275* ⊕ *www.naplesgarden.org* ⊠ *$12.95* ☾ *Fri.-Wed. 9–5, Thurs. 8–5.*

FAMILY **Naples Zoo at Caribbean Gardens.** The lush 44-acre zoo got its start as a botanical garden in 1919 and has since drawn visitors curious to see lions, tigers, bears, leopards, gazelles—and a wildly popular giraffe herd added in 2011. For an extra fee you can feed the gentle, eyelash-batting giants or, in the winter season only, ride aboard dromedary camels. Other exhibits include the cult-favorite honey badgers (only four U.S. zoos have them), whose innocuous-sounding name belies their ferocious ways; a "Snakes Live" interactive area; a pair of endangered Madagascar fossas; and the "Primate Expedition Cruise" that sails past islands populated with monkeys and lemurs. Youngsters can amuse themselves in three play zones, and there are daily meet-the-keeper times, alligator feedings, and live animal shows. ⊠ *1590 Goodlette-Frank Rd.* ☎ *239/262–5409* ⊕ *www.napleszoo.org* ⊠ *$19.95; giraffe feeding and camel rides $5 each* ☾ *Daily 9–5; gates close at 4.*

Fodor'sChoice ★ **Patty & Jay Baker Naples Museum of Art.** This cool, contemporary museum in the Naples Philharmonic Center for the Arts displays provocative, innovative pieces, including renowned miniatures, antique walking sticks, modern American and Mexican masters, and traveling exhibits. Dazzling installations by glass artist Dale Chihuly include a fiery cascade of a chandelier and an illuminated ceiling layered with many-hued glass bubbles, glass corkscrews, and other shapes that suggest the sea; alone, this warrants a visit. In 2010, the multimillion-dollar donation of a massive 12-piece Louise Nevelson sculpture installation greatly boosted the museum's importance. ✉ *5833 Pelican Bay Blvd.* ☎ *239/597–1900, 800/597–1900* ⊕ *www.thephil.org* 🎫 *$8* ☉ *Oct.– June, Tues.–Sat. 10–4, Sun. noon–4.*

FAMILY **Rookery Bay Environmental Learning Center.** In the midst of 110,000-acre Rookery Bay National Estuarine Research Reserve, the center dramatically interprets the Everglades environment and local history with interactive models, aquariums, original art, a film, tours, and classes (check Web site for times). It's on the edge of the estuary, about five minutes east of Marco's north bridge on Collier Boulevard. In 2009 the center debuted a $1 million, 440-foot pedestrian bridge that spans the reserve's creek from the center's second floor, and connects with a half-mile nature trail that can be followed by guided or self-guided tour. Kayak and boat tours are also available through advance registration. New exhibits include an interactive research boat, a display on the importance of the Gulf of Mexico to coastal communities, and another on global climate change. ✉ *300 Tower Rd.* ☎ *239/417–6310* ⊕ *www. rookerybay.org* 🎫 *$5* ☉ *Weekdays 9–4; Nov.–Apr., also Sat. 9–4.*

WORTH NOTING

Palm Cottage. Houses in 19th-century South Florida were often built of a concrete-like material made of sand and seashells called tabby mortar. For a fine example of such construction, stop by Palm Cottage, built in 1895 and one of the Lower Gulf Coast's few surviving tabby homes. The historically accurate interior contains simple furnishings typical of the period. Next door to the cottage, Norris Gardens was designed to reflect turn-of-the-last-century garden trends. Docent tours of the home are included with admission; for an extra $6, join the weekly two-hour walking tour of the garden and historic district (reservations are required for the historic district tours, which are held on Wednesday mornings). ✉ *137 12th Ave. S* ☎ *239/261–8164* ⊕ *www. napleshistoricalsociety.org* 🎫 *$10* ☉ *Tues.–Sat. 1–4.*

FAMILY **Sun-N-Fun Lagoon.** This is a splashy water park across from the children's museum along the eastern edge of town. Interactive water features throughout such as dumping buckets and spray guns will delight younger kids, and there's a Tadpole Pool geared to those age six and under. The whole family will go for the diving pool, lazy river, and slides. The park is generally closed from October to President's Day weekend (except during some local school breaks). ✉ *North Collier Regional Park, 15000 Livingston Rd.* ☎ *239/252–4021* ⊕ *www. napleswaterpark.com* 🎫 *$12* ☉ *Memorial Day–late Aug., daily 10–5; weekends 10–5 in fall and spring (check website for specific schedules).*

BEACHES

FAMILY **City of Naples Beach.** There's something here for everyone just west of the 3rd Street South shopping area, but what gets the most attention by far is the historic pier that extends deep into the gulf and has the best free dolphin-viewing seats around. Sunsets are a nightly ritual, and dodging anglers' poles is par for the course. The concession stand sells food for humans as well as for fishy friends, and on the sand below, teenagers hold court at the volleyball nets and families picnic on blankets, while a handful of people can always be seen swooping up cockles, fighting conchs, and coquinas. For a charming landscape away from the commotion, head south on Gulf Shore Boulevard and take your pick of the public access points. They may not have the amenities of the pier, but the solitude can't be beat. **Amenities:** showers; toilets; parking (fee); food and drink. **Best for:** sunsets; swimming. ⊠ *12th Ave. S at Gulf Shore Blvd.* ☎ *239/213–3062* ⊠ *Parking 25¢ per 10 min* ☉ *Daily 7–sunset.*

Clam Pass Beach Park. A quiet day at the beach gets an adventurous start when you board a tram and careen down a ¾-mile boardwalk through shaded mangroves and a network of canals. At the end is a pretty, secluded patch of sand that still has notable activities because of the family-vacation-magnet Waldorf Astoria Naples just a few steps from the public parking lot. The surf is calm, perfect for swimming, and aside from the usual lying out, shelling, and sand-castle building, you can spring for a kayak and meander around the marsh for a different kind of water experience. **Amenities:** food and drink; showers; toilets; water sports; parking (fee). **Best for:** solitude; swimming. ⊠ *465 Seagate Dr.* ☎ *239/353–0404* ⊕ *www.collierparks.com* ⊠ *Parking $8* ☉ *Daily 8–sunset.*

Fodor'sChoice ★ **Delnor-Wiggins Pass State Park.** This wide, virtually untouched expanse— about 166 acres—of open beach makes visitors feel transported from the bustling high-rises and resorts just a few blocks south. A full roster of eco-inclined features, like a designated fishing zone, hard-bottom reef (one of the only ones in the region and close enough to swim up to), boat dock, and observation tower, hook anglers, nature lovers, and water sports enthusiasts drawn to the peaceful, laid-back vibe. Moms and dads love the educational displays on the local environment and the ranger-led sea turtle and birding programs, not to mention the picnic tables, grills, and plenty of shade offshore. Take note, however, that everything is BYO; the park doesn't have any rentals or concessions. **Amenities:** showers; toilets; parking (fee). **Best for:** snorkeling; solitude; walking. ⊠ *11135 Gulf Shore Dr. N* ☎ *239/597–6196* ⊕ *www.floridastateparks.org/delnorwiggins* ⊠ *$6 per vehicle with up to 8 people, $4 for single drivers, $2 for pedestrians and bicyclists* ☉ *Daily 8–sunset.*

FAMILY **Lowdermilk Park.** Do you prefer your beach loud and active with a big dose of good old-fashioned fun? Kids running around in the surf, volleyballers hitting the sand, and tykes getting up close and personal with the park's most colorful residents, the red-throated Muscovy ducks, are all part of the Lowdermilk experience. Shallow waters and little-to-no wave action beg for a dip from even the most hesitant swimmer, and thatched umbrellas dotting the shoreline complete the happy tiki vibe and are yours for the taking—assuming you can snag one (they are strictly first come, first served). Even more, a food stand, two playgrounds, and some casual eateries down the strand at the Naples Beach Hotel make digging your feet into the sand a no-brainer. **Amenities:** parking (fee); toilets; showers; food and drink. **Best for:** swimming; walking. ⊠ *1301 Gulf Shore Blvd. N* ☎ *239/213–3029* ⊠ *Parking 25¢ per 10 min* ☉ *Daily 8–sunset.*

Vanderbilt Beach. If a day at the shore just doesn't seem quite complete without a piña colada and serious people-watching, this place is for you. The white powdery sand often looks like a kaleidoscope, with multihued towels and umbrellas dotting the landscape in front of the nearly 3 miles of tony north Naples condos and luxe resorts, including the Ritz-Carlton and LaPlaya. If you walk far enough—which many people do—you come across eye candy of a different kind: the architecturally stunning megamansions of Bay Colony perched up on the dunes. A covered public parking garage gives easy access, and the beach really comes alive at sunset with onlookers. **Amenities:** water sports; food and drink; parking (fee); toilets; showers. **Best for:** partiers; sunsets; walking. **TIP→ Stroll up to Gumbo Limbo at the Ritz for the best Floribbean, yet surprisingly not wallet-busting, lunches and panoramic views from a shaded deck.** ✉ *100 Vanderbilt Beach Rd.* ☎ *239/252–4000* 🌐 *www.collierparks.com* 🎟 *Parking $8* 🕐 *Daily 8–sunset.*

WHERE TO EAT

$$$$ SEAFOOD 🍴 **Baleen.** The mood cast in this well-appointed dining room and the romantic gulf-view patio that spills out from it onto the sand feels like the perfect Florida restaurant experience. There's only one small problem: lighting is so low at dinner that you can't read the menu, even with its built-in flashlight. Too bad, because that means you also miss the effect of the beautifully presented dishes: Asian pear–and-arugula salad, black grouper with tamarind glaze, grilled scallops paired with polenta and serrano chilies, Grand Marnier crème brûlée, and the like. (Thankfully, there's a great prix-fixe option.) At breakfast, the housemade corned beef hash is divine. For lunch, the lobster Cobb salad is a popular choice. [$] *Average main: $37* ✉ *La Playa Beach & Golf Resort, 9891 Gulf Shore Dr.* ☎ *239/598–5707, 800/237–6883* 🌐 *www.laplayaresort.com* ✍ *Reservations essential.*

$$ ITALIAN 🍴 **Barbatella.** This trattoria with an edge was the most buzzed-about opening in 2012; it's still just as popular. The restaurant has three dining spaces to suit any whim: the wine bar, with sleek eclectic decor, has a communal table, green ceiling medallions, crystal chandeliers wrapped in birdcages, and a wine dispenser that allows guests to sip their way through 32 bottles (Italian, of course) by the 1-, 3-, or 6-ounce glass. The brick room, with 150-year-old recycled floors, is more casual and open to the kitchen; and the central patio is shaded and relaxed. The menu, straight-up Italian and expertly done, stars refined versions of classics, including bruschetta, fried calamari, lasagna, and wood-fired pizza. Don't miss the house's sweetest treat: a gelateria that's open to passersby on 3rd Street South is a partnership with artisan-chocolate king Norman Love. [$] *Average main: $20* ✉ *1290 3rd St. S* ☎ *239/263–1955* 🌐 *www.barbatellanaples.com.*

$$$ SEAFOOD 🍴 **The Bay House.** On a quiet side street just north of the Immokalee and U.S. 41 is one of the area's best restaurants for casual fine dining—and breathtaking scenery. Here, the spotlight is on a serene, hidden expanse of twisted mangrove trees and flowing canals. Beautifully restored rowboats and modern chandeliers hang from the ceiling of the main dining room, which is packed almost every night in season. The food is a serious celebration of the sea with Southern accents, like locally caught fish with shrimp hash and green tomato jam. Adjacent

Tierney's Tavern & Claw Bar shares the same kitchen but has lower prices and greater appeal for landlubbers. ■ TIP→ Saturday lunches are surprisingly quiet and a perfect time to snag one of the coveted tables closest to the windows. $ *Average main: $28* ⊠ *799 Walkerbilt Rd.* ☎ *239/591–3837* ⊕ *www.bayhousenaples.com* ⌂ *Reservations essential* ⊘ *No lunch May–Nov.*

$$$
MIDLE EASTERN

✕ **Bha! Bha! Persian Bistro.** Long considered one of Naples's best ethnic restaurants, its loyal fans flocked to a tiny north Naples strip mall year in and year out to indulge in classic and fusion Middle Eastern cooking. On the eve of its 15th birthday came a well-deserved present: a brand-new location on bustling 5th Avenue South. Expect a few tweaks to the menu, but all of the old favorites have made the move, including plum lamb with tomato-pomegranate sauce, mango-garlic shrimp (which was featured in *Bon Appetit*), and spicy beef in saffron sauce with cucumber yogurt. $ *Average main: $25* ⊠ *865 5th Ave. S* ☎ *239/594–5557* ⊕ *www.bhabhapersianbistro.com.*

$$$$
ECLECTIC

✕ **Chops City Grill.** Count on high-quality cuisine that fuses, as its name suggests, chopstick cuisine and steak-house mainstays. Sophisticated yet resort-wear casual, it draws everyone from young businesspeople to local retirees. Sushi and Pacific Rim inspirations such as shrimp spring rolls rub elbows with beef carpaccio and watermelon salad with goat cheese and pecans. Grilled seafood and fine cuts of meat like dry-aged rib eyes and strip steaks come with side options such as "wild" sherry-laced mushrooms and four-cheese mac. For dessert, sip a frothy Chocolate Kiss martini. Dine alfresco or inside with a view of the kitchen. $ *Average main: $32* ⊠ *837 5th Ave. S* ☎ *239/262–4677* ⊕ *www.chopscitygrill.com* ⌂ *Reservations essential* ⊘ *No lunch.*

$$
CUBAN

✕ **Fernández The Bull.** Intrepid palates venture several miles inland to get a taste of authentic, home-cooked Cuban specialties at this simple storefront café. Stick to the basics, and don't miss the lemony *lechon asado* (slow-roasted pork that's grilled and basted with garlic) or *ropa vieja* (shreds of flank steak simmered in tomato sauce with heaps of peppers and onions). In chichi Naples, the prices are good, and the portions are better: one entrée is enough for dinner and lunch the next day, as all are served with salads, big slabs of toasted garlic bread, and two sides. The bar is wine-and-beer only; the mojitos are *faux*-jitos but still pretty tasty. $ *Average main: $17* ⊠ *1201 Piper Blvd., No. 10* ☎ *239/254–9855* ⊕ *www.fernandezthebull.com.*

$
AMERICAN

✕ **Old Naples Pub.** Local blue- and white-collar workers gather with shoppers for affordable sandwiches and seafood in the vaulted, vine-twisted courtyard of this traditional pub, which has been tucked away from shopping traffic at 3rd Street Plaza since the late 1980s. It strikes one as an everybody-knows-your-name kind of place, with jars of pickles on the tables and friendly bartenders. Taste any of 25 kinds of beer and order fried "ungrouper" sandwiches (made with "mild flaky white filet" as grouper becomes rarer), burgers, crispy chicken salad, and nachos, as well as such not-so-traditional pub grub as grilled fresh catch-of-the-day and fried gator tail. There's musical entertainment Wednesday and Sunday year-round. $ *Average main: $15* ⊠ *255 13th Ave. S* ☎ *239/649–8200* ⊕ *www.naplespubs.com* ⌂ *Reservations not accepted.*

$$$$ ✕ **Sea Salt.** Naples's hottest upscale restaurant draws a crowd of con-
MEDITERRANEAN noisseurs to its modern coral-rock dining room that spills out onto
Fodor's Choice the sidewalk. Venetian-born Chef Fabrizio Aielli puts a New World
★ spin on traditional Italian on his nightly changing menu. Everyone
gets a sea-salt sampler. The best way to start is to dabble in charcute-
rie and European cheese. The finest quality meats and seafood go into
dishes including Wagyu beef and Kurobuta pork, grilled local black
grouper, and dry-packed scallops with lemon-caper oil. At lunch,
choose between creative sandwiches and salads. $ *Average main:*
$34 ✉ *1186 3rd St. S* ☎ *239/434–7258* ⊕ *www.seasaltnaples.com*
⌕ *Reservations essential.*

$$$ ✕ **Tommy Bahama Restaurant and Bar.** Here Naples takes a youthful curve.
CARIBBEAN Island music sounds on the umbrella-shaded courtyard at this eatery,
the prototype for a small national chain. It has that trademark rattan
look that identifies the casual Tommy Bahama label in clothing and fur-
niture stores across the world. Indoors and out, everybody's munching
sandwiches, salads, and grilled seafood and meats with a tropical flair,
like shrimp and scallops in curry-coconut sauce and blackberry-brandy
barbecued ribs. $ *Average main: $28* ✉ *1220 3rd St. S* ☎ *239/643–6889*
⊕ *www.tommybahama.com.*

$$$ ✕ **USS Nemo.** Don't be fooled by the tacky glowing sign from the high-
SEAFOOD way: most Neapolitans swear this is *the* place for seafood in town, which
Fodor's Choice is why you should still make a reservation even in the heat of summer.
★ The food is in the vein of fine dining but served in a whimsical setting with portholes, antique bronze diving gear, and colorful sculptures
of fish. Speaking of fish, almost all are locally caught and reach new
depths of deliciousness with eclectic, often Asian-inspired preparations.
The house signature miso-broiled sea bass with citrus-ginger butter
strikes the right balance between sweet and savory; the ginger-steamed
halibut with soy-lime dressing and the herb-grilled tuna with warm
goat cheese and lobster risotto are also winners. $ *Average main: $24*
✉ *3745 Tamiami Trail N* ☎ *239/261–6366* ⊕ *www.ussnemorestaurant.*
com ⌕ *Reservations essential* ⊘ *No lunch weekends.*

WHERE TO STAY

For expanded reviews, facilities, and current deals, visit Fodors.com.

$$$$ 🏨 **Bellasera Hotel.** This downtown hotel is just far enough "off Fifth" to
HOTEL be away from the dining-and-shopping foot traffic but close enough for
convenience, and it feels like a lovely Italian villa with its red tile roofs
and burnt-ochre stucco. **Pros:** spacious accommodations; near restaurants; free bikes for guests; first-come, first-served private cabanas at
pool. **Cons:** must take shuttle to beach; on a busy highway. $ *Rooms*
from: $249 ✉ *221 9th St. S* ☎ *239/649–7333, 888/612–1115* ⊕ *www.*
bellaseranaples.com ↪ *10 studios, 30 1-bedroom suites, 48 2-bedroom*
suites, 12 3-bedroom suites ⧉ *No meals.*

$$$$ 🏨 **Edgewater Beach Hotel.** At this all-suite property at the north end of
HOTEL scenic Gulf Shore Boulevard with a relaxed, contemporary atmosphere,
the rooms are large and come with nice touches like fully equipped
kitchens and dining room tables. **Pros:** beautiful beach; quiet; exquisite
views. **Cons:** far from shopping; surrounded closely by high-rises; no
tubs in some rooms. $ *Rooms from: $389* ✉ *1901 Gulf Shore Blvd. N*

☎ *239/403–2000, 888/564-1308* 🌐 *www.edgewaternaples.com* 🛏 *97 1-bedroom suites, 28 2-bedroom suites* 🍴 *No meals.*

$$$$ HOTEL 🏨 **Inn on Fifth.** You can't top this luxe hotel if you want to plant yourself in the heart of Naples nightlife and shopping, and its $15-million expansion across the street in 2012 added 32 new club-level suites with their own private lobby and roof deck. **Pros:** central location; metro vibe; spa has free sauna for guests. **Cons:** pool is eye-level with power lines; beach is a long stroll or shuttle ride away. [$] *Rooms from: $319* ✉ *699 5th Ave. S* ☎ *239/403–8777, 888/403–8778* 🌐 *www.innonfifth.com* 🛏 *117 rooms* 🍴 *No meals.*

$$$$ RESORT Fodor's Choice ★ 🏨 **LaPlaya Beach & Golf Resort.** LaPlaya bespeaks posh and panache down to the smallest detail—note the Balinese-style spa, marble bathrooms, and a stuffed sea turtle toy to cuddle during your stay. **Pros:** right on the beach; high-end amenities; beautiful rooms, which were renovated in 2012. **Cons:** golf course is off property; no locker rooms in spa. [$] *Rooms from: $399* ✉ *9891 Gulf Shore Dr.* ☎ *239/597–3123, 800/237–6883* 🌐 *www.laplayaresort.com* 🛏 *180 rooms, 9 suites* 🍴 *No meals.*

$$$ RESORT FAMILY 🏨 **Naples Bay Resort.** This place, a boater's dream, has the class, polish, and services associated with a property its size and scope (20 prime canal-front acres) but has the feel of a boutique hotel. **Pros:** on-site marina; free shuttle to beach; walking distance to downtown; $5 water taxi to other bayside hot spots. **Cons:** tennis courts and most pools a trek from main building; no beach; some highway noise. [$] *Rooms from: $169* ✉ *1500 5th Ave. S* ☎ *239/530–1199, 866/605–1199* 🌐 *www.naplesbayresort.com* 🛏 *20 rooms, 29 1-bedroom suites, 36 2-bedroom suites, 108 cottages (minimum 6-night stay in cottages)* 🍴 *No meals.*

$$$$ RESORT FAMILY 🏨 **The Naples Beach Hotel & Golf Club.** Family-owned and -managed since 1946 (the existing hotel dates from the early 1970s), this resort is a piece of Naples history—and its stretch of powdery sand has lots of action at all times, and is home to a sprawling casual restaurant and lively bar. **Pros:** terrific beach scene; golf course and driving range on property; complimentary kids' program. **Cons:** expensive nightly rates; showing its age; have to cross street to reach spa. [$] *Rooms from: $375* ✉ *851 Gulf Shore Blvd. N* ☎ *239/261–2222, 800/237–7600* 🌐 *www.naplesbeachhotel.com* 🛏 *267 rooms, 42 suites, 10 efficiencies* 🍴 *No meals.*

$$$$ RESORT 🏨 **Ritz-Carlton Golf Resort, Naples.** Ardent golfers with a yen for luxury will find their dream vacation at Naples's most elegant golf resort where Ritz style prevails, but in a more contemporary vein than at its sister resort, the Ritz-Carlton, Naples. **Pros:** best golf academy in area; two championship courses at the front door; plush setting; access to Ritz spa and beach via shuttle. **Cons:** 10-minute drive to gulf; expensive rates; farther inland than most properties. [$] *Rooms from: $299* ✉ *2600 Tiburón Dr.* ☎ *239/593–2000* 🌐 *www.ritzcarlton.com* 🛏 *295 rooms* 🍴 *No meals.*

$$$$ RESORT FAMILY Fodor's Choice ★ 🏨 **Ritz-Carlton, Naples.** This is a regal Ritz-Carlton, with marble statues, antique furnishings, and 19th-century European oil paintings, and a short stroll from the lobby is a beautiful white-sand beach dense with seashells. **Pros:** flawless service; fun tiki bar and water-sport options; near north Naples shopping and restaurants; private, ultra-indulgent spa (guests and members only). **Cons:** high price tag; hike to downtown;

valet parking only; extra charge for beach rentals. $ *Rooms from: $499* ✉ *280 Vanderbilt Beach Rd.* ☎ *239/598–3300* ⊕ *www.ritzcarlton.com* ⌐ *450 rooms* ⊚ *No meals.*

$$$$

HOTEL

⌂ **Trianon Old Naples.** Refined ladies and gents will feel at home in this classy boutique hotel that's right smack in the central historic district, yet enrobed in an aura of privacy two quiet residential blocks south of Fifth Avenue's bustle. **Pros:** can't-beat location for urbanites; large rooms; continental breakfast included. **Cons:** limited facilities; must drive to beach. $ *Rooms from: $235* ✉ *955 7th Ave. S* ☎ *239/435–9600, 877/482–5228* ⊕ *www.trianon.com* ⌐ *55 rooms, 3 suites* ⊚ *Breakfast.*

$$$$

RESORT

FAMILY

Fodor's Choice

★

⌂ **Waldorf Astoria Naples.** Beach access, a golf club, and top-shelf luxury are all yours at this ultramodern high-rise formerly known as the Naples Grande; it has a big following with families because of its immense free-form pool with a 100-foot waterslide. **Pros:** indulgent spa; great tennis, golf, and kayaking; attentive service; selection of eateries. **Cons:** not directly on the beach; golf facility is 6 miles away. $ *Rooms from: $299* ✉ *475 Seagate Dr.* ☎ *239/597–3232, 888/722–1267* ⊕ *www. waldorfastorianaples.com* ⌐ *395 rooms, 79 suites* ⊚ *No meals.*

NIGHTLIFE AND THE ARTS

THE ARTS

Naples Players. Musicals and dramas are performed year-round; winter shows often sell out well in advance. ✉ *Sugden Community Theatre, 701 5th Ave. S* ☎ *239/263–7990* ⊕ *www.naplesplayers.org.*

Philharmonic Center for the Arts. This 1,473-seat performance center hosts plays, concerts, and exhibits year-round, the bulk from September to May. It's home to the 85-piece Naples Philharmonic Orchestra, which presents both classical and pop concerts. The Miami City Ballet performs here during its winter season. ✉ *5833 Pelican Bay Blvd.* ☎ *239/597–1900, 800/597–1900* ⊕ *www.thephil.org.*

NIGHTLIFE

Avenue Wine Café. Young, casual oenophiles camp out here; there's also an impressive craft-beer list as well as cigars. ✉ *483 5th Ave. S* ☎ *239/403–9463.*

Burn by Rocky Patel. At this part cigar bar, part dance club, you can expect pretty young things grooving to a house DJ. ✉ *9110 Strada Pl.* ☎ *239/653–9013* ⊕ *www.burnbyrockypatel.com.*

Osetra. A hint of SoBe on the Gulf Coast serves champagne and caviar in a sleek setting. ✉ *469 5th Ave. S* ☎ *239/776–7938* ⊕ *www.osetranaples.com.*

The Pub. Long lists of brews, flat-screens, and fun British decor attract a lively crowd to this popular outpost of a small, family-run chain. ✉ *9118 Strada Pl.* ☎ *239/594–2748* ⊕ *www.experiencethepub.com.*

Silverspot Cinema. More than a plush movie theater; the Silverspot is a place to sip specialty cocktails in the lounge before showtime or instead of watching the show. ✉ *9118 Strada Pl., 2nd fl.* ☎ *239/592–0300* ⊕ *www.silverspot.net.*

Vergina. The mature crowd hits the dance floor for Gloria Gaynor and the Bee Gees. ✉ *700 5th Ave. S* ☎ *239/659–7008* ⊕ *www. verginarestaurant.com.*

8

SHOPPING

SHOPPING AREAS

Tin City. Near 5th Avenue South, a collection of tin-roof former boat docks along Naples Bay has more than 30 boutiques, eateries, and souvenir shops, with everything from jewelry and T-shirts to jet ski rentals and seafood. ⊠ *1200 5th Ave. S* ⊕ *www.tin-city.com.*

Village on Venetian Bay. Stroll along the classy boutiques, nearly 30 in all, that line the water's edge, and grab a bite at one of the excellent restaurants, all with fantastic views. ⊠ *4200 Gulf Shore Blvd. N* ⊕ *www. venetianvillage.com.*

Waterside Shops. Only in South Florida can you find more than four dozen upscale stores plus eateries wrapped around a series of waterfalls, waterways, and shaded open-air promenades. Saks 5th Avenue and Nordstrom are the main anchors; Burberry, Cartier, Ralph Lauren, and St. John are in the mix. ⊠ *5415 Tamiami Trail N* ☎ *239/598–1605* ⊕ *www.watersideshops.com.*

SPECIALTY SHOPS

Gattle's. This downtown shop stocks pricey-but-pretty linens. ⊠ *1250 3rd St. S* ☎ *239/262–4791, 800/344–4552* ⊕ *www.gattles.com.*

Marissa Collections. *The* destination in Naples for ultra-high-end designer women's wear. ⊠ *1167 3rd St. S* ☎ *239/263–4333* ⊕ *www.marissa-collections.com.*

New to You. The most upscale clothes sometimes go to this consignment shop. ⊠ *933 Creech Rd.* ☎ *239/262–6869.*

Options. Naples's ladies who lunch often donate their year-old Armani castoffs and fine collectibles to this terrific thrift shop whose proceeds benefit the Shelter for Abused Women & Children. ⊠ *968 2nd Ave. N* ☎ *239/434–7115* ⊕ *www.naplesshelter.org/thriftstore.*

Regatta. Among 5th Avenue South's selection with a decidedly local flair, this shop sells personal and home accessories with a sense of humor and style. ⊠ *760 5th Ave. S* ☎ *239/262–3929.*

SPORTS AND THE OUTDOORS

BIKING

Naples Cyclery. For daily rentals, rates range from $6 to $32 for two hours and selections include two- and four-passenger surreys, tandems, and more; weekly rentals are also available. ⊠ *Pavilion Shopping Center, 813 Vanderbilt Beach Rd.* ☎ *239/566–0600* ⊕ *www.naplescyclery.com.*

BOATING AND FISHING

Mangrove Outfitters. Take a guided boat and learn to cast and tie flies. ⊠ *4111 Tamiami Trail E* ☎ *239/793–3370, 888/319–9848* ⊕ *www. mangroveoutfitters.com.*

Naples Watersports at Port-O-Call Marina. A 19-foot center-console boat and several 22-foot deck boats start at $130 for two hours. ⊠ *550 Port-O-Call Way* ☎ *239/774–0479* ⊕ *www.naples-boatrentals.com.*

FAMILY **Pure Naples.** Half-day deep-sea and backwater fishing trips depart twice daily. Sightseeing cruises and thrilling jet tours are also available, along with Jet Ski and boat rentals and private charters. ⊠ *Tin City, 1200 5th Ave. S* ☎ *239/263–4949* ⊕ *www.purenaples.com.*

GOLF

Lely Resort Golf and Country Club. There are two 18-hole championship courses open to the public—Flamingo Island and the Mustang—plus a John Jacobs' school; greens fees $169/$49. ⊠ *8004 Grand Lely Blvd.* ☎ *239/793–2600* ⊕ *www.lely-resort.net.*

The Naples Beach Hotel & Golf Club. This club has 18 holes, weekly clinics, a driving range, and a putting green. The region's oldest course, a par 72, it was built in 1929, last redesigned in 1998, and refurbished in 2011; greens fees (includes cart) $125/$55. ⊠ *851 Gulf Shore Blvd. N* ☎ *239/435–2475* ⊕ *www.naplesbeachhotel.com.*

Riviera Golf Club. This affordable 18-hole executive course has greens fees of $45/$35 (includes cart); 9-holes and later tee times are less. ⊠ *48 Marseille Dr.* ☎ *239/774–2011* ⊕ *www.rivieragolf.com.*

Tiburón Golf Club. There are two 18-hole Greg Norman–designed courses, the Black and the Gold, and a Rick Smith golf academy. Challenging and environmentally pristine, the links include narrow fairways, stacked sod wall bunkers, coquina sand, and no roughs; greens fees $190/$75 (includes cart and tax). ■ TIP➜ If you're not a guest of either Ritz-Carlton, book tee times well in advance. ⊠ *Ritz-Carlton Golf Resort, 2620 Tiburón Dr.* ☎ *239/593–2201* ⊕ *www.tiburongcnaples.com.*

MARCO ISLAND

20 miles south of Naples via Rte. 951.

High-rises dominate part of the shores of Marco Island, which is connected to the mainland by two bridges. Yet because of its distance from downtown Naples, it retains an isolated feeling much appreciated by those who love this corner of the world. Some natural areas have been preserved, and the down-home fishing village of Goodland, a 20-minute drive from historic Old Marco, resists change. Fishing, boating, sunning, swimming, and tennis are the primary activities here.

GETTING HERE AND AROUND

From Naples, Collier Boulevard (Route 951) takes you to Marco Island. If you're not renting a car, taxi rides cost about $100 from the regional airport in Fort Myers, and Collier Area Transit (CAT) runs regular buses through the area. Key West Express operates a ferry from Marco Island (from Christmas through Easter) and Fort Myers Beach (year-round) to Key West. The cost for the round-trip (less than four hours each way) is $146 from either Fort Myers Beach or Marco Island.

Contacts Collier Area Transit (CAT) ☎ *239/252–7777* ⊕ *www.colliergov.net.* **Key West Express** ⊠ *951 Bald Eagle Dr.* ☎ *239/394–9700, 888/539–2628* ⊕ *www.keywestexpress.us.*

VISITOR INFORMATION

Contacts Marco Island Area Chamber of Commerce ⊠ *1102 N. Collier Blvd.* ☎ *239/394–7549, 800/788–6272* ⊕ *www.marcoislandchamber.org.* **Naples, Marco Island, Everglades Convention and Visitors Bureau** ⊠ *2800 Horseshoe Dr. N, Naples* ☎ *800/688–3600, 239/225–1013* ⊕ *www.paradisecoast.com.*

8

EXPLORING

Marco Island Historical Museum. Marco Island was once part of the ancient Calusa kingdom. The Marco Cat, a statue found in 1896 excavations, has become symbolic of the island's prehistoric significance. The original is part of the Smithsonian Institution's collection, but a replica of the Marco Cat is among displays illuminating the ancient past at this museum, which opened in January 2011. Three rooms examine the island's history with dioramas, artifacts, and signage: the Calusa Room, Pioneer Room, and Modern Marco Room. A fourth will host changing exhibits, and there will be more developments to come. Outside, the yard was built to look like a Calusa village atop a shell mound with a water feature and *chickee* structure. ✉ *180 S. Heathwood Dr.* ☎ *239/642–1440* 🌐 *www.colliermuseums.com* 🎟 *Free* 🕒 *Tues.–Sat. 9–4.*

BEACHES

FAMILY **Tigertail Beach.** On the northwest side of the island is 2,500 feet of both developed and undeveloped areas. Once gulf front, in recent years a sand spit known as Sand Dollar Island has formed, which means the stretch especially at the north end has become mud flats—great for birding. There's still plenty of sand further south and across the lagoon on the sand spit, and it's still got a broad base of fans flocking there for its varied facilities, including playgrounds, a butterfly garden, volleyball nets, and kayak and umbrella rentals. Beach wheelchairs are also available for free use. **TIP→ The Conservancy of Southwest Florida conducts free educational beach walks at Tigertail Beach every weekday from 8:30 to 9:30 from January to mid-April.** **Amenities:** food and drink; showers; toilets; water sports; parking (paid). **Best for:** sunset; walking; swimming. ✉ *490 Hernando Dr.* ☎ *239/252–4000* 🌐 *www.collierparks.com* 🎟 *Parking $8* 🕒 *Daily 8–sunset.*

WHERE TO EAT

$$ ITALIAN Fodor's Choice ★ 🍴 **Arturo's.** This place is huge, with expansive Romanesque dining rooms and more seating on the patio. Still, it fills up year-round with a strong well-dressed following that appreciates a fun attitude and serious Italian cuisine done comprehensively and traditionally. Start with the plump mussels marinara, then choose from a lengthy list of classic Italian entrées, including homemade pasta. The stuffed pork chop, a nightly special, is a winner, as is the New York–style cheesecake. [$] *Average main: $20* ✉ *844 Bald Eagle Dr.* ☎ *239/642–0550* 🌐 *www.arturosmarcoisland.com* 👔 *Reservations essential* 🕒 *No lunch.*

$ AMERICAN 🍴 **Crazy Flamingo.** Burgers, conch fritters, and chicken wings draw mostly locals to this neighborhood bar, where there's counter service only and seating indoors and outdoors on the sidewalk. Try the peel-and-eat shrimp, sushi, mussels marinara, chicken bistro salad, or fried grouper basket. [$] *Average main: $11* ✉ *Marco Island Town Center, 1035 N. Collier Blvd.* ☎ *239/642–9600* 🌐 *www.thecrazyflamingo.com.*

$$ SEAFOOD 🍴 **Old Marco Lodge Crab House.** Built in 1869, this waterfront restaurant is Goodland's oldest landmark. Boaters often cruise in and tie up dockside to sit on the veranda and dine on local seafood and pasta entrées. The crab-cake sandwich is a popular lunch option. For dinner, start with a wholesome bowl of vegetable crab soup and then a trip to the

salad bar (included in the price of entrées). The menu has all manner of seafood dishes, including a teriyaki shrimp wrap, a basket of fried oysters, and a soft-shell crab sandwich. There's also steak and chicken dishes for landlubbers. Save room for the authentic key lime pie. [$] *Average main: $18* ✉ *401 Papaya St., Goodland* ☎ *239/642–7227* 🌐 *www.oldmarcolodge.com* 🕒 *Closed July–Sept.*

$$$ ITALIAN 🍴 **Sale e Pepe.** Marco's best dining view comes also with some of its finest cuisine. The name means "salt and pepper," an indication that this palatial restaurant with terrace seating overlooking the beach adheres to the basics of Southern Italian cuisine. Pastas, sausages, and ice cream are made right here in the kitchen. Simple, artfully presented dishes—butternut squash ravioli, cornish hen with grilled oyster mushrooms, yellow-pepper-and-shrimp soup, baked salmon with lobster sauce, chianti-braised short ribs, and tomato-crusted Atlantic salmon—explode with home-cooked, long-simmered flavors. With the exception of a handful of pizzas, lunch is more traditional, less Italian. [$] *Average main: $25* ✉ *Marco Beach Ocean Resort, 480 S. Collier Blvd.* ☎ *239/393–1400* 🌐 *www.sale-e-pepe.com.*

$$ SEAFOOD 🍴 **Snook Inn.** On the water with live entertainment in the tiki bar and a loaded salad bar: no wonder this place has been a casual favorite for locals and visitors for decades. Signature items include the spicy conch chowder, beer-battered grouper sandwich, Caribbean BBQ baby back ribs, and grouper in a bag with mushroom crab sauce. [$] *Average main: $21* ✉ *1215 Bald Eagle Dr., Old Marco* ☎ *239/394–3313* 🌐 *www.snookinn.com* ✍ *Reservations not accepted.*

$$$ ECLECTIC 🍴 **Verdi's American Bistro.** There's a Zen feel to this intimate bistro built on creative American-Italian-Asian fusion cuisine. You might start with steamed littleneck clams in garlic butter or duck potstickers, then move on to entrées such as grilled swordfish with pumpkin seeds, miso-glazed shrimp, pasta pomodoro, or the New Zealand rack of lamb. Cuban coffee crème brûlée and deep-dish apple strudel are among the tempting desserts. [$] *Average main: $27* ✉ *Sand Dollar Plaza, 241 N. Collier Blvd.* ☎ *239/394–5533* 🌐 *www.verdisbistro.com* 🕒 *May–July and Oct.–Dec., closed Sun. and Mon. Closed Aug. and Sept. No lunch.*

8

WHERE TO STAY

For expanded reviews, facilities, and current deals, visit Fodors.com.

$$ HOTEL 🏨 **The Boat House Motel.** For a great location at a good price, check into this modest, but appealing, two-story motel at the north end of the island on a canal close to the Gulf. **Pros:** away from busy beach traffic; affordable; boating docks and access. **Cons:** no beach; hard to find; tight parking area. [$] *Rooms from: $132* ✉ *1180 Edington Pl.* ☎ *239/642–2400, 800/528–6345* 🌐 *www.theboathousemotel.com* 🛏 *20 rooms, 3 apartments, 1 2-bedroom house* 🍽 *No meals.*

$$$$ RESORT 🏨 **Hilton Marco Island Beach Resort and Spa.** This 11-story hotel is smaller and more conservative than the Marriott—but it seems less busy and crowded—and rooms, redesigned starting in 2012 with a contemporary beachy style, are spacious and have private balconies with full or partial ocean views. **Pros:** gorgeous, wide beach; complete business services; exclusive feel. **Cons:** a little stuffy; charges for Wi-Fi and self-parking;

business focus. $ *Rooms from: $299* ⊠ *560 S. Collier Blvd.* ☎ *239/394–5000, 800/445–8667* ⊕ *www.hiltonmarcoisland.com* ⇨ *271 rooms, 22 suites, 4 penthouses* ⚹⊙⚹ *No meals.*

$$$$
RESORT
Fodor's Choice
★

🖼 **Marco Beach Ocean Resort.** One of the island's first condo hotels, this 12-story class act has luxurious one- and two-bedroom suites decorated in elegant neutral tones with the finest fixtures; all rooms face the water and look down onto the crescent-shape rooftop pool (on the fifth floor). **Pros:** gourmet dining; intimate; on beach; sophisticated crowd. **Cons:** steep prices; squeezed between high-rises; near a busy resort. $ *Rooms from: $249* ⊠ *480 S. Collier Blvd.* ☎ *239/393–1400, 800/715–8517* ⊕ *www.marcoresort.com* ⇨ *83 1-bedroom and 15 2-bedroom suites* ⚹⊙⚹ *No meals.*

$$$$
RESORT
FAMILY

🖼 **Marco Island Marriott Beach Resort.** A circular drive and manicured grounds with rock waterfalls front this hilltop, beachfront resort made up of twin 11-story towers and villa-like suites, two large pools, and the widest stretch of sand on the island. **Pros:** top-notch amenities; great spa and restaurants; appeals to children and adults; two private golf courses. **Cons:** huge size; lots of convention business; paid parking across the street in an uncovered lot. $ *Rooms from: $379* ⊠ *400 S. Collier Blvd.* ☎ *239/394–2511, 800/438–4373* ⊕ *www.marcoislandmarriott.com* ⇨ *664 rooms, 63 suites* ⚹⊙⚹ *No meals.*

$$$
RENTAL

🖼 **Olde Marco Island Inn & Suites.** This Victorian with tin roofs and royal-blue shutters and awnings used to be the only place to stay on the island when lodging back then was in the circa-1883 historic building that now holds the restaurant; today guests check into newer hotel sections with comfortable condo suites. **Pros:** quiet part of the island; full kitchen in every room; free Wi-Fi; laundry facilities; free covered parking. **Cons:** must drive to beach; annexed to a shopping center; office closes at night. $ *Rooms from: $169* ⊠ *100 Palm St.* ☎ *239/394–3131, 877/475–3466* ⊕ *www.oldemarcoinn.com* ⇨ *51 suites, 2 penthouses* ⚹⊙⚹ *No meals.*

SPORTS AND THE OUTDOORS

FISHING

Sunshine Tours. Try a deep-sea ($99 per person for half-day) or back-country ($60 per person for three hours) fishing charter with this outfitter. ⊠ *Rose Marina, 951 Bald Eagle Dr.* ☎ *239/642–5415* ⊕ *www.sunshinetoursmarcoisland.com.*

ORLANDO AND
ENVIRONS

WELCOME TO ORLANDO AND ENVIRONS

TOP REASONS TO GO

★ **Magic and Fantasy:** Unleash your inner child, in the glow of Cinderella Castle, at WDW's Magic Kingdom. Fireworks transform the night skies—and you—at this park and at Epcot. And, over at Universal's Islands of Adventure we have just, two words: Harry Potter.

★ **Around:** Visit Epcot's 11 countries, complete with perfect replicas of foreign monuments, unique crafts, and traditional cuisine.

★ **Amazing Animals:** Safari through Africa in Disney's Animal Kingdom, get splashed by Shamu at SeaWorld, kiss a dolphin at Discovery Cove, and watch gators wrestle at Gatorland.

★ **Shopping Opps:** Hit the national chains at Orlando's upscale malls, or browse Winter Park's unique Park Avenue boutiques. Don't forget the mouse ears: Main Street U.S.A. and Downtown Disney are filled with the best classic souvenirs and some quirkier items as well.

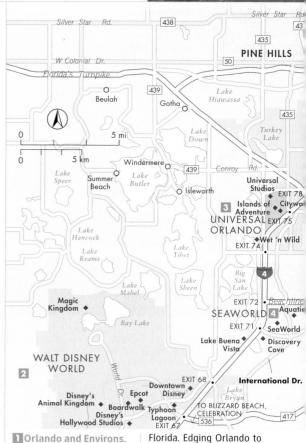

1 Orlando and Environs. Once you've exhausted the theme parks, or have been exhausted by them, turn your attention to a wealth of offerings, including museums, parks, and gardens, in Winter Park, Kissimmee, and elsewhere. Thanks to Disney World, Orlando is the gateway for many visitors to central Florida. Edging Orlando to the south is Kissimmee, with home-grown attractions like Gatorland. Looking for more laid-back local flavor? You'll find it just 20 miles northeast of Orlando in the charming Winter Park suburb.

GETTING ORIENTED

Central Florida runs from Tampa/St. Petersburg in the west through Orlando to the coastal attractions of Daytona Beach and Cape Canaveral on the east coast. Orlando is more or less equidistant, about 90 minutes by car to the Gulf of Mexico. Walt Disney World is not, contrary to advertising, in Orlando, but lies about 25 miles southwest of the city.

9

2 **Walt Disney World.**
Walt Disney's original decree that his parks be ever-changing, along with some healthy competition from Universal Studios and SeaWorld, has kept the Disney Imagineers dreaming up new entertainment and installing higher-tech thrills and attractions.

3 **Universal Orlando.**
While Disney creates a fantasy world for those who love fairy tales, Universal Orlando is geared to older kids, adults, and anyone who enjoys pop culture. Movie and TV fans love this place. Two other parks—Islands of Adventure (IOA) and Wet 'n Wild—add to the fun.

4 **SeaWorld and Discovery Cove.** Less glitzy than Walt Disney World or Universal, SeaWoarld and Discovery Cove are worth a visit for a low-key, relaxing, ocean-theme experience. If you want to get more keyed up, pay a call on SeaWorld's Aquatica water park.

Updated by
Rona Grindin,
Jennifer Green-
hill-Taylor, and
Jennie Hess

Most Orlando locals look at the theme parks as they would an unruly neighbor: it's big and loud, but it keeps a nice lawn. Central Florida's many theme parks can become overpowering for even the most enthusiastic visitor, and that's when an excursion into the "other" Orlando—the one the locals know and love—is in order.

There are so many day trips. If the outdoors is your thing, you can swim or canoe at Wekiwa Springs State Park or one of the area's many other sparkling springs, where the water remains a refreshing 72°F no matter how hot the day. Alternatively, you can hike, horseback ride, canoe, and camp in the Ocala National Forest.

If museums are your thing, charming Winter Park has the Charles Hosmer Morse Museum of American Art with its huge collection of Tiffany glass, and the Cornell Fine Arts Museum on the oak-tree-covered Rollins College campus. While in Winter Park, you can indulge in some high-end shopping or dining on Park Avenue or take a leisurely boat tour of the lakefront homes.

Got kids to educate and entertain? Check out WonderWorks or the Orlando Science Center, where you can view live gators and turtles. Even more live gators (some as long as 14 feet) can be viewed or fed (or even eaten) at Gatorland, just south of Orlando.

Do the kids prefer rockets and astronauts? Don't miss a day trip to Kennedy Space Center, where you can tour a rocket forest, sit in a space capsule, or climb aboard a shuttle.

Kissimmee is a 19th-century cattle town south of Orlando that proudly hangs on to its roots with a twice-yearly rodeo where real cowboys ride bulls and rope cattle. The town sits on Lake Tohopekaliga, a favorite spot for airboat rides or fishing trips.

PLANNING

Orlando is a diverse town. The Downtown area, though small, is dynamic, thanks to an ever-changing skyline of high-rises, sports venues, museums, restaurants, nightspots, a history museum, and several annual cultural events—including film festivals and a world-renowned theater fest. Downtown also has a central green, Lake Eola Park, which offers a respite from otherwise frantic touring.

Neighborhoods such as Thornton Park (great for dining) and College Park (great antiques shopping along Lake Ivanhoe) are fun to wander. Not too far to the north, you can come in contact with natural Florida—its manatees, gators, and crystal clear waters in spring-fed lakes.

Closer to the theme-park action, International Drive, the hub of resort and conference hotels, offers big restaurants and even bigger outlet-mall bargains. Sand Lake Road, between the two, is Orlando's Restaurant Row, with plenty of exciting dining prospects.

GETTING HERE AND AROUND

Orlando is spread out. During rush hour, car traffic crawls along the often-crowded Interstate 4, which runs to both coasts. If you're heading east, you can also take Route 528 (aka the Beachline), a toll road that heads directly for Cape Canaveral and points along the Space Coast; no such option leads west.

If you avoid rush-hour traffic, traveling to points of interest shouldn't take too much time out of your vacation. Winter Park is no more than 20 minutes from Downtown; International Drive and the theme parks are about 30 minutes away in heavier traffic. Orlando International Airport is only 9 miles south of Downtown, but it will take about 30 minutes via a circuitous network of highways (Interstate 4 west to Florida's Turnpike south to Route 528 east).

ESSENTIALS

Visitor Information Orlando Visitors Bureau ☎ *407/363–5872, 800/972–3304* ⊕ *www.visitorlando.com.*

EXPLORING

Updated by
Jennie Hess

Use the coordinate (⊕ 1:B2) at the end of each review to locate a site on the Where to Explore, Eat, and Stay in the Orlando Area *map.*

CENTRAL ORLANDO

Fodor'sChoice
★
Harry P. Leu Gardens. A few miles outside of downtown—on the former lakefront estate of a citrus entrepreneur—is this 50-acre garden. Among the highlights are a collection of historical blooms (many varieties of which were established before 1900), ancient oaks, a 50-foot floral clock, and one of the largest camellia collections in eastern North America (in bloom November–March). Mary Jane's Rose Garden, named after Leu's wife, is filled with more than 1,000 bushes; it's the largest formal rose garden south of Atlanta. The simple 19th-century Leu House Museum, once the Leu family home, preserves the furnishings

and appointments of a well-to-do, turn-of-the-20th-century Florida family. ⊠ *1920 N. Forest Ave., Lake Ivanhoe* ☎ *407/246–2620* ⊕ *www. leugardens.org* 🖾 *$10, free 1st Mon. of month* ⊘ *Garden daily 9–5; guided house tours daily on hr and ½ hr 10–3:30.*

FAMILY **Lake Eola Park.** This beautifully landscaped 43-acre park is the verdant heart of downtown Orlando, its mile-long walking path a gathering place for families, health enthusiasts out for a run, and culture mavens exploring area offerings. The well-lighted playground is alive with children, and ducks, swans, and native Florida birds call the lake home. A farmers' market takes up residence on Sunday afternoon.

The lakeside Walt Disney Amphitheater is a dramatic site for concerts, ethnic festivals, and spectacular July 4 fireworks. Don't resist the park's biggest draw: a ride in a swan-shaped pedal boat. Up to five adults can fit comfortably into each. (Children under 16 must be accompanied by an adult.)

The Relax Grill, by the swan-boat launch, is a great place for a snack. There are also several good restaurants in the upscale Thornton Park neighborhood along the park's eastern border. The ever-expanding skyline rings the lake with modern high-rises, making the peace of the park even more welcome. After a lightning strike in 2009, the landmark fountain was revamped and features an LED light and music show every night at 8 and 9:30. ⊠ *195 N. Rosalind Ave., Downtown Orlando* ☎ *407/246–4485 park, 407/246–4485 swan boats* 🖾 *Swan boat rental $15 per ½ hr* ⊘ *Park daily 6 am–midnight; swan boats Sun.–Tues. 10–7, Wed.–Sat. 10–10.*

Mennello Museum of American Folk Art. One of the few museums in the United States devoted to folk art has intimate galleries, some with lovely lakefront views. Look for the nation's most extensive permanent collection of Earl Cunningham paintings as well as works by many other self-taught artists. There's a wonderful video about Cunningham and his "curio shop" in St. Augustine. Temporary exhibitions have included the works of Wyeth, Cassatt, and Michael Eastman. At the museum shop you can purchase folk-art books, toys, and unusual gifts. The Mennello is the site of the annual Orlando Folk Festival, held the second weekend of February. ⊠ *900 E. Princeton St., Lake Ivanhoe* ☎ *407/246–4278* ⊕ *www.mennellomuseum.org* 🖾 *$5* ⊘ *Tues.–Sat. 10:30–4:30, Sun. noon–4:30.*

FAMILY **Orange County Regional History Center.** Exhibits here take you on a journey back in time to discover how Florida's Paleo-Indians hunted and fished the land, what the Sunshine State was like when the Spaniards first arrived, and how life in Florida was different when citrus was king. Visit a cabin from the late 1800s, complete with Spanish moss–stuffed mattresses and mosquito netting over the beds. Seminole Indian displays include interactive activities, and the Tourism Before Disney exhibit previews Florida's destiny as a future vacation mecca. ⊠ *65 E. Central Blvd., Downtown Orlando* ☎ *407/836–8500, 800/965–2030* ⊕ *www.thehistorycenter.org* 🖾 *$9* ⊘ *Mon.–Sat. 10–5, Sun. noon–5.*

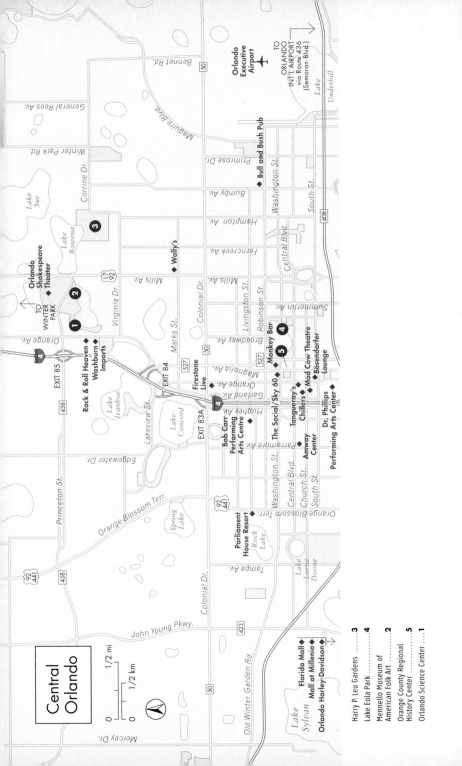

Central Orlando

0   1/2 mi

0   1/2 km

TO
WINTER
PARK

Orange Av.

Rock & Roll Heaven ◆
Washburn
Imports ◆

Orlando
Shakespeare
Theater ◆

Wally's ◆

Bull and Bush Pub ◆

Firestone
Live ◆

Bob Carr
Performing
Arts Centre ◆

The Social/Sky 60 ◆
Tanqueray's ◆
Chillers ◆

Monkey Bar ◆
Mad Cow Theatre ◆
Bösendorfer
Lounge ◆

Dr. Phillips
Performing Arts Center ◆

Amway
Center ◆

Parliament
House Resort ◆

Florida Mall ◆
Mall at Millenia ◆
Orlando Harley-Davidson ◆

TO
ORLANDO
INT'L AIRPORT
via Route 436
(Semoran Blvd)

Orlando
Executive
Airport

The 300-seat Dr. Phillips CineDome, a movie theater with an eight-story screen at the Orlando Science Center, offers large-format iWERKS films.

Orlando Science Center. With all the high-tech glitz and imagined worlds of the theme parks, is it worth visiting Orlando's reality-based science center? If you're a kid crazy about science, the answer is an overwhelming "yes." With exhibits about the human body, mechanics, computers, math, nature, the solar system, and optics, the science center has something for every child's inner geek.

The four-story internal atrium is home to live gators and turtles and is a great spot for simply gazing at what Old Florida once looked like. The 300-seat Dr. Phillips CineDome, a movie theater with a giant eight-story screen, offers large-format iWERKS films and planetarium programs. The Crosby Observatory and Florida's largest publicly accessible refractor telescope are here, as are several smaller telescopes; some weekends you can safely view spots and flares on the sun's surface.

Adults like the science center, too, thanks to events like the annual Science of Wine and Cosmic Golf Challenge; evenings of stargazing in the Crosby Observatory, live music, art, and film; and Otronicon, the annual interactive technology expo. ⊠ *777 E. Princeton St., Lake Ivanhoe* ☎ *407/514–2000, 888/672–4386* ⊕ *www.osc.org* 🎟 *$27; parking $5; tickets include all permanent and special exhibits, films, live science presentations, and planetarium shows* ☽ *Daily 10–5.*

INTERNATIONAL DRIVE

FAMILY **Fun Spot America.** Four go-kart tracks offer a variety of driving experiences. Though drivers must be at least 10 years old and meet height requirements, parents can drive younger children in two-seater cars on several of the tracks, including the Conquest Track. Nineteen rides range from the dizzying Paratrooper to an old-fashioned Revolver Ferris Wheel to the twirling toddler Teacups. Fun Spot recently expanded from 5 to 15 acres and now features Central Florida's only wooden roller coaster as well as the Freedom Flyer steel suspension family coaster, a kiddie coaster, and what's billed as the world's second-tallest (250 feet) SkyCoaster—part skydive, part hang-glide. The tallest, at 300 feet, is located at sister park Fun Spot USA, in Kissimmee. There's also an arcade. From Exit 75A, turn left onto International Drive, then left on Fun Spot Way. ✉ *5700 Fun Spot Way, I-Drive area* ☎ *407/363–3867* ⊕ *www.funspotattractions.com* ✇ *$39.95 for all rides (online discounts available) or pay per ride; admission for nonriders free; arcade extra; parking free* ☼ *Apr.–Oct., daily 10 am–midnight; Nov.–Mar., weekdays noon–11, weekends 10 am–midnight.*

Ripley's Believe It or Not! Odditorium. A 10-foot-square section of the Berlin Wall. A pain and torture chamber. Two African fertility statues that women swear have helped them conceive. These and almost 200 other oddities (shrunken heads included) speak for themselves in this museum-cum-attraction in the heart of tourist territory on International Drive. The building itself is designed to appear as if it's sliding into one of Florida's notorious sinkholes. Give yourself an hour or two to soak up the weirdness, but remember: this is a looking, not touching, experience; it might drive antsy youngsters—and their parents—crazy. ■ TIP→ **Buy tickets online ahead of time, and you can get discounts.** ✉ *8201 International Dr., I-Drive area* ☎ *407/351–5803* ⊕ *www. ripleysorlando.com* ✇ *$19.99; parking free* ☼ *Daily 9 am–midnight; last admission at 11 pm.*

FAMILY **WonderWorks.** The building seems to be sinking into the ground. Not only that, but it seems to be sinking into the ground at a precarious angle and upside down. Many people stop to take pictures in front of the topsy-turvy facade, complete with upended palm trees and broken skyward-facing sidewalks. Inside, the upside-down theme continues only as far as the lobby. After that, it's a playground of 100 interactive experiences—some incorporating virtual reality, others educational (similar to those at a science museum), and still others pure entertainment. You can experience an earthquake or a hurricane, land a space shuttle using simulator controls, make giant bubbles in the Bubble Lab, play laser tag in the enormous laser-tag arena and arcade, design and ride your own roller coaster, lie on a bed of real nails, and play baseball with a virtual Major League batter. ✉ *9067 International Dr., I-Drive area* ☎ *407/351–8800* ⊕ *www.wonderworksonline.com* ✇ *$24.99; laser tag and Outta Control Magic Comedy Dinner Show extra (online discounts available); parking $3–$6* ☼ *Daily 9 am–midnight.*

9

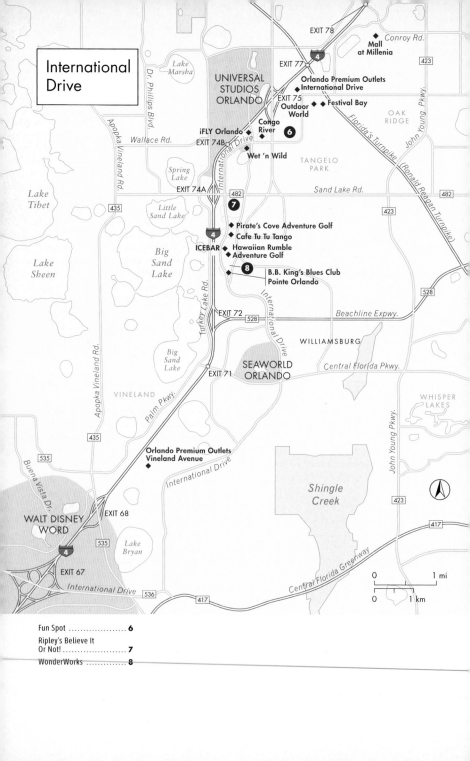

International Drive

EXIT 78

Conroy Rd.

Mall at Millenia

423

EXIT 77

EXIT 75

UNIVERSAL STUDIOS ORLANDO

Orlando Premium Outlets
International Drive

Outdoor World

Festival Bay

OAK RIDGE

iFLY Orlando

Congo River **6**

EXIT 74B

Wet 'n Wild

TANGELO PARK

Wallace Rd.

Spring Lake

Lake Tibet

435

Little Sand Lake

EXIT 74A

482

Sand Lake Rd.

482

7

423

Big Sand Lake

◆ Pirate's Cove Adventure Golf

◆ Cafe Tu Tu Tango

ICEBAR ◆ Hawaiian Rumble

◆ Adventure Golf

8

B.B. King's Blues Club
Pointe Orlando

528

Lake Sheen

Turkey Lake Rd.

EXIT 72

528

Beachline Expwy.

WILLIAMSBURG

Big Sand Lake

EXIT 71

SEAWORLD ORLANDO

Central Florida Pkwy.

WHISPER LAKES

VINELAND

Palm Pkwy.

435

John Young Pkwy.

Orlando Premium Outlets
Vineland Avenue

International Drive

Shingle Creek

423

535

Buena Vista Dr.

WALT DISNEY WORD

EXIT 68

535

Lake Bryan

417

Central Florida Greenway

EXIT 67

International Drive

536

417

0 ——— 1 mi

0 ——— 1 km

Dr. Phillips Blvd.

Lake Marsha

Apopka Vineland Rd.

Florida's Turnpike

John Young Pkwy. (Ronald Reagan Turnpike)

Apopka Vineland Rd.

International Drive

KISSIMMEE

18 miles south of Orlando, 10 miles southeast of Walt Disney World (WDW).

Although Kissimmee is primarily known as the gateway to Disney (technically, the vast Disney property of theme parks and resorts lies in both Osceola and Orange counties), its non-WDW attractions just might tickle your fancy. They range from throwbacks to old-time Florida to dinner shows for you and 2,000 of your closest friends. Orlando used to be prime cattle country, and the best sampling of what life was like is here during the Silver Springs Rodeo in February and June.

With at least 100,000 acres of freshwater lakes, the Kissimmee area brings anglers and boaters to national fishing tournaments and speedboat races. A 50-mile-long series of lakes, the Kissimmee Waterway, connects Lake Tohopekaliga—a Native American name that means "Sleeping Tiger"; locals call it Lake Toho—with huge Lake Okeechobee in South Florida, and from there, to both the Atlantic Ocean and the Gulf of Mexico.

FAMILY **Gatorland.** This campy attraction near the Orlando–Kissimmee border on U.S. 441 has endured since 1949 without much change, despite competition from the major parks. Over the years, the theme park and registered conservancy has gone through some changes while retaining its gator-rasslin' spirit. Kids get a kick out of this unmanufactured, old-timey thrill ride.

The Gator Gulley Splash Park is complete with giant "egrets" spilling water from their beaks, dueling water guns mounted atop giant gators, and other water-park splash areas. There's also a small petting zoo and an aviary. A free train ride is a high point, taking you through an alligator breeding marsh and a natural swamp setting where you can spot gators, birds, and turtles. A three-story observation tower overlooks the breeding marsh, swamped with gator grunts, especially come sundown during mating season.

For a glimpse of 37 giant, rare, and deadly crocodiles, check out the Jungle Crocs of the World exhibit. To see eager gators leaping out of the water to catch their food, come on cool days for the Gator Jumparoo Show (summer heat just puts them to sleep). The most thrilling is the first one in the morning, when the gators are hungriest. There's also a Gator Wrestlin' Show, and although there's no doubt who's going to win the match, it's still fun to see the handlers take on those tough guys with the beady eyes. In the educational Upclose Encounters show, the show's host handles a variety of snakes. Recent park additions include Panther Springs, featuring brother-and-sister endangered panthers, and the Screamin' Gator Zip Line (additional cost). This is a real Florida experience, and you leave knowing the difference between a gator and a croc. ✉ *14501 S. Orange Blossom Trail, between Orlando and Kissimmee* ☎ *407/855–5496, 800/393–5297* ⊕ *www.gatorland. com* ➔ *$24.99; discount coupons online* ☉ *Daily 10–5.*

Kissimmee's Lake Tohopekaliga (affectionately known as Lake Toho) is famous with fishers the world over. It's also great for wildlife spotting—an especially exhilarating experience when done from an airboat.

LEGOLAND

50 miles southwest of Orlando.

The quiet town of Winter Haven is home to numerous lakes and a waterskiing school. From 1936 until 2009, it was also home to the Sunshine State's first theme park, Cypress Gardens. Today the spot holds the world's largest LEGOLAND, set on 150 acres and built using nearly 56 million LEGOs. In addition to its 1:20-scale miniature reproductions of U.S. cities, the park features more than 50 rides, shows, and attractions throughout 10 different zones, as well as the marvelous botanical gardens from the original park. Just opened mid-2013, the World of Chima presented by Cartoon Network invites guests into a fantastical world of animal tribal habitats anchored by an interactive water ride, the Quest for CHI. In Chima's new Speedorz Arena, participants compete to win a supply of the mystical CHI energy source. A 4-D movie and Chima-character meet and greets round out the experience.

The Danish toy company's philosophy is to help children "play well." And play they do, as LEGOLAND attractions are very hands-on. Kids can hoist themselves to the top of a tower, power a fire truck, or navigate a LEGO robot. Sights include huge LEGO dragons, wizards, knights, pirates, castles, roller coasters, racetracks, villages, and cities.

The cityscapes in Miniland USA fascinate children and adults, who delight in discovering what's possible when you have enough bricks. Miniland opens with Kennedy Space Center, where a 6-foot shuttle waits on the launch pad. Miami Beach features bikini-clad bathers and art deco hotels; St. Augustine and its ancient fort play into LEGO's pirate theme; Key West's Mallory Square is accurate right down to the trained cats leaping through rings of fire. The rest of the United States is not ignored: New York City, Las Vegas, San Francisco, and Washington D.C. appear in intricate detail. Visitors spend hours looking for amusing details hidden in each city, like New York's purse snatcher.

Among other highlights are LEGO Kingdoms, whose castle towers over a jousting area and a roller coaster where knights, damsels, dragons, and ogres are found; Land of Adventure, where you can explore hidden tombs and hunt for treasure; and the Imagination Zone, showcasing LEGO Mindstorms robots, where a giant head of Albert Einstein invites kids to explore and invent. Things get wild in LEGO Technic, the most active of the park's zones, where Test Track, Aquazone Wave Racers, and Technicycle let the family expend some energy. And Pirates' Cove provides a chance to sit in the shade and watch a full-size pirate battle, with actors wearing LEGO suits defending the huge ship from attacking pirates on water skis.

LEGOLAND Water Park features a wave pool; Build-a-Raft, where families construct a LEGO vessel and float down a lazy river; a 375-foot pair of intertwined waterslides that plunge riders into a pool; and a DUPLO toddler water play area. Not to be forgotten, Cypress Gardens, at the heart of the park, preserves one of Florida's treasures. Families can wander the lush, tropical foliage and gasp at one of the world's largest banyan trees.

The trip to Winter Haven is worth it. The rides, interactive games, gardens, water park, and other attractions will amuse and engage. Round-trip transportation from Orlando Premium Outlets, on Vineland Avenue, leaves at 9 and costs $5. ⊠ *1 Legoland Way, Winter Haven* ☎ *877/350–5346* ⊕ *www.legoland.com* 🏷 *$79; parking $12* ☉ *Hrs vary seasonally.*

BOK TOWER GARDENS

57 miles southwest of Orlando, 42 miles southwest of WDW.

Fodor'sChoice
★

You'll see citrus groves as you ride south along U.S. 27 to the small town of Lake Wales and the Bok Tower Gardens. This appealing sanctuary of plants, flowers, trees, and wildlife has been something of a local secret for years. Shady paths meander through pine forests with silvery moats, mockingbirds and swans, blooming thickets, and hidden sundials. The majestic, 200-foot Bok Tower is constructed of coquina—from seashells—and pink, white, and gray marble. The tower houses a carillon with 60 bronze bells that ring out each day at 1 and 3 pm during 30-minute recitals that might include early-American folk songs, Appalachian tunes, Irish ballads, or Latin hymns. The bells are also featured in recordings every half hour after 10 am, and sometimes even moonlight recitals.

The landscape was designed in 1928 by Frederick Law Olmsted Jr., son of the planner of New York's Central Park. The grounds include the 20-room, Mediterranean-style Pinewood Estate, built in 1930 and open for self-guided touring. January through April, guides lead you on a

60-minute tour of the gardens (included in the admission price); tours of the inside of the tower are a benefit of membership ($100 and up).

Take Interstate 4 to Exit 55 and head south on U.S. 27 for about 23 miles. Proceed past Eagle Ridge Mall, then turn left after two traffic lights onto Mountain Lake Cut Off Road, and follow the signs. ⊠ *1151 Tower Blvd., Lake Wales* ☎ *863/676–1408* ⊕ *www.boktower. org* ⊠ *$12; Pinewood Estate tour $6; 50% off admission Sat. 8–9 am* ⊙ *Daily 8–6.*

WEKIWA SPRINGS STATE PARK

13 miles northwest of Orlando, 28 miles north of WDW.

FAMILY   "Wekiva" is a Creek Indian word meaning "flowing water"; *wekiwa*
Fodor'sChoice   means "spring of water." The river, springs, and surrounding 6,400-acre
★   Wekiwa Springs State Park are well suited to camping, hiking, picnicking, swimming, canoeing, and fishing. The area is also full of Florida wildlife: otters, raccoons, alligators, bobcats, deer, turtles, and birds.

Canoe trips can range from a simple hour-long paddle around the lagoon to observe a colony of water turtles to a full-day excursion through the less congested parts of the river, which haven't changed much since the area was inhabited by the Timacuan Indians. You can rent canoes ($17.98 for two hours and $3.20 per hour after that) in the town of Apopka, near the park's southern entrance.

The park has 60 campsites: some are "canoe sites" that you can reach only via the river, and others are "trail sites," meaning you must hike a good bit of the park's 13½-mile trail to reach them. Most, however, are for the less hardy—you can drive right up to them. Sites go for $24 a night with electric and water hookups.

To get here, take Interstate 4 Exit 94 (Longwood) and turn left on Route 434. Go 1¼ miles to Wekiwa Springs Road; turn right and go 4½ miles to the entrance, on the right. ⊠ *1800 Wekiva Circle* ☎ *407/884– 2008, 800/326–3521 campsites, 407/884–4311 canoe rentals* ⊕ *www. floridastateparks.org* ⊠ *$2 per pedestrian or bicycle; $6 per vehicle* ⊙ *Daily 8–dusk.*

WINTER PARK

6 miles northeast of Orlando, 20 miles northeast of WDW.

This peaceful, upscale community may be just outside the hustle and bustle of Orlando, but it feels like a different country. The town's name reflects its early role as a warm-weather haven for those escaping the frigid blasts of Northeast winters. From the late 1880s until the early 1930s, wealthy industrialists and their families would travel to Florida by rail on vacation, and many stayed, establishing grand homes and cultural institutions. The lovely, 8-square-mile village retains its charm with brick-paved streets, historic buildings, and well-maintained lakes and parkland. Even the town's bucolic 9-hole golf course is on the National Register of Historic Places.

Wildlife-rich Wekiwa Springs State Park is a great place to camp, hike, picnic, canoe, fish, swim, or snorkel.

On Park Avenue you can spend a few hours sightseeing, shopping, or both. The street is lined with small boutiques and fine restaurants and bookended by world-class museums: the Charles Hosmer Morse Museum of American Art, with the world's largest collection of artwork by Louis Comfort Tiffany, and the Cornell Fine Arts Museum, on the campus of Rollins College (the oldest college in Florida).

TOURS

Scenic Boat Tour. Head east from Park Avenue and, at the end of Morse Boulevard, you'll find the launching point for this tour, a Winter Park tradition since 1938. The one-hour cruise takes in 12 miles of waterways, including three lakes and narrow, oak- and cypress-shaded canals built in the 1800s as a transportation system for the logging industry. A well-schooled skipper shares stories about the moguls who built their mansions along the shore and points out wildlife and remnants of natural Florida still surrounding the expensive houses. Cash or check only is accepted. ⊠ *312 E. Morse Blvd.* ☎ *407/644–4056* ⊕ *www. scenicboattours.com* ✉ *$12* ⊙ *Daily 10–4.*

EXPLORING

Fodor's Choice ★ **Charles Hosmer Morse Museum of American Art.** The world's most comprehensive collection of work by Louis Comfort Tiffany—including immense stained-glass windows, lamps, watercolors, and desk sets—is in this museum, which also contains American decorative art and paintings from the mid-19th to the early 20th centuries.

Among the draws is the 1,082-square-foot Tiffany Chapel, originally built for the 1893 World's Fair in Chicago. It took craftsmen 2½ years to painstakingly reassemble the chapel here. Many of the works were rescued from Tiffany's Long Island estate, Laurelton Hall, after a 1957 fire destroyed much of the property. The 12,000-square-foot Laurelton Hall wing, opened in 2011, allows for much more of the estate's collection to be displayed at one time. Exhibits in the wing include architectural and decorative elements from Laurelton's dining room, living room, and Fountain Court reception hall. There's also a re-creation of the striking Daffodil Terrace, so named for the glass daffodils that serve as the capitals for the terrace's marble columns. ⊠ *445 N. Park Ave.* ☎ *407/645–5311* ⊕ *www.morsemuseum.org* ⊠ *$5; free Nov.–Apr., Fri. 4–8* ⊘ *Tues.–Sat. 9:30–4, Sun. 1–4; Nov.–Apr., Fri. until 8.*

WHERE TO EAT

Updated by
Rona Gindin

You'll find burger-and-fries combos everywhere in Orlando, yet the ambitious chefs behind Orlando's theme-park and independent restaurants provide loads of better options—much better. Locally sourced foods, creative preparations, and clever international influences are all the rage here. Theme-park complexes have some of the best restaurants in town, although you may opt for a rental car to seek out the local treasures.

The signs of Orlando's dining progress is most evident in the last place one would look: Disney's fast-food outlets. Every eatery on Disney property offers a tempting vegetarian option, and kiddie meals come with healthful sides and drinks unless you specifically request otherwise. Disney now offers the option of preordering gluten-, egg-, and lactose-free cakes from BabyCakes NYC and having them waiting at Disney restaurants.

Around town, locals flock to the Ravenous Pig, a gastropub where the menu changes every day; Luma on Park, a suave home of thoughtfully created cutting-edge meals; and any number of dining establishments competing to serve the very finest steak. Orlando's culinary blossoming began in 1995, when Disney's signature California Grill debuted, featuring farm-to-table cuisine and wonderful wines by the glass. Soon after, celebrity chefs started opening up shop.

Orlando's destination restaurants can be found in the theme parks, as well as in the outlying towns. Sand Lake Road is now known as Restaurant Row for its eclectic collection of worthwhile tables. Here you'll find fashionable outlets for sushi and seafood, Italian and chops, Hawaiian fusion and upscale Mexican. Heading into the residential areas, the neighborhoods of Winter Park (actually its own city), Thornton Park, and College Park are prime locales for chow. Scattered throughout Central Florida, low-key ethnic restaurants specialize in the fare of Turkey, India, Peru, Thailand, Vietnam—you name it. Prices in these family-owned finds are usually delightfully low.

Use the coordinate (✛ 1:B2) at the end of each review to locate a site on the Where to Explore, Eat, and Stay in the Orlando Area map.

MEAL PLANS

Disney Magic Your Way Plus Dining Plan allows you one table-service meal, one counter-service meal, and one snack per day of your trip at more than 100 theme-park and resort restaurants, provided you stay in a Disney hotel. For more money, you can upgrade the plan to include more; to save, you can downgrade to a counter-service-only plan Used wisely, a Disney dining plan is a steal, but be careful to buy only the number of meals you'll want to eat. Moderate eaters can end up turning away appetizers and desserts to which they're entitled. Plan ahead, and use "extra" meals to your advantage by swapping two table-service meals for a Disney dinner show, say, or an evening at a high-end restaurant like California Grill.

Universal Meal Deal is a lunch-through-closing, all-you-can-eat offer at participating walk-up eateries inside Universal Studios and Islands of Adventure. Daily prices are $26 and $13 (both parks), and $22 and $11 (one park) for ages 10 and over and kids under 10, respectively. All-you-can-drink soft drinks are $11 daily for all.

RESERVATIONS

Reservations are strongly recommended throughout the theme parks. Indeed, make reservations for Disney restaurants and character meals at both Universal and Disney at least 90 (and up to 180) days out. And be sure to ask about the cancellation policy—at a handful of Disney restaurants, for instance, you may be charged penalties if you don't give 24 to 48 hours' notice.

For restaurant reservations within Walt Disney World, call ☎ 407/939–3463 (WDW–DINE) or book online at ⊕ www.disneyworld.com/dining. You can also get plenty of information on the website, including the meal periods served, price range, and specialties of all Disney eateries. Menus for all restaurants are posted online and tend to be up-to-date. For Universal Orlando reservations, call ☎ 407/224–9255 (theme parks and CityWalk) or ☎ 407/503–3463 (hotels). Learn about the complex's 50-plus restaurants at ⊕ www.universalorlando.com/dining.

In our reviews, reservations are mentioned only when they're essential or not accepted. Unless otherwise noted, the restaurants listed are open daily for lunch and dinner.

9

WALT DISNEY WORLD AREA

MAGIC KINGDOM

$$$ ✕ **Be Our Guest.** Traverse a bridge flanked by gargoyles and gas lamps
BRASSERIE to reach the Beast's castle, home of this massive new restaurant with
Fodor'sChoice a *Beauty and the Beast* theme, French flair, and the Magic Kingdom's
★ first and only wine and beer served at dinner. The 500-seat restaurant has three rooms: a gilded ballroom, whose ceiling sports cherubs with the faces of Imagineers' children; the tattered West Wing, with a slashed painting that changes from prince to beast during faux storms; and the Rose Gallery. Decor comprises French provincial furniture, suits of armor, and heavy drapes. Food, scratch-prepared on-site, includes pan-seared salmon, grilled steak, and maybe a pork rack with red wine au jus. The signature kids' soft drink comes in a light-up castle cup, and desserts, while sweet, are made without refined sugar. Be sure to accept a dollop of "the gray stuff—it's delicious." Lunch is a no-reservations fast-casual affair with the likes of quinoa salad and a braised pork stew with mashed potatoes, ordered on a touch screen and delivered to the table. $ *Average main: $23* ⊠ *Fantasyland* ☎ *407/939–3463* ⊕ *www.disneyworld.com* ⟟ *Reservations essential* ✛ *2:B1.*

$$$$ ╳ **Cinderella's Royal Table.** Cinderella and other Disney princesses appear
AMERICAN at this eatery in the castle's old mead hall; you should book reservations up to 180 days in advance to be sure to see them. The Fairytale Breakfast offers all-you-can-eat options such as lobster and crab cakes, and caramel apple–stuffed French toast. The Fairytale Lunch and Dinner, prix-fixe table-service meals, include entrées like gnocchi or pork shank with seasonal vegetables. When you arrive at the Cinderella Castle, a photographer snaps a shot of your group in the lobby. A package of photographs will be delivered to your table during your meal. Ⓢ *Average main: $59* ⊠ *Cinderella Castle* ☎ *407/939–3463* ⊕ *www. disneyworld.com* ⚭ *Reservations essential* ✛ *2:B1.*

$$$$ ╳ **Liberty Tree Tavern.** This "tavern" is dry, but it's a prime spot on the
AMERICAN parade route, so you can catch a good meal while you wait. Order Colonial-period comfort food for lunch like hearty pot roast cooked with a Cabernet wine–and-mushroom sauce, or turkey and dressing with mashed potatoes. Dinner is the family-style Patriot's Platter, with turkey, roast beef, pork, and sides. The restaurant is decorated in lovely Williamsburg colors with Early American–style antiques and lots of brightly polished brass. Each of the six dining rooms commemorates a historical U.S. figure, like Betsy Ross or Benjamin Franklin. Ⓢ *Average main: $38* ⊠ *Liberty Square* ☎ *407/939–3463* ✛ *2:B1.*

EPCOT

$$$$ ╳ **Akershus Royal Banquet Hall.** This restaurant has character buffets at all
SCANDINAVIAN three meals, with an array of Disney princesses, including Ariel, Belle, Jasmine, Snow White, Mulan, Mary Poppins, and even an occasional cameo appearance by Cinderella. The breakfast menu is American, but lunch and dinner find an ever-changing assortment of Norwegian specialties. Appetizers are offered buffet style, and usually include herring, goat-milk cheese, peppered mackerel, and gravlax (cured salmon served with mustard sauce) or *fiskepudding* (a seafood mousse with herb dressing). For your main course, chosen à la carte, you might try traditional ground pork and beef *kjottkake* (dumplings) or pan-seared salmon. Aquavit, wine, and specialty drinks are offered. All meals are fixed price. Ⓢ *Average main: $52* ⊠ *Norway Pavilion* ☎ *407/939–3463* ⊕ *www.disneyworld.com* ⚭ *Reservations essential* ✛ *2:E4.*

$$$ ╳ **Biergarten.** Oktoberfest runs 365 days a year here. The cheerful, some-
GERMAN times raucous, crowds are what you would expect in a place with an oompah band. The menu and level of frivolity are the same at lunch and dinner. Mountains of sauerbraten, bratwurst, chicken or pork schnitzel, German sausage, spaetzle, apple strudel, Bavarian cheesecake, and Black Forest cake await you at the all-you-can-eat buffet. Patrons pound pitchers of all kinds of beer and wine on the long communal tables—even when the yodelers, singers, and dancers aren't egging them on. Prices change seasonally. Ⓢ *Average main: $40* ⊠ *Germany Pavilion* ☎ *407/939–3463* ⊕ *www.disneyworld.com* ⚭ *Reservations essential* ✛ *2:E4.*

$$$ ╳ **Les Chefs de France.** What some consider the best restaurant at Dis-
FRENCH ney was created by three of France's most famous chefs: Paul Bocuse, Gaston Lenôtre, and Roger Vergé. Classic escargots, a good starter, are prepared in a casserole with garlic butter; you might follow up with roasted breast and leg of duck confit, or grilled beef tenderloin with

green pepper sauce. Make sure you finish with profiteroles drizzled with chocolate sauce. The three-course prix-fixe menu is a great value. An Audio-Animatronics Remy, from the movie *Ratatouille,* makes the rounds atop a roving chef's cart. [$] *Average main: $27* ✉ *France Pavilion* ☎ *407/939–3463* 🌐 *www.disneyworld.com* ✥ *2:D4.*

$$$$ FRENCH Fodor's Choice ★ 🍴 **Monsieur Paul.** A mere staircase away from Epcot's busy World Showcase, Monsieur Paul is a subdued and sophisticated fine dinery. It's owned by Chef Jerome Bocuse and named for his world-famous father, the Culiniary Institute of America's Chef of the Century, Paul Bocuse. The restaurant is expensive and sophisticated—in odd juxtaposition to the rumpled clothing and sneakers of most diners—and a delightful diversion from the theme park's bustle. The menu is overtly French while incorporating the best of America. For example, the signature fish dish, which has "scales" of potato, braised fennel, and rosemary sauce, is made with Florida red snapper instead of the original's red mullet. Escargot is presented in large raviolis and a parsley cream. The namesake salad tops curly greens with dry-aged ham, braised leeks, a Parmesan crisp, and celery cream, and the seared scallops and roasted duck breast are especially interesting entrées. Although the service isn't as polished as the menu, it is heartening to hear the waitstaff converse in French. [$] *Average main: $36* ✉ *France Pavilion* ☎ *407/939–3463* 🌐 *www.disneyworld.com* ⏲ *No lunch* ✥ *2:D4.*

$$$ BRITISH 🍴 **Rose & Crown.** If you're an Anglophile and you love a beer so thick you could stand a spoon up in your mug, this is the place to soak up both the suds and British street culture. "Wenches" serve up traditional English fare—fish-and-chips, cottage or shepherd's pie (ground beef or lamb with onions, carrots, and peas, topped with mashed potatoes and cheddar cheese), and, at times, the ever-popular bangers and mash (sausage over mashed potatoes). Scotch egg makes a good appetizer. Vegetarians can always find one item adapted for them, such as vegetable pie 'n' mash. For dessert, try the sticky toffee pudding. The terrace has a splendid view of IllumiNations. [$] *Average main: $23* ✉ *United Kingdom Pavilion* ☎ *407/939–3463* 🌐 *www.disneyworld.com* ✥ *2:D4.*

$$$ PIZZA 🍴 **Via Napoli.** When the Patina Restaurant Group decided to open a second Italian eatery in Epcot (the first was Tutto Italia Ristorante), they opted to specialize in authentic Neapolitan wood-fired pizza, importing the mozzarella from Italy and using only San Marzano tomatoes. The result is crusty, thin pies topped with your choice of pepperoni; portobello and crimini mushrooms; or eggplant, artichokes, cotto ham, and mushrooms. The eggplant parmigiana is an outstanding alternative. [$] *Average main: $23* ✉ *Italy Pavilion* ☎ *407/939–3463* 🌐 *www.disneyworld.com* ✥ *2:E4.*

DISNEY'S HOLLYWOOD STUDIOS

$$ AMERICAN FAMILY 🍴 **50's Prime Time Café.** Who says you can't go home again? If you grew up in middle America in the 1950s, just step inside. While *I Love Lucy* and *The Donna Reed Show* clips play on a television screen, you can feast on meat loaf, pot roast, or fried chicken, all served on a Formica tabletop. At $16, the meat loaf is one of the best inexpensive, filling dinners in any local theme park. Enjoy it with a malted-milk shake or root-beer float (or a bottle of wine). The place offers some

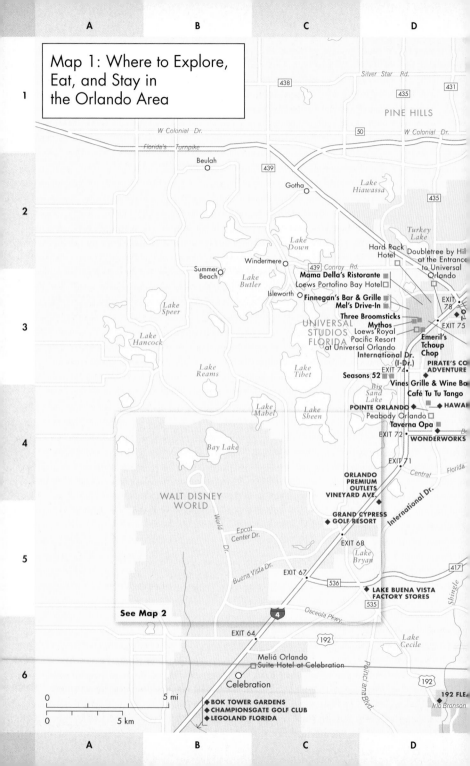

Map 1: Where to Explore, Eat, and Stay in the Orlando Area

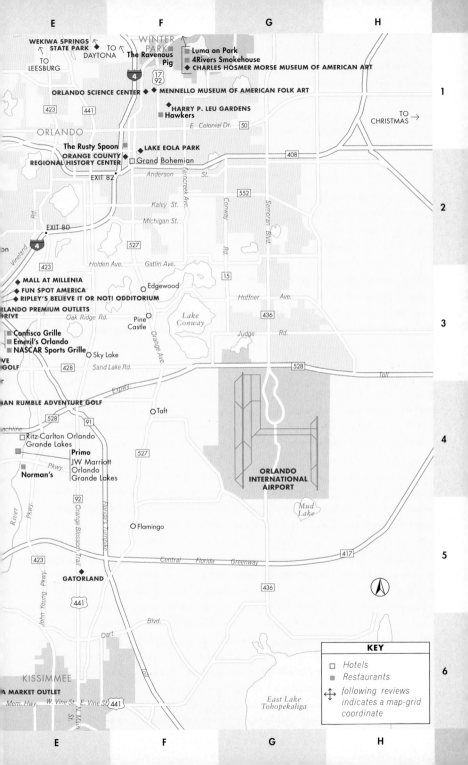

BEST BETS FOR ORLANDO AND THE PARKS DINING

Orlando is not all fast food. Quality restaurants operate within the parks, Downtown Disney, and several Orlando neighborhoods. Here are our top recommendations, organized by price, cuisine, and experience. The restaurants we consider the very best are indicated in the listings with the Fodor's Choice logo.

Fodor's Choice ★

Be Our Guest, p. 499
Boma—Flavors of Africa, p. 506
Emeril's Orlando, p. 512
Flying Fish, p. 507
4Rivers Smokehouse, p. 516
Hawkers, p. 516
Jiko, p. 508
Luma on Park, p. 517
Monsieur Paul, p. 501
Norman's, p. 514
Primo, p. 515
The Ravenous Pig, p. 517
The Rusty Spoon, p. 516
Todd English's blue-zoo, p. 508
Victoria & Albert's, p. 509

By Price

$

Confisco Grill, p. 512
4Rivers Smokehouse, p. 516
Mel's Drive-In, p. 509

$$

50s Prime Time Café, p. 501
Hawkers, p. 516
Mama Melrose's Ristorante Italiano, p. 505
Mythos, p. 512

$$$

Be Our Guest, p. 499
Boma—Flavors of Africa, p. 506
Emeril's Tchoup Chop, p. 513
Kouzzina by Cat Cora, p. 508
Luma on Park, p. 517
The Ravenous Pig, p. 517
The Rusty Spoon, p. 516

$$$$

California Grill, p. 507
Emeril's Orlando, p. 512
Flying Fish, p. 507
Jiko, p. 508
Monsieur Paul, p. 501
Norman's, p. 514
Primo, p. 515
Todd English's blue-zoo, p. 508
Victoria & Albert's, p. 509

By Cuisine

AMERICAN

California Grill, p. 507
Cinderella's Royal Table, p. 500
50s Prime Time Café, p. 501
Luma on the Park, p. 517
The Ravenous Pig, p. 517
The Rusty Spoon, p. 516
Victoria & Albert's, p. 509
Wolfgang Puck Grand Café, p. 506

ITALIAN

La Luce by Donna Scala, p. 515
Mama Melrose's Ristorante Italiano, p. 505
Primo, p. 515

SEAFOOD

Flying Fish, p. 507
Sunset Sam's Fish Camp, p. 514
Todd English's blue-zoo, p. 508

By Experience

BEST BUFFET

Boma—Flavors of Africa, p. 506
Chef Mickey's, p. 507

BEST DISNEY RESTAURANT

Be Our Guest, p. 499
Boma—Flavors of Africa, p. 499
California Grill, p. 507
Jiko, p. 508
Monsieur Paul, p. 501
Victoria & Albert's, p. 509

BEST OFF-SITE RESTAURANT

Luma on Park, p. 517
Norman's, p. 514
Primo, p. 515
The Ravenous Pig, p. 517

fancier dishes, like the olive oil–poached salmon, which is a good choice for lighter eaters. If you're not feeling totally wholesome, go for Dad's Electric Lemonade (rum, vodka, blue curaçao, sweet-and-sour mix, and Sprite), which is worth every bit of the $10.75 price tag. Just like Mother, the menu admonishes, "Keep your elbows off the table." [$] *Average main: $18* ✉ *Echo Lake* ☎ *407/939–3463* 🌐 *www.disneyworld.com* ✣ *2:D5.*

$$$$ AMERICAN 🍴 **Hollywood Brown Derby.** At this reproduction of the famous 1940s Hollywood restaurant, the walls are lined with movie-star caricatures, just as in Tinseltown. The specialty is the Cobb salad, which by legend was invented by Brown Derby founder Robert Cobb; the salad consists of finely chopped lettuce enlivened by loads of tomato, bacon, turkey, blue cheese, chopped egg, and avocado, all tossed table-side. Other menu choices include grilled salmon with beets and fillet of beef with corn-pancetta risotto. Dining with an Imagineer is a special option; you will have lunch or dinner with one of Disney's creative engineers while enjoying a set-price four-course meal including soup, salad, entrée, and dessert. If you request the Fantasmic! dinner package, make a reservation for no later than two hours before the start of the show. [$] *Average main: $35* ✉ *Hollywood Blvd.* ☎ *407/939–3463* 🌐 *www.disneyworld.com* ✣ *2:D5.*

$$ ITALIAN 🍴 **Mama Melrose's Ristorante Italiano.** To replace the energy you've no doubt depleted by miles of theme-park walking, you can load up on carbs at this casual Italian restaurant that looks like an old warehouse. Good main courses include spaghetti with meatballs, and grilled tuna with vegetable risotto and olive-caper butter. Wood-fired flatbreads are available as an entrée choice here (a great bargain at $13 and up) with toppings ranging from grilled chicken with sweet onion relish to mushroom. The sangria, available by the carafe, flows generously. Ask for the Fantasmic! dinner package if you want priority seating for the show. [$] *Average main: $21* ✉ *Streets of America* ☎ *407/939–3463* 🌐 *www.disneyworld.com* ✣ *2:D5.*

$$ AMERICAN 🍴 **Sci-Fi Dine-In Theater Restaurant.** If you don't mind zombies leering at you while you eat, then head to this enclosed faux drive-in, where you can sit in a fake candy-color '50s convertible and watch trailers from classics like *Attack of the Fifty-Foot Woman* and *Teenagers from Outer Space*. The menu includes choices like steak and garlic-mashed potatoes, an Angus or veggie burger, sautéed shrimp with pasta, and a huge Reuben sandwich with fries or cucumber salad. The hot-fudge sundaes are delicious. [$] *Average main: $21* ✉ *Commissary La.* ☎ *407/939–3463* 🌐 *www.disneyworld.com* ✣ *2:D5.*

DISNEY'S ANIMAL KINGDOM

$ FAST FOOD 🍴 **Flame Tree Barbecue.** This counter-service eatery is one of the relatively undiscovered gems of Disney's culinary offerings. There's nothing fancy here, but you can dig into ribs and pulled pork sandwiches. For something with a lower calorie count, try the smoked turkey served with cranberry mayo or a great barbecued chicken served with baked beans and cole slaw. The outdoor tables, set beneath intricately carved wood pavilions, make great spots for a picnic, and they're not usually crowded. [$] *Average main: $9* ✉ *Discovery Island* ✍ *Reservations not accepted* ✣ *2:B5.*

$$$
ASIAN

╳ Yak & Yeti. The location of this pan-Asian cuisine, sit-down eatery—the only full-service restaurant inside Disney's Animal Kingdom—certainly makes sense. It's just at the entrance to the Asia section, in a two-story, 250-seat building that is pleasantly faux-Asian, with cracked plaster walls, wood carvings, and tile mosaic tabletops. Standout entrées include seared miso salmon, roasted duck with orange-wasabi glaze, and tempura shrimp with coconut-ginger rice and chili-plum sauce. Also tasty, if not authentically Asian, are the baby back ribs with a hoisin barbecue sauce and sweet chili slaw. $ *Average main: $22* ⊠ *Asia* ☎ *407/939–3463* ⊕ *www.disneyworld.com* ⊹ *2:B5.*

DOWNTOWN DISNEY

$$$
IRISH

╳ Raglan Road Irish Pub. An authentic Irish pub in Downtown Disney seems oxymoronic, particularly when that pub seats 600 people. But if Irish grub's your thing, Raglan's is the place to go. The shepherd's pie served here is of higher quality than the usual version, prepared with beef and lamb and jazzed up with house spices. And you don't have to settle for plain fish-and-chips (though you can for $19); there's also baked salmon with smoked salmon and maple glaze; shiitake risotto; and lamb shanks braised with rosemary jus. Three massive and ornate bars, all imported from Ireland and all more than a century old, help anchor the pub. The entertainment alone makes this place worth the visit. The house bands play nightly, and a trio of Irish dancers performs most evenings and during Sunday brunch. $ *Average main: $22* ⊠ *Pleasure Island, 1640 E. Buena Vista Dr.* ☎ *407/938–0300* ⊕ *www. raglanroadirishpub.com* ⊹ *2:F4.*

$$$
AMERICAN

╳ Wolfgang Puck Grand Café. There are lots of choices here, from wood-oven pizza at the informal Puck Express to fine-dining meals in the upstairs formal dining room. There's also a sushi bar and an informal café; the café is quite literally a happy medium, and may be the best bet for families hoping for a bit of elegance without the pressure of a formal dinner. At Express try the butternut squash soup or the Margherita pizza. At the café, midprice entrées like bacon-wrapped meat loaf and pumpkin ravioli with brown butter and Parmesan are winners, and you can always try the pizza pie that made Puck famous: smoked salmon with dill cream, red onion, chili oil, and chives. The dining room offers creative entrées plus classic Wiener schnitzel. Three- and four-course menus are priced at $52 (Austrian) and $57 (Californian), respectively. $ *Average main: $27* ⊠ *1482 E. Buena Vista Dr., West Side* ☎ *407/938–9653* ⊕ *www.wolfgangpuckcafeorlando.com* ⊹ *2:F4.*

WDW RESORTS

$$$
AFRICAN
Fodor'sChoice
★

╳ Boma—Flavors of Africa. Boma takes Western-style ingredients and prepares them with an African twist—then invites guests to walk through an African marketplace–style dining room to help themselves at the extraordinary buffet. The dozen or so serving stations have entrées such as roasted pork, Durban-style chicken, spice-crusted beef, and fish served with tamarind and other robust sauces; intriguing salads; and some of the best hummus this side of the Atlantic. Don't pass up the soups, as the coconut-curry seafood stew is excellent. The zebra dome dessert is chocolate mousse covered with white chocolate and striped with dark chocolate. All meals are prix fixe, and prices change seasonally. The South African wine list is outstanding. $ *Average main: $43* ⊠ *Animal Kingdom Lodge, 2901 Osceola Pkwy., Animal Kingdom Resort Area* ☎ *407/939–3463* ⊕ *www.disneyworld.com* ⌲ *Reservations essential* ⊗ *No lunch* ✛ *2:A5.*

$$$$
AMERICAN

✕ **California Grill.** The view from the surrounding Disney parks from this 15th-floor restaurant—the World's signature dining establishment since 1995—is as stunning as the food, especially after dark, when you can watch the nightly Magic Kingdom fireworks. The entire space and menu underwent major transformations in 2013, from new furnishings and chandeliers, to kitchen equipment such as a cast-iron plancha designed specifically for cooking fish. Expect locally sourced foods where possible, such as Cape Canaveral shrimp cooked with the heads on in a wood-fired oven, and house-made sausages. Sushi remains a highlight alongside creative globally inspired entrées. A 12-course "omakase" tasting menu is available. $ *Average main: $41* ⊠ *Contemporary Resort, 4600 N. World Dr., Magic Kingdom Resort Area* ☎ *407/939–3463* ⊕ *www.disneyworld.com* ⌲ *Reservations essential* ⊗ *No lunch* ✛ *2:C1.*

$$$
AMERICAN

✕ **Chef Mickey's.** This is the holy shrine for character meals, with Mickey, Minnie, or Goofy around for breakfast and dinner. Folks come here for entertainment and comfort food, not a quiet spot to read the *Orlando Sentinel.* The breakfast buffet includes "pixie-dusted" French toast, mountains of pancakes, and even a breakfast pizza. The dinner buffet doesn't disappoint with Thai-curry chicken, roasted ham, and changing specials like beef tips with mushrooms or salmon. Finish off your meal at the all-you-can-eat dessert bar of sundaes and chocolate cake. $ *Average main: $44* ⊠ *Contemporary Resort, 4600 N. World Dr., Magic Kingdom Resort Area* ☎ *407/939–3463* ⊕ *www.disneyworld. com* ⊗ *No lunch* ✛ *2:C1.*

$$
AMERICAN

✕ **ESPN Club.** Not only can you watch sports on a big-screen TV here (the restaurant has about 100 monitors), but you can also periodically see ESPN programs being taped in the club itself and be part of the audience of sports-radio talk shows. Food ranges from a variety of half-pound burgers, made with Angus chuck, to an excellent Reuben with plenty of corned beef, sauerkraut, and cheese. If you want an appetizer, try the Macho Nachos, crispy corn tortilla chips piled high with spicy chili, shredded cheddar cheese, sour cream, spicy salsa, nachos cheese sauce, and sliced jalapeños. This place is open quite late by Disney standards—until 1 am daily. Beware, the place can be pretty loud during any broadcast sports event, especially football games. $ *Average main: $16* ⊠ *BoardWalk Inn, 2101 Epcot Resorts Blvd., Epcot Resort Area* ☎ *407/939–3463* ⊕ *www.disneyworld.com* ✛ *2:D5.*

$$$$
SEAFOOD
Fodor's Choice
★

✕ **Flying Fish.** One of Disney's best restaurants, Flying Fish is whimsically decorated with murals, along the upper portion of the walls, that pay tribute to Atlantic seaboard spots of the early 1900s. This is a place where you put on your "resort casual" duds to "dine," as opposed to putting on your flip-flops and shorts to "chow down." The chefs take the food so seriously that the entire culinary team takes day trips to

9

local farms to learn their foodstuffs' origins. Flying Fish's best dishes include potato-wrapped red snapper, which is so popular it has been on the menu for several years, and oak-grilled salmon. Groups of up to six can sit at the counter that directly faces the exhibition kitchen for a five-course wine tasting menu. $ *Average main: $34* ✉ *BoardWalk Inn, 2101 Epcot Resorts Blvd., Epcot Resort Area* ☎ *407/939–2359* ⊕ *www.disneyworld.com* ❍ *No lunch* ✚ *2:D5.*

$$$$
AFRICAN
Fodor's Choice
★

✕ **Jiko.** The name of this restaurant means "the cooking place" in Swahili, and it is certainly that. The dining area surrounds two big, wood-burning ovens and a grill area where you can watch cooks in North African–style caps working on your meal. The menu here is more African-inspired than purely African, but it does include authentic flavors in entrées like peri-peri chicken flatbread and spiced pumpkin soup. Menu items often change, but entrées might include maize-crusted fish with tomato-butter sauce or chermoula-roasted Nigerian prawns with orange-olive salad. The restaurant offers more than 65 wines by the glass, including a large selection of South African vintages; vegetarian, vegan, and gluten-free menus are also available. Ask about the wine-and-dine experiences and the Wanyama vehicle safari-dinner combo (only for hotel guests). $ *Average main: $36* ✉ *Animal Kingdom Lodge, 2901 Osceola Pkwy., Animal Kingdom Resort Area* ☎ *407/939–3463* ⊕ *www.disneyworld.com* 🍽 *Reservations essential* ❍ *No lunch* ✚ *2:A5.*

$$$
MEDITERRANEAN

✕ **Kouzzina by Cat Cora.** Celebrity-chef Cat Cora and Disney joined forces to open an upbeat family-oriented Greek restaurant along the BoardWalk. From an exhibition *kouzzina* (Greek for kitchen), the culinary team puts out hearty portions of Cora's family favorites, including the familiar starter *spanakopita* (spinach pie) and an amazing side dish of brussels sprouts sautéed with capers. Entrées range from a sweet cinnamon-stewed chicken to a whole fish pan-roasted with braised greens, olives, fennel, and smoked chili. End with the *loukoumades* (donuts with warm honey) or baklava. For another option, try the five-course meal with wine pairings that is the Chef's Menu at CoraNation Room. $ *Average main: $24* ✉ *BoardWalk Inn, 2101 Epcot Resorts Blvd., Epcot Resort Area* ☎ *407/939–3463* ⊕ *www.disneyworld.com* ❍ *No lunch* ✚ *2:D5.*

$$
AMERICAN

✕ **Olivia's Café.** This is like a meal at Grandma's—provided she lives in Key West and likes to gussy up her grub with trendy twists. The menu ranges from a seafood pasta with sundried tomato to grilled pork chops with a Jamaican barbecue sauce and a side of smoked-cheddar mac 'n' cheese. Desserts are indulgent, such as the banana-bread-pudding sundae with bananas Foster topping and vanilla ice cream. The outdoor seating, which overlooks a waterway, is a nice place to dine any time the midsummer heat is not bearing down. $ *Average main: $21* ✉ *Old Key West Resort, 1510 N. Cove Rd., Downtown Disney Resort Area* ☎ *407/939–3463* ⊕ *www.disneyworld.com* ✚ *2:E4.*

$$$$
SEAFOOD
Fodor's Choice
★

✕ **Todd English's bluezoo.** Celebrity chef Todd English oversees this cutting-edge seafood eatery, a sleek, modern restaurant that resembles an underwater dining hall, with blue walls and carpeting, aluminum fish suspended from the ceiling, and bubble-like lighting fixtures. The menu is creative and pricey, with entrées like the two-pound Maine

"Cantonese lobster," fried and tossed in a sticky soy glaze, and the daily "dancing fish," cooked on an upright rotisserie with a roasted garlic-caper marinade. If you don't care for fish, you can opt for seasonal pork or steak preparations. The children's menu is especially good. $ *Average main: $45 ⊠ Walt Disney World Dolphin, 1500 Epcot Resorts Blvd., Epcot Resort Area ☎ 407/934–1111 ⊕ www.thebluezoo. com* ⊗ *No lunch* ⊹ *2:D4.*

$$$$ ✕**Victoria & Albert's.** At this ultraposh award-winning Disney restaurant,
MODERN a well-polished service team will anticipate your every need during a
AMERICAN gourmet extravaganza. This is one of the plushest fine-dining experi-
Fodor'sChoice ences in Florida, with an ambience so sophisticated that children under
★ 10 aren't on the guest list. The seven-course, prix-fixe menu changes daily, and you'd do well to supplement the $135 tab with a $65 wine pairing. Appetizer choices may include Maine lobster with watermelon radish, kohlrabi (a type of cabbage), and vanilla aïoli. Entrées may feature duck three ways with salsify (a root vegetable with an oysterlike flavor) and squash puree followed by Japanese Wagyu strip loin with oxtail jus. For most of the year, there are two seatings, at 5:45 and 9 pm. In July and August, however, there's generally just one seating at 6:30. For a more luxe experience, reserve a table in the intimate Queen Victoria Room or at the Chef's Table, which has more courses (10) and a bigger bill ($210). $ *Average main: $173 ⊠ Grand Floridian, 4401 Floridian Way, Magic Kingdom Resort Area ☎ 407/939–3862 ⊕ www. victoria-alberts.com* ⌕ *Reservations essential* 🏛 *Jacket required* ⊗ *No lunch* ⊹ *2:B1.*

UNIVERSAL ORLANDO AREA

UNIVERSAL STUDIOS

$$ ✕**Finnegan's Bar & Grill.** In an Irish pub that would look just right in
IRISH downtown New York during the Ellis Island era, Finnegan's offers classic Irish comfort food like shepherd's pie, corned beef and cabbage, bangers and mash (sausage and mashed potatoes), and fish-and-chips, plus Guinness on tap. If shepherd's pie isn't your thing, opt instead for a steak, burger, entrée salad, or sandwich. Irish folk music, sometimes live, completes the theme. $ *Average main: $16 ⊠ New York ☎ 407/224–3613 ⊕ www.universalorlando.com* ⊹ *1:D3.*

$ ✕**Mel's Drive-In.** At the corner of Hollywood and Vine is a flashy '50s
AMERICAN eatery with a pink-and-white 1956 Ford Crown Victoria parked out in front. For burgers and fries, this is one of the best choices in the park, and it comes complete with a roving doo-wop group during peak seasons. You're on vacation, so go ahead and have that extra-thick shake or the decadent chili-cheese fries. Mel's is also a great place to meet up, in case you decide to go your separate ways in the park. $ *Average main: $9 ⊠ Hollywood ☎ 407/363–8766 ⊕ www.universalorlando.com* ⌕ *Reservations not accepted* ⊹ *1:D3.*

9

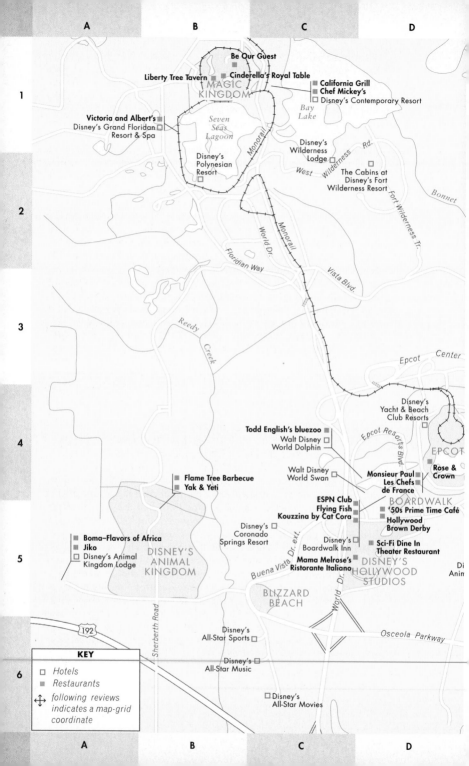

Be Our Guest

Liberty Tree Tavern **Cinderella's Royal Table**

MAGIC
KINGDOM

California Grill
Chef Mickey's
Disney's Contemporary Resort

Victoria and Albert's
Disney's Grand Floridian
Resort & Spa

*Seven
Seas
Lagoon*

*Bay
Lake*

Disney's
Polynesian
Resort

Disney's
Wilderness
Lodge

The Cabins at
Disney's Fort
Wilderness Resort

West *Wilderness* *Rd.*

Monorail

Bonnet

Floridian Way

World Dr.

Monorail

Vista Blvd.

Reedy

Creek

Epcot   Center

Disney's
Yacht & Beach
Club Resorts

EPCOT

Todd English's bluezoo
Walt Disney
World Dolphin

Epcot Resorts Blvd.

**Rose &
Crown**

Walt Disney
World Swan

Monsieur Paul
**Les Chefs
de France**

Flame Tree Barbecue
Yak & Yeti

ESPN Club
Flying Fish
Kouzzina by Cat Cora

BOARDWALK

'50s Prime Time Café

**Hollywood
Brown Derby**

Disney's
Coronado
Springs Resort

Disney's
Boardwalk Inn

**Sci-Fi Dine In
Theater Restaurant**

Boma–Flavors of Africa
Jiko
Disney's Animal
Kingdom Lodge

DISNEY'S
ANIMAL
KINGDOM

Buena Vista Dr. ext.

**Mama Melrose's
Ristorante Italiano**

DISNEY'S
HOLLYWOOD
STUDIOS

Di
Anim

BLIZZARD
BEACH

World Dr.

Osceola   Parkway

Sherberth Road

192

Disney's
All-Star Sports

KEY

□ *Hotels*
■ *Restaurants*
↔ *following reviews
indicates a map-grid
coordinate*

Disney's
All-Star Music

Disney's
All-Star Movies

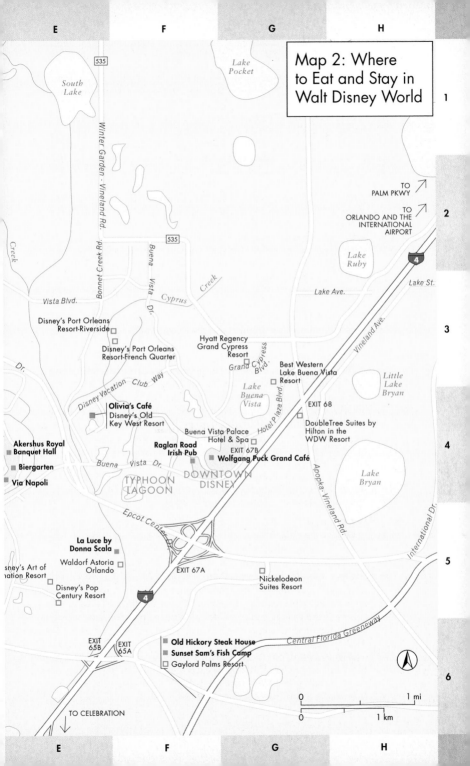

ISLANDS OF ADVENTURE

$ AMERICAN 🍴 **Confisco Grille.** You could walk right past this full-service restaurant without noticing it, but if you want a good meal and sit-down service, don't pass by too quickly. This is one of the better eateries inside the theme parks. The menu changes often, but typical entrées include pad Thai, grilled or blackened fresh fish of the day with mashed potatoes and sautéed spinach in a lemon-butter-cilantro sauce, and penne puttanesca—the vodka-cream tomato sauce is enhanced with sausage, kalamata olives, fried pepperoncini, and roasted garlic. Wash it all down with refreshing sangria, available by glass, pitcher, and half pitcher. [$] *Average main: $13* ✉ *Port of Entry* ☎ *407/224–4012* 🌐 *www.universalorlando.com* ✥ *1:D3.*

$$ ECLECTIC 🍴 **Mythos.** The name may be Greek, but the dishes are eclectic. The seasonally changing menu usually includes such mainstays as pad Thai with barbecue plum-roasted pork and cedar-plank salmon with citrus butter. The building itself—which looks like a giant rock formation from the outside and a huge cave (albeit one with plush upholstered seating) from the inside—is enough to grab your attention, but so do sandwiches like crab sliders and buffalo chicken wraps. Mythos also has a waterfront view of the big lagoon in the center of the theme park. When it's slow in the park, the restaurant is open only for lunch. [$] *Average main: $15* ✉ *Lost Continent* ☎ *407/224–4012* 🌐 *www.universalorlando.com* ✥ *1:D3.*

$ BRITISH 🍴 **Three Broomsticks.** Now Harry Potter fans can taste pumpkin juice (with hints of honey and vanilla) and butterbeer (sort of like bubbly butterscotch cream soda; some say it tastes like shortbread cookies). They're on the menu along with British foodstuffs at this Hogsmeade restaurant modeled after the fantasy books. Rickety staircases and gaslit chandeliers set the tone for the counter-service restaurant, where families gobble down ample portions of shepherd's pie, fish-and-chips, chargrilled ribs, and smoked chicken. In the adjacent Hog's Head pub, a faux hog's head sneers now and then. [$] *Average main: $12* ✉ *Wizarding World of Harry Potter* ☎ *407/224–4233* 🌐 *www.universalorlando.com* ✍ *Reservations not accepted* ✥ *1:D3.*

CITYWALK

$$$$ CAJUN Fodor's Choice ★ 🍴 **Emeril's Orlando.** The popular eatery is a culinary shrine to Emeril Lagasse, the famous TV chef who occasionally makes an appearance. And although the modern interior of the restaurant with its 30-foot ceilings, blond woods, second-story wine loft, and lots of galvanized steel looks nothing like the French Quarter, the hardwood floors and linen tablecloths create an environment befitting the stellar nature of the cuisine. Entrées may include andouille-crusted pan-roasted redfish with creole meunière sauce, pork chop with horseradish jus, and blackened Atlantic salmon with red pepper–truffle butter sauce. Reservations are usually essential, but there's a chance of getting a walk-in seating if you show up for lunch (11:30 am) or early for dinner (5:30 pm). [$] *Average main: $39* ✉ *6000 Universal Blvd.* ☎ *407/224–2424* 🌐 *www.emerils.com* ✍ *Reservations essential* ✥ *1:D3.*

$$ **✕ NASCAR Sports Grille.** Filled with race-car simulator games as well
AMERICAN as arcade and racing memorabilia, this eatery might not look like the place to grab a sublime meal, but that's not the case. This theme restaurant has a reputation as a good place for grub. Selections worth trying include the Southern-style pot roast and the slow-roasted baby back rib platter; the Talladega cheeseburger with a side of fries is a cut above the standard theme-park burger. $ *Average main: $18* ✉ *6000 Universal Blvd.* ☎ *407/224–7223* ⊕ *www.nascarsportsgrilleorlando.com* ✛ 1:D3.

UNIVERSAL HOTELS

$$$ **✕ Emeril's Tchoup Chop.** The bold interior decor—with lots of bamboo,
SOUTH PACIFIC bright glazed tile, an exposition kitchen, and a long zero-edge pool with porcelain lily pads running the length of the dining room—is just as ambitious as the food at Emeril Lagasse's Pacific-influenced restaurant. Following the theme of the Royal Pacific Resort, Lagasse fuses his signature bold flavors with Polynesian tastes. Entrées change regularly, but representative dishes include hot iron-seared yellowfin tuna steak with Thai sticky rice and smoked bacon with wasabi-butter infusion; sake-braised beef short ribs with caramelized onion mashed potatoes and a Burgundy-veal reduction; and cilantro-cashew pesto-marinated tofu with crispy rice cake and citrus soy. $ *Average main: $29* ✉ *Loews Royal Pacific Resort, 6300 Hollywood Way* ☎ *407/503–2467* ⊕ *www. emerils.com* ⚱ *Reservations essential* ✛ 1:D3.

$$$ **✕ Mama Della's Ristorante.** This playfully themed Italian restaurant hap-
ITALIAN pens to have excellent food. The premise is that you're eating at a home-turned-restaurant owned by an Italian woman. That woman, Mama Della, is played by an actress, whose warmth enhances the experience (as does the serenade by an accordianist, guitar player, and vocalist). The menu features Italian classics like chicken parmigiana and lasagna as well as more ambitious dishes like salmon with tomato marmalade and braised lamb with eggplant caponata. Outdoor seating on the patio provides a view of the hotel's nightly *Musica Della Notte* (Music of the Night) opera show. $ *Average main: $29* ✉ *Loews Portofino Bay Hotel, 5601 Universal Blvd.* ☎ *407/503–3463* ⊕ *www.loewshotels.com* ⊗ *No lunch* ✛ 1:D3.

ORLANDO METRO AREA

KISSIMMEE

$$$$ **✕ Old Hickory Steakhouse.** This upscale steak house is designed to look
STEAKHOUSE like rustic cabins in the Everglades. Beyond the playful facade is a polished restaurant with a classic steak-house menu—bone-in rib eye, porterhouse, and filet mignon, supplemented by rack of lamb, pork chop, and Atlantic salmon, all priced for the hotel's convention-goers. The chef gets creative with appetizers like a warm pear-and-goat-cheese tart, but most are standards such as onion soup, shrimp cocktail, and tomato-onion salad. Artisanal cheese plates are on the menu, and desserts are interesting, such as fudge-dipped derby pie. $ *Average main: $50* ✉ *Gaylord Palms Resort, 6000 W. Osceola Pkwy., I–4 Exit 65* ☎ *407/586–1600* ⊕ *www.gaylordhotels.com* ⊗ *No lunch* ✛ 2:F6.

9

$$$

SEAFOOD

✕ **Sunset Sam's Fish Camp.** Sunset Sam's looks gimmicky—its bar and dining room encircle two 60-foot masts—yet the food is both excellent and affordable. Starters are big enough to be a meal and include crab bisque and tempura-fried oysters. Entrées are pricey but not exorbitant and might be herb-crusted fish with a Basque sauce of olives, capers, and roasted red and yellow peppers, or rice-crusted fish with coconut sticky rice and ginger–passion fruit sauce. Entrée sandwiches and salads, priced below $20, are a wallet-friendly option. For dessert, go for the traditional key lime tart. $ *Average main: $25 ⊠ Gaylord Palms Resort, 6000 W. Osceola Pkwy., I–4 Exit 65 ☎ 407/586–1101 ⊕ www. gaylordhotels.com ✛ 2:F6.*

INTERNATIONAL DRIVE

$$$

ECLECTIC

✕ **Café Tu Tu Tango.** The food here is served tapas-style—everything is appetizer size but plentiful, and relatively inexpensive. If you want a compendium of cuisines at one go, try the black-bean soup with cilantro sour cream, guava barbecue-glazed pork ribs, Hungarian-sausage flatbread, and spiced alligator bites. The wine list includes more than 50 wines from several countries, with all but a handful by the bottle and the glass. The restaurant is designed to resemble an artist's loft; artists paint at easels while diners take a culinary trip around the world. Belly dancers, flamenco dancers, Bolivian dancers, and African drummers are among the entertainers who perform in the evening. Thanks to a new patio, diners can now share their small plates alfresco. $ *Average main: $22 ⊠ 8625 International Dr. ☎ 407/248–2222 ⊕ www.cafetututango. com ⌕ Reservations not accepted ✛ 1:D4.*

$$$

GREEK

✕ **Taverna Opa.** This high-energy Greek restaurant bills itself as offering "fun with a capital F." Here the ouzo flows like a mountain stream, the Greek music almost reaches the level of a rock concert, and the roaming belly dancers actively encourage diners to take part in the mass Zorba dancing, which often happens on the tops of dining tables. The only thing missing is the Greek restaurant tradition of throwing dinner plates, made up in part by the throwing of torn-up paper napkins, which sometimes reaches near-blizzard level. The food, by the way, is also excellent. Standouts include traditional staples like spanakopita, *saganaki* (the traditional flaming cheese appetizer), *avegolemono* (lemony chicken-rice soup), and perhaps the most famous Greek entrée, moussaka. The best dessert is the baklava. $ *Average main: $26 ⊠ Pointe Orlando, 9101 International Dr. ☎ 407/351–8660 ⊕ www.opaorlando.com ✛ 1:D4.*

SOUTH ORLANDO

$$$$

ECLECTIC

Fodor'sChoice

★

✕ **Norman's.** Celebrity-chef Norman Van Aken brings impressive credentials to the restaurant that bears his name, as you might expect from the headline eatery in the Ritz-Carlton Orlando Grande Lakes. Van Aken's culinary roots go back to the Florida Keys, where he's credited with creating "Floribbean" cuisine, a blend that is part Key West and part Caribbean—although he now weaves in flavors from all continents. The Orlando operation is a formal, sleek restaurant with marble floors, starched tablecloths, waiters in ties and vests, and a creative, if expensive, menu. In addition to exceptional ceviches and a signature appetizer called Down Island French toast made with Curacao-marinated foie gras, favorites include a Mongolian-marinated veal chop, pan-cooked Florida snapper with citrus butter, and pork Havana with "21st-century mole sauce." A six-course tasting menu is $95, more with beverage pairings. [$] *Average main: $46* ✉ *Ritz-Carlton Orlando Grande Lakes, 4000 Central Florida Pkwy.* ☎ *407/393–4333* 🌐 *www.normans.com* 🕑 *No lunch* ✥ *1:E4.*

$$$$ ITALIAN Fodor's Choice ★ 🍴 **Primo.** James Beard Award winner Melissa Kelly cloned her Italian-organic Maine restaurant in an upscale Orlando hotel and brought her farm-to-table sensibilities with her. Here the daily dinner menu pays tribute to Sicily's lighter foods made with produce grown in the hotel garden. Homemade pasta is tossed Bolognese-style with beef, pork, or duck. Dry-aged prime New York strip steak is enhanced with mushroom and sweetbread ragù. Desserts are just as special, with the likes of warm Belgian chocolate *budino* (pudding) cake or hot zeppole tossed in cinnamon and sugar. [$] *Average main: $37* ✉ *JW Marriott Orlando Grande Lakes, 4040 Central Florida Pkwy.* ☎ *407/393–4444* 🌐 *www.primorestaurant.com* 🕑 *No lunch* ✥ *1:E4.*

LAKE BUENA VISTA

$$$ ITALIAN 🍴 **La Luce by Donna Scala.** Having made a name for herself at California's Bistro Don Giovanni, Donna Scala brought the same Italian cuisine with a Napa Valley farm-fresh flair to this upscale Hilton at the edge of Disney World. The art changes with the seasons, and a chalk mural is updated periodically. Equal effort goes into the menu, where pastas are made fresh. Try the ricotta gnocchi with Gorgonzola dolce cream sauce, the porcini-rubbed rib eye, or a simple seared salmon fillet with chive-butter sauce. [$] *Average main: $27* ✉ *Hilton Orlando Bonnett Creek, 14100 Bonnet Creek Resort La., Bonnet Creek* ☎ *407/597–3600* 🌐 *www.laluceorlando.com* 🕑 *No lunch* ✥ *2:F5.*

SAND LAKE ROAD

$$ AMERICAN 🍴 **Seasons 52.** Parts of the menu change every week at this innovative restaurant that serves different foods at different times of year, depending on what's in season. Meals here tend to be healthful (butter is banned) yet hearty and very flavorful. The beef chili starter is to die for. For an entrée, you might have wood-roasted pork tenderloin with polenta, cremini mushrooms, and a Dijon glaze, or caramelized grilled sea scallops with sun-dried tomato–mushroom pearl pasta. An impressive wine list with dozens of selections by the glass complements the menu. For dessert, have mini-indulgence classics like pecan pie, rocky road, carrot cake, and key lime pie served in petite portions. Although the cuisine is haute, the prices are modest—not bad for a snazzy, urbane bistro and wine bar. It has live music nightly to boot. Another Seasons is located in Altamonte Springs. [$] *Average main: $21* ✉ *Plaza Venezia, 7700 Sand Lake Rd., I–4 Exit 75A* ☎ *407/354–5212* 🌐 *www.seasons52.com* ✥ *1:D3.*

$$$$ STEAKHOUSE 🍴 **Vines Grille & Wine Bar.** Live jazz and blues music fills the night at the bar section of this dramatically designed restaurant, but the food and drink in the snazzy main dining room are headliners in their own right. The kitchen bills itself as a steak house, but it really is far more than that. Entrées range from a porterhouse (alas, no longer dry-aged) to pan-seared Chilean sea bass with lobster risotto and Thai-basil *beurre blanc,* from a one-pound Wagyu burger with truffle fries to beef short

9

rib osso bucco. Be sure to start with the grilled octopus, which is simply prepared with red onions, capers, and roasted fennel. The wine list here is extensive, and the cocktails are serious business, too. The crowd tends to dress up, but jackets and ties are not required. [$] *Average main: $48* ✉ *The Fountains, 7533 W. Sand Lake Rd.* ☎ *407/351–1227* 🌐 *www.vinesgrille.com* ⏲ *No lunch* ✣ *1:D3.*

CENTRAL ORLANDO

$$ ASIAN Fodor's Choice ★

🍴 **Hawkers.** Hipsters, families, and business groups dine side by side at this popular restaurant, a laid-back spot that specializes in serving Asian street food. Travel the continent with $3 to $7.50 appetizer-size portions of scratch-made specialties from Malaysia, Singapore, Thailand, and Vietnam. Musts for adventurous diners include roti canai, a flaky bread with a chicken-curry dip; curry laksa, a noodle soup with exotic flavors; and stir-fried udon noodles. More timid eaters adore the marinated beef skewers with Malaysian satay sauce, peanuty chilled sesame noodles, smoky hot iron mussels, and any of the Americanized (but flavorful) lettuce wraps. [$] *Average main: $15* ✉ *1103 Mills Ave., Mills 50 District* ☎ *407/237–0606* 🌐 *www.facebook.com/hawkersstreetfare* ✣ *1:F1.*

$$$ SOUTHERN Fodor's Choice ★

🍴 **The Rusty Spoon.** Lovingly raised animals and locally grown produce are the menu foundation at this Downtown gastropub, an ideal spot for a business lunch or a pre–basketball game, -theater, or -concert dinner. The wood-and-brick dining room is a comfortable backdrop to hearty American meals with a Southern bent. Creatively stuffed eggs and buttermilk-soaked Vidalia onion rings are top starters. The salads—with ultrafresh greens—are always sensational. All pastas are made from scratch, whether a butternut squash lasagna or a winter pappardelle with wilted escarole, parsnips, toasted walnuts, and fried sage. The Dirty South seafood stew is a Dixie take on bouillabaisse. End with a very grown-up take on s'mores. One Sunday a month, there's brunch. [$] *Average main: $22* ✉ *55 W. Church St., Downtown Orlando* ☎ *407/401–8811* 🌐 *www.therustyspoon.com* ⏲ *No lunch Sun.* ✣ *1:F1.*

WINTER PARK

$ BARBECUE Fodor's Choice ★

🍴 **4Rivers Smokehouse.** Obsessed with Texas-style barbecue brisket, John Rivers decided to turn his passion into a business upon retiring from the corporate world. The result is the über-popular 4Rivers, which turns out barbecue standards like pulled pork and cornbread, plus more unusual items like the addicting bacon-wrapped smoked jalapeño peppers, the Six Shooter with cheese grits, and a sausage-filled pastry called *kolache*. Old-time soft drinks such as Frostie Root Beer and Cheerwine are for sale, along with desserts like the kiddie favorite Chocolate Awesomeness, an indulgent layering of chocolate cake, chocolate pudding, Heath Bar, whipped cream, and chocolate and caramel sauces. Additional 4Rivers are located north of Disney in Winter Garden and Longwood, with more on the way. [$] *Average main: $14* ✉ *1600 W. Fairbanks Ave.* ☎ *407/474–8377* 🌐 *www.4rsmokehouse.com* ✍ *Reservations not accepted* ⏲ *Closed Sun.* ✣ *1:F1.*

Luma on Park in Winter Park sources nearly all their ingredients from local producers.

$$$ MODERN AMERICAN Fodor's Choice ★ 🍴 **Luma on Park.** Indisputably one of the Orlando area's best restaurants, Luma on Park is a popular spot for progressive American cuisine served in a fashionable setting. Every ingredient is carefully sourced from local producers when possible, and scratch preparation—from pastas to sausages to pickled rhubarb—is the mantra among its dedicated clique of chefs. The menu changes daily. You might discover chestnut agnolotti with Maine lobster or a cauliflower-onion tart as starters, followed by tilefish with tangerine-fennel broth or a duck breast with kale, toasted pine nuts, parsnip puree, and pickled white asparagus. The wine cellar is a high point, holding 80 varieties, all available by the half glass, glass, and bottle. The restaurant offers a three-course, prix-fixe dinner Sunday through Tuesday for $35 per person, $45 with wine pairings. [$] *Average main: $26* ✉ *250 S. Park Ave., Park Ave.* ☎ *407/599–4111* 🌐 *www.lumaonpark.com* ✍ *Reservations essential* 🕒 *No lunch Mon.–Thurs.* ✥ *1:F1.*

$$$ MODERN AMERICAN Fodor's Choice ★ 🍴 **The Ravenous Pig.** A trendy, vibrant gastropub in one of Orlando's most affluent enclaves, the Pig is arguably Orlando's most popular foodie destination. Run by husband-and-wife chefs James and Julie Petrakis, the restaurant dispenses delicacies such as pork porterhouse with heirloom-tomato panzanella, chimichurri verde, and charred scallion vinaigrette, and grilled Canaveral cobia with roasted salsify-and-potato hash, grapefruit nage, and caramelized endive marmalade. The menu changes daily and always includes less expensive pub fare like lobster tacos and homemade pretzels with a taleggio-porter fondue. All charcuterie is made in house, from spiced orange salami to game-bird terrine. The signature dessert is the Pig Tails, essentially a basket full of piping hot, pig tail–shape doughnuts with a

9

chocolate-espresso dipping sauce. $ *Average main: $25* ✉ *1234 N. Orange Ave., Orange Ave.* ☏ *407/628–2333* ⊕ *www.theravenouspig. com* ⌅ *Reservations essential* ⊘ *Closed Sun. and Mon.* ✛ *1:F1.*

WHERE TO STAY

Updated
by Jennifer
Greenhill-Taylor

With tens of thousands of lodging choices available in the Orlando area, from tents to deluxe villas, there is no lack of variety in price or amenities. Narrowing down the possibilities can be part of the fun.

More than 50 million visitors come to the Orlando area each year, making it the most popular tourism destination on the planet. More upscale hotels are opening as visitors demand more luxurious surroundings, such as luxe linens, tasteful and refined decor, organic toiletries, or ergonomic chairs and work desks. But no matter what your budget or desires, lodging comes in such a wide range of prices, themes, color schemes, brands, meal plans, and guest-room amenities, you will have no problem finding something that fits.

Resorts on and off Disney property combine function with fantasy, as befits visitor expectations. Characters in costume perform for the kids, pools are pirates' caves with waterfalls, and some, like the Gaylord Palms, go so far as to re-create Florida landmarks under a gargantuan glass roof, giving visitors the illusion of having visited more of the state than they expected.

The area around the expanded Orange County Convention Center is going more upscale as the center draws more and more savvy conventioneers who bring their families along to visit the theme parks. Central Florida has weathered the tough economic times of the past few years so well, in fact, that prices are on the rise, and hotels are expanding.

Many hotels are joining the trend toward green lodging, bringing recycling, water conservation, and other environmentally conscious amenities to the table. Best of all, the sheer number and variety of hotel rooms means you can still find relative bargains throughout the Orlando area, even on Disney property, by researching your trip well, calling the lodgings directly, negotiating packages and prices, and shopping wisely.

RESERVATIONS

WDW Central Reservations Office. You can book many accommodations—Disney-owned hotels and some non-Disney-owned hotels—through the WDW Central Reservations Office. The website now allows you to compare prices at the various on-site resorts. ☏ *407/934–7639* ⊕ *www. disneyworld.com.*

WDW Special Request Reservations. People with disabilities can call WDW Special Request Reservations. ☏ *407/939–7807.*

When booking by phone, expect a robot first, then a real person.

Walt Disney Travel Co. Packages can be arranged through the Walt Disney Travel Co. Avoid checkout headaches by asking about the resort fee in advance. Many hotels and resorts, on property or off, charge this fee, and few tell you until checkout. ☏ *407/934–7639* ⊕ *www. disneyworld.com.*

WHERE SHOULD WE STAY?

	VIBE	PROS	CONS
Disney	Thousands of rooms at every price; convenient to Disney parks; free transportation all over WDW complex.	Perks like early park entry and Magical Express, which lets you circumvent airport bag checks.	Without a rental car, you likely won't leave Disney. On-site buses, although free, can take a big bite of time out of your entertainment day; convenience comes at a price.
Universal	On-site hotels offer luxury and convenience. There are less expensive options just outside the gates.	Central to Disney, Universal, SeaWorld, malls, and I–4; free water taxis to parks from on-site hotels.	On-site hotels are pricey; expect heavy rush-hour traffic during drives to and from other parks.
I-Drive	A hotel, convention center, and activities bonanza. A trolley runs from one end to the other.	Outlet malls provide bargains galore; diners enjoy world-class restaurants; it's central to parks; many hotels offer free shuttles.	Transportation can be pricey, in cash and in time, as traffic is often heavy. Crime is up, especially after dark, although area hotels and businesses have increased security.
Kissimmee	It offers mom-and-pop motels and upscale choices, restaurants, and places to buy saltwater taffy.	It's just outside Disney, very close to Magic Kingdom. Lots of Old Florida charm and low prices.	Some of the older motels here are a little seedy. Petty crime in which tourists are victims is rare— but not unheard of.
Lake Buena Vista	Many hotel and restaurant chains here. Adjacent to WDW, which is where almost every guest in your hotel is headed.	Really close to WDW; plenty of dining and shopping options; easy access to I–4.	Heavy peak-hour traffic. As in all neighborhoods near Disney, a gallon of gas will cost 10%–15% more than elsewhere.
Central Orlando	Parts of town have the modern high-rises you'd expect. Other areas have oak tree–lined brick streets winding among small, cypress-ringed lakes.	Lots of locally owned restaurants and some quaint B&Bs. City buses serve the parks. There's good access to I–4.	You'll need to rent a car. And you will be part of the traffic headed to WDW. Expect the 25-mile drive to take at least 45 minutes.
Orlando International Airport	Mostly business and flight-crew hotels and car-rental outlets.	Great if you have an early flight or just want to shop in a mall. There's even a Hyatt on-site.	Watching planes, buses, taxis, and cars arrive and depart is all the entertainment you'll get.

9

ABOUT OUR REVIEWS

Prices: Prices in the hotel reviews are the lowest cost of a standard double room in high season, excluding taxes, service charges, and meal plans (except at all-inclusives). Prices for rentals are the lowest per-night cost for a one-bedroom unit in high season.

Maps: *Throughout the chapter, you'll see mapping symbols and coordinates (✛ 3:F2) after property names or reviews. Maps are within the chapter. The first number after the ✛ symbol indicates the map number. After that is the property's coordinate on the map grid.*

DISNEY AND UNIVERSAL RESORT PERKS

DISNEY PERKS

Extra Magic Hours. You get special early and late-night admission to certain Disney parks on specified days. Call ahead for details so you can plan your early- and late-visit strategies.

Free Parking. Parking is free for Disney hotel guests at Disney hotel and theme-park lots.

Magical Express. If you're staying at a select Disney hotel, this free airport service means you don't need to rent a car or think about finding a shuttle or taxi or worry about baggage handling.

At your hometown airport, you check your bags in and won't see them again till you get to your Disney hotel. At Orlando International Airport you're met by a Disney rep, who leads you to a coach that takes you to your hotel. Your luggage is delivered separately and usually arrives in your room an hour or two after you do. If your flight arrives before 5 am or after 10 pm, you will have to pick up your luggage and deliver it to the coach.

On departure, the process works in reverse (though only on some participating airlines, so check in advance). You get your boarding pass and check your bags at the hotel. At the airport you go directly to your gate, skipping check-in. You won't see your bags until you're in your hometown airport. Participating airlines include American, Delta, JetBlue, Southwest, United, and US Airways.

Charging Privileges. You can charge most meals and purchases throughout Disney to your hotel room.

Package Delivery. Anything you purchase at Disney—at a park, a hotel, or in Downtown Disney—can be delivered to the gift shop of your Disney hotel for free.

Priority Reservations. Disney hotel guests get priority reservations at Disney restaurants and choice tee times at Disney golf courses up to 30 days in advance.

Guaranteed Entry. Disney theme parks sometimes reach capacity, but on-site guests can enter even when others would be turned away.

UNIVERSAL PERKS

Head-of-the-Line Access. Your hotel key lets you go directly to the head of the line for most Universal Orlando attractions. Unlike Disney's Fastpass program, you don't need to use this at a specific time; it's always good. Hotel guests also get early admission to the often-crowded Harry Potter attraction.

Priority Seating. Many of Universal's restaurants offer priority seating to those staying at on-site hotels.

Charging Privileges. You can charge most meals and purchases throughout Universal to your hotel room.

Delivery Services. If you buy something in the theme parks, you can have it sent directly to your room, so you don't have to carry it around.

Free Loaners. Some on-site hotels have a "Did You Forget?" closet that offers everything from kids' strollers to dog leashes to computer accessories. There's no fee for using this service.

WALT DISNEY WORLD

Disney-operated hotels are fantasies unto themselves. Each is designed according to a theme (quaint New England, the relaxed culture of the Polynesian Islands, an African safari village, and so on), and each offers the same perks: free transportation from the airport and to the parks, the option to charge all of your purchases to your room, special guest-only park-visiting times, and much more. If you stay on-site, you'll have better access to the parks and be more immersed in the Disney experience.

MAGIC KINGDOM RESORT AREA

$$$$
RESORT

The Cabins at Disney's Fort Wilderness Resort. The cabins in this 700-acre campground right across the lake from the Magic Kingdom don't exactly constitute roughing it, as they are small, air-conditioned log homes that accommodate four grown-ups and two youngsters. **Pros:** lots of traditional camping activities and a real campground community feel; you can save money by cooking, but you don't have to, as there is a three-meals-a-day restaurant and nightly barbecue; free Internet and Wi-Fi. **Cons:** shuttle to parks is free, but slow; pricey for what is really just a mobile home encased in logs; coin-op laundry is pricey, too. $ *Rooms from: $419* ✉ *4510 N. Fort Wilderness Trail* ☎ *407/824–2900* ⌐ *421 cabins* ⦿ *No meals* ✛ *2:D2.*

$$$$
RESORT

Disney's Contemporary Resort. You're paying for location at this sleek, modern resort in the heart of WDW, as the monorail runs right through the lobby, making park hopping a breeze, and offering quick respite for families in search of relief from the midday heat. **Pros:** easy access to parks via monorail; Chef Mickey's, the epicenter of the character-meal world, is here; a launching point for romantic Bay Lake cruises. **Cons:** a mix of conventioneers and vacationers means it can be too frenzied for the former and too staid for the latter; if you don't like lots of kids around, look elsewhere. $ *Rooms from: $546* ✉ *4600 N. World Dr.* ☎ *407/824–1000* ⌐ *1,013 rooms, 25 suites* ⦿ *No meals* ✛ *2:C1.*

$$$$
RESORT
Fodor's Choice
★

Disney's Grand Floridian Resort & Spa. On the shores of the Seven Seas Lagoon, this red-roofed Victorian emulates the style of the great railroad resorts of the past with beautifully appointed guest rooms, rambling verandas, delicate, white-painted gingerbread woodwork, and brick chimneys. **Pros:** old-Florida ambience; on the monorail route; Victoria & Albert's, one of Disney's best restaurants, offers an evening-long experience in dining; if you're a couple with no kids, this is definitely the most romantic on-property hotel. **Cons:** pricey; convention clientele and vacationing singles may be more comfortable than families with young children. $ *Rooms from: $652* ✉ *4401 Floridian Way* ☎ *407/824–3000* ⌐ *867 rooms, 90 suites* ⦿ *No meals* ✛ *2:B1.*

$$$$
RESORT

Disney's Polynesian Resort. You may not think you're in Fiji, but families with kids can have fun pretending here, especially after hearing the drumming and chanting that occasionally fills the three-story atrium of the Great Ceremonial House—aka the lobby—or, in the case of the adults in the party, downing a few of the tropical drinks available at the bar. **Pros:** on the monorail; great atmosphere; free Wi-Fi. **Cons:** pricey;

9

not good for those bothered by lots of loud children. $ *Rooms from: $596* ⊠ *1600 Seven Seas Dr.* ☎ *407/824–2000* ⤳ *847 rooms, 5 suites* ꠵ *No meals* ✛ *2:B2.*

$$$$
RESORT ꠵ **Disney's Wilderness Lodge.** The architects outdid themselves with this seven-story hotel modeled after majestic turn-of-the-20th-century lodges of the American Northwest. **Pros:** impressive architecture; boarding point for romantic cruises or free water taxi to Magic Kingdom; elegant dining options; children's activity center. **Cons:** no direct bus to Magic Kingdom. $ *Rooms from: $427* ⊠ *901 Timberline Dr.* ☎ *407/824–3200* ⤳ *727 rooms, 31 suites* ꠵ *No meals* ✛ *2:C2.*

EPCOT RESORT AREA

$$
RESORT ꠵ **Disney's Art of Animation Resort.** This brightly colored three-story value resort is a kid's version of paradise: each of its four wings features images from *Finding Nemo, Cars, The Lion King,* or *The Little Mermaid,* and in-room linens and carpeting match the wing's theme. **Pros:** direct transportation to airport; free parking; images that kids adore; free Wi-Fi. **Cons:** can be crowded; standard rooms fill up fast. $ *Rooms from: $180* ⊠ *1850 Animation Way* ☎ *407/934–7639* ⤳ *1,984 rooms, 1,120 suites* ꠵ *No meals* ✛ *2:E5.*

$$$$
RESORT ꠵ **Disney's Yacht and Beach Club Resorts.** These big Crescent Lake inns next door to Epcot seem straight out of a Cape Cod summer, with their nautical decor, waterfront locale, rocking chair porches, and family-friendly water-based activities. **Pros:** location, location, location—it's easy to walk or hop a ferry to Epcot, the BoardWalk, or Hollywood Studios; free Wi-Fi. **Cons:** distances within the hotel—like from your room to the front desk—can seem vast; high noise factor. $ *Rooms from: $502* ⊠ *1700 Epcot Resorts Blvd.* ☎ *407/934–8000 Beach Club, 407/934–7000 Yacht Club* ⤳ *1,213 rooms, 112 suites* ꠵ *No meals* ✛ *2:D4.*

ANIMAL KINGDOM RESORT AREA

$
RESORT
FAMILY
Fodor's Choice
★ ꠵ **Disney's All-Star Sports, All-Star Music, and All-Star Movies Resorts.** Stay here if you want the quintessential Disney-with-your-kids experience, or if you're a couple that feels all that pitter-pattering of little feet is a reasonable tradeoff for a good deal on a room. **Pros:** unbeatable price for a Disney property. **Cons:** no kids' clubs or programs, possibly because this is on the bottom tier of Disney hotels in terms of room rates; distances between rooms and on-site amenities can seem vast. $ *Rooms from: $152* ⊠ *1701 W. Buena Vista Dr.* ☎ *407/939–5000 Sports, 407/939–6000 Music, 407/939–7000 Movies* ⤳ *1,700 rooms, 215 family suites at Music; 1,920 rooms at Movies and Sports* ꠵ *No meals* ✛ *2:C6.*

$$$$
RESORT
Fodor's Choice
★ ꠵ **Disney's Animal Kingdom Lodge.** Giraffes, zebras, and other wildlife roam three 11-acre savannas separated by the encircling arms of this grand hotel, designed to resemble a "kraal" or animal enclosure in Africa. **Pros:** extraordinary wildlife and cultural experiences; excellent on-site restaurants: Jiko, Boma, and Sanaa. **Cons:** shuttle to parks other than Animal Kingdom can take more than an hour; guided savanna tours available only to guests on the concierge level, where the least expensive room is $100 a night higher than the least expensive rooms in other parts of the hotel. $ *Rooms from: $457* ⊠ *2901 Osceola Pkwy.* ☎ *407/938–3000* ⤳ *972 rooms, 499 suites and villas* ꠵ *No meals* ✛ *2:A5.*

$$ 🛎 **Disney's Coronado Springs Resort.** Popular with convention-goers who
RESORT love the huge meeting spaces, and with families who appreciate its
Fodor's Choice casual Southwestern architecture; lively, Mexican-style food court; and
★ elaborate swimming pool, colorful Coronado Springs Resort also offers
a moderate price. **Pros:** great pool with a play-area arcade for kids
and a bar for adults; lots of outdoor activities, free Wi-Fi. **Cons:** some
accommodations are a long trek from the restaurants; standard rooms
are on the small side; as in many Disney lakefront properties, the lake
is for looking at and boating on, not for swimming in. $\boxed{\$}$ *Rooms from:*
$243 ✉ *1000 W. Buena Vista Dr.* ☎ *407/939–1000* 📞 *1,917 rooms*
🍴 *No meals* ✛ *2:C5.*

DOWNTOWN DISNEY RESORT AREA

$$ 🛎 **Disney's Port Orleans Resort–French Quarter.** Ornate Big Easy–style row
HOTEL houses with wrought iron–clad balconies cluster around magnolia-
shaded squares in this relatively quiet resort, which appeals to couples
more than families. **Pros:** authentic, or as authentic as Disney can make
it, fun, New Orleans–style; moderate price; lots of water recreation
options, including boat rentals; free Wi-Fi. **Cons:** even though there
are fewer kids here, public areas can still be quite noisy; shuttle service
is slow; food court is the only on-site dining option. $\boxed{\$}$ *Rooms from:*
$239 ✉ *1251 Riverside Dr.* ☎ *407/934–5000* 📞 *1,008 rooms* 🍴 *No*
meals ✛ *2:F3.*

$$ 🛎 **Disney's Port Orleans Resort–Riverside.** Buildings in this family-friendly,
RESORT moderately priced resort look like Southern plantation–style mansions
(in the Magnolia Bend section) and rustic bayou dwellings (in the Alli-
gator Bayou section), and you can usually pick which section you want.
Pros: carriage rides; river cruises; lots of recreation options for kids.
Cons: shuttle to parks can be slow; no shortage of extremely noisy
youngsters. $\boxed{\$}$ *Rooms from: $239* ✉ *1251 Riverside Dr.* ☎ *407/934–*
6000 📞 *2,048 rooms* 🍴 *No meals* ✛ *2:F3.*

OTHER ON-SITE DISNEY HOTELS

Although not operated by the Disney organization, the Swan and the
Dolphin, just outside Epcot; Shades of Green, near the Magic Kingdom;
and the hotels along Hotel Plaza Boulevard near Downtown Disney call
themselves "official" Walt Disney World hotels. Whereas the Swan,
Dolphin, and Shades of Green have the special privileges of on-site
Disney hotels, such as free transportation to and from the parks and
early park entry, the Downtown Disney resorts may use Disney trans-
portation, but don't have all the same perks.

EPCOT RESORT AREA
Take I–4 Exit 64B or 65.

$$$ 🛎 **Walt Disney World Dolphin.** A pair of 56-foot-tall sea creatures book-
RESORT end this 25-story glass pyramid, a luxe resort designed, like the adjoin-
ing Swan, by world-renowned architect Michael Graves. **Pros:** access
to all facilities at the Swan; easy walk or boat ride to BoardWalk and
Epcot; excellent on-site restaurants. **Cons:** self-parking is $10 a day;
a daily resort fee covers Wi-Fi and Internet access, use of health club,

and local phone calls; room-charge privileges stop at the front door and don't extend to the Disney parks. $ *Rooms from: $280* ✉ *1500 Epcot Resorts Blvd.* ☎ *407/934–4000, 800/227–1500* ⊕ *www.swandolphin. com* ⤳ *1,509 rooms, 112 suites* ❖❉ *No meals* ✛ *2:D4.*

$$$ 🔲 **Walt Disney World Swan.** With Epcot and Hollywood Studios close by,
RESORT   guests here can hit the parks in the morning, return for a swim or nap on a hot afternoon, and go back to the parks refreshed and ready to play until the fireworks. **Pros:** charge privileges and access to all facilities at the Dolphin (but not inside Disney World); easy walk to BoardWalk; free boats to BoardWalk and Epcot; good on-site restaurants. **Cons:** long bus ride to Magic Kingdom; daily resort fee. $ *Rooms from: $294* ✉ *1200 Epcot Resorts Blvd.* ☎ *407/934–3000, 800/325–3535* ⊕ *www. swandolphin.com* ⤳ *756 rooms, 55 suites* ❖❉ *No meals* ✛ *2:D4.*

DOWNTOWN DISNEY RESORT AREA
Take I–4 Exit 68.

$$ 🔲 **Best Western Lake Buena Vista Resort.** Only a few minutes' walk from
RESORT   Downtown Disney, this resort offers luxury linens, flat-screen TVs, free
Fodor's Choice   Wi-Fi and parking, and, in many rooms, a bird's-eye view of the nightly
★   Disney World fireworks. **Pros:** free Wi-Fi and parking, not to mention no resort fee, make this one of the best bargains on Hotel Row; close to Downtown Disney. **Cons:** inconvenient to Universal and Downtown Orlando; transportation to the parks can eat up time. $ *Rooms from: $199* ✉ *2000 Hotel Plaza Blvd.* ☎ *407/828–2424, 800/348–3765* ⊕ *www. lakebuenavistaresorthotel.com* ⤳ *325 rooms* ❖❉ *No meals* ✛ *2:G3.*

$ 🔲 **Buena Vista Palace Hotel & Spa.** This large and amenity-filled hotel
RESORT   caters to business and leisure guests and gets kudos as much for its on-site charms as for its location, just yards from Downtown Disney. **Pros:** easy walk to Downtown Disney; good restaurants and bars on-site; kids' activities; pool is heated; spa is large and luxurious. **Cons:** inconvenient to Universal and Downtown Orlando; daily resort fee for Wi-Fi and fitness center. $ *Rooms from: $158* ✉ *1900 E. Buena Vista Dr.* ☎ *407/827–2727* ⊕ *www.buenavistapalace.com* ⤳ *1,014 rooms* ❖❉ *No meals* ✛ *2:G4.*

$$ 🔲 **DoubleTree Suites by Hilton in the WDW Resort.** Price and location make
HOTEL   this all-suites, Hilton-owned hotel a good choice for families and business travelers, as there are amenities for both, and it's a quick, free bus ride to any of the Disney parks. **Pros:** family and business traveler amenities; separate pools for kids, adults; free shuttle to Disney attractions; quick access to I–4. **Cons:** of the properties on Hotel Plaza Boulevard, this is the farthest away from Downtown Disney; inconvenient to Universal and Downtown Orlando; daily fee for parking, Wi-Fi. $ *Rooms from: $246* ✉ *2305 Hotel Plaza Blvd.* ☎ *407/934–1000, 800/222–8733* ⊕ *www.doubletreeguestsuites.com* ⤳ *229 units* ❖❉ *No meals* ✛ *2:G4.*

UNIVERSAL ORLANDO AREA
Universal Orlando's on-site hotels were built in a little luxury enclave that has everything you need, so you never have to leave Universal property. In minutes, you can walk from any hotel to CityWalk, Universal's dining and entertainment district, or take a ferry that cruises the adjacent artificial river.

Early in 2014, Universal is scheduled to open Cabana Bay Beach Resort, with 900 family suites and 900 standard rooms adjacent to Islands of Adventure and its popular Harry Potter attraction. The more affordable, motor court–style resort was designed to evoke 20th-century driving vacations with a hip, retro look.

$$ HOTEL **DoubleTree by Hilton at the Entrance to Universal Orlando.** The name is a mouthful, but it's an accurate description for this hotel, which caters to business-trippers and pleasure seekers alike, thanks to a location right at the Universal Orlando entrance and not far from the Convention Center. **Pros:** three on-site restaurants; within walking distance of Universal, shops, and restaurants; free shuttle to Universal; on I-Drive trolley route. **Cons:** fee for parking; on a fast-lane tourist strip; need a car to reach Disney and Downtown Orlando. [$] *Rooms from: $190* ✉ *5780 Major Blvd.* ☎ *407/351–1000, 800/327–2110* 🌐 *www.doubltreeorlando.com* 🛏 *742 rooms, 19 suites* 🍴 *No meals* ✣ *1:D3.*

$$$$ HOTEL **Hard Rock Hotel.** Music rules in this California Mission–style building, where guests can pretend they are rock stars as their hotel key card lets them skip the lines at Universal and grants early admission to Islands of Adventure's Wizarding World of Harry Potter. **Pros:** shuttle, water taxi, or short walk to Universal and CityWalk; preferential treatment at Universal rides; charge privileges extend to the other on-property Universal hotels. **Cons:** rooms and meals are pricey; steep fees for parking, gym, and in-room Wi-Fi; loud rock music in public areas, even the pool, but that's why you're here, right? [$] *Rooms from: $392* ✉ *5800 Universal Blvd.* ☎ *407/503–7625, 800/232–7827* 🌐 *www.hardrockhotelorlando.com* 🛏 *621 rooms, 29 suites* 🍴 *No meals* ✣ *1:D3.*

$$$$ HOTEL Fodor's Choice ★ **Loews Portofino Bay Hotel at Universal Orlando.** The charm and romance of Portofino, Italy—destination of Europe's rich and famous—are conjured up at this lovely luxury resort, whose 2013 renovation brought cool modern decor in aqua and cream, a spiffed-up exterior, and new beds, furniture, and TVs. **Pros:** Italian villa atmosphere; large spa; short walk or ferry ride to CityWalk, Universal Studios, and Islands of Adventure; guests skip lines at Universal rides; kids' activities; shuttles to SeaWorld. **Cons:** rooms and meals are pricey; daily fee for in-room high-speed Internet or Wi-Fi as well as for parking. [$] *Rooms from: $369* ✉ *5601 Universal Blvd.* ☎ *407/503–1000, 800/232–7827* 🌐 *www.loewshotels.com/Portofino-Bay-Hotel* 🛏 *750 rooms, 49 suites* 🍴 *Breakfast* ✣ *1:D3.*

$$$ RESORT Fodor's Choice ★ **Loews Royal Pacific Resort at Universal Orlando.** The entrance—a broad, covered footbridge high above a tropical stream—sets the tone for the Pacific Rim theme of this hotel, which lies amid 53 acres of lush shrubs, soaring bamboo, orchids, and palms. **Pros:** preferential treatment at Universal rides; early admission to Islands of Adventure (Wizarding World of Harry Potter); serene, Zen garden vibe. **Cons:** rooms can feel cramped; steep fees for in-room Internet access, fitness center, and parking are unwarranted, given rates. [$] *Rooms from: $342* ✉ *6300 Hollywood Way* ☎ *407/503–3000, 800/232–7827* 🌐 *www.universalorlando.com* 🛏 *1,000 rooms, 113 suites* 🍴 *No meals* ✣ *1:D3.*

9

BEST BETS FOR
ORLANDO AND THE PARKS LODGING

With thousands of hotels to choose from, ask yourself first what your family truly wants to do in Orlando during your visit. This invariably leads to an on-property versus off-property debate, and more questions. To assist you, here are our top recommendations by price (any property listed here has at least some rooms in the noted range) and experience. The very best properties—those that provide a particularly remarkable experience in their price range—are designated in the listings with the Fodor's Choice logo.

By Experience

BEST BUDGET

Art of Animation Resort, p. 522

Best Western Lake Buena Vista, p. 524

BEST POOLS

Hyatt Regency Grand Cypress Resort, p. 528

JW Marriott Orlando Grande Lakes, p. 527

Loews Portofino Bay Hotel at Universal Orlando, p. 525

Ritz-Carlton Orlando Grande Lakes, p. 527

MOST KID-FRIENDLY

Disney's All-Star Resorts, p. 522

Disney's Contemporary Resort, p. 521

Nickelodeon Suites Resort, p. 528

Fodor's Choice ★

Best Western Lake Buena Vista Resort, p. 524

Disney's All-Star Resorts, p. 522

Disney's Animal Kingdom Lodge, p. 522

Disney's Coronado Springs Resort, p. 523

Disney's Grand Floridian Resort & Spa, p. 521

Hyatt Regency Grand Cypress Resort, p. 528

Loews Portofino Bay Hotel at Universal Orlando, p. 525

Loews Royal Pacific Resort at Universal Orlando, p. 525

Meliá Orlando Suite Hotel at Celebration, p. 527

Nickelodeon Suites Resort, p. 528

Ritz-Carlton Orlando Grande Lakes, p. 527

Waldorf Astoria Orlando, p. 528

By Price

$

Disney's All-Star Resorts, p. 522

$$

Best Western Lake Buena Vista Resort, p. 524

Disney's Art of Animation Resort, p. 522

Disney's Coronado Springs Resort, p. 523

Meliá Orlando Suite Hotel at Celebration, p. 527

Nickelodeon Suites Resort, p. 528

$$$

Hyatt Regency Grand Cypress Resort, p. 528

Loews Royal Pacific Resort at Universal Orlando, p. 525

$$$$

Disney's Animal Kingdom Lodge, p. 522

Disney's Grand Floridian Resort & Spa, p. 521

Loews Portofino Bay Hotel at Universal Orlando, p. 525

Ritz-Carlton Orlando Grande Lakes, p. 527

Waldorf Astoria Orlando, p. 528

ORLANDO METRO AREA

KISSIMMEE, CELEBRATION, AND POINTS SOUTH

$$$
RESORT
🖫 **Gaylord Palms Resort.** Built in the style of a grand turn-of-the-20th-century Florida mansion, this resort is meant to inspire awe: inside its enormous atrium, covered by a 4-acre glass roof, are re-creations of Florida destination icons such as the Everglades, Key West, and old St. **Pros:** you could have a great vacation without ever leaving the grounds; free shuttle to Disney. **Cons:** daily resort fee; rooms can be pricey; not much within walking distance (although the hotel is so big that you can take quite a hike inside the building); shuttles to Universal and Sea-World are available for a fee. $ *Rooms from: $259* ✉ *6000 W. Osceola Pkwy., I–4 Exit 65, Kissimmee* ☎ *407/586–0000* ⊕ *www.gaylordpalms. com* ⤳ *1,406 rooms, 86 suites* ❍ *No meals* ✛ *2:F6.*

$$
HOTEL
Fodor's Choice
★
🖫 **Meliá Orlando Suite Hotel at Celebration.** Much like a European boutique hotel in style and service, the Meliá Orlando is very human in scale and crisply minimalist in decor. **Pros:** shuttle to Celebration, Disney parks, Universal, and SeaWorld; golf privileges at Celebration Golf; spa privileges at Celebration Day Spa. **Cons:** busy U.S. 192 is close by; daily resort fee; need a car to go anywhere besides Celebration and the parks. $ *Rooms from: $229* ✉ *225 Celebration Pl., Celebration* ☎ *866/404–6662, 407/964–7000* ⊕ *www.solmelia.com* ⤳ *240 suites* ❍ *Breakfast* ✛ *1:B6.*

INTERNATIONAL DRIVE

$$$$
RESORT
🖫 **Peabody Orlando.** This deluxe, high-rise conference hotel offers anything a full-service resort customer could want, with richly appointed rooms, two pools with cabanas, a comprehensive spa and health center the size of your local Y, two large restaurants, and a 360-seat glass-walled lounge overlooking the pool. **Pros:** no resort fee; good spa; close to shops and more restaurants. **Cons:** pricey; check-in can take a while if a convention is arriving; long walk from end to end, so wear comfy shoes. $ *Rooms from: $400* ✉ *9801 International Dr.* ☎ *407/352–4000, 800/732–2639* ⊕ *www.peabodyorlando.com* ⤳ *1,641 rooms, 193 suites, 5 penthouse suites* ❍ *No meals* ✛ *1:D4.*

SOUTH ORLANDO

$$$
RESORT
🖫 **JW Marriott Orlando Grande Lakes.** With more than 70,000 square feet of meeting space, this hotel caters to a convention clientele, but it also has a European-style spa, a Greg Norman–designed golf course, and a lazy river–style pool complex, giving this lush resort family and leisure appeal. **Pros:** pool is great for kids and adults; shares amenities with the Ritz, including huge spa; golf course; free shuttle to SeaWorld and Universal. **Cons:** fees for parking and in-room Wi-Fi; things are spread out on the grounds; need a car to reach Disney or shopping. $ *Rooms from: $339* ✉ *4040 Central Florida Pkwy.* ☎ *407/206–2300, 800/576–5750* ⊕ *www.grandelakes.com* ⤳ *1,000 rooms, 64 suites* ❍ *Multiple meal plans* ✛ *1:E4.*

$$$$
RESORT
Fodor's Choice
★
🖫 **Ritz-Carlton Orlando Grande Lakes.** Orlando's only Ritz-Carlton is a particularly extravagant link in the luxury chain, with exemplary service that extends from the porte-cochere entrance to the 18-hole golf course, restaurants, children's programs, and 40-room spa. **Pros:** truly luxurious; impeccable service; great spa; golf course; shares amenities

9

with Marriott. **Cons:** pricey; need a car to reach theme parks, area shops, and restaurants. $ *Rooms from: $369* ✉ *4012 Central Florida Pkwy.* ☎ *407/206–2400, 800/576–5760* ⊕ *www.ritzcarlton.com* ⇥ *581 rooms, 64 suites* ¶◎¶ *Multiple meal plans* ✦ *1:E4.*

LAKE BUENA VISTA

$$$
RESORT
Fodor'sChoice
★

Hyatt Regency Grand Cypress Resort. Sitting amid 1,500 palm-filled acres just outside Disney's back gate, this huge luxury resort hotel has a private lake with watercraft, three golf courses, and miles of trails for strolling, bicycling, jogging, and horseback riding. **Pros:** huge pool; lots of recreation options, for kids and adults, including equestrian center; free Wi-Fi. **Cons:** need a car or taxi to get to Downtown Orlando; steep resort fee. $ *Rooms from: $275* ✉ *1 Grand Cypress Blvd.* ☎ *407/239–1234, 800/233–1234* ⊕ *www.hyattgrandcypress.com* ⇥ *815 rooms* ¶◎¶ *No meals* ✦ *2:G3.*

$$
RESORT
FAMILY
Fodor'sChoice
★

Nickelodeon Suites Resort. This 24-acre Nickelodeon-themed resort is so kid-friendly that you can barely take a step without bumping into images of SpongeBob, Dora the Explorer, Jimmy Neutron, or other Nick characters. **Pros:** extremely kid-friendly; Disney, Universal, and SeaWorld shuttles included in resort fee; discounts (up to 50% off standard rates) for active-duty military; mini-golf course. **Cons:** daily resort fee of $30; not within walking distance of Disney or Downtown Disney; way too frenetic for folks without kids. $ *Rooms from: $246* ✉ *14500 Continental Gateway* ☎ *407/387–5437, 866/462–6425* ⊕ *www.nickhotel.com* ⇥ *777 suites* ¶◎¶ *No meals* ✦ *2:G5.*

$$$$
RESORT
Fodor'sChoice
★

Waldorf Astoria Orlando. While it doesn't duplicate the famed Waldorf Astoria Hotel in New York, this Waldorf echoes the original with imagination and flair, from the iconic clock in the center of the circular lobby to tiny, black-and-white accent tiles on guest room floors. **Pros:** lavish and luxurious hotel with spa and golf, next to Disney; free transportation to Disney parks. **Cons:** pricey, but you knew that; if you can bear to leave your cabana, you'll need a car to see anything else in the area; steep daily resort fee. $ *Rooms from: $450* ✉ *14200 Bonnet Creek Resort La., Bonnet Creek* ☎ *407/597–5500* ⊕ *www.waldorfastoriaorlando.com* ⇥ *328 rooms, 169 suites* ¶◎¶ *Breakfast* ✦ *2:F5.*

CENTRAL ORLANDO

$$$
HOTEL

Grand Bohemian Hotel. Decorated in a sophisticated and eclectic "Bohemian" style, this European-style property is Downtown Orlando's only Four Diamond luxury hotel. **Pros:** art gallery; quiet, adult-friendly atmosphere; great restaurant; sophisticated entertainment; short walk to Amway Center, arts center, and Downtown restaurants and clubs. **Cons:** kids may find it boring; meals are pricey. $ *Rooms from: $339* ✉ *325 S. Orange Ave., Downtown Orlando* ☎ *407/313–9000, 866/663–0024* ⊕ *www.grandbohemianhotel.com* ⇥ *212 rooms, 35 suites* ¶◎¶ *No meals* ✦ *1:F2.*

Beloved music club The Social is the heart of Downtown Orlando's nightlife scene—appropriate given its location on Orange Avenue, the main nightlife artery.

NIGHTLIFE

Updated by
Jennie Hess

Outside of Downtown Disney and Universal's CityWalk, the focal point of Orlando nightlife is Downtown. If you stand on the corner of Orange Avenue and Church Street long enough, you can watch all types of gussied-up reveler walk by. The bars and clubs here hop even after the 2 am last call.

CENTRAL ORLANDO

BARS

Sky Sixty. You have to head up to the roof using the side staircase of the Social nightclub to reach this breezy hot spot. The great view of busy Orange Avenue is accompanied by dance-friendly DJ beats and cool mojitos. Score a cozy cabana seat for prime people-watching. Sunday Funday features mimosa and other drink discounts. ⊠ *60 N. Orange Ave., Downtown Orlando* ☎ *407/246–1599* ⊘ *Thurs.–Sat. 10 pm–2 am, Sun. 5–11.*

Wally's. One of Orlando's oldest bars (circa 1954), this longtime local favorite is a hangout for a cross section of cultures and ages. Some would say it's a dive, but that doesn't matter to the students, bikers, lawyers, and barflies who land here to drink surrounded by the go-go-dancer wallpaper and '60s-era interior. Just grab a stool at the bar to take in the scene and down a cold one. ⊠ *1001 N. Mills Ave., Downtown Orlando* ☎ *407/896–6975* ⊕ *www.wallysonmills.com* ⊘ *Mon.–Sat. 7:30 am–2 am.*

MUSIC CLUBS

Firestone Live. Based in an old automotive repair shop, this multilevel, high-energy club draws international music acts. Something's always going on to make the crowd hop: DJ mixes, big band, jazz, hip-hop, rock. Often the dance floor is more like semicontrolled chaos than a place to just listen, so be prepared. Hours and prices vary by event; check the website. ✉ *578 N. Orange Ave., Downtown Orlando* ☎ *407/872–0066* ⊕ *www.firestonelive.net.*

Fodor's Choice ★ **The Social.** Beloved by locals, the Social is a great place to see touring and area musicians. Up to seven nights a week you can sip trademark martinis while listening to anything from indie rock to rockabilly to undiluted jazz. Several now-national acts got their start here, including Matchbox Twenty, Seven Mary Three, and other groups that don't have numbers in their names. Hours vary. ✉ *54 N. Orange Ave., Downtown Orlando* ☎ *407/246–1419* ⊕ *www.thesocial.org* 🍴 *$5–$30, depending on entertainment.*

INTERNATIONAL DRIVE AREA

MUSIC CLUB

B.B. King's Blues Club. The blues great was doing quite well as a musician before becoming a successful entrepreneur, with blues clubs in Memphis, Nashville, Las Vegas, and West Palm Beach as well as Orlando. Like the others, this club has music at its heart. There's a dance floor and stage for live performances by the B.B. King All-Star Band or visiting musicians. You can't really experience Delta blues without Delta dining, so the club doubles as a restaurant with fried dill pickles, catfish bites, po'boys, ribs, and other comfort foods. Oh, yeah, and there's a full bar. ✉ *Pointe Orlando, 9101 International Dr., I-Drive area* ☎ *407/370–4550* ⊕ *www.bbkingclubs.com* ⊗ *Fri. and Sat. 11 am–2 am, Sun.–Thurs. 11–midnight.*

NIGHTCLUBS

ICEBAR. Thanks to the miracle of refrigeration, this is Orlando's coolest bar—literally and figuratively. Fifty tons of pure ice is kept at a constant 27°F and has been cut and sculpted by world-class carvers into a cozy (or as cozy as ice can be) sanctuary of tables, sofas, chairs, and a bar. The staff loans you a thermal cape and gloves (upgrade to a fur coat for $10), and when you enter the frozen hall your drink is served in a glass made of crystal-clear ice. There's no cover charge if you just want to hang out in the Fire Lounge or outdoor Polar Patio, but you will pay $19.95 to spend as much time as you can handle in the subfreezing ICEBAR. There's no beer or wine inside; it's simply too cold. ✉ *Pointe Orlando, 8967 International Dr., I-Drive area* ☎ *407/426–7555* ⊕ *www.icebarorlando.com* ⊗ *Fri. and Sat. 7 pm–2 am, Sun.–Wed. 7–midnight, Thurs. 7–1.*

SPORTS AND THE OUTDOORS

Updated by
Jennie Hess

There are many ways to enjoy the outdoors here. You can navigate the more than 2,000 lakes and waterways, perhaps on a sportfishing excursion—something to consider in what is one of the bass-fishing capitals of the world. You can also take to the air in a glider or hot-air balloon, or stay firmly planted hiking or biking a trail.

BALLOONING

Fodor's Choice
★

Bob's Balloons. Bob's offers one-hour rides over protected marshland and even flies over the Disney area if wind and weather conditions are right. You meet at Champions Gate, near Disney World, at dawn, where Bob and his assistant take you by van to the launch site. It takes about 15 minutes to get the balloon in the air, and then you're off on an adventure that definitely surpasses Peter Pan's Flight in the Magic Kingdom.

You'll see farm and forest land for miles, along with horses, deer, wild boar, cattle, and birds flying *below* you. Bob may take you as high as 1,000 feet, and you may be able to see such landmarks as the Animal Kingdom's Expedition Everest mountain and Epcot's Spaceship Earth sphere. Several other balloons are likely to go up near you—there's a tight-knit community of ballooners in the Orlando area—so you'll view these colorful sky ornaments from an unparalleled sightline. There are seats in the basket, but you'll probably be too thrilled to sit down. Check the website for specials and call Bob to reserve. ☎ 407/466–6380, 877/824–4606 ⊕ www.bobsballoons.com ☞ $175 per person.

GOLF

If golf is your passion, you already know that Arnold Palmer and Gary Player—in fact, almost half of the PGA tour—make Orlando their off-road home. It's not by accident that the Golf Channel originates from here. The Bay Hill Invitational and several LPGA tourneys (the headquarters is in Daytona) come to Orlando every year. And with more than 80 public and private courses, there's ample opportunity for you to play on world-class courses such as Grand Cypress or Champions Gate.

MINIATURE GOLF

FAMILY
Fodor's Choice
★

Hawaiian Rumble Adventure Golf. Who can resist golfing around an erupting volcano? Hawaiian Rumble combines a tropical setting with waterfalls, tunnels, tiki gods, and flame-belching mountains. There's also a location in the Lake Buena Vista area. ⊠ 8969 International Dr., I-Drive area ☎ 407/351–7733 ⊕ www.hawaiianrumbleorlando.com ☞ $9.95–$11.95 ⊙ Sun.–Thurs. 9 am–11:30 pm, Fri. and Sat. 9 am–midnight.

FAMILY

Pirate's Cove Adventure Golf. Two 18-hole courses wind around artificial mountains, through caves, and into lush foliage. The beginner's course is called Captain Kidd's Adventure; the more advanced course is Blackbeard's Challenge. There's another Pirate's Cove on International Drive. ⊠ 12545 State Rd. 535, Lake Buena Vista ☎ 407/827–1242 ⊕ www.piratescove.net ☞ $10.45–$14.95 ⊙ Daily 9 am–11 pm.

9

SKYDIVING

Fodor's Choice ★ **iFLY Orlando.** OK, you technically aren't skydiving, but you come pretty close in a 12-foot-high, 1,000-horsepower wind tunnel that lets you experience everything skydivers do, but closer to the ground. The experience starts with instruction, after which you suit up and hit the wind tunnel, where you soar like a bird under your instructor's watchful eye. It's all so realistic that skydiving clubs come to hone their skills. The attraction is safe for anyone under 250 pounds and older than 3. You can purchase a video of your "jump" for $24.95. ⊠ *6805 Visitors Circle, I-Drive area* ☎ *407/903–1150* ⊕ *www.skyventureorlando.com* ☎ *$59.95 and up, depending on package* ☉ *Daily 10–10.*

SHOPPING

Updated by
Jennie Hess

Visitors from as far away as Britain and Brazil often arrive in Orlando with empty suitcases for their purchases. Although shopping has all but disappeared from Downtown, the metro area is filled with options. There really is something for everyone—from high-end fashion to outlet-mall chic, from the world's largest flea market to a boutique-filled town, from an antique treasure to a hand-hewn Florida find.

The east end of the Lake Ivanhoe area of College Park is an antique fan's dream, with more than a dozen small shops (including an antiques store–restaurant) running south from Princeton Street along North Orange Avenue.

The simultaneously glitzy and kitschy International Drive has almost 500 designer outlet stores and odd, off-brand electronics shops. The factory outlets on the north end of the Drive once consisted of shops with merchandise piled on tables; today the shops here are equal to their higher-priced first-run cousins. The strip also has plenty of restaurants and, for those in your group who don't feel like shopping, movie theaters.

CENTRAL ORLANDO

MALLS

Fodor's Choice ★ **Mall at Millenia.** "Deluxe" is the word for this mall, a high-end collection of designer shops, including Gucci, Burberry, Chanel, Jimmy Choo, Hugo Boss, Cartier, Tiffany, and Ferragamo. You'll also find Neiman Marcus, Bloomingdale's, and an Apple store, but the biggest attraction may be the adjacent IKEA. A few minutes northeast of Universal, the mall is easy to reach via Interstate 4 Exit 78. ⊠ *4200 Conroy Rd., South Orlando* ☎ *407/363–3555* ⊕ *www.mallatmillenia.com* ☉ *Mon.–Sat. 10–9, Sun. 11–7.*

INTERNATIONAL DRIVE AREA

MALLS

Pointe Orlando. What was once an enclosed shopping center is now a dining, shopping, and entertainment hot spot—one that's within walking distance of five top hotels and the Orange County Convention Center. In addition to WonderWorks and the enormous Regal IMAX theater, the complex has specialty shops such as Armani Exchange, Tommy Bahama, Chico's, Tommy Hilfiger, Hollister, Charming Charlie, and Victoria's Secret. Restaurants have become a reason to visit, with the very high-end Capital Grille, the Oceanaire Seafood Room, Cuba Libre Restaurant and Rum Bar, The Pub, Marlow's Tavern, the popular Funky Monkey Wine Company, B.B. King's Blues Club, and Taverna Opa. Parking ($3 for 15 minutes–two hours, $6 daily) can be validated by the movie theater and many of the restaurants. ⊠ *9101 International Dr., I-Drive area* ☎ *407/248–2838* ⊕ *www.pointeorlando.com* ⊗ *Mon.–Sat. noon–10, Sun. noon–8; restaurant hrs vary.*

FACTORY OUTLETS

Orlando Premium Outlets International Drive. This is a prime destination for international shoppers who can find shoes, clothing, cosmetics, electronics, and household goods at a fraction of their home-country prices. The massive complex at the north tip of International Drive includes Saks Fifth Avenue OFF 5TH, Coach, Kate Spade New York, Victoria's Secret Outlet, and a Disney outlet. Searching for bargains works up an appetite, and there are plenty of places to eat here, either in the well-lit food court or in one of several sit-down and highly regarded restaurants. ⊠ *4951 International Dr., I-Drive area* ☎ *407/352–9600* ⊕ *www. primeoutlets.com* ⊗ *Mon.–Sat. 10 am–11 pm, Sun. 10–9.*

Orlando Premium Outlets Vineland Avenue. This outlet capitalizes on its proximity to Disney (it's at the confluence of Interstate 4, State Road 535, and International Drive). It's easier to see from the highway than to enter, and parking is tedious and scarce, but smart shoppers have lunch on International Drive and take the I-Ride Trolley right to the front entrance (it runs every 15 minutes). The center's design makes this almost an open-air market, so walking can be pleasant on a nice day. You'll find Prada, Gap, Nike, Adidas, Tory Burch, Polo Ralph Lauren, Giorgio Armani, Burberry, Tommy Hilfiger, Reebok, and about 100 other stores. ⊠ *8200 Vineland Ave., I-Drive area* ☎ *407/238–7787* ⊕ *www.premiumoutlets. com/orlando* ⊗ *Mon.–Sat. 10 am–11 pm, Sun. 10–9.*

WALT DISNEY
WORLD

WELCOME TO WALT DISNEY WORLD

TOP REASONS TO GO

★ **Nostalgia:** Face it— Mickey and Company are old friends. And you probably have childhood pictures of yourself in front of Cinderella Castle. Even if you don't, nobody does yesteryear better: head to Main Street, U.S.A., or Hollywood Boulevard and see.

★ **Memories in the Making:** Who doesn't want to snap photos of Sis on the Dumbo ride or of Junior after his Splash Mountain experience? The urge to pass that Disney nostalgia on to the next generation is strong.

★ **The Thrills:** For some this means roller coasting to an Aerosmith soundtrack or simulating space flight; for others it's about cascading down a waterslide or going on safari.

★ **The Chills:** If the Pirates of the Caribbean cave doesn't give you goose bumps, try the Haunted Mansion or Twilight Zone Tower of Terror.

★ **The Spectacle:** The list is long—fireworks, laser-light displays, arcade games, parades . . .

1 Magic Kingdom. Disney's emblematic park is home to Space Mountain, Pirates of the Caribbean, and an expanded Fantasyland full of new experiences.

2 Epcot. Future World's focus is science, technology, and hands-on experiences. In the World Showcase, you can tour 11 countries without getting jet-lagged.

3 Disney's Hollywood Studios. Attractions at this re-creation of old-time Hollywood include Rock 'n' Roller Coaster Starring Aerosmith and Twilight Zone Tower of Terror.

4 Disney's Animal Kingdom. Amid a 403-acre wildlife preserve are an Asian-themed water ride, an African safari ride, a runaway train coaster, and shows.

5 Blizzard Beach. Water thrills range from steep flume rides to tubing expeditions in the midst of a park that you'd swear is a slowly melting ski resort. There's plenty for little ones, too.

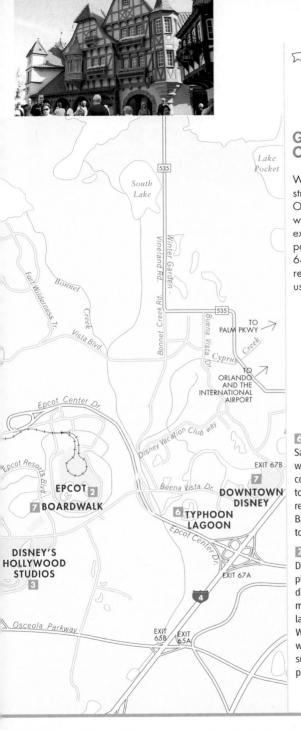

GETTING ORIENTED

Walt Disney World straddles Orange and Osceola counties to the west of Interstate 4. Four exits will get you to the parks and resort areas: 64B, 65, 67, and 68. To reach hotels along I-Drive, use Exit 72, 74A, or 75A.

6 Typhoon Lagoon.
Sandy beaches, oceanlike waves, and a themed water coaster invite castaways to enjoy a day of fun and relaxation. Take the kids on Bay Slides and don snorkels to explore Shark Reef.

7 Disney's Other Worlds.
Downtown Disney is the place to go for shopping, dining, and great entertainment from morning through late night. Disney's Board-Walk is a nostalgia trip, with bicycles built for two, surreys with a fringe on top, pizza, bars, and a dance hall.

10

Updated by
Jennie Hess

Mickey Mouse. Tinker Bell. Cinderella. What would childhood be like without the magic of Disney? When kids and adults want to go to *the* theme park, they're heading to Disney. Here you're walking amid people from around the world and meeting characters like Snow White and Donald Duck while rides whirl nonstop and the irrepressible "It's a Small World" tune and lyrics run through your head. You can't help but believe dreams really do come true here.

The **Magic Kingdom** is the heart and soul of the Walt Disney World empire. It was the first Disney outpost in Florida when it opened in 1971, and it's the park that launched Disney's presence in France, Japan, and Hong Kong. For a landmark that wields such worldwide influence, the 142-acre Magic Kingdom may seem small—indeed, Epcot is more than double the size of the Magic Kingdom, and Animal Kingdom is almost triple the size when including the park's expansive animal habitats. But looks can be deceiving. Packed into six different "lands" are nearly 50 major crowd pleasers, and that's not counting all the ancillary attractions: shops, eateries, live entertainment, character meet-and-greet spots, fireworks shows, and parades.

Nowhere but at **Epcot** can you explore and experience the native food, entertainment, culture, and arts and crafts of countries in Europe, Asia, North Africa, and the Americas. What's more, employees at the World Showcase pavilions actually hail from the countries the pavilions represent.

Epcot, or "Experimental Prototype Community of Tomorrow," was the original inspiration for Walt Disney World. Walt envisioned a future in which nations coexisted in peace and harmony, reaping the miraculous harvest of technological achievement. The Epcot of today is both more and less than his original dream. Less, because the World Showcase presents views of its countries that are, as an Epcot guide once put it, "as Americans perceive them"—highly idealized. But this is a minor quibble in the face of the major achievement: Epcot is that rare paradox—a successful educational theme park that excels at entertainment, too.

Disney's Hollywood Studios were designed to be a trip back to Tinseltown's golden age, when Hedda Hopper, not tabloids, spread celebrity gossip and when the girl off the bus from Ohio could be the next Judy Garland.

The result is a theme park that blends movie-production capabilities and high-tech wonders with breathtaking rides and nostalgia. The park's old-time Hollywood atmosphere begins with a rosy-hued view of the moviemaking business presented in a dreamy stage set from the 1930s and '40s, amid sleek art moderne buildings in pastel colors, funky diners, kitschy decorations, and sculptured gardens populated by roving actors playing, well, roving actors. There are also casting directors, gossip columnists, and other colorful characters.

Thanks to a rich library of film scores, the park is permeated with music, all familiar, all evoking the magic of the movies, and all constantly streaming from the camouflaged loudspeakers at a volume just right for humming along. The park icon, a 122-foot-high Sorcerer Mickey Hat that serves as a gift shop and Disney pin-trading station, towers over Hollywood Boulevard.

Disney's Animal Kingdom explores the stories of all animals—real, imaginary, and extinct. Enter through the Oasis, where you hear exotic background music and find yourself surrounded by gentle waterfalls and gardens alive with exotic birds, reptiles, and mammals.

At 403 acres and several times the size of the Magic Kingdom, Animal Kingdom is the largest in area of all Disney theme parks. Animal habitats take up much of that acreage. Creatures here thrive in careful re-creations of landscapes from Asia and Africa. Throughout the park, you'll also learn about conservation in a low-key way.

Amid all the nature are thrill rides, a 3-D show (housed in the "root system" of the iconic Tree of Life), two first-rate musicals, and character meet and greets. Cast members are as likely to hail from Kenya or South Africa as they are from Kentucky or South Carolina. It's all part of the charm. New park areas based on the movie *Avatar* are expected to open in 2015, a fitting addition since the film's theme of living in harmony with nature reflects the park's eco-philosophy.

10

Typhoon Lagoon and **Blizzard Beach** are two of the world's best water parks. What sets them apart? It's the same thing that differentiates all Disney parks—the detailed themes. Whether you're cast away on a balmy island at Typhoon Lagoon or washed up on a ski resort–turned–seaside playground at Blizzard Beach, the landscaping and clever architecture will add to the fun of flume and raft rides, wave pools, and splash areas. Another plus: The vegetation has matured enough to create shade. The Disney water parks give you that lost-in-paradise feeling on top of all those high-speed, wedgie-inducing waterslides. They're so popular that crowds often reach overflow capacity in summer. If you're going to Disney for five days or more between April and October, add the Water Park Fun & More option to your Magic Your Way ticket.

PLANNING

ADMISSION

At the gate, the per-person, per-day price is $89 for adults (ages 10 and older) and $83 for children (ages 3–9). You can buy tickets at the Ticket and Transportation Center (TTC) in the Magic Kingdom, from booths at other park entrances, in all on-site resorts if you're a guest, at the Disney store in the airport, and at various other sites around Orlando. You can also buy them in advance online—the best way to save time and money.

If you opt for a multiday ticket, you'll be issued a nontransferable pass that uses your fingerprint for ID. Slide your pass through the reader, just like people with single-day tickets, and also slip your finger into the V-shaped reader. A new option, the MyMagic+ wristband, serves as park ticket, attraction Fastpass, and even hotel room key.

OPERATING HOURS

Walt Disney World operates 365 days a year. Opening and closing times vary by park and by season, with the longest hours during prime summer months and year-end holidays. The parking lots open at least an hour before the parks do.

In general, openings hover around 9 am, though certain attractions might not start up till 10 or 11 am. Closings range between 5 and 8 pm in the off-season and between 8 and 10, 11, or even midnight in high season. Downtown Disney and BoardWalk shops stay open as late as 11 pm.

EXTRA MAGIC HOURS

The Extra Magic Hours program gives Disney resort guests free early and late-night admission to certain parks on specified days—check ahead (⊕ *www.disneyworld.disney.go.com/calendars*) for information about each park's "magic hours" days to plan your early- and late-visit strategies.

PARKING AND IN-PARK TRANSPORT

Parking at Disney parks is free to resort guests; all others pay $14 for cars and $15 for RVs and campers. Parking is free for everyone at Typhoon Lagoon, Blizzard Beach, Downtown Disney, and the Board-Walk. Trams take you between the theme-park lots (*note your parking location!*) and turnstiles. Disney's buses, boats, and monorails whisk you from resort to park and park to park. If you're staying on Disney property, you can use this system exclusively. Either take a Disney bus or drive to Typhoon Lagoon and Blizzard Beach. Once inside the water parks, you can walk, swim, slide, or chill out. Allow up to an hour for travel between parks and hotels on Disney transportation.

FASTPASS

Fastpass helps you avoid lines, and it's included in regular park admission. Insert your theme-park ticket into the machines near several attractions. Out comes your Fastpass, printed with a one-hour window of time during which you can return to get into the fast line. *Don't forget to take your park ticket back, too.* You can't make a Fastpass appointment for another attraction until you're within the window of time for your first appointment. It's best to make appointments only for the most popular attractions and to make new ones as soon as existing ones mature. Strategy is everything.

Disney has recently expanded the Fastpass program to allow park guests to reserve Fastpasses in advance—in fact, before they even enter the parks. The technology is slated to become available just as we go to press, so we don't have as many details as we'd like, but what we do know is this: (1) Guests can prebook a limited number of Fastpasses so you need to use them strategically. (2) Fastpasses can be reserved through the app My Disney Experience or online. (3) For the first time, guests can get Fastpasses for some designated character greetings, parades, and shows. It is rumored but not confirmed that these "experience" Fastpasses are in their own category and thus will not affect your ability to get a Fastpass for a popular ride. (4) Best Fastpass practices are explained by the program. It will direct you to the attractions where Fastpass is most helpful. If these attractions don't meet your family's specific needs—your kids are too young to ride coasters, for example—the program will also help you customize your Fastpass selections.

DISNEY STRATEGIES

Keep in mind these essential strategies, tried and tested by generations of Disney fans.

■ **Buy tickets before leaving home.** It saves money and gives you time to look into all the ticket options. It also offers an opportunity for you to consider vacation packages and meal plans.

■ **Make dining reservations before leaving home.** If you don't, you might find yourself eating fast food (again) or leaving Disney for dinner. On-site restaurants, especially those featuring character appearances, book up months ahead.

■ **Arrive at least 30 minutes before the parks open.** We know, it's your vacation and you want to sleep in. But you probably want to make the most of your time and money, too. Plan to be up by 7:30 am each day to get the most out of your park visits. After transit time, it'll take you 15–20 minutes to park, get to the gates, and pick up your park guide maps and *Times Guide*.

■ **See top attractions in the morning.** And we mean *first thing*. Decide in advance on your can't-miss attractions, find their locations, and hotfoot it to them before 10 am.

■ **Use Fastpass.** Yes, use the Fastpass. It's worth saying twice. The system is free and easy, and it's your ticket to the top attractions with little or no waiting in line.

■ **Use Baby Swap.** Disney has a theme-park "rider switch" policy that works like this: one parent waits with the baby or toddler while the other parent rides the attraction. When the ride ends, they switch places with minimal wait.

■ **Build in rest time.** Start early and then leave the parks around 3 or 4 pm, thus avoiding the hottest and often most crowded period. After a couple of hours' rest at your hotel, head back for a nighttime spectacle or to ride a big-ticket ride (lines often are shorter around closing time).

■ **Create an itinerary, but leave room for spontaneity.** Don't try to plot your trip hour by hour. If you're staying at a Disney resort, find out which parks have Extra Magic Hours on which days.

10

■ **Eat at off hours.** To avoid the mealtime rush hours, have a quick, light breakfast at 7 or 8 am, lunch at 11 am, and dinner at 5 or 6 pm.

OTHER DISNEY SERVICES

If you can shell out $275–$315 an hour (with a six-hour minimum), you can take a customized **VIP Tour** with guides who help you park-hop and get good seats at parades and shows. These tours don't help you skip lines, but they make navigating easy. Groups can have up to 10 people; book up to three months ahead.

Character meals. Mickey, Belle, or other characters sign autographs and pose for photos. Book through Disney's dining reservations line up to 180 days out; these hugging-and-feeding frenzies are wildly popular.

WDW Tours. Reserve with WDW Tours up to 180 days in advance for behind-the-scenes tours. Participant age requirements vary, so be sure to check before you book. ☎ *407/939–8687.*

DISNEY CONTACTS

Cruise Line: ☎ *800/370–0097* ⊕ *www.disneycruise.com*

Dining Reservations: ☎ *407/939–3463*

Extra Magic Hours: ⊕ *www.disneyworld.disney.go.com/calendars*

Fairy-Tale Weddings: ☎ *321/939–4610* ⊕ *www.disneyweddings.disney.go.com*

Golf Reservations: ☎ *407/939–4653*

Guest Info: ☎ *407/824–4321*

VIP Tours: ☎ *407/560–4033*

WDW Travel Company: ☎ *407/828–8101*

Web: ⊕ *www.disneyworld.disney.go.com*

THE MAGIC KINGDOM

Whether you arrive at the Magic Kingdom via monorail, boat, or bus, it's hard to escape that surge of excitement or suppress that smile upon sighting the towers of Cinderella Castle or the spires of Space Mountain. So what if it's a cliché by now? There's magic beyond the turnstiles, and you aren't going to miss one memorable moment.

Most visitors have some idea of what they'd like to see and do during their day in the Magic Kingdom. Popular attractions like Space Mountain and Splash Mountain are on the lists of any thrill seeker, and the recently expanded Fantasyland is Destination One for parents of small children. Visitors who steer away from wilder rides are first in line at the Jungle Cruise or Pirates of the Caribbean in Adventureland.

It's great to have a strategy for seeing the park's attractions, grabbing a bite to eat, or scouring the shops for souvenir gold. But don't forget that Disney Imagineers—the creative pros behind every themed land and attraction—are famous for their attention to detail. Your experience will be richer if you take time to notice the extra touches—from the architecture to the music to the costumes. The same genius is evident

TOP ATTRACTIONS

FOR AGES 7 AND UP	FOR AGES 6 AND UNDER
Big Thunder Mountain Railroad	Country Bear Jamboree
Buzz Lightyear's Space Ranger Spin	Dumbo the Flying Elephant
Haunted Mansion	The Magic Carpets of Aladdin
Pirates of the Caribbean	The Many Adventures of Winnie the Pooh
Space Mountain	Under the Sea: Journey of the Little Mermaid
Splash Mountain	

even in the landscape, from the tropical setting of Adventureland to the red-stone slopes of Frontierland's Big Thunder Mountain Railroad.

Wherever you go, watch for Hidden Mickeys—silhouettes and abstract images of Mickey Mouse—tucked by Imagineers in every corner of the Kingdom. For instance, at the Haunted Mansion, look for him in the place settings in the banquet scene.

Much of the Magic Kingdom's pixie dust is spread by the people who work here, the costumed cast members who do their part to create fond memories for each guest who crosses their path. Maybe the grim ghoul who greets you solemnly at the Haunted Mansion will cause you to break down and giggle. Or the sunny shop assistant will help your daughter find the perfect sparkly shoes to match her princess dress. You get the feeling that everyone's in on the fun; in fact, you wonder if they ever go home!

PLANNING

GETTING ORIENTED

The park is laid out on a north–south axis, with Cinderella Castle at the center and the various lands surrounding it in a broad circle.

As you pass underneath the railroad tracks, symbolically leaving behind the world of reality and entering a world of fantasy, you'll immediately notice the adorable buildings lining Town Square and Main Street, U.S.A., which runs due north and ends at the Hub (also called Central Plaza), in front of Cinderella Castle. If you're lost or have questions, cast members are available at almost every turn to help you.

PARK AMENITIES

Guest Relations. To the left in Town Square as you face Main Street, **City Hall** houses Guest Relations, the Magic Kingdom's principal information center (☎ 407/824–4521). Here you can search for misplaced belongings or companions, ask questions of staffers, and pick up a guide map and a *Times Guide* with schedules of events and character-greeting information. ■ TIP➜ If you're trying for a last-minute lunch or dinner reservation, you may be able to book it at City Hall.

10

Adventure Number 1: Being shipwrecked with the Swiss Family Robinson and exploring their treehouse.

Lockers: Lockers ($7 or $9 plus $5 deposit) are in an arcade under the Main Street railroad station. If you're park-hopping, use your locker receipt to get a free locker at the next park.

Lost People and Things: Instruct your kids to talk to anyone with a Disney name tag if they lose you. **City Hall** also has a lost and found and a computerized message center, where you can leave notes for your companions in the Magic Kingdom and other parks.

VISITING TIPS

■ Try to come toward the end of the week, because most families hit the Magic Kingdom early in a visit.

■ Ride a star attraction during a parade; lines ease considerably. (But be careful not to get stuck on the wrong side of the parade route when it starts, or you may never get across.)

■ At City Hall, near the park's Town Square entrance, pick up a guide map and a *Times Guide*, which lists showtimes, character-greeting times, and hours for attractions and restaurants.

■ Book character meals early. Main Street, U.S.A.'s Crystal Palace, A Buffet with Character has breakfast, lunch, and dinner with Winnie the Pooh, Tigger, and friends. All three meals at the Fairy Tale Dining experience in Cinderella Castle are extremely popular—so much so that you should reserve your spot six months out. The same advice goes for booking the full-service dinner at the new Be Our Guest restaurant in the Beast's Castle in Fantasyland.

EXPLORING THE MAGIC KINGDOM

MAIN STREET, U.S.A.

With its pastel Victorian-style buildings, antique automobiles ahoohga-oohga-ing, sparkling sidewalks, and an atmosphere of what one writer has called "almost hysterical joy," Main Street is more than a mere conduit to the other enchantments of the Magic Kingdom. It's where the spell is first cast.

You emerge from beneath the Walt Disney World Railroad Station into a realization of one of the most tenacious American dreams. The perfect street in the perfect small town in a perfect moment of time is burnished to jewel-like quality, thanks to a four-fifths-scale reduction, nightly cleanings with high-pressure hoses, and constant repainting. And it's a very sunny world, thanks to an outpouring of welcoming entertainment: live bands, barbershop quartets, and background music from Disney films and American musicals played over loudspeakers. Horse-drawn trolleys and omnibuses with their horns tooting chug along the street. Vendors in Victorian costumes sell balloons and popcorn. And Cinderella's famous castle floats whimsically in the distance where Main Street disappears.

Although attractions with a capital A are minimal on Main Street, there are plenty of inducements—namely, shops—to while away your time and part you from your money. The largest of these, the Emporium, is often the last stop for souvenir hunters at day's end, so avoid the crowds and buy early. You can pick up your purchases later at Package Pick-Up or have them delivered to your Disney hotel or mailed home.

If you can't resist an interactive challenge while making your way through the park, head first to the Firehouse, next to City Hall, to join the legendary wizard Merlin in the Sorcerers of the Magic Kingdom role-playing game. For no extra charge, you can take ownership of special cards with "magic spells" that help you search for symbols and bring down Disney villains like Yzma and Kronk from the Disney film *The Emperor's New Groove*. Don't worry—you'll have time between fireball battles and cyclone spells to ride Space Mountain.

10

The Harmony Barber Shop lets you step back in time for a haircut ($15 for children 12 and under, $18 for anyone older). Babies or tots get free Mickey Ears, a souvenir lock of hair, and a certificate if it's their first haircut ever, but you pay $19 for the experience. Tweens like to get colored hair gel or "pixie dust" applications (about $8 a pop). At the Town Square Theater (formerly Exposition Hall), presented by Kodak, Mickey Mouse meets you for photos and autographs. And, for the first time in Disney history, you can pick up a Fastpass appointment for such meet and greets. While you're here, stock up on batteries and memory cards or disposable cameras.

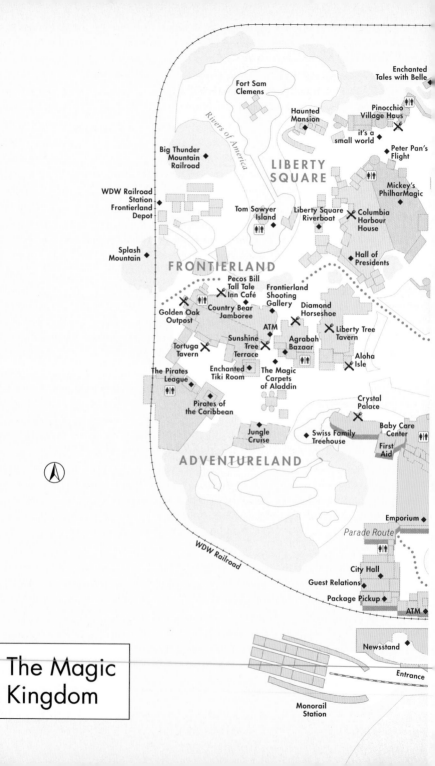

Enchanted
Tales with Belle

Fort Sam
Clemens

Haunted
Mansion

Pinocchio
Village Haus

it's a
small world

Peter Pan's
Flight

Big Thunder
Mountain
Railroad

LIBERTY
SQUARE

Mickey's
PhilharMagic

WDW Railroad
Station
Frontierland
Depot

Tom Sawyer
Island

Liberty Square
Riverboat

Columbia
Harbour
House

Splash
Mountain

FRONTIERLAND

Hall of
Presidents

Pecos Bill
Tall Tale
Inn Café

Frontierland
Shooting
Gallery

Diamond
Horseshoe

Golden Oak
Outpost

Country Bear
Jamboree

ATM

Agrabah
Bazaar

Liberty Tree
Tavern

Tortuga
Tavern

Sunshine
Tree
Terrace

Aloha
Isle

The Pirates
League

Enchanted
Tiki Room

The Magic
Carpets
of Aladdin

Crystal
Palace

Pirates of
the Caribbean

Jungle
Cruise

Swiss Family
Treehouse

Baby Care
Center

First
Aid

ADVENTURELAND

Rivers of America

Emporium

Parade Route

WDW Railroad

City Hall

Guest Relations

Package Pickup

ATM

Newsstand

Entrance

The Magic
Kingdom

Monorail
Station

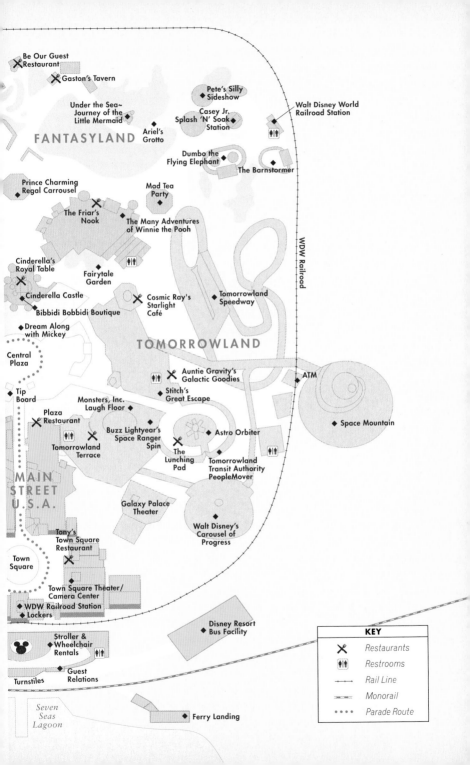

Be Our Guest Restaurant

Gaston's Tavern

Pete's Silly Sideshow

Under the Sea~ Journey of the Little Mermaid

Casey Jr. Splash 'N' Soak Station

Walt Disney World Railroad Station

FANTASYLAND

Ariel's Grotto

Dumbo the Flying Elephant

The Barnstormer

Prince Charming Regal Carrousel

Mad Tea Party

The Friar's Nook

The Many Adventures of Winnie the Pooh

Cinderella's Royal Table

Fairytale Garden

Cinderella Castle

Cosmic Ray's Starlight Café

Tomorrowland Speedway

Bibbidi Bobbidi Boutique

Dream Along with Mickey

TOMORROWLAND

Central Plaza

Auntie Gravity's Galactic Goodies

ATM

Tip Board

Stitch's Great Escape

Plaza Restaurant

Monsters, Inc. Laugh Floor

Space Mountain

Buzz Lightyear's Space Ranger Spin

Astro Orbiter

Tomorrowland Terrace

The Lunching Pad

Tomorrowland Transit Authority PeopleMover

MAIN STREET U.S.A.

Galaxy Palace Theater

Tony's Town Square Restaurant

Walt Disney's Carousel of Progress

Town Square

Town Square Theater/ Camera Center

WDW Railroad Station

Lockers

Disney Resort Bus Facility

Stroller & Wheelchair Rentals

Guest Relations

Turnstiles

Seven Seas Lagoon

Ferry Landing

WDW Railroad

KEY	
✗	Restaurants
🛉🛉	Restrooms
—•—	Rail Line
⋈	Monorail
••••	Parade Route

MAGIC KINGDOM

NAME	Height Req.	Type of Entertainment	Duration	Crowds	Audience	Tips
Adventureland						
Enchanted Tiki Room	n/a	Show	12 mins.	Light	All Ages	Come when you need a refresher in a/c.
Jungle Cruise	n/a	Cruise	10 mins.	Heavy	All Ages	Use Fastpass or come during the parade.
The Magic Carpets of Aladdin	n/a	Thrill Ride for Kids	3 mins.	Heavy	All Ages	Visit while waiting for Frontierland Fastpass appointment.
Pirates of the Caribbean	n/a	Cruise	10 mins.	Moderate	All Ages	A good destination in the heat of the afternoon.
Swiss Family Treehouse	n/a	Walk-through	Up to you	Moderate	All Ages	Visit while waiting for Jungle Cruise Fastpass.
Fantasyland						
★ Dumbo the Flying Elephant	n/a	Thrill Ride for Kids	2 mins.	Heavy	Small Kids	Come at rope drop. New circus tent offers shade.
it's a small world	n/a	Cruise	11 mins.	Moderate	All Ages	Tots may beg for a repeat ride; it's worth it.
Mad Tea Party	n/a	Thrill Ride for Kids	2 mins.	Moderate	Small Kids	Come in the early morning. Skip it if wait is 30 mins.
★ The Many Adventures of Winnie the Pooh	n/a	Thrill Ride for Kids	3½ mins.	Heavy	All Ages	Use Fastpass. Come early, late in the afternoon, or after dark.
★ Mickey's PhilharMagic	n/a	3-D Film	12 mins.	Heavy	All but Small Kids	Use Fastpass or arrive early or during a parade.
Prince Charming Regal Carrousel	n/a	Thrill Ride for Kids	2 mins.	Moderate to Heavy	Families	Come while waiting for Peter Pan's Flight Fastpass, during afternoon parade, or after dark.
Peter Pan's Flight	n/a	Thrill Ride for Kids	2½ mins.	Heavy	All Ages	Try evening or early morning. Use Fastpass first.
Frontierland						
★ Big Thunder Mountain Railroad	At least 40"	Thrill Ride	4 mins.	Absolutely!	All but Small Kids	Use Fastpass. Most exciting at night when you can't anticipate the curves.
Country Bear Jamboree	n/a	Show	17 mins.	Heavy	All Ages	Visit before 11 am. Stand to the far left lining up for the front rows.
★ Splash Mountain	At least 40"	Thrill Ride with Water	11 mins.	Yes!	All but Small Kids	Use Fastpass. Get in line by 9:45 am, or ride during meal or parade time. You may get wet.

			Up to you	Light to Moderate	Kids and Tweens	
Tom Sawyer Island	n/a	Playground	Up to you	Light to Moderate	Kids and Tweens	Afternoon refresher. It's hard to keep track of toddlers here.

Liberty Square

Hall of Presidents	n/a	Show/Film	25 mins.	Moderate	All but Small Kids	Come in the morning or during the parade.
★ Haunted Mansion	n/a	Thrill Ride	8 mins.	Moderate	All Ages	Nighttime adds extra fear factor.
Liberty Square Riverboat	n/a	Cruise	15 mins.	Light to Moderate	All Ages	Good for a break from the crowds.

Main Street U.S.A.

Walt Disney World Railroad	n/a	Railroad	21 mins.	Moderate to Heavy	All Ages	Board with small children for an early start in Frontierland or Fantasyland and or hop on midafternoon.

Tomorrowland

Astro-Orbiter	n/a	Thrill Ride for Kids	2 mins.	Moderate to Heavy	All Ages	Skip unless there's a short line.
★ Buzz Lightyear's Space Ranger Spin	n/a	Interactive Ride	5 mins.	Heavy	All Ages	Come in the early morning and use Fastpass. Kids will want more than one ride.
Monster's Inc. Laugh Floor	n/a	Film with special effects	15 mins.	Moderate to Heavy	All Ages	Come when you're waiting for your Buzz Lightyear or Space Mountain Fastpass.
★ Space Mountain	At least 44"	Thrill Ride	2½ mins.	You Bet!	All but Small Kids	Use Fastpass, or come at the beginning or the end of day or during a parade.
Stitch's Great Escape	At least 40"	Simulator Exp.	20 mins.	Moderate to Heavy	All but Small Kids	Use Fastpass. Visit early after Space Mountain, Splash Mountain, Big Thunder Mountain, or during a parade.
Tomorrowland Indy Speedway	54" to drive	Thrill Ride for Kids	5 mins.	Moderate	All but Small Kids	Come in the evening or during a parade; skip on a first-time visit; 32" height requirement to ride shotgun.
Tomorrowland Transit Authority PeopleMover	n/a	Railroad	10 mins.	Light	All Ages	Come with young kids if you need a restful ride.
Walt Disney's Carousel of Progress	n/a	Show	20 mins.	Light to Moderate	All Ages	Skip on a first-time visit unless you're heavily into nostalgia.

ADVENTURELAND

From the scrubbed brick, manicured lawns, and meticulously pruned trees of the Central Plaza, an artfully dilapidated wooden bridge leads to the jungles of Adventureland. Here, South African cape honeysuckle droops, Brazilian bougainvillea drapes, Mexican flame vines cling, spider plants clone, and three varieties of palm trees sway. The bright, all-American sing-along tunes that fill the air along Main Street and Central Plaza are replaced by the recorded repetitions of trumpeting elephants, pounding drums, and squawking parrots. The architecture is a mish-mash of the best of Thailand, the Middle East, the Caribbean, Africa, and Polynesia, arranged in an inspired disorder that recalls comic-book fantasies of far-off places.

Once contained within the Pirates of the Caribbean attraction, Captain Jack Sparrow and the crew of the Black Pearl are brazenly recruiting new hearties at the Pirates League, adjacent to the ride entrance. You can get pirate makeovers (for lots of doubloons) here. On a nearby stage furnished with pirate booty, the captain instructs scurvy dog recruits on brandishing a sword at Captain Jack Sparrow's Pirate Tutorial (several shows a day). And that's not all! The new "A Pirate's Adventure: Treasures of the Seven Seas" sends park guests on an interactive quest with a pirate map and talisman to complete "raids" through Adventureland as they fight off pirate enemies along the way. Shiver me timbers—it's a pirate's life for ye!

FRONTIERLAND

Frontierland evokes the American frontier and is planted with mesquite, twisted Peruvian pepper trees, slash pines, and cacti. The period seems to be the latter half of the 19th century, and the West is being won by Disney cast members dressed in checked shirts, leather vests, cowboy hats, and brightly colored neckerchiefs. Banjo and fiddle music twangs from tree to tree, and snackers walk around munching turkey drumsticks so large that you could best an outlaw single-handedly with one. (Beware of hovering seagulls that migrate to the parks during cooler months—they've been known to snatch snacks.)

The screams that drown out the string music aren't the result of a cowboy surprising an Indian. They come from two of the Magic Kingdom's more thrilling rides: Splash Mountain, an elaborate flume ride; and Big Thunder Mountain Railroad, a roller coaster. The Walt Disney World Railroad tunnels past a colorful scene in Splash Mountain and drops you off between it and Thunder Mountain.

FANTASYLAND

Walt Disney called this "a timeless land of enchantment," and Fantasyland does conjure pixie dust. Perhaps that's because the fanciful gingerbread houses, gleaming gold turrets, and, of course, the rides based on Disney-animated movies.

Many of these rides, which could ostensibly be classified as rides for children, are packed with enough delightful detail to engage the adults who accompany them. Fantasyland has always been the most heavily trafficked area in the park, and its rides and shows are almost always crowded.

The good news is that Fantasyland has added several new attractions and will open even more between the time of this writing and sometime

Coasting down Splash Mountain in Frontierland will put some zip in your doo-dah and some water on your clothes.

in 2014. Once completed, it will be the largest expansion in the park's history. Dumbo the Flying Elephant now is double the size, flying above circus-themed grounds that also include the new Great Goofini coaster, starring Goofy as stuntman. There's also a new Walt Disney World Railroad station in Fantasyland. And a circus-themed Casey Jr. Splash 'N' Soak Station provides waterplay respite for kids. Ariel of *The Little Mermaid* invites you to her own state-of-the-art attraction, Under the Sea: Journey of the Little Mermaid. Disney princesses welcome you for a dance or celebration in the glittering Princess Fairytale Hall. You can be part of the show when you join Belle, Lumiere, and Madame Wardrobe of *Beauty and the Beast* at the Enchanted Tales with Belle attraction for a story performance. Meanwhile, Beast may be brooding in his castle, where the Be Our Guest dining room welcomes lunch and dinner guests. The Seven Dwarfs Mine Train, a musical ride, is expected to sway with each twist and turn of the track when it opens in 2014.

You can enter Fantasyland on foot from Liberty Square or Tomorrowland, but the classic introduction is through Cinderella Castle. As you exit the castle's archway, look left to discover a charming and often overlooked touch: Cinderella Fountain, a lovely brass casting of the castle's namesake, who's dressed in her peasant togs and surrounded by her beloved mice and bird friends.

From the southern end of Liberty Square, head toward the park hub and stop at the designated Kodak PictureSpot for one of the park's best, unobstructed ground-level views of Cinderella Castle. It's a great spot for that family photo.

Few can resist being captivated by the chubby, happy, shiny, flying elephants of Fantasyland's Dumbo ride.

TOMORROWLAND

The "future that never was" spins boldly into view as you enter Tomorrowland, where Disney Imagineers paint the landscape with whirling spaceships, flashy neon lights, and gleaming robots. This is the future as envisioned by sci-fi writers and moviemakers in the 1920s and '30s, when space flight, laser beams, and home computers were fiction, not fact. Retro Jetsonesque styling lends the area lasting chic.

Gamers who want a break from the crowds can find their favorite video challenges in the arcade attached to Space Mountain. SEGA race car, NASCAR, and Fast and Furious Super Bikes games draw tweens and teens; Lil' Hoops give young kids a manageable basketball challenge. Though Tomorrowland Transit Authority (TTA) PeopleMover isn't a big-ticket ride, it's a great way to check out the landscape from above as it zooms in and out of Space Mountain and curves around the entire land.

TOP MAGIC KINGDOM SPECTACLES

Fodor's Choice
★

Main Street Electrical Parade. The Main Street parade, with 23 illuminated floats, 80 performers, and a half-million lights in all, first debuted at Disneyland in California in 1972. It lights up Magic Kingdom nights with plenty of power and its distinctive synthesizer-infused "Baroque Hoedown" musical theme. The lead float features Tinker Bell showering guests with 25,000 pixie-dusted points of light, and a Fireworks Finale float is the longest in the parade at 118 feet. Check *Times Guide;* the parade sometimes runs twice in one night and occasionally not at all. ■TIP→ **Take your place on the curb at least 40 minutes**

before the parade begins. ☞ *Duration: 16 mins. Crowds: Heavy. Audience: All Ages.*

FodorsChoice ★ **Wishes.** When the lights dim on Main Street and orchestral music fills the air, you know this fireworks extravaganza is about to begin. In Wishes, Jiminy Cricket's voice comes to life and tries to convince you that your wishes really can come true. He gets plenty of support from the Disney stars of classic films such as *Pinocchio, Fantasia, Cinderella,* and *The Little Mermaid.* Portions of famous film songs play over loudspeakers, and you hear the voices of film characters like Peter Pan and Aladdin as more than 680 individual fireworks paint the night sky. Oh, and don't worry that Tinker Bell may have been sealed in her jar for the night—she comes back to fly above the crowd in grand pixie-dust style. Check the *Times Guide* for performance time, which varies seasonally. ■**TIP**➜ **Find a place near the front of the park for a quick postshow exit.** ☞ *Duration: 12 mins. Crowds: Heavy. Audience: All Ages.*

TOP ATTRACTIONS
The American Adventure
IllumiNations
Mission: SPACE
Soarin'
Test Track

EPCOT

Walt Disney said that Epcot would "take its cue from the new ideas and new technologies that are now emerging from the creative centers of American industry." He wrote that Epcot, never completed, always improving, "will never cease to be a living blueprint of the future, a showcase to the world for the ingenuity of American free enterprise."

But the permanent settlement that Disney envisioned wasn't to be. Epcot opened in 1982—16 years after his death—as a showcase, ostensibly, for the concepts that would be incorporated into the real-life Epcots of the future. (Disney's vision *has* taken an altered shape in the self-contained city of Celebration, an urban planner's dream opened in 1996 on Disney property near Kissimmee.)

Epcot, the theme park, has two key areas: Future World, where most pavilions are collaborations between Walt Disney Imagineering and U.S. corporations and are designed to demonstrate technological advances through innovative shows and attractions; and the World Showcase, where shops, restaurants, attractions, and live entertainment create microcosms of 11 countries from four continents.

For years, Epcot was considered the more staid park, a place geared toward adults. But after its 10th anniversary, Epcot began to evolve into a livelier, more child-friendly park, with interactive fun at Innoventions and such "wow" attractions as Future World's Test Track, Mission: SPACE, and Soarin'.

There's something for everyone here. The World Showcase appeals to younger children with the Kidcot Fun Stop craft stations and the Norway pavilion's Princess Storybook Dining. Soarin', in The Land

10

pavilion, is a family favorite. And the Seas with Nemo & Friends—with one of the world's largest saltwater aquariums—is a must-see for all. The hottest new ticket? The greatly improved Test Track presented by Chevrolet, where you can design your own custom concept car, then put it through its high-speed paces.

Wear comfortable shoes—there's *a lot* of territory to cover here. Arrive early, and try to stay all day, squeezing in extras like high-tech games at Innoventions and a relaxing meal. If you enter through International Gateway before 11 am, cast members will direct you to Future World, which usually opens two hours before World Showcase.

PLANNING

GETTING ORIENTED

Epcot is composed of two areas: Future World and the World Show-case. The inner core of Future World's pavilions has the Spaceship Earth geosphere and a plaza anchored by the computer-animated Fountain of Nations. Bracketing it are the crescent-shape Innoven-tions East and West, with hands-on, high-tech exhibits, and immersion entertainment.

Six pavilions compose Future World's outer ring. Each of the three east pavilions has a ride and the occasional postride showcase; a visit rarely takes more than 30 minutes. The blockbuster exhibits on the west side contain rides and interactive displays; each exhibit can take up to 90 minutes for the complete experience.

World Showcase pavilions are on the promenade that circles the World Showcase Lagoon. Each houses shops, restaurants, and friendly foreign staffers; some have films or displays. Mexico and Norway offer tame rides. Live entertainment is scheduled at every pavilion except Norway.

Disney's monorail and buses drop you off at the main entrance in front of Future World. But if you're staying at one of the Epcot resorts (the BoardWalk, Yacht Club, Beach Club, Dolphin, or Swan), you can use the International Gateway entrance between World Showcase's France and U.K. pavilions.

PARK AMENITIES

Guest Relations: To the right of the ticket windows at the park entrance and to the left of Spaceship Earth inside the park is the place to pick up schedules and maps. You also can get maps at the park's International Gateway entrance and most shops. Guest Relations will also assist with dining reservations, ticket upgrades, and services for guests with disabilities.

Epcot Lost and Found. Located in the Guest Relations lobby east of Space-ship Earth. ☒ *Future World* ☎ *407/560–7500.*

Lockers: Lockers ($7 and $9, with $5 refundable deposit) are at the International Gateway and to the west of Spaceship Earth. Coin-operated lockers also are at the bus information center by the bus parking lot.

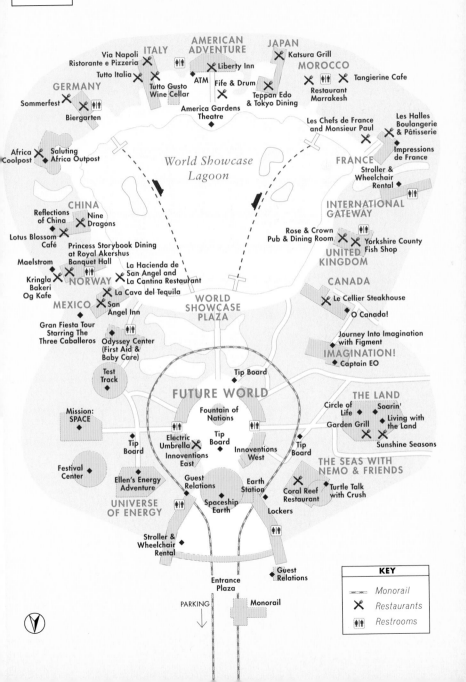

Epcot

WORLD SHOWCASE

ITALY
Via Napoli Ristorante e Pizzeria
Tutto Italia
Tutto Gusto Wine Cellar

AMERICAN ADVENTURE
Liberty Inn
ATM
Fife & Drum
America Gardens Theatre

JAPAN
Katsura Grill
Teppan Edo & Tokyo Dining

MOROCCO
Restaurant Marrakesh
Tangierine Cafe

GERMANY
Sommerfest
Biergarten

Africa Coolpost
Saluting Africa Outpost

World Showcase Lagoon

Les Chefs de France and Monsieur Paul

Les Halles Boulangerie & Pâtisserie

Impressions de France

FRANCE
Stroller & Wheelchair Rental

CHINA
Reflections of China
Nine Dragons
Lotus Blossom Café

INTERNATIONAL GATEWAY

Rose & Crown Pub & Dining Room
Yorkshire County Fish Shop

UNITED KINGDOM

Princess Storybook Dining at Royal Akershus Banquet Hall
Maelstrom
Kringla Bakeri Og Kafe
NORWAY

La Hacienda de San Angel and La Cantina Restaurant

CANADA
Le Cellier Steakhouse
O Canada!

La Cava del Tequila

MEXICO
San Angel Inn

Gran Fiesta Tour Starring The Three Caballeros

Odyssey Center (First Aid & Baby Care)

WORLD SHOWCASE PLAZA

Journey Into Imagination with Figment
IMAGINATION!
Captain EO

Test Track

Tip Board

FUTURE WORLD

THE LAND
Circle of Life
Garden Grill
Soarin'
Living with the Land
Sunshine Seasons

Mission: SPACE

Fountain of Nations

Electric Umbrella
Tip Board
Innoventions East
Innoventions West

Tip Board

Tip Board

THE SEAS WITH NEMO & FRIENDS

Festival Center

Ellen's Energy Adventure

Guest Relations

Earth Station

Coral Reef Restaurant
Turtle Talk with Crush

UNIVERSE OF ENERGY

Spaceship Earth

Lockers

Stroller & Wheelchair Rental

Guest Relations

Entrance Plaza

PARKING

Monorail

KEY

Monorail

✕ Restaurants

🚻 Restrooms

EPCOT

NAME

Future World

Name	Height Req.	Type of Entertainment	Duration	Crowds	Audience	Tips
Captain EO (Imagination!)	n/a	3-D Film	14 mins.	Moderate to Heavy	All Ages	Come in the early morning or just before closing. Take off the 3-D glasses if little kids get scared.
Journey into Imagination with Figment (Imagination!)	n/a	Ride-Through	8 mins.	Light	Small Kids	Ride while waiting for Captain EO Fastpass. Warn toddlers about darkness at the end of the ride.
Ellen's Energy Adventure (Universe of Energy)	n/a	Ride-Through	45 mins.	Moderate	All Ages	Best seats are to the far left and front of the theater.
Innoventions	n/a	Walk-Through	Up to you	Moderate to Heavy	All Ages	Come anytime.
The Circle of Life (The Land)	n/a	Film	20 mins.	Moderate to Heavy	All but Small Kids	Come early or for your toddler's afternoon nap.
Living with the Land (The Land)	n/a	Cruise	14 mins.	Moderate	All but Small Kids	The line moves quickly, so come anytime.
Soarin' (The Land)	At least 40"	Simulator Ride	5 mins.	Heavy	All but Small Kids	Use Fastpass, or come early, or just before closing.
★ The Seas with Nemo & Friends	n/a	Ride- and Walk-Through	Up to you	Moderate to Heavy	Small Kids	Get Nemo fans here early in the morning.

	Name		Type	Duration	Crowds	Ages	Comments
★	Mission: SPACE	At least 44"	Thrill Ride	4 mins.	You Bet!	All but Small Kids	Come before 10 am or use Fastpass. Don't ride on a full stomach.
	Spaceship Earth	n/a	Ride-Through	15 mins.	Moderate to Heavy	All Ages	Ride while waiting for Mission: SPACE Fastpass appointment or just before closing.
★	Test Track	At least 40"	Thrill Ride	5 mins.	Heavy	All but Small Kids	Come in morning with Fastpass unless you want to customize your car. The ride can't function on wet tracks, so don't come after a downpour.
	World Showcase						
★	The American Adventure Show	n/a	Show/Film	20 mins.	Heavy	All Ages	Arrive 10 mins. before the Voices of Liberty or the Spirit of America Fife & Drum Corps are slated to perform.
	America Gardens Theatre	n/a	Live Show	Varies	Varies	Varies	Arrive more than an hour or so ahead of time for holiday and celebrity performances.
	Gran Fiesta Tour Starring the Three Caballeros	n/a	Cruise	9 mins.	Light to Moderate	All Ages	Especially good if you have small children.
	Impressions de France	n/a	Film	20 mins.	Moderate	All but Small Kids	Come anytime.
	Maelstrom	n/a	Thrill Ride for Kids with Water	10 mins.	Moderate to Heavy	All Ages	Use Fastpass for after lunch or dinner.
	O Canada!	n/a	Film	14 mins.	Moderate to Heavy	All Ages	Come when World Showcase opens or in the evening. No strollers permitted.
	Reflections of China	n/a	Film	14 mins.	Moderate	All Ages	Come anytime. No strollers permitted.

★ **Fodor's** Choice

Lost People and Things: Instruct children to speak to someone with a Disney name tag if you become separated. Guest Relations (aka Guest Services) has a computerized message center for contacting companions in any of the parks.

Stroller Rentals: You can rent strollers on the east side of the Entrance Plaza and at the International Gateway. Singles are $15 daily, $13 for multiday rental; doubles cost $31 daily, $27 for multiple days. Even preschoolers will be glad for a stroller in this large park.

VISITING TIPS

■ Epcot is so vast and varied that you really need two days to explore. With just one day, you'll have to be highly selective.

■ Go early in the week, when others are at Magic Kingdom.

■ If you like a good festival, visit during the International Flower & Garden Festival (early to mid-March through May) or the International Food & Wine Festival (late September through mid-November).

■ Once through the turnstiles at either the main Future World entrance or the back World Showcase entrance, make a beeline for the popular Mission: SPACE and Test Track (for fast-paced thrills) or the Seas with Nemo & Friends and Soarin' (for family fun). Or get a Fastpass and return later.

EXPLORING EPCOT

FUTURE WORLD

Future World's inner core is composed of the iconic Spaceship Earth geosphere and, beyond it, a plaza anchored by the awe-inspiring computer-animated Fountain of Nations, which shoots water 150 feet skyward. Bracketing it are the crescent-shape Innoventions East and West.

Six pavilions compose Future World's outer ring. On the east side, they are the Universe of Energy, Mission: SPACE, and Test Track. Each pavilion presents a single, self-contained ride and an occasional postride showcase; a visit rarely takes more than 30 minutes, but it depends on how long you spend in the postride area. On the west side are the Seas with Nemo & Friends, the Land, and Imagination! These blockbuster exhibits contain both rides and interactive displays; you could spend at least 1½ hours at each of these pavilions, but there aren't enough hours in the day, so prioritize.

WORLD SHOWCASE

Nowhere but at Epcot can you explore a little corner of nearly a dozen countries in one day. As you stroll the 1 miles around the 40-acre World Showcase Lagoon, you circumnavigate the globe-according-to-Disney by experiencing native food, entertainment, culture, and arts and crafts at pavilions representing countries in Europe, Asia, North Africa, and the Americas. Pavilion employees are from the countries they represent—Disney hires them as part of its international college program.

Instead of rides, you have solid film attractions at the Canada, China, and France pavilions; several art exhibitions; and the chance to try your foreign language skills with the staff. Each pavilion also has a designated Kidcot Fun Stop, open daily from 11 am or noon until about 8 or 9, where youngsters can try a cultural crafts project. Live entertainment is an integral part of the experience, and you'll enjoy watching the incredibly talented Jeweled Dragon Acrobats in China, singing along with terrific British rock band impersonators in the United Kingdom and the Off Kilter band in Canada, or laughing along with some improv fun in the Italy courtyard.

Dining is another favorite pastime at Epcot, and the World Showcase offers tempting tastes of the authentic cuisines of the countries here.

TOP EPCOT SPECTACLE

Fodor's Choice
★

IllumiNations: Reflections of Earth. This marvelous nighttime spectacular takes place over the World Showcase Lagoon every night before closing. Be sure to stick around for the lasers, lights, flames, fireworks, fountains, and music that fill the air over the water. The show's Earth Globe—a gigantic, spherical, video-display system rotating on a 350-ton floating island—is three stories tall with 180,000 light-emitting diodes. It houses six computer processors and 258 strobe lights and projects images celebrating the diversity and unified spirit of humankind. The globe opens like a lotus flower in the grand finale, revealing a huge torch that rises 40 feet into the air as additional flames spread light across the lagoon. Nearly 2,800 fireworks shells paint colorful displays across the night sky.

Although there's generally good viewing from all around the lagoon, some of the best spots are in front of the Italy pavilion, on the bridge between France and the United Kingdom, on the promenade in front of Canada, at the World Showcase Plaza, and at La Hacienda de San Angel and La Cantina de San Angel in Mexico. **For people with disabilities:** During the show, certain areas along the lagoon's edge at Showcase Plaza, Canada, and Germany are reserved for guests using wheelchairs. ■TIP→ **For best views (and if you have young children), find your place 45 minutes in advance.** ⌨ *Duration: 13 mins. Crowds: Heavy. Audience: All Ages.*

NIGHTLIFE

BARS

Cava del Tequila. Set inside the Mexico pavilion, this intimate bar serves tasty tapas, tequila flights, and some of the best margaritas anywhere, including the Cava Organic Skinny Lime Margarita. ⊠ *World Showcase, Mexico.*

Rose & Crown Pub. Great piano sets by the Hat Lady and, on busy nights, four-to-six-deep at the bar guarantees good times at this United Kingdom watering hole. The fish-and-chips are first rate, and the Trio of United Kingdom Cheeses includes aged Irish cheddar and Stilton. Grab a beer or a cordial and let the fun begin! ⊠ *World Showcase, United Kingdom.*

The Temple of Quetzalcoatl (ket-zel-co-WAH-tal) at Teotihuacán (tay-o-tee-wah-CON), just outside Mexico City, is the model for the pyramid at the Mexico pavilion.

Tutto Gusto. This cool, cozy wine cellar adjoining Tutto Italia is the ideal place to kick back at a table or on a sofa and sip a bubbly Prosecco or a glass of Italian wine while noshing on antipasto or tapas-size pastas. For quicker service, head straight for the bar. ⊠ *World Showcase Italy pavilion.*

DISNEY'S HOLLYWOOD STUDIOS

The first thing you notice when you pass through the Hollywood Studios turnstiles is the laid-back California attitude. Palm-lined Hollywood Boulevard oozes glamour—but in a casual way that makes you feel as if you belong, even without your slinky Michael Kors jersey and Jimmy Choos.

When the park opened in May 1989 as Disney-MGM Studios, officials welcomed the first guests and VIPs to "the Hollywood that never was and always will be." Attending the lavish, red-carpet affair were Tinseltown icons such as Bette Midler and Warren Beatty. Disney explains the 2008 name change to Hollywood Studios as a way to "better reflect not only the golden age of Tinseltown, but all that today's Hollywood has to offer in movies, music, theater, and television."

Unlike the first movie theme park—Universal Studios in California—Hollywood Studios combined Disney detail with MGM's motion-picture legacy and Walt Disney's own animated classics. Imagineers built the park with real film and television production in mind, and during its first decade, the Studios welcomed films like *Ernest Saves Christmas* and TV shows like *Wheel of Fortune* to its soundstages.

TOP ATTRACTIONS

AGES 8 AND UP
The American Idol Experience.

Indiana Jones Epic Stunt Spectacular!

The Magic of Disney Animation.

Rock 'n' Roller Coaster Starring Aerosmith.

Star Tours: The Adventures Continue.

Toy Story Midway Mania!

Twilight Zone Tower of Terror

AGES 7 AND UNDER
Beauty and the Beast—Live on Stage

Disney Junior—Live on Stage!

Honey, I Shrunk the Kids Movie Set Adventure

Muppet*Vision 3-D

The Animation Studios, too, were busy. Stories such as *Aladdin* and *Lilo & Stitch* came to life on the easels and computers of Disney's Florida animators. Though production has mostly halted at the park, you can enjoy plenty of attractions that showcase how filmmakers practice their craft. Want to see how special effects are created? Visit the Studio Backlot Tour. If you're wowed by action-film stunts, you can learn the tricks of the trade at the Indiana Jones Epic Stunt Spectacular! or the Lights, Motors, Action! Extreme Stunt Show. No trip to the Studios would be complete without a tour of the Magic of Disney Animation, where you can sit down and draw a character like Mickey or Donald.

In a savvy effort to grab a big piece of the pop-culture pie, in late 2008 Disney opened its own *American Idol* attraction, where performers earn audience votes to compete in an end-of-day contest for a spot in the TV show's regional audition process. Imagineers continue to "bring it" with big-hit attractions such as Toy Story Midway Mania! and new twists on old favorites like the 2011 3-D debut of the Star Tours simulator ride.

PLANNING

GETTING ORIENTED

The park is divided into sightseeing clusters. **Hollywood Boulevard** is the main artery to the heart of the park, and is where you find the glistening replica of Graumann's Chinese Theater.

Encircling it are **Sunset Boulevard**, the **Animation Courtyard**, **Mickey Avenue**, **Pixar Place**, **Commissary Lane**, the **Streets of America area**, and **Echo Lake**.

The entire park is 135 acres, and has just 20 major attractions (compared with Magic Kingdom's 40-plus). It's small enough to cover in a day and even repeat a favorite ride or two.

If you're staying at one of the Epcot resorts (BoardWalk, Yacht or Beach Club, Swan, or Dolphin), getting to the Entrance Plaza on a motor launch is part of the fun. Disney resort buses also drop you at the entrance.

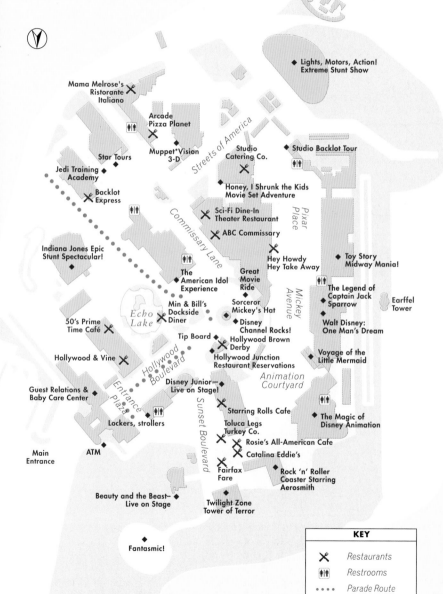

Disney's Hollywood Studios

Catastrophe Canyon
on Studio Backlot Tour

Lights, Motors, Action!
Extreme Stunt Show

Mama Melrose's
Ristorante
Italiano

Arcade
Pizza Planet

Muppet*Vision
3-D

Studio
Catering Co.

Studio Backlot Tour

Streets of America

Star Tours

Jedi Training
Academy

Backlot
Express

Honey, I Shrunk the Kids
Movie Set Adventure

Pixar
Place

Sci-Fi Dine-In
Theater Restaurant

ABC Commissary

Indiana Jones Epic
Stunt Spectacular!

Commissary Lane

Hey Howdy
Hey Take Away

Toy Story
Midway Mania!

The
American Idol
Experience

Great
Movie
Ride

Mickey
Avenue

The Legend of
Captain Jack
Sparrow

Earffel
Tower

Echo
Lake

Min & Bill's
Dockside
Diner

Sorceror
Mickey's Hat

Walt Disney:
One Man's Dream

50's Prime
Time Café

Disney
Channel Rocks!

Voyage of the
Little Mermaid

Tip Board

Hollywood Brown
Derby

Hollywood & Vine

Hollywood
Boulevard

Hollywood Junction
Restaurant Reservations

Animation
Courtyard

Guest Relations &
Baby Care Center

Entrance
Plaza

Disney Junior—
Live on Stage!

Sunset Boulevard

Starring Rolls Cafe

The Magic of
Disney Animation

Lockers, strollers

Toluca Legs
Turkey Co.

Main
Entrance

ATM

Rosie's All-American Cafe

Catalina Eddie's

Fairfax
Fare

Rock 'n' Roller
Coaster Starring
Aerosmith

Beauty and the Beast—
Live on Stage

Twilight Zone
Tower of Terror

Fantasmic!

KEY

✖	Restaurants
🚻	Restrooms
••••	Parade Route

DISNEY'S HOLLYWOOD STUDIOS

NAME	Height Req.	Type of Entertainment	Duration	Crowds	Audience	Tips
Animation Courtyard						
Disney Junior—Live on Stage!	n/a	Show	22 mins.	Moderate to Heavy	Small Kids	Come first thing in the morning, when your child is most alert and lines are shorter.
The Magic of Disney Animation	n/a	Tour	15+ mins.	Moderate	All Ages	Come in the morning or late afternoon. Toddlers may get bored.
Voyage of the Little Mermaid	n/a	Show	17 mins.	Heavy	All Ages	Come first thing in the morning. Otherwise, wait until after 5.
Echo Lake						
The American Idol Experience	n/a	Show	25 mins./ 45 mins.	Yes!	All but Small Kids	Check *Times Guide*, for showtimes. Arrive at least 30 minutes early for seats inside the theater.
Indiana Jones Epic Stunt Spectacular!	n/a	Show	30 mins.	Moderate to Heavy	All but Small Kids	Come at night, when the idol's eyes glow. Sit up front to feel the heat of a truck on fire.
Sounds Dangerous—Starring Drew Carey	n/a	Show	12 mins.	Moderate	All but Small Kids	Arrive 15 minutes before show. You sit in total darkness.
Star Tours 3-D—The Adventure Continues	At least 40"	Simulator Exp.	5 mins.	Heavy	All but Small Kids	Come before closing, early morning, or get a Fastpass. Keep to the left in line for the best seats.
Hollywood Boulevard						
Great Movie Ride	n/a	Ride/Tour	22 mins.	Moderate	All but Small Kids	Come while waiting for Fastpass appointment. Lines out the door mean 25-min. wait—or longer.

Mickey Avenue

Attraction	Height	Type	Duration	Crowds	Audience	Comments
Walt Disney: One Man's Dream	n/a	Walk-Through/Film	20+ mins.	Light to Moderate	All but Small Kids	See this attraction while waiting for a Fastpass appointment.

Pixar Place

Attraction	Height	Type	Duration	Crowds	Audience	Comments
Toy Story Midway Mania!	n/a	Interactive Ride	7 mins.	Heavy	All Ages	Come early; use Fastpass.

Streets of America

Attraction	Height	Type	Duration	Crowds	Audience	Comments
Honey, I Shrunk the Kids Movie Set Adventure	n/a	Playground	Up to you	Moderate	Small Kids	Come after you've done several shows and your kids need to cut loose. Keep an eye on toddlers who can quickly get lost in the caves and slides.
Lights, Motors, Action! Extreme Stunt Show	n/a	Show	33 mins.	Heavy	All but Small Kids	For the best seats, line up for the show while others are lining up for the parade.
Muppet*Vision 3-D	n/a	3-D Film	25 mins.	Moderate to Heavy	All Ages	Arrive 10 mins. early. And don't worry—there are no bad seats.
Studio Backlot Tour	n/a	Tour	35 mins.	Moderate	All but Small Kids	People sitting on the left can get wet. Come early; it closes at dusk.

Sunset Boulevard

Attraction	Height	Type	Duration	Crowds	Audience	Comments
Beauty and the Beast— Live on Stage!	n/a	Show	30 mins.	Moderate to Heavy	All Ages	Come 30 mins. before showtime for good seats. Performance times vary, so check ahead.
★ Rock 'n' Roller Coaster Starring Aerosmith	At least 48"	Thrill Ride	1 min., 22 secs.	Huge	All but Small Kids	Ride early, then use Fastpass for another go later.
★ Twilight Zone Tower of Terror	At least 40"	Thrill Ride	10 mins.	You Bet!	All but Small Kids	Use Fastpass. Come early or late evening.

★ Fodor'sChoice

If you're staying off-property and driving, your parking ticket will remain valid for parking at another Disney park later in the day—provided, of course, you have the stamina.

PARK AMENITIES

Disney's Hollywood Studios Lost and Found. Report lost or found articles at Guest Relations. ⊠ *Hollywood Blvd.* ☎ 407/560–4666.

Guest Relations: You'll find it just inside the turnstiles on the left side of the Entrance Plaza. The **Studios Tip Board**, with updated information on events and attraction wait times, is at the corner of Hollywood and Sunset boulevards. ■ TIP→ Behind the Tip Board is the Hollywood Junction information window, where you can make dining reservations, pick up maps and guides, or get answers to your questions.

Lockers: You can rent lockers at the Crossroads of the World kiosk in the center of the Entrance Plaza. The cost is $7 or $9 with a $5 refundable key deposit. The lockers themselves are at Oscar's Super Service.

Lost People and Things: Instruct your kids to go to a Disney staffer with a name tag if they can't find you. If you lose them, ask any cast member for assistance; logbooks of lost children's names are kept at Guest Relations, which also has a computerized message center where you can leave notes for companions.

Stroller Rentals: Oscar's Super Service rents strollers. Single strollers are $15 daily, $13 for more than one day; doubles are $31 daily, $27 multiday.

VISITING TIPS

■ Visit early in the week, when most people are at Magic Kingdom and Animal Kingdom.

■ Check the Tip Board periodically for attractions with short wait times to visit between Fastpass appointments.

■ Be at the Fantasmic! amphitheater at least an hour before showtime if you didn't book the dinner package.

■ Need a burst of energy? On-the-run hunger pangs? Grab a slice at Pizza Planet at **Streets of America**. Alternatively, **Hollywood Scoops ice cream** on Sunset is the place to be on a hot day.

■ If you're planning on a fast-food lunch, eat before 11 or after 2:30. There are quick-bite spots all over the park and several stands along Sunset. Get a burger (meat or vegetarian) or chicken strips at **Rosie's All-American Café**, a slice of pizza from **Catalina Eddie's**, or a hunk of smoked bird at **Toluca Legs Turkey Co.**

EXPLORING DISNEY'S HOLLYWOOD STUDIOS

HOLLYWOOD BOULEVARD

With its palm trees, pastel buildings, and flashy neon, Hollywood Boulevard paints a rosy picture of 1930s Tinseltown. There's a sense of having walked right onto a movie set of old, with art deco storefronts and roving starlets and nefarious agents—actually costumed actors known as the Citizens of Hollywood. Throughout the park, characters

from Disney movies new and old—from *Mickey Mouse* to *Toy Story* friends—pose for photos and sign autographs.

SUNSET BOULEVARD

This avenue honors Hollywood with facades derived from the Cathay Circle, the Beverly Wilshire Theatre, and other City of Angels landmarks. As you turn onto Sunset Boulevard from Hollywood Boulevard, you'll notice the Hollywood Junction information window, where questions are answered and reservations can be made for restaurants throughout the park.

ANIMATION COURTYARD

As you exit Sunset Boulevard, veer right through the high-arched gateway to the Animation Courtyard. Straight ahead are *Disney Junior—Live on Stage!*, the Magic of Disney Animation, and *Voyage of the Little Mermaid.*

PIXAR PLACE

Pixar Place has a fresh look tied to one of the park's biggest attractions, Toy Story Midway Mania! Where TV- and film-production soundstages once stood, warm brick facades welcome you to the land of Woody and Buzz. Open-air kiosks invite you to browse for themed toys and souvenirs. The brick Camera Department building is the place to mix and mingle with characters from the blockbuster movie *Toy Story.* Check schedules on your *Times Guide.*

STREETS OF AMERICA

It's fun to tour the New York and San Francisco sets here on foot, so that you can check out the windows of shops and apartments, the taxicabs, and other details. If you're lucky (or smart enough to check the *Times Guide* show schedule), you'll join the street party for a performance by Mulch, Sweat & Shears—Live in Concert, as they play a 30-minute set of rock classics or rockin' seasonal tunes during holidays.

ECHO LAKE

In the center of an idealized slice of Southern California is a cool, blue lake—an oasis fringed with trees, benches, and things like pink-and-aqua, chrome-trimmed restaurants with sassy waitresses and black-and-white TVs at the tables; the shipshape Min & Bill's Dockside Diner; and Gertie, an emotive dinosaur that dispenses ice cream (seasonally) as well as Disney souvenirs and the occasional puff of smoke. (Look for Gertie's giant footprints in the sidewalk.) The hot ticket here is the American Idol Experience, where you can act out your own *American Idol* ambitions. You'll also find two of the park's longest-running attractions, the Indiana Jones Epic Stunt Spectacular! and Star Tours, where a 3-D attraction transformation jazzes up the galaxy.

ANIMAL KINGDOM

If you're thinking, "Oh, it's just another zoo, let's skip it," think again. Walt Disney World's fourth theme park, opened in 1998, takes its inspiration from humankind's enduring love for animals and pulls out all the stops. Your day will be packed with unusual animal encounters, enchanting entertainment, and themed rides that'll leave you breathless.

A large chunk of the park is devoted to animal habitats, especially the forest and savanna of Africa's Kilimanjaro Safaris. Towering acacia trees and tall grasses sweep across the land where antelopes, giraffes, and wildebeests roam. A lion kopje, warthog burrows, a zebra habitat, and an elephant watering hole provide ample space for inhabitants.

TOP ATTRACTIONS

Africa

Kilimanjaro Safaris

Asia

Expedition Everest

Camp Minnie-Mickey

Festival of the Lion King

DinoLand U.S.A.

DINOSAUR.

Finding Nemo: The Musical

Discovery Island

Tree of Life: It's Tough to Be a Bug!

About 94 acres contain foliage like hibiscus and mulberry, perfect for antelope and many other species. The largest groups of Nile hippos and African elephants in North America live along the winding waterway that leads to the savanna. The generously landscaped Pangani Forest Exploration Trail provides roaming grounds for troops of gorillas and authentic habitats for meerkats, birds, fish, and other creatures.

Beyond the park's Africa territory, similar large spaces are set aside for the homes of Asian animals like tigers and Komodo dragons, as well as for creatures such as Galápagos tortoises and a giant anteater.

Disney Imagineers didn't forget to include their trademark thrills, from the Kali River Rapids ride in Asia to the fast-paced DINOSAUR journey in DinoLand U.S.A. Expedition Everest, the park's biggest thrill attraction, is a "runaway" train ride on a faux rugged mountain complete with icy ledges, dark caves, and a yeti legend.

The only downside to the Animal Kingdom layout is that walking paths and spaces can get very crowded and hot in the warmest months. Your best bet is to arrive very early and see the animals first before the heat makes them (and you) woozy.

Just before the park opens, Minnie Mouse, Pluto, and Goofy arrive at the iconic Tree of Life in a safari vehicle to welcome the first guests into the heart of the park. Let the adventure begin!

10

PLANNING

GETTING ORIENTED

Animal Kingdom's hub is the Tree of Life, in the middle of Discovery Island. The park's lands, each with a distinct personality, radiate from Discovery Island. To the southwest is Camp Minnie-Mickey, a character-greeting location and live-show area. North of the hub is Africa, where Kilimanjaro Safaris travel across extensive savanna. In the northeast corner is Rafiki's Planet Watch with conservation activities.

Asia, with thrills like Expedition Everest and Kali River Rapids, is east of the hub, and DinoLand U.S.A. brings *T. rex* and other prehistoric creatures to life in the park's southeast corner.

If you're staying on-site, you can take a Disney bus to the Entrance Plaza. If you drive, the $14 parking fee allows you to park at other Disney lots throughout the day.

Although this is technically Disney's largest theme park, most of the land is reserved for the animals. Pedestrian areas are actually quite compact, with relatively narrow passageways. The only way to get around is on foot or in a wheelchair or electronic convenience vehicle (ECV).

PARK AMENITIES

Animal Kingdom Lost and Found. To retrieve lost articles on the same day, visit or call Lost and Found, which is at Guest Relations. ⊠ *Oasis* ☎ *407/938–2785.*

Guest Relations: Guest Services will help with tickets at a window to the left just before you pass through the turnstile. Once you've entered, Guest Relations staffers in the Oasis can provide park maps, schedules, and answers to questions. They can also assist with dining reservations, ticket upgrades, and services for guests with disabilities.

Lockers: Lockers are in Guest Relations (aka Guest Services) in the Oasis. Rental fees are $7 to $9 (depending on size) for a day plus a $5 key deposit.

Lost People and Things: Instruct your kids to speak to someone with a Disney name tag if you become separated. Lost children are taken to the baby-care center, where they can watch Disney movies, or to Guest Relations, whichever is closer. If you do lose your child, contact any cast member immediately and Disney security personnel will be notified.

Stroller Rentals: Garden Gate Gifts in the Oasis rents strollers. Singles are $15 daily, $13 for more than one day; doubles run $31 daily, $27 for multiday.

VISITING TIPS

■ Try to visit during the week. Pedestrian areas are compact, and the park can feel uncomfortably packed on weekends.

■ Plan on a full day here. That way, while exploring Africa's Pangani Forest Exploration Trail, say, you can spend 10 minutes (rather than just two) watching vigilant meerkats stand sentry or tracking a mama gorilla as she cares for her infant.

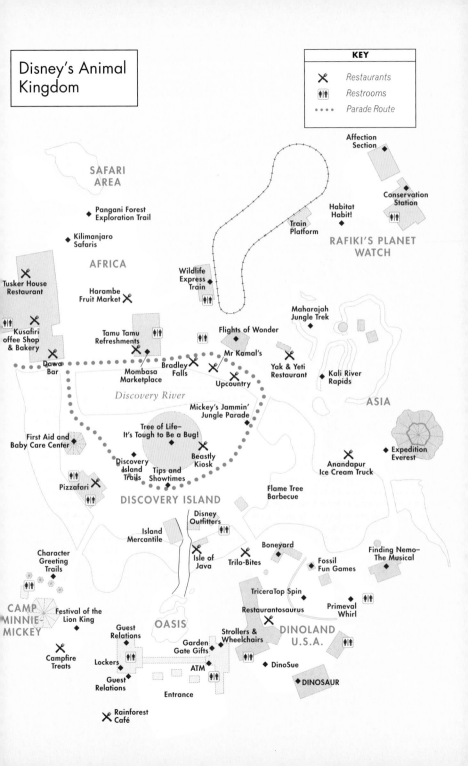

Disney's Animal Kingdom

KEY

✗ — Restaurants
🚻 — Restrooms
•••• — Parade Route

SAFARI AREA

◆ Pangani Forest Exploration Trail

◆ Kilimanjaro Safaris

AFRICA

✗ Tusker House Restaurant

✗ Kusafiri offee Shop & Bakery

Harambe ✗ Fruit Market

Dawa Bar

Tamu Tamu Refreshments

Mombasa Marketplace

Bradley Falls

Wildlife Express Train

Train Platform

RAFIKI'S PLANET WATCH

Affection Section ◆

Conservation Station ◆

Habitat Habit! ◆

Flights of Wonder ◆

Mr Kamal's

Upcountry ✗

Maharajah Jungle Trek ◆

Yak & Yeti Restaurant ✗

Kali River Rapids ◆

ASIA

Discovery River

Mickey's Jammin' Jungle Parade

Tree of Life— It's Tough to Be a Bug! ◆

First Aid and Baby Care Center

Beastly Kiosk ✗

Expedition Everest ◆

Anandapur Ice Cream Truck ✗

Discovery Island Trails

Tips and Showtimes

Pizzafari ✗

DISCOVERY ISLAND

Flame Tree Barbecue

Disney Outfitters

Island Mercantile

Isle of Java ✗

Trilo-Bites ✗

Boneyard ◆

Fossil Fun Games ◆

Finding Nemo— The Musical

TriceraTop Spin

Restaurantosaurus

Primeval Whirl ◆

DINOLAND U.S.A.

CAMP MINNIE-MICKEY

Festival of the Lion King ◆

Character Greeting Trails

OASIS

Guest Relations

Garden Gate Gifts

Strollers & Wheelchairs

Campfire Treats ✗

Lockers

Guest Relations

ATM

DinoSue ◆

DINOSAUR ◆

Entrance

Rainforest Café ✗

ANIMAL KINGDOM

NAME	Height Req.	Type of Entertainment	Duration	Crowds	Audience	Tips
Africa						
★ Kilimanjaro Safaris	n/a	Riding Tour	20 mins.	Moderate to Heavy	All Ages	Do this first thing in the morning or use Fastpass. If you arrive at the park late morning, save it for day's end, when it's not so hot.
Pangani Forest Exploration Trail	n/a	Zoo/Aviary	Up to you	Light to Moderate	All Ages	Come while waiting for your safari Fastpass; try to avoid coming at the hottest time of day, when the gorillas like to nap.
Asia						
★ Expedition Everest	At least 44"	Thrill Ride	2½ mins.	Huge	All but Small Kids	Use Fastpass. This is the park's biggest thrill ride.
Flights of Wonder	n/a	Show	25 mins.	Light	All Ages	Arrive 15 mins. before showtime, and find a shaded seat beneath one of the awnings—the sun can be brutal.
Kali River Rapids	At least 38"	Thrill Ride	7 mins.	Heavy	All but Small Kids	Use your Fastpass or come during the parade. You'll get wet.
Maharajah Jungle Trek	n/a	Zoo/Aviary	Up to you	Light to Moderate	All Ages	Come anytime.
Camp Minnie-Mickey						
★ Festival of the Lion King	n/a	Show	25 mins.	Light	All Ages	Arrive 30-40 mins. before showtime. Sit in one of the front rows to increase your kid's chance of being chosen.
DinoLand U.S.A.						
Boneyard	n/a	Playground	Up to you	Moderate to Heavy	Small Kids	Play here while waiting for DINOSAUR Fastpass, or come late in the day.

	Name	Height	Type	Duration	Crowds	Audience	Comments
★	DINOSAUR	At least 40"	Thrill Ride	4 mins.	Heavy	All but Small Kids	Come first thing in the morning or at the end of the day, or use Fastpass.
	Finding Nemo–The Musical	n/a	Show	40 mins.	Heavy	All Ages	Arrive 40 mins. before showtime. Take little kids here while big kids wait for Expedition Everest.
	Fossil Fun Games	n/a	Arcade/Fair	Up to you	Light	All but Small Kids	Bring a pocketful of change and a stash of ones.
	Primeval Whirl	At least 48"	Thrill Ride	2½ mins.	Heavy	All Ages	Kids may want to ride twice. Take your first spin early, then use Fastpass if the wait is more than 20 mins.
	TriceraTop Spin	n/a	Thrill Ride for Kids	2 mins.	Heavy	Small Kids	Ride early while everyone else heads for the safari or while waiting for your Fastpass appointment for DINOSAUR.

Discovery Island

	Name	Height	Type	Duration	Crowds	Audience	Comments
★	Tree of Life—It's Tough to Be a Bug!	n/a	3-D film	20 mins.	Moderate to Heavy	All but Small Kids	Do this after Kilimanjaro Safaris. Fastpass is available. Small children may be frightened.

Rafiki's Planet Watch

	Name	Height	Type	Duration	Crowds	Audience	Comments
	Affection Section	n/a	Petting Yard	Up to you	Light	Families	Pet exotic goats and other rare domesticated animals.
	Conservation Station	n/a	Walk-Through	Up to you	Light to Moderate	All Ages	Wait for the critter encounter and learn how to protect endangered species.
	Habitat Habit!	n/a	Trail Walk	Up to you	Light	All Ages	Watch cotton-top tamarins along this discovery trail.
	Wildlife Express Train	n/a	Train Ride	5 mins.	Moderate	All Ages	Head straight to Affection Section with little kids to come face-to-face with domesticated critters.

■ Arrive a half hour before the park opens as much to see the wild animals at their friskiest (morning is a good time to do the safari ride) as to get a jump on the crowds.

■ For updates on line lengths, check the Tip Board, just after crossing the bridge into Discovery Island.

■ Good places to rendezvous include the outdoor seating area of Tusker House restaurant in Africa, in front of DinoLand U.S.A.'s Boneyard, and at the entrance to *Festival of the Lion King* at Camp Minnie-Mickey.

EXPLORING ANIMAL KINGDOM

THE OASIS
This entrance makes you feel as if you've been plunked down in the middle of a rain forest. Cool mist, the aroma of flowers, playful animals, and colorful birds enliven a miniature landscape of streams and grottoes, waterfalls, and glades fringed with banana leaves and jacaranda. On mornings when mists shroud the landscape, it's the scene setter for the rest of your day. It's also where you can take care of essentials before entering. Here you'll find guide maps, stroller and wheelchair rentals, Guest Relations, and an ATM.

DISCOVERY ISLAND
The park hub and site of the Tree of Life, this island is encircled by Discovery River, which isn't an actual attraction but makes for attractive views from the bridge to Harambe and another between Asia and DinoLand U.S.A. The island's whimsical architecture, with wood carvings from Bali, lends charm and a touch of fantasy. The Discovery Island Trails that lead to the Tree of Life provide habitats for African crested porcupines, lemurs, Galápagos tortoises, and other creatures you won't want to miss. It's hard to tear the kids from the glass panel in a cave-like observation area where you can see river otters frolic underwater and above.

You'll discover some great shops and good counter-service eateries here, and the island is also the site of the daily Mickey's Jammin' Jungle Parade. Visitor services that aren't in the Oasis are here, on the border with Harambe, including the baby care center and the first aid center.

ASIA
Meant to resemble an Asian village, this land is full of remarkable rainforest scenery and ruins. Groupings of trees grow from a crumbling tiger shrine, and massive towers—representing Thailand and Nepal—are the habitat for gibbons, whose hooting fills the air.

AFRICA
This largest of the lands is an area of forests and grasslands, predominantly an enclave for wildlife from the continent. Harambe, on the northern bank of Discovery River, is Africa's starting point. Inspired by several East African coastal villages, this Disney town has so much detail that it's mind-boggling to try to soak it all up. Signs on the apparently peeling stucco walls of the buildings are faded, as if bleached by

On Asia's Expedition Everest, you'll chug, twist, turn, and plunge up, through, and down Mt. Everest on nearly a mile of track. Oh, yeah, and beware of the yeti!

the sun, and everything has a hot, dusty look. For souvenirs with both Disney and African themes, browse through the Mombasa Marketplace and

CAMP MINNIE-MICKEY

This Adirondacks-style land hosts performances of the *Festival of the Lion King.* It's also the place to meet the Disney characters for autographs and photo ops at four meet-and-greet trails.

TYPHOON LAGOON AND BLIZZARD BEACH

The beauty of Disney's water parks is that you can make either experience fit your mood. Like crowds? Head for the lounge chairs along the Surf Pool at Typhoon Lagoon or Melt-Away Bay at Blizzard Beach. Prefer peace? Walk past lush foliage along each park's circular path until you spot a secluded lean-to or tree-shaded patch of sand.

According to Disney legend, Typhoon Lagoon was created when the lush Placid Palms Resort was struck by a cataclysmic storm. It left a different world in its wake: surfboard-sundered trees, once-upright palms imitated the Leaning Tower of Pisa, and part of the original lagoon was cut off, trapping thousands of tropical fish—and a few sharks. Nothing, however, topped the fate of *Miss Tilly,* a shrimp boat from "Safen Sound, Florida," which was hurled high in the air and became impaled on Mt. Mayday, a magical volcano that periodically tries to dislodge *Miss Tilly* with huge geysers.

Ordinary folks, the legend continues, would have been crushed by such devastation. But the resourceful residents of Placid Palms were made of hardier stuff—and from the wreckage they created 56-acre Typhoon Lagoon, the self-proclaimed "world's ultimate water park."

With its oxymoronic name, Blizzard Beach promises the seemingly impossible—a seaside playground with an alpine theme. As with its older cousin, Typhoon Lagoon, Disney Imagineers have created a legend to explain the park's origin.

TOP ATTRACTIONS

Typhoon Lagoon

Crush 'n' Gusher

Storm Slides

Typhoon Lagoon Surf Pool

Blizzard Beach

Slush Gusher

Summit Plummet

Tike's Peak

The story goes that after a freak winter storm dropped snow over the western side of Walt Disney World, entrepreneurs created Florida's first downhill ski resort. Sauna-like temperatures soon returned. But as the 66-acre resort's operators were ready to close up shop, they spotted a playful alligator sliding down the 120-foot-tall "liquid ice" slopes. The realization that the melting snow had created the world's tallest, fastest, and most exhilarating water-filled ski and toboggan runs gave birth to the ski resort–water park.

TYPHOON LAGOON

GETTING ORIENTED

The layout is so simple. The wave and swimming lagoon is at the park's center. Note that the waves are born in the Mt. Mayday side and break on the beaches closest to the entrance. Any attraction requiring a gravitational plunge starts around the summit of Mt. Mayday. Shark Reef and Ketchakiddee Creek flank the head of the lagoon, to Mt. Mayday's right and left, respectively, as you enter. The Crush 'n' Gusher water coaster is due right of Singapore Sal's.

You can take WDW bus transportation or drive to Typhoon Lagoon. There's no parking charge. Once inside, your options are to walk, swim, or slide.

WDW Information. Call WDW Information or check www.disney-world.com's park calendars for days of operation. ✉ *Blizzard Beach* ☎ *407/824–4321.*

WHAT TO EXPECT

You can speed down waterslides with names like Crush 'n' Gusher and Humunga Kowabunga or bump through rapids and falls at Mt. Mayday. You can also bob along in 5-foot waves in a surf pool the size of two football fields or, for a mellow break, float in inner tubes along the 2,100-foot Castaway Creek. Go snorkeling in Shark Reef, rubberneck as fellow human cannonballs are ejected from the Storm Slides, or hunker down in a hammock or lounge chair and read a book. Ketchakiddee

Creek, for young children, replicates adult rides on a smaller scale. It's Disney's version of a day at the beach—complete with friendly Disney lifeguards. Most people agree that kids under 7 and older adults prefer Typhoon Lagoon. Bigger kids and teens like Blizzard Beach.

During the off-season between October and April, Typhoon Lagoon closes for several weeks for routine maintenance and refurbishment.

PARKS AMENITIES

Dressing Rooms and Lockers: There are thatched-roof dressing rooms and lockers to the right on your way into the park. It costs $8 a day to rent a small locker and $10 for a large one; there's also a $5 deposit. There are restrooms in every nook and cranny. Most have showers and are much less crowded than the dressing rooms. If you forgot your towel, rent ($2) or buy one at Singapore Sal's.

Guest Services: The staff at Typhoon Lagoon's Guest Services window outside the entrance turnstiles, to your left, can answer many questions. ■ TIP➔ A chalkboard inside gives water temperature and surfing information.

Lost People and Things: Ask about your misplaced people and things at the Guest Services window near the entrance turnstiles. Lost children are taken to an area by the Tip Board near the front of the park, where Disney cast members entertain them with games.

Private Patios: The park has a dozen premium, roped-off Beachcomber Shacks (patios, really) that groups of as many as six can rent. They generally offer shade and sun as well as plush loungers and other chairs, a table with an umbrella, and an ice chest with two bottles of water per guest (up to six). Each guest also gets two beach towels and a refillable soft-drink mug. The whole group gets a locker to share and an attendant to take and deliver food orders (cost of meals not included). The patios cost $300 during peak season (usually March through October) and $175 the rest of the year. Reserve (☏ 407/939–8687) well in advance or arrive very early to book one at High 'N Dry. In summer, any patio that isn't prebooked sells out within a half hour of the park opening.

VISITING TIPS

■ In summer, come first thing in the morning (early birds can ride several times before the lines get long), late in the afternoon when park hours run later, or when the weather clears after a thundershower (rainstorms drive away crowds). Afternoons are also good in cooler weather, as the water is a bit warmer. To make a whole day of it, avoid weekends, when locals and visitors pack in.

■ Women and girls should wear one-piece swimsuits unless they want to find their tops somewhere around their ears at the bottom of the waterslide.

■ Invest in sunscreen and water shoes. Plan to slather sunscreen on several times throughout the day. An inexpensive pair of water shoes will save tootsies from hot sand and walkways and from restroom floors.

■ Arrive 30 minutes before opening so you can park, buy tickets, rent towels, and snag inner tubes before the crowds descend and, trust us, it gets very crowded.

10

From the wreckage—like that shown here—in the wake of a storm, Placid Palms Resort residents created 56-acre Typhoon Lagoon. Or so the story goes…

BLIZZARD BEACH

GETTING ORIENTED

The park layout makes it fairly simple to navigate. Once you enter and rent a locker, you'll cross a small bridge over Cross Country Creek before choosing a spot to park your towels and cooler. To the left is the Melt-Away Bay wave pool. Dead ahead you can see Mt. Gushmore, a chairlift to the top, and the park's many slopes and slides.

If thrills are your game, come early and line up for Summit Plummet, Slush Gusher, and Downhill Double Dipper before wait times go from light to moderate (or heavy). Anytime is a good time for a dip in Melt-Away Bay or a tube trip around Cross Country Creek. Parents with young children should claim their spot early at Tike's Peak, to the park's right even before you cross the bridge.

You can take WDW bus transportation or drive to Blizzard Beach. There's no charge for parking. Once inside, your options are to walk, swim, or slide. (*For more information, see WDW Information, under Getting Oriented in Typhoon Lagoon.*)

WHAT TO EXPECT

Disney Imagineers have gone all out here to create the paradox of a ski resort in the midst of a tropical lagoon. Lots of verbal puns and sight gags play with the snow-in-Florida motif. The centerpiece is Mt. Gushmore, with its 120-foot-high Summit Plummet. Attractions have names like Teamboat Springs, a white-water raft ride. Themed speed slides include Toboggan Racers, Slush Gusher, and Snow Stormers.

Between Mt. Gushmore's base and its summit, swim-skiers can also ride a chairlift converted from ski-resort to beach-resort use—with multihued umbrellas and snow skis on their undersides. Older kids and devoted waterslide enthusiasts generally prefer Blizzard Beach to other water parks.

PARKS AMENITIES

Dressing Rooms and Lockers: Dressing rooms, showers, and restrooms are in the village area, just inside the main entrance. There are other restrooms in Lottawatta Lodge, at the Ski Patrol Training Camp, and just past the Melt-Away Bay beach area. Lockers are near the entrance, next to Snowless Joe's Rentals, and near Tike's Peak (the children's area and the most convenient if you have little swim-skiers in tow). It costs $8 to rent a small locker and $10 for a large one, and there's a $5 deposit. Note that there are only small lockers at Tike's Peak. The towels for rent ($2) at Snowless Joe's are tiny. If you forgot yours, you're better off buying a proper one at the Beach Haus.

Guest Services: Disney staffers at Blizzard Beach's Guest Services window, to the left of the ticket booth as you enter the park, can answer most of your questions. Get free life vests or rent towels and lockers at **Snowless Joe's.** Inner tubes, rafts, and slide mats are provided at the rides. Buy beach gear or rent towels or lockers at **Beach Haus. Shade Shack** is the place for a new pair of sunglasses.

Lost People and Things: Instruct youngsters to let a lifeguard know if they get lost. The lost-children station is beneath a large beach umbrella near the front of the park. And don't worry about the kids—a Disney cast member will keep them busy with activities.

Private Patios: The park has 14 Polar Patios to rent to groups of as many as six people. For $300 a day in peak season (usually March through October) and $175 off-peak, you get plush loungers, chairs, a table with umbrella, refillable beverage mugs, an ice chest with two water bottles per person, a group locker, and an attendant who will take your orders for and deliver lunch and snacks (food costs extra). It's best to book a patio ahead of time (☏407/939–8687). If you arrive early enough, there might be an open patio; check at the Shade Shack.

10

DISNEY'S OTHER WORLDS

Budget a few hours to explore Disney's "other" places. Several are no-admission-required charmers; one is a high-tech, high-cover-charge gaming wonderland.

DISNEY'S BOARDWALK

In the good ol' days, Americans escaped their city routines for breezy seaside boardwalks. Disney's BoardWalk is within walking distance of Epcot, across Crescent Lake from Disney's Yacht and Beach Club Resorts, and fronting a hotel of the same name. You may be drawn to its good restaurants (including Kouzzina, developed by Iron Chef Cat Cora ⇨ *Where to Eat*), bars, shops, surreys, and performers. After sunset, the mood is festive. ■TIP→ If you're here when Epcot is ready to close, you can watch the park fireworks from the bridge that connects BoardWalk to the Yacht and Beach Club Resorts.

NIGHTLIFE

Atlantic Dance Hall. This high-energy Top 40 dance club has a huge screen showing videos requested by the crowd. The parquet dance floor is set off by furnishings of deep blue, maroon, and gold, and the ceiling glows with gold stars and twinkling lights. Signature cocktails are in demand, and you can sip a cognac or choose from a selection of popular beers to inspire your dance floor moves. ⊠ *BoardWalk, Epcot Resort Area* ☎ *407/939–2444* ☜ *No cover* ⊙ *Tues.–Sat. 9 pm–1:45 am.*

Big River Grille & Brewing Works. Disney World's only brewpub has intimate tables where brew masters tend to their potions. You can order an $8.25 sampler with up to five 2½-ounce shots of whatever's on tap that day, usually including Red Rocket, Southern Flyer Light Lager, Gadzooks Pilsner, and Steamboat Pale Ale. Upscale pub grub and sandwiches pair well. There's also a sidewalk café. ⊠ *BoardWalk, Epcot Resort Area* ☎ *407/560–0253* ☜ *No cover* ⊙ *Daily 11:30 am–midnight.*

ESPN Club. The sports motif here is carried into every nook and cranny— the main dining area looks like a sports arena, with a basketball-court hardwood floor and a giant scoreboard that projects the day's big game. While you watch, munch on wings, nachos, and linebacker-sized burgers. There are more than 100 TVs throughout (even in the restrooms). The place is packed for big games; call ahead to see if special seating rules are in effect. ⊠ *BoardWalk, Epcot Resort Area* ☎ *407/939–1177* ☜ *No cover* ⊙ *Daily 11:30 am–1 am.*

Jellyrolls. In this rockin', boisterous piano bar, comedians act as emcees and play dueling grand pianos nonstop. The steady stream of conventions at Disney makes this the place to catch CEOs doing the conga to Barry Manilow's "Copacabana"—if that's your idea of a good time. ⊠ *BoardWalk, Epcot Resort Area* ☎ *407/560–8770* ☜ *$12 cover* ⊙ *Daily 7 pm–1:45 am.*

DOWNTOWN DISNEY

EXPLORING

East of Epcot and close to Interstate 4 (I–4) along a large lake, this shopping, dining, and entertainment complex has three areas: the Marketplace, West Side, and the connecting district, Pleasure Island. You can rent lockers, strollers, or wheelchairs, and there are two Guest Relations (aka Guest Services) centers.

DisneyQuest. In a five-story virtual-reality mini-theme park in Downtown Disney's West Side, DisneyQuest lets you pay a hefty cover to participate in high-tech virtual adventures and play video games. To be fair, you can play all day, and there are cutting-edge games and interactive adventures that make the admission worthwhile. It's also a great place for teens and older tweens (children under 10 must be accompanied by an adult).

All attractions are wheelchair accessible, but most require transfer from wheelchair to the attraction itself. You can, however, wheel right onto Pirates of the Caribbean: Battle for Buccaneer Gold, Aladdin's Magic Carpet Ride, and Mighty Ducks Pinball Slam. Rent wheelchairs at the DisneyQuest Emporium or at Downtown Disney Marketplace Guest Relations ($12 per day for hand operated, plus $100 refundable credit-card deposit); electric chairs are $50 plus deposit at the Marketplace location only. Guide dogs are permitted in all areas but aren't allowed to ride several attractions. Strollers are *not* permitted.

Four attractions have height requirements: Cyberspace Mountain (51 inches), Buzz Lightyear's AstroBlaster (51 inches), Mighty Ducks Pinball Slam (48 inches), and Pirates of the Caribbean (35 inches). Little ones 2–7 can enjoy a Kids' Area on the fourth floor, where they can play smaller versions of video and other games like air hockey, basketball, and bowling.

Lost and Found is at the admissions window, film can be purchased at the Emporium, and cash is available at ATMs inside the House of Blues merchandise shop not far from the DisneyQuest entrance. ⊠ *West Side* ☎ 407/828–4600 💲 *$44 adults, $38 children 3–9, excluding sales tax* ⊙ *Sun.–Thurs. 11:30 am–10 pm, Fri. and Sat. 11:30 am–11 pm.*

Marketplace. In the Marketplace, the easternmost Downtown Disney area, you can meander along winding sidewalks and explore hidden alcoves. Children love to splash in fountains that spring from the pavement and ride the miniature train and old-time carousel ($2). Toy stores entice with creation-stations and too many treasures to comprehend. There are plenty of spots to grab a bite or sip a cappuccino along the lakefront. The Marketplace is open from 9:30 am to 11 pm.

Pleasure Island. When it was a hopping nightlife destination, this area offered a mix of bars, comedy clubs, and dance spots. But the nightclubs are long closed, and the Island has become more of a family-oriented dining and entertainment district. Raglan Road Irish Pub & Restaurant offers great food by Raglan Road's Irish celebrity chef Kevin Dundon, live Irish music, and traditional dance performances every night. Paradiso 37 also welcomes diners, and the upscale cigar bar Fuego Cigars by Sosa serves wine and spirits. Other restaurants and shops beckon as you stroll from the Marketplace to West Side.

West Side. The main attractions in the hip West Side are the House of Blues music hall, Cirque du Soleil, the new Splitsville Luxury Lanes, and DisneyQuest virtual indoor theme park and arcade. You can also take a ride in the Characters in Flight helium balloon tethered here ($18 ages 10 and up, $12 ages 3–9), shop in boutiques, or dine in such restaurants as the Wolfgang Puck Café and Planet Hollywood. Shops open at 9:30 or 10:30 am, and closing time is between 11 pm and 2 am. The Splitsville entertainment center offers plenty of fresh fun with 30 bowling lanes on two floors, weekend DJs, and upscale eats like filet sliders and sushi.

10

NIGHTLIFE

Bongos Cuban Café. Latin rhythms provide the beat at this enterprise with a pre-Castro theme owned by pop singer Gloria Estefan. Four bars are especially busy on weekends, when a Latin band kicks it up a notch with *muy caliente* music. Samba, tango, salsa, and merengue rhythms roll throughout the week. ⊠ *West Side* ☎ *407/828–0999* ◷ *Sun.–Thurs. 11–11, Fri. and Sat. 11 am–2 am.*

House of Blues. The restaurant serves up live blues performances Friday and Saturday and rib-sticking Mississippi Delta cooking all week long. The attached concert hall has showcased such artists as Aretha Franklin, David Byrne, Steve Miller, Willie Nelson, and Journey. ⊠ *West Side* ☎ *407/934–2583* ▦ *Covers vary* ◷ *Daily, performance and restaurant times vary.*

UNIVERSAL ORLANDO

with Wet 'n Wild

WELCOME TO UNIVERSAL ORLANDO

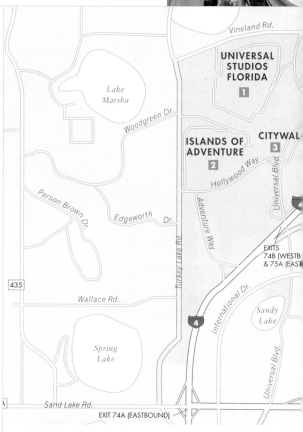

TOP REASONS TO GO

★ **The Variety:** Universal Orlando is much more than just a single Hollywood-themed amusement park. It's also the fantasy-driven Islands of Adventure (IOA) theme park; the clubs and restaurants of the CityWalk entertainment complex; and the upscale, on-site Hard Rock Hotel, Portofino Bay, and Royal Pacific resorts. Nearby Wet 'n Wild water park is also affiliated with Universal.

★ **Theme-Park Powerhouse:** Neither SeaWorld nor any of Disney's four theme parks can match the energy at Universal Studios and Islands of Adventure. Wild rides, clever shows, constantly updated attractions, and an edgy attitude all push the envelope here.

★ **Party Central:** Throughout the year, Universal hosts festive park-wide events such as Mardi Gras, Halloween Horror Nights, Grinchmas, the Summer Concert Series, and the Rock the Universe Christian-music celebration.

1 Universal Studios Florida. The centerpiece of Universal Orlando is a creative and quirky tribute to Hollywood past, present, and future. Overall, the collection of wild rides, quiet retreats, live shows, street characters, and clever movies (both 3-D and 4-D) are as entertaining as the

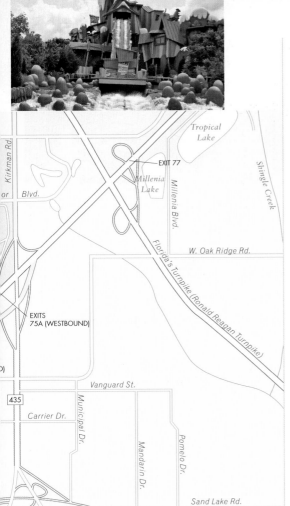

GETTING ORIENTED

Universal Orlando is tucked into a corner created by the intersection of Interstate 4 and Kirkman Road (Highway 435), midway between Downtown Orlando and the Walt Disney World Resort. Here you'll be about 15 minutes from each and just 10 minutes from SeaWorld.

motion pictures they celebrate (and they're always adding something new).

2 Islands of Adventure. Certainly the most significant addition to any Orlando theme park came in 2010 when IOA introduced an entire land dedicated to Harry Potter, which, in turn, sparked

a substantial surge in attendance. Also at IOA are Spider-Man, the Hulk, velociraptors, the Cat in the Hat, and dozens of other characters that give guests every reason to head to the islands.

3 CityWalk. Even when the parks are closed (especially when the parks are

closed), locals and visitors come to this sprawling entertainment and retail complex to watch movies; dine at theme restaurants; shop for everything from cigars to surf wear; and stay up late at nightclubs celebrating the French Quarter, Jamaica, and Latin America.

By Gary
McKechnie

Universal Orlando's personality is revealed the moment you arrive on property. Mood music, cartoonish architecture, abundant eye candy, subtle and overt sound effects, whirling and whizzing rides plus a throng of fellow travelers will follow you to nearly every corner of the park. For peace and quiet, seek out a sanctuary at one of the resort hotels.

At a breathless pace, there's a chance you could visit both Universal parks in a single day, but you'd have to invest in an Express Pass. Otherwise you'll spend a good portion of that day waiting in line at the premium attractions. Allow two days, perhaps three; a day for each park and a "pick-up" day to return to your favorites at a leisurely pace. Which attractions are the main attractions? At IOA, it's definitely the Wizarding World of Harry Potter (especially the high-volume/low-capacity Ollivanders wand shop), and at Universal Studios you'll find long lines at the Mummy and the Simpsons.

Universal Studios appeals primarily to those who like loud, fast, high-energy attractions—generally teens and adults. Covering 444 acres, it's a rambling montage of sets, shops, and soundstages housing themed attractions, reproductions of New York and San Francisco, and some genuine moviemaking paraphernalia.

When Islands of Adventure (IOA) first opened in 1999, it took attractions to a new level. Most—from Marvel Super Hero Island and Toon Lagoon to Seuss Landing and the Lost Continent—are impressive; some even out-Disney Disney. And in 2010, IOA received well-deserved worldwide attention when it opened the 20-acre Wizarding World of Harry Potter.

PLANNING

GETTING HERE AND AROUND

East on Interstate 4 (from WDW and Tampa), exit at Universal Boulevard (75A); take a left into Universal Orlando, and follow the signs. Heading west on Interstate 4 (from Downtown or Daytona, even), exit at Universal Boulevard (74B), turn right, and follow Hollywood Way.

Both Universal Studios and IOA require a lot of walking—a whole lot of walking. Start off by using the parking area's moving walkways as much as possible. Arrive early at either park, and you may be able to complete a single lap that will get you to the main attractions.

OPERATING HOURS

Universal Studios and IOA are open 365 days a year, from 9 am to 7 pm, with hours as late as 10 pm in summer and at holidays. Wet 'n Wild is also open 365 days a year, weather permitting, but with widely varying hours. Usually it's open from 9 to 6—sometimes earlier, often times much later, with summer hours from 9:30 am until 9 pm. Call for exact hours during holiday periods.

PARKING

Universal's two garages total 3.4 million square feet, so *note your parking space.* The cost is $15 for cars and motorcycles ($5 after 6 pm and free after 10), $20 for RVs and preferred parking. Although moving walkways get you partway, you could walk up to a half mile to reach the gates. Valet parking ($15 for up to two hours, $30 for more than two hours) is much closer.

ADMISSION

The at-the-gate, per-person, per-day rate for either Universal Studios Florida or IOA is $89 (ages 10-plus) and $83 for children (ages 3–9).

EXPRESS PASSES

The Express Pass ranges in price from about $20 off-season to $80 in peak season and as high as $100 around Christmas. Why so much? This pass gets you to the front of most lines and saves a tremendous amount of time. If crowds are thin and lines are moving fast, skip this pass. Also, if you're a guest at a Universal hotel, this perk is free; your room key card serves as the pass.

MEAL DEALS

All-you-can-eat, daylong meal deals are good at three sit-down restaurants in Universal (Mel's Drive-In, Louie's Italian, and Monsters Café) and three in IOA (Circus McGurkus Cafe Stoo-pendous, Comic Strip Cafe, the Burger Digs). The cost is $21.99 a day for adults, $10.99 daily for kids; an extra $10.99 a day buys all-you-can-drink soda in a souvenir cup.

UNIVERSAL STRATEGIES

■ **Arrive early.** Come as early as 8 am if the parks open at 9. Seriously. Better to share them with hundreds of people than with thousands.

■ **Visit on a weekday.** Crowds are lighter, especially fall through spring, when kids are in school

■ **Don't forget anything in your car.** Universal's parking areas are at least a half mile from park entrances, and a round-trip hike will eat up valuable time. Consider valet parking. It costs $30 for more than two hours before 6 pm (almost twice as much as regular parking), but it puts you much closer to Universal's park entrances and just steps from CityWalk.

■ **Know the restrictions.** A few things aren't allowed in the parks: alcohol and glass containers; hard-sided coolers; soft-sided coolers larger than 8½ inches wide by 6 inches high by 6 inches deep; and coolers, suitcases, and other bags with wheels. But if your flight's leaving later, they will check your luggage at the parks (unless you just leave them in your car).

■ **Look into the Express Pass.** Jumping to the front of the line with this pass really is worth the extra cost on busy days—unless you stay at a resort hotel, in which case front-of-line access is one of the perks. A very valuable perk.

■ **Ride solo.** At Universal some rides have a Single Rider line that moves much faster than regular lines.

■ **Get expert advice.** The folks at Guest Services (aka Guest Relations) have great insight. The reps can even create a custom itinerary free of charge.

■ **Check out Child Swap.** At certain Universal attractions, one parent can enter the attraction, take a spin, and then return to take care of the baby while the other parent rides without having to wait in line again.

FOR PEOPLE WITH DISABILITIES

The *Studio Guide for Guests with Disabilities* (aka *Rider's Guide*) details attractions with special entrances and viewing areas, interpreters, Braille scripts, and assistance devices. In general, if you can transfer from your wheelchair unassisted or with the help of a friend, you can ride many attractions. Some rides have carts that accommodate manual wheelchairs, though not motorized wheelchairs or electronic convenience vehicles (ECVs).

CONTACTS

Universal ☎ *407/363–8000* ⊕ *www.universalorlando.com*

Universal Dining and Tickets ☎ *407/224–7840*

Universal (Loews Resorts) Room Reservations ☎ *877/819–7884*

Universal Vacation Packages ☎ *800/407–4275*

Wet 'n Wild ☎ *407/351–1800 or 800/992–9453* ⊕ *www.wetnwild.com*

UNIVERSAL STUDIOS

Inspired by the California original and opened in Orlando in 1990 (when the city assumed it would become "Hollywood East"), Universal Studios celebrates the movies. The park is a jumble of areas and attractions. But the same is true of back-lot sets at a film studio. Suspend any disbelief you might have, and just enjoy the motion-picture magic.

At Production Central large soundstages house attractions based on TV programs and films like *Shrek*, *Despicable Me*, and *Twister*. Because it's right near the entrance it may be the park's most crowded area.

Here you see first-hand that not every film or program based in New York is actually shot in New York. Cleverly constructed sets mean that nearly every studio can own its own Big Apple. Universal is no exception. As you explore Production Central, a collection of sparkling public buildings, well-worn neighborhoods, and back alleys are the next best thing to Manhattan itself.

As you enter the area known as San Francisco, you're roughly one-third of the way through the park. The crowds spread out, and the pace seems to slow. You can stop to see a show starring Beetlejuice or dine at the waterfront Lombard's Seafood Grille.

There's not much shaking between San Francisco and World Expo and its two large attractions—MEN IN BLACK: Alien Attack and the Simpsons Ride. The scarcity of rides here is, however, offset by the abundant attractions at Woody Woodpecker's KidZone. It matches the energy of toddlers and the under-10 crowd with diversions that include a junior-size roller coaster, a mini–water park, and a chance to meet E.T. and Barney the dinosaur. In Hollywood, quiet parks and flashy Rodeo Drive really do make you think you've stepped into vintage Tinseltown.

All in all, Universal Studios fulfills its promise: to put you in the movies.

PLANNING

GETTING ORIENTED

On a map, the park appears neatly divided into six areas positioned around a huge lagoon. There's Production Central, which covers the entire left side of the Plaza of the Stars; New York, with street performances at 70 Delancey; San Francisco; futuristic World Expo; Woody Woodpecker's KidZone; and Hollywood.

What's tricky is that—because it's designed like a series of movie sets—there's no straightforward way to tackle the park. You'll probably make some detours and do some backtracking. To save time and shoe leather, ask theme park hosts for itinerary suggestions and time-saving tips. Here are a few of our own suggestions.

TOURING TIPS

We highly recommend you purchase your tickets online because it gives you plenty of time to consider your many options and includes a discount. Entering Universal Studios can be overwhelming as you and thousands of others flood through the turnstiles at once. Pick up a map in the entryway to CityWalk or by the park turnstiles and spend a few minutes reviewing it. Map out a route, find show schedules, and select restaurants. If a host is nearby, ask for insider advice on what to see first.

The "right" way. Upon entering, avoid the temptation to go left toward the towering soundstages, looping the park clockwise. Instead, head right—bypassing shops, restaurants, and some crowds to primary attractions like the Simpsons Ride and MEN IN BLACK: Alien Attack.

Universal Studios

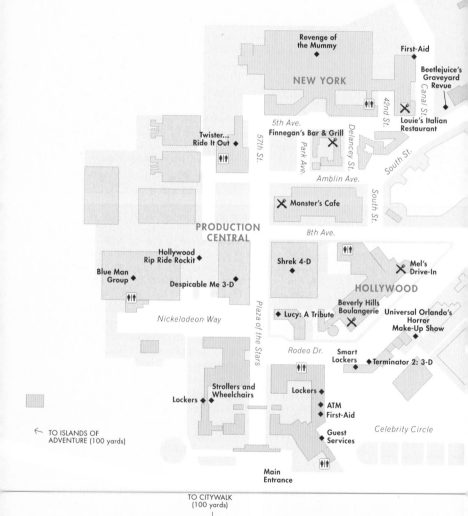

NEW YORK

Revenge of
the Mummy

First-Aid

Beetlejuice's
Graveyard
Revue

Louie's Italian
Restaurant

Canal St.

42nd St.

5th Ave.
Finnegan's Bar & Grill

Twister...
Ride It Out

57th St.

Park Ave.

Delancey St.

South St.

Amblin Ave.

Monster's Cafe

South St.

**PRODUCTION
CENTRAL**

8th Ave.

Hollywood
Rip Ride Rockit

Blue Man
Group

Despicable Me 3-D

Shrek 4-D

Mel's
Drive-In

HOLLYWOOD

Beverly Hills
Boulangerie

Universal Orlando's
Horror
Make-Up Show

Nickelodeon Way

Plaza of the Stars

Lucy: A Tribute

Rodeo Dr.

Smart
Lockers

Terminator 2: 3-D

Strollers and
Wheelchairs

Lockers

Lockers

ATM
First-Aid

Celebrity Circle

← TO ISLANDS OF
ADVENTURE (100 yards)

Guest
Services

Main
Entrance

TO CITYWALK
(100 yards)
↓

Midway
Grill

Disaster!

SAN FRANCISCO

The Embarcadero

San Francisco
Pastry Co.

Amity Ave.

Lombard's
Seafood Grille

Richter's Burger Co.

The
Lagoon

Smart Lockers

MEN IN BLACK:
Alien Attack

WORLD EXPO

The Simpsons
Ride

Exposition Blvd.

Sunset Blvd.

International
Food and Film
Festival

Animal Actors
on Location!

A Day in the
Park with Barney

WOODY WOODPECKER'S
KIDZONE

E.T. Adventure

Fievel's Playland

Curious George
Goes to Town

Woody
Woodpecker's
Nuthouse Coaster

TO VINELAND RD. →

KEY	
✕	*Restaurants*
🚻	*Restrooms*

UNIVERSAL STUDIOS

NAME	Height Req.	Type of Entertainment	Duration	Crowds	Audience	Tips
Hollywood						
Lucy: A Tribute	n/a	Walk-Through	15 mins.	Light	Adults	Save this for a hot afternoon or for on your way out.
Terminator 2 3-D	n/a	3-D Film/ Simulator Exp.	21 mins.	Heavy	All but Small Kids	Come first thing in the morning or use Express Pass.
★ Universal Orlando's Horror Make-Up Show	n/a	Show	25 mins.	Moderate	All but Small Kids	Come in the afternoon or evening. Young children may be frightened; older children eat up the blood-and-guts comedy.
Production Central						
★ Hollywood Rip Ride Rockit!	At least 51"	Thrill Ride	2 mins.	You Bet!	All but Small Kids	Come early, late, or use a Express Pass. Be patient.
Shrek 4-D	n/a	3-D Film	12 mins.	Heavy	All Ages	Come early or late, or use Express Pass.
New York						
Revenge of the Mummy	At least 48"	Thrill Ride	3 mins.	Heavy	All but Small Kids	Use Express Pass, or come first thing in the morning.
Twister…Ride It Out	n/a	Show/ Simulator Exp.	3 mins.	Heavy	All but Small Kids	Come first thing in morning or at closing. This "ride" involves standing and watching the action unfold.
San Francisco/Amity						
Beetlejuice's Graveyard Revue	n/a	Show	25 mins.	Light to Moderate	All but Small Kids	You can use Express Pass here, but there's really no need as there's little chance of a wait.
Disaster!	n/a	Thrill Ride	20 mins.	Heavy	All but Small Kids	Come early, before closing, or use Universal Express Pass. This is loud.
JAWS	n/a	Thrill Ride with Water	7 mins.	Moderate	All but Small Kids	Come after dark for a more terrifying ride. Use Express Pass if needed.

Woody Woodpecker's KidZone

A Day in the Park with Barney	n/a	Show	20 mins.	Light	Small Kids	Arrive 10–15 mins. early on crowded days for a good seat—up close and in the center. Can use Express Pass.
Animal Actors on Location!	n/a	Show	20 mins.	Moderate to Heavy	All Ages	Stadium seating, but come early for a good seat. Express Pass accepted.
Curious George Goes to Town	n/a	Playground with Water	Up to you	Moderate	Small Kids	Come in late afternoon or early evening. Bring a towel.
E.T. Adventure	At least 34"	Thrill Ride for Kids	5 mins.	Moderate to Heavy	All Ages	Come early morning or use Express Pass.
Fievel's Playland	n/a	Playground with Water	Up to you	Light to Moderate	Small Kids	Generally light crowds, but there are waits for the waterslide. On hot days come late.
Woody Woodpecker's Nuthouse Coaster	At least 36"	Thrill Ride for Kids	1½ mins.	Moderate to Heavy	Small Kids	Come at park closing, when most little ones have gone home. Try Express Pass.

World Expo

MEN IN BLACK: Alien Attack	At least 42"	Thrill Ride	4½ mins.	Heavy	All but Small Kids	Solo riders can take a faster line, so split up. This ride spins. Use Express Pass.
★ The Simpsons Ride	40"	Thrill Ride/ Simulator Exp.	6 mins.	Heavy	All but Small Kids	Use Express Pass.

★ **Fodor's**Choice

TOP ATTRACTIONS

AGES 7 AND UP Hollywood Rip Ride Rockit MEN IN BLACK: Alien Attack Revenge of the Mummy Shrek 4-D The Simpsons Ride Terminator 2: 3-D Twister...Ride It Out	Universal Orlando's Horror Make-Up Show **AGES 6 AND UNDER** Animal Actors on Location! Curious George Goes to Town A Day in the Park with Barney

Photo ops. Universal Studios posts signs that indicate photo spots and show how best to frame your shot.

Rendezvous. Good meeting spots include Lucy: A Tribute, near the entrance; Mel's Drive-In, midway through the park on the right, and Beetlejuice's Graveyard Revue midway through the park on the left.

PARK AMENITIES

Guest Services: Get strategy advice *before* visiting by calling Guest Services at ☎ *407/224–4233.*

Lockers: Daily rates for lockers near the park entrance are $8 for a small unit and $10 for a larger one. There are free lockers near the entrances of some high-speed attractions (such as MEN IN BLACK: Alien Attack and Revenge of the Mummy), where you can stash your stuff before your ride; they're available to you for up to 90 minutes total.

Lost People and Things: If you plan to split up, be sure everyone knows where and when to reconnect. Staffers take lost children to **Guest Services** near the main entrance. This is also where you might find lost personal items.

Stroller Rentals: Just inside the main entrance, there are strollers for $15 (single) and $25 (double) a day. You can also rent small kiddie cars ($18) or large ones ($28) by the day.

Wheelchair Rentals: You can rent manual wheelchairs ($12 per day) at the parking garages and inside the main entrance. Because there are limited quantities of electronic convenience vehicles (ECVs, available in the park for $50), reserve one in advance. A photo ID and a $50 deposit on a credit card are required for wheelchairs.

EXPLORING UNIVERSAL STUDIOS

PRODUCTION CENTRAL

Expect plenty of loud, flashy, rollicking rides that appeal to tweens, teens, and adults. Clear the turnstiles and go straight. You can use Express Pass at all attractions but Hollywood Rip Ride Rockit.

NEW YORK

Universal has gone all out to re-create New York's skyscrapers, commercial districts, ethnic neighborhoods, and back alleys—right down to the cracked concrete. Hidden within these structures are restaurants, arcades, gift shops, and key attractions. And, although they're from Chicago, the Blues Brothers drive from the Second City to New York City in their Bluesmobile for free performances at 70 Delancey. Here you can use Express Pass at Revenge of the Mummy and *Twister.*

SAN FRANCISCO

This area celebrates the West Coast with the wharves and warehouses of San Francisco's Embarcadero and Fisherman's Wharf districts. *Use your Express Pass at both attractions.*

WORLD EXPO

At the far end of the park is a futuristic set of buildings containing two of Universal Studios' most popular attractions, MEN IN BLACK: Alien Attack and the Simpsons Ride, which offer fast admission with Express Pass.

HOLLYWOOD

The quintessential tribute to the golden age of the silver screen, this area to the right of the park entrance celebrates icons like the Brown Derby, Schwab's Pharmacy, and art deco Hollywood. There are only a few attractions here, and all except Lucy accept Universal Express Pass.

ISLANDS OF ADVENTURE

More so than just about any other theme park, Islands of Adventure has gone all out to create settings and attractions that transport you from reality into the surreal. What's more, no one island here has much in common with any other, so in a way, a visit here is almost like a visit to half a dozen different parks.

IOA's unique nature is first revealed when you arrive at the Port of Entry and are greeted by a kaleidoscope of sights and a cacophony of sounds. It's all designed to put you in the frame of mind for adventure.

When you reach the central lagoon, your clockwise journey commences with Marvel Super Hero Island and its tightly packed concentration of roller coasters and thrill rides. Of special note is the amazingly high-tech and dazzling Amazing Adventures of Spider-Man. In just minutes you'll have experienced a day's worth of sensations—and you've only just begun.

Stepping into Toon Lagoon is like stepping into the pages of a comic book, just as entering the upcoming island, Jurassic Park, is like entering a research center where reconstituted dinosaur DNA is being used to create a new breed of *brontosaurus.*

Islands of Adventure

THE WIZARDING WORLD OF HARRY POTTER

Flight of the Hippogriff

Hagrid's Hut

Harry Potter and the Forbidden Journey

Dragon Challenge

Three Broomsticks

Hogsmeade Village

Fire Eater's Grill

Eighth Voyage of Sindbad

Mythos

LOST CONTINENT

Poseidon's Fury

First Aid

Jurassic Park River Adventure

Thunder Falls Terrace

Camp Jurassic

Guest Services

The Burger Digs

Pteranodon Flyers

Jurassic Park Discovery Center

JURASSIC PARK

Dudley Do-Right's Ripsaw Falls

Blondie's

TOON LAGOON

Comic Strip Cafe

Popeye & Bluto's Bilge-Rat Barges

Me Ship, The Olive

Captain America Diner

MARVEL SUPER HERO ISLAND

Amazing Adventures of Spider-Man

SEUSS LANDING

The High in the Sky Seuss Trolley Train Ride!

If I Ran the Zoo

Circus McGurkus Cafe Stoo-pendous

Doctor Doom's Fearfall

Cafe 4

Incredible Hulk Coaster

Caro-Seuss-el

Confisco Grill

One Fish, Two Fish, Red Fish, Blue Fish

Storm Force Accelatron

Smart Lockers

The Cat in the Hat

PORT OF ENTRY

Lockers

Guest Services and First Aid

Strollers and Wheelchairs

KEY

✗ Restaurants

🛉🛉 Restrooms

In the Jurassic Park Discovery Center, your kids might just learn something about dinosaurs that they didn't already know.

You move from the world of science into the world of magic when you segue into the Wizarding World of Harry Potter. For the first time anywhere, you—and not just a few fortunate actors—can wander through the magnificently fictional, yet now very realistic, realm of the young wizard and his Hogwarts classmates and tutors. Beyond belief.

But that's not the end of it. In the Lost Continent the mood is that of a Renaissance fair, where crafters work inside colorful tents. It's as pronounced an atmosphere as that of the final island, Seuss Landing, which presents the incredible, topsy-turvy world of Dr. Seuss. It's a riot of colors and shapes and fantastic wildlife that pay tribute to the good doctor's vivid imagination.

PLANNING

GETTING ORIENTED

Getting your bearings at IOA is far easier than at its sister park, Universal Studios. Brochures in a multitude of languages are in a rack a few steps beyond the turnstiles. The brochures include a foldout map that will acquaint you with the park's simple layout (it's a circle).

And, ahead by the lagoon, boards are posted with up-to-the-minute ride and show information—including the length of lines at the major attractions.

You pass through the turnstiles and into the Port of Entry plaza, a bazaar that brings together bits and pieces of architecture, landscaping, music, and wares from many lands—Dutch windmills, Indonesian pedicabs, African masks, restrooms marked "Loo's Landing," and Egyptian figurines that adorn a massive archway inscribed with the notice "The Adventure Begins." From here, themed islands—arranged around a large lagoon—are connected by walkways that make navigation easy. When you've done the full circuit, you'll recall the fantastic range of sights, sounds, and experiences and realize there can be truth in advertising. This park really *is* an adventure.

TOURING TIPS

Hosts. Just about any employee is a host, whether they're at a kiosk or attraction or turnstile. Ask them about their favorite experiences—and for suggestions for saving time.

TOP ATTRACTIONS

11

Ages 7 and Up

Amazing Adventures of Spider-Man

Dudley Do-Right's Ripsaw Falls

Eighth Voyage of Sindbad

Harry Potter and the Forbidden Journey

Ages 6 and Under

The Cat in the Hat

Flight of the Hippogriff

Popeye & Bluto's Bilge-Rat Barges

Photo Ops. Islands of Adventure posts signs that indicate picture spots and show how best to frame your shot.

Retreat. Explore little-used sidewalks and quiet alcoves to counter IOA's manic energy.

Split the difference. If the park's open late, split the day in half. See part of it in the morning, head off-site to a restaurant for lunch (your parking ticket is good all day) then head to your hotel for a swim or a nap (or both). Return in the cooler, less crowded evening.

ISLANDS OF ADVENTURES PLANNER

PARK AMENITIES

Guest Services. Guest Services is right near the turnstiles, both before and after you enter Islands of Adventure (IOA). ☎ *407/224–6350.*

Lockers: There are $8-a-day lockers across from Guest Services at the entrance; for $10 a day you can rent a family-size model. You have unlimited access to both types throughout the day—although it's a hike back to retrieve things. Scattered strategically throughout the park—notably at the Incredible Hulk Coaster, Jurassic Park River Adventure, and Forbidden Journey—are so-called Smart Lockers. These are free for the first 45 to 75 minutes, $2 per hour afterward, and max out at $14 per day. Stash backpacks and cameras here while you're being drenched on a watery ride or going through the spin cycle on a twisty one.

Lost People and Things: If you've misplaced something, head to Guest Services in the Port of Entry. This is also where park staffers take lost children.

Stroller Rentals: You can rent strollers ($15 per day for singles, $25 for doubles) at the Port of Entry to your left after the turnstiles. You can also rent kiddie cars—small ones for $18, and large ones for $28.

NAME	Height Req.	Type of Entertainment	Duration	Crowds	Audience	Tips
Jurassic Park						
Camp Jurassic	n/a	Playground	Up to you	Light to Moderate	All Ages	Come anytime.
Jurassic Park Discovery Center	n/a	Walk-Through	Up to you	Light	Small Kids to Teens	Come anytime.
Jurassic Park River Adventure	At least 42"	Thrill Ride with Water	6 mins.	Heavy	All but Small Kids	Use Express Pass. Come early or late.
Pteranodon Flyers	36" to 56"	Thrill Ride for Kids	2 mins.	Heavy	All Ages	Skip this on your first visit. 36" to 48" can ride but must do so with an adult.
Lost Continent						
Eighth Voyage of Sindbad	n/a	Show	25 mins.	Heavy	All but Small Kids	Stadium seating for everyone, but arrive at least 15 mins. early. Don't sit too far up front. Use Express Pass.
Poseidon's Fury	n/a	Walk-through Simulator Exp.	20 mins.	Heavy	All but Small Kids	Come at the end of the day. Stay to the left for best spot. Get in first row each time. Express Pass accepted.
Marvel Super Hero Island						
★ The Amazing Adventures of Spider-Man	At least 40"	Simulator Exp.	4½ mins.	Absolutely	All but Small Kids	Use Express Pass, or come early or late in day. Don't miss the bad guys in the wanted posters. Try it twice if you can.
Doctor Doom's Fearfall	At least 52"	Thrill Ride	1 min.	Light to Moderate	All but Small Kids	Use Express Pass, or come later in the day. Regardless, come with an empty stomach.
Incredible Hulk Coaster	At least 54"	Thrill Ride	2¼ mins.	Yes!	All but Small Kids	Come here first. Effects are best in the morning. The front row is best.

Attraction	Height	Type	Duration	Crowds	Age	Comments
Storm Force Accelatron	n/a	Thrill Ride	2 mins.	Light	All but Small Kids	Come whenever—except right after eating.
Seuss Landing						
Caro-Seuss-el	n/a	Thrill Ride for Kids	2 mins.	Moderate	All Ages	Use Express Pass, or end your day here.
The Cat in the Hat	n/a	Thrill Ride for Kids	4½ mins.	Heavy	All Ages	Use Express Pass here, or come early or at the end of the day.
High in the Sky Seuss Trolley Train Ride!	At least 34"	Railroad	3 mins.	Heavy	All Ages	Kids love trains, so plan to get in line! 34" to 48" can ride but must do so with an adult. Express Pass accepted.
If I Ran the Zoo	n/a	Playground with Water	Up to you	Heavy	Small Kids	Come toward the end of your visit.
One Fish, Two Fish, Red Fish, Blue Fish	n/a	Thrill Ride for Kids	2+ mins.	Heavy	Small Kids	Use Express Pass, or come early or late in day. Skip it on your first visit.
Toon Lagoon						
Dudley Do-Right's Ripsaw Falls	At least 44"	Thrill Ride with Water	5½ mins.	Heavy	All but Small Kids	Ride the flume in late afternoon to cool down, or at day's end. There's no seat where you can stay dry. Express Pass accepted.
Me Ship, The Olive	n/a	Playground	Up to you	Heavy	Small Kids	Come in the morning or at dinnertime.
Popeye and Bluto's Bilge-Rat Barges	At least 42 "	Thrill Ride with Water	5 mins.	Heavy	All but Small Kids	Come early in the morning or before closing. You will get wet. Express Pass accepted.
The Wizarding World of Harry Potter						
Dragon Challenge	At least 54"	Thrill Ride	3 mins.	Heavy	All but Small Kids	Use Express Pass. Avoid if you're prone to motion sickness.
Flight of the Hippogriff	At least 36"	Thrill Ride for Kids	1 min.	Moderate	Small Kids	Keep an eye on the line, and come when there's an opening. Express Pass accepted.
Harry Potter and the Forbidden Journey	At least 48"	Walk-Through/Ride-Through/Thrill Ride	50 mins.	Yes!	All but Small Kids	Come early and use Express Pass. Steer clear if you have a queasy stomach.

EXPLORING ISLANDS OF ADVENTURE

MARVEL SUPER HERO ISLAND

The facades on Stanley Boulevard (named for Marvel's famed editor and co-creator Stan Lee) put you smack in the middle of an alternatively pleasant and apocalyptic comic-book world—complete with heroes, villains, and cartoony colors and flourishes. Although the spiky, horrific towers of Doctor Doom's Fearfall and the vivid green of the Hulk's coaster are focal points, the Amazing Adventures of Spider-Man is the must-see attraction. At various times Doctor Doom, Spider-Man, and the Incredible Hulk are available for photos, and sidewalk artists are on hand to paint your face like your favorite hero (or villain). All rides here accept Universal Express Pass.

TOON LAGOON

The main street, Comic Strip Lane, makes use of cartoon characters that are recognizable to anyone—anyone born before 1940, that is. Pert little Betty Boop, gangly Olive Oyl, muscle-bound Popeye, Krazy Kat, Mark Trail, Flash Gordon, Pogo, and Alley Oop are all here, as are the relatively more contemporary Dudley Do-Right, Rocky, Bullwinkle, Beetle Bailey, Cathy, and Hagar the Horrible. With its colorful backdrops, chirpy music, hidden alcoves, squirting fountains, and highly animated scenery, Toon Town is a natural for younger kids (even if they don't know who these characters are). All attractions here accept Universal Express Pass except Me Ship, The Olive.

JURASSIC PARK

Pass through the towering gates of Jurassic Park and the music becomes slightly ominous, the vegetation tropical and junglelike. All of this, plus the high-tension wires and warning signs, does a great job of re-creating the Jurassic Park of Steven Spielberg's blockbuster movie (and its insipid sequels). The half-fun, half-frightening Jurassic Park River Adventure (the only attraction here that uses Universal Express Pass) is the standout, bringing to life key segments of the movie's climax.

THE WIZARDING WORLD OF HARRY POTTER

In mid-2010, Islands of Adventure fulfilled the fantasy of Harry Potter devotees when it unveiled the biggest theme-park addition since the arrival of Disney's Animal Kingdom in 1998. At the highly publicized premiere, even the actors from the Potter film franchise were amazed. Having performed their roles largely before a green screen, they had never seen anything like this. Neither have you. It's fantastic and unbelievable. The movie-magic-perfect re-creations of mythical locales such as Hogwarts, Hogsmeade Village, and Diagon Alley are all here, while playing supporting roles are a handful of candy shops, souvenir stores, and restaurants expertly and exquisitely themed to make you believe you've actually boarded the *Hogwarts Express* and arrived in the incredible fantasy world of J. K. Rowling. Wands, candy, novelties, and more are unique to this magical land. Expect to be impressed . . . and to wait in line. Even if you owned a wand and were a real wizard, the only attractions in this land that accept the Universal Express Pass are Flight of the Hippogriff and Dragon Challenge. In fact, the land is so popular that in peak season it sometimes reaches capacity, and you have to wait for others to leave before you can enter.

The Cat and his Hat, McGurkus and the Circus, and fish both red and blue are among the attractions geared to the under-7 set at Seuss Landing.

LOST CONTINENT

Just beyond a wooden bridge, huge mythical birds guard the entrance to a land where trees are hung with weathered metal lanterns, and booming thunder mixes with chimes and vaguely Celtic melodies. Farther along the path, the scene looks similar to a Renaissance fair. Seers and fortune-tellers practice their trade in tents, and, in a huge theater, Sindbad leaps and bounces all over Arabia. This stunt show and Poseidon let you bypass lines using Universal Express Pass.

SEUSS LANDING

This 10-acre tribute to Dr. Seuss puts you in the midst of his classic children's books. This means spending quality time with the Cat, Things 1 and 2, Horton, the Lorax, and the Grinch. From topiary sculptures to lurching lampposts to curvy fences (there was never a straight line in any of the books) to buildings that glow in lavenders, pinks, peaches, and oranges, everything seems surreal. It's a wonderful place to wrap up a day. Even the Cat would approve. All rides here except If I Ran the Zoo accept Express Pass.

CITYWALK

With an attitude that's distinctly non-Disney, Universal has created nightlife for adults who want to party. The epicenter here is CityWalk, a 30-acre entertainment and retail complex at the hub of promenades that lead to both Universal parks.

When it comes to retail, much of the merchandise includes things you can find elsewhere—and most likely for less. But when you're swept up in the energy of CityWalk and dazzled by the degree of window-shopping (not to mention the fact that you're on vacation and you're more inclined to spend), chances are you'll want to drop into stores selling everything from surfwear and cigars to tattoos and timepieces.

In addition to stores, the open and airy gathering place includes an over-the-top discotheque, a theater for the fabulous and extremely popular Blue Man Group, and a huge hall where karaoke's king. There's a New Orleans bar, a Jamaican reggae lounge, a casual Key West hang-out and, as of 2012, Hollywood Drive-In Golf, a pair of 1950s sci-fi movie–themed miniature golf courses. On weeknights you find families and conventioneers; weekends a decidedly younger crowd parties until the wee hours.

Clubs have individual cover charges, but it's far more economical to pay for the whole kit and much of the caboodle. Choose a Party Pass (a one-price-all-clubs admission) for $11.99; a Party Pass-and-a-Movie for $15.98 (tax included); a Movie-and-a-Meal for $21.95 ; or a Party Pass-and-a-Meal for $21.

At AMC Universal Cineplex, with its 20 screens (including IMAX), there's certain to be something you like—including nightly midnight movies. Meals (tax and gratuity included) are served at Jimmy Buffett's Margaritaville, the Hard Rock Cafe, NASCAR Sports Grille, and others. And as if these deals weren't sweet enough, after 6 pm the $15 parking fee drops to $5. Nevertheless, it's a long haul from the garage to CityWalk—if you prefer, simply call a cab. They run at all hours. ☎ *407/354–3374, 407/363–8000 Universal main line* ⊕ *www. citywalkorlando.com.*

NIGHTLIFE

With the wide range of nightlife you'll find at Universal, you may get the feeling that you're vacationing not in Orlando, but in New York City. CityWalk's stores open by midmorning, and its restaurants come to life between lunchtime and late afternoon. Eateries that double as nightclubs (such as Pat O'Brien's, Latin Quarter, and the Red Coconut Club) start charging a cover before dusk and apply age restrictions (usually 21) around 9 pm. For details on a particular establishment, check with Guest Services.

BARS AND CLUBS

Bob Marley—A Tribute to Freedom. Modeled after the King of Reggae's home in Kingston, Jamaica (even down to the A/C window units), this club is like a museum. It contains more than 100 photographs and paintings showing pivotal moments in Marley's life. Though the place does serve meals, most patrons are at the cozy bar or by the patio, where they can be jammin' to a (loud) live band that plays nightly. For a nice souvenir, pose by the wonderful Marley statue outside the club. Legendary Thursdays feature drink specials for everyone, and Sunday is ladies' night from 9 pm until closing. ⊠ *CityWalk* ☎ *407/224–2692* 🖼 *$7 after 9 pm* ☉ *Daily 4 pm–2 am.*

CityWalk's Rising Star. Here you and other hopeful (and hopeless) singers can really let loose. Instead of singing to recorded music, you're accompanied by a band complete with backup singers—in front of a live audience. Backup singers are on hand every night, while the live band plugs in Tuesday through Saturday. ⊠ *6000 Universal Blvd., #717* ☎ *407/224–2425* ✉ *$7, no charge to sing* ⊙ *Nightly 8 pm–2 am.*

the groove. In this cavernous hall images flicker rapidly on several screens, and the lights, music, and mayhem appeal to a mostly under-30 crowd. Prepare for lots of fog, swirling lights, and sweaty bodies. The '70s-style Green Room is filled with beanbag chairs and everything you threw out when Duran Duran hit the charts. The Blue Room is sci-fi Jetson-y, and the Red Room is hot and romantic in a bordello sort of way. The music is equally diverse: Top 40, hip-hop, R&B, techno and the occasional live band. ⊠ *6000 Universal Blvd.* ☎ *407/224–2692* ✉ *$7* ⊙ *Daily 9 pm–2 am.*

Jimmy Buffett's Margaritaville. Buffett tunes fill the air at the restaurant here and at the Volcano, Land Shark, and 12 Volt bars. Inside there's a miniature Pan Am Clipper suspended from the ceiling, music videos projected onto sails, limbo and hula-hoop contests, a huge margarita blender that erupts "when the volcano blows," and live music nightly—everything that Parrotheads need to roost. Across the promenade, another full-size seaplane (emblazoned with 'Jimmy Buffett, Captain') is the setting for the Lone Palm Airport, a nice outdoor waterfront bar. ⊠ *6000 Universal Studios Plaza, #704* ☎ *407/224–2692* ⊕ *www.margaritavilleorlando.com* ✉ *$7 after 10 pm* ⊙ *Daily 11:30 am–2 am.*

Latin Quarter. Although this is largely a Brazilian steak house, after 10 pm on Thursday through Saturday it transforms into a hot club with a DJ spinning Latin and reggae tunes. A cool design, based on Aztec, Incan, and Mayan architecture—there's even an Andes mountain range, complete with waterfalls—surrounds the dance floor. If you can get your hips working overtime, pick a rumba from 1 to 10 and swivel (or tango or merengue or salsa . . .). ⊠ *6000 Universal Blvd.* ☎ *407/224–2692* ✉ *$7; price may vary for certain performances* ⊙ *Mon.–Thurs. 5 pm–2 am, Fri. and Sat. noon–2 am.*

Pat O'Brien's. An exact reproduction of the legendary New Orleans original, this comes complete with flaming fountain and dueling pianists who are playing for highly entertained regulars and visitors—even on weekday afternoons. Outside, the cozy and welcoming Patio Bar has a wealth of tables and chairs, allowing you to do nothing but enjoy the outdoors and your potent, rum-based Hurricanes in the Orlando version of the Big Easy. ⊠ *6000 Universal Blvd.* ☎ *407/224–2692* ⊕ *www.patobriens.com* ✉ *$7 after 9 pm* ⊙ *Patio Bar daily 4 pm–2 am; piano bar daily 5 pm–2 am.*

Red Coconut Club. Paying tribute to kitsch design of the 1950s, the interior here is part Vegas lounge, part Cuban club, and part Polynesian tiki bar. There's a full bar, signature martinis, an extensive wine list, and VIP bottle service. Hang out in the lounge, on the balcony, or at the bar. On a budget? Take advantage of the daily happy hours and gourmet appetizer menu. A DJ (Sunday–Wednesday) or live music (Thursday–Saturday) pushes the energy with tunes ranging from Sinatra to rock. Thursday is ladies' night. ⊠ *6000 Universal Blvd.* ☎ *407/224–2425* ◻ *$7 after 9 pm* ☉ *Sun.–Wed. 8 pm–2 am, Thurs.–Sat. 6 pm–2 am.*

SHOWS

Blue Man Group. At their own venue, the Sharp-Aquos Theatre, the Blue Men continue to pound out new music, sketches, and audience interaction that is nothing like you've ever seen. Attempting to understand the apps on a GiPad (a gigantic iPad), they may appear clueless and perplexed about cutting-edge technology, which for them can be as basic as a can of paint. But they're always excited when they can drum out rhythms on lengths of PVC pipes and throw a rave party finale for all in attendance. Three levels of admission (Poncho, Tier 1, and Tier 2) hint at how messy things can get when the Blue Men cut loose. If you have the time and a little extra in your vacation budget, this is a must. ⊠ *CityWalk* ☎ *407/258–3626* ◻ *Adults $69 advance purchase, $84 at box office; children 9 and under from $29* ☉ *Daily showtimes vary; call for schedule.*

SHOPPING

This 30-acre entertainment and retail complex is at the hub of promenades that lead to Universal Studios and Islands of Adventure. Shops here sell fine jewelry, cool beachwear, fashionable clothing, and stylish accessories. The best stores are near the entrance/exit of the complex.

Cigarz. For years, this perfectly themed cigar sanctuary has lured cigar aficionados with an impressive range of cigars preserved in a well-stocked humidor, as well as a good selection of pipes, lighters, and accessories. A cozy bar has become a popular gathering spot for in-the-know locals and soon-to-be friends. FYI: Smoking's permitted. ⊠ *600 Universal Blvd., Suite 740* ☎ *407/370–2999* ⊕ *cigarzcitywalk.com.*

Fresh Produce. Featuring fashions that look right at home in sunny Florida, this boutique showcases comfortable and colorful swimwear, blouses, Capri slacks, dresses, footwear, beach gear, and accessories designed for coastal comfort. ⊠ *CityWalk.*

PiQ. Although it's a small shop, there's enough room to hold hundreds of fun and mind-bending toys and books and games for kids (and adults) to teach them about math and physics and sometimes just plain fun stuff—like beer steins. ⊠ *6000 Universal Blvd., Suite 745J* ⊕ *www.piqproducts.com.*

Quiet Flight. Granted, the closest beach is about 60 miles east, but you can still get outfitted like a surfer at this shop, which sports an inventory featuring brand names such as Billabong, Quicksilver, Hurley, and Oakley. In addition to shorts and shirts, Quiet Flight also sells sandals, watches, sunglasses (Ray-Ban, Prada, and D&G among the featured names), and . . . surfboards! ⊠ *CityWalk.*

WET 'N WILD

When you were a kid, chances are all you needed for unlimited summer fun was a simple inflatable pool and a garden hose or sprinkler. Well, about the same time that you were growing up, so were water parks. They started with a few simple slides and are now the aquatic equivalents of megamalls.

TOP ATTRACTIONS

Bomb Bay

Brain Wash

Disco H20

Lazy River

The Storm

Surf Lagoon

It all began in 1977 with Wet 'n Wild, created by George Millay, who was also one of the founders of SeaWorld. Although it's now far from alone, Wet 'n Wild remains extremely popular, thanks to its quality, service, and ability to create more heart-stopping waterslides, rides, and tubing adventures than its competitors. Indeed, new rides seem to be added like clockwork, old ones improved, and settings developed for the comfort of guests. There's a complete water playground for kids, numerous high-energy slides for adults, a lazy-river ride, and some quiet, sandy beaches on which you can stretch out and get a tan.

Speaking of high energy, this is a park that requires a lot of it. A day here is often a marathon of climbing steps, sliding, swimming, and splashing, though you may not notice just how much your stamina is being drained as you scamper from slide to slide. Plan to take breaks: laze in a beach chair and eat high-protein meals and snacks to maintain your strength. You can bring in a cooler for a picnic or eat at a restaurant in one of several food courts.

If you're not a strong swimmer, don't worry. There are plenty of low-key attractions, and all of the ride entrances are marked with warnings to let you know which ones are safe for you. Plus, during peak season, there are as many as 200 lifeguards on duty daily. Also note that all the pools (if not the rides) are ADA-compliant and are heated in cooler weather. This, combined with Orlando's temperate climate, means that Wet 'n Wild is one of the few water parks in the country to stay open year-round.

Surf's up!

PLANNING

GETTING ORIENTED

If you arrive early, when crowds are light to moderate, you should have plenty of time to do each ride once, and possibly twice or more. With the Surf Lagoon at 12 o'clock, head counterclockwise to the most thrilling experiences (Bomb Bay, Der Stuka, the Storm) first. By the time you've circled the park and are worn out, your kids should still have plenty of energy to deplete at Blastaway Beach.

Brain Wash is one of Wet 'n Wild's most thrilling slides.

PARK AMENITIES

Guest Services: Get maps and other information at Guest Services, to the left as you enter.

Lockers: There are dressing rooms with three different-size lockers (personal $6/$3 deposit, standard $9/$3 deposit, family $11/$3 deposit) as well as showers and restrooms to the left of the entrance gates. Additional restrooms are on the island inside the lazy river and near the First-Aid Stand and the Surge.

Lost People and Things: The Lost and Found is at Guest Services, to the left just after you enter the park. This is also where lifeguards and other staffers take lost children.

Wheelchair Rentals: Near the entrance, you can rent modified wheelchairs (they have large tires that can handle the sand) for $5 per day with a $25 refundable deposit. Note that although many of the paths are flat and accessible, none of the rides accommodates people using wheelchairs.

ESSENTIALS

Admission: Basic admission is about $49 for adults (ages 10 and up) and $43 for children (but look for discount coupons in flyers and magazines displayed in stores and restaurants throughout the I-Drive area). Full price covers admission for any or all of the next 14 consecutive days. Other money-saving options include the FlexTicket, which bundles Wet 'n Wild with parks and attractions at Universal Orlando, SeaWorld, and Busch Gardens.

General Information. Call Wet 'n Wild or visit online. ☎ *407/351–3200 recorded information, 407/351–1800 park operations* ⊕ *www.wetnwildorlando.com.*

Parking: Costing $12 for cars, vans, and motorcycles and $16 for RVs and cars with trailers, parking is in a large lot along Universal Boulevard.

TOURING TIPS

■ Want to save a bundle? Admission drops to half price during the afternoon; exactly when depends on closing time but can be as late as 5 pm in the summer. Call ahead for the magic hour. Even better, if you pay for a full-price ticket, you can return for free for 14 consecutive days. It's a great deal for families in town for an extended stay. You can see the big three (Disney, Universal, SeaWorld) during the day and return here in the evening.

■ When you arrive, it's a good idea to pick up a map, scan the park layout, and stake out a spot on the beach before heading on or in. To claim a prime beach spot, arrive 30 minutes before the park opens, or visit on a cloudy day. If it looks like rain all day, though, head elsewhere.

■ Men should wear a true bathing suit, and women should opt for a one-piece rather than a bikini. Cutoff shorts and garments with rivets, metal buttons, buckles, or zippers aren't allowed.

■ Wading slippers are a good idea—hot sidewalks and sandpaper-like pool bottoms can do a number on your feet—but put them in a locker or carry them when taking a plunge, since they can catch on slides.

■ Items too large to carry should be stashed in a locker. Some picnic tables have lockable containers (secured to the umbrella stand) that are just large enough to hold smaller items such as keys, glasses, and cell phones.

■ For extra privacy, a quiet oasis in the middle of the lazy river features cabanas with a fan, chaise lounges, and a fridge stocked with a dozen bottles of water. It's a nice base for stowing your things, but the privilege costs an extra $150. Don't want to get up? Servers will bring food to you.

■ Be patient with the lines here. Just when you think you've arrived, you discover there's another level or two to go.

■ To bypass lines at the popular rides, get an Express Pass (available seasonally), accepted at most rides. Prices change based on park attendance and time of day, so call ☎ *407/351–1800* for details. A limited number of passes are sold each day—all the more reason to get here early.

■ Okay. So you remembered your swimsuit and towel. But what about sunscreen? You can buy it and other necessities or souvenirs at the **Breakers Beach Shop,** near the park entrance. And if you did forget a towel, renting one here costs $4 with a $3 deposit. Rent a three-pack, though, and you save $2.

SEAWORLD

With Discovery Cove and Aquatica

WELCOME TO SEAWORLD ORLANDO

TOP REASONS TO GO

★ **Animal magnetism:** If you love animals—slick, shiny, feathery, or furry—SeaWorld, Discovery Cove, and Aquatica are where you want to be. No robotic wildlife here; just well-cared-for and talented dolphins, whales, seals, otters, penguins, cats, dogs . . .

★ **A slower pace:** The shows and natural settings of SeaWorld and Discovery Cove let you enjoy a theme-park vacation without racing from one attraction to the next. Living in the moment is the lesson here.

★ **Getting smarter:** No one leaves these parks without learning a little something about nature through shows, backstage tours, instructional signage, and well-versed educators and naturalists who are always ready to answer questions.

★ **Memories in the making:** Chances are SeaWorld and Discovery Cove will afford you the chance to pet a penguin, feed a dolphin, or watch a 5-ton whale leap out of the water. You can't forget things like that.

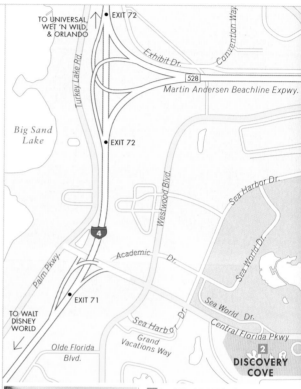

1 SeaWorld. With the exception of a handful of thrill rides, the original park (which opened in 1973 to reroute visitors heading to the then recently opened Walt Disney World) maintains a slow and easy pace. Here it's all about clever shows, shaded sidewalks, and plenty of opportunities to enjoy the natural grace and intriguing personalities of marine life and other animals.

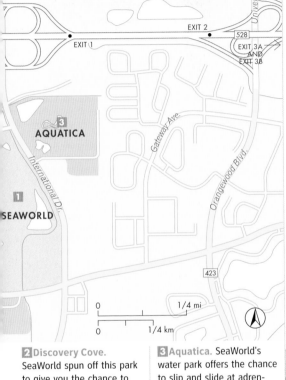

TO WET 'N WILD &
UNIVERSAL STUDIOS

12

GETTING ORIENTED

SeaWorld is just off the intersection of Interstate 4 and the Beachline Expressway, equidistant from Universal Orlando and the Walt Disney World Resort, which are only about five minutes away. SeaWorld is also a mere 10 minutes from Downtown Orlando and 15 minutes from the airport. Discovery Cove is its own oasis across the street from SeaWorld. Aquatica, a little ways down the road from both, is the first of the three that you'll see after exiting the expressway.

2 Discovery Cove.
SeaWorld spun off this park to give you the chance to enjoy a lot more time (and to spend a little more cash) with the animals. A trip to this aquatic oasis feels like a trip to the islands; a daylong, all-inclusive experience that includes breakfast and lunch, drinks, a private beach, snorkeling equipment, and—for approximately an extra $100—the chance to swim with dolphins. Paradise.

3 Aquatica. SeaWorld's water park offers the chance to slip and slide at adrenaline-rush speeds, relax in the current of two wave pools, laze on a wide beach, and take the wee ones to pint-size play areas of their very own. All in all, there's something for everyone, showcased in a tropical, tiki-themed setting.

By Gary
McKechnie

Just as Walt Disney World and Universal Orlando are much more than just a single park, the same is true of SeaWorld. The original park—which includes the Shamu shows as well as presentations featuring dolphins and seals—has expanded to include Discovery Cove (an immersive tropical retreat), and Aquatica (a water park loaded with aquatic excitement). So, as you plan your vacation, consider that SeaWorld can easily fill a single day or, if you're really eager to take to the waters, perhaps a day or two more.

There's a whole lot more to SeaWorld and Discovery Cove than being splashed by Shamu. You can see manatees face-to-snout, learn to love a shark, swim with dolphins, and be spat at by a walrus. These two parks celebrate all the mammals, birds, fish, and reptiles that live in and near the ocean.

Then there's Aquatica, a wild water park that takes its cues from Sea-World and Discovery Cove in design and mood—marine-life motifs are everywhere. It also gives competitor water parks a run for their money with thrilling slides, broad beaches, calming rivers, and an area for small kids.

The park also takes some tips from the tropics. Right after you clear the parking lot, you see a tropical pastiche of buildings. Yup. That's definitely an island vibe you're detecting. Upon entering Aquatica, you feel as if you've left Central Florida for the Caribbean or Polynesia, even.

You might be drawn to the series of superfast waterslides (some of which conclude by sending you into serene streams), or you might feel the pull of the white-sand beaches beside the twin wave pools, where you can laze in the sun, venturing out every so often to try a ride or climb into an inner tube and float down a river. Whether you're spending the day at SeaWorld, Discovery Cove, or Aquatica, just go with it. Get into a groove, relax, and enjoy yourself at some of the most pleasant theme parks in Orlando.

PLANNING

GETTING HERE AND AROUND

Heading west on Interstate 4 (toward Disney) take Exit 72; heading east, take Exit 71. After that you'll be going east on the Beachline Expressway (aka Route 528), and the first right-hand exit leads you to International Drive. Turn left, and you'll soon see the entrance to Aquatica on your left. Sea Harbor Drive—leading to SeaWorld's entrance—will be on your right. To reach Discovery Cove, follow International Drive past Aquatica ½ mile to the Central Florida Parkway and turn right. The park's entrance will be on your left.

OPERATING HOURS

SeaWorld opens daily at 9 am and usually closes at 7 pm, with extended hours during the summer and holidays. Hours at Discovery Cove also vary seasonally, although it's generally open daily from 8 to 5:30, with check-in beginning 30 minutes earlier—which is not a bad idea considering Discovery Cove serves a complimentary breakfast until 10 am. Aquatica is open at 9 am, with closing times varying between 5 and 9 pm, depending on the season. Allow a full day to see each attraction.

ADMISSION

SeaWorld, Discovery Cove, Aquatica, and Busch Gardens Tampa Bay fall under the SeaWorld Parks & Entertainment umbrella, and you can save by buying combo tickets. Regular one-day tickets to **SeaWorld** cost $89 (adults) and $81 (children ages 3–9), excluding tax, but if you order in advance over the phone or online, you'll save $10 per ticket. Combo-park admission prices are as follows:

Flex Ticket (14 days at SeaWorld/Aquatica/Busch Gardens Tampa) *$345/$325*

SeaWorld/Aquatica *$129 adults/$121 children*

SeaWorld/Busch Gardens Tampa *$139/$131*

SeaWorld/Aquatica/Busch Gardens Tampa *$159/$151*

Aquatica admission is $55 (adults) and $50 (children 3–9), but if you order online you'll save around $10 per ticket. Add a Banana Beach all-you-can-eat option, and the online price is $55 adults, $50 children.

Reserve **Discovery Cove** visits well in advance—attendance is limited to about 1,000 a day. Tickets (with a dolphin swim) start at about $229 (off-season) but are generally around $289. Forgo the dolphin swim and save approximately $100. Keep in mind, this park has what they call "dynamic pricing" (i.e., prices change by season and/or without notice). Admission is less expensive the earlier you book, so call well in advance. Either way, the fee includes access to all beach and snorkeling areas and the free-flight aviary; meals and snacks; use of a mask, snorkel, swim vest, towel, locker, and sunscreen; parking; and a pass for 14 days of unlimited admission to SeaWorld Orlando and Aquatica. Upgrade to an "ultimate" pass (about $20), which includes admission (and free transportation) to Busch Gardens Tampa.

Quick Queue Passes. SeaWorld's Quick Queue passes (≈ *$15–$35 per person, depending on the season*) get you to the front of the line at major attractions and shows for one admission each. The higher price unlimited pass is good for unlimited admissions. Neither Discovery Cove nor Aquatica has such a pass.

All-Day Dining Deal. Available at select SeaWorld restaurants (Voyager's Smokehouse, Seaport Pizza, Terrace Garden Buffet, the Spice Mill, Seafire Inn, and Mango Joe's), and for multiple meals, adults will pay from $32.99 and kids from $17.99 to chow down on an entrée, side dish, drink, and dessert. Skip it if you plan on having just one meal in the park.

SEAWORLD STRATEGIES

Avoid weekend and school-holiday visits. These are the busiest times, so plan around them if you can.

Wear sneakers or water shoes—no heels or slip-on sandals. It may not seem like it, but there'll be a whole lot of walking as you roam from one end of the park to the other, stand in line, and walk through attractions.

Pack dry clothes. You can get wet just by being toward the front at the Shamu show or riding Journey to Atlantis. Alternatively, carry a rain poncho.

Budget for food for the animals. Participating in animal feedings is a major part of the SeaWorld experience, although it comes at a price: A small carton of fish costs $5.

Pick up a map/show schedule inside the entrance. SeaWorld has its show schedule down to a science. If you start by catching the show closest to the entrance, shortly after that one's over, guests are moving farther into the park to grab a seat at the next performance. So spend a few minutes planning so you can casually stroll from show to show and have time for learning, testing out thrill rides, *and* enjoying a leisurely meal.

Be open to learning. SeaWorld's trainers and educators are always at the ready to share information about the park's wildlife.

DISCOVERY COVE STRATEGIES

Make reservations well in advance. Prized June dates, for instance, can sell out in March. If there aren't openings when you call, though, don't despair. Call back often to inquire about cancellations.

Think about your eyewear. Park masks don't accommodate glasses, but there are a limited number of near- and far-sighted prescription masks (first-come, first-served) available. Just step into a booth and you'll be able to try on a few different pairs with different magnifications. If you don't mind risking lost contacts, just wear those beneath a nonprescription mask.

Don't bring your own wet suit or fins. Every guest must wear a Discovery Cove–issued wet suit or vest—not a bad idea, as the water can be cold.

Leave belongings in your locker. The plastic passes you're given are all you need to pick up your meals, soft drinks, and—if you're over 21—alcoholic drinks.

SeaWorld Orlando

← TO AQUATICA

TO DISCOVERY COVE →

Turtle Trek

Dolphin Cove

Stingray Lagoon

First Aid

Journey to Atlantis

Blue Horizons (Whale & Dolphin Theater)

KEY WEST

Pelican Preserve

Key West at SeaWorld

Captain Pete's Island Eats

Cypress Bakery

Kraken

Penguin Encounter

Seaport Pizza

Manta

Information and Reservations

Guest Services, Information

Reservations and Show Schedules

Main Entrance/Exit

Pacific Point Preserve

Clyde and Seamore Take Pirate Island (Sea Lion & Other Stadium)

Antarctic Market

Voyager Smokehouse

Dolphin Nursery

Lockers

Pet Care Center

Shark's Underwater Grill

Shark Encounter

Spice Mill Cafe

Sky Tower

Pearl Dive

The Waterfront

Pets Ahoy

Seafire Inn

A'Lure, the Call of the Ocean (Nautilus Theater)

Paddle boats

One Ocean (Shamu Stadium)

Dine with Shamu

Lagoon

Atlantis Bayside Stadium

The Terrace Garden Buffet

Arcade

Games Area

Sea Carousel

First Aid

Baby Care Center

Shamu's Happy Harbor

Coconut Cove Snacks

Mango Joe's Café

Wild Arctic

KEY

✕ Restaurants

🚻 Restrooms

ℹ Tourist information

Be flexible when it comes to weather. If the weather on your reserved day looks like it'll be an all-day downpour, attempts will be made to reschedule your visit while you're in town. If that's not possible, you'll have to settle for a refund.

Have a dolphin relay a message. The Special Occasion Package enlists the help of a bottlenose dolphin to deliver love notes, wedding proposals, birthday or anniversary greetings, and the like.

> **TOP ATTRACTIONS**
>
> Clyde and Seamore Take Pirate Island
>
> Journey to Atlantis
>
> Kraken
>
> Manta
>
> One Ocean
>
> Pets Ahoy

AQUATICA STRATEGIES

■ **Buy tickets in advance.** Tickets bought ahead of time online or at another SeaWorld park allow early entry (and discounts) to Aquatica, which, in turn, increases your chances of hitting all the big-deal flume and tube rides—possibly more than once.

■ **Be open to animal encounters.** The Commerson's dolphins of Dolphin Plunge have scheduled feeding times, and you can see macaws perched on tree limbs and small mammals on display in Conservation Cabanas—usually attended to by knowledgeable educators.

■ **Pack beach supplies.** You'll save a few bucks by having your own towels, lotion, water shoes, and snacks.

■ **Take care of yourself.** Fight fatigue by eating a good breakfast, drinking plenty of water, and nibbling on high-energy snacks. Avoid sunburn by reapplying sunscreen often—even the waterproof stuff washes off.

■ **Save your soles.** Water shoes protect your feet from hot sand and sidewalks and the rough surfaces in some pools.

CONTACTS

Aquatica ☎ 888/800–5447 ⊕ www.aquaticabyseaworld.com

Busch Gardens Tampa ☎ 888/800–5447 ⊕ www.buschgardens.com/bgt

Discovery Cove ☎ 877/557–7404 ⊕ www.discoverycove.com

SeaWorld ☎ 888/800–5447 ⊕ www.seaworld.com

Parking. Parking is $15 for a car or motorcycle, $20 for an RV or camper. For $20 you can pull into one of the six Preferred Parking rows closest to the front gate. At Aquatica, cars and motorcycles are charged $12, RVs $16—although if you already have your parking slip from that day at SeaWorld, it's free. Parking is free at Discovery Cove.

SEAWORLD ORLANDO AND DISCOVERY COVE

SeaWorld

NAME	Height Req.	Type of Entertainment	Duration	Crowds	Audience	Tips
A'Lure, the Call of the Ocean	n/a	Show	20 mins.	Heavy	All Ages	Plenty of seats, but arrive 15 mins. early for a wide selection.
Blue Horizons	n/a	Show	20 mins.	Heavy	All Ages	Arrive 20 mins. before showtime.
Dolphin Nursery	n/a	Aquarium	Up to you	Light	All Ages	Come during a Shamu show so the kids can be up front.
Journey to Atlantis	At least 42"	Thrill Ride with Water	6 mins.	Heavy	All but Small Kids	You can make a beeline here first thing or come about an hour before closing. But the best time for this is at night.
Key West at SeaWorld	n/a	Walk-Through/Aquarium	Up to you	Light to Moderate	All Ages	If too crowded, wander until crowds disperse.
★ Kraken	At least 54"	Thrill Ride	6 mins.	Heavy	All but Small Kids	Get to the park when it opens and head straight to Kraken; otherwise, hit it near closing time or during a Blue Horizons show.
Manatees Rescue	n/a	Aquarium	Up to you	Light to Moderate	All Ages	Come during a Shamu show but not right after a dolphin show.
★ Manta	At least 54"	Thrill Ride with Water	6 mins.	You Bet!	All but Small Kids	Come first thing or late in the day, or purchase a Quick Queue pass for front-of-ride access.
Pacific Point Preserve	n/a	Aquarium	Up to you	Light	All Ages	Come anytime.
Penguin Encounter	n/a	Aquarium	Up to you	Moderate to Heavy	All Ages	Come during dolphin and sea lion shows, and before you've gotten soaked at Journey to Atlantis, or you'll freeze.
Pets Ahoy	n/a	Show	15–20 mins.	Moderate to Heavy	All Ages	Gauge the crowds, and come here early if necessary.
★ Sea Lion & Otter Stadium	n/a	Show	40 mins.	Heavy	All Ages	Sit toward the center for the best view, and don't miss the pre-show mime. Plenty of seats.

					Small Kids	
Shamu's Happy Harbor	n/a	Playground with Water	Up to you	Heavy	All Ages	Don't come first thing in morning, or you'll never drag your child away. Bring a towel to dry them off.
★ Shamu Stadium (One Ocean)	n/a	Show	25 mins.	Moderate to Heavy	All Ages	Show itself lasts 25 minutes, but there's a 30-minute pre-show; plan accordingly.
Shark Encounter	n/a	Aquarium	Up to you	Light to Moderate	All Ages	Come during the sea lion show.
Sky Tower	48"	Tour/ Thrill Ride	6 mins.	Light	All Ages	Come whenever there's no line. Note the extra $4 charge, though.
Stingray Lagoon	n/a	Aquarium	Up to you	Moderate to Heavy	All Ages	Walk by if it's crowded, but return before dusk.
Turtle Point	n/a	Zoo	Up to you	Light	All Ages	Come anytime.
Wild Arctic	At least 42"	Simulator Exp./ Aquarium	5+ mins.	Moderate to Heavy	All Ages	Come during a Shamu show. You can skip the ride if you just want to see the mammals.
Discovery Cove						
Beaches	n/a	Beach Area	Up to you	Light	All Ages	Arrive early and head to the far side for a private spot.
★ Dolphin Lagoon	n/a	Pool	45–60 mins.	n/a	All but Small Kids	Be mindful of your appointment time.
Explorer's Aviary	n/a	Aviary	Up to you	Light to Moderate	All Ages	Come early, when the birds are most active.
Tropical Reef	n/a	Aquarium/ Pool Area	Up to you	Light to Moderate	All Ages	Monitor crowds and come when they're lightest. Popular with teens.
Wind-Away River	n/a	Aquarium	Up to you	Light to Moderate	All Ages	When it gets hot, slip into the water. Popular with teens.

★ Fodor's Choice

SEAWORLD

Just as you wouldn't expect to arrive at Disney and see nothing but Mickey Mouse, don't expect to arrive at SeaWorld and see only Shamu. Only a few steps into the park you'll find baby dolphins and their mothers, a pool filled with stingrays, colorful flamingos, rescued sea turtles, rescued pelicans, and even resuced manatees. SeaWorld's objective is to educate as well as entertain.

You'll see how lumbering manatees live and what they look like up close; watch otters and seals perform slapstick routines based on their natural behaviors; learn about the lives of giant tortoises and sea turtles; and be absolutely amazed at the scope of marine life celebrated throughout the park.

Then there are the attractions, each and every one designed not only to showcase the marine world but also to demonstrate ways in which humans can protect the earth's waters and wildlife. And, because there are more exhibits and shows than rides, the difference between SeaWorld and other theme parks is that you can go at your own pace, without that hurry-up-and-wait feeling. It's also worth noting that because shows, attractions, and exhibits are based primarily on nature and animals, designers have created a natural layout as well, with winding lanes and plenty of places to relax by the waterfront or beside bouquets of flowers. There's never a nagging urge to race through anything; indeed, the entire park encourages you to slow down and move at a casual pace.

PLANNING

GETTING ORIENTED

SeaWorld's performance venues, attractions, and activities surround a 17-acre lagoon, and the artful landscaping, curving paths, and concealing greenery sometimes lead to wrong turns. But armed with a map that lists showtimes, it's easy to plan an approach that lets you move fluidly from one show and attraction to the next and still have time for rest stops and meal breaks.

TOURING TIPS

Before investing in front-of-the-line Quick Queue passes (✉ $15–$35), remember that there are only a handful of big-deal rides, and space is seldom a problem at shows.

If you bring your own food, remove all straws and lids before you arrive—they can harm fish and birds.

Arrive at least 30 minutes early for the Shamu show, which generally fills to capacity. Prepare to get wet in the "splash zone" down front.

In Discovery Cove make the aviary one of your first stops, since the 250-plus birds within will be more active in the morning. Check-in starts at around 7:30 am.

At Discovery Cove's Explorer's Aviary, you can attract exotic birds with fruit or feed. You might even get one (or two) to hop onto your shoulder. Get the camera ready.

PARKS AMENITIES

Guest Services: Ticket booths have become the new Guest Services center. If you ordered your tickets online, have questions about dining or attractions, or just need tickets to begin with, you can find it here.

Information and Reservation Center: Right inside the entrance you can pick up the park map—which also has info on showtimes, services, and amenities—make dinner reservations; and buy tickets for Discovery Cove, Aquatica, and park tours.

Lockers: One-time-use, coin-op lockers ($1) are near flip-over coasters like Kraken and Manta, Journey to Atlantis, and Shamu's Happy Harbor as well as inside SeaWorld's main entrance. Also near the entrance, next to Shamu's Emporium, are day lockers ($7 small, $10 large per day). At Discovery Cove free lockers await you near the cabanas.

Lost People and Things: SeaWorld's Main Information Center operates as the park's Lost and Found. Lost children are brought here, and it's the place to report lost children. A parkwide paging system also helps reunite parents with kids. At Discovery Cove lost kids and items eventually find their way to the check-in lobby.

ANIMAL ENCOUNTERS AND TOURS

SeaWorld has several programs that put you closer to the animals. Up-Close and Behind-the-Scenes tours last 60 to 90 minutes and cost about $10 to $50. The six-hour VIP Tour starts at around $100 for adults and $80 for children.

You can book tours up to three months in advance. For a list, check the Sea-World website (⊕ *www.seaworld.com*) or call the park (☎ *407/351–3600*).

DISCOVERY COVE

If you were pleasantly surprised by the pace at SeaWorld, believe it or not, it's even slower at Discovery Cove. Here your mission is to spend an entire day doing nothing but savoring a 32-acre tropical oasis. It's a task made easier by an all-inclusive admission that covers all meals, towels, a wet suit, masks, sunscreen, and the option of springing for the highlight of the day: a unique swimming experience with a bottlenose dolphin.

Even without a dolphin encounter, you can have a great time splashing around coral reefs, swimming into a spacious aviary, floating down a quiet river, and lazing on a sandy beach beneath lovely palms. New in 2012, Freshwater Oasis is a tropical rain-forest environment of sparkling clear springs offering face-to-face encounters with playful otters and curious marmoset monkeys, while thanks to a special diving helmet, SeaVenture lets you walk underwater through a reef filled with tropical fish and rays, which you can literally reach out and touch.

PLANNING

GETTING ORIENTED

Thanks to Discovery Cove's daily cap on crowds, it may seem as if you have the park to yourself. Navigating the grounds is simple; signs point to swimming areas, cabanas, or the free-flight aviary—aflutter with exotic birds and accessible via a walkway or (even better) by swimming to it beneath a waterfall.

TOURING TIP

In Discovery Cove make the aviary one of your first stops, since the 250-plus birds within will be more active in the morning. Remember that check-in starts at 7:30 am, and the waterways open around 9 am.

PARK AMENITIES

Guest Services: You can get information on meals, cabanas, lockers, dolphin swims, merchandise, souvenir photos, and other aspects of the park at the **Discovery Cove Check-In**

Lost People and Things: Lost kids and items are usually turned over to Discovery Cove attendants, who bring them to the attendants at the Check-In Lobby.

ANIMAL ENCOUNTERS

Trainer for a Day. This opportunity (from $398) rivals SeaWorld's Marine Mammal Keeper Experience. General admission includes meals, wet suits, and diving gear; this tour adds a gift bag, waterproof camera, trainer T-shirt, 30-minute dolphin swim, photo session with two dolphins, and an almost exclusive (only eight guests in the entire lagoon) interaction that includes a "double-foot push" (two dolphins propel you across the lagoon by the soles of your feet). Ready for more? Head to the dolphin back area and talk to trainers about how they teach and care for these amazing animals. Call ahead to arrange a tour. ☎ *407/351–3600, 877/557–7404.*

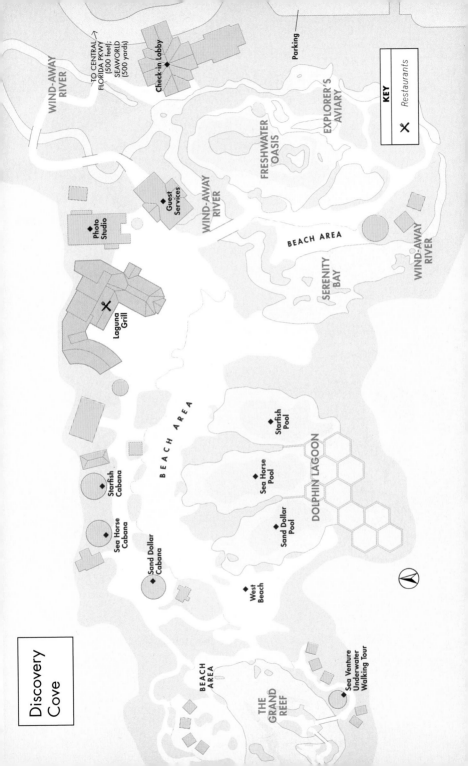

Discovery Cove

WIND-AWAY RIVER

TO CENTRAL
FLORIDA PKWY
(500 feet);
SEAWORLD
(500 yards)

Check-in Lobby

Parking

Photo
Studio

Guest
Services

WIND-AWAY RIVER

FRESHWATER
OASIS

EXPLORER'S
AVIARY

BEACH AREA

Laguna
Grill

SERENITY
BAY

WIND-AWAY
RIVER

BEACH AREA

Starfish
Cabana

Sea Horse
Cabana

Sand Dollar
Cabana

BEACH AREA

West
Beach

Sand Dollar
Pool

Sea Horse
Pool

Starfish
Pool

DOLPHIN LAGOON

BEACH
AREA

THE GRAND
REEF

Sea Venture
Underwater
Walking Tour

KEY

✕ Restaurants

DID YOU KNOW?

You can "swim" with the dolphins even if you didn't book a dolphin swim at Discovery Cove. Just take the Dolphin Plunge, a waterslide that jettisons you into a clear tube running through the pool inhabited by Commerson's dolphins.

AQUATICA

Just across International Drive from SeaWorld, Aquatica is the 60-acre water park that does a wonderful job angling water-park lovers away from Disney's Typhoon Lagoon and Blizzard Beach and Universal's Wet 'n Wild. And, sure, Aquatica has all the slides you'd expect, but it also has plenty of whimsical SeaWorld touches.

Aquatica takes cues from SeaWorld and Discovery Cove in design and mood. The park also takes its cues from the tropics. Right after you clear the parking lot, you see a tropical pastiche of buildings. Yup. That's definitely an island vibe you're detecting. Upon entering, you feel as if you've left Central Florida for the Caribbean or Polynesia, even.

Go with it. Get into a groove, and relax and enjoy yourself. You might be drawn to the series of superfast waterslides (some of which conclude by sending you into serene streams). Or you might feel the pull of the white-sand beaches beside the twin wave pools, where you can laze in the sun, venturing out every so often to try a ride or climb into an inner tube and float down a river.

Ideally you'll have arrived with some snacks and drinks to combat the fatigue you'll feel after scaling to the tops of all those watery thrill rides. If not, fear not—there are plenty of places to find food and drink.

You should also be toting beach towels, sunscreen, and water shoes. Again, if not, fear not—there are a number of shops and kiosks where you can buy (or rent) all of this stuff and more.

Many of the rides have height restrictions, so if you're traveling with kids, have their heights checked at the Information Center, which you'll see right when you enter the park. Each child will be issued a colored wristband that alerts attendants to which rides are appropriate for him or her (or just look for the height requirement signage at the entrance to each attraction—and check our reviews). If you or your child isn't comfortable in the water, this is also a good place to inquire about swimming lessons, which they offer.

After stashing excess supplies in a locker and generally settling in, it's time to explore. Unless it's peak season, several hours should be enough to visit each ride and attraction once or twice. It will also allow for some downtime, lazing on the beach, or enjoying a leisurely meal.

PLANNING

GETTING ORIENTED

Initially, you might find it hard to get your bearings amid the towering slides, Caribbean palms, winding sidewalks, and the seemingly random layout of restaurants, rides, slides, and facilities. And there are no paper maps, only posted diagrams throughout the park. But in reality, the park is fairly easy to navigate—its layout forms a simple circle. The services (restaurants, changing rooms, shops) form a core around which the attractions are situated.

At the entrance, turn right and you'll be at the premier attraction, Dolphin Plunge; but after that you may want to do an about-face and head straight to the shores of the beach at Cutback Cove. This way, you can set up a base and then work your way to other attractions around the circle while remaining conveniently close to meals at Waterstone Grill and the Banana Beach Cookout.

TOURING TIPS

Be aware of the sun. Avoid sunburn by reapplying sunscreen (they suggest SPF 30) often—even waterproof sunblock washes off. For even more sun protection, rent a cabana (about $60).

Be aware of your feet. Wear sandals or water shoes (or even socks) to protect your feet from hot sand, sidewalks, and rough pool surfaces. At the major thrill rides, a "sneaker keeper" offers a place to stash your footwear while you experience the ride.

Buy tickets in advance. Prepurchased tickets get you early entrance, and this head start will enable you to hit the major flume and tube rides more than once.

Commune with nature. You can catch Commerson's dolphins at feeding times; spot macaws on tree limbs; or see small mammals in the Conservation Cabanas, where docents answer questions. A variety of animals are on display around the park.

PARK AMENITIES

Information: The Main Information Center is at the park entrance, just past the ticket kiosks. Also at the entrance are an ATM, telephones, and restrooms. This is where you can (and should) pick up a park map (or a couple in case one gets wet) and plan your approach. On the walkways outside the information center and leading into the park, attendants are stationed to help you get your bearings and point out where to find strollers and wheelchairs, help you with lost-and-found inquiries, and describe combination-ticket packages.

Lockers: There are three areas with unlimited-access lockers to rent for a day. One is near the splashdown area at Walhalla Wave and HooRoo Run; two others are at the center and far end of the park, where there are also nursing facilities. You pay $15 for a small locker (enough for one backpack) and $30 for a large one (for about two backpacks); there's also a $5 deposit, which is refunded when you leave. The central locker area also rents towels for $4 ($1 of which is refunded upon return).

Lost People and Things: Lost items and people are taken to a small tent called the "Concierge Cabana," which is right by the entrance to the beach area.

NORTHEAST
FLORIDA

WELCOME TO NORTHEAST FLORIDA

TOP REASONS TO GO

★ **Get out and play:**
Beautiful beaches and a wealth of state and national parks mean swimming, sunbathing, kayaking, fishing, hiking, bird-watching, and camping opportunities are all nearby.

★ **Golfer's paradise:**
"Above par" describes the golf scene, from award-winning courses to THE PLAYERS Championship to the World Golf Hall of Fame.

★ **Start your engines:**
Few things get racing fans as revved up as tours of Daytona International Speedway, home of the Daytona 500, Coke Zero 400, and Rolex 24 at Daytona.

★ **Be in the now:**
Whether you want a yoga retreat or the ultimate in sybaritic pampering, the oceanfront spas at Amelia Island and Ponte Vedra Beach make this region the place to be.

★ **The rest is history:**
The nation's oldest city, St. Augustine, is a must-see for anyone interested in history.

1 Jacksonville. With a metro-area population of 1.3 million, Jacksonville has the social and cultural appeal of a big city (think pro sports teams, fine dining, museums, nightlife, and shopping) but the down-to-earth charm of a small town. At Amelia Island/Fernandina Beach, just to the north, you'll find a historic downtown, beautiful beaches, and two superlative resorts: the Omni Amelia Island Plantation Resort and the Ritz-Carlton.

2 St. Augustine. You don't have to be a history buff to enjoy America's oldest city, founded in 1565. Foodies, golfers, art lovers, and beach bums generally find plenty to do here, too.

3 Daytona Beach and Inland Towns. The Daytona 500, Bike Week, and spring break put it on the map, but places like New Smyrna Beach, the Ocala National Forest, and Ocala are popular with vacationing families, too. Gainesville is home to the University of Florida and its Gators.

4 The Space Coast.
This area includes Canaveral National Seashore; the Kennedy Space Center; Cocoa, offering quiet appeal; and Cocoa Beach, the ultimate surf and bodyboard destination.

GETTING ORIENTED

Northeast Florida has historic port cities like Amelia Island/Fernandina Beach and St. Augustine and inland towns like Micanopy and Gainesville, as well as the urban hub of Jacksonville. About two hours south of Jacksonville, on Interstate 95, Titusville is the entry point for the Kennedy Space Center. It marks the northern perimeter of the Space Coast, which includes Cocoa and Melbourne. If you take U.S. 1, it lengthens the trip, but the scenery makes up for the inconvenience. Route A1A/Atlantic Avenue is the main road on all the barrier islands. In many places on A1A, you can see the area's beautiful beaches from your car window.

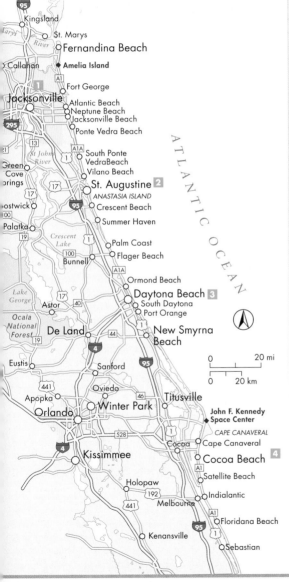

Updated by Sharon Hoffmann and Steve Master

For many travelers, Florida is about fantasy, thanks in no small part to Central Florida's make-believe kingdoms. But the northeastern part of the state—you could call it "authentic Florida"—has its own allure, with unspoiled beaches and rivers, historic small towns, and urban arts and culture.

Northeastern Florida's beaches have wide, shell-strewn expanses of soft sand and breakers just the right height for kids to jump. Thanks to the temperate climate and waters warmed by the Gulf Stream, these beaches are a year-round playground—when it's too cold to swim, you can still enjoy surf-fishing or just strolling the shoreline looking for shells and sharks' teeth.

Sun and surf aren't the only reasons to explore northeastern Florida, though. There's historic St. Augustine and its horse-drawn carriages, Daytona and its classic spring-break flavor, and Space Coast and its sense of discovery. Along the way is an array of little towns—from Fernandina and its shrimp fleets to Micanopy and its antiques stores—that invite quiet exploration.

There's city life in the northeast, too. In the last decade or so, Jacksonville has revitalized its institutions and infrastructure. And with the revitalization has come an arts renaissance—from virtuoso productions in the theaters of the Times-Union Center for the Performing Arts to world-class exhibits in the Museum of Contemporary Art.

So, even if the ultimate reason for your Florida sojourn is Mickey and his friends, there's no reason to miss the northeast. Indeed, you'll find some authentic benefits—among them, a dearth of crowds and lines and an abundance of southern hospitality, plus good value for the money.

PLANNING

WHEN TO GO

It's not 90°F and sunny here every day. In winter the weather is fair, averaging in the low 50s in Jacksonville and low 60s in Cocoa Beach, but the temperature sometimes dips below freezing for a day or two. Summer temperatures hover around 90, but the humidity makes it seem hotter, and late-afternoon thunderstorms are frequent. April and May are good months to visit, because the ocean is beginning to warm up and the beaches aren't yet packed. Fall is usually pleasant, too.

GETTING HERE AND AROUND

AIR TRAVEL

Jacksonville International Airport (JAX) is the region's air hub. A welcome center with information on local attractions, including St. Augustine and Amelia Island, is on the ground floor at the foot of the escalator near baggage claim. It's open daily 9 am–10 pm.

Daytona Beach International (DAB) and Gainesville Regional (GNV) are smaller operations with fewer flights; that said, they may be more convenient in certain travel situations.

Although Orlando isn't part of the area, visitors to northeastern Florida often choose to arrive at Orlando International Airport (MCO), because cheaper flights are usually available. Driving east from Orlando on tollroad 528 (aka the Beachline Expressway) brings you to Cocoa Beach in about an hour. To reach Daytona from Orlando, take the Beachline Expressway to Interstate 95 and drive north for an hour or so.

CAR TRAVEL

East–west traffic travels the northern part of the state on Interstate 10, a cross-country highway stretching from Jacksonville, Florida, to Santa Monica, California. Farther south, Interstate 4 connects Florida's west and east coasts. Signs on Interstate 4 designate it an east–west route, but actually the road rambles northeast from Tampa to Orlando, then heads north–northeast to Daytona. Two interstates head north–south on Florida's peninsula: Interstate 95 on the east coast and Interstate 75 on the west.

If you want to drive as close to the Atlantic as possible, choose Route A1A, but accept the fact that it will add considerably to your drive time. It runs along the barrier islands, changing its name several times along the way.

The Buccaneer Trail, which overlaps part of Route A1A, goes from St. Augustine north to Mayport, through marshlands and beaches, and then finally into Fort Clinch State Park. The extremely scenic Route 13, also known as the William Bartram Trail, runs from Jacksonville to East Palatka along the east side of St. Johns River through tiny hamlets. U.S. 17 travels the west side of the river, passing through Green Cove Springs and Palatka. Route 40 runs east–west through the Ocala National Forest, giving a nonstop view of stately pines and bold wildlife.

ABOUT THE RESTAURANTS

The ocean, St. Johns River, and numerous lakes and smaller rivers teem with fish, and so, naturally, seafood dominates local menus. Northeast Florida also has fine-dining restaurants, and its ethnic eateries include some excellent Middle Eastern places. And then there are the barbecue joints—more of them than you can shake a hickory chip at.

ABOUT THE HOTELS

For the busy seasons—during summer in and around Jacksonville and during summer and holiday weekends all over Florida—reserve well ahead for top properties. Jacksonville's beach hotels fill up quickly for PGA's THE PLAYERS Championship in mid-May. Daytona Beach presents similar problems during the Daytona 500 (late-February), Bike Week (late February–early March), spring break (March), and the Coke Zero 400 (early July).

St. Augustine stays busy all year. In fall rates are low and availability is high, but it's also hurricane season. Although the area hasn't been hit directly since 1964, it's possible for threatening storms to disrupt plans.

HOTEL AND RESTAURANT COSTS

Prices in the restaurant reviews are the average cost of a main course at dinner or, if dinner isn't served, at lunch. Prices in the hotel reviews are the lowest cost of a standard double room in high season. Prices don't include taxes (6%, more in some counties, and 1%–5% tourist tax for hotel rooms).

TOURS

TourTime, Inc. This company offers custom group and individual motorcoach tours of Jacksonville, Amelia Island, Jekyll Island, and St. Augustine, as well as river cruises and trips to Silver Springs, Kennedy Space Center, Orlando, Okefenokee Swamp, and Savannah. Prior arrangements are required. ☎ *904/282–8500* ⊕ *www.tourtimeinc.com.*

JACKSONVILLE

399 miles north of Miami, on I–95.

Jacksonville is an underrated vacation spot. It offers appealing downtown riverside areas, handsome residential neighborhoods, a thriving arts scene, and, for football fans, the NFL's Jaguars and the NCAA Gator Bowl.

Although the city has become the largest in area of the continental United States (841 square miles), its Old South flavor remains, especially in the Riverside/Avondale historic district. Here moss-draped oak trees frame prairie-style bungalows and Tudor Revival mansions, and palm trees, Spanish bayonet, and azaleas populate the landscape.

EXPLORING JACKSONVILLE

GETTING HERE AND AROUND

The main airport for the region is Jacksonville International Airport. Free shuttles run from the terminal to all parking lots (except the garage) around the clock, and transportation service into the city is available from numerous companies in vehicles that range from taxis

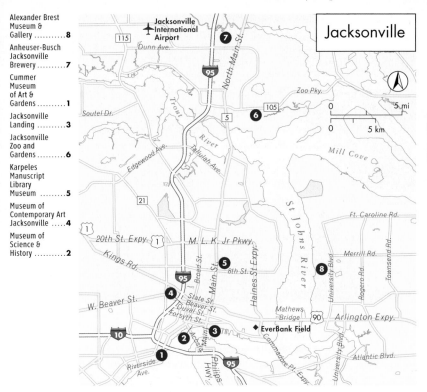

to vans to elegant limousines. Check beforehand on prices, which vary widely, and on which credit cards are accepted. The average cost per person from airport to downtown is $35 to $45; it's $45 to $55 for trips to the beaches. The larger companies usually operate 24/7, but the smaller (and often less expensive ones) may be by appointment only.

Connecting the north and south banks of the St. Johns River, the S.S. *Marine* water taxi runs between several locations, including Crowne Plaza Jacksonville Riverfront and Jacksonville Landing. The one-way trip takes about five minutes. During football season the water taxi also makes trips to EverBank Field on game days and for special events. The water taxi runs Sunday, Wednesday, and Thursday 11:30–9, Friday and Saturday 11–11 (except during rain or other bad weather), with special hours on game days and for special events. One-way fare is $3; special-event fare is $5.

Jacksonville Transportation Authority buses and shuttles serve the city and its beaches. The city also operates a small monorail system that links the convention center and a few downtown areas to several other stations across the river on the Southbank and San Marco. It costs only 35 cents and runs weekdays from 6 am to 11 pm.

Rainbox Lorikeet might pop by and say hello while you're touring the Jacksonville Zoo.

Contacts **Carey Jacksonville** ☎ *904/221–5466.* **Gator City Taxi** ☎ *904/355–8294.* **Jacksonville International Airport (JAX)** ☎ *904/741–4902* ⊕ *www.flyjax.com.* **Jacksonville Transportation Authority (JTA)** ☎ *904/630–3100* ⊕ *www.jtafla.com.* **S.S. Marine Taxi** ☎ *904/733–7782* ⊕ *www.jaxwatertaxi.com.* **Yellow Cab–Jacksonville** ☎ *904/999–9999.*

VISITOR INFORMATION
Contact **Visit Jacksonville** ✉ *208 N. Laura St., Suite 102, Downtown* ☎ *904/798–9111, 800/733–2668* ⊕ *www.visitjacksonville.com.*

EXPLORING

Jacksonville was settled along both sides of the twisting St. Johns River, and a number of attractions are on or near its banks. Both sides of the river, which is spanned by myriad bridges, have downtown areas and waterfront complexes of shops, restaurants, parks, and museums.

You can reach some attractions by water taxi or Skyway Express monorail system—scenic alternatives to driving back and forth across the bridges. That said, a car is generally necessary.

In addition to the visitor information center at the airport, there's one at the Jacksonville Landing marketplace and another in Jacksonville Beach at the Beaches Historical Museum (425 Beach Boulevard), open Tuesday through Saturday 10–4:30.

TOP ATTRACTIONS

Cummer Museum of Art & Gardens. The Wark Collection of early-18th-century Meissen porcelain is just one reason to visit this former riverfront estate, which includes 13 permanent galleries with more than 5,500 items spanning more than 8,000 years, and 3 acres of riverfront gardens reflecting northeast Florida's blooming seasons and indigenous varieties. Art Connections allows kids to experience art through hands-on, interactive exhibits. The Thomas H. Jacobsen Gallery of American Art focuses on works by American artists, including Max Weber, N.C. Wyeth, and Paul Manship. ⊠ *829 Riverside Ave., Riverside* ☎ *904/356–6857* ⊕ *www.cummer.org* ⊠ *$10, free Tues. 4–9* ⊘ *Tues. 10–9, Wed.–Fri. 10–4, Sat. 10–5, Sun. noon–5.*

Jacksonville Landing. During the week, this riverfront market caters to locals and tourists alike, with specialty shops, full-service restaurants—including a sushi bar, Italian bistro, and a steak house—and an internationally flavored food court. The Landing hosts more than 250 weekend events each year, ranging from the good clean fun of the Lighted Boat Parade and Christmas Tree Lighting to the just plain obnoxious Florida/Georgia game after-party, as well as live music (usually of the local cover-band variety) in the courtyard. ⊠ *2 W. Independent Dr., Downtown* ☎ *904/353–1188* ⊕ *www.jacksonvillelanding. com* ⊠ *Free* ⊘ *Mon.–Thurs. 10–8, Fri. and Sat. 10–9, Sun. noon–5:30; restaurant hrs vary.*

FAMILY

Fodor's Choice ★

Jacksonville Zoo and Gardens. What's new at the zoo? Plenty. Not only has it seen the births of a rare Amur leopard and a greater kudu calf, but it now offers Tuxedo Coast, a controlled environment for a group of Magellanic penguins. Among the other highlights are rare waterfowl and the African Reptile Building, which showcases some of the world's most venomous snakes. Wild Florida is a 2½-acre area with black bears, bald eagles, white-tailed deer, and other animals native to Florida. The African Loop has elephants, white rhinos, and two highly endangered leopards, among other species of African birds and mammals. The Range of the Jaguar, winner of the Association of Zoos and Aquarium's Exhibit of the Year, includes 4 acres of exotic big cats as well as 20 other species of animals. Play Park contains a Splash Ground, forest play area, two mazes, and discovery building; Stingray Bay has a 17,000-gallon pool where visitors can pet and feed the mysterious creatures; and Butterfly Hollow is a flower-filled "fairy world" open seasonally. Parking is free. ⊠ *370 Zoo Pkwy., off Heckscher Dr. E* ☎ *904/757–4463* ⊕ *www.jaxzoo.org* ⊠ *$14.95* ⊘ *Daily 9–5.*

Fodor's Choice ★

Museum of Contemporary Art Jacksonville. In this loftlike downtown building, the former headquarters of the Western Union Telegraph Company, a permanent collection of 20th-century art shares space with traveling exhibitions. The museum encompasses five galleries and ArtExplorium, a highly interactive educational exhibit for kids, as well as a funky gift shop and Café Nola, open for lunch on weekdays and for dinner on Thursday. MOCA Jacksonville also hosts film series and workshops throughout the year, and packs a big art-wallop into a relatively small 14,000 square feet. Sunday is free for families; a once-a-month Art Walk is free to all. ⊠ *Hemming Plaza, 333 N. Laura St.*

13

☎ 904/366–6911 ⊕ *www.mocajacksonville.org* ✉ *$8* ◷ *Tues., Wed., Fri., and Sat. 11–5, Thurs. 11–9, Sun. noon–5; Art Walk 1st Wed. of month 5–9.*

WORTH NOTING

FAMILY **Alexander Brest Museum & Gallery.** This Jacksonville University museum features one of the finest collections of ivory anywhere, dating from the early 17th to the late 19th century. ⊠ *Jacksonville University, Phillips Fine Arts Bldg., 2800 University Blvd. N, Arlington* ☎ *904/256–7371* ⊕ *arts.ju.edu* ✉ *Free* ◷ *Mon.–Thurs. 9–4.*

Anheuser-Busch Jacksonville Brewery Tour. Guided tours give a behind-the-scenes look at how barley, malt, rice, hops, and water form the King of Beers. Or you can hightail it through the self-guided tour and head straight to the free beer tastings (if you're 21 years or older, that is). ⊠ *111 Busch Dr.* ☎ *904/696–8373* ⊕ *www.budweisertours.com* ✉ *Free* ◷ *Mon.–Sat. 10–4; guided tours, call for availability.*

Karpeles Manuscript Library Museum. File this one under "hidden treasure," given that even many residents have never visited Karpeles. That's too bad, because this 1921 neoclassical building on the outskirts of downtown has displayed some priceless documents: the original draft of the Bill of Rights, the Emancipation Proclamation signed by Abraham Lincoln, handwritten manuscripts of Edgar Allan Poe and Charles Dickens, and musical scores by Beethoven and Mozart. Manuscript exhibits change every four months or so and coincide with bi-monthly art exhibits. Also on the premises is an antique-book library, with volumes dating from the late 1800s. ⊠ *101 W. 1st St.* ☎ *904/356–2992* ⊕ *www.karpeles.com* ✉ *Free* ◷ *Tues.–Fri. 10–3, Sat. 10–4.*

FAMILY **Museum of Science & History.** Also known locally as MOSH, this museum is home to the Bryan-Gooding Planetarium. As a next-generation planetarium, it can project 3-D laser shows that accompany the ever-popular weekend Cosmic Concerts. For those taking in the planetarium shows, the resolution is significantly sharper than that of the biggest 1080p hi-def TV currently on the market. Whether you're a kid taking in the awe of the new *Dinosaurs at Dusk*, or an adult falling into darkness during *Black Holes: The Other Side of Infinity,* the experience is awesome.

MOSH also has a wide variety of interactive exhibits and programs that include JEA Science Theater, where you can participate in live science experiments; JEA PowerPlay: Understanding our Energy Choices, where you can energize the future city of MOSHtopia as you learn about alternative energy resources and the science of energy; the Florida Naturalist's Center, where you can interact with northeast Florida wildlife; and the Currents of Time, where you'll navigate 12,000 years of Northeast Florida history, from the region's earliest Native American settlers to modern day events. Nationally acclaimed traveling exhibits are featured along with signature exhibits on regional history. ⊠ *1025 Museum Circle* ☎ *904/396–6674* ⊕ *www.themosh.org* ✉ *Museum $10, museum and planetarium $15, Cosmic Concerts $5; Fri. $5 all admissions* ◷ *Mon.–Thurs. 10–5, Fri. 10–8, Sat. 10–6, Sun. noon–5.*

WHERE TO EAT

$$ AMERICAN 🍴 **bb's.** Sleek yet cozy, this hip bistro is as popular with corporate types looking to close a deal as it is with young lovebirds seemingly on the verge of popping the question (though shouting the question might be more appropriate, considering how loud the dining room can get on weekends). The concrete floors and a stainless-steel wine bar provide an interesting backdrop for comfort-food-inspired entrées and daily specials that might include char-grilled beef tenderloin, pan-seared diver scallops with house-made parsnip pierogies, or linguini with catalan-style black angus meatballs. On the lighter side, grilled pizzas, sandwiches, and salads, especially the warm goat-cheese salad, are favorites. Although a wait is common, you can pass the time sizing up the display of diet-destroying desserts. [$] *Average main: $20* ✉ *1019 Hendricks Ave., San Marco, Southbank* ☎ *904/306–0100* 🌐 *www.bbsrestaurant.com* 🕒 *Closed Sun.*

$$ AMERICAN 🍴 **Biscottis.** The local artwork on the redbrick walls is a mild distraction from the jovial yuppies, soccer moms, and metrosexuals—all of whom are among the crowd jockeying for tables in this midsize restaurant. Elbows almost touch, but no one seems to mind. The menu offers the unexpected: wild mushroom ravioli with a broth of corn, leek, and dried apricot; or curry-grilled swordfish with cucumber-fig bordelaise sauce. Be sure to sample from Biscottis's decadent desserts (courtesy of "b the bakery"). Brunch, a local favorite, is served until 3 on weekends. [$] *Average main: $21* ✉ *3556 St. Johns Ave.* ☎ *904/387–2060* 🌐 *www.biscottis.net* ✍ *Reservations not accepted.*

$$$ ECLECTIC 🍴 **Bistro Aix.** When a Jacksonville restaurant can make Angelinos feel like they haven't left home, that's saying a lot. With its slick leather booths, 1940s brickwork, olive drapes, and intricate marbled globes, Bistro Aix (pronounced "X") is just that place. Regulars can't get enough of the creamy onion soup or escargot appetizers, prosciutto and goat cheese salad, or entrées like oak-grilled fish Aixoise, steak frites, or mushroom and fontina wood-fired pizza. Most items (salads included) come in full or lighter-appetite portions, and you'll definitely want to save room for dessert. Aix's in-house pastry team ensures no sweet tooth leaves unsatisfied, with offerings such as profiteroles (mini cream puffs filled with vanilla ice cream and topped with chocolate and caramel sauce) and warm chocolate banana walnut bread pudding. Call for preferred seating. [$] *Average main: $24* ✉ *1440 San Marco Blvd., San Marco* ☎ *904/398–1949* 🌐 *www.bistrox.com* ✍ *Reservations essential* 🕒 *No lunch weekends.*

$$ SEAFOOD 🍴 **Clark's Fish Camp.** It's out of the way, but every mile will be forgotten once you step inside this former bait shop overlooking Julington Creek. Clark's has more than 160 appetizers and entrées, including the usual—shrimp, catfish, and oysters—and the unusual—ostrich, rattlesnake, and kangaroo. In keeping with the more bizarre entrées is the decor, best described as early American taxidermy: hundreds of stuffed critters gaze upon you in the main dining room, and preserved lions, gazelles, baboons, even a rhino, keep a watchful eye in the bar. One person's kitschy may be another's creepy. Be careful not to park illegally—tickets are expensive. [$] *Average main: $20* ✉ *12903 Hood Landing Rd., Mandarin* ☎ *904/268–3474* 🌐 *www.clarksfishcamp.com* 🕒 *No lunch weekdays.*

$ AMERICAN 🍴 **European Street Café.** Wicker baskets and lofty shelves brimming with European confections and groceries like Toblerone and Nutella fill practically every inch of space not occupied by café tables. The menu is similarly overloaded, with nearly 100 deli sandwiches and salads. Notable are raspberry-almond chicken salad and the Blue Max, with pastrami, corned beef, Swiss cheese, sauerkraut, hot mustard, and blue-cheese dressing. This quirky spot is favored by area professionals looking for a quick lunch, as well as the under-forty set doing 23-ounce curls with one of the restaurant's 20-plus beers on tap (plus more than 100 in bottles). The San Marco and Beach Boulevard locations offer live music several nights a week. [$] *Average main: $9* ✉ *2753 Park St.* ☎ *904/384–9999* 🌐 *www.europeanstreet.com* ✍ *Reservations not accepted* [$] *Average main: $9* ✉ *1704 San Marco Blvd., San Marco* ☎ *904/398–9500* 🌐 *www.europeanstreet.com* [$] *Average main: $9* ✉ *5500 Beach Blvd., Southside* ☎ *904/398–1717* 🌐 *www.europeanstreet.com.*

$$$ ECLECTIC Fodor's Choice ★ 🍴 **Matthew's.** No one can accuse chef Matthew Medure of resting on his laurels. Widely praised for culinary creativity and dazzling presentation at his signature San Marco restaurant, Medure has transitioned from French-influenced to Italian-inspired cuisine, complete with a pasta course and a create-your-own cheese and charcuterie spread "for the table." While the regulars (and there are many) are sure to miss their favorites, new menu items such as house-made rigatoni with clams and andouille sausage, arctic char with a basil-pistachio crust, and the veal-and-shortrib meatball appetizer are more than worthy substitutes. Complement your meal with one of 450 wines (topping out at more than $1,000 per bottle). And for those worried that Medure has done away with his famous warm soufflé, relax. Some things are sacred. [$] *Average main: $23* ✉ *2107 Hendricks Ave., San Marco* ☎ *904/396–9922* 🌐 *www.matthewsrestaurant.com* ✍ *Reservations essential* ⏲ *Closed Sun. No lunch.*

WHERE TO STAY

For expanded reviews, facilities, and current deals, visit Fodors.com.

$ HOTEL 🏨 **Hotel Indigo.** Despite the name, don't expect this Southside hotel to be moody and blue: it's bright, bold, and visually different from any other Jacksonville property. **Pros:** reasonable rates; free Wi-Fi throughout; 24-hour business center; loaner PC. **Cons:** wood floors can be noisy; convenient to business parks but not downtown and its sights; lots of traffic at rush hour. [$] *Rooms from: $80* ✉ *9840 Tapestry Park Circle, Southside* ☎ *904/996–7199, 877/270–1392* 🌐 *www.hotelindigo.com* 🛏 *96 rooms, 4 suites* 🍴 *No meals.*

$$$ HOTEL 🏨 **Hyatt Regency Jacksonville Riverfront.** It doesn't get much more convenient than this 19-story, downtown, waterfront hotel within walking distance of Jacksonville Landing, EverBank Field, Florida Theatre, Times-Union Center, corporate office towers, and the county courthouse. **Pros:** riverfront location; rooftop pool and hot tub; free Wi-Fi in public areas; 24-hour gym and business center. **Cons:** not all rooms are riverfront; slow valet service; no minibars; fee for in-room Wi-Fi. [$] *Rooms from: $159* ✉ *225 E. Coastline Dr., Downtown* ☎ *904/588–1234* 🌐 *www.jacksonville.hyatt.com* 🛏 *963 rooms, 21 suites* 🍴 *No meals.*

$$ ⊞ **Omni Jacksonville Hotel.** Jacksonville's most luxurious and glamorous
HOTEL   hotel last underwent a major update in 2011—right down to new flat-
FAMILY screen HD TVs in its chic, spacious guest rooms—with more work in
2012. **Pros:** four-diamond onsite restaurant; downtown location; large
rooms; rooftop pool; great kids' offerings. **Cons:** congested valet area;
restaurant pricey; can be chaotic when there's a show at the Times-
Union Center across the street. $ *Rooms from: $119* ⊠ *245 Water St.*
☎ *904/355–6664, 800/843–6664* ⊕ *www.omnijacksonville.com* ⤲ *354
rooms, 4 2-bedroom suites* ¶⊙¶ *No meals.*

$$$ ⊞ **Riverdale Inn.** In the early 1900s, Jacksonville's wealthiest residents
B&B/INN built mansions along Riverside Avenue—dubbed the Row—and the
three-story Riverdale Inn is only one of two such homes remaining.
Pros: close to area restaurants and shops; private baths. **Cons:** small
rooms; limited parking; strict cancellation policy. $ *Rooms from:*
$150 ⊠ *1521 Riverside Ave., Riverside* ☎ *904/354–5080* ⊕ *www.*
riverdaleinn.com ⤲ *10 rooms, 3 suites* ¶⊙¶ *Breakfast.*

$ ⊞ **St. Johns House.** You can enjoy the grace and elegance of the past and
B&B/INN all the modern amenities at this surprisingly inexpensive B&B. **Pros:**
historic home; beautiful Riverside location near parks, restaurants,
and river; elegant antique furnishings. **Cons:** only open six months a
year. $ *Rooms from: $99* ⊠ *1718 Osceola St., Riverside* ☎ *904/384–*
3724 ⊕ *www.stjohnshouse.com* ⤲ *3 rooms* ⊙ *Closed Mar., June–Oct.*
¶⊙¶ *Breakfast.*

NIGHTLIFE

Club TSI Discotheque. Billing itself as the city's premier underground
venue, TSI hosts local and national indie performers like Break Science, Derek Van Scoten, Archnemesis, and Elliot Lipp. ⊠ *333 E. Bay*
St., Downtown ☎ *904/424–3531* ⊕ *www.clubtsi.com.*

Comedy Zone. The area's premier comedy club is inside the Ramada
Inn Mandarin. ⊠ *3130 Hartley Rd.* ☎ *904/292–4242* ⊕ *www.*
comedyzone.com.

Eclipse. This dance club serves up a mix of moods and music styles
for the twentysomething set. ⊠ *4219 St. Johns Ave.* ☎ *904/387–3582*
⊕ *www.eclipsejax.com.*

The Grotto. Wine snobs, rejoice! Here you can enjoy more than 70 wines
by the glass. ⊠ *2012 San Marco Blvd., San Marco* ☎ *904/398–0726*
⊕ *www.grottowine.com.*

Harmonious Monks. This place claims to have "the world's most talented waitstaff." They certainly might be the most energetic, performing
throughout the night and encouraging customers to dance on the bar.
⊠ *10550 Old St. Augustine Rd., Mandarin* ☎ *904/880–3040* ⊕ *www.*
harmoniousmonks.net.

Jack Rabbits. It's the place to catch the latest and greatest indie bands and
budding rock stars. ⊠ *1528 Hendricks Ave.* ☎ *904/398–7496.*

Latitude 30. This place could be called a pleasure complex, offering "luxury bowling," a game arcade, billiards, casual restaurants, sports bars,
and "cinegrille" movie screening rooms, all at one 50,000-square-foot

DID YOU KNOW?

The Jacksonville Jazz Festival takes place in a five-block area centered on Laura Street in the heart of downtown. Festival highlights include performances by renowned jazz musicians, and jazz piano and youth jazz talent competitions.

facility. ⊠ *10370 Phillips Hwy., Southside* ☎ *904/365–5555* ⊕ *www. latthirty.com* ✉ *Admission free; bowling $4–$5 game; others vary* ⊙ *Sun.–Wed. 11 am–midnight, Thurs.–Sat. 11 am–2 am.*

Mark's. This self-proclaimed "neighborhood lounge with a dash of dance club style" attracts beautiful people to a fairly classy bar with a small dance floor and a popular happy hour. ⊠ *315 E. Bay St., Downtown* ☎ *904/355–5099* ⊕ *www.marksjax.com.*

Metro. It's more than just a gay bar: it's like eight gay bars rolled into one, including a piano bar, dance club, lounge, and drag-show cabaret. ⊠ *859 Willow Branch Ave., Riverside* ☎ *904/388–8719* ⊕ *www.metrojax.com.*

13

Plush. At 12,000 square feet, Plush is certainly Jacksonville's largest nightclub. It's also the loudest. ⊠ *845 University Blvd. N* ☎ *904/743– 1845* ⊕ *www.plushjax.com.*

Square One. The upscale singles' scene here is complemented by live music on weekends. ⊠ *1974 San Marco Blvd., San Marco* ☎ *904/306–9004.*

SHOPPING

DISTRICT

Five Points. This small but funky shopping district less than a mile south-west of downtown has new and vintage-clothing boutiques, shoe stores, and antiques shops. It also has a handful of eateries and bars, not to mention some of the city's most colorful characters. ⊠ *Intersection of Park, Margaret, and Lomax Sts., Riverside* ⊕ *www.5pointsjax.com.*

MALLS

San Marco Square. Dozens of interesting apparel, home, and jewelry stores and restaurants are in 1920s Mediterranean revival–style buildings. ⊠ *San Marco and Atlantic Blvds., San Marco* ⊕ *www.mysanmarco.com.*

The Shoppes of Avondale. The highlights here include upscale clothing and accessories boutiques, art galleries, home-furnishings shops, a choco-latier, and trendy restaurants. ⊠ *St. Johns Ave., between Talbot Ave. and Dancy St., Avondale* ⊕ *www.shoppesofavondale.com.*

St. Johns Town Center. Some of the shops at this huge outdoor "life-style center" aren't found anywhere else in northeast Florida, includ-ing Anthropologie, Apple, Lucky Brand Jeans, and Sephora, as well as the Cheesecake Factory, P.F. Chang's China Bistro, and Maggiano's Little Italy. ⊠ *4663 River City Dr., Southside* ☎ *904/998–7156* ⊕ *www. stjohnstowncenter.com.*

MARKET

Riverside Arts Market. The unique location—under the Fuller-Warren Bridge, a block from the Cummer Museum of Art & Gardens—might be as much of a draw as the merchandise. Regardless, since its first Sat-urday in 2009, RAM has attracted larger and larger crowds of singles, couples, families, and their dogs. They all come to shop for locally created art and crafts, sample food from vendors that include some excellent area restaurants, and check out street performers or the live music shows on the riverfront stage.

Quality is high in every aspect—artists and vendors all go through a fairly rigorous application/audition process—and what there is to see or hear or eat varies from week to week. Sometimes there's also a farmers' market, with licensed farmers and growers selling everything from just-laid eggs and local honey to salad greens that were still in the earth the day before. Inside the Children's Activity Center tent, several organizations offer free educational arts activities to kids.

Because it's sheltered by the bridge, RAM goes on rain or shine. Free parking is available at Fidelity National Financial and other adjacent businesses, and a "bike valet" service encourages people to travel on two wheels. ⊠ *715 Riverside Ave., Riverside* ☎ *904/349–2449* ⊕ *www. riversideartsmarket.com* ⊠ *Free* ⊙ *Mar.–Dec., Sat. 10–4.*

SPORTS AND THE OUTDOORS

BASEBALL

FAMILY **Jacksonville Suns.** The AA minor-league affiliate of the Miami Marlins plays at the $34 million Baseball Grounds of Jacksonville. The Suns were Southern League champions in 2009 and 2010. ⊠ *301 A. Philip Randolph Blvd., Downtown* ☎ *904/358–2846* ⊕ *www.jaxsuns.com.*

BOAT TOURS

River Cruises. Relaxing lunch and dinner-dancing cruises and private sightseeing charters are offered aboard this operation's *Annabelle Lee* and *Lady St. Johns* paddleboats; schedules and prices vary. ⊠ *1501 Riverplace Blvd., Southbank* ☎ *904/306–2200* ⊕ *www.jaxrivercruises.com.*

JACKSONVILLE AREA

JACKSONVILLE BEACHES

Atlantic Beach is 20 miles east of Jacksonville, on U.S. 90 (Beach Blvd.).

Perhaps because the Intracoastal Waterway isn't all that wide where it separates the mainland from the beaches, people here aren't likely to think of themselves as "islanders." But they are, indeed, living on a barrier island, functioning with its own rhythms and led by its own elected officials. And, although there's only one island, there are four beaches/beach communities, each with its own mayor and city officials, tax base, and local legislation. They are, from north to south, Atlantic Beach, Neptune Beach, Jacksonville Beach, and Ponte Vedra Beach. Technically, Ponte Vedra, which is home to the PGA Tour, is just across the border between Duval County and St. Johns County, but the four communities are all considered "Jacksonville's beaches."

Oceanfront properties here can be worth millions, but a few blocks from the beach, things become more affordable. That means kids grow up and go to school together, and then stick around to live in and govern the towns together. Instead of pouring money into attractions designed to rake in tourism dollars, locals are likely to concentrate on stodgy subjects like good schools and parks. Because of this, some visitors might find area beaches to be a little calmer and quieter than they expected.

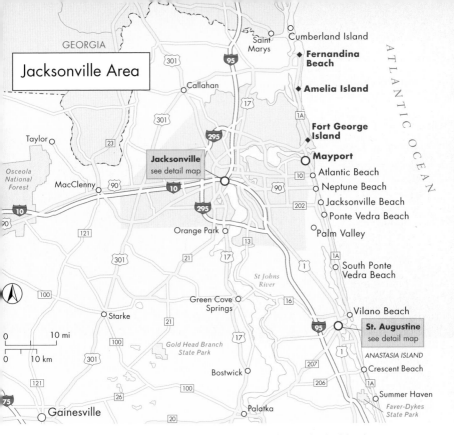

Jacksonville Area

But there's a real sense of community—that and a laid-back pace. You might want to embrace it all. In fact, many vacationers like the easy pace so much that they decide to make the area their permanent home.

EXPLORING

FAMILY **Adventure Landing and Shipwreck Island Water Park.** With go-karts, two miniature-golf courses, laser tag, batting cages, kiddie rides, and an arcade, Adventure Landing is more like an old-time boardwalk than a high-tech amusement park. But when the closest theme park is more than two hours away, you make do. The largest family-entertainment center in northeast Florida also encompasses Shipwreck Island Water Park, which features a lazy river for tubing, a 500,000-gallon wave pool, and three extreme slides—the Rage, HydroHalfpipe, and Eye of the Storm. ⊠ *1944 Beach Blvd., Jacksonville Beach* ☎ *904/246–4386* ⊕ *www.adventurelanding.com* ⊠ *Adventure Landing free (fees for rides and games), Shipwreck Island $27.99* ⊘ *Adventure Landing: Sun.– Thurs. 10–10, Fri. and Sat. 10 am–midnight; Shipwreck Island: late Mar.–late Sept., hrs vary.*

Beaches Historical Museum. This museum has exhibits about the history of the beaches communities, the St. Johns River, the fishing and shrimping industry, and the area's settlers. Its gift shop is a good place to find Florida souvenirs of every variety, from tasteful to pure kitsch. Admission

Beaches make great places to drop a line and see if the fish are biting.

here includes a guided tour of the adjacent Pablo Historical Park with its 1911 steam locomotive, railroad foreman's house, and the Mayport Depot. ⊠ *381 Beach Blvd., Jacksonville Beach* ☎ *904/241–5657* ⊕ *www.beachesmuseum.org* ▧ *$5* ☽ *Tues.–Sat. 10–4:30.*

J. Johnson Gallery. Built by photographer and art collector Jennifer Johnson, this stunning Mediterranean building just a block from the ocean in Jacksonville Beach hosts contemporary art exhibits you'd expect to find only in the nation's largest and most sophisticated cities. Exhibits like "Multiplicity" and "Contemporary Complexities" include work by emerging artists as well as established names. The gallery also presents experimental and project work. ⊠ *177 4th Ave. N, Jacksonville Beach* ☎ *904/435–3200* ⊕ *www.jjohnsongallery.com* ▧ *Free* ☽ *Tues.– Fri. 10–5, Sat. 1–5.*

BEACHES

Atlantic Beach. If you're looking for sun-soaked relaxation, head for Atlantic Beach, where you can sink your feet into its white, sugary sands or catch some waves in the warm surf. You can even rejuvenate with some prime pampering at the One Ocean resort's spa. Hotel guests and those wandering in from the beach can both use this luxurious oceanfront hotel's beach rental services, which offer umbrellas, lounge chairs, boogie boards, kayaks, and surfboards for a fee. Beachgoers with canine companions are welcome at Atlantic Beach during the day and evening as long as the dog is leashed. Atlantic Beach and next-door Neptune Beach share the trendy Town Center, which has lots of tempting dining and shopping within a block of the beach. **Amenities:** food and drink; lifeguards (seasonal); showers; water sports. **Best for:** sunrise; surfing;

swimming; walking. ⊠ *Beach Ave., between 18th and 20th Sts.; Dewees Ave., between 1st and 16th Sts.; Ahern St. and Atlantic Blvd., Atlantic Beach.*

Jacksonville Beach. Enjoy the waves at one of Jacksonville's busier beaches, which stretches along the coast for 4.1 miles. A boardwalk and a bevy of beachfront restaurants and shops are also draws, so expect moderate crowds during spring and summer school breaks. The municipal Seawalk Pavilion hosts outdoor movies, concerts, and festivals, and the 2-acre Oceanfront Park (1st Street South, between 5th Avenue South and 6th Avenue South) has a small playground, volleyball court, and picnic areas. Anglers can fish without a license from the wheelchair-accessible 1,320-foot fishing pier ($4, $1 spectator; daily 6 am–10 pm), which also has free fish-cleaning stations, a bait-and-tackle shop, and free parking. The historic Casa Marina Hotel, which opened its doors here in 1925, has a popular Sunday brunch. **Amenities:** toilets; showers; food and drink; lifeguards (seasonal); parking (free). **Best for:** partiers; sunrise; surfing; swimming. ⊠ *1st St., between Seagate and S. 16th Aves., Jacksonville Beach* ☎ *904/241–1515 fishing pier* ☉ *Daily 8–5.*

Neptune Beach. Nestled between Atlantic and Jacksonville beaches, this is a great destination for those wishing to combine a day at the beach with other activities. The beach, with its light beige sand, is a great family spot, as it tends to be less crowded than Jacksonville Beach. And because Neptune and Atlantic beaches share Atlantic Avenue's Town Center, with its assortment of restaurants, galleries, stores, and boutiques, beachgoers can escape the sun when they're ready for great food, shopping, and live entertainment. Slider's Bar and Grill is a local favorite, or stop in Pete's Bar for a beer so you can say you were there. **Amenities:** showers; food and drink; lifeguards (seasonal). **Best for:** sunrise; swimming; walking. ⊠ *Strand St., between Atlantic Blvd. and Gaillardia Pl., Oak St. and Rose Pl., North St. and 20th Ave., Neptune Beach.*

Ponte Vedra Beach. Although this upscale coastal community 18 miles southeast of downtown Jacksonville is primarily known for its golf courses and swanky homes, it also has beautiful beaches that attract wealthy residents, as well as a number of resorts: the Ponte Vedra Inn & Club, the Lodge & Club, and the Sawgrass Marriott. Public beach access for nonresort guests is minimal in most areas because of heavily restricted parking. However, thanks to its free public parking, Mickler's Landing, south of most residences, is the most popular beach access point. It's also famous for producing sharks' teeth. **Amenities:** showers; toilets; lifeguards (seasonal); parking (free). **Best for:** solitude; sunrise; walking. ⊠ *East of intersection of A1A S and Ponte Vedra Blvd., Ponte Vedra Beach.*

WHERE TO EAT

ATLANTIC BEACH

$ ITALIAN 🍴 **Al's Pizza.** The beach locations of this popular restaurant defy all expectations of a neighborhood pizza joint. Bright colors and geometric patterns accent the dining room, which manages to look retro (soda-fountain chairs) and modern (steel columns) at the same time. The menu is fairly predictable; there's pizza by the slice and by the pie, plus standbys like lasagna and ravioli. The clientele, too, is typical beachgoer, with lots of young surfer dudes and dudettes and sunburned families, as well as a fair representation of older Atlantic Beach couples, who come for the food more than the scene. Service is quick, but finding parking at peak hours can be a problem. Check behind the restaurant as well as out front. There's also a branch in Ponte Vedra Beach. [$] *Average main: $10* ✉ *303 Atlantic Blvd.* ☎ *904/249–0002* 🌐 *www.alspizza.com* ✍ *Reservations not accepted.*

$$ SEAFOOD 🍴 **The Fish Company Restaurant and Oyster Bar.** If you want fresh fish, this is the place. Owners Bill and Ann Pinner have lots of street cred: among other area culinary achievements, they helped establish the Ragtime Tavern as an institution. Options include perfectly blended crab cakes, oh-so-lightly fried Mayport shrimp (never a heavy batter that might cover up the flavor), seafood salads, and delicious sides. And there are offerings for meat lovers in the family, too. There's also a raw bar, outdoor seating, and a full drinks bar with happy-hour prices 2–7 Monday through Saturday and all day on Sunday. [$] *Average main: $21* ✉ *725-12 Atlantic Blvd.* ☎ *904/246–0123* 🌐 *www.thefishcojax.com* ✍ *Reservations not accepted.*

$$$ ECLECTIC Fodor's Choice ★ 🍴 **Ocean 60.** Despite being a block from the Atlantic Ocean, this lively restaurant–wine bar–martini room has gone largely undiscovered by visitors, who might think fine dining and flip-flops don't mix. Those who do stumble upon it, however, are pleasantly surprised to find that a casual aura befits Ocean 60's eclectic seasonal menu, with signature items like salmon gratin (seared salmon topped with a parmesan and tomato gratin served over butternut squash risotto), rosemary grilled rib eye, and crepes Florentine. Things are anything but laid-back on Thursday, Friday, and Saturday nights, however, thanks to live music and potent cocktails. [$] *Average main: $22* ✉ *60 Ocean Blvd.* ☎ *904/247–0060* 🌐 *www.ocean60.com* ⏲ *Closed Sun.*

$$ AMERICAN 🍴 **Ragtime Tavern & Seafood Grill.** A New Orleans theme prevails at this loud place that attracts a lively crowd ranging in age from 21 to midlife crisis. Grouper oscar (seared and topped with crabmeat, asparagus, and Béarnaise sauce) and Ragtime shrimp (deep-fried fresh shrimp rolled in coconut) are specialties (as are microbrews made on the premises), or try a po'boy sandwich or fish sizzled on the grill. [$] *Average main: $20* ✉ *207 Atlantic Blvd.* ☎ *904/241–7877* 🌐 *www.ragtimetavern.com.*

JACKSONVILLE BEACH

$ AMERICAN FAMILY 🍴 **Ellen's Kitchen.** Once upon a time, Ellen's Kitchen was a breakfast and lunch place inside Silver's Drug Store at First and Atlantic, a landmark from time immemorial. Silver's is no more, and Ellen's long ago relocated to a shopping strip, but it's still an institution, and probably

13

will be for generations. It's also a great place to bring the kids, thanks to the kid-friendly menu, very reasonable prices, and relaxed atmosphere. Sure, you can get your eggs over easy and your bacon crisp, but if you want to be mistaken for a local, ask for a Hippie or a Surfer, two poached-egg-on-English-muffin creations that are far better than anybody's eggs Benedict. If it's hollandaise sauce you're craving, though, the crab cake Benedict is brunch perfection. Breakfast is served until the doors close at 2 pm, but the lunch menu is also fairly extensive. Don't expect too much chat from your server at "rush hour" on weekend mornings—everyone's usually working at warp speed. Regardless, though, the staffers do their best to please, no matter how crowded. ⓢ *Average main: $6* ⊠ *1824 3rd St. S* ☎ *904/246–1572* ⚑ *Reservations not accepted* ☾ *No dinner.*

$
AMERICAN
╳ **European Street Café.** This colorful, quirky, family-owned eatery has a menu with an ambitious list of sandwiches, salads, and soups; an overflowing gourmet-food section; a mind-boggling beer list; and cookies big enough to knock someone unconscious. Thirsty locals belly up to the impressive, hand-carved bar for monthly beer tastings and daily happy hour (2–7 pm). More mature crowds prefer to sip their zinfandel in the bustling dining room. ⓢ *Average main: $9* ⊠ *992 Beach Blvd.* ☎ *904/249–3001* ⊕ *www.europeanstreet.com* ⚑ *Reservations not accepted.*

$$
CUBAN
FAMILY
╳ **Mambo's Cuban Bistro.** So you think you can't dance? Don't let that stop you from checking out the Salsa Thursdays here. In addition to authentic Cuban cuisine daily, Mambo's offers live music and free dance lessons some evenings. Mambo's draws raves from a mix of the young and the restless, who love the music and dancing, and families, who insist that even Miami doesn't offer better Cuban cooking. Mojitos from the full bar are lauded, too, but the highest praise goes to desserts from *tres leches* (cake soaked in evaporated milk, condensed milk, and heavy cream) to guava flan. ⓢ *Average main: $18* ⊠ *311 3rd St. N, Suite 103* ☎ *904/853–6360* ⊕ *www.mamboscubanbistro.com.*

$
BARBECUE
╳ **Mojo Kitchen BBQ Pit & Blues Bar.** True barbecue aficionados know that the country's really divided into four territories: North Carolina, Memphis, Kansas City, and Texas, each renowned for its own barbecue style. Owner Todd Lineberry did some serious research into each region before deciding his restaurants would honor all four traditions—along with some original flavor. In addition to great barbecue, you'll find Deep South sides like cheese grits and fried green tomatoes as well as some truly delicious sweet tea and banana pudding. The beach location brings both young and old, blue collar and no-collar (plus pukashells), all ready to chow down on generous portions, with a backdrop of bright, bold-color walls and edgy portraits of blues royalty. Mojo's appreciation for the blues doesn't end with the interior design. There's good recorded blues at all times, and on occasion, some great live blues as well. ⓢ *Average main: $14* ⊠ *1500 Beach Blvd.* ☎ *904/247–6636* ⊕ *www.mojobbq.com* ⚑ *Reservations not accepted.*

PONTE VEDRA BEACH

$$$$ MODERN AMERICAN

🍴 **Augustine Grille.** The atmosphere at this Sawgrass Marriott restaurant is polished but informal, the service is attentive but not intrusive, and the menu is exquisite. Executive chef Brett Smith subscribes to the farm-to-table philosophy that focuses on sourcing food from regional farms and dairies who practice organic farming techniques. You can order an old favorite (for many, that means steak, a fillet or KC strip), seasonal fresh fish, or experiment with small-plate tasting combinations. Options might include lobster Napolean, scallop ceviche, bacon mac and cheese, and farm tomato with mozzarella and basil. If you're feeling truly adventurous, put yourself into the chef's hands with the five-course tasting menu, to which you can also add wine pairings. [$] *Average main: $38* ✉ *Sawgrass Marriott, 1000 PGA Tour Blvd.* ☎ *904/285–7777* 🌐 *www.sawgrassmarriott.com/dining/augustine_grille.asp* ✍ *Reservations essential* ⏲ *No lunch. Closed Sun.*

WHERE TO STAY

For expanded reviews, facilities, and current deals, visit Fodors.com.

ATLANTIC BEACH

$$$ RESORT FAMILY

🏨 **One Ocean.** Atlantic Beach's only high-rise oceanfront hotel captures the serenity of the ocean through a color palette of sea-foam green, sand, and sky blue, and reflective materials like glass and marble. **Pros:** exceptional service; walking distance to restaurants and shops; all rooms have floor-to-ceiling ocean view; 24-hour room service. **Cons:** tiny bathroom; no self-parking on property; resort fee. [$] *Rooms from: $219* ✉ *1 Ocean Blvd.* ☎ *904/249–7402* 🌐 *www.oneoceanresort.com* 🛏 *190 rooms, 3 suites* 🍽 *No meals.*

NEPTUNE BEACH

$$ HOTEL

🏨 **Sea Horse Oceanfront Inn.** This bright-pink-and-aqua '50s throwback caters to budget-minded guests seeking an ultracasual, laid-back vibe. **Pros:** beach access with private walk-over; popular bar on-site; walking distance to restaurants and shops; free breakfast baskets available at front desk. **Cons:** no-frills; no room service. [$] *Rooms from: $129* ✉ *120 Atlantic Blvd.* ☎ *904/246–2175, 800/881–2330* 🌐 *www.jacksonvilleoceanfronthotel.com* 🛏 *37 rooms, 1 suite.*

PONTE VEDRA BEACH

$$$$ RESORT FAMILY Fodor's Choice ★

🏨 **The Lodge & Club.** This Mediterranean-revival oceanfront resort—with its white-stucco exterior and Spanish roof tiles—is luxury lodging at its best. **Pros:** high-end accommodations; excellent service; private beach. **Cons:** most recreation facilities are a few blocks away at Ponte Vedra Inn & Club; gratuity charge automatically added to bill nightly. [$] *Rooms from: $319* ✉ *607 Ponte Vedra Blvd.* ☎ *904/273–9500, 800/243–4304* 🌐 *www.pontevedra.com* 🛏 *42 rooms, 24 suites* 🍽 *No meals.*

$$$$ RESORT FAMILY Fodor's Choice ★

🏨 **Ponte Vedra Inn & Club.** Considered northeast Florida's premier resort for decades, this 1928 landmark continues to wow guests with its stellar service and large guest rooms housed in white-brick, Spanish-style buildings lining the beach. **Pros:** accommodating, friendly staff; private beach; adults-only pool. **Cons:** charge for umbrellas and chaises on the beach; crowded pool at some times of year. [$] *Rooms from: $279* ✉ *200 Ponte Vedra Blvd.* ☎ *904/285–1111, 800/234–7842* 🌐 *www.pontevedra.com* 🛏 *217 rooms, 33 suites* 🍽 *No meals.*

$$$ RESORT FAMILY Fodor's Choice ★ **Sawgrass Marriott Golf Resort & Spa.** Here you can laze about in the highly regarded spa or by one of four swimming pools, get active out on a golf course, or fish in a freshwater lake or pond. **Pros:** championship golf courses; beautiful surroundings; readily available shuttle; efficient staff. **Cons:** beach not within walking distance; no free parking; fee for in-room Wi-Fi. [$] *Rooms from: $239* ✉ *1000 PGA Tour Blvd.* ☎ *904/285–7777, 800/457–4653* 🌐 *www.sawgrassmarriott.com* 🛏 *508 rooms, 24 suites, 80 villas* 🍴 *No meals.*

NIGHTLIFE

JACKSONVILLE BEACH

Free Bird Live. This medium-size (it holds 700) concert venue owned by Judy Van Zant (widow of Lynyrd Skynyrd's Ronnie Van Zant) draws some complaints about its standing-room-only tickets and slow bar service. But it also gets raves for the chance to see great blues, rock, funk, rockabilly, and jam bands in an intimate setting. ✉ *200 1st St. N* ☎ *904/246–2473* 🌐 *www.freebirdlive.com* 🎟 *Admission varies by show.*

Lynch's Irish Pub. Hoist a pint o' Guinness and enjoy live local music. ✉ *514 N. 1st St.* ☎ *904/249–5181* 🌐 *www.lynchsirishpub.com.*

Penthouse Lounge. If you'd rather gawk at sports stars in person than on the tube, head to this oceanfront spot, where local NFL and PGA stars have been known to congregate. ✉ *Casa Marina Hotel, 691 N. 1st St.* ☎ *904/270–0025* 🌐 *www.casamarinahotel.com.*

Sneakers Sports Grille. With nearly 80 TVs and an impressive menu (by sports-bar standards anyway), this is the go-to sports bar at the beach. ✉ *111 Beach Blvd.* ☎ *904/482–1000* 🌐 *www.sneakerssportsgrille.com.*

NEPTUNE BEACH

Pete's Bar. The oldest bar in the Jacksonville area is also notable for the cheapest drinks, cheapest pool tables, and most colorful clientele. Authors like John Grisham and James W. Hall have written about this hole-in-the-wall, probably because it's across from the BookMark, a great independent bookstore where writers love to give readings. ✉ *117 1st St.* ☎ *904/249–9158.*

SHOPPING

The BookMark. It may be small in size, but this book shop is big in prestige. Thanks to its knowledgeable owners, many famous authors love this place and always include it on their publicity tours. Once you've bought books here a time or two, the staff will be able to recommend ones you'll like with amazing accuracy. ✉ *220 1st St., Neptune Beach* ☎ *904/241–9026* 🌐 *www.bookmarkbeach.com* 🕒 *Mon.–Wed. 10–7, Thurs.–Sat. 10–8, Sun. 11–5.*

SPORTS AND THE OUTDOORS

BIKING

Champion Cycling. You can rent beach cruisers by the hour or the day. ✉ *1303 N. 3rd St., Jacksonville Beach* ☎ *904/241–0900* 🌐 *www.championcycling.net.*

Ponte Vedra Bicycles. This outfitter includes free bike maps with your rental. ✉ *250 Solana Rd., Ponte Vedra Beach* ☎ *904/273–0199.*

GOLF

Every May millions of golf fans watch golf's most elite competitors vie for the prestige of winning THE PLAYERS Championship. The event—considered by many to be the sport's "unofficial fifth major"—takes place each year at the Tournament Players Club (TPC) Sawgrass in Ponte Vedra Beach, 20 miles southeast of Jacksonville. Designed and built for major tournament golf, TPC has an elevated seating area that gives more than 40,000 fans a great view of the action. And while you're in the area, be sure to visit the World Golf Hall of Fame a few miles down the road in St. Augustine.

Tournament Players Club Sawgrass. There are two courses here: the Stadium Course (with its world-renowned Island Green), which hosts THE PLAYERS Championship each year, and the Pete Dye–designed Valley Course. In conjunction with the Sawgrass Marriott, TPC offers packages like the Tour Player Experience, which not only provides access to the TPC's player area, but also gives you a caddie who wears your name on the back of his golf shirt just like he does when caddying for the pros. How cool is that? If you want to play a round of golf and aren't staying at the Marriott, check out the Resort Day Passes. ⊠ *110 Championship Way, Ponte Vedra Beach* ☎ *904/273–3235, 800/457–4653* ⊕ *www.tpc.com/sawgrass.*

MAYPORT

20 miles northeast of downtown Jacksonville, on Rte. A1A/105.

Dating back more than 300 years, this is one of the oldest fishing communities in the United States. It has several excellent and very casual seafood restaurants and a commercial shrimp-boat fleet. It's also home to one of the largest naval facilities in the country, Naval Station Mayport.

GETTING HERE AND AROUND

St. Johns River Ferry. The arrival of the *Jean Ribault* ferry in 1948 made everyday life here more convenient—and fun. The 153-vessel continues to delight passengers young and old as they embark on the 10-minute cruise across the river between Mayport and Fort George Island. The cost is $5 per motorcycle, $6 per car. Pedestrians enjoy the ride for just $1 each way. Call for departure times. ☎ *904/241–9969* ⊕ *www.stjohnsriverferry.com.*

EXPLORING

Fodor's Choice ★ **Kathryn Abbey Hanna Park.** This 450-acre oceanfront park just north of Atlantic Beach is beloved by surfers, swimmers, campers, hikers, and especially bikers, who regularly hit the many off-road bike trails from novice right up to those named Grunt and Misery. You can rent canoes, kayaks, or paddleboats to go out on the 60-acre freshwater lake. Younger kids delight in the lakefront playground and a water park with fountains and squirting hoses. There are restrooms, picnic areas, and grills throughout, and from Memorial Day to Labor Day lifeguards supervise all water activities. ⊠ *500 Wonderwood Dr.* ☎ *904/249–4700* ⊠ *$3 per vehicle* ☉ *Apr.–Oct., daily 8–8; Nov.–Mar., daily 8–6.*

FORT GEORGE ISLAND

25 miles northeast of Jacksonville, on Rte. A1A/105.

One of the oldest inhabited areas of Florida, Fort George Island is lush with foliage, natural vegetation, and wildlife. A 4-mile nature and bike trail meanders across the island, revealing shell mounds dating as far back as 5,000 years.

EXPLORING

Kingsley Plantation. Built in 1792 by Zephaniah Kingsley, an eccentric slave trader, this is the oldest remaining cotton plantation in the state. The ruins of 23 tabby (a concretelike mixture of sand and crushed shells) slave houses, a barn, and the modest Kingsley home are open to the public via self-guided tours and reachable by bridge. ⊠ *Rte. A1A– Heckscher Dr.* ☎ *904/251–3537* ⊕ *www.nps.gov/timu* ⊠ *Free* ⊗ *Daily 9–5; plantation house weekends only; call ahead for reservations.*

Talbot Island State Parks. These parks, including Big and Little Talbot islands, have 17 miles of gorgeous beaches, sand dunes, and golden marshes that hum with birds and native waterfowl. Come to picnic, fish, swim, snorkel, or camp. Little Talbot Island, one of the few undeveloped barrier islands in Florida, has river otters, marsh rabbits, raccoons, alligators, and gopher tortoises. Canoe and kayak rentals are available, and the north area is considered the best surfing spot in northeast Florida. A 4-mile nature trail winds across Little Talbot, and there are several smaller trails on Big Talbot. ⊠ *12157 Heckscher Dr.* ☎ *904/251–2320* ⊕ *www.floridastateparks.org/littletalbotisland* ⊠ *$5 per vehicle, up to 8 people; $4 single occupants, motorcyclists; $2 pedestrians, bicyclists* ⊗ *Daily 8–sunset.*

AMELIA ISLAND AND FERNANDINA BEACH

35 miles northeast of Jacksonville.

At the northeasternmost reach of Florida, Amelia Island has beautiful beaches with enormous sand dunes along its eastern flank, a state park with a Civil War fort, sophisticated restaurants, interesting shops, and accommodations that range from bed-and-breakfasts to luxury resorts. The town of Fernandina Beach is on the island's northern end; a century ago casinos and brothels thrived here, but those are gone. Today there's little reminder of the town's wild days, though one event comes close: the Isle of Eight Flags Shrimp Festival, held during the first weekend of May.

TOURS

Amelia River Cruises and Charters. Narrated tours glide near the area's marshes, rivers, and wilderness beaches. ⊠ *1 N. Front St.* ☎ *904/261– 9972, 877/264–9972* ⊕ *www.ameliarivercruises.com.*

VISITOR INFORMATION

Contact Amelia Island Convention and Visitors Bureau ⊠ *102 Centre St.* ☎ *904/277–0717* ⊕ *www.ameliaisland.com.*

EXPLORING

Amelia Island Historic District. This district in Fernandina Beach has more than 50 blocks of buildings listed on the National Register of Historic Places; 450 ornate structures built before 1927 offer some of the nation's finest examples of Queen Anne, Victorian, and Italianate homes. Many date from the haven's mid-19th-century glory days. Pick up a self-guided-tour map at the chamber of commerce, in the old train depot—once a stopping point on the first cross-state railroad—and take your time exploring the quaint shops, restaurants, and boutiques that populate the district, especially along Centre Street.

FAMILY
Fodor's Choice
★

Fort Clinch State Park. One of the country's best-preserved and most complete 19th-century brick forts, Fort Clinch was built to discourage further British intrusion after the War of 1812 and was occupied in 1863 by the Confederacy; a year later it was retaken by the North. During the Spanish-American War it was reactivated for a brief time, but no battles were ever fought on its grounds (which explains why it's so well preserved). Wander through restored buildings, including furnished barracks, a kitchen, and a repair shop. Living-history reenactments of Civil War garrison life are scheduled throughout the year. The 1,086-acre park surrounding the fort has full-facility camping, nature trails, carriage rides, a swimming beach, and surf and pier fishing. Nature buffs enjoy the variety of flora and fauna, especially since Fort Clinch is the only state park in northeast Florida designated by the Florida Fish and Wildlife Conservation Commission as a viewing destination for the eastern brown pelican, green sea turtle, and loggerhead sea turtle. ⊠ *2601 Atlantic Ave.* ☎ *904/277–7274* ⊕ *www.floridastateparks.org/fortclinch* ⊠ *$6 per vehicle, up to 8 people; $4 motorcycles; $2 pedestrians, bicyclists* ☉ *Daily 8–sunset; fort 9–5.*

BEACHES

There are a number of places on Amelia Island where driving on the beach is allowed in designated areas, including Seaside Park, Peters Point, Burney Park, and Amelia Island State Park. If you have a four-wheel-drive vehicle (and a lot of beach equipment to haul), you may want to try this. Be warned, though: it's easier to get stuck than you might think, and towing is expensive. You also need to watch the tides carefully if you don't want your car floating out to sea. And unless you're a county resident or disabled, you must buy a permit, which is available at the Nassau County Historic Courthouse (⊠ *416 Centre St., Fernandina Beach* ☎ *904/491–6430*), Hall's Beach Store (⊠ *2012 S. Fletcher Ave., Fernandina Beach* ☎ *904/310–6124*), and several other locations. All city beaches have free admission.

Huguenot Memorial Park. Though it's officially a Jacksonville city park, this popular spot on the northern side of the St. Johns River is usually grouped with Amelia's beaches. Among a handful of places where driving on the beach is permitted, it's unusual in that no special permit is required. Families with lots of beach equipment like the option of parking close to the water, but it takes vigilance to avoid soft sand and incoming tides. The ocean side offers good surfing, Boogie boarding, and surf fishing. On the western side is a shallow, sheltered lagoon that's a favorite with windsurfers, paddleboarders, and parents of small children. The

park is also an important stop for migrating birds, so at certain times of the year, some areas are closed to vehicles. **Amenities:** showers; toilets; lifeguards (seasonal); parking (free). **Best for:** surfing; swimming; windsurfing. ✉ *10980 Heckscher Dr.* ☎ *904/251-3335* 💲 *$3 per car up to 6 people; $1 each additional person* ⊙ *Apr.–Oct., daily 8–8; Nov.–Mar., daily 8–6.*

Main Beach. Of all Fernandina Beach access points (there are 40), this is likely to be the most crowded—but also the most fun for kids and teens. Not only are there sand volleyball courts, a beachfront playground, picnic tables, and barbecue grills at the park itself, but there's old-school fun to be had at the adjacent skate park and vintage miniature-golf course, whose concession stand sells cold drinks, ice cream, and snow cones. A casual restaurant and bar are right on the beach. **Amenities:** showers; toilets; food and drink; lifeguards (seasonal); parking (free). **Best for:** swimming. ✉ *Atlantic Ave. and S. Fletcher Ave*

Peters Point Beach. At the south end of the island, this beach allows you free access to the same gorgeous sands used by vacationers at the Ritz-Carlton. It has a large parking area, a picnic area, barbecue grills, and three lifeguard towers. **Amenities:** showers; toilets; lifeguards (seasonal); parking (free). **Best for:** sunrise; surfing; swimming; walking. ✉ *1974 S. Fletcher Ave*

Seaside Park Beach. Like Main Beach to the north and Peters Point to the south, Seaside Park allows limited beach driving if you have a permit, but beware—vehicles here frequently get stuck and have to be towed. There are several picnic tables and dune walkovers to the beach. It's a great place to fish or to ride bikes at low tide. Bikes and other beach equipment can be rented at Hall's Beach Store (✉ *2021 S. Fletcher Ave.*). Also nearby, Sliders Seaside Grill is a venerable oceanfront restaurant where you can enjoy food and drinks inside or at the tiki bar overlooking the beach, often with live music. **Amenities:** showers; toilets; food and drink; lifeguards (seasonal); parking (free). **Best for:** surfing; swimming; walking. ✉ *Sadler Rd. and S. Fletcher Ave*

Talbot Islands State Parks Beaches. A few miles south of Fernandina Beach, the Talbot Islands State Parks system consists of seven parks, three of which have beach settings. All of the oceanfront parks have picnic areas and a small admission charge but free parking. **Little Talbot** is popular for swimming and beachcombing. Sand dollars are often found at the far north end. **Big Talbot,** with its Boneyard Beach of wind-twisted trees, is not recommended for swimming but is a photographer's paradise. **Amelia Island State Park** is best known for letting you horseback ride on the

---

A BANNER BEACH

Fernandina Beach is also known as the "Isle of Eight Flags," a moniker derived from the fact that it's the only American site to have been under eight different flags (French, Spanish, British, Patriots, Green Cross of Florida, Mexican Revolutionary, National Flag of the Confederacy, and United States). Every May the Isle of Eight Flags Shrimp Festival celebrates another of Fernandina's claims to fame: birthplace of the modern shrimping industry.

beach as well as for the adjacent George Crady fishing pier. Kayak and canoe tours can be booked through the parks system's vendor, Kayak Amelia. **Amenities:** showers; toilets; lifeguards (seasonal); parking (free). **Best for:** solitude; sunrise; swimming; walking. ⊠ *Rte. A1A, south of Fernandina Beach* 🚗 *Little Talbot, $5 per vehicle; Big Talbot, $3 per vehicle for the Bluffs picnic area; Amelia Island, $2 per person.*

WHERE TO EAT

$$
ECLECTIC

✕ **Kelley's Courtyard Café.** Few places embody the charm of the historic district like this casual courtyard restaurant, where guests and tourists alike gather as much for the garden setting as the eclectic cuisine. There's an indoor seating area, too, but most prefer the umbrella- and palm-shaded courtyard tables surrounding a soothing brick fountain. The rotating dinner menu might include sweet potato soup, seafood enchiladas, or blue cheese–crusted filet mignon. Lunch offers a tasty respite from shopping, with refreshing salads, wraps, and signature sandwiches such as a BLT with spinach and goat cheese. Wines by the glass (mostly $6) are reasonable for a tourist town. And if there's such a thing as a destination dessert, Granny Mutt's blueberry squares with vanilla ice cream would certainly qualify. $ *Average main: $19* ⊠ *19 S. 3rd St.* ☎ *904/432–8213* ⊕ *www.kelleyscourtyardcafe.com* ⊙ *Closed Sun.*

$$$$
ECLECTIC

✕ **PLAE.** Short for People Laughing and Eating, PLAE has an extensive wine list and an upscale but eclectic menu with French and Mediterranean influences. The mussels, say patrons, should not be missed. Adventurous diners love to order the Chef's Plate, not knowing exactly what delights the chef has prepared for the evening until they appear at the table. PLAE's atmosphere varies greatly depending on your seating choice. Indoors has a sleek, contemporary ambience with intimate, high-backed booths. Dining on the outdoor patio provides a view over the beautiful natural surroundings of the adjacent golf course. Although PLAE's location at the Spa & Shops at Omni Amelia Island Plantation makes it a favorite with Plantation visitors, it's an independently owned restaurant and equally popular with locals. $ *Average main: $26* ⊠ *Omni Amelia Island Plantation, 80 Amelia Village Circle* ☎ *904/277–2132* ⊕ *www.plaefl.net* 🍴 *Reservations essential.*

$$$$
ECLECTIC
Fodor's Choice
★

✕ **Salt.** The Ritz-Carlton restaurant's inventive cuisine highlights seasonal ingredients that might include Florida snapper with Calypso beans and clams, or Darling Downs Wagyu rib eye cooked on a wood-burning grill. The wine list has more than 300 bottles (24 by the glass), service is nothing short of impeccable, and there's a view of the Atlantic from every table. For a unique dining experience, reserve A Seat in the Kitchen, a private dining room within the kitchen, where you can watch the chefs at work and enjoy a personalized five-course meal. To learn the secrets of Salt's cuisine, consider taking one of the two-day Salt cooking school sessions. They've proven so popular, the Ritz-Carlton has expanded the schedule to several a year. Long pants and collared shirts are recommended (for dining, we mean; cooking students get their own Ritz-Carlton aprons). $ *Average main: $44* ⊠ *Ritz-Carlton, 4750 Amelia Island Pkwy.* ☎ *904/277–1000* ⊕ *www.ritzcarlton.com* 🍴 *Reservations essential* ⊙ *Closed Mon. No lunch.*

13

$$$ ✕**Sliders Seaside Grill.** After the condo-building boom of the last decade
SEAFOOD or so, not many oceanfront restaurants remain, but thankfully this is
FAMILY one of them. Indeed there aren't many places where you can enjoy an
ocean view like this—a surf break offshore makes it a good place to
watch surfers do their thing—and even fewer with a moderately priced
menu that allows for an affordable family outing. These are some of
the reasons Sliders has evolved into a local favorite, but another is its
award-winning Florida seafood dishes, including shrimp and grits, and
Apalachicola oysters in season. Sliders also has three bars and live music
every night, including the region's favorite reggae band, Pili Pili, on
Wednesday. $ *Average main: $19* ✉ *1998 S. Fletcher Ave.* ☎ *904/277–
6652* ⊕ *www.slidersseaside.com.*

$$$$ ✕**Verandah Restaurant.** Although it's at the Amelia Island Plantation,
SEAFOOD this family-friendly restaurant is open to nonresort guests, many of
whom drive in from Jacksonville. The dining room has a casual vibe,
with plush, roomy booths and tables overlooking the tennis facility, but
the menu is all business. Start with the crab cake—nearly 100% blue
crab—or deviled eggs topped with pecanwood smoked bacon. Fresh
seafood entrées are a highlight, including the Florida fish muddle (fresh
catch with Mayport shrimp and clams) and line-caught pink snapper
with Cohen Farm's pecans and local strawberries. And if you luck out
and find she-crab soup on the menu (it's seasonal and not always avail-
able), order yourself the biggest bowl or bucket they have. $ *Aver-
age main: $32* ✉ *Omni Amelia Island Plantation, 39 Beach Lagoon,
Amelia Island* ☎ *904/261–6161* ⊕ *www.omnihotels.com/FindAHotel/
AmeliaIsland/Dining.aspx* ⟨ *Reservations essential* ⊗ *No lunch.*

WHERE TO STAY

For expanded reviews, facilities, and current deals, visit Fodors.com.

$$ ⊞**Amelia Hotel at the Beach.** Across the street from the beach, this mid-
HOTEL size inn is not only convenient but an economical and family-friendly
FAMILY alternative to the area's luxury resorts and romantic and kid-unfriendly
B&Bs. **Pros:** complimentary breakfast; free Wi-Fi; comfy beds. **Cons:**
small pool; not all rooms have balconies; no on-site restaurant. $ *Rooms
from: $139* ✉ *1997 S. Fletcher Ave.* ☎ *904/206–5600, 877/263–5428*
⊕ *www.ameliahotel.com* ⟿ *86 rooms* ❘⊙❘ *Breakfast.*

$$$ ⊞**Elizabeth Pointe Lodge.** Guests at this oceanfront inn, built to resemble
B&B/INN an 1890s sea-captain's house, can't say enough about the impeccable
personal service, legendary breakfasts, and enjoyable evening social
hour. **Pros:** beachfront location; hospitable staff; 24-hour desk atten-
dant; convenient to recreation possibilities. **Cons:** pricey for a B&B;
not all rooms are oceanfront; must reserve well in advance in high
season. $ *Rooms from: $225* ✉ *98 S. Fletcher Ave.* ☎ *904/277–4851,
800/772–3359* ⊕ *www.elizabethpointelodge.com* ⟿ *24 rooms, 1 2-bed-
room cottage* ❘⊙❘ *Breakfast.*

$ ⊞**Florida House Inn.** Under new ownership, the recently restored inn has
B&B/INN a rambling two-story clapboard main building, more than 150 years old,
that is full of character. **Pros:** breakfast included; outstanding service;
walk to restaurants and shops; free Wi-Fi; bridal suite. **Cons:** bar can be
noisy. $ *Rooms from: $100* ✉ *22 S. 3rd St.* ☎ *904/491–3322, 800/258–
3301* ⊕ *www.floridahouseinn.com* ⟿ *17 rooms, 1 suite* ❘⊙❘ *Breakfast.*

$$$$
RESORT
FAMILY
Fodor'sChoice
★
Omni Amelia Island Plantation Resort and the Villas of Amelia Island Plantation. Rebranded, and "reimagined" by the Omni hotel chain, this resort has been transformed by an $85-million renovation and expansion, including 155 new oceanfront rooms and stunning oceanfront Beach Club pools. **Pros:** family-friendly; variety of outdoor activities; shuttle service throughout property; kids' programs; "green" practices; largest poolscape in Northern Florida. **Cons:** some facilities require a golf cart or shuttle ride; quality of villas inconsistent; 11 am checkout. $ *Rooms from: $299* ✉ *6800 1st Coast Hwy.* ☎ *904/261–6161, 800/843–6664* ⊕ *www.omnihotels.com* ⤳ *404 rooms, more than 300 1-, 2-, and 3-bedroom villas* ⊖ *No meals.*

$$$
HOTEL
Residence Inn Amelia Island. Discerning, value-driven travelers love this newer all-suites property for its great location, modern design features, and family-friendly amenities. **Pros:** proximity to beach and restaurants; complimentary breakfast; free Wi-Fi; bike rental on property; pet friendly (restrictions). **Cons:** no on-site restaurant or room service; historic district not within walking distance. $ *Rooms from: $145* ✉ *2301 Sadler Rd.* ☎ *904/277–2440* ⊕ *www.residenceinnameliaisland. com* ⤳ *133 rooms* ⊖ *Breakfast.*

$$$$
RESORT
FAMILY
Fodor'sChoice
★
The Ritz-Carlton, Amelia Island. Guests know what to expect from the Ritz—elegance, superb comfort, excellent service—and the Amelia Island location is no exception. **Pros:** fine-dining restaurant; world-class spa; private beach access; accommodating staff; great programs, activities, and amenities for kids, teens, and families. **Cons:** fee for Wi-Fi; no self-parking ($20 per day valet); a drive to sites and other restaurants. $ *Rooms from: $299* ✉ *4750 Amelia Island Pkwy.* ☎ *904/277–1100* ⊕ *www.ritzcarlton. com/ameliaisland* ⤳ *446 rooms, 50 suites* ⊖ *No meals.*

NIGHTLIFE

Falcon's Nest. The 7,000-square-foot, aviation-theme club in Amelia Island Plantation has a dance floor and outdoor deck. ✉ *Omni Amelia Island Plantation, 39 Beach Lagoon, Amelia Island* ☎ *904/261–6161* ⊕ *www.omnihotels.com/ameliaisland.*

O'Kane's Irish Pub. It's St. Patrick's Day every day here. ✉ *318 Centre St.* ☎ *904/261–1000* ⊕ *www.okanes.com.*

Palace Saloon. Florida's oldest continuously operating bar entertained the Rockefellers and Carnegies at the turn of the 20th century but now caters to common folk. It also operates a package store, the only one in downtown Fernandina. ✉ *117 Centre St.* ☎ *904/491–3332* ⊕ *www. thepalacesaloon.com.*

The Surf Restaurant & Bar. Locals like to congregate on the outdoor deck here for drinks and good old-fashioned bar food (burgers, wings, nachos). The restaurant has an extensive menu. ✉ *3199 S. Fletcher Ave.* ☎ *904/261–5711* ⊕ *www.thesurfonline.com.*

SHOPPING

Amelia SanJon Gallery. One of a cluster of "Ash and Third" galleries, the Amelia SanJon offers watercolors, acrylic paintings, fused-glass art, custom jewelry, and large-scale, welded sculptures. ✉ *218-A Ash St.* ☎ *904/491–8040* ⊕ *www.ameliasanjongallery.com.*

13

Book Loft. Popular for its readings and book signings, this old-fashioned bookstore fits perfectly in an old-fashioned town. In keeping with Fernandina's emphasis on its pirate heritage, the store includes kid-friendly pirate volumes like *The Pirate of Kindergarten* and *Do Pirates Change Diapers?* ✉ *214 Centre St.* ☎ *904/261–8991.*

Celtic Charm. In addition to the obvious coffee cup with shamrocks and Irish-blessing plaque, this shop carries wonderful clothing—such as colorful and artistic Bill Baber Scottish sweaters—as well as Galway Irish crystal and Donegal Town Hana hats. ✉ *310 Centre St.* ☎ *904/277–8009* ⊕ *www.celticcharmamelia.com.*

Fantastic Fudge. Right there in the window, resting in splendor on several marble-topped tables, are huge blocks of fudge just calling your name—enough fudge to put every citizen of the town into a coma—not to mention hand-dipped chocolates, caramel corn, and so on. Indeed, if you hang out at one of the tables in front of this confectionery/ice cream shop, you'll see just about every kind of person imaginable pause by the door, sigh, and give in to temptation. The service is fast and friendly, and the ice cream is excellent, too. ✉ *218 Centre St.* ☎ *904/277–4801* ⊕ *www.fantasticfudge.com.*

Gallery C. Up a wildly painted staircase, this gallery owned by artist Carol Winner displays and sells one-of-a-kind semiprecious jewelry and mixed-media creations, as well as stunning paintings of local nature scenes. ✉ *218-B Ash St.* ☎ *904/583–4676* ⊕ *www.carolwinnerart.com.*

Lindy's Jewelry. For tasteful jewelry that reflects beach life, Lindy's is a good place to shop. Those who collect charms will love the Fernandina Beach and Cumberland Island map charms to commemorate their vacation. ✉ *202 Centre St.* ☎ *904/277–4880* ⊕ *www.lindysjewelry.com.*

Sea Jade. Inside, it's funny T-shirts and cheap souvenirs; outside, it's fishnet floats and stunning shells in all their natural beauty, heaped up in old-fashioned wooden baskets. Whether you want to buy sand dollars or saltwater taffy, if it's beach-related, there's a good chance you'll find it here. ✉ *208 Centre St.* ☎ *904/277–2977.*

Slightly Off Centre Gallery & Gifts. Just a block off the main drag, this store sells artistic ceramics as well as vivid photographs, paintings, pottery, and metalwork. ✉ *218-C Ash St.* ☎ *904/277–1147.*

SPORTS AND THE OUTDOORS

HORSEBACK RIDING

Kelly Seahorse Ranch. At this ranch within the Amelia Island State Park, you can arrange horseback rides on the beach. ✉ *7500 1st Coast Hwy., Amelia Island* ☎ *904/491–5166* ⊕ *www.kellyranchinc.net* ⊙ *Closed Mon.*

KAYAKING

Kayak Amelia. This outfitter takes adventurous types on guided tours of salt marshes and Fort George River and also rents equipment for those looking to create their own adventures. Reservations are required. ✉ *13030 Heckscher Dr., Amelia Island* ☎ *904/251–0016* ⊕ *www.kayakamelia.com.*

ST. AUGUSTINE

35 miles south of Jacksonville, on U.S. 1.

Along the banks of the shining Matanzas River lies St. Augustine, the nation's oldest city. It shows its age with charm, its history revealed in the narrow cobblestone streets, the horse-drawn carriages festooned with flowers, and the coquina bastions of the Spanish fort that guard the bay like sentinels. Founded in 1565 by Spanish explorers, St. Augustine is the site of the fabled Fountain of Youth, but travelers find additional treasures in the Historic District, which was built in the Spanish Renaissance Revival style. Terra-cotta roofs and narrow balconies overhang a wonderful hodgepodge of shops and eateries that can be happily explored for weeks.

St. Augustine also has miles of beaches on Anastasia Island to the east. From the idyllic, unspoiled beaches of Anastasia State Park to the more boisterous St. Augustine Beach, travelers have a full range of options when it comes to enjoying an ocean outing.

VISITOR INFORMATION

Centrally located between the south and north ends of St. Augustine's Historic District, the St. Augustine & St. Johns County Visitor Information Center is a smart place to start your day. You can park in the multistoried garage here ($1.25 per hour, $7.50 per day), as well as pick up maps, get information on and advice about attractions and restaurants, and hop aboard the sightseeing trolley.

Contacts St. Augustine, Ponte Vedra, & the Beaches Visitors and Convention Bureau ⊠ *29 Old Mission Ave.* ☎ *904/829–1711, 800/653–2489* ⊕ *www.floridashistoriccoast.com* ⊙ *Daily 8:30–5:30.* **St. Augustine & St. Johns County Visitor Information Center** ⊠ *10 W. Castillo Dr.* ☎ *904/825–1000* ⊙ *Daily 8:30–5:30.*

TOURS

Old Town Trolley Tour. These fully narrated tours ($23 adults/$10 children) cover more than 100 points of interest and are, perhaps, the best way to take in the Historic District. Your pass is good for three days and, with parking at a premium and meters closely watched, it's nice to be able to park at one of the main stations (free) and get on and off at any of 22 stops throughout town. There are even shuttles to the beach. In the evening a macabre slant is added on the Ghosts and Graveyards Tour ($26 adults/$14 children), which includes visits to the Old Jail and Lighthouse. ⊠ *167 San Marco Blvd.* ☎ *904/829–3800* ⊕ *www.historictours.com/staugustine.*

St. Augustine Transfer Company. The nation's oldest continually operated carriage company (since 1877) knows quite a few things about the city's history. Guides fill you in on horse-drawn carriage tours ($80 per carriage for up to four adults) that are as calming as they are informative. For a different slant, consider the Ghostly Gatherings evening carriage excursion ($25 adults/$18 children). ☎ *904/829–2391* ⊕ *www.staugustinetransfer.com.*

Built to protect Spain's St. Augustine, the Castillo de San Marcos still stands along the shore.

EXPLORING

St. Augustine's neighborhoods are fairly compact. Most include a stretch of waterfront—whether ocean, river, or creek—which, along with Mediterranean architectural details like curves, archways, and red-tile roofs gives the city its relaxed semitropical aura. Neighborhoods range from centuries old to mere decades, but all have sights worthy of attention.

It can be confusing to see references to the "Old City," "Old Town," and "Historic District." The Old City, like the Big Apple, refers not to a neighborhood but to the entire city of St. Augustine. Old Town is a small neighborhood, with the Plaza de la Constitución at its northern border, a row of shops and restaurants along King Street, many award-winning B&Bs, and the Oldest House museum toward the south. Old Town is actually within a larger neighborhood, the Historic District, a 144-block area filled with many of the city's most popular attractions, including museums, parks, restaurants, nightspots, shops, and historic buildings.

St. Augustine's Uptown is filled with the shops, restaurants, and galleries along San Marco Boulevard, as well as museums, parks, and historic structures, all of which attract crowds. The narrow streets and hustle and bustle make for a vibrant atmosphere.

Heading east across the Bridge of Lions, you enter Anastasia Island, much of which is within city limits. In the 1920s, real estate developer D.P. Davis had big plans for a Mediterranean-style development here, but the Florida land boom went bust. Today Davis Shores has a mélange of styles and a casual beach vibe.

TOP ATTRACTIONS

FAMILY

Fodor's Choice

★

Castillo de San Marcos National Monument. The focal point of St. Augustine, this massive and commanding structure was completed by the Spaniards in 1695 (English pirates were handy with a torch back then), and it looks every day of its three centuries. The fort was constructed of coquina, a soft limestone made of broken shells and coral that, unexpectedly, could absorb the impact of British cannonballs. (Unlike solid stone, the softer coquina wouldn't shatter when hit by large munitions.) The fort was also used as a prison during the Revolutionary and Civil wars.

13

Park rangers provide an introductory narration, after which you're on your own to explore the moat, turrets, and 16-foot-thick walls. Garrison rooms depict the life of the era, and special cannon-firing demonstrations are held several times a day Friday through Sunday year-round. Children 15 and under are admitted free and must be accompanied by an adult. Save the receipt, since admission is valid for seven days. ⊠ *11 S. Castillo Dr.* ☎ *904/829–6506* ⊕ *www.nps.gov/casa* ⊠ *$7* ◷ *Daily 8:45–5:15, last ticket sold at 5.*

Cathedral Basilica of St. Augustine. This cathedral has the country's oldest written parish records, dating from 1594. The circa-1797 structure underwent changes after a fire in 1887 as well as restoration work in the mid 1960s. If you're around for the holidays, stop in for Christmas Eve's gorgeous midnight mass, conducted amid banks of flickering candles that reflect off gilded walls. Regular Sunday masses are held throughout the year at 7, 9, 11, and 5. ⊠ *38 Cathedral Pl.* ☎ *904/824–2806* ⊕ *www. thefirstparish.org* ⊠ *Donations welcome* ◷ *Daily 7–4:45.*

FAMILY

Colonial Quarter. After being closed to the general public for yearlong renovations, the Colonial Quarter, formerly known as the Spanish Quarter, is now an even more appealing attraction. The 2-acre living history museum gives visitors a vivid sense of life in 16th-, 17th-, and 18th-century St. Augustine. The De Mesa–Sanchez House dates from the 1740s and the other buildings—including a soldier's home, print shop, blacksmith's shop, and gunsmith—are replicas, mostly built on the original foundations. Costumed reenactors help make the history come alive. New additions to the complex include a 35-foot watchtower from which you have a panoramic view of the city. You can also dig for replica artifacts, create a leather medallion, take part in a musket drill, watch a 16th-century ship being built, and more. A family-style show, *The Colonial Crew Revue*, requires a separate admission. The complex also includes two restaurants: the Taberna del Caballo and the Bull and Crown British Publick House. ⊠ *33 St. George St.* ☎ *904/825–6830* ⊕ *colonialquarter.com/* ⊠ *Admission $12.99, Colonial Crew Revue $29.99* ◷ *Daily 9–8.*

Dow Museum of Historic Houses. An entire city block of historic homes is not a typical gift from a philanthropist, but that's what Kenneth Worcester Dow gave today's visitors to St. Augustine. Dow was not a St. Augustine native, but when he arrived in the 1930s, he bought the Prince Murat House (Murat was a nephew of Napoleon Bonaparte and also the crown prince of Naples, Italy), one of the city's oldest surviving colonial structures. Over the next two decades, Dow acquired the block's other nine historic homes and in 1989 donated them, along with his collections of art and antiques, but it took more than a decade to restore the buildings and open seven of them to the public. The houses were built between 1790 and 1910, demonstrating Florida history from the colonial era to the period when Henry Flagler established St. Augustine as a luxury resort location. The museum entrance is through the Star General Store, originally a dry-goods emporium built in 1899, which now houses the museum's gift shop. Both guided and self-guided tours are available. ⊠ *149 Cordova St.* ☎ *904/823–9722* ⊕ *www.moas.org/dowmuseum* 🎫 *$8.95* ⊙ *Mon.– Sat. 10–4:30, Sun. 11–4:30.*

NEED A BREAK?

St. George Tavern. Although they serve food (sandwiches, mostly), the appeal of this joint is that, in a city of historic recreations, this is the real deal: a noisy, packed, active bar where smokers smoke, drinkers drink, locals gather, and strangers blend right in. ⊠ *116-A St. George St.* ☎ *904/824–4204.*

Lightner Museum. In his quest to turn Florida into an American Riviera, Henry Flagler built two fancy hotels in 1888: the Ponce de León, which became Flagler College, and the Alcazar, which closed during the Great Depression, was purchased by publisher Otto Lightner in 1946, and was donated to the city in 1948. It's now a museum with three floors of furnishings, costumes, and Victorian art glass, and not-to-be-missed ornate antique music boxes (demonstrations daily at 11 and 2). The Lightner Antiques Mall is on three levels of what was once the hotel's indoor pool. City staff occupy other floors since, apparently, the guest rooms of a former grand hotel also make nice municipal-government offices. ⊠ *75 King St.* ☎ *904/824–2874* ⊕ *www.lightnermuseum.org* 🎫 *$10* ⊙ *Museum daily 9–5, last admission at 4.*

Old Jail Museum. At this 19th-century prison, felons were detained and released or detained and hanged from the gallows in back. After learning the history of local crime and punishment and seeing displays of weapons and other artifacts, you can browse the surfeit of souvenirs in Cracker Bob's Trading Post and the adjacent Old Store Museum. Note that the museum is at the starting point for the Old Town Trolley Tour. ⊠ *167 San Marco Ave.* ☎ *904/829–3800* 🎫 *$9* ⊙ *Daily 9–4:30.*

Ponce de León Hall, Flagler College. Originally one of two posh hotels Henry Flagler built in the 1880s, this building—which is now part of a small liberal-arts college—is a riveting Spanish Renaissance–revival structure with towers, turrets, and stained glass by Louis Comfort Tiffany. The former Hotel Ponce de León is a National Historic Landmark, having hosted U.S. presidents Grover Cleveland, Theodore Roosevelt, and Warren Harding. Visitors can view the building free or take a guided tour offered daily through Flagler's Legacy Tours. ⊠ *74 King St.* ☎ *904/829–6481, 904/823–3378 tour information* ⊕ *legacy.flagler. edu* 🎫 *Tours $10* ⊙ *Tours daily 10 and 2 when school's in session, on hr 10–3 when school's out.*

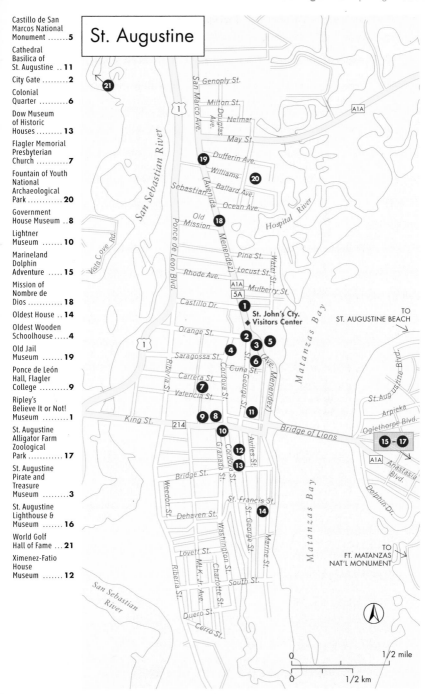

St. Augustine

FAMILY **St. Augustine Alligator Farm Zoological Park.** Founded in 1893, the Alligator Farm is one of Florida's oldest (and, at times, smelliest) zoological attractions and is credited with popularizing the alligator in the national consciousness and helping to fashion an image for the state. In addition to oddities like Maximo, a 15-foot, 1,250-pound saltwater crocodile, and a collection of rare albino alligators, the park is also home to Land of Crocodiles, the only place in the world to see all 23 species of living crocodilians. Traversing the treetops in Crocodile Crossing is an inventive, ambitious, and expensive ($65) zipline/rope course with more than 50 challenges and 10 ziplines. It's the only attraction of its kind through a zoological park. In many places, a thin cable is all that keeps you from becoming croc cuisine. Reptiles are the main attraction, but there's also a wading-bird rookery, an exotic-birds and mammals exhibit, and nature trails. Educational presentations are held throughout the day, and kids love the wild-animal shows. ⊠ *999 Anastasia Blvd.* ☎ *904/824–3337* ⊕ *www.alligatorfarm. com* ✉ *$22.95* ⊙ *Daily 9–5.*

St. Augustine Lighthouse & Museum. It's unusual to find a lighthouse tucked into a residential neighborhood. This 1874 version replaced an earlier one built when the city was founded in 1565. Although its beacon no longer guides ships, it does draw thousands of visitors each year. The visitor center has a museum with exhibits on the U.S. Coast Guard, historic boat building, maritime archaeology, and the life of a lighthouse keeper—whose work involved far more than light housekeeping. You have to climb 219 steps to reach the peak, but the wonderful view and fresh ocean breeze are well worth it. Children must be at least 44" tall to make the ascent. ⊠ *81 Lighthouse Ave.* ☎ *904/829–0745* ⊕ *www. staugustinelighthouse.org* ✉ *$9.75* ⊙ *Daily 9–6.*

FAMILY **St. Augustine Pirate and Treasure Museum.** Inside this small museum established by entrepreneur and motivational speaker Pat Croce is a collection of more than 800 pirate artifacts, including one of only two Jolly Rogers (skull-and-crossbone flags) known to have actually flown above a ship. Exhibits include a mock-up of a tavern, a captain's quarters, and a ship's deck. You'll learn about the lives of everyday and famous pirates, their navigation techniques, their weaponry, and the concoctions they drank (including something called Kill Devil, which is rum mixed with gunpowder). You'll get to touch an actual treasure chest; see piles of gold, jade, emeralds, and pearls; and leave knowing full well that there were pirates before Captain Jack Sparrow. ⊠ *12 S. Castillo Dr.* ☎ *877/467–5863, 904/819–1444* ⊕ *www.thepiratemuseum.com* ✉ *$12.99* ⊙ *Daily 9–8.*

WORTH NOTING

Anastasia State Park. This park draws families who like to hike, bike, swim, camp, and play on the beach to its 1,700 protected acres of bird sanctuary and 4 miles of secluded beachfront. ⊠ *1340-A Rte. A1A S* ☎ *904/461–2033* ⊕ *www.floridastateparks.org/anastasia* ✉ *$8 per vehicle; $2 pedestrians, bicyclists* ⊙ *Daily 8–sunset.*

City Gate. At the northernmost end of the colorful shops and sites of St. George Street, the gate is a relic from the days when the Castillo's

The "Oldest Wooden Schoolhouse" is made of cedar and cypress wood and dates to the early 18th century.

moat ran westward to the river, and the Cubo Defense Line (defensive wall) protected against approaches from the north. The old coquina gates set the tone for St. George Street, a historic lane filled with old-world balconies and quaint little shops. ⊠ *St. George and Orange Sts.*

Flagler Memorial Presbyterian Church. To look at a marvelous Venetian Renaissance–style structure, head to this church, built by Flagler in 1889 as a memorial to his daughter Jenny, who died during childbirth. In addition to Jenny, this is the final resting place for Flagler himself; his first wife, Mary; and their granddaughter Marjorie. The dome of this stunning sanctuary towers more than 100 feet and is topped by a 20-foot Greek cross. ⊠ *36 Sevilla St.* ☎ *904/829–6451* ⊕ *www.memorialpcusa. org* ☉ *Sanctuary Mon.–Sat. 9–3:35; Sun. services, hrs vary.*

Fountain of Youth National Archaeological Park. This once-dated attraction continues to undergo a major rejuvenation. There are still fun elements from the original "Old Florida" (admittedly somewhat kitschy), but there's much that's new and exciting, too. The timing is appropriate—in 2013, the park celebrated the 500th anniversary of Ponce de León's arrival. The 15-acre waterfront site is also the location where Spanish explorer Pedro Menéndez de Avilés, in 1565, established the first and oldest continuous European settlement in what's now the United States. Excavations have also shown it was the site of a Franciscan mission to the Timucuan Indians. The park includes a replica of the mission, a Timucuan village and burial grounds, a boatyard in which a 16th-century-style boat is being constructed, and a new observation platform over the marsh. Other highlights include cannon firings, Navigators Planetarium, a gift shop and snack bar, and the springhouse where you can still quench your thirst from "the fountain of youth." ⊠ *11 Magnolia Ave.* ☎ *904/829–3168, 800/356–8222* ⊕ *www.fountainofyouthflorida. com* 🎫 *$12* ⊗ *Daily 9–5.*

Ft. Matanzas National Monument. As you drive south on Anastasia Island, you head toward what was, in the 1700s, St. Augustine's farthest reaches. With Castillo de San Marcos guarding the town, in 1740 the Spanish created the relatively small Ft. Matanzas to defend their southern flank. A short ferry ride across the Matanzas River takes you to this national monument.

> **HOPE SPRINGS ETERNAL**
>
> Whether St. Augustine's world-renowned Fountain of Youth has curative powers is debatable—as is the legend of Ponce de León himself. Many scholars believe he came ashore closer to Melbourne, 150 miles south, in 1513. Still, those caught in the trap of folklore are still tempted to drink the foul-smelling water, which packs a dose of 42 minerals, including iron and—not surprising—sulfur.

Although it's only 15 miles from town, the fort feels eerily remote, and it takes little imagination to picture the demanding lives of the soldiers sent here to protect the young colony. Ferry shuttles are free and run on the half hour from 9:30 to 4:30, but you need to pick up a boarding pass from the visitor center. ⊠ *8635 Rte. A1A S* ☎ *904/471–0116* ⊕ *www.nps.gov/foma* 🎫 *Free* ⊗ *Daily 9–5:30.*

Government House Museum. This historical building has been a hospital, a courthouse, a customs house, a post office, and, during the American Revolution, the home of the British governors. And it was from here, in 1821, that the Spanish governor ceded control of East Florida to the United States to conclude 256 years of colonial control. After a major renovation, the building reopened in fall 2013 with a new exhibit, "First Colony: Our Spanish Origins." The exhibit presents the story of the founding of St. Augustine and focuses on the Hispanic aspect of American history. A new gift shop is also being added. ⊠ *48 King St.* ☎ *904/825–5034* ⊕ *www.staugustine.ufl.edu* 🎫 *Free* ⊗ *Thurs.–Mon. 10–4.*

Marineland Dolphin Adventure. The world's first oceanarium was constructed in 1938, 18 miles south of St. Augustine. This National Register of Historic Places designee, now part of the Georgia Aquarium, has come a long way from marine film studio to theme park to its current iteration as dolphin research, education, and entertainment center. The formal dolphin shows are history, but you can have a far more memorable experience with interactive programs that allow you to swim with and feed the animals, become a dolphin trainer for a day, or create dolphin art. Programs start at $29 a day (for the simple "touch-and-feed" option) and go as high as $450 (for "trainer for a day"). General admission allows you to observe the dolphins through 6-foot-by-10-foot acrylic windows. The 1.3-million-gallon facility is home to 13 dolphins, including Nellie, who was born here on February 27, 1953, making her the oldest dolphin in human care. Reservations are required. ⊠ *9600 Ocean Shore Blvd.* ☎ *904/471–1111, 877/933–3402* ⊕ *www. marineland.net* 🎫 *$9.95* ⊗ *Daily 9–4:30.*

Mission of Nombre de Dios. The site, north of the Historic District, commemorates where America's first mass was celebrated. A 208-foot-tall stainless-steel cross (purportedly the world's tallest) allegedly marks the spot where the mission's first cross was planted in 1565. Also on the property is the Shrine of Our Lady of La Leche, the first shrine devoted to Mary in the United States. The landscape is exquisitely maintained, and the mission is crisscrossed with paths. A museum and gift shop are also on the property. ⊠ *27 Ocean Ave.* ☎ *904/824–2809, 800/342–6529* ⊕ *www.missionandshrine.org* ✉ *Donations welcome* ☉ *Site weekdays 9–5, weekends 10–5; museum Thurs.–Sat. 10–4, Sun. noon–4.*

13

Oldest House. Known as the Gonzalez-Alvarez House, Florida's oldest surviving Spanish-colonial dwelling is a National Historic Landmark. The current site dates from the early 1700s, but there's been a structure here since the early 1600s. Much of the city's history is seen in the building's modifications and additions, from the coquina blocks—which came into use to replace wood soon after the town burned in 1702—to the house's enlargement during the British occupation. The complex also includes the Manucy Museum; the Page L. Edwards Gallery and its rotating exhibits; a gift shop; and an ornamental garden. ⊠ *14 St. Francis St.* ☎ *904/824–2872* ⊕ *www.oldesthouse.org* ✉ *$8* ☉ *Sun.–Fri.10–5, tours every ½ hr until 4:30.*

Oldest Wooden Schoolhouse. This tiny 18th-century building of cypress and cedar served not only as a schoolhouse but also as a tearoom, a farmhouse, and a guardhouse and sentry shelter during the Seminole Wars. In 1939, members of the Class of '64 (1864, that is) dressed out the school as they remembered it, and today automated mannequins instruct you on the education of 150 years ago. Apparently teachers had more leeway then because miscreants were given "time out" in a cubby beneath the stairs. And the heavy chain wrapped around the building? It was to hold the structure down during hurricanes. Kids will like the school bell and wishing well in the charming courtyard garden. ⊠ *14 St. George St.* ☎ *888/653–7245* ⊕ *www.oldestwoodenschoolhouse.com* ✉ *$4.50* ☉ *Sun.–Thurs. 9–5, Fri. and Sat. 9–8.*

Plaza de la Constitución. At the foot of the Bridge of Lions, this central area of the original settlement was laid out in 1598 by decree of Spain's King Philip II. At its core is a monument to the Spanish constitution of 1812, and at its east end is a portico dating from early American days. This is where products and, regrettably, people were sold, earning the area the twin names of "public market" and "slave market." Today, it's the gathering spot for holiday events, art shows, and evening concerts. Toward the bridge, look for the life-size statue of Ponce de León. The man who "discovered" Florida in 1513 was, apparently, all of 4' 11". ⊠ *St. George St. and Cathedral Pl.*

FAMILY **Ripley's Believe It or Not! Museum.** The nation's first Ripley's museum is, appropriately enough, in a historic structure—Castle Warden, an 1887 Moorish Revival–style mansion. Like its younger siblings, this odditorium is packed with plenty of unusual items including Robert Ripley's personal collections; a mummified cat; a death mask of Abraham Lincoln; a scale model of the original Ferris Wheel created from an Erector set; and life-size models of Robert Wadlow, the world's tallest man, and Robert Hughes, the world's fattest man. ✉ *19 San Marco Ave.* ☎ *904/824–1606* ⊕ *www.ripleys.com/staugustine* 🏷 *$14.99* ⊙ *Daily 9–8.*

World Golf Hall of Fame. This stunning tribute to the game of golf is the centerpiece of World Golf Village, an extraordinary complex that includes 36 holes of golf, a golf academy, several accommodations options, a convention center, spa, and a variety of restaurants, including Murray Bros. Caddyshack. The Hall of Fame features an adjacent IMAX theater and houses a variety of exhibits combining historical artifacts and personal memorabilia with the latest in interactive technology. Stand up to the pressures of the TV camera and crowd noise as you try to sink a final putt, take a swing on the museum's simulator, or snap a photo as you walk across a replica of St. Andrews's Swilcan Burn Bridge. Once you're sufficiently inspired, see how you fare on the 18-hole natural-grass putting course. Admission includes a chance to score a hole-in-one on a 132-yard hole. If you do, you win a prize, such as admission to THE PLAYERS Championship. ✉ *1 World Golf Pl.* ☎ *904/940–4123* ⊕ *www.worldgolfhallof fame.org* 🏷 *$19.50 (includes museum, round on 18-hole putting course, and shot at hole-in-one challenge). IMAX $13 features, $8.50 documentaries* ⊙ *Mon.–Sat. 10–6, Sun. noon–6.*

Ximenez-Fatio House Museum. Built as a merchant's house and store in 1798, the place became a boardinghouse in the 1800s and has been restored to look like it did during its inn days—romantic yet severe, with balconies that hearken back to Old Spain and sparely appointed rooms. Docents lead you around the property; be sure to look at the fascinating St. Augustine street scenes, painted in 1854 by an itinerant artist. Amazingly, much of what you see in the paintings is extant. ✉ *20 Aviles St.* ☎ *904/829–3575* ⊕ *www.ximenezfatiohouse.org* 🏷 *$7* ⊙ *Tues.–Sat. 11–4.*

BEACHES

Anastasia State Park Beach. If you don't mind paying a bit for beach access, this park offers some outstanding choices. At one end of the beach, there's a playground and snack bar, where you can order sandwiches and cold drinks or rent a beach chair, umbrella, surfboard, or other beach paraphernalia. If you walk north along the beach, however, all traces of civilization seem to vanish. An offshore break makes the park a good surfing spot, there's a boat launch, and canoes and kayaks can be rented. The campgrounds are very popular, too. **Amenities:** showers; toilets; food and drink; lifeguards (seasonal); parking (free); water sports. **Best for:** solitude; surfing; swimming; walking. ✉ *1340-A Rte. A1A S* 🏷 *$8 per vehicle; $2 motorcycles, pedestrians.*

Butler Park Beach. In the days of racial segregation, Butler Beach, located south of St. Augustine and north of Crescent Beach, was an African-American beach. Today it is a small town that still provides access to the beachfront. **Amenities:** lifeguards (seasonal); parking (free); showers; toilets. **Best for:** swimming; walking. ✉ *Rte. A1A, south of St. Augustine Beach.*

Crescent Beach. A 15 minute-drive beyond the area's big tourist destinations, this quieter, less crowded spot offers wide, white-sand beaches with good shelling, making it particularly popular with beachcombers. Adding to the laid-back atmosphere are some good restaurants, where visitors can enjoy the beach from a distance, glass in one hand and plate of fresh seafood in the other. **Amenities:** lifeguards (seasonal); parking (free); showers; toilets. **Best for:** solitude; swimming; walking. ⊠ *South of Rtes. A1A and 206.*

North Beach. Just five minutes from St. Augustine, this site (aka Usina Beach) includes boat ramps, two campsites, and a picnic area with grills. If you'd rather opt for a restaurant than a picnic, you're in the right spot—a variety of eateries overlook the ocean or the Intracoastal Waterway. **Amenities:** lifeguards (seasonal); parking (free); showers; toilets. **Best for:** solitude; walking. ⊠ *Rte. A1A, north of Vilano Beach.*

13

St. Augustine Beach. Just south of Anastasia State Park, this beach has a livelier setting, thanks to the restaurants, bars, and shops along Beachfront Avenue and the 4-acre St. Johns County Ocean Pier Park. The park includes a playground, small splash park, sand volleyball courts, and a covered pavilion, where from May to September a series of Music by the Sea concerts are offered free. Speaking of free, the beach doesn't charge a fee, but the popular fishing pier does ($3). In addition, there are some areas designated for driving on the beach. **Amenities:** lifeguards (seasonal); parking (free); showers; toilets. **Best for:** swimming. ⊠ *Old A1A/Beach Blvd., south of Rte. 312.*

WHERE TO EAT

$ ✕ **Bull & Crown British Publick House.** A replica of an 18th-century "publick
BRITISH   house," this recently opened pub features both British fare and local favorites. Since the restaurant was built on the homesite of Francisco Pellicer—a Minorcan carpenter who lived on St. George Street—it's only natural that you'd find a number of Minorcan-influenced dishes, from wings basted in datil-pepper sauce to a seafood pilau. Be sure to try the Gató d' Ametlla, an almond cake topped with butter-almond ice cream. The pub also offers beer and wine, a range of appetizers and hearty salads, a small number of entrées, and soups and sandwiches. Both indoor and courtyard seating are available. $ *Average main: $12* ⊠ *53 St. George St.* ☎ *904/342–2869* ⊕ *www.colonialquarter.com/dine/bull-and-crown-publick-house* ♨ *Reservations not accepted* ☉ *Sun.–Thurs. 11–11, Fri. and Sat. 11–midnight.*

$ ✕ **The Bunnery Bakery & Café.** Hidden among the art galleries and trinket
CAFÉ   shops of St. George Street is this cozy little restaurant, which is very popular at breakfast and nearly as popular during lunch. There's nothing fancy—just high-back booths and a menu of pancakes, bacon, eggs, cinnamon buns, salads, and sandwiches. It's the perfect spot when you want something familiar in a new place. $ *Average main: $7* ⊠ *121 St. George St.* ☎ *904/829–6166* ⊕ *www.bunnerybakeryandcafe.com* ♨ *Reservations not accepted* ☉ *No dinner.*

$$$ ECLECTIC 🍴 **Collage.** Foodies seeking a new dining experience in the Oldest City head here for "artful global cuisine" in a warm and intimate setting. Tucked away on Hypolita Street in the Historic District, the 48-seat restaurant highlights local seafood, which, depending on the success of the fishermen, will include several fish entrées each day. The ever-changing menu also often has steak, lamb, or veal selections. For dessert, the bougainvillea, an original dessert inspired by the colorful flowering plants that frame the building, is made of strawberries, ice cream, and cabernet-vanilla sauce served in a leaf-shape phyllo cup. [$] *Average main: $29* ✉ *60 Hypolita St.* ☎ *904/829–0055* 🌐 *www.collagestaug.com* 🕒 *No lunch.*

$$ MODERN AMERICAN FAMILY 🍴 **The Floridian.** Although vegetarians flock to this artsy and inspired eatery for the veggie-centric menu, there's plenty to tantalize omnivores as well. Delicious Southern food with flair ranges from fried green tomato bruschetta to 'N Grits, with many dishes offering a choice of meat, tofu, or tempeh. Some gluten-free dishes are also available. The produce featured at this farm-to-table establishment is at the peak of freshness and plays a starring role in the Winter Salad and Florida Sunshine Salad. Attire is casual, and the oceanic hues and funky decor put you at ease. Kids' needs are handled with flexible good nature. It's a deservedly popular spot, especially on the weekends, but reservations are accepted. [$] *Average main: $15* ✉ *39 Cordova St.* ☎ *904/829–0655* 🌐 *www.thefloridianstaug.com* 🕒 *No lunch Tues.*

$$$$ ECLECTIC Fodor's Choice ★ 🍴 **95 Cordova.** On the first floor of the Casa Monica Hotel, this restaurant serves classic cuisine with an international flair. Sup in one of three dining rooms, including the main room with intricate Moroccan-style chandeliers, wrought-iron chairs, and heavy wood columns, or the Sultan's Room, a gold-dipped space accented with potted palms and a silk-draped ceiling. Innovative dishes with New World, Middle Eastern, and Asian flavors change seasonally and highlight local seafood and produce. Among the dinner items are several types of steak, roast duckling, corn-crusted mahimahi, crab and shrimp ravioli, and ahi tuna with a Thai peanut sauce. The tasting menu offers six international courses paired with outstanding wines. [$] *Average main: $32* ✉ *95 Cordova St.* ☎ *904/810–6810* 🌐 *www.casamonica.com* ✍ *Reservations essential.*

$$ SEAFOOD 🍴 **O.C. White's Seafood & Spirits.** Dining outside is a treat at this bustling little spot across from the marina. Set in the circa-1791 General Worth house, it has a homelike feel with a balanced clientele of locals, students, and visitors. Favorites include coconut shrimp, blue-crab cakes, and Caribbean jerk chicken. Beef lovers may want to try the 20-ounce porterhouse or the 12-ounce New York strip. From upstairs, you have a great marina view; in the courtyard you might enjoy the perfume of blooming jasmine. Call ahead for "preferred seating." [$] *Average main: $19* ✉ *118 Av. Menendez* ☎ *904/824–0808* 🌐 *www.ocwhitesrestaurant.com* ✍ *Reservations not accepted.*

$ SEAFOOD 🍴 **O'Steen's.** Across the Bridge of Lions from downtown, this hole-in-the-wall restaurant is recognizable for the line of customers who wait patiently for fried shrimp (the specialty), oysters, scallops, hush puppies, fried chicken, coleslaw, biscuits and cornbread with gravy, and banana cream pie. Needless to say it's been a popular local eatery for generations. [$] *Average main: $14* ✉ *205 Anastasia Blvd.* ☎ *904/829–6974* 🌐 *www.osteensrestaurant.com* ✍ *Reservations not accepted* 💳 *No credit cards* 🕒 *Closed Sun. and Mon.*

$ TAPAS 🍴 **Taberna del Caballo.** Contemporary tapas, chilled sangria, and servers in 18th-century costumes make the Taberna del Caballo, opened in February 2012, an excellent addition to the St. Augustine dining scene. Built on the foundations of the de Hita House and the Gonzalez House, the restaurant is connected to the newly renovated Colonial Quarter on St. George Street (formerly known as the Spanish Quarter). In addition to sangria, wine, and beer, the Taberna serves appetizers, salads, sandwiches, a modest number of entrées, and desserts. All sandwiches are served on authentic Cuban bread from Segunda Central Bakery in Ybor City—the mojo pork panini and Cuban are both outstanding. There's additional seating in a lovely courtyard. [$] *Average main: $13* ✉ *37 St. George St.* ☎ *904/342–2867* 🌐 *www.colonialquarter.com/dine/taberna-del-caballo* ✍ *Reservations not accepted.*

13

WHERE TO STAY

For expanded reviews, facilities, and current deals, visit Fodors.com.

$$$ B&B/INN FAMILY 🏨 **Bayfront Marin House Bed and Breakfast.** Children are rarely permitted at B&Bs, but this is a charming exception, thanks to separate entrances, several units large enough to accommodate families, and the warm welcome of the inn's owners, Mike and Sandy Weber. **Pros:** personal service; child- and pet-friendly; waterfront location; porches and balconies with river views; moderate prices outside high season. **Cons:** parking a block away; dining area small if weather forces breakfast indoors. [$] *Rooms from: $169* ✉ *142 Av. Menendez* ☎ *904/824–4301* 🌐 *www.bayfrontmarinhouse.com* 🛏 *15 units* 🍽 *Breakfast.*

$$$ B&B/INN 🏨 **Bayfront Westcott House.** A bit more elegant and formal than the average B&B, this inn wows guests with a combination of English and American antiques and a wealth of complimentary food, from extravagant breakfasts to wine and canapés in the early evening. **Pros:** great views, most from private balconies; romantic rooms; Wi-Fi. **Cons:** parking a short distance away; carriage house rooms not as elegant as main house. [$] *Rooms from: $159* ✉ *146 Av. Menendez* ☎ *904/825–4602, 800/513–9814* 🌐 *www.westcotthouse.com* 🛏 *16 rooms* 🍽 *Breakfast.*

$$$ B&B/INN 🏨 **Carriage Way Bed and Breakfast.** When it comes to location, the Victorian-era Carriage Way has the best of both worlds; it's far enough from the Historic District to avoid tourist noise but close enough to have easy access to excellent restaurants (try the nearby Floridian) and shops. **Pros:** great location; free on-site parking; personal attention; excellent breakfasts. **Cons:** some small rooms; no TVs in rooms. [$] *Rooms from: $149* ✉ *70 Cuna St.* ☎ *904/829–2467, 800/908–9832* 🌐 *www.carriageway.com* 🛏 *9 rooms, 1 cottage* 🍽 *Breakfast.*

$$ B&B/INN **Casablanca Inn Bed & Breakfast on the Bay.** Breakfast comes with scenic views of the Matanzas Bay at this restored 1914 Mediterranean-revival stucco-and-stone house, just north of the Bridge of Lions in the Historic District. **Pros:** comfy beds; friendly staff; free early evening snacks and beverages. **Cons:** some rooms have no view; street noise in some rooms. [$] *Rooms from: $129* ✉ *24 Av. Menendez* ☎ *904/829–0928, 800/826–2626* 🌐 *www.casablancainn.com* 🛏 *21 rooms, 2 suites* 🍴 *Breakfast.*

$$ B&B/INN **Casa de Solana.** There's a reason you feel like you're stepping back in time when you enter this 1820s-era inn made of coquina and handmade bricks: It's on the oldest street in the oldest European-settled city in the country. **Pros:** excellent service; delicious breakfast; location. **Cons:** some small rooms; free parking is four blocks away; "forced" socialization. [$] *Rooms from: $139* ✉ *21 Aviles St.* ☎ *904/824–3555* 🌐 *www.casadesolana.com* 🛏 *10 rooms* 🍴 *Breakfast.*

$$$ HOTEL Fodor's Choice ★ **Casa Monica Hotel.** Hand-stenciled Moorish columns and arches, handcrafted chandeliers, and gilded iron tables decorate the lobby of this late-1800s Flagler-era masterpiece. **Pros:** location; affordable off-season rates; flat-screen TVs in all rooms. **Cons:** busy lobby; expensive ($24) parking; small rooms. [$] *Rooms from: $179* ✉ *95 Cordova St.* ☎ *904/827–1888, 800/648–1888* 🌐 *www.casamonica.com* 🛏 *127 rooms, 11 suites.*

$$$$ HOTEL FAMILY **Hilton St. Augustine Historic Bayfront.** In the heart of historic St. Augustine, this Spanish-colonial-inspired hotel overlooking Matanzas Bay has 19 separate buildings in a village setting. **Pros:** location; comfortable beds; great for families. **Cons:** expensive valet parking only ($21); late-night noise at street level. [$] *Rooms from: $319* ✉ *32 Av. Menendez* ☎ *904/829–2277, 800/445–8667* 🌐 *www.staugustinehistoricbayfront.hilton.com* 🛏 *72 rooms.*

$$$ B&B/INN **Inn on Charlotte Bed & Breakfast.** Innkeeper Rodney Holeman says guests comment that staying at his inn reminds them of visiting a friend or family member's home, assuming that person offers an elegant two-course breakfast and cozy rooms with whirlpool tubs. **Pros:** location; excellent service; free parking. **Cons:** tight parking in compact lot; weekend street noise. [$] *Rooms from: $174* ✉ *52 Charlotte St.* ☎ *904/829–3819, 800/355–5508* 🌐 *www.innoncharlotte.com* 🛏 *8 rooms.*

$ B&B/INN **Old City House Inn & Restaurant.** Touches of Paris, Venice, and India are just a few of the surprises within this small two-story inn's coquina walls, where the rooms are decorated to reflect international cities or themes. **Pros:** location; romantic; free Wi-Fi; on-site restaurant. **Cons:** thin walls; may have to share room with a ghost! [$] *Rooms from: $100* ✉ *115 Cordova St.* ☎ *904/826–0113* 🌐 *www.oldcityhouse.com* 🛏 *7 rooms, 2 suites* 🍴 *Breakfast.*

$$ RESORT Fodor's Choice ★ **Renaissance Resort at World Golf Village.** If you want to be within walking distance of all World Golf Village has to offer, this AAA Four Diamond resort is an excellent choice. **Pros:** breakfast buffet; large bathrooms; free shuttle to golf courses, spa, and downtown St. Augustine. **Cons:** small pool; no pets; daily fee for Internet/phone. [$] *Rooms from: $139* ✉ *500 S. Legacy Trail* ☎ *904/940–8000, 888/740–7020* 🌐 *www.worldgolfrenaissance.com* 🛏 *271 rooms, 30 suites* 🍴 *Multiple meal plans.*

$$$
B&B/INN
⌐ **St. Francis Inn Bed & Breakfast.** If the walls of this late-18th-century house in the Historic District—and the oldest inn in the Oldest City—could talk, they would tell of slave uprisings, buried doubloons, and Confederate spies. **Pros:** warm hospitality; family-friendly cottage; Southern breakfast buffet; short walk to Historic District attractions. **Cons:** small rooms; small pool. $ *Rooms from: $189* ⌧ *279 St. George St.* ☎ *904/824–6068, 800/824–6062* ⊕ *www.stfrancisinn.com* ⤺ *12 rooms, 4 suites, 1 2-bedroom cottage.*

13

NIGHTLIFE

A1A Aleworks. The Aleworks always seems to be filled with students and visitors taste-driving the microbrews and other selections from the full bar. Seats on the second-story balcony provide a great view of the marina and bay across the street. It's a little like being on Bourbon Street—but clean. ⌧ *1 King St.* ☎ *904/829–2977* ⊕ *www.A1Aaleworks.com.*

Mill Top Tavern. The rustic Mill Top is famous for its live, local music. ⌧ *19½ St. George St.* ☎ *904/829–2329* ⊕ *www.milltoptavern.com.*

The Original Cafe Eleven. This live music haven sets the stage for local groups, and tries to book national acts at least once a month. They also serve breakfast, lunch, and dinner seven days a week. ⌧ *501 Rte. A1A Beach Blvd.* ☎ *904/460–9311* ⊕ *www.originalcafe11.com.*

Scarlett O'Hara's. It's a popular and convenient spot to stop for lunch or dinner (preferably enjoyed on the front porch); later in the evening it turns up the volume with blues, jazz, disco, Top 40, or karaoke. Whatever's playing, it's always packed. ⌧ *70 Hypolita St.* ☎ *904/824–6535* ⊕ *www.scarlettoharas.net.*

Tini Martini Bar. The veranda overlooking Matanzas Bay at this Casablanca Inn bar is the perfect place to enjoy a cocktail, people-watch, and listen to live music. ⌧ *Casablanca Inn, 24 Av. Menendez* ☎ *904/829–0928* ⊕ *www.tini-martini-bar.com.*

Tradewinds. It's been showcasing bands—from country and western to rock and roll—since 1964. Thanks to the music, beer, and margaritas, you may feel as if you're in Key West. ⌧ *124 Charlotte St.* ☎ *904/826–1590* ⊕ *www.tradewindslounge.com.*

The World Famous Oasis Deck and Restaurant. If you're staying on Anastasia Island, this is your best nightlife bet. It has 24-ounce draft beers, beach access, and what many locals consider the best burgers in town. ⌧ *4000 Rte. A1A S, at Ocean Trace Rd.* ☎ *904/471–3424* ⊕ *www.worldfamousoasis.com.*

SHOPPING

One of the most pleasing pastimes in St. Augustine is a stroll along St. George Street, a pedestrian mall with shoulder-to-shoulder art galleries and one-of-a-kind shops selling candles, home accents, handmade jewelry, aromatherapy products, pottery, books, and clothing. There are also restaurants, clubs, and a veritable orchestra of street musicians.

Several blocks north of the Castillo and the popular St. George Street, a string of shops—galleries, antiques, a bookstore—line both sides of San Marco Avenue. Although this strip isn't as eclectic as it used to be, you'll still find some interesting independent stores.

MALLS

Prime Outlets. Several miles outside of the city, Prime Outlets has more than 60 name-brand stores including Gucci, Saks 5th Avenue's OFF 5TH, and Michael Kors. ⊠ *500 Belz Outlet Blvd.* ☎ *904/826–1311* ⊕ *www.staugoutlets.com.*

St. Augustine Premium Outlets. Just north of St. Augustine, off Interstate 95, is this collection of 85 designer and brand-name outlet stores. ⊠ *2700 State Rd. 16* ☎ *904/825–1555* ⊕ *www.premiumoutlets.com.*

SPECIALTY SHOPS

Whetstone Chocolate Factory. Chocolate fans won't want to miss a stop at Whetstone. Once upon a time the company operated a large factory in St. Augustine. They've scaled back to a small operation next door to their retail shop, but you can still take a quick-paced behind-the-scenes tour (reservations recommended). ⊠ *139 King St., Vilano Beach* ☎ *904/217–0275* ⊕ *www.whetstonechocolates.com* ⌂ *$8* ⊙ *Tours: weekdays at 11, 1, 2:15, 3:30, Sat. at 10, 11:15, 1, 2:15, 3:30, Sun. at 1, 2:15, 3:30.*

SPORTS AND THE OUTDOORS

BIKING

Solano Cycle. Here you can rent bicycles, scooters, and "scoot coups," which look like the offspring of a scooter and a bumper car and are $49 for the first hour (one-hour minimum) and $69 for two. ⊠ *32 San Marco Ave.* ☎ *904/825–6766* ⊕ *www.solanocycle.com.*

BOAT TOURS

EcoTours. Amidst America's most enduring human history, EcoTours investigates St. Augustine's natural history. Scenic cruises, kayak tours, and catamaran excursions on Matanzas Bay offer a chance to see bottlenose dolphins, bird habitats, lakes, creeks, and saltwater marshes. Along the way are incredible photo ops of the city and the Castillo from the water. ⊠ *111 Av. Menendez* ☎ *904/377–7245* ⊕ *www. staugustineecotours.com.*

FAMILY **The Pirate Ship Black Raven.** Whether you prefer Captain Hook or Captain Jack Sparrow, it's a pirate's life for everyone aboard the Black Raven, even if you're only sailing on the Mantanzas River. This "floating performance theater" hosts live pirate shows that include sea chanties, black powder cannon firings, sword-fighting lessons for kids (with harmless foam blades), and treasure hunts on weekends. This is just entertainment, not historical education, so expect the jokes to be cheap and cheesy. However, the atmosphere's lively and the river's lovely. Kids can trade their "letters of marque" to get a share of the booty—if, that is, the crew and the kids can manage to get their treasure back from Blackbeard. There are also adults-only evening cruises—the ship includes a fully licensed bar, so grown-ups can live out the fantasy of "yo-ho-ho and a bottle of rum." Cruises can be cancelled for inclement weather, so call to check before making final travel plans. ✉ *St. Augustine Municipal Marina, 111 Av. Menendez* ☎ *904/826–0000, 877/578–5050* ⊕ *www.blackravenadventures.com* ⊟ *$29.95.*

Schooner *Freedom.* Cutting a sharp profile, this 72-foot replica of a 19th-century blockade-runner sails from the marina for excursions across Matanzas Bay. You can relax and savor the breeze, or you can help the crew prepare to set sail. There are two-hour day ($35 per person) and sunset ($45) sails as well as a 75-minute twilight/after dark sail ($35). Precise times vary by season. Reservations are advised. ✉ *111 Av. Menendez* ☎ *904/810–1010* ⊕ *www.schoonerfreedom.com.*

FISHING

Sea Love Charters. Tackle and bait are included on this outfit's half- or full-day deep-sea fishing trips. ✉ *Cat's Paw Marina, 220 Nix Boat Yard Rd.* ☎ *904/824–3328* ⊕ *www.sealovefishing.com.*

GOLF

Pine Course at the Grand Club. Greens fees at this Arnold Palmer–designed course 30 minutes south of downtown range from $35 to $45 depending on season; $26 for nine holes. ✉ *400 Pine Lakes Pkwy., Palm Coast* ☎ *386/445–0852* ⊕ *www.thegrandclub.com.*

World Golf Village. The World Golf Hall of Fame complex has two 18-hole layouts named for and partially designed by golf legends Sam Snead, Gene Sarazen, Arnold Palmer, and Jack Nicklaus. Greens fees at the Slammer & Squire are $109 to $129; $129 to $169 at the King & Bear. ✉ *1 World Golf Pl.* ☎ *904/940–4000, 904/940–6100 Slammer & Squire, 904/940–6200 King & Bear* ⊕ *www.worldgolfhalloffame.com.*

WATER SPORTS

Smile High Parasail. Beneath huge canopies you can sit three abreast and soak in a commanding view of the city and the sea. Call in advance for weather conditions, and know that the higher the altitude, the higher the cost. ✉ *111 Av. Menendez* ☎ *904/819–0980, 888/300–0812* ⊕ *www.smilehighparasail.com.*

Surf Station. Here you can rent surfboards, skimboards, and body-boards. ✉ *1020 Anastasia Blvd.* ☎ *904/471–9463, 800/460–6394* ⊕ *www.surf-station.com.*

DAYTONA BEACH AND INLAND TOWNS

The section of the coast around Daytona Beach offers considerable variety, from the unassuming bedroom community of Ormond Beach to the spring-break and auto-racing capital of Daytona Beach. (Go 75 miles to the south, and you've got speeding rockets instead of speeding cars.)

Peaceful little inland towns are separated by miles of two-lane roads, running through dense forest and flat pastureland and skirting one lake after another. There's not much to see but cattle and the state's few hills. Gentle and rolling, they're hardly worth noting to people from true hill country, but they're significant enough in Florida for much of this area to be called the "hill and lake region."

DAYTONA BEACH

65 miles south of St. Augustine.

Best known for the Daytona 500, Daytona has been the center of automobile racing since cars were first raced along the beach here in 1902. February is the biggest month for race enthusiasts, and there are weekly events at the International Speedway. During race weeks, bike weeks, spring-break periods, and summer holidays, expect extremely heavy traffic. On the mainland, near the inland waterway, several blocks of Beach Street have been "streetscaped," and shops and restaurants open onto an inviting, broad brick sidewalk.

GETTING HERE AND AROUND

Several airlines have regular service to Daytona Beach International Airport, which is next to Daytona International Speedway on International Speedway Boulevard, an east–west artery that stretches from I–95 to the beaches. The average drive time from the airport to beachside hotels is 20 minutes; Yellow Cab–Daytona Beach makes the trip for $12–$40.

DOTS Transit Service has scheduled service ($35 one-way, $65 round-trip) connecting Daytona Beach, DeLand, Deltona, and the Orlando International Airport, which serves more airlines and has more direct flights but is about a 70-mile commute via Interstate 4 and SR 417. (Allow at least 90 minutes.) Note that DOTS doesn't serve the Daytona airport. Indeed, outside of a few hotel shuttles, there's no shuttle service between the Daytona airport and town.

Daytona Beach has an excellent bus network, Votran, which serves the beach area, airport, shopping malls, and major arteries, including service to DeLand and New Smyrna Beach and the Express Link to Orlando. Exact fare is required for Votran ($1.25) if using cash.

Contacts Daytona Beach International Airport (*DAB*) ⊠ *700 Catalina Dr.* ☎ *386/248–8069* ⊕ *www.flydaytonafirst.com.* **DOTS Transit Service** ⊠ *1034 N. Nova Rd.* ☎ *386/257–5411, 800/231–1965* ⊕ *www.dots-daytonabeach.com.* **Votran** ⊠ *950 Big Tree Rd., South Daytona Beach* ☎ *386/756–7496* ⊕ *www.votran.org.* **Yellow Cab–Daytona Beach** ⊠ *114 Reva St.* ☎ *386/255–5555, 888/333–3356* ✍ *www.daytonataxi.com.*

VISITOR INFORMATION

Contact Daytona Beach Area Convention and Visitors Bureau ⊠ *126 E. Orange Ave.* ☎ *800/544–0415* ⊕ *www.daytonabeach.com.*

EXPLORING

Casements. Built in 1912 for Reverend Harwood Huntington and named for its hand-crafted casement windows, it was purchased by John D. Rockefeller Sr. in 1918 as a winter retreat. Once considered the richest man in the world, Rockefeller entertained famous friends such as Henry Ford, Will Rogers, and Henry Flagler at the home while remaining an active member of the Ormond Beach community. After Rockefeller's death in 1937, the property was bought and sold numerous times and is now a cultural center and museum. The waterfront estate and its formal gardens host daily tours and an annual lineup of events and exhibits;

there's also a permanent exhibit of Hungarian folk art and Boy Scout memorabilia. ✉ *25 Riverside Dr., Ormond Beach* ☎ *386/676–3216* ⊕ *www.ormondbeach.org* 💵 *Donations accepted* ⊙ *Call for hrs and tour times.*

Halifax Historical Museum. Memorabilia from the early days of beach automobile racing are on display here, as are historic photographs, Native American and Civil War artifacts, a postcard exhibit, and a video that details city history. There's a shop for gifts and antiques, too. Admission is by donation on Thursday and on Saturday, kids 12-and-under are free. ✉ *252 S. Beach St.* ☎ *386/255–6976* ⊕ *www.halifaxhistorical.org* 💵 *$5* ⊙ *Tues.–Fri. 10:30–4:30, Sat. 10–4.*

HURRY UP AND WAIT

To snowbirds, a trip to Daytona Beach in mid-February might sound like a great idea. Just don't plan it for the weekend of the Daytona 500. Assuming you can even find a hotel room, it'll probably cost you double the usual rate. If you plan on leaving your hotel room, you'll most likely get stuck in bumper-to-bumper traffic. And when you get to your destination, it might not be open.

13

FAMILY **Museum of Arts & Sciences.** This behemoth museum has displays of Chinese art and an eye-popping complete skeleton of a giant ground sloth that's 130,000 years old. The museum also boasts a new Visible Storage Building, one of the most significant collections of Cuban art outside of Cuba, a large Coca-Cola and Americana collection, a rare Napoleonic exhibit, and one of the more expansive collections of American art in the Southeast. Kids love the Charles and Linda Williams Children's Museum, which features interactive science, engineering, and physics exhibits; a nature preserve with half a mile of boardwalks and nature trails; and a planetarium with daily laser-light shows. ✉ *352 S. Nova Rd.* ☎ *386/255–0285* ⊕ *www.moas.org* 💵 *$12.95* ⊙ *Tues.–Sat. 9–5, Sun. 11–5.*

OFF THE
BEATEN
PATH

Ponce de León Inlet Light Station. At the southern tip of the barrier island that includes Daytona Beach is the sleepy town of Ponce Inlet, with a small marina, a few bars, and casual seafood restaurants. Boardwalks traverse delicate dunes and provide easy access to the beach, although storms have caused serious erosion. Marking this prime spot is the bright-red, century-old Ponce de León Inlet Light Station, a National Historic Monument and museum, the tallest lighthouse in the state and the third-tallest in the country. Climb to the top of the 175-foot-tall lighthouse tower for a bird's-eye view of Ponce Inlet. ✉ *4931 S. Peninsula Dr., Ponce Inlet* ☎ *386/761–1821* ⊕ *www.ponceinlet.org* 💵 *$5* ⊙ *Sept.–May, daily 10–6; May–Sept., daily 10–9; last admission 1 hr before closing.*

BEACH

Daytona Beach. At the World's Most Famous Beach you can drive right onto the sand (at least from one hour after sunrise to one hour before sunset), spread out a blanket, and have all your belongings at hand (with the exception of alcohol, which is prohibited). All that said, heavy traffic during summer and holidays makes it dangerous for

If the action on Daytona Beach is too much for you, soar above it by parasailing.

children, and families should be extra careful or stay in the designated car-free zones. The speed limit is 10 mph, and there's a $5 fee, collected at the beach ramps, for driving on the sands every month but December and January.

The wide, 23-mile-long beach can get crowded in the "strip" area (between International Speedway Boulevard and Seabreeze Boulevard) with its food vendors, beachfront bars, volleyball matches, and motorized water sports enthusiasts. Those seeking a quieter experience can head north or south in either direction toward car-free zones in more residential areas. The hard-packed sand that makes the beach suitable for driving is also perfect for running and cycling. There's also excellent surf fishing directly from the beach. **Amenities:** food and drink; lifeguards; parking (some with fee); showers; toilets; water sports. **Best for:** sunrise; surfing; swimming; walking. ▐ TIP➔ Signs on Route A1A indicate car access via beach ramps. Sand traps aren't limited to the golf course, though—cars can get stuck. ⊠ *Rte. A1A* ⊕ *www.daytonabeach.com.*

WHERE TO EAT

$$
SEAFOOD

✕ **Aunt Catfish's on the River.** Don't be surprised if your server introduces herself as your cousin, though you've never seen her before in your life. You see, everybody is "cousin" at Aunt Catfish's (as in, "Can I get you another mason jar of sweet tea, Cousin?"). The silly Southern hospitality is only one of the draws at this wildly popular seafood restaurant just south of Daytona. The main lure, of course, is the food: mouthwatering plates of fresh seafood and other Southern favorites. Hot cinnamon rolls, hush puppies, baked beans, cheese grits, and slaw come with every entrée and can be a meal in themselves. Bring your appetite and your patience—a wait is practically guaranteed. Sunday brunch lures empty stomachs with made-to-order eggs and French toast, and a chocolate fountain. $ *Average main: $18* ☒ *4009 Halifax Dr., Port Orange* ☎ *386/767–4768* ⊕ *www.auntcatfishontheriver.com* ⚑ *Reservations not accepted.*

$ ✕ **Daytona Brickyard.** It's not just the locals who swear that the Brickyard's charbroiled sirloin burgers are the best they've ever tasted—devotees have been known to drive from Georgia just for lunch. Given its name and location in the heart of NASCAR country, the popular bar and grill is covered in racing memorabilia. Dang, even the floor and the tablecloths are black-and-white checkered. But don't mistake the racing theme to mean the place merely serves greasy bar food to Joe Sixpacks. It also feeds T-bone and New York strip steaks to doctors. $ *Average main: $12* ☒ *747 International Speedway Blvd.* ☎ *386/253–2270* ⊕ *www.brickyardlounge.com* ⚑ *Reservations not accepted.*

AMERICAN

$$$ ✕ **Hyde Park Prime Steakhouse.** This chophouse provides an upscale alternative to Daytona's more prevalent shorts-and-flip-flop joints. The lively dining room—done in dark wood with soft lighting and splashes of colorful artwork—is complemented by dramatic ocean views. Attentive servers carry chalkboards detailing specials such as lobster mac and cheese. But steaks, especially the cuts named after race-car drivers, and mouthwatering sides (don't miss the potatoes Gruyère gratin) are the main attractions. The 22-ounce bone rib eye named after beefy Tony Stewart is, appropriately, the thickest, showing that these guys know their NASCAR. The popular Steak Earnhardt is a filet mignon over bordelaise crowned with lobster, béarnaise (yes, it has two sauces), asparagus, and mushroom caps. An expansive wine list includes more than 40 options by the glass. And don't let this restaurant chain's Ohio roots fool you—the key lime pie is absolutely Florida-worthy. $ *Average main: $40* ☒ *Hilton Resort, 100 N. Atlantic Ave.* ☎ *386/226–9844* ⊕ *www.hydeparkrestaurants.com* ⊗ *No lunch.*

STEAKHOUSE

$$$ ✕ **Martini's Chophouse.** Local beautiful people seem to flock to this trendy South Daytona eatery and lounge as much for the scene as for the food. The bar area, done in gray with splashes of lime green, is a modern meeting place for the after-work crowd, and the outdoor deck and bar attract a livelier bunch. Those who do deign to dine appreciate the chef's use of homegrown herbs and creative sauces in dishes such as Bahamian lobster sautee and natural grass-fed filet mignon with Amish blue cheese, tempura onion rings, and mashed potatoes, which can be enjoyed in the sleek dining room or in the garden, complete with a 20-foot lighted waterfall and fire pit. $ *Average main: $23* ☒ *1815 S. Ridgewood Ave., South Daytona Beach* ☎ *386/763–1090* ⊕ *www.martinischophouse.com* ⊗ *Closed Sun. and Mon. No lunch.*

CONTEMPORARY
Fodor'sChoice
★

WHERE TO STAY

For expanded reviews, facilities, and current deals, visit Fodors.com.

$$$ RESORT **Hilton Daytona Beach Oceanfront Resort.** Perched on the only traffic-free strip of beach in Daytona, this high-rise is as popular with families as it is with couples. **Pros:** spacious rooms; beach access. **Cons:** inconvenient self-parking; extra charges. [$] *Rooms from: $129* ✉ *100 N. Atlantic Ave.* ☎ *386/254–8200, 866/536–8477* 🌐 *www.daytonahilton.com* 🛏 *744 rooms, 52 suites* 🍴 *No meals.*

$$$ RESORT FAMILY **Perry's Ocean Edge Resort.** Perhaps more than any other property in Daytona, Perry's has a die-hard fan base, many of whom started coming to the oceanfront resort as children, then returned with their children and their children's children. **Pros:** spacious rooms; helpful staff; nice pools; family-friendly. **Cons:** small bathrooms; slow elevators; limited TV channels. [$] *Rooms from: $129* ✉ *2209 S. Atlantic Ave.* ☎ *386/255–0581, 800/447–0002* 🌐 *www.perrysoceanedge.com* 🛏 *170 rooms, 30 suites* 🍴 *Breakfast.*

$$$ RESORT Fodor's Choice ★ **The Shores Resort & Spa.** Rustic furniture and beds swathed in mosquito netting are a nod to Old Florida at this 11-story beachfront resort, but there's nothing rustic about the amenities, including a luxury four-poster bed and a 42-inch plasma TV in every room. **Pros:** beachfront; spa; friendly staff; 24-hour room service. **Cons:** expensive restaurant; crowded pool; not all rooms have balconies. [$] *Rooms from: $139* ✉ *2637 S. Atlantic Ave., Daytona Beach Shores* ☎ *386/767–7350, 866/934–7467* 🌐 *www.shoresresort.com* 🛏 *212 rooms, 2 suites.*

$$$ RESORT FAMILY Fodor's Choice ★ **Wyndham Ocean Walk Resort.** Kids definitely won't be bored at this all-suites high-rise beachfront resort with four swimming pools, a waterslide, lazy river, game room, indoor miniature-golf course, activities center, and the only traffic-free beach in Daytona Beach. **Pros:** family-friendly; beachfront; great facilities; in-room washers and dryers; spacious accommodations. **Cons:** no room service; very slow elevators. [$] *Rooms from: $149* ✉ *300 N. Atlantic Ave.* ☎ *386/323–4800, 888/743–2323* 🌐 *www.oceanwalk.com* 🛏 *200 1-, 2-, and 3-bedroom suites* 🍴 *No meals.*

NIGHTLIFE

BARS

Boot Hill Saloon. Despite its reputation as a biker bar, this place welcomes nonbikers and even nonbiker tourists! ✉ *310 Main St.* ☎ *386/258–9506* 🌐 *www.boothillsaloon.com.*

Ocean Walk Village. Lively and always hopping, Ocean Walk is a cluster of shops, restaurants, and bars (the Mai Tai Bar is a good bet) stretching along Atlantic Avenue and the ocean. ✉ *250 N. Atlantic Ave.* ☎ *386/258–9544* 🌐 *www.oceanwalkshoppes.com.*

The Oyster Pub. Sports fans and oyster lovers congregate by the thousands here. ✉ *555 Seabreeze Blvd.* ☎ *386/255–6348* 🌐 *www.oysterpub.com.*

DANCE CLUBS

Razzle's Nightclub. DJs play high-energy dance music 8 pm–3 am. ✉ *611 Seabreeze Blvd.* ☎ *386/257–6236* 🌐 *www.razzlesnightclub.com.*

The Florida Trail goes through Ocala National Forest, taking hikers past hardwoods, pines, and prairies.

SHOPPING

Daytona Flea and Farmers' Market. One of the largest flea markets in the South draws residents from all over the state as well as visitors to the state. ✉ *2987 Bellevue Ave.* ☎ *386/253–3330* ⊕ *www. daytonafleamarket.com.*

Destination Daytona. This 100-acre biker enclave is complete with an expansive Harley-Davidson dealership; retail shops; a restaurant; bars; a tattoo parlor; a hotel; and a pavilion used for concerts, conventions—even biker-inspired weddings. ✉ *1635 N. U.S. 1, Ormond Beach* ⊕ *www.destinationdaytona.com.*

The Pavilion at Port Orange. Just off Interstate 95 (Port Orange exit), this outdoor shopping complex houses a 14-screen Hollywood Theaters; numerous restaurants; and retailers like the Southern department store, Belk, and ULTA beauty and cosmetics. ✉ *5501 S. Williamson Blvd., Port Orange* ⊕ *www.thepavilionatportorange.com.*

SPORTS AND THE OUTDOORS

BIRD-WATCHING

Tomoka State Park. With more than 160 species to see, this scenic park is perfect for bird-watching. It also has wooded campsites, bicycle and walking paths, and kayak and canoe rentals on the Tomoka and Halifax rivers. It's on the site of a Timucuan Indian settlement discovered in 1605 by Spanish explorer Alvaro Mexia. ✉ *2099 N. Beach St., 3 miles north of Ormond Beach* ☎ *386/676–4050* ⊕ *www. floridastateparks.org/tomoka* ✉ *$5 per vehicle, up to 8 people; $2 pedestrians* ⊙ *Daily 8–sunset.*

Continued on page 688

by John Blodgett
and Steve Masler

THE RACE IS ON IN DAYTONA

It's morning on race day. Check the weather—rain or shine? The race won't run if it's raining, but bring a poncho just in case, and pack some sunscreen, too (maybe even throw in a beach umbrella). Oh, and don't forget your binoculars and ear plugs. Fill your cooler with snacks and drinks—yes, it's allowed. Got your waterproof padded seat? Good. If you have a radio scanner, bring it to listen in on the pit crews; if you don't, you can rent one at the track for $50 ($30 for Sprint customers). This handheld device, in addition to its scanning capabilities, provides live video feeds, driver statistics, and auto replay.

You're here! Welcome to Daytona International Speedway—the storied race track that is home to one of America's most famous races, the Daytona 500. Hope you like crowds, because you'll be jostling with upward of 200,000 fellow race fanatics. The gate generally opens at 8 AM, with the race starting at 1 PM. The hours in between are one of the best times to seek autographs from your favorite racers in their garages near the Sprint FANZONE (drivers also can be approached throughout race weekend as they hang out at their respective souvenir haulers).

Watching the race is a sensory experience: 43 cars powered by 800 or more horsepower make

DAYTONA ROARS
ALL YEAR LONG

As the headquarter city for the National Association for Stock Car Auto Racing, better known as NASCAR, Daytona celebrates auto racing year-round. So while the Daytona 500 happens just one day out of 365, there's plenty for you to see and do every day at the speedway's 480-acre complex. You can go to other races, go on a tour, or, as part of the Richard Petty Driving Experience, maybe even jump into a stock car yourself. Major races are held during nine weekends, and an assortment of other races take place throughout the year. On non-race days the Speedway is host to R&D of racing vehicles, car shows, and other events. For motorcycles, there's the Daytona 200 and the Daytona Supercross by Honda.

for a constant roar; there's the smell of hot rubber, fuel, and exhaust; and, if you happen to be down low by the track itself, you might be pelted by flecks of tire as the pack blasts by at speeds approaching 190 mph. Every so often, let your binoculars wander—you might just see a past champion or other celebrity.

A few hours later the adrenaline-packed race is finished and your ears will be ringing (unless you remembered plugs). Now it's time to cheer the victor and wait in line to go find your car. This is when you grab another beverage from your cooler and relive the race with the fans next to you.

THE LAPS ALONG THE WAY

For more than 50 years, the world's top NASCAR drivers have competed in the Daytona 500, considered by many to be the sport's premier race.

The first official Daytona 500 was held on February 22, 1959, with 59 cars in front of 41,000 fans. It has been held each year in late February ever since. In the half century that followed, cash awards have grown from $68,000 to $18 million, with fewer drivers—43—but triple the fans—200,000. Every year the 500-mi (200-lap) race marks the beginning of NASCAR's premier Sprint Cup series and generally offers the greatest monetary reward. Winning the Daytona 500 has been equated with a Super Bowl victory, and much as in that sport, the final moments can be the most memorable and most important.

GETTING TICKETS

For tickets to the Daytona 500 or any other races held at the speedway, contact the Daytona Speedway ticket office (✉ 1801 W. International Speedway Blvd., Daytona Beach ☎ 800/PIT-SHOP [748–7467] ⊕ www.daytonainternationalspeedway.com). Single ticket prices to the Daytona 500 range from $65 to $185, primo seats go quickly, so the sooner you order the better. Grandstand seats typically sell out days or weeks in advance.

NASCAR'S FINEST

David Pearson
"The Silver Fox"
105 NASCAR wins
retired in 1986.

Dale Earnhardt
"The Intimidator"
"Ironhead"
Killed during the
2001 Daytona 500.

Richard Petty
"King Richard,"
Most NASCAR wins
(200) and Daytona
victories (7).

Jimmie Johnson
Won his fifth
consecutive Sprint
Cup championship
in 2010.

13

IN FOCUS THE RACE IS ON

Getting out and inspecting the track first hand is just one part of a Daytona Speedway tour.

You don't have to wait until race days to explore the World Center of Racing. Some of the best exploring can be done when the engines are silent. Narrated tours give you a look at the hallowed grounds where Fireball Roberts, Bobby Allison, Richard Petty, and Dale Earnhardt turned a regional sport into an international phenomenon.

The 70-minute All Access Tour ($22; hourly 10–3) brings you into the ritzy Daytona 500 Club and the Houston Lawing Press Box in the Sprint Tower, which features views not only of the 2.5-mile tri-oval, but also of the Atlantic Ocean nearby. You'll also visit the drivers' meeting room, the NASCAR Sprint Cup garages, Gatorade Victory Lane, and Sprint FANZONE. There are three dramatic photo opportunities on the tour: Victory Lane, the start/finish line, and the daunting 31-degree banking in Turns 3 and 4.

Other options include the 30-minute Speedway Tour ($15; 11:30, 1:30, and 4) and the three-hour VIP Tour ($50; by reservation on select days). ✉ 1801 W. International Speedway Blvd. ☎ 800/748–7467 ⊕ www.daytonainternationalspeedway.com.

If you're not satisfied with merely viewing the historic speedway, driving opportunities are also available through the Richard Petty Driving Experience. You can ride shotgun—or, for more dough, drive yourself—in a stock car on Daytona International Speedway. You suit up, helmet and all, and slide into the car through the window, just like you're Jimmie Johnson. Be sure to get a photo afterward so your friends believe you when you tell them how you zoomed around at speeds in excess of 150 mph! Ride-alongs cost $135; call for driving prices and to reserve a ride. ☎ 800-BE PETTY (800/237–3389).

LADIES WELCOME

Stock-car racing has long been a male-dominated sport, but icons such as Dale Earnhardt Jr. and Jeff Gordon have been, on occasion, overshadowed by women. Danica Patrick, the pint-sized, telegenic driver of Indy Car fame made her NASCAR debut at Daytona in a 2010 Nationwide Series race. Patrick, who made her Sprint Cup debut in 2012, is among a growing number of women entering motorsports but one of only a few to break into NASCAR.

BOATING

Cracker Creek. At this eco-adventure park you can rent kayaks, canoes, hydrobikes, and pontoon boats or take ecotours or a Pirate Cruise on scenic Spruce Creek. There are also on-site picnic facilities. ⊠ *1795 Taylor Rd., Port Orange* ☎ *386/304–0778* ⊕ *www.oldfloridapioneer. com* ⊘ *Wed.–Sun. 8–5; canoeing and kayaking by reservation only.*

FISHING

Sea Spirit Fishing. Four- to 12-hour private and group charters are options with this operator. ⊠ *Inlet Harbor Marina, 133 Inlet Harbor Rd., Ponce Inlet* ☎ *386/763–4388* ⊕ *www.seaspiritfishing.com.*

GOLF

Indigo Lakes Golf Club. Greens fees to play the 18 holes here are $30–$49. ⊠ *312 Indigo Dr.* ☎ *386/254–3607* ⊕ *www.indigolakesgolf.com.*

LPGA International. LPGA Qualifying School is played here. There are two 18-hole links-style courses, Legends and Champions, with greens fees running $35–$79. ⊠ *1000 Champions Dr.* ☎ *386/523–2001* ⊕ *www.lpgainternational.com.*

Pelican Bay South Country Club. In addition to featuring two 18-hole courses, this club offers a pro shop, club rentals, and a restaurant. Greens fees are $35–$50. ⊠ *350 Pelican Bay Dr.* ☎ *386/756–0034* ⊕ *www.pelicanbaycc.com.*

Spruce Creek Golf & Country Club. There's an 18-hole course here, along with practice and driving ranges, rental clubs, a pro shop, and a restaurant. Greens fees are $34–$40. ⊠ *1900 Country Club Dr., Port Orange* ☎ *386/756–6114* ⊕ *www.sprucecreekgolf.com.*

MANATEE SPOTTING

Blue Spring State Park. January and February are the top months for sighting sea cows at this designated manatee refuge, but they begin to head here in November, as soon as the water gets cold enough (below 68°F). Your best bet for spotting a manatee is to walk along the boardwalk. The park, which is 30 miles southwest of Daytona Beach on Interstate 4, was once a river port where paddle wheelers stopped to take on cargoes of oranges. Home to the largest spring on the St. Johns River, the park offers hiking, camping, and picnicking facilities. It also contains a historic homestead that's open to the public. ⊠ *2100 W. French Ave., Orange City* ☎ *386/775–3663* ⊕ *www. floridastateparks.org/bluespring* ⊠ *$6 per vehicle, up to 8 people; $2 pedestrians, bicyclists* ⊘ *Daily 8–sunset.*

FAMILY **Manatee Scenic Boat Tours.** This Ponce Inlet operator takes you on narrated cruises of the Intracoastal Waterway. Kids will love looking for the creatures also known as "sea cows," and your guide might tell you how (sun-delirious?) sailors may have mistaken them for mermaids. ⊠ *133 Inlet Harbor Rd.* ☎ *386/761–2027, 800/881–2628* ⊕ *www. manateecruise.com.*

WATER SPORTS

Daytona Beach Parasail. Catch air with this Ponce Inlet outfitter. ⊠ *4936 S. Peninsula Dr., Ponce Inlet* ☎ *386/547–6067* ⊕ *www.daytona-parasailing.com.*

Maui Nix. This is one of several outfitters that rent surf and boogie boards. ⊠ *635 N. Atlantic Ave.* ☎ *386/253–1234* ⊕ *www.mauinix.com/store.*

Salty Dog Surf Shop. You can rent surfboards or boogie boards here. ⊠ *700 E. International Speedway Blvd.* ☎ *386/258–0457* ⊕ *www. saltydogsurfshop.com.*

NEW SMYRNA BEACH

13

19 miles south of Daytona Beach, 56 miles northeast of Orlando.

The long, dune-lined beach of this small town abuts the Canaveral National Seashore. Behind the dunes sit beach houses, small motels, and an occasional high-rise (except at the extreme northern tip, where none is higher than seven stories). Canal Street, on the mainland, and Flagler Avenue, with many beachside shops and restaurants, have both been "streetscaped" with wide brick sidewalks and stately palm trees. The town is also known for its internationally recognized artists' workshop and some of the best surfing on the East Coast.

EXPLORING

Arts on Douglas. In a warehouse that has been converted into a stunning 5,000-square-foot, high-ceiling art gallery, Arts on Douglas has a new exhibit of works by a Florida artist every month. Representing more than 50 Florida artists, the gallery has hosted exhibits on the handmade jewelry of Mary Schimpff Webb and landscape and still-life oils by Barbara Tiffany. The gallery also holds an opening reception every first Saturday of the month from 4 to 7 pm. ⊠ *123 Douglas St.* ☎ *386/428–1133* ⊕ *www.artsondouglas.net* ⌑ *Free* ☉ *Tues.–Fri. 10–5, Sat. 11–3, and by appointment.*

Atlantic Center for the Arts. With exhibits that change every two months, the Atlantic Center for the Arts has works of internationally known artists. Mediums include sculpture, mixed materials, video, drawings, prints, and paintings. Intensive three-week residencies are periodically run by visual-, literary-, and performing-master artists such as Edward Albee, James Dickey, and Beverly Pepper. ⊠ *1414 Art Center Ave.* ☎ *386/427–6975* ⊕ *www.atlanticcenterforthearts.org* ⌑ *Free* ☉ *Tues.– Fri. 10–4, Sat. 10–2.*

Canaveral National Seashore. Miles of grassy windswept dunes and a virtually empty beach await you at this remarkable 57,000-acre park on a barrier island with 24 miles of undeveloped coastline spanning from New Smyrna to Titusville. The unspoiled area of hilly sand dunes, grassy marshes, and seashell-sprinkled beaches is a large part of NASA's buffer zone and is home to more than 1,000 species of plants and 300 species of birds and other animals. Surf and lagoon fishing are available, and a hiking trail leads to the top of an American Indian shell midden at Turtle Mound. For an additional charge, visitors can take a pontoon-boat tour ($20) or participate in the turtle-watch interpretive program ($14). Reservations are required. A visitor center is on Route A1A at Apollo Beach. Weekends are busy, and parts of the park are closed when mandated by NASA launch operations at the Kennedy Space Center, so call ahead. ⊠ *Visitor information,*

7611 S. Atlantic Ave. ☎ *386/428–3384* 🌐 *www.nps.gov/cana* 🎟 *$5 cars; $1 pedestrians, bicycles* 🕒 *Nov.–Mar., daily 6–6; Apr.–Oct., daily 6 am–8 pm.*

Smyrna Dunes Park. In this park, on a barrier island at the northernmost tip of New Smyrna Beach peninsula, 1½ miles of boardwalks crisscross sand dunes and delicate dune vegetation to lead to beaches and a fishing jetty. Botanical signs identify the flora, and there are picnic tables and an information center. It's also one of the few county parks where pets are allowed (on leashes, that is). ✉ *2995 N. Peninsula Ave.* ☎ *386/424–2935* 🌐 *www.volusia.org/parks/smyrnadunes.htm* 🎟 *$5 per vehicle, up to 8 people* 🕒 *Daily sunrise–sunset.*

BEACHES

Apollo Beach. In addition to typical beach activities, visitors to this beach on the northern end of Canaveral National Seashore can also ride horses here (with a permit), hike self-guided trails, and tour the historic Eldora Statehouse. From I–95, take Exit 220 and head east. **Amenities:** lifeguards (seasonal); parking (fee); toilets. **Best for:** solitude; swimming; walking. ✉ *Rte. A1A at southern end of New Smyrna Beach* ☎ *386/428–3384* 🎟 *$5 per vehicle for national seashore.*

New Smyrna Beach. This public beach extends 7 miles from the northernmost part of New Smyrna's barrier island south to the Canaveral National Seashore. It's mostly hard-packed white sand, and at low tide can be stunningly wide. The beach is lined with heaps of sandy dunes, but because they're endangered, it's against the law to walk on or play in them or to pick the sea grass, which helps to stabilize the dunes. From sunrise to sunset cars are allowed on certain sections of the beach (speed limit: 10 mph). In season there's a nominal beach-access fee for cars. **Amenities:** food and drink; lifeguards; parking (some with fee); showers; toilets; water sports. **Best for:** sunrise; surfing; swimming; walking. ✉ *Rte. A1A.*

WHERE TO EAT

$$ SEAFOOD 🍴 **J.B.'s Fish Camp and Restaurant.** Better known simply as J.B.'s, this local landmark is on the eastern shore of the Indian River (i.e., the middle of nowhere). Crowds gather around the picnic-style tables inside and out, or belly up to the bar to dine on mounds of spicy seafood, Cajun alligator, J.B.'s famous crab cakes, and blue crabs by the dozen. It's a great place to catch the sunset, and there's live music weekend afternoons. Five bucks says at least one person at your table says their hush puppies are the best he's ever eaten. [$] *Average main: $16* ✉ *859 Pompano Ave.* ☎ *386/427–5747* 🌐 *www.jbsfishcamp.com* ✍ *Reservations not accepted.*

$$$ SEAFOOD 🍴 **Norwood's Seafood Restaurant.** Fresh local fish and shrimp are the specialties at this bustling New Smyrna Beach landmark, open since 1946. Built as a gas station, the building later served as a general store and piggy-bank factory, but the remodeled interior belies this backstory; the place is replete with wood, from the chairs and booths to the walls and rafters. Order steak, blackened chicken breast, or pasta. Prices are reasonable, and more than 3,000 bottles of wine are on hand. Don't be fooled by the fancy wine list and linen tablecloths; you can still wear shorts (business casual, however, is the norm). [$] *Average main: $20* ✉ *400 2nd Ave.* ☎ *386/428–4621* 🌐 *www.norwoods.com.com* ✍ *Reservations not accepted.*

$$$ CUBAN 🍴 **Spanish River Grill.** Michele and Henry Salgado own this modern Cuban and Spanish eatery, which many locals think is the best restaurant in New Smyrna Beach. Though many consider the cuisine to represent fine dining, overall the restaurant is casual and unpretentious. Henry combines his Cuban grandmother's recipes with local ingredients for knockout results. Start with fried-green plantains or clams tossed with homemade salsa verde and white wine. For the main course, try the incredible paella or a chimichurri-marinated filet. Be sure to save room for one of Michele's desserts. Sunday sees a brunch from 11 to 3. [$] *Average main: $20* ✉ *737 E. 3rd Ave.* ☎ *386/424–6991* 🌐 *www.thespanishrivergrill.com* ✍ *Reservations not accepted* ⏲ *Closed Mon. No lunch Tues.–Thurs.*

13

WHERE TO STAY

For expanded reviews, facilities, and current deals, visit Fodors.com.

$$$ B&B/INN 🏨 **Riverview Hotel and Spa.** A landmark since 1885, this former bridge tender's home is set back from the Intracoastal Waterway at the edge of the north causeway, which still has an operating drawbridge. **Pros:** on-site spa and dining; hospitable staff; homey feel. **Cons:** small rooms in main house; strict cancellation policy; blocks from the beach. [$] *Rooms from: $179* ✉ *103 Flagler Ave.* ☎ *386/428–5858, 800/945–7416* 🌐 *www.riverviewhotel.com* 🛏 *17 rooms, 1 suite* 🍽 *Breakfast.*

OCALA NATIONAL FOREST

Eastern entrance 40 miles west of Daytona Beach, northern entrance 52 miles south of Jacksonville.

Ocala National Forest. This breathtaking 383,000-acre national forest off Route 40 has lakes, springs, rivers, hiking trails, campgrounds, and historic sites. It also has the largest off-highway vehicle trail system in the Southeast and three major recreational areas: Alexander Springs, Salt Springs, and Juniper Springs. To get here, take Interstate 4 east to Exit 92, and head west on Route 436 to U.S. 441, which you take north to Route 19 north. ✉ *Visitor center, 17147 Rte. 40 E, Salt Springs* ☎ *352/625–2520* 🌐 *www.fs.fed.us/r8/florida* 🎟 *Alexander Springs, Salt Springs, Juniper Springs: $5–$5.50.*

Alexander Springs. In this recreation area you'll find a stream and a campground. ✉ *Off Rte. 40 via Rte. 445 S* 🎟 *$5.50.*

Salt Springs. The draw here is a natural saltwater spring where Atlantic blue crabs come to spawn each summer. ✉ *Visitor center, 14100 Rte. 19* 🎟 *$5.50.*

Juniper Springs. Here you'll find a stone waterwheel house, a campground, a natural-spring swimming pool, and hiking trails. The 7-mile Juniper Springs run is a narrow, twisting, and winding canoe ride, which, although exhilarating, isn't for the novice. ✉ *14100 Rte. 40 N* 🎟 *$5.*

Silver Springs. The 350-acre natural theme park at the western edge of the Ocala National Forest has the world's largest collection of artesian springs. The state's first tourist attraction, it was established in 1890. Today the park presents wild-animal displays, glass-bottom-boat tours on the Silver River, a Jeep safari through 35 acres of wilderness, and walks through natural habitats. Exhibits include the Panther Prowl, which lets you watch and photograph the endangered Florida panther, and the Big Gator Lagoon, a 1-acre cypress swamp with more than 30 alligators. Other attractions include the Fort King River Cruise and the Lighthouse Ride, a combination carousel/gondola ride that gives a bird's-eye view of the park. Take Route 40 east from I–75 Exit 352 or west from I–95 Exit 268. ⊠ *5656 E. Silver Springs Blvd., Silver Springs* ☎ *352/236–2121* ⊕ *www.silversprings.com* ☜ *$34.99* ⊗ *Mid-Feb.–mid-Aug., daily 10–5; mid-Aug.–late Sept., Fri.–Sun. 10–5.*

Wild Waters. This is a great place to cool off, thanks to a 450,000-gallon wave pool, a 220-foot-long speed flume, the Alligator Ambush extreme tube slide, and a multilevel kids area. ⊠ *5656 E. Silver Springs Blvd., Silver Springs* ☎ *352/236–2121* ⊕ *www.wildwaterspark.com* ☜ *$14* ⊗ *Apr.–Sept., hrs vary.*

SPORTS AND THE OUTDOORS

CANOEING

Juniper Springs Canoe Rentals. This operator inside the national forest offers canoe rentals. ⊠ *26701 Florida 40, Silver Springs* ☎ *877/444–6777.*

FISHING

Captain Tom's Custom Charters. Charter fishing trips offered by this company range from two hours to a full day. You can arrange sightseeing cruises as well. Trips are by reservation only. ☎ *352/236–0872* ⊕ *www.captaintomcustomcharters.net.*

HORSEBACK RIDING

Adopt a Horse Club. Located within the Ocala National Forest, this outfitter offers trail riding and lessons (walk, gait, and canter) for all ages. ⊠ *22651 S.E. Rte. 42, Umatilla* ☎ *352/821–4756, 800/731–4756* ⊕ *www.adoptahorseclub.com.*

GAINESVILLE

98 miles northwest of Daytona Beach.

The University of Florida (UF) anchors this sprawling town. Visitors are mostly Gator football fans and parents of students, so the styles and costs of accommodations are aimed at budget-minded travelers rather than luxury-seeking vacationers. The surrounding area encompasses several state parks and interesting gardens and geological sites.

GETTING HERE AND AROUND

Gainesville Regional Airport is served by American, Delta, United, and US Airways. From the airport, taxi fare to the center of Gainesville is about $20; some hotels provide free airport pickup.

Contact Gainesville Regional Airport (*GNV*) ⊠ *3400 N.E. 39th Ave.* ☎ *352/373–0249* ⊕ *www.gra-gnv.com.*

VISITOR INFORMATION

Contact Gainesville/Alachua County Visitors and Convention Bureau ⊠ *30 E. University Ave.* ☎ *352/374–5260, 866/778–5002* ⊕ *www.visitgainesville.com.*

EXPLORING

Devil's Millhopper Geological State Park. Scientists surmise that thousands of years ago an underground cavern collapsed and created this geological wonder that is designated as a National Natural Landmark. You pass a dozen small waterfalls as you head down 236 steps to the bottom of this botanical wonderland: exotic subtropical ferns and trees growing in a 500-foot-wide, 120-foot-deep sinkhole. You can pack a lunch to enjoy in one of the park's picnic areas. And bring Spot, too; just keep him on a leash. Guided walks with a park ranger are offered Saturday mornings at 10. ⊠ *4732 Millhopper Rd., off U.S. 441* ☎ *352/955–2008* ⊕ *www.floridastateparks.org/ devilsmillhopper* ⊠ *$4 per vehicle, up to 8 people; $2 pedestrians and bicyclists* ⊙ *Wed.–Sun. 9–5.*

LATER, GATORS

Depending on what time of year you visit, Gainesville's population could be plus or minus 50,000. Home to one of the largest colleges in the country, the University of Florida, Gainesville takes on a different personality during the summer, when most students return home. During the fall and spring terms, the downtown streets are teeming with students on bikes, scooters, and foot, but in summer it's much more laid-back.

13

FAMILY **Florida Museum of Natural History.** On the campus of the University of Florida, the state's official museum of natural history and the largest natural-history museum in the Southeast has holdings of more than 34 million objects and specimens. In addition to active collections in anthropology, archaeology, botany, mammalogy, and ornithology, the museum features several interesting replicas, including nearly complete fossil skeletons of a mastodon and mammoth from the last Ice Age as well as a full-size model of a Florida cave and mangrove forest. The Butterfly Rainforest houses 60 to 80 species in a 6,400-square-foot, screened, free-flight vivarium. Butterfly releases take place weekdays at 2, and weekends at 2, 3, and 4, weather permitting. ⊠ *University of Florida Cultural Plaza, S.W. 34th St. and Hull Rd.* ☎ *352/846–2000* ⊕ *www.flmnh.ufl.edu* ⊠ *Free; Butterfly Rainforest $10.50* ⊙ *Mon.–Sat. 10–5, Sun. 1–5.*

FAMILY **Marjorie Kinnan Rawlings Historic State Park.** One of America's most cherished authors found inspiration in this out-of-the-way hamlet about 20 miles outside of Gainesville. The 90-acre park, set amid aromatic citrus groves, has a playground for kids and short hiking trails, where you might see owls, deer, and Rawlings' beloved "red birds." But the main attraction is the restored Florida Cracker–style home, where Rawlings wrote classics such as *The Yearling* and *Cross Creek* and entertained the likes of poet Robert Frost, author Thornton Wilder, and actor Gregory Peck. Although the house is guarded closely by spirited roosters, guided tours ($3) are offered seasonally. ⊠ *18700 S. County Rd. 325, Hawthorne* ☎ *352/466–3672* ⊕ *www. floridastateparks.org/marjoriekinnanrawlings* ⊠ *$3 per car; house tour an additional $3* ⊙ *Daily 9–5; house tours Oct.–July, Thurs.– Sun. at 10, 11, 1, 2, 3, and 4.*

Samuel P. Harn Museum of Art. This 112,800-square-foot museum has five main collections: Asian, with works dating back to the Neolithic era; African, encompassing costumes, domestic wares, and personal adornments; Modern, featuring the works of Georgia O'Keeffe, William Morris Hunt, Claude Monet, and George Bellows; Contemporary, with original pieces by Yayoi Kusama and El Anatsui; and Photography, including the work of Jerry N. Uelsmann, a retired University of Florida professor. ⊠ *University of Florida Cultural Plaza, S.W. 34th St. and Hull Rd.* ☎ *352/392–9826* ⊕ *www.harn.ufl.edu* ⊠ *Free* ☉ *Tues.–Fri. 11–5, Sat. 10–5, Sun. 1–5.*

WHERE TO EAT

$
ECLECTIC
✕ **Bistro 1245.** You can get high-quality meals at bargain-basement prices at this trendy yet surprisingly down-to-earth restaurant, which shares a roof with Leonardo's by the Slice. Some call the small dining room cramped, while others find the close quarters romantic. However you look at it, the menu is full of comfort foods with a twist, such as maple-roasted chicken breast, spicy shrimp pasta, a seared-tuna club sandwich, and bison sirloin. In keeping with the bistro's lack of pretention, you're invited to pick your own wine from the restaurant's wine rack. For a lighter meal and a lighter price, order from the lunch menu in the evening. $ *Average main: $13* ⊠ *1245 W. University Ave.* ☎ *352/376–0000* ⊕ *www.leonardosgainesville.com.*

$$
LATIN AMERICAN
✕ **Emiliano's Café.** Linen tablecloths and art deco–style artwork create a casual, elegant feel at this Gainesville institution serving Pan-Latin cuisine for more than 20 years. Dine indoors or beneath the stars at the sidewalk café. Start with the Gallician stew (a family recipe) or the black-bean soup, and then move on to one of the chef's signature dishes—Spanish saffron rice with shrimp, clams, mussels, fresh fish, chicken, artichoke hearts, peas, asparagus, and pimientos. Emiliano's also offers an extensive tapas menu with nearly 40 items to mix and match, and tempting desserts like the original chipotle brownie cake. Live jazz fills the air Monday and Wednesday nights. $ *Average main: $15* ⊠ *7 S.E. 1st Ave.* ☎ *352/375–7381* ⊕ *www.emilianoscafe.com.*

$
ITALIAN
✕ **Leonardo's by the Slice.** It's ironic that the kitschy pizza joint with a '50s flair is surrounded by a white-picket fence, since most of its patrons and employees are far from conventional. College students, especially the pierced and tatted kind, flock to the Gainesville landmark not only because it's cheap but because it has the best pizza in town. Available in thick or thin varieties, by the pie and, of course, by the slice, Leonardo's pizza comes in a handful of varieties (like veggie, pepperoni, Greek, and spinach tomato). It also offers calzones, salads, and pasta such as baked ziti and fettuccini Alfredo, with no nonpizza entrée over $8.25. $ *Average main: $12* ⊠ *1245 W. University Ave.* ☎ *352/378–2001* ⊕ *www. leonardosgainesville.com* ⌣ *Reservations not accepted.*

$$$
EUROPEAN
Fodor'sChoice
★
✕ **Paramount Grill.** This tiny, fine-dining restaurant may have single-handedly changed the perception of Gainesville from a college town fueled by pizza, chicken wings, and pitchers of beer to an up-and-coming culinary destination with imaginative menus driven by fresh Florida produce. What Paramount lacks in size and glitz it makes up for with its ever-changing menu. Try the organic beet salad and such entrées as

sesame-roasted domestic red snapper with coconut milk and lemon-grass basmati rice, or grilled butcher-cut pork chops with white-cheddar polenta. If you miss lunch here, try the Sunday brunch. $ *Average main: $28* ⊠ *12 S.W. 1st Ave.* ☎ *352/378–3398* ⊕ *www.paramountgrill.com* ⊘ *No lunch Sat.*

WHERE TO STAY

For expanded reviews, facilities, and current deals, visit Fodors.com.

$$
B&B/INN

🏠 **Herlong Mansion.** Spanish moss clings to the stately oak trees surrounding this restored 1880s mansion in the town of Micanopy, 11 miles north of Gainesville. **Pros:** large private bathrooms; gourmet breakfast; evening wine-and-cookies reception. **Cons:** no phones in rooms; no TVs in some rooms; some small and windowless rooms; 14-day cancellation policy. $ *Rooms from: $119* ⊠ *402 N.E. Cholokka Blvd., Micanopy* ☎ *352/466–3322, 800/437–5664* ⊕ *www.herlong.com* ⤳ *10 rooms, 2 cottages* ¶◯¶ *Breakfast.*

$$
HOTEL

🏠 **Hilton University of Florida Conference Center Gainesville.** With 25,000 square feet of meeting space, the University of Florida's flagship hotel caters most obviously to business travelers, but its location on the southwest corner of campus also makes it a good choice for UF visitors. **Pros:** proximity to college; free Internet; spacious rooms. **Cons:** spotty service; overrated restaurant; signs of wear and tear. $ *Rooms from: $109* ⊠ *1714 S.W. 34th St.* ☎ *352/371–3600* ⊕ *www.hilton.com* ⤳ *245 rooms, 3 suites* ¶◯¶ *No meals.*

$$$
B&B/INN

🏠 **Laurel Oak Inn.** Guests at this 1885 Queen Anne–style dwelling say they're so comfortable and at ease they feel like they're in a home, not an inn. **Pros:** three-course breakfast; location; hospitable staff. **Cons:** processing fee for cancellations; not family-friendly; no pool. $ *Rooms from: $140* ⊠ *221 S.E. 7th St.* ☎ *352/373–4535* ⊕ *www.laureloakinn.com* ⤳ *5 rooms* ¶◯¶ *Breakfast.*

$$$
B&B/INN
Fodor's Choice
★

🏠 **Magnolia Plantation Inn.** Among only a handful of French Second Empire buildings in the southeastern United States, this inn conists of a main house, built in 1885, and nine adorable cottages. **Pros:** friendly service; breakfast; nightly social hour. **Cons:** small rooms; seven-day cancellation policy; some uncomfortable beds. $ *Rooms from: $145* ⊠ *309 S.E. 7th St.* ☎ *352/375–6653, 800/201–2379* ⊕ *www.magnoliabnb.com* ⤳ *5 rooms, 9 cottages* ¶◯¶ *Breakfast.*

$$
B&B/INN

🏠 **Sweetwater Branch Inn Bed & Breakfast.** Modern conveniences such as hair dryers, Internet, and business services mix with Southern charm and hospitality, all wrapped up in two grand Victorian homes surrounded by lush tropical gardens. **Pros:** Southern-style breakfast; Jacuzzi suites. **Cons:** occasional noise issues; frequent on-site weddings. $ *Rooms from: $139* ⊠ *625 E. University Ave.* ☎ *352/373–6760, 800/595–7760* ⊕ *www.sweetwaterinn.com* ⤳ *12 rooms, 7 cottages* ¶◯¶ *Breakfast.*

SPORTS AND THE OUTDOORS

AUTO RACING

Auto Plus Raceway. The site of professional and amateur auto and motor-cycle races, including Gatornationals in March, is also home to Frank Hawley's Drag Racing School (☎ *866/480–7223* ⊕ *www.frankhawley.com*). ⊠ *11211 N. County Rd. 225* ☎ *352/377–0046* ⊕ *www.autoplusraceway.com.*

13

THE SPACE COAST

South of the Daytona Beach area and Canaveral National Seashore are Merritt Island National Wildlife Refuge and the John F. Kennedy Space Center. This area is also home to the laid-back town of Cocoa Beach, which attracts visitors on weekends year-round because it's the closest beach to Orlando, 50 miles to the east.

VISITOR INFORMATION
Contact **Space Coast Office of Tourism** ⊠ *430 Brevard Ave., Suite 150, Cocoa* ☎ *877/572–3224, 321/433–4470* ⊕ *www.visitspacecoast.com.*

TITUSVILLE

34 miles south of New Smyrna Beach, 67 miles east of Orlando.

It's unusual that such a small, easily overlooked community could accommodate what it does, namely the magnificent Merritt Island National Wildlife Refuge and the entrance to the Kennedy Space Center, the nerve center of the U.S. space program (⇨ *See In-Focus feature, "Soaring High at Kennedy Space Center").*

EXPLORING
American Police Hall of Fame & Museum. You know police officers deserve your respect, and you'll be reminded why at this intriguing attraction. In addition to memorabilia like the Robocop costume and Blade Runner car from the films, informative displays offer insight into the dangers officers face every day: drugs, homicides, and criminals who can create knives from dental putty and guns from a bicycle spoke (really). Other historical exhibits include invitations to hangings, police patches, how you collect evidence at a crime scene, and a rotunda where more than 8,000 names are etched in marble to honor police officers who have died in the line of duty. The 24-lane shooting range provides rental guns (Tuesday to Friday noon–8, weekends noon–6). ⊠ *6350 Horizon Dr.* ☎ *321/264–0911* ⊕ *www.aphf.org* 🎟 *$13* ⊗ *Daily 10–6.*

Valiant Air Command Warbird Museum & Tico Airshow. Although its exterior looks sort of squirrelly, what's inside here is certainly impressive. Aviation buffs won't want to miss memorabilia from World Wars I and II, Korea, and Vietnam, as well as extensive displays of vintage military flying gear and uniforms. There are posters that were used to identify Japanese planes, plus there's a Huey helicopter and the cockpit of an F-106 that you can sit in. In the north hangar it looks like activity day at the senior center as a volunteer team of retirees busily restores old planes. It's an inspiring sight, and a good place to hear some war stories. The lobby gift shop sells real flight suits, old flight magazines, bomber jackets, books, models, and T-shirts. ⊠ *6600 Tico Rd.* ☎ *321/268–1941* ⊕ *www.vacwarbirds.org* 🎟 *$18* ⊗ *Daily 9–5.*

BEACHES
Playalinda Beach. The southern access for the Canaveral National Seashore, remote Playalinda Beach has pristine sands and is the longest stretch of undeveloped coast on Florida's Atlantic seaboard. Hundreds of giant sea turtles come ashore here from May through August to lay

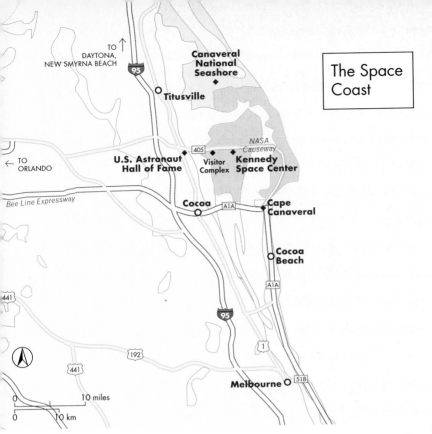

their eggs. Fourteen parking lots anchor the beach at 1-mile intervals. From Interstate 95, take Exit 249 and head east. Bring bug repellent in case of horseflies, and note that you may see some unauthorized clothing-optional activity. **Amenities:** lifeguards (seasonal); parking (fee); toilets. **Best for:** solitude; swimming; walking. ✉ *Northern end of Rte. 402/Beach Rd.* ☎ *321/867–4077* ⊕ *www.nps.gov/cana* ✉ *$5 per vehicle for national seashore.*

WHERE TO EAT

$$ ✕ **Dixie Crossroads.** This sprawling restaurant is always crowded and **SEAFOOD** festive, but it's not just the rustic setting that draws the throngs—it's the seafood. The specialty is the difficult-to-cook rock shrimp, which are served fried, broiled, or steamed. Diners with a hearty appetite can opt for the all-you-can-eat rock shrimp, small shrimp, tilapia, or catfish. You might have to wait (up to 90 minutes) for a table, but if you don't have time to wait, you can order takeout or use the call-ahead seating option. And a word to the wise: as tempting as those corn fritters dusted with powdered sugar are, don't fill up on them. $ *Average main: $21* ✉ *1475 Garden St., 2 miles east of I–95 Exit 220* ☎ *321/268–5000* ⊕ *www.dixiecrossroads.com* ✍ *Reservations not accepted.*

WHERE TO STAY

For expanded reviews, facilities, and current deals, visit Fodors.com.

$$ HOTEL **Hampton Inn Titusville.** Proximity to the Kennedy Space Center and reasonable rates make this four-story hotel a top pick for an overnight near the center. **Pros:** free Internet; extra-comfy beds; convenient to I–95. **Cons:** thin walls; no restaurant on-site; no room service. [$] *Rooms from: $101* ✉ *4760 Helen Hauser Blvd.* ☎ *321/383–9191* 🌐 *www.hamptoninn.com* 🛏 *86 rooms, 4 suites* 🍴 *Breakfast.*

SPORTS AND THE OUTDOORS

Fodor's Choice ★ **Merritt Island National Wildlife Refuge.** Owned by the National Aeronautics and Space Administration (NASA), this 140,000-acre refuge, which adjoins the Canaveral National Seashore, acts as a buffer around Kennedy Space Center while protecting 1,000 species of plants and 500 species of wildlife, including 15 considered federally threatened or endangered. It's an immense area dotted by brackish estuaries and marshes and patches of land consisting of coastal dunes, scrub oaks, pine forests and flatwoods, and palm and oak hammocks. You can borrow field guides and binoculars at the visitor center (5 miles east of U.S. 1 in Titusville on State Road 402) to track down falcons, ospreys, eagles, turkeys, doves, cuckoos, owls, and woodpeckers, as well as loggerhead turtles, alligators, and otters. A 20-minute video about refuge wildlife and accessibility—only 10,000 acres are developed—can help orient you.

You might take a self-guided tour along the 7-mile Black Point Wildlife Drive. On the Oak Hammock Foot Trail you can see wintering migratory waterfowl and learn about the plants of a hammock community. If you exit the north end of the refuge, look for the Manatee Observation Area just north of the Haulover Canal (maps are at the visitor center). They usually show up in spring and fall. There are also fishing camps, fishing boat ramps, and six hiking trails scattered throughout the area. Most of the refuge is closed 24 hours prior to a launch. ✉ *Rte. 402, across Titusville Causeway* ☎ *321/861–0667, 321/861–0669 visitor center* 🌐 *www.fws.gov/merrittisland* 🎫 *Free* 🕒 *Daily sunrise–sunset; visitor center weekdays 8–4:30, weekends 9–5.*

COCOA

17 miles south of Titusville.

Not to be confused with the seaside community of Cocoa Beach, the small town of Cocoa sits smack-dab on mainland Florida and faces the Intracoastal Waterway, known locally as Indian River. There's a planetarium and a museum, as well as a rustic fish camp along the St. Johns River, a few miles inland.

Folks in a rush to get to the beach tend to overlook Cocoa's Victorian-style village, but it's worth a stop and is perhaps Cocoa's most interesting feature. Within the cluster of restored turn-of-the-20th-century buildings and cobblestone walkways you can enjoy several restaurants, indoor and outdoor cafés, snack and ice-cream shops, and more than 50 specialty shops and art galleries. The area hosts music performances in the gazebo, arts-and-crafts shows, and other family-friendly events throughout the year. To get to Cocoa Village, head east on Route 520—named King Street in Cocoa—and when the streets get narrow and the road curves, make a right onto Brevard Avenue; follow the signs for the free municipal parking lot.

EXPLORING

FAMILY **Brevard Museum of History & Natural Science.** This is the place to come to see what the lay of the local land looked like in other eras. Hands-on activities draw children, who especially migrate toward the Imagination Center, where they can act out history or reenact a space shuttle flight. Not to be missed is the Windover Archaeological Exhibit of 7,000-year-old artifacts indigenous to the region. In 1984, a shallow pond revealed the burial ground of more than 200 American Indians who lived in the area about 7,000 years ago. Preserved in the muck were bones and, to the archaeologists' surprise, the brains of these ancient people. Nature lovers appreciate the museum's butterfly garden and the nature center with 22 acres of trails encompassing three distinct ecosystems—sand pine hills, lake lands, and marshlands. ⊠ *2201 Michigan Ave.* ☎ *321/632–1830* ⊕ *www.brevardmuseum.org* ⊉ *$6* ⊘ *Thurs.–Sat. 10–4.*

WHERE TO EAT

$$$ ✕ **Café Margaux.** Eclectic, creative, and international is the best way to
ECLECTIC describe the cuisine and decor at this charming Cocoa Village spot. The
Fodor's Choice menu blends French, Italian, and Asian influences with dishes like lol-
★ lipop pork chop over English pea and orzo risotto, sweet onion-crusted fresh red snapper, and braised veal scallopini, and also features more exotic fare such as duck and ostrich. Themed dining rooms are elaborately decorated with dramatic but not necessarily coordinating window treatments, wallpaper, and artwork. Ⓢ *Average main: $27* ⊠ *220 Brevard Ave.* ☎ *321/639–8343* ⊕ *www.margaux.com* ⊘ *Closed Sun.*

SHOPPING

Cocoa Flea Market. With more than 1,000 booths, this is, essentially, the largest outdoor shopping center in Brevard County. The market is open Friday, Saturday, and Sunday from 8 to 4. ⊠ *5605 N. U.S. 1* ☎ *321/631–0241.*

Cocoa Village. You could spend hours browsing in the more than 50 boutiques here, along Brevard Avenue and Harrison Street (the latter has the densest concentration of shops). Although most stores are of the gift and clothing variety, the village is also home to 11 antiques shops, 13 art galleries, restaurants, a tattoo parlor, and a spa. ⊠ *Rte. 520 and Brevard Ave.* ☎ *321/631–9075.*

WORD OF MOUTH

"We have been to KSC several times. Keep to the basic tour. The Astronaut Hall of Fame is also nice. My children's only complaint was that they showed pretty much the same film at each stop. I would recommend staying at the Hilton on Cocoa Beach; it is in a quieter area with a nice beach. There are lots of good restaurants in the area."

—cbr

13

Super Flea & Farmers' Market. You're sure to find a bargain at one of the 900 booths at this market, which is held every Friday, Saturday, and Sunday from 9 to 4. ⊠ *4835 W. Eau Gallie Blvd., Melbourne* ☎ *321/242–9124* ⊕ *www.superfleamarket.com.*

SPORTS AND THE OUTDOORS
BOATING

Twister Airboat Rides. If you haven't seen the swampy, alligator-ridden waters of Florida, then you haven't really seen Florida. This thrilling wildlife tour goes where eagles and wading birds coexist with water moccasins and gators. The Coast Guard–certified deluxe airboats hit speeds of up to 45 mph and offer unparalleled opportunities to photograph native species. The basic tour lasts 30 minutes, but 60- and 90-minute ecotours are also available at an additional cost by reservation only. Twister Airboat Rides is inside the Lone Cabbage Fish Camp, about 9 miles west of Cocoa's city limits, 4 miles west of Interstate 95. ⊠ *8199 Rte. 520, at St. Johns River* ☎ *321/632–4199* ⊕ *www.twisterairboatrides.com* ⊠ *$22* ☉ *Daily 10–4:30.*

CAPE CANAVERAL

5 miles east of Cocoa via Rte. A1A.

The once-bustling commercial fishing area of Cape Canaveral is still home to a small shrimping fleet, charter boats, and party fishing boats, but its main business these days is as a cruise-ship port. This isn't the spiffiest place around, but what is becoming quite clean and neat is the north end of the port, where the Carnival, Disney, and Royal Caribbean cruise lines set sail. Port Canaveral is now Florida's second-busiest cruise port for multiday cruises, which makes this a great place to catch a glimpse of these giant ships.

BEACHES

Jetty Park. A wonderful taste of the real Florida, this 4½-acre beach and oceanfront campground has picnic pavilions, bike paths, and a 1,200-foot-long fishing pier that doubles as a perfect vantage point from which to watch a liftoff from Cape Canaveral. Lifeguards are on duty all year, and beach wheelchairs are available for rent. A jetty constructed of giant boulders adds to the landscape, and a walkway that crosses it provides access to a less populated stretch of beach. Real and rustic, this is Florida without the theme-park varnish. **Amenities:** food and drink; lifeguards; parking (fee); showers; toilets; water sports. **Best for:** sunrise; surfing; swimming; walking. ⊠ *400 Jetty Rd.* ☎ *321/783–7111* ⊕ *www.jettyparkbeachandcampground.com* ⊠ *$5–$10 cars, $7–$15 RVs.*

WHERE TO EAT

$ ✕ **Seafood Atlantic.** Locals think of this casual waterfront seafood mar-
SEAFOOD ket/eatery as a well-kept secret, but more and more cruise patrons
are making their way here for a pre- or postcruise treat. The market
is connected to the restaurant, guaranteeing not only freshness but
an array of choices. You don't just order a fish sandwich or plate of
steamed shrimp; you choose from at least four varieties of fish (try
the Golden Tile in season) and several varieties of shrimp (the Royal
Reds may be the best you've ever tasted). Seating is alfresco, with
views of the inland waterway and nearby cruise ships. Best for lunch
or an early dinner, the restaurant closes at 8 on Friday and Saturday, earlier other nights. $ *Average main: $12* ✉ *520 Glen Cheek
Dr.* ☎ *321/784–1963* ⊕ *www.seafoodatlantic.net* ⌂ *Reservations not
accepted* ⊘ *Closed Tues.*

$$ ✕ **Thai Thai III.** The mouthwatering photos on the menu aren't just a
THAI marketing ploy. The pictures don't do the real stuff justice. Locals
and cruise-ship vacationers frequent this casual Thai/Japanese eatery
within walking distance of cruise-port hotels. Seafood is an emphasis
here, with specialties like lobster pad Thai and snapper with ginger
and scallion. The Thai curries, noodles, and soups can be prepared
"Thai hot," but "medium" packs a subtle punch, too. On the sushi
side, try the Beauty and the Beast roll: half tuna, half eel, with avo-
cado, asparagus, scallions, and roe. Decor is eclectic and relaxing,
with brightly painted walls and low-hanging sconces. Don't fret if you
see a crowd out front. The place does a brisk take-out business. $ *Av-
erage main: $16* ✉ *8660 Astronaut Blvd.* ☎ *321/784–1561* ⊕ *www.
thaithai3.com.*

WHERE TO STAY

For expanded reviews, facilities, and current deals, visit Fodors.com.

$$ ⌂ **Radisson Resort at the Port.** For cruise-ship passengers who can't wait
HOTEL to get under way, this splashy resort, done up in pink and turquoise,
already feels like the Caribbean. **Pros:** cruise-ship convenience;
pool area; free shuttle. **Cons:** rooms around the pool can be noisy;
loud air-conditioning in some rooms; no complimentary breakfast.
$ *Rooms from: $120* ✉ *8701 Astronaut Blvd.* ☎ *321/784–0000,
888/201–1718* ⊕ *www.radisson.com/capecanaveralfl* ⌐ *284 rooms,
72 suites* ⦿| *No meals.*

$$$ ⌂ **Residence Inn Cape Canaveral/Cocoa Beach.** Billing itself as the closest
HOTEL all-suites hotel to the Kennedy Space Center, this four-story Residence
Inn, painted cheery yellow, is also convenient to other area attractions
such as Port Canaveral, the Cocoa Beach Pier, the Brevard Zoo, and
Cocoa Village, and is only an hour from the Magic Kingdom. **Pros:**
helpful staff; free breakfast buffet; pet-friendly. **Cons:** less than pictur-
esque views; street noise in some rooms. $ *Rooms from: $179* ✉ *8959
Astronaut Blvd.* ☎ *321/323–1100, 800/331–3131* ⊕ *www.marriott.
com* ⌐ *150 suites* ⦿| *Breakfast.*

Continued on page 712

The astronauts prepare for the launch
of Endeavour STS-118 on Pad 39-A.

SOARING HIGH

by John Blodgett
and Steve Master

AT THE KENNEDY SPACE CENTER

Ever since the National Aeronautics and Space Administration (NASA) was founded, in 1958, the United States has been working on missions that launch us heavenward. When these dreams are about to become reality, and until 2011, when it was time for blastoff, Kennedy Space Center in Cape Canaveral, Florida, was where the action could be found.

NASA FROM COAST TO COAST

The Vehicle Assembly Building housed the space shuttle before a launch.

You've heard the words: "Houston, the *Eagle* has landed." And *Apollo 13's* "Houston, we have a problem." But have you wondered, "Why are they talking to Houston if they left from Florida?"

NASA actually has operations at centers scattered across the United States. Its major centers are in Florida, Texas, and California. NASA's Launch Operations Center, known as the Kennedy Space Center, in Cape Canaveral, Florida, is where the famous countdowns are heard as a mission prepares for launch. You could say this is like NASA's big airport for outbound flights.

Once a mission (with a crew inside) is airborne, Houston takes over. In addition to operating all manned space flights, the Lyndon B. Johnson Space Center in Houston, Texas, is home base for American astronauts. They train here in laboratories that simulate weightlessness and other space-related concepts.

Not to be left out, the West Coast also gets a piece of the space-action pie. At Moffet Field, in California's Silicon Valley, the Ames Research Center is research and development central for NASA technology. If a mission can't happen because the technology isn't there yet, it's the job of the Ames Research Center to figure it out. Also in California is the Dryden Flight Research Center, at Edwards Air Force Base in Southern California. The center is where a lot of smart people who know a lot about aerodynamics get to test out their ideas; it's also where space shuttle orbiters land.

So, in a nutshell, you could say California is the brains of NASA's operations, Texas is its heart, and Florida is its wings.

NASA TIMELINE

OCT. 1958: NASA begins operating with 8,000 employees and $100 million. Ten days later, *Pioneer* I takes off.

MAY 1961: Alan B. Shepard, Jr., becomes the first person in space.

FEB. 1962: John Glenn is the first American to orbit the Earth.

JUNE 1965: Edward H. White II is the first American to walk in space.

DEC. 1968: Three astronauts orbit the moon aboard *Apollo 8*.

JULY 1969: *Apollo 11* brings man to the moon.

JULY 1976: *Viking 1* lands on Mars.

APRIL 1981: First space shuttle orbiter launches two astronauts into space.

JAN. 1986: Space shuttle *Challenger* explodes 73 seconds after launch; seven onboard astronauts die.

APRIL 1990: Hubble telescope launches.

JULY 1997: Mars Pathfinder lands on the red planet.

JULY 1999: Eileen Collins is the first woman to command a space shuttle mission.

FEB. 2002: Mars Odyssey begins mapping the red planet.

FEB. 1, 2003: Space shuttle *Columbia* explodes over Texas 15 minutes before scheduled landing; seven astronauts on board die.

JULY 2004: Cassini–Huygens spacecraft begins orbiting Saturn.

MAY 2010: Shuttle *Atlantis* delivers new Russian module and critical spare parts to International Space Station.

DID YOU KNOW?

Known as the Moon Rockets, the Saturn Vs stood over 363 feet high. NASA sent more than a dozen of these expendable rockets skyward between 1967 and 1973. See one at the Apollo/Saturn V Center.

THE KENNEDY SPACE CENTER

The 140,000-acre Kennedy Space Center is one of central Florida's most popular sights. The must-see attraction gives you a hands-on opportunity to learn about the past, present, and future of America's space program. View old rockets and other artifacts from space flight operations, talk with astronauts during Q&As, experience a simulated launch, and become part of the awed crowd on launch days as you watch the blastoff from a viewing site on the grounds or nearby.

VISITOR COMPLEX

Space Walk of Honor

Space Education

Children's Play Dome

Rocket Garden

Early Space Exploration

Early Space Exploration

PARKING

VISITOR COMPLEX

Kennedy Space Center Visitor Complex is the starting place for your visit. It's home to several attractions and is also where you can board the bus for tours of the center beyond the visitor complex.

EXHIBITS

The **Early Space Exploration** display highlights the rudimentary yet influential Mercury and Gemini space programs; **Robot Scouts** is a walk-through exhibit of unmanned planetary probes; and the **Exploration Space: Explorers Wanted** exhibit immerses visitors in exploration beyond Earth. Don't miss the outdoor **Rocket Garden,** with walkways winding beside rockets, from early Atlas spacecraft to a Saturn IB. The most moving exhibit is the **Astronaut Memorial.** The 70,400-pound black-granite tribute to astronauts who lost their lives in the name of space exploration stands 42½ feet high by 50 feet wide.

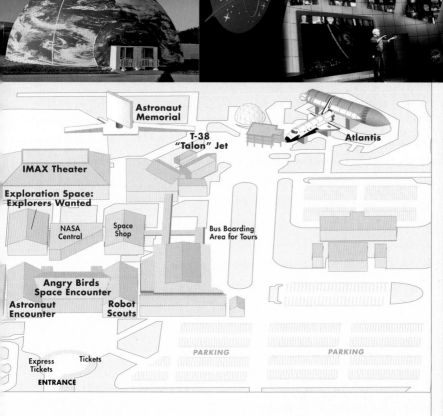

Astronaut Memorial

T-38 "Talon" Jet

Atlantis

IMAX Theater

Exploration Space: Explorers Wanted

NASA Central

Space Shop

Bus Boarding Area for Tours

Angry Birds Space Encounter

Astronaut Encounter

Robot Scouts

PARKING

PARKING

Express Tickets

Tickets

ENTRANCE

INTERACTIVE SHOWS AND RIDES

Astronaut Encounter Theater has two daily programs where NASA astronauts share their adventures in space travel and show a short film. More befitting Walt Disney World or Universal Studios (complete with the health warnings), the **Shuttle Launch Experience** is the center's spectacular attraction. Designed by a team of astronauts, NASA experts, and renowned attraction engineers, the 44,000-square-foot structure uses a sophisticated motion-based platform, special-effects seats, and high-fidelity visual and audio components to simulate the sensations experienced in an actual space-shuttle launch, including MaxQ, Solid Rocker Booster separation, main engine cutoff, and External Tank separation. The journey culminates with a breathtaking view of Earth from space. For those under 44 inches, **Children's Play Dome** enables kids to play among the next generation of spacecraft, climb a moon-rock wall, and crawl through rocket tunnels.

MOVIES

At the world's only back-to-back twin **IMAX Theater** the dream of space flight comes to life on a movie screen five stories tall with dramatic footage shot by NASA astronauts during missions. Realistic 3-D special effects will make you feel like you're in space with them. Films alternate throughout the year.

BEYOND THE VISITOR COMPLEX

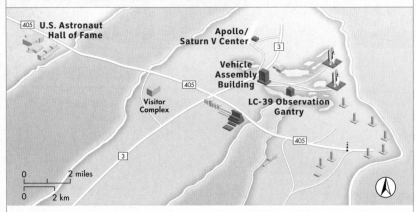

405 U.S. Astronaut
Hall of Fame

Apollo/
Saturn V Center **3**

Vehicle
Assembly
Building **405**

LC-39 Observation
Gantry

Visitor
Complex

405

3

0   2 miles

0   2 km

SPACE CENTER TOURS

To explore the remainder of the space center, you will need to take a tour by bus. Buses depart every 15 minutes from the Visitor Complex; the tour duration is two hours, but you can get off and back on again at will at various sites. Bus stops include the **Launch Complex 39 Observation Gantry,** which has an unparalleled view of the launchpads and the **Apollo/Saturn V Center,** with a don't-miss presentation at the Firing Room Theater, where the launch of America's first lunar mission, 1968's *Apollo VIII,* is re-created with a ground-shaking, window-rattling lift-off. The **Apollo/Saturn V Center** features one of the three remaining Saturn V moon rockets. This bus tour is included with admission; four others are available for additional fees (*see Add-Ons*).

U.S. ASTRONAUT HALL OF FAME

The original Mercury 7 team and the later Gemini, Apollo, Skylab, and shuttle astronauts contributed to make the United States Astronaut Hall of Fame the world's premium archive of astronauts' personal stories. Authentic memorabilia and equipment from their collections tell the story of human space exploration. This stand-alone attraction

is across the river from the Kennedy Space Center; admission to it is included with your Visitor Complex ticket.

You can see one-of-a-kind items like Wally Schirra's relatively archaic Sigma 7 Mercury space capsule, Gus Grissom's spacesuit (colored silver only because NASA thought silver looked more "spacey"), and a flag that made it to the moon. The exhibit First of the Moon focuses on crew selection for Apollo 11 and the Soviet Union's role in the space race. One of the more challenging activities at the hall of fame is a space-shuttle simulator that lets you try your hand at landing the craft—and afterward replays a side view of your rolling and pitching descent. Don't miss Simulation Station, an area with interactive exhibits about space travel. There are also videos of historic moments.

ADD-ONS

The following tours and programs are available for extra cost beyond admission and should be reserved in advance.

■ **KSC:** For the first time since the 1980s, guests may see where rockets were built inside the Vehicle Assembly Building on the KSC Up-Close Tour ($25) for a limited time. They can walk the Transfer Aisle and look inside one of four high bays.

■ See how far the space program has come on the **Cape Canaveral: Then and Now Tour** ($21). It puts you up close to the original launch pads, brings you to the Air Force Space and Missile Museum, and lets you watch the active unmanned rocket program.

■ During **Lunch With an Astronaut** ($24.99), astronauts talk about their experiences and engage in Q&A (kids often ask "How do you eat/sleep/relieve yourself in space?").

■ If you want to live the life of an astronaut, you can enroll in the **Astronaut Training Experience** (ATX) at the U.S. Astronaut Hall of Fame. The half-day program combines hands-on training and preparation for the rigors of space flight. NASA astronauts helped design the program, and you'll hear first-hand from them as you progress through an exciting day at the busiest launch facility on Earth. The $145 cost includes flight training simulators, a full-scale space shuttle mission simulation, a meet-and-greet with a NASA astronaut, and ATX Gear. Age restrictions apply. Reserve your spot well in advance.

Cape Canaveral Then and Now Tour.

PLANNING YOUR TRIP

GETTING HERE

Kennedy Space Center Visitor Complex and the U.S. Astronaut Hall of Fame are near Titusville on Cape Canaveral, about a 45-minute drive from Orlando. From Orlando International Airport, take the north exit to 528 East (the Beachline Expressway) and drive east to the exit marked "407, Titusville, Kennedy Space Center." Take 407 until you reach Rte. 405 (Columbia Boulevard/ NASA Parkway) and then turn right. After approximately 1 mi you will see the U.S. Astronaut Hall of Fame on your right. Continue another 5 mi until you reach the visitor complex, your starting point for all tours.

BUDGETING YOUR TIME

Plan to spend a full day at the Visitor Complex and hall of fame, or at the very least, several hours.

ADMISSION

Your $50 (plus tax) admission ticket grants you one day's admission to Kennedy Space Center Visitor Complex and related tours as well as a second day's free admission to the U.S. Astronaut Hall of Fame, which is just across the causeway.

CONTACT INFORMATION

✉ Off Rte. 405
☎ 877/313–2610
🌐 www.kennedyspacecenter.com
🎫 $43
🕐 Daily 9 am; closing times vary. (Call ahead for restrictions if you're visiting on a launch day.)

SHUTTLE COMPONENTS

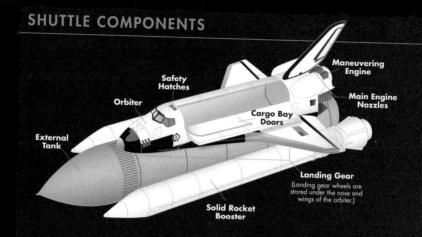

Maneuvering Engine

Safety Hatches

Orbiter

Main Engine Nozzles

Cargo Bay Doors

External Tank

Landing Gear
(Landing gear wheels are stored under the nose and wings of the orbiter.)

Solid Rocket Booster

ROCKET VS. SHUTTLE

When the space shuttle orbiter *Columbia* blasted off on April 12, 1981, NASA launched its Space Transportation System—a planned fleet of manned, reusable spacecraft that could transport crew, cargo, and experiments into space and return to Earth to land like an aircraft. The system was a radical departure from the days when manned lunar modules were thrust into space at the tip of a disposable rocket, to return to the planet by parachute and then be plucked from the ocean. (Shuttles were launched piggyback on a huge, single-use fuel tank; its two solid rocket boosters returned via parachute.) Modern traditional rockets are used only to deploy instruments like unmanned probes into space.

EXTERNAL TANK—provided a platform for the shuttle and fuel for the three main shuttle engines that transported the shuttle into space. It separated from the shuttle within the first 10 minutes of the flight and disintegrated upon reentry.

SOLID ROCKET BOOSTER—one of two rockets used to launch the shuttle into space. Each returned to Earth via parachute to be restored for use on a future mission.

ORBITER—another name for the space shuttle, which rode piggyback on the fuel tank until it could launch into space under its own rocket power. The crew was inside.

PAYLOAD BAY DOORS—the two long doors on the back of the orbiter that opened to allow payload to be deployed into space by means of a manipulating arm.

LANDING GEAR—the retractable wheels under the nose and wings of the orbiter, which allowed it to land like a typical aircraft.

ENTRY HATCH—this door allowed astronauts to enter the shuttle, and doubled as an escape hatch.

MANEUVERING ENGINES—a number of smaller orbiter engines, on the nose and in the tail section, which allowed the craft to make fine positioning adjustments while in space.

MAIN ENGINE NOZZLES—the three engines at the rear of the orbiter that propelled the craft to space.

BLASTOFF!

From Kennedy Space Center's launch pads most unmanned space flights and all manned space missions have found their origin, with many of them being momentous events—the first satellite launched into space, the first man in space, that giant leap onto the moon's surface. Over the years many flights have become rather routine, happening fairly frequently, but hundreds of spectators still line the cape's nearby roads to watch the countdown, the great explosions of rocket power, and the always-exciting liftoff—proving that NASA routine is never boring.

With the retirement of the Shuttle fleet, a new era at NASA brims with possibilities such as space tourism, commercial space transportation, and expanded frontiers in space. The future of manned space flight remains unclear, but unmanned vehicles such as Atlas and Falcon 9 rockets remain a spectacle to behold at Cape Canaveral. Tickets are available for viewing a launch from within the Kennedy Space Center at the visitor complex ($40–$50); prices include admission to the center. Popular off-site vantage points include:

- Along the Indian River on Hwy. 1, especially in Titusville

- Beach Line Expressway (Rte. 528), especially where it crosses over the Indian or Banana Rivers

- Rte. A1A in Cocoa Beach

- Jetty Park at Port Canaveral, just south of the Cape Canaveral Air Force Station border (park admission is $5)

SHOPPING

Cove Marketplace. Whether you're at Port Canaveral for a cruise or are just passing through, this retail marketplace on the south side of the harbor has enough shops, restaurants, and entertainment venues to keep you occupied. Since most of the bars and eateries are located on the public waterfront area, you'll have a view of the cruise ships—and their colorful passengers. ⊠ *Glen Cheek Dr. and Scallop Dr., Port Canaveral* ⊕ *www.portcanaveral.com/covemarketplace* 🖃 *Free* ☉ *Hrs vary by business.*

COCOA BEACH

5 miles south of Cape Canaveral, 58 miles southeast of Orlando.

After crossing a long and high bridge just east of Cocoa Village, you drop down upon a barrier island. A few miles farther and you'll reach the Atlantic Ocean and picture-perfect Cocoa Beach at Route A1A.

In the early 1960s Cocoa Beach was a sleepy, little-known town. But in 1965 the sitcom *I Dream of Jeannie* premiered. The endearing show centered on an astronaut, played by Larry Hagman, and his "Jeannie" in a bottle, Barbara Eden, and was set in Cocoa Beach. Though the series was never shot in Florida, creator Sidney Sheldon paid homage to the town with local references to Cape Kennedy (now known as the Kennedy Space Center) and Bernard's Surf restaurant. Today the town and its lovely beach are mecca to Florida's surfing community.

ESSENTIALS

Visitor Information Cocoa Beach Convention and Visitors Bureau ⊠ *8501 Astronaut Blvd., Suite 4, Cape Canaveral* ☏ *321/454–2022, 877/321–8474* ⊕ *www.visitcocoabeach.com.*

EXPLORING

Cocoa Beach Pier. By day, it's a good place to stroll—if you don't mind weather-worn wood and sandy, watery paths. Although most of the pier is free to walk on, there's a $1 charge to enter the fishing area at the end of the 800-foot-long boardwalk, and a $5 fishing fee. You can rent rods and reels here for an additional $10. By night, visitors and locals—beach bums and surfers among them—head here to party. Come on Friday night for the Boardwalk Bash, with live acoustic and rock-and-roll music; Wednesday and Saturday also see live music. ■TIP→ The pier is a great place to watch launches from Kennedy Space Center. ⊠ *401 Meade Ave.* ☏ *321/783–7549* ⊕ *www.cocoabeachpier.com.*

BEACH

Cocoa Beach. This is one of the Space Coast's nicest beaches—and the place where the great professional surfer Kelly Slater got his start. The beach boasts one of the steadiest surf breaks on the East Coast and has wide stretches that are excellent for biking, jogging, power walking, and strolling. In some places there are dressing rooms, showers, playgrounds, picnic areas with grills, snack shops, and surfside parking lots. Beach vendors offer necessities, and lifeguards are on duty in the summer.

The Cocoa Beach Pier is a magnet for nightlife in Cocoa Beach after dark.

A popular entry road, Route 520 crosses the Banana River into Cocoa Beach. At its east end, 5-acre **Alan Shepard Park**, named for the famous astronaut, aptly provides excellent views of launches from Kennedy Space Center. Facilities here include 10 picnic pavilions, shower and restroom facilities, and more than 300 parking spaces. Beach vendors carry necessities for sunning and swimming. Parking is $7, $10 on weekends and holidays March through Labor Day. Shops and restaurants are within walking distance. Another enticing Cocoa Beach entry point is 10-acre **Sidney Fischer Park**, in the 2100 block of Route A1A in the central beach area. It has showers, playgrounds, changing areas, picnic areas with grills, snack shops, and plenty of well-maintained, inexpensive parking lots ($5 for cars). **Amenities:** food and drink; lifeguards (summer); parking (fee); showers; toilets; water sports. **Best for:** sunrise; surfing; swimming; walking. ⊠ *Rte. A1A from Cape Canaveral to Patrick Air Force Base.*

WHERE TO EAT

$$$ ╳ **Heidelberg.** As the name suggests, the cuisine here is definitely German, **GERMAN** from the sauerbraten served with potato dumplings and red cabbage to the beef Stroganoff and spaetzle to the classically prepared Wiener schnitzel. All the soups and desserts are homemade; try the Viennese-style apple strudel and the rum-zapped almond-cream tortes. Elegant interior touches include crisp linens and fresh flowers. There's live music Wednesday through Saturday evenings. You can also dine inside the jazz club, Heidi's, next door. Ⓢ *Average main: $27* ⊠ *7 N. Orlando Ave., opposite City Hall* ☎ *321/783–6806* ⊕ *www.heidisjazzclub.com* ⊗ *Closed Mon. and Tues.; no lunch.*

$ 🍴 **Oh Shucks Seafood Bar.** At the only open-air seafood bar on the beach,
SEAFOOD at the entrance of the Cocoa Beach Pier, the main item is oysters, served on the half shell. You can also grab a burger here, crab legs by the pound, or Oh Shucks's most popular item, coconut beer shrimp. Some diners complain that the prices don't jibe with the ultracasual atmosphere (e.g., plastic chairs), but they're also paying for the "ex-Pierience." During high season, there's live entertainment on Wednesday, Friday, Saturday, and Sunday. [$] *Average main: $12* ✉ *401 Meade Ave., Cocoa Beach Pier* ☎ *321/783–7549* 🌐 *www.cocoabeachpier.com.*

WHERE TO STAY

For expanded reviews, facilities, and current deals, visit Fodors.com.

$$ 🏨 **Best Western Oceanfront Hotel & Suites.** Families love this Best Western
HOTEL for its affordable suites; everyone loves it for its location—just a half block from the Cocoa Beach Pier—and great views of launches from Kennedy Space Center. **Pros:** free Internet; complimentary breakfast. **Cons:** not all rooms have an ocean view; small bathrooms; noise from the pier. [$] *Rooms from: $113* ✉ *5600 N. Atlantic Ave.* ☎ *321/784–4343, 800/367–1223* 🌐 *www.bestwesterncocoabeach.com* 🛏 *208* 🍽 *Breakfast.*

$$ 🏨 **DoubleTree by Hilton Cocoa Beach Oceanfront.** Proximity to the beach
HOTEL and comforts like in-room microwaves and refrigerators—and DoubleTree's famous chocolate-chip walnut cookies—make this six-story hotel a favorite of vacationing families, particularly Orlandoans on weekend getaways. **Pros:** private beach access; comfy beds; complimentary parking. **Cons:** extra charge for beach-chair rental; loud air-conditioning in some rooms; slow elevators; no breakfast with standard room. [$] *Rooms from: $147* ✉ *2080 N. Atlantic Ave.* ☎ *321/783–9222* 🌐 *www.cocoabeachdoubletree.com* 🛏 *148 rooms, 12 suites.*

$$ 🏨 **Hilton Cocoa Beach Oceanfront.** You can't get any closer to the beach
HOTEL than this seven-story oceanfront hotel. **Pros:** beachfront; friendly staff; clean. **Cons:** small pool and bathrooms; no balconies; room windows don't open; breakfast not included with standard rate. [$] *Rooms from: $124* ✉ *1550 N. Atlantic Ave.* ☎ *321/799–0003* 🌐 *www.hiltoncocoabeach.com* 🛏 *285 rooms, 11 suites.*

$$$ 🏨 **Inn at Cocoa Beach.** This charming oceanfront inn has spacious, indi-
B&B/INN vidually decorated rooms with four-poster beds, upholstered chairs, and balconies or patios; most have ocean views. **Pros:** quiet; romantic; honor bar. **Cons:** no on-site restaurant; "forced" socializing. [$] *Rooms from: $145* ✉ *4300 Ocean Beach Blvd.* ☎ *321/799–3460, 800/343–5307 outside Florida* 🌐 *www.theinnatcocoabeach.com* 🛏 *50 rooms* 🍽 *Breakfast.*

$$$ 🏨 **The Resort on Cocoa Beach.** Even if the beach weren't in its back-
RESORT yard, this family-friendly, oceanfront property offers enough activities
FAMILY and amenities—from tennis and basketball courts to a game room and
Fodor's Choice ★ 50-seat movie theater—to keep everyone entertained. **Pros:** full kitchens; in-room washers and dryers; large balconies. **Cons:** check-in not until 4 and checkout at 10; not all rooms are oceanfront; slow elevators. [$] *Rooms from: $196* ✉ *1600 N. Atlantic Ave.* ☎ *321/783–4000* 🌐 *www.theresortoncocoabeach.com* 🛏 *124 suites* 🍽 *No meals.*

NIGHTLIFE

The Cocoa Beach Pier has several nightspots as well as live-music sessions a couple of nights a week.

Heidi's Jazz Club. Local and nationally known jazz musicians (Boots Randolph and Mose Allison have taken the stage) play Tuesday through Sunday, with showcase acts appearing on weekends. ✉ *7 Orlando Ave. N* ☎ *321/783–4559.*

SPORTS AND THE OUTDOORS

13

KAYAKING

Adventure Kayak of Cocoa Beach. Specializing in manatee encounters, this outfitter organizes one- and two-person kayak tours of mangroves, channels, and islands. Tours launch from various locations in the Cocoa Beach area. Rates run about $30 per person. ✉ *599 Ramp Rd.* ☎ *321/480–8632* ⊕ *www.kayakcocoabeach.com.*

SURFING

Cocoa Beach Surf Company. The world's largest surf complex has three floors of boards, apparel, sunglasses, and anything else a surfer, wannabe-surfer, or souvenir-seeker could need. Also on-site are a 5,600-gallon fish and shark tank and the Shark Pit Bar & Grill. Here you can also rent surfboards, bodyboards, and wet suits, as well as umbrellas, chairs, and bikes. And staffers teach grommets (dudes) and gidgets (chicks)—from kids to seniors—how to surf. There are group, semi-private, and private lessons available in one-, two-, and three-hour sessions. Prices range from $40 (for a one-hour group lesson) to $120 (three-hour private). All gear is provided. ✉ *4001 N. Atlantic Ave.* ☎ *321/799–9930.*

Fodor's Choice ★ **Ron Jon Surf Shop.** It's impossible to miss Ron Jon: it takes up nearly two blocks along Route A1A and has a giant surfboard and an art deco facade painted orange, blue, yellow, and turquoise. What started in 1963 as a small T-shirt and bathing-suit shop has evolved into a 52,000-square-foot superstore that's open every day 'round the clock. The shop rents water-sports gear as well as chairs and umbrellas, and it sells every kind of beachwear, surf wax, plus the requisite T-shirts and flip-flops. ✉ *4151 N. Atlantic Ave., Rte. A1A* ☎ *321/799–8820* ⊕ *www.ronjonsurfshop.com.*

MELBOURNE

20 miles south of Cocoa Beach.

Despite its dependence on the high-tech space industry, this town is decidedly laid-back. Most of the city is on the mainland, but a small portion trickles onto a barrier island, separated by the Indian River Lagoon and accessible by several inlets, including the Sebastian.

EXPLORING

FAMILY
Fodor's Choice ★ **Brevard Zoo.** At the only Association of Zoo and Aquariums–accredited zoo built by a community, you can stroll along the shaded boardwalks and get a close-up look at rhinos, giraffes, cheetahs, alligators, crocodiles, giant anteaters, marmosets, jaguars, eagles, river otters, kangaroos, exotic birds, and kookaburras. Alligator, crocodile, and river-otter

feedings are held on alternate afternoons—and no, the alligators don't dine on the otters. Stop by Paws-On, an interactive learning playground with a petting zone, wildlife detective training academy, and the Indian River Play Lagoon. Hand-feed a giraffe in Expedition Africa or a lorikeet in the Australian Free Flight Aviary, and step up to the Wetlands Outpost, an elevated pavilion that's a gateway to 22 acres of wetlands through which you can paddle kayaks and keep an eye open for the 4,000 species of wildlife that live in these waters and woods. Adventurers seeking a chimp's-eye view can zipline through the zoo on Treetop Trek. ⊠ *8225 N. Wickham Rd.* ☎ *321/254–9453* ⊕ *www.brevardzoo. org* ⊠ *$15, including train and giraffe and lorikeet food $19.50, Treetop Trek $22–$54* ◔ *Daily 9:30–5, last admission 4:15.*

BEACHES

Paradise Beach. Small and scenic, this 1,600-foot stretch of sand is part of a 10-acre park north of Indialantic, about 20 miles south of Cocoa Beach on Route A1A. It has a refreshment stand, volleyball courts, outdoor showers, a beachfront park with pavilions, grills, picnic tables, and lifeguards in summer. **Amenities:** food and drink; lifeguards (seasonal); parking; showers; toilets. **Best for:** sunrise; surfing; swimming; walking. ⊠ *2301 N. Rte. A1A.*

Satellite Beach. The sands of this sleepy little community just south of Patrick Air Force Base, about 15 miles south of Cocoa Beach on Route A1A, are cradled between the balmy Atlantic Ocean and biologically diverse Indian River Lagoon. It's a popular spot for family vacations because of its slow pace and lack of crowds as well as its beachfront park with playground, five pavilions, and picnic facilities. **Amenities:** food and drink; lifeguards; parking; showers; toilets; water sports. **Best for:** sunrise; surfing; swimming; walking. ⊠ *Rte. A1A, Satellite Beach.*

SPORTS AND THE OUTDOORS

BASEBALL

Space Coast Stadium. Even though they play in our nation's capital during the regular season, the Washington Nationals, formerly the Montreal Expos, use this stadium for their spring training site. For the rest of the season, the facility is home to the Brevard County Manatees (☎ *321/633–9200*), one of the Milwaukee Brewers' minor-league teams. ⊠ *5800 Stadium Pkwy., Viera* ☎ *321/633–4487* ⊕ *www.viera.com.*

GOLF

Baytree National Golf Links. Greens fees are $21–$65 at this 18-hole course. ⊠ *8207 National Dr.* ☎ *321/259–9060* ⊕ *www.baytreenational.com.*

Viera East Golf Club. This is a public, 18-hole course. Greens fees are $29–$52. ⊠ *2300 Clubhouse Dr., Viera* ⊹ *5 miles from Melbourne* ☎ *321/639–6500* ⊕ *www.vieragolf.com.*

THE PANHANDLE

WELCOME TO
THE PANHANDLE

TOP REASONS
TO GO

★ **Snowy white beaches:**
Most of the Panhandle's
Gulf Coast shoreline is
relatively unobstructed
by high-rise condos and
hotels, and the white-
powder sand is alluring.

★ **Lots of history:**
Spanish, Native American,
and, later, French and
English influences shaped
the direction of this region
and are well represented
in architecture, historic
sites, and museums.

★ **Slower pace:**
The Panhandle is some-
times referred to as "LA,"
or Lower Alabama.
Southern through and
through, the pace here is
as slow as molasses—a
fact Tallahassee plays up
by claiming to be "Florida
with a Southern accent."

★ **Capital sites:** As the
state capital (chosen
because it was midway
between the two earlier
Spanish headquarters
of St. Augustine and
Pensacola), Tallahassee
remains intriguing thanks
to its history, historical
museums, universities, and
quiet country charm.

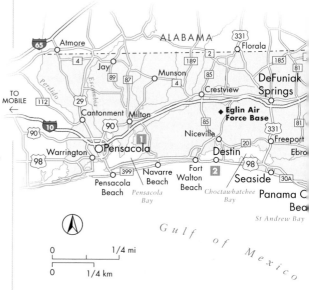

1 **Around Pensacola Bay.**
By preserving architecture
from early Spanish settlements, Pensacola earns
points for retaining the
influence of these early
explorers. The downtown
district is compact, plus
there's the city's Naval
Air Museum and beaches
nearby. Inland are some
small towns with Old
Florida appeal.

GETTING ORIENTED

The Panhandle is a large area, and there are a number of airports to access the largest cities. Two major east–west routes offer alternatives to Interstate 10. Roughly parallel to its modern cousin, U.S. 90 is an early byway that goes from Tallahassee through small Old Florida towns like Marianna and DeFuniak Springs on its way to Pensacola. From Pensacola, U.S. 98 generally skirts along the Gulf of Mexico through seaside towns and communities like Fort Walton Beach, Destin, Panama City Beach, and Apalachicola, providing some breathtaking waterfront drives.

14

2 **The Emerald Coast.**
A nature reserve spans thousands of square miles of Gulf Coast land, and miles of shoreline between Pensacola and Destin is nearly void of development. The area is known for its blue-green waters and sugarlike sand beaches made of Appalachian quartz crystals. Panama City offers unique attractions.

3 **Tallahassee.** In the state capital you can see the old and new capitols, visit the state's historical museum, attend an FSU football game, and go for a country ride down canopied roads.

By Ashley Wright

The sugar-white sands of the Panhandle's beaches stretch 227 miles from Pensacola east to Apalachicola. Sprinkle in clear emerald waters, towering dunes, and laid-back small towns where the fish are always biting and the folks are friendly, and you have a region with local color that's beloved by Floridians and visitors alike.

There are sights in the Panhandle, but sightseeing isn't the principal activity. The region is better known for its rich history, ample fishing and diving, and its opportunities for relaxation. Here it's about Southern drawls, a gentle pace, fresh seafood, and more grits and old-fashioned hospitality than anywhere else in the state. Sleepy beach towns offer world-class golf, deep-sea fishing, relaxing spa treatments, and unbeatable shopping.

There's glamour here, too. Look for it in winning resorts throughout the region and in the abundance of nightlife, arts, and culture—from local symphonies to boutique art galleries—particularly in the more metropolitan areas. And then there's the food: from fresh catches of the day to some of the nation's finest oysters to mom-and-pop favorites offering fried seafood goodness.

Jump in a car, rent a bike, or buy a spot on a charter boat—you're never too far from outdoor adventure, with more miles of preserved coastline than anywhere else in the state. Destin is, after all, dubbed "The World's Luckiest Fishing Village" and the sport of YOLO Boarding (this region's term for the popular paddleboarding craze) has invaded the area in full force, offering a unique waterborne view of all the region's unspoiled, natural beauty.

Don't forget to veer off the beach roads and venture into some of the area's picturesque historic districts. Pensacola is known as America's first settlement, and the rest of the region follows suit with rich history dating from the first settlers. The state's capital, Tallahassee, has its own unique history woven of politics, varying cultures, and innovation. Between the local charm, natural splendor, outdoor adventures, and miles of coastline, it's no wonder that the Panhandle is so beloved.

PLANNING

WHEN TO GO

Peak season is Memorial Day to Labor Day, with another spike during spring break. Inland, especially in Tallahassee, high season is during the fall (football) and March to April. Vendors, attractions, and other activities are in full swing in the summer. There's a "secret season" that falls around October and November: things quiet down as students go back to school, but restaurants and attractions keep normal hours and the weather is moderate.

TOP FESTIVALS

Destin Fishing Rodeo. Anglers young and old compete in offshore and inshore categories throughout October. ⊠ *Destin* ☎ *850/837–6734* ⊕ *www.destinfishingrodeo.org.*

Florida Seafood Festival. In November, Apalachicola celebrates the oyster harvest with oyster-shucking and -eating contests. ⊠ *Apalachicola* ☎ *888/653–8011* ⊕ *www.floridaseafoodfestival.com.*

Pensacola Jazzfest. Groove to the sounds of America's indigenous musical form during this early April event downtown. ⊠ *Pensacola* ☎ *850/433–8382* ⊕ *www.jazzpensacola.com.*

Pensacola Seafood Festival. Fried, broiled, battered, grilled, or served gourmet—the fish options abound at this September event in downtown Pensacola. And while that's the main course, side dishes to this family-friendly festival are arts and crafts, cooking demonstrations, children's activities, and live entertainment. ⊠ *Pensacola* ☎ *850/433–6512* ⊕ *www.fiestaoffiveflags.org/seafoodfestival.*

Springtime Tallahassee. Held in late March or early April, the capital city's major cultural event has handmade works, stages with entertainment, and a crowd-pleasing parade. ⊠ *Tallahassee* ☎ *850/224–5012* ⊕ *www.springtimetallahassee.com.*

GETTING HERE AND AROUND

AIR TRAVEL

In May 2010 the Northwest Florida Beaches International Airport (ECP) debuted on the east shore of Panama City's West Bay with flights to six U.S. cities through Southwest Airlines and Delta. In addition, there are airports with regularly scheduled passenger service in Pensacola and Tallahassee, as well as a public airport—Northwest Florida Regional Airport—in Fort Walton Beach on the Eglin Air Force Base. Many major carriers operate out of at least one of these airports.

Contacts Northwest Florida Beaches International Airport ☎ *850/763–6751* ⊕ *www.iflybeaches.com.* **Northwest Florida Regional Airport** ☎ *850/651–7160* ⊕ *www.flyvps.com.* **Pensacola International Airport** ☎ *850/436–5000* ⊕ *www.flypensacola.com.* **Tallahassee Regional Airport** ☎ *850/891–7800* ⊕ *www.talgov.com/airport.*

CAR TRAVEL

The main east–west arteries across the top of the state are Interstate 10 and U.S. 90. Interstate 10 can be monotonous, but U.S. 90 routes you along the main streets of several county seats. U.S. 98 snakes eastward along the coast, splitting into 98 and 98A at Inlet Beach before rejoining at Panama City and continuing on to Port St. Joe and Apalachicola. The view of the gulf from U.S. 98 can be breathtaking, especially at sunset.

If you need to get from one end of the Panhandle to the other in a timely manner, drive inland to Interstate 10, where the speed limit runs as high as 70 mph in places. Major north–south highways that weave through the Panhandle are (from east to west) U.S. 231, U.S. 331, Route 85, and U.S. 29. From U.S. 331, which runs over a causeway at the east end of Choctawhatchee Bay between Route 20 and U.S. 98, the panorama of barge traffic and cabin cruisers on the twinkling waters of the Intracoastal Waterway will get your attention.

HOTELS

Many of the lodging selections here revolve around extended-stay options: resorts, condos, and time-shares that allow for a week or more in simple efficiencies, as well as fully furnished homes. There are also cabins, such as the ones that rest between the dunes at Grayton Beach. In any case, these are great for families and get-togethers, allowing you to do your own housekeeping and cooking, and explore the area without tour guides.

Local visitors' bureaus often act as clearinghouses for these types of properties, and you can also search online for vacation rentals. On the coast, but especially inland, the choices seem geared more toward mom-and-pop motels in addition to the usual line of chain hotels. ▦TIP➡ During the summer and over holiday weekends, always reserve ahead for top properties.

RESTAURANTS

An abundance of seafood is served at coastal restaurants: oysters, crab, shrimp, scallops, and a variety of fish. Of course, that's not all there is on the menu. This part of Florida still impresses diners with old-fashioned comfort foods such as meat loaf, fried chicken, beans and cornbread, okra, and fried green tomatoes. You'll also find small-town seafood shacks where you can dine on local favorites such as deep-fried mullet, cheese grits, coleslaw, and hush puppies. Restaurants, like resorts, vary their operating tactics off-season, so call first if visiting during winter months.

HOTEL AND RESTAURANT COSTS

Prices in the restaurant reviews are the average cost of a main course at dinner or, if dinner isn't served, at lunch. Prices in the hotel reviews are the lowest cost of a standard double room in high season. Prices don't include taxes (6%, more in some counties) and 1%–5% tourist tax for hotel rooms.

PENSACOLA BAY

Nestled on the Gulf of Mexico at Florida's northwest tip, this region takes visitors back in time thanks to its rich cultural heritage. In 1559, Don Tristan de Luna first "discovered" the area, which today is divided into four distinct parts: North Pensacola, the walkable downtown historic district, Pensacola Beach, and Perdido Key. The historic district is the heart of the area. Just across the bay, Pensacola Beach is on Santa Rosa Island, while Perdido Key is further west, hugging the Alabama state line.

PENSACOLA

59 miles east of Mobile, Alabama, via I–10.

Pensacola consists of four distinct districts—Seville, Palafox, East Hill, and North Hill—though they're easy to explore as a unit. Stroll down streets mapped out by the British and renamed by the Spanish, such as Cervantes, Palafox, Intendencia, and Tarragona.

An influx of restaurants and bars has brought new nightlife to the historic districts, especially Palafox Street, which is now home to a thriving entertainment scene. Taste buds water over fresh coastal cuisine from a number of award-winning, locally owned and operated restaurants, and the downtown entertainment district offers fun for any age throughout the year—festivals, events at bars and concert venues, and a growing Mardi Gras celebration.

At the southern terminus of Palafox Street is Plaza DeLuna, a 2-acre park with open grounds, interactive water fountains, and an amphitheater. It's a quiet place to sit and watch the bay, fish, or enjoy the city's Thursday-evening sunset celebration.

GETTING HERE AND AROUND

Pensacola International Airport has dozens of daily flights and is served by AirTran, American Airlines (American Eagle), Delta, United, and US Airways. From Pensacola International Airport via Yellow Cab it costs about $14 to get downtown or about $32 to reach Pensacola Beach.

In Pensacola and Pensacola Beach, Escambia County Area Transit provides regular citywide bus service ($1.75), downtown trolley routes, tours through the historic districts, and free trolley service to the beach from mid-May to Labor Day on Friday, Saturday, and Sunday evening as well as Saturday afternoon.

Contacts Escambia County Area Transit (*ECAT*) ☎ *850/595–3228* ⊕ *www.goecat.com.* **Pensacola International Airport** ☎ *850/436–5000* ⊕ *www.flypensacola.com.* **Yellow Cab** ☎ *850/433–3333.*

VISITOR INFORMATION

Contacts Pensacola Visitor Information Center ✉ *1401 E. Gregory St.* ☎ *850/434–1234, 800/874–1234* ⊕ *www.visitpensacola.com.*

EXPLORING

TOP ATTRACTIONS

Fodor'sChoice ★ **Pensacola Naval Air Station.** Locals almost unanimously suggest this as *the* must-see attraction of Pensacola. As you drive near it, don't be alarmed if you're suddenly struck with the shakes—they're probably caused by the U.S. Navy's Blue Angels' aerobatic squadron buzzing overhead. This is their home base, and they practice maneuvers here on Tuesday and Wednesday mornings at 8:30 from March to November.

14

Then stay late—the pilots stick around after the show to shake hands and sign autographs. During the show, cover your ears as the six F/A 18s blast off in unison for 45 minutes of thrills and skill. Watching the Blue Angels practice their aerobatics is one of the best "free" shows in all of Florida (your tax dollars are already paying for these jets). It's also home to the National Flight Academy, which teaches the principles of Science, Technology, Engineering, and Math (STEM) during an immersive experience for students age 11–17. ✉ *1750 Radford Blvd.* ☎ *850/452–3604, 850/452–3606.*

TOP GUN

The National Museum of Naval Aviation is one of only two locations nationwide that feature "Top Gun," four real F-14 military flight-training simulators with all the actual controls. Experience mock air-to-air combat, practice carrier landings, or simply cruise over Las Vegas; Iraq; Miramar, California; and other simulated sites during a 20-minute joyride. The $25 experience includes "cockpit orientation training."

National Museum of Naval Aviation. Within the Pensacola Naval Air Station, this 300,000-square-foot museum has more than 140 historic aircraft. Among them are the NC-4, which in 1919 became the first plane to cross the Atlantic; the famous World War II fighter the F-6 *Hellcat*; and the Skylab Command Module.

Other attractions include an atomic bomb (it's defused, we promise), and the restored Cubi Bar Café—a very cool former airmen's club transplanted here from the Philippines. Relive the morning's maneuvers in the 14-seat motion-based simulator as well as an IMAX theater playing *Fighter Pilot, The Magic of Flight,* and other educational films. Pensacola, also known as the "Cradle of Naval Aviation," celebrated the 100th Anniversary of Naval Aviation in 2011. ✉ *1750 Radford Blvd.* ☎ *850/452–3604* ⊕ *www.navalaviationmuseum.org* ✉ *Free, IMAX film $8.75, children 5–12 $8.25, 4 and under free* ⊙ *Daily 9–5.*

Seville Square Historic District. Established in 1559, this is the site of Pensacola's first permanent Spanish settlement (it beat St. Augustine's by six years). Its center is Seville Square, a live oak–shaded park bounded by Alcaniz, Adams, Zaragoza, and Government streets. Roam these brick streets past honeymoon cottages and homes set in a parklike setting. Many buildings have been converted into restaurants, offices, and shops that overlook broad Pensacola Bay and coastal road U.S. 98, which provides access to the Gulf Coast and beaches. ☎ *850/595–5985.*

Historic Pensacola Village. Within the Seville Square Historic District is this complex of several museums and historic homes whose indoor and outdoor exhibits trace the area's history back 450 years. The Museum of Industry (✉ *200 E. Zaragoza St.*), in a late-19th-century warehouse, is home to permanent exhibits dedicated to the lumber, maritime, and shipping industries—once mainstays of Pensacola's economy. A reproduction of a 19th-century streetscape is displayed in the Museum of Commerce (✉ *201 E. Zaragoza St.*).

Also in the village are the Julee Cottage (⊠ *210 E. Zaragoza St.*), the "first home owned by a free woman of color"; the 1871 Dorr House (⊠ *311 S. Adams St.*); and the 1805 French-Creole Lavalle House (⊠ *205 E. Church St.*).

Strolling through the area gives you a good (and free) look at many architectural styles, but to enter some of the buildings you must purchase an all-inclusive ticket at the Village gift shop in the Tivoli High House—which was once in the city's red-light district but now is merely a calm reflection of a restored home. A guided tour (at 11, 1, and 2:30 and lasting 60–90 minutes) lets you experience the history of Pensacola as you visit the Lavalle House, Dorr House, Old Christ Church, and 1890s Lear-Rocheblave House. ⊠ *Tivoli High House, 205 E. Zaragoza St.* ⊕ *www.historicpensacola.org* 🎟 *$6* ⊘ *Tues.–Sat. 10–4.*

14

FAMILY **T.T. Wentworth, Jr. Florida State Museum.** Even if you don't like museums, this one is worth a look. Housed in the elaborate, Renaissance revival–style former city hall, it has an interesting mix of exhibits illustrating life in the Florida Panhandle over the centuries. One of these, the City of Five Flags, provides a good introduction to Pensacola's history. Mr. Wentworth was quite a collector (as well as a politician and salesman), and his eccentric collection includes a mummified cat (creepy) and the size 37 left shoe of Robert Wadlow, the world's tallest man (not creepy, but a really big shoe). A wide range of both permanent and traveling exhibits include a rare collection of dollhouses, Black Ink (a look at African-Americans' role in printing), Hoops to Hips (a review of fashion history), Civil War exhibits, and a kid-size interactive area with a ship and fort where kids can play and pretend to be colonial Pensacolans. ⊠ *330 S. Jefferson St.* ☎ *850/595–5990* ⊕ *www.historicpensacola.org* 🎟 *Free* ⊘ *Tues.–Sat. 10–4.*

WORTH NOTING

Palafox Historic District. Palafox Street is the main stem of historic downtown Pensacola and the center of the Palafox Historic District. The commercial and government hub of Old Pensacola is now an active cultural and entertainment district, where locally owned and operated bars and restaurants attract flocks of locals and visitors. The opulent, renovated Spanish Renaissance–style Saenger Theater, Pensacola's 1925 movie palace, hosts performances by the local symphony and opera, as well as national acts, and the Bear Block is a former wholesale grocery with wrought-iron balconies that are a legacy from Pensacola's creole past.

On Palafox between Government and Zaragoza streets is a statue of Andrew Jackson, which commemorates the formal transfer of Florida from Spain to the United States in 1821. While in the area, stop by Veterans Memorial Park, just off Bayfront Parkway near 9th Avenue. The ¾-scale replica of the Vietnam Memorial in Washington, D.C., honors the more than 58,000 Americans who lost their lives in the Vietnam War.

Pensacola Museum of Art. Pensacola's city jail once occupied the 1906 Spanish revival–style building that is now the secure home for the museum's permanent collection of paintings, sculptures, and works on paper by 20th- and 21st-century artists—and we do mean secure:

you can still see the actual cells with their huge iron doors. Traveling exhibits have focused on photography (Wegman, Leibovitz, Ansel Adams), Dutch masters, regional artists, and the occasional art-world icon, such as Andy Warhol or Salvador Dalí. ✉ *407 S. Jefferson St.* ☎ *850/432–6247* 🌐 *www.pensacolamuseumofart.org* 🎟 *$5* 🕒 *Tues.–Fri. 10–5, Sat. noon–5.*

BEACHES

Perdido Key State Park. Part of Gulf Islands National Seashore, this state park is on Perdido Key, a 247-acre barrier island. Its beach, now referred to as Johnson Beach, was one of the few beaches open to African-Americans during segregation. Today the park offers primitive camping year-round. It is within walking distance of dining and nightlife on the key and is a short drive from Alabama. **Amenities:** showers; toilets. **Best for:** sunsets; swimming; walking. ✉ *5 miles southwest of Pensacola off Rte. 292, Perdido Key* 🌐 *www.floridastateparks.org/perdidokey* 🎟 *$3 per vehicle.*

WHERE TO EAT

$$$ SEAFOOD

🍴 **Fish House.** Come one, come all, come hungry, and come at 11 am to witness the calm before the lunch storm. By noon the Fish House is packed with professionals, power players, and poseurs. The wide-ranging menu of fish dishes is the bait, and each can be served in a variety of ways: ginger-crusted, grilled, blackened, pecan-crusted, or Pacific-grilled, which puts any dish over the top. The attentive service, bay-front setting, and signature "Grits a Ya-Ya" (fresh gulf shrimp on a bed of smoked Gouda-cheese grits smothered with a portobello mushroom sauce) keeps diners in the net. Steaks, delicious homemade desserts, a sushi bar, more than 300 varieties of wine, and a full-service bar don't hurt the popularity of this restaurant either. [$] *Average main: $28* ✉ *600 S. Barracks St.* ☎ *850/470–0003* 🌐 *www.fishhousepensacola.com.*

$$$ ECLECTIC

🍴 **Global Grill.** Come hungry to this trendy downtown Pensacola restaurant, and fill your eyes, plate, and belly from the selection of more than 40 different tapas, 11 entrées, and eight salads. Among the tapas are the high-demand lamb lollipops, Israeli couscous, sundried tomato au jus, spicy seared tuna with five-pepper jelly, and the andouille-Manchego empanadas with cucumber cream. To jazz things up, entrées like filet mignon, gulf shrimp, duck breast, fresh fish, and New York strip compete with the light appetizers. [$] *Average main: $26* ✉ *27 S. Palafox St.* ☎ *850/469–9966* 🌐 *www.dineglobalgrill.com* ✍ *Reservations essential* 🕒 *Closed Sun. and Mon. No lunch.*

$$ IRISH

Fodor's Choice ★

🍴 **McGuire's Irish Pub.** Since 1977 this authentic Irish pub has promised its patrons "feasting, imbibery, and debauchery" seven nights a week. A sense of humor pervades the place, evidenced by the range of prices on hamburgers—$10–$100 depending on whether you want it topped with cheddar or served with caviar and champagne. Beer is brewed on the premises, and the wine cellar has more than 8,500 bottles. Menu items include corned beef and cabbage, great steaks, and a hickory-smoked prime rib. In an old firehouse, the pub is replete with antiques, moose heads, Tiffany-style lamps, and Erin-go-bragh memorabilia. As for the "richness" of the decor—on the walls and ceiling are nearly

Like an Old West town with a Victorian twist, historic Pensacola is eye candy for architecture buffs.

$1 million in bills signed and dated by "Irishmen of all nationalities." [$] *Average main: $20* ✉ *600 E. Gregory St.* ☎ *850/433–6789* 🌐 *www.mcguiresirishpub.com.*

WHERE TO STAY

For expanded reviews, facilities, and current deals, visit Fodors.com.

$$$ HOTEL 🏨 **Crowne Plaza–Pensacola Grand Hotel.** On the site of the restored historic Louisville & Nashville (L&N) railroad passenger depot, the Crowne Plaza has a 15-story glass tower, attached to the train depot by a glass atrium, and incredible views of historic Pensacola. **Pros:** great location near downtown; amenities perfect for business travelers. **Cons:** it's a box; there are more intimate choices closer to downtown. [$] *Rooms from: $188* ✉ *200 E. Gregory St.* ☎ *850/433–3336, 800/348–3336* 🌐 *www.pensacolagrandhotel.com* 🛏 *200 rooms, 10 suites.*

$$ B&B/INN 🏨 **New World Inn.** If you like your inns small, warm, and cozy, with the bay on one side and a short two-block walk to the downtown historic area on the other, then this is the inn for you. **Pros:** perfect location downtown; unique boutique hotel. **Cons:** not well suited for kids or large families. [$] *Rooms from: $109* ✉ *600 S. Palafox St.* ☎ *850/432–4111* 🌐 *www.newworldlanding.com* 🛏 *14 rooms, 1 suite* 🍴 *Breakfast.*

$$$ HOTEL 🏨 **Residence Inn by Marriott.** In the downtown bay-front area, this immaculately kept all-suites hotel is perfect for extended stays, whether for business or pleasure. **Pros:** self-serve meal and dining options make a family retreat easier. **Cons:** ordinary hotel style. [$] *Rooms from: $179* ✉ *601 E. Chase St.* ☎ *850/432–0202* 🌐 *www.marriott.com* 🛏 *78 suites* 🍴 *Breakfast.*

NIGHTLIFE

Pensacola offers a wide variety of lively places to enjoy once the sun goes down, from Irish pubs to local watering holes that were once the haunts of old naval heroes. You can sample homegrown concoctions at upscale martini bars and the tunes of local and national music acts at numerous live-music venues.

Hopjacks Pizza Kitchen and Taproom. This restaurant and bar has one of the Panhandle's most extensive selections of specialty beers—more than 150, including 36 on tap. A second location has opened at 204 Nine Mile Road in North Pensacola. ⊠ *10 S. Palafox St.* ☎ *850/497–6073* ⊕ *www.hopjacks.com.*

Hub Stacey's. On the corner by Seville Square, this friendly neighborhood pub has bottled beer, numerous drink specials, sidewalk tables, and a good vibe as well as delicious grub. ⊠ *312 E. Government St.* ☎ *850/469–1001* ⊕ *www.hubstaceys.com.*

McGuire's Irish Pub. Those of Irish descent and anyone else who enjoys cold home-brewed ales, beers, or lagers will feel at home in this restaurant and microbrewery. Its 8,500-bottle wine cellar includes vintages ranging from $14 to $20,000. If you want a quiet drink, steer clear on Friday and Saturday nights—when crowds abound and live entertainment enlivens the masses. ⊠ *600 E. Gregory St.* ☎ *850/433–6789* ⊕ *www.mcguiresirishpub.com.*

Seville Quarter. In the heart of the Historic District is Pensacola's equivalent of New Orleans's French Quarter. In fact, you may think you've traveled to Louisiana when you enter any of its seven bars and two courtyards offering an eclectic mix of live music. College students pack the place on Thursday, tourists come on the weekend, and military men and women from six nearby bases are stationed here nearly all the time. This is a classic Pensacola nightspot. ⊠ *130 E. Government St.* ☎ *850/434–6211* ⊕ *www.sevillequarter.com.*

SHOPPING

The Pensacola area is home to varied shopping. The Palafox and Seville historic districts are enjoyable areas for browsing or buying; here boutiques sell trendy clothing and imported and eclectic home furnishings. Meanwhile, the area's main shopping staple, the Cordova Mall, contains national chain stores.

Cordova Mall. Ten miles north of the historic districts, this mall is anchored by large stores such as Dillard's, Best Buy, and World Market. There are also more than 125 specialty shops and a food court. ⊠ *5100 N. 9th Ave.* ☎ *850/477–5355.*

SPORTS AND THE OUTDOORS
CANOEING AND KAYAKING

The Pensacola Bay area is known as the "Canoe Capital of Florida," and the pure sand-bottom Blackwater River is a particularly nice place to paddle. You can rent canoes and kayaks from a number of local companies as well as from outfits on nearby Perdido Key, home to the picturesque Perdido Watershed.

Adventures Unlimited. This outfitter on Coldwater Creek rents light watercraft as well as campsites and cabins along the Coldwater and Blackwater rivers in the Blackwater State Forest. Though prime canoe season lasts roughly from March through mid-November, Adventures Unlimited rents year-round. ⊠ *Rte. 87* 🕾 *850/623–6197, 800/239–6864* ⊕ *www.adventuresunlimited.com.*

Blackwater Canoe Rental. Canoe and kayak rentals for exploring the Blackwater River are available from this outfitter northeast of Pensacola off Interstate 10 Exit 31. ⊠ *6974 Deaton Bridge Rd., Milton* 🕾 *850/623–0235, 800/967–6789* ⊕ *www.blackwatercanoe.com.*

> **DEEPWATER SPILL**
>
> The beaches of northwest Florida were threatened by the Deepwater Horizon Oil Spill that unraveled in the early months of 2010. Some areas did report pollution in local waterways, but with the capping of the well, many of the area's beaches have cleaned up and reported very limited disturbances. Isolated impacts may still occur, mainly in the form of scattered tar balls; state and local emergency management officials ensure they're removed quickly and efficiently. The beaches largely remain as pure-white and the waters as emerald as they ever were.

14

FISHING

With 52 miles of coastline and a number of inland waterways, the Pensacola area is a great place to drop a line. Bottom fishing is best for amberjack and grouper; offshore trolling trips search for tuna, wahoo, and sailfish; and inshore charters are out to hook redfish, cobia, and pompano. For a complete list of local fishing charters, visit ⊕ *www.pensacolafishing.com.*

Beach Marina. For a full- or half-day deep-sea charter, try the Beach Marina, which represents several charter outfits. ⊠ *655 Pensacola Beach Blvd.* 🕾 *877/650–3474.*

GOLF

The bay area has a number of award-winning and picturesque golf courses. Some offer beach views, and others are local haunts.

Club at Hidden Creek. This 18-hole course is in Santa Rosa County, 20 miles from Pensacola. Greens fees are $25.95–$52.95 (with cart). ⊠ *3070 PGA Blvd., Navarre* 🕾 *850/939–1939* ⊕ *www.hiddengolf.com.*

Lost Key Golf Club. A public, par-71, 18-hole Arnold Palmer Signature Design Course, this was the first golf course in the world to be certified as an Audubon International Silver Signature Sanctuary. Greens fees are $30–$115 (with cart). ⊠ *625 Lost Key Dr.* 🕾 *850/549–2160, 888/256–7853* ⊕ *www.lostkey.com.*

Perdido Bay Golf Club. The 18-hole course here is well-kept. Greens fees are $29–$49 (with cart). ⊠ *1 Doug Ford Dr.* 🕾 *850/492–1223* ⊕ *www.perdidobaygolf.com.*

SCUBA DIVING

USS *Oriskany.* Also called the Mighty O, this retired aircraft carrier was sunk 24 miles off the Pensacola Pass in 2006 to serve as the superstructure of the world's largest artificial reef. The "island" is accessible just 67 feet down, and the flight deck can be reached at 137 feet. A number of dive shops offer charter trips to take divers to the site. ☎ *850/455–7702.*

PENSACOLA BEACH

5 miles south of Pensacola via U.S. 98 to Rte. 399 (Bob Sikes) Bridge.

One of the longest barrier islands in the world, Pensacola Beach offers a low-key, family-friendly feel with many local hangouts, fishing galore, and historic Fort Pickens. Connected to Pensacola by two long bridges, the island offers both a gulf-front and "sound" side for those seeking a calmer seaside experience. Public beaches abound in the area, including Casino Beach at the tip of Pensacola Beach Road, which offers live entertainment at its pavilion in the summer, as well as showers and bathrooms. Quietwater Beach Boardwalk, across the street from Casino Beach, also offers boutique shopping, eateries, and nightlife.

Long home to chain hotels as well as locally owned motels, the beach has opened a number of condominiums and resorts in recent years. Don't miss renting a bike or taking a drive to explore both Fort Pickens Road and J. Earle Bowden Way (connecting Pensacola Beach to the Navarre Beach area), which have reopened after many years of being closed to vehicular traffic. They offer breathtaking, unobstructed views of the gulf.

EXPLORING

Fort Pickens. Constructed of more than 21 million locally made bricks, this fort, dating back to 1834, once served as a prison for Apache chief Geronimo. A National Park Service plaque describes the complex as a "confusing jumble of fortifications," but the real attractions here are the beach, nature exhibits, a large campground, an excellent gift shop, and breathtaking views of Pensacola Bay and the lighthouse across the inlet. It's the perfect place for a picnic lunch and a bit of history, too. ✉ *Fort Pickens Rd., at western tip of island* ☎ *850/934–2635* 💲 *$8 per car* ☉ *Daily 7 am–10 pm.*

BEACHES

Casino Beach. Named for the Casino Resort, the island's first tourist spot when it opened in 1931 (the same day as the first Pensacola Beach Bridge), this beach offers everything from seasonal live entertainment to public restrooms and showers. You can also lounge in the shade of the Pensacola Beach Gulf Pier. Casino Beach has the most parking for beach access on the island and is just a short stroll from dining, entertainment, and major hotels such as the Margaritaville Beach Hotel and Holiday Inn Resort Beachfront Hotel. **Amenities:** food and drink; lifeguards (seasonal); parking (free); showers; toilets. **Best for:** swimming; walking. ✉ *735 Pensacola Beach Blvd.*

Langdon Beach. The Panhandle is home to the Florida District of the Gulf Islands National Seashore, the longest tract of protected seashore in the United States. At the Ft. Pickens area of the park on the gulf-side tip of Santa Rosa Island, this beach is one of the top spots to experience the unspoiled beauty and snow-white beaches this area is known for. Keep an eye out for wildlife of the flying variety; the Fort Pickens area is known for its nesting shorebirds. A large covered pavilion is great for picnicking and a few minutes of shade. **Amenities:** lifeguards; parking (no fee); showers; toilets; water sports. **Best for:** solitude; snorkeling; sunrise; sunset; walking. ⊠ *Fort Pickens Rd., 3 miles west of Pensacola Beach on west end of Santa Rosa Island* ⊕ *www.nps.gov/guis/index.htm.*

WHERE TO EAT

$$
SEAFOOD ✕ **Flounder's Chowder and Ale House.** The wide and peaceful gulf spreads out before you at this casual restaurant where, armed with a fruity libation, you're all set for a night of "floundering" at its best. Funkiness comes courtesy of an eclectic collection of objets d'art; tastiness is served in specialties such as seafood nachos and the shrimp-boat platter. Most signature dishes are charbroiled over a hardwood fire, and to cater to those who love the sea but not seafood, the extensive menu reveals more choices. Live entertainment is presented every night in season, with performances limited to weekends off-season. $ *Average main: $16* ⊠ *800 Quietwater Beach Blvd.* ☎ *850/932–2003* ⊕ *www.flounderschowderhouse.com.*

$$$
SEAFOOD ✕ **Grand Marlin Restaurant and Oyster Bar.** This restaurant offers unforgettable views of Santa Rosa Sound and Pensacola Bay along with mouthwatering fresh local cuisine. Top-notch seafood shares the menu—printed daily—with specials. A creative oyster bar carries the finest oysters from Apalachicola, East Bay, and beyond, shucked to order. $ *Average main: $21* ⊠ *400 Pensacola Beach Blvd.* ☎ *850/677–9153* ⊕ *www.thegrandmarlin.com.*

WHERE TO STAY

For expanded reviews, facilities, and current deals, visit Fodors.com.

$$$
HOTEL ▦ **Hilton Pensacola Beach Gulf Front.** The name is fitting; right on the gulf, this hotel offers incredible views at one of the beach's most affordable prices. **Pros:** impeccably well kept; great dining; affordable. **Cons:** chain hotel. $ *Rooms from: $157* ⊠ *12 Via De Luna* ☎ *850/916–2999, 866/916–2999* ⊕ *www.pensacolabeachgulffront.hilton.com* ⤳ *272 units* ⦿⃝ *No meals.*

$$$
RESORT ▦ **Holiday Inn Resort Pensacola Beach.** Known for its 250-foot lazy river and cascading waterfall, this gulf-front hotel is one of the most family-friendly on the beach. **Pros:** indoor pool; beach-view fitness center. **Cons:** non-gulf-front rooms have views of the parking lot. $ *Rooms from: $200* ⊠ *14 Via de Luna* ☎ *850/932–5331* ⊕ *www.myholidayinnbeachresort.com* ⤳ *206 rooms* ⦿⃝ *No meals.*

$$$$
HOTEL ▦ **Margaritaville Beach Hotel.** This tropical getaway, inspired by the lyrics of Jimmy Buffett, gives you the relaxed, fun Margaritaville experience with the amenities of a top-notch hotel that oozes barefoot elegance. **Pros:** clean, inviting atmosphere; lots of dining options; local spa services available. **Cons:** somewhat off the beaten path to other local dining and nightlife. $ *Rooms from: $299* ⊠ *165 Fort Pickens Rd.* ☎ *850/916–9755* ⊕ *www.margaritavillehotel.com* ⤳ *162 rooms* ⦿⃝ *Multiple meal plans.*

14

SPORTS AND THE OUTDOORS

DOLPHIN-SPOTTING CRUISES

Chase-N-Fins. Climb aboard this 50-foot navy utility launch, which cruises Pensacola Bay along Ft. Pickens, Pensacola Pass, and the Lighthouse at Pensacola Naval Air Station in search of friendly dolphins. Cruises cost $25. ✉ *655 Pensacola Beach Blvd.* ☎ *850/492–6337, 800/967–6789* ⊕ *www.chase-n-fins.com.*

FISHING

Pensacola Beach Gulf Pier. The 1,471-foot-long pier touts itself as the "the most friendly pier around." It hosts serious anglers who find everything they'll need here—from pole rentals to bait—to land that big one, but those looking to catch only a beautiful sunset are welcome, too. Check the pier's website for the latest reports on what's biting. ✉ *41 Fort Pickens Rd.* ☎ *850/934–7200* ⊕ *www.fishpensacolabeachpier.com* ⬚ *$7.50 fishers, $1.25 observers.*

DAYTRIPS FROM PENSACOLA

Inland, where the northern reaches of the Panhandle butt up against the back porches of Alabama and Georgia, you'll find a part of Florida that goes a long way toward explaining why the state song is "Swannee River" (and why its parenthetical title is "Old Folks at Home"). Stephen Foster's musical genius notwithstanding, the inland Panhandle area is definitely more Dixie than Sunshine State, with few lodging options other than the chain motels that flank the Interstate 10 exits and a decidedly slower pace of life than you'll find on the tourist-heavy Gulf Coast.

But the area's natural attractions—hills and farmland, untouched small towns, pristine state parks—make for great day trips from the coast should the sky turn gray or the skin red. Explore underground caverns where eons-old rock formations create bizarre scenes, visit one of Florida's up-and-coming wineries, or poke around small-town America in DeFuniak Springs. Altogether, the inland area of the Panhandle is one of the state's most satisfyingly soothing regions.

DEFUNIAK SPRINGS

77 miles northeast of Pensacola on U.S. 90 off I–10.

This scenic spot has a rather unusual claim to fame: at its center lies a nearly perfectly symmetrical spring-fed lake, one of only two such naturally circular bodies of water in the world (the other is in Switzerland). A sidewalk encircles Lake DeFuniak (also called Circle Lake), which is dotted by pine and shade trees, creating a very pleasing atmosphere for a long-distance mosey. In 1848 the Knox Hill Academy was founded here, and for more than half a century it was the only institution of higher learning in northwestern Florida.

In 1885 the town was chosen as the location for the New York Chautauqua educational society's winter assembly. The Chautauqua programs were discontinued in 1922, but DeFuniak Springs attempts to revive them, in spirit at least, by sponsoring a countywide Chautauqua Festival in April. Christmas is a particularly festive time, when the sprawling Victorian houses surrounding the lake are decorated to the nines.

There's not a tremendous amount to see here, but if you have the good sense to travel U.S. 90 to discover Old Florida, at least take the time to travel Circle Drive to see its beautiful Victorian homes. Also take a little time to walk around the small downtown area and drop in its bookstores, cafés, and small shops.

EXPLORING

Chautauqua Winery. Open since 1989, this winery and its vintages have slowly won respect from oenophiles wary of what was once considered to be an oxymoron at best: "Florida wine." The winery has won honors in national and international competitions, with wines that vary from dry, barrel-fermented wines to Southern favorites like sweet muscadine and blueberry wines. Fourteen vats ranging in size from 1,500 to 6,000 gallons generate a total of 70,000 gallons of wine. Take a free tour to see how ancient art blends with modern technology; then retreat to the tastefully decorated tasting room and gift shop. ✉ *I–10 and U.S. 331* ☎ *850/892–5887* 🌐 *www.chautauquawinery.com.*

TAKE A TOUR

Circle Drive. Some of the finest examples of Victorian architecture in the state can be seen while you are walking or motoring around Circle Drive, the road that wraps around Circle Lake. The circumference is marked with beautiful Victorian specimens like the Walton-DeFuniak Public Library, the Dream Cottage, and the Pansy Cottage. Most of the other notable structures are private residences, but you can still admire them from the street.

WHERE TO STAY

For expanded reviews, facilities, and current deals, visit Fodors.com.

$$ HOTEL

🏨 **Hotel DeFuniak.** You can't miss this sweet, Depression-era two-story red-brick structure on a quiet corner a few blocks from peaceful Lake DeFuniak—just look for the two-tone 1937 Buick permanently moored out front. **Pros:** applause for the owners who created a sweet little retreat in the heart of downtown. **Cons:** DeFuniak can be eerily empty and quiet at night. [$] *Rooms from: $105* ✉ *400 E. Nelson Ave.* ☎ *850/892–4383, 877/333–8642* 🌐 *www.hoteldefuniak.com* 🛏 *8 rooms, 3 suites* 🍴 *Breakfast.*

FALLING WATERS STATE PARK

35 miles east of DeFuniak Springs via U.S. 90 and Rte. 77.

This site of a Civil War–era whiskey distillery and, later, an exotic plant nursery (some species still thrive in the wild) is best known for also being the site of the Falling Waters Sink. The 100-foot-deep cylindrical pit provides the background for a waterfall, and there's an observation deck for viewing this natural phenomenon. The water freefalls 67 feet to the bottom of the sink, but where it goes after that is a mystery. ✉ *1130 State Park Rd., Chipley* ☎ *850/638–6130* 🌐 *www.floridastateparks.org/fallingwaters* 🎟 *$5 per vehicle, up to 8 people* 🕒 *Daily 8–sunset.*

FLORIDA CAVERNS STATE PARK

13 miles northeast of Falling Waters off U.S. 90 on Rte. 166.

A short drive from the center of Marianna, a cute and pristine community, you can see what's behind or—more accurately—what's beneath it all. Ranger-led cave tours reveal stalactites, stalagmites, soda straws, columns, rim stones, flowstones, and "waterfalls" of solid rock at these underground caverns, where the temperature hovers at an oh-so-pleasant 68°F year-round. Some of the caverns are off-limits to the public or open for scientific study by permit only, but you can still see enough to fill a half-day or more—and be amazed that caverns of this magnitude exist in the Sunshine State. Don't forsake the quiet, preserved, and peaceful woodlands, which encompass 10 distinct communities including upland glade, hardwood forests, floodplains, forests, and swamps. There are also hiking trails, campsites, and areas for swimming, horseback riding, and canoeing on the Chipola River. ⊠ *3345 Caverns Rd., off U.S. 90 on Rte. 166, Marianna* ☎ *850/482–9598, 800/326–3521 for camping reservations* ⊕ *www.floridastateparks.org/floridacaverns* ⊠ *Park $5 per vehicle, up to 8 people; caverns $8* ⊙ *Daily 8–sunset; cavern tours Thurs.–Mon. 9–4.*

THE EMERALD COAST

On U.S. 98, several towns, each with its own personality, are strung along the shoreline from Pensacola southeast to St. George Island. The side-by-side cities of Destin and Fort Walton Beach seemingly merge into one sprawling destination and continue to spread as more condominiums, resort developments, shopping centers, and restaurants crowd the skyline each year. The view changes drastically—and for the better—farther along the coast as you veer off 98 and enter Route 30A, the main coastal road that leads to a quiet stretch known as the Beaches of South Walton. Here building restrictions prohibit high-rise developments, and the majority of dwellings are privately owned homes, most of which are available to vacationers.

Continuing southeast on U.S. 98, you come to Panama City Beach, whose Miracle Strip, once crammed with carnival-like amusement parks, junk-food vendors, T-shirt shops, and go-kart tracks, has been nearly replaced by up-to-date shopping and entertainment complexes and new condos that have given the area a much-needed face-lift. Farther east, past the up-and-coming sleeper cities of Port St. Joe and Mexico Beach, is the quiet blue-collar town of Apalachicola, Florida's main oyster fishery. Watch oystermen ply their trade, using long-handled tongs to bring in their catch. Cross the Apalachicola Bay via the Bryant Patton Bridge to St. George Island. This unspoiled 28-mile-long barrier island offers some of America's most scenic beaches, including St. George Island State Park, which has the longest beachfront of any state park in Florida.

GETTING HERE AND AROUND

Northwest Florida Regional Airport, on Highway 85 in North Eglin, is served by American Airlines (American Eagle), Delta (Delta Connection), United Airlines (Express Jet), and US Airways. From here you can take a number of car and cab services, including Checker Cab, to destinations such as Fort Walton Beach ($18) or Destin ($24).

Contacts **Checker Cab** ☎ *850/650–8294.* **Northwest Florida Regional Airport** ☎ *850/651–7160* ⊕ *www.flyvps.com.*

VISITOR INFORMATION

Contacts **Emerald Coast Convention and Visitors Bureau** ☎ *850/651–7131, 800/322–3319* ⊕ *www.emeraldcoastfl.com.*

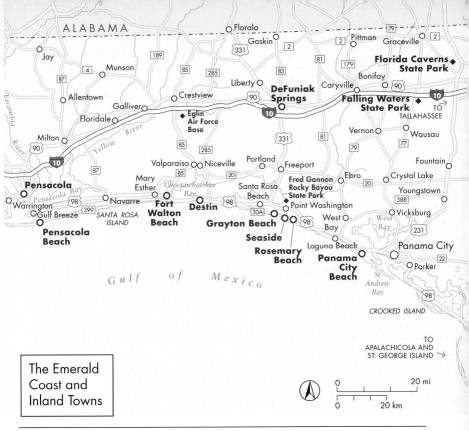

The Emerald
Coast and
Inland Towns

0 _____ 20 mi

0 _____ 20 km

FORT WALTON BEACH

46 miles east of Pensacola via U.S. 98.

This coastal town dates from the Civil War but had to wait more than 75 years to come into its own. Patriots loyal to the Confederate cause organized Walton's Guard (named in honor of Colonel George Walton, onetime acting territorial governor of West Florida) and camped at a site on Santa Rosa Sound, later known as Camp Walton. In 1940 fewer than 90 people lived in Fort Walton Beach, but within a decade the city became a boomtown, thanks to New Deal money for roads and bridges and the development of Eglin Field during World War II.

Although off-limits to civilians, Eglin Air Force Base, which encompasses 724 square miles of land with 10 auxiliary fields and 21 runways, is Fort Walton Beach's main source of income. Tourism runs a close second. Despite inland sprawl, the town has a cute little shopping district with independent merchants along U.S. 98.

EXPLORING

Air Force Armament Museum. The collection at this museum just outside the Eglin Air Force Base's main gate contains more than 5,000 armaments (aka missiles, bombs, and aircraft) from World Wars I and II and the Korean and Vietnam wars. Included are uniforms, engines, weapons, aircraft, and flight simulators. You can't miss the museum—there's a squadron of aircraft including a B-17 Flying Fortress, an SR-71 Blackbird, a B-52, a B-25, and helicopters parked on the grounds in front. A continuously playing 32-minute movie, *Arming the Future*, features current weapons and Eglin's history and its role in their development. ✉ *100 Museum Dr. (Rte. 85), Eglin Air Force Base* ☎ *850/651–1808* 🌐 *www.afarmamentmuseum.com* 🎟 *Free* 🕒 *Mon.–Sat. 9:30–4:30.*

Eglin Air Force Base Reservation. With 810 miles of creeks and plenty of challenging, twisting wooded trails, this 1,045-square-mile base appeals to outdoors enthusiasts who want to hunt, fish, canoe, and swim. You can buy a day pass to hike or mountain bike on the Timberlake Trail. Obtain permits from the Jackson Guard. ✉ *107 Rte. 85 N, Niceville* ☎ *850/882–4164* 🌐 *www.eglin.af.mil* 🎟 *$10 for Timberlake Trail* 🕒 *Trail Mon.–Thurs. 7–4:30, Fri. 7–6, Sat. 7:30–12:30.*

FAMILY **Gulfarium.** This marine adventure park has been a beloved attraction for locals and visitors alike for almost 60 years. In fact, it is the oldest continuously operating marine park in Florida. Species exhibited here include otters, penguins, alligators, harbor seals, and sharks. The summer of 2012 brought a number of fresh offerings, and now you can meander through renovated exhibits and get up close and personal with marine life thanks to several new interactive experiences, from swimming with our watery friends to feedings. For the not so faint of heart, the Stingray Bay Snorkel offers a chance to swim with the creatures as well as sharks, but for an even more intensive experience, there's a five-hour one-on-one with a marine-mammal trainer. ✉ *1010 Miracle Strip* ☎ *850/243–9046, 800/247–8575* 🌐 *www.gulfarium.com* 🎟 *$19.95, animal encounters extra* 🕒 *Daily 9–4:30.*

BEACHES

John Beasley Park. This tranquil seaside park rests among the rolling dunes on Okaloosa Island. Two dune walkovers lead to the beach, where there are a dozen covered picnic tables, pavilions, changing rooms, and freshwater showers—plus lifeguards in summer. The city's hottest nightlife is just down the road, but families can enjoy the scenic beauty. There is also an emphasis on wheelchair beach access. **Amenities:** lifeguards; parking; showers; toilets. **Best for:** sunset; walking. ✉ *Okaloosa Island.*

WHERE TO EAT

$$ AMERICAN 🍴 **Angler's.** Unless you sit in the water, you can't dine any closer to the gulf than at this casual beachside bar and grill next to the Gulfarium. Located at the entrance to Okaloosa Island Pier (and within a complex of other nightclubs and restaurants), Angler's houses the requisite sports bar with televisions broadcasting sports events, including in the elevators and bathrooms. Outside, a volleyball net tempts diners onto the sands. Snack on nachos and quesadillas, sample fresh-catch dishes such as king crab and prawns, or try the smoked tuna dip, a lightly smoked yellowfin tuna dip served with warm, crisp tortilla strips. The waterfront setting is the image of a picturesque Gulf Coast eatery. [$] *Average main: $19* ✉ *1030 Miracle Strip Pkwy.* ☎ *850/796–0260* 🌐 *www.anglersbeachside.com.*

$$$ ✕ **Pandora's Steakhouse and Lounge.** On the Emerald Coast, the name
STEAKHOUSE Pandora's is synonymous with prime rib. Steaks are cooked over a
wood-burning grill, and you can order your prime rib regular or extra-
thick cut; fish aficionados should try the char-grilled yellowfin tuna
or one of the daily specials. Cozy up in an alcove to enjoy your meal
in peace or head to the lounge, where the mood turns a bit more gre-
garious, with live entertainment Wednesday through Saturday. $ *Av-
erage main: $26* ✉ *1226 Santa Rosa Blvd.* ☎ *850/244–8669* ⊕ *www.
pandorassteakhouse.com* ⊗ *Closed Mon. No lunch.*

WHERE TO STAY

For expanded reviews, facilities, and current deals, visit Fodors.com.

$$ ⊞ **Aunt Martha's Bed and Breakfast.** Although it has been pampering and
B&B/INN charming its guests since 2001, Aunt Martha's can transport you back
half a century to when Florida was still a sleepy little state. **Pros:** quiet
sanctuary on the waterfront but with access to dining, shopping, and
sites. **Cons:** not suited for kids and families; primarily for romance and
privacy. $ *Rooms from: $105* ✉ *315 Shell Ave. SE* ☎ *850/243–6702*
⊕ *www.auntmarthasbedandbreakfast.com* ⊸ *5 rooms.*

$$$ ⊞ **Ramada Plaza Beach Resort.** If your family loves the water, splash
RESORT down at this beachside extravaganza, where activity revolves around
a 194,000-gallon pool (allegedly the area's largest) with a spectacular
swim-through waterfall that tumbles down from an island oasis; there's
also a separate kiddie pool, a beachwear and beach-toy shop, and an
800-foot private beach. **Pros:** extravagant offerings for a family-friendly
vacation; the pool may please the kids more than the gulf. **Cons:** may
be too busy for romance travelers or seniors seeking peace and quiet.
$ *Rooms from: $179* ✉ *1500 Miracle Strip Pkwy. SE* ☎ *850/243–9161,
800/874–8962* ⊕ *www.ramadafwb.com* ⊸ *335 rooms, 18 suites.*

NIGHTLIFE

The Boardwalk. This massive dining-and-entertainment complex at the
entrance to the Okaloosa Island Pier includes several restaurants (Crab
Trap, Oyster House, Floyd's Shrimp House, and Angler's) as well as
an assortment of nightclubs. ✉ *1450 Miracle Strip Pkwy.* ⊕ *www.
theboardwalkoi.com.*

Howl at the Moon. Dueling pianos and furious sing-alongs make
this Boardwalk spot extremely popular. The show starts at 8 pm and
rocks until 2. ✉ *1450 Miracle Strip Pkwy., Suite 203* ☎ *850/301–0111.*

SPORTS AND THE OUTDOORS

FISHING

Okaloosa Island Pier. Don't miss a chance to go out to the end of this
¼-mile-long pier. It costs two bucks to walk the plank, $7.50 if you'd
like to fish. (You can buy bait and tackle, and rent poles.) ✉ *1030 Mir-
acle Strip Pkwy. E* ☎ *850/244–1023* ⊕ *www.okaloosaislandpier.com.*

GOLF

Fort Walton Beach Golf Club. This 36-hole municipal course has links
(Oaks and Pines) that lie about 400 yards from each other and are
considered by many to be among Florida's best public layouts. Greens
fees are $18–$41 with a shared cart. ✉ *Rte. 189* ☎ *850/833–9528.*

14

Shalimar Pointe Country Club. There's a pleasing mix of water and bunkers at this 18-hole course. Greens fees are $28–$45 (with cart); if you book online you can save a little money. ⊠ *302 Country Club Dr., Shalimar* ☎ *850/651–1416* ⊕ *www.shalimarpointe.com.*

SCUBA DIVING

Discovery Dive World. Run by military veterans, this full-service snorkeling and dive shop offers a variety of gear and lessons, though they specialize in spear fishing. ⊠ *92 S. John Sims Pkwy., Valapariso* ☎ *850/678–5001* ⊕ *www.discoverydiveworld.com.*

DESTIN

8 miles east of Fort Walton Beach via U.S. 98.

Fort Walton Beach's "neighbor" lies on the other side of the strait that connects Choctawhatchee Bay with the Gulf of Mexico. Destin takes its name from its founder, Leonard A. Destin, a Connecticut sea captain who settled his family here sometime in the 1830s. For the next 100 years, Destin remained a sleepy little fishing village until the strait, or East Pass, was bridged in 1935. Then recreational anglers discovered its white sands, blue-green waters, and abundance of some of the most sought-after sport fish in the world. More billfish are hauled in around Destin each year than from all other gulf ports combined, giving credence to its nickname, the World's Luckiest Fishing Village.

But you don't have to be the rod-and-reel type to love Destin. There's plenty to entertain the sand-pail set as well as senior citizens, and there are many nice restaurants, which you'll have an easier time finding if you remember that the main drag through town is referred to as both U.S. 98 and Emerald Coast Parkway. The name makes sense, but part of what makes the gulf look so emerald in these parts is the contrasting whiteness of the sand on the beach. Actually, it's not sand—it's pure, powder-soft Appalachian quartz that was dropped off by a glacier a few thousand years back. Since quartz doesn't compress (and crews clean and rake the beach each evening), your tootsies get the sole-satisfying benefit of soft, sugary "sand." Sand so pure it squeaks.

ESSENTIALS

Visitor Information Destin Chamber of Commerce ☎ *850/837–6241* ⊕ *www.destinchamber.com.*

EXPLORING

FAMILY **Big Kahuna's Lost Paradise.** The water park is the big draw here, with the Honolulu Half Pipe (a perpetual surfing wave), flume rides, steep and slippery slides, and assorted other methods of expending hydroenergy appealing to travelers who prefer freshwater thrills over the gulf, which is just across the street. This complex also has dry family-friendly attractions: 54 holes of miniature golf, two go-kart tracks, an arcade,

Live oaks draped with Spanish Moss are most common in the Panhandle.

thrill rides, and an amphitheater. ✉ *1007 U.S. 98 E* ☎ *850/837–8319* 🌐 *www.bigkahunas.com* 🎫 *Grounds free, water park $37.99, miniature golf $6.99, go-karts $6.99, Sky Coaster or Cyclone $16.99* ⏲ *Early May–Labor Day, days and hrs vary; land activities also spring break.*

BEACHES

Crab Island. All of the sugary, white-sand beaches of Destin and the surrounding Emerald Coast garner worldwide attention, but this is the locals' favorite. Actually a sandbar in East Pass rather than an island, Crab Island draws water-lovers and boaters, who wade the sandbar or drop anchor in droves on fair-weather days, especially weekends. People are friendly, so it's a great place to make new friends, and the shallow waters are good for families. A food barge comes around the "island" seasonally. **Amenities:** food and drink, water sports. **Best for:** partiers, snorkeling, swimming. ✉ *North side of East Pass and Marler Bridge.*

WHERE TO EAT

$$$ SEAFOOD 🍴 **Marina Café.** A harbor view, impeccable service, and sophisticated fare create one of the finest dining experiences on the Emerald Coast. An ocean motif is expressed in shades of aqua, green, and sand accented with marine tapestries and sea sculptures. The chef calls his creations contemporary Continental, offering diners a choice of thick USDA steaks, classic creole, Mediterranean, or Pan Asian dishes. One regional specialty is the popular pan-seared yellow-edge grouper with a blue-crab-meat crust. A special sushi menu is available, the wine list is extensive, and happy hour runs from 5 to 7. [$] *Average main: $24* ✉ *404 U.S. 98 E* ☎ *850/837–7960* 🌐 *www.marinacafe.com* ⏲ *No lunch.*

WHERE TO STAY

For expanded reviews, facilities, and current deals, visit Fodors.com.

$$$$ RESORT **Emerald Grande at HarborWalk Village.** Even locals seek out the views at this harborfront destination within a destination, with luxurious hotel accommodations and a full menu of amenities, including a full-service spa, marina, health club, and indoor/outdoor pools. **Pros:** great for larger families and groups; many top-rated amenities are part of the complex. **Cons:** very family-oriented, so it's not ideal for a romantic couple's getaway; must water-taxi to the beach. [$] *Rooms from: $487* ✉ *10 Harbor Blvd.* ☎ *800/676–0091* 🌐 *www.emeraldgrande.com* 🛏 *269 rooms.*

$$$$ RESORT Fodor's Choice ★ **Sandestin Golf and Beach Resort.** This place is its own little world—with shopping, charter fishing, spas, salons, tennis, water sports, golf, and special events—so it's no wonder newlyweds, conventioneers, and families all find something for them at this 2,400-acre resort. **Pros:** everything you'd ever need in a resort—and more. **Cons:** lacks the personal touches of a modest retreat. [$] *Rooms from: $239* ✉ *9300 Emerald Coast Pkwy. W* ☎ *850/267–8000, 800/277–0800* 🌐 *www.sandestin.com* 🛏 *1,400 rooms, condos, villas, and town homes.*

NIGHTLIFE

AJ's Seafood & Oyster Bar. Folks come by boat and car to this supercasual bar and restaurant overlooking the marina. Nightly live music means young lively crowds pack the dance floor. ✉ *116 U.S. 98 E* ☎ *850/837–1913* 🌐 *www.ajs-destin.com.*

Harbor Docks. Affiliated with Pensacola's Dharma Blue, this favorite with the local seafaring set has been around since 1979. The incredibly casual feel is marked by picnic tables and hibachi grills. There's live music Thursday through Saturday. There's also a sushi bar. ✉ *538 U.S. 98 E* ☎ *850/837–2506* 🌐 *www.harbordocks.com.*

Hog's Breath Saloon. The festive atmosphere is enhanced by good live music from a solo performer during the week and more musicians on the weekend. The food—steaks, burgers, salads—isn't bad, either. ✉ *541 U.S. 98 E* ☎ *850/837–5991.*

Nightown. This nightclub has an expansive dance floor, VIP access with bottle service, seven bars, live music, pool tables, and plenty of drink specials and themed evenings. It's open Wednesday through Saturday until 4 am. ✉ *140 Palmetto St.* ☎ *850/837–7625* 🌐 *www.nightown.com.*

Sandestin Village of Baytowne Wharf. You can find funky blues, great sushi, and a set of dueling pianos here any night of the week. Music guests have included Graffiti & the Funky Blues Shack and John Wehner's Village Door Nightclub. ✉ *9300 Emerald Coast Pkwy. W* ☎ *800/622–1038.*

SHOPPING

Destin Commons. Don't call it a mall. Call it an "open-air lifestyle center." More than 70 high-end specialty shops are here, as well as a 14-screen theater, Hard Rock Cafe, miniature train, and nautical theme park for kids. ✉ *4300 Legendary Dr.* ☎ *850/337–8700* 🌐 *www.destincommons.com.*

Market at Sandestin. The two dozen or so upscale shops in this elegant Sandestin complex peddle everything from expensive chocolates to designer clothes. ⊠ *9300 Emerald Coast Pkwy. W* ☎ *850/267–8092*.

Shops at Grand Boulevard at Sandestin Town Center. This town center–style shopping and dining complex is on the area's main thoroughfare, just a hop, skip, and jump from the Sandestin Resort. For the high-end shopper, the center offers everything from Fusion Art Glass Gallery to Brooks Brothers Country Club. A number of boutiques, such as Hello, Sunshine and Magnolia House, carry fare you can't find anywhere else. Dining options include Mitchell's Fish Market, P. F. Chang's China Bistro, and Cantina Laredo Gourmet Mexican Food. ⊠ *600 Grand Blvd.* ☎ *850/654–5929* ⊕ *www.grandboulevard.com*.

Silver Sands Factory Stores. One of the Southeast's largest retail designer outlets has more than 100 shops selling top-name merchandise. ⊠ *10562 Emerald Coast Pkwy. W* ☎ *850/654–9771* ⊕ *www.silversandsoutlet.com*.

SPORTS AND THE OUTDOORS

FISHING

Destin has the largest charter-boat fishing fleet in the state. You can also pier-fish from the 3,000-foot-long Destin Catwalk and along East Pass Bridge.

Adventure Charters. This company represents more than 90 charter services that offer deep-sea, bay-bottom, and light-tackle fishing excursions. ⊠ *East Pass Marina, 288 U.S. 98 E* ☎ *850/837–1995* ⊕ *www.destinfishingservice.com*.

Destin Dockside. It's a great place to pick up bait, tackle, and most anything else you'd need for a day of fishing. ⊠ *East Pass Marina, 288 U.S. 98 E* ☎ *850/428–3313* ⊕ *www.boatrentalsindestin.com*.

HarborWalk Marina. At this rustic-looking waterfront complex you can get bait, gas, tackle, and food. Party-fishing-boat excursions cost as little as $55, a cheaper alternative to chartering or renting your own boat. ⊠ *66 Harbor Blvd. (U.S. 98 E)* ☎ *850/337–8250* ⊕ *www.harborwalk-destin.com*.

GOLF

Indian Bayou Golf Club. The club has 27 holes; greens fees are $32–$64 (with cart). ⊠ *1 Country Club Dr. E, off Airport Rd., off U.S. 98* ☎ *850/837–6191* ⊕ *www.indianbayougolf.com*.

Kelly Plantation Golf Club. Designed by Fred Couples and Gene Bates, this semiprivate 18-hole course runs along Choctawhatchee Bay; greens fees are $59–$139 (with cart). ⊠ *307 Kelly Plantation Dr.* ☎ *850/650–7600* ⊕ *www.kellyplantationgolf.com*.

Regatta Bay Golf and Country Club. Here you'll find an 18-hole, semiprivate course. Greens fees are $59–$129. ⊠ *465 Regatta Bay Blvd.* ☎ *850/337–8080* ⊕ *www.regattabay.com*.

Sandestin Golf and Beach Resort. For sheer number of holes, Sandestin tops the list with 72 (four courses). Prices change seasonally, but peak greens fees are: Baytowne Golf Club at Sandestin, $54–$89; Burnt Pines Course, $109–$155; Links Course, $49–$75; and the Raven Golf Club, $79–$129. ⊠ *9300 U.S. 98 W* ☎ *850/267–8211* ⊕ *www.sandestin.com*.

14

SCUBA DIVING

Although visibility here (about 50 feet) isn't on par with the reefs of the Atlantic Coast, divers can explore artificial reefs, wrecks, and a limestone shelf at depths of up to 90 feet.

Emerald Coast Scuba. You can take diving lessons, arrange excursions, and rent all the necessary equipment through this operation. ⊠ *503 Harbor Blvd.* ☎ *850/837–0955* ⊕ *www.divedestin.com.*

BEACHES OF SOUTH WALTON

The 26-mile stretch of coastline between Destin and Panama City Beach is referred to as the Beaches of South Walton. From the middle of this mostly residential stretch of the Panhandle you can see the monolithic condos of Destin and Panama City Beach in either direction, like massive bookends in the distance, flanking the area's low-slung, less imposing structures. A decidedly laid-back, refined mood prevails in these parts, where vacation homes go for millions and selecting a dinner spot is usually the day's most challenging decision.

Accommodations consist primarily of private-home rentals, the majority of which are managed by local real-estate firms. Also scattered along Route 30A are a growing number of boutiques selling everything from fine art and unique hand-painted furniture to jewelry, gifts, and clothes.

ESSENTIALS

Visitor Information Beaches of South Walton Visitor Information Center
☎ *850/267–1216, 800/822–6877* ⊕ *www.beachesofsouthwalton.com.*

GRAYTON BEACH

18 miles east of Destin via U.S. 98 on Rte. 30A (Exit 85).

Inland, pine forests and hardwoods surround the area's 14 dune lakes, giving anglers ample spots to drop a line and kayakers a peaceful refuge. Grayton Beach, the oldest community in this area, was founded in 1890. You can still see some of the old weathered-cypress homes scattered along narrow, crushed-gravel streets. The secluded off-the-beaten-path town has been noticed with the addition of adjacent WaterColor, a high-end development of vacation homes with a stylish boutique hotel as its centerpiece. The architecture is tasteful, development is carefully regulated—no buildings taller than four stories are allowed—and bicycles and kayaks are the preferred methods of transportation. Stringent building restrictions, designed to protect the pristine beaches and dunes, ensure that Grayton maintains its small-town feel and look.

EXPLORING

Eden Gardens State Park. Scarlett O'Hara could be at home here on the lawn of an antebellum mansion amid an arcade of moss-draped live oaks in nearby Point Washington. Tours of the mansion are given every hour on the hour, and furnishings inside the spacious rooms date as far back as the 17th century. The surrounding grounds—the perfect setting for a picnic lunch—are beautiful year-round, but they're nothing short of spectacular in mid-March, when the azaleas and dogwoods are in full bloom. ⊠ *Rte. 395, Point Washington* ☎ *850/267–8320* 🖼 *Gardens $4, mansion tours $4* ☉ *Daily 8–sunset; mansion tours Thurs.–Mon. 10–3.*

Continued on page 749

GONE FISHIN'

by Gary McKechnie

My favorite uncle has a passion for fishing.

It was one I didn't really understand—I'm more of a motorcycle guy, not a fishing pole–toting one. But one day he piqued my curiosity by telling me that fishing has many of the same enticements as motorcycling. Come again? He beautifully described the peaceful process of it all—how the serenity and solitude of the sport wash away concerns about work and tune him into the wonder of nature, just like being on a bike (minus the helmet and curvy highways).

I took the bait, and early one morning a few weeks later, my Uncle Bud and I headed out in a boat to a secluded cove on the St. Johns River near DeLand. We'd brought our rods, line, bait, and tackle—plus hot chocolate and a few things to eat. We didn't need much else. We dropped in our lines and sat silently, watching the fog hover over the water.

There was a peaceful stillness as we waited (and waited) for the fish to bite. There were turtles sunning themselves on logs and herons perched in the trees. We waited for hours for just a little nibble. I can't even recall now if we caught anything, but it didn't matter. My uncle was right: it was a relaxing way to spend a Florida morning.

REEL TIME

Florida is recognized as the "Fishing Capital of the World" as well as the "Bass Capital of the World." It's also home to some of the nation's most popular crappie tournaments.

Florida and fishing have a bond that goes back to thousands of years before Christ, when Paleo-Indians living along Florida's rivers and coasts were harvesting the waters just as readily as they were harvesting the land. Jump ahead to the 20th century and along came amateur anglers like Babe Ruth, Clark Gable, and Gary Cooper vacationing at central Florida fishing camps in pursuit of bream, bluegill, and largemouth bass, while Ernest Hemingway was scouring the waters off Key West in hopes of snagging marlin, tarpon, and snapper. Florida was, and is, an angler's paradise.

A variety of fish and plentiful waterways—7,800 lakes and 1,700 rivers and creeks, not to mention the gulf and the ocean—are just two reasons why Florida is the nation's favorite fishing spot. And let's not forget the frost-free attributes: unlike their northern counterparts, Florida anglers have yet to

When he wasn't writing, Ernest Hemingway loved to fish in the Florida Keys. He's shown here in Key West in 1928.

drill through several feet of ice just to go fishing in the wintertime. Plus, a well-established infrastructure for fishing—numerous bait and tackle shops, boat rentals, sporting goods stores, public piers, and charters—makes it easy for experts and first-time fishermen to get started. For Floridians and the visitors hooked on the sport here, fishing in the Sunshine State is a sport of sheer ease and simplicity.

An afternoon on the waters of Charlotte County in southwest Florida.

CASTING WIDE

The same way Florida is home to rocket scientists and beach bums, it's home to a diverse variety of fishing methods. What kind will work for you depends on where you want to go and what you want to catch.

From the Panhandle south to the Everglades, fishing is as easy as finding a quiet spot on the bank or heading out on freshwater lakes, tranquil ponds, spring-fed rivers, and placid inlets and lagoons.

Perhaps the biggest catches are found offshore—in the Atlantic Ocean, Florida Straits, or the Gulf of Mexico. For saltwater fishing, you can join a charter, be it a private one for small groups or a large party one; head out along the long jetties or public piers that jut into the ocean; or toss your line from the shore into the surf (known as surf casting). Some attempt a tricky yet effective form of fishing called net casting: tossing a circular net weighted around its perimeter; the flattened net hits the surface and drives fish into the center of the circle.

Surf casting on Juno Beach, about 20 mi north of Palm Beach.

FRESHWATER FISHING VS. SALTWATER FISHING

FRESH WATER

With nearly 8,000 lakes to choose from, it's hard to pick the leading contenders, but a handful rise to the top: Lake George, Lake Tarpon, Lake Weohyakapka, Lake Istokpoga, Lake Okeechobee, Crescent Lake, Lake Kissimmee, Lake George, and Lake Talquin. Florida's most popular freshwater game fish is the large-mouth bass. Freshwater fishermen are also checking rivers and streams for other popular catches, such as spotted bass, white bass, Suwannee bass, striped bass, black crappie, bluegill, redear sunfish, and channel catfish.

SALT WATER

The seas are filled with some of the most challenging (and tasty) gamefish in America. From piers, jetties, private boats, and charter excursions, fishermen search for bonefish, tarpon, snook, redfish, grouper, permit, spotted sea trout, sailfish, cobia, bluefish, snapper, sea bass, dolphinfish (the short, squat fish, not Flipper), and sheepshead.

Tarpon

Florida Largemouth Bass

Striped Bass

Black Crappie

Channel Catfish

Bluegill

Redear Sunfish

Bonefish

Dolphinfish (Mahi-Mahi)

Red Snapper

Sheepshead

Snook

Sailfish

(top six) freshwater, (bottom six) saltwater

HERE'S THE CATCH

The type of fish you're after will depend on whether you fish in Florida's lake, streams, and rivers, or head out to sea. The Panhandle has an abundance of red snapper, while Lake Okeechobee is the place for bass fishing— although the largemouth bass is found throughout the state (they're easiest to catch in early spring, when they're in shallower wa- ters). If you're looking for a good charter, Destin has a very large charter-boat fishing fleet. In the Florida Keys, you can fish by walking out in the very shallow water for hundreds of yards with the water only up to your knees; the fish you might reel in this way include bonefish, tarpon, and permit.

CHARTING THE WATERS

TYPE OF TRIP	COST	PROS	CONS
LARGE PARTY BOAT	Approx. $40/person for 4 hrs.	The captain's fishing license covers all passengers; you keep whatever you catch.	Not much privacy, assistance, or solitude: boats can hold as many as 35 passengers.
PRIVATE CHARTER	Roughly $1,200 for up to six people for 9 hrs.	More personal attention and more time on the water.	Higher cost ($200 per person instead of $40); tradition says you split the catch with the captain.
GUIDED TRIP FOR INLAND WATERS	Around $300–$400 for one or two people for 6 hrs.	Helpful if your time is limited and you want to make sure you go where the fish are biting.	Can be expensive and may not be as exciting as deep-sea fishing.
GOING SOLO	Cost for gear (rod, line, bait, and tackle) and license ($30–$100 depending on where you fish and if you need gear).	Privacy, flexibility, your time and destination are up to you; you can get fishing tips from your fellow anglers.	If you require a boat, you need to pay for and operate it yourself, plus pay for gear and a fishing license and find a fishing spot!

14

IN FOCUS GONE FISHIN'

With a little hunting (by calling marinas, visiting bait and tackle stores, asking at town visitor centers), you can find a fishing guide who will lead you to some of the best spots on Florida's lakes and rivers. The guide provides the boat and gear, and his or her license should cover all passengers. A guide is not generally necessary for freshwater fishing, but if you're new to the sport, it might be a worthwhile investment.

On the other hand, if you're looking for fishing guides who can get you into the deep water for tarpon, redfish, snook, snapper, and dolphinfish, your best bet is to hang out at the marinas along the Florida coast and decide whether price or privacy is more important. If it's price, choose one of the larger party boats. If you'd prefer some privacy and the privilege of creating an exclusive passenger list, then sign up for a private charter. The average charter runs about nine hours, but some companies offer overnight and extended trips, too. Gear is provided in both charter-boat methods, and charters also offer the service of cleaning your catch. All guided trips encourage tipping the crew.

Most people new to the sport choose to do saltwater fishing via a charter party boat. The main reasons are expert guidance, convenience, and cost. Plus, fishing with others can be fun. Charter trips depart from marinas throughout Florida.

CREATING A FLOAT PLAN

If you're fishing in a boat on your own, let someone know where you're headed by providing a float plan, which should include where you're leaving from, a description of the boat you're on, how many are in the boat with you, what survival gear and radio equipment you have onboard, your cell phone number, and when you expect to return. If you don't return as expected, your friend can call the Coast Guard to search for you. Also be sure to have enough life jackets for everyone on board.

RULES AND REGULATIONS

To fish anywhere in (or off the coast of) Florida, you need a license, and there are separate licenses for freshwater fishing and saltwater fishing.

For non-residents, either type of fishing license cost $47 for the annual license, $30 for the 7-day one, or $17 for a 3-day license. Permits/tags are needed for catching snook ($10), crawfish/lobster ($5), and tarpon ($51.50). License and permit costs help generate funds for the Florida Fish and Wildlife Conservation Commission, which reinvests the fees into ensuring healthy habitats to sustain fish and wildlife populations, to improve access to fishing spots, and to help ensure public safety.

You can purchase your license and permits at county tax collectors' offices as well as wherever you buy your bait and tackle, such as Florida marinas, specialty stores, and sporting goods shops. You can also buy it online at ⊕ www.myfwc.com/license and have it mailed to you; a surcharge is added to online orders.

If you're on a charter, you don't need to get a license. The captain's fishing license covers all passengers. Also, some piers have their own saltwater fishing licenses that cover you when you're fishing off them for recreational purposes—if you're pier fishing, ask the personnel at the tackle shop if the pier is covered.

RESOURCES

For the latest regulations on gear, daily limits, minimum sizes and seasons for certain fish, and other fishing requirements, consult the extraordinary **Florida Fish and Wildlife Conservation Commission** (☎ 850/488–4676 ⊕ www.myfwc.com).

WEB RESOURCES
Download the excellent, and free, Florida Fishing PDF at www.visitflorida.com/guides. Other good sites:
www.floridafishinglakes.net
www.visitflorida.com/fishing
www.floridasportsman.com

BEACHES

Fodor's Choice ★ **Grayton Beach State Park.** This is the place to see what Florida looked like when only American Indians lived here. One of the most scenic spots along the Gulf Coast, this 2,220-acre park is composed primarily of untouched Florida woodlands within the Coastal Lowlands region. It also has salt marshes, rolling dunes covered with sea oats, crystal-white sand, and contrasting blue-green waters. The park has facilities for swimming, fishing, and snorkeling, and there's an elevated boardwalk that winds over the dunes to the beach, as well as walking trails around the marsh and into the piney woods. Notice that the "bushes" you see are actually the tops of full-size slash pines and Southern magnolias, an effect created by the frequent shifting of the dunes. Even if you're just passing by, the beach here is worth a stop. Thirty fully equipped cabins and a campground provide overnight options. **Amenities:** fishing; parking (fee); showers; toilets; water sports. **Best for:** snorkeling; sunrise; swimming; walking. ✉ *357 Main Park Rd., off Rte. 30A* ☎ *850/267–8300* ⊕ *www.floridastateparks.org/ graytonbeach* 💲 *$5 per vehicle, up to 8 people; $2 pedestrians/cyclists* ⊙ *Daily 8–sunset.*

> ### WORD OF MOUTH
>
> "You might want to look into the cabins at the state park on Grayton Beach. This is the 'real' Florida, with a beach ranked among the best in the nation."
>
> —FlaAnn

14

WHERE TO EAT

$$$ ECLECTIC Fodor's Choice ★ ╳ **Fish Out of Water.** Time your appetite to arrive at sunset and you'll witness the best of both worlds: sea oats lumbering on gold-dusted dunes outside and a stylish interior that sets new standards of sophistication for the entire Panhandle. Colorful, handblown-glass accent lighting that "grows" out of the hardwood floors, plush taupe banquettes, oversize handmade lamp shades, and a sleek bar area create an atmosphere worthy of the inventive cuisine. Menus are seasonal, but often range in influences from Southern (Low Country shrimp and scallops with creamy grits) to classic Continental, but all are convincingly wrought and carefully presented. The extensive wine list keeps pace with the menu offerings. 💲 *Average main: $26* ✉ *34 Goldenrod Circle, 2nd fl. of WaterColor Inn, Santa Rosa Beach* ☎ *850/534–5050* ⊕ *www.watercolorresort.com* ⊙ *No lunch.*

$$ SEAFOOD ╳ **Picolo Restaurant and Red Bar.** You could spend weeks here just taking in all the funky-junky, eclectic toy-chest memorabilia—from Marilyn Monroe posters to flags to dolls—dangling from the ceiling and tacked to every available square inch of wall. The contemporary menu is small, although it includes what you'd expect to find in the Panhandle: crab cakes, shrimp, and crawfish, to name a few. It also serves breakfast. In season, it can feed hundreds of people a day, so expect a wait. Blues and jazz musicians play nightly in the Red Bar. You can't make up a place like this. 💲 *Average main: $20* ✉ *70 Hotz Ave., Santa Rosa Beach* ☎ *850/231–1008* ⊕ *www.theredbar.com* ▭ *No credit cards.*

If you saw *The Truman Show,* you may recognize several places in Seaside, where the movie was filmed.

WHERE TO STAY

$$ RENTAL

Cabins at Grayton Beach State Park. Back-to-nature enthusiasts and families love to visit these stylish accommodations set among the sand pines and scrub oaks of this pristine state park. **Pros:** rare and welcome preservation of Old Florida; pure peace and quiet; what a gulf vacation is meant to be. **Cons:** if you're accustomed to abundant amenities, you won't find them here. [$] *Rooms from: $130* ✉ *357 Main Park Rd., Santa Rosa Beach* ☎ *800/267–8300* ⇒ *30 cabins.*

$$$$ HOTEL Fodor's Choice ★

WaterColor Inn and Resort. Nature meets seaside chic at this boutique property, the crown jewel of the area's latest—and largest—planned communities. **Pros:** perhaps the ultimate vacation experience on the gulf; upscale and fancy. **Cons:** you may feel like it caters exclusively to Ivy Leaguers and CEOs, which might make it hard to relax. [$] *Rooms from: $333* ✉ *34 Goldenrod Circle, Santa Rosa Beach* ☎ *850/534–5000* 🌐 *www.watercolorresort.com* ⇒ *60 rooms* 🍴 *Breakfast.*

NIGHTLIFE

Red Bar. The local watering hole presents red-hot blues or jazz acts every night. On Friday and Saturday nights it's elbow-to-elbow at the truly funky and colorful bar, which would be right at home on Miami's South Beach or in New York City's Greenwich Village. ✉ *70 Hotz Ave., Santa Rosa Beach* ☎ *850/231–1008.*

SHOPPING

Shops of Grayton. In the eight cottages of this colorful complex you can buy gifts, artwork, and antiques. ✉ *Rte. 283, 2 miles south of U.S. 98.*

SPORTS AND THE OUTDOORS

YOLO Board. The biggest craze in the region is YOLO ("You Only Live Once") Boarding, or stand-up paddling, on what looks like a surfboard. It can be found at many resorts in the region and privately through YOLO Board. ✉ *250 WaterColor Blvd., Santa Rosa Beach* ☎ *850/622–5760* 🌐 *www.yoloboard.com.*

SEASIDE

2 miles east of Grayton Beach on Rte. 30A.

This thriving planned community with old-fashioned Victorian architecture, brick streets, restaurants, retail stores, and a surfeit of art galleries was the brainchild of Robert Davis. Dubbed New Urbanism, the development style was designed to promote a neighborly, old-fashioned lifestyle. There's much to be said for an attractive, billboard-free village where you can park your car and walk everywhere you need to go. Pastel-color homes with white-picket fences, front-porch rockers, and captain's walks are set along redbrick streets, and all are within walking distance of the town center and its unusual cafés and shops. The community is so reminiscent of a storybook town that producers chose it for the set of the 1998 film *The Truman Show,* starring Jim Carrey.

The community has come into its own in the last few years, achieving a comfortable, lived-in look and feel that had escaped it since its founding in the late 1970s. Some of the once-shiny tin roofs are starting to rust around the edges and the foliage has matured, creating pockets of privacy and shade. There are also more signs of a real neighborhood with bars and bookstores added to the mix. Still, although Seaside's popularity continues to soar, it retains a suspicious sense of *Twilight Zone* perfection that can weird out some visitors.

Other planned neighborhoods, variations on the theme pioneered by Seaside's founders, have carved out niches along the dozen miles of Route 30A east to Rosemary Beach. The focus in Rosemary Beach is on preserving the local environment (the landscape is completely made up of indigenous plants) and maintaining its small-town appeal. A nascent sense of community is sprouting at the Town Green, a perfect patch of manicured lawn fronting the beach, where locals gather with their wineglasses to toast the sunset. In total, the Beaches of South Walton touts 15 of these New Urbanism–style beach communities and resorts.

WHERE TO EAT

$$$ EUROPEAN 🍴 **Bud & Alley's.** This down-to-earth beachside bistro (named for a pet cat and dog) has been a local favorite since 1986. Tucked in the dunes by the gulf, the rooftop Tarpon Club bar makes a great perch for a sunset toast (guess the exact moment the sun will disappear and win a drink). Daily salad specials are tangy introductions to such entrées as grilled black grouper, seared diver scallops with creamy grits, a marinated pork chop with sweet-potato hash browns, and a taco and pizza bar. [$] *Average main: $30* ✉ *2236 E. Rte. 30A* ☎ *850/231–5900* 🌐 *www.budandalleys.com.*

$$$$ EUROPEAN 🍴 **Café Thirty-A.** About a mile and half east of Seaside in a beautiful Florida-style home with high ceilings and a wide veranda, this restaurant has an elegant look—bolstered by white linen tablecloths—and impeccable service. The menu changes nightly and includes such entrées

as wood-oven-roasted wild king salmon, sesame-crusted rare yellowfin tuna, and grilled Hawaiian butterfish. Even if you're not a Southerner, you should try the appetizer of grilled Georgia quail with creamy grits and sage fritters. With nearly 20 creative varieties, the martini menu alone is worth the trip. [$] *Average main: $32* ✉ *3899 E. Rte. 30A, Seagrove Beach* ☎ *850/231–2166* 🌐 *www.cafethirtya.com* ✍ *Reservations essential* ⏲ *No lunch.*

$$$ SEAFOOD 🍴 **Great Southern Cafe.** Jim Shirley, founder of Pensacola's very popular Fish House, brought Grits a Ya Ya to this restaurant on Seaside's town square. Breakfast is served from 8 to 11, when the menu segues to regional fare, including gulf shrimp, Apalachicola oysters, and fresh sides such as collards, okra, black-eyed peas, fried green tomatoes, and sweet potatoes. Oysters and po'boys stuffed with shrimp bring a little of N'awlins to the beach. Beer and wine and a full liquor bar are here to boot. [$] *Average main: $24* ✉ *83 Central Sq.* ☎ *850/231–7327* 🌐 *www.thegreatsoutherncafe.com.*

WHERE TO STAY

For expanded hotel reviews, visit Fodors.com.

$$$ RENTAL 🏨 **Seaside Cottage Rental Agency.** When residents aren't using their pricey one- to six-bedroom, porticoed, faux-Victorian cottages, they rent them out. **Pros:** gulf breezes blowing off the water; unspoiled sugar-white beaches a short stroll away. **Cons:** not much here for those who want the comforts of a full-service hotel. [$] *Rooms from: $198* ✉ *2311 E. Rte. 30A, Santa Rosa Beach* ☎ *850/231–2222, 866/966–2565 reservations* 🌐 *www.cottagerentalagency.com* 🛏 *275 units.*

SHOPPING

Seaside's central square and open-air market, along Route 30A, offer a number of unusual and whimsical boutiques carrying clothing, jewelry, and arts and crafts. In the heart of Seaside there's a collection of small shops and artists' galleries in an area called Ruskin Place that has everything from toys and pottery to fine works of art.

Perspicacity. This shop sells simply designed women's clothing and accessories perfect for easy, carefree, beach-town casualness. ✉ *178 Market St.* ☎ *850/231–5829.*

SPORTS AND THE OUTDOORS

Butterfly Bike & Kayak. A few miles from Seaside in Seagrove Beach, this outfitter rents bikes, kayaks, scooters, and golf carts and has free delivery and pickup. ✉ *3657 E. Rte. 30A* ☎ *850/231–2826* 🌐 *www.butterflybikerentals.com.*

SeaOats Beach Service. Whether it's a beach fire or surf lessons, this local couple's love for the beach shows through in a wide variety of luxury beach services. They don't have a brick-and-mortar store, but will meet you on the beach instead. ☎ *850/951–3632* 🌐 *www.seaoatsbeachservice.com.*

YOLO Board. The biggest craze in the region is YOLO ("You Only Live Once") Boarding, or stand-up paddling, on what looks like a surfboard. It can be found at many resorts in the region and privately through YOLO Board. ✉ *250 WaterColor Blvd., Santa Rosa Beach* ☎ *850/622–5760* 🌐 *www.yoloboard.com.*

PANAMA CITY BEACH

21 miles southeast of Seaside off U.S. 98.

In the early 2000s a dizzying number of high-rises built along the Miracle Strip—about two dozen in total—led to the formation of a new moniker for this stretch of the Panhandle: the "Construction Coast." This spate of invasive growth turned the main thoroughfare, Front Beach Road, into a dense mass of traffic that peaks in spring and between June and August, when college students descend en masse from neighboring states. The bright side of the changing landscape is that many of the attractions that gave parts of this area a seedy reputation (i.e., strip joints and dive bars) were driven out and replaced by new retailers and the occasional franchise "family" restaurant or chain store.

The one constant in this sea of change is the area's natural beauty, which, in some areas at least, manages to excuse its gross over-commercialization. The shoreline in town is 17 miles long, so even when a mile is packed with partying students, there are 16 more where you can toss a beach blanket and find the old motels that managed to survive. What's more, the beaches along the Miracle Strip, with their powder-soft sand and translucent emerald waters, are some of the finest in the state; in one sense, anyway, it's easy to understand why so many condos are being built here.

Cabanas, umbrellas, sailboats, WaveRunners, and floats are available from any of dozens of vendors along the beach. To get an aerial view, for about $30 you can strap yourself beneath a parachute and go parasailing as you're towed aloft behind a speedboat a few hundred yards offshore. And St. Andrews State Park, at the southeast end of the beaches, is treasured by locals and visitors alike. The incredible white sands, navigable waterways, and plentiful marine life that once attracted Spanish conquistadors today draw invaders of the vacationing kind—namely families, the vast majority of whom hail from nearby Georgia and Alabama. ■ TIP→ When coming here, be sure to set your sights for Panama City Beach. Panama City is its beachless inland cousin.

GETTING HERE AND AROUND

The Northwest Florida Beaches International Airport opened in May 2010 on the east shore of Panama City's West Bay, with routes operated by Delta and Southwest. From the airport to the beach area, depending on the location of your hotel, it's about $15–$27 by taxi. Try Yellow Cab or Checker Cab.

When navigating Panama City Beach by car, don't limit yourself to Front Beach Road—the stop-and-go traffic will drive you nuts. You can avoid the congestion by following parallel roads like Back Beach Road and U.S. 98. Also, anywhere along this long stretch of beachfront, look for "sunrise" signs, which indicate an access point to the beach. They're a treasure to find, especially when you happen across one in the midst of a quiet residential neighborhood and know that a private, quiet beach experience is just a few feet away. The Baytown Trolley serves Bay County, including downtown Panama City and the beaches ($1.50, $3 for an all-day pass).

Get up close and personal with intriguing seashells on undeveloped Shell Island.

Contacts Baytown Trolley ☎ *850/769–0557* ⊕ *www.baytowntrolley.org.*
Checker Cab ☎ *850/236–6666.* **Northwest Florida Beaches**
International Airport ☎ *850/763–6751* ⊕ *www.iflybeaches.com.*
Yellow Cab ☎ *850/763–4691.*

VISITOR INFORMATION

Contacts Panama City Beach Convention and Visitors Bureau
✉ *17001 Back Beach Rd.* ☎ *850/233–5070, 800/722–3224*
⊕ *www.visitpanamacitybeach.com.*

EXPLORING

FAMILY **Gulf World Marine Park.** It's certainly no SeaWorld, but with a tropical garden, tropical-bird theater, plus alligator and otter exhibits, the park is still a winner with kids. The stingray-petting pool and the shark-feeding and scuba demonstrations are big crowd pleasers, and the old favorites—performing sea lions, otters, and bottlenose dolphins—still hold their own. If you're particularly interested, consider a specialty program, such as Trainer for a Day, which takes you behind the scenes to assist in food preparation and training sessions and lets you make an on-stage appearance in the Dolphin Show. The $250, six-hour program includes a souvenir photo, lunch, and trainer T-shirt. ✉ *15412 Front Beach Rd.* ☎ *850/234–5271* ⊕ *www.gulfworldmarinepark.com* ✉ *$28* ☉ *Late May–early Sept., daily 9–7; call for hrs at other times.*

FAMILY **St. Andrews State Park.** At the southeastern tip of Panama City Beach, Fodor's Choice the hotels and condos and traffic stop, and there suddenly appears a ★ pristine 1,260-acre park that offers a peek at what the entire beach area looked like before developers sank their claws into it. Here are beaches, pinewoods, and marshes with places to swim, pier-fish, and hike on clearly marked nature trails. A rock jetty creates a calm, shallow play area that is perfect for young children. There are also camping facilities and a snack bar. Board a ferry to Shell Island—a 700-acre barrier island in the Gulf of Mexico with some of the best shelling between here and southwest Florida's Sanibel Island. ⊠ *4607 State Park La.* ☎ *850/233–5140* ⊕ *www.floridastateparks.org* ✉ *$8 per vehicle, up to 8 people* ⊙ *Daily 8–sunset.*

FAMILY **Shipwreck Island Waterpark.** Once part of the now-defunct Miracle Strip Amusement Park operation, this 6-acre water park has everything from speedy slides and tubes to the slow-moving Lazy River. Oddly enough, admission is based on height: 50 inches, $33; between 35 and 50 inches, $28; under 35 inches, free. Wear flats. ⊠ *12201 Middle Beach Dr.* ☎ *850/234–3333* ⊕ *www.shipwreckisland.com* ✉ *$33* ⊙ *Mid-Apr.– May, weekends and some weekdays 10:30–4:30; June–early Aug., daily 10:30–5; mid-Aug.–early Sept., Sat. and some other days, 10:30–4:30.*

BEACHES

Mexico Beach. Just over 30 miles east of Panama City along scenic U.S. 98, this jewel of a beach is refreshingly free of the high-rises that populate many parts of Panama City Beach itself. Home to colorful, gracefully aging beach houses, the beach offers seclusion and a slower pace than its neighbor to the west. **Amenities:** food and drink; parking. **Best for:** solitude. ⊠ *U.S. 98, 35 miles east of Panama City Beach, Mexico Beach* ☎ *888/723–2546.*

Panama City Beach. With 27 miles of shoreline, the beaches of Panama City offer the same pure white sand and emerald-green waters as its neighbors. Here, however, the coastline is dotted with high-rises rather than unspoiled nature. On the plus side, there are plenty of places to play, swim, splash, and feast, and there's no excuse for getting bored or hungry. Although it was once known as party central, Panama City Beach is becoming more family-friendly. **Amenities:** lifeguards; parking; showers; toilets; water sports. **Best for:** partiers; swimming. ⊠ *Front Beach Rd., between U.S. 98 and St. Andrews State Park* ☎ *800/722–3224.*

WHERE TO EAT

$$ ╳ **Billy's Steamed Seafood Restaurant, Oyster Bar, and Crab House.** Join the
SEAFOOD throng of locals who really know their seafood. Then roll up your sleeves and dig into some of the gulf's finest blue crabs and shrimp seasoned to perfection with Billy's special recipe. Homemade gumbo, crawfish, shrimp, crab claws, fish tacos, whole lobsters, and the day's catch as well as sandwiches and burgers round out the menu. It's no-frills dining, but you may get a kick out of hanging out with some real Florida folks who consider table manners optional. $ *Average main: $16* ⊠ *3000 Thomas Dr.* ☎ *850/235–2349* ⊕ *www.billysoysterbar.com* ⊙ *Closed early Jan.*

$$$ ╳ **Boar's Head.** An exterior that looks like an oversize thatch-roof cot-
AMERICAN tage sets the mood for dining in this ersatz-rustic restaurant and tavern. Inside you'll find the dark woods and dim lighting of steak restaurants of the 1970s, which is understandable considering that Boar's Head opened in 1978. From opening day, prime rib has been the number-one

people pleaser—with blackened seafood and broiled shrimp with crab-meat stuffing always a close second. Its motto: "Good food, simply prepared." $ *Average main: $25* ✉ *17290 Front Beach Rd.* ☎ *850/234–6628* ⊕ *www.boarsheadrestaurant.com* ☾ *Closed Mon. No lunch.*

$$$ ✗**Boatyard.** The same folks who operate Schooners on the beach side
SEAFOOD   opened this larger, more stylish establishment overlooking a marina on the Grand Lagoon. For dinner, choose from the five-spice seared tuna, spicy bowtie pasta with shrimp, or the aptly named Fried Shrimp You Can't Live Without. The shrimp and grits is a knockout (this is definitely the South). There are a kids' menu, an extensive wine list, a full bar, and flat-screen televisions, and the upstairs deck area is a great place to get away from the beach for a long, lazy lunch or romantic sunset dinner. Boatyard kicks into high gear at sundown, transforming into one of the hottest nightspots in town. $ *Average main: $23* ✉ *5325 N. Lagoon Dr.* ☎ *850/249–9273* ⊕ *www.boatyardclub.com.*

$$$ ✗**Capt. Anderson's.** Come early to watch the boats unload the catch of
SEAFOOD   the day on the docks and to beat the long line that forms each after-noon at this noted restaurant with a real family feel. Here since 1953, it doesn't seem to have changed much and that's a good thing. A nauti-cal theme is reinforced by tables made of hatch covers in the attached bar, which attracts longtime locals. The Greek specialties aren't limited to feta cheese and shriveled olives. Charcoal-broiled grouper, amber-jack, and yellowfin tuna; crab-stuffed jumbo shrimp; stuffed fillet of grouper; whole oven-broiled stuffed Florida lobster; and steaks are prominent on the menu as well. If you're visiting in the off-season, call to make sure it's adhering to the posted hours before venturing out. $ *Average main: $30* ✉ *5551 N. Lagoon Dr.* ☎ *850/234–2225* ⊕ *www.captainandersons.com* ⌒ *Reservations not accepted* ☾ *Closed Sun. and Nov.–Jan. No lunch.*

$$$ ✗**Schooners.** Thanks to a clientele that's mostly local, this beachfront
SEAFOOD   spot—which is really tucked away down a small avenue—bills itself as the "last local beach club," and more boldly, "the best place on Earth." It's actually a perfect spot for a casual family lunch or early dinner: kids can have burgers and play on the beach while Mom and Dad enjoy grown-up drinks and more substantial fare such as homemade gumbo, steak, or simply prepared seafood like crab-stuffed shrimp, gulf-fresh grouper, and grilled tuna steaks. One sign of Schooners' casual atmo-sphere is the ceremonial firing of the cannon when the sun disappears into the gulf, a crowd favorite that fires up an all-around good vibe. Late-night folks pile in for live music and dancing. $ *Average main: $17* ✉ *5121 Gulf Dr.* ☎ *850/235–3555* ⊕ *www.schooners.com.*

WHERE TO STAY

For expanded reviews, facilities, and current deals, visit Fodors.com.

$$$ 🏨**Edgewater Beach Resort.** You can sleep at least four and as many as
RESORT   eight in the luxurious one-, two-, and three-bedroom apartments in beachside towers and golf course villas. **Pros:** variety of lodging options; 110 acres of beautiful beachfront property. **Cons:** overwhelming for those looking for a quiet getaway. $ *Rooms from: $219* ✉ *11212 Front Beach Rd.* ☎ *855/874–8686 information, 877/278–0544 reservations* ⊕ *www.edgewaterbeachresort.com* ⇲ *520 apartments.*

$$$ HOTEL **Legacy by the Sea.** Nearly every room at this 14-story, pastel-peach hotel has a private balcony with commanding gulf views. **Pros:** shopping, dining, and attractions are within walking distance; all the amenities a family (or college kids) need. **Cons:** in the heart of a crowded and congested district; can be difficult to access in peak seasons. [$] *Rooms from: $143* ✉ *15325 Front Beach Rd.* ☎ *850/249–8601, 888/886–8917* 🌐 *www.legacybythesea.com* 🛏 *139 rooms and suites* 🍴 *Breakfast.*

$$$ RESORT Fodor's Choice ★ **Wyndham Bay Point Resort.** Across the Grand Lagoon from St. Andrews State Park, this expansive property exudes elegance. **Pros:** quiet and away from the madness of Panama City Beach; complete range of services and activities. **Cons:** may be too expansive and generic for those seeking a small, intimate resort. [$] *Rooms from: $159* ✉ *4114 Jan Cooley Dr.* ☎ *850/236–6000, 877/999–3223 reservations* 🌐 *www.wyndham.com/hotels/ECPWR/main.wnt* 🛏 *316 rooms, 60 1- and 2-bedroom golf villas.*

14

NIGHTLIFE

Boatyard. This multilevel, indoor-outdoor waterfront nightclub and restaurant presents a regular lineup of bands, ranging from blues to steel drums to classic rock. DJs round out the entertainment roster. ✉ *5325 N. Lagoon Dr.* ☎ *850/249–9273* 🌐 *www.boatyardclub.com.*

Club La Vela. Among the offerings that guarantee a full-tilt party here are a slate of concerts (acts have included Aerosmith, Creed, and Ludacris); international DJs; 48 bar stations; swimming pools; a tropical waterfall; and dance halls with names like Thunderdome, Underground, Night Gallery, Rock Arena, and the Pussykat Lounge. At spring-break time this club is transformed into a whirlpool of libido. ✉ *8813 Thomas Dr.* ☎ *850/234–1061, 850/234–3866* 🌐 *www.clublavela.com.*

Pineapple Willy's. This eatery and bar is geared to families and tourists—as well as sports fans. The signature rum drink, the Pineapple Willy, was the inspiration for its full slate of tropical drinks and the hangout's tiki attitude. ✉ *9875 S. Thomas Dr.* ☎ *850/235–0928* 🌐 *www.pwillys.com.*

SHOPPING

Pier Park. Occupying a huge swath of land that was once an amusement park, this diverse 900,000-square-foot entertainment/shopping/dining complex creates the downtown that Panama City Beach lacked. Anchor stores including Dillard's, JCPenney, and Target keep things active during the day, and clubs like Jimmy Buffett's Margaritaville and the 16-screen Grand Theatre keep things hopping after dark. Other stores, such as Ron Jon Surf Shop and Fresh Market, offer even more reason to see this vibrant and enjoyable complex. ✉ *600 Pier Park Dr.* ☎ *850/236–9974* 🌐 *www.simon.com/Mall/?id=1204.*

SPORTS AND THE OUTDOORS

CANOEING

Econfina Creek Canoe Livery. Rentals for a trip down Econfina Creek—known as Florida's most beautiful canoe trail—are supplied by this outfitter. Single kayaks are $40; double kayaks and canoes rent for $50. No checks or credit cards. ✉ *Strickland Rd., north of Rte. 20, Youngstown* ☎ *850/722–9032* 🌐 *www.canoeeconfinacreek.net.*

GOLF

Hombre Golf Club. This 27-hole club occasionally hosts professional tours. Greens fees are $25–$54 with cart. ✉ *120 Coyote Pass* ☎ *850/234–3673* ⊕ *www.hombregolfclub.com.*

Wyndham Bay Point Resort. There are two courses open to the public at this country club: the Nicklaus Course and the Meadows Course. Greens fees are $22–$62. ✉ *4200 Marriott Dr.* ☎ *850/235–6950, 877/235–6950* ⊕ *www.baypointgolf.com.*

SCUBA DIVING

Snorkeling and scuba diving are extremely popular in the clear waters here. If you have the proper certification, you can dive among dozens of ships sunk by the city to create artificial reefs.

Panama City Dive Center. Here you can arrange for instruction, gear rental, and charters. Two-day "Wreck Daze," for those interested in wreck diving, include boat accommodations and guides. ✉ *4823 Thomas Dr.* ☎ *850/235–3390* ⊕ *www.pcdivecenter.com.*

APALACHICOLA

65 miles southeast of Panama City Beach off U.S. 98.

It feels like a long haul between Panama City Beach and here. Add an odd name and a town's below-the-radar reputation to that long drive and you may be tempted to skip Apalachicola. But you shouldn't. It's a weirdly fascinating town that, for some reason, has a growing cosmopolitan veneer. And that makes it worth a visit.

Meaning "land of the friendly people" in the language of its original Native American inhabitants, Apalachicola—known in these parts as simply Apalach—lies on the Panhandle's southernmost bulge. European settlers began arriving in 1821, and by 1847 the southern terminus of the Apalachicola River steamboat route was a bustling port town. Although the town is now known as the Oyster Capital of the World, oystering became king only after the local cotton industry flagged—the city's extra-wide streets, built to accommodate bales of cotton awaiting transport, are a remnant of that trade—and the sponge industry moved down the coast after depleting local sponge colonies.

But the newest industry here is tourism, and visitors have begun discovering the Forgotten Coast, as the area is known, flocking to its intimate hotels and bed-and-breakfasts, dining at excellent restaurants, and browsing in unique shops selling anything from handmade furniture to brass fixtures recovered from nearby shipwrecks. If you like oysters or want to go back in time to the Old South of Gothic churches and spooky graveyards, Apalachicola is a good place to start.

VISITOR INFORMATION

Contacts Apalachicola Bay Chamber of Commerce ☎ *850/653–9419* ⊕ *www.apalachicolabay.org.*

Twenty percent of the state's shrimp and 10% of the country's oysters come from Apalachicola Bay.

WHERE TO EAT

$ SEAFOOD 🍴 **Apalachicola Seafood Grill.** Where will you find the world's largest fish sandwich? Right here in downtown Apalachicola. Here since 1908, this is where the locals go for lunch and dinner, noshing on blue-crab cakes, seafood gumbo, fresh grouper, shrimp, and hamburgers. The decor is iconic diner, with a giant flamingo on the ceiling for that added Florida charm. [$] *Average main: $15* ✉ *100 Market St.* ☎ *850/653–9510* ⏲ *No dinner Sun.*

$$ SEAFOOD 🍴 **Boss Oyster.** "Shut up and shuck." That's the advice from this rustic Old Florida restaurant—and it should know, since many consider this the top oyster restaurant in Florida's oyster capital. Located at the Apalachicola River Inn, this is where you can eat your oysters fried, Rockefeller-style, on the half shell, or Greek, Mexican, English, with garlic, with shrimp, with crab, with hot peppers, with—oh, just eat 'em with gusto at this laid-back eatery overlooking the Apalachicola River. In addition to oysters, it lays down jumbo gulf shrimp, blue crabs, bay scallops, and fresh gulf grouper. Eat alfresco at picnic tables or inside in the busy, rustic dining room, but don't let the modest surroundings fool you—oysters aren't cheap here or anywhere in Apalach. The menu also includes such staples as steak and pizza. [$] *Average main: $20* ✉ *123 Water St.* ☎ *850/653–9364* 🌐 *www.apalachicolariverinn.com/boss.html.*

$$$ AMERICAN 🍴 **Owl Café.** Located in a behemoth clapboard building on a prime corner in downtown Apalachicola, this old-fashioned, charming lunch-and-dinner spot pleases modern palates, both in the white-linen elegance of the dining room and in the colorful garden terrace. The food is an artful blend of old and new as well: the chicken wrap seems as much at home on the lunch menu as the crab quesadillas. Dinner seafood

specials are carefully prepared and include lump-crab cakes, Atlantic salmon, and authentic jambalaya. Fine wines for adults and special menu selections for children along with a cluttered gift shop make this a family-friendly place. At night, the mood shifts to a casual lounge setting with a full bar—and if the liquor bar lacks enough choices there's a 3,000-bottle wine cellar featuring 250 selections from around the world. [$] *Average main: $21* ✉ *15 Ave. D* ☎ *850/653–9888* 🌐 *www.owlcafeflorida.com.*

> **WORD OF MOUTH**
>
> "St. George Island for a day at the beach is great. Great fresh seafood!"
>
> —MollyinFL

$$$ LATIN AMERICAN 🍴 **Tamara's Café.** Mixing Florida flavors with South American flair, Tamara, a native Venezuelan, opened this colorful bistro more than a decade ago. Now owned by her daughter and son-in-law, the restaurant resides in a 1920s-era building, complete with stamped-tin ceiling and original brick walls. For starters, try the creamy black-bean soup or the pleasantly spicy oyster stew; for dinner choose from seafood paella, prosciutto-wrapped salmon with mango-cilantro sauce, or margarita chicken and scallops with a tequila-lime glaze. All entrées come with black beans and rice, fresh vegetables, and focaccia bread, but if you still have room for dessert, try the fried-banana split or the *tres leches* (cake soaked in three types of milk), a South American favorite. The chef, who keeps watch over the dining room from an open kitchen, is happy to accommodate most any whim. [$] *Average main: $23* ✉ *71 Market St.* ☎ *850/653–4111* 🌐 *www.tamarascafe.com.*

WHERE TO STAY

For expanded reviews, facilities, and current deals, visit Fodors.com.

$$$ HOTEL 🏨 **The Consulate.** These four elegant suites, on the second story of the former offices of the French consul, range in size from 650 to 1,650 square feet and combine a 19th-century feel with 21st-century luxury. **Pros:** large rooms; more character than you'd find in a chain hotel. **Cons:** a bit pricey, especially for Apalachicola. [$] *Rooms from: $155* ✉ *76 Water St.* ☎ *850/408–0556* 🌐 *www.consulatesuites.com* 🛏 *4 suites.*

$$ B&B/INN 🏨 **Coombs Inn.** A combination of neighboring homes and a carriage house, this entire complex was created with Victorian flair. **Pros:** clean and comfortable; on-site, friendly owner who's happy to assist with travel tips and suggestions. **Cons:** be prepared to meet and greet other guests at the inn; if you favor complete privacy, a hotel may suit you better. [$] *Rooms from: $119* ✉ *80 6th St.* ☎ *850/653–9199* 🌐 *www.coombshouseinn.com* 🛏 *23 rooms* 🍽 *Breakfast.*

$$ B&B/INN 🏨 **Gibson Inn.** One of a few inns on the National Register of Historic Places still operating as a full-service facility, this turn-of-the-20th-century hostelry in the heart of downtown is easily identified by its wraparound porches, intricate fretwork, and widow's walk. **Pros:** smack dab in the center of town; peaceful veranda. **Cons:** may get a little busy when weddings are taking place in the main lobby. [$] *Rooms from: $120* ✉ *51 Ave. C* ☎ *850/653–2191* 🌐 *www.gibsoninn.com* 🛏 *28 rooms, 2 suites.*

SHOPPING

The best way to shop in Apalachicola is just to stroll around the tiny downtown area. There are always new stores joining old favorites, and somewhere along the way you'll find something that'll pique your interest.

Grady Market. On the first floor of the Consulate Inn is a collection of more than a dozen boutiques, including several antiques dealers and the gallery of Richard Bickel, known for his stunning black-and-white photographs of local residents. ⊠ *76 Water St.* ☎ *850/653–4099* ⊕ *www. gradymarket.com.*

ST. GEORGE ISLAND

14

8 miles southeast of Apalachicola via Bryant Patton Bridge off U.S. 98.

Cross the long, long bridge leading east out of Apalachicola and then look to your right for another lengthy span that takes you south to pristine St. George Island. Sitting 5 miles out in the Gulf of Mexico, the island is bordered by both Apalachicola Bay and the gulf, offering the best of both to create a nostalgic seaside retreat.

The rich bay is an angler's dream, whereas the snowy-white beaches and clear gulf waters satisfy even the most finicky beachgoer. Indulge in bicycling, hiking, canoeing, and snorkeling, or find a secluded spot for reading, gathering shells, or bird-watching. Accommodations mostly take the form of privately owned, fully furnished condos and single-family homes.

EXPLORING

Fodor's Choice ★ **St. George Island State Park.** This is Old Florida at its undisturbed best. On the east end of the island are 9 miles of undeveloped beaches and dunes—the longest beachfront of any state park in Florida. Sandy coves, salt marshes, oak forests, and pines provide shelter for many birds, including bald eagles and ospreys. Spotless restrooms and plentiful parking make a day at this park a joy. ⊠ *1900 E. Gulf Beach Dr.* ☎ *850/927–2111* ⊕ *www.floridastateparks.org/stgeorgeisland* ⊠ *$6 per vehicle, up to 8 people* ⊙ *Daily 8–sunset.*

WHERE TO EAT

$
PIZZA

✕ **BJs.** In any other locale you might think twice before dining at a restaurant that advertises "kegs-to-go" on the menu, but this is an island, so establishments tend to wear several hats (some even sell live bait). Fear not. This simple beach shack serves solid, if predictable, sandwiches (grilled chicken, turkey club, BLT), salads (Caesar, tuna, fried chicken), and appetizers (buffalo wings, cheese sticks, onion rings), but the pizza is definitely worth stopping for. Pies range from white pizza with chicken and bacon to shrimp-and-mozzarella to build-your-own personal pie (choose from 15 toppings). Beer and wine are available, and there are pool tables to pass the time while you wait for your order. $ *Average main: $7* ⊠ *105 W. Gulf Beach Dr.* ☎ *850/927–2805* ⊕ *www.sgipizza.com* ⊚ *Reservations not accepted.*

$$
SEAFOOD

✕ **Blue Parrot.** You'll feel like you're sneaking in the back door as you climb the side stairs leading to an outdoor deck overlooking the gulf (this is Apalach's only restaurant on the beach). Or if you can, grab a table indoors. During special-event weekends, the place is packed, and service may be a little slow. The food is hard to beat if you're not looking for anything fancy. Baskets of shrimp, oysters, and crab cakes—fried or char-grilled and served with fries—are more than one person can handle. Daily specials are listed on the blackboard. $ *Average main: $20* ✉ *68 W. Gorrie Dr.* ☎ *850/927–2987* ⊕ *www.blueparrotcafe.net.*

TALLAHASSEE

103 miles east of Panama City, 78 miles northeast of Apalachicola.

Tallahassee is Florida with a Southern accent. It maintains a tranquillity quite different from the sun-and-surf coastal towns. The only Southern capital spared in the Civil War, Tallahassee has preserved its history. Vestiges of the city's colorful past are found throughout. For example, in the capitol complex, the turn-of-the-20th-century Old Capitol building is strikingly paired with the New Capitol skyscraper.

The canopies of ancient oaks and spring bowers of azaleas line many streets; among the best "canopy roads" are St. Augustine, Miccosukee, Meridian, Old Bainbridge, and Centerville, all dotted with country stores and antebellum plantation houses. Between March and April, flowers bloom, the legislature is in session, and the Springtime Tallahassee festival is in full swing.

GETTING HERE AND AROUND

Just 14 miles south of the Georgia border and nearer to Atlanta than Miami, Tallahassee is midway between Jacksonville and Pensacola. Tallahassee Regional Airport is served by American, Delta, United Express, and US Airways. From the airport to downtown is around $20 via City Taxi or Yellow Cab.

Contacts **City Taxi** ☎ *850/562–4222.* **Tallahassee Regional Airport** ☎ *850/891–7800* ⊕ *www.talgov.com/airport.* **Yellow Cab** ☎ *850/575–1022.*

VISITOR INFORMATION

Contacts **Tallahassee Area Convention and Visitors Bureau** ☎ *850/606–2305, 800/628–2866* ⊕ *www.visittallahassee.com.*

EXPLORING

DOWNTOWN

FAMILY **Challenger Learning Center.** Visitors of all ages can't help but get excited about math and science exploration at this museum that features a space mission simulator, an IMAX 3-D theater, and the Downtown Digital Dome Theatre and Planetarium. Every kid, and kid at heart, can also reenact a space mission with the Challenger Learning Center Space Mission Simulator. The next best thing to actual space flight, the simulator features a Mission Control room designed after NASA Johnson Space Center and an orbiting space station modeled after the laboratory on the International Space Station. ✉ *200 S. Duval St.* ☎ *850/645–7796, 850/644–4629 IMAX* ⊕ *www.challengertlh.com* 🎫 *Planetarium $5, IMAX $5.50–$10* ☉ *Show times vary.*

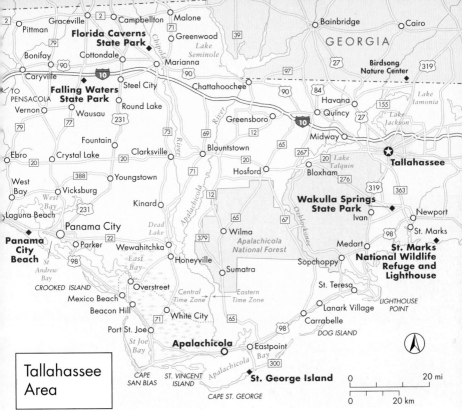

Tallahassee Area

Museum of Florida History. If you thought Florida was founded by Walt Disney, stop in here. The displays explain the state's past by highlighting the unique geological and historical events that have shaped the state. Exhibits include a mammoth armadillo grazing in a savanna, the remains of a giant mastodon found in nearby Wakulla Springs, and a dugout canoe that once carried American Indians into Florida's backwaters. Florida's history also includes settlements by the Spanish, British, French, and Confederates who fought for possession of the state.

Gold bars, weapons, flags, maps, furniture, steamboats, and other artifacts underscore the fact that although most Americans date the nation to 1776, Florida's residents were building settlements hundreds of years earlier. If this intrigues you, one floor up is the Florida State Archives and Library, where there's a treasure trove of government records, manuscripts, photographs, genealogical records, and other materials. ■TIP➜ **It was in these archives that researchers found footage of a young Jim Morrison appearing in a promotional film for Florida's universities.** ✉ *500 S. Bronough St.* ☎ *850/245–6400, 850/245–6600 library, 850/245–6700 archives* ⊕ *www.museumoffloridahistory.com* 🎟 *Free* ☾ *Weekdays 9–4:30, Sat. 10–4:30, Sun. noon–4:30.*

DID YOU KNOW?

There are many types of speleothems (cave formations). The two you hear spelunkers say the most are probably stalactites and stalagmites. Formed from dripping water, stalactites (shown here at Florida Caverns State Park) are conical formations that hang down from a cave ceiling. Formations that go the other direction—from the ground up, because of mineral deposits—are called stalagmites.

New Capitol. In the 1960s, when there was talk of relocating the capital to a more central location like Orlando, Panhandle legislators got to work and approved the construction of a 22-story skyscraper that would anchor the capital right where it was. It's perfectly placed at the crest of a hill, sitting prominently behind the low-rise Old Capitol. The governor's office is on the first floor, along with the Florida Artists Hall of Fame, a series of plaques that pay tribute to Floridians such as Ray Charles, Burt Reynolds, Tennessee Williams, Ernest Hemingway, and Marjorie Kinnan Rawlings.

The House and Senate chambers on the fifth floor provide viewer galleries for when the legislative sessions take place (March to May). Catch a panoramic view of Tallahassee and the surrounding countryside all the way into Georgia from the fabulous 22nd-floor observation deck. Although budget cuts have stopped scheduled guided tours, a free brochure can get you around; if you're traveling in a group you can call ahead to have a guide usher you. To pick up information about the area, stop at the Florida Visitors Center on the plaza level, and check out the plaque on the north wall facing the elevators. It's dedicated to Senator Lee Wissenborn ". . . whose valiant effort to move the Capitol to Orlando was the prime motivation for the construction of this building." ⊠ *400 S. Monroe St.* ☎ *850/488–6167* ⊕ *www.myfloridacapitol. com* ⊡ *Free* ⊙ *Visitor center weekdays 8–5.*

Old Capitol. The centerpiece of the capitol complex, this 1842 structure has been added to and subtracted from several times. Having been restored, the jaunty red-and-white-striped awnings and combination gas-electric lights make it look much as it did in 1902. Inside, it houses a must-see museum of Florida's political history as well as the old Supreme Court chambers and Senate Gallery—a very interesting peek into the past. ⊠ *S. Monroe St. at Apalachee Pkwy.* ☎ *850/487–1902* ⊡ *Free* ⊙ *Self-guided tours weekdays 9–4:30, Sat. 10–4:30, Sun. noon–4:30; call for guided tours.*

AWAY FROM DOWNTOWN

Alfred B. Maclay Gardens State Park. Starting in December, the grounds at this 1,200-acre estate are afire with azaleas, dogwood, Oriental magnolias, spring bulbs of tulips and irises, banana shrubs, honeysuckle, silverbell trees, pansies, and camellias. Allow half a day to wander past the reflecting pool into the tiny walled garden and around the lakes and woodlands. The Maclay residence (open January through April) is furnished as it was in the 1920s; picnic areas, gardens, and swimming and boating facilities are open to the public. ⊠ *3540 Thomasville Rd.* ☎ *850/487–4556* ⊡ *$6 per vehicle, up to 8 people; garden extra $6 per person Jan.–Apr. (blooming season), free rest of year* ⊙ *Daily 8–sunset.*

Fodor'sChoice
★

Edward Ball Wakulla Springs State Park. Known for having one of the deepest springs in the world, this very picturesque and highly recommended park remains relatively untouched, retaining the wild and exotic look it had in the 1930s, when the films *Tarzan* and *Creature from the Black Lagoon* were shot here. Even if they weren't, you'd want to come here and see what Florida really looks like. Beyond the lodge is the spring where glass-bottom boats set off deep into the lush, jungle-lined

Guided tours are given daily at Florida's Old Capitol in Tallahassee. It sits in front of the 22-story New Capitol.

waterways to catch glimpses of alligators, snakes, nesting limpkins, and other waterfowl. It costs $50 to rent a pontoon boat and go it alone—it may be worth it since an underground river flows into a pool so clear you can see the bottom more than 100 feet below. The park is 15 miles south of Tallahassee on Route 61. If you can't pull yourself away from this idyllic spot, spend the night in the 1930s Spanish Mediterranean–style lodge. ⊠ *550 Wakulla Park Dr., Wakulla Springs* ☎ *850/926–0700* ⊕ *www.floridastateparks.org/wakullasprings* ✉ *$6 per vehicle, up to 8 people; boat tour $8* ⊙ *Daily 8–sunset; boat tours daily 9:30–4:30.*

Mission San Luis Archaeological and Historic Site. Long before New England's residents began gaining a foothold in North America, the native Apalachee Indians as well as Spanish missionaries settled here. On the site of a 17th-century Spanish mission and Apalachee Indian town, this museum focuses on the archaeology of the late 1600s, when the Apalachee village here had a population of at least 1,400. By 1704, however, threatened by Creek Indians and British forces, the locals burned the village and fled. About once a year, researchers conduct digs, and then they spend the rest of the year analyzing their findings. If you're here when they are, you can watch them dig. Otherwise, you'll have to be content with roaming around the re-creation of a 17th-century Spanish village and speaking with the living-history guides, who offer tours by advance arrangement. Even without seeing researchers digging for clues, this is still a cool experience and a great way to learn about Florida's impressive history. A 24,000-square-foot, state-of-the-art visitor center offers an expanded exhibit hall and gift shop. ⊠ *2100 W. Tennessee St.* ☎ *850/245–6406* ⊕ *www.missionsanluis.org* ✉ *$5* ⊙ *Tues.–Sun. 10–4.*

St. Marks National Wildlife Refuge and Lighthouse. As its name suggests, this attraction is of both natural and historical interest. Natural salt marshes, tidal flats, and freshwater pools used by early natives set the stage for the once-powerful Fort San Marcos de Apalache, which was built nearby in 1639. Stones salvaged from the fort were used in the lighthouse, which is still in operation. In winter the 100,000-acre-plus refuge on the shores of Apalachee Bay is the resting place for thousands of migratory birds of more than 300 species, but the alligators seem to like it year-round (keep your camera ready). The visitor center has information on more than 75 miles of marked trails. Hardwood swamps and pine woodlands also provide habitat for wood ducks, black bears, otters, raccoons, deer, armadillos, coyotes, feral hogs, fox squirrels, gopher tortoises, and woodpeckers. Twenty-five miles south of Tallahassee, the refuge can be reached via Route 363. ✉ *1255 Lighthouse Rd., St. Marks* ☎ *850/925–6121* 🌐 *saintmarks.fws.gov* 🎟 *$5 per vehicle* 🕒 *Refuge daily sunrise–sunset; visitor center weekdays 8–4, weekends 10–5.*

FAMILY **Tallahassee Museum.** Not exactly a museum, this is really an expansive, bucolic park that showcases a peaceful and intriguing look at Old Florida, located about 20 minutes from downtown. The theme and presentation here is of a working 1880s pioneer farm that offers daily hands-on activities for children, such as soap-making and blacksmithing. A boardwalk meanders through the 52 acres of natural habitat that make up the zoo, which has such varied animals as panthers, bobcats, white-tailed deer, bald eagles, red wolves, hawks, owls, otters, and black bears—many of which were brought here injured or orphaned. Also on-site are nature trails, a one-room schoolhouse dating from 1897, and an 1840s Southern plantation manor, where you can usually find someone cooking on weekends. It's peaceful, pleasing, and educational. ✉ *3945 Museum Dr.* ☎ *850/575–8684* 🌐 *www.tallahasseemuseum.org* 🎟 *$9* 🕒 *Mon.–Sat. 9–5, Sun. 12:30–5.*

WHERE TO EAT

$$$ ITALIAN 🍴 **Andrew's 228.** Part of a smart complex in the heart of the political district, this two-story "urban Tuscan villa" (contradiction noted) is the latest of owner Andy Reiss's restaurant incarnations to occupy the same space (the last was Andrew's Second Act). Leaning toward upscale, the menu includes a range of chicken, steak, pasta, and fish dishes such as grouper picatta, pesto salmon, wild-mushroom risotto, chicken marsala, and double-cut pork chops. If you're so inclined, try the specialty $6 martini. [$] *Average main: $26* ✉ *228 S. Adams St.* ☎ *850/222–3444* 🌐 *www.andrewsdowntown.com* 🕒 *Closed Sun. No lunch.*

$$$ SOUTHERN 🍴 **Avenue Eat and Drink.** Elegant yet unpretentious, this cozy restaurant offers an eclectic mix of Southern fusion food that delights taste buds in small bites and larger plates. You can't go wrong with tuna two ways or the melt-in-your-mouth boneless short ribs served with mashed parsnip and potatoes with a rosemary-Cabernet reduction. There is an extensive wine selection and a specialty martini menu. [$] *Average main: $28* ✉ *115 E. Park Ave.* ☎ *850/224–0115* 🌐 *www.avenueeatanddrink.com.*

$ ✕**Hopkins' Eatery.** Locals in the know flock here for superb salads, home-
AMERICAN made soups, and sandwiches—expect a short wait at lunchtime—via simple counter service. Kids like the traditional peanut butter–and-jelly sandwich (with bananas and sprouts, if they dare); adults might opt for a chunky chicken melt, smothered beef, or garden vegetarian sub. The spearmint iced tea is a must-have, as is a slice of freshly baked chocolate cake. A second location on North Monroe Street offers the same menu; a third location has also opened at 1208 Capital Circle SE. $ *Average main: $6* ⊠ *1415 Market St.* ☎ *850/668–0311* ⊕ *www.hopkinseatery. com* ☉ *Closed Sun. No dinner Sat.* $ *Average main: $6* ⊠ *1660-9 N. Monroe St.(in Lake Ella Plaza)* ☎ *850/386–4258.*

$$ ✕**The Mockingbird.** At this cozy café, contemporary gourmet dining
CONTEMPORARY meets Southern staples set against a backdrop of eclectic artwork and local musicians' tunes. The brunch is infamous, and locals flock here to partake of such favorites as huevos rancheros and shrimp and grits. The chef teases palates with creative specials on a regular basis. Prices are reasonable and drink specials are always on tap. $ *Average main: $18* ⊠ *1225 N. Monroe St.* ☎ *850/222–4956* ⊕ *www. mockingbirdtallahassee.com.*

14

WHERE TO STAY

For expanded reviews, facilities, and current deals, visit Fodors.com.

$$ 🛏 **Aloft Tallahassee Downtown.** This urban-chic hotel provides the tree-
HOTEL lined downtown district with a bit of trendy fun courtesy of loft-style rooms with bright, minimalist decor. **Pros:** convenient to downtown, universities, and nightlife/restaurants. **Cons:** small, utilitarian rooms; lobby can get packed from the bar on weekend nights. $ *Rooms from: $139* ⊠ *200 N. Monroe St.* ☎ *850/513–0313, 866/513–0313* 🛏 *162 rooms.*

$$$ 🛏 **Governors Inn.** Only a block from the capitol, this plushly restored
B&B/INN historic warehouse is abuzz during the week with politicians, press, and lobbyists. **Pros:** well run and well placed, a few steps from museums, restaurants, and the capitol; the rooms and lobby are warm and inviting. **Cons:** during session and football season, the district can get crowded and busy, and accessing the area may be a challenge. $ *Rooms from: $169* ⊠ *209 S. Adams St.* ☎ *850/681–6855* ⊕ *www.thegovinn. com* 🛏 *41 rooms, 8 suites* ⍾ *Breakfast.*

$$ 🛏 **Hotel Duval.** Part of the Autograph Collection, this boutique hotel,
HOTEL a renovated version of the landmark 1951 Duval Hotel, sets a high
Fodor's Choice standard for any who choose to follow. **Pros:** top-level amenities; good
★ restaurants. **Cons:** not suited to families; small rooms. $ *Rooms from: $109* ⊠ *415 N. Monroe St.* ☎ *850/224–6000* ⊕ *www.hotelduval.com* 🛏 *108 rooms, 9 suites.*

NIGHTLIFE

There are endless options for after-dark entertainment for Tallahassee's government and university populations. When you're in town, be sure to check the college newspapers for the latest developments.

Floyd's Music Store. Floyd's hosts local and touring acts, such as Daughtry and Kenney Chesney. Other performers, from dueling pianos to assorted DJs, round out the schedule. ⊠ *666-1 W. Tennessee St.* ☎ *850/222–3506* ⊕ *www.floydsmusicstore.com.*

Level 8 Lounge. This rooftop lounge oozes a sleek, chic sophistication that matches the boutique hotel to which it's attached. Enjoy panoramic views of the capital city while you sip a drink from the custom drink menu (try the Cougarita) or nibble on small bites from the bar menu. ⊠ *Hotel Duval, 415 N. Monroe St.* ☎ *850/224–6000.*

Midtown Filling Station. Comfort food and cold drinks abound at this gastropub in Midtown. Get a Dang Hippie burger or enjoy a Boiled Peanut of the Day while enjoying a good brew and live music. ⊠ *1122 Thomasville Rd.* ☎ *850/224–8272.*

The Moon. For decades, this has been one of the capital city's most active nightclubs, capable of changing its music to suit the tastes of the new students attending FSU. Live bands and DJs have kept this club going since 1985 and will likely sustain its collegiate appeal for years to come. ⊠ *1105 E. Lafayette St.* ☎ *850/878–6900, 850/222–6666 event line* ⊕ *www.moonevents.com.*

Waterworks. With its retro-chic tiki-bar fittings, Waterworks attracts the college art crowd, jazz fans, and hipsters of all ages for cocktails and DJ-spun dance music. On Friday night there's a banjo player, a retro-cool treat. ⊠ *1133 Thomasville Rd.* ☎ *850/224–1887* ⊕ *www.waterworkstallahassee.com.*

SHOPPING

Market District. Hop off I–10 at Exit 203 to head to this shopping and dining district filled with locally owned specialty shops, salons, cafés, and restaurants. My Favorite Things and Cotton Colors are popular, as are many other stores scattered around the area in smaller enclaves. Not to worry, though—most are within walking distance of one another. The Market District is the place for a taste of true local culture. It's slightly west of Thomasville Road at the intersection of Timberline Road and Market Street. ⊠ *Timberline Rd. at Market St.* ⊕ *www.themarketdistricttallahassee.com.*

Midtown District. This area mixes a little bit of Southern charm with city chic, offering everything from the stylish and cutting-edge fashions of Cole Couture and Divas and Devils to luxury beauty and spa services at Kanvas. Shops adorn the sides of North Monroe Street heading toward downtown, as well as some of the side streets. If you get hungry picking up purchases, try the delicious treats at Lucy & Leo's Cupcakery, featured on *Cupcake Wars.* ⊠ *Between North Moore St. and Thomasville Rd., between W. 7th Ave. and W. 4th Ave.*

TRAVEL SMART
FLORIDA

GETTING HERE AND AROUND

▌ AIR TRAVEL

Average flying times to Florida's international airports are 3 hours from New York, 4 hours from Chicago, 2¾ hours from Dallas, 4½–5½ hours from Los Angeles, and 8–8½ hours from London.

AIRPORTS

Florida has 21 commercial airports, the busiest being Orlando International Airport (MCO), Miami International Airport (MIA), Tampa (TPA), and Fort Lauderdale–Hollywood International Airport (FLL). Note, though, that flying to alternative airports can save you time and money. Take, for example, Fort Lauderdale, which is close to Miami, and Sarasota Bradenton International (SRQ), which is close to Tampa. FLL is a 30-minute drive from MIA (and as close to certain neighborhoods of Miami). And what you might lose in driving time between Sarasota and downtown Tampa, you'll make up for in spades with shorter security lines and fewer in-terminal navigation woes at SRQ.

▌▌▌TIP➔ Flying to secondary airports can save you money—sometimes even when there are additional ground transportation costs—so price things out before booking.

Airport Information **Daytona Beach International Airport (DAB)** ☎ 386/248–8069 ⊕ www.flydaytonafirst.com. **Fort Lauderdale–Hollywood International Airport (FLL)** ☎ 866/435–9355 ⊕ www.broward.org/airport. **Jacksonville International Airport (JAX)** ☎ 904/741–4902 ⊕ www.flyjax.com. **Key West International Airport (EYW)** ☎ 305/809–5200 ⊕ www.eywairport.com. **Miami International Airport (MIA)** ☎ 305/876–7000 ⊕ www.miami-airport.com. **Orlando International Airport (MCO)** ☎ 407/825–2001 ⊕ www.orlandoairports.net. **Palm Beach International Airport (PBI)** ☎ 561/471–7420 ⊕ www.pbia.org. **Northwest Florida Beaches International Airport (ECP)**

☎ 850/763–6751 ⊕ www.iflybeaches.com. **Sarasota Bradenton International Airport (SRQ)** ☎ 941/359–5200 ⊕ www.srq-airport.com. **Southwest Florida International Airport (RSW)** ☎ 239/590–4800 ⊕ www.flylcpa.com. **St. Petersburg–Clearwater International Airport (PIE)** ☎ 727/453–7800 ⊕ www.fly2pie.com. **Tampa International Airport (TPA)** ☎ 813/870–8700 ⊕ www.tampaairport.com.

GROUND TRANSPORTATION

There's SuperShuttle service from several Florida airports: Miami, Orlando, Sarasota, St. Petersburg/Clearwater, and Tampa. That said, most airports have some type of shuttle service or another.

Buying a round-trip ticket and reserving for the return trip can sometimes save you money, and it makes departure that much easier. Otherwise book a shuttle from your hotel to the airport at least 24 hours in advance. Expect to be picked up 2½ hours before your scheduled departure.

Cab fares from Florida's larger airports into town average $35 to $55. Note that in some cities airport cab fares are a single flat rate; in others, flat-rate fares vary by zone; and in others still, the fare is determined by the meter. Private car service fares run between $50 and $150, depending on the locale and the type of vehicle.

Shuttle Service **SuperShuttle** ☎ 800/258–3826 ⊕ www.supershuttle.com.

FLIGHTS

AirTran. Miami, Fort Lauderdale, Fort Myers, Jacksonville, Key West, Orlando, Pensacola, Sarasota, Tampa, and West Palm Beach. ☎ 800/247–8726 ⊕ *www.airtran.com.*

American Airlines. Fort Lauderdale, Fort Myers, Fort Walton Beach, Gainesville, Jacksonville, Key West, Miami, Orlando, Pensacola, Tallahassee, Tampa, and West

Palm Beach. ☎ *800/433–7300* ⊕ *www. aa.com.*

Delta. Daytona Beach, Fort Lauderdale, Fort Myers, Fort Walton Beach, Gainesville, Jacksonville, Key West, Melbourne, Miami, Orlando, Panama City, Pensacola, Sarasota, Tallahassee, Tampa, and West Palm Beach. ☎ *800/221–1212 for U.S. reservations, 800/241–4141 for international reservations* ⊕ *www.delta.com.*

Frontier. Fort Lauderdale, Fort Myers, Orlando, and Tampa. Charges for a carry-on bag if you don't book on the airline's website. ☎ *800/432–1359* ⊕ *www. frontierairlines.com.*

JetBlue. Tampa, Fort Lauderdale, Sarasota, Fort Myers, Jacksonville, West Palm Beach, and Orlando. ☎ *800/538–2583* ⊕ *www.jetblue.com.*

Southwest. Fort Lauderdale, Fort Myers, Jacksonville, Orlando, Panama City, Tampa, and West Palm Beach. ☎ *800/435–9792* ⊕ *www.southwest.com.*

Spirit Airlines. Fort Lauderdale, Fort Myers, Orlando, Tampa, and West Palm Beach. This is one of a few airlines that charges ($50) for a carry-on bag. ☎ *800/772–7117* ⊕ *www.spirit.com.*

United. Daytona, Fort Lauderdale, Fort Myers, Fort Walton Beach, Gainesville, Jacksonville, Key West, Melbourne, Miami, Orlando, Pensacola, Tallahassee, Tampa, and West Palm Beach. ☎ *800/864–8331 for U.S. reservations, 800/538–2929 for international reservations* ⊕ *www.united.com.*

US Airways. Daytona Beach, Fort Lauderdale, Fort Myers, Fort Walton Beach, Gainesville, Jacksonville, Key West, Melbourne, Miami, Pensacola, Sarasota, Tallahassee, Tampa, and West Palm Beach. ☎ *800/428–4322 for U.S. and Canadian reservations, 800/622–1015 for international reservations* ⊕ *www.usairways.com.*

▌CAR TRAVEL

Three major interstates lead to Florida. I–95 begins in Maine, runs south through the Mid-Atlantic states, and enters Florida just north of Jacksonville. It continues south past Daytona Beach, the Space Coast, Vero Beach, Palm Beach, and Fort Lauderdale, ending in Miami.

I–75 begins in Michigan at the Canadian border and runs south through Ohio, Kentucky, Tennessee, and Georgia, then moves south through the center of the state before veering west into Tampa. It follows the west coast south to Naples, then crosses the state through the northern section of the Everglades, and ends in Miami.

California and most Southern and Southwestern states are connected to Florida by I–10, which moves east from Los Angeles through Arizona, New Mexico, Texas, Louisiana, Mississippi, and Alabama. It enters Florida at Pensacola and runs straight across the northern part of the state, ending in Jacksonville.

FROM–TO	MILES	HOURS +/-
Pensacola–Panama City	100	2
Tallahassee–Panama City	100	2
Tallahassee–Jacksonville	165	3
Jacksonville–St. Augustine	40	0:45
Gainesville–Orlando	115	2
Cape/Port Canaveral–Orlando	60	1
Orlando–Tampa	85	1:30
Fort Lauderdale–Miami	30	0:30
Miami–Naples	125	2:15
Miami–Key Largo	65	1
Miami–Palm Beach	70	1:15
Key Largo–Key West	100	2

RENTAL CARS

Unless you plan to plant yourself at a beach or theme-park resort, you really need a car to get around in most parts of Florida. Rental rates usually start at $35 a day/$160 a week, plus tax ($2 per day), though rates have been going up lately. In Florida you must be 21 to rent a car, and rates are higher if you're under 25.

RULES OF THE ROAD

Speed limits are generally 60 mph on state highways, 30 mph within city limits and residential areas, and 70 mph on interstates and Florida's Turnpike. Be alert for signs announcing exceptions. Children younger than four years old must be strapped into a separate carrier or child seat; children four through five can be secured in a separate carrier, an integrated child seat, or by a seat belt. The driver will be held responsible for passengers under the age of 18 who aren't wearing seat belts, and all front-seat passengers are required to wear seat belts.

Electronic tolls are becoming more common, and there's often no way of paying them in cash. Renting a toll pass may be a good idea in some areas (especially around Orlando).

Florida's Alcohol/Controlled Substance DUI Law is one of the toughest in the United States. A blood-alcohol level of .08 or higher can have serious repercussions even for a first-time offender.

CAR RENTAL RESOURCES

Local Agencies		
Continental (Fort Lauderdale and Orlando)	800/221–4085 or 954/332–1125	www.continental-car.com
Sunshine Rent A Car (Fort Lauderdale)	888/786–7446 or 954/467–8100	www.sunshine-rentacar.com
Major Agencies		
Alamo	877/222–9075	www.alamo.com
Avis	800/331–1212	www.avis.com
Budget	800/218–7992	www.budget.com
Hertz	800/654–3131	www.hertz.com
National Car Rental	800/227–7368	www.national-car.com

▌ FERRY TRAVEL

Ferries are few and far between in Florida, but if you would like to avoid traffic to the Keys and make the trip less of a hassle, Key West Express ferries people from Fort Myers Beach on a daily basis (and Marco Island in season) to the historic seaport in Key West, which is within walking distance of all major attractions as well as many hotels. The trip, just under four hours, is much cheaper than airfare and doesn't require months-in-advance booking.

Contact Key West Express ☎ *888/539–2628* ⊕ *www.keywestexpress.us.*

ESSENTIALS

▌ ACCOMMODATIONS

In the busy seasons, reserve ahead for the top properties. In general, the peak seasons are during the Christmas holidays and from late January through Easter in the southern half of the state, during the summer along the Panhandle and around Jacksonville and St. Augustine, and in both time frames in Orlando and Central Florida. Holiday weekends at any point during the year are packed; if you're considering home or condo rentals, minimum-stay requirements go up in these periods, too. Fall is the slowest season, with only a few exceptions (Key West is jam-packed for Fantasy Fest at Halloween). Rates are low and availability is high, but this is also the prime time for hurricanes.

Children are welcome generally everywhere in Florida; however, the buck stops at spring breakers. Hotels are fair game—and some even cater to them—but almost all rental agencies won't lease units to anyone under 25 without a guardian present.

Pets, although allowed at hotels more and more often (one upscale chain, Kimpton, celebrates its pet-friendliness with treats in the lobby and doggie beds for rooms), often carry an extra flat-rate fee for cleaning and de-allergen treatments, and are not a sure thing. Inquire ahead if Fido is coming with you.

APARTMENT AND HOUSE RENTALS

The state's reputation for visiting snowbirds (northerners who "flock" to Florida in the winter) has caused private home and condo rentals to be a booming business and at times a better option for vacationers, particularly families who want to have some extra space and cooking facilities. In some destinations, home and condo rentals are more readily available than hotels. Fort Myers, for example, doesn't have many luxury hotel properties downtown. Everything aside from beach towels is provided during a stay, but some things to consider are that sizeable down payments must be made at booking (15% to 50%), and the full balance is often due before arrival. Check for any cleaning fees (usually not more than $150). If being on the beach is of utmost importance, carefully screen properties that tout "water views," because they might actually be of bays, canals, or lakes rather than of the Gulf of Mexico or the Atlantic.

Finding a great rental agency can help you weed through the junk. Target offices that specialize in the area you want to visit, and have a personal conversation with a representative as soon as possible. Be honest about your budget and expectations. For example, let the rental agent know if having the living room couch pull double duty as a bed is not OK. Although websites listing rentals directly from home owners are growing in popularity, there's a higher chance of coming across Pinocchios advertising "gourmet" kitchens that have one or two nice gadgets but fixtures from 1982. To protect yourself, talk extensively with the owners in advance, see if there's a system in place for accountability should something go wrong, and make sure there's a 24-hour phone number for emergencies.

Contacts American Realty of Captiva. Lower Gulf Coast (Captiva Island) ☏ 800/547–0127 ⊕ www.captiva-island.com. **Endless Vacation Rentals.** Unused time-share units from all major Florida cities and regions. ☏ 877/782–9387 ⊕ www.evrentals.com. **Florida Keys Rental Store.** Florida Keys ☏ 800/585–0584, 305/451–3879 ⊕ www.floridakeysrentalstore.com. **Freewheeler Vacations.** Florida Keys ☏ 866/664–2075, 305/664–2075 ⊕ www.freewheeler-realty.com. **Interhome.** Daytona Beach, Miami, Orlando, Sarasota, Florida Keys, Lower Gulf Coast, Tampa Bay Area ☏ 954/791–8282, 800/882–6864 ⊕ www.interhomeusa.com. **ResortQuest.** Panhandle ☏ 800/336–4853 ⊕ www.resortquest.com.

Sand Key Realty. Tampa Bay Area (beaches) ☎ 800/257–7332, 727/443–0032 ⊕ www. sandkey.com. **Suncoast Vacation Rentals.** Panhandle (St. George Island) ☎ 800/341–2021 ⊕ www.uncommonflorida.com. **Villas International.** Miami, Orlando, Broward County, Florida Keys, Lower Gulf Coast, Palm Beach County, Tampa Bay Area ☎ 415/499–9490, 800/221–2260 ⊕ www.villasintl.com.

BED-AND-BREAKFASTS

Small inns and guesthouses in Florida range from modest, cozy places with home-style breakfasts and owners who treat you like family, to elegantly furnished Victorian houses with four-course breakfasts and rates to match. Since most B&Bs are small, they rely on various agencies and organizations to get the word out and to help coordinate reservations.

Reservation Services Florida Bed & Breakfast Inns ☎ 877/303–3224 ⊕ www.florida-inns.com.

HOTELS AND RESORTS

Wherever you look in Florida, you'll find lots of plain, inexpensive motels and luxurious resorts, independents alongside national chains, and an ever-growing number of modern properties as well as quite a few classics. In fact, since Florida has been a favored travel destination for some time, vintage hotels are everywhere: there are grand edifices like the Breakers in Palm Beach, Boca Raton Resort & Club in Boca Raton, the Biltmore Hotel in Coral Gables, and Casa Marina in Key West.

All hotels listed have a private bath unless otherwise noted.

▌EATING OUT

Smoking is banned statewide in most enclosed indoor workplaces, including restaurants. Exemptions are permitted for stand-alone bars where food takes a backseat to the libations.

One caution: Raw oysters are a potential problem for people with chronic illness of the liver, stomach, or blood, or who have immune disorders. All Florida restaurants

FLORIDA'S SCENIC TRAILS

Florida has some 8,000 miles of land-based routes (plus another 4,000 miles for paddling!). About 1,400 miles of these connect to create the Florida Trail, one of only 11 National Scenic Trails in the United States. Info on top segments is available at ⊕ www.floridatrail.org, and you can find a searchable list of all trails at ⊕ www.visitflorida.com/trails.

that serve raw oysters must post a notice in plain view warning of the risks associated with consuming them.

FLORIBBEAN FOOD

A true marriage of Floridian, Caribbean, and Latin cultures yields the homegrown cuisine known as "Floribbean." (Think freshly caught fish with tropical fruit salsa.) A trip to the Tampa area or South Florida, however, isn't complete without a taste of Cuban food. The cuisine is heavy, including dishes like *lechon asado* (roasted pork) that are served in garlic-based sauces. The two most typical dishes are *arroz con frijoles* (the staple side dish of rice and black beans) and *arroz con pollo* (chicken in sticky yellow rice).

Key West is famous for its key lime pie (the best is found here) and conch fritters. Stone-crab claws, a South Florida delicacy, can be savored from October through May.

MEALS AND MEALTIMES

Unless otherwise noted, the restaurants listed in this guide are open daily for lunch and dinner.

RESERVATIONS AND DRESS

We discuss reservations only when they're essential (there's no other way you'll ever get a table) or when they're not accepted. It's always smart to make reservations when you can, particularly if your party is large or if it's high season. It's critical to do so at popular restaurants (book as far ahead as possible, often 30 days, and reconfirm on arrival).

We mention dress only when men are required to wear a jacket or a jacket and tie. Expect places with dress codes to truly adhere to them.

Contacts OpenTable ⊕ *www.opentable.com.*

▌HEALTH

Sunburn and heat prostration are concerns, even in winter. So hit the beach or play tennis, golf, or another outdoor sport before 10 am or after 3 pm. If you must be out at midday, limit exercise, drink plenty of nonalcoholic liquids, and wear a hat. If you feel faint, get out of the sun and sip water slowly.

Even on overcast days, ultraviolet rays shine through the haze, so use a sunscreen with an SPF of at least 15, and have children wear a waterproof SPF 30 or higher.

While you're frolicking on the beach, steer clear of what look like blue bubbles on the sand. These are Portuguese men-of-war, and their tentacles can cause an allergic reaction. Also be careful of other large jellyfish, some of which can sting.

If you walk across a grassy area on the way to the beach, you'll probably encounter the tiny, light-brown, incredibly prickly sand spurs. If you get stuck with one, just pull it out.

▌HOURS OF OPERATION

Many museums are closed Monday but have late hours on another weekday and are usually open on weekends. Some museums have a day when admission is free. Popular attractions are usually open every day but Thanksgiving and Christmas Day. Watch out for seasonal closures at smaller venues; we list opening hours in this guide, but if you're visiting during a transitional month (for example, May in the southern part of the state), it's always best to call before showing up.

▌MONEY

Prices throughout this guide are given for adults. Substantially reduced fees are almost always available for children, students, and senior citizens.

CREDIT CARDS

We cite information about credit cards only if they aren't accepted at a restaurant or a hotel. Otherwise, assume that most major credit cards are acceptable.

Reporting Lost Cards American Express ☎ *800/528–4800* ⊕ *www.americanexpress. com.* **Diners Club** ☎ *800/234–6377* ⊕ *www. dinersclub.com.* **Discover** ☎ *800/347–2683* ⊕ *www.discovercard.com.* **MasterCard** ☎ *800/622–7747* ⊕ *www.mastercard.com.* **Visa** ☎ *800/847–2911* ⊕ *www.visa.com.*

▌PACKING

Northern Florida is much cooler in winter than southern Florida, so pack a heavy sweater. Even in summer, ocean breezes can be cool, so it's good to have a lightweight sweater or jacket.

Aside from an occasional winter cold spell (when the mercury drops to, say, 50), Miami and the Naples–Fort Myers areas are warm year-round and extremely humid in summer. Be prepared for sudden storms all over in summer, and note that plastic raincoats are uncomfortable in the high humidity. Often storms are quick, usually in the afternoons, and the sun comes back in no time. (This also means that it's best to get in your beach time earlier in the day; if it's nice in the morning in August, go to the beach. Don't wait.)

Dress is casual throughout the state—sundresses, sandals, or walking shorts are appropriate. Palm Beach is more polos and pearls, Miami is designer jeans, and elsewhere the Tommy Bahama-esque look dominates. Even beach gear is OK at a lot of places, but just make sure you've got a proper outfit on (shirt, shorts, and shoes). A very small number of restaurants request that men wear jackets and ties, but most don't. Where there are dress codes, they tend to be fully adhered to. Funnily enough, the strictest places are golf and tennis clubs. Many ask that you wear whites or at least special sport shoes and attire. Be prepared for air-conditioning working in overdrive anywhere you go.

You can generally swim year-round in peninsular Florida from about New Smyrna Beach south on the Atlantic coast and from Tarpon Springs south on the Gulf Coast. Bring a sun hat and sunscreen.

▌ SAFETY

Stepped-up policing of thieves who prey on tourists in rental cars has helped address what was a serious issue in the early 1990s. Still, visitors should be especially wary when driving in strange neighborhoods and leaving the airport, especially in the Miami area. Don't assume that valuables are safe in your hotel room; use in-room safes or the hotel's safety-deposit boxes. Try to use ATMs only during the day or in brightly lighted, well-traveled locales. Don't leave valuables unattended while you walk the beach or go for a dip. And never leave anything of value in a car; thefts from parked cars are on the rise in Florida, and visitors have reported the loss of their belongings while stopped for lunch or dinner as they travel to or from the airport.

If you're visiting Florida during the June through November hurricane season and a hurricane is imminent, be sure to follow directions from local authorities.

▌ TAXES

Florida's sales tax is 6% or higher, depending on the county, and local sales and tourist taxes can raise what you pay considerably. Miami Beach hoteliers, for example, collect 13% for city and resort taxes. It's best to ask about additional costs up front to avoid a rude awakening.

▌ TIME

The western portion of the Panhandle is in the Central time zone, and the rest of Florida is in the Eastern time zone.

▌ TIPPING

Tip airport valets or hotel bellhops $1 to $3 per bag (there is also usually a charge to check bags outside the terminal, but this isn't a tip). Maids should get $1 to $2 per night per guest, more at expensive resorts, left each morning since your cleaner could change from day to day. Room service waiters still receive a 15% tip despite hefty room-service charges and service fees, which don't usually go to the waiters. A doorman or parking valet should get $1 to $3. Waiters should get 15% to 20% (on the before tax amount). Bartenders get $1 or $2 per round of drinks. Golf caddies get 15% of the greens fee.

▌ VISITOR INFORMATION

There are Florida welcome centers on I–10 (near Pensacola), I–75 (near Jennings), I–95 (near Yulee, north of Jacksonville), and U.S. 231 (near Campbellton), and in the lobby of the New Capitol in Tallahassee. Contact **Visit Florida** ☎ 850/488–5607, 866/972–5280 ⊕ www.visitflorida.com.

INDEX

PHOTO CREDITS

NOTES

NOTES

ABOUT OUR WRITERS

Tampa Bay and Naples updater and beach lover Kate Bradshaw lives in the small Gulf Coast town of St. Pete Beach and writes for various Tampa Bay news, environmental, and entertainment outlets. On weekends, you may spot her strumming her guitar at a local beach haunt. Born in the Chicago area, Kate has lived in Hawaii, New Zealand, and New Mexico, among other places. She is proud to now be a Florida resident, and with her coverage for Fodor's, hopes to convey to visitors all the beauty and wonder of her adopted home.

After being hired sight unseen by a South Florida newspaper, Fort Lauderdale–based freelance travel writer and editor Lynne Helm arrived from the Midwest anticipating a few years of palm-fringed fun. More than a quarter century later (after covering the state for several newspapers, consumer magazines, and trade publications), she's still enamored of Florida's sun-drenched charms. Lynne updated the Everglades chapter.

Updating the Florida Keys and much of the Lower Gulf Coast is Miami native, Jill Martin. As a freelance writer, she has blogged more than 1,000 articles for the state's tourism website, Visit Florida, and also writes for various travel sites and print magazines. She has appeared on numerous TV and radio shows as a Florida travel expert and is the creator of Sunshine Brain Games, a trivia card game all about Florida. She resides full time in the Redland and part time on Sanibel.

Northeast Florida updater Steve Master can hear the engines roar, literally, from his Port Orange, Florida, home, 10 miles south of famed Daytona International Speedway. Steve spent 20 years as a sports writer for the *Daytona Beach News Journal*, where he won many awards, including a 2007 national honor from the Associated Press Sports Editors. He has written commentary for *NASCAR Illustrated* and covered travel for Orbitz Worldwide. Currently, he's an assistant professor of communication at Embry-Riddle Aeronautical University in Daytona Beach.

Paul Rubio's insatiable quest to discover and learn has taken him to the far corners of the world—more than 80 countries and counting. A Harvard-trained economist with a double masters degree, he took on his passion for travel writing full time in 2008 and hasn't looked back. Paul, who updated the Fort Lauderdale, Palm Beach, and Miami chapters, currently contributes to *Ocean Home Magazine, Palm Beach Illustrated,* and *Weddings Illustrated* as well as other Fodor's guides, jetsetter.com, and various outlets of Modern Luxury Media.

St. Augustine updater Sharon Weightman Hoffmann is a writer and researcher who has lived in the Jacksonville Beaches area for more than 20 years. She's also an editor whose recent assignments as a "book doctor" have ranged from a memoir of early radio to a Christian vampire novel. Sharon was assisted by Jaimie Wilson, a distance learning developer and a writer who has covered many aspects of the arts and pop culture from fine dining and the symphony to skateboarding and square-dancing. Sharon, Jaimie, and co-author Alex van der Tuuk have written a biography of blues musician Blind Blake.

Panhandle updater Ashley Wright is a northwest Florida native and a master-of-all-trades in the publishing world, including (but certainly not limited to) writing, editing, graphic design, and photography. She contributes to a number of local and regional publications and loves sharing the hidden treasures of her native coast with travelers both near and far.

The Orlando and Walt Disney World chapters were updated by a talented team of writers, including Rona Gindin (Where to Eat), Jennifer Greenhill-Taylor, (Where to Stay), Jennie Hess (all of Disney World), Gary McKechnie (Universal and SeaWorld), and Megan Peck (Orlando and environs sights and attractions).